Chives

A member of the onion family, versatile chives are among the most popular of all seasonings.

Cinnamon

Virtually all the cinnamon sold in the United States is the full-bodied, pungent cassia variety.

Cloves

Famous for spicy fragrance, these nail-shaped buds are imported from Madagascar and Zanzibar.

Coriander

One of the first spices known to man, coriander is grown in Morocco, Europe and South America.

Cumin

The slightly bitter taste of cumin is used most widely to accent the flavor of Mexican-style dishes.

Curry Powder

A ground blend of as many as 16 spices, curry gives the characteristic flavor of Indian curry cookery.

Dill Seed

A member of the parsley family, this warm, slightly sharp seed is imported in abundance from India.

Fennel

Believed by the ancients to be one of the nine sacred herbs, fennel has a pleasant anise-like flavor.

Fenugreek

Fenugreek, a small seed of the pea family, tastes like burnt sugar, and is for commercial use only.

Filé

An important spice in authentic Creole cookery, filé is made from powdered sassafras leaves.

Garlic

Formerly used to ward off evil spirits, flavorful garlic is used widely in French and Italian cooking.

Ginger

One of the few spices that grow below ground, ginger has an interesting spicy-sweet, pungent flavor.

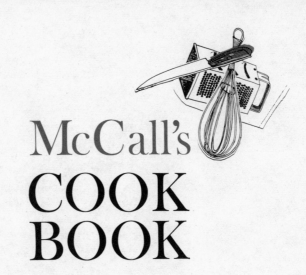

McCall's
COOK
BOOK

By the Food Editors of McCall's

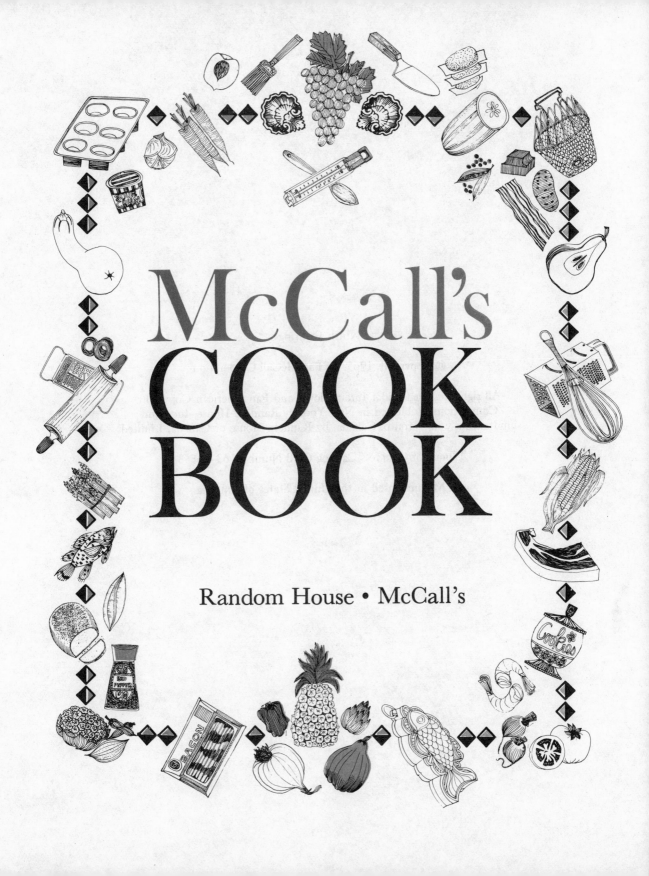

McCall's COOK BOOK

Random House • McCall's

CONTENTS

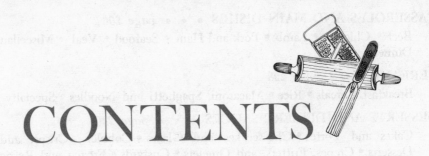

v

ILLUSTRATIONS BY RICHARD ROSENBLUM

MUFFIN PHOTOGRAPH BY TOSH MATSUMOTO

ALL OTHER PHOTOGRAPHS BY PAUL DOME STUDIOS

1

Introduction to Cooking

Here is your book, the one your thousands of letters have asked us to publish. It has taken us years to do, checking and rechecking countless recipes to bring you only the best, only the interesting, only the perfect. Now we can say, without a shadow of a doubt, that every single one of them, if you follow the directions to the letter, will work for you exactly as well as it did for us, even if you have never cooked before.

It's true that preparing three meals a day remains the homemaker's biggest chore, and one she strives to accomplish with variety, originality, skill, and economy. But cooking is something even beyond that. It is one of the really creative arts, and a deeply satisfying, deeply personal one, since it is done for the ones we love.

Social customs radiate from the service of food in the home. So does the most fundamental kind of social status. Thus, the woman who can cook well and serve food graciously is a successful homemaker.

Our book starts from the beginning with the beginner, and everything is simply stated, not merely so it can be understood, but so it cannot be misunderstood. We tell you how to tackle a recipe. We give you the easiest method—McCall's own step-by-step way. We define cooking terms precisely, tell you how to measure, how to set a table, how to plan meals for any occasion, and much, much more. Our chapters are arranged alphabetically, and there is an easy index, so you can find whatever you wish without delay. Just as we hope you will learn from us, we have learned from you, from the recipes and short cuts and tips and traditions you have been kind enough to tell us about. Without your help, truly, this book could not have been written.

Your friends in McCALL'S
FOOD DEPARTMENT

Beginners, Begin Here!

As a new cook, you are greatly to be envied, because you have such a wonderfully exciting experience ahead of you. Cooking can, and should, be a creative joy—and once you learn to cook really well, not only will you get a great deal of personal satisfaction out of it, but you will also contribute to the happiness of your family. Undoubtedly, you will shed some tears of frustration along the way; but once you achieve your first perfect cake and serve your first dinner party perfectly, you will be a new woman, ready to meet any new recipe.

Before you can cook intelligently, you will need to know: (1) How to tackle a recipe. (2) How to measure correctly. (3) The common food weights and measures. (4) About oven temperatures. (5) Cooking terminology. (6) Definitions of common food terms.

Obviously, you are not going to pick up all this information in one fell swoop. You will learn as you cook, until one fine day you'll discover you have all these important facts neatly pigeonholed in your mind.

HOW TO TACKLE A RECIPE

1. Read the recipe all the way through before you turn a hand. Every word!

2. Check your supplies, to see if you have all the ingredients called for.

3. See if you have the right equipment to work with. Nothing is more frustrating than to be in the middle of a recipe and find you haven't the right pan or pot.

4. If you aren't familiar with an ingredient listed, look it up, so you'll recognize it the next time.

5. At this point, get out all ingredients and all equipment.

6. Do as much preparation prior to combining ingredients as you possibly can—following exactly, of course, recipe directions.

7. Last but not least, follow the recipe to the letter. It is only the experienced cook who can take liberties with or make changes in a recipe. All recipes published today are thoroughly tested, and the directions given should be followed meticulously.

You'll be a happier cook if you . . .

· Make it a habit to trim, peel, scrape foods over waxed paper or paper towels. Saves work in the long run.

· Keep a damp cloth close at hand. Cooking is more fun and more successful when your hands and kitchen are tidy.

· Wash pots, pans, utensils as you work.

· Wipe off your range each time you use it.

· Preheat your oven for all baking—unless recipes say not to.

· Wipe off tops of salad-oil, catsup, chili-sauce, mustard bottles or jars every time you use them.

· Do not cut or increase recipes unless you are skilled enough to recognize the difference in pan sizes and/or cooking time necessitated by the change.

HOW TO MEASURE CORRECTLY

1. Use only standard measuring cups and spoons. Any recipe you follow has been tested with standard equipment.

2. Make all measurements level.

3. In measuring dry ingredients or fats, use the standardized metal cups that come in nests and hold ¼, ⅓, ½, and 1 cup.

4. In measuring dry ingredients (flour, confectioners' sugar, etc.), heap the cup or spoon to overflowing; then level off excess with a straight-edge knife or spatula.

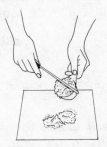

5. In measuring fats, bring to room temperature if stored in refrigerator; then press firmly into spoon or cup, and level off with straight-edge knife or spatula. One stick of butter or margarine measures ½ cup, or 8 tablespoons. Many wrappers have a printed measuring guide. Tape one to your kitchen ruler for handy reference.

6. When measuring liquids, use the standard glass liquid measuring cup, with lip, marked off in quarters and thirds. Always place cup on a flat surface, and measure at eye level.

7. When recipe calls for sifted flour, sift before you measure. Never pack the flour down by banging the cup on the table.

8. Brown sugar should always be packed firmly into the measuring cup or spoon, then leveled off with knife or spatula. If lumpy, roll with rolling pin before measuring.

9. When measuring molasses, syrup, or honey, pour liquid into cup or spoon. Do not dip measuring utensil into the heavy liquid. Scrape out thoroughly, with a rubber scraper, all liquid that clings to inside.

10. If confectioners' sugar looks lumpy, it is advisable to roll it with a rolling pin before measuring. If recipe calls for sifted confectioners' sugar, press through sieve to sift.

Memorize the following common weights and measures to save time and assure accuracy. Make sure all measurements are level.

COMMON FOOD WEIGHTS AND MEASURES

Dash	Less than ⅛ teaspoon
1 tablespoon	3 teaspoons
4 tablespoons	¼ cup
5⅓ tablespoons	⅓ cup
8 tablespoons	½ cup
12 tablespoons	¾ cup
16 tablespoons	1 cup
1 fluid ounce	2 tablespoons
1 cup	½ pint (liquid)
2 cups	1 pint
2 pints (4 cups)	1 quart
4 quarts	1 gallon
8 quarts	1 peck (dry)
4 pecks	1 bushel
16 ounces	1 pound

ABOUT OVEN TEMPERATURES

In the old days, the cook stuck her hand in the oven to "feel" the temperature. Happily, the modern cook doesn't have to guess at the temperature of her oven, because, in nine cases out of ten, her range has oven-heat control.

However, to those cooks whose ovens do not have heat control, we strongly recommend the purchase of a tested, proven oven thermometer.

We cannot overemphasize the need for correct oven temperature if you are going to cook successfully. Nor can we stress too strongly the need to follow the temperature indicated in the recipe. Many a good roast or cake has been ruined because the oven temperature was not correct.

Once a year, at least, have your oven checked by the utility company that serves your area, because even the best range goes off the beam occasionally and needs an expert to get it back on.

If you have the manufacturer's booklet about your range, study it—because the people who made the range know best how you should treat it for maximum service.

Although modern recipes give exact oven temperatures, it is just as well for you to know what these different temperatures mean:

Temperature (Degrees F)	Term
250 to 275 · · · · · · · · · ·	Very slow
300 to 325 · · · · · · · · · ·	Slow
350 to 375 · · · · · · · · · ·	Moderate
400 to 425 · · · · · · · · · ·	Hot
450 to 475 · · · · · · · · · ·	Very hot
500 to 525 · · · · · · · · · ·	Extremely hot

BASIC TOP-OF-THE-RANGE COOKING TERMINOLOGY

Boiling is probably used in more recipes, and misunderstood by more cooks, than any other cooking term. Many a cook mistakenly thinks, for instance, that the harder food boils, the quicker it's done. The explanations below should help.

Bring to the boiling point, or *bring to a boil,* signifies the step before cooking. You'll know that water or any liquid is reaching that point when bubbles appear at the bottom, rise to the top, and then break. When all liquid is in motion, it has come to a boil.

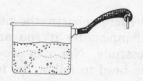

Boil means to cook at the boiling point. When this point is reached, adjust heat to maintain it. This is the term recipes use most often—the one that retains flavor and color of vegetables; saves fuel; avoids scorched pans. And boiling harder won't cook faster.

Boil rapidly means the point at which liquid goes into rapid motion; the surface breaks into small, lumpy waves. A rapid boil won't cook food faster; but for some uses, it is better: to start cereals (keeps particles separated) and to evaporate soup or jam.

Full, rolling boil means the point at which the liquid rises in the pan, then tumbles into waves that can't be stirred down. It usually happens in heavy sugar mixtures, like candy or frosting, in jelly making when jelly is almost done or when liquid pectin is added.

Simmer means to cook just below the boiling point; adjust the heat to maintain this stage. In simmering, the food cooks so slowly the surface moves slightly; no bubbles show.

Steam means to cook by steam in a closed container. Dumplings and puddings are examples. You can cook by steam under pressure in less time than usual, with a pressure cooker.

Blanch means to remove skins from fruits, vegetables, or nuts by letting them stand in boiling water until skins peel off easily. Occasionally, it is necessary to drain off the first water and add more boiling water.

Poach means to cook eggs, fish, vegetables in liquid at or below simmering, or cook eggs over water in a special pan.

Steep means to let a food stand in hot liquid, below boiling, to extract flavor, color, or both.

Parboil means to cook food in a boiling liquid until partially done. This is usually a preliminary step to further cooking. Beans and ham, for instance, are parboiled, later baked.

Scald means to heat liquids like milk almost to boiling; tiny bubbles will appear at edge. Or when freezing or canning vegetables, heat by steam or in boiling water.

OTHER COOKING TERMINOLOGY

Bake: To cook by dry heat, usually in the oven. When applied to meats and vegetables, this is called roasting.

Barbecue: To roast meats very slowly on a spit or rack over heat, basting with a seasoned sauce.

Baste: To moisten foods (usually roasting meats) while cooking, with meat drippings, melted fat, or sauces, to prevent drying and to add flavor.

Beat: To work a mixture smooth with a regular, hard, rhythmic movement.

Blend: To mix thoroughly two or more ingredients.

Braise: To brown meat or vegetables in a small amount of hot fat and cook slowly, tightly covered. In some recipes, you add other liquids after the initial browning.

Broil: To cook directly under a flame or heating unit or over an open fire or grill.

Brush: To spread food with butter or margarine or egg, using a small brush.

Candy: To cook fruit in a heavy sugar syrup until transparent, then drain and dry. (Orange peel, for example.) Also, to cook vegetables with sugar or syrup, to give a coating or glaze when cooked.

Caramelize: To melt sugar slowly over very low heat until sugar is liquid, brown, and caramel flavored.

Coat: To roll foods in flour, nuts, sugar, crumbs, etc., until all sides are evenly covered; or to dip first into slightly beaten egg or milk, then to cover with whatever coating is called for in recipe.

Coddle: To cook slowly and gently in water just below the boiling point. Eggs are frequently coddled.

Combine: To mix all ingredients.

Cook: To prepare food by applying heat in any form.

Cream: To beat shortening until smooth, creamy, and light, with wooden spoon or beater. Usually applied to shortening when combined with sugar; *e.g.,* in making cakes.

Crisp: To make firm and brittle in very cold water or in refrigerator (lettuce, other greens, for example).

Cut: (1) To break up food into pieces, with a knife or scissors. (2) To combine shortening with dry ingredients by working together with two knives used scissor fashion, or with pastry blender. Usually applied to pastry making.

Devil: To coat with a hot seasoning, such as mustard or a hot sauce. Eggs are "deviled" when the yolk is mixed with hot seasonings.

Dissolve: To make a liquid and a dry substance go into solution.

Dot: To scatter small amounts of butter, nuts, chocolate, and so forth over the surface of a food.

Dredge: To coat food with some dry ingredient, such as seasoned flour or sugar.

Dust: To sprinkle a food or coat lightly with flour or sugar.

Flambé: To cover a food with brandy or cognac, etc.; then light, and serve flaming; *e.g.,* plum pudding.

Fold: To combine two ingredients—more often than not, beaten egg whites and batter —very gently with a wire whisk or rubber scraper, using an under-and-over motion, until thoroughly mixed.

Fricassee: To braise fowl, veal, or other meat, cut into pieces, in a small amount of liquid.

Fry: (1) To cook in a small amount of fat on top of stove; also called "sauté" and "pan-fry." (2) To cook a food in a deep layer of hot fat, called "deep-frying." The aim is to produce foods with a crisp golden-brown crust and a thoroughly cooked interior without letting them absorb too much fat. The kind, quantity, and temperature of the fat are important in accomplishing this result.

Garnish: To decorate any foods. Nuts, olives, parsley, and so forth are called garnishes when used to give a finish to a dish.

Glacé: To coat with a thin sugar syrup cooked to the crack stage.

Glaze: To cover with aspic; to coat with a thin sugar syrup; to cover with melted fruit jelly. Cold meats, fish, fruit, etc., are often glazed.

Grill: See "Broil."

Knead: To work and press dough hard with the heels of your hands, so the dough becomes stretched and elastic. Usually done to bread and other yeast doughs.

Marinate: To soak food, mainly meat, in acid such as lemon juice or tomato juice, or in an oil-acid mixture like French dressing. Acts as a tenderizer, steps up flavor.

Melt: To heat solid food, like sugar or fat, until it becomes liquid.

Mix: To stir, usually with a spoon, until ingredients are thoroughly combined.

Pan-broil: To cook, uncovered, on a hot surface, usually a skillet. The fat is poured off as it accumulates.

Pan-fry: To cook or fry on top of range in a hot, uncovered skillet with little or no fat. Steaks, chops, potatoes are frequently cooked this way.

Pare: To cut away coverings of vegetables and fruits.

Peel: To strip or slip off outer coverings of some vegetables or fruit.

Plank: To bake or broil meat, fish, vegetables on a wooden or metal plank.

Pot-roast: To brown meat in a small amount of fat, then finish cooking in a small amount of liquid. Done in a deep, heavy, covered kettle or Dutch oven to tough cuts of meat.

Preheat: To heat oven to stated temperature before product goes in.

Purée: To work fruits or vegetables through a sieve or food mill or blend in an electric blender until food is pulpy. Sauces, soups, baby foods, vegetables are often puréed.

Reduce: To boil a liquid until you have a small, concentrated amount.

Roast: To cook meat or vegetables in an oven by dry heat. See "Bake."

Sauté: To fry foods until golden and tender, in a small amount of fat on top of range. See "Fry."

Scallop: To arrange foods in layers in a casserole, with a sauce or liquid, and then bake. Usually has a topping of bread crumbs.

Score: To cut narrow gashes, part way through fat, in meats before cooking; *e.g.*, in steaks to prevent curling, or to cut diamond-shaped gashes part way through fat in ham just before glazing.

Scramble: To stir or mix foods gently while cooking, as eggs.

Sear: To brown surface of meat over high heat, either on top of range or in oven.

Shirr: To break eggs into a dish with cream or crumbs; then bake.

Sift: To put one or more dry ingredients through a fine sieve.

Skewer: To thread foods, such as meat, fish, poultry, vegetables, on a wooden or metal skewer, so they hold their shape during cooking.

Sterilize: To heat in boiling water or steam for at least 20 minutes, until living organisms are destroyed.

Stew: To cook foods, in enough liquid to cover, very slowly—always below the boiling point.

Stir: To mix, usually with a spoon or fork, until ingredients are worked together.

Toast: To brown and dry the surface of foods with heat, such as bread and nuts.

Toss: To tumble ingredients lightly with a lifting motion.

Whip: To rapidly beat eggs, heavy cream, etc., in order to incorporate air and expand volume.

CUTTING TERMINOLOGY

Chop means to cut food into smaller pieces, usually with large knife and cutting board. One hand holds knife tip on board; the other moves blade up and down, cutting through the food.

Mince means to cut food in pieces, but finer than chopped. Mincing takes the same steps: Use cutting board and sharp knife, chopping knife and wooden bowl, or scissors—just do it longer.

Grind means to put food through chopper. Choppers have two or three blades. Use a blade with smaller holes to grind foods fine; one with larger holes for coarse chopping or grinding.

Flake means to break or pull apart a food, like chicken or fish, that divides naturally. All you do is follow these divisions, pulling at them gently with one or two forks. Or flake with your fingers.

Cube means to cut a solid into little cubes from about ½ inch to 1 inch.

Dice means to cube but to make the cubes smaller—less than ½ inch. Use a cutting board and a very sharp knife, or a special cubing gadget, if you prefer.

Grate means to tear off coarse-to-fine particles of food with a hand grater or mechanical device. Degrees of fineness vary from hard cheese through lemon peel to powdered nutmeg.

Sliver means to cut or split into long, thin strips, with a knife on a cutting board. The term applies to almonds and to pimiento pieces used for decoration.

Shred means to cut or tear in long, narrow pieces. The fineness varies—recipes often say that foods should be "finely" or "coarsely" shredded. Use a hand or mechanical shredder; cut crisp vegetables, like cabbage, to shreds with a sharp knife.

Julienne means to cut potatoes or vegetables into matchlike sticks.

DEFINITIONS OF COMMON FOOD TERMS

A la king: Food, such as fowl and bland meats, served in a rich cream or white sauce.

A la mode: Pie or cake served with a garnish of ice cream on top.

Appetizer: A small, tasty portion of food served before dinner or as a first course.

Aspic: Meat or vegetable jelly, sometimes with gelatine added, used as a garnish or to mold meats, fish, fowl, or vegetables.

Au gratin: Food mixed with cream or white sauce, covered with bread crumbs or grated cheese, and baked or broiled until the surface is browned.

Au jus: Meat served in its natural juices.

Au lait: Beverage made and served with milk. Coffee, for example.

Au naturel: Food plainly cooked or served in its natural state.

Bar-le-Duc: Fruit preserve made from white or red currants.

Batter: Any mixture of dry ingredients and liquid that is stirred or beaten and can be poured or dropped from a spoon.

Bavarian: A dessert pudding made with a gelatine-and-cream base.

Béarnaise: Hollandaise sauce with shallots, tarragon, chervil, and other seasonings added.

Béchamel: Cream sauce made with chicken and veal stock.

Bisque: (1) A rich cream soup, usually made from fish or shellfish. (2) A rich frozen dessert made from cream, macaroons, and nuts.

Blanquette: A meat or vegetable stew made with a cream or white sauce.

Bombe: A melon or round mold lined with one kind of ice cream and filled with another kind of ice cream or sherbet.

Bouillabaisse: Hearty French soup made with large pieces of fish and shellfish.

Brochette: Small spit or skewer used for broiling meat cubes.

Canapé: An appetizer of highly seasoned food, usually served on little pieces of crisp toast or crackers.

Caviar: Prepared, salted roe (or eggs) of sturgeon and other large fish. Usually served as an appetizer.

Charlotte: A molded dessert, usually made with gelatine and flavored whipped cream, with cake or ladyfingers outlining the mold.

Chaud-froid: Literally "hot-cold." Gelatine sauce made with white-sauce base, used to coat cold meat, poultry, and fish.

Chiffonade: A mixture of finely chopped fresh herbs, used to season soups and salads.

Chowder: A soup or stew made with fish, shellfish—such as clams or lobster—and/or vegetables.

Cobbler: A deep-dish fruit pie made with top covering of rich pastry or biscuit dough.

Compote: A variety of stewed fruit served cold in a syrup.

Condiment: A seasoning, such as salt, pepper, spices, herbs. Relishes are also spoken of as condiments.

Conserve: Fruit preserve made with more than one fruit, often with nuts and raisins added.

Court bouillon: A richly flavored stock made from fish.

Crepe: A thin, rich pancake, served with filling and sauce as a main dish or dessert.

Croquettes: Finely chopped or ground meat, fish, fowl, etc., mixed with thick cream sauce, shaped into patties or cones, dipped into egg and cracker crumbs, and fried until crisp on the outside.

Croutons: Fried or toasted cubes of bread. Used frequently in soups and salads.

Demitasse: Small cups of strong coffee, served after dinner.

Dough: A mixture of dry ingredients, such as flour, and liquid that is stiff enough to handle or knead. Bread and biscuit dough are examples.

Éclair: A small, finger-shape pastry, filled with custard or whipped cream.

Entrée: (1) The main dish of an American family meal. (2) At a formal dinner, a small serving of food, usually fish, served before the main course.

Filet mignon: Tender, cross-cut slice of beef, from the tenderloin.

Fondant: A type of candy made from sugar syrup, which is kneaded to creaminess.

Fondue: A cheese luncheon or supper dish. (1) American version is made with eggs, cheese, milk and is thickened with crumbs.

(2) Swiss version is like a rich cheese sauce, made with cheese, thickening agent (cornstarch or potato flour), and wine.

Fritters: Mixture of vegetables, fruit, or meat and batter, fried crisp in hot fat.

Goulash: A thick meat stew flavored with vegetables and paprika. Usually associated with Hungarian cookery.

Grenadine: Syrup used for sweetening mixed drinks; made from pomegranate juice.

Gumbo: A richly flavored soup thickened with okra.

Hollandaise: A sauce made with eggs, butter, lemon juice or vinegar. Served hot or cold, with vegetables or fish.

Hors d'oeuvres: Appetizer course; usually small pieces of finger food.

Ice: A frozen dessert made from fruit juices, sugar, and water. Sometimes gelatine or egg whites are added.

Kirsch: Cherry liqueur, mainly produced in Switzerland.

Kisses: Tiny dessert meringues. See "Meringue."

Leavening agent: Gas-forming ingredient used in baking (such as baking powder and yeast), producing lightness and volume.

Légumes: Vegetable seeds (peas, beans, lentils), usually referred to as such in the dried state.

Macaroons: Small cakes made from egg whites, sugar, and ground almonds or almond paste.

Macédoine: A combination of different fruits or vegetables.

Marguerite: A salted cracker spread with boiled frosting, sprinkled with nuts, coconut, or chocolate pieces, and baked until golden.

Marinade: An acid (tomato or lemon juice) or a mixture of oil and acid (French dressing), in which food is soaked to develop flavor and tenderness.

Marrons: Chestnuts; usually preserved or glacéed.

Marzipan: A candylike paste made with finely ground almonds and sugar.

Meringue: A mixture of stiffly beaten egg whites and sugar, used as a pie topping or baked alone and served as dessert with ice cream, fruit, or flavored whipped cream.

Minestrone: A thick Italian soup made with vegetables and pasta.

Mocha: A coffee or coffee-chocolate combination of flavors, used in desserts and beverages.

Mousse: (1) A dessert of sweetened, frozen whipped cream, with fruit and nuts. (2) A vegetable or meat dish, thickened with gelatine and served as a main dish.

Pancakes: A batter cake fried on both sides on a griddle. Sometimes called "griddlecakes."

Parfait: A dessert of ice cream, fruit, and whipped cream; or a frozen mixture of egg whites or yolks, cooked with hot syrup and combined with whipped cream.

Pâté de fois gras: A smooth, richly seasoned paste made from goose livers.

Patty shell: A shell made from puff paste or pastry and filled with creamed shellfish, chicken, and the like.

Petits fours: Very small, iced-all-over cakes. Served at tea parties or as a dessert accompaniment for ice cream or fruit.

Pilaf: A main dish made with meat, fish, or fowl and rice, vegetables, and spices.

Rabbit or *rarebit:* A mixture of cheese, eggs, seasonings, and white sauce, usually served over toast.

Ragout: A thick, well-seasoned French stew made with meat, vegetables, herbs.

Ramekins: Small, individual casserole dishes.

Ravioli: Large noodles filled with finely minced meat, vegetables, or cheese, then cooked in boiling stock or water.

Relish: A highly seasoned food accompaniment, like chutney, India relish, or olives. Used to enhance the flavor of other foods.

Rissole: A nicely seasoned meat mixture, wrapped in rich pastry and fried in deep fat.

Roux: A cooked mixture of butter and flour, used to thicken soups and sauces.

Sherbet: A frozen mixture of fruit juice, sugar, egg whites, water or milk. Served as dessert or as a meat accompaniment.

Smörgasbord: Swedish appetizer or entrée course, consisting of a large variety of foods, usually set up as buffet.

Soufflé: A puffy, airy, hot dish made light with egg whites mixed gently with white sauce. Usually cheese, fish, meat, etc., are added. Also a dessert, most frequently made with chocolate or fruit.

Stock: The richly flavored liquid in which meat, fish, fowl, or vegetables have been cooked. Used in sauces, soups, and general cookery.

Timbale: A baked, unsweetened custard in which finely chopped meats, fish, fowl, vegetables have been mixed.

Torte: Very rich layers of cake made with crumbs, eggs, nuts, and topped with whipped cream and fruit.

Truffles: Fungus that grows underground; used for garnishing and flavoring.

Tutti-frutti: A mixture of many kinds of fruit.

Velouté: Rich white sauce made with ham, chicken, or veal stock, seasoned with bouquet garni.

Vinaigrette: Sauce made of oil, vinegar, and seasonings.

Vol-au-vent: Patties of puff paste, to be filled with meat, fish, or poultry.

White sauce: A combination of butter, flour, milk, cream, or stock, seasoned and cooked until smooth and creamy.

COMMON CAN SIZES

Know the common can sizes and approximate number of servings in each, in order to buy canned foods economically and wisely. Most common canned foods are packed in more than one size can; scan the labels to determine the number of servings or cups contained in each can.

Can Size Number	Approximate Net Weight (Check Label)	Approximate Cups	Principal Products	Average Servings
6 ounce	6 oz	3 cups (diluted)	Frozen fruit-juice concentrates	6
5–6 ounce	5–6 oz	¾ cup	Fruit and vegetable juices, natural strength	1–2
8 ounce	8 oz	1 cup	Fruits and vegetables	2
No. 1 (Picnic)	10½ oz to 12 oz	1¼ cups	Condensed soups, fruits, vegetables, and fruit juices	3
12 ounce (Vacuum)	12 oz	1½ cups	Vacuum-packed corn, vegetables	3–4
No. 300	14 to 16 oz	1¾ cups	Pork and beans, cranberry sauce, blueberries	3–4
No. 303	16 to 17 oz	2 cups	Fruits and vegetables, ready-to-serve soups	4

COMMON CAN SIZES (Continued)

Can Size Number	Approximate Net Weight (Check Label)	Approximate Cups	Principal Products	Average Servings
No. 2	1 lb, 4 oz, or 1 pt, 2 fl oz	2½ cups	Juice, vegetables, fruits	6
No. 2½	1 lb, 13 oz	3½ cups	Fruits, some vegetables (tomatoes, pumpkin, sauerkraut)	7
No. 3 cylinder or 46 fl oz	3 lb, 3 oz or 1 qt, 14 fl oz	5¾ cups	"Economy family size" fruit and vegetable juices, pork and beans, whole chicken	10–12
No. 10	6½ lb to 7 lb, 5 oz	12–13 cups	Institutional size for fruits, vegetables	25

Basic Cooking Utensils

The utensils and tools you use for cooking are your best kitchen friends. They determine to a great extent your cooking success or failure. Consider these points when buying utensils:

1. Buy things of good quality—you'll be using these utensils for a long time.

2. Consider your needs, and buy to suit them. If you are not heavy coffee drinkers, for instance, buy a smaller-size coffee maker.

3. Buy matched sets of utensils or tools if what you want is included in the set—if not, buy various kinds to suit your needs.

4. Select utensils of standard sizes. These will generally have their size and/or capacity stamped on the bottom or indicated on a label.

5. Some things such as paring knives and spoons are used in different parts of the kitchen at the same time—save time and steps by having duplicates of these. We call it storage at the point of first use.

6. Buy enough basic cooking utensils (see below) to start with, and add to these as you need them and as your cooking skills increase.

PANS FOR TOP-OF-RANGE USE

1 coffee maker, size to suit family
1 double boiler—1½ quarts
1 Dutch oven—4–6 quarts
1 small frying pan—7–8" top diameter
1 large frying pan with fitted cover—9–10" diameter
1 griddle
3 saucepans with covers—
1 quart, 2 quarts, 3 quarts

1 teakettle—2½ quarts

PANS FOR OVEN USE

1 shallow baking dish—1½ quarts
2 layer-cake pans—8" or 9" x 1½" deep
1 square cake pan—8" x 8" x 2" or 9" x 9" x 1¾"
2 casseroles—1½ quarts, 3 quarts
2 cookie sheets—15½" x 12"
6 custard cups—5 or 6 ounce
2 loaf pans—9" x 5" x 3"

1 muffin pan with 6 to 12 individual cups
1 oblong pan—13" x 9½" x 2"
1 pie plate—9" diameter
1 shallow roasting pan with rack
1 tube pan—10" x 4"

PREPARATION AND MEASURING TOOLS

1 biscuit cutter
1 bottle opener and corkscrew
1 bread or cutting board
1 can opener
1 colander
1 flour sifter
1 French cook's knife
1 fruit reamer
1 set assorted graters
1 jar opener
1 pair kitchen shears
1 ladle
1 long-handled, slotted metal spoon
1 long-handled, 2-tined kitchen fork
1 nest mixing bowls—4 sizes
1 minute timer
1 narrow spatula—¾" wide
1 pair tongs
1 pancake turner
1 paring knife
1 pastry blender
1 pastry brush
1 potato masher
1 rolling pin
1 rotary beater
2 rubber scrapers—one narrow, one wide
1 slicing knife (8–9" blade)
1 set standard dry measuring cups
2 standard liquid measuring cups—1 cup and
  4 cups
1 set standard measuring spoons
1 medium-large strainer
1 small strainer
1 vegetable brush
1 vegetable peeler
1 wire rack
1 wooden spoon

NICE TO HAVE

apple corer
baster

bread knife with serrated or scalloped edge
butter-ball paddles
cake tester
assorted cutters for cookies, doughnuts, biscuits
food grinder or chopper
French wire whisk
funnel
garlic press
grapefruit knife
ice-cream spade
jelly-roll pan—15½" x 10½" x 1"
knife sharpener
melon-ball cutter
molds—large and individual for puddings and
  salads
mortar and pestle for crushing garlic, herbs,
  and seeds
nutmeg grater
pastry cloth and rolling-pin cover
pepper mill
poultry pins
slicer for eggs, tomatoes
soufflé dish
strawberry huller
thermometers—roast meat, deep-fry, candy

FOR STORAGE

bins for fruits and vegetables
bread box
canister set
cookie jar
covered cake plate
juice jug
refrigerator dishes with covers
waxed paper, saran, aluminum foil, plastic
  sandwich wrap

FOR CLEANUP

dishcloths and/or sponges
dish drainer
dish-draining rack
dishpan
dish towels
garbage can
paper towels
pot holders
wastebasket

The Right Way to Carve

What you need in the way of equipment to carve any type of meat or bird are a long carving knife or slicer, a short auxiliary knife, and a two-pronged fork. The knives should be sharp enough to slice easily.

Because a roast continues to cook after it leaves the heat, remove it from the oven just before it is done, and let it stand a few minutes. The juices settle; it will carve more easily and be tastier. Be sure that hot meat goes to the table on a hot platter and cold meat on a cold platter.

HOW TO CARVE A STANDING RIB ROAST

1. Place the roast on a platter or on a wooden board, cut side up, with the rib side of the roast at the carver's left.

3. Release this first slice by cutting vertically along the full length of the rib bone with the point of the carving knife.

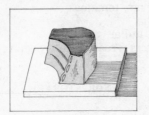

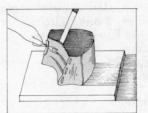

2. Plunge the fork between the two top ribs, to get a firm grip on the roast. (A fork that is equipped with a hand guard is a good protection.) Beginning at the outside edge of the roast, draw the carving knife (its blade should be 8 or 9 inches long) across the roast to the rib side.

4. The first slice is usually fairly thick. Remaining slices, however, may vary from ⅛ to ¼ inch thick, depending on personal preference. Lift off each slice as it is cut, with the aid of an auxiliary fork, to a serving platter or to an individual dinner plate.

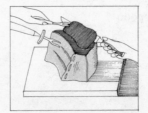

How to Carve Roast Turkey

1. Turkey is placed with legs to carver's right. Plunge fork into bird just below breast, to give firm support, being careful not to puncture breast. With carving knife, slice thigh and leg from body.

4. Carve thin slices (parallel to breastbone) the full sweep of the breast, from top to bottom. Slice enough breast meat for first servings.

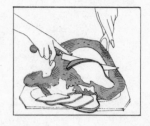

2. Pull thigh and leg away—joint should give easily. If necessary, cut through joint at socket, using a sharp, small auxiliary knife. Lift to small platter, to carve later.

5. Holding leg in left hand, separate it from thigh, with small knife.

3. Grasp wing in left hand; pull from body as far as possible. Work knife through joint; twist wing from body. Place on small platter.

6. Holding thigh with fork, cut long, thin slices, with auxiliary knife.
Then, holding leg in hand, carve thick slices. Include white and dark meat in each serving. Carve other side of turkey for second servings.

17

How to Carve Leg of Lamb

1. Leg of lamb is placed so that the thick, meaty section is on the side nearest the carver. (If a left leg, shank will be at carver's left; if right, at his right.) Insert fork firmly in the large end of leg; cut 2 or 3 lengthwise slices from the thin side of the leg (the side away from the carver).

2. Turn lamb so it rests on the surface just cut; the thick, meaty section will be in an upright position.

3. Insert fork firmly into the thick, meaty section. Starting at the shank end, cut slices (¼ inch thick) down to large leg bone, cutting as many slices as needed.

4. With fork still in place, run knife along leg bone to release all the slices.

5. Then cut more slices from underside.

How to Carve a Whole Ham

1. Ham is placed so that the bone end (shank) is at carver's right, fat side up. Insert fork into the heavy end of ham (butt). Cut 2 or 3 slices, parallel to the length of the ham, from the thin side. (Thin side of ham will face carver if the ham is a left one; it will face away from carver if ham is a right one.)

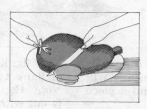

2. Using fork and hand, turn ham so it rests on cut surface. Cut a small wedge-shape piece from the shank end of ham; remove piece to side of platter.

4. Insert knife at the wedge-shape cut at shank end. Run knife parallel to leg bone to release slices.

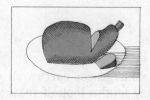

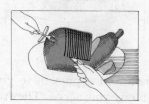

3. With fork steadying ham, start slicing at the wedge-shape cut, cutting thin horizontal slices down to leg bone. (Use long, sawing motions to cut.)

5. For more servings, turn ham back to its original position, fat side up. Cut additional slices at right angles to the bone.

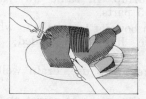

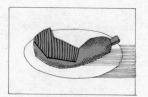

How to Carve Porterhouse Steak

1. Steak is placed on wooden board, or on platter with wooden insert, so that the flank end of steak is at carver's left. With point of knife, cut around T-shape bone. Remove bone to small platter placed beside the carver for that purpose.

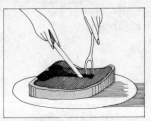

2. Cutting across the entire width of the steak, cut into 1-inch-wide slices. (Each serving will consist of a piece of the tenderloin and a piece of the sirloin.)

3. If flank end is to be served, cut across width of flank as shown.
Note: Contrary to most carving rules, a steak is cut with the grain.

Garnishes

Here we make you a present to give flowery sparkle to foods you serve. They're made of vegetables your grocer carries all year. Inexpensive, they lend a look of luxury.

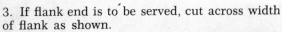

TURNIP DAISIES

1. Wash a medium white turnip; pare.
2. Cut crosswise into ⅛-inch slices.
3. With paring knife, divide each slice into fourths by cutting out thin slivers, from center section to edge. Be careful not to cut through center of turnip. In same way, divide each fourth into 5 parts.
4. Place in bowl of ice water to which a little lemon juice has been added; refrigerate, covered.
5. When ready to use, drain well on paper towels.
6. Place a tiny piece of carrot and tomato in center of each daisy.

SCALLOPED RADISH FLOWERS

1. Wash as many large radishes as desired; cut off both ends.
2. With tip of paring knife, outline scallops around top edge of each radish.
3. Carefully scrape off red part within scalloped area.
4. Place in ice water until ready to use.
5. Before using, drain well on paper towels.

TOMATO ROSES

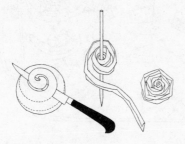

1. Wash as many small tomatoes as desired.
2. Cover with boiling water; let stand 1 minute. Remove, and let cool.
3. With paring knife, starting from bottom of tomato, remove skin in one spiral by cutting, circular-fashion, around tomato.
(Slice peeled tomatoes, and use in a salad.)
4. Wind skin loosely around a wooden skewer, folding back edges of skin as you wind, to give petal effect.
5. Carefully remove wooden skewer. Refrigerate roses until ready to use.

CELERY CURLS

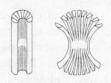

1. Wash celery stalks carefully; remove leaves. Cut stalks into as many 1½-inch pieces as desired.
2. With paring knife, cut very thin, ½-inch-long slices at each end of celery pieces, leaving ½ inch intact in center.
3. Place immediately in ice water, to curl. Refrigerate, covered, at least 1 hour.
4. Before using, drain well on paper towels.

TURNIP-AND-CARROT FLOWERS

1. Wash a medium white turnip; pare.
2. Cut crosswise into ⅛-inch slices.
3. With tip of paring knife, divide each slice into eighths by cutting out thin slivers from center section to edge. Be careful not to cut through center of turnip.
4. Trim each eighth to a point.
5. Place in bowl of ice water to which a little lemon juice has been added; refrigerate, covered.
6. Repeat steps 1 through 5, using a large carrot.
7. When ready to use, drain all flowers well on paper towels.
8. Secure carrot flower to center of turnip flower with part of a toothpick. Place a caper in center.
Note: Turnip and carrot flowers may be used separately, if desired.

2

Appetizers

An appetizer, by its very name, should tempt the appetite, not destroy it. In other words, it should be a teaser, not an appeaser, of the appetite. It should be easy to nibble, look tempting, and be easy to prepare.

How many varieties should you serve before dinner? That's a purely personal question; but we've noticed that most clever hostesses serve no more than four to six kinds, usually four cold ones and two hot ones. The cocktail party is something else again, and here the variety can be as great as you choose.

Dips are understandably popular, both with guests and with hostesses. They are tasty, exciting to eat, and really not much trouble to prepare, especially if you have a blender to make them smooth as silk.

Dips, hot and cold, are many and varied. Even more varied is the choice of food you can use as dippers. There are crackers of every kind. Or why not fix a colorful tray of crisp vegetable relishes—carrot sticks, celery sticks, cucumber sticks, cauliflowerets, or green-pepper strips—sprinkled with onion or garlic salt. We promise you that these will make a special hit with any calorie-conscious guests.

AVOCADO DIP

MAKES ABOUT 1½ CUPS

2 medium ripe avocados
 (about 1 lb)
½ teaspoon onion salt
½ teaspoon garlic salt
1 tablespoon lemon juice
Few drops liquid hot-
 pepper seasoning
4 slices crisp-cooked bacon,
 coarsely chopped
1 hard-cooked egg, sieved
Crisp potato or corn chips

1. Cut avocados in half lengthwise; remove pits, and peel. Cut into chunks; blend, covered, in electric blender at high speed, until very smooth. Measure 1⅓ cups purée.

2. In small bowl, combine well purée with rest of ingredients, except egg and potato chips.

3. Refrigerate, covered, until well chilled.

4. To serve: Sprinkle with egg. Surround bowl with potato chips.

BEAN DIP MEXICANA

MAKES ABOUT 2 CUPS

2 cans (1-lb size)
    kidney beans
¼ cup salad oil

1 cup grated Cheddar
    cheese
½ teaspoon salt
1½ teaspoons chili powder

1. Drain beans, reserving liquid.
2. Heat oil in skillet. Add beans, and mash with a potato masher. Add ⅓ cup bean liquid, to help make a smoother mixture.
3. Stir in cheese, salt, and chili powder; cook, stirring, until cheese melts.
4. Serve hot, with corn chips. If mixture gets too stiff for dipping, add a little more bean liquid.

CREAMY COCKTAIL DIP

MAKES ABOUT 1½ CUPS

1 cup dairy sour cream
½ cup catsup
1 tablespoon grated onion
2 teaspoons finely chopped
    chives

½ teaspoon bottled steak
    sauce
1 teaspoon prepared
    horseradish

1. Combine all ingredients. Blend well.
2. Refrigerate.

SPRING DIP

MAKES ABOUT 3 CUPS

¼ cup heavy cream
2 cups creamed cottage
    cheese
¼ cup grated raw carrot
¼ cup thinly sliced green
    onions

¼ cup finely chopped
    green pepper
6 radishes, sliced very thin
Dash freshly ground black
    pepper
Dash dill weed

1. Stir cream into cottage cheese. Add remaining ingredients, and mix well.
2. Refrigerate.

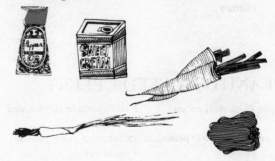

HERB DIP

MAKES ABOUT 1¾ CUPS

½ cup dairy sour cream
1 cup mayonnaise or
    cooked salad dressing
1 teaspoon chopped capers
1 teaspoon dill weed
1 teaspoon dried tarragon
    leaves

1 tablespoon chopped
    chives
1 tablespoon chopped
    parsley
¼ teaspoon paprika
Salt to taste
Pepper to taste

1. Combine all ingredients.
2. Refrigerate.

Finger Foods, Cold

Finger Foods, Cold. One secret of a good cocktail party is finger foods that really are finger foods—bite-size tidbits that hold together, don't crumble or drip when they are eaten. If you serve them on a toothpick, they should be firm enough to hold on a pick.

As with other canapés, it's better to put a few at a time on a platter, and then refill it, than to serve an enormous array that gets soggy and unappetizing. All our appetizers in this section can be made ahead of time and refrigerated.

ANCHOVY-STUFFED EGGS

MAKES 24 HALVES

12 hard-cooked eggs
2 teaspoons anchovy paste
6 tablespoons mayonnaise
   or cooked salad
   dressing
2 teaspoons sugar
2 tablespoons finely
   chopped parsley

1. Cut eggs in half lengthwise, and remove yolks.
2. Using fork, mash yolks. Mix in remaining ingredients smoothly.
3. With a pastry tube, fill whites with yolk mixture.

CHUTNEY EGGS

MAKES 24 HALVES

12 hard-cooked eggs
6 slices crisp-cooked bacon
¼ cup finely chopped
   chutney
3 tablespoons mayonnaise
   or cooked salad
   dressing

1. Cut eggs in half lengthwise, and remove yolks.
2. With fork, mash yolks. Crumble bacon fine; add to mashed yolks, along with chutney and mayonnaise.
3. With a pastry tube, fill whites with yolk mixture.

PEANUT-STUFFED CELERY

MAKES 8

2 pkg (3-oz size) cream
   cheese
¼ cup creamy-style peanut
   butter
2 tablespoons light cream
1 tablespoon finely chopped
   onion
½ teaspoon curry powder
8 stalks celery
½ cup chopped salted
   peanuts

1. In small bowl, with wooden spoon, cream cheese and peanut butter until well combined. Blend in cream, onion, and curry powder.
2. Fill celery stalks. Sprinkle with peanuts.
3. Refrigerate 30 minutes before serving.

LAMB TIDBITS

MAKES 3 DOZEN

1½ cups ground cooked
   lamb
2 tablespoons butter or
   margarine, melted
3 tablespoons chopped
   chutney
¾ teaspoon curry powder
¾ teaspoon prepared
   mustard
½ teaspoon salt
½ cup chopped blanched
   almonds

1. Combine lamb, butter, chutney, curry powder, mustard, and salt; mix well.
2. Shape into ½-inch balls. Roll in chopped almonds; refrigerate.
3. Serve cold, speared on wooden picks.

CHICKEN SALAD IN TOAST CUPS

½ cup finely chopped
    cooked or canned
    chicken
3 tablespoons finely
    chopped celery
1 pimiento, finely chopped

½ pkg (8-oz size) cream
    cheese
¼ teaspoon salt
Dash pepper
15 slices white bread
¼ cup butter or margarine

MAKES 30

1. Thoroughly mix all ingredients, except bread and butter. Makes 1 cup.
2. Preheat oven to 350F.
3. Cut out 30 (2-inch) rounds of bread. Brush both sides with melted butter; press into 1¾-inch muffin-pan cups.
4. Bake 10 to 15 minutes, or until golden around edges. Cool.
5. Fill each little cup with about 1½ teaspoons chicken-salad filling.

HAM-AND-CHEESE RIBBONS

4 slices process American
    cheese
6 slices spiced ham

4 slices process Muenster
    cheese
1 tablespoon prepared
    horseradish, drained

MAKES 17 HORS D'OEUVRES

1. Stack, in order, one slice each of: American cheese, ham, Muenster cheese, ham, American cheese, ham, Muenster cheese, spreading ¼ teaspoon horseradish between slices. Trim edges.
2. Repeat with rest of ingredients, to make another stack.
3. Cut one stack into 4 squares; then cut each square in half diagonally to form triangles.
4. Cut other stack into 3 strips; then cut each strip into 3 squares. Refrigerate until ready to serve.

SAVORY STEAK SLICES

1½ lb flank steak*
⅓ cup soy sauce
⅓ cup dry white wine
2 tablespoons salad oil

Watercress sprigs
¼ cup sliced radishes
Party-rye-bread slices,
    lightly buttered

MAKES ABOUT 20 OR 40 HORS-D'OEUVRE SERVINGS

1. Trim excess fat from steak. If flank steak is very wide—5 inches or more—halve lengthwise.
2. Combine soy sauce and white wine in large, shallow dish. Place flank steak in mixture to marinate.
3. Refrigerate steak, covered, 24 hours, turning occasionally.
4. Brush steak lightly on all sides with oil; place in broiler pan, without rack.
5. Broil steak, 6 inches from heat, 1 minute on each side. Turn steak, and broil 5 minutes longer: turn, and broil 5 more minutes, or until medium rare.
6. Let cool; brush surface of steak with pan juices. Refrigerate, lightly covered, until serving.
7. To serve: Cut steak into thin diagonal slices; arrange on serving board or platter. Garnish with watercress sprigs and sliced radishes. Place basket of bread slices nearby.
* Use U. S. Prime or Choice grade of beef.

COCKTAIL MACADAMIAS

MAKES 1¼ CUPS

1 jar (7 oz) Macadamia nuts
2 tablespoons butter or
  margarine, melted
½ teaspoon seasoned salt

¼ teaspoon liquid
  hot-pepper seasoning
¼ teaspoon paprika
¼ teaspoon garlic salt

1. Preheat oven to 375F.
2. In shallow baking pan, toss nuts with butter, seasoned salt, hot-pepper seasoning, and paprika.
3. Bake 10 minutes.
4. Drain nuts on paper towels. Sprinkle with garlic salt. Serve slightly warm.

COCKTAIL NIBBLERS

MAKES 4 QUARTS

1 pkg (5 oz) pretzel sticks
2 cans (8-oz size) salted
  peanuts
1 pkg (6 oz) bite-size
  shredded-rice biscuits
1 pkg (7 oz) crisp oat cereal

1½ cups butter or
  margarine
¼ cup Worcestershire
  sauce
1 tablespoon garlic salt
1 tablespoon onion salt
1 tablespoon celery salt

1. Preheat oven to 350F.
2. Break pretzel sticks into small pieces. Mix with peanuts and cereals in large roasting pan.
3. Melt butter in small saucepan. Stir in Worcestershire, garlic, onion, and celery salts.
4. Pour over cereal mixture; mix thoroughly.
5. Bake 20 minutes, stirring occasionally.
Note: Three tablespoons seasoned salt may be substituted for garlic, onion, and celery salts.

COCKTAIL CREAM PUFFS

MAKES ABOUT 35

⅓ cup butter or margarine
¾ cup sifted all-purpose
  flour

¼ teaspoon salt
3 eggs

1. Preheat oven to 400F.
2. In saucepan, heat ¾ cup water and butter to boiling.
3. Stir in flour and salt briskly; beat until mixture forms a ball and leaves side of pan. Remove from heat.
4. Beat in eggs, one at a time, beating hard after each addition.
5. Drop, by teaspoonfuls, onto a greased cookie sheet.
6. Bake 30 minutes. Cool on wire rack.
7. Split; fill with chicken or crab salad.
Or use 1 stick cream-puff mix, prepared according to package instructions. Shape and bake as above.

SPANISH OLIVES

MAKES ABOUT 30

1 can (9 oz) large green
  olives
½ cup vinegar
¼ cup salad oil

1 green chili pepper,
  chopped
1 clove garlic, minced
1 teaspoon dried oregano
  leaves

1. Put olives, with liquid from can, into large jar. Add remaining ingredients, and shake well.
2. Refrigerate several days, shaking jar occasionally. (These will keep several weeks in refrigerator.)

Finger Foods, Hot

Finger Foods, Hot. Don't plan on serving more than one or two hot appetizers unless you have someone helping you in the kitchen. The broiled appetizers should be served as soon as they have been made, piping hot. The others can be kept warm in the oven. If you have one of those handsome electric skillets, or a chafing dish, or a candle-warmer dish, you can use it to great advantage here.

CHEESE-CORN CRISPS

MAKES 4 DOZEN

1 cup yellow cornmeal
2 tablespoons butter or
    margarine
1 teaspoon salt
1 cup boiling water
½ cup grated Parmesan
    cheese
2 tablespoons grated onion
Poppy, sesame, or caraway
    seed

1. Preheat oven to 400F. Grease large cookie sheets.
2. In medium bowl, combine cornmeal, butter, and salt with boiling water.
3. Stir in cheese and onion until well combined.
4. Drop batter by ½ teaspoonfuls, 1 inch apart, onto prepared cookie sheets. With spatula, flatten each to a circle about 1½ inches in diameter.
5. Sprinkle with poppy seed. Bake 20 minutes, or until golden-brown. Partially cool on wire rack. Serve warm.
Note: Crisps can be reheated to regain crispness and flavor.

CHEESE FONDUE

MAKES ABOUT 3 CUPS

1 clove garlic, split in half
1 lb natural Swiss cheese,
    grated
Dash salt
Dash pepper
1½ to 2 cups dry white
    wine
4 tablespoons cornstarch
2 tablespoons kirsch
1 loaf French or Italian
    bread

1. For making fondue, use a rather deep baking dish with a glazed interior, flameproof-glass saucepan, or crockery utensil. *Never use a metal pan.*
2. Rub side and bottom of baking dish with garlic. Put cheese, salt, and pepper into dish; add enough wine almost to cover.
3. Cook, over medium heat and stirring constantly, just until cheese melts—no longer. Cheese and wine won't be blended yet.
4. Now make a smooth paste of cornstarch, kirsch, and about 2 tablespoons water. Using wire whip, stir cornstarch mixture into melted cheese and wine.
5. Cook, over medium heat and stirring, 2 to 3 minutes, or until fondue is as creamy and thick as medium white sauce.
6. Cut bread into 1-inch cubes.
7. To serve: Set fondue over a chafing-dish flame or candle warmer. Each bread cube should be speared with a fork and dipped into warm fondue.

27

HORSERADISH MEATBALLS

MAKES 44

2 egg yolks, or 1 whole egg
½ cup packaged dry bread
    crumbs
2 tablespoons prepared
    horseradish

1 cup water chestnuts,
    finely chopped
1 lb ground chuck

1. Preheat oven to 350F.
2. In medium bowl, beat ½ cup water with egg yolks. Stir in bread crumbs, horseradish, and water chestnuts. Add ground chuck; gently mix, with hands.
3. Shape into 1-inch balls. Place in shallow pan, and bake 12 minutes.
4. Serve with Hot Marmalade-Soy Dip.
Or bake only 10 minutes. Cool; broil on hibachi to desired doneness.

HOT MARMALADE-SOY DIP

MAKES ABOUT 1 CUP

⅓ cup orange marmalade
1 clove garlic, minced
¼ cup soy sauce

2 tablespoons lemon juice
⅓ cup water

1. Mix all ingredients; cook to boiling point.
2. Serve hot, as a dip for various meatballs.

DILL PASTRIES

MAKES ABOUT 3½ DOZEN

1 pkg (10 oz) piecrust mix
2 teaspoons dill weed

1 egg
1 teaspoon coarse salt

1. Combine piecrust mix and dill in medium bowl.
2. Combine egg and 2 tablespoons water in small bowl, beating well with fork. Gradually add egg mixture to piecrust mix, tossing with fork until pastry leaves side of bowl.
3. Divide pastry in half. On lightly floured surface, form each half into a roll about 5½ inches long and 1½ inches in diameter.
4. Wrap each roll in foil; refrigerate 2 hours.
5. Preheat oven to 400F.
6. Cut rolls into ¼-inch slices. (Or cut as many slices as you need, and refrigerate rest until ready to use.)
7. Place on ungreased cookie sheets; bake 12 to 15 minutes, or until golden. Remove from cookie sheets. Sprinkle with salt. Serve warm

CHILI MEATBALLS

MAKES 44

2 egg yolks, or 1 whole egg
½ cup packaged dry bread
    crumbs
1 cup grated Cheddar
    cheese

1½ teaspoons chili powder
2 teaspoons salt
1 lb ground chuck
Paprika

1. Preheat oven to 350F.
2. In medium bowl, beat ½ cup water with egg yolks. Stir in bread crumbs, cheese, chili powder, and salt. Add chuck; mix with hands.
3. Shape into 1-inch balls. Place in shallow pan, and bake 12 minutes.
4. For added eye appeal, sprinkle with paprika just before serving.
5. Serve with Hot! Pepper Dip.
Or bake only 10 minutes. Cool; broil on hibachi to desired doneness.

HOT! PEPPER DIP

MAKES ABOUT 2 CUPS

4 hot cherry peppers,
  minced
½ cup stuffed green olives,
  minced
½ cup pitted ripe olives,
  minced

1 cup peanut oil
3 drops liquid hot-pepper
  seasoning
½ teaspoon salt

1. Combine all ingredients. Bring to a boil; then remove from heat.
2. Serve hot, as a dip for meatballs, etc.

QUICHE TARTLETS

MAKES 43 TARTLETS, EACH 2½ TO 3 INCHES
WIDE AND ½ INCH DEEP

Pastry:
2½ cups sifted all-purpose
  flour
1½ teaspoons salt
1 cup shortening
6 to 8 tablespoons ice
  water
1 egg yolk, beaten

Filling:
16 slices bacon; or 1 cup
  sliced stuffed green
  olives; or 6 medium
  onions, sliced
1½ cups (6 oz) grated
  natural Swiss cheese
4 eggs
2 cups light cream
¾ teaspoon salt
Dash nutmeg
Dash cayenne
Dash pepper

1. Make Pastry: Sift flour and salt into a bowl. Using pastry blender or 2 knives, cut half of shortening into flour mixture until mixture looks like coarse cornmeal. Cut in remaining shortening until mixture is size of large peas.
2. Sprinkle ice water (1 tablespoon at a time) over different parts of flour mixture, mixing quickly, with a fork, after each addition; blend just until mixture holds together. Turn out on waxed paper, and press into a ball.
3. Roll out one fourth of dough at a time. Carefully fit pastry into tartlet pans.
4. Combine egg yolk and 2 tablespoons water. Before filling tartlet shells, brush with this mixture, to prevent a soggy crust.
5. Preheat oven to 400F.
6. Make Filling: For Bacon Quiche: Fry bacon until crisp. Drain on paper towels; crumble into bits. Put 1 teaspoon crumbled bacon in each pastry-lined tartlet pan.
7. For Olive Quiche: Put a few olive slices into each pastry-lined pan.
8. For Onion Quiche: Sauté sliced onions in 2 tablespoons butter or margarine until golden; drain. Put about 1 teaspoon onion into each pastry-lined tartlet pan.
9. Sprinkle 1 heaping teaspoon cheese into each tartlet. Then beat eggs. Beat in cream, salt, nutmeg, cayenne, and pepper. Pour 1 to 1½ tablespoons of this mixture over cheese in each tartlet.
10. Bake at 400F for 8 minutes; reduce heat to 350F; bake 5 to 8 minutes longer, or until filling puffs up and is golden-brown. Serve hot. *Note:* These can be baked early in the day. Do not brown completely, however. At serving time, brown at 400F for 3 to 5 minutes. Serve hot.

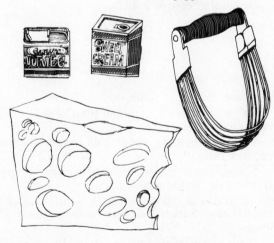

MUSTARD SPARERIBS

MAKES HORS D'OEUVRES FOR 8

2 lb spareribs
½ cup lemon juice
¼ teaspoon pepper

2 teaspoons dry mustard
2 teaspoons sugar
½ cup prepared mustard

1. Have butcher crack spareribs across middle. At home, with kitchen shears, cut spareribs into finger-length pieces.

2. In a flat pan, mix ½ cup water, lemon juice, pepper, mustard, and sugar. Marinate spareribs in this mixture at least 2 hours (turn once during marinating).

3. Drain spareribs; arrange on broiler rack. Spread ribs with mustard mixture.

4. Place rack 4 to 5 inches from heat; broil 10 minutes. Turn ribs, and broil 5 minutes.

5. Serve hot.

PIZZA SNACKS

MAKES 8

4 English muffins
3 tablespoons butter or
    margarine
¼ cup catsup
¼ lb sliced salami (16
    slices)

1 pkg (8 oz) sliced process
    American cheese
1 teaspoon dried oregano
    leaves

1. With fork, split muffins in half. Spread with butter.

2. Toast lightly under broiler; then remove.

3. Brush each with catsup; top with 2 slices salami and 1 slice of cheese, cut in half and overlapped to fit.

4. Sprinkle with oregano, and place under broiler until cheese is bubbly.

SABLÉS

MAKES 20

1 cup sifted all-purpose
    flour
½ cup soft butter or
    margarine
1 cup grated Parmesan
    cheese

1 teaspoon salt
Dash pepper
Dash cayenne
1 egg, slightly beaten

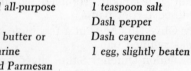

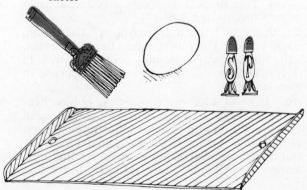

1. Preheat oven to 400F.

2. In medium bowl, combine flour and butter, using pastry blender or fork.

3. Add cheese, salt, pepper, and cayenne, mixing with fork.

4. Sprinkle mixture with 2 tablespoons water; using hands, shape into a ball.

5. On unfloured board, roll to ¼-inch thickness. Using 2-inch biscuit cutter, cut into rounds.

6. Place on ungreased cookie sheet. Brush each with beaten egg.

7. Bake 12 to 15 minutes, or until golden-brown.

8. Cool on wire rack. Serve warm or cold, as appetizer or with soup or salad.

Canapés

Canapés. A beautiful beginning for a party is a trayload of canapés. They're so good that guests will return to them often and unapologetically, so be sure you have the makings for many. Our canapé butters will help prevent sogginess; but don't make too many canapés too far ahead. At parties where you have no one to help, why not put the canapé material in bowls, provide bread, or toast—let guests spread their own?

CANAPÉ SPREADS

Use one or more of these as a spread for canapés. They are especially nice as a base for sliced ham, turkey, roast beef, tongue, tomatoes, cucumbers, or radishes. Spread on toast rounds.

Caper Butter: Combine ⅓ cup soft butter or margarine and 1½ tablespoons finely chopped bottled capers, mixing well. Makes about ⅓ cup.

Watercress Butter: Combine ⅓ cup soft butter or margarine, 3 tablespoons finely chopped watercress, 1½ teaspoons lemon juice, and ⅛ teaspoon Worcestershire sauce, mixing until well combined. Makes about ⅓ cup.

Chive Butter: Combine ⅓ cup soft butter or margarine, 2 tablespoons finely chopped chives, and 1½ teaspoons lemon juice, mixing well. Makes about ⅓ cup.

Curry Butter: Combine ⅓ cup soft butter or margarine and ½ teaspoon curry powder, mixing well. Makes ⅓ cup.

Mustard Mayonnaise: Combine 1 teaspoon prepared mustard, ⅓ cup mayonnaise or cooked salad dressing, and a dash of garlic powder, mixing well. Makes ⅓ cup.

Chili Mayonnaise: Combine 2 tablespoons chili sauce and ⅓ cup mayonnaise or cooked salad dressing, mixing well. Makes about ½ cup.

Horseradish Cream Cheese: Combine 1 package (8 oz) soft cream cheese and 2 tablespoons prepared horseradish (drained), mixing well. Makes about 1 cup.

Garlic Cream Cheese: Combine 1 package (8 oz) soft cream cheese, ¼ cup mayonnaise or cooked salad dressing, and ¼ teaspoon garlic powder, mixing well. Makes about 1 cup.

DEVILED-EGG SPREAD

MAKES ABOUT ¾ CUP

3 hard-cooked eggs
1 tablespoon onion powder
2 teaspoons soft butter or margarine
1 teaspoon lemon juice
2 tablespoons mayonnaise or cooked salad dressing
¼ teaspoon dry mustard
½ teaspoon salt
Dash cayenne

1. Press eggs through coarse sieve.
2. Combine with rest of ingredients, mixing well.

EGG-RELISH SPREAD

MAKES ABOUT ¾ CUP

3 hard-cooked eggs
1½ tablespoons sweet-pickle relish, drained
3 tablespoons mayonnaise or cooked salad dressing

1. Press eggs through coarse sieve.
2. Combine with rest of ingredients, mixing well.

BLUE-CHEESE SPREAD

MAKES 1¾ CUPS

½ lb natural blue cheese, sieved
2 pkg (3-oz size) cream cheese
¼ teaspoon Worcestershire sauce
¼ teaspoon paprika
Dash salt
Dash cayenne
3 tablespoons port

1. Let cheeses warm to room temperature.
2. Combine with remaining ingredients in large electric-mixer bowl. Beat, at high speed, until thoroughly combined and smooth.
To store: Fill small crocks; seal tops with melted paraffin. Keep refrigerated.

CHEDDAR IN SHERRY

MAKES 1¼ CUPS

2 tablespoons soft butter or margarine
1 teaspoon dry mustard
Few grains cayenne
½ lb Cheddar cheese
5 tablespoons sherry

1. Cream butter with mustard and cayenne.
2. Grate cheese very finely. Mix with sherry.
3. Add butter mixture, and blend thoroughly.

CHEESE-BOWL SPREAD

MAKES 3 CUPS

1 cup grated natural sharp Cheddar cheese
1 pkg (12 oz) pot cheese
2 tablespoons prepared horseradish
3 green onions, finely chopped
3 tablespoons mayonnaise or cooked salad dressing
2 tablespoons dairy sour cream

1. Combine all ingredients.
2. Transfer to serving bowl, and set in center of plate. Surround with small, thin pumpernickel, rye-bread slices, or salted whole-wheat crackers.

HAM-AND-SWISS-CHEESE CANAPÉS

MAKES 24

12 white-bread slices
Butter or margarine
12 thin slices boiled ham
6 thin slices process Swiss cheese
Prepared mustard

1. Spread bread lightly with butter.
2. Top each of 6 slices bread with 1 slice ham, then 1 slice cheese; spread with mustard; top with another ham slice and bread slice.
3. Refrigerate at least 1 hour.
4. To serve: Trim off crusts; cut each sandwich into 4 triangles.
5. Sauté in hot butter in skillet until golden on both sides. Serve hot.

CHEESE PÂTÉ PINEAPPLE

2 pkg (3-oz size) cream
    cheese
⅔ cup prepared mustard
2½ lb natural sharp
    Cheddar cheese,
    grated

1 jar (2 oz) small pimiento-
    stuffed olives, drained
1 fresh green pineapple
    frond

MAKES ENOUGH TO SPREAD ABOUT 180 CRACKERS

1. In large bowl of electric mixer, combine cream cheese and mustard. Beat, at medium speed, until well blended.

2. At low speed, gradually beat in grated cheese to combine well.

3. Turn mixture out onto wooden board. With hands, knead until smooth and pliable.

4. Refrigerate cheese mixture until chilled and able to be molded—about ¾ hour.

5. With hands, roll cheese mixture into a cylinder. Place on cookie sheet so that back of pineapple will rest flat against it.

6. Mold into pineapple shape, about 5½ inches long, 15 inches at widest part, 10½ inches at narrowest part.

7. Cut olives crosswise into ¼-inch-thick slices. On surface of cheese, carefully arrange olive slices in straight horizontal rows, arranging them so that vertical rows run on diagonal.

8. Using a wooden pick, make diagonal lines between rows of olive slices, ⅛ inch deep.

9. Cover with saran. Refrigerate, still on cookie sheet, until serving time (overnight, if desired).

10. To serve, with broad spatula, carefully remove cheese from cookie sheet to serving platter, standing upright on broadest end. (Flat side of cheese-pineapple becomes the back.)

11. Place pineapple frond on top. Surround with small crackers. Let stand at room temperature about 30 minutes before serving.

GOUDA CUP

1 (12 oz) Gouda cheese
3 tablespoons beer
1 teaspoon bottled steak
    sauce

Dash liquid hot-pepper
    seasoning

MAKES ¾ CUP

1. Cut a wide circle in waxy red top of cheese, and peel off cut section. Scoop out cheese, leaving red covering and ¼-inch cheese shell.

2. Refrigerate shell. Let scooped-out cheese soften at room temperature.

3. With fork, thoroughly mash cheese (or put through electric blender). Blend with remaining ingredients. Let stand 1 hour, to blend flavors.

4. Pile cheese mixture into chilled Gouda cup; shape top to look like a cone. Cover with saran or foil, and refrigerate. Flavor is improved if mixture is allowed to age a few days.

5. To serve: Let cheese cup come to room temperature. Surround with pumpernickel triangles or crackers.

FONDUE AMÉRICAINE

½ cup soft butter or
    margarine
1 small clove garlic, crushed
½ teaspoon dry mustard
12 white-bread slices, crusts
    removed
2 cups grated sharp
    Cheddar cheese
2 tablespoons grated onion

1 teaspoon salt
½ teaspoon Worcestershire
    sauce
⅛ teaspoon pepper
Dash cayenne
4 eggs
2⅓ cups milk
⅔ cup dry white wine

1. In small bowl, combine butter, garlic, and mustard; beat with wooden spoon to mix well.

2. Spread bread slices with butter mixture; cut each into thirds.

3. Line bottom and side of a 9-inch pie plate with some of bread slices, buttered side down. Reserve rest of bread.

4. In large bowl, toss cheese with onion, salt, Worcestershire sauce, pepper, and cayenne until well combined.

5. Sprinkle cheese mixture evenly over bread slices in pie plate. Cover with rest of bread, buttered side up.

6. In medium bowl, beat eggs with rotary beater. Add 1⅓ cups milk and wine; beat until well combined. Pour slowly over bread in pie plate.

7. Let stand 30 minutes. Gradually pour rest of milk over bread. Refrigerate, covered, overnight.

8. Next day, preheat oven to 350F, about 1½ hours before serving. Bake 1¼ hours, or until puffy and golden-brown on top. Let stand several minutes; then serve in small squares.

Appetizers as a First Course

Appetizers as a First Course. These make extra-special beginnings to a sit-down dinner. Serve the fruit dishes nested in individual meat-pie casseroles full of crushed ice. Serve vegetable, fish, and liver appetizers on your boldest plates (and there's no reason colorful fruit or salad plates wouldn't do just as well), with larger, contrasting plates underneath.

What to serve depends on the kind of dinner that follows. For a dinner that includes poultry, ham, or veal, a fruit cocktail is excellent. For a mild dinner, a spicier appetizer. For a light entrée, a more substantial appetizer.

CAVIAR: THE TASTE OF LUXURY

The best quality of fresh caviar is made with a minimum of salt. The word "Malossol" on a jar is not, as some may think, the name of a variety of fresh caviar; literally, it means "little salt" in Russian, or mildly salted.

What makes caviar so expensive is that it is extremely perishable and must be refrigerated with utmost care on its journey from Iran or Russia, home of the sturgeon. If the temperature goes below 28 degrees, it will freeze and be ruined; above 32 degrees, it spoils.

BELUGA, a gray caviar, largest grained, is the costliest food in the world—$40 a pound.

OSETRA, a smaller caviar, is lower in price.

SEVRUGA, prized by experts, is the smallest. PRESSED CAVIAR, lowest priced and popular with many connoisseurs, is made of small eggs of Beluga that drop out during grading and are pressed into a mass, thick as marmalade.

RED CAVIAR, made from salmon roe, is not a "true" caviar, like sturgeon caviar; but it is appetizing, delicious, and modestly priced. Caviar of whatever variety should be served well chilled, in a well-chilled crystal or china dish in a bed of finely chopped ice. A tablespoonful, or two generous teaspoonfuls, of caviar would make one good average serving.

Purists eat it without any embellishments—just slices of dark bread and sweet butter. Other caviar lovers may add trimmings, like a sprinkling of hard-cooked eggs, the yolks and whites chopped separately; sour cream; chopped onion; warm toast, crisp crackers. Top jellied madrilène with a dab of caviar. Mix pressed caviar with softened cream cheese, and serve on buttered toast fingers. Mold a six-inch ball of cream cheese, and spread with pressed caviar. Cut in wedges. Mix a dollop of caviar with salad dressing. Try caviar on plain omelets or egg salad.

Make a "jelly roll" of caviar on long, thin slices of bread, rolled up and cut crosswise. Traditionally, chilled dry champagne or ice-cold vodka is served with any caviar.

AVOCADO COCKTAIL

MAKES 6 SERVINGS

2 large ripe avocados (about 1½ lb)
½ cup catsup
¾ to 1 teaspoon prepared horseradish
1 teaspoon Worcestershire sauce
2 tablespoons lemon juice
¼ teaspoon salt
Dash liquid hot-pepper seasoning

1. Cut avocados in half lengthwise; remove pits, and peel. Cut into cubes; measure 3 cups.
2. Spoon ½ cup avocado cubes into each of 6 sherbet glasses.
3. Combine remaining ingredients in small bowl; stir to mix well.
4. Spoon evenly over avocado; refrigerate until well chilled—at least ½ hour.

CANTALOUPE COCKTAIL

MAKES 8 SERVINGS

1 can (6 oz) frozen lemon-and-lime concentrate, thawed
4 cups cantaloupe balls
8 mint sprigs

1. Combine concentrate with 1 can cold water; mix well. Refrigerate until well chilled—about 1 hour.
2. Divide melon balls into 8 cocktail glasses.
3. Pour on lemon-and-lime. Garnish with mint.

STRAWBERRY-MELON CUP

MAKES 6 SERVINGS

4 cups cantaloupe or Persian-melon balls
2 cups sliced fresh strawberries
2 tablespoons sugar
¼ cup sherry
6 mint sprigs

1. Combine all ingredients, except mint, in medium bowl. Refrigerate, covered, until thoroughly chilled, stirring once.
2. Spoon into 6 dessert dishes. Garnish with mint sprigs.

PROSCIUTTO AND MELON

MAKES 6 SERVINGS (2 WEDGES PER PERSON)

¼ lb sliced prosciutto
  (Italian ham)

1 (2½-lb) honeydew melon
1 lemon
1 lime

1. Cut prosciutto into 1-inch strips.
2. Cut melon in half; scoop out seeds and fibers. Cut half into six wedges; remove rind.
3. Roll each melon wedge in strip of ham. Serve garnished with lemon and lime wedges.

WINTER PEARS IN WINE

MAKES 6 SERVINGS

2 cups sugar
1 cup rosé wine

⅛ teaspoon red food color
6 medium pears

1. Combine sugar, wine, food color, and 2 cups water in large saucepan; heat, stirring, until sugar is dissolved.
2. Pare pears, leaving stems on.
3. Add to sugar syrup; bring to boiling. Reduce heat; simmer, covered, 30 to 45 minutes, or until pears are tender when pierced with fork.
4. Serve, warm or cold, in wine syrup.

ANTIPASTO SALAD PLATTER

MAKES 8 SERVINGS

4 medium tomatoes, sliced
Bottled Italian-style
  dressing
Crisp lettuce leaves
½ lb domestic Bel Paese
  cheese, sliced

2 cans (2-oz size) anchovy
  fillets, drained
1 can (8 oz) pitted ripe
  olives, drained
1 bottle (4½ oz) artichoke
  hearts in olive oil,
  drained

1. Sprinkle tomato slices lightly with dressing; refrigerate until well chilled—about 1 hour.
2. Then, on lettuce leaves on large platter, place tomato slices and rest of ingredients, in individual mounds. Guests make their own selection.

PICKLED MUSHROOMS

MAKES 6 SERVINGS

1 tablespoon salt
1 lb fresh button
  mushrooms
½ cup chopped onion
1 clove garlic, finely
  chopped
¼ cup chopped parsley
2 bay leaves

⅛ teaspoon pepper
½ teaspoon dried thyme
  leaves
2 cups white wine
2 cups white vinegar
½ cup olive or salad oil
2 tablespoons lemon juice

1. Add salt to 6 cups cold water. Wash mushrooms in this; drain.
2. Combine remaining ingredients in large saucepan. Add mushrooms; bring to boiling point.
3. Then reduce heat, and simmer, covered, 8 to 10 minutes, or until mushrooms are tender. Cool.
4. Refrigerate, covered, at least 1 hour, or until ready to use.

MARINATED ARTICHOKE HEARTS

3 tablespoons lemon juice
⅓ cup salad oil
3 tablespoons vinegar
3 tablespoons olive oil
2 teaspoons salt

Dash pepper
½ teaspoon sugar
1 clove garlic
1 can (15 oz) artichoke
    hearts, drained

1. In a jar, combine all ingredients except artichoke hearts. Shake well.

2. Pour over artichoke hearts. Marinate at least 3 hours.

3. To serve: Drain, and then serve on greens or spear on wooden picks.

LIVER PÂTÉ

1 lb liverwurst
⅛ teaspoon dried thyme
    leaves
1 tablespoon
    Worcestershire sauce
⅛ teaspoon mace

1 teaspoon cloves
1½ tablespoons sherry
1 tablespoon grated onion
¼ teaspoon pepper
¼ cup soft butter or
    margarine

1. Peel casing from liverwurst. In medium bowl, mash meat with fork until smooth.

2. Add remaining ingredients, except butter; mix well.

3. Blend in butter until well combined.

4. Cover tightly; refrigerate until ready to use.

CHICKEN-LIVER PÂTÉ

2 tablespoons butter or
    margarine
½ lb chicken livers
2 eggs, hard-cooked
2 pkg (3-oz size) cream
    cheese

1 tablespoon finely chopped
    parsley
¾ teaspoon salt
⅛ teaspoon pepper
1 tablespoon cognac

1. Heat butter in medium skillet. Add chicken livers; cook, stirring occasionally, over medium heat, 10 minutes, or until tender. Drain.

2. Mix livers and eggs through food grinder (or put in blender, a little at a time; blend, covered, at high speed).

3. With wooden spoon, work cream cheese until light and fluffy.

4. Mix cheese into liver mixture along with remaining ingredients. Serve with hot toast or crackers.

HERRING IN DILL SAUCE

1 cup prepared mustard
1 cup olive oil
¼ cup vinegar
3 tablespoons lemon juice
½ cup chopped fresh dill
1 teaspoon pepper

1½ teaspoons salt
1½ teaspoons whole
    allspice
2 tablespoons sugar
8 salt-herring fillets
Fresh dill sprigs

1. Combine mustard and oil in small bowl; beat, with rotary beater, until as thick as mayonnaise.

2. Gradually beat in vinegar and lemon juice, then dill, pepper, salt, allspice, and sugar.

3. Rinse herring; drain well on paper towels. Place in large glass bowl; cover with sauce.

4. Refrigerate, covered, at least 3 days.

5. Garnish with dill sprigs, and serve as first course.

HERRING IN SOUR CREAM

2 cans (6-oz size) matjes-
herring fillets, or 3
matjes-herring fillets
1 medium onion

24 whole black peppers
2 bay leaves
¾ cup dairy sour cream
¼ cup sauterne

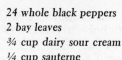

1. Rinse fillets in cold water; drain; dry on paper towels. Cut crosswise into 1-inch pieces. Then slice onion into thin rings.

2. In medium bowl, layer onion rings, black peppers, bay leaves, herring pieces.

3. Combine sour cream, wine. Pour over herring mixture, mixing gently to combine.

4. Refrigerate, covered, 8 hours, or overnight. *Note:* Herring in Sour Cream may be stored, covered, in refrigerator 3 days.

PICKLED HERRING

2 (1-lb) salt herring
¾ teaspoon allspice
2 bay leaves
½ teaspoon ginger
½ teaspoon mustard seed

1 teaspoon prepared
horseradish
2 cups sliced sweet red
onion
1 cup white vinegar
½ cup sugar

1. Cut off herring heads, and clean herring.

2. Refrigerate in cold water, covered, overnight.

3. Next day, drain. Remove all bones; then cut herring crosswise into ½-inch slices.

4. In medium saucepan, combine ⅓ cup water and all ingredients except herring. Cook, stirring, over low heat until sugar is dissolved. Bring to boiling point; boil, covered, 5 minutes. Let cool to room temperature.

5. In 1-quart jar, alternately layer herring pieces and pickling mixture, so herring and onion slices are well distributed.

6. Refrigerate, covered, at least 3 days.

7. Serve herring along with pickling mixture.

OYSTERS ROCKEFELLER

Rock salt
¾ cup butter
or margarine
¼ cup finely chopped
onion
¼ cup finely chopped
celery
¼ cup finely chopped
parsley
¼ clove garlic, finely
chopped
½ cup packaged dry bread
crumbs

½ cup finely chopped
watercress, packed
½ cup finely chopped
raw spinach,
packed
Pinch anise
¼ teaspoon salt
⅛ teaspoon liquid-hot-
pepper seasoning
2 dozen oysters on the half
shell

1. Preheat oven to 450F.

2. Into each of 6 (8-inch) pie plates place a layer of rock salt, ½ inch deep; set aside.

3. In medium skillet, in ¼ cup hot butter or margarine, sauté onion, celery, parsley, and garlic until onion is golden—about 5 minutes.

4. Add rest of butter and crumbs; stir, over medium heat, until butter melts.

5. Add watercress, spinach, anise, salt, and hot-pepper seasoning; cook, stirring, 1 minute.

6. Pour off liquid from oysters. Spread each oyster with 1 tablespoon vegetable mixture, covering each oyster completely.

7. Sprinkle rock salt lightly with water, to dampen. Arrange 4 oysters in each pie plate.

8. Bake, uncovered, 10 minutes. Serve oysters hot, right in pie plate.

Beverages

E ver stop to think that it's always beverage time, always beverage weather? Morning, noon, night, and the hours in between; summer, winter; surrounded by family, entertaining friends, or relaxing alone.

You can be as festive, as ceremonial, as casual as you please with beverages. Here come the beverages, one and all, for one and all.

Coffee

Coffee's not only the key to a pleasant way to start the day or end it, not only a quick, gratifying pick-me-up on a busy morning or a warm greeting when friends meet—in short, it's not only a marvelous beverage, but a fascinating flavor, unlike any other flavor in the world.

What's the key to a really satisfying cup of coffee, one that's full-bodied and just plain good? The secret of perfect coffee (no matter which method you use: drip, vacuum, percolator, espresso) is as simple as this: Fresh coffee, exactly measured; fresh water; a thoroughly clean coffee maker; immediate service. Directly after your coffee is brewed, throw away the grounds. After you open your vacuum can or paper bag of coffee, best use it up within a week. If coffee has

gone stale, don't use it. The right-size coffee maker is important: If you're a two-cup family, use a small coffee maker, and save the large one for company.

Best way to measure your coffee is to use a standard measuring scoop or its equivalent.

Two level tablespoonfuls of coffee to three quarters of a standard liquid measuring cup (*not a coffee cup*) of water. Concerning grinds: A drip grind is good, unless the coffee maker specifies differently. Brew it just under the boiling point, but never let your coffee boil.

In the coffee shops that have sprung up all over the country, you will see more kinds of coffee than you ever thought existed. If their names baffle you, here's what a few of them mean:

Cappuccino is a beverage composed of equal parts of steaming coffee and steaming milk, poured into a cup, sugared, and sprinkled with nutmeg. Good!

Viennese coffee is always topped with whipped cream; sometimes it's spiced.

Caffè Espresso is pressurized with steam. There are small, simple espresso makers for home use.

Turkish coffee is a sweet, heavy brew of pulverized coffee.

American, French, Italian describe the kind of roast. Italian coffee is roasted longest.

COFFEE MADE IN A PERCOLATOR

MAKES 8 SERVINGS

6 cups fresh cold water   *1 cup percolator or drip-grind coffee*

1. Fill bottom section of an 8-cup percolator with water.

2. Measure the coffee into basket, placed on stem. Insert stem in pot.

3. Over medium heat, percolate coffee 10 minutes, timing from point when liquid first shows color.

4. Immediately remove basket with coffee grounds; replace cover.

5. If coffee is not served at once, keep hot over very low heat; do not let it boil.

COFFEE MADE IN A DRIP COFFEEPOT

MAKES 8 SERVINGS

1 cup drip-grind coffee   *6 cups boiling water*

1. Assemble an 8-cup drip coffeepot: Put coffee section in place. (If using filter paper, insert before putting in coffee.) Measure coffee into coffee section. Place water section on top of coffee section.

2. Pour boiling water into water section. Cover; let stand until all water has dripped through coffee.

3. Detach water and coffee sections; discard grounds; replace cover.

4. If coffee is not served at once, keep hot over very low heat; do not let it boil.

CAFFÈ ESPRESSO

Use dark-roast Italian coffee, fine grind, with fresh cold water in a special caffè-espresso pot. Follow manufacturer's directions. Serve hot in demitasse cups, with a twist of lemon peel in each, if desired.

COFFEE MADE IN A VACUUM-TYPE COFFEE MAKER

6 cups fresh cold water   1 cup silex or drip-grind
coffee

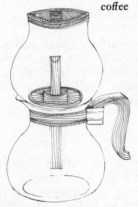

MAKES 8 SERVINGS

1. Fill lower bowl of an 8-cup vacuum-type coffee maker with water.
2. Attach upper bowl securely to lower bowl, adjusting filter. Measure coffee into upper bowl; cover.
3. Over medium heat, bring water to boiling (most of water will rise to upper bowl). Stir several times; let stand over heat about 2 minutes.
4. Remove from heat; let coffee return to lower bowl. Immediately detach upper bowl with coffee grounds. Cover coffee.
5. If coffee is not served at once, keep hot over very low heat; do not let it boil.

CAMPFIRE COFFEE

1 cup coffee (coarse grind)   1 egg, slightly beaten

MAKES 8 CUPS

1. Bring 2 quarts fresh cold water to a full, rolling boil.
2. Meanwhile, combine coffee and egg, mixing well; turn into double thickness of cheesecloth that has been dampened with water. (Cheesecloth should be large enough so coffee will only half fill it.)
3. Tie cheesecloth with strong cord, to form a sack (cord should be long enough to fasten to handle of pan).
4. Submerge sack of coffee in boiling water, tying securely to handle of pan.
5. Let simmer 10 minutes, pushing sack up and down in water several times.
6. Lift sack; let drain over pan; then discard. Serve coffee hot.

ORANGE-SPICE COFFEE

1 tablespoon sugar
6 whole cloves
2 (1½-inch) cinnamon
    sticks

Peel of 1 small orange
1½ cups hot strong coffee

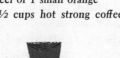

MAKES 6 SERVINGS

1. In small saucepan, combine sugar, cloves, cinnamon, and peel with ½ cup hot water; heat for 5 minutes.
2. Strain mixture into medium bowl, discarding spices and orange peel.
3. Stir hot coffee into spice liquid; let stand about 1 minute.
4. Strain coffee into demitasse cups.

SPICED COFFEE CREAM

½ cup evaporated milk,
    undiluted
¼ teaspoon vanilla extract
1½ tablespoons
    confectioners' sugar

½ teaspoon cinnamon
2 cups hot coffee
Nutmeg

1. In ice-cube tray, freeze evaporated milk just until ice crystals form ½ inch from edge of tray.
2. Turn into small bowl along with vanilla, sugar, and cinnamon.
3. With portable electric mixer, at medium speed, beat until thick and fluffy.
4. Fill 6 demitasse cups one fourth full. Fill each with coffee (milk will rise to top). Sprinkle with nutmeg.

COFFEE FOR A CROWD

2 gallons plus ½ cup fresh
    cold water
Cheesecloth*

1 lb regular-grind coffee
3 eggs, slightly beaten
3 eggshells, crushed

1. In large kettle, bring 2 gallons water to full, rolling boil.
2. Meanwhile, soak cheesecloth (or sugar sack large enough so coffee will only half fill it); rinse well.
3. In medium bowl, combine coffee, eggs, shells, and ½ cup cold water; mix well. (Eggs and shells will clarify coffee.)
4. Put coffee mixture into sack; tie with strong cord long enough to fasten to handle of kettle.
5. When water has boiled, reduce heat to just below boiling point. Tie sack to kettle handle; submerge.
6. Over low heat, brew coffee 10 minutes, pushing sack up and down in water several times.
7. Remove sack, letting all liquid drain into kettle. Keep coffee hot.
* Cheesecloth should be 1 yard wide and 2 yards long; fold it to make double thickness 1 yard square.

Tea

When you consider what the earliest American settlers did with tea, it is a great wonder that it ever became the popular beverage it is today.

There are many ways to make teatime in your home an occasion of style and enchantment, high in inventiveness, but low in actual cost.

Serve tea in an Oriental mood, with the bright drama of unusual colors . . . unusual accessories . . . the incense of green tea rising from a red lacquer pot . . . somewhere, close at hand, a bowl of litchi nuts in their fabulous shells . . . the sparkle of crystallized ginger.

The friendly tea, iced, served in amber

glasses with golden brioche, ready to melt a spread of sweet butter; pottery plates, green as all outdoors; flowers from your own garden; a time for welcoming new neighbors or old friends.

HOW TO BREW A CUP OF TEA

It might be well to point out the way to make a good cup of tea. You must, of course, have freshly boiled water. The teapot itself should be heated with boiling water before you make the tea. Allow one teaspoonful of tea (or 1 tea bag) per person and one for the pot. Add the briskly boiling water, and let the tea steep 3 or 4 minutes. To make tea in a cup, simply place a tea bag in the cup, and pour on boiling water. Let steep until color is right. In these modern days, many people are discovering how simple it is to make perfectly delicious tea with instant tea. Measure 1 level teaspoonful into a cup; add the briskly boiling water.

Because China tea is so delicate, it is served without milk. This is also true of the teas flavored with spices. With other teas, you may or may not add milk—as you prefer. Many people like their tea with a slice of lemon, sometimes stuck with cloves. Others add a dash of rum. Whatever you do, it's most important that freshly made tea be served while it is piping hot.

ICED TEA

MAKES 3 CUPS—
3 OR 4 SERVINGS

¼ cup tea leaves   *Crushed ice or ice cubes*
3 cups cold water

1. Combine tea leaves and water in a glass pitcher; refrigerate, covered, at least 12 hours.
2. Strain. Serve over ice.
Note: Or dissolve 3 to 4 teaspoons instant tea in 3 cups cold water.

HOT TEA FOR 50

MAKES ABOUT 50 CUPS

1½ qt cold water   ¼ lb tea leaves

1. Concentrate: In teakettle, bring 1½ quarts fresh cold water to full, rolling boil. Remove from heat.
2. Add loose tea leaves; stir to immerse leaves. Cover.
3. Let stand 5 minutes. Strain into teapot. Makes about 1 quart.
4. To serve: Have ready a large pot of very hot water. Pour 1 to 2 tablespoons concentrate into teacup. Fill cup with hot water. By varying amount of concentrate, you can vary tea strength.

ORANGE ICED TEA

3 oranges, washed   2 cups tea, chilled
¼ cup sugar   Ice cubes
½ cup boiling water   3 fresh mint sprigs

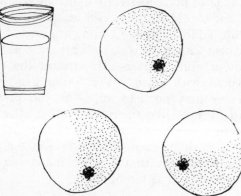

1. With sharp knife, cut peel from 1 orange in a continuous spiral. Cut spiral into 3 long, narrow strips; set aside.
2. Slice peeled orange and 2 unpeeled oranges into large bowl. Add sugar; crush with potato masher until sugar is dissolved.
3. Add water; crush slices again. Let steep 15 minutes.
4. Strain orange syrup. Combine with tea.
5. Fill 3 tall glasses with ice cubes. Add orange tea.
6. Twist long orange-peel strips around 3 straws; insert in glasses. Garnish each glass with mint sprig.

SPICED ICED TEA

6 whole cloves   2 teaspoons lemon juice
8 whole allspice   1¾ cups tea, chilled
½ cup sugar   Ice cubes
1¼ cups orange juice,
    chilled

1. In medium saucepan, combine spices and sugar with 1¼ cups water; bring to boiling. Reduce heat; simmer for 20 minutes.
2. Let cool; then strain.
3. Add the juices and tea. Serve over ice cubes in 4 tall glasses.

Hot Chocolate

All the young people and the old ones and, in fact, everybody who loves the taste of chocolate can thank Cortez. When he returned to Spain from his explorations of Mexico, he took with him the secret of a new beverage, which the natives of the New World called "chocolatl." The new flavor found great favor among Europeans, and the use of chocolate spread rapidly. It is well to understand the use of the various terms:

Cacao is used in the trade to refer to the raw beans.

Chocolate is the manufactured product when it appears in solidified form, such as bars.

Cocoa is the pulverized bean, from which part of the cocoa butter has been removed, and is a soft, brown powder.

Chocolate drinks are good, nutritious, quick.

OLD-FASHIONED HOT CHOCOLATE

2 squares unsweetened
   chocolate
3 tablespoons sugar

Dash salt
3 cups milk
Whipped cream (optional)

1. In saucepan, over very low heat, melt chocolate in 1 cup water, stirring constantly until blended.
2. Stir in sugar and salt; bring to boiling, stirring. Reduce heat, and simmer 3 minutes.
3. Gradually add milk; heat thoroughly.
4. Just before serving, beat with rotary beater. Serve at once, topped with whipped cream, if desired.

For Mocha Chocolate: Substitute 1 cup strong coffee for 1 cup water.

For Orange Chocolate: Mix 1 tablespoon grated orange rind with sugar.

For Mint Chocolate: Add ¼ teaspoon peppermint extract just before serving.

SPICED COCOA

1½ cups sweetened cocoa
½ teaspoon cinnamon
¼ teaspoon nutmeg
2 tablespoons sugar

2 cups boiling water
3 cups milk
8 marshmallows

1. Combine cocoa, cinnamon, nutmeg, and sugar in large saucepan. Gradually stir in water, then milk.
2. Heat carefully, stirring often; be careful not to scorch.
3. Serve the cocoa hot, topped with marshmallows.

COCOA SYRUP

½ cup sifted unsweetened
   cocoa
1 cup sugar

⅛ teaspoon salt
1 cup boiling water
1 teaspoon vanilla extract

1. In medium saucepan, combine cocoa with sugar and salt. Gradually add water, stirring until smooth.
2. Cook, stirring, over medium heat, until mixture reaches boiling point. Boil, without stirring, for 1 minute.
3. Let mixture cool. Stir in vanilla.
4. Refrigerate, covered, until ready to use.

HOT COCOA IN A HURRY

MAKES 1 SERVING

1 cup milk 2 tablespoons Cocoa Syrup

1. In small saucepan, heat milk until bubbles form around edge.
2. Add Cocoa Syrup, stirring until well combined.
3. To serve: Pour into mug; top with marshmallow or whipped cream.

Hot Mocha Cocoa: To HOT COCOA IN A HURRY, add ½ teaspoon instant coffee.

ICED COCOA

1 cup milk 2 tablespoons Cocoa Syrup

1. In small bowl, with rotary beater, beat cold milk with Cocoa Syrup, until well combined. If desired, add 1 tablespoon crème de cacao.
2. To serve, pour over ice in a tall glass.

Fruit Drinks and Carbonated Drinks

What can we say about icy-cold beverages in tall, dewed glasses with, perhaps, a bit of fruit here and there? Beverages like these on a steaming-hot day are the very essence of refreshment.

There are many interesting variations and combinations that use canned and packaged fruits, fruit juices, nectars, and ready-mixed juices. Iced drinks, we think, look best in high glasses. Exception, punch. Whether hot or cold, punch is most properly served from a punch bowl into small cups with handles.

Fancy ice cubes give a lovely party touch, and they are very easy. Before freezing them, add a little green or red food color. Or add curls of lemon or orange peel; whole maraschino cherries with their stems; thin slices of orange, lemon, lime. It's best to use freshly boiled water if you want clear cubes. If you don't want to run the risk of diluting your beverage, why not use leftover fruit drinks, and freeze them in the ice-cube trays? Or freeze canned unsweetened pineapple juice or reconstituted pineapple juice, or other fruit beverages.

Store canned juice in a cool, dry spot. Keep unopened frozen juices in the freezer.

BANANA COOLER

MAKES 2 SERVINGS

4 ice cubes, broken
Juice of 1 lime
2 teaspoons confectioners'
 sugar

5 tablespoons white rum, or
 5 tablespoons
 pineapple juice
1 ripe medium banana, cut
 into chunks

1. In electric blender, combine half the ice, the lime juice, sugar, white rum or pineapple juice, and banana.
2. Blend, with cover on, at high speed 1 minute, or until smooth.
3. Add remaining ice; blend 1 minute more. Serve in stem glasses.

FRESH LEMONADE

3 lemons
¾ cup sugar
Ice cubes

Maraschino cherries with
    stems, drained

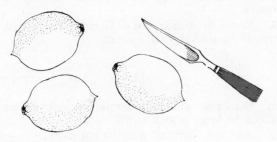

1. With a sharp knife, very thinly slice lemons crosswise. Discard end slices and seeds.
2. Put lemon slices into a large bowl or sturdy pitcher. Add the sugar.
3. With a wooden spoon or potato masher, pound until the sugar is dissolved and slices are broken.
4. Add 1 tray of ice cubes and 2 cups cold water. Stir until very cold.
5. To serve: Pour lemonade, along with lemon slices, into glasses. Garnish each glass with a cherry.

FRUIT COOLER

1⅓ cups tea, chilled
3 tablespoons sugar
¼ cup lemon juice
⅔ cup orange juice, chilled

1 can (12 oz) apricot nectar,
    chilled
1 bottle (7 oz) ginger ale,
    chilled
Ice cubes
6 fresh mint sprigs

1. In a 1-quart pitcher, combine tea, sugar, juices, and nectar; stir to mix well.
2. Gradually add ginger ale. Serve over ice in tall glasses, each garnished with mint sprig.

LEMON-AND-LIME MIST

½ cup lemon juice
¼ cup lime juice
⅔ cup granulated sugar

1¼ cups chilled club soda
½ cup chopped ice
Tropical flowers

1. In electric blender, combine juices, sugar, soda, and ice; blend at high speed, covered, ½ minute.
2. Pour into chilled glasses; garnish each with flower.
Daiquiris: Reduce sugar to ¼ cup. Omit soda; add 1¼ cups white rum to fruit juices before blending. MAKES 8 (3-OZ) SERVINGS

MULLED PINEAPPLE JUICE

1 can (46 oz) unsweetened
    pineapple juice
1 (2-inch) stick cinnamon

⅛ teaspoon nutmeg
⅛ teaspoon allspice
Dash ground cloves

1. Combine all ingredients in medium saucepan; bring to boiling.
2. Cover; reduce heat, and simmer 30 minutes to blend flavors. Serve warm.

SHERRY COBBLER

1 can (6 oz) frozen orange-
    juice concentrate
¼ cup sugar

1 cup dry sherry
Ice cubes

1. Dilute orange juice as label directs.
2. Add sugar and sherry, mixing well. Pour over ice cubes in tall glasses.

AUTUMN GOLD PUNCH

2 cans (12-oz size) apricot
    nectar
1½ cups orange juice
¾ cup lemon juice

1½ quarts sweet cider
20 maraschino cherries
    (optional)

1. In large pitcher, combine nectar, orange and lemon juices, and cider.
2. Refrigerate until well chilled—at least 2 hours.
3. Serve in punch cups. Garnish each with maraschino cherry, if desired.

PINK PARTY PUNCH

4 cans (6-oz size) raspberry-
    lemon-punch
    concentrate, partially
    thawed
1½ qt club soda, chilled

2 bottles (1-pt, 8-oz size)
    rosé wine, chilled
1 cup cognac
1 lemon, thinly sliced

1. Combine all ingredients, except lemon slices, in large punch bowl.
2. Add ice. Garnish with lemon slices.

CHRISTMAS PUNCH

1 orange
About 12 whole cloves
2 bottles (⅘-qt size) claret
1 lemon, sliced
1 (1½-inch) cinnamon stick

½ cup blanched whole
    almonds
½ cup dark raisins
½ cup sugar
½ cup cognac or brandy

1. Preheat oven to 400F.
2. Wash orange; with sharp knife, score skin into diamond pattern. Stud each diamond with a clove.
3. Place in shallow baking pan; bake, uncovered, 30 minutes.
4. Meanwhile, in large saucepan, combine claret, lemon slices, cinnamon stick, almonds, raisins, and ¼ cup sugar.
5. Add baked orange; over low heat, bring to simmering. Simmer, uncovered, 15 to 20 minutes, stirring occasionally.
6. Remove cinnamon stick. Pour punch into punch bowl.
7. Combine rest of sugar and the cognac in small saucepan; heat very gently.
8. Light with match; while it is flaming, pour into punch bowl.

FESTIVE WINE PUNCH

2½ cups orange juice
1 cup unsweetened
    pineapple juice
½ cup sifted confectioners'
    sugar
2 tablespoons grated lemon
    peel

1 qt dry white wine or
    champagne
1 tablespoon honey
6 whole cloves
½ teaspoon cinnamon
½ teaspoon nutmeg
2 trays ice cubes
1½ qt ginger ale, chilled

1. In large bowl, combine all ingredients, except ice cubes and ginger ale, with 2 cups cold water.
2. Refrigerate, covered, at least 3 hours.
3. To serve: Strain punch mixture over ice cubes in punch bowl. Stir in ginger ale.

FRUIT PUNCH NOËL

4 cups apple cider	1 lemon
2 cups bottled cranberry juice	36 whole cloves
	10 sugar lumps (optional)
1 cup orange juice	1 teaspoon cinnamon
1 can (12 oz) apricot nectar	(optional)

1. In a large saucepan, combine cider, cranberry juice, orange juice, and apricot nectar.
2. Wash lemon; cut thinly into 12 slices. Insert 3 cloves in each slice; add to fruit juices.
3. Over very low heat, bring just to simmer—15 to 20 minutes. Pour into punch bowl.
4. In small bowl, toss sugar lumps with cinnamon. Drop a sugar lump into each punch cup.

SHERRY PUNCH BOWL

2 cans (6-oz size) frozen lemonade concentrate	⅓ cup lemon juice
	1 qt dry sherry

1. Dilute lemonade as label directs.
2. Combine all ingredients in large bowl; cover, and refrigerate. This punch may be stored several days before serving.

GOLDEN PUNCH

2 bottles (⅘-qt size) champagne	¼ cup Cointreau
	¼ cup light corn syrup
1 bottle (⅘ qt) sauterne	1 cup sliced hulled strawberries
1 qt club soda	
2 trays ice cubes	Mint sprigs
¼ cup brandy	

1. Refrigerate champagne, sauterne, and soda until well chilled.
2. Put ice cubes into large punch bowl.
3. Combine brandy, Cointreau, and corn syrup, mixing well; pour over ice.
4. Add champagne, sauterne, and soda; mix well.
5. Garnish with strawberries and mint sprigs.

PLANTER'S PUNCH

1 cup lime juice	8 dashes angostura bitters
1 cup orange juice	1 tray ice cubes
1 cup granulated sugar	Orange and lime slices
1 jar (8 oz) maraschino cherries	

1. In blender or drink shaker, combine lime juice, orange juice, sugar, 1½ teaspoons maraschino-cherry juice, and bitters.
2. Blend, at low speed—or shake—1 minute.
3. Pour over ice cubes in pitcher; stir well. Let stand 10 minutes.
4. Strain into chilled glasses or small ceramic coconut shells. Garnish each with cherry, orange and lime slice speared on fancy pick.

Note: Or add 1 cup dark rum to fruit juices before blending.

ORANGE-CRANBERRY PUNCH

MAKES 3 OR 4 SERVINGS

1 bottle (1 pt) cranberry
   juice, chilled
½ pint soft orange sherbet

Few drops red food color
   (optional)
2 to 3 tablespoons sugar
1 bottle (7 oz) ginger ale,
   chilled

1. Combine cranberry juice and ¾ cup sherbet in large bowl; beat with rotary beater or spoon until sherbet is melted.

2. Add food color, sugar to taste, and ginger ale; stir to mix well.

3. Spoon rest of sherbet into 3 or 4 tall glasses. Pour punch over sherbet. Serve at once.

SPICED CIDER

MAKES 8 SERVINGS

1 qt cider
¼ cup sugar
Dash salt

12 whole cloves
2 (4-inch) cinnamon sticks
8 whole allspice

1. Combine all ingredients in 2-quart saucepan. Bring to boil, stirring, until sugar is dissolved.

2. Cool; refrigerate, covered, several hours.

3. Just before serving, reheat slowly. Strain to remove spices. Serve hot, in mugs or punch cups, along with cookies.

VIRGINIA SYLLABUB

MAKES 16 (4-OZ) SERVINGS

1 cup sherry or Madeira
1 cup sugar
1 qt heavy cream

2 tablespoons lemon juice
2 teaspoons grated lemon
   peel

1. In punch bowl, combine sherry with sugar, stirring until sugar dissolves.

2. In large bowl, whip cream just until soft peaks form. Add lemon juice and lemon peel.

3. Gradually stir whipped cream into sherry mixture. Serve at once.

Milk Shakes and Floats

These can be enjoyed by anyone, but mostly, we think, by the small fry. In fact, they may enjoy making some of these drinks themselves, in the family blender.

ICE-CREAM MILK SHAKES

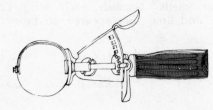

Peanut-Butter: In electric blender,* blend at high speed, for 1 minute, 1 cup milk and 2 tablespoons creamy peanut butter. Add 2 No. 16 (or medium) scoops vanilla ice cream; then blend 1 minute longer. This makes 2 cups.

*All milk shakes can be made using a rotary beater or a portable electric mixer and 1-quart measure or medium bowl.

Strawberry: Substitute 2 tablespoons strawberry jam for peanut butter.

Raspberry: Substitute 2 tablespoons raspberry jam for peanut butter.

Pineapple: Substitute 3 tablespoons drained, canned crushed pineapple for peanut butter.

Chocolate: Substitute 1 tablespoon canned chocolate syrup for peanut butter.

Banana: Substitute ½ medium-size ripe banana, cut in small pieces, for peanut butter.

Gingersnap: Omit peanut butter. Break 6 gingersnaps into pieces. Add milk, and let soak a few minutes, until soft. Add ice cream, and continue as directed above.

MAPLE MILK SHAKE

MAKES 4 SERVINGS

2 cups milk
½ cup maple syrup
1 pint soft vanilla ice cream

1. In large bowl, with rotary beater, beat all ingredients until well combined.
2. Serve at once in glasses.

MOCHA FROSTED

MAKES 3 OR 4 SERVINGS

2 cups strong coffee,*
    chilled
¾ cup chocolate milk
1½ cups soft coffee ice
    cream

1. Combine coffee, milk, and 1 cup ice cream in medium bowl; beat with rotary beater just until smooth.
2. Pour into 3 or 4 tall glasses. Top with rest of ice cream.
* Use 2 tablespoons instant coffee, dissolved in 2 cups boiling water.

LEMON-ORANGE COOLER

MAKES 4 SERVINGS

⅓ cup frozen orange-juice
    concentrate, thawed
    and undiluted
3 tablespoons honey
¾ cup crushed ice
2 cups milk
½ cup lemon sherbet

1. Combine orange concentrate and honey in 1-quart measure; stir until well mixed.
2. Add ice and milk; mix well.
3. Spoon sherbet into 4 tall glasses; fill with orange mixture. Serve at once.

FROSTED STRAWBERRY FLOAT

MAKES 4 SERVINGS

½ pint box fresh
    strawberries
¼ cup sugar
3 cups milk, chilled
½ pint strawberry ice
    cream

1. Gently wash berries in cold water. Drain, and hull.
2. Crush, with a potato masher, in medium bowl. Stir in sugar.
3. Gradually add milk, beating with rotary beater. Spoon in ice cream; stir until it starts to melt. Serve in tall glasses.

Sodas

These are enjoyed by anybody old enough to send a tall spoon down into a tall glass to raise a dollop of something ice-cold and creamy. Of course, you must know that we are speaking of ice-cream sodas. Exception: Some of them use sherbets, instead.

SODA SUGGESTIONS

MAKES 1 SERVING

CHOCOLATE-MINT SODA

In a large glass, combine ⅔ cup milk, 1 tablespoon canned chocolate syrup, few drops peppermint extract; stir well, with a long spoon. Add 2 scoops vanilla ice cream. Fill to top with ginger ale; stir well. Top with 2 tablespoons whipped cream. Streak with 1 teaspoon chocolate syrup.

ORANGE-SHERBET FREEZE

Put 2 scoops orange sherbet in a large glass. Spoon on 2 teaspoons orange marmalade. Fill to top with ginger ale; stir well, with a long spoon. Top with 2 tablespoons drained canned mandarin-orange sections.

DOUBLE STRAWBERRY SODA

Put 2 scoops strawberry ice cream in a large glass. Spoon 1 tablespoon strawberry jam over ice cream. Fill to top with ginger ale; stir well, with a long spoon.

ROOT-BEER FLOAT

Put 2 scoops ice cream (any flavor) in a large glass. Fill to top with root beer; stir well, with a long spoon.

PINEAPPLE-LEMON SODA

Put 2 scoops lemon sherbet and ¼ cup drained pineapple chunks in a large glass. Fill to top with ginger ale, stir well, with a long spoon.

Eggnogs

Eggnog starts the year and finishes it. It is the beverage of friendship and good wishes, of certain ceremony, too. When eggnogs were invented, centuries ago, they were served at any time of the year. Later, they became an important holiday drink, particularly popular on Christmas, New Year's, Easter, Independence Day, and—in early American years—election day.

Our recipes include eggnogs that may be mixed with spirits and some that need no fortifying at all. Even a child can drink them! A word here about dairy eggnogs: They are quick and excellent.

COFFEE EGGNOG

2 eggs, separated
⅓ cup sugar
⅓ cup instant coffee
Dash salt
1 tablespoon vanilla extract

2 cups milk, chilled
1 cup heavy cream,
    whipped
Shaved unsweetened
    chocolate

1. In small bowl of electric mixer, at high speed, beat egg whites until soft peaks form.
2. Gradually beat in sugar until stiff peaks form.
3. In large bowl, beat egg yolks until lemon-colored. Gradually beat in coffee, salt, vanilla, milk, and ¾ cup water.
4. Stir in egg-white mixture and whipped cream; mix well.
5. Serve well chilled, with chocolate sprinkled over each serving.

ENGLISH EGGNOG

6 egg yolks
1 cup granulated sugar
1 pt cognac

1 cup light rum
2 qt light cream
6 egg whites
½ cup confectioners' sugar

1. In large bowl, beat egg yolks until thick. Gradually add granulated sugar, beating until light.
2. Slowly stir in cognac and rum. Add 1½ quarts cream and about half the egg whites, beating until very well combined.
3. Beat remaining egg whites until foamy. Gradually add confectioners' sugar, beating well after each addition. Continue beating until soft peaks form when beater is slowly raised.
4. Gently stir egg whites and remaining cream into egg-yolk mixture.
5. Refrigerate, covered, until ready to serve.

SPICY EGGNOG

½ cup sugar
Dash allspice
¼ teaspoon cinnamon
⅛ teaspoon nutmeg

3 eggs, separated
2 cups milk, chilled
1 cup light cream, chilled
Nutmeg

1. Combine sugar, allspice, cinnamon, and ⅛ teaspoon nutmeg.
2. In large bowl of electric mixer, at high speed, beat egg whites until soft peaks form.
3. Gradually beat in half of sugar mixture until stiff peaks form.
4. In small bowl, beat egg yolks until lemon-colored. Gradually beat in remaining sugar mixture until thick and smooth.
5. Thoroughly fold into whites. Stir in milk and cream; mix well.
6. Serve well chilled, each serving sprinkled with nutmeg.

Wine Service and Selection

You don't have to be an expert in order to serve the right wine at the right time. Basically, there are four types of wine: appetizer wines, dessert wines, dinner wines, and sparkling wines. Although there are hundreds of wines and books devoted to their selection, we'll tell you about the essentials, so you can serve wines with confidence.

The appetizer wines, as their name implies, are served as a before-meal appetite stimulant. They may be served straight, in mixed drinks, or on-the-rocks. Usually they are served chilled. The flavors are dry and blend well with hors d'oeuvres and tidbits. The best known are Sherry, ranging from Fino through Pale Dry, and Vermouth, herb-flavored cocktail wine, both Dry and Sweet.

The dessert wines may also be served as refreshment when friends drop in, or as nightcaps. They are especially good with poundcakes and fruitcakes, nuts and cheese. Usually they are served at cool room temperature. The dessert wines include the Ports, Ruby, Tawny, and White; Muscatel; Cream Sherry; Tokay; and Sweet Sauterne.

The dinner wines are Red, White, and Rosé. Red dinner wines are best with steaks, roasts, stews, chops, game, cheeses, and spaghetti. They are usually served at cool room temperature. The fragrance of a red wine is improved if the cork is removed half an hour before serving. The red wines include Burgundy, Claret, and Chianti.

White dinner wines are served well chilled. They are especially good with white meats, salads, fish, cheese and mushroom dishes, and poultry. The white wines include Sauterne, Rhine Wine, and Chablis.

The increasingly popular Rosé is an all-purpose wine. It is served well chilled.

Sparkling wines are traditionally festive. They include Champagne, Pink Champagne, and Sparkling Burgundy.

Storing Wines Wines are best stored in a cool, dry spot, away from sunlight, where temperatures are as uniform as possible. Ideally, the temperature should stay between 50 and 60F. Corked bottles should be stored on their sides, so that corks are kept moist and airtight. Wines with screw tops may be stored upright.

White table wines are at their best as soon as you buy them; but if storage conditions are favorable, they can be kept for a few years before they begin to lose quality. Red table wines improve steadily in flavor for several years. Most dessert wines continue improving for as many years as you keep them. If you do keep a table wine in a bottle ten years or more, watch it—some corks shrink with age; excess air may get into the bottle as wine evaporates.

When you keep wines for years, you should expect a sediment to deposit on the sides or bottoms of the bottles. The deposit is harmless, but for appearance' sake, the wine should be poured slowly to avoid disturbing the sediment. For this, a wine basket is helpful. If there is too much sediment, the wine should be decanted; that is, poured carefully from the old bottle into another bottle or decanter. A light is held behind the bottleneck, so the clarity may be checked.

NUMBER OF SERVINGS IN A BOTTLE

The average serving of dinner wine or Champagne is 3 to 3½ fluid ounces; of cocktail or dessert wine, 2 to 2½ ounces. These bottles give you these approximate servings:

Size	Ounces	Dinner Wine—Champagne	Cocktail—Dessert Wine
Fifth (⅘ qt)	25.6	8 servings	8 to 12 servings
Tenth (⅘ pt)	12.8	4 servings	4 to 6 servings
Split	6.4	2 servings	
Pint	16	5 servings	5 to 7 servings
Quart	32	10 servings	10 to 14 servings
½ gallon	128	20 servings	20 to 30 servings
Gallon	64	40 servings	40 to 60 servings

Quick Breads

4

"Quick bread" is a term used to describe bread leavened by baking powder or baking soda, instead of yeast. Tea breads, biscuits, pancakes, and dumplings are all quick breads—quick to make because no rising period is required.

Tea Breads

It's hard to buy these sweet breads, so if you want to serve them, you'll have to make them. Use them when you entertain, particularly at afternoon teas or luncheons when a fruit salad is the main course. Whole loaves may be wrapped in a moistureproof, vapor-proof material, like saran or foil, and stored in the refrigerator for short periods or in the freezer.

PEANUT-BUTTER BREAD

2¼ cups sifted all-purpose flour
4 teaspoons baking powder
½ teaspoon salt
¾ cup creamy-style peanut butter
½ cup sugar
1 teaspoon vanilla extract
1¾ cups milk

1. Preheat oven to 350F. Grease a 9-by-5-by-3-inch loaf pan.

2. Sift flour with baking powder and salt; set aside.

3. In large bowl, with portable electric mixer or wooden spoon, beat peanut butter, sugar, and vanilla until well combined. Gradually add milk, beating until well blended.

4. Add flour mixture, beating until smooth.

5. Pour into pan; bake 1 hour, or until cake tester inserted in center comes out clean.

6. Let cool in pan 10 minutes. Remove from pan; cool completely on wire rack. To serve, cut into thin slices.

BANANA NUT BREAD

2½ cups sifted all-purpose
　　flour
3 teaspoons baking powder
½ teaspoon salt
1 cup sugar
¼ cup soft butter
　　or margarine
1 egg, beaten

1 cup mashed ripe bananas
　　(3 small bananas)
2 tablespoons grated orange
　　peel, or 1 tablespoon
　　grated lemon peel
½ cup milk
1 cup coarsely chopped
　　walnuts or pecans

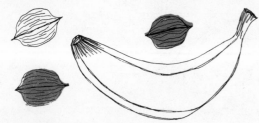

1. Preheat oven to 350F. Grease a 9-by-5-by-3-inch loaf pan.
2. Sift flour with baking powder and salt; set aside.
3. In medium bowl, with portable electric mixer or wooden spoon, beat sugar, butter, and egg until smooth.
4. Add bananas, orange peel, and milk, mixing well. Add flour mixture, beating just until smooth. Stir in nuts.
5. Pour batter into prepared pan; bake about 1 hour, or until cake tester inserted in center comes out clean.
6. Let cool in pan 10 minutes. Remove from pan; cool completely on wire rack. To serve, cut into thin slices.

DATE NUT BREAD

1 pkg (8 oz) pitted dates,
　　coarsely chopped
1½ cups boiling water
2¾ cups sifted all-purpose
　　flour
1 teaspoon baking powder
1½ teaspoons baking soda
1 teaspoon salt

1 egg, beaten
1 cup sugar
2 tablespoons butter or
　　margarine, melted
1 teaspoon vanilla extract
1 cup coarsely chopped
　　walnuts

1. In small bowl, combine dates with boiling water; let cool to room temperature.
2. Meanwhile, preheat oven to 350F. Grease a 9-by-5-by-3-inch loaf pan.
3. Sift flour with baking powder, soda, and salt; set aside.
4. In medium bowl, with wooden spoon or rotary beater, beat egg, sugar, butter, and vanilla until smooth.
5. Add cooled date mixture, mixing well. Then add flour mixture, beating with wooden spoon until well combined. Stir in nuts.
6. Turn batter into prepared pan; bake about 1 hour, or until cake tester inserted in center comes out clean.
7. Let cool in pan 10 minutes. Remove from pan; cool completely on wire rack. To serve, cut into thin slices.

HONEY-MARMALADE NUT BREAD

2½ cups sifted all-purpose
　　flour
1 tablespoon baking
　　powder
1 teaspoon salt
½ cup honey
2 tablespoons soft butter or
　　margarine

3 eggs, beaten
1 cup orange marmalade
1 tablespoon grated orange
　　peel
1 cup finely chopped
　　walnuts or pecans

1. Preheat oven to 350F. Grease a 9-by-5-by-3-inch loaf pan.
2. Sift flour with baking powder and salt; set aside.
3. In medium bowl, with wooden spoon, beat honey, butter, and eggs until smooth.
4. Stir in marmalade and orange peel, mixing well. Add flour mixture, stirring until well combined. Stir in nuts.
5. Turn into prepared pan; bake about 1 hour, or until cake tester inserted in center comes out clean.
6. Let cool in pan 10 minutes. Remove from pan; cool completely on wire rack. To serve, cut into thin slices.

McCALL'S BEST NUT BREAD

2½ cups sifted all-purpose flour

3 teaspoons baking powder

½ teaspoon salt

1 egg, beaten

1 teaspoon vanilla extract

¾ cup sugar

¼ cup butter or margarine, melted, or salad oil

1¼ cups milk

1 cup finely chopped walnuts or pecans

1. Preheat oven to 350F. Grease a 9-by-5-by-3-inch loaf pan.
2. Sift flour with baking powder and salt.
3. In large bowl, combine egg, vanilla, sugar, and butter. Using wooden spoon or portable electric mixer, beat until well blended. Add milk, blending well.
4. Add flour mixture, beating until smooth. Stir in nuts.
5. Pour batter into prepared pan; bake 60 to 65 minutes, or until cake tester inserted in center comes out clean.
6. Let cool in pan 10 minutes. Remove from pan; cool completely on wire rack. To serve, cut into thin slices.

SHAPE VARIATIONS

1. Divide batter evenly among 4 greased 5½-by-3¼-by-2¼-inch pans; bake at 375F, 25 minutes, till cake tester inserted in center comes out clean. Let cool in pans 10 minutes. Remove from pans; cool completely on wire rack. To serve, cut into thin slices.
2. Divide batter evenly among 6 greased 10½-oz cans, filling half full. Bake at 375F, 35 minutes, till cake tester inserted in center comes out clean. Cool in cans 10 minutes. Remove from cans; cool completely on wire rack. To serve, cut into thin slices.
3. Divide batter evenly among 4 greased 1-lb, 4-oz cans, filling half full. Bake at 375F, 40 minutes, till cake tester inserted in center comes out clean. Cool in cans 10 minutes. Remove from cans; cool completely on wire rack. To serve, cut into thin slices.

FLAVOR VARIATIONS

Kumquat-Pecan Nut Bread: Use pecans, reducing amount to ½ cup. Add ½ cup finely chopped preserved kumquats to batter, along with nuts in Best Nut Bread recipe. Bake as directed.

Lemon-Prune Nut Bread: Omit milk in Best Nut Bread recipe. Combine ½ cup chopped, pitted, dried prunes with 1¼ cups boiling unsweetened prune juice; let cool. Use in place of milk. Add 1 tablespoon grated lemon peel along with nuts. Bake as directed.

Candied-Fruit Nut Bread: Instead of walnuts or pecans, add 1 cup finely chopped mixed candied fruit and ½ cup sliced Brazil nuts to Best Nut Bread recipe. Bake as directed.

Cherry-Raisin Nut Bread: Use walnuts reducing amount in Best Nut Bread recipe to ½ cup. Combine ¼ cup finely chopped, drained maraschino cherries, ½ cup seedless raisins, and ½ teaspoon almond extract with vanilla. Add to batter along with nuts. Bake as directed.

PINEAPPLE-WALNUT BREAD

1 can (1 lb, 4½ oz) crushed pineapple

2 cups sifted all-purpose flour

½ cup sugar

3 teaspoons baking powder

1 teaspoon salt

½ teaspoon baking soda

⅓ cup finely chopped dates

¾ cup finely chopped walnuts

1 egg, beaten

¼ cup butter or margarine, melted

1½ teaspoons vanilla extract

1. Preheat oven to 350F.
2. Lightly grease a 9-by-5-by-3-inch loaf pan. Drain pineapple very well.
3. Sift flour with sugar, baking powder, salt, and baking soda into large bowl.
4. Add dates and walnuts; mix well. Add egg, pineapple, butter, and vanilla; with wooden spoon, stir just until blended. Turn into pan.
5. Bake 1 hour, or until cake tester inserted in center comes out clean. Cool in pan 15 minutes. Remove from pan; cool completely on wire rack. To serve: Slice thinly. Spread with softened cream cheese.

CRANBERRY NUT BREAD

1 cup fresh cranberries
2 cups sifted all-purpose
 flour
¾ cup sugar
3 teaspoons baking powder
¼ teaspoon salt

½ cup walnuts, chopped
2 eggs
1 cup milk
¼ cup butter or margarine,
 melted
1 teaspoon vanilla extract

1. Preheat oven to 350F. Grease a 9-by-5-by-3-inch loaf pan. Wash cranberries, removing stems; chop coarsely.

2. Sift flour with sugar, baking powder, and salt into large bowl. Stir in cranberries and walnuts.

3. In small bowl, with rotary beater, beat eggs with milk, butter, and vanilla.

4. Make well in center of cranberry mixture. Pour in egg mixture; with fork, stir just until dry ingredients are moistened.

5. Turn into prepared pan; bake 55 minutes, or until golden-brown on top and cake tester inserted in center comes out clean.

6. Cool in pan 10 minutes. Remove from pan; cool on wire rack. Serve thinly sliced.

MAKES 1 LOAF—6 TO 8 SERVINGS

IRISH SODA BREAD

4 cups sifted all-purpose
 flour
1 tablespoon baking soda
1 tablespoon sugar
2½ teaspoons salt

¼ teaspoon cream of tartar
1½ cups buttermilk
1 tablespoon butter or
 margarine, melted

1. Preheat oven to 375F. Grease well a large cookie sheet.

2. In large bowl, combine flour with soda, sugar, salt, and cream of tartar; mix well.

3. Add buttermilk; with fork, stir just until dry ingredients are moistened.

4. Turn out dough onto lightly floured board. Knead lightly until smooth—about 1 minute.

5. Shape dough into a ball; place on cookie sheet. With hands, flatten into a 7-inch circle. With sharp knife, cutting ¼ inch deep, mark into quarters.

6. Bake 30 to 40 minutes, or until top is golden-brown and loaf sounds hollow when rapped with knuckle.

7. Remove loaf to wire rack. Brush top with butter; cool completely.

IRISH OATMEAL BREAD

3 cups sifted all-purpose
 flour
1¼ cups quick rolled oats
1½ tablespoons baking
 powder
1 tablespoon salt

1 egg
¼ cup honey
1½ cups milk
1 tablespoon butter or
 margarine, melted

1. Preheat oven to 350F. Grease a 9-by-5-by-3-inch loaf pan.

2. In large bowl, mix flour, oats, baking powder, salt.

3. In medium bowl, using rotary beater, beat egg with honey and milk to combine well.

4. Pour egg mixture into oat mixture, stirring with wooden spoon just until dry ingredients are moistened—mixture will not be smooth.

5. Spread batter in prepared pan; bake 1 hour and 15 minutes, or until top is brown and cake tester inserted in center comes out clean.

6. Turn out loaf onto wire rack. While still warm, brush top with melted butter.

QUICK BREADS

Muffins are easy to make—and so are other sweet breads and coffeecakes. Though the sweet muffin is a delectable mate to a cup of coffee, it need not be confined to breakfast. Serve cheese muffins for lunch, corn muffins for supper, fruit muffins for tea.

PASTA

A meal's not really a meal in Italy without pasta, and the habit could be catching here, too. It takes many forms, many tastes. Have it to open a meal, perhaps; to thicken a soup; to serve in a salad; to star as a main dish.

Muffins

They are absurdly easy to make. What is known as the "muffin method"—that is, adding all the liquid ingredients to all the dry —is often used for other quick breads and for simple cakes, as well.

Muffins keep well, so if you don't eat all you've made for a meal, wrap the remainder in saran or foil, and refrigerate or freeze them, to serve at another meal. But be sure to heat them before serving.

PERFECT MUFFINS

2 cups sifted all-purpose
    flour
¼ cup sugar
3 teaspoons baking powder
½ teaspoon salt

1 cup milk
⅓ cup salad oil or melted
    shortening
1 egg, slightly beaten

1. Preheat oven to 400F. Grease bottoms of 14 (2½-inch) muffin-pan cups, or 11 (3-inch) muffin-pan cups; or line each with paper liner.

2. Sift flour with sugar, baking powder, and salt into large bowl.

3. Measure milk in 2-cup measure. Add oil and egg; beat with fork to mix well.

4. Make a well in center of flour mixture. Pour in milk mixture all at once; stir quickly, with fork, just until dry ingredients are moistened. Do not beat. Batter will be lumpy.

5. Using ¼-cup measuring cup (not quite full), quickly dip batter into muffin cups, filling each slightly more than half full. (Dip only once for each muffin cup.)

6. Bake 20 to 25 minutes, or until golden and cake tester inserted in center comes out clean.

7. Loosen edge of each muffin with spatula; turn out. Serve hot.

4.

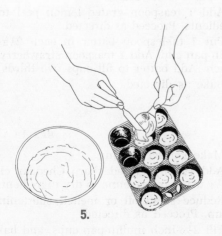

5.

7.

BLUEBERRY MUFFINS

MAKES 16 TO 18

1. Make Perfect Muffins; use ⅓ cup sugar.
2. Add 1 cup fresh blueberries (washed and well drained), or ¾ cup well-drained canned or thawed frozen blueberries, to dry ingredients. Proceed as directed.
3. Fill 2½-inch muffin-pan cups. Lightly sprinkle tops with sugar, and bake.

CINNAMON-SUGAR MUFFINS

MAKES 14

1. Make Perfect Muffins. Fill 2½-inch muffin-pan cups.
2. Combine 2 teaspoons cinnamon and ¼ cup sugar, mixing well. Sprinkle about 1 teaspoon mixture on each muffin just before baking. Bake as directed.

RAISIN MUFFINS

MAKES 14 TO 16

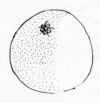

1. Make Perfect Muffins.
2. Add 1 tablespoon grated orange peel and ½ cup seedless raisins to dry ingredients. Proceed as directed.
3. Fill 2½-inch muffin-pan cups, and bake.

STRAWBERRY-JAM MUFFINS

MAKES 12 TO 14

1. Make Perfect Muffins.
2. Add 1 teaspoon grated lemon peel to dry ingredients. Proceed as directed.
3. Put 1 tablespoon batter in each 2½-inch muffin-pan cup. Add 1 teaspoon strawberry jam to each. Add batter to fill cups two thirds full.
4. Bake as directed.

CHEESE MUFFINS

MAKES 14 TO 16

1. Make Perfect Muffins.
2. Add ½ cup grated sharp Cheddar cheese and ¼ teaspoon cayenne to dry ingredients.
3. Reduce salad oil or melted shortening to ¼ cup. Proceed as directed.
4. Fill 2½-inch muffin-pan cups, and bake.

BACON MUFFINS

1. Make Perfect Muffins.
2. Add ½ cup coarsely chopped crisp-cooked bacon to dry ingredients.
3. Reduce salad oil or melted shortening to ¼ cup. Proceed as directed.
4. Fill 2½-inch muffin-pan cups, and bake.

APRICOT MUFFINS

1. Make Perfect Muffins.
2. Add 2 teaspoons grated orange peel and ½ cup finely chopped dried apricots to dry ingredients. Proceed as directed.
3. Fill 2½-inch muffin-pan cups, and bake.

MARASCHINO-CHERRY MUFFINS

1. Make Perfect Muffins, adding ½ cup very-well-drained and finely chopped maraschino cherries to dry ingredients. Proceed as directed.
2. Fill 2½-inch muffin-pan cups, and bake.

COCONUT MUFFINS

1¾ cups sifted all-purpose
    flour
½ cup sugar
3 teaspoons baking powder
1 teaspoon salt

1 cup canned flaked
    coconut
1 cup milk
¼ cup butter or margarine,
    melted
1 egg, slightly beaten

1. Preheat oven to 400F. Grease bottoms of 12 (2½-inch) muffin-pan cups, or line each with paper liner.
2. Sift flour with sugar, baking powder, and salt into large bowl. Add coconut; mix well.
3. Measure milk in 2-cup measure. Add butter and egg; beat with fork to mix well.
4. Make a well in center of flour mixture. Pour in milk mixture all at once; stir quickly, with fork, just until dry ingredients are moistened. Do not beat. Batter will be lumpy.
5. Quickly dip batter into muffin-pan cups, filling not quite two thirds full. Bake 20 to 25 minutes, or until golden.
6. Loosen edge of each muffin with spatula; turn out. Serve hot.

CORN MUFFINS

1 cup sifted all-purpose
    flour
2 tablespoons sugar
3 teaspoons baking powder
½ teaspoon salt

1 cup yellow cornmeal
1 cup milk
¼ cup salad oil or melted
    shortening
1 egg, slightly beaten

1. Preheat oven to 425F. Grease bottoms of 12 (2½-inch) muffin-pan cups, or line each with paper liner.

2. Sift flour with sugar, baking powder, and salt into large bowl. Add cornmeal; mix well.

3. Measure milk in 2-cup measure. Add oil and egg; beat with fork to mix well.

4. Make a well in center of flour mixture. Pour in milk mixture all at once; stir quickly, with fork, just until dry ingredients are moistened. Do not beat. Batter will be lumpy.

5. Quickly dip batter into muffin-pan cups, filling not quite two thirds full. Bake 15 to 20 minutes, or until golden.

6. Loosen edge of each muffin with spatula; turn out. Serve hot.

BUTTERMILK BRAN MUFFINS

1 cup sifted all-purpose
    flour
2 teaspoons baking powder
½ teaspoon baking soda
1 teaspoon salt
3 cups whole-bran cereal

½ cup seedless raisins
⅓ cup shortening
½ cup sugar
1 egg
1 cup buttermilk

1. Preheat oven to 400F. Grease bottoms of 12 (3-inch) muffin-pan cups, or line each with paper liner.

2. Sift flour with baking powder, soda, and salt into medium bowl. Add bran and raisins; mix well.

3. In large bowl of electric mixer, at medium speed, cream shortening with sugar until light and fluffy. Beat in egg.

4. Using fork, stir flour mixture into shortening mixture alternately with buttermilk, stirring only until dry ingredients are moistened. Do not beat. Batter will be lumpy.

5. Quickly dip batter into muffin-pan cups, filling not quite two thirds full. Bake 20 to 25 minutes, or until golden.

6. Loosen edge of each muffin with spatula; turn out. Serve hot.

OATMEAL-RAISIN MUFFINS

1 cup milk
1 cup quick-cooking oats
1 cup sifted all-purpose
    flour
¼ cup sugar
3 teaspoons baking powder

½ teaspoon salt
1 egg
¼ cup salad oil or melted
    shortening
½ cup seedless raisins

1. Combine milk and oats in small bowl; let stand 1 hour.

2. Preheat oven to 400F. Grease bottoms of 14 (2½-inch) muffin-pan cups, or line each with paper liner.

3. Sift flour with sugar, baking powder, and salt onto sheet of waxed paper.

(Oatmeal-Raisin Muffins continued)

4. In medium bowl, using fork, beat egg with salad oil. Stir in milk mixture.

5. Add flour mixture and raisins, quickly stirring, with fork, just until dry ingredients are moistened. Do not beat. Batter will be lumpy.

6. Quickly dip batter into muffin-pan cups, filling not quite two thirds full. Bake 20 to 25 minutes, or until golden.

7. Loosen edge of each muffin with spatula; turn out. Serve hot.

DATE-NUT MUFFINS

MAKES 12

2 cups sifted all-purpose
    flour
¼ cup sugar
3 teaspoons baking powder
1 teaspoon salt
1 cup finely chopped dates

¼ cup finely chopped
    walnuts
1 cup milk
¼ cup salad oil or melted
    shortening
1 egg

1. Preheat oven to 400F. Grease bottoms of 12 (3-inch) muffin-pan cups, or line each with paper liner.

2. Sift flour with sugar, baking powder, and salt into medium bowl. Add dates and nuts.

3. Measure milk in 2-cup measure. Add oil and egg; beat with fork to mix well.

4. Make a well in center of dry ingredients. Pour in milk mixture all at once; stir quickly, with fork, just until dry ingredients are moistened. Do not beat. Batter will be lumpy.

5. Quickly dip batter into muffin-pan cups, filling not quite two thirds full. Bake 20 to 25 minutes, or until golden.

6. Loosen edge of each muffin with spatula; turn out. Serve hot.

HONEY WHOLE-WHEAT MUFFINS

good 10/72

MAKES 12

1 cup sifted all-purpose
    flour
2 teaspoons baking powder
½ teaspoon salt
½ cup unsifted whole-
    wheat flour
½ cup milk
1 egg, well beaten

½ cup honey
½ cup coarsely chopped
    cooked prunes
1 teaspoon grated orange
    peel
¼ cup salad oil or melted
    shortening

1. Preheat oven to 400F. Grease bottoms of 12 (2½-inch) muffin-pan cups, or line each with paper liner.

2. Sift all-purpose flour with baking powder and salt into large bowl. Stir in whole-wheat flour; mix well.

3. Combine milk and rest of ingredients in medium bowl; beat well with wooden spoon.

4. Make a well in center of dry ingredients. Pour in milk mixture all at once; stir quickly, with fork, just until dry ingredients are moistened. Do not beat. Batter will be lumpy.

5. Quickly dip batter into muffin-pan cups, filling not quite two thirds full. Bake 20 to 25 minutes, or until nicely browned.

6. Loosen edge of each muffin with spatula; turn out. Serve hot.

63

Biscuits

If you read the funny papers, you know that a bride's biscuits are supposed to be heavy as lead. McCALL's step-by-step method for biscuits gives you the kind of perfection you hope you'll get and seldom do. Biscuits should be served as soon as they are baked, piping hot, so butter can melt into them deliciously.

PERFECT BAKING-POWDER BISCUITS

2 cups sifted all-purpose flour	1 teaspoon salt
3 teaspoons baking powder	1/3 cup shortening
	About 3/4 cup milk

MAKES 8 (2½-INCH) BISCUITS

1. Preheat oven to 450F. Sift flour with baking powder and salt into medium bowl.
2. Cut shortening into flour mixture, with a pastry blender or 2 knives (used scissors-fashion), until mixture resembles coarse cornmeal.
3. Make a well in the center. Pour in 2/3 cup milk all at once. Stir quickly round the bowl, with a fork. If mixture seems dry, add a little more milk, to form dough just moist enough (but not wet) to leave side of bowl and form ball.
4. Turn out dough onto a lightly floured surface, to knead. Gently pick up dough from side away from you; fold over toward you; press out lightly with palm of hand. Give the dough a quarter turn. Repeat ten times.
5. Gently roll out dough, from center, to ½- to ¾-inch thickness.
6. With floured 2½-inch biscuit cutter, cut straight down into dough, being careful not to twist cutter.
7. Place on ungreased cookie sheet; bake 12 to 15 minutes.

1.

2.

4.

6.

VARIATIONS

Buttermilk Biscuits: Substitute buttermilk for milk. Reduce baking powder to 2 teaspoons, and add ¼ teaspoon baking soda to sifted dry ingredients. Make Perfect Baking-Powder Biscuits.

Cheese Biscuits: Adding ¾ cup grated sharp Cheddar cheese to sifted dry ingredients, make Perfect Baking-Powder Biscuits.

Nut Biscuits: Adding ½ cup finely chopped walnuts or pecans to sifted dry ingredients, make Perfect Baking-Powder Biscuits.

Curry Biscuits: Adding ½ teaspoon curry powder to sifted dry ingredients, make Perfect Baking-Powder Biscuits.

Caraway Biscuits: Adding 2 teaspoons caraway seed to sifted dry ingredients, make Perfect Baking-Powder Biscuits.

Bacon Biscuits: Sauté 6 bacon slices until crisp. Drain well on paper towels; crumble. Adding bacon to sifted dry ingredients, make Perfect Baking-Powder Biscuits.

Herb Biscuits: Adding ¼ cup chopped parsley or chives to sifted dry ingredients, make Perfect Baking-Powder Biscuits.

Onion Biscuits: In 2 tablespoons butter or margarine, sauté ¼ cup finely chopped onion until golden—about 5 minutes. Adding onion with milk, make Perfect Baking-Powder Biscuits.

Drop Biscuits: Make Perfect Baking-Powder Biscuits, increasing milk to 1 cup. Do not knead or roll out. Drop dough, by tablespoonfuls, onto lightly greased cookie sheet; bake at 450F for 10 minutes, or until golden-brown. Makes 20.

SOUR-CREAM BISCUITS

MAKES 8 (2½-INCH) BISCUITS

2 cups sifted all-purpose
    flour
3 teaspoons baking powder
½ teaspoon baking soda
1 teaspoon sugar
1 teaspoon salt
½ cup shortening
1 cup dairy sour cream

1. Preheat oven to 450F.
2. Sift flour with baking powder, soda, sugar, and salt into medium bowl.
3. Cut in shortening, with pastry blender or 2 knives (used scissors-fashion), until mixture resembles coarse cornmeal.
4. Add sour cream, stirring only until mixture is moistened.
5. Turn out dough onto lightly floured surface. Knead about 10 times, to form a soft, smooth dough.
6. Gently roll out dough, from center, to ¾-inch thickness.
7. With floured 2½-inch biscuit cutter, cut straight down into dough, being careful not to twist cutter.
8. Place on ungreased cookie sheet; bake 10 to 12 minutes. Serve hot.

SAVORY TOPPING FOR MEAT PIE

4 tablespoons butter or margarine
¾ cup finely chopped onion
⅓ cup milk
1 cup packaged biscuit mix
¼ cup finely chopped parsley

1. Preheat oven to 425F.
2. In 2 tablespoons hot butter in small skillet, cook onion until tender. Set aside to cool.
3. Pour milk, all at once, into biscuit mix in medium bowl; stir, with fork, to make a soft dough. With spoon, beat about 15 strokes. Mixture will be sticky.
4. Turn out dough onto lightly floured surface. Roll out to a 10-by-5-inch rectangle.
5. Melt remaining butter; use to brush surface of dough. Spread onion evenly over dough. From long side, roll up jelly-roll fashion. Moisten edge; seal.
6. Cut crosswise into 10 (1-inch) slices. Place on top of any hot meat-pie filling in a 2½-quart casserole.
7. Bake 12 to 15 minutes, or until golden.

CHEESE-AND-OLIVE BISCUITS

1 jar (5 oz) olive-pimiento-cheese spread
2 tablespoons butter or margarine
Perfect Baking-Powder Biscuit dough, or 3 cups packaged biscuit mix

1. Preheat oven to 450F.
2. In small saucepan, over very low heat, melt cheese spread and butter, stirring until smooth. Remove from heat.
3. Make Baking-Powder Biscuits, as recipe or package label directs. Arrange on lightly greased cookie sheet.
4. Spread biscuit tops with cheese mixture; bake 12 to 15 minutes. Serve hot. Makes 8 (2½-inch) biscuits.

FRESH-CORN DROP BISCUITS

2 cups sifted all-purpose flour
1 tablespoon baking powder
1 teaspoon salt
1 cup corn kernels, cut from fresh, cooked ears
2 eggs, slightly beaten
¾ cup heavy cream

1. Preheat oven to 400F. Lightly grease a cookie sheet.
2. Sift flour, baking powder, and salt into medium bowl. Stir in corn until well coated.
3. Combine eggs and cream. Add, all at once, to flour mixture, stirring only until dry ingredients are moistened.
4. Drop by tablespoonfuls onto cookie sheet; bake 15 minutes, or until golden-brown. Makes 12 to 14.

Doughnuts

McCall's perfect doughnuts are tender, light, fragrant. We warn you that once you have learned to make them—and you will very shortly—your family will never permit you to forget—they'll want them again and again. Incidentally, we give you glazes and frostings to go over the doughnuts and make them look just as pretty as a picture.

PERFECT DOUGHNUTS

MAKES 22 (3-INCH) DOUGHNUTS
AND DOUGHNUT HOLES

3 eggs (¾ cup)
1 cup sugar
2 tablespoons soft butter or
    margarine
3¾ cups sifted all-purpose
    flour
2 teaspoons baking powder

1 teaspoon baking soda
1 teaspoon salt
¾ teaspoon nutmeg or
    mace
⅔ cup buttermilk
Salad oil or shortening
    for deep-frying

1. In large bowl of electric mixer, at high speed, beat eggs with sugar and butter until very light and fluffy—about 2 minutes. Scrape side of bowl occasionally.

2. Meanwhile, sift flour with baking powder, soda, salt, and nutmeg; set aside.

3. At low speed, gradually beat buttermilk into egg-sugar mixture.

4. Add flour mixture gradually; beat, at low speed, just until combined and smooth. Dough will be soft.

5. Cover bowl with saran or waxed paper; refrigerate until well chilled—about 1 hour.

6. Now remove half the chilled dough to a very-well-floured pastry cloth (keep rest in refrigerator until ready to use). Turn over dough, to coat with flour.

7. Roll out ⅓ inch thick. Cut with floured 3-inch doughnut cutter, dipping cutter into flour between each cutting.

8. With wide spatula, transfer cut doughnuts to top edge of pastry cloth.

9. Press trimmings together; reroll, and cut. Let rest, uncovered, 10 minutes.

10. Meanwhile, in electric skillet or heavy saucepan, slowly heat salad oil (from 1½ to 2 inches deep) to 375F on deep-frying thermometer.

11. Gently drop doughnuts and "holes," 3 or 4 at a time, into hot oil. (Adding too many doughnuts at one time would cool oil; doughnuts would absorb it and be greasy.)

12. As they rise to surface, turn with slotted utensil. Continue frying doughnuts and holes until golden-brown on both sides—about 3 minutes in all.

13. With slotted utensil, lift doughnuts from hot oil; hold over skillet a few seconds, to drain slightly.

14. Drain well on paper towels. Frost warm doughnuts, or sprinkle with cinnamon-sugar.

7.

12.

13.

14.

FRENCH CRULLERS

2 tablespoons sugar
½ teaspoon salt
¼ cup butter or margarine
1¼ cups sifted all-purpose
    flour

4 eggs
1 teaspoon vanilla extract
Confectioners' sugar
Shortening or salad oil for
    deep-frying

1. Cut out 14 (3-inch) foil circles; grease one side of each very well.

2. In a 2½-quart saucepan, combine sugar, salt, butter, and 1 cup water. Bring to a full, rolling boil (butter will melt).

3. Remove from heat. Quickly add flour all at once; beat with wooden spoon until smooth.

4. Return to medium heat, stirring vigorously, about 1 minute—until it forms a ball and cleans side of pan.

5. Remove from heat. Add eggs, one at a time, beating vigorously with wooden spoon 2 minutes after each addition. Beat in vanilla. Mixture should be smooth and shiny.

6. Turn mixture into a large pastry bag with a No. 6 star tube in place. Using outer edge of foil rounds as a guide, press mixture onto foil to form circles about 3 inches in diameter. Overlap ends of circles slightly.

7. Let stand at room temperature 20 minutes.

8. Meanwhile, in electric skillet or deep-fat fryer, slowly heat oil (1½ to 2 inches) to 365F on deep-frying thermometer.

9. Fry crullers: Place crullers, foil and all, in hot oil, a few at a time. Crullers will separate from foil. Remove foil from oil. Turn each cruller as soon as it rises to top. Fry about 7 minutes in all, until nicely browned, turning several times.

10. Lift out crullers, one by one, with slotted spoon. Hold over fryer a few seconds to drain. Then drain crullers on wire rack.

11. Serve warm, sprinkled lightly with confectioners' sugar or spread with a glaze.

CHOCOLATE GLAZE FOR DOUGHNUTS

MAKES ABOUT ¾ CUP

2 squares unsweetened
    chocolate
2 tablespoons butter or
    margarine

¼ cup milk
1 cup sifted confectioners'
    sugar
1 teaspoon vanilla extract

1. Over hot, not boiling, water, melt chocolate and butter.

2. In small saucepan, slowly heat milk until bubbles form around edge of pan.

3. In small bowl, using fork, beat chocolate with hot milk, sugar, and vanilla until smooth.

VANILLA GLAZE FOR DOUGHNUTS

MAKES 2½ CUPS, ENOUGH FOR
2 DOZEN DOUGHNUTS

¼ cup milk
1 teaspoon vanilla extract

2 cups sifted confectioners'
    sugar

In medium bowl, blend milk and vanilla into sugar until smooth.

VANILLA FROSTING

4 cups sifted confectioners'
    sugar

5 tablespoons milk
2 teaspoons vanilla extract

MAKES ENOUGH FOR 2 DOZEN DOUGHNUTS

1. In medium bowl, combine all ingredients, stirring with fork until smooth and well combined.

2. Spread each warm doughnut with 2 tablespoons frosting. If desired, garnish tops with chopped nuts, plain or toasted coconut, or nonpareils.

VARIATIONS

Orange Frosting: Substitute 2 tablespoons grated orange peel for vanilla extract.

Cherry Frosting: Substitute ¼ cup maraschino-cherry juice and ¼ cup chopped maraschino cherries for milk and vanilla.

Chocolate Frosting: Blend 2 squares melted unsweetened chocolate into Vanilla Frosting.

Browned-Butter Frosting: Omit vanilla, and blend in ¼ cup browned butter (heat ¼ cup butter over very low heat just until golden, not scorched).

WHOLE-WHEAT DOUGHNUTS

3 eggs (¾ cup)
1 cup light-brown sugar,
    firmly packed
2 tablespoons soft butter or
    margarine
2 cups sifted all-purpose
    flour
4 teaspoons baking powder

1 teaspoon salt
½ teaspoon cinnamon
1½ cups unsifted whole-
    wheat flour
¾ cup milk
Salad oil or shortening
Granulated or confection-
    ers' sugar

MAKES ABOUT 2 DOZEN

1. In large bowl of electric mixer, at high speed, beat eggs with brown sugar and butter until very light and fluffy—about 2 minutes.

2. Meanwhile, sift all-purpose flour with baking powder, salt, and cinnamon. Stir in whole-wheat flour.

3. At low speed, add flour mixture to egg mixture alternately with milk; beat just until combined and smooth. Dough will be soft.

4. Cover bowl with saran or waxed paper; refrigerate until well chilled—about 1 hour.

5. Remove half the chilled dough to well-floured pastry cloth (keep rest in refrigerator until ready to use). Turn over dough, to coat with flour. Then roll out ⅓ inch thick.

6. Cut with floured 3-inch doughnut cutter. With wide spatula, transfer cut doughnuts to top edge of pastry cloth. Press dough trimmings together; reroll, and cut. Let rest, uncovered, 10 minutes.

7. Meanwhile, in electric skillet or heavy saucepan, slowly heat salad oil (1½ to 2 inches) to 375F on deep-frying thermometer.

8. Gently drop doughnuts, 3 or 4 at a time, into hot oil. As they rise to surface, turn over with slotted utensil. Fry until golden-brown on both sides—about 3 minutes in all.

9. With slotted utensil, lift doughnuts from oil; hold over skillet a few seconds, to drain slightly. Drain well on paper towels. Dip warm doughnuts in granulated or confectioners' sugar.

POTATO DOUGHNUTS

MAKES ABOUT 2 DOZEN

3 cups sifted all-purpose
    flour
4 teaspoons baking powder
1 teaspoon salt
1 teaspoon nutmeg or mace
3 eggs (¾ cup)
1 cup granulated sugar

¼ cup soft butter or
    margarine
1 cup cold unseasoned
    mashed potatoes
¼ cup milk
Salad oil or shortening
Cinnamon-sugar

1. Sift flour with baking powder, salt, and nutmeg; set aside.
2. In large bowl of electric mixer, at high speed, beat eggs with sugar and butter until very light and fluffy—about 2 minutes.
3. At low speed, beat in potatoes. Then beat in half the dry ingredients along with milk, then the rest of the dry ingredients. Dough will be soft. Refrigerate, covered with saran or waxed paper, until well chilled—about 1 hour.
4. Remove half the chilled dough to well-floured pastry cloth (keep rest in refrigerator until ready to use). Turn over dough, to coat with flour. Then roll out ⅓ inch thick.
5. Cut with floured 3-inch doughnut cutter. With wide spatula, transfer cut doughnuts to top edge of pastry cloth. Press dough trimmings together; reroll, and cut. Let rest, uncovered, 10 minutes.
6. Meanwhile, in electric skillet or heavy saucepan, slowly heat salad oil (1½ to 2 inches) to 375F on deep-frying thermometer.
7. Gently drop doughnuts, 3 or 4 at a time, into hot oil. As they rise to surface, turn over with slotted utensil. Fry until golden-brown on both sides—about 3 minutes in all.
8. With slotted utensil, lift doughnuts from oil; hold over skillet a few seconds, to drain slightly. Drain well on paper towels. Dip warm doughnuts in cinnamon-sugar.

OLD-FASHIONED CRULLERS

MAKES ABOUT 32

3 eggs (¾ cup)
1 cup granulated sugar
½ cup soft butter or
    margarine
4 cups sifted all-purpose
    flour
1½ teaspoons baking
    powder

1 teaspoon salt
½ teaspoon ground
    cardamom, or ¾
    teaspoon nutmeg or
    mace
¼ cup milk
Salad oil or shortening
Confectioners' sugar

1. At high speed, in large bowl of electric mixer, beat eggs with granulated sugar and butter until very light and fluffy—about 3 minutes.
2. Meanwhile, sift flour with baking powder, salt, and cardamom; set aside.
3. At low speed, beat milk into egg mixture.
4. Then add half the flour mixture gradually; beat until combined and smooth. With wooden spoon, beat in rest of flour mixture. Dough will be a little stiff. Cover bowl with saran or waxed paper; refrigerate until well chilled—about 1 hour.
5. Remove half the chilled dough to well-floured pastry cloth (keep rest in refrigerator until ready to use). Turn over dough, to coat with flour. Then roll out into a 12-by-8-inch rectangle.

(Old-Fashioned Crullers continued)

6. With sharp knife or pastry wheel, cut dough in half lengthwise, to make two 12-by-4-inch rectangles.

7. Cut each crosswise into 8 (1½-inch) strips. Cut a 1-inch slit lengthwise in center of each strip. Pull one end through slit.

8. Meanwhile, in electric skillet or heavy sauce-pan, slowly heat salad oil (1½ to 2 inches) to 375F on deep-frying thermometer.

9. Gently drop crullers, 3 or 4 at a time, into hot oil. As they rise to surface, turn over with slotted utensil. Fry until golden-brown on both sides—about 3 minutes in all.

10. With slotted utensil, lift crullers from oil; hold over skillet a few seconds, to drain slightly. Drain well on paper towels. Cool completely on wire rack; then sprinkle with confectioners' sugar.

Pancakes and Waffles

Betty Botter, nursery-rhyme batter problem girl, would have only one trouble with our recipes for pancakes and waffles—deciding which to choose first. Our advice to you: Try them all. Men, particularly, favor the griddlecake (call it flannel cake, flapjack, hot cake, or whatever you wish). As for waffles, what a treat well-favored, well-flavored waffles are for a Sunday breakfast—and what a wonderful way to start a week!

BUCKWHEAT BUTTERMILK PANCAKES

1 cup sifted all-purpose flour	1 cup unsifted buckwheat flour
½ teaspoon salt	1 egg, well beaten
1 teaspoon baking powder	¼ cup butter or margarine, melted; or ¼ cup salad oil
1 teaspoon baking soda	
2 tablespoons sugar	2 cups buttermilk

MAKES ABOUT 16 (4-INCH) PANCAKES

1. Into medium bowl, sift all-purpose flour with salt, baking powder, soda, and sugar. Stir in buckwheat flour; set aside.

2. In small bowl, combine egg, butter, and buttermilk, mixing well. Add to flour mixture, mixing only until combined. Batter will be lumpy.

3. Meanwhile, slowly heat griddle or heavy skillet. To test temperature, drop a little cold water onto hot griddle; water should roll off in drops.

4. Use ¼ cup batter for each pancake; cook until bubbles form on surface and edges become dry. Turn; cook 2 minutes longer, or until nicely browned on underside. Serve warm.

Note: For thinner pancakes, increase buttermilk to 2¼ cups.

71

OLD-FASHIONED FLAPJACKS

3 eggs
1 cup sifted all-purpose
    flour
3 teaspoons baking powder
½ teaspoon salt
2 teaspoons granulated
    sugar ·

1 teaspoon light-brown
    sugar
½ cup buttermilk
2 tablespoons butter or
    margarine, melted

1. In large bowl of electric mixer, at high speed, beat eggs until light and fluffy—about 2 minutes.
2. Into eggs, sift flour with baking powder, salt, and granulated sugar. Add brown sugar; beat until smooth.
3. Stir in buttermilk and butter just until combined; do not overbeat.
4. Meanwhile, slowly heat griddle or heavy skillet. To test temperature, drop a little cold water onto hot griddle; water should roll off in drops.
5. Use ¼ cup batter for each flapjack; cook until bubbles form on surface and edges become dry. Turn; cook 2 minutes longer, or until nicely browned on underside.

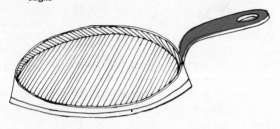

BLUEBERRY PANCAKES

1. To Old-Fashioned Flapjacks Batter, gently add 1 pkg (12 oz) thawed frozen blueberries, drained; or 1¼ cups fresh blueberries. Stir just until combined. Be careful not to break berries as you stir.
2. Cook pancakes as directed in flapjack recipe.

SOUR-CREAM PANCAKES

1 cup sifted all-purpose
    flour
½ teaspoon baking powder
½ teaspoon baking soda
½ teaspoon salt

½ cup dairy sour cream
½ cup milk
2 eggs
3 tablespoons butter or
    margarine, melted

1. Sift flour with baking powder, soda, and salt. Combine sour cream and milk, stirring well.
2. In large bowl of electric mixer, at high speed, beat eggs until light and fluffy.
3. At low speed, alternately blend in flour mixture and sour-cream mixture, beginning and ending with flour. Then blend in melted butter.
4. Meanwhile, slowly heat griddle or heavy skillet. To test temperature, drop a little cold water onto hot griddle; water should roll off in drops.
5. Use a scant ¼ cup batter for each pancake; cook until bubbles form on surface and edges become dry. Turn; cook 2 minutes longer, or until nicely browned on underside. Serve with whipped butter and Strawberry Sauce.*

* See this chapter.

GRIDDLECAKES

1 cup sifted all-purpose
　　flour
2 teaspoons baking powder
½ teaspoon salt
2 tablespoons sugar

1 egg
1 cup milk
3 tablespoons butter or
　　margarine, melted

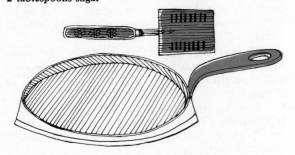

MAKES 8 (4-INCH) GRIDDLECAKES

1. Sift flour with baking powder, salt, and sugar into medium bowl.

2. With rotary beater, beat egg. Add milk and butter; beat until well mixed.

3. Pour into dry ingredients; beat only until combined—batter will be lumpy.

4. Meanwhile, slowly heat griddle or heavy skillet. To test temperature, drop a little cold water onto hot griddle; water should roll off in drops.

5. Use about ¼ cup batter for each griddle-cake; cook until bubbles form on surface and edges become dry. Turn; cook 2 minutes longer, or until nicely browned on underside. Serve with whipped butter.*

VARIATIONS

MAKES 12 (4-INCH) GRIDDLECAKES

Apple Griddlecakes: Add 1 cup pared, thinly sliced apple to Griddlecakes batter; cook as above. Serve with Spicy Applesauce.*

MAKES 10 (4-INCH) GRIDDLECAKES

Pecan or Walnut Griddlecakes: Add ½ cup chopped pecans or walnuts to Griddlecakes batter; cook as above. Serve with whipped butter and Sour-Cream Topping.*

MAKES 12 (4-INCH) GRIDDLECAKES

Banana Griddlecakes: Sift ⅛ teaspoon nutmeg with Griddlecakes dry ingredients. Add to batter 1 cup mashed banana and 2 teaspoons lemon juice; cook as above. Serve with whipped butter and Hot Maple Syrup.*

MAKES 12 (4-INCH) GRIDDLECAKES

Rice Griddlecakes: Sift ½ teaspoon cinnamon with Griddlecakes dry ingredients. Add to batter 1 cup cooked white rice; cook as above. Serve with Praline-Butter Sauce.*

MAKES 10 (4-INCH) GRIDDLECAKES

Honey-Spice Griddlecakes: Sift ¾ teaspoon cinnamon, ¼ teaspoon ginger, and ⅛ teaspoon nutmeg with Griddlecakes dry ingredients. Add to batter ½ cup uncooked, quick-cooking oats and 2 tablespoons honey; cook as above. Serve with whipped butter and Orange-Maple Syrup or Praline-Butter Sauce.*

MAKES 10 (4-INCH) GRIDDLECAKES

Whole-Wheat Griddlecakes: Reduce milk in Griddlecakes to ¾ cup plus 2 tablespoons. Add to batter 2 tablespoons light molasses and ½ cup crushed bite-size shredded-wheat biscuits; cook as above. Serve with whipped butter and Hot Maple Syrup.*

* See this chapter.

CORNMEAL PANCAKES

1 cup yellow cornmeal
2 tablespoons sugar
1 teaspoon salt
1 cup boiling water
½ cup sifted all-purpose
    flour

2 teaspoons baking powder
1 egg
½ cup milk
2 tablespoons butter or
    margarine, melted

1. Combine cornmeal, sugar, and salt in large bowl. Slowly stir in boiling water; cover, and let stand 10 minutes.
2. Sift flour with baking powder; set aside.
3. In small bowl, beat egg, milk, and butter until smooth. Pour into cornmeal batter, along with flour mixture, stirring quickly only until combined.
4. Meanwhile, slowly heat griddle or heavy skillet. To test temperature, drop a little cold water onto hot griddle; water should roll off in drops.
5. Use ¼ cup batter for each pancake; cook until bubbles form on surface and edges become dry. Turn; cook 2 minutes longer, or until nicely browned on underside.
6. Serve with whipped butter and Orange-Maple Syrup, or Spicy Applesauce.*

* See this chapter.

H. R. M.'S FAVORITE WAFFLES

4 eggs
2 cups sifted all-purpose
    flour
1 teaspoon salt
1 teaspoon baking soda

1 teaspoon baking powder
2 cups buttermilk; or 1 cup
    dairy sour cream,
    mixed with 1 cup
    milk
1 cup melted butter

1. Preheat waffle iron.
2. Beat eggs until light.
3. Sift together flour, salt, soda, and baking powder.
4. Add flour mixture and buttermilk alternately to beaten eggs, beginning and ending with flour mixture. Add melted butter; blend thoroughly.
5. For each waffle, pour batter into center of lower half of waffle iron until it spreads to 1 inch from edge—about ½ cup.
6. Lower cover on batter; cook as manufacturer directs, or until waffle iron stops steaming. Do not raise cover during baking.
7. Carefully loosen edge of waffle with fork; remove. Serve hot.

PECAN WAFFLES

2 cups sifted cake flour
2 teaspoons baking powder
½ teaspoon salt
2 egg yolks

1¼ cups milk
6 tablespoons salad oil
2 egg whites
½ cup chopped pecans

1. Preheat waffle iron.
2. Sift flour with baking powder and salt; set aside.
3. In medium bowl, with rotary beater, beat egg yolks, milk, and salad oil until well combined. Gradually add flour mixture, a little at a time, beating after each addition; beat only until smooth.

(*Pecan Waffles continued*)

4. In small bowl, beat egg whites until stiff peaks form when beater is raised. With rubber scraper, gently fold egg whites into batter just until combined. Stir in pecans.

5. For each waffle, pour batter into center of lower half of waffle iron until it spreads to 1 inch from edge—about ½ cup.

6. Lower cover on batter; cook as manufacturer directs, or until waffle iron stops steaming. Do not raise cover during baking.

7. Carefully loosen edge of waffle with fork; remove. Serve hot.

Toppings

Special sauces and butters complement the flavor of pancakes and waffles, and will earn you compliments when you serve them.

You'll find a wide variety of syrups on your grocer's shelf. But you'll want to try these easy recipes, too.

BLUEBERRY SAUCE

1 can (14½ oz) blueberries   2 tablespoons light corn
      syrup

MAKES 2 CUPS

1. Drain blueberry liquid into small saucepan. Stir in corn syrup.

2. Bring to a boil; reduce heat, and simmer 10 minutes. Stir in blueberries. Serve warm.

STRAWBERRY SAUCE

1 pkg (12 oz) thawed frozen   2 teaspoons cornstarch
    sliced strawberries   1 teaspoon lemon juice

MAKES ABOUT 1½ CUPS

1. Drain strawberries, reserving liquid. In medium saucepan, combine 1 tablespoon strawberry liquid and the 2 teaspoons cornstarch; stir until smooth.

2. Add remaining liquid, the berries, and lemon juice; bring to boiling, stirring. Sauce will be slightly thickened and translucent. Serve warm.

HOT MAPLE SYRUP

1 cup dark-brown sugar,   2 tablespoons butter or
    firmly packed   margarine
¼ teaspoon maple flavoring

MAKES 1 CUP

1. Combine sugar and ½ cup water in medium saucepan; bring to boiling.

2. Boil, uncovered, 5 minutes. Add maple flavoring and butter; stir until butter melts. Serve hot.

ORANGE-MAPLE SYRUP

MAKES 2¼ CUPS

1½ cups maple-flavored syrup
1 cup butter or margarine
1½ teaspoons grated orange peel

1. Combine all ingredients in medium saucepan; bring to boiling.
2. Reduce heat; simmer, uncovered, 3 minutes. Serve hot.

ORANGE BUTTER

MAKES ⅔ CUP

½ cup butter
2 teaspoons grated orange peel
6 tablespoons confectioners' sugar

Work butter until very soft. Stir in orange peel and sugar until smooth. Serve at room temperature.

UNCLE JOHN'S WHIPPED BUTTER

MAKES ABOUT 1 CUP

¼ lb sweet or salt butter

1. Let butter stand, at room temperature, in small bowl of electric mixer 30 minutes.
2. Beat at low speed until smooth; then beat at high speed until light and fluffy (about 10 minutes in all).
3. Mound high in small bowl. Serve at room temperature.

PRALINE-BUTTER SAUCE

MAKES 1 CUP

½ cup butter or margarine
½ cup light-brown sugar, firmly packed
¼ cup chopped pecans

1. In small bowl of electric mixer, at high speed, beat butter until light and fluffy.
2. Gradually beat in sugar until very light and fluffy.
3. Add pecans. Serve at room temperature.

SPICY APPLESAUCE

MAKES 1⅓ CUPS

1 can (1 lb) applesauce
1 tablespoon butter or margarine
½ teaspoon nutmeg
½ teaspoon cinnamon

1. Combine all ingredients in small bowl; blend thoroughly.
2. Serve warm or cold.

SOUR-CREAM TOPPING

MAKES 1⅔ CUPS

1½ cups dairy sour cream
2 tablespoons honey
2 tablespoons light-brown sugar
⅛ teaspoon nutmeg

1. Combine all ingredients in small bowl; blend thoroughly.
2. Serve at room temperature.

Cornbread

Certain meals seem to demand cornbread, and when they do, stir up a batter of McCall's own, or a lovely variation thereof, and serve piping hot!

JOHNNYCAKE

MAKES 9 SERVINGS

1 cup sifted all-purpose
   flour
2 tablespoons sugar
3 teaspoons baking powder
½ teaspoon salt
1 cup yellow cornmeal
1 egg, beaten
¼ cup salad oil or
   shortening, melted
1 cup milk

1. Preheat oven to 425F. Grease an 8-by-8-by-2-inch baking pan.
2. Sift flour with sugar, baking powder, and salt. Add cornmeal, mixing well; set aside.
3. In medium bowl, combine egg, salad oil, and milk, mixing well. Add flour mixture, stirring only until flour mixture is moistened.
4. Spoon batter into prepared pan; bake 20 to 25 minutes, or until golden-brown. To serve, cut into squares. Serve hot, with butter.

CORNBREAD RING

MAKES 6 TO 8 SERVINGS

1. Preheat oven to 425F. Grease a 5½-cup ring mold very well.
2. Prepare batter as directed above. Pour into prepared ring mold; bake 20 to 25 minutes, or until golden-brown.
3. Run a spatula around edge of mold; then invert cornbread onto serving platter. Fill center as desired. Serve hot.

CORNSTICKS

MAKES ABOUT 14

1. Preheat oven to 425F. Grease cornstick pans very well. Place in oven while preparing batter as directed above.
2. Spoon batter into prepared pans, filling about three fourths full; bake 10 to 15 minutes, or until golden-brown. Serve hot.

CORN MUFFINS

MAKES 12

1. Preheat oven to 425F. Grease 12 (2½-inch) muffin-pan cups.
2. Prepare batter as directed above. Spoon batter into prepared muffin-pan cups, filling about two thirds full.
3. Bake 15 to 20 minutes, or until golden-brown. Serve hot.

SOUTHERN SPOON BREAD

MAKES 8 SERVINGS

1 cup yellow or white
   cornmeal
1 teaspoon salt
2 cups boiling water
2 tablespoons butter or
   margarine

1 cup milk
3 egg whites
3 egg yolks, slightly beaten
1 teaspoon baking powder

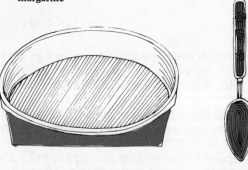

1. Preheat oven to 375F. Grease a 1½-quart casserole or a 12-by-8-by-2-inch baking dish.
2. In medium saucepan, gradually stir cornmeal and salt into boiling water. Cook, over medium heat, stirring constantly, until consistency of thick mush. Remove from heat.
3. Add butter and milk; beat until smooth. Let cool to room temperature.
4. Meanwhile, beat egg whites until stiff peaks form when beater is raised; set aside.
5. Using same beaters, beat egg yolks until thick and lemon-colored.
6. Stir egg yolks and baking powder into cooled cornmeal mixture, mixing well. Then gently fold in egg whites until well combined.
7. Turn into prepared casserole; bake 40 to 50 minutes, or until golden-brown and puffy.
8. To serve, spoon from casserole (or, if baked in oblong dish, cut into squares), and serve hot, with butter.

DOUBLE CORNBREAD

MAKES 9 SERVINGS

1 cup sifted all-purpose
   flour
1 cup yellow cornmeal
4 teaspoons baking powder
1 teaspoon salt
¼ cup sugar

2 eggs, slightly beaten
1 cup milk
3 tablespoons butter or
   margarine, melted
1 can (8¾ oz) cream-style
   corn (1 cup)

1. Preheat oven to 425F. Grease a 9-by-9-by-1¾-inch baking pan.
2. Sift flour with cornmeal, baking powder, salt, and sugar; set aside.
3. In medium bowl, combine eggs, milk, butter, and corn. Add flour mixture, stirring only until flour mixture is moistened.
4. Spoon batter into prepared pan; bake 25 to 30 minutes, or until cake tester inserted in center comes out clean and top is golden-brown. To serve, cut into squares. Serve hot.

CRISPY BUTTERMILK CORNSTICKS

MAKES ABOUT 12

½ cup sifted all-purpose
   flour
1 cup yellow cornmeal
1 tablespoon sugar
1 teaspoon salt

1½ teaspoons baking
   powder
1 cup buttermilk
2 tablespoons salad oil
1 egg

1. Preheat oven to 400F. Grease cornstick pans very well.
2. Sift flour with cornmeal, sugar, salt, and baking powder into medium bowl.
3. Make a well in center of ingredients. Pour in buttermilk, oil, and egg; with rotary beater, beat until smooth.
4. Fill prepared pans, using about 3 tablespoons mixture for each cornstick.
5. Bake 25 minutes, or until tops are golden-brown. Serve hot.

Coffeecakes

The ones we've included here are easier to make than our equally delicious yeast coffeecakes, particularly those that start with a base of packaged biscuit mix. They're rich enough to serve as a simple dessert, or with afternoon coffee, or to after-dinner guests. The guests probably won't believe you made them; but that's part of the fun, isn't it?

STREUSEL CINNAMON COFFEECAKE

Streusel Mixture:
½ cup light-brown sugar, firmly packed
2 teaspoons cinnamon
1 teaspoon nutmeg
½ cup finely chopped walnuts
2 tablespoons butter or margarine, melted

Coffeecake:
1 egg, slightly beaten
¼ cup granulated sugar
1 cup milk
2½ cups packaged biscuit mix
2 tablespoons butter or margarine, melted

MAKES 8 OR 9 SERVINGS

1. Preheat oven to 375F. Grease a 9-by-9-by-1¾-inch pan.
2. Make Streusel Mixture: Combine all ingredients in small bowl; set aside.
3. Make Coffeecake: In medium bowl, with rotary beater, beat egg, sugar, and milk until well blended. Add biscuit mix and butter, mixing until well combined.
4. Add half of Streusel Mixture to batter, stirring just until blended.
5. Turn batter into prepared pan. Sprinkle rest of Streusel Mixture evenly over top.
6. Bake 20 to 25 minutes, or until top is golden-brown. Cool partially on wire rack. To serve, cut into squares while still warm.

BLUEBERRY CRUMBCAKE

1 pkg (12 oz) thawed frozen blueberries, undrained
1 tablespoon cornstarch
1 teaspoon grated lemon peel
2 cups packaged biscuit mix
2 tablespoons sugar
2 tablespoons butter or margarine

1 egg
¼ cup milk

Topping:
½ cup packaged biscuit mix
¼ cup sugar
1 teaspoon cinnamon
2 tablespoons butter or margarine

MAKES ABOUT 10 SERVINGS

1. In small saucepan, combine blueberries, cornstarch, and lemon peel. Cook, stirring, over medium heat, until mixture begins to boil and becomes thickened and translucent. Let cool.
2. Preheat oven to 400F. Grease a 9-inch round layer-cake pan.
3. In medium bowl, combine biscuit mix and sugar. With pastry blender or 2 knives, cut in butter until mixture resembles coarse cornmeal.
4. Add egg and milk, stirring until thoroughly combined.
5. Pat dough on bottom and side of prepared pan. (It will come three quarters of the way up side.) Pour blueberry mixture into pan.
6. Make Topping: In small bowl, combine all ingredients; toss lightly, with fork, until mixture is crumbly. Sprinkle evenly over blueberry mixture.
7. Bake 20 minutes, or until topping is golden. Cool on wire rack. To serve, cut into wedges, and serve warm or cold.

PRUNE-AND-APRICOT COFFEECAKE

¾ cup dried prunes

¾ cup dried apricots

2 cups sifted all-purpose flour

2 teaspoons baking powder

½ teaspoon salt

⅔ cup light-brown sugar, firmly packed

1 tablespoon flour

1 tablespoon cinnamon

¾ cup soft shortening

¾ cup granulated sugar

2 eggs

¾ cup milk

1 teaspoon vanilla extract

6 tablespoons butter or margarine, melted

⅓ cup chopped walnuts

1. Lightly grease and flour a 9-inch tube pan. Preheat oven to 350F.

2. Let prunes and apricots stand in hot water, to cover, 5 minutes. Drain; chop finely; set aside.

3. Into medium bowl, sift 2 cups flour with baking powder and salt; set aside.

4. In small bowl, combine brown sugar with 1 tablespoon flour and the cinnamon, mixing well.

5. In large bowl of electric mixer, at medium speed, beat shortening with granulated sugar until light and fluffy. Beat in eggs, one at a time, beating well after each addition.

6. At low speed, beat in flour mixture (in 3 additions) alternately with milk and vanilla extract (in 2 additions); beat just to combine.

7. With rubber scraper, gently fold in fruit.

8. Turn one third of batter into prepared pan, spreading evenly. Sprinkle with one third of brown-sugar mixture, then with 2 tablespoons melted butter. Repeat layering twice. Sprinkle top with chopped nuts.

9. Bake 55 minutes, or until cake tester inserted in center comes out clean. Let cool in pan on wire rack about 25 minutes.

10. Gently remove from pan. Serve warm.

EVERYDAY COFFEECAKE

Batter:

1½ cups sifted all-purpose flour

2½ teaspoons baking powder

½ teaspoon salt

1 egg

¾ cup sugar

⅓ cup butter or margarine, melted

½ cup milk

1 teaspoon vanilla extract

Topping:*

2 tablespoons sugar

1 teaspoon cinnamon

1. Preheat oven to 375F. Grease an 8-by-8-by-2-inch baking pan, or a 9-by-1½-inch layer-cake pan.

2. Make Batter: Sift flour with baking powder and salt; set aside.

3. In medium bowl, with rotary beater, beat egg until frothy; then beat in sugar and butter until well combined. Add milk and vanilla.

4. With wooden spoon, beat in flour mixture until well combined.

5. Pour into prepared pan. Sprinkle with Topping—sugar combined with cinnamon. Bake 25 to 30 minutes, or until cake tester inserted in center comes out clean. Cool partially, in pan, on wire rack. To serve, cut into squares or wedges while still warm.

* *Crumb-Topped Coffeecake:* In small bowl, combine ½ cup sugar, ¼ cup sifted all-purpose flour, ¼ cup soft butter or margarine, and 1 teaspoon cinnamon; mix lightly, with fork, until crumbly. Sprinkle over prepared batter in pan. Bake as above.

STREUSEL LAYERED COFFEECAKE

Streusel Layer:
½ cup light-brown sugar,
    firmly packed
2 tablespoons soft butter or
    margarine
2 tablespoons all-purpose
    flour

1 teaspoon cinnamon
½ cup coarsely chopped
    walnuts (optional)

*Everyday Coffeecake
    batter*

MAKES ABOUT 9 SERVINGS

1. Preheat oven to 375F. Grease an 8-by-8-by-2-inch baking pan, or a 9-by-1½-inch layer-cake pan.
2. Make Streusel Layer: In small bowl, combine all ingredients; mix with fork, until crumbly.
3. Make batter as directed for Everyday Coffeecake. Turn half batter into prepared pan. Sprinkle evenly with half Streusel Layer. Repeat with remaining batter and layer.
4. Bake 25 to 30 minutes, or until cake tester inserted in center comes out clean. Cool partially, in pan, on wire rack. Serve warm.

COFFEE KUCHEN

3 cups sifted all-purpose
    flour
3 teaspoons baking powder
¼ teaspoon salt
1¼ teaspoons cinnamon
1 cup granulated sugar
1 cup light-brown sugar,
    firmly packed

3 tablespoons instant coffee
½ cup butter or margarine
½ cup shortening
1 cup milk
⅛ teaspoon baking soda
2 eggs, slightly beaten

MAKES 10 SERVINGS

1. Preheat oven to 350F. Lightly grease and flour a 9-inch tube pan.
2. Into large bowl, sift flour with baking powder, salt, cinnamon, sugars, and coffee.
3. Using pastry blender or 2 knives, cut butter and shortening into flour mixture until it resembles small peas. Set aside 1 cup for topping.
4. Combine milk with baking soda and eggs; mix well. With wooden spoon, stir all at once into flour-fat mixture just until combined.
5. Turn into prepared tube pan. Sprinkle evenly with reserved flour-fat mixture.
6. Bake 55 to 60 minutes, or until cake tester inserted in center comes out clean.
7. Let cool, in pan, on wire rack 10 minutes. Remove from pan; serve warm.

Dumplings

A good old-fashioned dumpling gives a hearty and tasty touch to soups and stews.

QUICK DUMPLINGS

1 egg, slightly beaten
½ cup milk
2 cups packaged biscuit mix

2 tablespoons chopped
    parsley or chives
    (optional)

MAKES ABOUT 10 DUMPLINGS

1. In medium bowl, combine egg and milk. Add biscuit mix and parsley; stir until blended.
2. Drop batter, by rounded tablespoonfuls, onto gently boiling stew in large Dutch oven or heavy skillet. Cook, uncovered, over low heat, 10 minutes. Cover tightly; cook 10 minutes.
3. Remove dumplings; keep warm while thickening stew. If desired, sprinkle dumplings with additional parsley. Serve along with stew.

81

POTATO DUMPLINGS

3 lb medium potatoes
Salt
Dash pepper
2 eggs
1 cup unsifted all-purpose
    flour
½ cup packaged dry bread
    crumbs
¼ teaspoon nutmeg
¼ cup chopped parsley

1. Cook unpeeled potatoes, covered, in boiling water just until tender—about 30 minutes. Drain; cool slightly; peel.

2. Put potatoes through ricer. Spread on paper towels, to dry well.

3. Then turn potatoes into large bowl. Lightly toss with 2½ teaspoons salt and the pepper. Make a well in center; break eggs into it.

4. Sift ¾ cup flour over eggs. Then add bread crumbs, nutmeg, and parsley. With hands, work mixture until it is smooth and holds together.

5. Shape into approximately 18 egg-size balls. Roll in remaining flour.

6. Meanwhile, in large saucepan, bring about 2 quarts lightly salted water to boiling point; reduce heat.

7. Drop in at one time just enough potato balls to fit comfortably in pan. Boil gently, uncovered, 2 minutes after they rise to surface. With slotted spoon, transfer dumplings to paper towels; drain. Serve hot, with Sauerbrauten.*

* See International Cookery Chapter.

FLUFFY EGG DUMPLINGS

1½ cups sifted all-purpose
    flour
2 teaspoons baking powder
¾ teaspoon salt
1 egg, well beaten
2 tablespoons melted
    shortening or salad oil
1 cup milk

1. Sift flour with baking powder and salt into medium bowl.

2. In small bowl, combine egg, shortening, and milk until well combined. Pour, all at once, into flour mixture, mixing only until dry ingredients are moistened.

3. Drop batter, by rounded tablespoonfuls, onto gently boiling stew in large Dutch oven or heavy skillet. Cook, uncovered, over low heat, 10 minutes. Cover tightly; cook 10 minutes longer.

4. Remove dumplings; keep warm while thickening stew. Serve dumplings along with stew.

VARIATIONS

Curry Dumplings: Make Fluffy Egg Dumplings as directed, adding ½ teaspoon curry powder to flour mixture.

Sage Dumplings: Make Fluffy Egg Dumplings as directed, adding ½ teaspoon rubbed sage to flour mixture.

Parsley or Chive Dumplings: Make Fluffy Egg Dumplings as directed, adding 2 tablespoons finely chopped parsley or chives to flour mixture.

Caraway Dumplings: Make Fluffy Egg Dumplings as directed, adding 1 teaspoon caraway seed to flour mixture.

Popovers

If you think that popovers are difficult to make, how surprised you'll be at the ease with which our spectacular beauties are produced! Serve them piping hot and puffy, right out of the oven. If you don't have an old-fashioned cast-iron popover pan, you can make them just as successfully in individual custard cups. Popovers are steam leavened; but if you like them on the dry side, pierce them with a fork five minutes before you take them out of the oven, to let some of the steam escape.

POPOVERS

MAKES 8

1 cup sifted all-purpose
    flour
½ teaspoon salt

2 eggs
1 cup milk

1.   Preheat oven to 400F. Grease 8 (5-oz) custard cups well.

2.   Sift flour with salt into medium bowl. Add eggs and milk; with rotary beater, beat just until smooth.

3.   Pour batter into prepared custard cups, filling each about half full. Bake, on large cookie sheet, 40 to 45 minutes, or until a deep golden-brown. Serve hot.

POPOVERS DE LUXE

MAKES 8

3 eggs
1 cup milk
3 tablespoons salad oil

1 cup sifted all-purpose
    flour
½ teaspoon salt

1.   Preheat oven to 400F. Lightly grease 8 (5-oz) custard cups.

2.   In medium bowl, with rotary beater, beat eggs, milk, and oil until well combined.

3.   Sift flour with salt over egg mixture; beat just until smooth.

4.   Pour batter into prepared custard cups, filling each about half full. Bake, on large cookie sheet, 45 to 50 minutes, or until deep golden-brown. Serve hot.

YORKSHIRE PUDDING

MAKES 8 SERVINGS

2 tablespoons roast-beef
    drippings or salad oil
2 eggs
1 cup milk

1 cup sifted all-purpose
    flour
½ teaspoon salt

1.   Preheat oven to 425F.

2.   Pour drippings into 10-inch pie plate; tilt to coat surface.

3.   In medium bowl, with rotary beater, beat eggs, milk, flour, and salt to make a smooth batter.

4.   Pour into prepared pie plate; bake 23 to 25 minutes, or until deep golden-brown. Serve immediately, with roast beef.

Yeast Breads

5

The fragrance of bread baking in the kitchen is so heavenly we think it should be bottled and sprayed about! There is something about baking her own bread that's deeply satisfying to a woman, and nothing makes a husband feel more flattered, more pampered.

While you're baking a loaf for dinner, multiply the recipe, and make one or two loaves to freeze. Bread properly cooled, wrapped tightly in moistureproof material, and stored in the freezer will keep its delicate moisture, remain free of mold, and retain its original fresh quality for several weeks. To thaw it, place the wrapped bread in a 350F oven for 45 minutes. Serve it still warm and thinly sliced, with curls of butter to melt into it.

Tips for Bread Bakers

Flour: Our bread recipes were tested using sifted all-purpose flour. If the unsifted type of flour is substituted, follow the manufacturer's directions on the package.

Yeast: Yeast is available in two forms—active dry and compressed. The active dry yeast keeps well for several months, but should be used before the expiration day on the package. Keep it, in its package, on a cool shelf. Dissolve active dry yeast in warm water (105 to 115F). Water that is too hot will kill yeast. Water that is too cold will slow down yeast action considerably.

Compressed yeast is more perishable. It will keep 1 to 2 weeks under refrigeration. Dissolve compressed yeast by crumbling it into lukewarm water (95F).

Yeast is a living plant that needs warmth to grow, so the water or milk in which you dissolve it must be warm; so must the bowl in which the dough is mixed.

In growing, yeast forms the gas that makes your bread light. Unlike baking powder, its action is continuous; so the flour mixture needs a framework capable of holding the

84

gas over a period of time. This framework is provided by the gluten in the flour.

Stirring or beating or kneading flour and liquid develops the gluten, and the gluten traps the leavening gas, so the bread rises.

Kneaded Breads: When all the ingredients have been combined, most recipes suggest kneading the dough. This is simply mixing and blending by hand a dough that is too stiff to mix with a spoon.

Doughs that are kneaded contain more flour than those that are not, and the gluten framework is strong enough to hold the gas in tiny pockets, so the resulting bread is fine and evenly textured, with a smoothly rounded top.

Kneading: Turn out dough onto lightly floured board or pastry cloth. With floured hands, pick up dough. Fold dough over toward you, then push it down and away from you, with heel of hand. Give dough a quarter turn; repeat kneading, developing a rocking rhythm. Continue kneading and turning 10 minutes, until dough is smooth and elastic and blisters appear on surface.

Rising: The room in which dough rises must be warm. The ideal temperature is 85F. Cover the dough with a towel, and keep it away from drafts. If your room is chilly, place the dough in an unlighted oven, with a large pan of hot water on the rack below the bowl, to hasten rising.

Crust: If bread is baked in a loaf pan, there will be a break between the sides and the top crust, and both sides of the bread will have a uniform, well-shaped appearance.

For a tender, soft crust, brush it with shortening after you take it from the oven, and cover it with a towel. For a crisp crust, omit the shortening, and let the bread cool without covering it. For a highly glazed crust, varnish the loaf, before baking, with an egg yolk beaten into a tablespoonful of water; use a pastry brush to apply it.

There are two kinds of yeast breads: kneaded and batter. This chapter has many recipes for both. We think you will be delighted with their taste and their variety.

McCALL'S BASIC WHITE BREAD

2 cups milk
3 tablespoons sugar
1 tablespoon salt
¼ cup butter or margarine
¼ cup warm water
   (105 to 115F)

2 pkg active dry yeast
6½ to 7 cups sifted
   all-purpose flour
2 tablespoons melted butter
   or margarine

1. In small saucepan, heat milk just until bubbles form around edge of pan. Remove from heat. Add sugar, salt, and ¼ cup butter, stirring until butter is melted. Let cool to lukewarm (a drop sprinkled on wrist will not feel warm).

2. If possible, check temperature of warm water with thermometer. Sprinkle yeast over water in large bowl, stirring until dissolved. Stir in milk mixture.

3. Add half the flour; beat, with wooden spoon, until smooth—about 2 minutes. Gradually add remaining flour, mixing it in with hand until dough is stiff enough to leave side of bowl.

4. Turn out dough onto lightly floured board. Cover with the bowl; let rest 10 minutes. Knead by folding dough toward you, then pushing down and away from you, with heel of hand. Give dough a quarter turn; repeat kneading, developing a rocking rhythm. Continue kneading and turning 10 minutes, or until dough is smooth and elastic and blisters appear on surface.

5. Place in lightly greased large bowl; turn dough to bring up greased side. Cover with towel; let rise in warm place (85F), free from drafts, about 1 hour, or until double in bulk. When two fingers poked into dough leave indentations, rising is sufficient. Punch down dough with fist; turn out onto lightly floured pastry cloth. Divide in half; shape each half into smooth ball. Cover with towel; let rest 10 minutes. Shape each portion into loaf, and place in pan, according to the shaping directions.

6. Brush top of each loaf with 1 tablespoon melted butter. Cover with towel; let rise in warm place (85F), free from drafts, until double in bulk, or until sides of dough reach tops of pans —about 1 hour.

7. Meanwhile, preheat oven to 400F.

8. Bake loaves 40 to 50 minutes—tops should be well browned and sound hollow when rapped with knuckle. Remove from pans immediately; cool well on wire rack, away from drafts.

Note: If a lighter-color crust is desired, cover top of loaves with brown paper or aluminum foil after bread has baked 25 minutes.

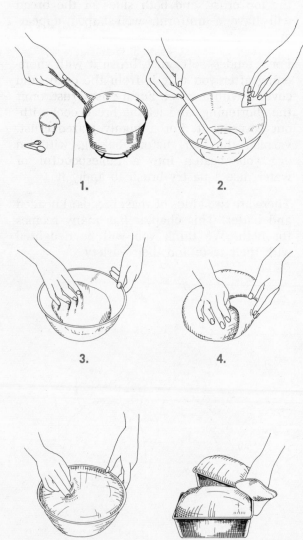

1.   2.

3.   4.

5.   8.

TO SHAPE LOAF

1. On lightly floured pastry cloth, stretch or roll dough until it is about 27 inches long (3 times as long as pan in which it well be baked).

2. Fold dough into thirds, pressing or rolling, to break any air pockets, until dough is a 7-inch square.

3. Fold dough into thirds, from opposite direction, pressing with fingers to break any air pockets.

4. Seal edge and ends of loaf by pinching together. Roll under palm of hand to smooth shape of loaf.

5. Place, seam side down, in lightly greased 9-by-5-by-3-inch pan.

6. Brush top of shaped loaf with melted butter. Cover with towel; let rise in warm place (85F), free from drafts, until double in bulk—about 1 hour. When a finger poked into dough leaves an indentation, rising is sufficient. Sides of dough should reach top of pan.

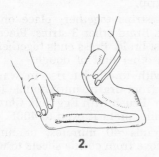

1.

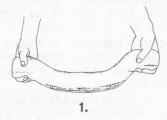

2.

3.

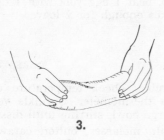

5.

4.

6.

SWISS EGG BREAD

1. Prepare McCall's Basic White Bread. Add 2 eggs, slightly beaten, to milk-yeast mixture before adding flour. Proceed as directed, increasing flour to 7 or 7¼ cups.

2. After dough has risen and been punched down, turn out on lightly floured pastry cloth. Shape into 2 braids or round loaves, or one of each, as below.

3. To shape braids: Divide dough in half. Cut one half into 6 parts. With palms of hands, roll each sixth on floured pastry cloth, to make a 12-inch strip.

4. Braid 3 strips together; place on greased cookie sheet. Braid other 3 strips. Place directly on top of first braid. Press ends together, to seal. Repeat with other half of dough.

5. Cover with towel; let rise in warm place (85F), free from drafts, until double in bulk— about 1 hour. Brush with Egg-Yolk Glaze, below.

6. Meanwhile, preheat oven to 400F.

7. Bake braids 40 minutes, or until deep-golden. Remove from cookie sheets to wire rack; cool thoroughly.

Egg-Yolk Glaze: In small bowl, using fork or small whip, beat 1 egg yolk with 1 tablespoon water. Makes enough for 2 loaves.

CARAWAY RYE BREAD

2 cups warm water
(105 to 115F)
2 pkg active dry yeast
1 tablespoon salt
¼ cup light molasses
2 tablespoons soft butter or
margarine

1 to 2 tablespoons caraway
seed, to taste
3½ cups sifted rye flour
3 to 3½ cups sifted
all-purpose flour
Cornmeal
1 egg white, slightly beaten
Caraway seed or coarse salt

1. If possible, check temperature of warm water with thermometer. Sprinkle yeast over water in large bowl, stirring until dissolved.

2. Add salt, molasses, butter, caraway seed, rye flour, and 1½ cups all-purpose flour; beat, with wooden spoon, till smooth—2 minutes.

3. Gradually add rest of all-purpose flour; mix in with hand until dough leaves side of bowl.

4. Turn dough onto lightly floured board. Dough will be stiff. Knead until smooth—about 10 minutes.

5. Place in lightly greased large bowl; turn to bring up greased side. Cover with towel; let rise in warm place (85F), free from drafts, until double in bulk—about 1 hour.

6. Grease large cookie sheet; sprinkle with cornmeal.

7. Punch down dough. Turn out onto lightly floured pastry cloth. Divide in half.

8. To make round loaves: Shape each half into a smooth ball; tuck edges under. Place, 5 inches apart, on prepared cookie sheet.

9. To make oval loaves: Shape each half into a ball. Roll each into a 10-inch loaf, tapering ends. Place, 3 inches apart, on cookie sheet.

10. Cover with towel; let rise in warm place (85F), free from drafts, until double in bulk—about 40 minutes.

11. Meanwhile, preheat oven to 375F.

12. Bake bread 50 minutes, or until loaf sounds hollow when rapped with knuckle. Remove to wire rack. Brush tops of loaves with egg white; sprinkle with caraway seed; cool.

CHEESE BREAD

1 cup milk
¼ cup sugar
1 tablespoon salt
½ cup warm water
    (105 to 115F)
2 pkg active dry yeast
¼ lb grated sharp Cheddar
    cheese

1 teaspoon dry mustard
⅛ teaspoon cayenne
4½ to 5 cups sifted
    all-purpose flour
1 tablespoon butter or
    margarine, melted

MAKES 1 LOAF

1. In small saucepan, heat milk just until bubbles form around edge of pan.

2. Add sugar and salt, stirring until dissolved; let cool to lukewarm.

3. If possible, check temperature of warm water with thermometer. Sprinkle yeast over water in large bowl, stirring until dissolved.

4. Stir in milk mixture, cheese, mustard, cayenne, and 2 cups flour; beat, with wooden spoon, until smooth—about 2 minutes.

5. Gradually add remaining flour; mix in last of it with hand until dough leaves side of bowl.

6. Turn dough onto lightly floured board. Knead until smooth—about 10 minutes.

7. Place in lightly greased large bowl. Brush top with melted butter. Cover with towel; let rise in warm place (85F), free from drafts, until double in bulk—about 2 hours.

8. Grease a 9-by-5-by-3-inch loaf pan.

9. Punch down dough; turn onto lightly floured pastry cloth. Shape into smooth ball. Cover with towel; let rest 10 minutes.

10. Roll the ball into a 12-by-8-inch rectangle. From long side, roll tightly, as for jelly roll; pinch edge, to seal. Place, seam side down, in prepared pan.

11. Cover with towel; let rise in warm place (85F), free from drafts, until double in bulk—about 1 hour.

12. Meanwhile, preheat oven to 400F.

13. Bake loaf 20 minutes. Cover with foil; bake 10 to 15 minutes, or till loaf sounds hollow when rapped with knuckle.

14. Remove from pan to wire rack; cool.

HERB CHEESE BREAD

Prepare Cheese Bread, omitting mustard and cayenne; substitute ½ teaspoon dried oregano leaves, ½ teaspoon dried basil leaves, and ½ teaspoon dried thyme leaves. Bake as directed.

HONEY-WHOLE-WHEAT BREAD

MAKES 2 LOAVES

1 cup milk
2 tablespoons sugar
1 tablespoon salt
¼ cup butter or margarine
½ cup honey
1½ cups warm water
   (105 to 115F)

2 pkg active dry yeast
2½ cups sifted all-purpose
   flour
5 cups unsifted whole-
   wheat flour
2 tablespoons melted butter
   or margarine

1. In small saucepan, heat milk until bubbles form around edge of pan; remove from heat.
2. Add sugar, salt, ¼ cup butter, and honey; stir till butter melts. Cool to lukewarm.
3. If possible, check temperature of warm water with thermometer. Sprinkle yeast over water in large bowl, stirring until dissolved. Stir in milk mixture.
4. Add all-purpose flour and 2½ cups whole-wheat flour; beat, with wooden spoon, until smooth—about 2 minutes. Gradually add remaining whole-wheat flour, mixing in last of it with hand until dough leaves side of bowl.
5. Turn out dough onto lightly floured board. Cover with the bowl; let rest 10 minutes.
6. Knead till smooth, elastic—10 minutes.
7. Place in lightly greased large bowl; turn dough to bring up greased side. Cover with towel; let rise in warm place (85F), free from drafts, until double in bulk—about 1¼ hours. When two fingers poked into dough leave indentations, the rising is sufficient.
8. Punch down dough with fist; turn out onto lightly floured pastry cloth. Divide in half; shape each half into a smooth ball. Cover with towel; let rest 10 minutes.
9. Shape each portion into loaf, according to directions for McCall's Basic White Bread, stretching or rolling dough only until it is 20 inches long, and place in lightly greased 9-by-5-by-3-inch pan.
10. Brush top of each loaf with 1 tablespoon melted butter. Cover with towel; let rise in warm place (85F), free from drafts, until double in bulk, or until sides of dough reach tops of pans—about 1¼ hours.
11. Meanwhile, preheat oven to 400F.
12. Bake loaves 40 to 50 minutes—tops should be well browned and sound hollow when rapped with knuckle. Remove from pans immediately; cool well on wire rack, away from drafts.

Note: If a lighter-color crust is desired, cover top of loaves with brown paper or foil after baking 25 minutes.

VARIATIONS

Honey-Nut: Add 1½ cups finely chopped walnuts with first addition of flours.

Molasses-Whole-Wheat: Substitute ½ cup light or dark molasses for honey.

Honey-Raisin: Add 1½ cups seedless raisins with first addition of flours. Increase rising time to 1½ hours. Before baking, brush each of the loaves with ½ tablespoon melted butter, and sprinkle each with 1 tablespoon sugar.

BREAD

Louis Bromfield said it this way: "...Bread is the king of the table and all else...is merely the court that surrounds the king. The courtiers are the soup, the meat, the vegetables, the salad...But Bread is King." There's something deeply satisfying about baking your own. It smells so wonderfully good, and there's hardly a better way to pamper your husband.

FRENCH BREAD

2 cups warm water
    (105 to 115F)
1 pkg active dry yeast
1 tablespoon salt
2 teaspoons sugar

1 tablespoon soft butter or
    margarine
5½ to 6 cups sifted
    all-purpose flour
Cornmeal

1. If possible, check temperature of warm water with thermometer. Sprinkle yeast over water in large bowl, stirring until dissolved.

2. Add salt, sugar, butter, and 2 cups flour; beat, with wooden spoon, until smooth—about 2 minutes.

3. Gradually add remaining flour; mix in last of it with hand until dough leaves side of bowl.

4. Turn dough onto lightly floured board. Knead until it is smooth and elastic—about 10 minutes. Dough will be stiff.

5. Place in lightly greased large bowl; turn dough over to bring up greased side. Cover with towel; let rise in warm place (85F), free from drafts, until double in bulk—about 1½ hours.

6. Lightly grease a large cookie sheet. Sprinkle with cornmeal.

7. Punch down dough; turn onto lightly floured pastry cloth. Divide in thirds.

8. Roll each into a 14-by-8-inch oblong. Beginning with wide side, roll tightly, as for jelly roll, tapering ends. Pinch edge, to seal.

9. Place the three rolls, 3 inches apart, on prepared cookie sheet. Brush each with cold water. With scissors, cut 4 diagonal slashes across each loaf.

10. Let rise, uncovered, in warm place (85F), free from drafts, until double in bulk—about 1½ hours.

11. Meanwhile, preheat oven to 400F.

12. Place shallow pan of water on oven bottom. Bake loaves 40 to 50 minutes, brushing with water every 20 minutes. Remove loaves to wire rack; cool.

Batter Breads

The newest and probably the easiest and quickest yeast breads to make are batter breads. Instead of being kneaded, the batters are beaten. The ingredients and mixing methods are similar to those of standard yeast breads, but the amount of liquid is higher in proportion to the amount of flour. This produces a dough that is relatively soft —soft enough, in fact, to beat with a spoon or an electric mixer.

Batter breads have a more open, lacy texture, and the top and break will be more uneven. In color, aroma, flavor, and all-around goodness, they are comparable to kneaded breads. However, they do not keep as well and are best when freshly baked.

ANADAMA BATTER BREAD

MAKES 1 LOAF

¾ cup boiling water
½ cup yellow cornmeal
3 tablespoons shortening
¼ cup light molasses
2 teaspoons salt
¼ cup warm water
    (105 to 115F)
1 pkg active dry yeast

1 egg
2¾ cups sifted all-purpose
    flour
¼ teaspoon salt
1 teaspoon yellow cornmeal
1 teaspoon soft butter or
    margarine

1. Lightly grease a 9-by-5-by-3-inch loaf pan.
2. In large bowl, pour boiling water over corn-meal. Stir in shortening, molasses, and salt; let cool to lukewarm.
3. If possible, check temperature of warm water with thermometer. Sprinkle yeast over warm water in large bowl of electric mixer, stirring until dissolved. Stir into cornmeal mixture.
4. Add egg and half the flour; beat 2 minutes at medium speed, frequently scraping down side of bowl and beaters with rubber scraper. Add rest of flour; beat 1 minute longer.
5. Spread batter evenly in prepared pan, using a buttered spatula to smooth top. Cover with towel; let rise in warm place (85F), free from drafts, until double in bulk—about 1½ hours. Then sprinkle top with salt and cornmeal.
6. Meanwhile, preheat oven to 375F.
7. Bake loaf 50 to 55 minutes, or until it sounds hollow when rapped with knuckle. Remove from pan to wire rack. Brush top with butter; cool completely.

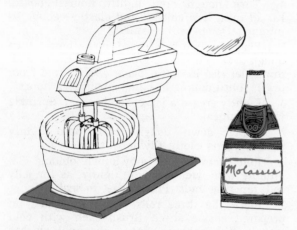

HERB-PARMESAN BREAD

MAKES 1 ROUND LOAF

2 cups warm water
    (105 to 115F)
2 pkg active dry yeast
2 tablespoons sugar
2 teaspoons salt
2 tablespoons soft butter or
    margarine

½ cup plus 1 tablespoon
    grated Parmesan
    cheese
1½ tablespoons dried
    oregano leaves
4¼ cups sifted all-purpose
    flour

1. If possible, check temperature of warm water with thermometer. Sprinkle yeast over water in large bowl of electric mixer. Let stand a few minutes; stir to dissolve yeast.
2. Add sugar, salt, butter, ½ cup cheese, oregano, and 3 cups flour. Beat, at low speed, until blended. At medium speed, beat until smooth— 2 minutes. Scrape down bowl and beaters.
3. With wooden spoon, gradually beat in rest of flour. Cover with waxed paper and towel.
4. Let rise in warm place (85F), free from drafts, about 45 minutes, or until quite light and bubbly and more than double in bulk.
5. Meanwhile, preheat oven to 375F. Lightly grease a 1½- or 2-quart casserole; set aside.
6. With wooden spoon, stir down batter. Beat vigorously ½ minute, or about 25 strokes. Turn into casserole. Sprinkle top of batter evenly with 1 tablespoon grated Parmesan cheese.
7. Bake 55 minutes, or until nicely browned. Turn out onto wire rack. Let cool, or serve slightly warm, in wedges.

OATMEAL BATTER BREAD

1½ cups boiling water
¾ cup rolled oats
¼ cup light molasses
1½ teaspoons salt
3 tablespoons butter or
    margarine

¼ cup warm water
    (105 to 115F)
1 pkg active dry yeast
4 cups sifted all-purpose
    flour
1 teaspoon soft butter or
    margarine

1. In medium bowl, pour boiling water over oats. Add molasses, salt, and 3 tablespoons butter, stirring to mix well; cool.
2. If possible, check temperature of warm water with thermometer. Sprinkle yeast over warm water in large bowl of electric mixer, stirring until dissolved.
3. Stir in oatmeal mixture. Gradually add 2 cups flour; at medium speed, beat 2 minutes. Mix in rest of flour by hand till well blended.
4. Cover with towel; let rise in warm place (85F), free from drafts, until double in bulk—about 30 minutes.
5. Grease a 9-by-5-by-3-inch loaf pan.
6. With wooden spoon, beat batter 25 vigorous strokes. Spread evenly in pan, using a buttered spatula to smooth top. Cover with towel; let rise in warm place (85F), free from drafts, until 1 inch from top of pan.
7. Meanwhile, preheat oven to 425F.
8. Bake loaf 40 to 50 minutes, or until it sounds hollow when rapped with knuckle. Remove from pan to wire rack. Brush top with 1 teaspoon butter; cool completely.

VIRGINIA SALLY LUNN

1 cup milk
2 tablespoons sugar
1 teaspoon salt
⅓ cup butter or margarine
½ cup warm water
    (105 to 115F)

1 pkg active dry yeast
3 eggs
4 cups sifted all-purpose
    flour

1. In small saucepan, heat milk until bubbles form around edge of pan; remove from heat.
2. Add sugar, salt, and butter, stirring until butter is melted; let cool to lukewarm.
3. If possible, check temperature of warm water with thermometer. Sprinkle yeast over water in large bowl of electric mixer; stir to dissolve.
4. Add milk mixture, eggs, and all of flour; at medium speed, beat till smooth—2 minutes.
5. Cover with waxed paper and towel; let rise in warm place (85F), free from drafts, until double in bulk and bubbly—about 1 hour.
6. Grease two 9-by-5-by-3-inch loaf pans.
7. With wooden spoon, beat batter vigorously ½ minute. Pour batter evenly into prepared pans. Cover with towel; let rise in warm place (85F), free from drafts, to within 1 inch of tops of pans—about 45 minutes.
8. Meanwhile, preheat oven to 350F.
9. Bake loaves 35 to 40 minutes, or until golden-brown. Remove from pans to wire rack. Serve hot, splitting into slices with two forks.

Almost every country in Europe has its favorite sweet bread. The German Stollen, sweet and filled with fruits, is one. Traditionally, it is served at Christmastime—thinly sliced, with coffee or perhaps a glass of wine. A cake called Kulich comes from Russia. It is a sweet bread, baked in tall, slender loaves. This also was a holiday bread. In Italy, the sweet bread is Panettone, a round loaf studded with citron and all sorts of other cut-up fruits. Spread with butter, to accompany a cup of steaming-hot coffee, American style or espresso, it is a wonderful treat on a Sunday afternoon.

CHRISTMAS KUCHEN

MAKES 1

1/2 cup milk
1 cup granulated sugar
1 teaspoon salt
1/2 cup butter or margarine
1 pkg active dry yeast
1/2 cup warm water
 (105 to 115F)
4 eggs, well beaten
1 tablespoon grated lemon
 peel

4 cups sifted all-purpose
 flour
1/4 cup slivered candied
 cherries
1/4 cup cubed candied
 pineapple
1/4 cup diced citron
1/4 cup diced candied lemon
 peel
Confectioners' sugar

1. Heat milk until bubbles form around edge of pan. Add granulated sugar, salt, and butter; stir until sugar is dissolved and shortening is melted. Let cool to lukewarm.

2. Meanwhile, sprinkle yeast over warm water in large bowl; stir until dissolved.

3. Add lukewarm milk mixture, eggs, lemon peel, and half the flour; beat, with spoon, until smooth. Stir in rest of flour; beat vigorously 2 minutes.

4. Cover with damp towel; let rise in warm place (85F), free from drafts, until light and bubbly—about 1 hour.

5. Stir down, with spoon. Stir in fruit. Pour into lightly greased 10-inch tube pan. Cover with damp towel; let rise until double in bulk— about 1 1/2 hours.

6. Meanwhile, preheat oven to 350F.

7. Bake Kuchen 45 minutes, or until golden-brown. Let cool, in pan, on wire rack.

8. Loosen from pan, and invert on serving plate. Sprinkle lightly with confectioners' sugar.

CHRISTMAS STOLLEN

MAKES 2

1 cup milk
1/2 cup granulated sugar
1 teaspoon salt
1/2 cup shortening
2 pkg active dry yeast
1/4 cup warm water
 (105 to 115F)
4 1/2 cups sifted all-purpose
 flour
1/2 teaspoon nutmeg
1 teaspoon cinnamon
1/2 cup seedless raisins

1/2 cup diced mixed candied
 fruit
1/4 cup slivered almonds

Frosting:
1 cup unsifted
 confectioners' sugar
2 tablespoons milk

8 to 10 candied cherries
Angelica

1. In large saucepan, heat milk until bubbles form around edge of pan. Remove from heat. Stir in granulated sugar, salt, and shortening; let cool until lukewarm.

2. Sprinkle yeast over warm water in large bowl; stir until dissolved. Then stir in milk mixture. Add 2 cups flour; beat until thoroughly combined and smooth.

3. Cover bowl with damp towel; let dough rise in warm place (85F), free from drafts, until double in bulk—about 30 minutes.

4. Sift remaining flour with nutmeg and cinnamon.

5. Stir raisins, fruit, and almonds into dough. Then stir in flour-spice mixture until well mixed.

(Christmas Stollen continued)

6. Turn dough onto lightly floured surface. Knead 10 minutes, or until smooth. Place in greased bowl; cover with damp towel; let rise in warm place until double in bulk—about 1 hour.

7. Punch down. Turn out onto lightly floured surface. Knead 5 minutes. Divide into 2 balls. Place on greased cookie sheets. Cover with damp towel; let rise in warm place until double in bulk—about 1 hour.

8. Meanwhile, preheat oven to 400F.

9. Bake Stollen 10 minutes. Reduce heat to 350F; bake 40 minutes more. Cool on wire rack.

10. Make Frosting: Combine sugar and milk in small bowl until smooth. Frost top of Stollen. Decorate with cherries and bits of angelica.

ITALIAN PANETTONE
(Christmas Bread)

1 cup warm water (105 to 115F)	5½ to 6 cups sifted all-purpose flour
2 pkg active dry yeast	1½ cups seedless raisins
½ cup sugar	1 cup chopped diced citron
2 teaspoons salt	½ cup sliced candied cherries
½ cup soft butter or margarine	2 tablespoons butter or margarine, melted
3 eggs	2 tablespoons sugar
1 egg, separated	

VARIATIONS

Antonio's Panettone: Add 1 teaspoon anise, or ½ teaspoon anise extract, along with fruit.

Frosted Panettone: Omit egg-white glaze and sugar. Combine 1 cup sifted confectioners' sugar with 2 teaspoons milk; spread over tops of cooled loaves. Decorate with toasted sliced almonds and sliced candied cherries.

MAKES 2 LOAVES

1. If possible, check temperature of warm water with thermometer. Sprinkle yeast over water in large bowl, stirring until dissolved.

2. Add ½ cup sugar, salt, ½ cup butter, 3 eggs, egg yolk, and 3 cups flour; beat, with wooden spoon, until smooth—about 2 minutes.

3. Stir in fruit. Gradually add remaining flour; mix in last of it with hand until dough leaves side of bowl.

4. Turn onto lightly floured board; roll to coat with flour. Knead until smooth—5 minutes.

5. Place in lightly greased large bowl; turn to bring up greased side. Cover with towel; let rise in warm place (85F), free from drafts, until double in bulk—about 1½ to 2 hours. (Fruited dough requires longer rising time.)

6. Meanwhile, grease two 8- or 9-inch layer-cake pans or 2 large cookie sheets.

7. Punch down dough; turn out onto lightly floured pastry cloth. Divide in half; shape each into a round loaf.

8. Place in prepared pans. Brush tops with 2 tablespoons melted butter. Cover with towel; let rise in warm place (85F), free from drafts, until double in bulk—1½ to 2 hours.

9. Meanwhile, preheat oven to 350F.

10. With sharp knife, cut a deep cross in top of each loaf. Combine egg white with 2 tablespoons water; brush over loaves. Sprinkle each with 1 tablespoon sugar. Bake 40 to 50 minutes, or until golden. Remove from pans immediately; cool well on wire rack, away from drafts.

KUGELHOPF

1 pkg active dry yeast
1 cup warm milk
(105 to 115F)
4 cups sifted all-purpose
flour
1 cup soft butter or
margarine
¾ cup granulated sugar
6 eggs
1 tablespoon cognac or
vanilla extract

½ teaspoon salt
1 tablespoon grated lemon
peel
1 cup seedless raisins
½ cup dried currants
½ cup chopped blanched
almonds
3 tablespoons
confectioners' sugar
3 tablespoons cinnamon

1. Sprinkle yeast over milk in large bowl; stir until dissolved.

2. With rotary beater, blend in 1 cup flour. Cover bowl with towel; let rise in warm place (85F) until double in bulk—about 1½ hours. Batter will be spongy.

3. Meanwhile, grease 9-inch tube pan.

4. Cream butter in large bowl of electric mixer, at medium speed. Gradually add granulated sugar, beating until light and fluffy. Beat in eggs, one at a time. Mix in cognac and salt.

5. At low speed, beat in yeast sponge and remaining flour until smooth. Stir in lemon peel, raisins, and currants.

6. Pour half of batter into prepared tube pan. Sprinkle with almonds. Top with remaining batter.

7. Cover with towel, and let batter rise in warm place until it fills pan—about 1½ hours.

8. Meanwhile, preheat oven to 350F.

9. Combine confectioners' sugar and cinnamon; sprinkle over surface of Kugelhopf. Bake 45 minutes, or until cake tester inserted in center comes out clean. Cool in pan, on wire rack, 20 minutes. Remove from pan; cool completely.

KULICH
(Russian Easter Bread)

1 cup warm water
(105 to 115F)
2 pkg active dry yeast
½ cup sugar
1 teaspoon salt
½ cup soft butter or
margarine
3 eggs
5 to 5½ cups sifted
all-purpose flour

½ cup seedless raisins
¼ cup finely chopped diced
citron
¼ cup finely chopped diced
candied orange peel
½ cup chopped blanched
almonds
1 teaspoon grated lemon
peel

1. If possible, check temperature of warm water with thermometer. Sprinkle yeast over water in large bowl, stirring until dissolved.

2. Add sugar, salt, butter, eggs, and 2½ cups flour; beat, with wooden spoon, until smooth—about 2 minutes. Stir in fruit, nuts, and lemon peel.

3. Gradually add remaining flour; mix in last of it with hand until dough leaves side of bowl.

4. Turn out dough onto lightly floured board. Cover with bowl; let rest 5 minutes. Knead until smooth—about 5 minutes.

5. Place in lightly greased large bowl; turn to bring up greased side. Cover with towel; let rise in warm place (85F), free from drafts, until double in bulk—1½ to 2 hours.

6. Meanwhile, grease well 3 cans (1 pint, No. 303; 1-lb coffee; or 1-lb shortening size may be used).

(*Kulich continued*)

7. Punch down dough; turn onto lightly floured pastry cloth. Divide into thirds; shape each into a smooth ball. Press each into can.
8. Cover with towel; let rise in warm place (85F), free from drafts, until double in bulk and slightly above tops of cans—50 to 60 minutes.
9. Meanwhile, preheat oven to 375F.
10. Bake bread 30 to 35 minutes, or until well browned. Place on wire racks; cool 5 minutes. Remove from cans; finish cooling on wire racks. While warm, frost with Kulich Icing, below.

Olga's Kulich: Omit lemon peel. Substitute 1 teaspoon vanilla extract, or 1 teaspoon ground cardamom, or 1 tablespoon grated orange peel.

KULICH ICING

MAKES 1 CUP

1 cup sifted confectioners'
    sugar
2 teaspoons milk

½ teaspoon lemon or
    almond extract
3 tablespoons multicolor
    decorettes

1. In small bowl, mix sugar, milk, and extract until smooth.
2. Spread over tops of warm loaves, dribbling down sides. Sprinkle with decorettes.

LUCIA BUNS

MAKES 36

1 cup milk
¼ to ½ teaspoon crumbled
    saffron threads, or ½
    teaspoon powdered
    saffron
¾ cup sugar
1 teaspoon salt
½ cup soft butter or
    margarine

¾ cup warm water
    (105 to 115F)
2 pkg active dry yeast
6½ cups sifted all-purpose
    flour
2 eggs
½ cup dark raisins
½ cup ground blanched
    almonds

1. In small saucepan, heat milk until bubbles form around edge of pan; remove from heat.
2. Add saffron, sugar, salt, and butter, stirring until butter is melted. Let cool to lukewarm.
3. If possible, check temperature of warm water with thermometer. Sprinkle yeast over it in large bowl; stir to dissolve. Add milk mixture.
4. Add 3½ cups flour; beat, with wooden spoon, until smooth—about 2 minutes.
5. Beat in eggs, raisins, and almonds. Gradually add remaining flour, mixing in last of it with hand until dough leaves side of bowl. (This is soft dough.)
6. Turn out dough onto lightly floured pastry cloth. Cover with bowl; let rest 10 minutes.
7. Turn dough, to coat with flour; knead until it is smooth—about 5 minutes.
8. Place in lightly greased large bowl; turn to bring up greased side. Cover with towel; let rise in warm place (85F), free from drafts, until double in bulk—1 to 1½ hours. Punch down. Turn out onto lightly floured pastry cloth.
9. Divide and shape as directed for Lucia Buns, page 98. The following recipe directions are for one third of dough—enough to work with at a time.

Cardamom Dough: Substitute ½ to 1 teaspoon ground cardamom and 1 tablespoon grated orange peel for the saffron.

(Lucia Buns, continued) MAKES 12

1. On lightly floured pastry cloth, roll one third of dough into a 10-inch square. Cut in half, to make two 10-by-5-inch rectangles; cut each rectangle crosswise into 12 strips.

2. With palm, roll each into a pencil-thin strip, 6 inches long. On lightly greased large cookie sheet, cross 2 strips to make an X; curl each end into a small coil. Press a raisin in center of each coil.

3. Cover with towel; let rise in warm place (85F), free from drafts, until double in bulk—40 to 50 minutes.

4. Meanwhile, preheat oven to 400F.

5. Brush buns with 1 egg yolk mixed with 1 tablespoon water; bake 12 to 15 minutes, or until golden-brown. Cool on wire rack.

S weet but not too sweet, light but chewy, and with happy surprises tucked away in it—a nugget of walnut, or a streak of ground almonds, or a plump brown raisin, or a sprinkling of cinnamon and sugar—there is something about coffeecake that's comfortingly old-fashioned.

BASIC SWEET DOUGH

¼ cup milk
¼ cup sugar
½ teaspoon salt
3 tablespoons butter or
    margarine

¼ cup warm water
    (105 to 115F)
1 pkg active dry yeast
1 egg, beaten
2¼ cups sifted all-purpose
    flour

1. In small saucepan, heat milk just until bubbles form around edge of pan; remove from heat. Add sugar, salt, and butter, stirring until butter is melted. Let cool to lukewarm (a drop sprinkled on wrist will not feel warm).

2. If possible, check temperature of warm water with thermometer. Sprinkle yeast over water in large bowl, stirring until dissolved. Stir in milk mixture.

3. Add egg and 1½ cups flour; beat, with wooden spoon, until smooth. Add rest of flour; beat until dough is smooth and leaves side of bowl.

4. Turn out dough onto lightly floured pastry cloth. Knead until dough is satiny and elastic and blisters appear on surface.

5. Place in lightly greased large bowl; turn to bring up greased side. Cover with towel; let rise in warm place (85F), free from drafts, until double in bulk—1 to 1½ hours.

6. Punch down dough with fist. Turn out onto lightly floured pastry cloth; knead 10 to 15 times.

7. Shape and fill, following directions for one of following variations.

APRICOT-FILLED COFFEECAKE

MAKES 1

Filling:
1 cup dried apricots
1 cup granulated sugar
¼ cup light-brown sugar,
     firmly packed
Dash cinnamon
Dash nutmeg

2 tablespoons butter or
     margarine, melted
½ cup chopped pecans

Icing:
½ cup confectioners' sugar
1 tablespoon milk
⅛ teaspoon vanilla extract

Coffeecake:
1 recipe Basic Sweet
     Dough, ready for
     shaping

¼ cup pecan halves

1. **Make Filling:** Simmer apricots, covered, in 1 cup water, with granulated sugar, until tender —10 minutes. Drain; reserve ¾ cup liquid.
2. Press apricots and reserved liquid through sieve, or purée in electric blender. Add brown sugar, cinnamon, and nutmeg; let cool.
3. **Make Coffeecake:** Butter an 8-inch spring-form pan.
4. Roll Basic Sweet Dough into a 32-by-8-inch strip. Brush with 1 tablespoon melted butter.
5. Reserve ⅓ cup apricot filling for later use, and spread remainder over entire surface of dough. Sprinkle with chopped pecans.
6. Roll dough from long side, forming a long rope; pinch edge to roll, to seal well.
7. With sealed edge down, spiral rope into spring-form pan, beginning in center of pan. Brush top with remaining butter. Cover with towel; let rise in warm place (85F), free from drafts, until double in bulk—about 1 hour.
8. Meanwhile, preheat oven to 350F.
9. Bake coffeecake 30 to 35 minutes, or until browned. Remove from pan at once; cool on wire rack.
10. **Make Icing:** Combine confectioners' sugar, milk, and vanilla.
11. Blend reserved apricot filling with 1 tablespoon warm water. Spoon along spiral crease on coffeecake. Top with pecans and icing.

CINNAMON SWIRLS

1 recipe Basic Sweet
     Dough, ready for
     shaping
4 tablespoons butter or
     margarine

¼ cup light-brown sugar,
     firmly packed
1 teaspoon cinnamon
2 tablespoons granulated
     sugar

MAKES 12

1. Lightly grease 12 (2-inch) muffin-pan cups.
2. Roll Basic Sweet Dough into a 12-by-8-inch rectangle. Spread with 2 tablespoons butter, softened. Combine brown sugar and ½ teaspoon cinnamon; sprinkle evenly over butter.
3. Roll dough tightly, from long side; pinch edge, to seal well. Cut into 12 slices.
4. Place a slice, cut side down, in each muffin cup. Brush with 1 tablespoon butter, melted. With a fork, gently pull up center of each roll.
5. Cover with towel; let rise in warm place (85F), free from drafts, until double in bulk— about 40 minutes.
6. Meanwhile, preheat oven to 350F.
7. Bake rolls 20 minutes, or until browned.
8. Combine remaining cinnamon and granulated sugar. Brush hot rolls with remaining butter, melted; sprinkle with cinnamon mixture.

HOT CROSS BUNS

1 recipe Basic Sweet
    Dough
½ teaspoon cinnamon
¼ teaspoon nutmeg
¼ cup currants
2 tablespoons finely
    chopped citron
    or lemon peel
    (optional)

Glaze:
¾ cup sifted con-
    fectioners' sugar
1 tablespoon milk
½ teaspoon vanilla
    extract

1. Make Basic Sweet Dough as recipe directs, adding cinnamon and nutmeg along with first addition of flour. Add currants and citron along with second addition of flour. Then knead dough and let rise as recipe directs.

2. To Shape: On lightly floured pastry cloth, using palms of hands, shape dough into a roll, 12 inches long.

3. Cut roll crosswise into 9 pieces. With fingertips, shape each piece into a ball; tuck edges underneath to make a smooth top.

4. Arrange in a greased 9-by-9-by-1¾-inch pan. With palm of hand, flatten each ball to a 2-inch round.

5. Cover with towel; let rise in warm place (85F), free from drafts, until double in bulk—about 1½ hours.

6. Preheat oven to 375F. Bake buns 20 to 25 minutes or until golden brown.

7. Meanwhile, make Glaze: In small bowl, combine all ingredients until smooth.

8. Brush tops of hot buns in pan, with some of glaze.

9. Let cool partially. With tip of spoon, drizzle cross on each bun with rest of glaze. Serve warm.

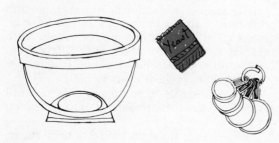

DANISH PASTRY

2 pkg active dry yeast
½ cup warm water
    (105 to 115F)
2½ (4-oz size) bars butter
    or margarine
½ cup sugar
¾ cup milk

3 eggs
4¼ cups sifted all-purpose
    flour
1 teaspoon ground
    cardamom
Prune Filling, below
¼ cup slivered blanched
    almonds

1. Sprinkle yeast over warm water in large bowl; stir until dissolved.

2. Cut each bar of butter into 4 lengthwise strips. On a sheet of foil, arrange strips close together in a single layer, to form a rectangle. Refrigerate until ready to use.

3. Stir ¼ cup sugar, the milk, and 2 eggs (slightly beaten) into yeast mixture. With wooden spoon, gradually beat in flour, then cardamom.

4. Turn out onto lightly floured surface. Knead 5 to 8 minutes, or until smooth and elastic. Lightly flour board as necessary.

5. Roll out dough into a 15-inch square. On half of dough, place chilled butter strips to within 1 inch of edges. Fold other half over butter; press edges together, to seal.

6. With folded side of dough at left, quickly roll out lengthwise into a 24-by-8-inch rectangle. From short side, fold into thirds. Repeat rolling and folding twice. (If butter should show through dough, sprinkle with a little flour.) Refrigerate, in foil, 30 minutes.

(*Danish Pastry continued*)

7. Then roll and fold pastry 3 times, as above. Wrap in foil; refrigerate 30 minutes.

8. Then again roll and fold pastry 3 times, as above. Wrap in foil; refrigerate 30 minutes.

9. Roll out half of dough into a 15-by-7-inch rectangle (other half in refrigerator). Place in lightly greased 15-by-10-by-1-inch jelly-roll pan.

10. Down 2 long sides, make parallel cuts 2½ inches long and ¾ inch apart. Spread uncut portion with ⅓ cup Prune Filling.

11. Combine remaining egg with 1 tablespoon water, for egg wash.

12. For a braidlike effect, fold cut strips at an angle across filling, alternating from side to side; fasten with a little egg wash. Lightly brush top of pastry with egg wash. Sprinkle with 2 tablespoons almonds and 2 tablespoons sugar.

13. Refrigerate, covered, 2 hours—pastry will then be risen and light.

14. Meanwhile, repeat with other half.

15. Preheat oven to 350F. Bake pastry 25 to 30 minutes, or until nicely browned. Cool slightly on wire rack. Serve warm. Cut each pastry crosswise into 15 (1-inch) pieces.

Note: Baked pastry may be cooled completely, then freezer-wrapped and frozen. To serve, reheat unthawed pastry in jelly-roll pan, at 325F, for 10 minutes. Cut into 15 pieces.

PRUNE FILLING

MAKES ⅔ CUP

¾ cup dried prunes, firmly packed
3 tablespoons sugar
¼ teaspoon ground cardamom
½ teaspoon vanilla extract
Dash salt

1. Cover prunes with cold water in small saucepan; bring to boiling. Reduce heat; simmer, covered, 30 minutes.

2. Drain prunes, reserving 3 tablespoons liquid. Cool; pit, and chop finely.

3. Combine chopped prunes, prune liquid, sugar, and cardamom in small saucepan; cook, stirring, 5 minutes, or until mixture is a thick purée. Add vanilla and salt. Let cool.

CINNAMON BUBBLE LOAF

MAKES 1 LOAF

Loaf:

½ cup warm water
   (105 to 115F)

1 pkg active dry yeast

¼ cup sugar

1 teaspoon salt

3 tablespoons soft butter or
   margarine

1 egg

2½ cups sifted all-purpose
   flour

Topping:

¼ cup butter or margarine,
   melted

¼ cup sugar

1 teaspoon cinnamon

¼ cup seedless raisins

¼ cup finely chopped
   walnuts or pecans

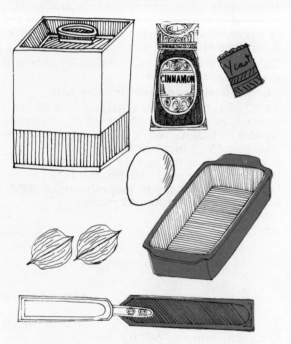

1. Make Loaf: If possible, check temperature of warm water with thermometer. Sprinkle yeast over water in large bowl; stir until dissolved.

2. Add sugar, salt, butter, egg, and 1½ cups flour; beat, with wooden spoon, until smooth— about 2 minutes.

3. Gradually add remaining flour; mix in last of it with hand until dough leaves side of bowl.

4. Turn out dough onto lightly floured board. Cover with bowl; let rest 5 minutes. Knead until smooth—about 5 minutes.

5. Place in lightly greased large bowl; turn to bring up greased side. Cover with towel; let rise in warm place (85F), free from drafts, until double in bulk—about 1 hour.

6. Punch down dough. Turn out onto lightly floured pastry cloth. Shape into roll 12 inches long. Cut into 20 pieces. Shape each into a smooth ball. Place 10 balls in bottom of well-greased 9-by-5-by-3-inch loaf pan.

7. For the Topping: Brush balls in pan with 2 tablespoons butter; sprinkle with 2 tablespoons sugar, ½ teaspoon cinnamon, 2 tablespoons raisins, and 2 tablespoons nuts. Arrange remaining 10 balls on top. Brush with rest of butter; sprinkle with rest of sugar, cinnamon, raisins, and nuts.

8. Cover with towel; let rise in warm place (85F), free from drafts, until double in bulk— 1 to 1¼ hours. Meanwhile, preheat oven to 375F.

9. Bake loaf 30 to 40 minutes. With spatula, loosen sides of loaf. Invert on serving plate; let stand 1 minute before removing pan. Serve slightly warm. Break rolls apart with 2 forks.

Roll Call! Response to fresh, home-baked rolls is immediate, we've noticed: eyes brighten, heads are raised, and noses sniff the air with blissful expectancy, while the little rolls are busy achieving a golden perfection in the kitchen. Take them to table, wrapped in a white napkin; watch your guests help themselves, roll after irresistible roll. Nothing makes a company meal more special.

REFRIGERATOR ROLLS

1¾ cups warm water
    (105 to 115F)
2 pkg active dry yeast
½ cup granulated sugar
1 tablespoon salt
1 egg, unbeaten

¼ cup soft butter or
    margarine
6 cups sifted all-purpose
    flour
1 tablespoon butter or
    margarine, melted

1. Pour warm water into a large bowl (first rinsed well in hot water). If possible, check temperature with thermometer. The water should be warm, not hot, on underpart of wrist. Sprinkle yeast over water; add sugar and salt; stir to dissolve completely.

2. Add egg, soft butter, and 3 cups flour. With wooden spoon, or electric mixer at medium speed, beat very hard 2 minutes, or until smooth. Gradually add 1 cup flour, beating hard after each addition. Using hands, work remaining 2 cups flour into the dough. Continue working dough, with hands, until smooth and elastic.

3. Brush top of the dough with melted butter; cover with a double thickness of saran or with a damp towel. Let rise in refrigerator at least 2 hours, or until double in bulk.

4. Punch down dough, and refrigerate. Store in refrigerator 1 to 3 days, punching it down once a day. Shape and bake as directed below.

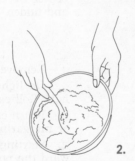
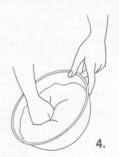

1.   2.   4.

MAKES 12

PARKERHOUSE ROLLS

1. Remove a third of dough from refrigerator.
2. On lightly floured surface, roll ⅜ inch thick.
3. Cut with 2½-inch biscuit cutter.
4. With dull edge of knife, press a crease just off center of each round. Brush lightly with melted butter or margarine. Fold over, so that larger part overlaps; press folded edge.
5. Place, 1 inch apart, on lightly greased cookie sheet. Cover with towel; let rise in warm place (85F), free from drafts, until double in bulk—about 1 hour.
6. Meanwhile, preheat oven to 400F. Brush rolls lightly with melted butter or margarine.
7. Bake 12 to 15 minutes, or until golden-brown. Serve hot.

BOWKNOTS

1. Remove a third of dough from refrigerator.

2. On lightly floured surface, with palms of hands, roll dough into a 12-inch rope. Divide into 12 pieces.

3. Roll each piece into an 8-inch strip; pull slightly. Tie each length loosely into a knot.

4. Place, 2 inches apart, on a greased cookie sheet; press ends on cookie sheet.

5. Cover with towel; let rise in warm place (85F), free from drafts, until double in bulk —about 1 hour.

6. Meanwhile, preheat oven to 400F. Brush rolls lightly with melted butter or margarine.

7. Bake 12 to 15 minutes, or until golden-brown. Serve hot.

Rosettes: Follow directions for shaping Bowknots. Then bring one end up and through center of knot; bring other end over the side and under. Let rise and bake as for Bowknots.

BUTTERHORNS

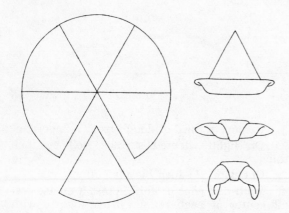

1. Remove a third of dough from refrigerator.

2. On lightly floured surface, divide dough in half. Roll each half into an 8-inch circle.

3. Brush each with 1 tablespoon melted butter or margarine. Cut each circle into 6 wedges.

4. Starting at wide end, roll up wedges, toward the point.

5. Place, 2 inches apart, points underneath, on greased cookie sheet.

6. Cover with towel; let rise in warm place (85F), free from drafts, until double in bulk— about 1 hour.

7. Meanwhile, preheat oven to 400F. Brush rolls lightly with melted butter or margarine.

8. Bake 12 to 15 minutes, or until golden-brown. Serve hot.

Crescents: Follow directions for shaping Butterhorns. Curve each roll before placing on cookie sheet. Let rise and bake as for Butterhorns.

CLOVERLEAVES

1. Remove a third of dough from refrigerator.

2. On lightly floured surface, divide dough in half. With palms of hands, roll each half into a 16-inch rope.

(*Cloverleaves continued*)

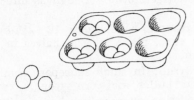

3. Cut each rope into 18 pieces. With finger-tips, shape each piece of dough into a smooth ball; tuck the edges under to make a smooth top.
4. Place 3 balls into each greased 2½-inch muffin-pan cup.
5. Cover with towel; let rise in warm place (85F), free from drafts, until double in bulk—about 1 hour.
6. Meanwhile, preheat oven to 400F. Brush rolls lightly with melted butter or margarine.
7. Bake 12 to 15 minutes, or until golden-brown. Brush with melted butter. Serve hot.

OLD-FASHIONED PAN ROLLS

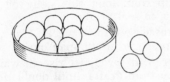

MAKES 12

1. Remove a third of dough from refrigerator.
2. On lightly floured surface, with palms of hands, roll into a 12-inch strip. Cut into 12 pieces.
3. With fingertips, shape each piece into a ball; tuck edges underneath, to make a smooth top. Arrange in a greased round 8- or 9-inch layer-cake pan.
4. Cover with towel; let rise in warm place (85F), free from drafts, until double in bulk—about 1 hour.
5. Meanwhile, preheat oven to 400F.
6. Bake rolls 15 to 20 minutes, or until golden-brown. Brush lightly with melted butter or margarine. Serve hot.

FAN-TANS

MAKES 12

1. Remove a third of dough from refrigerator.
2. On lightly floured surface, roll into a 15-by-8-inch rectangle.
3. Spread with 2 tablespoons melted butter or margarine.
4. With sharp knife, cut dough crosswise into 5 (about 1½-inch) strips.
5. Stack strips; cut stack into 12 (1¼-inch) pieces.
6. Place, cut side up, in greased 2½-inch muffin-pan cups.
7. Cover with towel; let rise in warm place (85F), free from drafts, until double in bulk—about 1 hour.
8. Meanwhile, preheat oven to 400F. Brush rolls lightly with melted butter or margarine.
9. Bake 12 to 15 minutes, or until golden-brown. Serve hot.

PECAN "STICKIES"

Refrigerator-Roll Dough
36 pecan halves

1 tablespoon light corn
   syrup

Syrup:
¼ cup light-brown sugar,
   firmly packed
2 tablespoons butter or
   margarine

2 tablespoons butter or
   margarine, melted
½ cup light-brown sugar,
   firmly packed

1. Make Refrigerator-Roll Dough as directed; refrigerate.

2. When ready to bake, grease 12 (2½-inch) muffin-pan cups; place 3 pecan halves in bottom of each.

3. Make Syrup: In small saucepan, combine brown sugar, butter, and corn syrup.

4. Cook, stirring, over medium heat, until butter melts. Spoon evenly into prepared muffin-pan cups.

5. Remove a third of dough from refrigerator.

6. On lightly floured surface, roll into a 10-by-14-inch rectangle.

7. Brush with melted butter; sprinkle with brown sugar.

8. Roll up from long side, jelly-roll fashion; pinch edge, to seal firmly.

9. Cut crosswise into 12 pieces. Place, cut side down, in prepared muffin-pan cups.

10. Cover with towel; let rise in warm place (85F), free from drafts, until double in bulk—about 1 hour.

11. Meanwhile, preheat oven to 375F.

12. Bake Stickies 20 to 25 minutes, or until golden-brown.

13. Invert pan on large cookie sheet; let stand 1 minute; then remove pan. Press the pecans into the Stickies. Serve warm.

BRIOCHE
(Refrigerator Method)

½ cup warm water
   (105 to 115F)
1 pkg active dry yeast
¼ cup sugar
1 teaspoon salt
1 teaspoon grated lemon
   peel

1 cup soft butter or
   margarine
6 eggs
4½ cups sifted all-purpose
   flour
1 egg yolk

1. If possible, check temperature of warm water with thermometer. Sprinkle yeast over water in large bowl of electric mixer; stir until dissolved.

2. Add sugar, salt, lemon peel, butter, 6 eggs, and 3 cups flour; at medium speed, beat 4 minutes. Add remaining flour; at low speed, beat until smooth—about 2 minutes.

3. Cover bowl with waxed paper and damp towel; let rise in warm place (85F), free from drafts, until double in bulk—about 1 hour. Refrigerate, covered, overnight.

4. Next day, grease 24 (3-inch) muffin-pan cups.

(*Brioche continued*)

5. Stir down dough with wooden spoon. Dough will be soft. Turn out onto lightly floured board; divide in half. Return half to bowl; refrigerate until ready to use.

6. Working quickly, shape three fourths of dough on board into a 12-inch roll. With floured knife, cut into 12 pieces. Shape each into ball; place in prepared muffin cup.

7. Divide other fourth of dough into 12 parts; shape into balls. With finger, press indentation in center of each large ball; fill with small ball.

8. Cover with towel; let rise in warm place (85F), free from drafts, until double in bulk— about 1 hour.

9. Meanwhile, shape refrigerated half of dough, and let rise, as directed.

10. Preheat oven to 400F.

11. Combine egg yolk with 1 tablespoon water; brush on Brioche. Bake 15 to 20 minutes, or until golden-brown. Serve hot or cold.

BRIOCHE BRAID

MAKES 2 BRAIDS

1. Prepare Brioche recipe. Refrigerate overnight.

2. Next day, grease 2 cookie sheets.

3. Stir down dough with wooden spoon. Dough will be soft. Turn out onto lightly floured board; divide in half. Return half to bowl; refrigerate until ready to use.

4. Working quickly, divide dough on board into thirds. Roll each, under palms, into a 12-inch roll. Place rolls, side by side, on prepared cookie sheet. Braid loosely; pinch ends, to seal.

5. Cover with towel; let rise in warm place (85F), free from drafts, until double in bulk— about 1 hour.

6. Meanwhile, shape refrigerated half of dough, and let rise, as directed. (If preferred, half may be shaped as Brioche, above.)

7. Preheat oven to 400F.

8. Combine egg yolk with 1 tablespoon water; brush on Braids. Bake 20 to 25 minutes, or until golden-brown. Cool on wire rack. Serve hot or cold.

RAISED DOUGHNUTS

MAKES ABOUT 20

½ cup milk
½ cup sugar
1 teaspoon salt
½ cup soft butter or
    margarine
½ cup warm water
    (105 to 115F)

2 pkg active dry yeast
2 eggs
4 cups sifted all-purpose
    flour
¾ teaspoon nutmeg or
    mace
Salad oil or shortening

1. Heat milk in small saucepan until bubbles form around edge of pan; remove from heat. Add sugar, salt, and butter; stir until butter is melted. Let cool to lukewarm.
2. If possible, check temperature of water with thermometer. In large bowl of electric mixer, sprinkle yeast over warm water; stir to dissolve.
3. Add milk mixture, eggs, 2 cups flour, and nutmeg; at medium speed, beat until smooth—about 2 minutes.
4. With wooden spoon, beat in remaining flour; beat until smooth. Dough will be soft.
5. Cover with towel; let rise in warm place (85F), free from drafts, until double in bulk—about 1 hour.
6. Punch down dough. Turn out onto well-floured pastry cloth; turn over, to coat with flour. Knead 10 times, until dough is smooth.
7. Cover with bowl; let rest 10 minutes.
8. Roll out dough ½ inch thick. Cut with floured 3-inch doughnut cutter. With wide spatula, move cut doughnuts to edge of pastry cloth.
9. Press remaining dough into ball; reroll, and cut. Cover with towel; let rise until double in bulk—about 45 minutes.
10. Meanwhile, in electric skillet or heavy saucepan, slowly heat salad oil (1½ to 2 inches) to 375F on deep-frying thermometer.
11. Gently drop doughnuts, 3 or 4 at a time, into hot oil. As they rise to surface, turn over with slotted utensil. Fry until golden-brown on both sides—about 3 minutes in all.
12. With slotted utensil, lift doughnuts from oil; hold over skillet a few seconds, to drain slightly. Drain well on paper towels; cool on wire rack.

SHAPING VARIATIONS

DOUBLE TWISTS
MAKES 24

1. After punching down dough, roll half of it into 12-by-7-inch rectangle.
2. With sharp, floured knife, cut into 12 (1-inch) strips. Fold each strip in half crosswise; pinch ends together. Pull to 4-inch length, and twist twice. Place twists at top edge of pastry cloth. Repeat with remaining dough.
3. Cover with towel; let rise until double in bulk—about 45 minutes. Fry as directed above.

BISMARCKS (Filled Doughnuts)
MAKES 24

1. Punch down dough; roll it ¼ inch thick.
2. Cut with floured 3-inch biscuit cutter. Place at top edge of pastry cloth. Press remaining dough into ball; reroll, and cut.
3. Cover with towel; let rise until double in bulk—about 45 minutes. Fry as directed above.
4. Cool on wire rack. Cut deep slit in side of each doughnut. Place teaspoonful of jelly or jam in center. Roll in granulated sugar.

HOMEMADE PIZZA

1 cup warm water
     (105 to 115F)
1 pkg active dry yeast
2 tablespoons shortening

¼ teaspoon salt
4 cups sifted all-purpose
     flour
2 teaspoons salad oil

1. If possible, check temperature of warm water with thermometer. Sprinkle yeast over water in large mixing bowl; stir until dissolved.

2. Add shortening, salt, and half the flour. Beat, with wooden spoon, until smooth—about 2 minutes.

3. Gradually add remaining flour, mixing with hand until dough is stiff enough to leave side of bowl.

4. Turn out dough onto lightly floured board. Cover with bowl; let rest 10 minutes. Knead 8 to 10 minutes, or until smooth and elastic.

5. Place in lightly greased medium bowl; turn dough, to bring up greased side. Cover with towel; let rise in warm place (85F), free from drafts, until double in bulk—about 1 hour. When two fingers poked into dough leave indentations, rising is sufficient.

6. Punch down dough with fist; turn out onto lightly floured pastry cloth.

7. Preheat oven to 450F. Spread oil over bottoms of 2 (12-inch) pizza pans.

8. Knead dough 3 to 5 minutes. Divide in half; roll each into a 12-inch circle.

9. Fit each circle into prepared pan, pressing edges onto side of pan. Spread with desired filling, below.

10. Place pans on cookie sheets. Bake pizza 25 minutes, or until crust is golden-brown and filling is bubbly.

PIZZA FILLING

1 tablespoon salad oil
¼ cup coarsely chopped
     onion
1 can (1 lb, 3 oz) whole
     tomatoes
1 can (8 oz) tomato sauce

1 small bay leaf
1 teaspoon salt
1 teaspoon sugar
1 teaspoon dried oregano
     leaves
Dash pepper

1. Slowly heat oil in 2-quart saucepan. In it, sauté onion until golden.

2. Drain tomatoes, reserving liquid. Crush tomatoes with pastry blender or fork.

3. In saucepan, combine tomato pulp and reserved liquid with remaining ingredients; over medium heat, bring to boiling. Reduce heat, and simmer, stirring occasionally, 30 minutes.

4. Remove bay leaf.

Note: Use 1⅓ cups Pizza Filling for each pizza.

P art of the enchantment of pizza, lies in its endless variations. On the next page you'll find some of our favorites.

Filling Variations

Cheese: Place 1 lb Mozzarella cheese, sliced, on Pizza Filling.

Anchovy: Drain 2-oz can anchovy fillets; arrange on Pizza Filling. Cover with 1 lb Mozzarella cheese, sliced.

SAUSAGE

Cut 1 lb sweet Italian sausage into ¼-inch slices. Sauté over medium heat until well browned. Drain; place over Pizza Filling. Cover with 1 lb Mozzarella cheese, sliced.

Onion: Slice 2 medium onions thinly; arrange on Pizza Filling. Sprinkle with 1 cup grated Parmesan cheese.

Mushroom: Drain 4 cans (3-oz size) sliced mushrooms. Place on Pizza Filling. Cover with 1 lb Mozzarella cheese, sliced.

SAUSAGE WITH GREEN PEPPER

Cut ½ lb sweet Italian sausage into ¼-inch slices. Sauté over medium heat until well browned. Drain; place on Pizza Filling. In same skillet, sauté 1 small green pepper, cut into strips, about 3 minutes. Sprinkle over Pizza Filling. Cover with 1 lb Mozzarella cheese, sliced.

Note: Pizza Fillings are sufficient for 2 (12-inch) pizzas.

Ways with Bakery Bread

There are ever so many ways of using the baked bread you buy at your grocer's, even stale bread, as you'll see in our recipes. As for fresh bread, the variety of things you can do to make it more interesting are limited only by your imagination—and ours!

CRISPY HERB BREAD

1 loaf unsliced white bread
1 cup soft butter or
   margarine
½ teaspoon paprika

2 teaspoons snipped fresh
   thyme or rosemary
   leaves*

* Or use 1 teaspoon dried thyme or rosemary leaves.

MAKES 16 SMALL SERVINGS

1. Preheat oven to 375F.
2. With serrated bread knife, completely trim crust from bread.
3. Cut loaf in half, lengthwise. Make a cut down center of each half, being careful not to cut all the way through.
4. Then make 3 cuts crosswise, being careful not to cut all the way through. Place on wire rack in shallow pan.
5. With wooden spoon, cream butter with paprika and thyme until well blended. Spread evenly over sides and top of bread.
6. Bake 15 minutes, or until crisp and golden. To serve, cut apart with scissors or knife.

GRILLED TOAST STICKS

9 slices bread
½ cup butter or margarine,
   melted

½ cup sugar
4 teaspoons cinnamon

MAKES 36

1. Preheat griddle to 360F.
2. Trim crusts from bread; cut each slice into 4 sticks. Brush with butter; roll in sugar combined with cinnamon.
3. Place on ungreased griddle; grill, turning often, until browned on all sides—about 2 minutes. Serve hot.

GARLIC FRENCH BREAD

MAKES ABOUT 12 SERVINGS

1 loaf French bread
½ cup soft butter or
   margarine
1 clove garlic, crushed
3 tablespoons grated
   Parmesan cheese

1 teaspoon dried marjoram
   leaves
¼ teaspoon pepper
Dash cayenne

1. Preheat oven to 350F.
2. At 1-inch intervals, make diagonal cuts in loaf; don't cut through bottom.
3. In small bowl, combine remaining ingredients until well blended. Spread mixture between bread slices.
4. Place bread on ungreased cookie sheet; sprinkle top with few drops water.
5. Bake about 10 minutes, or until butter is melted and bread is hot. Serve immediately.

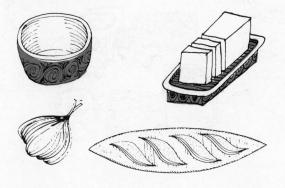

QUICK PATTY SHELLS

1. Preheat oven to 350F.
2. Cut a loaf of day-old, unsliced white bread, crosswise, into as many 1½-inch slices as desired. Trim crust completely.
3. Carefully hollow out center of each slice, leaving ½-inch-thick side walls and base.
4. Brush with melted butter or margarine. Place on ungreased cookie sheet; bake 15 to 20 minutes, or until golden. Fill as desired.

CROUTONS

1. Trim crusts from as many day-old white-bread slices as desired. Cut each into ⅓-inch cubes.
2. Sauté in melted butter or margarine until golden on both sides.

Cakes

Whether you say it *kake* as the Swedish do, or *torta* like the Italians, or *gateau* as the French do, or *kuchen* as they say in Germany, there isn't an occasion that is not made a little happier by cake.

If you're planning to do much baking (and we hope you will now), you'll find an electric mixer a marvelous investment. One thing, though—DON'T OVER-BEAT. Timing is of utmost importance when you use a mixer. If the recipe says, "Beat for two minutes," do just that, and at the specified speed. Over-beating would beat out the air and make your cake fall. Even when you add the various ingredients, turn off the mixer between additions. Those few extra seconds of beating could spoil your cake.

For the best cakes, read the recipe carefully all the way through before you start. In cake baking, there isn't room for the cook's imagination, so follow the recipe to the letter if you want a perfect result. Don't guess! Accurate measurements are essential. Use standard measuring cups, spoons, and cake pans.

Have your oven checked regularly for accuracy. Correct temperatures are also essential for successful baking.

The ingredients of a cake are something like the instruments in an orchestra. Each plays a specific part: one makes the cake rise; another gives it tender-ness; another makes it brown beautifully. And of course you know that the best cakes start with the best ingredients.

Flour is the basic ingredient that gives body to your cake. Some packaged cake flours already contain baking powder and salt (self-rising flour); when this type of flour is used, follow the directions on the package.

Sugar gives flavor and tenderness to your cake. It is necessary for browning and good texture.

Shortening adds richness and makes your cake tender. It prolongs freshness and distributes the flavoring. Shortenings differ in action, so use the one the recipe specifies.

Baking powder controls much of the height, grain, and texture of the cake. It is called a leavening agent; other leavening agents are soda and air.

Soda is generally used in recipes calling for sour cream, buttermilk, or molasses.

Eggs and the other ingredients together contribute to the framework of the cake. They also add flavor and increase volume, especially in cakes where egg whites are beaten separately and folded into the batter.
Use only fresh eggs—eggs that have thick whites and yolks that don't spread when eggs are broken.
Whole eggs and egg whites beat more easily if they are at room temperature when you beat them. If your kitchen is very warm, keep eggs refrigerated until ready to use.

Liquid, usually sweet milk or buttermilk, dissolves the sugar and salt and develops the starch and gluten in the flour.

Notes on Cakes

1. All our cakes were developed using sifted flour. If the unsifted type is substituted, follow manufacturer's directions.

2. Our cake recipes were tested using double-acting baking powder.

3. When a recipe calls for shortening, use one of the soft emulsifier types, such as Snowdrift, Crisco, Spry, or Fluffo.

4. Do not substitute shortening in recipes that specifically call for butter or margarine.

5. Our cake recipes were tested using large eggs.

6. Make sure all ingredients are at room temperature.

7. For best results, use only pans that are the size recommended in the recipe. To measure pans: For diameter, width, or length, measure across the top of pan with ruler, from one inside edge to the other. For depth, measure inside of sidewall.

8. To ensure even and delicate browning of cakes, use metal cake pans with a bright, shiny finish. If using metal cake pans with a dull finish or oven-glass cake dishes, decrease oven temperature 25 degrees, to prevent overbrowning.

9. If baking a single cake, place on rack in center of oven. If baking two layers, place both on same rack in center of oven, being careful pans do not touch sides of oven or each other. If baking three layers, adjust oven racks to divide oven into thirds; do not place one pan directly over another.

10. Do not open oven door to test cake until minimum baking time has elapsed.

TO REMOVE CAKES FROM PANS

Layer cakes: Carefully run a knife or metal spatula around edge of cake, to loosen from pan; invert on wire rack; remove pan. Then place another wire rack on top of cake; invert again, so cake cools right side up.

Tube cakes: Using an up-and-down motion, run a knife or metal spatula carefully around edge of cake and around tube, to loosen cake from pan. If tube pan does not have a lift-out bottom, hit pan sharply on table; then invert pan, and turn out cake.

TO CUT CAKES

Angel-food, chiffon, and sponge cakes:
Use a knife with a serrated edge. Cut cake gently, back and forth, with a sawing motion.

Frosted layer cakes: Use a knife with a thin, sharp edge. Rinse knife in hot water after making each cut.

TO FREEZE CAKES

Kinds to freeze: All types of unfrosted cake and cupcake may be frozen.

Frosted cakes: Cakes frosted with butter or fudge frostings may be frozen successfully. Do not freeze cakes with whipped-cream or fluffy frostings. Freeze cakes, unwrapped, until frosting is firm; then wrap in freezer wrap; label, and freeze. If possible, place wrapped cake in a box when freezing, to prevent crushing.

Unfrosted cakes: Wrap completely cooled cakes in freezer wrap; label, and freeze. When freezing layer cakes, wrap each layer separately. If possible, place wrapped cake in a box when freezing, to prevent crushing.

Length of storage: Unfrosted cakes may be stored in freezer 2 to 3 months. Frosted cake may be stored only 1 to 2 months.

TO THAW CAKES

Unfrosted layers: Let stand, still wrapped, at room temperature about 1 hour. Let larger cakes stand, still wrapped, about 2 hours.

Frosted cakes: Remove freezer wrap. Let stand at room temperature until thawed—about 2 hours.

TO STORE CAKES

Cover loosely with moistureproof wrap; or place under a "cake saver" or large, inverted bowl. Always store cakes with whipped-cream or cream fillings in refrigerator.

Conventional cakes are those made by the "creaming method," working sugar into softened butter or margarine until the mixture is light and fluffy, then adding whole eggs, one at a time, and beating the batter thoroughly to incorporate more air.

McCALL'S BEST CHOCOLATE LOAF CAKE

1 cup boiling water
2 squares unsweetened chocolate, cut-up
2 cups sifted all-purpose flour
¼ teaspoon salt
1 teaspoon baking soda
½ cup soft butter or margarine
1 teaspoon vanilla extract
1¾ cups light-brown sugar, firmly packed
2 eggs
½ cup dairy sour cream

1. In small bowl, pour boiling water over chocolate; let cool.

2. Meanwhile, preheat oven to 325F. Grease well and flour a 9-by-5-by-3-inch loaf pan.

3. Sift flour with salt and soda; set aside.

4. In large bowl of electric mixer, at high speed, beat butter, vanilla, sugar, and eggs until light and fluffy—about 5 minutes—occasionally scraping side of bowl with rubber scraper.

5. At low speed, beat in flour mixture (in fourths), alternately with sour cream (in thirds), beginning and ending with flour mixture.

6. Beat in chocolate mixture just until combined.

(*McCall's Best Chocolate Loaf Cake continued*)

7. Pour batter into prepared pan. Bake 60 to 70 minutes, or until cake tester inserted in center comes out clean.

8. Cool in pan 15 minutes. Remove from pan; cool thoroughly on wire rack. Serve plain, with ice cream and chocolate sauce, or frost as desired.

CLOVE CAKE

3 cups sifted all-purpose flour	1 cup seedless raisins
1 tablespoon cloves	1 cup soft butter or margarine
1 tablespoon cinnamon	2¼ cups sugar
1 teaspoon baking powder	5 eggs
½ teaspoon baking soda	1 cup buttermilk or sour milk*
⅛ teaspoon salt	

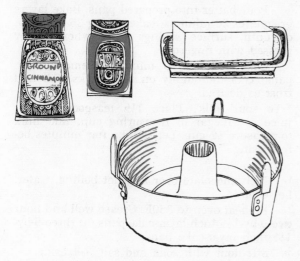

1. Preheat oven to 350F. Grease well a 10-inch tube pan.

2. Sift 2¾ cups flour with cloves, cinnamon, baking powder, soda, and salt; set aside. Toss remaining flour with raisins.

3. In large bowl of electric mixer, at medium speed, beat butter until creamy. Gradually add sugar, beating until light—about 5 minutes.

4. In small bowl of mixer, beat eggs until very light and fluffy. Blend into sugar mixture at medium speed, using rubber scraper to clean side of bowl.

5. At low speed, alternately blend into sugar-egg mixture the dry ingredients (in thirds) and milk (in halves), beginning and ending with dry ingredients. Beat only until blended. Stir in floured raisins.

6. Pour batter into prepared tube pan; bake 60 to 65 minutes, or until cake tester inserted in center comes out clean.

7. Cool cake in pan, on wire rack, 20 minutes. Gently loosen, with a spatula; turn out of pan onto rack. Cool completely—takes about 1 hour. This is a large, moist cake that keeps well.

* To sour milk: Put 1 tablespoon lemon juice or vinegar in measuring cup. Add milk to make 1 cup. Let stand a few minutes before using.

OLD-FASHIONED MOLASSES CAKE

1½ cups sifted all-purpose flour	¼ teaspoon salt
	1 egg, beaten
1½ teaspoons baking soda	½ cup butter or margarine, melted
½ teaspoon cinnamon	
½ teaspoon ginger	1 cup light molasses
¼ teaspoon cloves	½ cup hot water

1. Preheat oven to 375F. Grease a 9-by-9-by-1¾-inch baking pan.

2. Sift flour with soda, spices, and salt; set aside.

3. In large bowl, with rotary beater or portable electric mixer, beat egg, butter, molasses, and water until combined.

4. Add flour mixture, beating until smooth.

5. Pour into prepared pan; bake 30 to 35 minutes, or until cake tester inserted in center comes out clean.

6. Cool partially, in pan, on wire rack. To serve, cut into squares while still warm.

COCOA DEVIL'S-FOOD CAKE

½ cup sifted unsweetened
    cocoa
1 cup boiling water
2¼ cups sifted all-purpose
    flour
½ teaspoon baking soda
1 teaspoon baking powder
½ teaspoon salt

½ cup soft butter or
    margarine
2 cups sugar
2 eggs
1 teaspoon vanilla extract
½ cup buttermilk or sour
    milk*

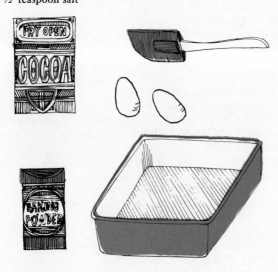

1. In small bowl, combine cocoa with boiling water, mixing well. Let cool.
2. Meanwhile, preheat oven to 350F. Grease well and flour two 8-by-1½-inch layer-cake pans; or two 8-by-8-by-2-inch baking pans; or a 13-by-9-by-2-inch baking pan.
3. Sift flour with soda, baking powder, and salt; set aside.
4. In large bowl of electric mixer, at high speed, beat butter, sugar, eggs, and vanilla until light and fluffy—about 5 minutes—occasionally scraping side of bowl and guiding mixture into beaters with rubber scraper.
5. At low speed, blend in flour mixture (in fourths), alternately with combined buttermilk and cocoa mixture (in thirds), beginning and ending with flour mixture; beat just until smooth.
6. Pour batter into prepared pans. Bake layers or squares 30 minutes; bake oblong 35 minutes; or until surface springs back when gently pressed with fingertip.
7. Cool in pans 10 minutes. Remove from pans; cool thoroughly on wire racks. Fill and frost as desired.

* To sour milk: Place 1½ teaspoons lemon juice or vinegar in measuring cup. Add milk to measure ½ cup. Let stand a few minutes before using.

McCALL'S BEST DEVIL'S-FOOD CAKE

3 squares unsweetened
    chocolate
2¼ cups sifted cake flour
2 teaspoons baking soda
½ teaspoon salt
½ cup soft butter or
    margarine

2½ cups light-brown sugar,
    firmly packed
3 eggs
2 teaspoons vanilla extract
½ cup sour milk*
    or buttermilk
1 cup boiling water

1. Melt chocolate over hot, not boiling, water. Let cool.
2. Preheat oven to 350F. Grease well and flour two 9-by-1½-inch layer-cake pans; or three 8-by-1½-inch layer-cake pans.
3. Sift flour with soda and salt; set aside.
4. In large bowl of electric mixer, at high speed, beat butter, sugar, eggs, and vanilla until light and fluffy—about 5 minutes—occasionally scraping side of bowl with rubber scraper.
5. At low speed, beat in chocolate.
6. Beat in flour mixture (in fourths), alternately with milk (in thirds), beginning and ending with flour mixture. Beat just until smooth—about 1 minute.
7. Beat in water just until mixture is smooth. Batter will be thin.
8. Pour batter into prepared pans; bake 30 to 35 minutes, or until surface springs back when gently pressed with fingertip.

(*McCall's Best Devil's-Food Cake continued*)

9. Cool in pans 10 minutes. Remove from pans; cool thoroughly on wire racks. Fill and frost as desired.

* To sour milk: Place 1½ teaspoons lemon juice or vinegar in measuring cup. Add milk to measure ½ cup. Let stand a few minutes before using.

MARBLE LOAF CAKE

1½ squares unsweetened chocolate	½ cup soft butter or margarine
2½ cups sifted cake flour	1½ cups sugar
¾ teaspoon salt	3 eggs
3 teaspoons baking powder	¾ teaspoon vanilla extract
	¾ cup milk

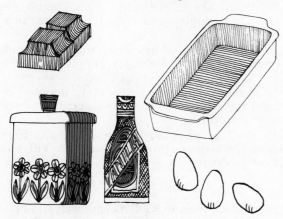

1. Melt chocolate over hot, not boiling, water. Let cool.

2. Preheat oven to 350F. Grease and flour a 9-by-5-by-3-inch loaf pan.

3. Sift flour with salt and baking powder; set aside.

4. In large bowl of electric mixer, at medium speed, beat butter and sugar until light.

5. Add eggs and vanilla, beating until very light and fluffy.

6. At low speed, beat in flour mixture (in fourths), alternately with milk (in thirds), beginning and ending with flour mixture.

7. In medium bowl, combine about one third batter with chocolate, mixing well.

8. Spoon plain and chocolate batters, alternately, into prepared pan. With spatula or knife, cut through batter, forming a Z.

9. Bake 65 minutes, or until cake tester inserted in center comes out clean.

10. Cool in pan 15 minutes. Remove from pan; cool thoroughly on wire rack. To serve, cut in thin slices.

NUT LAYER CAKE

2¼ cups sifted cake flour	3 eggs
1½ teaspoons baking powder	⅔ cup milk
½ teaspoon salt	⅛ teaspoon vanilla extract
Dash mace	⅛ teaspoon almond extract
⅔ cup shortening	½ cup chopped walnuts, pecans, or pistachio nuts
1⅓ cups sugar	

1. Preheat oven to 350F. Grease well and flour two 8-by-1½-inch layer-cake pans.

2. Sift flour with baking powder, salt, and mace; set aside.

3. In large bowl of electric mixer, at medium speed, beat shortening until creamy. Gradually add sugar, beating until light and fluffy.

4. Add eggs, one at a time, beating after each addition; then beat until very light and fluffy.

5. At low speed, beat in flour mixture (in fourths), alternately with milk (in thirds), beginning and ending with flour mixture. Mix only until smooth. Stir in extracts and nuts.

6. Pour batter into prepared pans; bake 35 to 40 minutes, or until surface springs back when gently pressed with fingertip.

7. Cool in pans 10 minutes. Remove from pans; cool on wire racks. Fill; frost as desired.

SOUR-CREAM LAYER CAKE

½ cup egg whites (about 4)
2½ cups sifted cake flour
1½ teaspoons baking
   powder
1 teaspoon baking soda
½ teaspoon salt
1½ cups sugar

½ cup soft butter
   or margarine
1 cup dairy sour cream
1 teaspoon vanilla extract,
   or 2 teaspoons grated
   lemon peel

1. In small bowl of electric mixer, let egg whites warm to room temperature—about 1 hour.
2. Meanwhile, preheat oven to 350F. Grease well and flour two 8-by-1½-inch layer-cake pans, or a 13-by-9-by-2-inch baking pan.
3. Sift flour with baking powder, soda, and salt; set aside.
4. At high speed, beat egg whites until foamy. Gradually beat in ½ cup sugar, beating well after each addition. Beat just until soft peaks form when beater is slowly raised; set aside.
5. In large bowl of electric mixer, at high speed, cream butter with rest of sugar until light and fluffy.
6. At low speed, beat in flour mixture (in fourths), alternately with sour cream (in thirds), beginning and ending with flour mixture.
7. Beat in egg whites and vanilla just until mixture is smooth—about 1 minute.
8. Pour into prepared pans; bake layers 30 to 35 minutes; bake oblong 35 to 40 minutes; or until surface springs back when gently pressed with fingertip.
9. Cool in pans 10 minutes. Remove from pans; cool thoroughly on wire rack. Fill and frost as desired.

McCALL'S BEST SPICECAKE

2½ cups sifted cake flour
1 teaspoon baking powder
1 teaspoon baking soda
1 teaspoon salt
1 teaspoon cinnamon
½ teaspoon cloves
⅛ teaspoon pepper

½ cup soft butter or
   margarine
½ cup light-brown sugar,
   firmly packed
1 cup granulated sugar
2 eggs
1 teaspoon vanilla extract
1¼ cups buttermilk

1. Preheat oven to 350F. Grease well and flour two 8-by-1½-inch layer-cake pans, or a 13-by-9-by-2-inch baking pan.
2. Sift flour with baking powder, soda, salt, cinnamon, cloves, and pepper.
3. In large bowl of electric mixer, at high speed, beat butter, sugars, eggs, and vanilla until light and fluffy—about 5 minutes—occasionally scraping side of bowl with rubber scraper.
4. At low speed, beat in flour mixture (in fourths), alternately with buttermilk (in thirds), beginning and ending with flour mixture. Beat just until smooth—about 1 minute.
5. Pour batter into prepared pans; bake layers 30 to 35 minutes; bake oblong 40 to 45 minutes; or until surface springs back when gently pressed with fingertip.
6. Cool in pans 10 minutes. Remove from pans; cool thoroughly on wire racks. Fill and frost as desired.

McCALL'S BEST YELLOW CAKE

3 cups sifted cake flour
2½ teaspoons baking
    powder
1 teaspoon salt
¾ cup soft butter or
    margarine

1½ cups sugar
3 eggs
1 teaspoon vanilla extract
1 cup milk

1.   Preheat oven to 350F. Grease well and flour three 8-by-1½-inch layer-cake pans, or two 9-by-1½-inch layer-cake pans.

2.   Sift flour with baking powder and salt; set aside.

3.   In large bowl of electric mixer, at high speed, beat butter, sugar, eggs, and vanilla until light and fluffy—about 5 minutes—occasionally scraping side of bowl and guiding mixture into beaters with rubber scraper.

4.   At low speed, beat in flour mixture (in fourths), alternately with milk (in thirds), beginning and ending with flour mixture; beat only until smooth.

5.   Pour batter into prepared pans; bake 30 to 35 minutes, or until surface springs back when gently pressed with fingertip.

6.   Cool in pans 10 minutes. Remove from pans; cool thoroughly on wire racks. Fill and frost as desired.

McCALL'S BEST WHITE CAKE

¾ cup egg whites (about 6)
2¾ cups sifted cake flour
3 teaspoons baking powder
½ teaspoon salt
1½ cups sugar

¾ cup soft butter or
    margarine
1 teaspoon vanilla extract
½ teaspoon almond extract
1 cup milk

1.   In small bowl of electric mixer, let egg whites warm to room temperature—about 1 hour.

2.   Meanwhile, preheat oven to 350F. Grease well and flour three 8-by-1½-inch layer-cake pans, or two 9-by-1½-inch layer-cake pans.

3.   Sift flour with baking powder and salt; set aside.

4.   At high speed, beat whites until foamy. Gradually beat in ½ cup sugar, beating well after each addition. Beat until soft peaks form when beater is slowly raised; set aside.

5.   In large bowl of electric mixer, at high speed, cream butter with rest of sugar and the extracts until light and fluffy.

6.   At low speed, beat in flour mixture (in fourths), alternately with milk (in thirds), beginning and ending with flour mixture.

7.   Beat in egg whites just until batter is smooth—about 1 minute.

8.   Pour batter into prepared pans; bake 25 to 30 minutes, or until surface springs back when gently pressed with fingertip.

9.   Cool in pans 10 minutes. Remove from pans; cool thoroughly on wire racks.

Oⁿe-bowl cakes are those in which the ingredients are mixed in one bowl, according to a strict formula, which eliminates guesswork and promises even an inexperienced cook a uniformly good result every time. Here, your electric mixer is worth its weight in diamonds!

BANANA CAKE

2¼ cups sifted cake flour
2½ teaspoons baking
    powder
½ teaspoon baking soda
½ teaspoon salt
1¼ cups sugar
½ cup shortening

1 cup mashed ripe bananas
    (2 or 3)
1 teaspoon vanilla extract
2 eggs
½ cup buttermilk or sour
    milk*

1. Preheat oven to 350F. Grease well and flour two 8-by-1½-inch layer-cake pans, or a 13-by-9-by-2-inch baking pan.

2. Into large bowl of electric mixer, sift flour with baking powder, soda, salt, and sugar.

3. Add shortening, bananas, and vanilla; at low speed, beat just until ingredients are combined.

4. At medium speed, beat 2 minutes, occasionally scraping side of bowl and guiding mixture into beaters with rubber scraper.

5. Add eggs and buttermilk; beat 2 minutes longer.

6. Pour batter into prepared pans; bake layers 30 to 35 minutes; oblong 40 to 45 minutes; or until surface springs back when gently pressed with fingertip.

7. Cool in pans 10 minutes. Remove from pans; cool thoroughly on wire racks. Fill and frost layers with sweetened whipped cream, and garnish with banana slices; or fill and frost as desired.

* To sour milk: Place 1½ teaspoons vinegar or lemon juice in a measuring cup. Add milk to measure ½ cup. Let stand a few minutes before using.

McCALL'S BEST RED DEVIL'S-FOOD CAKE

1¾ cups sifted cake flour
1½ cups sugar
⅓ cup sifted unsweetened
    cocoa
1¼ teaspoons baking soda
1 teaspoon salt

½ cup shortening
1 cup buttermilk or sour
    milk*
2 eggs
1 teaspoon vanilla extract

1. Preheat oven to 350F. Grease well and flour two 8-by-1½-inch layer-cake pans, or a 13-by-9-by-2-inch baking pan.

2. Into large bowl of electric mixer, sift flour with sugar, cocoa, soda, and salt.

3. Add shortening and buttermilk. At medium speed, beat 2 minutes, occasionally scraping side of bowl and guiding mixture into beaters with rubber scraper.

(McCall's Best Red Devil's-Food Cake continued)

4. Add eggs and vanilla; beat 2 minutes longer.

5. Pour batter into prepared pans; bake layers 30 to 35 minutes; oblong 40 to 45 minutes; or until surface springs back when gently pressed with fingertip.

6. Cool in pans 10 minutes. Remove from pans; cool thoroughly on wire racks.
Fill and frost as desired.

* To sour milk: Place 1 tablespoon vinegar or lemon juice in measuring cup. Add milk to measure 1 cup. Let stand a few minutes before using.

BURNT-SUGAR CAKE

Syrup:
½ cup sugar
½ cup boiling water

Cake:
2½ cups sifted cake flour

1 cup sugar
3 teaspoons baking powder
1 teaspoon salt
½ cup shortening
2 eggs
1 teaspoon vanilla extract

1. Make Syrup: Melt sugar in small, heavy skillet, over very low heat. Shake pan slightly as sugar melts. Heat, stirring constantly, until dark-golden. Remove from heat.

2. Gradually stir in boiling water. Over low heat, cook, stirring constantly, until sugar is dissolved.

3. Pour syrup into measuring cup; add water to make 1 cup liquid. Set aside to cool—about 1 hour.

4. Meanwhile, preheat oven to 350F. Grease well and flour two 8-by-1½-inch layer-cake pans, or two 9-by-1½-inch layer-cake pans.

5. Make Cake: Into large bowl of electric mixer, sift flour with sugar, baking powder, and salt.

6. Add shortening and ¾ cup syrup. At medium speed, beat 2 minutes, occasionally scraping side of bowl and guiding mixture into beaters with rubber scraper.

7. Add eggs, vanilla, and rest of syrup; beat 2 minutes longer.

8. Pour batter into prepared pans; bake 30 to 35 minutes, or until surface springs back when gently pressed with fingertip.

9. Cool in pans 10 minutes. Remove from pans; cool thoroughly on wire racks. Fill and frost as desired.

SOUR-CREAM FUDGE CAKE

2 squares unsweetened
    chocolate
2 cups sifted cake flour
1½ cups sugar
1 teaspoon baking soda

1 teaspoon salt
½ cup shortening
1 cup dairy sour cream
2 eggs
1 teaspoon vanilla extract

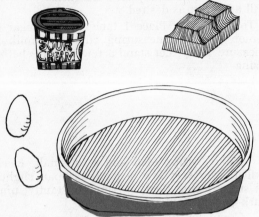

1. Preheat oven to 350F. Grease well and flour two 8-by-1½-inch layer-cake pans, or a 13-by-9-by-2-inch baking pan.

2. Melt chocolate over hot, not boiling, water; let cool.

3. Into large bowl of electric mixer, sift flour with sugar, soda, and salt.

4. Add shortening and sour cream. At medium speed, beat 2 minutes, occasionally scraping side of bowl and guiding mixture into beaters with rubber scraper.

5. Add eggs, vanilla, chocolate, and ¼ cup hot water; beat 2 minutes longer.

6. Pour batter into prepared pans; bake layers 30 to 35 minutes; oblong 35 to 40 minutes; or until surface springs back when gently pressed with fingertip.

7. Cool in pans 10 minutes. Remove from pans; cool thoroughly on wire racks. Fill and frost as desired.

McCALL'S BEST GOLD CAKE

2½ cups sifted cake flour
1½ cups sugar
1 teaspoon salt
3 teaspoons baking powder
½ cup shortening
1¼ cups milk

5 egg yolks (½ cup)
1 teaspoon vanilla extract,
    or 2 teaspoons grated
    lemon peel, or 1
    tablespoon grated
    orange peel

1. Preheat oven to 350F. Grease well and flour three 8-by-1½-inch layer-cake pans, or two 9-by-1½-inch layer-cake pans, or a 13-by-9-by-2-inch baking pan.

2. Into large bowl of electric mixer, sift flour with sugar, salt, and baking powder.

3. Add shortening and ¾ cup milk. At medium speed, beat 2 minutes, occasionally scraping side of bowl and guiding mixture into beaters with rubber scraper.

4. Add egg yolks, vanilla, and remaining milk; beat 2 minutes longer.

5. Pour batter into prepared pans; bake layers 30 to 35 minutes; oblong 35 to 40 minutes; or until surface springs back when gently pressed with fingertip.

6. Cool in pans 10 minutes. Remove from pans; cool thoroughly on wire racks. Fill and frost as desired.

OLD-FASHIONED APPLESAUCE CAKE

2½ cups sifted all-purpose
    flour
1¾ cups sugar
¼ teaspoon baking powder
1½ teaspoons baking soda
1½ teaspoons salt
1 teaspoon cinnamon
½ teaspoon cloves
½ teaspoon allspice

½ teaspoon nutmeg
½ cup shortening
1 can (15 oz) applesauce
    (1¾ cups)
3 eggs (⅔ cup)
1 cup seedless raisins,
    chopped
1 cup finely chopped
    walnuts

MAKES 16 SERVINGS

1. Preheat oven to 350F. Grease well and flour a 13-by-9-by-2-inch baking pan.

2. Sift flour, sugar, baking powder, baking soda, salt, and spices into large bowl of electric mixer. Add shortening and applesauce; beat 1 minute, at low speed, just to combine.

3. At medium speed, beat 2 minutes, constantly cleaning side of bowl with rubber scraper and guiding batter into beaters.

4. Add eggs; beat 2 minutes.

5. Combine raisins and walnuts; fold into batter with rubber scraper.

6. Turn batter into prepared pan; bake 45 minutes, or until cake tester inserted in center comes out clean.

7. Let cake cool completely in pan on wire rack. To serve, cut into 16 rectangles. Frost as desired.

FAVORITE ONE-EGG CAKE

2 cups sifted cake flour
1 cup sugar
2½ teaspoons baking
    powder
1 teaspoon salt

⅓ cup shortening
1 cup milk
1 egg
1 teaspoon vanilla extract

1. Preheat oven to 350F. Grease well and flour two 8-by-1½-inch layer-cake pans, or a 9-by-9-by-1¾-inch baking pan.

2. Into large bowl of electric mixer, sift flour with sugar, baking powder, and salt.

3. Add shortening and milk. At medium speed, beat 2 minutes, occasionally scraping side of bowl and guiding mixture into beaters with rubber scraper.

4. Add egg and vanilla; beat 2 minutes longer.

5. Pour batter into prepared pans; bake layers 25 to 30 minutes; square 30 to 35 minutes; or until surface springs back when gently pressed with fingertip.

6. Cool in pans 10 minutes. Remove from pans; cool thoroughly on wire racks. Fill and frost as desired.

BOSTON CREAM PIE

1. Bake two 8-inch Favorite One-Egg Cake layers.

2. Prepare half Rich Vanilla Cream Filling* recipe. Use to put cooled layers together.

3. Pour Chocolate Glaze* on top of cake, letting it run down side.

* See Frostings and Fillings Chapter.

SILVERY WHITE CAKE

4 egg whites
2¼ cups sifted cake flour
1½ cups sugar
3½ teaspoons baking
    powder
1 teaspoon salt
½ cup shortening

1 cup milk
1½ teaspoons vanilla
    extract, or 1 teaspoon
    vanilla extract plus ¼
    teaspoon almond
    extract

1. In small bowl, let egg whites warm to room temperature—about 1 hour.

2. Meanwhile, preheat oven to 350F. Grease well and flour two 8-by-1½-inch layer-cake pans, or two 9-by-1½-inch layer-cake pans, or a 13-by-9-by-2-inch baking pan.

3. Into large bowl of electric mixer, sift flour with sugar, baking powder, and salt.

4. Add shortening, ¾ cup milk, and vanilla. At low speed, beat only until ingredients are combined.

5. At medium speed, beat 2 minutes, occasionally scraping side of bowl and guiding mixture into beaters with rubber scraper.

6. Add unbeaten egg whites and rest of milk; beat 2 minutes longer.

7. Pour batter into prepared pans; bake layers 30 to 35 minutes; oblong 35 to 40 minutes; or until surface springs back when gently pressed with fingertip.

8. Cool in pans 10 minutes. Remove from pans; cool thoroughly on wire racks. Fill and frost as desired.

TWO-EGG YELLOW CAKE

2 cups sifted all-purpose
    flour
1½ cups sugar
3 teaspoons baking powder
1 teaspoon salt

½ cup shortening
1 cup milk
1 teaspoon vanilla extract
2 eggs

1. Preheat oven to 350F. Grease well and flour two 8-by-1½-inch layer-cake pans, or a 13-by-9-by-2-inch baking pan.

2. Into large bowl of electric mixer, sift flour with sugar, baking powder, and salt.

3. Add shortening, milk, and vanilla. With mixer at medium speed, beat 2 minutes, occasionally scraping side of bowl with rubber scraper and guiding mixture into beaters.

4. Add eggs; beat 2 minutes longer.

5. Pour batter into prepared pans; bake layers 30 to 35 minutes; oblong 35 to 40 minutes; or until surface springs back when gently pressed with fingertip.

6. Cool in pans 10 minutes. Remove from pans; cool thoroughly on wire racks. Fill and frost as desired.

Poundcake, delicious and moist, traces its name to its ingredients. Look in an old colonial cookbook. You'll discover that the recipe calls for "ye pound" of each of the basic ingredients—sugar, butter, flour, eggs. Poundcake, thinly sliced, is especially delicious with a dish of berries or a glass of port.

McCALL'S BEST POUNDCAKE

MAKES ABOUT 30 SERVINGS

1¼ cups egg whites (9 egg whites)

3 cups sifted all-purpose flour

1 teaspoon baking powder

½ teaspoon salt

2 cups sugar

9 egg yolks

2 cups soft butter or margarine

2 teaspoons vanilla or almond extract

1. In large bowl of electric mixer, let egg whites warm to room temperature—about 1 hour.

2. Meanwhile, preheat oven to 350F. Grease well and flour a 10-inch tube pan, or two 9-by-5-by-3-inch loaf pans.

3. Sift flour with baking powder and salt; set aside.

4. At high speed of electric mixer, beat egg whites until foamy. Gradually beat in 1 cup sugar, ¼ cup at a time, beating after each addition. Continue beating until soft peaks form when beater is slowly raised. Gently transfer egg whites to medium bowl.

5. In same bowl of electric mixer, at high speed, beat egg yolks with remaining sugar, butter, and vanilla until light and fluffy—about 5 minutes.

6. At low speed, beat in flour mixture just until smooth and well combined.

7. At low speed, gradually beat in egg whites just until blended, scraping side of bowl and guiding batter into beaters with rubber scraper.

8. Turn batter into prepared pan; bake tube 65 to 70 minutes; bake loaf 60 to 65 minutes; or until cake tester inserted in center comes out clean.

9. Cool in pan on wire rack 15 minutes. Remove from pan; cool thoroughly on wire rack.

10. Serve plain, or frost as desired. To serve, cut into thin slices.

SPICE POUNDCAKE

3 cups sifted all-purpose
　　flour
½ teaspoon baking powder
½ teaspoon baking soda
¼ teaspoon salt
2 teaspoons cinnamon
1 teaspoon cloves

1 cup soft butter or
　　margarine
2 cups sugar
4 eggs
1 teaspoon vanilla extract
1 cup buttermilk

1. Preheat oven to 350F. Grease well and flour a 10-inch tube pan.

2. Sift flour with baking powder, soda, salt, cinnamon, and cloves; set aside.

3. In large bowl of electric mixer, at medium speed, beat butter with sugar until light.

4. Add eggs and vanilla; beat until very light and fluffy.

5. At low speed, beat in flour mixture (in fourths), alternately with buttermilk (in thirds), beginning and ending with flour mixture; beat only until combined.

6. Turn into prepared pan. Bake 60 to 65 minutes, or until cake tester inserted in center comes out clean.

7. Cool in pan, on wire rack, 15 minutes. Then turn out on rack; cool completely. To serve, slice thinly.

Walnut Spice Poundcake: Stir 1 cup finely chopped walnuts into batter before turning into prepared pan.

WALNUT POUNDCAKE

5 eggs
1½ cups sifted all-purpose
　　flour
½ teaspoon baking powder
1 cup butter or margarine

½ teaspoon vanilla extract
1 cup sugar
¾ cup finely chopped wal-
　　nuts

1. Preheat oven to 325F. Grease well and flour 9-by-5-by-3-inch loaf pan.

2. Separate eggs, putting whites in large bowl.

3. Sift flour with baking powder; set aside.

4. In large bowl of electric mixer, at medium speed, cream butter and vanilla until light. Gradually add ½ cup sugar, beating until very light and fluffy.

5. Then add egg yolks, one at a time, beating well after each addition.

6. At low speed, beat in flour mixture only until combined. Stir in walnuts.

7. Beat egg whites, with rotary beater or portable electric mixer, just until soft peaks form when beater is slowly raised.

8. Add remaining sugar, 2 tablespoons at a time, beating until stiff peaks form when beater is slowly raised.

9. With wire whisk or rubber scraper, using an under-and-over motion, gently fold egg whites into batter just until combined.

10. Pour batter into prepared pan; bake 1 hour and 10 minutes, or until cake tester inserted in center comes out clean.

11. Cool in pan, on wire rack, 15 minutes. Then turn out on rack; cool completely. To serve, slice thinly.

Fruitcakes are ceremonial cakes, served traditionally on important holidays and at important occasions, like weddings. Though there may be women who enjoy the ancient tradition of shelling and mincing barrels of nuts and tubs of candied fruits, today most prefer to buy the nuts already shelled and the fruits already prepared. Fruitcakes improve with storage. Because they keep well, it is proportionately less trouble to make a large amount than a small one, especially if you intend the fruitcakes as gifts.

NO-BAKE FESTIVE FRUITCAKE

4 cups miniature
  marshmallows
8 cups graham-cracker
  crumbs
2 cups seedless raisins
1 pkg (8 oz) pitted dates,
  finely chopped
1½ cups diced mixed
  candied fruit
1½ cups walnuts, coarsely
  chopped
½ teaspoon cinnamon
½ teaspoon nutmeg
¼ teaspoon cloves
6 tablespoons orange juice
1 cup evaporated milk,
  undiluted

MAKES TWO
2¼-POUND FRUITCAKES

1. Line two 9-by-5-by-3-inch loaf pans with waxed paper; set aside.
2. In large bowl, combine all ingredients except orange juice and evaporated milk; mix well, using hands if necessary.
3. Add remaining ingredients; mix well, with hands, until graham-cracker crumbs are moistened.
4. Pack mixture evenly into loaf pans; cover with foil; refrigerate at least 2 days before serving.

WHITE FRUITCAKE

1¼ cups light raisins
1 can (4 oz) shredded
  coconut
1¼ cups coarsely chopped
  candied cherries
1¼ cups cubed candied
  pineapple
⅔ cup coarsely chopped
  pitted dates
1 cup dried currants
1 jar (8 oz) diced mixed
  candied fruit
1¼ cups coarsely chopped
  pecans
1¼ cups coarsely chopped
  walnuts
¾ cup coarsely chopped
  blanched almonds
2¾ cups sifted all-purpose
  flour
¾ cup soft butter or
  margarine
1 cup sugar
Dash salt
5 eggs
½ cup orange juice

MAKES A
7-POUND FRUITCAKE

1. Lightly oil a 10-inch tube pan. Line bottom and side with heavy brown wrapping paper; then lightly oil paper.
2. In very large bowl, toss fruits and nuts until well mixed. Sift ¼-cup flour over them; toss, coating evenly.
3. Preheat oven to 275F.
4. In large bowl of electric mixer, at medium speed, cream butter until light. Gradually add sugar, beating until light and fluffy.
5. Add salt. Add eggs, one at a time, beating after each addition; then beat until very light and fluffy.
6. At low speed, alternately blend in remaining flour (in fourths) and orange juice (in thirds), beginning and ending with flour.
7. Pour batter over fruit-nut mixture. With hands, mix until fruits and nuts are distributed through batter.
8. Turn into prepared pan, packing lightly; bake 3 hours, or until cake tester inserted in center comes out clean.
9. Cool cake completely in pan on wire rack. Then remove from pan, and peel off paper. Glaze, if desired.

CHRISTMAS FRUITCAKE

MAKES 3½-POUND LOAF

1 jar (8 oz) diced candied
pineapple

1 jar (4 oz) candied
cherries, halved

2 tablespoons chopped
candied citron

2 tablespoons chopped
candied lemon peel

2 tablespoons chopped
candied orange peel

1⅓ cups light raisins

⅔ cup dark raisins

⅓ cup currants

⅔ cup blanched almonds,
coarsely chopped

1 cup walnuts, coarsely
chopped

1½ cups sifted all-purpose
flour

¼ teaspoon allspice

¼ teaspoon cinnamon

¼ teaspoon baking soda

3 eggs

2 tablespoons brandy

3 tablespoons applesauce

½ teaspoon almond extract

¼ cup soft butter or
margarine

½ cup granulated sugar

½ cup light-brown sugar,
firmly packed

16 blanched almonds,
halved (optional)

1. Lightly grease an 11-by-4½-by-2¾-inch angel-food loaf pan. Line bottom and sides of pan with oiled, heavy brown paper; grease again.

2. In large bowl, combine pineapple, cherries, citron, lemon and orange peels, light and dark raisins, currants, almonds, walnuts, and ½ cup flour. Toss to mix well; set aside.

3. Sift rest of flour with allspice, cinnamon, and baking soda; set aside.

4. In small bowl, with fork, beat eggs until they are light. Beat in the brandy, applesauce, and almond extract.

5. In large bowl of electric mixer, at medium speed, beat butter with sugars until light and fluffy. Gradually beat in egg mixture.

6. At low speed, gradually beat in flour-spice mixture, beating only until combined. Preheat oven to 275F.

7. Turn fruit-and-nut mixture into batter; mix with hands or with wooden spoon or rubber scraper, to combine well.

8. Turn batter into prepared pan; press down well with rubber scraper, to make surface smooth and even.

9. If desired, arrange almond halves on batter in a pattern.

10. Bake about 2½ hours, or until cake tester inserted in center comes out clean. Let cool in pan on wire rack 30 minutes.

11. Turn out of pan. Let cool completely on wire rack. Store. Then glaze as desired.

Note: This basic recipe can be baked in different-size pans. Refer to the baking chart.

BAKING CHART FOR CHRISTMAS FRUITCAKE

Pan Size	Amount of Batter	Oven Temperature	Baking Time	Yield
11-by-4½-by-2¾-inch angel-food loaf pan	Recipe	275F	2½ hr	1 loaf cake
9-by-5-by-3-inch loaf pan	Recipe	275F	3 hr	1 loaf cake
10-inch tube pan	Recipe doubled	275F	3 hr, 15 min	1 large tube cake
2 (1-lb) coffee cans	Recipe (½ batter for each pan)	275F	2 hr	2 small round cakes
7 (4½-by-2½-by-1½-inch) individual loaf pans	Recipe (¾ cup batter for each pan)	275F	1 hr	7 small loaves
11 (5-oz) custard cups (unlined, greased)	Recipe (½ cup batter for each custard cup)	250F	1 hr, 10 min	11 cupcakes
160 foil bonbon cups (ungreased)	Recipe (1 teaspoon batter for each cup)	275F	½ hr	160 bonbons

Foam-type cakes are light-as-air cakes, including chiffon, angel, and sponge-cakes. Delicate in texture, these cakes are traditional party fare. All have one thing in common—stiffly beaten egg whites, on which their fluffiness depends.

Angel cakes. These are the lightest and tenderest of the foam cakes and call for the most egg whites.

Chiffon cakes. Enriched with egg yolks and salad oil, these combine the lightness of angel cake and the richness of a cake made with shortening. They require the dual leavening of egg whites and baking powder.

Spongecakes. Creamy yellow in color, these use both egg yolks and egg whites.

Important tip: Never grease the cake pan in which any foam-type cake is to be baked. If it has been used before to bake a cake with shortening, scour it, and dry it thoroughly before using it for a foam-type cake.

McCALL'S BEST ANGEL-FOOD CAKE

1¾ cups egg whites
    (12 to 14)
1¼ cups sifted cake flour
1¾ cups sugar
½ teaspoon salt

1½ teaspoons cream of
    tartar
1 teaspoon vanilla extract
½ teaspoon almond extract

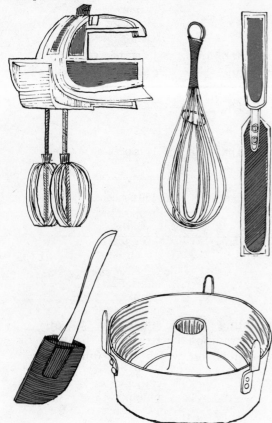

1. In large bowl, let egg whites warm to room temperature—about 1 hour.

2. Meanwhile, preheat oven to 375F.

3. Sift flour with ¾ cup sugar; resift 3 times; set aside.

4. With portable electric mixer, at high speed, beat egg whites with salt and cream of tartar until soft peaks form when beater is slowly raised.

5. Gradually beat in remaining sugar, ¼ cup at a time, beating well after each addition. Continue beating until stiff peaks form when beater is slowly raised.

6. With rubber scraper or wire whisk, gently fold extracts into egg whites until combined.

7. Sift flour mixture, one fourth at a time, over egg whites. With wire whisk or rubber scraper, using an under-and-over motion, gently fold in each addition with 15 strokes, rotating bowl a quarter of a turn after each addition.

8. Then fold an additional 10 strokes; flour mixture should be blended into egg whites.

9. With rubber scraper, gently push batter into ungreased 10-inch tube pan. With spatula or knife, cut through batter twice.

10. With rubber scraper, gently spread batter in pan until it is smooth on top and touches side of pan.

11. Bake, on lower oven rack, 35 to 40 minutes, or until cake tester inserted in center comes out clean.

12. Invert pan over neck of bottle; let cake cool completely—about 2 hours.

13. With spatula, carefully loosen cake from pan; remove. Serve plain, or frost as desired.

ANGEL-FOOD LOAF CAKES

1. Preheat oven to 375F. Prepare as directed above. Divide batter evenly between two ungreased 9-by-5-by-3-inch loaf pans.

2. Bake 30 to 35 minutes, or until cake tester inserted in center comes out clean.

3. Invert cakes by hanging each pan between 2 other pans. Let cool completely—about 1 hour.

Cherry-Pecan Angel-Food Cake: Just before turning batter into pan, fold in, ¼ cup at a time, ½ cup very-well-drained maraschino cherries mixed with ½ cup finely chopped pecans. Bake and cool as directed.

McCALL'S BEST DAFFODIL CAKE

White Batter:
1¾ cups egg whites
   (12 to 14)
1¼ cups sifted cake flour
1¾ cups sugar
½ teaspoon salt
1½ teaspoons cream of
   tartar

1½ teaspoons vanilla
   extract

Yellow Batter:
5 egg yolks
2 tablespoons cake flour
2 tablespoons sugar
1 tablespoon grated orange
   peel

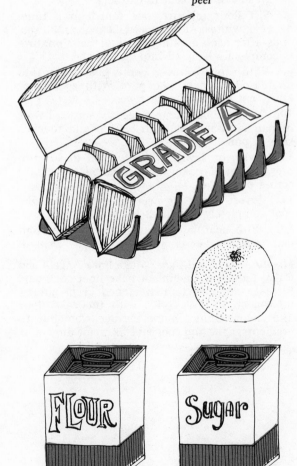

MAKES 20 SERVINGS

1. In large bowl, let egg whites warm to room temperature—about 1 hour.

2. Meanwhile, preheat oven to 375F.

3. Make White Batter: Sift flour with ¾ cup sugar; resift 3 times. Set aside.

4. With portable electric mixer, at high speed, beat egg whites with salt and cream of tartar until soft peaks form when beater is slowly raised.

5. Gradually beat in remaining sugar, ¼ cup at a time, beating well after each addition. Continue beating until stiff peaks form when beater is slowly raised.

6. With rubber scraper or wire whisk, gently fold vanilla into egg whites until well combined.

7. Sift flour mixture, one fourth at a time, over egg whites. With wire whisk or rubber scraper, using an under-and-over motion, gently fold in each addition with 15 strokes, rotating bowl a quarter of a turn after each addition.

8. Then fold an additional 10 strokes; flour mixture should be completely blended into egg whites. Put one third batter into medium bowl.

9. Make Yellow Batter: In small bowl, combine egg yolks with cake flour and sugar. With portable electric mixer, at high speed, beat until thick and lemon-colored. Stir in orange peel.

10. With rubber scraper or wire whisk, using an under-and-over motion, gently fold egg-yolk mixture into one third batter, with 15 strokes.

11. For marbled effect, spoon batters alternately into an ungreased 10-inch tube pan, ending with white batter on top. With spatula or knife, cut through batter twice.

12. With rubber scraper, gently spread batter in pan until it is smooth on top and touches side of pan.

13. Bake, on lower oven rack, 35 to 40 minutes, or until cake tester inserted in center comes out clean.

14. Invert pan over neck of bottle; let cake cool completely—about 2 hours.

15. With spatula, carefully loosen cake from pan; remove. Serve plain, or frost as desired.

EASY ANGEL-FOOD CAKE

MAKES 16 SERVINGS

1½ cups egg whites
(about 12)
1¼ cups sifted cake flour
1½ cups sugar
¼ teaspoon salt

1½ teaspoons cream of
tartar
1 teaspoon vanilla extract
¼ teaspoon almond extract

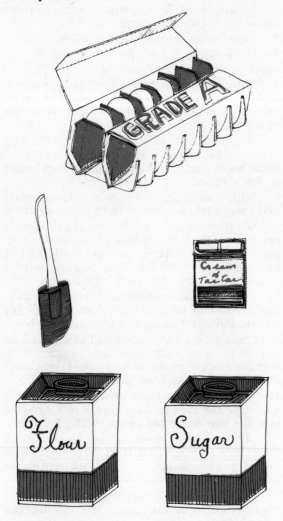

1. In large bowl of electric mixer, let egg whites warm to room temperature—about 1 hour.

2. Meanwhile, preheat oven to 375F.

3. Sift flour with ¾ cup sugar; resift 3 times; set aside.

4. With electric mixer, at medium speed, beat egg whites with salt and cream of tartar until soft peaks form when beater is slowly raised.

5. Gradually beat in remaining sugar, 3 tablespoons at a time, beating well after each addition.

6. At high speed, beat until stiff peaks form when beater is slowly raised.

7. At low speed, beat in extracts.

8. Sift flour mixture, one fourth at a time, over egg whites. At low speed, beat about 30 seconds after each addition, or until flour mixture is completely blended into egg whites.

9. With rubber scraper, gently push batter into ungreased 10-inch tube pan. With spatula or knife, cut through batter twice.

10. With rubber scraper, gently spread batter in pan until it is smooth on top and touches side of pan.

11. Bake, on lower oven rack, 35 to 40 minutes, or until cake tester inserted in center comes out clean.

12. Invert pan over neck of bottle; let cake cool completely—about 2 hours.

13. With spatula, carefully loosen cake from pan; remove. Serve plain, or frost as desired.

Mocha Angel-Food Cake: Make Easy Angel-Food Cake, reducing amount of cake flour to 1 cup. Sift ¼ cup sifted unsweetened cocoa and 1 tablespoon instant coffee with the cake flour and sugar. Omit almond extract. Combine ingredients, bake and cool cake as recipe directs.

APRICOT CHIFFON CAKE

MAKES 10 TO 12 SERVINGS

1 cup egg whites (7 or 8)
1⅓ cups dried apricots
2¼ cups sifted cake flour
1½ cups sugar
3 teaspoons baking powder
1 teaspoon salt
½ cup salad oil
5 egg yolks
1 teaspoon grated lemon peel
½ teaspoon cream of tartar

1. In large bowl of electric mixer, let egg whites warm to room temperature—about 1 hour.

2. Meanwhile, make apricot purée: In medium saucepan, combine apricots with 1¼ cups water; bring to boiling.

3. Remove from heat; let stand, covered, 10 minutes. Drain, reserving cooking liquid.

4. Press apricots through food mill or sieve, or blend in blender. Measure purée. Add enough reserved liquid to make 1 cup; mix well, and set aside.

5. Preheat oven to 325F. Sift flour with sugar, baking powder, and salt into another large bowl. Make a well in center.

6. Add, in order, salad oil, egg yolks, ⅔ cup water, lemon peel, and apricot purée; beat, with wooden spoon, until smooth.

6.

7. With electric mixer at high speed, beat egg whites with cream of tartar until very stiff peaks form when beater is slowly raised. Do not underbeat.

8. With wire whisk or rubber scraper, using an under-and-over motion, gently fold egg-yolk mixture into egg whites just until blended.

7.

9. Pour into an ungreased 10-inch tube pan; bake 55 minutes.

10. Increase the oven temperature to 350F; bake 10 minutes longer, or until cake tester inserted in center comes out clean.

11. Invert pan over neck of bottle; let cake cool completely—about 1½ hours.

12. With spatula, carefully loosen cake from pan; remove. Place upside down on cake plate.

13. If desired, spoon Apricot Glaze* over top of cake, letting some drizzle down side. Decorate top and side with slivered almonds.

* See Cake Frostings and Fillings Chapter.

8.

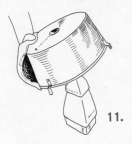

11.

MOCHA CHIFFON CAKE

MAKES 10 TO 12 SERVINGS

1 cup egg whites (7 or 8)
2 teaspoons instant coffee
½ cup sifted unsweetened
    cocoa
¾ cup boiling water
1¾ cups sifted cake flour
1¾ cups sugar

1½ teaspoons baking soda
1 teaspoon salt
½ cup salad oil
7 egg yolks
2 teaspoons vanilla extract
½ teaspoon cream of tartar

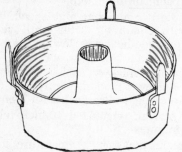

1. In large bowl of electric mixer, let egg whites warm to room temperature—about 1 hour. Meanwhile, preheat oven to 325F.

2. Combine coffee and cocoa in small bowl. Add boiling water, stirring until smooth. Let cool.

3. Sift flour with sugar, soda, and salt into large bowl. Make well in center.

4. Pour in salad oil, egg yolks, vanilla, and cooled coffee mixture. With spoon or portable electric mixer, beat just until smooth.

5. Sprinkle cream of tartar over egg whites; with mixer at high speed, beat until very stiff peaks form when beater is slowly raised. Do not underbeat.

6. Pour batter over egg whites; with rubber scraper or wire whisk, using an under-and-over motion, gently fold into egg whites just until blended.

7. Turn into ungreased 10-inch tube pan; bake 60 minutes, or until cake tester inserted in center comes out clean.

8. Invert pan over neck of bottle; let cake cool completely—about 1½ hours.

9. With spatula, carefully loosen cake from pan; remove. Serve plain, or frost as desired.

COCONUT CHIFFON LOAF CAKE

MAKES 10 TO 12 SERVINGS

½ cup egg whites (3 or 4)
1 cup sifted cake flour
⅔ cup sugar
1¼ teaspoons baking
    powder
½ teaspoon salt

¼ cup salad oil
3 egg yolks
2 teaspoons coconut extract
½ teaspoon vanilla extract
¼ teaspoon cream of tartar
½ cup flaked coconut

1. Let egg whites warm to room temperature in large bowl of electric mixer—about 1 hour. Meanwhile, preheat oven to 325F.

2. Sift flour with sugar, baking powder, and salt into another large bowl. Make well in center.

3. Add, in order, oil, egg yolks, ⅓ cup water, coconut and vanilla extracts; beat, with spoon, until smooth.

4. In large bowl of electric mixer, at high speed, beat egg whites with cream of tartar until stiff peaks form when beater is slowly raised.

5. With wire whisk or rubber scraper, using an under-and-over motion, gently fold egg-yolk mixture, along with coconut, into egg whites just until blended.

6. Pour into ungreased 9-by-5-by-3-inch loaf pan; bake 50 minutes, or until cake tester inserted in center comes out clean.

(*Coconut Chiffon Loaf Cake continued*)

7. Invert cake by hanging pan between 2 other pans; let cool completely—about 1 hour.
8. With sharp knife, cut edges of cake from sides of pan; hit pan sharply on table; turn out cake.
9. To serve: Slice cake into ¾-inch slices.

HOT-MILK SPONGECAKE

½ cup milk
1 cup sifted all-purpose
    flour
1 teaspoon baking powder

¼ teaspoon salt
3 eggs (⅔ cup)
1 cup sugar
1 teaspoon vanilla extract

1. In small saucepan, heat milk until bubbles form around edge of pan. Remove from heat; set aside.
2. Preheat oven to 350F.
3. Sift flour with baking powder and salt; set aside.
4. In small bowl of electric mixer, at high speed, beat eggs until thick and lemon-colored. Gradually add sugar, beating until mixture is smooth and well blended—about 5 minutes.
5. At low speed, blend in flour mixture just until smooth.
6. Add warm milk and vanilla, beating just until combined.
7. Pour batter immediately into an ungreased 9-by-9-by-1¾-inch baking pan or two greased and floured 8-by-1½-inch layer-cake pans; bake 25 to 30 minutes, or until cake tester inserted in center comes out clean.
8. Invert square cake by hanging between 2 other pans; let cool completely. Remove from pan. Let layer cakes cool in pans 10 minutes. Remove from pans; cool thoroughly on wire racks. Serve plain, or frost as desired.
Note: If a larger cake is desired, double amounts of ingredients above. Use large bowl of electric mixer. Bake in an ungreased 10-inch tube pan 35 to 40 minutes. Invert pan over neck of bottle; let cake cool completely.

HOT-MILK SPONGE CUPCAKES

1. Preheat oven to 375F.
2. Prepare cake batter.
3. Quickly spoon evenly into 24 ungreased or paper-lined 2½-inch cupcake cups.
4. Bake 15 minutes, or until cake tester inserted in center comes out clean. Remove to wire rack; cool completely. Frost as desired.

FRESH-ORANGE SPONGECAKE

MAKES 12 SERVINGS

6 egg whites
1¾ cups sifted all-purpose
   flour
½ teaspoon salt
1½ cups sugar

6 egg yolks
6 tablespoons fresh orange
   juice
1 tablespoon grated orange
   peel

1. In large bowl of electric mixer, let egg whites warm to room temperature—about 1 hour.

2. Meanwhile, preheat oven to 350F.

3. Sift flour with salt; set aside.

4. With electric mixer, at medium speed, beat egg whites until foamy. Gradually beat in ½ cup sugar, beating after each addition.

5. Continue beating until soft peaks form when beater is slowly raised. Set aside.

6. In small bowl of electric mixer, at high speed and with the same beaters, beat egg yolks until thick and lemon-colored.

7. Gradually beat in remaining sugar; continue beating until mixture is smooth and well blended.

8. At low speed, blend in flour mixture, guiding mixture into beaters with rubber scraper.

9. Add orange juice and orange peel, beating just until combined—about 1 minute.

10. With wire whisk or rubber scraper, using an under-and-over motion, gently fold egg-yolk mixture into egg whites just until blended.

11. Pour batter into an ungreased 10-inch tube pan; bake 35 to 40 minutes, or until cake tester inserted in center comes out clean.

12. Invert pan over neck of bottle; let cake cool completely—about 1 hour.

13. With spatula, carefully loosen cake from pan; remove. Serve plain, or frost as desired.

Cupcakes, finger cakes—these small cakes are easy to make, fun to decorate. And how infinitely useful they are. Serve them as snacks; slip them into the lunchbox. Keep them, if you can manage to, for unexpected parties when friends drop in.

DATE-NUT CUPCAKES

MAKES 24

1 pkg (8 oz) pitted dates, finely chopped
1½ cups sifted all-purpose flour
1 teaspoon baking powder
½ teaspoon baking soda
½ teaspoon salt
½ cup soft butter or margarine
1 cup sugar
2 eggs
1 cup finely chopped walnuts

1. Pour 1 cup hot water over dates in small bowl; let stand 20 minutes.

2. Meanwhile, preheat oven to 375F. Grease and flour bottoms of 24 (2½-inch) cupcake cups; or place paper liners in cupcake cups.

3. Sift flour with baking powder, soda, and salt; set aside.

4. In large bowl of electric mixer, at high speed, beat butter with sugar and eggs until light and fluffy—about 5 minutes.

5. At low speed, beat in flour mixture (in fourths), alternately with date mixture (in thirds), beginning and ending with flour mixture. Beat just until combined. Stir in walnuts.

6. Spoon batter evenly into prepared cupcake cups, filling two thirds full. Bake 20 to 25 minutes, or until surface springs back when gently pressed with fingertip.

7. Remove to wire rack; cool completely. Serve plain, or frost as desired.

McCALL'S BEST CHOCOLATE CUPCAKES

MAKES 16 (2½-INCH) CUPCAKES
OR 12 (3-INCH) CUPCAKES

1 cup sifted all-purpose flour
¼ cup sifted unsweetened cocoa
¾ cup sugar
¾ teaspoon baking soda
1 teaspoon salt
⅓ cup shortening
½ cup buttermilk or sour milk*
1 teaspoon vanilla extract
1 egg

1. Preheat oven to 375F. Grease and flour bottoms of 16 (2½-inch) cupcake cups or 12 (3-inch) cupcake cups; or place paper liners in cupcake cups.

2. Into large bowl of electric mixer, sift flour with cocoa, sugar, soda, and salt.

3. Add shortening, buttermilk, and vanilla.

4. At low speed, beat 30 seconds, scraping side of bowl with rubber scraper. At medium speed, beat 2 minutes.

5. Add egg; continue beating 1 minute longer.

6. Spoon batter evenly into prepared cupcake cups, filling about half full.

7. Bake about 20 minutes, or until surface springs back when gently pressed with fingertip.

8. Remove to wire rack; cool thoroughly. Frost as desired.

* To sour milk: Place 1½ teaspoons vinegar or lemon juice in measuring cup. Add milk to measure ½ cup. Let stand a few minutes before using.

McCALL'S BEST GOLD CUPCAKES

1¼ cups sifted cake flour
¾ cup sugar
1¾ teaspoons baking powder
½ teaspoon salt
¼ cup shortening
⅔ cup milk

1 teaspoon vanilla extract, or 1 teaspoon grated lemon peel, or 2 teaspoons grated orange peel
3 egg yolks

1. Preheat oven to 375F. Grease and flour bottoms of 16 (2½-inch) cupcake cups; or place paper liners in cupcake cups.
2. Into large bowl of electric mixer, sift flour with sugar, baking powder, and salt.
3. Add shortening, milk, and vanilla.
4. At low speed, beat 30 seconds, scraping side of bowl with rubber scraper. At medium speed, beat 2 minutes.
5. Add egg yolks; continue beating 1 minute longer, or until batter is smooth.
6. Spoon batter evenly into prepared cupcake cups, filling about half full.
7. Bake about 20 minutes, or until surface springs back when gently pressed with fingertip.
8. Remove to wire rack; cool completely. Frost as desired.

Snowy Coconut Balls: Make McCall's Best Gold Cupcakes; let cool. Remove paper liners, if necessary. Insert fork in bottom of cupcake. Holding by fork, frost top and side of cupcake with Four-Minute Frosting.* Then roll in flaked coconut, coating well.

* See Frostings and Fillings Chapter.

GOLD PETITS-FOURS CAKE

1. Preheat oven to 350F. Grease well and flour an 11-by-7-by-1½-inch baking pan.
2. Make batter for McCall's Best Gold Cupcakes. Pour batter into prepared pan; bake 20 to 25 minutes, or until surface springs back when gently pressed with fingertip.
3. Cool in pan 10 minutes. Remove; cool completely on wire rack.

LADYFINGERS

3 egg whites
½ cup sifted all-purpose flour
⅛ teaspoon salt

⅔ cup sifted confectioners' sugar
3 egg yolks
½ teaspoon vanilla extract
Confectioners' sugar

1. In medium bowl, let egg whites warm to room temperature—about 1 hour.
2. Preheat oven to 350F. Cover 2 large cookie sheets with heavy brown wrapping paper.
3. Sift flour with salt and ⅓ cup sugar.
4. With portable electric mixer, at high speed, beat egg whites until foamy. Gradually add ⅓ cup confectioners' sugar, beating well after each addition. Continue to beat until stiff peaks form when beater is slowly raised.

(Ladyfingers continued)

5.   In small bowl, with portable electric mixer at low speed, beat egg yolks until thick and lemon-colored—about 5 minutes. Add vanilla, stirring until well blended.

6.   At low speed, beat egg yolks into egg whites just until blended.

7.   Add flour mixture; continue beating, at low speed, until batter is smooth and well blended.

8.   From tip of spoon, drop batter onto paper on cookie sheet, in 4-by-1-inch strips, 2 inches apart. Or fill pastry bag with batter; force batter through plain tip onto cookie sheet, in 4-inch strips, 2 inches apart. Sprinkle with a little confectioners' sugar.

9.   Bake 12 to 15 minutes, or until light-golden.

10.   Immediately slide brown paper from cookie sheet onto dampened surface; let stand 30 seconds. With spatula, remove ladyfingers to wire rack; let cool. Serve plain, or put together, sandwich fashion, with frosting or jelly.

RAISIN-SPICE CUPCAKES

MAKES 16

2 cups sifted all-purpose
   flour
1 teaspoon baking soda
½ teaspoon salt
1 teaspoon cinnamon
1 teaspoon cloves
1 teaspoon nutmeg
½ cup soft butter or
   margarine

1 cup light-brown sugar,
   firmly packed
1 egg
1 cup milk
1 cup seedless raisins
½ cup finely chopped nuts
   (optional)

1.   Preheat oven to 375F. Grease and flour bottoms of 16 (2½-inch) cupcake cups.

2.   Sift flour with soda, salt, cinnamon, cloves, and nutmeg; set aside.

3.   In large bowl of electric mixer, at high speed, beat butter, sugar, and egg until light and fluffy.

4.   At low speed, beat in flour mixture (in fourths), alternately with milk (in thirds), beginning and ending with flour mixture. Beat just until combined.

5.   Stir in raisins and nuts.

6.   Spoon batter evenly into prepared cupcake cups, filling two thirds full.

7.   Bake about 25 minutes, or until surface springs back when gently pressed with fingertip.

8.   Remove to wire rack; cool completely. Serve plain, or frost as desired.

Raggedy Ann Cupcakes: Frost with Cupcake Butter Frosting.* Make eyes, nose, and mouth from drained maraschino or candied cherries. Turn each cupcake on side, and place inside colorful paper liner, so liner forms a bonnet for Raggedy Ann.

* See Frostings and Fillings Chapter.

McCALL'S BEST WHITE CUPCAKES

¼ cup egg whites (about 2)
1¼ cups sifted cake flour
¾ cup sugar
1½ teaspoons baking powder
½ teaspoon salt
⅓ cup shortening
1 teaspoon vanilla extract, or ½ teaspoon almond extract
½ cup milk

1. In small bowl, let egg whites warm to room temperature—about 1 hour.
2. Preheat oven to 375F. Grease and flour bottoms of 12 (2½-inch) cupcake cups; or place paper liners in cupcake cups.
3. Into large bowl of electric mixer, sift flour with sugar, baking powder, and salt.
4. Add shortening, vanilla, and milk.
5. At low speed, beat 30 seconds, scraping side of bowl with rubber scraper.
6. At medium speed, beat 2 minutes. Add unbeaten egg whites; continue beating 1 minute longer.
7. Spoon batter evenly into prepared cupcake cups, filling half full.
8. Bake about 20 minutes, or until surface springs back when gently pressed with fingertip.
9. Remove to wire rack; cool completely. Frost as desired.

WHITE PETITS-FOURS CAKE

1. Preheat oven to 350F. Grease well and flour an 11-by-7-by-1½-inch baking pan.
2. Make batter for McCall's Best White Cupcakes. Pour batter into prepared pan; bake 20 to 25 minutes, or until surface springs back when gently pressed with fingertip.
3. Cool in pan 10 minutes. Remove; cool completely on wire rack.

Ladies' Luncheon Cupcakes: Make McCall's Best White Cupcakes; let cool. Remove paper liners. Spread top of each cupcake with tart red jelly. Insert fork in bottom of cupcake. Holding by fork, frost side with Four-Minute Frosting.* Then roll in finely chopped pecans, so side is well coated.

* See Frostings and Fillings Chapter.

Coconut-Jelly Cupcakes: Remove paper liners. Spread tops and sides of cupcakes with tart red jelly. Sprinkle with flaked coconut.

One-Egg Cupcakes, or One-Egg Petits-Fours Cake: Substitute 1 whole egg for egg whites. Bake as directed for Best White Cupcakes or White Petits-Fours Cake.

Men of every age, from four to ninety-four, adore frosted cakes. A beautiful frosting on a cake will get a woman more compliments from them than a beautiful gown. As a matter of fact, frosting does for a cake exactly what a stunning gown does for a woman. Though it's true that frostings (and we include icings, glazes, and toppings) preserve the moisture and freshness of a cake and give it flavor, their chief function is glamour.

How to Frost a Layer Cake

1. Be sure both cake and frosting are cool.
2. Brush off all loose crumbs with a pastry brush; trim off any ragged edges with kitchen scissors.
3. Select a cake plate or tray that will set off the cake to the best advantage. It should be flat and at least 2 to 3 inches larger in diameter than the cake.
4. Cut 4 strips of waxed paper, each 10 by 3 inches. Place strips, overlapping, around edge of cake plate. Invert a cake layer in the center of the cake plate. If there is a difference in thickness of the layers, use the thicker or thickest for the bottom.
5. Using a flexible metal spatula, spread top of bottom layer smoothly with frosting or filling, almost to the outer edge.
6. Place the next layer, right side up, on first layer. Repeat with other layers. If layers have a tendency to slide, anchor them with wooden picks or wooden skewers until the filling has set, before frosting side and top of cake.
7. Spread side of cake with a thin coating of frosting, to set crumbs. Then spread frosting from top edge down over the side, making sure cake is completely covered. If frosting is fluffy or creamy type, swirl as you spread.
8. Pile the remaining frosting on top, and spread it lightly to the edge, swirling it as you spread.
9. If you wish to sprinkle the top and side with grated chocolate, coconut, or finely chopped nuts, this should be done while the frosting is still moist.
10. When cake frosting is set, carefully pull out waxed-paper strips.

U ncooked frostings are the simplest of all frostings to make. They are made with confectioners' sugar, shortening, liquid, and whatever flavoring you wish. For a smooth frosting, it is imperative that the sugar be sifted. For the beginner, uncooked frostings are quick to make, easy to spread. And they stay moist.

COCOA CREAM FROSTING

⅓ cup light cream or evaporated milk, undiluted

¼ cup soft butter or margarine

¼ teaspoon salt

½ cup sifted unsweetened cocoa

1 teaspoon vanilla extract, or ½ teaspoon rum extract

3 cups sifted confectioners' sugar

1. In small saucepan, heat cream until bubbles form around edge of pan. Let cool slightly.
2. In medium bowl, combine butter, salt, cocoa, vanilla, ¼ cup hot cream, and 1½ cups sugar.
3. With portable electric mixer at medium speed, or wooden spoon, beat mixture until smooth.
4. Gradually add remaining sugar, beating until smooth and fluffy. If frosting seems too thick to spread, gradually beat in a little more hot cream. Makes enough to fill and frost an 8-inch or 9-inch two-layer cake.

Note: If frosting is too thin, set in bowl of ice water. Beat until thick enough to spread.

COFFEE BUTTER FROSTING

⅓ cup soft butter or margarine

3½ cups sifted confectioners' sugar

1 tablespoon instant coffee

3 tablespoons hot milk

1 teaspoon vanilla or rum extract or brandy flavoring

1. In medium bowl, combine butter, sugar, coffee, and 2 tablespoons hot milk and the vanilla.
2. With portable electric mixer at medium speed, or wooden spoon, beat mixture until smooth and fluffy.
3. If frosting seems too thick to spread, gradually beat in a little more hot milk. Makes enough to fill and frost an 8-inch or 9-inch two-layer cake.

Mocha-Spice Frosting: Make Coffee Butter Frosting, reducing amount of sugar to 3 cups; add 1 teaspoon cinnamon, ½ teaspoon nutmeg and 2 tablespoons sifted unsweetened cocoa.

CUPCAKE BUTTER FROSTING

2½ to 3 cups sifted
   confectioners' sugar
2 tablespoons soft butter
   or margarine

1 egg
1 teaspoon vanilla extract,
   or ½ teaspoon
   almond extract

1. In medium bowl, with portable electric mixer at medium speed, or wooden spoon, beat 2½ cups sugar, butter, egg, and vanilla until smooth and easy to spread. If frosting is too thin, gradually beat in more confectioners' sugar.

2. Makes 1 cup—enough for 24 cupcakes.

Pink Peppermint: Omit vanilla extract. Add ¼ teaspoon peppermint extract and a few drops red food color.

Wintergreen: Omit vanilla extract. Add ¼ teaspoon wintergreen extract and a few drops green food color.

Orange: Omit vanilla extract. Add 1 tablespoon grated orange peel.

Coffee: Add 1 teaspoon instant coffee.

DE LUXE CHOCOLATE FROSTING

4 squares unsweetened
   chocolate
3½ cups sifted confec-
   tioners' sugar

1 egg, or 3 egg yolks
½ cup soft butter or
   margarine
1 teaspoon vanilla extract

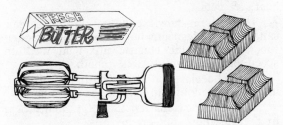

1. Melt chocolate over hot water. Let cool.

2. In medium bowl, combine chocolate, sugar, and ½ cup hot water. With portable electric mixer at medium speed, or rotary beater, beat until smooth and well combined.

3. Add egg, butter, and vanilla; continue beating until frosting is thick.

4. Set bowl of frosting in ice water. With wooden spoon, stir frosting until of spreading consistency. (If it becomes too thick to spread, dip bowl in hot water; then stir until of spreading consistency.)

5. Makes enough to fill and frost an 8-inch or 9-inch two-layer cake.

PEANUT-BUTTER FROSTING

2 tablespoons soft butter
   or margarine
½ cup creamy or chunk-
   style peanut butter

3 cups sifted
   confectioners' sugar
1 teaspoon vanilla extract
¼ to ⅓ cup milk or light
   cream

1. In small bowl, combine butter, peanut butter, sugar, vanilla, and ¼ cup milk.

2. With portable electric mixer at medium speed, or wooden spoon, beat frosting until creamy and of spreading consistency. If frosting seems too thick to spread, gradually beat in a little more milk.

3. Makes enough to fill and frost an 8-inch or 9-inch two-layer cake.

143

RICH ORANGE FROSTING

2 tablespoons soft butter
    or margarine
2 egg yolks
1 tablespoon grated orange
    peel

4 cups sifted
    confectioners' sugar
2 to 3 tablespoons orange
    juice

 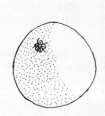 

1. In small bowl of electric mixer, combine butter, egg yolks, orange peel, sugar, and 2 tablespoons orange juice.

2. With mixer at medium speed, beat until frosting is smooth and easy to spread. If frosting seems too thick to spread, gradually beat in a little more orange juice.

3. Makes enough to frost top and side of a 10-inch tube cake.

Rich Orange Glaze: Prepare half recipe, adding enough orange juice so glaze can be poured over top of a 10-inch tube cake and run unevenly down sides.

VANILLA BUTTER-CREAM FROSTING

⅓ cup soft butter or
    margarine
3½ cups sifted
    confectioners' sugar
3 to 4 tablespoons light
    cream or milk

1½ teaspoons vanilla
    extract, or 1 teaspoon
    vanilla extract and ¼
    teaspoon almond
    extract

1. In medium bowl, with portable electric mixer at medium speed, or wooden spoon, beat butter with sugar, 3 tablespoons cream, and vanilla until smooth and fluffy. If frosting seems too thick to spread, gradually beat in a little more cream.

2. Makes enough to fill and frost an 8-inch or 9-inch two-layer cake; or to frost a 13-by-9-by-2-inch cake.

QUICK FUDGE FROSTING

2 squares unsweetened
    chocolate
¼ cup soft butter or
    margarine
3 cups sifted
    confectioners' sugar
⅛ teaspoon salt

¼ cup hot light cream or
    evaporated milk,
    undiluted
1 teaspoon vanilla extract,
    or ½ teaspoon rum
    extract

1. Melt chocolate over hot water. Remove from heat; let cool.

2. In medium bowl, combine butter, sugar, salt, and 3 tablespoons hot cream. With wooden spoon, or portable electric mixer at medium speed, beat until mixture is smooth.

3. Add chocolate; continue beating until frosting is thick enough to spread. Add vanilla.

4. If frosting seems too thick, gradually beat in a little more hot cream.

5. Makes enough to fill and frost an 8-inch or 9-inch two-layer cake.

TOASTED-PECAN FROSTING

¼ cup butter or margarine
4½ cups (1 lb) sifted
    confectioners' sugar
¼ cup light cream

1 teaspoon vanilla extract
¾ cup finely chopped
    toasted* pecans

1. In large bowl of electric mixer, at medium speed, cream butter until light.

2. Gradually add sugar, alternately with cream, beating until smooth and creamy. Stir in vanilla and pecans.

(Toasted-Pecan Frosting continued)

3. Makes enough to fill and frost an 8-inch or 9-inch two-layer cake.

* To toast: Cover shelled nuts with cold water; bring to boil, and simmer 3 minutes. Drain well. Place in shallow baking pan; bake at 350F for 15 to 20 minutes, or until they are golden.

COCOA CREAM FILLING AND FROSTING

2 cups heavy cream	½ cup sifted unsweetened
1 cup sifted	cocoa
confectioners' sugar	⅛ teaspoon salt

1. Combine all ingredients in medium bowl. Refrigerate, covered, 30 minutes.

2. With portable electric mixer at high speed, or rotary beater, beat mixture until stiff. Refrigerate until ready to use.

3. Makes enough to fill and frost an angel-food or chiffon cake split crosswise into 3 layers; or to spoon over individual slices of an angel-food or chiffon cake.

Mocha Cream Filling and Frosting: Combine 2 tablespoons instant coffee with rest of ingredients.

CHOCOLATE SOUR-CREAM FROSTING

1 pkg (6 oz) semisweet-	½ cup dairy sour cream
chocolate pieces	Dash salt

1. Melt chocolate pieces in top of double boiler, over hot water. Remove top of double boiler from hot water.

2. Add sour cream and salt. With portable electric mixer at medium speed, or rotary beater, beat frosting until creamy and of spreading consistency.

3. Makes enough to frost top and side of an 8-inch or 9-inch two-layer cake; or top of a 13-by-9-by-2-inch cake; or top and side of a 10-inch tube cake.

Note: To make enough frosting to fill and frost an 8-inch or 9-inch two-layer cake, use 1½ pkg (6-oz size) semisweet-chocolate pieces and ¾ cup dairy sour cream.

SPICED COFFEE FROSTING

2 pkg (6½-oz size) fluffy-	½ teaspoon cinnamon
white-frosting mix	¼ teaspoon nutmeg
4 teaspoons instant coffee	1 cup boiling water

1. In small bowl of electric mixer, combine frosting mix with coffee, cinnamon, and nutmeg.

2. Add boiling water; beat, at low speed, until mixture is smooth. Then, at high speed, beat just until frosting stands in very stiff peaks when beater is raised.

3. Use to fill and frost two 8-inch cake layers.

TO FROST AND DECORATE
   GRAND-SLAM CAKE

1. Cut 4 strips of waxed paper, each 10 by 3 inches. Place strips, overlapping, around edge of cake plate. Invert a cake layer on paper.

2. Put layers together with 2 cups Spiced Coffee Frosting. Using spatula, spread side of cake with thin coat of frosting, to set crumbs. Then spread with enough additional frosting to hide seams and make sides straight and smooth.

3. Insert 7 evenly spaced wooden picks around top edge of cake, to mark for top decoration. Frost top smoothly. Opposite each pick, place a large mound of frosting. With metal spatula, smoothly form each mound into a cylinder radiating from center. Remove picks.

4. Make Chocolate Silhouettes: Melt ½ cup semisweet-chocolate pieces · in top of double boiler over hot, not boiling, water. Stir in 1½ tablespoons shortening, mixing well.

5. Pour onto waxed paper on cookie sheet, tilting to let mixture flow evenly over as wide an area as possible. Refrigerate until firm.

6. With cookie cutters (1½ to 2 inches wide) for 4 playing-card suits, cut out 10 to 12 silhouettes. Carefully place silhouettes at intervals around side of cake. If desired, sprinkle top of cake with ¼ cup coarsely chopped pecans.

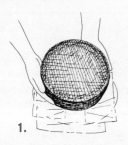

1.

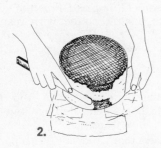

2.

3.

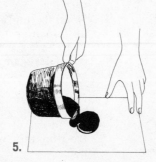

5.

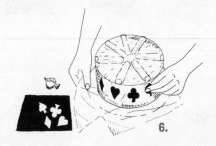

6.

Cooked frostings, the royalty of frostings, are more difficult to make than uncooked, but worth the effort. They include:

Fudge frosting: Rich, candylike in appearance and texture.

Cooked white frosting: Under this category, when frosting is made in the top part of a double boiler, it is known as 7-Minute, or Double-Boiler, Frosting. The ingredients are all combined in the top part of a double boiler and beaten continuously over hot water until the desired stiffness is reached. Adding corn syrup or cream of tartar prevents sugar crystals from forming and keeps the frosting from becoming grainy.

Boiled white frosting: A sugar-syrup base is cooked to the right consistency and added to beaten egg whites, then beaten until the frosting is stiff enough to hold its form when the beater is slowly raised. These are sometimes called White Mountain Frostings.

SEAFOAM FROSTING

2 egg whites (¼ cup)
1½ cups light-brown sugar,
    firmly packed
¼ teaspoon cream of tartar,
    or 1 tablespoon light
    corn syrup
1 teaspoon vanilla extract,
    or ½ teaspoon maple
    flavoring

1. In top of double boiler, combine egg whites, sugar, cream of tartar, and ⅓ cup water.
2. Cook over rapidly boiling water (water in bottom should not touch top of double boiler), beating constantly with portable electric mixer at medium speed, or rotary beater, until soft peaks form when beater is slowly raised—about 7 minutes.
3. Remove from boiling water. Add vanilla; continue beating until frosting is thick enough to spread—about 2 minutes.
4. Makes enough to fill and frost an 8-inch or 9-inch two-layer cake; or to frost a 13-by-9-by-2-inch cake.

EASY WHITE-FUDGE FROSTING

½ cup butter or margarine
1 cup granulated sugar
¼ cup milk
1¾ to 2 cups sifted
    confectioners' sugar
1 teaspoon vanilla extract,
    or ½ teaspoon
    almond extract

1. Melt butter in small saucepan, over medium heat. Remove from heat.
2. Add granulated sugar and milk, stirring until well blended.
3. Over medium heat, bring to boiling, stirring. Remove from heat; let cool slightly.
4. With portable electric mixer at medium speed, or wooden spoon, gradually beat 1¾ cups confectioners' sugar into warm mixture, beating well after each addition, until frosting is thick enough to spread and barely holds its shape. If frosting seems too thin to spread, gradually beat in a little more confectioners' sugar. Add vanilla.
5. Makes enough to frost top and side of an 8-inch or 9-inch two-layer cake; or top of a 13-by-9-by-2-inch cake.

SEVEN-MINUTE FROSTING

2 egg whites (¼ cup)
1½ cups granulated sugar

1 tablespoon light corn
    syrup, or ¼ teaspoon
    cream of tartar
1 teaspoon vanilla extract

1. In top of double boiler, combine egg whites, sugar, corn syrup, and ⅓ cup water.

2. With portable electric mixer or rotary beater, beat about 1 minute to combine ingredients.

3. Cook over rapidly boiling water (water in bottom should not touch top of double boiler), beating constantly, about 7 minutes, or until stiff peaks form when beater is slowly raised.

4. Remove from boiling water. Add vanilla; continue beating until frosting is thick enough to spread—about 2 minutes.

5. Makes enough to fill and frost an 8-inch or 9-inch two-layer cake; or to frost a 13-by-9-by-2-inch cake.

Coffee Spice: Beat in 2 teaspoons instant coffee, 1 teaspoon cinnamon, and ½ teaspoon nutmeg along with vanilla.

Half 'n' Half: Substitute ¾ cup light-brown sugar, firmly packed, for ¾ cup of the granulated sugar.

Pink Peppermint: Omit vanilla. Add ½ teaspoon peppermint extract and few drops red food color. Fold in ¼ cup finely crushed peppermint candy.

Coconut: Reduce vanilla to ½ teaspoon, and add ½ teaspoon coconut flavoring. Sprinkle top and side of cake with 1 can (3½ oz) flaked coconut.

Four-Minute Frosting: Make Seven-Minute Frosting, halving each ingredient and beating over boiling water only 4 minutes. Makes enough to frost 12 cupcakes; or top of an 8-inch or 9-inch square cake.

EASY CARAMEL FROSTING

½ cup butter or margarine
1 cup light-brown sugar, firmly packed
⅓ cup light cream or evaporated milk, undiluted

2 to 2½ cups sifted confectioners' sugar
1 teaspoon vanilla extract, or ½ teaspoon maple extract

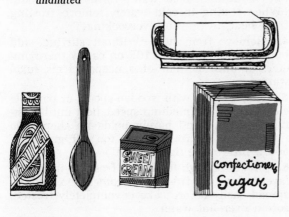

1. Melt butter in small saucepan, over low heat. Remove from heat.

2. Add brown sugar, stirring until smooth. Over low heat, bring to boiling, stirring; boil, stirring, 1 minute. Remove from heat.

3. Add cream; over low heat, return just to boiling. Remove from heat; let cool to 110F on candy thermometer, or until bottom of saucepan feels lukewarm.

4. With portable electric mixer at medium speed, or wooden spoon, beat in 2 cups confectioners' sugar until frosting is thick. If frosting seems too thin to spread, gradually beat in a little more confectioners' sugar. Add vanilla.

5. Set in bowl of ice water; beat until frosting is thick enough to spread and barely holds its shape.

6. Makes enough to frost top and side of an 8-inch or 9-inch two-layer cake; or top of a 13-by-9-by-2-inch cake.

OLD-FASHIONED FUDGE FROSTING

1½ cups sugar
1½ tablespoons light corn syrup
½ cup milk
2 squares unsweetened chocolate

2 tablespoons butter or margarine
1 teaspoon vanilla extract, or ½ teaspoon rum extract

1. In medium saucepan, combine sugar, corn syrup, milk, and chocolate. Over low heat, cook, stirring, until sugar is dissolved and chocolate melted.

2. Over medium heat, bring to boiling, stirring occasionally.

3. Reduce heat, and simmer, without stirring, to 234F on candy thermometer, or until a little in cold water forms a soft ball. (When testing in cold water, remove frosting from heat, to prevent overcooking.)

4. Remove from heat. Without stirring, add butter, and let cool to 110F on candy thermometer, or until bottom of saucepan feels lukewarm.

5. Add vanilla; with wooden spoon, or portable electric mixer at medium speed, beat until frosting is creamy and barely holds its shape. Do not overbeat. (If frosting gets too stiff, gradually add a little more milk.)

6. Makes enough to frost a 9-inch square cake; or side and top of an 8-inch two-layer cake; or a 13-by-9-by-2-inch cake. (If frosting becomes too stiff to spread easily before cake is completely frosted, soften over hot water.)

Note: To fill and frost an 8-inch or 9-inch two-layer cake, double recipe, using large saucepan.

PENUCHE FROSTING

1½ cups light-brown sugar,
firmly packed
1½ cups granulated sugar
⅛ teaspoon salt
1 tablespoon light corn
syrup

1 cup light cream
2 tablespoons butter or
margarine
1 teaspoon vanilla extract

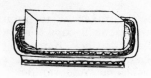

1. In large saucepan, combine sugars, salt, corn syrup, and cream. Over low heat, cook, stirring, until sugars are dissolved.

2. Over medium heat, bring to boiling, stirring occasionally.

3. Continue cooking, over medium heat, without stirring, to 234F on candy thermometer, or until a little in cold water forms a soft ball. (When testing in cold water, remove frosting from heat, to prevent overcooking.)

4. Remove from heat. Without stirring, add butter, and let cool to 110F on candy thermometer, or until bottom of saucepan feels lukewarm.

5. Add vanilla; with wooden spoon, or portable electric mixer at medium speed, beat until frosting is creamy and barely holds its shape. Do not overbeat. (If frosting gets too stiff, gradually add a little more light cream.)

6. Makes enough to fill and frost a 9-inch two-layer cake. (If frosting becomes too stiff to spread easily before cake is completely frosted, soften over hot water.)

Note: To frost an 8-inch two-layer cake or a 13-by-9-by-2-inch cake, make half the recipe, using a medium saucepan.

OLD-FASHIONED BOILED FROSTING

(White Mountain)

2 egg whites (¼ cup)
2 cups sugar
⅛ teaspoon salt
1 teaspoon vinegar

1 teaspoon vanilla extract,
or 1 teaspoon grated
lemon peel

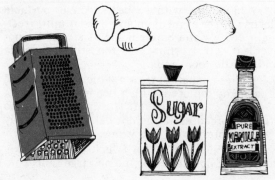

1. In small bowl of electric mixer, let egg whites warm to room temperature.

2. In medium saucepan, combine sugar, salt, and vinegar with 1 cup water. Cook, stirring, over medium heat, until sugar is dissolved and syrup is clear.

3. Continue cooking, over medium heat, without stirring, to 242F on candy thermometer, or until a little spins a thin thread, 6 to 8 inches long, when dropped from tip of spoon.

4. Meanwhile, with mixer at medium speed, beat egg whites until soft peaks form when beater is slowly raised.

5. With mixer at high speed, gradually pour hot syrup, in a thin stream, over egg whites, beating constantly.

6. Add vanilla; continue beating until stiff peaks form when beater is slowly raised and frosting is thick enough to spread.

7. Makes enough to fill and frost an 8-inch or 9-inch two-layer cake.

G lazes are quick and easy substitutes for frostings. The thin coating helps to keep the cake moist but requires no technique to apply. Traditionally, glazes are used to decorate chiffon or angel-food cakes but they may also be used on cookies or fruitcakes.

APRICOT GLAZE

MAKES ABOUT ⅔ CUP

1 cup apricot preserves
1 teaspoon grated lemon
    peel
2 teaspoons lemon juice
½ teaspoon almond extract

1. Heat preserves in small saucepan, stirring, just until melted.
2. Stir in rest of ingredients; strain. Refrigerate until cooled completely—about 30 minutes.

COFFEE GLAZE

MAKES ABOUT ¾ CUP

2 tablespoons milk or light
    cream
2 tablespoons soft butter or
    margarine
1½ teaspoons instant coffee
½ teaspoon vanilla extract
2 cups sifted confectioners'
    sugar

1. In small saucepan, heat milk until bubbles form around edge of pan; let cool slightly.
2. In small bowl, combine butter, coffee, vanilla, sugar, and hot milk. With portable electric mixer at medium speed, or rotary beater, beat until mixture is smooth and well combined.

CHOCOLATE GLAZE

MAKES ABOUT ½ CUP

2 tablespoons butter or
    margarine
1 square unsweetened
    chocolate
1 cup sifted confectioners'
    sugar
2 tablespoons boiling water

1. Melt butter and chocolate over hot water. Remove from heat; let cool.
2. In small bowl, combine chocolate mixture with remaining ingredients.
3. With rotary beater, beat just until mixture is smooth and well combined. (Glaze seems thin, but will thicken on standing.)

GLAZE FOR FRUITCAKES

MAKES ½ CUP

1¼ cups sifted
    confectioners' sugar
2 tablespoons soft butter or
    margarine
¼ teaspoon vanilla extract
1½ to 2 tablespoons milk

1. In small bowl, combine sugar, butter, vanilla, and 1½ tablespoons milk.
2. With wooden spoon, beat until mixture is smooth. If thinner glaze is desired, add remaining milk.

151

Toppings, nut or cream, can transform any cake into a glamorous quick dessert for any occasion. Toppings can serve the double purpose of frosting and sauce.

BROILED COCONUT TOPPING

¼ cup soft butter or margarine

¼ cup light cream or evaporated milk, undiluted

½ cup light-brown sugar, firmly packed

1 cup flaked or shredded coconut

1. In small bowl, combine all ingredients; mix well.
2. Spread evenly over top of hot 8-inch or 9-inch square cake.
3. Run under broiler, 4 inches from heat, 2 to 3 minutes, or until topping is bubbly and golden. Cool cake in pan on wire rack; serve slightly warm.

BROILED NUT TOPPING

¼ cup soft butter or margarine

2 tablespoons milk or undiluted evaporated milk

½ cup light-brown sugar, firmly packed

1 cup finely chopped walnuts or pecans

1. In small bowl, combine all ingredients; mix well.
2. Spread evenly over top of hot 8-inch or 9-inch square cake.
3. Run under broiler, 4 inches from heat, 2 to 3 minutes, or until topping is bubbly and golden. Cool cake in pan on wire rack; serve slightly warm.

ORANGE-CREAM TOPPING

3 egg yolks

½ cup sugar

1½ teaspoons grated orange peel

¼ cup orange juice

½ cup heavy cream

MAKES ABOUT 1½ CUPS

1. In top of double boiler, with rotary beater, beat egg yolks until light.
2. Add sugar, orange peel and juice; cook, over boiling water, stirring constantly, until mixture thickens and coats a metal spoon. Cool thoroughly.
3. Whip cream until stiff. Fold into cooled orange mixture.
4. Refrigerate in covered container. (Keeps for several days.) Delicious on angel-food cake, poundcake, fruit cup, or fruit cobbler.

SOUR-CREAM TOPPING

MAKES ABOUT 1 CUP

1 cup dairy sour cream

2 tablespoons confectioners' sugar

1 teaspoon grated orange peel

Combine all ingredients. Refrigerate.

Fillings can be the same as the frosting used on the outside of your layer cake. Or you can make them out of a soft, sweet cooked or uncooked mixture that spreads easily between layers. Either way, they hold your cake together, make it a delectable surprise to bite into. We suggest you try all of the following.

CHOCOLATE-CUSTARD FILLING

1 pkg (6 oz) semisweet-
   chocolate pieces
½ cup soft butter or
   margarine
⅔ cup sifted
   confectioners' sugar
2 egg yolks
1 teaspoon vanilla extract
2 egg whites

1. Melt chocolate in top of double boiler, over hot water. Remove from heat; let cool.
2. In small bowl of electric mixer, at medium speed, beat butter until light. Add sugar gradually, beating until very light and fluffy.
3. Add egg yolks, one at a time, beating after each addition.
4. Gradually beat in chocolate. Add vanilla.
5. With rotary beater, beat egg whites just until stiff peaks form. With rubber scraper, using an under-and-over motion, fold egg whites into chocolate mixture just until blended.

FRESH-ORANGE FILLING

¾ cup sugar
2½ tablespoons cornstarch
⅛ teaspoon salt
½ cup orange juice
2 tablespoons grated orange
   peel
2 tablespoons lemon juice
2 tablespoons butter or
   margarine

1. In small saucepan, combine sugar with cornstarch and salt.
2. Gradually stir in orange juice and ½ cup water; over medium heat, bring to boiling, stirring. Boil 1 minute. Remove from heat.
3. Stir in remaining ingredients. Cool well.

LEMON FILLING

4 egg yolks
½ cup sugar
¼ cup lemon juice
2 teaspoons grated lemon
   peel
1 tablespoon heavy cream

1. In top of double boiler, with rotary beater, beat egg yolks with sugar until smooth.
2. Stir in lemon juice and peel; cook over boiling water, stirring, 5 to 8 minutes, or until mixture thickens.
3. Remove from heat. Stir in cream; cool. Makes filling for an 8-inch two-layer cake.

RICH VANILLA-CREAM FILLING

½ cup sugar
¼ cup cornstarch
¼ teaspoon salt
2 cups milk
4 egg yolks, slightly
   beaten
1 teaspoon vanilla extract

1. In medium saucepan, combine sugar with cornstarch and salt.
2. Gradually add milk; over medium heat, bring to boiling, stirring. Remove from heat.
3. Add half of hot mixture to egg yolks; mix well. Gradually return to saucepan, stirring.
4. Over medium heat, bring to boiling, stirring. Remove from heat. Add vanilla. Cool completely before using to fill cake.

Coconut-Cream Filling: Add ½ cup flaked coconut and ½ teaspoon almond extract along with vanilla.

Chocolate-Cream Filling: Increase sugar to ¾ cup. Combine ¼ cup sifted unsweetened cocoa with sugar, cornstarch, and salt.

No home, we say, is complete without a recipe for a very special cake to honor a very special occasion. It may be an occasion as important as a birthday party for a child, a Sweet Sixteen party, a graduation . . . or that greatest of all events, a wedding.

Our Humpty-Dumpty Cake will brighten many an occasion—particularly the birthday of a child. We guarantee excitement when it makes its appearance.

HUMPTY-DUMPTY CAKE

MAKES 24 SERVINGS

Cake:
2 pkg (1-lb, 1-oz size)
     poundcake mix
4 eggs
2 squares unsweetened
     chocolate, grated

Frosting:
1 pkg (13 oz) creamy-fudge-
     frosting mix

Several long, thin wooden
     skewers

Decoration:
5 egg whites
10 cups sifted
     confectioners' sugar
Blue, green, yellow, and red
     food color
2 blue drinking straws, cut
     in half crosswise

1. Preheat oven to 300F. Lightly grease and flour 2 (1½-quart size) heatproof bowls (6¾ inches in diameter) and 1 (10-oz) custard cup.

2. Make Cake: Make both packages of pound-cake mix together, as label directs, using the 4 eggs and amount of water specified on package. Swirl chocolate into batter just to combine.

3. Put ¾ cup batter in custard cup. Divide remaining batter into 2 bowls.

4. Bake cakes at same time. Bake small cake 55 minutes and large ones 1 hour and 20 minutes, or until tester inserted in center comes out clean.

5. Let cool, in cup and bowls, 10 minutes. With sharp knife, loosen edges; turn out on wire racks; cool completely.

6. From top of each cake, cut a thin slice crosswise, to make cakes level. Brush off any loose crumbs. Cut the 2 large cakes in half crosswise, as in diagram.

(Humpty-Dumpty Cake continued)

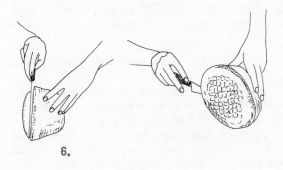

6.

9.

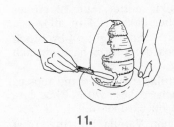

11.

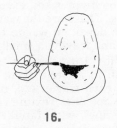

16.

7. Make creamy-fudge frosting as package label directs.

8. Put 2 halves of each of the 2 large cakes together, using ¼ cup frosting between halves.

9. To make egg shape (see diagram), invert 1 large cake on top of other, putting together with ½ cup frosting. Invert small cake on top, putting together with rest of frosting. Insert a wooden skewer through center of cakes, from top to bottom, to make secure. Place on serving plate.

10. To decorate: In large bowl of electric mixer, at high speed, beat 3 egg whites just until soft peaks form when beater is raised. Gradually beat in 6 cups confectioners' sugar, beating until stiff peaks form. (If necessary, add a little more sugar, to make this frosting stiff enough to spread and cling.)

11. Using small metal spatula, spread frosting over entire cake, covering seams and rounding out to give an oval shape. Occasionally dip spatula in hot water, so frosting will be easier to spread. Let set completely—at least 4 hours.

12. In large bowl of electric mixer, at high speed, beat remaining egg whites just until soft peaks form when beater is raised. Gradually beat in 4 cups confectioners' sugar, beating until stiff peaks form. (If necessary, add a little more sugar, to make frosting stiff enough to spread and cling.)

13. Using small metal spatula, spread frosting evenly over first coating, covering entire cake and making frosting as smooth as possible. Occasionally dip spatula in hot water, so frosting will be easier to spread.

14. To make frosting very smooth, brush lightly with soft pastry brush, moistened with a little hot water. Don't make frosting too wet.

15. Let dry 1 hour. With small wooden skewer, lightly mark position of eyes, nose, and mouth. Also, outline collar and tie. Let dry completely —several hours.

16. Then, with soft paintbrush dipped in appropriate food color, paint cake.

17. Insert wooden skewers in cake, for arms and legs. Place half a blue straw over each.

18. To serve: With a sharp knife, slice down through cake, cutting a quarter at a time. Cut each quarter into 3 slices; cut each slice in half.

Note: Cake is easier to frost if baked one day, wrapped in foil, and stored. Frost next day.

"**D**ear McCall's," a mother wrote us, "please come to the aid of the party of an about-to-be-eight-years-old boy, who has freckles and a passion for anything even remotely related to the Old West. Why are all birthday cakes slanted toward little girls? Doesn't anyone believe Birthday Boys are people, too?" Well, we do, and here's our Wagon-Train Birthday Cake to prove it.

WAGON-TRAIN BIRTHDAY CAKE

MAKES TRAIN OF 8 COVERED WAGONS

3 pkg (1-lb, 3-oz size)
    yellow-cake mix
Chocolate Frosting
Vanilla Frosting
Decorator's Frosting

Thin cardboard
32 (2-inch) round
    commercial cookies
16 waffle cream wafers
16 or 32 small plastic horses

1. Preheat oven to 350F. Grease and lightly flour a 9-by-9-by-1¾-inch baking pan and two 15½-by-10½-by-1-inch baking pans.

2. Prepare each package of cake mix separately, according to package directions. Pour into prepared pans—batter from one package to a pan.

3. Bake square cake 50 to 55 minutes and the others 22 to 25 minutes, or until surface springs back when gently pressed with fingertip.

4. Meanwhile, make three frostings; set aside.

5. Cool cakes, in pans, about 8 minutes. Then remove from pans; cool thoroughly on wire racks.

6. With sharp or serrated knife, slice about ¼ inch from top of square cake, to make it level. Turn cut side down. Cut cake into 8 pieces, each about 4 by 2 inches; set aside.

7. With 3-inch cookie cutter, cut 12 circles from each of the other cakes (24 in all).

8. Assemble cakes: Cut eight 4-by-2-inch pieces of thin cardboard, to form base of each wagon.

9. Using small spatula, frost sides and tops of the eight 4-by-2-inch cakes with Chocolate Frosting. Place each on cardboard.

10. With 1 tablespoon Vanilla Frosting, frost top of each of 16 circles. Immediately stack 2 frosted circles; top with unfrosted circle, to make 8 small three-layer cakes.

11. Turn each on side, and cut off a lengthwise ¼-inch slice, to make a flat base.

12. Now frost cakes, except base, with Vanilla Frosting. These are the wagon tops. Place them, flat side down, on wagon bases, flush with base at rear and leaving a small seat area at front.

13. With 1 teaspoon Chocolate Frosting for each, fill in a circle about size of a quarter on rear of each wagon top, near bottom, to simulate the opening. Texture frosting out from edge of "opening" with fanlike strokes; accentuate with lines of Decorator's Frosting.

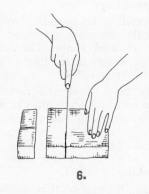

6.

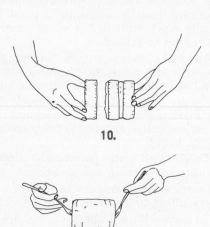

10.

12.

(*Wagon-Train Cake continued*)

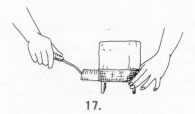

17.

18.

14.   On smooth backs of round cookies, using Decorator's Frosting in pastry tube, outline edge of wheel, hub, and spokes.

15.   Assemble wagon train on table centerpiece from which it is to be served. With sharp knife, cut waffle cream wafers to 2½ inches.

16.   Stand 2 wafers on long side in parallel position, 3½ inches apart, to form 2 axles for wagon. Put remaining wafers in position for wagon train, leaving enough room between wagons for horses.

17.   Using small pancake turner, lift wagons, on cardboard bases, into position on axles.

18.   Place cookie wheels against axles; adhere with a dab of Decorator's Frosting.

19.   Arrange horses in front of wagons. If desired, add figures for drivers.

CHOCOLATE FROSTING

½ cup unsweetened cocoa
½ cup soft shortening
1 pkg (1 lb) confectioners'
  sugar, sifted

3 tablespoons milk
1 teaspoon vanilla extract

1.   Blend cocoa with 6 tablespoons hot water in small bowl.

2.   Cream shortening well in large bowl of electric mixer.

3.   Gradually add sugar, alternately with combined cocoa mixture and milk.

4.   Add vanilla. Store in medium bowl, covered with damp cloth, until ready to use.

VANILLA FROSTING

1 cup soft butter or
  margarine
7 cups sifted confectioners'
  sugar (1½ pkg, 1-lb
  size)

⅓ cup milk
2 teaspoons vanilla extract

1.   Cream butter, in large bowl of electric mixer, until smooth and fluffy.

2.   Gradually add sugar, alternately with combined milk and vanilla. Store in medium bowl, covered with damp cloth, until ready to use.

DECORATOR'S FROSTING

1 egg white
Dash salt
¼ teaspoon cream of tartar

¼ teaspoon vanilla extract
About 1¼ cups sifted
  confectioners' sugar

1.   In small bowl of electric mixer, beat egg white, salt, and cream of tartar until stiff peaks form. Stir in vanilla.

2.   Then gradually beat in enough confectioners' sugar to make frosting just thick enough so it later can be used for writing.

3.   Store in small bowl, covered with damp cloth, until ready to use.

4.   To use: Spoon into bag of pastry tube, using small, plain tip with opening about 1/16 inch in diameter. (Or make cone by folding and rolling heavy paper; tape together. Cut off the cone's tip end, to make 1/16-inch opening.)

Ow pretty can a cake be? Try our basket cake, in two variations, and find out. And/or our delicious, delovely, divine decorated Petits Fours.

PINK POSY CAKE

MAKES 14 SERVINGS

2 (9-inch) Silvery-White-
    Cake layers*
Basic Decorating Frosting,
    follows
Red food color
No. 48 decorating tip
No. 4 small decorating tip

Flowers:
12 small purple gumdrops
2 small yellow gumdrops
Granulated sugar
96 large pink gumdrops
6 large green gumdrops

Pink birthday candles

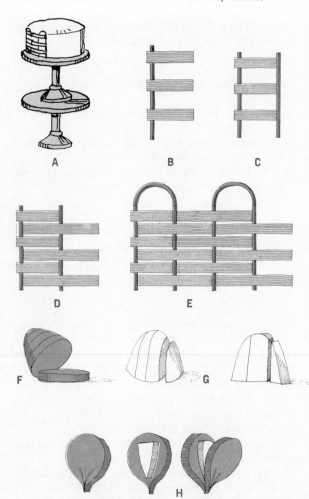

1.   On serving plate, put 2 cake layers together, using about ½ cup Decorating Frosting.

2.   Frost top and side of cake, using about 1¾ cups frosting, smoothing over with a metal spatula.

3.   In small bowl, combine 1 cup frosting with red food color, just enough to tint frosting a delicate pink. Turn into a pastry bag with a No. 48 ribbon decorating tip.

4.   Turn remaining ¼ cup frosting into a pastry bag with a No. 4 small decorating tip.

5.   Mark around outer edge of cake to divide into 32 even sections. Place cake plate on cake stand or inverted bowl, to raise to eye level. (See diagram A.)

6.   Using the No. 4 decorating tip, make a vertical line down side of cake to mark one section. (See diagram B.)

7.   Using the No. 48 decorating tip, overlapping the vertical line, make 3 horizontal basket weaves on side of cake. (See diagram B.) Also make second vertical line with No. 4 decorating tip. (See diagram C.)

8.   Between each of the 3 horizontal basket weaves, make 3 more, extending to overlap second vertical line. (See diagram D.)

9.   Continue alternating horizontal basket weave around side of cake and vertical lines down cake to give a woven effect. (See diagram E.)

10.   Using No. 4 decorating tip, make a loop to join pairs of 2 vertical lines around top of cake. (See diagram E.) Refrigerate cake.

11.   Make Flowers: Slice each purple gumdrop horizontally into 4 circles. (See diagram F.) Cut each yellow gumdrop into 4 vertical slices; then cut crosswise in thirds, making 12 strips. (See diagram G.)

12.   With fingers dipped in sugar, flatten purple circles to make petals, pinching one side of each to give a tapered effect.

13.   Insert a yellow strip between 2 purple "petals," pinching tapered ends together at base to join "petals." (See diagram H.) Makes 24 violets.

158

(Pink Posy Cake continued)

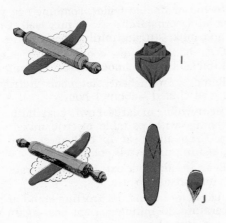

14. For roses: On well-sugared board, roll out each pink gumdrop to form a long strip. Roll up each strip lengthwise; stand on end. Makes 96 roses. (See diagram I.)

15. For leaves: Also on well-sugared board, roll out each green gumdrop to form a long strip. With tip of sharp knife, cut out leaves of varying sizes. Makes about 18 leaves. (See diagram J.)

16. To decorate cake: Fill basket with "flowers," pressing into frosting to hold them firm. Then arrange some of the flowers to spill over edge and down one side of cake.

17. Insert green leaves between some of the flowers.

18. Refrigerate cake 2 hours, or until serving. Just before serving, insert candles into cake.

19. To serve cake, remove a few flowers for each serving as cake is being cut.

Day before: If desired, flowers may be made and refrigerated. Also, cake layers may be made, frosted, and refrigerated. Several hours before serving, arrange flowers on cake. Refrigerate until serving.

* See Cake Chapter.

SUGARPLUM CAKE

MAKES 14 SERVINGS

1 lb red or green grapes
1 egg white, slightly beaten
1 cup superfine granulated sugar
2 (9-inch) Silvery-White-Cake-layers*
Basic Decorating Frosting, follows

1½ squares unsweetened chocolate, melted and cooled
No. 48 decorating tip
2 teaspoons instant coffee
1 teaspoon boiling water
No. 4 small decorating tip

1. Frost cake and make basket weave design around side as directed in Pink Posy Cake. Refrigerate cake.

2. Wash and dry 1 lb. red or green grapes very well. With scissors, cut into small clusters.

3. Brush grapes well with 1 egg white, slightly beaten. Roll in 1 cup superfine granulated sugar. Let dry completely on wire rack.

4. Just before serving, arrange grapes attractively on top of cake.

5. To serve cake, remove a few grape clusters for each serving as cake is being cut.

Day before: If desired, grapes may be frosted, then refrigerated. Also, cake layers may be baked, frosted, and refrigerated. Just before serving, arrange grapes on cake.

* See Cake Chapter.

Note: Strawberries may be used in season.

BASIC DECORATING FROSTING

4 egg yolks
½ cup sugar
2 teaspoons cornstarch
½ cup milk

1¼ cups butter or
    margarine
¾ cup shortening
3 teaspoons almond extract

MAKES ABOUT 3½ CUPS

1. In top of double boiler, combine egg yolks, sugar, and cornstarch; stir to mix well. Gradually add milk, stirring until smooth.

2. Over boiling water, cook mixture, stirring, until thickened and smooth—15 to 20 minutes.

3. Remove from heat; let cool. Refrigerate until well chilled—about 1 hour.

4. Meanwhile, in large bowl, beat butter and shortening, with portable electric mixer, until fluffy. Gradually beat in chilled custard mixture, beating until well combined.

5. Beat in almond extract. Refrigerate, covered, until ready to use.

6. Just before using, let frosting stand at room temperature 30 minutes; then beat again until soft and smooth.

DECORATED PETITS FOURS

Gold, White, or One-Egg
    Petits-Fours Cake*
Apricot Glaze

Fondant Frosting
Frosting Flowers and
    Leaves

MAKES 32

1. With sharp knife, trim edges from cake. Cut cake into 4 lengthwise strips.

2. Cut 2 strips into 6 squares each.

3. Cut remaining 2 strips into 5 rectangles each. Then cut each rectangle diagonally in half, to make 20 triangles in all.

4. Insert fork in top of cake. Holding by fork, dip each cake into Apricot Glaze, covering top and sides completely.

5. Place cakes, uncoated side down, 1 inch apart, on wire racks, placed on cookie sheet; let stand until glaze is set—about 1 hour.

6. Using very large spoon, pour enough Fondant Frosting over cakes, one at a time, to run over top and sides evenly. Cookie sheet underneath will catch excess frosting.

7. Scrape frosting from cookie sheet. Return to double boiler; reheat just enough to make frosting thin again.

8. Let cakes dry completely on wire racks—about 1 hour. Repeat frosting if necessary; let dry.

9. Then decorate. Or freeze in freezer until firm; then freezer-wrap; store in freezer until ready to use.

10. About 4 hours before serving, let petits fours stand at room temperature, uncovered, to thaw. Place frozen Frosting Flowers and Leaves on top of petits fours.

11. Let thaw completely before serving.

* See Cake Chapter.

APRICOT GLAZE FOR PETITS FOURS

¾ cup apricot preserves   ¾ cup Simple Syrup*

MAKES ENOUGH FOR 32 PETITS FOURS

1. In small saucepan, over low heat, heat preserves until bubbles form around edge of pan.

2. Remove from heat; press preserves through sieve. Add Simple Syrup, stirring until well combined.

3. Keep warm, over hot water, until ready to use; or reheat before using, to make glaze thin enough to pour.

* To make Simple Syrup:

MAKES 1 CUP

1. In small saucepan, combine 1 cup sugar with 1 cup water. Over medium heat, cook, stirring, until sugar is dissolved.

2. Bring to boiling, without stirring; boil, uncovered, 10 minutes. Let cool.

3. Refrigerate, covered, until ready to use.

FONDANT FROSTING FOR PETITS FOURS

2¾ cups granulated sugar   4 to 4½ cups sifted
Dash salt   confectioners' sugar
¼ teaspoon cream of tartar   ½ teaspoon almond extract

MAKES ENOUGH FOR 32 PETITS FOURS

1. In medium saucepan, combine granulated sugar, salt, and cream of tartar with 1½ cups water. Over low heat, cook, stirring, until sugar is dissolved.

2. Over medium heat, cook, without stirring, to 226F on candy thermometer.

3. Transfer to top of double boiler; let cool to lukewarm (110F on candy thermometer).

4. With wooden spoon, gradually beat in just enough confectioners' sugar to make frosting thick enough to coat spoon but thin enough to pour. Add almond extract.

5. Keep frosting over hot, not boiling, water, to keep thin enough to pour, until ready to use. If frosting is too thin, add a little more confectioners' sugar; if too thick, thin out with a little Simple Syrup or water.

FROSTING FLOWERS AND LEAVES

1 egg white
2¼ to 2½ cups sifted
   confectioners' sugar
Green, yellow, red, and blue
   food color

No. 65 decorating tip
No. 15 decorating tip
No. 4 small decorating tip
Waxed paper, cut into 52
   (2-inch) squares

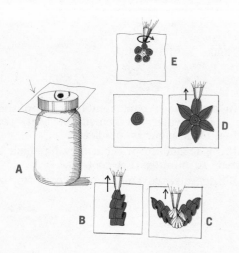

1. In medium bowl, with portable electric mixer, beat egg white with 2 cups sugar until well blended and thick.

2. Beat in enough additional sugar to make a mixture that will stand in stiff peaks when beater is slowly raised.

3. In each of 4 custard cups, place 2 tablespoons frosting. Keep covered with damp paper towels to prevent drying.

4. Color one portion of frosting chartreuse: Add 6 drops green and 2 drops yellow food color; mix well. Place frosting in small pastry bag with No. 65 decorating tip.

5. With a small amount of frosting, "glue" a waxed-paper square to the flat top of a small jar. (Diagram A.)

6. Onto waxed paper, pipe one leaf. (See diagram B.) Remove waxed paper with leaf. Continue to make 20 leaves.

7. Also, pipe a pair of leaves onto waxed-paper square. (See diagram C.) Continue to make 22 pairs of leaves.

8. Color second portion of frosting yellow: Add 10 drops yellow food color; mix well. Place frosting in small pastry bag with a No. 15 decorating tip.

9. In center of a pair of leaves, pipe 3 star flowers close together. (See diagram C.) Continue to make 11 yellow flower sprays.

10. Color third portion of frosting lavender: Add 4 drops red and 2 drops blue food color; mix well. Place frosting in small pastry bag with No. 65 decorating tip.

11. In center of a pair of leaves, pipe 1 lavender flower. (See diagram D.) Flowers may be piped separately, if desired. Continue to make 11 lavender flower sprays.

12. Color last portion of frosting pink: Add 2 drops red food color; mix well. Place frosting in small pastry bag with a No. 4 small decorating tip.

13. Onto square of waxed paper, pipe 3 daisies on one square. (See diagram E.) Continue to make 10 daisy clusters.

14. Arrange flowers on waxed-paper squares on a large tray. If desired, use at once. Or freeze until firm; then freezer-wrap tray. Store in freezer until ready to use.

(*Frosting Flowers and Leaves continued*)

15. To set flowers in place: Peel off waxed paper. Place yellow and lavender sprays in center of 22 petits fours.

16. Place a cluster of pink flowers and 2 individual leaves in center of each of remaining petits fours.

Note: Any leftover frosting may be used to make flowers, then frozen for later use.

W ant a truly lovely, light-as-foam cake for a sweet girl graduate, a Valentine party, or an engagement shower? Make our sweetheart of a cake, filled with heavenly strawberry filling and topped with real live roses.

SWEETHEART CAKE

MAKES 12 SERVINGS

1 pkg (15 oz) angel-food-
*   cake mix*
Strawberry Filling, below
3 cups heavy cream
Small silver dragees

1 paper doily, cut into heart
*   shape*
6 small pink roses and
*   several rosebuds*
9-inch narrow pink velvet
*   ribbon*

1. Preheat oven to 375F. Line bottom of heart-shape pan (12-cup or No. 4 size) with waxed paper.

2. Make angel-food cake as package label directs; turn into pan.

3. Bake, on lowest shelf of oven, 35 to 45 minutes. Cool completely, in pan, on wire rack.

4. Meanwhile, make Strawberry Filling.

5. With sharp knife, gently loosen side of cake from pan. Turn out onto serving plate; remove paper from bottom.

6. With wooden picks, mark depth of cake into thirds. With a serrated knife, slice off top third crosswise; reserve.

7. With fork, hollow out center third of cake, leaving a ½-inch-wide edge all around. Remove picks.

8. Pour Strawberry Filling into hollow. Refrigerate cake, uncovered, until filling is firm—at least 30 minutes. Set reserved layer on top.

9. To frost and decorate: In medium bowl, beat cream with rotary beater just until stiff.

10. With two thirds of whipped cream, smoothly frost top and side of cake.

11. With rest of cream in pastry bag, using No. 6 decorating tip, pipe double row of rosettes, one on top of the other, around top edge of cake, to outline heart shape. Also, pipe row of rosettes around base and down point of heart. Top each rosette with silver dragee. Refrigerate several hours, or until ready to serve.

12. Just before serving, put doily on cake, and arrange ribbon-tied roses and rosebuds. Lift off doily and flowers before cutting cake.

STRAWBERRY FILLING

1 pkg (10 oz) thawed
    frozen sliced
    strawberries
1 cup hot water
1 pkg (6 oz) strawberry-
    flavored gelatin

½ cup finely chopped
    almonds
½ cup heavy cream
¼ cup kirsch, or
    ½ teaspoon almond
    extract

1. Drain strawberries, reserving ½ cup juice. Crush with potato masher.

2. Pour hot water over gelatin in bowl, stirring until gelatin is dissolved. Stir in reserved strawberry juice, the berries, and almonds.

3. Refrigerate until consistency of unbeaten egg white—at least 1 hour.

4. In small bowl, beat cream with rotary beater just until stiff.

5. With wire whisk or rubber scraper, gently fold kirsch and whipped cream into gelatin mixture until well combined. Refrigerate until slightly jelled, not firm—about 30 minutes.

We cannot think of a nicer way to please a bride who's to be married at home than to make the wedding cake for the reception. And we cannot think of a prettier, easier way to make it than our own step-by-step method. We tell you how to make the fruitcake, the layers (enough for 80 servings), the simply beautiful frosting and flower decorations, and even give directions for cutting. The eating's up to the guests, however.

WEDDING CAKE

Bride's Fruitcake
3 (13-by-9-by-2-inch)
    Wedding-Cake
    Layers
2 (8-by-8-by-2-inch)
    Wedding-Cake
    Layers
14-inch cardboard square,
    covered with foil; or
    14-inch-square silver
    platter

Creamy Frosting
    (two and a half times
    recipe)
7-inch and 4-inch cardboard
    squares, covered with
    foil
No. 18 decorating tip
    in pastry bag
8 waxed or frosting roses
White porcelain figurine

MAKES **80** SERVINGS

At least one week before serving, bake Bride's Fruitcake, and store. Two days before serving, bake all the Wedding-Cake Layers. Wrap well in foil; refrigerate.

1. The day before serving, assemble the cake. To make bottom tier: Cut one 13-by-9-by-2-inch Wedding-Cake Layer in half lengthwise. Using 14-inch cardboard square as a base, fit together lengthwise one whole 13-by-9-by-2-inch layer with half a layer (cut side in), to form a 13-inch square; "glue" together with Creamy Frosting. Frost top lightly. Over this, arrange the other 13-by-9-by-2-inch layer with the other half layer, reversing the position of whole and half layers. Frost top and sides completely. Let stand until frosting is dry.

2. To make middle tier: On 7-inch cardboard square, frost together two 8-inch Wedding-Cake Layers; center on bottom tier. Frost top. Let stand until dry.

1.

(Wedding Cake continued)

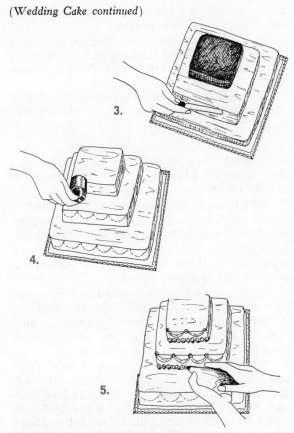

3.

4.

5.

BRIDE'S FRUITCAKE
(Make at least a week ahead)

1 cup sifted all-purpose
    flour
¼ teaspoon baking powder
¼ teaspoon salt
¼ teaspoon cinnamon
¼ teaspoon nutmeg
⅛ teaspoon cloves
¼ cup soft shortening

½ cup light-brown sugar,
    firmly packed
1 egg
¼ cup light molasses
1 cup diced mixed candied
    fruit
¼ cup slivered almonds
½ cup seedless raisins
Sherry or brandy

3. To make top tier: Place fruitcake on 4-inch cardboard square; then center on middle tier. Completely frost tops and sides of all three tiers.

4. To decorate cake: Frost cake again, making tops and sides very smooth. With 2-inch biscuit cutter, make scallop outlines on sides; 2 on each side of top tier, 4 on middle tier, 5 on bottom tier. With frosting in pastry bag and No. 18 decorating tip, trace biscuit-cutter outlines, to make scallops. Start with the top tier.

5. Make rosettes to join the scallops: Force frosting through decorating tip while making a sharp, full twist. (Practice on waxed paper first. Keep frosting in large bowl of electric mixer; beat often, to keep it plastic.) Also, make rosettes, in same fashion, around base of top and middle tiers.

6. Make ruching to edge top of all tiers: Force frosting through same decorating tip in heavy stream, reversing direction every half inch, to form overlapping folds.

7. Make swags at corners by forcing diminishing stream of frosting upward. Make double row of little rosettes around base of cake.

8. Place waxed or frosting roses at corners of middle and bottom tiers, mounding on a little frosting to give more height. Set the porcelain figurine in place. (If you serve the fruitcake, servings will be 96.)

MAKES 4-INCH SQUARE CAKE

1. Preheat oven to 300F. Make foil pan (see directions page 166). Fit into 9-by-5-by-3-inch loaf pan.

2. Sift flour with baking powder, salt, and spices; set aside.

3. In large bowl of electric mixer, at medium speed, beat shortening with sugar, egg, and molasses until light and fluffy.

4. At low speed, blend in flour mixture just until combined.

5. With wooden spoon, stir in candied fruit, almonds, and raisins.

6. Turn into prepared foil pan; bake 1¾ to 2 hours, or until cake tester inserted in center comes out clean. Let cool, in pan, on wire rack.

7. Remove foil, and wrap cake completely in cheesecloth soaked in sherry or brandy. Store in airtight container. Sprinkle with sherry or brandy every 3 days.

HOW TO MAKE FOIL PAN

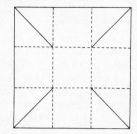

1. In center of 11-inch square of heavy-duty foil, measure a 4-inch square.
2. Cut diagonally from outer corners to corners of 4-inch square. Fold sides upright, overlapping corners, to make a 4-inch pan. Secure corners with paper clips.
3. Put foil pan at end of 9-by-5-by-3-inch loaf pan, to support side walls; place custard cup to support exposed wall.

WEDDING-CAKE LAYERS
(Make two days ahead)

2½ cups sifted cake flour
2½ teaspoons baking powder
1 teaspoon salt
4 egg whites, at room temperature
1½ cups sugar

½ cup soft butter or margarine
1 cup milk
1½ teaspoons rose water, or 1 teaspoon almond extract

1. Preheat oven to 350F. Lightly grease and then flour a 13-by-9-by-2-inch baking pan, or two 8-by-8-by-2-inch baking pans.
2. Sift flour, baking powder, salt; set aside.
3. In small bowl of electric mixer, at medium speed, beat egg whites until foamy throughout.
4. Gradually add ½ cup sugar, beating well after each addition; beat until soft peaks form when beater is slowly raised.
5. In large bowl, at high speed, cream butter with remaining sugar until light and fluffy.
6. At low speed, alternately blend in flour mixture (in fourths) and milk (in thirds), beginning and ending with flour mixture.
7. Then blend in egg whites and rose water just until mixture is smooth—about 1 minute.
8. Turn into prepared pan. Bake 13-by-9-by-2-inch layer 35 to 40 minutes; 8-by-8-by-2-inch layers 30 minutes; or until surface springs back when gently pressed with fingertip.
9. Cool cake, in pan, on wire rack 10 minutes. Invert on rack; remove pan; cool completely.
Note: You will need three times recipe, or 3 packages white-cake mix, to make three 13-by-9-by-2-inch layers. Also, you will need one recipe, or 1 package white-cake mix, to make two 8-by-8-by-2-inch layers.

CREAMY FROSTING

½ cup soft butter or margarine
½ cup shortening
2 pkg (1-lb size) confectioners' sugar

½ cup light cream
3 teaspoons rose water, or 2 teaspoons vanilla extract

1. In large bowl of electric mixer, at low speed, beat butter and shortening until light and fluffy.
2. Beat in sugar, 1 cup at a time, alternately with light cream, beating until smooth after each addition.
3. Add rose water; continue beating until smooth and of spreading consistency.
4. Keep frosting covered with damp cloth, to prevent drying out. Beat again just before using.
Note: Recipe makes enough to frost three-tier cake once. You will need one and a half times recipe to refrost and decorate cake.

WAXED ROSES*

Paraffin　　　　　　　*8 white roses*

1. Melt paraffin in a coffee can over very low heat. Paraffin should measure halfway up side of can.
2. Quickly dip roses, one by one, in warm paraffin, to coat blossom completely.
3. Let stand upright in glass tumbler until dry and firm. Then remove the stems.

* Or purchase 8 frosting roses from bakery or confectioner's.

SILVER-ANNIVERSARY CAKE

MAKES 80 SERVINGS

1. Bake and decorate Wedding Cake, as directed. Omit the porcelain figurine.
2. With frosting in pastry bag, using plain tip for writing, make the numerals 25 on top of cake. Outline with silver dragees. Outline scallops with silver dragees.
3. Place two silver leaves, one on each side, at base of each waxed or frosting rose.
4. Cut according to diagram. (If you serve the fruitcake, servings will be 96.)

GOLDEN-ANNIVERSARY CAKE

MAKES 80 SERVINGS

1. Bake and decorate Wedding Cake, as directed. Omit figurine and white roses. Use yellow roses, waxed or frosting.
2. Tint ½ cup Creamy Frosting a deep yellow. With frosting in pastry bag, using plain tip for writing, make the numerals 50 on top of cake.
3. Place 2 gold leaves, one on each side, at base of each rose.
4. Cut according to diagram. (If you serve the fruitcake, servings will be 96.)

HOW TO CUT WEDDING CAKE

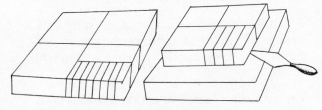

Carefully lift off top tier (fruitcake) and figurine, with cardboard support. After the reception, fruitcake should be freezer-wrapped, then frozen, to be served on the first anniversary.

Middle tier: Cut into quarters. Then cut each quarter into 4 slices. When middle tier has been served, remove cardboard support. Makes 16 servings.

Bottom tier: Cut into quarters. Halve each quarter; cut each eighth into 8 slices. Makes 64 servings.

Cookies

Cookies are popular the world round. As a matter of fact, they have a very national character. We in this country have made use of many of the recipes brought to us by settlers, early and late. Our repertoire of cookies is, therefore, rich and varied.

There are dropped cookies, rolled cookies, refrigerator cookies and molded cookies, bar cookies—all easy to make—all keep well in a jar or a covered tin.

MAKING COOKIES

1. Our cookie recipes were tested using sifted all-purpose flour. If the unsifted type of flour is substituted, just follow manufacturer's directions on the package.
2. The back of any large baking pan may be substituted for a cookie sheet. Use greased or ungreased, as recipe directs.
3. If you are baking one sheet of cookies at a time, place oven rack in center of oven. If you are baking two sheets, place racks to divide oven into thirds. If tops of cookies do not brown properly, move to a higher rack the last few minutes of baking.
4. Bright, shiny baking sheets ensure delicately browned cookies. They should be at least an inch shorter and narrower than the oven, to allow for circulation of heat.
5. Check cookies when minimum baking time is up. To cool, remove with wide spatula to wire racks. Do not overlap.

STORING COOKIES

Line bottom of container with waxed paper; place a sheet of waxed paper between each two layers of cookies. Store different types of cookie in separate containers.

Soft Cookies: Store in container with tight-fitting lid. Slices of apple or orange in container help keep cookies moist. Change fruit often.

Crisp Cookies: Store in container with loose-fitting lid. If cookies lose their crispness, heat at 300F about 5 minutes before serving.

Bar Cookies: Store in pan. Cover tightly.

FREEZING COOKIES

Drop- or rolled-cookie dough: Pack in freezer containers; label, and freeze. To use, thaw dough in refrigerator until it is easy to handle. Prepare and bake as recipe directs.

Refrigerator-cookie dough: Form dough into a roll. Wrap in foil or saran; seal; label, and freeze. To use, cut frozen dough into slices, and bake as recipe directs.

Baked cookies: All types of cookie may be frozen. Wrap cooled cookies in foil or saran; seal; label, and freeze. Fragile cookies should be packed in freezer containers; label, and freeze. To thaw: Let stand, unwrapped, at room temperature 15 minutes.

MAILING COOKIES

Select only cookies that will hold up in the mail. Bar and drop cookies are particularly good for mailing.

Wrap each cookie separately in waxed paper or saran. Or put in pairs, and wrap each pair.

Line heavy-cardboard box with foil or waxed paper. Pack cookies in box. Stuff corners and any spaces with crushed waxed paper, cotton or marshmallows so cookies are secure; place crushed waxed paper on top of cookies. Cover; secure with tape. Wrap in heavy brown paper; tie securely. Clearly print address and return address. Attach "Fragile" sticker.

Drop cookies are made from a soft dough and dropped from the spoon directly onto the baking sheet. Actually, "dropped" is a little misleading, as the mixture must be stiff enough to be pushed from the spoon. Dropped cookies can be soft, with a cake-like texture; crisp; or even brittle. Their shape is irregular, as they spread on the cookie sheet. You can make them in a wide variety of delicious flavors.

BANANA-OATMEAL COOKIES

MAKES ABOUT 3½ DOZEN

1½ cups sifted all-purpose flour
1 teaspoon salt
½ teaspoon baking soda
½ teaspoon nutmeg
¾ teaspoon cinnamon
¾ cup soft butter or margarine
1 cup sugar

1 egg
1 cup mashed ripe bananas (about 3)
1 teaspoon vanilla extract
1½ cups raw quick-cooking oats
½ cup coarsely chopped walnuts

1. Sift flour with salt, soda, nutmeg, and cinnamon; set aside.

2. In large bowl, with wooden spoon or portable electric mixer at medium speed, beat butter, sugar, and egg until light and fluffy.

3. Beat in bananas and vanilla until smooth.

4. Gradually stir in flour mixture and oats until well combined. Stir in nuts. Refrigerate 30 minutes.

5. Meanwhile, preheat oven to 400F. Lightly grease cookie sheets.

6. Drop batter by rounded teaspoonfuls, 2 inches apart, onto cookie sheets.

7. Bake 12 to 15 minutes, or until golden. Remove to wire rack; cool.

CHOCOLATE-CHIP COOKIES

MAKES ABOUT 4 DOZEN

1 cup plus 2 tablespoons
    sifted all-purpose flour
½ teaspoon baking soda
½ teaspoon salt
½ cup granulated sugar
¼ cup light-brown sugar,
    firmly packed
1 egg

1 teaspoon vanilla extract
½ cup soft butter or
    margarine
½ cup coarsely chopped
    walnuts or pecans
1 pkg (6 oz) semisweet-
    chocolate pieces

1. Preheat oven to 375F.
2. Into large bowl, sift flour with soda and salt.
3. Add sugars, egg, vanilla, and butter. With wooden spoon, or portable electric mixer at medium speed, beat until smooth and well combined—about 1 minute.
4. Stir in nuts and chocolate pieces.
5. Drop by teaspoonfuls, 2 inches apart, onto ungreased cookie sheets.
6. Bake 10 to 12 minutes, or until golden. Remove to wire rack; cool.

GLAZED CHOCOLATE COOKIES

MAKES ABOUT 4 DOZEN

1¼ cups sifted all-purpose
    flour
¼ teaspoon salt
¼ teaspoon baking soda
½ cup soft butter or
    margarine
1 cup light-brown sugar,
    firmly packed
1 egg
1 teaspoon vanilla extract
2 squares unsweetened
    chocolate, melted

½ cup buttermilk
1 cup coarsely chopped
    walnuts or pecans

Glaze:
3 cups sifted confectioners'
    sugar
¼ cup light cream
1 teaspoon vanilla extract
1 square unsweetened
    chocolate, melted

1. Preheat oven to 375F. Sift together flour, salt, and soda; set aside.
2. In large bowl of electric mixer, at medium speed, beat butter, sugar, egg, and vanilla until light and fluffy.
3. Beat in chocolate.
4. At low speed, beat in flour mixture alternately with buttermilk until well combined.
5. Stir in nuts. Mixture will be soft.
6. Drop by slightly rounded teaspoonfuls, 2 inches apart, onto ungreased cookie sheets.
7. Bake 8 to 10 minutes. Remove to wire rack; cool partially.
8. Meanwhile, make Glaze: In medium bowl, combine sugar, cream, and vanilla. With spoon, beat until smooth. Add melted chocolate; mix well. (If glaze is too stiff to spread easily, add a little more cream.)
9. Glaze top of cookies while slightly warm.

GLAZED GINGER COOKIES

MAKES ABOUT 4 DOZEN

2½ cups sifted all-purpose
    flour
½ teaspoon salt
1 teaspoon baking powder
¼ teaspoon baking soda
1 teaspoon cinnamon
½ teaspoon cloves
1 teaspoon ginger
½ cup shortening
½ cup light-brown sugar,
    firmly packed

1 egg
½ cup light molasses
1 tablespoon vinegar
½ cup seedless raisins
    (optional)

Glaze:
2 cups sifted confectioners'
    sugar
2 to 3 tablespoons milk

1. Sift flour with salt, baking powder, soda, cinnamon, cloves, and ginger; set aside.
2. In large bowl, with wooden spoon, or portable electric mixer at medium speed, beat shortening, sugar, and egg until light and fluffy.
3. Stir in molasses, vinegar, and ½ cup water. Mixture will look curdled.
4. Gradually stir in flour mixture until smooth. Stir in raisins. Refrigerate 30 minutes.

as in cake

...and in chocolate, coconut, cheese, and cherry. A child's delight, an adult's dream, a dieter's secret vice. If a wife makes good cake, she's a good wife; if a mother makes good cake, she's a great mother. Little else is needed. You can make a good cake.

magic carpet of cake decoration

With cake, you can let your imagination fly. By using molds ingeniously, you can come up with a variety of shapes, each guaranteed to win praise from your audience. But inventive as you can be with forms, so much more inventive can you be with cake decorations, frosting, and props. We don't say that you should create an original work of art every time you bake a cake. On the contrary, the cakes we're recommending here take skill, patience, and time to make, and should be made to honor only the most important events. They should be dazzling show-off cakes, witty or ethereal or sentimental, to suit the day. They should be the grand climaxes to extra-special meals or parties; they should be made with love as well as skill. And if you approach them in this spirit, we're sure you won't regret a minute of the time it takes you. Your own sense of artistic achievement and, more important, the pleasure of the person you make the cake for are more than enough compensation. In fact, you may be tempted to try another elaborate cake again soon!

What kinds of cake can you make? Take a look at the ones we've pictured here. First, there's the "Sweetheart Cake," perfect for a girl sweet sixteen or older, or whenever there's a romantic mood to the party. This time, we've used, among other things, angel-food-cake mix, pink velvet ribbon, and roses. We love this cake, and so will you. Next comes our "Humpty-Dumpty Cake," ideal for a child's birthday; or fun as a centerpiece, to be consumed later as a party dessert; or as the star of an Easter table, amid all the eggs you can dye. Ours is made of poundcake mix, and you'll find we've used such nonedibles as drinking straws and thin wooden skewers to help make the effect. Third, there's our "Pink Posy Cake," guaranteed to be the sensation of any girl's birthday party. Our basket is made of buttery cream frosting. It's filled with tiny pink gumdrop flowers, illuminated with flickering candles, one for each year and one to grow on. And if this cake will delight a little girl, then our "Wagon Train" will enthrall her brother. It's not nearly so difficult to

make as it looks. The basic ingredient is a yellow-cake mix, to which we've added cookies, wafers, three kinds of frosting, and the horsepower to pull them all. Next, there's our "Grand-Slam Cake," as exciting as winning all thirteen tricks at bridge. This cake boasts of a frosting of coffee and spice and everything nice. Serve it to the boss's wife the first time she comes for an afternoon of cards. Finally, of course, there's the "Wedding Cake," brightest star in our galaxy and, if the bride is to be married at home, the most appreci-ated cake you'll ever make. Here, the basic cake is a white cake; but the top layer is a fruitcake, designed to be saved and eaten on the first anniversary. The fruitcake is the only cake of all you can't make from a packaged mix. For the skill and fun come not so much in the cake as in the decorations. And you, of course, are free to experiment with your own. You'll find unexpected inspiration in colorful candies and flowers, toy counters, and miniatures from antiques shops, so much so, you may never make a plain cake again!

(Glazed Ginger Cookies continued)

5. Meanwhile, preheat oven to 375F. Lightly grease cookie sheets.

6. Drop by slightly rounded teaspoonfuls, 2 inches apart, onto cookie sheets.

7. Bake 10 to 12 minutes, or until set. Remove to wire rack; cool partially.

8. Make Glaze: In medium bowl, combine sugar and milk; stir until smooth.

9. Spread top of cookies with glaze while still slightly warm. Decorate, if desired, with additional raisins.

DOUBLE-CHOCOLATE DROPS

1 pkg (6 oz) semisweet-
   chocolate pieces
1 cup sifted all-purpose
   flour
½ teaspoon baking soda
½ teaspoon salt

½ cup soft butter or
   margarine
½ cup sugar
1 egg
½ cup coarsely chopped
   walnuts or pecans

MAKES ABOUT 3 DOZEN

1. In top of double boiler, over hot, not boiling, water, melt ½ cup chocolate pieces. Let cool.

2. Sift together flour, soda, and salt; set aside.

3. In large bowl of electric mixer, at medium speed, beat butter, sugar, and egg until light and fluffy.

4. At low speed, beat in melted chocolate and ¼ cup warm water.

5. Then beat in flour mixture, just until combined.

6. With spoon, stir in remaining chocolate pieces and nuts. Refrigerate 30 minutes.

7. Meanwhile, preheat oven to 375F. Lightly grease cookie sheets.

8. Drop batter by teaspoonfuls, 3 inches apart, onto cookie sheets.

9. Bake 10 to 12 minutes. Remove to wire rack; cool.

FRUITCAKE COOKIES

2½ cups sifted all-purpose
   flour
1 teaspoon baking soda
1 teaspoon salt
1 teaspoon cinnamon
1 cup soft butter or
   margarine
1½ cups sugar
2 eggs
4 pkg (8-oz size) pitted
   dates, coarsely
   chopped

2 jars (4-oz size) cubed candied pineapple,
   finely chopped
1 cup candied cherries,
   quartered
1 can (3½ oz) toasted
   sliced almonds,
   coarsely chopped
1 cup toasted Brazil nuts,*
   coarsely chopped

MAKES ABOUT 8 DOZEN

1. Preheat oven to 400F. Sift flour with baking soda, salt, and cinnamon; set aside.

2. In large bowl, with wooden spoon, or portable electric mixer at medium speed, beat butter, sugar, and eggs until light and fluffy.

3. Stir in flour mixture until well combined. Add fruits and nuts, mixing well.

4. Drop by level tablespoonfuls, 2 inches apart, onto ungreased cookie sheets.

5. Bake 8 to 10 minutes, or until golden-brown. Let stand 1 minute. Remove to wire rack; cool.

* To toast Brazil nuts: Cover shelled nuts with cold water; bring to boil, and simmer 3 minutes. Drain well. Place in shallow baking pan; bake at 350F for 15 to 20 minutes, or until golden.

HERMITS

3½ cups sifted all-purpose
    flour
1 teaspoon baking soda
1 teaspoon salt
1 teaspoon nutmeg
1 teaspoon cinnamon
1 cup soft butter or
    margarine

2 cups light-brown sugar,
    firmly packed
2 eggs
½ cup cold black coffee
1¾ cups seedless raisins
1¾ cups chopped dried
    apricots

1. Sift together flour, soda, salt, and spices; set aside.
2. In large bowl of electric mixer, at medium speed, cream butter with sugar until light and fluffy. Add eggs; beat until well combined.
3. At low speed, beat in coffee. Then beat in dry ingredients, a third at a time.
4. With spoon, stir in raisins and apricots until well mixed. Refrigerate 1 hour.
5. Meanwhile, preheat oven to 400F. Lightly grease cookie sheets.
6. Drop by rounded teaspoonfuls, 2 inches apart, onto cookie sheets.
7. Bake 8 to 10 minutes, or until hermits are nicely browned. Remove to wire rack; cool.

PEANUT-BUTTER DROPS

1½ cups sifted all-purpose
    flour
1 teaspoon baking soda
½ teaspoon salt
1 teaspoon ginger
½ teaspoon cloves
¾ cup shortening

¾ cup chunk-style peanut
    butter
1 cup light-brown sugar,
    firmly packed
2 eggs
2 tablespoons milk
1 cup salted Spanish
    peanuts

1. Preheat oven to 375F. Sift flour with soda, salt, ginger, and cloves; set aside.
2. In large bowl, with wooden spoon, or portable electric mixer at medium speed, beat shortening, peanut butter, and sugar until light and fluffy.
3. Add eggs and milk; beat until smooth.
4. Stir in flour mixture and peanuts until thoroughly combined.
5. Drop by rounded teaspoonfuls, 2 inches apart, onto ungreased cookie sheets.
6. Bake 10 to 12 minutes, or until golden-brown. Let stand 1 minute before removing from cookie sheets. Remove to wire rack; cool.

RAISIN-SPICE DROPS

3 cups sifted all-purpose
    flour
1 teaspoon baking soda
1 teaspoon salt
1 teaspoon cinnamon
½ teaspoon cloves
1 cup shortening
1½ cups light-brown
    sugar, firmly packed
3 eggs

1 teaspoon vanilla extract
2 cups seedless raisins
1 cup coarsely chopped
    walnuts

Glaze:
3 cups sifted confectioners'
    sugar
¼ cup milk
1 teaspoon vanilla extract

1. Sift flour with soda, salt, cinnamon, and cloves; set aside.
2. In large bowl of electric mixer, at medium speed, beat shortening, sugar, eggs, and vanilla until light and fluffy.
3. At low speed, beat in flour mixture until well combined.
4. Stir in raisins and walnuts. Refrigerate 30 minutes.
5. Meanwhile, preheat oven to 375F. Lightly grease cookie sheets.
6. Drop batter by rounded teaspoonfuls, 2 inches apart, onto cookie sheets.

(Raisin-Spice Drops continued)

7. Bake 10 to 12 minutes, or until lightly browned. Remove to wire rack; cool partially.

8. Make Glaze: In medium bowl, combine sugar with milk and vanilla; stir until smooth.

9. Use to glaze tops of slightly warm cookies. Decorate with raisins or nuts, if desired.

TOASTED OATMEAL COOKIES

MAKES ABOUT 4 DOZEN

¾ cup butter or
    margarine
2½ cups raw rolled oats
½ cup sifted all-purpose
    flour
1 teaspoon cinnamon

½ teaspoon salt
½ teaspoon baking soda
1 cup light-brown sugar,
    firmly packed
1 egg
1 teaspoon vanilla extract

1. Preheat oven to 375F.

2. In medium skillet, over medium heat, heat butter until lightly browned. Be careful not to burn. Add oats; sauté, stirring constantly, until golden—about 5 minutes. Remove from heat; cool.

3. Meanwhile, sift flour with cinnamon, salt, and soda; set aside.

4. In large bowl, combine sugar, egg, and vanilla. With wooden spoon, or portable electric mixer at medium speed, beat until light.

5. Stir in rolled oats and flour mixture until well combined.

6. Drop by slightly rounded teaspoonfuls, 3 inches apart, onto ungreased cookie sheets.

7. Bake 10 to 12 minutes, or until golden. Remove to wire rack; cool.

Rolled cookies are made from dough stiff enough to roll thin. Thorough chilling of the dough is one of the first principles of successful rolled cookies, so keep this in mind if you plan to serve rolled cookies to company and leave yourself enough time. If the dough is not well chilled, it will be too soft to roll without adding more flour, and that will make the cookies less tender. The dough should be handled a little at a time, leaving the rest to chill in the refrigerator. If you're in a hurry, roll dough into an oblong, and cut, with sharp knife or pastry wheel, into squares or diamonds.

LEBKUCHEN ROUNDS

MAKES 36

3 cups sifted all-purpose
    flour
½ teaspoon baking soda
½ teaspoon salt
1 teaspoon allspice
1 teaspoon nutmeg
1 teaspoon cinnamon
1 teaspoon cloves
1 jar (4 oz) citron,* finely
    chopped

1 can (4 oz) walnuts, finely
    chopped
1 cup honey
¾ cup light-brown sugar,
    firmly packed
1 egg
1 tablespoon lemon juice
2 teaspoons grated lemon
    peel
2 cups sifted confectioners'
    sugar

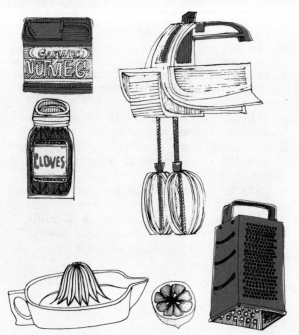

1. Sift flour with baking soda, salt, and spices; set aside. Toss citron with walnuts; set aside.

2. Warm honey in small saucepan. Remove from heat.

3. In large bowl, using portable electric mixer at medium speed, beat brown sugar and egg until smooth and fluffy.

4. Add lemon juice and honey; beat until well blended. Beat in lemon peel and 1 cup flour mixture; beat until smooth.

5. Using wooden spoon, stir in rest of flour mixture until well combined. Then stir in fruit-nut mixture.

6. Refrigerate dough, covered, overnight.

7. Next day, preheat oven to 375F. Lightly grease cookie sheets.

8. On lightly floured surface, roll out dough, one half at a time, ¼ inch thick. (Refrigerate remaining half until ready to roll out.)

9. Using floured 2-inch, round cookie cutter, cut out cookies. Place, 2 inches apart, on prepared cookie sheets; bake 15 minutes. Remove to wire rack; cool slightly.

10. Meanwhile, make glaze: Combine confectioners' sugar with 3 tablespoons water; stir until smooth.

11. Brush glaze on warm cookies. Decorate with bits of candied cherry and angelica, if desired. Cool completely.

12. Store, tightly covered, 2 to 3 weeks before using. (To make cookies more moist, store with cut piece of apple.)

* Or use ½ cup mixed candied fruit, finely chopped.

SWISS CINNAMON CRISPS

MAKES 64

3 cups sifted all-purpose
    flour
½ teaspoon salt
1 tablespoon cinnamon
1 cup soft butter or
    margarine
½ cup light-brown sugar,
    firmly packed

¾ cup granulated sugar
1 egg

Topping:
2 tablespoons milk
1 egg
½ cup granulated sugar
1 tablespoon cinnamon

1. Sift flour with salt and cinnamon; set aside.

2. In large bowl, with wooden spoon, or portable electric mixer at medium speed, beat butter, sugars, and egg until light and fluffy.

3. Gradually add flour mixture, stirring until smooth and well combined.

4. With rubber scraper, form dough into a ball. Wrap in waxed paper or foil; refrigerate 1 hour.

5. Divide dough into 4 parts. Refrigerate until ready to roll out.

(Swiss Cinnamon Crisps continued)

6. Meanwhile, preheat oven to 375F. Make Topping: In small bowl, with rotary beater, combine milk and egg. In another small bowl, combine sugar and cinnamon; set aside.

7. On lightly floured surface, roll dough, one part at a time, into a 9-by-7-inch rectangle. With floured sharp knife or pastry wheel, cut into 16 rectangles.

8. Using spatula, place, 1½ inches apart, on ungreased cookie sheets. Brush top of cookies lightly with egg mixture; then sprinkle with sugar mixture.

9. Bake 10 to 12 minutes, or until set and golden-brown. Remove to wire rack; cool.

OLD-FASHIONED SUGAR COOKIES

MAKES 4 DOZEN

4 cups sifted all-purpose
    flour
1 teaspoon baking powder
½ teaspoon baking soda
½ teaspoon salt
½ teaspoon nutmeg
1 cup soft butter or
    margarine
1½ cups sugar

1 egg
½ cup dairy sour cream
1 teaspoon vanilla extract

Topping:
¼ cup sugar
Raisins or blanched almonds
    (optional)

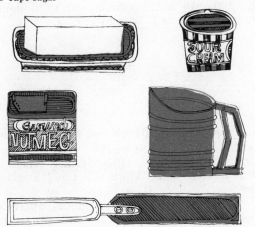

1. Sift flour with baking powder, soda, salt, and nutmeg; set aside.

2. In large bowl of electric mixer, at medium speed, beat butter, sugar, and egg until light and fluffy.

3. At low speed, beat in sour cream and vanilla until smooth.

4. Gradually add flour mixture, beating until well combined.

5. With rubber scraper, form dough into a ball. Wrap in waxed paper or foil; refrigerate several hours, or overnight.

6. Divide dough into 4 parts. Refrigerate until ready to roll out.

7. Meanwhile, preheat oven to 375F. Lightly grease cookie sheets.

8. On well-floured surface, roll dough, one part at a time, ¼ inch thick.

9. With floured, 2½-inch, round or scalloped cookie cutter, cut out cookies. Using spatula, place, 2 inches apart, on cookie sheets.

10. Sprinkle tops of cookies with sugar. Place a raisin or almond in the center of each, if desired. Reroll trimmings, and cut.

11. Bake 10 to 12 minutes, or until golden. Remove to wire rack; cool.

OLD-FASHIONED FILLED COOKIES

3 cups sifted all-purpose
    flour
1 teaspoon baking powder
½ teaspoon salt
¾ cup soft butter or
    margarine
1½ cups sugar
2 eggs
1 teaspoon vanilla extract,
    or 1 tablespoon
    grated lemon peel

Filling:
1 pkg (8 oz) pitted dates,
    cut up; or 1 cup
    seedless raisins
½ cup sugar
1 teaspoon grated lemon
    peel
¼ cup lemon juice
½ cup coarsely chopped
    walnuts

1. Sift flour with baking powder and salt; set aside.

2. In large bowl, with wooden spoon, or portable electric mixer at medium speed, beat butter, sugar, eggs, and vanilla until light and fluffy.

3. Gradually stir in flour mixture until smooth and well combined.

4. Using rubber scraper, form dough into a ball. Wrap in waxed paper or foil; refrigerate several hours, or overnight.

5. Divide dough into 4 parts; refrigerate until ready to use.

6. Meanwhile, make Filling: In small saucepan, combine dates and sugar with ½ cup water. Cook, stirring and over medium heat, until mixture has thickened—about 5 minutes. Remove from heat. Stir in lemon peel, lemon juice, and walnuts. Cool completely.

7. Preheat oven to 375F. Lightly grease cookie sheets.

8. On lightly floured surface, roll dough, one part at a time, ⅛ inch thick. With floured, 2½-inch, round or scalloped cookie cutter, cut out cookies. Reroll trimmings, and cut.

9. Using spatula, place half the cookies, 2 inches apart, on cookie sheets. Spread 1 teaspoon filling over each cookie; cover with another cookie. With floured fork, seal edges firmly; also prick center of top.

10. Bake 10 to 12 minutes, or until lightly browned. Remove to wire rack; cool.

FILLED TURNOVERS

1. Prepare cookie dough and filling as above.

2. On lightly floured surface, roll dough, one part at a time, into a 10-by-12-inch rectangle. With floured, sharp knife, cut into 12 rectangles.

3. Using spatula, place, 2 inches apart, on cookie sheets. Spread 1 teaspoon filling on half of each; fold over. With floured fork, seal edges firmly; prick center of tops.

4. Bake as above. Remove to wire rack; cool.

BROWN-SUGAR SHORTBREAD COOKIES

1 cup soft butter or
margarine
½ cup light-brown sugar,
firmly packed

2½ cups sifted all-purpose
flour

1.   In large bowl, with portable electric mixer at medium speed, or wooden spoon, beat butter with sugar until light and fluffy.

2.   With wooden spoon, stir in flour until smooth and well combined. Dough will be stiff.

3.   Refrigerate dough, covered, several hours.

4.   Preheat oven to 300F.

5.   Divide dough into 2 parts; refrigerate until ready to roll out.

6.   On lightly floured surface, roll out dough, one part at a time, ⅓ inch thick.

7.   Using 1½- or 2-inch fancy cookie cutters, cut out cookies. Place, 1 inch apart, on ungreased cookie sheets.

8.   Bake cookies 25 minutes, or until light-golden. Remove to wire rack; cool.

SHORTBREAD STARS

1.   Make Brown-Sugar Shortbread Cookies, substituting granulated sugar for light-brown sugar.

2.   Use 1½- or 2-inch star-shape cookie cutters to cut out cookies. Bake as directed above.

SWEDISH KRINGLER

2 cups sifted all-purpose
flour
1 cup butter or margarine
3 tablespoons milk

2 egg yolks
1 egg white, slightly beaten
Granulated sugar

1.   Sift flour into medium bowl. Cut in butter, with pastry blender or 2 knives, until mixture resembles coarse cornmeal.

2.   Add milk and egg yolks. With fork, blend just until dough holds together.

3.   Turn out dough onto waxed paper or foil. With rubber scraper or hands, shape into a 6-inch square. Wrap; refrigerate at least 1 hour.

4.   Divide dough into 4 parts. Refrigerate until ready to roll out.

5.   Meanwhile, preheat oven to 375F. On lightly sugared surface, roll out dough, one part at a time, into a 6-by-3-inch rectangle. Cut crosswise into 10 parts.

6.   With hands, roll each part into a 9-inch, pencil-thin strip. Place, 2 inches apart, on ungreased cookie sheets; shape each into a "pretzel."

7.   Brush lightly with a mixture of egg white and 1 tablespoon water; sprinkle with sugar.

8.   Bake 10 to 12 minutes, or until light-golden. Remove to wire rack; cool.

SPRINGERLE

4 cups sifted all-purpose
   flour
1 teaspoon baking powder
½ teaspoon salt
4 eggs

2 cups granulated sugar
2 teaspoons grated lemon
   peel
2 tablespoons anise seed
Confectioners' sugar

1. Sift flour with baking powder and salt, twice; set aside.

2. In large bowl of electric mixer, at high speed, beat eggs until thick and lemon-colored— about 5 minutes.

3. At medium speed, gradually beat in granulated sugar, 2 tablespoons at a time, beating after each addition. Continue to beat until mixture is thick and smooth—about 10 minutes— occasionally cleaning side of bowl with rubber scraper.

4. Add flour mixture and lemon peel to egg mixture; stir with wooden spoon until smooth and well combined.

5. Refrigerate dough, covered, overnight. Also, refrigerate Springerle rolling pin.

6. Lightly grease 2 large cookie sheets; sprinkle each with 1 tablespoon anise seed.

7. Divide dough into 3 parts; refrigerate until ready to roll out.

8. Sprinkle pastry cloth or wooden board lightly with confectioners' sugar. Roll over dough, one part at a time, on pastry cloth, coating lightly with sugar.

9. With regular rolling pin, roll out dough to a rectangle 8 inches long and 5½ inches wide.

10. Remove Springerle pin from refrigerator; coat surface lightly with confectioners' sugar. Starting from long side, slowly roll pin once, firmly and evenly, over surface of dough, to make designs. (If dough sticks to pin while rolling, peel off with spatula.)

11. With sharp, floured knife, carefully cut along lines in dough, to make individual cookies.

12. With wide spatula, transfer to prepared cookie sheets. Let stand, uncovered, at room temperature, overnight.

13. Next day, preheat oven to 325F. Bake cookies 15 minutes, or just until light-golden. Remove to wire rack; cool completely.

14. Store in tightly covered container 2 to 3 weeks before using.

MORAVIAN SPICE COOKIES

Cookie Dough:

4 cups sifted all-purpose
    flour
¾ teaspoon baking soda
½ teaspoon salt
1 teaspoon ginger
1 teaspoon nutmeg
1 teaspoon cinnamon
½ teaspoon allspice
½ teaspoon cloves

½ cup light-brown sugar,
    firmly packed
½ cup soft butter or
    margarine
1 cup light molasses

Frosting:

⅓ cup egg white
3¾ to 4 cups sifted
    confectioners' sugar

1. Make Cookie Dough: Sift flour with baking soda, salt, and spices; set aside.

2. In large bowl, with portable electric mixer at medium speed, beat brown sugar, butter, and molasses until well combined.

3. With wooden spoon, stir in flour mixture; then mix with hands until well combined. Form dough into a ball. Wrap in waxed paper or saran; refrigerate overnight.

4. Next day, preheat oven to 375F. Lightly grease cookie sheets.

5. Divide dough into 4 parts. Refrigerate until ready to roll out.

6. On lightly floured surface, roll out dough, one part at a time, ⅛ inch thick.

7. Using 5-inch gingerbread-man cutter, cut out 12 cookies. Use assorted smaller cutters to cut out rest of cookies.

8. Place cookies, 1 inch apart, on prepared cookie sheets. Bake 6 to 8 minutes, or until cookies are lightly browned. Remove to wire rack; let cool.

9. Meanwhile, make Frosting: In medium bowl, with portable electric mixer at medium speed, beat egg white with 3¾ cups sugar, to make a smooth, stiff frosting. If frosting seems too thin, beat in a little more sugar. Cover with damp cloth until ready to use.

10. To decorate cookies: Pipe frosting through No. 4 small tip for writing, following outline of cookies. Decorate centers of cookies as desired.

Refrigerator cookies are made from a stiff dough that must be chilled in the refrigerator until it is firm, so that it can be sliced as thin and even as possible. The great advantage of refrigerator cookies is that the dough, once made, can be kept on hand in the refrigerator almost indefinitely, and the cookies sliced and baked as you need them. Refrigerator cookies are always crisp, buttery, and flavorful—their special taste, of course, depending on the ingredients you use. They're easy to make, convenient to have.

VANILLA-NUT ICEBOX COOKIES

MAKES ABOUT 9 DOZEN IN ALL

2 cups sifted all-purpose
    flour
1½ teaspoons baking
    powder
½ teaspoon salt
⅔ cup soft butter or
    margarine

1 cup sugar
1 egg
1 teaspoon vanilla extract
1 cup finely chopped
    walnuts, pecans, or
    unsalted peanuts

1.

2.

3.

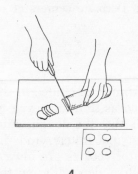

4.

1. On sheet of waxed paper, sift flour with baking powder and salt; set aside. In large bowl, with wooden spoon, or portable electric mixer at medium speed, beat butter until light. Gradually beat in sugar. Add egg and vanilla; continue beating until very light and fluffy.

2. At low speed, beat in half the flour mixture; mix in rest, with hands, to form a stiff dough. Add chopped nuts, mixing to combine well.

3. Turn out dough onto lightly floured surface. Divide in half. With hands, shape each half into a roll 7 inches long. Wrap each roll in saran or foil. Refrigerate until firm—about 8 hours, or overnight—before slicing and baking. (Rolls of cookie dough may be stored in refrigerator as long as 10 days. Slice and freshly bake as many as desired.)

4. Preheat oven to 375F. With sharp knife, cut as many ⅛-inch slices as desired for baking at one time. Rewrap rest of roll; refrigerate. Place slices, 2 inches apart, on ungreased cookie sheets. Bake 8 to 10 minutes, or until lightly browned. With spatula, lift cookies from cookie sheets to wire rack. Let cool completely.

Chocolate Nut: Melt 3 squares unsweetened chocolate over hot, not boiling, water. Cool; add to butter mixture. Then proceed as above.

Lemon Pecan: Omit vanilla; add 1 tablespoon grated lemon peel to creamed butter mixture. Use finely chopped pecans. Proceed as above.

Orange Coconut: Omit vanilla extract; add 1 tablespoon grated orange peel to creamed butter mixture. Omit nuts; use 1 can (3½ oz) flaked coconut, or ½ package (7-oz size) grated coconut. Proceed as above.

TART SHELLS

1. For each shell, cut 6 slices icebox-cookie dough, ⅛ inch thick. Let stand at room temperature about 10 minutes, to soften.
2. Fit one slice in bottom of ungreased 3-inch muffin-pan cup. Place 5 slices, overlapping, around side. Gently press slices together to conform to pan shape.
3. Prick shell with fork. Bake at 350F for 15 to 20 minutes, or until lightly browned. (If shells puff during baking, prick again with fork.)
4. Let cool in pan on wire rack 15 minutes. Carefully lift out of pan. Use as a tart shell for ice cream, sliced fresh strawberries, or a cream filling.

PIE SHELL

1. Slice icebox-cookie dough ⅛ inch thick. Press 33 slices, overlapping, in 8-inch pie plate, to form a pie shell.
2. Prick well with fork. Bake at 375F for 10 minutes, or until browned.
3. Let cool in pie plate on wire rack. Fill with a packaged pie-filling mix.

BROWN-SUGAR ICEBOX COOKIES

3½ cups sifted all-purpose flour
1 teaspoon baking soda
½ teaspoon salt
1 cup soft butter or margarine
2 cups light-brown sugar, firmly packed
2 eggs
1 teaspoon vanilla extract
1 cup finely chopped walnuts or pecans

MAKES ABOUT 16 DOZEN IN ALL

1. Sift flour with baking soda and salt; set aside.
2. In large bowl of electric mixer at medium speed, beat butter until light. Gradually beat in sugar. Add eggs and vanilla; continue beating until very light and fluffy.
3. At low speed, beat in half the flour mixture until smooth. Mix in rest, with hands, to form a stiff dough. Add nuts, mixing to combine well.
4. Turn out dough onto lightly floured surface. Divide in thirds. With hands, shape each third into a roll 8 inches long.
5. Wrap each in saran or foil. Refrigerate until firm—about 8 hours, or overnight—before slicing and baking. (Rolls may be stored in refrigerator a week or 10 days. Bake fresh as desired.)
6. Preheat oven to 375F. With sharp knife, cut as many ⅛-inch slices as desired for baking at one time. Rewrap rest of roll; refrigerate.
7. Place slices, 2 inches apart, on ungreased cookie sheets. Bake 7 to 10 minutes, or until lightly browned. Remove to wire rack; cool.

181

DATE-NUT PINWHEELS

MAKES ABOUT 9 DOZEN IN ALL

2 cups sifted all-purpose
    flour
1½ teaspoons baking
    powder
½ teaspoon salt
1 teaspoon cinnamon
½ teaspoon ginger
½ teaspoon nutmeg
⅔ cup soft butter or
    margarine
1 cup sugar

1 egg
1 teaspoon vanilla extract

Filling:
1 pkg (8 oz) pitted dates,
    cut up
½ cup sugar
2 teaspoons grated lemon
    peel
½ cup finely chopped
    walnuts

1. Sift flour with baking powder, salt, cinnamon, ginger, and nutmeg; set aside.

2. In large bowl, with wooden spoon, or portable electric mixer at medium speed, beat butter until light. Gradually beat in sugar. Add egg and vanilla; continue beating until very light and fluffy.

3. At low speed, gradually add half of flour mixture. Mix in rest, with hands, to form a stiff dough. Refrigerate 1 hour.

4. Meanwhile, make Filling: In small saucepan, combine dates and sugar with ½ cup water. Cook, stirring, over medium heat, until mixture thickens—about 5 minutes. Remove from heat. Stir in lemon peel and nuts. Cool completely.

5. Divide dough in half. On a lightly floured surface, roll each half into an 8-by-10-inch rectangle. Spread each rectangle with half the date-nut mixture.

6. From long side, roll each, jelly-roll fashion. Gently press edge, to seal.

7. Wrap separately, seam side down, in saran or foil. Refrigerate until firm—about 8 hours, or overnight—before baking. (Rolls may be stored in refrigerator a week or 10 days. Bake fresh as needed.)

8. Preheat oven to 375F. Lightly grease cookie sheets.

9. With sharp knife, cut as many ⅛-inch slices as desired for baking at one time. Rewrap rest of roll; refrigerate.

10. Place slices, 2 inches apart, on cookie sheets. Bake 8 to 10 minutes, or until lightly browned. Let stand 1 minute. Remove to wire rack; cool.

Orange-Fig Filling: In small saucepan, combine 1¼ cups finely chopped figs and ¼ cup sugar with ¾ cup water. Cook, stirring, over medium heat until mixture is thickened—about 10 minutes. Remove from heat. Stir in 1 tablespoon grated orange peel and ½ cup finely chopped walnuts. Cool completely. Use instead of Date-Nut Filling.

PEANUT-BUTTER PINWHEELS

2 cups sifted all-purpose
    flour
1 teaspoon baking soda
½ teaspoon salt
1 cup soft butter or
    margarine
1 cup light-brown sugar,
    firmly packed
1 cup chunk-style peanut
    butter

1 egg
1 teaspoon vanilla extract

Filling:
1 pkg (6 oz) semisweet-
    chocolate pieces
1 teaspoon butter or
    margarine

MAKES ABOUT 9 DOZEN IN ALL

1. Sift flour with soda and salt; set aside.

2. In large bowl, with wooden spoon, or portable electric mixer at medium speed, beat butter until light. Gradually beat in sugar, beating until light and fluffy.

3. Beat in peanut butter, egg, and vanilla.

4. At low speed, gradually add half of flour mixture. Mix in rest, with hands, to form a stiff dough. Refrigerate 30 minutes.

5. Meanwhile, make Filling: Melt chocolate over hot, not boiling, water. Add butter; cool.

6. Divide dough in half. On lightly floured surface, roll each half into an 8-by-10-inch rectangle. Spread each with half the filling.

7. From long side, roll each tightly, jelly-roll fashion. Gently press edge, to seal.

8. Wrap separately, seam side down, in saran or foil. Refrigerate until firm—about 8 hours, or overnight—before slicing and baking. (Rolls may be stored in refrigerator a week or 10 days. Bake fresh as needed.)

9. Preheat oven to 375F. Grease cookie sheets.

10. With sharp knife, cut as many ⅛-inch slices as desired. Rewrap roll; refrigerate.

11. Place slices, 1½ inches apart, on cookie sheets. Bake 6 to 8 minutes, or until lightly browned. Remove to wire rack; cool.

PETTICOAT TAILS

2½ cups sifted all-purpose
    flour
½ teaspoon baking soda
¼ teaspoon salt
1½ cups soft butter

1½ cups sifted
    confectioners' sugar
1 teaspoon vanilla extract or
    rose water

MAKES ABOUT 8½ DOZEN

1. Sift flour with soda and salt; set aside.

2. In large bowl, with wooden spoon, or portable electric mixer at medium speed, beat butter, sugar, and vanilla until light and fluffy.

3. Add flour mixture; mix well, with hands, to make a soft dough. Refrigerate 30 minutes.

4. Turn out dough onto lightly floured surface. Divide in half. With hands, shape each into a roll 8 inches long.

5. Wrap each in waxed paper or foil; refrigerate until firm—several hours, or overnight—before baking. (Rolls may be stored in refrigerator a week or 10 days; bake fresh as needed.)

6. Preheat oven to 375F. With sharp knife, cut as many ⅛-inch slices as desired for one baking. Rewrap roll; refrigerate.

7. Place slices, 1 inch apart, on ungreased cookie sheets; bake 8 to 10 minutes, or until lightly browned. Let stand 1 minute. Remove to wire rack; cool.

OATMEAL ICEBOX COOKIES

MAKES ABOUT 7 DOZEN IN ALL

1 cup sifted all-purpose
    flour
½ teaspoon baking soda
½ teaspoon salt
½ teaspoon cinnamon
½ cup soft butter or
    margarine

½ cup granulated sugar
½ cup light-brown sugar,
    firmly packed
1 egg
2 tablespoons honey
1½ cups rolled oats

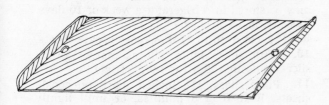

1. Sift flour with baking soda, salt, and cinnamon; set aside.
2. In large bowl, with wooden spoon, or portable electric mixer at medium speed, beat butter until light. Gradually beat in sugars. Add egg and honey; continue beating until very light and fluffy.
3. At low speed, gradually add half the flour mixture. Mix in rest, with hands, to form a stiff dough.
4. Add oats, mixing to combine well. Refrigerate 30 minutes.
5. Divide dough in half. On lightly floured surface, shape each half into a roll 7 inches long. Wrap in saran or foil; refrigerate until firm—about 8 hours, or overnight. (Rolls may be stored in refrigerator a week or 10 days. Bake fresh as desired.)
6. Preheat oven to 375F. With sharp knife, cut as many ⅛-inch slices as desired for baking at one time. Rewrap rest of roll; refrigerate.
7. Place slices, 2 inches apart, on ungreased cookie sheets. Bake 8 to 10 minutes, or until lightly browned. Remove to wire rack; let cool.

Molded Cookies have somewhat the symmetrical form of rolled cookies. The stiff cookie doughs are shaped, sometimes with the palms of the hands, into small balls. The more elaborate are forced through a cookie press in many and fancy shapes. Most of the doughs should be refrigerated at least an hour before using, so they can be handled easily.

ALMOND LACE WAFERS

MAKES ABOUT 2 DOZEN

½ cup ground blanched
    almonds
½ cup butter or margarine

½ cup sugar
1 tablespoon flour
2 tablespoons milk

1. Preheat oven to 375F. Grease generously and flour well 2 cookie sheets.
2. Combine all ingredients in a small saucepan. Cook, stirring and over low heat, until butter melts.
3. Drop by teaspoonfuls, 4 inches apart, onto cookie sheets. (Bake only 4 or 5 at a time.)
4. Bake 6 minutes, or until cookies are light-brown and centers are bubbling. Let stand 1 minute.

(Almond Lace Wafers continued)

5. Working quickly, roll each wafer around the handle of a wooden spoon.

6. Gently slide cookie off handle. Place, seam side down, on wire rack; cool. If cookies become too crisp to roll, return to oven for a minute or two.

7. Regrease and reflour cookie sheets before baking each batch.

COCONUT COOKIES

1¾ cups sifted all-purpose
    flour
½ teaspoon baking powder
¼ teaspoon salt
½ cup soft butter or
    margarine
1½ cups sugar

2 eggs
1 teaspoon vanilla extract
1 can (3½ oz) flaked
    coconut
½ cup finely chopped
    almonds

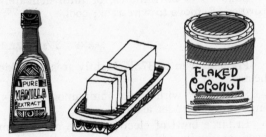

MAKES ABOUT 5 DOZEN

1. Sift flour with baking powder and salt; set aside.

2. In large bowl, with wooden spoon, or portable electric mixer at medium speed, beat butter and sugar until light and fluffy. Beat in eggs and vanilla until smooth.

3. Add flour mixture; stir just until combined. Refrigerate 1 hour.

4. Meanwhile, preheat oven to 400F. Lightly grease cookie sheets. Combine coconut and almonds on sheet of waxed paper.

5. Drop dough by slightly rounded teaspoonfuls onto coconut mixture; roll to coat completely. Using hands, roll dough into balls. Place, 2 inches apart, on cookie sheet.

6. Bake 12 to 15 minutes, or until golden. (Cookies will flatten during baking.) Remove to wire rack; cool.

CREAM-CHEESE COOKIES

1 pkg (3 oz) soft cream
    cheese
1 cup soft butter
    or margarine
1 cup sugar
1 egg yolk
1 teaspoon vanilla extract
2½ cups sifted all-purpose
    flour

Glaze:
2 tablespoons butter or
    margarine
3 squares semisweet
    chocolate
Chocolate or multicolored
    nonpareils

MAKES ABOUT 9 DOZEN

1. Refrigerate ungreased cookie sheets until ready to use. Preheat oven to 375F.

2. In large bowl, with wooden spoon, or portable electric mixer at medium speed, beat cheese, butter, sugar, egg yolk, and vanilla until light and fluffy.

3. Stir in flour to make a soft dough.

4. Fill cookie press. Force dough through ribbon disk of cookie press in 2-inch strips onto cookie sheets, 1½ inches apart.

5. Bake 8 to 10 minutes, or until golden around edges. Remove to wire rack; cool.

6. Meanwhile, make Glaze: Over hot, not boiling, water, melt butter and chocolate; mix well.

7. Dip ends of cookies in chocolate mixture, then in nonpareils. Return to wire rack to let glaze set.

FINNISH LOGS

¾ cup soft butter or
    margarine
⅓ cup sugar
1 teaspoon almond extract
2 cups sifted all-purpose
    flour

¼ teaspoon salt
1 egg, slightly beaten
¼ cup finely chopped
    unblanched almonds
1 teaspoon sugar

1. Preheat oven to 350F. Lightly grease cookie sheets.
2. In large bowl, with wooden spoon, beat butter, ⅓ cup sugar, and almond extract until light and fluffy.
3. Add flour and salt; mix well with hands.
4. Turn out dough onto lightly floured surface. With hands, shape into a roll 6 inches long. With sharp knife, cut roll crosswise into 6 parts.
5. With hands, shape each part into a roll 12 inches long and ¾ inch in diameter. Cut each roll into 6 (2-inch) pieces.
6. Place, 1 inch apart, on cookie sheets. Brush tops lightly with egg; then sprinkle with mixture of almonds combined with 1 teaspoon sugar.
7. Bake 15 to 20 minutes, or until delicately browned. Remove to wire rack; cool.

GINGER-SUGAR COOKIES

2 cups sifted all-purpose
    flour
2 teaspoons baking soda
1 teaspoon cinnamon
1 teaspoon cloves
1 teaspoon ginger

¼ teaspoon salt
1⅓ cups sugar
¾ cup soft shortening
¼ cup light molasses
1 egg

1. Preheat oven to 375F. Lightly grease cookie sheets.
2. Sift flour with soda, cinnamon, cloves, ginger, and salt; set aside.
3. In large bowl of electric mixer, at medium speed, gradually add 1 cup sugar to shortening, creaming until very light and fluffy—about 5 minutes. Blend in molasses and egg.
4. At low speed, beat in flour mixture just until well mixed, scraping down side of bowl with rubber scraper. Refrigerate 1 hour.
5. Pinch off pieces of dough; shape into 1¼-inch balls. Roll in remaining sugar.
6. Place, 2½ inches apart, on cookie sheets; bake 8 to 10 minutes, or until golden-brown. Remove to wire rack; cool. These cookies will have a crinkled surface.

JEWEL COOKIES

½ cup soft butter or
    margarine
¼ cup light-brown sugar,
    firmly packed
1 egg yolk
1 teaspoon vanilla extract

1 cup sifted all-purpose
    flour
1 egg white, slightly beaten
1 cup finely chopped
    walnuts or pecans
2 tablespoons currant jelly

1. In medium bowl, with wooden spoon, beat butter, sugar, egg yolk, and vanilla until smooth.
2. Stir in flour just until combined. Refrigerate 30 minutes.
3. Meanwhile, preheat oven to 375F. Using hands, roll dough into balls 1 inch in diameter. Dip in egg white; then roll in walnuts.

ICEBOX COOKIES

Best way to win a child's (or husband's) heart is with fresh-baked cookies. And with our icebox-cookie dough in the refrigerator, you'll always have a supply, ready to slice and bake. They'll think it's magic. But perfect cookies are easy to make. To see how, read on!

FLAMING

Finish your dinner in a blaze of glory. Dramatic, impressive, easy to make, there's nothing more exciting than the dessert that comes to table wreathed in a flickering flame of brandy or rum.

(Jewel Cookies continued)

4. Place, 1 inch apart, on ungreased cookie sheets. With thimble or thumb, press center of each cookie.

5. Bake 10 to 12 minutes, or until a delicate golden-brown. Remove to wire rack; cool.

6. Place ¼ teaspoon jelly in center of each cookie. (Diced candied fruit may be used, instead of jelly, if desired.)

OLD-FASHIONED JUMBLES

MAKES ABOUT 5 DOZEN

3 cups sifted all-purpose
    flour
½ teaspoon salt
1 tablespoon cinnamon
1 cup soft butter or
    margarine
1 cup sugar
2 eggs
1 teaspoon vanilla extract
Salad oil
Granulated sugar

1. Sift flour with salt and cinnamon; set aside.

2. In large bowl, with wooden spoon, or portable electric mixer at medium speed, beat butter, 1 cup sugar, eggs, and vanilla until creamy and smooth.

3. Gradually add flour mixture, stirring until well blended. Refrigerate 1 hour.

4. Meanwhile, preheat oven to 375F. Lightly grease cookie sheets.

5. Using hands, roll dough into balls 1¼ inches in diameter. Place on cookie sheet, 2 inches apart. Flatten with bottom of glass brushed with salad oil, then dipped in sugar. (Redip bottom of glass in sugar frequently.)

6. Bake 10 to 12 minutes, or until light-brown. Remove to wire rack; cool.

PECAN BALLS

MAKES ABOUT 20

1 cup sifted all-purpose
    flour
½ cup soft butter
    or margarine
1 cup finely chopped pecans
    or hazelnuts
2 tablespoons granulated
    sugar
⅛ teaspoon salt
1 teaspoon vanilla extract
Confectioners' sugar

1. In large bowl, combine all ingredients except confectioners' sugar. With hands, mix until thoroughly blended. Refrigerate 30 minutes.

2. Meanwhile, preheat oven to 375F. Using hands, roll dough into balls 1¼ inches in diameter. Place, 1 inch apart, on ungreased cookie sheets.

3. Bake 15 to 20 minutes, or until cookies are set but not brown. Let stand 1 minute before removing from cookie sheets. Remove to wire rack; cool slightly.

4. Roll in confectioners' sugar while still warm; cool completely. Just before serving, re-roll in sugar.

PFEFFERNUESSE

6 cups sifted all-purpose
   flour
2 teaspoons baking powder
½ teaspoon salt
½ teaspoon black pepper
½ teaspoon mace
½ teaspoon nutmeg
1 teaspoon cloves
1 teaspoon allspice
3 teaspoons cinnamon
¼ teaspoon ground anise

⅛ teaspoon ground
   cardamom
5 eggs
2 cups light-brown sugar,
   firmly packed
3 tablespoons black coffee
1 cup ground blanched
   almonds
1 teaspoon grated lemon
   peel
1 jar (4 oz) diced citron
½ cup confectioners' sugar

MAKES ABOUT 4 DOZEN

1. Sift flour with baking powder, salt, pepper, and spices into large bowl; set aside.
2. In large bowl of electric mixer, at high speed, beat eggs until fluffy—about 5 minutes. Gradually beat in brown sugar.
3. At low speed, alternately beat in flour mixture, in fourths, and coffee, in thirds.
4. Fold in almonds, lemon peel, and citron.
5. Wrap dough in waxed paper or foil; refrigerate until well chilled—at least 2 hours.
6. Meanwhile, preheat oven to 300F. Lightly grease cookie sheets.
7. Roll dough into balls, using 1 tablespoon dough for each.
8. Place, on cookie sheets; bake 18 to 20 minutes. Remove to wire rack; cool. Roll in confectioners' sugar.

SPRITZ COOKIES

2 cups sifted all-purpose
   flour
¼ teaspoon salt
¾ cup soft butter
   or margarine

½ cup sugar
1 egg yolk
1 teaspoon vanilla extract,
   or ¼ teaspoon
   almond extract

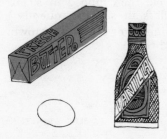

MAKES ABOUT 3½ DOZEN

1. Refrigerate ungreased cookie sheets until ready to use. Preheat oven to 375F.
2. Sift flour with salt; set aside.
3. In large bowl, with wooden spoon, or portable electric mixer at medium speed, beat butter, sugar, egg yolk, and vanilla until light and fluffy.
4. Beat in flour mixture just until combined.
5. Fill cookie press. Force dough through desired disk of press onto cookie sheet, 1½ inches apart. (If dough is too soft to hold its shape when pressed, refrigerate 30 minutes.)
6. Bake 8 to 10 minutes, or just until cookies are set but not brown. Remove to wire rack; cool.

KRIS KRINGLES

½ cup soft butter or
   margarine
½ cup sugar
3 hard-cooked egg yolks,
   sieved
1 raw egg yolk
¼ to ½ teaspoon
   ground cardamom

1 tablespoon grated lemon
   peel
2 cups sifted all-purpose
   flour
1 egg white
½ cup finely chopped
   blanched almonds
2 tablespoons sugar

MAKES 4 DOZEN

1. Preheat oven to 375F. Lightly grease cookie sheets.
2. In medium bowl, with wooden spoon, beat butter, ½ cup sugar, egg yolks, cardamom, and lemon peel.
3. Stir in flour, to form a stiff dough; then mix with hands to blend.
4. Divide dough in 2 parts. On lightly floured surface, roll out each part into a 7-by-6-inch rectangle.
5. Cut each rectangle in half lengthwise; then cut crosswise into 12 strips. You will have 48 strips in all.

(Kris Kringles continued)

6. With palms of hands, roll each strip 4 inches long. Form each into a ring; pinch ends, to seal.

7. Place on cookie sheet. Brush with egg white beaten with 1 tablespoon water. Sprinkle with almonds combined with 2 tablespoons sugar.

8. Bake 10 to 12 minutes, or until golden. Remove to wire rack; let cool completely.

B ar cookies have a rich, cakelike texture. Easy to make, they store and ship well. They are made in a large pan, cooled, and then cut into squares or bars. Best known, and best loved, of the bar cookies are brownies; we've added some that are less known but equally good.

APPLESAUCE-SPICE SQUARES

MAKES 35

2 cups sifted all-purpose
    flour
2 teaspoons baking soda
¾ teaspoon cinnamon
¼ teaspoon cloves
¼ teaspoon nutmeg
½ cup soft butter or
    margarine

1 cup granulated sugar
1 egg
1 teaspoon vanilla extract
1½ cups canned applesauce
1 cup coarsely chopped
    walnuts or pecans
1 cup light or dark raisins
Confectioners' sugar

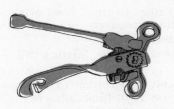 

1. Preheat oven to 350F. Lightly grease a 15½-by-10½-by-1-inch pan.

2. Sift flour with soda, cinnamon, cloves, and nutmeg; set aside.

3. In large bowl of electric mixer, at medium speed, cream butter with granulated sugar until light and fluffy.

4. Add egg and vanilla; beat well, scraping down side of bowl with rubber scraper.

5. At low speed, beat in flour mixture just until combined.

6. Add applesauce, walnuts, and raisins; stir, with spoon, until well mixed.

7. Turn into prepared pan; bake 25 minutes, or just until surface springs back when gently pressed with fingertip. Cool on wire rack. Sprinkle with confectioners' sugar. Cut into squares.

BROWNIES

MAKES 16

2 squares unsweetened
    chocolate
½ cup butter or margarine
¾ cup sifted all-purpose
    flour
½ teaspoon baking powder

¼ teaspoon salt
2 eggs
1 cup sugar
1 teaspoon vanilla extract
1 cup coarsely chopped
    walnuts

1. Preheat oven to 350F. Lightly grease an 8-by-8-by-2-inch pan.

2. Melt chocolate with butter over hot, not boiling, water. Cool.

3. Sift flour, baking powder and salt; set aside.

4. In large bowl, with wooden spoon, or portable electric mixer at medium speed, beat eggs and sugar until light.

5. Beat in chocolate mixture and vanilla.

6. Stir in flour mixture and nuts.

7. Spread evenly in prepared pan; bake 25 to 30 minutes. Cool 10 minutes.

8. With sharp knife, cut into squares.

BROWN-SUGAR BROWNIES

MAKES 20

1⅓ cups sifted all-purpose flour

1 teaspoon baking powder

½ teaspoon salt

½ cup soft butter or margarine

1 cup light-brown sugar, firmly packed

1 egg

1 teaspoon vanilla extract

½ cup coarsely chopped walnuts

1. Preheat oven to 350F. Lightly grease a 9-by-9-by-1¾-inch pan.
2. Sift flour with baking powder and salt; set aside.
3. In large bowl, with wooden spoon, or portable electric mixer at medium speed, beat butter, sugar, egg, and vanilla until smooth.
4. Stir in flour mixture and nuts until well blended. Spread evenly in prepared pan.
5. Bake 25 to 30 minutes, or until surface springs back when gently pressed with fingertip. Cool slightly.
6. With sharp knife, cut into bars while still warm.

Chocolate Brown-Sugar Brownies: Stir in one package (6 oz) semisweet-chocolate pieces along with nuts. Bake in lightly greased 13-by-9-by-2-inch pan 30 minutes. Cool slightly. Cut into bars while still warm. Makes 24.

DELICIOUS PRUNE BARS

MAKES 24

Cookie Crust:

½ cup soft butter or margarine

½ cup light-brown sugar, firmly packed

1 cup sifted all-purpose flour

Prune Filling:

1¼ cups dried prunes (about 20)

⅓ cup light-brown sugar, firmly packed

2 tablespoons cornstarch

⅛ teaspoon salt

1 tablespoon grated orange peel

¼ cup orange juice

1 cup coarsely chopped walnuts

2 eggs

1 can (3½ oz) flaked coconut

1. Preheat oven to 350F.
2. Make Cookie Crust: In small bowl of electric mixer, at medium speed, cream butter with sugar until light and fluffy.
3. At low speed, beat in flour. Mixture will be creamy.
4. Pat dough evenly into bottom of a 9-by-9-by-1¾-inch pan; bake 10 to 12 minutes, or until light-golden. Let cool at least 15 minutes.
5. Meanwhile, make Prune Filling: In medium saucepan, over medium heat, cook prunes in just enough water to cover 30 minutes. Drain, reserving 2 tablespoons liquid.
6. Remove pits; with scissors, cut prunes into quarters.
7. Combine in saucepan with reserved liquid, sugar, cornstarch, salt, orange peel and juice; bring to boiling. Reduce heat; simmer, stirring constantly, 2 to 3 minutes, or until thickened. Stir in walnuts. Spread over cooled crust.
8. In small bowl, beat eggs just until frothy. Stir in coconut.
9. Spread evenly over prune mixture; bake 25 minutes. Cool slightly.
10. With sharp knife, cut into bars while still warm.

FILLED OATMEAL-DATE BARS

MAKES 32

Date Filling:
2 pkg (8-oz size) pitted
   dates, cut up
½ cup granulated sugar
¼ cup lemon juice
½ cup coarsely chopped
   walnuts

½ teaspoon baking soda
½ teaspoon salt
¾ cup soft butter or
   margarine
1 cup light-brown sugar,
   firmly packed
1½ cups raw quick-cooking
   oats

Oatmeal Crust:
1½ cups sifted all-purpose
   flour

1. Make Date Filling: In small saucepan, combine dates and sugar with 1 cup water. Over medium heat, cook, stirring constantly, until mixture is thickened—about 5 minutes. Remove from heat. Stir in lemon juice and nuts; cool.
2. Meanwhile, preheat oven to 375F. Lightly grease a 13-by-9-by-2-inch pan.
3. Make Oatmeal Crust: Sift flour with soda and salt; set aside.
4. In medium bowl, with wooden spoon, or portable electric mixer at medium speed, beat butter and sugar until light and fluffy. Add flour mixture and oats. With hands, mix until well combined.
5. Press half oatmeal mixture, evenly, into bottom of prepared pan. Spread with filling. Cover with remaining oatmeal mixture; press lightly with hands.
6. Bake 25 to 30 minutes, or until golden. Cool slightly.
7. Cut into bars while still warm.

Filled Oatmeal-Mincemeat Bars: In small bowl, combine 2 cups prepared mincemeat, ½ cup coarsely chopped walnuts, and 1 tablespoon grated orange peel. Use instead of Date Filling.

DREAM BARS

MAKES 30

Cookie Crust:
½ cup soft butter or
   margarine
½ cup light-brown sugar,
   firmly packed
1 cup sifted all-purpose
   flour

1 teaspoon vanilla extract
3 tablespoons all-purpose
   flour
¼ teaspoon salt
1 teaspoon baking powder
1 can (3½ oz) flaked
   coconut
1 cup coarsely chopped
   walnuts or pecans

Filling:
2 eggs
1 cup light-brown sugar,
   firmly packed

1. Preheat oven to 350F.
2. Make Cookie Crust: In small bowl, cream butter and sugar, with wooden spoon, until smooth.
3. With hands, work in flour until mixture is smooth.
4. Pat into bottom of a 13-by-9-by-2 inch pan; bake 10 minutes, or until golden. Cool on wire rack.
5. Meanwhile, make Filling: In small bowl of electric mixer, at medium speed, beat eggs until light.
6. Gradually beat in sugar. Add vanilla, flour, salt, and baking powder, beating just until combined.
7. Stir in coconut and walnuts.
8. Spread evenly over cooled crust; bake 25 minutes, or until golden and firm to the touch. Cool slightly.
9. With sharp knife, cut into bars while still warm.

DATE-NUT BARS

½ cup sifted all-purpose
    flour
1 teaspoon baking powder
¼ teaspoon salt
2 eggs
1 cup granulated sugar

1 pkg (8 oz) pitted dates,
    finely chopped
1 cup coarsely chopped
    walnuts
Confectioners' sugar

1. Preheat oven to 350F. Lightly grease a 13-by-9-by-2-inch pan.
2. Sift flour with baking powder and salt; set aside.
3. In small bowl of electric mixer, at medium speed, beat eggs until light.
4. Gradually add granulated sugar, beating until smooth and fluffy.
5. At low speed, beat in flour mixture until well combined.
6. Stir in dates and nuts; mix thoroughly. Spread evenly in prepared pan.
7. Bake 25 to 30 minutes, or until golden. Cool slightly.
8. With sharp knife, cut into 30 bars while still warm. Let cool completely in pan before removing. To serve, roll in confectioners' sugar.

CHOCOLATE-BUTTERSCOTCH PICNIC BARS

2 cups sifted all-purpose
    flour
1 teaspoon baking soda
1 teaspoon salt
2 teaspoons cinnamon
¾ cup butter, margarine, or
    shortening

1 cup sugar
2 eggs
½ cup chopped walnuts
1 pkg (6 oz) semisweet-
    chocolate pieces
1 pkg (6 oz) butterscotch
    pieces

1. Preheat oven to 350F. Lightly grease an 11½-by-7½-by-2-inch disposable foil pan, or 13-by-9-by-2-inch baking pan.
2. Sift flour with soda, salt, and cinnamon; set aside.
3. In large bowl of electric mixer, at medium speed, cream butter with sugar until light and fluffy. Beat in eggs.
4. At low speed, beat in flour mixture just until combined. Stir in nuts. Divide dough in half. Stir chocolate into one half and butterscotch into other.
5. Spread chocolate mixture in half of prepared pan and butterscotch mixture in other half; bake 30 minutes.
6. Let cool, in pan, on wire rack. Cut into bars.

SCOTCH OATMEAL SHORTBREAD

3 cups raw quick-cooking
    oats
⅔ cup sugar
½ cup sifted all-purpose
    flour

½ teaspoon salt
¾ cup butter or margarine
1 teaspoon vanilla extract

1. Preheat oven to 350F. Lightly grease a 13-by-9-by-2-inch pan.
2. In large bowl, combine oats, sugar, flour, and salt.
3. With pastry blender or 2 knives, cut in butter until mixture resembles coarse cornmeal. Stir in vanilla; mix well.
4. With hands, press mixture evenly into prepared pan.

(*Scotch Oatmeal Shortbread continued*)

5. Bake 25 to 30 minutes, or until golden. Cool slightly.

6. Cut into bars while still warm. Let cool thoroughly in pan before removing.

GUMDROP BARS

1½ cups sifted all-purpose flour

1 teaspoon baking powder

½ teaspoon salt

1 teaspoon cinnamon

⅓ cup soft shortening

1 cup light-brown sugar, firmly packed

1 egg

2 teaspoons vanilla extract

¼ cup evaporated milk, undiluted

1 cup small, soft gumdrops,* cut into small pieces

½ cup coarsely chopped walnuts

Confectioners' sugar

MAKES 20

1. Preheat oven to 350F. Lightly grease a 9-by-9-by-1¾-inch pan.

2. Sift flour with baking powder, salt, and cinnamon; set aside.

3. In large bowl, with wooden spoon, or portable electric mixer at medium speed, beat shortening, brown sugar, egg, and vanilla until fluffy.

4. Beat in half the flour mixture along with evaporated milk until smooth.

5. Stir in remaining flour mixture.

6. Add gumdrops combined with walnuts; mix well.

7. Spread evenly in prepared pan; bake 25 to 30 minutes, or until cake tester inserted in center comes out clean. Cool slightly.

8. Cut into bars while still warm. Sprinkle lightly with confectioners' sugar.

* You may use gumdrops of any flavor except licorice.

TOFFEE BARS

Cookie Crust:

½ cup soft butter or margarine

½ cup light-brown sugar, firmly packed

1 egg yolk

1 teaspoon vanilla extract

½ cup sifted all-purpose flour

½ cup raw quick-cooking oats

Topping:

3 squares semisweet chocolate

1 tablespoon butter or margarine

½ cup coarsely chopped walnuts or pecans

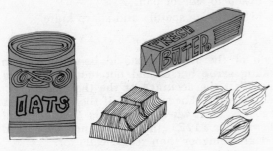

MAKES 24

1. Preheat oven to 375F. Lightly grease a 13-by-9-by-2-inch pan.

2. Make Cookie Crust: In large bowl, with wooden spoon, or portable electric mixer at medium speed, beat butter, sugar, egg yolk, and vanilla until smooth.

3. Add flour and oats; stir until well combined.

4. Press mixture evenly in bottom of prepared pan.

5. Bake 15 minutes, or until golden. Cool slightly.

6. Meanwhile, make Topping: Melt chocolate and butter over hot, not boiling, water.

7. Spread over warm cookie crust; sprinkle with nuts.

8. With sharp knife, cut into bars while still warm. Let cool completely in pan before removing.

For teatime, cut each bar in half, to make 48 small bars.

193

Candy and Confections

10

Do-it-yourself candy is as much fun to make as it is to eat. Family memories are made of it. No one who has ever had a taffy pull will ever forget it. And sweet in the mind are the memories of evenings making fudge and peanut brittle.

Cooked Candies

The most important ingredient in cooked candies is granulated sugar. The sugar is dissolved in a liquid and cooked to a specific concentration for each variety of candy.

The boiling temperature indicates the concentration of the solution: that is, the longer it is cooked, the more concentrated it becomes and the higher the temperature reached. For this reason, we strongly urge the use of a candy thermometer to measure the temperature accurately and to prevent under- or overcooking the candy.

In the temperature chart for candies given in this chapter, you will find cold-water tests listed as alternates to the thermometer readings recommended. To make these cold-water tests: Drop about ½ teaspoon hot syrup into 1 cup very cold water. Shape the syrup with the fingers of one hand, to determine whether it has reached the desired temperature.

Equipment for Candy-Making at Home

1. Heavy-aluminum or stainless-steel saucepan.
2. Long-handled wooden spoon, for stirring and beating.
3. Candy thermometer—should have a clamp to fasten to side of pan.
4. Medium-size spatula and sharp knife.

To Use Candy Thermometer

Bulb of thermometer should be immersed in boiling syrup but should not touch bottom of pan. Test the accuracy of the thermometer in boiling water. For example: If the thermometer registers 214F when water boils (boiling point of water is 212F), the candy must be cooked 2 degrees higher than recipe calls for.

TEMPERATURES AND TESTS FOR SYRUP AND CANDIES*

Product	Temperature of Syrup (Degrees F)	Test	Description of Test
Syrup	230 to 234	Thread	Syrup spins a 2-inch thread when dropped from fork or spoon
Fondant Fudge Penuche	234 to 240	Soft ball	Syrup, when dropped into very cold water, forms a soft ball, which flattens on removal from water
Caramels	244 to 248	Firm ball	Syrup, when dropped into very cold water, forms a firm ball, which does not flatten on removal from water
Divinity Marshmallows Popcorn balls	250 to 266	Hard ball	Syrup, when dropped into very cold water, forms a ball, which is hard enough to hold its shape, yet plastic
Butterscotch Taffies	270 to 290	Soft crack	Syrup, when dropped into very cold water, separates into threads, which are hard but not brittle
Brittle Glace	300 to 310	Hard crack	Syrup, when dropped into very cold water, separates into threads, which are hard and brittle
Barley sugar	320	Clear liquid	Sugar liquefies
Caramel	338	Brown liquid	Liquid becomes brown

* From American Home Economics Association "Handbook of Food Preparation"

Here are your old friends—pralines, divinity, meringues (those lovely kisses), old-fashioned fudge, peanut brittle, and other pleasures.

CANDIED FRUIT SQUARES

MAKES 49 SQUARES

1⅔ cups chopped walnuts
½ cup granulated sugar
½ cup light-brown sugar, firmly packed
⅔ cup light corn syrup

2 cans (4-oz size) shredded coconut
1 jar (4 oz) diced mixed candied fruit, drained
½ teaspoon salt
1 teaspoon vanilla extract

1. Grease a 9-by-9-by-1¾-inch pan. Sprinkle bottom with ⅔ cup nuts. In heavy, 2-quart saucepan, combine sugars, corn syrup, and ⅓ cup water. Heat, stirring, to dissolve sugar.

2. Cook, without stirring, to 248F on candy thermometer. Remove from heat; stir in 2¾ cups coconut, and rest of ingredients.

3. Spread in pan. Top with rest of coconut. Refrigerate, covered, overnight.

APRICOT-NUT BALLS

MAKES ABOUT 7 DOZEN

3 cups sugar
½ teaspoon salt
1½ cups dairy sour cream
1 cup chopped dried
   apricots

2 teaspoons vanilla extract
1½ cups finely chopped
   walnuts

1. In heavy 3-quart saucepan, combine sugar, salt, sour cream, and apricots. Cook, over medium heat, stirring, until sugar is dissolved and mixture begins to boil.

2. Continue to cook, stirring occasionally, to 236F on candy thermometer, or until a little in cold water forms a soft ball.

3. Let cool 10 minutes. Stir in vanilla and ½ cup nuts; then cool 1 hour.

4. With wooden spoon, beat mixture vigorously 1 minute. Refrigerate 30 minutes.

5. Form mixture into balls, ¾ inch in diameter; roll in rest of nuts. Store, covered, in refrigerator.

BASIC VANILLA CARAMELS

MAKES 1 POUND

1 cup granulated sugar
½ cup light-brown sugar,
   firmly packed
½ cup light corn syrup

½ cup heavy cream
1 cup milk
¼ cup butter or margarine
1 teaspoon vanilla extract

1. Line a 9-by-5-by-3-inch loaf pan with foil. Lightly butter foil. In medium saucepan, combine all ingredients except vanilla.

2. Cook, stirring, over low heat, until sugars are dissolved.

3. Over medium heat, cook, uncovered and stirring occasionally, to 248F on candy thermometer, or until a little in cold water forms a firm ball.

4. Remove from heat; stir in vanilla. Turn into prepared pan; let cool.

5. With sharp knife, cut into 36 pieces. Wrap each individually in waxed paper.

Coffee Caramels: Proceed as above, adding 2 tablespoons instant coffee to sugar mixture.

BASIC FONDANT

MAKES 1 POUND

2 cups sugar
2 tablespoons light corn
   syrup

1 teaspoon vanilla extract

1. In small saucepan, combine sugar, corn syrup, and 1 cup water.

2. Over low heat, stir until sugar is dissolved.

3. Bring to boiling; cover, and boil 3 minutes.

4. Boil, uncovered, without stirring, to 238F on candy thermometer, or until a small amount in cold water forms a soft ball.

5. As crystals form, wipe them from side of pan with damp cloth.

(Basic Fondant continued)

6. Pour out onto marble slab or large platter that has been rinsed or wiped with cold water.

7. Let syrup cool to 110F, or lukewarm.

8. With wooden spoon, work mixture to center of slab until a creamy white mass forms.

9. Knead with hands, to produce a smooth mixture.

10. Place in small bowl or jar; cover tightly with damp cloth. Store in cool place 2 to 3 days, to ripen.

11. When ready to use, knead in vanilla extract.

CARAMEL-NUT ROLL

MAKES ABOUT 2 POUNDS

Filling:

6 tablespoons butter or margarine

3 cups sifted confectioners' sugar

Dash salt

¼ teaspoon rum extract

2 tablespoons hot milk

1 cup light-brown sugar, firmly packed

¼ cup cold milk

1 tablespoon light corn syrup

⅓ cup finely chopped unblanched filberts

Caramel Coating:

½ lb vanilla caramels

1 tablespoon milk

⅔ cup finely chopped unblanched filberts

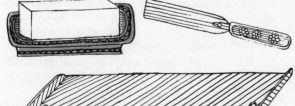

1. Make Filling: In small bowl of electric mixer, cream 4 tablespoons butter until light. Add confectioners' sugar, salt, rum extract, and hot milk; beat until smooth and fluffy. Set aside.

2. In small saucepan, combine brown sugar, remaining 2 tablespoons butter, cold milk, and corn syrup.

3. Cook, over medium heat, stirring occasionally, to 248F on candy thermometer, or until a small amount in cold water forms a firm ball.

4. In a thin stream, pour hot syrup into confectioners'-sugar mixture, beating at high speed until mixture becomes thick.

5. Turn out on well-buttered cookie sheet; let stand about 5 minutes, or until slightly cooled.

6. Sprinkle with ⅓ cup chopped nuts; using hands, knead nuts into mixture. Form into a roll 14 inches long.

7. Wrap in waxed paper; refrigerate until firm —about 4 hours.

8. Make Caramel Coating: In top of double boiler, heat caramels over boiling water until melted. Add milk, stirring until smooth.

9. With a knife or small spatula, spread some of caramel over top and sides of chilled roll, coating evenly. Press some filberts into caramel.

10. Turn roll over, and spread with rest of caramel. Also, press remaining filberts into caramel.

11. Refrigerate roll 2 to 3 hours, or until firm.

12. Let stand at room temperature a few minutes before slicing. Cut roll into 24 slices.

CARAMEL-NUT SQUARES

MAKES ABOUT 2½ POUNDS

1½ cups granulated sugar
½ cup light-brown sugar, firmly packed
Dash salt
2 cups light corn syrup

½ cup butter or margarine
1⅔ cups evaporated milk, undiluted
1 teaspoon vanilla extract
1 cup finely chopped pecans

1. Lightly butter a 9-by-9-by-1¾-inch pan.

2. In 4-quart saucepan, mix sugars, salt, and syrup.

3. Over high heat, bring to boiling, stirring occasionally, to 245F on candy thermometer, or until a small amount in cold water forms a firm ball. Remove from heat to test.

4. Continue to boil over high heat. Add butter. Add milk gradually, stirring constantly. Over medium heat, continuing to stir, bring to 244F on candy thermometer, or until a small amount in cold water forms a firm ball. This should take about 30 minutes.

5. Remove from heat. Add vanilla and nuts; mix well. Let stand until mixture stops bubbling.

6. Pour into buttered pan; cool to room temperature. Refrigerate until hardened—about 2 hours.

7. When ready to serve, loosen caramel from sides of pan with metal spatula or broad knife.

8. Invert pan on cutting board. Place a hot, wet dishcloth over bottom of pan. Repeat with cloth until caramel is loosened and unmolds onto board.

9. Cut caramels, with a sharp knife dipped into hot water, into 1-inch pieces.

CREAM PRALINES

MAKES 1 POUND

1 cup dark-brown sugar, firmly packed
1 cup granulated sugar

⅔ cup evaporated milk, undiluted
½ teaspoon vanilla extract
1½ cups pecan halves

1. Butter a large cookie sheet generously.

2. Mix sugars and milk in medium saucepan.

3. Cook, over medium heat, stirring constantly, to 234F on candy thermometer, or until a small amount in cold water forms a soft ball.

4. Remove from heat. Add vanilla and pecans; stir with wooden spoon.

5. Immediately drop candy, by tablespoonfuls, onto prepared cookie sheet or waxed paper, to form patties.

Note: If candy becomes too stiff while you are forming patties, stir in a small amount of cold water.

DIVINITY FUDGE

MAKES 24 PIECES

2½ cups sugar
½ cup light corn syrup
2 egg whites
¼ teaspoon salt

2 teaspoons vanilla extract
1 cup coarsely chopped
    walnuts
12 candied cherries, halved

1. In a 1-quart heavy saucepan, combine sugar and corn syrup with ½ cup water. Over low heat, cook, stirring, until sugar is dissolved. Cover; cook 1 minute, or until sugar crystals on side of pan melt.

2. Uncover; bring to boiling, without stirring, to 238F on candy thermometer, or until a small amount in cold water forms a soft ball.

3. Meanwhile, in large bowl of electric mixer, at high speed, beat egg whites with salt until stiff peaks form when beater is slowly raised.

4. In a thin stream, pour half of hot syrup over egg whites, beating constantly, at high speed, until stiff peaks form when beater is raised.

5. Continue cooking rest of syrup to 256F on candy thermometer, or until a small amount in cold water forms a hard ball.

6. In a thin stream, pour hot syrup into meringue mixture, beating constantly with a wooden spoon.

7. Beat in vanilla and walnuts; continue beating until mixture is stiff enough to hold its shape—about 5 minutes.

8. Turn into a lightly greased 11-by-7-by-1¼-inch baking pan. Do not scrape saucepan. Let stand until firm.

9. With sharp knife, cut into 24 pieces. Top each with a cherry half.

MERINGUES

MAKES ABOUT 6 DOZEN

4 egg whites
1¼ cups sugar
⅓ cup coarsely chopped
    walnuts

⅓ cup coarsely chopped
    pitted dates
⅓ cup coarsely chopped
    candied cherries

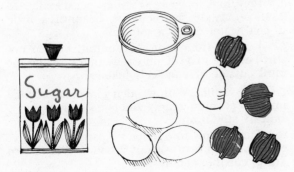

1. Preheat oven to 300F.

2. In large bowl of electric mixer, let egg whites warm to room temperature—about 1 hour.

3. With mixer at high speed, beat whites just until soft peaks form when beater is slowly raised.

4. Add sugar, 2 tablespoons at a time, beating well after each addition. Continue beating until stiff peaks form when beater is slowly raised.

5. Fold in rest of ingredients.

6. Drop mixture by teaspoonfuls, 1 inch apart, onto lightly greased cookie sheets; bake 25 to 30 minutes, or just until faintly colored.

7. Cool on wire rack. Then store in air-tight container.

MOCHA-NUT LOGS

MAKES 40

1 cup light-brown sugar,
   firmly packed
⅓ cup evaporated milk,
   undiluted
2 tablespoons light corn
   syrup

1 pkg (6 oz) semisweet-
   chocolate pieces
1 teaspoon instant coffee
2 teaspoons vanilla extract
1 cup chopped walnuts

1. In heavy 1-quart saucepan, combine brown sugar, evaporated milk, and corn syrup. Over medium heat, bring mixture to a full boil, stirring constantly. Boil 2 minutes, stirring.

2. Remove from heat. Add chocolate pieces, coffee, and vanilla, stirring until chocolate melts.

3. With wooden spoon, beat until mixture is thick and smooth. Stir in nuts.

4. Divide mixture in half. Shape each half into a "log," 10 inches long. Wrap each in waxed paper.

5. Refrigerate about 2 hours, or until firm. To serve, cut each "log" into 20 slices.

PEANUT BRITTLE

MAKES 1½ POUNDS

2 cups sugar
½ cup light corn syrup
2 cups unsalted peanuts

1 teaspoon butter or
   margarine
¼ teaspoon baking soda

1. Combine sugar, corn syrup, and 1 cup water in medium saucepan; stir, over low heat, until sugar is dissolved.

2. Continue cooking, without stirring, to 238F on candy thermometer, or until a little in cold water forms a soft ball—takes about 15 minutes.

3. Add peanuts; cook until syrup turns golden —about 10 minutes. Add butter and soda, stirring just enough to mix.

4. Pour onto greased cookie sheet, forming a large square of brittle. Cool; then break into pieces.

OLD-FASHIONED CHOCOLATE FUDGE

MAKES 1¾ POUNDS

3 cups sugar
¼ teaspoon salt
½ cup sifted unsweetened
   cocoa; or 3 squares
   unsweetened
   chocolate, cut up
1 cup milk; or ½ cup
   undiluted evaporated
   milk combined with
   ½ cup water

2 tablespoons light corn
   syrup
3 tablespoons butter or
   margarine
1 teaspoon vanilla extract
1 cup coarsely chopped
   walnuts or pecans

1. Lightly butter an 8-by-8-by-2-inch or 9-by-9-by-1¾-inch pan.

2. In heavy 3-quart saucepan, combine sugar, salt, cocoa, milk, and corn syrup. Cook, stirring, over medium heat, until sugar dissolves.

3. Continue to cook, stirring occasionally, to 234F on candy thermometer, or until a little in cold water forms a soft ball.

4. Remove from heat. Add butter, but do not stir. Let cool to 110F on candy thermometer, or until outside of pan feels lukewarm.

5. Add vanilla. With wooden spoon, beat fudge until it becomes creamy and is no longer glossy. Quickly stir in nuts.

6. Turn evenly into prepared pan. Refrigerate, covered, until firm—about 2 hours. With sharp knife, cut into squares.

TAFFY APPLES

2 cups sugar
2 cups light corn syrup
2 bottles (1¾-oz size)
   cinnamon candies
   (⅓ cup)

½ teaspoon red food color
½ teaspoon cinnamon
6 medium red eating apples
6 wooden skewers

1. Butter a cookie sheet generously.
2. In medium saucepan, combine sugar, corn syrup, and cinnamon candies with 1 cup water.
3. Over medium heat, stirring constantly, cook until sugar and candies dissolve. Do not boil.
4. Add food color and cinnamon, stirring well.
5. Boil to 300F, without stirring.
6. Meanwhile, wash apples, and dry. Remove stems, and firmly insert wooden skewers at stem ends.
7. When temperature reaches 300F, remove taffy from heat. Dip apples quickly into taffy until well coated.
8. Place on prepared cookie sheet, skewer end up, to let taffy harden. Let stand at room temperature until serving.
Note: It is essential to work rapidly once taffy reaches correct temperature.

FIVE-MINUTE FUDGE

1 can (6 oz) evaporated
   milk, undiluted
1⅔ cups sugar
½ teaspoon salt
½ cup chopped walnuts

1½ cups diced
   marshmallows
1½ cups semisweet-
   chocolate pieces
1 teaspoon vanilla extract

1. Grease a 9-by-9-by-1¾-inch pan.
2. In medium saucepan, combine evaporated milk with sugar and salt; bring to boiling. Reduce heat, and simmer, stirring constantly, 5 minutes.
3. Remove from heat. Add remaining ingredients, stirring until marshmallows melt.
4. Pour into prepared pan; let cool. To serve, cut into squares.

Uncooked Candies

These candies are especially popular with beginners, because they are so quickly and easily made. They don't require the skill and patience that cooked candies demand.

COCONUT ECLIPSES

2 tablespoons butter or
   margarine
1 teaspoon vanilla extract
2 cups sifted confectioners'
   sugar

½ cup instant nonfat dry
   milk
2⅔ cups flaked coconut
3 squares semisweet
   chocolate

1. Melt butter in saucepan; add 2 tablespoons water and vanilla.
2. Combine confectioners' sugar and nonfat dry milk; stir into butter mixture, ½ cup at a time; mix well after each addition. Blend in coconut.
3. Drop teaspoonfuls of mixture onto cookie sheet covered with waxed paper. Let stand until firm—15 minutes.
4. Melt chocolate over hot, not boiling, water. Remove from hot water; let stand, to cool slightly.
5. Dip bottom of each piece of candy into chocolate. Place upside down on waxed paper to dry.

BRANDY BALLS

1 can (6 oz) evaporated
   milk, undiluted
1 pkg (6 oz) semisweet-
   chocolate pieces
2½ cups crushed vanilla
   wafers (about 64)

½ cup sifted confectioners'
   sugar
1¼ cups chopped pecans
⅓ cup brandy

1. In heavy 2-quart saucepan, combine evaporated milk and chocolate pieces. Cook, stirring, over medium heat, until chocolate melts and mixture is smooth and thickened.

2. Remove from heat. Add crushed wafers, sugar, ½ cup pecans, and brandy, mixing well.

3. Let stand at room temperature 30 minutes.

4. Shape mixture into balls 1 inch in diameter. Roll in remaining pecans. Refrigerate 1 hour, or until firm.

CHOCOLATE CLUSTERS

1 pkg (6 oz) semisweet-
   chocolate pieces
¼ cup light corn syrup
1 cup raisins

1 cup salted peanuts
Red cinnamon candies
Angelica

1. In top of double boiler, combine chocolate pieces, corn syrup, and 1 tablespoon water. Over hot, not boiling, water, heat until chocolate melts. Remove from heat; divide in half.

2. Add raisins to half the chocolate mixture and peanuts to the other half.

3. Drop by teaspoonfuls onto cookie sheet covered with waxed paper. Top with candies and angelica. Refrigerate, to harden chocolate slightly, 1 hour.

COCONUT PASTEL BONBONS

1 pkg (3 oz) soft cream
   cheese
2½ cups sifted
   confectioners' sugar
¼ teaspoon vanilla extract

Dash salt
Few drops green food color
⅓ to ½ cup packaged
   grated coconut

1. In medium bowl, with wooden spoon, beat cream cheese until smooth. Gradually beat in confectioners' sugar, blending thoroughly. Beat in vanilla and salt. Add just enough food color to tint a delicate green.

2. Refrigerate, covered, 1 hour. Shape into balls, using a teaspoon of mixture for each.

3. Roll in coconut; flatten top slightly with fingers. Place on cookie sheet, covered with waxed paper; refrigerate several hours, or until firm.

MAKE-BELIEVE APPLES

1 pkg (8 oz) pitted dates
1 cup seedless raisins
1 cup dried figs
1 cup walnut pieces
1 teaspoon grated orange
   peel

1 tablespoon orange juice
½ teaspoon cinnamon
Confectioners' sugar
Red sugar
28 whole cloves
Citron or angelica

1. Put fruits, walnuts, and orange peel through coarse blade of food chopper.

2. Combine mixture with orange juice and cinnamon in medium bowl; knead, with hands, until well blended.

3. Form into 28 (1-inch) balls. Roll lightly in confectioners' sugar. Then roll one side of each very lightly in red sugar.

4. Insert whole clove in each apple, to form stem. Close to stem, insert citron pieces, for leaves. Store, covered, in refrigerator.

FONDANT-FILLED FRUITS

⅓ cup soft butter or
   margarine
⅓ cup light corn syrup
½ teaspoon salt
1 teaspoon vanilla extract

1 pkg (1 lb) confectioners'
   sugar, sifted
20 large pitted prunes
1 pkg (11 oz) apricot halves
   (56)
½ cup granulated sugar

1. Combine butter, syrup, salt, and vanilla in large mixing bowl; blend well.
2. Add confectioners' sugar all at once; mix, with spoon, until stiff.
3. Turn onto board; knead until well blended and smooth.
4. Use about 1¼ cups fondant to fill prunes.
5. Fill apricot halves, putting 2 halves together with 1 rounded teaspoon of fondant.
6. Roll prunes and apricots in granulated sugar.
7. Store, covered, in refrigerator.

PASTEL FONDANT PATTIES

⅓ cup soft butter or
   margarine
⅓ cup light corn syrup
½ teaspoon salt
1 lb confectioners' sugar
¼ teaspoon wintergreen
   extract

Green food color
¼ teaspoon peppermint
   extract
Red food color
¼ teaspoon lemon extract
Yellow food color
¼ teaspoon vanilla extract

1. Combine butter, syrup, and salt in large mixing bowl. With wooden spoon, beat until well blended.
2. Add confectioners' sugar all at once; beat until stiff. Turn mixture out onto wooden board; knead with hands until it is well blended and smooth.
3. Divide fondant into 4 equal portions. Make an indentation in center of each.
4. To first portion, add wintergreen extract and one or two drops of green food color, just enough to tint a delicate green. Knead with hands to blend well.
5. To second portion, add peppermint extract and one or two drops of red food color, just enough to tint a delicate pink. Knead with hands to blend well.
6. To third portion, add lemon extract and one or two drops of yellow food color, just enough to tint a delicate yellow. Knead with hands to blend well.
7. To last portion, add vanilla extract. Knead with hands to blend well.
8. Roll out each portion, one at a time, ⅛ inch thick. With biscuit cutter or fancy cookie cutter, cut into circles 1¼ inches in diameter.
9. Refrigerate on cookie sheets until firm.

Note: Patties may be made several days before serving. Refrigerate them, covered, until ready to serve.

Glacéed Fruits and Nuts

For a tea party, for a cool-looking conclusion to a warm, wintry dinner, we recommend our candied fruit peels, our coated and flavored nuts. They're lovely to look at, good to eat, easy to do. Though they are often associated with the holiday season, there's no reason in the world you shouldn't serve them all year round. These sophisticated sweets are a pleasant tidbit to pass after dessert, a thoughtful gift to take to a friend.

CANDIED ORANGE PEEL

MAKES ABOUT 1 POUND

2½ lb navel oranges   3 cups sugar
   (4 large)

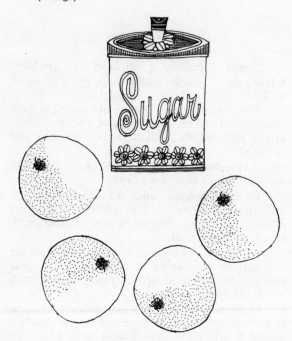

1. With sharp knife, remove peel from each orange in quarters; scrape out any pulp (peel should be about ¼ inch thick).
2. In 2 quarts water in large saucepan or kettle, simmer peel, covered, 30 to 40 minutes, or until tender. Drain, reserving cooking liquid. Set peel aside.
3. In same saucepan, combine 2 cups sugar and 1 cup reserved liquid; cook, over medium heat, stirring constantly, until sugar is dissolved.
4. Continue cooking, without stirring, to 238F on candy thermometer, or until a little in cold water forms a soft ball.
5. Add orange peel; simmer gently, stirring occasionally, about 30 minutes, or until peel becomes translucent. (To prevent scorching during cooking, lift peel off bottom of pan several times.)
6. Drain peel. While still hot, roll in rest of sugar, coating all sides very well.
7. Cool on wire rack; let dry 24 hours.
8. Then, with scissors, cut into ¼-inch-wide strips. Store, covered, in refrigerator.

Candied Grapefruit* Peel: Follow recipe for Candied Orange Peel, substituting grapefruit (2 large) for oranges. Cook as directed above; do not reserve cooking liquid. Combine the 2 cups sugar with 1 cup water. Makes ½ pound. * Use only thick-skinned fruit.

Candied Lemon* Peel: Follow recipe for Candied Orange Peel, substituting 2 lb lemons for oranges. Halve lemons crosswise; carefully remove pulp. Cook as directed above; do not reserve cooking liquid. Combine the 2 cups sugar with 1 cup water. Makes about ¾ pound. * Use only thick-skinned fruit.

ORANGE WALNUTS

1½ cups sugar
½ cup fresh orange juice

1 tablespoon grated orange peel
3 cups walnut halves

1. Combine sugar and orange juice in medium saucepan. Cook, over medium heat, stirring constantly, until sugar is dissolved.

2. Continue cooking, without stirring, to 238F on candy thermometer, or until a little in cold water forms a soft ball.

3. Remove from heat. Add orange peel and walnuts.

4. With wooden spoon, stir gently until mixture becomes creamy.

5. Turn onto waxed paper; with fork, separate walnuts. Let dry.

SPICED WALNUTS

1 cup sugar
1 teaspoon salt
2 teaspoons cinnamon

½ teaspoon nutmeg
¼ teaspoon cloves
2 cups walnut halves

1. Combine sugar, salt, cinnamon, nutmeg, cloves, and ½ cup water in medium saucepan; cook, over medium heat, stirring constantly, until sugar is dissolved.

2. Continue cooking, without stirring, to 238F on candy thermometer, or until a little in cold water forms a soft ball.

3. Remove from heat. Add walnuts; stir gently until mixture becomes creamy.

4. Turn onto waxed paper; with fork, separate walnuts. Let dry.

SUGAR-AND-HONEY PECANS

1½ cups sugar
¼ teaspoon salt
¼ cup honey

½ teaspoon vanilla extract
3 cups pecan halves

1. Combine sugar, salt, honey, and ½ cup water in medium saucepan; cook, over medium heat, stirring constantly, until sugar is dissolved.

2. Continue cooking, without stirring, to 244F on candy thermometer, or until a little in cold water forms a firm ball.

3. Remove from heat. Add vanilla and pecans; stir gently until mixture becomes creamy.

4. Turn onto waxed paper; with fork, separate pecans. Let dry.

Casseroles 11 and Main Dishes

When you can't think of what else to serve, compose a casserole. It's the hostess' best friend and the busy homemaker's helper, because usually the preparations can be finished ahead of time and the final heating can be done in the oven, without extra attention.

Modern homemakers think of the casserole as a combination of protein (meat, fish, cheese, or eggs), an extender like pasta or rice, all bound together with a sauce. Since the casserole is a bake-and-serve dish, there's less trouble serving, less washing up to do afterward.

BOILED DINNER

MAKES 6 TO 8 SERVINGS

3- to 4-lb fresh brisket of
    beef
¼ teaspoon whole black
    peppers
2 bay leaves
6 whole cloves
¼ teaspoon liquid hot-
    pepper seasoning
1 tablespoon salt

4 onions, peeled and halved
    (1 lb)
4 carrots, pared and halved
    (½ lb)
4 potatoes, pared and
    halved (1½ lb)
4 parsnips, pared and
    halved (1 lb)
1 head cabbage (2 lb), cut
    in eighths

1. Wipe beef with damp paper towels.

2. In large kettle, place beef with seasonings. Cover with water (about 2 quarts).

3. Bring to boiling. Cover; reduce heat; simmer 2¼ hours, or until almost tender.

4. Add vegetables. Return to boiling; simmer 25 to 30 minutes, or until vegetables and beef are tender.

5. To serve: Drain well. Slice brisket across grain in thin slices. Serve with vegetables and Hot Horseradish Sauce,* if desired.

* See Sauces and Gravies Chapter.

BEEF PIE

2 lb beef chuck or round,
    cut in 1¼-inch cubes
7 tablespoons unsifted
    all-purpose flour
3 tablespoons shortening
⅔ cup tomato juice
½ teaspoon Worcestershire
    sauce
2 teaspoons salt

Dash pepper
1 bay leaf
2 whole cloves
4 medium carrots
8 small white onions
3 medium potatoes
1 stalk celery
⅔ cup peas, fresh or frozen

1. Coat meat well with 4 tablespoons flour.
2. Over medium heat, slowly heat shortening in Dutch oven. In it, brown meat cubes well, turning on all sides.
3. Add 3 cups water, tomato juice, Worcestershire, salt, pepper, bay leaf, and cloves. Cover; simmer 1½ hours, or until just tender.
4. Meanwhile, prepare vegetables: Peel carrots, and cut in chunks. Peel onions; leave whole. Pare potatoes; cube. Cut celery in chunks.
5. When meat has cooked 1½ hours, add vegetables. Cook 30 minutes, or until vegetables are tender.
6. Meanwhile, preheat oven to 425F.
7. To thicken gravy: Remove vegetables and meat; set aside. In small bowl, blend remaining flour and 3 tablespoons water.
8. Blend quickly into cooking liquid; cook, over medium heat, stirring constantly, until mixture boils and thickens.
9. Combine vegetables, meat, and gravy in 2½-quart casserole.
10. Top with Herbed Crust.* Slash steam vents. Fold under edge of crust; seal to edge of casserole; crimp.
11. Bake 30 minutes, or until golden-brown.
* See Pies and Small Pastries Chapter.

STEAK-AND-KIDNEY PIE

1½ lb beef round, 1 inch
    thick
6 lamb kidneys
¼ cup unsifted all-purpose
    flour
1½ teaspoons salt
¼ teaspoon ginger
⅛ teaspoon cinnamon

6 bacon slices, diced
1 teaspoon prepared
    mustard
8 small white onions
1 can (10½ oz) beef
    bouillon, undiluted
Pastry for one-crust pie

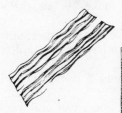

1. Cut beef into 1-inch cubes.
2. Wash kidneys; remove outer membrane and excess fat and tubes. Cut kidneys into quarters.
3. Combine flour, salt, ginger, and cinnamon; use to coat beef and kidneys.
4. Sauté bacon in Dutch oven or heavy skillet. Add beef and kidneys; brown well on all sides.
5. Remove from heat. Add any remaining flour mixture, mustard, onions, and bouillon diluted with enough water to measure 2 cups.
6. Simmer, covered, 1 hour.
7. Meanwhile, preheat oven to 425F.
8. Prepare pastry; roll out to 8-inch circle.
9. Turn beef-and-kidney mixture into 1½-quart casserole. Adjust pastry over top of casserole; make several air vents in pastry top.
10. Bake 40 minutes.

BEEF STEW

6 tablespoons shortening

3 lb beef chuck, round, or rump, cut in 1½-inch cubes

2 medium onions, coarsely chopped

1 cup red wine

2 bouillon cubes

1 clove garlic, finely chopped

2 tablespoons finely chopped parsley

1 bay leaf

⅛ teaspoon dried thyme leaves

1½ tablespoons salt

¼ teaspoon pepper

6 medium potatoes

6 medium carrots

10 small white onions

3 stalks celery

2 medium green peppers

2 medium tomatoes; or 1 can (8 oz) tomatoes, undrained

1. Over medium heat, slowly heat shortening in Dutch oven. In it, brown meat cubes well, turning on all sides. Remove, and set aside.

2. In Dutch oven, sauté onions until tender.

3. Return meat to pan; add 4 cups water, the wine, bouillon cubes, garlic, parsley, bay leaf, thyme, salt, and pepper. Cover; simmer 1½ hours, or until just tender.

4. Meanwhile, prepare vegetables: Peel potatoes and carrots; halve. Peel onions. Cut celery in 3-inch sections. Remove seeds and ribs from peppers; cut in chunks. Quarter fresh tomatoes.

5. When meat has cooked 1½ hours, add potatoes, carrots, onions, and celery. Cook 1 hour, or until meat and vegetables are tender.

6. Twenty minutes before end of cooking time, add peppers and tomatoes.

Note: Gravy will be thin. If desired, thicken with ¼ cup flour blended smoothly into ¼ cup water. Stir quickly into pan liquid. Cook, stirring, until it boils and thickens.

HEARTY POT ROAST WITH VEGETABLES

3½- to 4-lb chuck pot roast, bone in

2 tablespoons flour

1 teaspoon salt

1 tablespoon shortening or salad oil

6 whole black peppers

1 bay leaf

6 medium carrots, pared

6 medium potatoes, pared

6 medium onions, peeled

1 can (1 lb, 3 oz) stewed tomatoes

1 lb fresh green beans, ends removed

2 green peppers, quartered

Gravy:

Pan liquid

¼ cup unsifted all-purpose flour

Salt

Pepper

1. Wipe roast well with damp paper towels. Combine flour and salt; rub into surface.

2. Slowly heat large Dutch oven. Add shortening; heat. In it, brown roast well on all sides, turning with tongs.

3. Add black peppers and bay leaf along with 1 cup water; simmer, covered, 1 hour (add more water, as necessary, to keep ½ to 1 inch liquid in bottom of Dutch oven during cooking period).

4. Turn roast. Add vegetables; simmer, covered, 45 minutes to 1 hour, or until roast and vegetables are tender.

5. Remove roast and whole vegetables to hot serving platter; keep warm.

6. Make Gravy: Press any remaining vegetables, with pan liquid, through coarse sieve. Skim off fat.

7. Add water to liquid to make 2½ cups. Return to Dutch oven; reheat.

8. Combine flour with ½ cup cold water, stirring until smooth. Slowly stir into hot liquid; bring to boiling, stirring.

9. Reduce heat, and simmer 5 minutes. Add salt and pepper to taste.

10. Pass gravy with the pot roast and vegetables.

HUNGARIAN GOULASH

MAKES 6 TO 8 SERVINGS

2 lb beef chuck, cut in
   1-inch cubes
3 tablespoons all-purpose
   flour
2 tablespoons salad oil
¼ cup chopped onion
1 bay leaf
2 whole cloves

1½ teaspoons salt
¼ teaspoon pepper
1 tablespoon paprika
1½ cups beef bouillon*
1 pkg (8 oz) medium
   noodles
2 tablespoons butter or
   margarine

1. Coat beef well with flour.
2. Slowly heat oil in Dutch oven, over medium heat. In it, brown beef well, turning on all sides.
3. Add onion; cook, stirring, until tender—about 5 minutes.
4. Add remaining ingredients except noodles and butter, stirring to mix well. Bring to boiling; cover; reduce heat; simmer 2 to 2¼ hours, or until meat is fork-tender.
5. Meanwhile, cook noodles as package directs. Drain; toss with butter.
6. Serve Goulash over hot, buttered noodles.

* If extra gravy is desired, increase bouillon to 2 cups.

BEEF CREOLE WITH POTATO PUFFS

MAKES 4 TO 6 SERVINGS

1 lb ground chuck
½ cup chopped onion
½ cup chopped green
   pepper
½ cup chopped celery
1 pkg (10 oz) frozen peas,
   partially thawed
1 tablespoon flour
1½ teaspoons chili powder
1 teaspoon salt
⅛ teaspoon pepper
1 cup catsup
1 tablespoon Worcester-
   shire sauce

Potato Puffs:
1½ cups mashed potatoes
1 egg, beaten
½ teaspoon salt
1 teaspoon grated onion
1 tablespoon parsley flakes
⅓ cup packaged dry bread
   crumbs
¼ cup unsifted all-purpose
   flour
½ teaspoon baking powder

1. Preheat oven to 375F.
2. In large skillet, over medium heat, slowly brown chuck, leaving it in large chunks.
3. Add onion, green pepper, and celery; cook, stirring until tender-crisp—about 5 minutes. Add peas.
4. Blend flour with chili powder, salt, and pepper. Stir quickly into meat mixture.
5. Add catsup and Worcestershire. Cover; simmer 5 minutes.
6. Meanwhile, make Potato Puffs: In medium bowl, combine all ingredients; beat to blend.
7. Turn meat mixture into 2-quart casserole. Drop potato puffs by tablespoonfuls onto hot meat mixture. Cover; bake 30 minutes.

HAMBURGER ITALIANO

MAKES 6 TO 8 SERVINGS

¼ cup butter or margarine
½ cup chopped onion
½ cup chopped green
   pepper
1½ lb ground chuck
1½ teaspoons salt
¼ teaspoon pepper
½ teaspoon dried oregano
   leaves

2 tablespoons
   Worcestershire sauce
1 pkg (8 oz) elbow macaroni
1 can (3 oz) button
   mushrooms, drained
1 can (10½ oz) tomato
   soup, undiluted
1 medium tomato, chopped
½ cup grated Parmesan
   cheese

1. Preheat oven to 375F.
2. In hot butter in large skillet, sauté onion and green pepper until tender—5 minutes.
3. Add beef; cook, stirring, over medium heat until browned—about 5 minutes. Add salt, pepper, oregano, and Worcestershire.
4. Meanwhile, cook macaroni as package label directs. Drain; turn into 2½-quart casserole.
5. Add beef mixture, mushrooms, tomato soup, and chopped tomato; toss to combine well.
6. Bake, covered, 40 minutes.
7. Remove cover; sprinkle with cheese. Bake 5 minutes longer, or until nicely browned.

HAMBURGER AND NOODLES STROGANOFF

½ pkg (4 oz) noodles
¼ cup butter or margarine
½ cup finely chopped onion
1 clove garlic, finely chopped
½ lb mushrooms, thickly sliced; or 1 can (6 oz) sliced mushrooms, drained
1 lb ground chuck

1 tablespoon flour
1 can (8 oz) tomato sauce
¼ cup Burgundy
1 can (10½ oz) beef bouillon, undiluted
1 teaspoon salt
¼ teaspoon pepper
1 cup dairy sour cream
½ cup grated Parmesan cheese

1. Preheat oven to 375F.
2. Cook noodles as package label directs. Drain.
3. Meanwhile, in hot butter in large skillet, sauté onion, garlic, and mushrooms until onion is golden—about 5 minutes.
4. Add beef; cook, stirring, until it is browned.
5. Remove from heat. Stir in flour, tomato sauce, Burgundy, bouillon, salt, and pepper.
6. Simmer 10 minutes, stirring occasionally. Blend in sour cream.
7. In lightly greased 2-quart casserole, layer a third of the noodles, then a third of the meat mixture. Repeat twice. Sprinkle with cheese.
8. Bake, uncovered, 25 minutes.

STUFFED-CABBAGE ROLLS

Cabbage:
1 large (about 2½ lb) head green cabbage
1 teaspoon salt

Stuffing:
½ cup butter or margarine
1 cup chopped onion
1 clove garlic, crushed
½ lb fresh mushrooms, sliced
½ lb ground chuck
½ lb ground veal
1½ cups cooked white rice

3 hard-cooked eggs, chopped
1 teaspoon salt
Dash pepper

Tomato Sauce:
¼ cup butter or margarine
¼ cup unsifted all-purpose flour
1 can (6 oz) tomato paste
½ teaspoon salt
Dash pepper
¼ teaspoon allspice

1. In large saucepan, bring 6 cups water to boiling point.
2. Add cabbage and salt; simmer 3 minutes— just long enough to make leaves pliable.
3. Drain, reserving 2 cups liquid. Remove 12 outer leaves from cabbage.
4. Make Stuffing: Melt ¼ cup butter in large skillet. Add onion, and sauté until golden.
5. Add rest of butter, along with garlic and mushrooms; sauté, stirring occasionally, about 4 minutes.
6. Add remaining stuffing ingredients; cook, uncovered, about 5 minutes, or until meat is no longer red.
7. Make Tomato Sauce: Melt butter in medium saucepan; remove from heat.
8. Stir in flour until smooth; then gradually stir in 2 cups reserved cabbage liquid.
9. Bring mixture to boiling point, stirring, over medium heat.
10. Remove from heat; stir in tomato paste, salt, pepper, and allspice.
11. Preheat oven to 350F.
12. Fill center of each cabbage leaf with ½ cup stuffing. Fold two sides over stuffing; roll up from end.
13. Arrange rolls, seam side down, in greased 3-quart casserole. Pour sauce over all.
14. Bake, uncovered, 25 minutes.

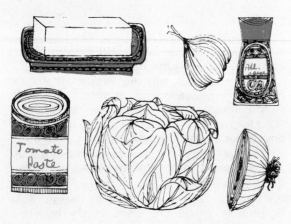

NEAPOLITAN BEEF

¼ cup salad oil

⅓ cup finely chopped
  onion

3 cloves garlic, crushed

1 cup pared, diced carrot

1½ cups diced celery

1½ lb ground chuck

1 can (6 oz) mushroom
  caps, drained

½ cup sherry

1 can (6 oz) tomato paste

1 can (1 lb, 3 oz) tomatoes

1 tablespoon salt

½ teaspoon pepper

½ teaspoon dried oregano
  leaves

½ teaspoon dried basil
  leaves

1 pkg (8 oz) small shell
  macaroni

1 pkg (10 oz) frozen
  chopped spinach

½ cup buttered fresh-bread
  cubes

1 cup grated sharp Cheddar
  cheese

Grated Parmesan cheese

1. In hot oil in large skillet, sauté onion, garlic, carrot, and celery until onion is golden—about 5 minutes.

2. Add beef; cook, stirring, until red disappears.

3. Add mushrooms, sherry, tomato paste, tomatoes, salt, pepper, oregano, and basil; simmer, uncovered, 1½ hours.

4. If desired, cool; cover, and refrigerate until needed.

5. About 45 minutes before serving time, preheat oven to 350F.

6. Cook macaroni and spinach according to package directions.

7. Reheat sauce. Add well-drained macaroni and spinach.

8. Turn into 3-quart casserole. Top with bread cubes and Cheddar cheese.

9. Bake, uncovered, 30 minutes, or until bubbly and browned.

10. Serve sprinkled with Parmesan cheese.

CHILI CON CARNE IN RED WINE

2 tablespoons salad or olive
  oil

1 cup finely chopped onion

2 cloves garlic, finely
  chopped

2 lb ground chuck

¼ cup boiling water

2 to 3 tablespoons chili
  powder

1 can (1 lb, 3 oz) tomatoes,
  undrained

2 teaspoons salt

2 teaspoons dried oregano
  leaves

1 teaspoon dried basil leaves

1 cup dry red wine

2 cans (15½-oz size) kidney
  beans, undrained

1. In hot oil in large skillet, sauté onion, garlic, and chuck until chuck is browned—about 5 minutes.

2. Pour boiling water over chili powder in small bowl, stirring until powder is dissolved.

3. Add to meat mixture, along with tomatoes, salt, oregano, and basil.

4. Simmer, covered and over very low heat, about 1 hour, stirring occasionally.

5. Stir in wine; simmer, uncovered, 20 minutes, stirring several times.

6. Add beans; heat slowly until thoroughly hot and most of liquid has evaporated. If desired, serve over Polenta Squares.*

Note: Chili con Carne may be made day before serving; but do not add beans. Refrigerate overnight. Next day, add beans, and proceed as directed.

* See Cereal Chapter.

SHEPHERD'S PIE

1 pkg (2 envelopes) instant
    mashed potatoes
1 tablespoon grated onion
1 egg, slightly beaten
2 cups finely chopped
    cooked beef
3 tablespoons finely
    chopped parsley
½ cup finely
    chopped celery

1 can (6 oz) mushroom
    stems and pieces,
    finely chopped
1½ teaspoons salt
¼ teaspoon pepper
⅓ cup hot milk
2 tablespoons grated
    Parmesan cheese
2 tablespoons butter

1. Prepare mashed potatoes according to package directions, adding grated onion to hot water required for potatoes. Beat in egg.
2. In a bowl, mix beef, 2 tablespoons parsley, celery, mushrooms, salt, pepper, and milk.
3. Preheat oven to 400F. Grease a 2-quart casserole.
4. Spoon half the potato mixture (about 2 cups) into bottom of casserole; cover with meat, and top evenly with remaining potatoes.
5. Sprinkle with cheese and remaining parsley; dot with butter.
6. Bake 20 to 25 minutes, or until surface is golden-brown.
7. If desired, serve with Creole Sauce.*
* See Sauces and Gravies Chapter.

CORNED-BEEF HASH WITH EGGS

2 tablespoons butter or
    margarine
¼ cup finely chopped
    onion
4 cups, or 2 cans (12-oz
    size), corned beef,
    coarsely chopped

2 medium boiled potatoes,
    diced
½ teaspoon salt
¼ teaspoon pepper
Dash ginger
Dash allspice
¾ cup tomato juice
6 eggs

1. Preheat oven to 350F.
2. In hot butter in small skillet, sauté onion until tender.
3. In bowl, combine the onion, corned beef, potatoes, salt, pepper, ginger, and allspice.
4. Spread evenly in greased 12-by-8-by-2-inch baking dish. Pour on tomato juice.
5. Bake 25 minutes. Remove from oven.
6. Using back of large spoon, space 6 shallow indentations in top of hash.
7. Break an egg into each indentation. Bake 8 to 10 minutes, or until eggs are just set. Serve immediately.

BAKED CHICKEN THERMIDOR

1 pkg (10 oz) frozen peas
2 cups cut-up cooked
    chicken
1 cup diced celery
1 can (5 oz) water
    chestnuts, drained
    and thinly sliced
½ cup canned toasted
    sliced almonds
2 tablespoons chopped
    green pepper
1 tablespoon grated onion

2 tablespoons chopped
    pimiento
2 tablespoons white wine
1 tablespoon lemon juice
½ teaspoon salt
½ cup milk
1 can (10½ oz) cream-of-
    chicken soup,
    undiluted
2 white-bread slices, cut
    into cubes
1 cup grated sharp Cheddar
    cheese (¼ lb)

1. Cook peas as package label directs; drain. Preheat oven to 375F.
2. In 2-quart casserole, combine peas, chicken, celery, water chestnuts, almonds, green pepper, onion, and pimiento.
3. Sprinkle with wine, lemon juice, and salt. Toss gently to mix well.
4. In small saucepan, combine milk and soup, stirring until smooth. Bring to boiling, stirring. Add to casserole mixture, combining well.
5. Sprinkle with bread cubes; bake 20 minutes, or until sauce is bubbly and bread cubes are toasted. Sprinkle with cheese; bake 5 minutes, or until cheese is melted.

BAKED CHICKEN-AND-VEGETABLE CASSEROLE

3-lb broiler-fryer, cut in
   serving pieces
½ cup unsifted all-purpose
   flour
2½ teaspoons salt
½ teaspoon pepper
½ cup butter or margarine
1 cup raw regular white rice
8 small white onions,
   peeled
½ lb fresh mushrooms,
   halved

1 medium eggplant, pared
   and cubed (1¼ lb)
1 can (4 oz) pimientos,
   drained and chopped
1 clove garlic, crushed
1 teaspoon monosodium
   glutamate
1 teaspoon dried tarragon
   leaves
½ cup chicken bouillon
½ cup red wine

1.   Wash chicken; dry with paper towels.
2.   Combine flour with 1 teaspoon salt and ¼ teaspoon pepper. Coat chicken well in seasoned flour.
3.   Heat butter slowly in 6-quart Dutch oven. In it, brown chicken well, turning on all sides (takes about 15 minutes).
4.   Meanwhile, preheat oven to 375F.
5.   Add rice, onions, mushrooms, eggplant, pimientos, garlic, monosodium glutamate, tarragon, remaining salt and pepper, and bouillon. Cover.
6.   Bake 35 to 40 minutes, or until chicken and vegetables are tender.
7.   Remove cover. Stir to mix well. Add wine. Bake 15 minutes.

CHICKEN POT PIE

5-lb stewing hen
3 celery tops
3 sprigs parsley
1 medium onion, peeled
   and quartered
10 whole black peppers
1 bay leaf
2½ teaspoons salt
1 teaspoon monosodium
   glutamate

¼ teaspoon dried rosemary
   leaves
6 carrots, pared and
   quartered (1 lb)
⅛ teaspoon pepper
¼ cup unsifted all-purpose
   flour
½ cup milk
1 pkg (10 oz) frozen peas,
   thawed
Pastry for one-crust pie

1.   In large kettle, combine chicken, celery, parsley, onion, peppers, bay leaf, 2 teaspoons salt, monosodium glutamate, and rosemary. Add 2 quarts water.
2.   Bring to boiling; cover; reduce heat, and simmer until chicken is tender—about 2 hours.
3.   Remove chicken; set aside.
4.   Strain stock. In 2 cups stock,* cook carrots, covered, until tender—about 20 minutes.
5.   Meanwhile, remove chicken from bones in large chunks. Place in 2-quart casserole; set aside.
6.   Preheat oven to 425F.
7.   Blend remaining salt, pepper, and flour in small bowl. Stir in milk until smooth.
8.   Quickly stir into stock with carrots. Add peas.
9.   Bring to boiling, stirring. Reduce heat; simmer about 8 minutes, or until sauce is thickened and peas are tender.
10.   Pour over chicken pieces in casserole; toss gently.
11.   Roll pastry to fit top of casserole with ½-inch overhang all around. Turn edge under; seal to rim of casserole; crimp. Slash vents in top. Bake 15 to 20 minutes, or until well browned.

   * Refrigerate any remaining stock for use in soups and sauces.

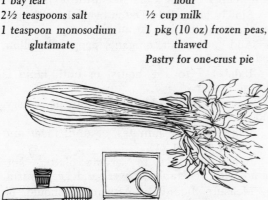

CHICKEN À LA KING

¼ lb fresh mushrooms
¼ cup butter or margarine, melted
½ green pepper, chopped
2 pimientos, chopped
3 tablespoons flour
½ teaspoon salt
1 cup chicken broth or bouillon
½ cup milk
Dash pepper
¼ teaspoon turmeric
1 teaspoon sugar
½ cup heavy cream
2 egg yolks, slightly beaten
2 cups cubed cooked chicken

1. Wash mushrooms; slice.
2. In hot butter in medium saucepan, sauté mushrooms, green pepper, and pimientos until mushrooms are tender—about 5 minutes.
3. Remove from heat; stir in flour and salt until smooth.
4. Blend in chicken broth and milk.
5. Cook, over low heat, stirring constantly, until mixture thickens and boils.
6. Stir in pepper, turmeric, and sugar.
7. Blend cream into egg yolks; stir into thickened sauce.
8. Add chicken; reheat gently.
9. Serve on toast triangles or biscuits.

BRAISED LAMB SHANKS

4 lamb shanks (3 lb)
3 to 4 tablespoons all-purpose flour
2 tablespoons salad oil
1 clove garlic, crushed
2 teaspoons salt
1 teaspoon dried oregano leaves
¼ teaspoon pepper
1 cup chicken bouillon
1 tablespoon lemon juice
4 carrots, pared and halved
4 small onions, peeled
2 stalks celery, quartered
2 potatoes, pared and quartered
¼ teaspoon liquid gravy seasoning (optional)

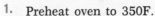

1. Preheat oven to 350F.
2. Remove excess fat from shanks. Wipe with damp paper towels. Coat well with flour.
3. Slowly heat oil in Dutch oven. In it, brown shanks well, turning on all sides.
4. Add garlic, salt, oregano, pepper, bouillon, and lemon juice; cover.
5. Bake 1¼ to 1½ hours, or until lamb is almost tender.
6. Turn shanks; add carrots, onions, celery, and potatoes; cover.
7. Bake 35 to 45 minutes, or until meat and vegetables are tender.
8. Remove shanks to serving platter; surround with vegetables; cover, and keep warm.
9. Measure liquid in casserole (should be about 1½ cups). Skim off excess fat, reserving 1 tablespoon in medium saucepan.
10. Blend 1 tablespoon flour into fat. Gradually stir in skimmed liquid and gravy seasoning.
11. Bring to boiling, stirring; boil 1 minute. Pour over shanks and vegetables.

Note: Veal shanks may be used instead of lamb. Increase first baking period ½ hour.

RAGOUT OF LAMB

MAKES 4 TO 6 SERVINGS

2-lb shoulder of lean lamb,
  cut in 1-inch cubes
3 tablespoons flour
½ cup butter or margarine
1 teaspoon salt
¼ teaspoon pepper
1½ teaspoons dried
  oregano leaves
1 can (13¾ oz) chicken
  broth
1 can (6 oz) tomato paste

1 teaspoon sugar
4 white turnips, quartered
8 small white onions,
  peeled
1 clove garlic, minced
4 small carrots, cut in strips
1 leek, cut in large cubes
1 pkg (8 oz) broad noodles
1 can (8½ oz) peas, drained
¼ cup finely chopped
  parsley

1. Lightly coat lamb cubes with flour. In 3 tablespoons butter, in Dutch oven or heavy kettle, brown lamb on all sides.
2. Add salt, pepper, oregano, chicken broth, and tomato paste; cover, and let simmer 45 minutes.
3. In small skillet, heat 3 tablespoons butter with sugar.
4. Add turnips, onions, and garlic; cook, over low heat, until vegetables are glazed and light-golden.
5. Meanwhile, preheat oven to 350F.
6. Add glazed vegetables, carrots, and leek to browned meat; cover, and bake 1 hour.
7. About 20 minutes before serving time, cook noodles according to package directions.
8. Also, add peas and parsley to lamb mixture.
9. To serve: Toss remaining 2 tablespoons butter with drained noodles. Arrange on heated serving platter, and top with Ragout of Lamb.

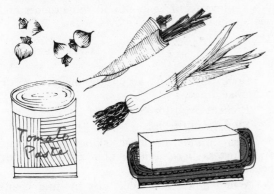

LAMB FRICASSEE

MAKES 6 SERVINGS

3-lb boned leg of lamb
½ cup unsifted all-purpose
  flour
1 teaspoon salt
¼ teaspoon pepper
⅓ cup olive oil
1 garlic clove
2 teaspoons instant minced
  onion
½ teaspoon paprika

¼ teaspoon dried rosemary
  leaves
3 tablespoons lemon juice
2 pkg (10-oz size) frozen
  artichoke hearts
1 tablespoon chopped
  parsley
4½ cups cooked white rice,
  drained

1. Wipe lamb with damp paper towels. Cut into 1-inch cubes, trimming off excess fat.
2. In large bowl, combine flour, salt, and pepper. Toss lamb cubes with flour mixture until well coated; set aside.
3. Slowly heat oil in large saucepan. Add garlic; sauté until browned. Remove, and discard.
4. Add lamb cubes to hot oil, about a third at a time; sauté, turning, until browned on all sides. Remove lamb as it browns.
5. In same saucepan, combine browned lamb, onion, paprika, rosemary, lemon juice, and 1½ cups water.
6. Over low heat, simmer, covered and stirring occasionally, 1 hour.
7. Add artichoke hearts; simmer over low heat 20 to 30 minutes longer, or until artichokes and lamb are tender.
8. Sprinkle lamb with parsley. Serve with rice.

CREAMED DRIED BEEF ON TOAST

1 can (3 oz) sliced
    mushrooms
¼ cup butter or margarine
¼ cup unsifted all-purpose
    flour

Dash pepper
About 1⅔ cups milk
1 jar (5 oz) dried beef
4 buttered toast slices

1. Drain mushrooms, reserving liquid; set aside.
2. Slowly heat butter in medium saucepan. Remove from heat. Add flour and pepper, stirring to make a smooth paste.
3. Combine reserved mushroom liquid with enough milk to make 2 cups. Gradually add milk mixture to flour mixture, stirring until smooth.
4. Over medium heat, bring mixture to boiling, stirring; reduce heat, and simmer 1 minute.
5. Remove from heat. Stir in mushrooms and beef; reheat gently. Serve over toast.

MIXED-BEAN CASSEROLE

1 pkg (10 oz) frozen lima
    beans
½ lb frankfurters
2 tablespoons butter or
    margarine
1 medium onion, chopped
1 clove garlic, minced
1 can (1 lb) kidney beans,
    drained
1 jar (1 lb, 6 oz) baked
    beans

1 teaspoon prepared
    mustard
1 tablespoon brown sugar
½ cup catsup
½ cup dry red wine
½ teaspoon salt
Dash pepper
½ cup crushed corn or
    potato chips

1. Cook lima beans according to package directions; drain.
2. Preheat oven to 350F.
3. Slice frankfurters.
4. Heat butter in large skillet, and sauté frankfurter slices, onion, and garlic, stirring occasionally.
5. When onion is tender, stir in lima beans and all remaining ingredients except chips.
6. Spoon mixture into a 2-quart casserole, and top with chips.
7. Bake 30 minutes.

PORK CASSEROLE MILANO

2 tablespoons salad oil
1 lb boneless pork loin, in
    1-inch strips
½ cup chopped onion
½ cup chopped celery
1 medium green pepper,
    cut into strips
1 can (3 oz) sliced
    mushrooms,
    undrained
1 teaspoon Worcestershire
    sauce
1 teaspoon salt
⅛ teaspoon pepper

½ teaspoon dried basil
    leaves
1 can (10½ oz) condensed
    cream-of-mushroom
    soup, undiluted
½ cup milk
1 pkg (8 oz) spaghetti
1 tomato, peeled and thinly
    sliced
1½ cups packaged
    croutons
2 tablespoons butter or
    margarine, melted
1 cup grated sharp Cheddar
    cheese

1. In hot oil in large skillet, brown pork strips well. Add onion, celery, and green pepper; sauté until tender.
2. Mix in sliced mushrooms and all the seasonings; simmer, covered, 25 minutes.
3. Blend in soup and milk; simmer, covered, for 5 minutes.
4. Meanwhile, preheat oven to 350F. In 3 quarts boiling, salted water, boil spaghetti, uncovered, 8 minutes. Drain.
5. In ungreased 2-quart casserole, combine pork mixture with drained spaghetti.
6. Overlap tomato slices around edge of casserole. Toss croutons with melted butter; sprinkle over tomatoes.
7. Bake 20 minutes. Top croutons with cheese; bake 10 minutes, or until cheese melts.

CRANBERRY BEANS WITH HAM SHANK

1 lb dried cranberry beans
4 teaspoons salt
1 bay leaf
1 small onion
2 whole cloves
1 ham shank, cracked
2 tablespoons butter or
   margarine

1 teaspoon pepper
2 cloves garlic, finely
   chopped
2 beef-bouillon cubes
1 cup boiling water
1 tablespoon soy sauce
3 tablespoons grated onion

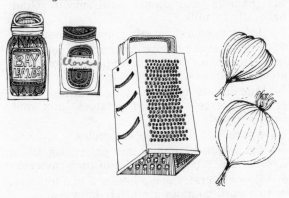

1. Cover beans with cold water; refrigerate, covered, overnight.
2. Next day, drain. Turn into 6-quart kettle.
3. Add 6 cups cold water, 3 teaspoons salt, bay leaf, onion stuck with cloves, and ham shank.
4. Bring to boiling point; reduce heat; then simmer, stirring several times, about 1½ hours, or until beans are tender.
5. Drain well; reserve liquid.
6. Trim meat from ham shank; cut into cubes.
7. In hot butter in medium skillet, sauté ham cubes until well browned.
8. Sprinkle with 1 teaspoon salt, the pepper, and garlic. Stir in bouillon cubes dissolved in boiling water. Add soy sauce.
9. Meanwhile, preheat oven to 375F.
10. Turn beans into 2-quart casserole. Stir in 1½ cups bean liquid, ham mixture, and grated onion. Bake 40 minutes, uncovered, or until top is brown and crusty.

BAKED LENTIL-AND-HAM CASSEROLE

2 cups lentils
3½-lb ham shank
1 onion, stuck with whole
   clove
2 bay leaves
2 bacon slices
12 small white onions,
   peeled
½ teaspoon dried thyme
   leaves

½ teaspoon dried
   marjoram leaves
2 teaspoons salt
½ teaspoon pepper
6 carrots, scraped and cut in
   chunks
1 cup Burgundy
¼ cup buttered fresh bread
   crumbs

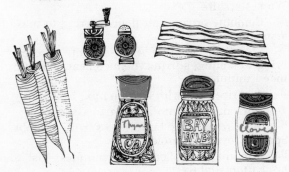

1. Combine lentils, ham shank, onion with clove, bay leaves, and 1 quart water in large saucepan; bring to boiling.
2. Reduce heat; simmer, covered, 30 minutes.
3. Drain lentils. Discard onion with clove and bay leaves.
4. Cut meat from ham shank into large chunks, trimming off excess fat.
5. Preheat oven to 350F.
6. Meanwhile, sauté bacon in medium skillet until crisp; then remove it, and crumble.
7. Sauté white onions in hot bacon fat, turning, until browned.
8. Mix thyme, marjoram, salt, and pepper.
9. Layer half of lentils in 2-quart casserole. Sprinkle with half of thyme mixture. Add ham, onions, carrots, and bacon. Add rest of lentils. Sprinkle with rest of thyme mixture. Pour Burgundy over top.
10. Bake, covered, 1½ hours, or until vegetables are tender.
11. Sprinkle with buttered crumbs; bake, uncovered, 15 minutes longer, or until golden.

LOBSTER-AND-ARTICHOKE CASSEROLES

4 (5- to 6-oz size) lobster
    tails, cooked
1 can (8 oz) artichoke
    hearts, drained
⅓ cup butter or margarine
1 green pepper, cut into
    strips
1 small onion, peeled and
    quartered
¼ cup unsifted all-purpose
    flour
1¾ teaspoons salt

½ teaspoon paprika
⅛ teaspoon pepper
2½ cups milk
1 egg, beaten
1 tablespoon bottled capers,
    drained
½ teaspoon Worcestershire
    sauce
1 teaspoon lemon juice
⅓ cup sherry
2 cups hot seasoned mashed
    potatoes

1. Remove lobster meat from shells; cut into bite-size chunks. Cut artichoke hearts in half; gently toss with lobster; set aside.

2. In hot butter in medium saucepan, sauté green pepper and onion until tender—about 5 minutes. Remove from heat. With slotted spoon, lift out vegetables; combine with lobster mixture.

3. Into same butter in saucepan, stir flour, salt, paprika, and pepper until smooth. Gradually stir in milk.

4. Bring to boiling, stirring; boil 1 minute.

5. Stir some of hot mixture into egg; pour back into saucepan. Cook, stirring, over low heat about 5 minutes, or until thickened.

6. Add lobster mixture along with rest of ingredients, except mashed potatoes; mix well. Gently reheat.

7. Spoon into 4 (15-oz) casseroles.

8. Put mashed potatoes into pastry bag, using a rosette tip; pipe around edge of each casserole.

9. Run casseroles under broiler 2 to 3 minutes, or just until potatoes are nicely browned.

SHRIMP-SUPREME CASSEROLE

2 lb medium raw shrimp
¼ cup butter or margarine
½ lb mushrooms, sliced
1 cup coarsely chopped
    onion
2 tomatoes, peeled and
    diced (1½ cups)
1½ teaspoons salt
¼ teaspoon pepper
⅛ teaspoon paprika

⅓ cup sherry
1 teaspoon Worcestershire
    sauce
½ cup light cream
2 tablespoons flour
4 cups drained cooked
    white rice
½ cup packaged dry bread
    crumbs

1. Shell shrimp; devein. Wash; dry well on paper towels. Set aside.

2. In 2 tablespoons hot butter in large skillet, sauté mushrooms, onion, and shrimp about 3 minutes, or just until shrimp turn pink.

3. Add tomatoes, salt, pepper, and paprika; simmer, covered, 5 minutes. Stir in sherry and Worcestershire.

4. Combine cream and flour, stirring to make a smooth paste.

5. Stir flour mixture into shrimp mixture; bring to boiling, stirring. Reduce heat, and simmer 1 minute.

6. Add rice; toss with fork, to mix; heat gently.

7. Turn mixture into a 2-quart casserole.

8. Melt remaining butter; toss with crumbs. Sprinkle over casserole.

9. Run under broiler a few minutes, just to brown top slightly.

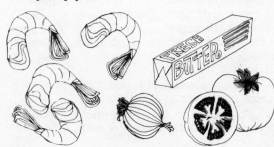

UNDER COVER
Many of the best casserole ideas come from abroad. But the best casseroles come from your own kitchen. Take some vegetables, a pinch of seasoning, and a dash of herbs; add a cup of this and a pound of that...and presto, a casserole! Easy to fix, wonderful to taste!

SERVE A
SALAD

Hail Caesar, chef, and all other salads! Served before, during, or just after the main course, salads have a special place in the hearts of food lovers. They're especially good in summer, often as the main attraction of an entire lunch, and they're pretty to look at as well as delicious to eat. You'll find all kinds here, along with many kinds of dazzling, delectable dressings.

(See chapter 21)

BAKED TUNA-AND-CHEESE CASSEROLE

1 cup elbow macaroni
2 cans (7-oz size) chunk-
    style tuna, drained
1 can (8 oz) diced carrots,
    drained
¼ cup slivered ripe olives
5 tablespoons butter or
    margarine
½ cup packaged seasoned
    dry bread crumbs

¼ cup sliced onion
¼ cup unsifted all-purpose
    flour
1½ teaspoons salt
⅛ teaspoon pepper
2½ cups milk
¾ cup grated sharp
    Cheddar cheese

MAKES 6 TO 8 SERVINGS

1. Cook macaroni as package label directs; drain.

2. Preheat oven to 375F. In 2-quart casserole, toss macaroni with tuna, carrots, and olives; mix well.

3. Melt butter in medium saucepan. Toss 1 tablespoon melted butter with bread crumbs in small bowl; set aside. In rest of hot butter, sauté onion until golden—about 5 minutes.

4. Remove from heat. Add flour, salt, and pepper, stirring until smooth. Gradually stir in milk.

5. Bring to boiling; boil 1 minute. Reduce heat. Add cheese, stirring until it is melted.

6. Pour cheese sauce over tuna mixture; toss to mix well.

7. Sprinkle buttered crumbs over top; bake 20 minutes, or until golden-brown and bubbly.

VEAL POT PIE

2 tablespoons salad oil
3 lb boneless veal, cut into
    3-inch cubes
2 teaspoons salt
¼ teaspoon pepper
3½ cups boiling water

Dumpling Squares:
1½ cups sifted all-purpose
    flour
½ teaspoon salt
1 teaspoon baking powder

1½ tablespoons butter or
    margarine
1 egg, beaten

1 large onion, coarsely
    chopped (¾ cup)
3 cups pared, diced
    potatoes (1 lb)
3 tablespoons chopped
    parsley
1 teaspoon paprika

MAKES 6 TO 8 SERVINGS

1. In hot oil in 4½- to 5-quart Dutch oven, brown veal well, turning on all sides—15 to 20 minutes in all. Sprinkle with salt and pepper.

2. Add water; bring to boiling; reduce heat, and simmer, covered, 45 minutes, or until veal is almost tender.

3. Meanwhile, make Dumpling Squares: Into medium bowl, sift flour with salt and baking powder. With pastry blender or 2 knives, cut in butter until particles are size of large peas.

4. With fork, quickly stir in egg and 3 to 4 tablespoons cold water. (Dough will be rather stiff, but should clean side of bowl.)

5. On lightly floured surface, roll dough ⅛ inch thick, to form a rectangle approximately 12 by 6 inches.

6. With sharp knife, cut dough into 1½-inch squares. Let stand, uncovered, several minutes.

7. Meanwhile, to veal in Dutch oven, add onion, potatoes, 2 tablespoons parsley, and paprika. Simmer, covered, 10 minutes.

8. Remove cover; drop half of dumpling squares, one by one, into simmering liquid. As they drop to the bottom of the Dutch oven, add the rest of the squares, stirring in carefully.

9. Simmer, covered, 25 minutes, or until dumplings are light and cooked through. Sprinkle top with more chopped parsley.

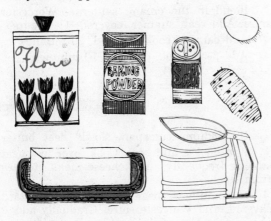

VEAL PAPRIKA

2 lb boned veal shoulder,
    cubed
3 tablespoons all-purpose
    flour
¼ cup butter or margarine
¼ cup chopped onion
1 cup chicken bouillon
½ teaspoon salt

½ teaspoon garlic salt
¼ teaspoon pepper
1 pkg (8 oz) medium
    noodles
1 tablespoon sesame seed
2 teaspoons paprika
¾ cup dairy sour cream

1. Coat veal cubes well in flour.
2. In Dutch oven, heat 2 tablespoons butter slowly. In it, brown veal well, turning on all sides.
3. Add onion; cook, stirring, until onion is tender—3 to 5 minutes.
4. Add bouillon, salt, garlic salt, and pepper.
5. Bring to boiling; cover; reduce heat; simmer 50 to 60 minutes, or until meat is fork-tender.
6. Meanwhile, cook noodles as package label directs. In remaining butter, sauté sesame seed. Drain noodles; toss with butter and sesame seed. Keep hot.
7. Blend paprika and sour cream into veal mixture. Heat gently.
8. Serve Veal Paprika over hot noodles.

VEAL STEW

6 tablespoons all-purpose
    flour
2 teaspoons salt
¼ teaspoon pepper
2 lb stewing veal, cubed
6 tablespoons butter or
    margarine
¾ cup chopped onion
¼ cup chopped parsley
½ lb mushrooms, sliced

2 chicken-bouillon cubes,
    dissolved in 2 cups
    boiling water
1 cup dairy sour cream
½ cup sauterne
1 teaspoon Worcestershire
    sauce
1½ cups sliced carrots
1 pkg (10 oz) thawed
    frozen peas

1. On waxed paper, combine 4 tablespoons flour with the salt and pepper. Thoroughly coat veal with mixture.
2. Melt butter in large skillet. Brown veal well on all sides. Remove from skillet; set aside.
3. Then add onion, parsley, and mushrooms; sauté, stirring, over medium heat until onion is golden—about 5 minutes. Remove from heat.
4. Stir in remaining flour. Blend in bouillon. Return to heat; cook, stirring, until thickened. Reduce heat.
5. Blend in the cream, sauterne, Worcestershire. Add veal; simmer, covered, 1½ hours.
6. Add carrots; cook, covered, 20 minutes.
7. Add peas; cook, covered, 10 minutes.

WELSH RABBIT

2 tablespoons butter
    or margarine
1 lb sharp Cheddar cheese,
    grated
½ cup light beer
1 egg

½ teaspoon salt
½ teaspoon dry mustard
Dash cayenne
1 teaspoon Worcestershire
    sauce
Toast slices

1. In medium saucepan, slowly heat butter.
2. Add cheese and beer. Cook, over low heat, stirring frequently, until cheese melts. Remove from heat.
3. In small bowl, beat egg with salt, mustard, cayenne and Worcestershire. Gradually add to cheese mixture, stirring until well combined.

(Welsh Rabbit continued)

4. Stir, over low heat, until mixture is heated through and smooth—about 5 minutes. Serve over toast.

Note: To keep rabbit warm, turn into top part of double boiler. Let stand over hot water until ready to serve.

EGG-AND-GREEN-BEAN CASSEROLE

MAKES 4 TO 6 SERVINGS

1 pkg (9 oz) frozen French-style green beans
¼ cup butter or margarine
¼ cup finely chopped onion
¼ cup unsifted all-purpose flour
2 cups milk
2 teaspoons salt
⅛ teaspoon pepper
Dash dried thyme leaves
Dash savory
1 tablespoon chopped parsley
6 hard-cooked eggs, sliced
¼ cup fine bread crumbs
½ cup grated Swiss cheese

1. Cook beans as package label directs; drain; set aside.
2. Preheat oven to 375F.
3. Melt butter in medium saucepan. In it, sauté onion until tender—about 3 minutes.
4. Remove from heat. Blend in flour, then milk. Add seasonings and parsley.
5. Bring to boiling, stirring; simmer 2 minutes.
6. Layer beans, eggs, and sauce in 1½-quart casserole.
7. Combine crumbs and cheese; sprinkle over top.
8. Bake 20 minutes.

STUFFED-PEPPER CASSEROLE

MAKES 6 SERVINGS

6 medium green peppers (1½ lb)
2 tablespoons butter or margarine, melted
½ cup chopped onion
½ cup chopped celery
1 can (1 lb, 3 oz) tomatoes, undrained
1 can (8 oz) tomato sauce
1 clove garlic, crushed
1 teaspoon dried basil leaves
1 teaspoon dried oregano leaves
2½ teaspoons salt
½ teaspoon pepper
1 egg
1 teaspoon Worcestershire sauce
1½ lb ground chuck
1½ cups cooked white rice

1. Cut off tops of peppers; remove ribs and seeds. Chop edible portion of tops; set aside. Wash peppers.
2. Place peppers in large kettle with 2 quarts salted water. Bring to boiling; cover; reduce heat, and simmer 5 minutes. Drain peppers; set aside.
3. In hot butter in medium skillet, sauté chopped green pepper, onion, and celery until tender—3 to 5 minutes.
4. Add tomatoes, tomato sauce, garlic, basil, oregano, 1½ teaspoons salt, and ¼ teaspoon pepper. Simmer, uncovered, 10 minutes.
5 Preheat oven to 350F.
6. Meanwhile, in large mixing bowl, combine egg, remaining salt and pepper, and Worcestershire. Beat with spoon to blend.
7. Add chuck, rice, and 1 cup of tomato mixture, mixing well.
8. Stuff peppers with meat mixture. Place in 3-quart casserole. Pour remaining tomato mixture over peppers.
9. Bake, uncovered, 1 hour.

We won't tell you that fritters have a long and honorable history, though they have; or that they are beloved in many countries and under many names, though they are. But we do want to say that nobody, absolutely nobody, has ever tasted better fritters than ours, and we have letters from our readers to prove it!

SAVORY BATTER

MAKES 1¾ CUPS

FOR MAIN-DISH FRITTERS

1½ cups sifted all-purpose
    flour
2¼ teaspoons baking
    powder
¾ teaspoon salt
1 egg white

2 egg yolks
¾ cup milk
1½ tablespoons salad oil
1 teaspoon grated lemon
    peel

1.   Sift flour with baking powder and salt.
2.   In small bowl, with rotary beater, beat egg white until stiff peaks form.
3.   In medium bowl, with same beater, beat egg yolks, milk, and salad oil until smooth.
4.   Gradually add flour mixture, beating until smooth.
5.   Then gently fold egg white into batter, along with grated lemon peel.

SHRIMP FRITTERS

MAKES ABOUT 36 FRITTERS,
OR 6 SERVINGS

1.   Make Savory Batter, adding ½ teaspoon curry powder.
2.   On paper towels, drain well 2 pounds cooked, cleaned, large shrimp (about 36).
3.   Meanwhile, in deep skillet or deep-fat fryer, slowly heat salad oil or shortening (at least 2 inches) to 375F on deep-frying thermometer.
4.   Dip shrimp into batter, coating evenly. Deep-fry a few at a time, turning once, 3 to 4 minutes, or until golden-brown on both sides.
5.   Drain well on paper towels.
6.   Serve hot, with soy sauce or Sour-Cream Tartar Sauce.*

Note: Small shrimp (2 pounds) may be substituted. Serve on wooden picks, as an hors d'oeuvre.

* See Sauces and Gravies Chapter.

CLAM FRITTERS

MAKES ABOUT 25 FRITTERS,
OR 5 OR 6 SERVINGS

1.   Make Savory Batter.
2.   Drain very well, on paper towels, 2 jars (6-oz size) whole clams.
3.   Meanwhile, in deep skillet or deep-fat fryer, slowly heat salad oil or shortening (at least 2 inches) to 375F on deep-frying thermometer.

(Clam Fritters continued)

4. Dip clams into batter, coating evenly. Deep-fry a few at a time, turning once, 4 to 5 minutes, or until golden-brown on both sides.

5. Drain well on paper towels.

6. Serve hot with lemon wedges and Sour-Cream Tartar Sauce.*

* See Sauces and Gravies Chapter.

CORN FRITTERS

MAKES ABOUT 15 FRITTERS,
OR 5 SERVINGS

1. Make Savory Batter, omitting lemon peel. Drain very well 1 can (12 oz) whole-kernel corn. Stir into batter until well combined.

2. Meanwhile, in deep skillet or deep-fat fryer, slowly heat salad oil or shortening (at least 2 inches) to 375F on deep-frying thermometer.

3. Into hot fat, drop corn mixture by large spoonfuls (about ¼ cup), a few at a time.

4. Deep-fry fritters, turning once, about 5 minutes, or until golden-brown on both sides.

5. Drain well on paper towels. Serve hot, with hot maple syrup and ham slices.

Crepes and Waffles

SUNDAY-MORNING CREPES

MAKES 12 CREPES

1½ cups sifted all-purpose
    flour
2 tablespoons sugar
1 teaspoon baking powder
½ teaspoon salt

2 eggs, beaten
2 cups milk
2 tablespoons butter or
    margarine

1. Sift flour with sugar, baking powder, and salt into medium bowl.

2. Combine eggs and milk; beat, with rotary beater, until well mixed. Pour into dry ingredients; beat until smooth.

3. Preheat oven to 300F.

4. For each pancake, melt ½ teaspoon butter in 8-inch skillet.

5. Pour in ¼ cup batter, rotating pan quickly to spread batter completely over bottom of pan.

6. Cook, over high heat, 1 minute; turn; cook 1 minute longer. Fold into quarters. Keep hot in oven while cooking remaining pancakes.

SUNDAY-BRUNCH CREPES

MAKES 6 SERVINGS

Sunday-Morning Crepes,
  see page 223
2 cans (5-oz size) boned
  chicken, drained; or
  1⅓ cups cooked
  chicken
2 tablespoons butter or
  margarine
2 tablespoons finely
  chopped onion
¼ cup finely chopped
  green pepper
1 tablespoon chopped
  pimiento

1 cup dairy sour cream
1 can (10½ oz) cream-of-
  chicken soup,
  undiluted
2 hard-cooked eggs,
  chopped
¼ teaspoon salt
Dash pepper
¼ teaspoon dried rosemary
  leaves
¼ cup milk
½ cup grated Parmesan
  cheese

1. Prepare crepes, but do not fold them; keep warm in oven.

2. Chop chicken fine; set aside in medium bowl.

3. Heat butter in small skillet. In it, sauté onion and green pepper about 5 minutes.

4. Add to chicken, along with pimiento, sour cream, 2 tablespoons soup, eggs, salt, pepper, and ⅛ teaspoon rosemary; mix well.

5. In saucepan, blend rest of soup and rosemary and the milk; heat.

6. Meanwhile, in center of each crepe, place about 2½ tablespoons chicken mixture. Fold two opposite sides over filling; roll up carefully.

7. Arrange crepes, seam side down, on large, ovenproof platter. Pour sauce over all. Sprinkle with cheese; run under broiler, to brown top.

CORNMEAL WAFFLES WITH CHILI

MAKES 5 LARGE WAFFLES

1 pkg (12 oz) corn-muffin
  mix
1 egg

1⅔ cups milk
¼ cup salad oil

1. Preheat waffle iron as manufacturer directs.

2. Pour corn-muffin mix into a bowl. Add egg, milk, and oil.

3. Beat, with rotary beater, until smooth.

4. Bake in preheated, oiled waffle iron until golden-brown. Serve topped with Chili con Carne.

CHILI CON CARNE

MAKES 5 SERVINGS

2 tablespoons butter or
  margarine
2 large onions, finely
  chopped
1 clove garlic, finely
  chopped
1 lb ground beef

2 teaspoons chili powder
1 teaspoon salt
½ teaspoon cumin seed
  (optional)
⅛ teaspoon pepper
1 can (8 oz) tomato sauce

1. In hot butter in large skillet with tight-fitting cover, sauté onion and garlic until tender —about 5 minutes.

2. Add beef; cook, stirring, until meat loses it red color.

3. Add remaining ingredients and ¼ cup water. Bring to boiling; reduce heat, and simmer, covered, 30 minutes.

If you think a broiler is simply for doing a short-order job on a lamb chop or a steak, here is a surprise for you: whole meals that you can slip under the heat and take right to the table a few minutes later. The secret: We use things that require little cooking—some fresh, some canned, some frozen.

CRANBERRY-GLAZED HAM LOAVES, GOLDEN POTATO PUFFS, AND LYONNAISE GREEN BEANS

MAKES 4 SERVINGS

Cranberry-Glazed Ham
    Loaves:
1 lb fully cooked ground
    ham
1 egg, beaten
3 tablespoons packaged dry
    bread crumbs
¼ cup milk
1 can (7 oz) jellied
    cranberry sauce
2 tablespoons orange juice
2 unpeeled orange slices,
    quartered
¼ cup light-brown sugar,
    firmly packed
2 teaspoons lemon juice

Golden Potato Puffs:
½ cup milk
½ teaspoon salt

1 packet (4 servings) instant
    mashed potatoes
⅛ teaspoon pepper
¼ cup grated process
    American cheese
1 egg
2 tablespoons cornflake
    crumbs
Paprika

Lyonnaise Green Beans:
1 can (1 lb) green beans
1 can (8 oz) small white
    onions
1 tablespoon butter or
    margarine

Salad oil

1. Make Cranberry-Glazed Ham Loaves: In medium bowl, combine ham, egg, 1 tablespoon crumbs, and milk; mix lightly. Shape the mixture into 4 loaves, each about 4 by 2½ by 1 inch.

2. Sprinkle rest of crumbs on waxed paper. Roll ham loaves in crumbs to coat evenly; refrigerate.

3. In small saucepan, break up cranberry sauce with spoon. Add orange juice, orange pieces, sugar, and lemon juice; mix well. Cook, stirring, over medium heat, until sugar is dissolved and mixture is slightly thickened—about 10 minutes.

4. Make Golden Potato Puffs: In 2-quart saucepan, bring 1¼ cups water, milk, and salt just to boiling. Add potatoes; beat well with fork. Beat in pepper, American cheese, and egg.

5. Combine cornflake crumbs and paprika on waxed paper. Drop potato mixture, in 4 mounds, onto crumb mixture; roll to coat well, forming puffs about 3 inches in diameter. Refrigerate puffs.

6. Make Lyonnaise Green Beans: Drain beans and onions, reserving ½ cup liquid from beans. Combine vegetables, reserved liquid, and butter in left side of broiler drip pan.

7. Brush broiler rack lightly with salad oil. Arrange ham loaves on right side of rack; set rack in place on drip pan.

8. Broil, 4 inches from heat, for 5 minutes, or until golden-brown.

9. Turn loaves; spoon cranberry glaze over each.

10. Place potato puffs on broiler rack with the ham loaves. Broil 5 minutes, or until cranberry glaze is bubbly and the potatoes are golden.

COMPANY PLANKED DINNER

MAKES 4 SERVINGS

Short Ribs of Beef:
2½ lb short ribs of beef
1 teaspoon salt
¾ teaspoon pepper
¼ teaspoon dried thyme
 leaves
2 bay leaves

Spicy Barbecue Sauce:
8 large mushrooms
6 tablespoons lemon juice
½ cup cider vinegar
1 tablespoon light brown
 sugar
¼ cup Worcestershire
 sauce
½ cup catsup
¼ cup chili sauce
½ teaspoon dry mustard

Herbed Tomato Halves:
2 medium tomatoes
½ cup packaged dry bread
 crumbs
2 tablespoons butter or
 margarine, melted

2 teaspoons dried oregano
 leaves
2 teaspoons salt
½ teaspoon pepper
1 tablespoon chopped
 parsley

Potato Ribbons:
2 packets (4-serving size)
 instant mashed
 potatoes
2 teaspoons salt
¼ teaspoon pepper
½ teaspoon nutmeg
2 tablespoons butter
 or margarine

Seasoned Corn:
2 cans (12-oz size) whole-
 kernel corn, drained
½ teaspoon seasoned salt
¼ teaspoon pepper

Watercress

1. Prepare Short Ribs of Beef: Wipe beef with damp paper towels. Place in large saucepan with 2 cups water and remaining beef ingredients.
2. Bring to boiling. Reduce heat; simmer, covered, 30 to 45 minutes, or until beef is tender.
3. Drain; let cool. Trim fat and bone from beef; cut beef into cubes. Thread cubes on 4 skewers (5 or 6 cubes each).
4. Meanwhile, prepare Barbecue Sauce: Wash mushrooms; remove stems. Toss caps with 5 tablespoons lemon juice until well coated. Make grooves in each cap to resemble a flower; set aside.
5. Chop stems finely.
6. In small saucepan, combine stems with remaining lemon juice and rest of ingredients.
7. Bring to boiling, stirring. Reduce heat; simmer, uncovered, about 45 minutes, or until sauce is thick enough to coat a spoon.
8. Prepare Herbed Tomato Halves: Cut tomatoes in half, crosswise; make small crisscross cuts in center of each half.
9. In small bowl, combine remaining ingredients; toss lightly with fork.
10. Top each tomato half with about 2 tablespoons crumb mixture.
11. Prepare Potato Ribbons: Prepare potatoes as package label directs, using amount of liquid specified on package, the salt, pepper, nutmeg, and butter. Fill a pastry bag with a No. 6 tip.
12. Make Seasoned Corn: Toss corn with salt and pepper, mixing well.
13. To assemble the dinners: Cover top of each of four hardwood planks (or one large one) with foil.
14. Arrange a skewer of beef cubes, 2 mushroom caps, and a tomato half on each plank; brush beef cubes well with Barbecue Sauce.
15. Broil, 6 inches from heat, 5 minutes, turning beef once and brushing with Sauce.
16. Remove beef skewers, mushrooms, and tomato halves; set aside; keep warm. Discard foil.
17. Make a border around each plank by forcing Potato Ribbons through decorating tip in overlapping folds.
18. Arrange beef cubes, mushroom caps, tomato halves, and Seasoned Corn on planks. Brush beef cubes with remaining Sauce.
19. Broil 5 minutes, or until mushrooms are tender and potatoes golden. Add watercress.

MIXED GRILL OF LAMB PATTIES AND SAUSAGE, PEACH HALVES WITH CHUTNEY, AND ZUCCHINI PARMESAN

Lamb Patties and Sausage:
1 lb lean lamb, ground
¼ cup cooked white rice
1 teaspoon salt
¼ teaspoon pepper
1 egg
2 tablespoons chopped celery
1 tablespoon dried mint flakes
2 tablespoons packaged dry bread crumbs
4 brown-and-serve sausages
Peach Halves with Chutney:
4 canned cling-peach halves, drained

2 tablespoons butter or margarine, melted
2 tablespoons chopped chutney

Salad oil

Zucchini Parmesan:
4 medium zucchini
Salt
3 tablespoons butter or margarine, melted
2 tablespoons lemon juice
3 tablespoons grated Parmesan cheese

1. Prepare Lamb Patties and Sausage: In medium bowl, gently toss lamb with rice, salt, pepper, egg, celery, and mint flakes. Lightly shape into four 4-by-2½-by-1-inch patties.

2. Coat patties evenly with crumbs.

3. Lightly press a sausage into each patty, so it is slightly embedded.

4. Make Peach Halves with Chutney: Brush peaches with butter. Fill hollow of each with ½ tablespoon chutney.

5. Brush broiler rack lightly with salad oil.

6. Arrange patties on rack, sausage side down. Broil, 4 inches from heat, for 8 to 10 minutes, or until nicely browned; turn. Place peaches on rack with patties; broil 5 minutes.

7. Meanwhile, make Zucchini Parmesan: Scrub zucchini; trim off ends. Cut each in half lengthwise; then halve crosswise. Cook in 1 inch boiling salted water, covered, 5 minutes, or until almost tender; drain.

8. Arrange zucchini, skin side down, on broiler rack with peaches and patties. Brush cut sides with butter; then sprinkle with lemon juice, salt, and cheese.

9. Broil all about 5 minutes, or until nicely browned.

HERB-BROILED CALVES' LIVER, BACON, AND ONIONS, AND SAVORY LIMA BEANS

Liver, Bacon, and Onions:
1 lb calves' liver, ½ inch thick
2 medium Spanish onions, peeled
Seasoned salt
Salad oil
3 tablespoons butter or margarine, melted
8 bacon slices, halved
2 tablespoons packaged dry bread crumbs
½ teaspoon dried thyme leaves

¼ teaspoon dried rosemary leaves

Savory Lima Beans:
1 can (1 lb) lima beans, drained
2 tablespoons chopped onion
¼ teaspoon salt
2 tablespoons catsup
2 tablespoons light-brown sugar
1 tablespoon butter or margarine, melted

1. Prepare Liver, Bacon, and Onions: Wash liver in cold water; drain. Cut into 4 pieces.

2. Cut each onion into 4 slices, each about ½ inch thick. Sprinkle with seasoned salt.

3. Lightly brush broiler rack with salad oil.

4. Brush liver and onions with half the melted butter. Arrange on broiler rack with bacon.

5. Combine bread crumbs, thyme, and rosemary leaves; mix well. Set aside.

6. Make Savory Lima Beans: Gently toss all ingredients in small, shallow pan. Place pan in broiler drip pan.

7. Set broiler rack in place on drip pan, so the liver is not directly over the beans.

8. Broil, 4 inches from heat, for 5 minutes; turn liver, bacon, and onions.

9. Brush liver and onions with rest of melted butter (1½ tablespoons). Sprinkle liver with crumb mixture; broil 5 minutes longer.

227

12 CEREALS

Cereals, ranging from breakfast foods to dinner pastas, represent one of the most economical and nutritious groups of food available. Cereal has a breakfast connotation for most people, but its family members are numerous and varied.

Scattered throughout this book are many recipes predominately of cereal that fall into other categories—desserts, confections, and cookies.

All cereal products should be stored, tightly covered, in a cool, dry place. Freshly ground grain cereals, sold regionally, are not processed, and they should be refrigerated.

Breakfast Cereals

Breakfast cereals are favorites for busy mornings. Ready-to-eat cereals, enriched with vitamins and minerals, combine with milk and a variety of fruits to form an endless succession of morning menus.

Cooked breakfast cereals have a stick-to-the-ribs quality just right for cold weather and for people with a heavy day's work. Here are some breakfast surprises to help overcome morning monotony.

HOT CEREAL WITH APRICOTS

MAKES 4 SERVINGS

3 cups boiling water
½ teaspoon salt
½ cup quick-cooking wheat
    cereal
⅔ cup coarsely chopped
    dried apricots
Brown sugar
Light cream

1. In boiling salted water, cook cereal as package label directs.
2. When mixture begins to thicken, stir in apricots; cook 5 minutes longer over low heat.
3. Serve hot, with brown sugar and cream.

BREAKFAST BOWL

1½ cups cornflakes
2 tablespoons butter or
    margarine, melted
Cinnamon sugar*
1½ cups cold milk
2 eggs

1½ teaspoons vanilla
    extract
1 cup whole strawberries,
    sliced; or ⅔ cup fresh
    blueberries

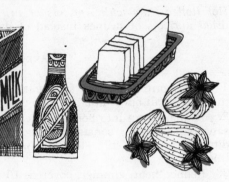

1. Preheat oven to 400F.
2. Spread cornflakes on cookie sheet; drizzle butter over surface; sprinkle generously with cinnamon sugar.
3. Bake until crisp—about 7 minutes.
4. Meanwhile, in small bowl, beat milk, eggs, and vanilla.
5. Divide hot cornflakes into 2 cereal bowls; top with strawberries. Serve with egg-milk mixture poured over.

* Combine 2 tablespoons sugar with ½ teaspoon cinnamon.

FRUIT-CEREAL SLICES

1 cup dates and raisins, or
    dried apricots

3 cups hot cooked cereal
    (cream of rice or
    cornmeal mush)
Light cream

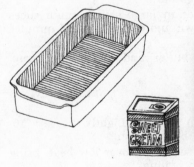

1. Soak fruit in 1 cup water, or enough to cover fruit, 3 to 4 hours. Drain. Cut, with scissors, into small pieces.
2. Grease well a 9-by-5-by-3-inch loaf pan.
3. Spread half of cereal in an even layer over bottom of loaf pan.
4. Cover with fruit; top with remaining cereal. Cover with saran.
5. Refrigerate overnight.
6. Next morning, preheat oven to 400F.
7. Heat cereal in pan 25 to 30 minutes, or until heated through.
8. Serve in thick slices, with light cream.

HOT CEREAL WITH PINEAPPLE

1 can (1 lb, 4½ oz)
    pineapple chunks

Dash salt
1 cup quick-cooking oats

1. Drain pineapple; measure liquid. Add water to make 1½ cups.
2. In medium saucepan, bring pineapple liquid and salt to boiling.
3. Add oats, and cook as package label directs.
4. Serve hot, topped with cold pineapple chunks. No sugar or milk needed.

HOT ROLLED OATS WITH DATES

MAKES 4 TO 6 SERVINGS

4 cups boiling water
1 teaspoon salt
2 cups quick-cooking oats

1 cup pitted chopped dates
Sugar
Milk

1. In boiling salted water in medium saucepan, cook oats as package label directs.
2. Stir in dates. Remove from heat; cover, and let stand 2 or 3 minutes.
3. Serve hot, with sugar and milk.

Hot Rolled Oats with Apricots or Prunes: Use dried apricots or prunes instead of dates.

SAUTÉED CORNMEAL SLICES

MAKES 6 SERVINGS

1 cup yellow cornmeal
1 teaspoon salt
½ teaspoon cinnamon
¼ teaspoon mace
3 cups boiling water

¼ cup unsifted all-purpose
   flour
3 tablespoons butter or
   margarine

1. Mix cornmeal with salt, cinnamon, and mace in small bowl. Stir in 1 cup cold water.
2. Pour mixture into boiling water in medium saucepan, stirring constantly. Cook, over medium heat and still stirring, until mixture thickens.
3. Reduce heat; simmer, covered, 10 minutes, stirring occasionally.
4. Pour into ungreased 9-by-5-by-3-inch loaf pan; cool.
5. Refrigerate until thoroughly chilled—about 4 hours, or overnight.
6. To serve, remove from pan. Cut into 12 slices; coat with flour.
7. In hot butter in large skillet, sauté slices until golden-brown and crisp—about 4 minutes on each side.
8. Serve with butter and hot maple syrup.

WHEAT-CEREAL BREAKFAST PUDDING

MAKES 6 SERVINGS

3¾ cups milk
Dash salt
½ cup quick-cooking wheat
   cereal

½ cup honey
½ cup raisins
2 eggs, separated

1. Preheat oven to 375F. Lightly grease a 10-by-6-by-1½-inch baking dish.
2. In medium saucepan, over low heat, bring milk and salt to boiling.
3. Slowly sprinkle in cereal, stirring. Cook, stirring constantly, until thickened—about 10 minutes. Remove from heat.
4. Stir in ¼ cup honey and the raisins.
5. In small bowl and using rotary beater, beat egg whites until stiff peaks form. Beat egg yolks in another small bowl.
6. Stir egg yolks into cereal; then fold in egg whites.
7. Pour into baking dish; spread remaining honey over surface.
8. Bake 25 minutes. Serve hot, cut in squares.

Rice

One of the oldest foods known to man, rice goes back to the centuries before recorded history. Thrifty housewives have known for ages that rice is ideal as an extender of casseroles and main dishes. But even gourmet cooks would favor rice at any price because it adapts itself so gracefully to any main dish made with a sauce.

RICE DO'S AND DON'TS

DO make sure water is boiling briskly before adding rice.

DO keep liquid above the boiling point while the rice is cooking; it prevents sogginess.

DO keep rice hot and fluffy in a covered dish in a very low oven, or in a sieve or colander over hot water (covered, of course), until you're ready to serve.

DON'T add cold liquid to boiling rice. If adding more liquid, it should be boiling.

DON'T stir rice with a spoon, or you'll mash the grains and make it gummy. Lift rice gently with a fork.

DON'T peek when boiling rice is in a tightly covered pot. It would let out the steam and lower the temperature.

OLD-FASHIONED FLUFFY WHITE RICE

MAKES 4 CUPS

1 tablespoon salt *1 cup raw long-grain white rice*

1. In large saucepan over high heat, bring to boiling 2 quarts cold water and the salt.
2. Slowly add rice; boil, uncovered, about 20 minutes, or until rice is tender.
3. Drain well. Fluff up with fork.

FLUFFY WHITE RICE

MAKES 4½ CUPS

1½ cups raw regular white rice *1½ tablespoons butter or margarine*
1½ teaspoons salt

1. In medium saucepan, combine 3 cups cold water with the rice, salt, and butter.
2. Bring to boiling, uncovered.
3. Reduce heat; simmer, covered, 12 to 14 minutes, or until rice is tender and water is absorbed.
4. Fluff up with fork.

OVEN-STEAMED RICE

OK 1/20/72

1½ cups raw regular white rice
1½ teaspoons salt
Dash pepper

2 tablespoons butter or margarine
3½ cups boiling water

1. Preheat oven to 350F.
2. In a 1½-quart, ungreased casserole with tight-fitting lid, combine rice, salt, and pepper. Dot top with butter.
3. Pour boiling water over rice, and stir until butter is melted.
4. Cover; bake 45 minutes (do not peek; do not stir). To serve, fluff up lightly with fork.

WHITE RICE WITH ONIONS

2 cups raw regular white rice
3 tablespoons butter or margarine

¾ cup thinly sliced green onions and tops

1. Cook rice as package label directs; drain if necessary.
2. Meanwhile, in hot butter in small skillet, sauté onions until tender—about 5 minutes.
3. Add to rice; toss lightly with fork until well mixed.

WHITE RICE WITH RAISINS

2 cups raw regular white rice
1 cup light or dark raisins

3 tablespoons butter or margarine

1. Cook rice as package label directs, drain if necessary.
2. Meanwhile, cover raisins with boiling water; let stand 10 minutes; drain.
3. With fork, stir raisins into drained cooked rice along with butter.

CURRIED RICE

1 tablespoon curry powder
1 teaspoon salt
2 tablespoons butter or margarine

2⅔ cups packaged precooked rice

1. In medium saucepan, combine curry powder, salt, and butter with 2⅔ cups water. Bring to boiling.
2. Stir in rice; cover, and remove from heat.
3. Let stand 5 minutes. Before serving, fluff up with fork.

RICE PILAF

½ cup butter or margarine
1 large onion, thinly sliced
1 cup sliced fresh
    mushrooms; or 1 can
    (6 oz) sliced
    mushrooms, drained

¼ cup finely chopped
    green pepper
1 cup raw regular white rice
Dash dried thyme leaves
2 cups canned chicken
    broth or chicken
    bouillon

1. Preheat oven to 350F.
2. In ¼ cup hot butter in skillet, cook onion over medium heat until golden.
3. Add mushrooms and green pepper; cook until tender. Remove vegetables, and set aside.
4. In same skillet, heat remaining butter. Add rice, and brown slightly, stirring, over low heat.
5. Then stir in vegetables and thyme.
6. Meanwhile, heat chicken broth to boiling point. Stir into rice-vegetable mixture; then turn into 1-quart casserole.
7. Cover, and bake 30 to 40 minutes, or until liquid is absorbed and rice is tender.

RICE-PRUNE PILAF

1 cup dried prunes (about
    16)
½ teaspoon salt
½ teaspoon dried thyme
    leaves

1 cup raw long-grain white
    rice
2 cans (10½-oz size)
    condensed onion
    soup, undiluted

1. Preheat oven to 350F.
2. Pit prunes. With scissors, cut into small pieces.
3. Combine all ingredients in 2-quart casserole; stir to combine well.
4. Bake, covered, about 1 hour, fluffing up with fork several times. Serve with pork, veal, ham, or poultry.

RICE-AND-SPINACH PILAF

1 can (13¾ oz) chicken
    broth
1½ teaspoons instant
    minced onion
2 chicken-bouillon cubes

3 tablespoons butter or
    margarine
3 cups packaged precooked
    rice
1¼ cups chopped fresh
    spinach

1. In medium saucepan, combine chicken broth with onion, bouillon cubes, butter, and 1¼ cups water. Bring to boiling.
2. Add rice. Cover, and remove from heat. Let stand 5 minutes.
3. Fluff up rice with fork. Add spinach; toss lightly to combine.

WILD RICE

½ cup wild rice

½ teaspoon salt

1. Wash rice several times; drain.
2. In medium saucepan, combine 3 cups cold water, salt, and rice; bring to boiling, covered. Boil, uncovered, 50 minutes, or until rice is tender.
3. Drain rice.
4. Return to saucepan; heat very slowly 10 to 15 minutes.

CASEROLE OF WILD RICE

1 tablespoon butter or
    margarine, melted
½ cup chopped celery
3 tablespoons finely
    chopped onion
4 chicken-bouillon cubes,
    dissolved in 1 qt
    boiling water

1 cup wild rice, washed
1 cup long-grain white rice
3 tablespoons soy sauce
½ teaspoon salt
1 tablespoon chopped
    parsley

1. Preheat oven to 350F.
2. In hot butter in small skillet, sauté celery and onion until tender—about 5 minutes.
3. Combine with remaining ingredients, except parsley, in 2-quart covered casserole.
4. Bake, covered, 40 minutes.
5. Remove cover; bake 15 minutes.
6. Garnish with parsley.

Macaroni, Spaghetti and Noodles

Whether it comes in the form of bows, shells, alphabets, numbers, spirals, stars, fluted ribbons, ridged tubes, or toy hats, pasta is a general term for macaroni products (macaroni, spaghetti and noodles). These are made of hard wheat flour and water. (Exception: Noodles, which have eggs, and occasionally spinach, added to the dough.)

BASIC DIRECTIONS FOR COOKING MACARONI, SPAGHETTI, NOODLES

1 tablespoon salt
3 qt boiling water

1 pkg (7 or 8 oz)
    macaroni, spaghetti,
    or noodles (3 cups)

1. In large kettle, bring salted water to a rapid boil. Add macaroni, breaking long pieces into short ones. You may leave long spaghetti whole; place one end in boiling water, and gradually coil in rest as it softens.
2. Bring back to boiling. Cook, uncovered, stirring occasionally with long fork to prevent sticking, just until tender—about 7 to 10 minutes. Do not overcook.
3. Drain in colander or sieve. Do not rinse.

Poppy-Seed Noodles: Cook 8-oz pkg noodles as directed above. Toss drained, hot noodles with ¼ cup melted butter and 1 tablespoon poppy seed.

HOMEMADE NOODLES

MAKES ABOUT 16 OUNCES

3 cups sifted all-purpose
    flour
1 teaspoon salt

4 egg yolks
7 to 8 tablespoons cold
    water

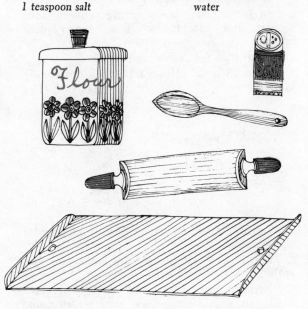

1. Sift flour with salt into medium bowl.
2. Make a well in center. Add egg yolks and 4 tablespoons cold water; beat vigorously with wooden spoon until well combined.
3. Gradually add 3 more tablespoons water, mixing well with hands. Dough will be stiff; but if it seems too stiff to knead, gradually add more water.
4. On lightly floured surface, knead dough until smooth and elastic—about 5 minutes Cover with bowl; let rest 30 minutes.
5. Divide dough into 4 parts. Keep covered with bowl until ready to roll out.
6. Roll each part into a 16-by-14-inch rectangle. Dough will be about 1/8 inch thick. Rectangle need not be perfect in shape. Work quickly, as dough will dry out.
7. Starting with long side, roll loosely, as for jelly roll. With thin, sharp knife, cut roll into 1/8-inch-wide strips for fine noodles, 1/3-inch-wide strips for broad noodles. Arrange on ungreased cookie sheets. Let dry overnight before cooking.

Note: Dried noodles can be stored in a covered glass jar in a cool place.

BAKED MACARONI AND CHEESE

MAKES 4 TO 6 SERVINGS

1 pkg (8 oz) elbow macaroni
2 cups grated sharp
    Cheddar cheese
    (1/2 lb)
1/4 cup butter or margarine

1/4 cup unsifted all-purpose
    flour
2 cups milk
1 teaspoon salt
1/8 teaspoon pepper

1. Preheat oven to 375F.
2. Cook macaroni as package label directs; drain.
3. In 1½-quart shallow baking dish, alternate macaroni (in 2 layers) with 1½ cups cheese (in 2 layers); set aside.
4. Meanwhile, prepare sauce: Melt butter in medium saucepan; remove from heat. Blend in flour; gradually stir in milk, then seasonings. Bring to boiling, stirring; boil 1 minute.
5. Pour sauce over macaroni and cheese in casserole. Top with remaining cheese.
6. Bake 15 to 20 minutes, or until cheese is melted and browned.

BAKED NOODLES WITH CHEESE

MAKES 4 TO 6 SERVINGS

1 pkg (8 oz) noodles
1 cup cottage cheese
1½ cups dairy sour cream

1 teaspoon Worcestershire
    sauce
1 teaspoon salt
⅛ teaspoon pepper

1. Preheat oven to 350F.
2. Cook noodles as package label directs; drain.
3. In large bowl, blend cottage cheese, sour cream, and seasonings. Toss gently with noodles.
4. Turn into 2-qt casserole; cover.
5. Bake 15 to 20 minutes, or until thoroughly hot.

SPAGHETTI WITH RED CLAM SAUCE

MAKES 1 QUART—
ENOUGH FOR 6 SERVINGS

2 cans (7½-oz size) minced
    clams
¼ cup olive oil
2 cloves garlic, crushed
2 tablespoons chopped
    parsley
¾ teaspoon dried oregano
    leaves

¼ teaspoon dried basil
    leaves
½ teaspoon salt
¼ teaspoon pepper
1 can (1 lb, 3 oz) tomatoes,
    undrained
1 can (8 oz) tomato sauce
1 pkg (8 oz) spaghetti,
    cooked and drained

1. Drain clams, reserving 1 cup liquid; set clams aside.
2. Slowly heat oil in medium saucepan. Add garlic; cook until golden.
3. Remove from heat. Add parsley, oregano, basil, salt, pepper, tomatoes, tomato sauce, and reserved clam liquid; mix well.
4. Simmer, uncovered, 45 minutes, stirring occasionally.
5. Add clams; reheat. Serve hot over spaghetti.

SPAGHETTI WITH WHITE CLAM SAUCE

MAKES 2 CUPS—ENOUGH FOR
3 OR 4 SERVINGS

2 jars (7½-oz size) minced
    clams
⅓ cup olive or salad oil
¼ cup butter or margarine
3 large cloves garlic, finely
    chopped

2 tablespoons finely
    chopped parsley
1½ teaspoons salt
1 pkg (8 oz) spaghetti,
    cooked and drained

1. Drain clams, reserving ¾ cup liquid; set aside.
2. Slowly heat olive oil and butter in medium skillet. Add garlic; sauté until golden—about 5 minutes.
3. Remove from heat. Stir in reserved clam liquid, parsley, and salt; bring to boiling. Reduce heat; simmer, uncovered, 10 minutes.
4. Add clams; simmer 3 minutes, or until heated through.
5. Serve hot over spaghetti.

Specialty Cereals

There are other cereals, less known in this country, whose interesting flavors deserve to be investigated. Such a one is bulgur, a nutty-tasting grain that, since Biblical days, has been widely used in the Middle East. Try it with your next leg of lamb.

BARLEY PILAF

MAKES 8 SERVINGS

½ cup butter or margarine
½ lb mushrooms, thinly sliced
½ cup coarsely chopped onion
1⅓ cups pearl barley

6 chicken-bouillon cubes, dissolved in 5 cups boiling water; or 5 cups canned chicken broth

1. Preheat oven to 350F.
2. In 2 tablespoons hot butter in medium skillet, sauté mushrooms until tender—4 to 5 minutes. Lift out mushrooms with slotted spoon, and set aside.
3. Heat remaining butter in same skillet. Add onion; sauté until golden—about 5 minutes.
4. Add barley; cook over low heat, stirring frequently, until barley is golden-brown—about 5 minutes.
5. Remove from heat. Stir in mushrooms and 2 cups bouillon.
6. Turn into 2-quart casserole; bake, covered, 30 minutes.
7. Stir in 2 more cups bouillon; bake, covered, 30 minutes, or until barley is tender.
8. Finally, stir in remaining cup bouillon; bake 20 minutes. Serve with veal or chicken.

BULGUR

MAKES 6 SERVINGS

2 tablespoons butter or margarine
1 cup chopped onion
1 teaspoon salt
1 cup bulgur
1 can (10½ oz) beef bouillon, undiluted

1 teaspoon Worcestershire sauce
1 bay leaf
⅛ teaspoon black pepper
Dash cayenne
¼ teaspoon dry mustard
3 green peppers, cut in strips (2½ cups)

1. Heat butter in heavy Dutch oven. In it, sauté onion until golden—3 to 5 minutes.
2. Add salt, bulgur, and 2 cups water; bring to boiling.
3. Reduce heat; cover, and simmer 20 minutes.
4. Add remaining ingredients; cook 10 minutes. If mixture seems too dry, add a little hot water during cooking. Serve hot.

FARINA DUMPLINGS

MAKES 20

⅓ cup sifted all-purpose
    flour
1 teaspoon baking powder
½ teaspoon salt
Dash pepper

⅔ cup farina
1 egg, beaten
¼ cup milk
1 tablespoon butter or
    margarine, melted

1.   Into medium bowl, sift flour with baking powder, salt, and pepper. Add farina, mixing well.

2.   Combine egg with milk and butter. Add to flour mixture, stirring until smooth.

3.   Meanwhile, in 3-quart saucepan, bring 6 cups lightly salted water to boiling.

4.   Drop farina mixture, by slightly rounded teaspoonfuls, into boiling water.

5.   Cover tightly; reduce heat; simmer 15 minutes.

6.   Drain dumplings well. Serve hot, with Hungarian goulash or stew.

Note: Or substitute 4 cans (14-oz size) clear chicken broth, or 3 cans (10½-oz size) condensed beef bouillon, diluted with 2 cups water, for the lightly salted boiling water. Serve dumplings with broth. Makes 6 servings.

Farina Dumplings Au Gratin: Melt ½ cup butter or margarine in large skillet. Stir in ⅔ cup packaged cornflake crumbs. Add drained dumplings; cook, turning occasionally, until dumplings are well coated with crumb mixture. Makes 20.

GOLDEN NOODLE NESTS

MAKES 10

9 egg whites
½ teaspoon cream of tartar
1 teaspoon salt

3 cans (3-oz size) Chinese
    noodles

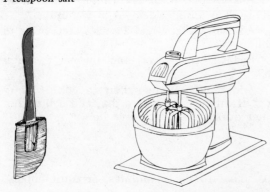

1.   Preheat oven to 425F. Grease 2 cookie sheets well.

2.   In large bowl of electric mixer, at high speed, beat egg whites with cream of tartar and salt just until soft peaks form when beater is slowly raised.

3.   With rubber scraper, gently fold noodles into egg-white mixture just until combined.

4.   For each nest, drop about ⅔ cup noodle mixture onto prepared cookie sheet. With back of spoon, shape into a nest 3 inches in diameter.

5.   Bake 10 to 12 minutes, or until golden-brown and crisp. Serve warm.

POLENTA SQUARES

1 teaspoon salt
1½ cups yellow cornmeal
2 eggs, beaten
1 cup grated sharp Cheddar
    cheese (¼ lb)

2 tablespoons butter or
    margarine, melted
⅓ cup grated Parmesan
    cheese

1. In 3½-quart heavy saucepan, bring 5 cups cold water and the salt to boiling. Add cornmeal very slowly, stirring constantly with long wooden spoon.

2. Reduce heat; simmer, uncovered and stirring occasionally, until cornmeal is very thick and leaves side of pan. Continue cooking, covered, 10 minutes.

3. Stir in eggs and Cheddar cheese, mixing until well combined.

4. Pour into lightly greased 9-by-9-by-1¾-inch baking dish; refrigerate until stiff enough to cut—this will take about 3 hours.

5. Just before serving, cut into 16 squares. Arrange in shallow baking pan or jelly-roll pan. Sprinkle with butter, then with Parmesan cheese.

6. Run under broiler until Polenta is heated through and top is golden-brown.

Note: Polenta may be made the day before and refrigerated overnight. Just before serving, proceed as directed above.

GNOCCHI WITH TOMATO

2½ cups milk
1 cup cream of wheat or
    white cornmeal
3 tablespoons butter or
    margarine

1 egg yolk
¼ teaspoon salt
1 can (8 oz) tomato sauce
½ cup grated Parmesan
    cheese

1. Lightly grease a 10-by-6-by-1½-inch baking dish.

2. In medium saucepan, heat milk just until film forms on surface; do not boil.

3. Over low heat, sprinkle in cream of wheat; cook, stirring, until mixture is thickened and heavy—about 5 minutes.

4. Remove from heat. With wooden spoon, beat in 1 tablespoon butter, egg yolk, and salt until mixture is smooth and well combined.

5. Spread evenly in prepared dish.

6. Refrigerate until firm—2 to 3 hours.

7. Meanwhile, preheat oven to 425F.

8. With sharp knife, cut gnocchi into 2-inch squares.

9. Arrange, overlapping, in 9-inch pie plate. Dot with remaining butter; spoon tomato sauce over top; sprinkle with cheese.

10. Bake 10 to 15 minutes, or until bubbly.

13

Desserts and Dessert Sauces

T he crowning touch to any meal, the most important course of all, according to man and boy, is the dessert. No matter how good everything else that precedes it, everybody looks forward to what the conclusion will be. Our desserts range from the divinely simple to the simply divine. In other words, from the basic custard to a towering, spectacular creation.

ALMOND CHIFFON ROLL

MAKES 8 SERVINGS

½ cup egg whites (3 or 4)
1 cup plus 2 tablespoons
    sifted cake flour
¾ cup granulated sugar
1½ teaspoons baking
    powder
½ teaspoon salt
¼ cup salad oil
2 egg yolks

2 teaspoons almond extract
½ teaspoon vanilla extract
¼ teaspoon cream of tartar
½ cup canned roasted
    diced almonds
Confectioners' sugar
1 quart peach ice cream,
    softened

1. In large bowl of electric mixer, let egg whites warm to room temperature—1 hour.

2. Preheat oven to 350F. Line bottom of ungreased 15½-by-10½-by-1-inch jelly-roll pan with waxed paper.

3. Sift flour with granulated sugar, baking powder, and salt into another large bowl.

4. Make a well in center. Add, in order, oil, egg yolks, ⅓ cup water, almond and vanilla extracts. Beat with spoon until smooth.

5. In large bowl of electric mixer, at high speed, beat egg whites with cream of tartar until stiff peaks form when beater is raised.

6. With wire whisk or rubber scraper, using an under-and-over motion, gently fold egg-yolk mixture, along with almonds, into egg whites just until combined.

(Almond Chiffon Roll continued)

7. Spread batter evenly in pan; then bake 20 minutes, or until surface springs back when gently pressed with fingertip.

8. Let cake cool in pan 5 minutes. With sharp knife, cut edges of cake from sides of pan.

9. Turn out cake and roll following Jelly-Roll instructions.

10. Unroll cake, and remove towel. Spread with ice cream; roll up again.

11. Freezer-wrap; store in freezer.

OLD-FASHIONED JELLY ROLL

MAKES 8 TO 10 SERVINGS

4 eggs
¾ cup sifted all-purpose or cake flour
1 teaspoon baking powder
¼ teaspoon salt
¾ cup sugar

1 teaspoon vanilla extract, or 1 tablespoon grated orange peel
Confectioners' sugar
1 cup currant jelly or strawberry or raspberry jam

1. In large bowl of electric mixer, let eggs warm to room temperature—about 1 hour.

2. Preheat oven to 400F. Lightly grease bottom of a 15½-by-10½-by-1-inch jelly-roll pan; then line with waxed paper.

3. Sift flour, baking powder, salt; set aside.

4. At high speed, beat eggs until thick and lemon-colored. Gradually beat in sugar, 2 tablespoons at a time; continue beating until very thick and light—about 5 minutes.

5. At low speed, blend in sifted dry ingredients and vanilla just until combined.

6. Turn into prepared pan; spread evenly. Bake 10 to 13 minutes, or until surface springs back when gently pressed with fingertip.

7. Meanwhile, onto clean towel, sift confectioners' sugar in a 15-by-10-inch rectangle.

8. With sharp knife, loosen sides of cake from pan. Turn out cake onto sugar; gently peel off waxed paper. Trim off crisp edges of cake.

9. Starting with long edge, roll cake in towel; place, seam side down, on wire rack until cool.

10. Gently unroll cake; remove towel. Spread cake with jelly (beaten with fork to spreading consistency), or fill with one of Jelly-Roll Fillings. Reroll.

11. Place, seam side down, on serving plate; cover loosely with foil. Chill at least 1 hour.

12. To serve, lightly sift confectioners' sugar over top. Slice on diagonal with serrated knife.

Spicecake Roll: Make Old-Fashioned Jelly Roll, above, sifting ½ teaspoon cloves, ½ teaspoon nutmeg, 1 teaspoon cinnamon, and 1 teaspoon ginger with dry ingredients. Proceed as above.

Jelly-Roll Fillings

MOCHA CREAM FILLING

MAKES ABOUT 2 CUPS

1 cup heavy cream
¼ cup sifted confectioners'
    sugar
2 tablespoons unsweetened
    cocoa
1 tablespoon instant coffee
1 teaspoon vanilla extract

1. Combine all ingredients in medium bowl.
2. Refrigerate, along with rotary beater, until well chilled—at least 40 minutes.
3. Beat cream mixture until stiff. Use three fourths to fill roll; spread rest over top. Decorate with finely chopped toasted almonds, if desired.

BANANA CREAM FILLING

MAKES ABOUT 2 CUPS

1 cup heavy cream
½ cup sifted confectioners'
    sugar
1 small ripe banana, diced
    (½ cup)
1 teaspoon lemon juice
¼ cup finely chopped
    pecans

1. Combine cream and sugar in medium bowl.
2. Refrigerate, along with rotary beater, until well chilled—at least 40 minutes.
3. In small bowl, lightly toss banana with lemon juice.
4. Beat cream mixture until stiff. Fold in banana to combine well. Use three fourths to fill roll; spread rest over top. Sprinkle with pecans.

CHOCOLATE-RUM FILLING

MAKES ABOUT 2 CUPS

1 cup heavy cream
¼ cup sifted confectioners'
    sugar
2 tablespoons unsweetened
    cocoa
1 teaspoon rum extract

1. Combine all ingredients in medium bowl.
2. Refrigerate, along with rotary beater, until well chilled—at least 40 minutes.
3. Beat cream mixture until stiff. Use three fourths to fill roll; spread rest over top. Decorate with chocolate curls, if desired.

COCONUT FILLING

MAKES ABOUT 2 CUPS

1 cup heavy cream
¼ cup sifted confectioners'
    sugar
1 teaspoon vanilla extract
½ teaspoon almond extract
¾ cup canned flaked
    coconut

1. Combine all ingredients, except coconut, in medium bowl.
2. Refrigerate, along with rotary beater, until well chilled—at least 40 minutes.
3. Beat cream mixture until stiff. Use three fourths to fill roll; sprinkle with ½ cup coconut. Spread rest of filling over top; sprinkle with rest of coconut.

CHOCOLATE ROLL

6 eggs

¾ cup sugar

⅓ cup unsweetened cocoa

1 teaspoon vanilla extract

½ teaspoon almond extract

Confectioners' sugar

MAKES 8 TO 10 SERVINGS

1. Separate egg yolks into small bowl and egg whites into large bowl of electric mixer. Let egg whites warm to room temperature—about 1 hour.

2. Preheat oven to 375F. Lightly grease bottom of a 15½-by-10½-by-1-inch jelly-roll pan; then line with waxed paper.

3. At high speed, beat egg whites just until soft peaks form when beater is slowly raised. Gradually beat in ¼ cup sugar, beating until stiff peaks form. Meringue will be shiny and moist.

4. With same beater, at high speed, beat egg yolks with rest of sugar until thick and lemon-colored—about 5 minutes. At low speed, beat in cocoa and extracts just until combined.

5. With wire whisk or rubber scraper, using an under-and-over motion, gently fold yolk mixture into egg whites just until combined.

6. Turn into prepared pan, spreading evenly. Bake 12 to 14 minutes, or just until surface springs back when gently pressed with fingertip.

7. Meanwhile, onto clean towel, sift confectioners' sugar in a 15-by-10-inch rectangle.

8. Turn out cake onto sugar; gently peel off waxed paper. With very sharp knife, trim edges.

9. Starting with long edge, roll up cake in towel, jelly-roll fashion. (Cake tends to crack slightly when rolled.) Place, seam side down, on wire rack 30 minutes, or until cool.

10. Meanwhile, make Mocha Cream Filling or one of the other Jelly-Roll Fillings.

11. Gently unroll cake; remove towel. Spread cake with filling; reroll.

12. Place, seam side down, on serving plate; cover loosely with foil. Refrigerate 1 hour, or until serving time.

13. To serve, slice on diagonal with serrated knife.

Chocolate Ice-Cream Roll: Fill roll with 1 pint slightly soft vanilla ice cream. Roll up as directed. Freezer-wrap, and freeze about 1 hour, or until serving time.

OLD-FASHIONED PINEAPPLE UPSIDE-DOWN CAKE

MAKES 8 SERVINGS

4 eggs, separated
½ cup butter or margarine
1 cup light-brown sugar,
    firmly packed
1 can (1 lb, 4½ oz)
    pineapple slices,
    drained
½ cup coarsely chopped
    pecans
10 maraschino cherries,
    drained and halved

1 cup sifted cake flour
1 teaspoon baking powder
¼ teaspoon salt
1 cup granulated sugar
1 tablespoon butter or
    margarine, melted
1 teaspoon almond extract
¾ cup heavy cream,
    whipped

1. Preheat oven to 325F. In large bowl of electric mixer, let egg whites warm to room temperature—about 1 hour.
2. In 10-inch heavy skillet with a heat-resistant handle, melt ½ cup butter over very low heat. Remove from heat.
3. Sprinkle brown sugar over butter. Arrange pineapple slices to cover bottom of skillet. Distribute pecans and cherries around pineapple; set aside.
4. Sift flour with baking powder and salt.
5. At high speed, beat egg whites just until soft peaks form when beater is slowly raised. Add granulated sugar gradually; beat well after each addition. Beat until stiff peaks form.
6. In small bowl of electric mixer, at high speed, beat egg yolks until very thick and yellow.
7. With a wire whisk or rubber scraper, using an under-and-over motion, gently fold egg yolks and flour mixture into whites until combined. Fold in 1 tablespoon butter and the almond extract.
8. Spread batter evenly over pineapple in skillet; bake 30 to 35 minutes, or until surface springs back when gently pressed with fingertip.
9. Loosen edge of cake; let stand 5 minutes. Invert on serving plate. Serve warm, with whipped cream.

MINIATURE BABAS

MAKES 16 SERVINGS

¼ cup warm water
    (105 to 115F)
1 pkg active dry yeast
2 tablespoons sugar
½ teaspoon salt
3 eggs
1¾ cups sifted all-purpose
    flour

¼ cup soft butter or
    margarine

Apricot-Rum Syrup:
1 can (12 oz) apricot nectar
¾ cup sugar
¼ cup lemon juice
¾ to 1 cup golden rum

1. Lightly grease 16 (2½-inch) muffin-pan cups. If possible, check temperature of warm water with thermometer.
2. Sprinkle yeast over water in small bowl of electric mixer, stirring until dissolved.
3. Add sugar, salt, eggs, and 1¼ cups flour. At medium speed, beat 4 minutes, or until smooth, scraping side of bowl and guiding mixture into beaters, with rubber scraper.
4. Add butter; beat 2 minutes, or until very well blended.
5. At low speed, beat in rest of flour; beat until smooth—about 2 minutes. Batter is thick.
6. Turn batter into prepared muffin cups, using 1 rounded tablespoon batter for each cup; cover with towel.

(*Miniature Babas continued*)

7. Let rise in warm place (85F), free from drafts, 1 hour, or until babas have risen to rims of muffin cups—more than double in bulk.

8. Preheat oven to 400F. Bake babas 15 to 18 minutes, or until deep golden-brown. Let cool several minutes in pan, on wire rack.

9. Meanwhile, make Apricot-Rum Syrup: In medium saucepan, combine apricot nectar with 1 cup water and the sugar. Bring to boiling, stirring until sugar is dissolved.

10. Reduce heat; simmer, uncovered, 15 minutes. Remove from heat; add lemon juice and rum.

11. Turn out babas; arrange in a 13-by-9-by-2-inch pan, tops up. Poke holes in babas, at ½-inch intervals, with cake tester.

12. Pour hot syrup over babas; let stand, basting occasionally, 1 hour, or until all syrup is absorbed.

13. Serve slightly warm, with sweetened whipped cream, if desired.

Note: Babas may be baked, soaked in syrup, then cooled completely. Freezer-wrap, pan and all; label, and freeze. To serve: Let stand at room temperature 1 hour; then reheat, foil-wrapped, 20 minutes at 350F. Serve as above.

COTTAGE PUDDING

MAKES 9 TO 12 SERVINGS

2 cups sifted all-purpose
    flour
3 teaspoons baking powder
¼ teaspoon salt
⅓ cup soft butter or
    margarine

⅔ cup sugar
2 eggs
1 teaspoon vanilla extract
1 cup milk

1. Preheat oven to 350F. Lightly grease a 9-by-9-by-1¾-inch pan.

2. Sift flour, baking powder, salt; set aside.

3. In large bowl of electric mixer, at medium speed, beat butter with sugar, eggs, and vanilla until light and fluffy—about 4 minutes.

4. At low speed, beat in flour mixture (in fourths) alternately with milk (in thirds), beginning and ending with flour mixture.

5. Turn into prepared pan. Bake 30 to 35 minutes, or until surface springs back when gently pressed with fingertip.

6. Let cake cool in pan, on wire rack, at least 5 minutes.

7. Cut into squares or rectangles. Serve warm, with Chocolate Sauce* or any fruit sauce.

Note: Or heat canned cherry- or blueberry-pie filling, and use as sauce.

* See this chapter.

TIPSY TORTE

Torte:
4 eggs, separated
½ cup sugar
1 cup sifted all-purpose
    flour
1 teaspoon baking powder
¼ teaspoon salt
1 teaspoon vanilla extract
⅓ cup butter or margarine,
    melted

Syrup:
2 cups sugar
½ cup sherry

Topping:
½ cup flaked coconut
½ cup heavy cream,
    whipped (optional)

1. Preheat oven to 375F. Make Torte: In medium bowl, with rotary beater, beat egg whites until they form soft peaks. Add ¼ cup sugar, and beat until stiff.

2. In small bowl, beat egg yolks until light and fluffy. Add remaining ¼ cup sugar, and beat well. Fold egg yolks into whites.

3. Sift together dry ingredients over egg mixture; fold in gently. Fold in vanilla and butter.

4. Pour into 1-quart casserole; bake 30 minutes, or until golden.

5. Meanwhile, make Syrup: In medium saucepan, combine sugar and 2 cups water; bring to boiling. Reduce heat, and simmer until syrup forms soft ball in cold water, 238F on candy thermometer—about 15 minutes.

6. Remove from heat; stir in sherry.

7. When torte is removed from oven, poke holes all through top, with ice pick or skewer.

8. Pour hot syrup over torte; when liquid is absorbed, sprinkle with coconut.

9. Serve warm or cold, with unsweetened whipped cream, if desired.

TRIFLE

2 cups heavy cream
2 cups milk
6 egg yolks
¼ cup light-brown sugar,
    firmly packed
6 tablespoons granulated
    sugar
1 tablespoon cornstarch
⅛ teaspoon salt

½ teaspoon vanilla extract
1 teaspoon almond extract
1 pkg (3 oz) ladyfingers
⅓ cup strawberry preserves
⅓ cup sherry
½ cup ground macaroons
2 tablespoons toasted
    slivered almonds
Candied cherries

1. In top of double boiler over simmering water, scald 1 cup cream and the milk.

2. In medium bowl, with rotary beater, beat egg yolks slightly.

3. Mix brown sugar, 4 tablespoons granulated sugar, the cornstarch, and salt. Beat sugar mixture into yolks.

4. Then quickly stir small amount of hot liquid into yolk mixture. Turn all of yolk mixture into top of double boiler; cook, stirring constantly, 15 minutes, or until mixture coats a metal spoon.

5. Remove from heat. Add vanilla and ½ teaspoon almond extract; cool.

6. Split ladyfingers; spread with preserves. In 2-quart serving dish, layer ladyfingers, sherry, macaroons, and custard; repeat twice.

7. Refrigerate until thoroughly chilled.

8. Just before serving, beat remaining 1 cup cream with remaining 2 tablespoons granulated sugar and ½ teaspoon almond extract, until stiff, use cream to garnish top of trifle.

9. Decorate with almonds and cherries.

Cheesecakes

Certain restaurants have built their reputation on a cheesecake. Why can't you do the same? Try our cool, smooth, rich cheese-cake, delicate in flavor, high in protein. Top it with a fruit glaze, and you can't ask for anything better—with a rather light dinner.

LINDY'S FAMOUS CHEESECAKE

MAKES 16 TO 20 SERVINGS

Crust:
1 cup sifted all-purpose flour
¼ cup sugar
1 teaspoon grated lemon peel
½ teaspoon vanilla extract
1 egg yolk
¼ cup soft butter or margarine

Filling:
5 pkg (8-oz size) cream cheese (2½ lb), at room temperature
1¾ cups sugar
3 tablespoons all-purpose flour
1½ teaspoons grated lemon peel
1½ teaspoons grated orange peel
¼ teaspoon vanilla extract
5 eggs
2 egg yolks
¼ cup heavy cream

1. Make Crust: In small bowl, combine flour, sugar, lemon peel, and vanilla. Make a well in center; add egg yolk and butter. With fingertips, mix until dough leaves side of bowl.
2. Form into a ball; wrap in waxed paper; refrigerate 1 hour.
3. Meanwhile, preheat oven to 400F. Lightly grease bottom and side of a 9-inch spring-form pan; remove side.
4. Remove one third of dough from refrigerator. Roll out directly on bottom of spring-form pan; trim dough even with edge.
5. Bake 8 to 10 minutes, or until golden. Cool.
6. Divide remaining dough into 3 parts. On lightly floured surface, roll each part into a strip 2½ inches wide.
7. Press strips to side of spring-form pan, joining ends of strips, to line inside completely. Trim dough so it comes only three quarters up side. Refrigerate until ready to fill.
8. Preheat oven to 500F.
9. Make Filling: In large bowl of electric mixer, combine cheese with sugar, flour, lemon peel, orange peel, and vanilla.
10. Add eggs and yolks, one at a time, beating after each addition. Beat only until mixture is well combined. Add cream, beating until well combined.
11. Assemble spring-form pan with baked crust on bottom and unbaked pastry around side. Pour in filling; bake 10 minutes.
12. Reduce oven temperature to 250F. Bake 1 hour longer.
13. Cool in pan, on wire rack. Then refrigerate 3 hours, or overnight.
14. To serve: Remove side of spring-form pan. Serve cheesecake plain or topped with one of the Glazes for Cheesecake.

McCALL'S BEST CHEESECAKE

MAKES 10 TO 12 SERVINGS

Crust:
¾ cup graham-cracker
    crumbs*
1 tablespoon sugar
1 tablespoon melted butter
    or margarine

Filling:
3 pkg (8-oz size) cream
    cheese, at room
    temperature

4 eggs
1 teaspoon vanilla extract
1 cup sugar

Topping:
2 cups dairy sour cream
1 tablespoon sugar
1 teaspoon vanilla extract

1. Preheat oven to 375F.
2. Make Crust: In medium bowl, combine crumbs, sugar, and butter, mixing well.
3. Spread evenly over bottom of a 9-inch spring-form pan, pressing lightly with finger-tips. Refrigerate while filling is prepared.
4. Make Filling: In large bowl of electric mixer, at medium speed, beat cheese until light.
5. Add eggs, vanilla, and sugar; continue beating until creamy and light.
6. Pour into crust in pan; bake 35 minutes.
7. Meanwhile, make Topping: In medium bowl, with wooden spoon, beat together cream, sugar, and vanilla.
8. Remove cheesecake from oven. Spread topping evenly over surface; bake 5 minutes.
9. Cool in pan, on wire rack. Then refrigerate 5 hours, or overnight.
10. To serve: Remove side of spring-form pan. Cut cheesecake into wedges.
* To make graham-cracker crumbs: With rolling pin, crush 10 graham crackers between 2 sheets of waxed paper.

CREAM-CHEESE PIE

MAKES 8 SERVINGS

Graham-Cracker Crust:
1 cup packaged graham-
    cracker crumbs
2 tablespoons sugar
¼ cup butter or margarine,
    melted

Filling:
4 pkg (3-oz size) soft cream
    cheese

2 eggs
¾ cup sugar
1 teaspoon vanilla extract
2 teaspoons grated lemon
    or orange peel

Sour-Cream Topping:
1½ cups dairy sour cream
¼ cup sugar
1 teaspoon vanilla extract

1. Preheat oven to 350F.
2. Make Graham-Cracker Crust: In small bowl, combine crumbs, sugar, and butter, stirring with fork to mix well. With back of metal spoon, press to bottom and side (not on rim) of 9-inch pie plate. Refrigerate.
3. Make Filling: Combine filling ingredients in small bowl of electric mixer. At medium speed, beat until smooth.
4. Turn into prepared crust; bake 35 minutes.
5. In small bowl, combine topping ingredients.
6. Spread pie with topping; bake 10 minutes.
7. Let cool completely on wire rack.
8. Serve as is or very well chilled—refrigerated 5 hours, or overnight.
9. If desired, garnish with seedless green grapes or strawberries.

Glazed Cream-Cheese Pie: Bake pie completely, omitting Sour-Cream Topping. Spread cooled pie with one of the Glazes for Cheesecake. Refrigerate 1 hour before serving.

REFRIGERATOR CHEESE PIE

MAKES 8 SERVINGS

Graham-Cracker Crust:
1 cup packaged graham-
    cracker crumbs
2 tablespoons sugar
¼ cup butter or margarine,
    melted

Filling:
½ cup sugar

1 envelope unflavored
    gelatine
¼ teaspoon salt
1 cup milk
2 eggs
1 tablespoon grated lemon
    peel
2 cups creamed cottage
    cheese

1. Make Graham-Cracker Crust: In small bowl, combine crumbs, sugar, and butter, stirring with fork to mix well. Reserve ¼ cup mixture for topping.

2. With back of metal spoon, press rest of crumb mixture to bottom and side (not on rim) of a 9-inch pie plate. Refrigerate while preparing filling.

3. Make Filling: In small saucepan, combine sugar, gelatine, salt, milk, and eggs.

4. Over medium heat, cook, stirring constantly, until custard forms a coating on metal spoon—about 5 minutes.

5. Remove from heat; stir in lemon peel. Refrigerate until mixture mounds when dropped from spoon—about 45 minutes.

6. Turn into large bowl of electric mixer. Add cheese. At high speed, beat until light and fluffy—3 minutes.

7. If filling is slightly thin, refrigerate 10 minutes. Turn into crust. Sprinkle reserved crumb mixture around edge of pie.

8. Refrigerate until firm—about 3 hours.

Glazed Refrigerator Cheese Pie: Omit crumb topping. Spread chilled pie with one of the Glazes for Cheesecake. Refrigerate 1 hour before serving.

Glazes for Cheesecakes

BLUEBERRY GLAZE

MAKES 1 CUP

1 pkg (10 oz) frozen
    blueberries, thawed
2 tablespoons sugar

2 tablespoons cornstarch
1 tablespoon lemon juice

1. Drain blueberries, reserving ½ cup liquid.

2. In small saucepan, combine sugar and cornstarch. Add reserved liquid, stirring until smooth.

3   Bring to boiling, stirring, over medium heat; boil 1 minute. Mixture will be thickened and translucent.

4. Remove from heat; let cool slightly. Add lemon juice and blueberries. Cool thoroughly before spreading over top of cooled cheesecake.

RED-CHERRY GLAZE

MAKES 1½ CUPS

1 can (1 lb) sour red
   cherries, packed in
   water
¼ cup sugar

1 tablespoon cornstarch
1 tablespoon lemon juice
2 drops red food color

1. Drain cherries, reserving ½ cup liquid. Set aside 1 cup cherries.
2. In small saucepan, combine sugar and cornstarch. Add reserved liquid, stirring until smooth.
3. Bring to boiling, stirring, over medium heat; boil 1 minute. Mixture will be thickened and translucent.
4. Remove from heat; let cool slightly. Add lemon juice, 1 cup cherries, and the food color. Cool thoroughly before spreading over top of cooled cheesecake.

PINEAPPLE GLAZE

MAKES 1 CUP

1 tablespoon sugar
2 teaspoons cornstarch
1 can (8¾ oz) crushed
   pineapple

1 tablespoon lemon juice
2 drops yellow food color

1. In small saucepan, combine sugar and cornstarch.
2. Stir in undrained pineapple and lemon juice.
3. Bring to boiling, stirring, over medium heat; boil 1 minute. Mixture will be thickened and translucent.
4. Stir in food color. Let cool thoroughly before spreading over top of cooled cheesecake.

COEUR À LA CRÈME

MAKES 8 SERVINGS

1 lb creamed cottage cheese
1 teaspoon salt

2 cups heavy cream
Strawberries

1. Line a 7-inch heart-shape basket (or a sieve) with cheesecloth.
2. In large bowl of electric mixer, at high speed, beat cheese and salt just until combined.
3. Gradually add cream, beating until very smooth. Pack cheese mixture firmly into basket; cover with waxed paper.
4. Place basket over large bowl; let drain overnight in refrigerator.
5. Unmold on serving plate. Surround with fresh whole strawberries.

Cobblers, Crisps, and Shortcakes

Once these were limited to the fresh-fruit season. But today, these old-fashioned favorites can be made any time during the year with canned or frozen fruits.

Our cobblers and crisps have homey charm. If you've never tried them, do. Served warm, the desserts in this group have a special melt-in-the-mouth quality.

FRENCH APPLE COBBLER

MAKES 6 TO 8 SERVINGS

Filling:

5 cups peeled, sliced tart
    apples
¾ cup sugar
2 tablespoons all-purpose
    flour
½ teaspoon cinnamon
¼ teaspoon salt
1 teaspoon vanilla extract
1 tablespoon soft butter or
    margarine

Batter:

½ cup sifted all-purpose
    flour
½ cup sugar
½ teaspoon baking powder
¼ teaspoon salt
2 tablespoons soft butter or
    margarine
1 egg, slightly beaten

Light or whipped cream

1. Preheat oven to 375F.
2. Make Filling: In medium bowl, combine apples, sugar, flour, cinnamon, salt, vanilla, and ¼ cup water.
3. Turn into a 9-by-9-by-1¾-inch baking pan. Dot apples with butter.
4. Make Batter: In medium bowl, combine all batter ingredients; beat with wooden spoon until smooth.
5. Drop batter in 9 portions on apples, spacing evenly. Batter will spread during baking.
6. Bake 35 to 40 minutes, or until apples are fork-tender and crust is golden-brown.
7. Serve warm, with cream.

FRESH-RHUBARB CRISP

MAKES 6 TO 8 SERVINGS

Topping:

1 cup sifted all-purpose
    flour
½ cup raw rolled oats
1 cup light-brown sugar,
    firmly packed
½ cup butter or margarine,
    melted

Rhubarb Filling:

4 cups cut rhubarb, in ½-
    inch pieces (about
    1¾ lb)
1 cup granulated sugar
¼ cup unsifted all-purpose
    flour
½ teaspoon cinnamon

1. Preheat oven to 375F. Make Topping: In large bowl, combine flour, oats, and brown sugar, mixing well. With fork, stir in butter to make a crumbly mixture.
2. Make Rhubarb Filling: In lightly greased 8-by-8-by-2-inch baking dish, combine rhubarb, granulated sugar, flour, cinnamon, and ½ cup water; stir to mix well.
3. Sprinkle topping evenly over filling; bake, uncovered, 35 minutes, or until topping is golden-brown and rhubarb is tender. Serve warm, with light cream or ice cream, if desired.

251

FRESH-PEACH CRISP

MAKES 6 SERVINGS

2½ lb fresh ripe peaches
    (about 8)
1 cup sifted all-purpose
    flour
1 cup sugar

¼ teaspoon salt
½ teaspoon cinnamon
½ cup soft butter or
    margarine

Light cream

1. Preheat oven to 375F. Lightly grease an 8-by-8-by-2-inch baking dish.
2. Wash peaches; peel. Cut in halves; remove pits. Slice peaches into prepared baking dish.
3. Sift flour with sugar, salt, and cinnamon into medium bowl.
4. With pastry blender or 2 knives, cut butter into flour mixture until mixture resembles coarse cornmeal. Sprinkle evenly over peaches.
5. Bake 45 to 50 minutes, or until topping is golden and peaches are tender.
6. Serve warm, with cream.

APPLE PANDOWDY

MAKES 6 TO 8 SERVINGS

4½ cups thinly sliced,
    pared, cored tart
    apples (about 1½ lb)
½ cup light molasses
3 tablespoons butter or
    margarine

Topping:
2 cups packaged biscuit mix
3 tablespoons sugar
½ teaspoon cinnamon
¼ teaspoon nutmeg
¾ cup milk

Light cream

1. Preheat oven to 375F. Lightly grease an 8-by-8-by-2-inch baking dish.
2. In medium saucepan, combine apple slices, molasses, butter, and ¼ cup water; bring to boiling, over medium heat, stirring occasionally. Turn into prepared baking dish.
3. Meanwhile, make Topping: Combine biscuit mix, sugar, cinnamon, and nutmeg in small bowl; mix well. Add milk, all at once, stirring just until dry ingredients are moistened.
4. Drop, by heaping teaspoonfuls, onto hot apple mixture; bake 20 minutes, or until topping is golden and firm to the touch.
5. Serve warm, with cream.

PEACH COBBLER

MAKES 6 SERVINGS

Fruit:
1 can (1 lb, 14 oz) sliced
    peaches, undrained
⅓ cup sugar
⅛ teaspoon nutmeg
1 tablespoon butter or
    margarine
1 tablespoon lemon juice

Topping:
1½ cups packaged biscuit
    mix
1 tablespoon sugar
1 tablespoon salad oil or
    melted shortening
1 egg
⅓ cup milk

1. Preheat oven to 425F.
2. Prepare Fruit: In medium saucepan, combine peaches with remaining fruit ingredients; cook, stirring, over low heat, until mixture boils. Keep hot.
3. Make Topping: In medium bowl, combine biscuit mix with sugar. In small bowl, with rotary beater, combine oil, egg, and milk.
4. Make well in center of biscuit mix. Add milk mixture; stir only until dampened.
5. Pour hot fruit into 2-quart baking dish. Drop topping, in 6 portions, onto hot fruit.
6. Bake 15 to 20 minutes, or until topping is firm and golden-brown.
7. Serve warm, with light cream, if desired.

DUTCH PEACH KUCHEN

Cake:
1 egg
¼ cup sugar
1¼ cups packaged biscuit
   mix
2 tablespoons soft butter or
   margarine
1 can (1 lb, 13 oz) sliced
   peaches, drained

Topping:
¼ cup packaged biscuit
   mix
¼ cup sugar
1 teaspoon cinnamon
¼ teaspoon nutmeg
¼ cup melted butter or
   margarine

1. Preheat oven to 375F. Grease a 8-by-8-by-2-inch pan.
2. Make Cake: In medium bowl, beat egg with fork.
3. Add sugar, biscuit mix, and butter; beat vigorously until mixture is smooth—about 1 minute.
4. Spread batter evenly in prepared pan. Arrange peaches over surface.
5. Make Topping: In small bowl, mix all topping ingredients, with fork, until well combined. Sprinkle evenly over peaches.
6. Bake 35 minutes, or until golden-brown.
7. Serve warm, with light cream, if desired.

OLD-FASHIONED PEACH SHORTCAKE

Filling:
2 lb fresh ripe peaches
   (about 6)
2 tablespoons granulated
   sugar*
¼ cup Cointreau
   (optional)*

Shortcake:
2 cups packaged biscuit
   mix
¼ cup granulated sugar
⅔ cup light cream
1 to 2 tablespoons butter or
   margarine

1 cup heavy cream
2 tablespoons confectioners'
   sugar

1. Make Filling: Wash peaches; peel. Cut in halves; remove pits. Slice peaches thinly into a medium bowl, or crush coarsely.
2. Sprinkle peaches with sugar and Cointreau. Refrigerate, covered, several hours or overnight, stirring occasionally.
3. Meanwhile, make Shortcake: Preheat oven to 450F. In large bowl, combine biscuit mix and granulated sugar.
4. Stir in light cream. With wooden spoon, beat 15 strokes.
5. Turn dough out onto lightly floured surface. Knead gently 10 times.
6. Divide dough in 2 parts. With lightly floured hands, pat one part evenly in bottom of an ungreased 8-inch layer-cake pan.
7. Dot with butter; pat remaining dough on top.
8. Bake 15 to 20 minutes, or until lightly browned. Cool completely on wire rack.
9. Turn shortcake out of pan. With sharp knife, carefully split shortcake crosswise, making 2 even 8-inch layers.
10. Just before serving, whip heavy cream with confectioners' sugar until stiff.
11. To assemble shortcake: Place one shortcake layer, cut side up, on serving platter. Top with half peach mixture and half whipped cream. Add remaining shortcake layer, cut side down; top with rest of peach mixture and whipped cream.

* If desired, adjust amounts to your taste.

STRAWBERRY SHORTCAKE

1 Tender Shortcake, recipe
   below
2 pt boxes fresh
   strawberries
1 cup sugar

½ cup heavy cream
1 teaspoon vanilla extract
2 tablespoons soft butter or
   margarine

1. While shortcake is baking, gently wash berries in cold water. Drain; hull.

2. Reserve 6 large berries. Slice remaining berries into medium bowl. Add sugar; stir gently. Set aside until ready to use.

3. In small bowl, whip cream until stiff. Stir in vanilla.

4. Split warm shortcake in half crosswise. Place bottom half, cut side up, on serving platter. Spread with butter. Spoon on half the sliced berries.

5. Top with other half of shortcake, cut side down. Spoon on rest of sliced berries and the whipped cream.

6. Garnish with whole berries.

TENDER SHORTCAKE

2¼ cups sifted cake flour
4 teaspoons baking powder
2 tablespoons sugar
½ teaspoon salt

⅓ cup shortening
1 egg, slightly beaten
⅔ cup milk

1. Lightly grease and flour an 8-inch round layer-cake pan. Preheat oven to 425F.

2. In medium bowl, sift flour with baking powder, sugar, and salt. With pastry blender or 2 knives, cut in shortening until mixture resembles coarse cornmeal.

3. Make well in center. Add egg and milk; stir quickly just until combined.

4. Spread in prepared pan; bake 15 minutes, or until golden.

5. Partially cool, in pan, on wire rack. Serve warm, with any desired fruit filling.

OLD-FASHIONED BERRY SHORTCAKE

Shortcake:
2 cups sifted all-purpose
   flour
¼ cup granulated sugar
3 teaspoons baking powder
½ teaspoon salt
½ cup butter or margarine
¾ cup milk

Berry Topping:
1½ qt raspberries, black-
   berries, or sliced
   strawberries
¾ cup granulated sugar
1 cup heavy cream
2 tablespoons confectioners'
   sugar

1. Make Shortcake: Preheat oven to 450F. Lightly grease an 8-by-8-by-2-inch pan.

2. Into medium mixing bowl, sift together flour, sugar, baking powder, and salt. With pastry blender or 2 knives, cut in butter until mixture resembles coarse cornmeal.

3. Make a well in center of flour mixture. Pour in milk all at once; mix with fork just until all flour is moistened. Dough will be lumpy.

4. Spoon dough into prepared pan; then press with fingers to fit pan.

5. Bake 12 to 15 minutes, or until golden and a cake tester inserted in center comes out clean.

6. Cool partially; cut into 9 squares. (Short-cakes can be served warm or cold.)

(Old-Fashioned Berry Shortcake continued)

7. Meanwhile, make Berry Topping: Set aside some good-looking berries for garnish. Then, in a bowl and using a potato masher, crush 3 cups berries. Stir in granulated sugar; add remaining uncrushed berries. Whip cream until stiff; fold in confectioners' sugar.

8. To serve: Split shortcake squares in half crosswise. Place bottom half on each serving plate; spoon on 3 tablespoons berry mixture. Top with other half; spoon on 1 tablespoon berry mixture. Finish with a heaping tablespoon whipped cream and berries reserved for garnish.

Cream Desserts

Sensational to look at and marvelous to taste are what party desserts must be. And the light, fluffy, creamy desserts in this section are exactly that.

BAVARIAN CREAM

MAKES 8 SERVINGS

1 envelope unflavored
   gelatine
1¼ cups milk
2 eggs, separated

Dash salt
6 tablespoons sugar
1 cup heavy cream
¼ teaspoon almond extract

1. Sprinkle gelatine over ¼ cup milk; let soften.

2. Heat remaining milk in top of double boiler, over direct heat, until tiny bubbles appear around edge.

3. Beat egg yolks with salt and 2 tablespoons sugar.

4. Add softened gelatine to egg-yolk mixture. Then add hot milk, stirring rapidly as you pour.

5. Return egg-milk combination to top of double boiler; cook, over simmering water and stirring constantly, until mixture coats a metal spoon. Remove from heat at once; cover to prevent film from forming.

6. Refrigerate until mixture is thicker than unbeaten egg white, or until it mounds slightly when lifted with a spoon.

7. Beat egg whites until they form soft peaks when beater is raised. Gradually add remaining sugar; beat until stiff.

8. Whip cream. Fold meringue and whipped cream into yolk mixture, with extract.

9. Rinse 1½-quart mold with cold water; fill with Bavarian Cream, and refrigerate until set.

10. To unmold: Run small spatula around edge of mold, to loosen. Invert over platter; shake gently to release. Serve with fruit, such as strawberries, peaches, or melon balls.

255

CHOCOLATE-COCONUT MOLD

MAKES 6 SERVINGS

2 cups milk
¼ cup sifted unsweetened
   cocoa
⅓ cup sugar
Dash salt
1 envelope unflavored
   gelatine

2 eggs, separated
½ teaspoon almond extract
⅓ cup flaked coconut,
   toasted
1 cup sweetened whipped
   cream

1. In top of double boiler, heat milk until film forms over surface.
2. Combine cocoa, sugar, salt, and gelatine in small bowl. Stir gradually into milk.
3. Place over boiling water; cook, stirring constantly, 5 minutes.
4. In small bowl, beat egg yolks slightly. Then quickly beat in a little hot cocoa mixture. Stir egg mixture quickly into remaining cocoa mixture.
5. Stirring constantly, continue to cook, over boiling water, 5 to 8 minutes, or until mixture coats a metal spoon. Cool completely.
6. Stir in almond extract and coconut.
7. In medium bowl, with rotary beater, beat egg whites until stiff peaks form.
8. Fold cocoa mixture into whites until all white patches disappear. Pour into 1-quart mold.
9. Refrigerate several hours, or until firm. Then unmold, and serve with sweetened whipped cream.

STRAWBERRY BAVARIAN CREAM

MAKES 6 TO 8 SERVINGS

2 pt boxes fresh
   strawberries
1 tablespoon lemon juice
¾ cup sugar

2 envelopes unflavored
   gelatine
2 cups heavy cream

1. Wash strawberries gently in cold water. Drain; hull.
2. In medium bowl, crush with potato masher; then press through sieve. Purée should measure 2 cups.
3. In medium bowl, combine purée, lemon juice, and sugar; stir to dissolve sugar.
4. Sprinkle gelatine over ½ cup cold water in small bowl. Place over hot water; stir to dissolve.
5. Blend gelatine into strawberry mixture.
6. Refrigerate, stirring occasionally, until consistency of unbeaten egg white.
7. In large bowl, with rotary beater, whip cream until stiff. Carefully fold berry mixture into cream.
8. Rinse 1½-quart mold with cold water. Fill with strawberry-cream mixture.
9. Refrigerate 2 hours, or until firm.
10. To unmold: Run small spatula around edge of mold, to loosen. Invert over platter; shake gently to release.

PINEAPPLE-TAPIOCA CREAM

1 can (6 oz) thawed frozen
    pineapple juice,
    undiluted
¼ cup sugar
3 tablespoons quick-cooking
    tapioca

¼ teaspoon salt
1 can (8¾ oz) crushed
    pineapple, undrained
⅓ cup heavy cream

1. Pour pineapple juice into a 2-cup measure; add water to make 2 cups.

2. Pour into medium saucepan. Stir in sugar, tapioca, and salt to combine well.

3. Over medium heat, bring to boiling, stirring. Remove from heat.

4. Let cool 20 minutes, stirring several times. Then stir in pineapple; refrigerate 30 minutes.

5. With rotary beater, whip cream in small bowl just until stiff enough to hold its shape. With rubber scraper, fold into tapioca until well combined.

6. Refrigerate until serving time.

VANILLA BLANC MANGE

2¼ cups milk
3 tablespoons cornstarch
⅓ cup sugar

¼ teaspoon salt
1 teaspoon vanilla extract

1. In medium saucepan, slowly heat 2 cups milk just until bubbles form around edge of pan.

2. In small bowl, combine cornstarch, sugar, salt, and remaining milk; stir to mix well.

3. Gradually stir cornstarch mixture into hot milk; bring to boiling, stirring. Boil 1 minute, stirring constantly.

4. Remove from heat. Add vanilla.

5. Turn into 6 individual dessert dishes; place piece of waxed paper directly on surface of each. Refrigerate 1 hour before serving. Serve with whipped cream or a fruit sauce.

Coconut Blanc Mange: Make Vanilla Blanc Mange, adding ½ cup flaked coconut to hot milk. Also, use ¼ teaspoon almond extract, and reduce vanilla extract to ½ teaspoon.

Mocha Blanc Mange: Make Vanilla Blanc Mange, adding 1 square unsweetened chocolate, halved, to milk along with 1 teaspoon instant coffee. Heat, stirring, until chocolate is melted. Proceed as directed, increasing sugar to ½ cup.

Chocolate Blanc Mange: Make Vanilla Blanc Mange, adding 2 squares unsweetened chocolate, halved, to milk. Heat, stirring, until chocolate is melted. Proceed as directed, increasing sugar to ½ cup.

257

SPANISH CREAM

MAKES 6 SERVINGS

1 envelope unflavored
  gelatine
Dash salt
½ cup sugar

2 egg yolks, slightly beaten
2 cups milk
1 teaspoon vanilla extract
2 egg whites

1. In small saucepan, combine gelatine, salt, and ¼ cup sugar. Blend in egg yolks and 1 cup milk, stirring until well combined.

2. Cook, over low heat, stirring constantly until gelatine dissolves and mixture coats a metal spoon—8 to 10 minutes. Remove from heat.

3. Stir in remaining milk and the vanilla. Turn into medium bowl.

4. Refrigerate until consistency of unbeaten egg whites. (Hasten chilling by placing bowl in larger one containing ice water.)

5. In small bowl, with rotary beater, beat egg whites until frothy. Gradually add remaining sugar, beating until soft peaks form.

6. Fold meringue into gelatine mixture. Pour into a 1-quart mold, or into 6 (5-oz) custard cups.

7. Refrigerate until firm—about 2 hours.

8. To serve: Loosen edge of mold with spatula. Invert over serving dish; shake gently to release. If desired, garnish with sweetened, whipped cream and chocolate curls or fresh strawberries.

Two-Layer Spanish Cream: Follow recipe above, but do not refrigerate gelatine mixture. Cool until slightly warm; then fold into meringue. Refrigerate mold until firm. Mixture will separate into 2 layers.

RICE CREAM WITH RASPBERRY SAUCE

MAKES 10 SERVINGS

2 jars (4-oz size) diced,
  mixed candied fruit,
  chopped
½ cup canned unsweetened
  pineapple juice
½ cup sugar
1 cup raw long-grain white
  rice
2 cups milk
2 teaspoons vanilla extract

2 envelopes unflavored
  gelatine
2 cups heavy cream,
  whipped

Sauce:
2 pkg (10-oz size) frozen
  raspberries, thawed
  and undrained
½ cup sugar

1. In small bowl, combine candied fruit with pineapple juice. Let stand 1 hour.

2. Meanwhile, in small saucepan, combine sugar with ½ cup water. Over medium heat, bring to boiling, stirring.

3. Add rice; boil gently, stirring, 5 minutes. Drain very well.

4. In top of double boiler, over boiling water, heat milk and vanilla until bubbles form around edge of pan.

5. Add drained rice; cook, covered, over boiling water and stirring occasionally, about 45 minutes, or until the rice is tender and most of the milk has been absorbed. Remove the top of the double boiler from boiling water.

6. Sprinkle gelatine over ½ cup cold water; let stand 5 minutes to soften.

(*Rice Cream with Raspberry Sauce continued*)

7. Stir gelatine into rice mixture; let cool.

8. Then gently fold fruit mixture and cooled rice mixture into whipped cream. Turn the whipped-cream mixture into 2-quart ring mold.

9. Refrigerate until firm—several hours or overnight.

10. Meanwhile, make Sauce: In medium saucepan, combine raspberries with sugar. Bring to boiling, stirring. Reduce heat, and simmer, uncovered, 5 minutes.

11. Blend raspberry mixture, in electric blender, covered, or put through sieve, to purée.

12. Refrigerate, covered, until well chilled.

13. To unmold pudding: Run a small spatula around edge of mold. Invert over serving platter; shake gently to release. If necessary, place a hot, wet dishcloth over mold; shake again.

14. Serve sauce with pudding.

Note: Do not use fresh or frozen pineapple juice in this recipe.

Crepes, Fritters, and Omelets

Crepes, as you no doubt know, are thin-as-tissue pancakes. Elsewhere in this cookbook, you'll find fritters that open a meal and that accompany a meal. Now we'd like to tell you about fritters to close a meal. Our sweet batter can be adapted to almost any fruit. And if you're wondering what in the world omelets are doing in the dessert section, let us tell you that these are puffy, sweet omelets, trimmed with jam or brandy and mocha.

SWEDISH PANCAKES

MAKES 8 TO 10 SERVINGS

1¼ cups sifted all-purpose
    flour
2 tablespoons sugar
½ teaspoon salt
3 eggs
3 cups milk
¼ cup butter or margarine,
    melted

Salad oil
1 jar (14¾ oz) lingon-
    berries, undrained; or
1 can (1 lb) jellied
    whole-cranberry
    sauce

1. Sift flour with sugar and salt into medium bowl. With rotary beater, beat in eggs, milk, and butter until mixture is smooth.

2. Slowly heat Swedish iron pancake pan (or heavy frying pan or griddle) until a drop of water will sizzle and roll off. Brush lightly with oil.

3. Stir batter just before using. Pour 1 tablespoonful into each section of pancake pan, tilting pan so batter covers each section completely. (Or use 1 tablespoon batter per pancake in frying pan or griddle.)

4. When surface of pancakes bubbles, turn quickly, and brown other side. Keep warm while rest of pancakes cook.

5. Meanwhile, heat lingonberries slightly. Serve warm, with pancakes.

CHEESE BLINTZES

MAKES 20 BLINTZES,
5 OR 6 SERVINGS

Filling:
½ pkg (8-oz size) cream
   cheese
½ cup creamed cottage
   cheese
2 egg yolks
2 tablespoons sugar
1 teaspoon vanilla extract

Blintzes:
2 eggs

2 tablespoons salad oil
1 cup milk
¾ cup sifted all-purpose
   flour
½ teaspoon salt
½ cup butter or margarine

1 cup dairy sour cream
1 pkg (10 oz) thawed frozen
   raspberries, undrained
   (optional)

1. Make Filling: Combine all ingredients in medium bowl; beat, with rotary beater, until smooth. Refrigerate, covered, until ready to use.

2. Make Blintzes: In medium bowl, with rotary beater, beat eggs, salad oil, and milk until well mixed. Add flour and salt; beat until very smooth.

3. Refrigerate, covered, 30 minutes. Batter should be consistency of heavy cream.

4. For each blintz, melt 1 teaspoon butter in 7-inch skillet. Pour in about 1½ tablespoons batter, rotating pan quickly, to spread batter completely over bottom of pan.

5. Cook, over medium heat, until lightly browned on one side; remove. Stack blintzes, browned side up, as you take them from skillet.

6. Place 1 tablespoon cheese filling on browned surface of each blintz. Fold two opposite sides over filling; then roll up carefully.

7. Melt rest of butter in large skillet. Sauté blintzes, seam side down, until golden-brown. Turn; sauté other side until golden-brown.

8. Serve hot, with sour cream and raspberries, if desired.

BASIC SWEET BATTER

MAKES 1½ CUPS

(FOR DESSERT FRITTERS)

1 cup sifted all-purpose
   flour
1 tablespoon sugar
1 teaspoon baking powder
1 teaspoon salt
2 eggs

½ cup milk
1 teaspoon salad oil
½ teaspoon vanilla extract
1 teaspoon grated lemon
   peel

1. Sift flour with sugar, baking powder, and salt.

2. In small bowl, with rotary beater, beat remaining ingredients until mixed.

3. Gradually add flour mixture, beating until smooth.

APPLE-RING FRITTERS

MAKES ABOUT 16 FRITTERS,
4 OR 5 SERVINGS

1. Make Basic Sweet Batter, adding ¼ teaspoon cinnamon to dry ingredients.

2. Peel and core 4 or 5 large apples; slice into ½-inch rings.

3. Meanwhile, in deep skillet or deep-fat fryer, slowly heat salad oil or shortening (at least 2 inches) to 375F on deep-frying thermometer.

(*Apple-Ring Fritters continued*)

4. Roll apple rings in flour; shake off excess. Then, with fingers, dip into batter, coating evenly.

5. Deep-fry a few at a time, turning once, 3 to 4 minutes, or until golden-brown on both sides. Drain on paper towels.

6. Serve hot, sprinkled with confectioners' sugar or cinnamon sugar.

APRICOT FRITTERS

MAKES ABOUT 20 FRITTERS,
5 OR 6 SERVINGS

1. Make half of Basic Sweet Batter.

2. On paper towels, drain very well 1 can (1 lb, 13 oz) unpeeled apricot halves.

3. Meanwhile, in deep skillet or deep-fat fryer, slowly heat salad oil or shortening (at least 2 inches) to 375F on deep-frying thermometer.

4. Roll apricot halves in flour; shake off excess. Then, with fingers, dip into batter, coating evenly.

5. Deep-fry a few at a time, turning once, 3 to 4 minutes, or until golden-brown on both sides. Drain on paper towels.

6. Serve hot, sprinkled with confectioners' sugar, with Almond Cream.*

* See this chapter.

BANANA FRITTERS

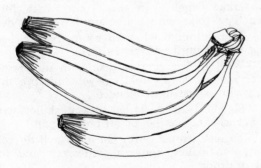

MAKES ABOUT 24 FRITTERS,
6 SERVINGS

1. Make Basic Sweet Batter.

2. Peel 3 large, not overly ripe bananas; slice on diagonal into ½-inch chunks. Sprinkle lightly with lemon juice (1 tablespoon in all) and nutmeg (½ teaspoon in all).

3. Meanwhile, in deep skillet or deep-fat fryer, slowly heat salad oil or shortening (at least 2 inches) to 375F on deep-frying thermometer.

4. Roll banana chunks in flour; shake off excess. Then, with fingers, dip into batter, coating evenly.

5. Deep-fry a few at a time, turning once, 3 to 4 minutes, or until golden-brown on both sides. Drain on paper towels.

6. Serve hot, sprinkled with confectioners' sugar, along with slightly thawed frozen sliced strawberries, or with Caramel or Rum Sauce.*

* See this chapter.

BEIGNETS
(FRENCH FRITTERS)

MAKES 6 BEIGNETS,
6 SERVINGS

Salad oil or shortening for
    deep-frying
1 stick (half of 8½-oz box)
    cream-puff mix

½ cup boiling water
2 eggs
Confectioners' sugar

1. In deep skillet or deep-fat fryer, slowly heat salad oil or shortening (at least 2 inches) to 400F on deep-frying thermometer.

2. Meanwhile, make cream-puff dough according to package-label directions for 1 stick cream-puff mix, using ½ cup boiling water and 2 eggs.

3. Spoon, by rounded tablespoonfuls, into hot oil.

4. Deep-fry 2 or 3 at a time, turning once, about 8 minutes, or until golden-brown and puffed. Drain on paper towels.

5. Serve hot, sprinkled with confectioners' sugar, with Caramel Sauce* or Cardinal Sauce.*

* See this chapter.

BRANDIED MOCHA OMELET

MAKES 1 OMELET,
2 SERVINGS

Filling:
¼ cup semisweet-chocolate
    pieces
2 tablespoons heavy cream
1 tablespoon brandy
1½ teaspoons sugar

Omelet:
3 egg yolks
2 teaspoons instant coffee
3 egg whites
2 tablespoons butter or
    margarine
1½ teaspoons sugar

1. Make Filling: Melt chocolate in top of double boiler, over hot, not boiling, water. Remove from heat.

2. Stir in cream, brandy, and sugar. Cover, and keep warm.

3. Make Omelet: In small bowl, with fork, beat egg yolks with coffee until well blended.

4. In medium bowl, with rotary beater, beat egg whites until stiff peaks form.

5. With rubber scraper, using an under-and-over motion, gently fold egg-yolk mixture into egg whites just until blended.

6. Slowly heat a 9-inch heavy skillet with heat-resistant handle, or an omelet pan.

7. To test temperature: Sprinkle a little cold water on skillet; water should sizzle and roll off in drops.

8. Add butter; heat until it sizzles briskly—it should not brown.

9. Quickly turn egg mixture, all at once, into skillet, spreading evenly over bottom of pan.

10. Cook, over medium heat, until omelet is golden-brown underneath.

(Brandied Mocha Omelet continued)

11. Then run under broiler, 6 inches from heat, about 2 minutes, or until top is golden-brown.

12. To turn out: Loosen edge with spatula. Invert onto serving plate, broiled side down.

13. Place 3 tablespoons filling in center; fold omelet in half.

14. Sprinkle with sugar. Spoon rest of filling over top.

PUFFY JAM OMELET

MAKES 1 OMELET,
2 SERVINGS

Filling:
¼ cup raspberry preserves
1 teaspoon lemon juice
¼ teaspoon grated lemon
　　peel
1 teaspoon kirsch

Omelet:
3 egg yolks
3 egg whites
2 tablespoons butter or
　　margarine
1 tablespoon sugar

1. Make Filling: In small saucepan, combine preserves, lemon juice and peel; simmer, uncovered and stirring occasionally, 5 minutes.

2. Remove from heat. Stir in kirsch; cover, and keep warm.

3. Make Omelet: In small bowl, with fork, beat egg yolks with 1 tablespoon water until blended.

4. In medium bowl, with rotary beater, beat egg whites until stiff peaks form.

5. With rubber scraper, using an under-and-over motion, gently fold egg-yolk mixture into egg whites just until blended.

6. Slowly heat a 9-inch heavy skillet with heat-resistant handle, or an omelet pan. To test temperature: Sprinkle a little cold water on skillet; water should sizzle and roll off in drops.

7. Add butter; heat until it sizzles briskly—it should not brown.

8. Quickly turn egg mixture, all at once, into skillet, spreading evenly over bottom of pan. Cook, over medium heat, until omelet is golden-brown underneath.

9. Then run under broiler, 6 inches from heat, about 2 minutes, or until top is golden-brown.

10. To turn out: Loosen edge with spatula. Invert onto serving plate, broiled side down.

11. Place filling in center; fold omelet in half. Sprinkle with sugar.

Custards

You can hardly name a meal that isn't the better for a light, delectable custard at the end of it. Whether it's a formal dinner, with your best china and silver, or a simple supper for a child, there is a dreamy, creamy custard to suit the occasion.

JUST-RIGHT BAKED CUSTARD

MAKES 5 SERVINGS

2 eggs
2 cups milk
¼ cup sugar
Dash salt

½ teaspoon vanilla extract
½ teaspoon lemon extract
Nutmeg

1. Preheat oven to 350F.
2. Beat eggs and milk together. Add sugar, salt, and extracts.* Mix well.
3. Ladle into 5 ungreased (6-oz) custard cups. Sprinkle with nutmeg.
4. Place in shallow pan. Pour hot water to ½-inch level around custard cups.
5. Bake 35 minutes, or until silver knife inserted ½ inch into center of custard comes out clean. Be careful not to overbake.

* Other flavorings can be used: ½ teaspoon almond, 1 teaspoon vanilla, etc.

FLOATING ISLAND

MAKES 6 SERVINGS

Custard:
2 cups milk
4 egg yolks
⅓ cup sugar
Dash salt
1 teaspoon vanilla extract

Meringue:
4 egg whites
¼ teaspoon cream of tartar
Dash salt
½ cup sugar
½ teaspoon vanilla extract
⅓ cup chopped toasted
    almonds (optional)

1. Several hours before serving, make Custard: In top of double boiler, over direct heat, heat milk until bubbles form around edge.
2. In medium bowl, beat egg yolks with sugar and salt until well blended.
3. Gradually pour hot milk into egg mixture, beating constantly. A wire whisk is handy.
4. Return mixture to top of double boiler; place over hot, not boiling, water. (Water in lower part of double boiler should not touch upper section.)
5. Cook, stirring constantly, until custard coats a metal spoon—about 10 minutes.
6. Pour custard into bowl; press waxed paper right on surface, to prevent formation of skin. When cool, stir in vanilla.
7. Refrigerate, covered, until well chilled—at least 2 hours.

(Floating Island continued)

8. Three hours before serving, make Meringue: In large bowl of electric mixer, let egg whites warm to room temperature—about 1 hour. Meanwhile, preheat oven to 350F. Butter generously and coat with sugar 6 (5-oz) custard cups.

9. At high speed, beat egg whites until foamy. Add cream of tartar and salt.

10. Beat, adding sugar gradually, until stiff peaks form when beater is raised.

11. Add vanilla; fold in almonds.

12. Spoon meringue into prepared custard cups, pressing gently to fill air pockets. Place custard cups in shallow pan containing 1 inch hot water.

13. Bake 15 minutes, or until meringue rises and becomes lightly browned.

14. Place on wire rack. Unmold at once into individual serving dishes. Cool; then refrigerate.

15. To serve, spoon custard around meringue. If desired, garnish with additional almonds or whole strawberries.

CARAMEL CRÈME BRÛLÉE

MAKES 6 SERVINGS

1 cup granulated sugar
4 eggs, slightly beaten
½ teaspoon salt
1 teaspoon vanilla extract

1 can (14½ oz) evaporated
   milk, undiluted
¼ cup light-brown sugar,
   firmly packed

1. Preheat oven to 350F.

2. In small, heavy skillet, over very low heat, melt ½ cup granulated sugar. Shake pan slightly until sugar melts; stir constantly, over low heat, just until light-golden.

3. Divide syrup evenly into 6 (5-oz) custard cups, coating bottoms completely; let cool.

4. Meanwhile, in medium bowl, combine eggs, remaining granulated sugar, the salt, vanilla, evaporated milk, and ¾ cup water; beat, with rotary beater, until thoroughly combined but not frothy.

5. Ladle mixture into custard cups. Set in shallow pan containing ½ inch hot water; bake 35 to 40 minutes, or until silver knife inserted ½ inch from edge comes out clean.

6. Remove from hot water at once. Let cool; then refrigerate until well chilled—2 hours, or overnight.

7. Sift brown sugar evenly over custards. Run under broiler, 3 inches from heat, 2 to 3 minutes, or just until sugar bubbles and melts but does not burn.

8. Refrigerate again, until well chilled. Nice served with fresh-pineapple wedges or strawberries or seedless green grapes.

CRÈME BRÛLÉE

2 cups heavy cream
5 eggs
5 tablespoons granulated
    sugar
¼ teaspoon vanilla extract
1 cup sifted light-brown
    sugar

1. Put cream in top of double boiler, over hot water, and heat until film forms over surface.
2. In bowl, beat eggs, granulated sugar, and vanilla. Slowly add hot cream, beating vigorously.
3. Return mixture to top of double boiler; cook, over simmering water and stirring constantly, until mixture coats a metal spoon. Don't overcook, or it will curdle.
4. Pour into 6 (½-cup) soufflé dishes or custard cups. Cool slightly.
5. Refrigerate 6 to 8 hours.
6. Before serving, sprinkle with brown sugar, and put under broiler 2 to 3 minutes, or until sugar bubbles. Watch carefully, so sugar doesn't burn.
7. Cool.

BAKED HONEY CUSTARD

4 eggs
½ cup honey
2½ cups milk
½ teaspoon salt
¼ teaspoon almond extract
Sesame seeds (optional)

1. Preheat oven to 350F.
2. Beat eggs just enough to blend thoroughly. Stir in honey, milk, salt, and almond extract; mix well.
3. Pour into 8 ungreased (5-oz) custard cups.
4. Place cups in shallow pan; pour hot water around them to depth of ½ inch.
5. Bake 30 to 35 minutes, or until silver knife inserted ½ inch from edge of custard comes out clean.
6. Cool; then chill in refrigerator. Sprinkle with sesame seeds, if desired. Serve cold.

Frozen and Refrigerator Desserts

When the weather is hot, a dessert out of the refrigerator is as welcome as a drop in the temperature. Why not have a variety of cold desserts on hand? Things like sherbets, or that cake you baked earlier, or glasses filled with frozen parfaits.

CRANBERRY SHERBET

2 cups fresh cranberries
1 teaspoon unflavored
    gelatine
2 tablespoons lemon juice
1 cup orange juice
1½ cups sugar
2 egg whites

1. Wash cranberries, removing stems. Turn into 2½-quart saucepan. Add 1½ cups water; simmer, covered, 10 minutes.
2. Meanwhile, sprinkle gelatine over 2 tablespoons cold water in medium bowl; let stand 5 minutes. Stir in lemon juice, orange juice, and sugar.

(*Cranberry Sherbet continued*)

3. Then press cranberries and liquid through a sieve, to remove skins and seeds. Add to gelatine mixture, stirring until gelatine and sugar are dissolved.

4. Pour into ice-cube tray; freeze just until mushy—about 1 hour.

5. Then beat egg whites, in small bowl of electric mixer at high speed, just until soft peaks form.

6. Turn cranberry mixture into large bowl of electric mixer; beat, at medium speed, until smooth. With rubber scraper, gently fold egg whites into cranberry mixture till combined.

7. Turn into 2 ice-cube trays; freeze until firm—about 2 hours.

8. Turn into large electric-mixer bowl; beat, at medium speed, until thick and smooth.

9. Return to ice-cube trays; freeze again until firm—about 30 minutes.

MAKES 6 TO 8 SERVINGS

CHERRY MOUSSE

1½ teaspoons unflavored gelatine
¼ cup sherry
1 cup coarsely chopped, pitted fresh Bing cherries
1 teaspoon grated lemon peel
1 tablespoon lemon juice
2 egg whites
½ cup sugar
1½ cups heavy cream

1. Sprinkle gelatine over sherry in top of double boiler; let stand 5 minutes, to soften. Stir, over hot water, until gelatine is dissolved.

2. Add cherries, lemon peel, and lemon juice; refrigerate until consistency of unbeaten egg white—about 40 minutes.

3. Meanwhile, beat egg whites, in medium bowl, just until foamy. Add sugar gradually, beating well after each addition; continue beating until stiff peaks form when beater is raised.

4. Beat cream until just stiff enough to hold its shape. Turn gelatine and egg whites into whipped cream; fold, using an under-and-over motion, until well combined.

5. Pour into 2 ice-cube trays; freeze until firm—about 2 hours.

MAKES 6 SERVINGS

FROZEN CHOCOLATE MOUSSE

1 tablespoon light corn syrup
¼ cup dark corn syrup
3 squares semisweet chocolate
2 teaspoons vanilla extract
½ teaspoon almond extract
2 cups heavy cream
½ cup canned buttered, toasted diced almonds

1. Combine syrups, 2 tablespoons water, and chocolate in small saucepan. Stir, over low heat, until chocolate melts.

2. Add extracts. Cool slightly.

3. In large bowl of electric mixer, combine chocolate mixture and cream. Refrigerate at least 30 minutes. (Chill beaters at same time.)

4. At high speed, beat mixture until thick and soft peaks form. Spoon into ice-cube tray.

5. Cover with foil; freeze several hours, or until firm. Serve sprinkled with almonds.

COFFEE PARFAIT

¾ cup sugar
4 egg yolks
2 cups heavy cream
2 teaspoons vanilla extract

2 tablespoons instant coffee
1 square unsweetened
    chocolate, grated
Whipped cream

1. Combine sugar and ⅓ cup water in small saucepan.
2. Cook, stirring, over low heat, until sugar is dissolved.
3. Bring to boiling; boil, uncovered and without stirring, to 230F on a candy thermometer.
4. Meanwhile, with portable electric mixer at low speed, beat egg yolks until thick and light. Pour sugar syrup in thin stream over egg yolks, beating constantly; refrigerate 30 minutes.
5. In medium bowl, beat cream with vanilla and coffee just until stiff. Fold into egg-yolk mixture along with chocolate until well combined.
6. Spoon into 6 parfait glasses. Cover top of each glass with foil; freeze until firm.
7. To serve: Remove foil. Garnish top of each parfait with whipped cream. If desired, sprinkle with candy coffee beans or grated chocolate.

MOCHA-MOUSSE DESSERT

Mocha Chiffon Cake*

Mocha Cream:
3 cups heavy cream
1 teaspoon unflavored
    gelatine

2 teaspoons instant coffee
2 teaspoons vanilla extract
1½ cups sifted
    confectioners' sugar
¾ cup unsweetened cocoa
¼ teaspoon salt

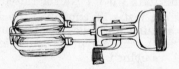

1. Prepare cake for filling: Cut 1-inch slice, crosswise, from top of cake; set aside.
2. With sharp knife, outline a cavity in cake, being careful to leave 1-inch-thick walls around center hole and side.
3. With a spoon, carefully remove cake from this area, being sure to leave 1-inch-thick base.
4. Reserve 1¼ cups crumbled cake.
5. Make Mocha Cream: Refrigerate cream, in large bowl, and rotary beater until very cold.
6. Sprinkle gelatine over 2 tablespoons cold water; let stand 5 minutes, to soften. Heat, stirring, over hot water until dissolved; let cool.
7. Dissolve coffee in vanilla. Add to chilled cream, along with sugar, cocoa, and salt.
8. Beat with chilled rotary beater, or portable electric mixer, until stiff enough to hold its shape.
9. Remove 2½ cups Mocha Cream. Stir in cooled gelatine.
10. Use to fill cavity in cake; replace top.
11. Mix ½ cup Mocha Cream with reserved cake pieces; use to fill center hole of cake.
12. Frost top and side of cake with remaining Mocha Cream. Refrigerate until well chilled.

* See Cakes Chapter.

FROZEN VANILLA MOUSSE

MAKES 6 TO 8 SERVINGS

1 (4-inch) piece vanilla
   bean, cut in quarters
½ cup light cream
½ cup milk

2 egg yolks
Dash salt
½ cup sugar
1 cup heavy cream

1. In top of double boiler, combine vanilla bean with light cream and milk. Heat slowly, over direct heat, just until bubbles form around edge of pan.
2. In small bowl, with rotary beater, beat egg yolks with salt until light. Gradually add sugar, beating until very light and fluffy.
3. Pour in a little light-cream mixture, stirring well; then add to mixture in double-boiler top.
4. Cook, stirring, over hot, not boiling, water (water in double-boiler base should not touch pan above) until slightly thickened and custard forms a coating on metal spoon—takes 12 to 15 minutes. Discard vanilla bean.
5. Cool custard; then refrigerate until cold—about 1 hour.
6. Turn refrigerator to coldest setting. Beat heavy cream in small bowl just until it holds its shape. Fold into chilled custard.
7. Pour into 1-quart ice-cube tray; freeze until almost firm—about 1 hour.
8. Turn into large bowl of electric mixer; beat, at high speed, until smooth. Return to ice-cube tray; freeze until firm—about 4 hours, or overnight.

GOLDEN PARFAIT

MAKES 6 TO 8 SERVINGS

¾ cup sugar
3 egg yolks
Dash salt

2 cups heavy cream
2 teaspoons vanilla extract

1. In medium saucepan, combine sugar with ⅓ cup water. Over low heat, cook, stirring, until sugar is dissolved.
2. Over medium heat, bring to boiling, stirring. Reduce heat, and boil gently, without stirring, to 230F on candy thermometer, or until a little spins a thread when dropped from spoon.
3. Meanwhile, in medium bowl, with portable electric mixer at medium speed, beat egg yolks and salt until light.
4. Gradually beat hot syrup, in a thin stream, into egg yolks. Continue beating until mixture begins to cool. Let cool completely.
5. Beat cream until stiff. Add vanilla.
6. With rubber scraper, gently fold whipped cream into egg-yolk mixture.
7. Spoon into 6 to 8 parfait glasses or a serving bowl. Cover with foil; freeze until firm.

STRAWBERRY PARFAIT

MAKES 6 SERVINGS

1½ pint boxes fresh
    strawberries
12 marshmallows
1 cup sugar

1 teaspoon lemon juice
2 cups heavy cream
1 tablespoon vanilla extract

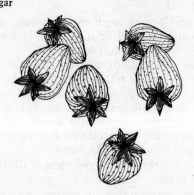

1. Gently wash berries in cold water. Drain; hull. Measure 2 cups; refrigerate rest.
2. In medium saucepan, combine 2 cups berries, the marshmallows, ¾ cup sugar, and the lemon juice. Over low heat, simmer 10 minutes, stirring occasionally. Do not scorch.
3. Remove from heat. Press through a sieve; cool.
4. In large bowl, beat cream until stiff. Stir in vanilla. Blend in strawberry purée. Pour into 2 ice-cube trays.
5. Freeze until mushy; stir thoroughly. Freeze until mushy; stir again. Freeze until firm.
6. To serve: Slice reserved strawberries; toss with remaining sugar. Divide frozen strawberry cream into 6 parfait glasses. Top with sliced berries.

FRESH-RASPBERRY SHERBET

MAKES 1¼ QUARTS

1 qt fresh raspberries
1 tablespoon lemon juice
1½ cups sugar
1 tablespoon light corn
    syrup

2 egg whites
¼ teaspoon salt
½ cup heavy cream,
    whipped

1. Wash and drain raspberries.
2. To purée berries, press through a food mill or sieve (or blend in electric blender, covered, about ½ minute). Measure 2½ cups purée. Stir in lemon juice.
3. In medium saucepan, combine sugar, corn syrup, and ⅔ cup water. Stir, over medium heat, until sugar is dissolved. Bring to a boil, without stirring; cook to 238F on candy thermometer, or until a little of mixture in cold water forms a soft ball.
4. In large bowl, with electric mixer at high speed, beat egg whites with salt until stiff peaks form when beater is raised.
5. Slowly pour syrup, in a thin stream, over whites, beating constantly until mixture is thick and shiny.
6. Meanwhile, set temperature control of refrigerator at coldest setting. Fold whipped cream into raspberry purée. Then fold into egg-white mixture until well blended.
7. Turn into 2 ice-cube trays; freeze until mushy—about 1 hour.
8. Turn into large bowl; beat until smooth. Return to ice-cube trays; freeze again until mushy—about 30 minutes.
9. Again beat mixture until smooth; refreeze until firm.
Note: Or use 1 quart fresh strawberries instead of raspberries.

Ice-Cream Desserts

We've come a long way from the old family freezer on the back porch, haven't we, when we can get our ice cream in five minutes from the drugstore or the supermarket. Lucky, too, for now you can make our ice-cream desserts at virtually the drop of a hat.

BAKED ALASKA

MAKES 12 SERVINGS

2 qt cherry-Burgundy ice
   cream

Cake:
1 pkg (9 oz) white-cake mix
1 egg
½ teaspoon almond extract

Meringue:
8 egg whites
⅛ teaspoon cream of tartar
⅛ teaspoon salt
1 cup sugar

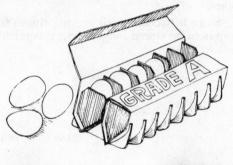

1. With foil, line bottom and sides of a 6-by-5-by-5-inch canister. Fill with ice cream, packing in firmly; freeze, covered, 24 hours.

2. Make Cake: Preheat oven to 350F. Lightly grease and flour bottom of an 8-by-8-by-2-inch pan.

3. Prepare cake mix as package label directs, using egg and amount of water specified on package. Stir in almond extract.

4. Turn batter into prepared pan; bake 25 minutes, or until surface springs back when gently pressed with fingertip.

5. Let cake stand in pan several minutes. Turn out onto wire rack; let cool completely.

6. Make Meringue: Meanwhile, let egg whites stand at room temperature 1 hour. In large bowl of electric mixer, at high speed, beat egg whites with cream of tartar and salt just until soft peaks form when beater is slowly raised.

7. Gradually beat in sugar, 2 tablespoons at a time, beating well after each addition. Continue beating until egg whites are shiny and stiff peaks form when beater is raised.

8. Put sheet of heavy brown paper on large cookie sheet; grease well. Place cake in center.

9. Working quickly, turn ice cream out of canister onto cake. Peel away foil.

10. With spatula, spread entire cake and ice cream with meringue, spreading down onto paper all around, to seal completely. Make swirls on top. Return to freezer until ready to serve—at least 2 hours.

11. Twenty minutes before serving, preheat oven to 425F. Bake the Alaska 8 to 10 minutes on lowest shelf of oven. Trim brown paper from edge of Alaska.

12. Remove to platter. Serve at once. (Or assemble the Alaska several days ahead, and freeze on cookie sheet. Bake as above.)

271

APRICOT-ICE-CREAM MOLD

MAKES 8 TO 10 SERVINGS

½ cup apricot preserves
½ cup seedless golden
    raisins
½ cup sliced toasted
    almonds
1 qt soft vanilla ice cream

1. Combine preserves, raisins, and almonds.
2. With spatula or back of large spoon, press a fourth of ice cream into bottom of a 5½-cup mold.
3. Then press three fourths of preserve mixture irregularly on side of mold. Pack in rest of ice cream. Fill any crevices with remaining preserve mixture.
4. Freeze in freezer overnight, or until ice cream is firm.
5. To unmold: Loosen edge with sharp knife. Invert mold on round of aluminum foil or serving platter. Place hot, damp cloth around mold, to melt ice cream slightly; then shake out ice cream.
6. Store in freezer until serving time (freezer-wrap if to be stored longer than several hours).

CHERRIES JUBILEE

MAKES 6 SERVINGS

1½ teaspoons grated
    orange peel
½ cup orange juice
½ cup sugar
1 can (1 lb, 14 oz) pitted
    Bing cherries, drained
½ teaspoon cornstarch
3 tablespoons brandy or
    cognac
1 qt vanilla ice cream

1. In medium saucepan, combine orange peel, orange juice, and sugar; cook, stirring, over low heat until sugar dissolves.
2. Add cherries; simmer, uncovered, 5 minutes.
3. Remove from heat. Drain, reserving liquid.
4. In small bowl, combine cornstarch and 1 tablespoon water until smooth.
5. Stir into reserved liquid in saucepan; bring to boiling, stirring. Reduce heat, and simmer 1 minute.
6. Add cherries; heat gently. Pour into metal serving bowl.
7. In small saucepan, heat brandy slightly over very low heat. Pour over cherries; light with match.
8. Serve, flaming, over vanilla ice cream.

CRANBERRIES JUBILEE

2 cups fresh cranberries
¾ teaspoon grated orange
    peel
½ cup orange juice

2 cups sugar
1 teaspoon cornstarch
½ cup cognac or brandy
1 qt vanilla ice cream

1. Wash cranberries; drain, and remove stems. Set aside.

2. In medium saucepan, combine orange peel, orange juice, and sugar with ½ cup water; stir, over low heat, to dissolve sugar.

3. Add cranberries; bring to boiling. Reduce heat; simmer, covered, 5 minutes, or until cranberries start to pop.

4. In small bowl, combine cornstarch with 2 tablespoons water.

5. Stir into cranberry mixture; bring to boiling, stirring. Reduce heat, and simmer 1 minute. Mixture will be slightly thickened and translucent.

6. Pour into metal serving bowl.

7. In small saucepan, heat cognac slightly over low heat. Pour over cranberry mixture; light with match.

8. Pass flaming cranberry sauce, to serve over ice cream.

ICE-CREAM BOMBE

1 pt soft vanilla ice cream

1½ pt soft raspberry
    sherbet

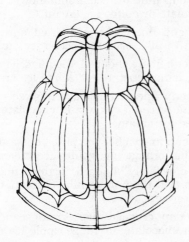

1. Chill well a 1¼-quart decorative mold.

2. Using back of spoon or rubber scraper, press ice cream evenly over interior of mold to make a shell. If ice cream becomes too soft, return to freezer for 15 minutes; then continue coating.

3. Freeze until firm—about 1 hour.

4. Fill center of mold with sherbet. Cover with waxed paper. Freeze several hours, or overnight.

5. To unmold: Wipe outside of mold with hot, damp cloth. Turn out onto chilled plate.

6. Serve at once, garnished with whipped cream and fruit, if desired.

Variations

1. Chocolate-ice-cream shell (1 pint) filled with crème-de-menthe cream (1½ cups heavy cream, whipped, with 6 tablespoons green crème de menthe folded in).

2. Chocolate-ice-cream shell (1 pint) filled with butter-almond ice cream (1½ pints).

3. Strawberry-ice-cream shell (1 pint) filled with orange sherbet (1½ pints).

ICE-CREAM COOKIE SUNDAES

MAKES 10 SERVINGS

Cookie Shells:
²⁄₃ *cup sifted all-purpose*
    flour
¼ *teaspoon baking powder*
¼ *cup soft butter or*
    margarine
¼ *cup sugar*
1 *teaspoon vanilla extract*

½ *teaspoon almond extract*
1 *tablespoon milk*
1 *egg white*
2 *tablespoons finely*
    chopped pecans

1½ *quarts vanilla ice cream*
Chocolate or fruit sauce

1. Preheat oven to 375F.

2. Make Cookie Shells: Sift flour with baking powder; set aside. In medium bowl, with wooden spoon, beat butter with sugar and extracts until smooth. Stir in flour mixture, milk, and egg white; mix until smooth. Stir in nuts.

3. On large, ungreased cookie sheet, drop slightly rounded tablespoonfuls of dough, 3 inches apart. With spatula, spread each to make a 4-inch circle. (Place only 4 on a cookie sheet.) Bake 1 sheet at a time.

4. Bake 7 to 8 minutes, or until edges are slightly brown—no longer.

5. To shape Cookie Shells: With broad spatula, remove cookies at once from sheet to inverted 6-ounce custard cups. With fingers, gently press each cookie around bottom of cup, to give slightly cupped shape to shells.

6. Let cool on cup. (If cookies get too hard to shape, return to oven a few minutes.)

7. To serve: Place cookie shells on serving plates. Fill with ice cream, mounding high. Top with sauce as desired.

Take a Pint of Ice Cream and . . .

To 1 pint slightly softened ice cream, fold in, or swirl through, one of the following:

1. ½ cup miniature marshmallows. Try them in chocolate or coffee ice cream.

2. ½ cup finely chopped dried apricots. Try them in vanilla, or butter-pecan ice cream.

3. ½ cup finely chopped dried figs. Try them in vanilla, lemon-custard, or coffee ice cream.

4. ½ cup finely chopped semisweet- or milk-chocolate pieces. Try them in chocolate, vanilla, or coffee ice cream.

5. ½ cup finely chopped pitted dates. Try them in vanilla, orange, or walnut ice cream.

6. ½ cup finely chopped, drained maraschino cherries. Try them in vanilla, coconut, or chocolate ice cream.

7. ½ cup crushed peppermint candies. Try them in chocolate, or fudge-ripple ice cream.

8. ½ cup canned or packaged flaked coconut. Try it in strawberry ice cream or in black-raspberry or pineapple sherbet.

In each case, return ice cream to pint container, or turn into ice-cube tray, and freeze until firm.

AN ICE-CREAM GARDEN

MAKES 5 SERVINGS

1.   Let 1 pint ice cream soften slightly.

2.   Line 5 (2½-inch) muffin-pan cups with packaged, colored paper liners. Fill to top with ice cream, and level off with a knife.

3.   Scatter chocolate sprinkles over surface, to resemble earth; or use canned or packaged flaked coconut, tinted green, to resemble grass. Insert a wooden pick in center of each "flower-pot."

4.   Place in freezer until serving time.

5.   To serve: Remove picks, and insert stem of small artificial flower in each hole. (Flower and stem should not be more than 3½ inches high.) Serve at once.

LEMON SHERBET WITH RASPBERRIES

MAKES 6 SERVINGS

1 qt lemon sherbet   *2 pkg (10-oz size) thawed*
frozen raspberries,
undrained

1.   Scoop sherbet into 6 sherbet dishes; top each with ⅓ cup raspberries and juice.

2.   Serve at once.

MINCEMEAT GLACÉ

MAKES 7 OR 8 SERVINGS

1 cup prepared mincemeat   *1 qt soft vanilla ice cream*
¼ cup slivered toasted
*   almonds*

1.   Drain mincemeat well. Mix with almonds.

2.   With spatula or back of large spoon, press a fourth of ice cream into bottom of a 5-cup mold.

3.   Then press three fourths of mincemeat mixture irregularly on side of mold. Pack in rest of ice cream. Fill any crevices with remaining mincemeat mixture.

4.   Freeze in freezer overnight, or until ice cream is firm.

5.   To unmold: Loosen edge with sharp knife. Invert mold on round of aluminum foil or serving platter. Place hot, damp cloth around mold, to melt ice cream slightly; then shake out ice cream.

6.   Store in freezer until serving time (freezer-wrap if to be stored longer than several hours).

MOCHA ICE-CREAM ROLL

MAKES 10 SERVINGS

¼ cup sifted cake flour
½ cup sifted unsweetened
    cocoa
1 teaspoon baking powder
¼ teaspoon salt
4 eggs
¾ cup granulated sugar
Confectioners' sugar

1½ pt soft coffee ice
    cream

Topping:
1½ cups heavy cream
¼ cup confectioners' sugar
1 tablespoon instant coffee
¼ teaspoon cinnamon

1. Preheat oven to 400F. Lightly grease a 15½-by-10½-by-1-inch jelly-roll pan. Line with lightly greased waxed paper.

2. Sift flour with cocoa, baking powder, and salt; set aside.

3. In large bowl of electric mixer, at high speed, beat eggs until thick and light. Beat in granulated sugar, 2 tablespoons at a time; then beat until very thick and light.

4. At low speed, beat in flour mixture just until combined—about 1 minute.

5. Turn into prepared pan; bake 13 to 15 minutes, or until surface springs back when gently pressed with fingertip.

6. Turn out onto dish towel sprinkled with confectioners' sugar. Roll up lengthwise, towel and all.

7. Let cool, seam side down, on wire rack.

8. Unroll cake, removing towel. Spread with ice cream; reroll.

9. Wrap in foil; freeze about 3 hours, or until firm.

10. Meanwhile, make Topping: In medium bowl, combine cream with rest of ingredients. Refrigerate at least 2 hours, or until serving time.

11. Beat topping until stiff.

12. To serve roll: Cut into 10 diagonal crosswise slices. Put mound of topping on each slice.

BRANDIED PEACH MELBA

MAKES 6 SERVINGS

3 fresh ripe peaches (about
    1 lb)
1 pkg (10 oz) thawed frozen
    raspberries

¼ cup brandy
1 qt vanilla ice cream

1. Wash peaches; peel. Cut peaches in halves; remove pits. Place peach halves in medium bowl.

2. Press raspberries and juice through sieve, or blend in electric blender, to make a purée.

3. Add brandy to purée, mixing well. Pour over peaches.

4. Refrigerate, covered, several hours, or overnight.

5. To serve: With slotted utensil, remove peach halves to individual serving plates. Place a scoop of ice cream in center of each. Spoon raspberry sauce over top.

FRESH-PEACH ICE CREAM

2 lb fresh ripe peaches
3 tablespoons lemon juice
1½ cups granulated sugar
2 eggs, separated

2 tablespoons
    confectioners' sugar
1 cup heavy cream

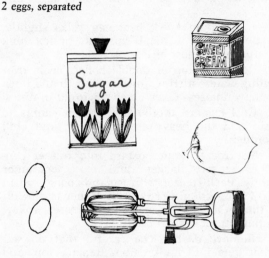

1. Set refrigerator control at coldest temperature.

2. Reserve 2 peaches for garnish. Peel remaining peaches; halve, and remove pits. Place peach halves in mixing bowl with lemon juice; crush with potato masher.

3. Stir in granulated sugar.

4. In medium bowl, with rotary beater, beat egg whites with confectioners' sugar until soft peaks form.

5. In small bowl, beat egg yolks well.

6. Fold yolks gently into whites, using wire whisk or rubber scraper.

7. Whip cream until it holds soft peaks; fold gently into egg mixture.

8. Fold in peaches. Pour into 1-quart ice-cube tray.

9. Freeze until firm around edges.

10. Transfer to bowl; beat with rotary beater until smooth and creamy. Return to tray.

11. Freeze until firm.

12. To serve: Peel and slice reserved peaches. Use to garnish servings.

BLENDER STRAWBERRY ICE CREAM

1 tablespoon grated lemon
    peel
1 tablespoon lemon juice
1 pkg (10 oz) frozen
    strawberries, thawed

⅔ cup sweetened
    condensed milk
1 cup heavy cream, whipped

1. Combine lemon peel, juice, and strawberries in blender. Blend, covered and at high speed, 20 seconds, or until smooth.

2. Reduce speed to low; remove cover; pour condensed milk in steady stream into strawberry mixture.

3. Fold strawberry mixture into whipped cream, using rubber scraper or wire whisk.

4. Pour mixture into ice-cube tray; cover with waxed paper. Freeze 2 to 3 hours, or until firm.

CAFÉ-SHERRY SUNDAES

1½ teaspoons instant
    coffee
¼ cup sweet sherry

1 cup light corn syrup
1 qt vanilla ice cream

1. In small saucepan, combine coffee and sherry, stirring until coffee is dissolved.

2. Add corn syrup; bring to boiling, stirring, over medium heat.

3. Serve warm, over ice cream.

BASIC VANILLA ICE CREAM
(Crank-freezer type)

MAKES 1 QUART,
6 SERVINGS

1½ cups half-and-half or
    top milk
¾ cup sugar
¼ teaspoon salt

4 egg yolks
1½ to 2 tablespoons vanilla
    extract
2 cups heavy cream

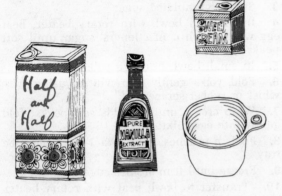

1. In top of double boiler, heat milk until film forms on surface. Do not boil. Stir in sugar and salt.

2. In medium bowl, beat egg yolks slightly. Gradually beat in small amounts of hot milk mixture until most of it is used.

3. Return to top of double boiler; cook, over boiling water, stirring, until as smooth and thick as mayonnaise—takes about 15 to 20 minutes.

4. Cool custard thoroughly. Stir in vanilla to taste and the heavy cream. Cover, and chill thoroughly.

5. To freeze: Pour custard into freezer container; insert dasher, and close container tightly. Pack freezer with ice and coarse salt in 8-to-1 proportion. Crank until dasher is difficult to turn. (If you use an electric freezer, follow manufacturer's instructions.)

6. Remove dasher (be careful that no salt water gets into ice cream). Replace top, and repack with ice and salt in 8-to-1 proportion. Mellow at least 2 hours.

VARIATIONS

Peppermint: Crush coarsely about ½ pound peppermint-stripe candy (you'll need 1¼ cups crushed candy). Prepare Basic Vanilla Ice Cream. When ice cream is frozen to semihardness, remove dasher. With a long wooden spoon, stir in candy. Pack down ice cream; replace cover, and mellow as in basic recipe.

Peach: Reduce vanilla in basic recipe to 1 tablespoon, and add ½ teaspoon almond extract. Prepare and freeze as directed. Peel and purée 2 large ripe peaches. Peel and coarsely chop 1 large peach. (You will need 2 cups of prepared peaches.) Remove dasher, and stir peaches into semihard ice cream. Pack down ice cream; replace cover, and mellow as in basic recipe.

Fruit and cheese are a classic Continental dessert combination that is finding more favor here since America has become so diet-conscious. Our section on fresh fruits tells you how to keep your favorite fruits in good shape until you are ready to use them.

But if you have a taste for sweeter desserts, we have them, made with almost any fruit you can name.

Selection and Storage of Fresh Fruits

Apples. Small quantities can be kept in the refrigerator. Larger quantities of firm, well-shaped apples should be kept in a cool, dry spot. To keep cut apples from turning brown, dip cut surface in lemon or pineapple juice.

Avocados. Keep unripened ones at room temperature, and they'll ripen in two to four days. When an avocado yields to gentle pressure of palms of hands, it's ripe and should be refrigerated. Wrap cut fruit in saran, to prevent discoloration.

Bananas. Keep both ripe and unripened at room temperature, away from light. Use bananas flecked with brown for eating; the green-tipped ones for cooking.

Cherries. Store, uncovered, in refrigerator. Do not wash until ready to eat; any dampness hastens mildew. Cherries are very perishable and should be used soon after buying.

Grapefruit. Best grapefruit has a smooth, tight skin and should feel heavy in the hand (this indicates lots of juice). As the grapefruit season progresses, fruit is noticeably sweeter (more sugar develops). This does not indicate degree of ripeness, since all grapefruit are tree-ripened. Store in refrigerator or a cool spot.

Grapes. Buy grapes that are attached tightly to the stem. They should be plump, firm, bright in color. Store in refrigerator. Wash just before eating.

Lemons and Limes. Select those heavy for their size, with waxy skin and moderate firmness. Keep in refrigerator. They last longer whole or cut, when wrapped in foil or saran.

Oranges. Buy oranges that are heavy for their size (indicates more juice), firm, and free from decay. Neither russeting nor green skin tone affects quality, since all oranges are tree-ripened. Should be stored in refrigerator or in a cool place.

Peaches. Peaches should be ripened at room temperature, away from light. When they yield to a slight pressure of thumb and forefinger, store in refrigerator. Do not wash before storing. If you prefer not-too-cold fruit, bring to room temperature for an hour or so before serving.

Pears. Pears are never tree-ripened. They are best when picked at a right stage of maturity and allowed to ripen at room temperature, away from light. When fruit responds to a slight pressure around the stem end, it is usually ready to eat. Pears need a rather humid atmosphere to ripen properly, and if air is dry from artificial heat, it's not a bad idea to keep a cup of water in the bottom of the fruit bowl. To deter ripening, refrigerate; but bring to room temperature to serve.

Plums. Select plump, fresh-looking, full-colored ones. Store in refrigerator. Wash just before serving.

Strawberries. Choose fruit that is bright, clean, and fresh-appearing. Do not wash strawberries until ready to use, and always wash before hulling. Drain well. Strawberries are highly perishable and ideally should be used soon after buying. If they must be kept briefly, empty them into a flat pan, and store, uncovered, in refrigerator.

BAKED APPLES WITH RAISINS

MAKES 6 SERVINGS

6 large baking apples
6 tablespoons packaged dry
  bread crumbs
6 tablespoons light-brown
  sugar, firmly packed
2 tablespoons butter or
  margarine, melted

¾ teaspoon cinnamon
¼ teaspoon nutmeg
2 tablespoons light or dark
  raisins
1½ cups boiling water

1. Preheat oven to 375F.
2. Wash and core apples; arrange in a greased 9-by-9-by-1¾-inch baking dish.
3. Combine remaining ingredients, except water; use to fill apples.
4. Pour boiling water around apples (use more, if necessary, to make ½ inch deep). Bake 50 minutes, or until tender, basting often with syrup in dish.
5. Cool. Serve with cream, if desired.

GLAZED APPLES

MAKES 4 TO 6 SERVINGS

2 lb tart cooking apples
½ cup sugar

Light cream

1. Wash, pare, and core apples. Cut each into 8 wedges.
2. Combine sugar and ¾ cup water in medium saucepan; bring to boiling, stirring until sugar is dissolved.
3. Add apples; bring to boiling. Then reduce heat; simmer, covered, 20 to 25 minutes; shake pan occasionally, to prevent apples from sticking. (Add a little more water, if necessary.)
4. Serve, warm or cold, with cream.

COUNTRY APPLESAUCE

MAKES ABOUT 3 CUPS

2 lb tart cooking apples

½ to ⅔ cup sugar, depend-
  ing on tartness of
  apples

1. Wash, core, and pare apples; cut into quarters. Measure about 7½ cups.
2. In medium saucepan, bring ½ cup water to boiling. Add apples; bring to boiling.
3. Reduce heat; simmer, covered, 20 to 25 minutes; stir occasionally. Add water, if needed.
4. Stir in sugar until well combined. Serve warm or cold.

Spiced Applesauce: Proceed as with Country Applesauce, but add 1 teaspoon lemon juice, ¼ teaspoon cinnamon, and ⅛ teaspoon nutmeg to apples along with sugar.

Sour-Cream Applesauce: To Country Applesauce, add ½ cup dairy sour cream combined with 1 tablespoon flour, and stir well. Bring to boiling, stirring constantly. Add ½ cup toasted, slivered almonds. Makes 3¾ cups.

BLACKBERRY FLUMMERY

1 qt blackberries
1¼ cups sugar
Dash salt

Dash cinnamon
2 tablespoons cornstarch

1. Wash and carefully pick over blackberries.
2. In saucepan, combine blackberries, ½ cup hot water, sugar, salt, and cinnamon; bring to boiling point. Reduce heat, and simmer gently until slightly syrupy—about 5 to 8 minutes.
3. Add 3 tablespoons water to cornstarch, stirring to make a smooth paste.
4. Blend this into hot blackberry mixture; cook, stirring, until mixture is slightly thickened and translucent—about 3 to 5 minutes. Cool.
5. Serve cold, with heavy cream, if desired.

MELON-BALL CUP

1 teaspoon grated lemon
      peel
2 teaspoons grated orange
      peel
2 tablespoons lemon juice
⅔ cup orange juice

⅓ cup sugar
⅛ teaspoon salt
3 cups honeydew-melon
      balls, chilled
Fresh mint sprigs

1. In small saucepan, combine lemon and orange peels and juices, sugar, and salt.
2. Bring to boiling, stirring until sugar is dissolved. Reduce heat; simmer, uncovered, 5 minutes.
3. Refrigerate syrup until well chilled—at least 2 hours.
4. Divide melon balls into 6 dessert dishes. Add syrup; garnish with mint.

MELON CHA-CHA-CHA

13-lb ripe watermelon   1 cup light rum

1. Cut a plug in center of melon (plug should be 2½ inches square and about 3 inches deep). Pour in rum.
2. Trim pink flesh from plug, leaving rind about ½ inch thick; replace.
3. Place melon in refrigerator, plug side up, and chill 6 to 8 hours, or until rum flavor permeates melon.
4. Cut in wedges.

FRESH ORANGE-COCONUT AMBROSIA

4 large navel oranges
6 tablespoons
      confectioners' sugar

1 cup grated fresh coconut,
      or 1 can (3½ oz)
      flaked coconut
3 tablespoons orange juice

1. Peel oranges, being careful to remove all outer white membrane. Cut oranges crosswise into slices about ⅛ inch thick.
2. Layer a third of slices in a serving bowl. Sprinkle with 2 tablespoons sugar, then with ⅓ cup coconut and 1 tablespoon orange juice. Repeat twice.
3. Refrigerate 1 hour.

MELON DELIGHT WITH FRESH-MINT SAUCE

Mint Sauce:
1 bunch fresh mint
¼ cup sugar
1 jar (10 oz) mint jelly

Fruit:
1 large fresh fully ripe
    pineapple
1 pt fresh strawberries
1 large honeydew melon

1. Make Sauce: Wash mint. Reserve 6 to 8 sprigs for garnish; remove stems from remainder. With scissors, snip mint leaves very fine—you'll have about ½ cup.

2. Combine snipped mint and sugar in a small bowl, and let stand 1 hour.

3. Melt jelly in top of double boiler, over boiling water. Blend in mint-sugar mixture and ¼ cup water.

4. Cover; let cool; then refrigerate until chilled.

5. Prepare Fruit: Cut off top of washed pineapple. Remove rind by cutting down pineapple in wide slices. Remove eyes by cutting V-shape wedges full length of pineapple, following diagonal pattern of eyes. Lift out wedges, and discard. Cut pineapple crosswise into ½-inch slices; remove core. Cut slices into chunks (you'll have about 4 cups).

6. Wash and hull strawberries; halve, if large. Combine with pineapple chunks.

7. Cut melon into 6 to 8 wedges. Scrape out seeds.

8. Heap each wedge with about 1 cup pineapple-strawberry mixture. Spoon about 2 tablespoons mint sauce over each portion. Garnish with sprig of mint.

BAKED FRESH PEACHES

6 fresh ripe peaches (about
    2 lb)
½ cup honey

3 tablespoons lemon juice
Heavy cream

1. Preheat oven to 350F. Wash peaches; peel. Cut in halves; remove pits.

2. Arrange peach halves in 2-quart casserole.

3. Combine honey and lemon juice with 1 cup water. Pour over peaches.

4. Bake, covered, 30 minutes, or until tender.

5. Serve warm or cold, with cream poured over.

FRESH PINEAPPLE IN SHELL

1 medium ripe pineapple
1 cup cut-up banana
1 pkg (10 oz) thawed frozen
    mandarin-orange
    sections, drained

¼ cup kirsch (optional)
4 fresh mint sprigs

1. With sharp knife, cut pineapple, right through frond, into quarters. Remove pineapple from shell; discard core. Cut pineapple into chunks.

2. In medium bowl, gently toss with banana and orange sections until well mixed.

3. Spoon into pineapple shells. Sprinkle each with 1 tablespoon kirsch; then garnish with mint sprig.

BAKED FRUIT FLAMBÉ

1 cup orange marmalade

4 teaspoons grated lemon peel

½ cup lemon juice

3 cups light-brown sugar, firmly packed

3 teaspoons cinnamon

2 cans (1-lb size) peach halves, drained

2 cans (1-lb size) pear halves, drained

2 jars (9½-oz size) pineapple sticks, drained

4 bananas, peeled and quartered

1 cup white rum

1. Preheat oven to 400F. In small saucepan, combine marmalade, lemon peel, and lemon juice; mix well. Bring just to simmering over low heat. Set aside.

2. Meanwhile, in medium bowl, combine brown sugar and cinnamon; mix well.

3. Dry fruit (except the banana quarters) well on paper towels. Dip all pieces of fruit in marmalade mixture, then in sugar mixture, coating completely.

4. Arrange the fruit in two 13½-by-9-by-2-inch baking dishes; bake for 15 minutes.

5. Just before serving, slowly heat rum in small saucepan. Ignite; pour flaming over fruit.

POACHED FRESH PEACHES

¼ cup apricot preserves

1 teaspoon grated orange peel

3 tablespoons sugar

4 fresh ripe peaches (about 1½ lb), peeled, halved, and pitted

1. In medium saucepan, combine preserves, orange peel, and sugar with ½ cup water.

2. Cook, stirring, over low heat, until mixture is syrupy and falls in heavy drops from side of spoon—about 5 minutes.

3. Add peach halves to syrup. Simmer, uncovered, about 10 minutes, or until peaches are tender.

4. Refrigerate, covered, several hours, or until well chilled. Serve peaches with syrup spooned over.

PEARS SABAYON

1 cup granulated sugar

4 fresh pears, pared, halved, and cored

Sauce:

4 egg yolks

1 cup confectioners' sugar

¼ cup sherry

¾ cup heavy cream

1. In 4-quart saucepan, combine granulated sugar and 3 cups water; heat until sugar dissolves.

2. Add pears; cover; simmer gently until tender—about 30 minutes. Remove from heat.

3. Carefully place pears, with about 1 cup syrup, in bowl; refrigerate several hours.

4. Make Sauce: In top of double boiler, with rotary beater or wire whisk, beat egg yolks, confectioners' sugar, and sherry until light.

5. Place over hot, not boiling, water; water should not touch bottom of double-boiler top. Cook, stirring constantly, 8 to 10 minutes.

6. Refrigerate several hours. Mixture thickens on standing.

7. In medium bowl, beat cream until soft peaks form when beater is raised. Carefully fold in chilled sauce.

8. Drain pears. Serve topped with sauce.

POACHED PLUMS

MAKES 4 TO 6 SERVINGS

1 lb fresh Italian plums
½ cup sugar

2 thin slices lemon

1. Wash plums. Cut in half; remove pits.
2. In medium saucepan, combine sugar and 1½ cups water. Bring to boiling; boil 5 to 6 minutes.
3. Add plums and lemon; return to boiling. Reduce heat, and simmer about 4 minutes.
4. Cool; refrigerate, covered, until well chilled.

PRUNES IN PORT, WITH CREAM

MAKES 8 SERVINGS

1½ cups port
1 pkg (16 oz) dried prunes
1 cup granulated sugar
2 teaspoons vanilla extract
1 cup heavy cream

1 tablespoon confectioners' sugar
¼ cup canned flaked coconut

1. Pour port over prunes in large bowl; refrigerate, covered, overnight.
2. Next day, combine prunes in wine with sugar and 1 cup water in medium saucepan; bring to boiling, covered.
3. Reduce heat, and simmer 30 minutes.
4. Remove from heat; stir in 1 teaspoon vanilla.
5. Turn into serving dish; refrigerate until well chilled—about 2 hours.
6. Just before serving, whip cream just until stiff. Fold in confectioners' sugar and rest of vanilla.
7. Garnish prunes with whipped cream. Then sprinkle with flaked coconut.

SPICED BAKED RHUBARB

MAKES 4 TO 6 SERVINGS

4 cups cut rhubarb, in
    1-inch pieces (about
    1¾ lb)

1 cup sugar
1-inch cinnamon stick
4 whole cloves

1. Preheat oven to 400F.
2. Place rhubarb in 2-quart casserole. Sprinkle with sugar; add cinnamon and cloves.
3. Bake, covered, 25 minutes, or until rhubarb is tender, not mushy.
4. Let stand, covered, on wire rack until cool.

STEWED RHUBARB

MAKES 4 TO 6 SERVINGS

1 cup sugar
4 cups cut rhubarb, in
    1-inch pieces (about
    1¾ lb)

1 teaspoon grated lemon
    peel (optional)

1. Combine sugar with ½ cup water in medium saucepan. Over medium heat, stir until sugar is dissolved and syrup comes to boiling.
2. Reduce heat. Add rhubarb and lemon peel; simmer, covered, 10 minutes, or until tender, not mushy.
3. Remove from heat. Let stand, covered, on wire rack until cool.

RHUBARB-AND-STRAWBERRY TAPIOCA

1 pkg (1 lb) thawed frozen
    rhubarb
1 pkg (10 oz) thawed frozen
    sliced strawberries

3 tablespoons quick-cooking
    tapioca
¼ teaspoon salt
Whipped cream

1. Drain rhubarb and strawberries, reserving liquid from both. Cut rhubarb into ¼-inch pieces.
2. Combine rhubarb and strawberry liquids with enough water to measure 2½ cups.
3. In medium saucepan, combine tapioca, salt, and liquid; bring to boiling, over medium heat, stirring occasionally.
4. Remove from heat. Stir in rhubarb and strawberries; let cool 15 minutes. Then stir to mix well.
5. Refrigerate, uncovered, until well chilled— about 2 hours.
6. To serve: Spoon into sherbet glasses. Let stand a few minutes at room temperature. Garnish with whipped cream.

STRAWBERRIES AU NATUREL

2 pt boxes fresh
    strawberries
⅔ cup plus 6 tablespoons
    dairy sour cream

⅓ cup plus 2 tablespoons
    light-brown sugar,
    firmly packed

1. Gently wash strawberries in cold water; drain well.
2. Hull berries; slice into large bowl.
3. Add ⅔ cup sour cream and ⅓ cup sugar; mix gently.
4. Divide into 6 serving dishes.
5. Top each with 1 tablespoon sour cream and 1 teaspoon sugar.
6. Chill 1 hour before serving.

STRAWBERRIES ROMANOFF

2 pt boxes fresh
    strawberries
1 cup confectioners' sugar
1 cup heavy cream

1 teaspoon almond extract
2 tablespoons Cointreau or
    orange juice

1. Gently wash strawberries in cold water. Drain; hull.
2. In medium bowl, sprinkle sugar over berries; toss gently.
3. Refrigerate 1 hour, stirring occasionally.
4. In chilled bowl, with rotary beater, whip cream until stiff. Add almond extract and Cointreau.
5. Fold into strawberries. Serve at once.

FRUIT-CHEESE-WINE COMBINATIONS

Fruit	Cheese	Wine
Apples	Camembert Gorgonzola Liederkranz Roquefort Sharp Cheddar	Burgundy Claret Port
Apricots	Cream cheese Jack Swiss	Light muscat Muscatel
Cherries	Jack Mild Cheddar	
Grapes	Baby Gouda Cream cheese Gruyère Liederkranz Swiss	Light muscat Medium sherry Muscatel Pink champagne Sweet sherry
Melon	Jack Mild brick Swiss	Light muscat Sweet sauterne
Oranges	Edam Gouda	Medium sherry Sweet sherry
Peaches	Camembert Cream cheese Mild brick Swiss	Champagne Light muscat Muscatel
Pears	Camembert Cheddar Cream cheese Gorgonzola Liederkranz Roquefort	Medium sherry Port Tokay

Gelatin Desserts

If you think gelatin desserts are strictly family affairs — particularly, families with children—look at our recipes for sophisticated, fruit-flavored beauties in colors brilliant as rubies and topazes. You will agree with us that they are elegant enough to climax a meal for your choicest guests—especially those who like a low-calorie sweet.

CHERRY-ALMOND FLIP

1 can (1 lb, 1 oz) pitted
    Bing cherries
1 pkg (3 oz) cherry-flavored
    gelatin

½ cup sherry
¼ cup slivered blanched
    almonds

1.   Drain cherries, reserving liquid. Add cold water to liquid to measure 1½ cups; bring to boiling.

2.   Pour hot liquid over gelatin in large bowl, stirring until gelatin is dissolved. Add sherry.

3.   Refrigerate until consistency of unbeaten egg white—about 1 hour.

4.   Fold in cherries and almonds.

5.   Spoon into 4 sherbet glasses; refrigerate until firm—about 1 hour. Serve with light or whipped cream, if desired.

LEMON FLUFF WITH RASPBERRIES

¾ cup boiling water
1 pkg (3 oz) lemon-flavored
    gelatin
2 teaspoons grated lemon
    peel
¼ cup lemon juice

1 cup ice water
3 egg whites
¼ cup sugar
2 pkg (10-oz size) thawed
    frozen raspberries
2 teaspoons cornstarch

1.   Pour boiling water over gelatin in large bowl, stirring until dissolved. Stir in lemon peel, lemon juice, and ice water.

2.   Refrigerate until consistency of unbeaten egg white—1 to 1½ hours.

3.   In medium bowl, beat egg whites with rotary beater just until soft peaks form when beater is slowly raised.

4.   Add sugar, 2 tablespoons at a time, beating well after each addition.

5.   With same beater, beat gelatin mixture until foamy. Add beaten egg whites to gelatin; beat until well combined.

6.   Turn into 8 (6-oz) custard cups; refrigerate until firm enough to unmold—about 1 hour.

7.   Meanwhile, drain raspberries, reserving 1 cup juice.

8.   In small saucepan, combine cornstarch and 2 tablespoons cold water, mixing until smooth.

9.   Stir in reserved raspberry juice; bring to boiling, stirring constantly—mixture should be thickened and translucent. Let cool completely.

10.   Then pour over drained raspberries. Refrigerate until serving time.

11.   To serve: Unmold each dessert on dessert plate (there will be a slight gelatin layer on the top). Pour raspberries over Lemon Fluff.

ORANGE-PINEAPPLE JUBILEE

MAKES 6 SERVINGS

1½ cups boiling water
1 pkg (3 oz) lemon-flavored
    gelatin
½ cup sherry
Dash salt

1 can (11 oz) mandarin-
    orange sections,
    drained
1 can (8¾ oz) pineapple
    tidbits, drained

1. Pour boiling water over gelatin in large bowl, stirring until gelatin is dissolved. Add sherry and salt.

2. Refrigerate until consistency of unbeaten egg white—about 1 hour.

3. Fold in orange and pineapple.

4. Spoon into 6 sherbet glasses; refrigerate until firm—about 1 hour. Serve topped with whipped cream, if desired.

JELLIED PEACH MEDLEY

MAKES 6 SERVINGS

½ cup boiling water
1 pkg (3 oz) peach-flavored
    gelatin
1½ cups canned pineapple
    juice

1 can (8 oz) apricot halves,
    drained
1 can (8 oz) sliced peaches,
    drained
½ cup packaged or canned
    flaked coconut

1. Pour boiling water over gelatin in large bowl, stirring until gelatin is dissolved. Add pineapple juice.

2. Refrigerate until consistency of unbeaten egg white—about 1 hour.

3. Meanwhile, cut apricots in half.

4. Fold apricots, peaches, and coconut into gelatin. Spoon into 6 sherbet glasses.

5. Refrigerate until firm—about 1 hour. Serve with light or whipped cream, if desired.

SNOW PUDDING

MAKES 6 SERVINGS

1 envelope unflavored
    gelatine
¾ cup sugar
Dash salt
¾ cup boiling water

1 teaspoon grated lemon
    peel
¼ cup lemon juice
3 egg whites

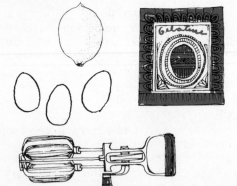

1. In large bowl, sprinkle gelatine over ½ cup cold water, to soften. Add ½ cup sugar, the salt, and boiling water; stir to dissolve gelatine.

2. Add lemon peel and juice, mixing well.

3. Refrigerate until consistency of unbeaten egg white—about 1 hour.

4. Beat egg whites until foamy. Gradually add remaining sugar, beating well after each addition. Continue beating until soft peaks form when beater is raised.

5. Beat gelatine mixture until foamy. With rubber scraper, using an under-and-over motion, gently fold beaten egg whites into gelatine mixture until well combined.

6. Turn mixture into a 1-quart mold; refrigerate until firm.

7. To unmold: Run a small spatula around edge of mold. Invert over serving platter; shake gently to release. If necessary, place a hot, damp dishcloth over mold; shake again to release. Serve with Pour Custard.*

* See this chapter.

JELLIED PRUNES WITH WALNUTS

1 envelope unflavored
    gelatine
1 cup boiling water
¼ cup sugar
1 tablespoon instant coffee
1 teaspoon lemon juice

1½ cups pitted cooked
    prunes, coarsely
    chopped
½ cup coarsely chopped
    walnuts
½ cup heavy cream,
    whipped
Grated orange peel

1. Sprinkle gelatine over ½ cup cold water in large bowl; let stand 5 minutes, to soften.
2. Add boiling water, sugar, and coffee, stirring until dissolved. Add lemon juice.
3. Refrigerate until consistency of unbeaten egg white—about 45 minutes.
4. Fold in prunes and walnuts. Spoon into 4 sherbet glasses.
5. Refrigerate until firm—about 20 minutes.
6. Serve with whipped cream and orange peel.

DOUBLE-RASPBERRY DELIGHT

1 cup boiling water
1 pkg (3 oz) black-raspberry-
    flavored gelatin
1 pkg (10 oz) frozen
    raspberries

½ cup canned pineapple
    juice*
1 medium-ripe banana,
    thinly sliced (¾ cup)

1. Pour boiling water over gelatin in large bowl, stirring until gelatin is dissolved.
2. Add raspberries and pineapple juice; stir until berries are thawed and gelatin is slightly thickened—about 5 minutes. Fold in banana.
3. Spoon into 6 sherbet glasses; refrigerate until firm—about 30 minutes. Serve topped with whipped cream, if desired.
* Do not use frozen pineapple juice.

Meringues

They look as fragile as eggshells and hard to make; yet anyone can make one of these elegant confections perfectly, and every time.

Our recipe is simple to follow. And we'll tell you the prettiest ways to fill your delicate meringue shells.

BAKED MERINGUE SHELL

3 egg whites
¼ teaspoon cream of tartar

¼ teaspoon salt
¾ cup sugar

1. Lightly butter bottom and side of a 9-inch pie plate.
2. In large bowl of electric mixer, let egg whites warm to room temperature—1 hour.
3. At high speed, beat egg whites with cream of tartar and salt just until very soft peaks form when beater is slowly raised.
4. Gradually beat in sugar, 2 tablespoons at a time, beating well after each addition. Continue beating until very stiff peaks form. Meringue should be shiny and moist.
5. Preheat oven to 275F. Spread two thirds of meringue on bottom of prepared pie plate. Use rest to cover side and mound around rim.
6. Bake 1 hour. Let cool in pan on wire rack.
7. To serve: Fill with ice cream and sauce.

INDIVIDUAL MERINGUE SHELLS

1. Make meringue mixture as directed in Baked Meringue Shell.
2. On heavy brown wrapping paper, placed on large cookie sheets, spoon heaping tablespoons of meringue to form 8 mounds, 3 inches apart.
3. With back of spoon, shape the center of each mound into a shell.
4. Bake 60 minutes. Turn off heat; let stand in oven until cool. Use in place of Meringue Shell.
5. To store meringues: Wrap cooled meringues in waxed paper. Store in cool, dry place. Do not place in air-tight container. Makes 8.

MAKES 8 SERVINGS

CHOCOLATE ANGEL PIE

Meringue Shell:
2 egg whites
⅛ teaspoon cream of tartar
½ cup sugar

½ teaspoon salt
1⅓ cups milk
3 squares unsweetened
    chocolate, chopped
3 eggs, separated
⅛ teaspoon cream of tartar
1 teaspoon vanilla extract

Chocolate-Chiffon Filling:
1 envelope unflavored
    gelatine
1 cup sugar

Whipped cream (optional)

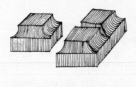

1. Make Meringue Shell: Preheat oven to 275F. Butter well a 9-inch pie plate.
2. In small bowl of electric mixer, at high speed, beat egg whites with cream of tartar until soft peaks form when beater is slowly raised. Slowly beat in sugar till stiff peaks form.
3. Spread meringue in prepared pie plate; bake 35 to 40 minutes, or until pale golden-brown. Cool, on wire rack, away from drafts.
4. Make Chocolate-Chiffon Filling: Combine gelatine, ½ cup sugar, and the salt in medium saucepan.
5. Gradually stir in milk. Add chocolate; over medium heat, stir until chocolate is melted.
6. Beat egg yolks slightly in small bowl. Into yolks, quickly beat hot chocolate mixture, a little at a time; then pour all of yolk-chocolate mixture into saucepan.
7. Cook, stirring constantly, until mixture thickens—3 to 5 minutes. Let cool.
8. In large bowl, with rotary beater, beat egg whites, cream of tartar, and vanilla until soft peaks form when beater is raised. Gradually beat in remaining sugar until stiff peaks form.
9. Carefully fold cooled chocolate mixture into egg-white mixture.
10. Pour into meringue shell. Refrigerate till firm—3 hours. Top with whipped cream.

MAKES 6 TO 8 SERVINGS

HEAVENLY LEMON PIE

Lemon Filling:
4 egg yolks
½ cup granulated sugar
1 tablespoon grated lemon
    peel
¼ cup lemon juice
½ cup heavy cream

9-inch Baked Meringue
    Shell

½ cup heavy cream,
    whipped
2 tablespoons
    confectioners' sugar

1. Make Lemon Filling: In top of double boiler, with rotary beater, beat egg yolks with granulated sugar until thick and light.
2. Stir in lemon peel and juice.
3. Cook, over hot, not boiling, water, stirring until thickened and smooth—10 minutes.

(Heavenly Lemon Pie continued)

4. Remove from heat. Let cool completely, stirring occasionally. (To hasten cooling, place top of double boiler in bowl of ice cubes.)

5. With rotary beater, beat cream in small bowl just until stiff. With rubber scraper, using an under-and-over motion, gently fold into cooled lemon mixture just until smooth.

6. Turn into meringue shell, spreading evenly. Cover top loosely with saran or foil; refrigerate overnight.

7. Just before serving, combine whipped cream with confectioners' sugar. Swirl over top.

Individual Lemon Pies: Use Lemon Filling in 8 Individual Meringue Shells. Refrigerate, lightly covered, overnight. To serve, garnish with whipped cream. Makes 8 servings.

FRESH-STRAWBERRY TORTE

MAKES 10 SERVINGS

Torte:
6 egg whites
¼ teaspoon salt
½ teaspoon cream of tartar
1½ cups sugar
¾ teaspoon vanilla extract
½ teaspoon almond extract

Filling:
1 pt box fresh
  strawberries
¼ cup sugar
1½ cups heavy cream,
  whipped

1. In large bowl of electric mixer, let egg whites warm to room temperature—1 hour.

2. Meanwhile, lightly grease bottom (not side) of 9-inch tube pan. Preheat oven to 450F.

3. Make Torte: With mixer at high speed, beat egg whites with salt and cream of tartar until soft peaks form when beater is raised.

4. Gradually beat in sugar, ¼ cup at a time, beating well after each addition. Continue beating until stiff peaks form. Beat in extracts.

5. Spread egg-white mixture evenly in prepared pan. Put pan in oven; turn off heat.

6. Let stand in oven several hours or overnight. Do not open oven door.

7. Run a small spatula around edge of torte; invert onto serving plate. Refrigerate several hours, or until well chilled.

8. Meanwhile, make Filling: Gently wash strawberries in cold water. Drain; hull. Reserve 5 large berries for garnish. Slice remaining berries into medium bowl. Add sugar; stir gently. Set aside until ready to use.

9. Split chilled torte in half crosswise. Spread bottom half with half of whipped cream; spoon on half the sliced berries.

10. Top with other half of torte, cut side down. Spoon on rest of sliced berries and whipped cream. Garnish with whole berries.

Note: Or use 1 package (10 oz) frozen whole strawberries, thawed and drained; omit sugar.

Soufflés

We've told you about our dinner soufflés in another chapter. And now we lift the curtain on the best sweet soufflés you've ever tasted.

To determine volume of soufflé dishes: Add water to soufflé dish just until it reaches inside ridge; do not fill dish to top.

BRANDIED-APRICOT SOUFFLÉ

MAKES 6 SERVINGS

4 egg whites
1 tablespoon butter or
    margarine
2 tablespoons plus ⅓ cup
    sugar

¼ teaspoon cream of tartar
¼ teaspoon salt
¼ cup brandy
1 cup apricot purée*
Brandy Sauce**

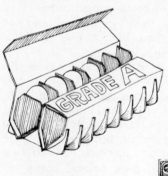

1. Preheat oven to 350F. In large bowl of electric mixer, let egg whites warm to room temperature—about 1 hour.

2. With butter, lightly grease bottom and side of 1½-quart, straight-side soufflé dish; sprinkle evenly with 2 tablespoons sugar.

3. With mixer at high speed, beat egg whites with cream of tartar and salt just until soft peaks form when beater is slowly raised.

4. Gradually add ⅓ cup sugar (about 2 tablespoons at a time), beating well after each addition; continue beating until very stiff peaks form when beater is slowly raised.

5. Combine brandy and apricot purée.

6. With rubber scraper, using an under-and-over motion, gently fold into beaten egg whites until well combined.

7. Turn into prepared soufflé dish. Set in pan containing about 1 inch hot water; bake 35 to 40 minutes.

8. Serve hot or cold, with Brandy Sauce** or whipped cream.

* To make apricot purée: In medium saucepan, combine 1½ cups dried apricots with just enough cold water to cover; bring to boil. Remove from heat; let stand, covered, 5 minutes. Drain, reserving liquid. Press apricots, along with ⅓ cup reserved liquid, through food mill or sieve (or blend in blender). Measure 1 cup purée.

** See this chapter.

BROWNIE SOUFFLÉ

5 eggs, separated
6½ tablespoons butter or
    margarine
1 cup sugar
5 tablespoons unsifted
    all-purpose flour
9 tablespoons unsweetened
    cocoa
1½ cups milk

1½ teaspoons vanilla
    extract
¼ teaspoon cream of tartar
¼ teaspoon salt
¾ cup coarsely chopped
    walnuts
1 pt very soft vanilla ice
    cream; or ½ pt heavy
    cream, whipped

1. Preheat oven to 350F. In large bowl of electric mixer, let egg whites warm to room temperature—about 1 hour.

2. With 1 tablespoon butter, lightly grease bottom and side of 1½-quart, straight-side soufflé dish; sprinkle evenly with 2 tablespoons sugar.

3. Make paper collar: Tear sheet of waxed paper 26 inches long; fold lengthwise in thirds. Lightly grease one side with ½ tablespoon butter; sprinkle evenly with 2 tablespoons sugar.

4. With string, tie collar (sugar side inside) around soufflé dish, to form 2-inch rim above top edge.

5. Melt remaining butter in medium saucepan; remove from heat. In small bowl, thoroughly combine flour and cocoa. Stir into butter. Gradually blend in milk.

6. Over low heat, cook to boiling point, stirring constantly (watch carefully—cocoa mixture can scorch easily). Mixture should be thick and smooth. Remove from heat; let cool about 10 minutes.

7. In medium bowl, beat egg yolks until thick and lemon-colored. Gradually beat in 6 tablespoons sugar and the vanilla. Gradually beat in cocoa mixture until well combined.

8. With electric mixer at high speed, beat egg whites with cream of tartar and salt just until soft peaks form when beater is slowly raised.

9. Gradually add remaining sugar (2 tablespoons at a time), beating well after each addition; continue beating until stiff peaks form when beater is slowly raised.

10. Turn cocoa mixture into egg whites; sprinkle with nuts. With wire whisk or rubber scraper, using an under-and-over motion, gently fold cocoa mixture into whites until well combined.

11. Turn into prepared soufflé dish. Set in pan containing about 1 inch hot water; bake 1 hour and 15 minutes.

12. Gently remove collar. Serve soufflé at once, with ice cream or whipped cream.

WALNUT-PRUNE WHIP
DE LUXE

5 egg whites
1½ cups dried prunes
2 tablespoons butter or
  margarine
2 tablespoons plus ½ cup
  sugar
¼ teaspoon cream of tartar

¼ teaspoon salt
2 teaspoons grated lemon
  peel, or 1 tablespoon
  grated orange peel
½ cup finely chopped
  walnuts

MAKES 6 SERVINGS

1. In large bowl of electric mixer, let egg whites warm to room temperature—about 1 hour.

2. In medium saucepan, combine prunes with just enough water to cover; over medium heat, bring to boiling. Remove from heat; let stand, covered, 10 minutes.

3. Drain prunes, reserving liquid; remove pits. Press prunes and liquid through food mill, or blend in blender to make a purée. Measure 1½ cups prune purée; set aside.

4. Preheat oven to 350F. Butter bottom and side of 2-quart casserole; then sprinkle with 2 tablespoons sugar, coating completely.

5. At high speed, beat egg whites with cream of tartar and salt just until soft peaks form when beater is slowly raised.

6. Gradually add ½ cup sugar (2 tablespoons at a time), beating well after each addition. Continue beating until stiff peaks form.

7. Combine prune purée with lemon peel and walnuts, mixing well.

8. With rubber scraper, using an under-and-over motion, gently fold prune mixture into egg whites just until combined.

9. Turn into prepared casserole; set in pan containing 1 inch hot water.

10. Bake 35 to 40 minutes, or until lightly browned. Serve warm, with whipped cream, if desired.

COLD LEMON-AND-LIME
SOUFFLÉ

3 egg whites
1 tablespoon butter or
  margarine
2 tablespoons unflavored
  gelatine
1½ cups boiling water
1¾ cups sugar

½ teaspoon salt
2 teaspoons grated lemon
  peel
1 cup lemon juice
½ cup lime juice
1 cup heavy cream

MAKES 6 TO 8 SERVINGS

1. In large bowl of electric mixer, let egg whites warm to room temperature—1 hour.

2. With butter, lightly grease bottom and side of 1½-quart, straight-side soufflé dish.

3. Sprinkle gelatine over 1 cup cold water in large bowl; let stand 5 minutes, to soften.

4. Stir in boiling water, 1½ cups sugar, and the salt; stir until gelatine and sugar are dissolved. Stir in lemon peel, lemon and lime juices.

5. Refrigerate until consistency of unbeaten egg white.

6. Then beat cream until stiff enough to hold its shape.

7. With mixer at high speed, beat egg whites just until soft peaks form when beater is slowly raised.

(Cold Lemon-and-Lime Soufflé continued)

8. Gradually beat in remaining sugar (2 table-spoons at a time), beating well after each addition; continue beating until stiff peaks form when beater is slowly raised.

9. Turn whipped cream and gelatine mixture into egg whites. With wire whisk or rubber scraper, using an under-and-over motion, gently fold together. Turn into soufflé dish.

10. Refrigerate four hours, or overnight.

11. Just before serving, decorate, if desired, with rosettes of whipped cream.

VANILLA SOUFFLÉ

MAKES 6 TO 8 SERVINGS

5 eggs, separated
1½ tablespoons plus ⅓ cup
   butter or margarine
¾ cup sugar
⅓ cup unsifted all-purpose
   flour
1⅓ cups milk
¼ teaspoon cream of tartar
¼ teaspoon salt
1½ teaspoons vanilla
   extract
Flaming Cherry Sauce*

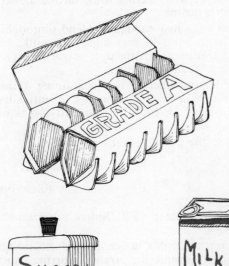

1. Preheat oven to 350F. In large bowl of electric mixer, let egg whites warm to room temperature—about 1 hour.

2. With 1 tablespoon butter, grease bottom and side of 1½-quart, straight-side soufflé dish; sprinkle evenly with 2 tablespoons sugar.

3. Make paper collar: Tear sheet of waxed paper 26 inches long; fold lengthwise in thirds. Grease one side with ½ tablespoon butter; sprinkle evenly with 2 tablespoons sugar.

4. With string, tie collar (sugar side inside) around soufflé dish, to form 2-inch rim above top edge.

5. Melt remaining butter in medium sauce-pan; remove from heat. Stir in flour until smooth; then stir in milk.

6. Bring to boiling point, stirring, over medium heat. Remove from heat; let cool 5 minutes.

7. With mixer at high speed, beat egg whites with cream of tartar and salt just until soft peaks form when beater is slowly raised.

8. Gradually add rest of sugar (2 tablespoons at a time), beating well after each addition; continue beating until stiff peaks form when beater is slowly raised.

9. In small bowl of mixer and at high speed, beat yolks with vanilla until light and fluffy.

10. Stir into white sauce until well mixed.

11. With wire whisk or rubber scraper, using an under-and-over motion, gently fold egg-yolk mixture into egg whites until well combined.

12. Turn into prepared soufflé dish. Set in pan containing 1 inch hot water; bake 1 hour.

13. Gently remove collar. Serve soufflé at once, with Flaming Cherry Sauce.*

* See this chapter.

Puddings

There comes a time in everyone's life when only an old-fashioned and homey pudding will fill the bill as a dessert. And we feature such favorites as Bread Pudding, Indian Pudding, Rice Pudding, as good as any your mother and grandmother ever made.

OLD-FASHIONED BREAD PUDDING

6 slices day-old white bread
2 tablespoons melted butter
    or margarine
2 tablespoons plus ½ cup
    sugar
1 teaspoon cinnamon
½ cup seedless raisins
4 eggs
2 cups milk
1 teaspoon vanilla extract

MAKES 8 SERVINGS

1. Preheat oven to 350F. Grease a 1½-quart baking dish.

2. Cut crusts from bread. Brush with melted butter; sprinkle with 2 tablespoons sugar and the cinnamon.

3. Cut each slice into quarters. Arrange in layers in prepared baking dish, sprinkling each layer with raisins.

4. Beat eggs just enough to blend thoroughly. Stir in remaining ½ cup sugar, the milk, and vanilla; continue stirring until sugar dissolves. Pour over bread and raisins.

5. Set baking dish in pan containing 1 inch hot water; bake 55 to 60 minutes, or until silver knife inserted ½ inch into custard comes out clean.

6. Serve the pudding warm or chilled.

CHOCOLATE-NUT BREAD PUDDING

1 square unsweetened
    chocolate
1¼ cups milk
1 egg
¼ cup sugar
⅛ teaspoon salt
½ teaspoon vanilla extract
1 cup white-bread cubes
2 tablespoons buttered,
    roasted diced almonds
Whipped cream

MAKES 4 SERVINGS

1. Preheat oven to 350F. Butter a 1-quart casserole.

2. In top of double boiler, heat chocolate and milk, over simmering water, stirring, until chocolate is melted.

3. In medium bowl, with rotary beater, beat egg until frothy. Gradually beat in sugar, salt, and vanilla.

4. Slowly beat in hot milk mixture. Stir in bread cubes and almonds. Pour into prepared casserole.

5. Place in shallow pan containing 1 inch cold water. Bake 1 hour, or until cake tester inserted in center comes out clean.

6. Serve warm, with whipped cream.

BUTTERSCOTCH BREAD PUDDING

3 slices white bread
2 teaspoons soft butter or
   margarine
1 cup light-brown sugar,
   firmly packed

3 eggs
1 cup evaporated milk,
   undiluted
Dash salt
½ teaspoon vanilla extract

MAKES 4 SERVINGS

1. Trim crusts from bread. Spread with butter, and cut into ½-inch squares.
2. Butter top section of double boiler. Pour in brown sugar; add bread cubes.
3. Beat eggs with remaining ingredients; then pour over bread cubes—don't stir.
4. Cover, and cook, over boiling water, 1 hour, or until silver knife inserted ½ inch into center comes out clean. (Add water to bottom of double boiler if necessary.)
5. Serve warm, with butterscotch sauce from bottom of pudding poured over.

FUDGE-PUDDING PIE

1 square unsweetened
   chocolate
½ cup soft butter or
   margarine
1 cup sugar
2 eggs

½ cup sifted all-purpose
   flour
½ cup finely chopped
   pecans
1 teaspoon vanilla extract
1 pt vanilla ice cream

MAKES 6 SERVINGS

1. Preheat oven to 350F. Lightly grease a 9-inch pie plate.
2. Melt chocolate in top of double boiler, over hot, not boiling, water.
3. Remove from heat. With portable electric mixer, beat in butter, sugar, and eggs well.
4. Gradually add flour, beating just until combined. Stir in nuts and vanilla.
5. Spread batter evenly in prepared pie plate; bake 25 minutes—do not overbake. Top will crack slightly.
6. Let cool on wire rack. To serve: Cut into wedges. Top each with ice cream.

STEAMED CARROT PUDDING

1½ cups sifted all-purpose
   flour
1½ teaspoons baking soda
1½ cups sugar
¾ teaspoon salt
1½ teaspoons cloves
1½ teaspoons cinnamon
1½ teaspoons nutmeg

3 tablespoons butter or
   margarine, melted
3 eggs, well beaten
1½ cups grated raw carrots
1½ cups grated raw
   potatoes
1½ cups coarsely chopped
   walnuts
1½ cups seeded raisins

MAKES 8 TO 10 SERVINGS

1. Thoroughly oil a 1½-quart mold.
2. Sift flour with soda, sugar, salt, and spices. Gradually stir butter into eggs in large bowl.
3. Then stir in flour mixture and remaining ingredients; mix well.
4. Turn into prepared mold; cover securely with aluminum foil or tight-fitting cover. Place on trivet in deep kettle.
5. Add enough boiling water to come halfway up side of mold.
6. Simmer, with cover on kettle, 2 hours. Remove mold from kettle. Cool pudding to lukewarm; remove from mold.
7. To store: Cool pudding completely. Wrap in aluminum foil. To serve: Unwrap pudding; steam 30 minutes, or until heated through. Serve with Vanilla Hard Sauce.*

* See this chapter.

FLAMING PLUM PUDDING

MAKES 12 SERVINGS

⅔ cup chopped suet (¼ lb)
2 tablespoons pared,
    chopped apple
2 tablespoons chopped
    candied orange peel
2 tablespoons chopped
    candied lemon peel
⅔ cup chopped candied
    citron
1½ cups raisins
1 cup currants
2 cups packaged dry bread
    crumbs
3 teaspoons cinnamon

1½ teaspoons ginger
¼ teaspoon nutmeg
½ teaspoon allspice
¼ teaspoon salt
1 cup sugar
⅓ cup raspberry preserves
4 eggs
2 tablespoons milk
6 tablespoons plus ¼ cup
    cognac
6 tablespoons dry white
    wine
Boiling water

1. In large bowl, combine well suet, fruits, bread crumbs, spices, salt, sugar, and preserves.
2. With rotary beater, beat eggs until foamy. Stir in milk, 6 tablespoons cognac, and wine.
3. With rubber scraper, fold egg mixture into fruit mixture until well combined.
4. Turn batter into a well-greased 2-quart pudding mold with tight-fitting cover.
5. Place mold on trivet in large kettle. Pour in enough boiling water to come halfway up side of mold. Cover kettle.
6. Steam pudding 4 hours. (Water in kettle should boil gently; add more water as needed.)
7. Remove pudding to wire rack; let cool 5 minutes. Invert on serving plate; lift off mold.
8. In small saucepan, warm rest of cognac slightly. Ignite with match; pour, blazing, over pudding. Serve with Vanilla Hard Sauce.*
* See this chapter.

BAKED INDIAN PUDDING

MAKES 8 SERVINGS

4½ cups milk
⅓ cup yellow cornmeal
1 tablespoon butter or
    margarine
¼ cup light-brown sugar,
    firmly packed

¼ cup dark molasses
½ teaspoon salt
1 teaspoon cinnamon
½ teaspoon ginger
⅛ teaspoon cloves
⅓ cup light cream

1. Preheat oven to 300F. In small bowl, combine 1 cup milk and the cornmeal; let stand.
2. In medium saucepan, slowly heat 2 cups milk until bubbles form around edge of pan.
3. Gradually stir cornmeal mixture into hot milk; cook, stirring, over medium heat, 10 minutes.
4. Add rest of milk, the butter, sugar, molasses, salt, and spices, stirring just until butter is melted.
5. Turn into ungreased 1½-quart casserole; bake, uncovered, 2 hours.
6. Stir in cream, combining well; bake, uncovered, 30 minutes.
7. Let cool on wire rack 1 hour before serving. Serve slightly warm, with vanilla ice cream or light cream.

LEMON-PECAN PUDDING

MAKES 6 SERVINGS

1½ tablespoons butter or
    margarine
¾ cup sugar
2 teaspoons grated lemon
    peel
¼ cup lemon juice
3 eggs, separated

3 tablespoons flour
⅓ cup finely chopped
    pecans
1 cup milk
⅛ teaspoon salt
Whipped cream (optional)

1. Preheat oven to 350F. Lightly grease 6 (6-oz) custard cups.
2. In medium bowl, with wooden spoon, mix butter and sugar. Stir in lemon peel and juice. Beat in egg yolks, one at a time.

(Lemon-Pecan Pudding continued)

3.   Combine flour and pecans. Add to sugar-egg mixture alternately with milk, beginning and ending with flour mixture.

4.   In small bowl, with rotary beater, beat egg whites with salt until stiff peaks form when beater is raised. Fold into batter.

5.   Pour into prepared custard cups. Place in shallow pan containing 1 inch cold water; bake about 50 minutes, or until nicely browned.

6.   Serve warm, topped with whipped cream, if desired.

STEAMED APPLE PUDDING

1½ cups sifted all-purpose
    flour
1 teaspoon baking soda
½ teaspoon salt
½ teaspoon cinnamon
½ teaspoon nutmeg
¼ teaspoon cloves
¼ cup soft butter or
    margarine

1 cup sugar
2 eggs, well beaten
4 pared medium apples,
    shredded (2⅓ cups)
½ cup dark raisins
Boiling water
Light cream

MAKES 6 TO 8 SERVINGS

1.   Grease well a 1½-quart, heatproof bowl.

2.   Into small bowl, sift flour with baking soda, salt, and spices; set aside.

3.   In large bowl, with wooden spoon, beat butter, sugar, and eggs until mixture is smooth and light. Stir in apples and raisins.

4.   Stir flour mixture into the fruit mixture, mixing well; turn into prepared bowl.

5.   Cover surface of pudding with double thickness of waxed paper. Cover top of bowl completely with foil; tie edge securely with twine.

6.   Place bowl on trivet in large kettle. Pour boiling water around bowl to come halfway up side.

7.   Cover kettle; bring to boiling. Reduce heat; boil gently 2 hours.

8.   Remove bowl to wire rack; let stand 5 minutes.

9.   With spatula, gently loosen edge of pudding from side of bowl. Invert on serving dish. Serve warm, with cream.

BAKED CREAMY RICE PUDDING

⅓ cup raw regular white
    rice
4 cups milk
½ cup sugar
½ teaspoon salt

1 teaspoon vanilla extract
¼ teaspoon nutmeg
    (optional)
½ cup seedless raisins

MAKES 6 TO 8 SERVINGS

1.   Preheat oven to 300F. Lightly butter a 1½-quart casserole.

2.   In prepared casserole, combine rice, milk, sugar, salt, vanilla, and nutmeg, mixing well.

3.   Bake, uncovered, 1 hour, stirring rice occasionally with fork, to prevent its settling to bottom and a brown crust's forming on top.

4.   Stir in raisins, mixing well. Bake 2 hours, stirring occasionally, or until rice is tender. Do not stir during last half hour of baking.

5.   Let cool on wire rack. Serve slightly warm or cold, with light cream, if desired.

SWEDISH RICE PORRIDGE

MAKES 6 TO 8 SERVINGS

2 tablespoons butter or
    margarine
1 cup raw regular white rice
4 cups milk
2-inch cinnamon stick
1 cup heavy cream

1 teaspoon salt
2 tablespoons sugar
1 teaspoon vanilla extract
1 blanched almond
1 cup raspberry preserves

1. Melt 1 tablespoon butter in a 3-quart saucepan. Add rice and 1 cup water; bring to boiling.
2. Boil, uncovered, 5 to 10 minutes, or until water is evaporated.
3. Add milk and cinnamon stick; simmer slowly, uncovered, 35 to 40 minutes, or until rice is tender; stir occasionally.
4. Gently stir in cream, salt, sugar, vanilla, rest of butter, and the almond.
5. Meanwhile, melt raspberry preserves in ¼ cup water over low heat. Strain.
6. Serve porridge warm, with raspberry sauce.

Note: This is a favorite Christmas Eve dessert. Traditionally, whoever is served the almond will marry before next Christmas.

Flans and Pastries

Light, spectacular flan—a sort of tart, with a creamy filling—is particularly pleasant in company with fresh fruits. We're happy to offer you a flan, a speciality of one of Manhattan's luxury restaurants. Some evening soon, try it on your most-knowing friends.

FOUR SEASONS FLAN

MAKES 8 SERVINGS

Flan Shell:
¼ cup soft butter
    or margarine
2 tablespoons sugar
3 tablespoons almond
    paste*
½ teaspoon grated lemon
    peel
1 egg white
¾ cup sifted all-purpose
    flour

Pastry Cream:
½ cup sugar
Dash salt
2 tablespoons cornstarch
2 cups milk or light cream

6 egg yolks, slightly beaten
1 teaspoon vanilla extract

4 baker's ladyfingers, split
2 teaspoons kirsch

Apricot Glaze:
½ cup apricot preserves

13 banana slices, cut
    diagonally, ⅛ inch
    thick
⅓ cup fresh raspberries
⅓ cup Thompson seedless
    grapes
8 fresh strawberries, halved
¼ cup fresh blueberries

1. Make Flan Shell: Grease and lightly flour an 8-by-1½-inch round layer-cake pan.
2. In small bowl of electric mixer, at medium speed, cream butter with sugar, almond paste, and lemon peel until light and well combined.
3. Add egg white; beat, at high speed, until smooth.
4. Gradually beat in flour, to make a smooth mixture.
5. Turn dough into prepared pan. With fingers, pat evenly onto bottom and side of pan. Refrigerate—1 hour or longer.
6. Preheat oven to 300F. Bake shell 50 minutes, or until light golden-brown.
7. Let cool 15 minutes, in pan, on wire rack. Then gently turn out onto rack, and let cool completely.

(*Four Seasons Flan continued*)

8. Make Pastry Cream: In heavy metal medium-size saucepan, combine sugar, salt, and cornstarch. Gradually add milk, stirring until smooth.

9. Cook, stirring, over medium heat, until mixture is thick and begins to boil—about 10 minutes. (Mixture should be bubbly throughout.) Boil 1 minute, stirring.

10. Remove from heat. Stir a little of hot mixture into egg yolks, mixing well. Pour back into rest of hot mixture in saucepan, mixing well.

11. Return to boiling, stirring constantly. Remove from heat.

12. Turn into medium bowl; stir in vanilla. Place sheet of waxed paper directly on surface of filling; refrigerate until well chilled.

13. Assemble flan about 1 hour before serving: Spread half the Pastry Cream over bottom of Flan Shell.

14. Arrange ladyfingers over surface; sprinkle ladyfingers with kirsch. Cover with rest of Pastry Cream.

15. Make Apricot Glaze: In small saucepan, heat apricot preserves with 2 tablespoons water, stirring, just until preserves are melted. Strain; let cool slightly.

16. Arrange fruits to cover surface completely, brushing lightly with Apricot Glaze. Overlap banana slices down center. Divide raspberries to make a row on each side of banana. Divide grapes to make a row on each side of raspberries. Divide strawberry halves to make a row on each side of grapes. Fill in area next to strawberries, on each side, with blueberries.

17. Brush fruit well with Apricot Glaze, to give a shiny effect. Refrigerate until serving.

Note: Well-drained canned fruit may be substituted for fresh fruit. Use 1 can (8 oz) apricot halves, 1 can (8 oz) peach slices, 1 can (8 oz) pineapple rings (each cut in sixths), 1 jar (4 oz) maraschino cherries and 1 can (8 oz) blueberries.

* For almond paste, you may use ¼ cup ground blanched almonds mixed with ½ teaspoon almond extract, if desired.

STRAWBERRY-MOUSSE FLAN

MAKES 6 SERVINGS

1½ cups fresh strawberries, washed
1 tablespoon lemon juice
½ cup sugar
1 envelope unflavored gelatine
½ cup heavy cream
1 egg white, beaten stiff
8-inch baked pie shell

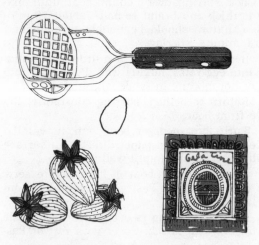

1. Set aside 6 large strawberries for garnish. Hull rest of berries; crush, with potato masher, in medium bowl.

2. Add lemon juice. Cover with sugar; let stand 30 minutes.

3. Sprinkle gelatine over ½ cup cold water in top of double boiler; let stand 5 minutes, to soften. Dissolve over hot water. Remove, and let cool.

4. Pour gelatine over crushed berries, stirring until sugar is dissolved; refrigerate until consistency of unbeaten egg white.

5. Beat ¼ cup cream until stiff. Gently fold into gelatine mixture, along with egg white, just until combined.

6. Turn into cooled pie shell. Refrigerate until firm—about 1½ hours.

7. To serve: Gently remove whole flan from pie plate to serving plate. Beat remaining cream until stiff.

8. Use to garnish top, along with reserved whole strawberries.

ORANGE-COCONUT FLAN

MAKES 6 SERVINGS

½ cup butter or margarine
3 tablespoons milk
1½ cups sifted confectioners' sugar
2 cans (3½-oz size) flaked coconut
2 large oranges, peeled
½ lemon, peeled
¼ cup granulated sugar
1 envelope unflavored gelatine
1 cup heavy cream, whipped
8 large-orange sections, drained

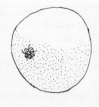

1. In small saucepan over low heat, melt butter in milk. Remove from heat.

2. Stir in confectioners' sugar and coconut until well mixed.

3. Spread on bottom and side (not on rim) of lightly buttered 8-inch pie plate.

4. Cut peeled oranges and lemon into chunks.

5. Put through coarse blade of food chopper, or blend in electric blender, to make a purée. Stir in granulated sugar.

6. Sprinkle gelatine over ½ cup cold water in top of double boiler; let stand 5 minutes, to soften. Dissolve over hot water; remove, and let cool.

7. Add orange-and-lemon purée, combining well; refrigerate until consistency of unbeaten egg white.

8. Fold in whipped cream. Turn into prepared shell; refrigerate until firm—about 1½ hours.

9. Before serving, garnish center with orange sections, arranged spoke fashion.

CREAM PUFFS

MAKES 12

½ cup butter or margarine
¼ teaspoon salt
1 cup sifted all-purpose
  flour

4 large eggs

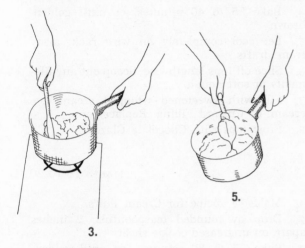

3.

5.

1. Preheat oven to 400F. In medium saucepan, slowly bring 1 cup water with butter and salt to boiling.

2. Remove from heat. With wooden spoon, beat in flour all at once.

3. Return to low heat; continue beating until mixture forms ball and leaves side of pan.

4. Remove from heat. Beat in eggs, one at a time, beating hard after each addition until mixture is smooth.

5. Continue beating until dough is shiny and satiny and breaks in strands.

6. Drop by rounded tablespoonfuls, 2 inches apart, onto ungreased cookie sheet.

7. Bake until puffed and golden-brown—45 to 50 minutes. Puffs should sound hollow when lightly tapped with fingertip.

8. Let cool completely on wire rack, away from drafts.

9. To serve: With sharp knife, cut off tops crosswise. Scoop out any filaments of soft dough.

10. Fill with sweetened whipped cream, ice cream, or Custard Filling. Replace tops.

11. Frost tops with Chocolate or Caramel Glaze. Serve with hot chocolate or butterscotch sauce.

9.

ÉCLAIRS

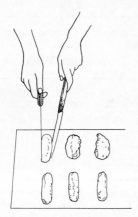

1. Make ½ recipe for Cream Puffs.
2. Drop by rounded tablespoonfuls, 3 inches apart, on ungreased cookie sheet.
3. With spatula, spread each ball of dough into a 4-by-1-inch strip.
4. Bake 35 to 40 minutes, or until golden-brown.
5. Let cool completely on wire rack, away from drafts.
6. Slice off tops lengthwise. Scoop out any filaments of soft dough.
7. Fill with sweetened whipped cream, ice cream, or Custard Filling. Replace tops.
8. Frost tops with Chocolate Glaze.

LITTLE PUFFS

1. Make ½ recipe for Cream Puffs.
2. Drop by rounded teaspoonfuls, 2 inches apart, on ungreased cookie sheet.
3. Bake 25 to 30 minutes, or until golden-brown.
4. Let cool completely on wire rack, away from drafts.
5. Cut off tops. Fill with sweetened whipped cream. Replace tops.
6. Frost tops with Chocolate Glaze.

CUSTARD FILLING

1½ cups milk
¼ cup sugar
1½ tablespoons cornstarch

2 egg yolks
1 teaspoon vanilla extract

MAKES ENOUGH FILLING FOR
6 CREAM PUFFS OR ÉCLAIRS

1. In small heavy saucepan, slowly heat milk just until bubbles form around edge of pan.
2. Meanwhile, in small bowl, combine sugar and cornstarch; stir to mix well. Stir into hot milk, all at once.
3. Cook, stirring, over medium heat, until mixture boils. Reduce heat, and simmer 1 minute.
4. Beat a small amount of hot mixture into egg yolks. Pour back into saucepan; cook, stirring, over medium heat, until mixture boils and thickens. Stir in vanilla.
5. Place waxed paper directly on surface of filling, to prevent film from forming. Refrigerate until ready to use.

SOUR-CREAM CUSTARD FILLING

MAKES ENOUGH FILLING FOR
6 CREAM PUFFS OR ÉCLAIRS

1 pkg (3⅝ oz) vanilla-
    pudding mix, or 1 pkg
    (4 oz) butterscotch-
    pudding and pie-
    filling mix

1½ cups milk
1 cup dairy sour cream
1 teaspoon vanilla extract
¼ teaspoon almond extract

1. Prepare pudding as package label directs, reducing milk to 1½ cups.
2. Turn into medium bowl; let cool completely.
3. Add sour cream and extracts; with rotary beater, beat until smooth. Refrigerate, covered, until ready to use.

CHOCOLATE GLAZE

MAKES 1 CUP

1 pkg (6 oz) semisweet-
    chocolate pieces
2 tablespoons shortening

2 tablespoons light corn
    syrup
3 tablespoons milk

1. In top of double boiler, over hot, not boiling, water, melt chocolate with shortening.
2. Add corn syrup and milk, stirring until smooth and well blended. Let cool slightly.
3. Pour warm glaze over cooled, filled cream puffs placed on wire rack, with pan underneath.

CARAMEL GLAZE

MAKES 1 CUP

½ lb caramels

1. Remove paper wrapping from caramels. Place caramels in top of double boiler with ¼ cup water.
2. Melt caramels over hot, not boiling, water.
3. Stir to mix well. Pour warm glaze over cooled, filled cream puffs placed on a wire rack, with pan underneath.

PUFF PASTRY

MAKES 1 POUND

2 bars (4-oz size) butter
1⅔ cups sifted all-purpose
   flour

½ teaspoon salt
½ cup ice water

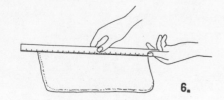

1. Cut each bar of butter into 3 lengthwise strips. On a sheet of foil, arrange strips close together in a single layer, to form a rectangle. Refrigerate until ready to use.

2. Into medium bowl, sift flour with salt. With fork, stir in ice water until well combined. Dough will be dry. Mix dough with hands until flour disappears. Shape into a ball.

3. On unfloured surface, knead dough until smooth and elastic—about 10 minutes. Cover with bowl; let rest 20 minutes.

4. On lightly floured surface, roll out dough into a 16-by-6-inch rectangle. Place chilled butter strips on half of dough, to within ½ inch of edges.

5. Fold other half of dough over butter; press edges together firmly with rolling pin or fingertips to seal. Refrigerate, in foil, 30 minutes.

6. With rolling pin, tap dough lightly several times, to flatten butter. With folded side of dough at left, on lightly floured surface, quickly roll out lengthwise into an 18-by-6-inch rectangle, pulling out corners to keep square.

7. From short side, fold dough into thirds, making sure edges and corners are even; press edges firmly to seal. You will have a 6-inch square. Refrigerate, in foil, 30 minutes.

8. Starting from center, with quick, light strokes, roll out dough, on lightly floured surface, lengthwise, into an 18-by-6-inch rectangle. Fold in thirds, as above. Refrigerate, in foil, 30 minutes.

9. Repeat rolling, folding, and chilling dough 4 times.

10. Refrigerate, in foil, until ready to use.
Note: Puff Pastry dough may also be freezer-wrapped and stored in freezer until used.

BOUCHÉES
(Patty Shells)

Puff Pastry   1 egg yolk

1. Line 2 cookie sheets with double thickness of heavy brown paper.

2. Remove chilled pastry from refrigerator. On lightly floured surface, roll out pastry into a 12-by-7-inch rectangle.

3. With plain or fluted, round 3-inch cookie cutter, cut out 8 pastry rounds. (Reroll trimmings, and cut out 2 more rounds, if desired.) Place, 3 inches apart, on cookie sheets.

4. With round 2-inch cookie cutter, mark center of each pastry round, cutting only halfway through. Refrigerate 30 minutes.

5. Meanwhile, preheat oven to 450F. Carefully brush top of each round with mixture of egg yolk beaten with 1½ teaspoons cold water. Do not let egg-yolk mixture run down sides of rounds; rounds would not puff.

6. Bake 15 minutes. Reduce temperature to 350F; bake 20 to 25 minutes, or until golden-brown.

7. With sharp knife, carefully cut around center section; remove top. Scoop out any uncooked pastry in center. Return shells and tops to oven; bake 5 minutes longer.

8. To serve, fill hot shells with creamed chicken, lobster, crabmeat, etc. Replace tops.

BRAIDS

Puff Pastry trimmings   *Poppy, sesame, or celery*
1 egg yolk   *seeds*

1. Line cookie sheet with double thickness of heavy brown paper.

2. On lightly floured surface, roll out pastry trimmings ⅛ inch thick. With sharp knife, cut into strips, 3 inches long and ½ inch wide.

3. Braid 3 strips together; press ends firmly. Place, 2 inches apart, on cookie sheet. Refrigerate 30 minutes.

4. Meanwhile, preheat oven to 450F. Brush braids with mixture of egg yolk beaten with 1½ teaspoons cold water. Sprinkle with seeds.

5. Bake 10 minutes. Reduce temperature to 350F; bake 10 minutes longer, or until golden-brown.

6. Remove to wire rack; cool. Serve as soup or salad accompaniment.

NAPOLEONS

Puff Pastry
Pastry Cream

Glaze:
1 cup sifted confectioners'
sugar

¼ teaspoon vanilla extract

1 square unsweetened
chocolate
2 teaspoons butter or
margarine

1. Line 2 cookie sheets with double thickness of heavy brown paper.
2. Remove half of chilled pastry from refrigerator. On lightly floured surface, roll into a 15-by-3-inch rectangle; trim edges. Refrigerate, on cookie sheet, 30 minutes.
3. Repeat with remaining pastry.
4. Meanwhile, make Pastry Cream as recipe directs.
5. Preheat oven to 450F. Prick pastry with fork; bake 15 minutes, or until pastry is puffed.
6. Reduce oven temperature to 350F. With wide spatula, turn pastry over; bake 15 minutes, or until golden.
7. With sharp knife, split pastry rectangles in half, to make 4. Arrange, cut sides up, on cookie sheets; bake 5 minutes longer. Remove to wire rack; cool completely.
8. Make Glaze: In small bowl, combine confectioners' sugar and vanilla with 1½ tablespoons hot water until smooth. (If glaze seems too thick, add a little more hot water.)
9. Place one pastry layer, cut side down, on rack on tray. Pour half of glaze evenly over surface. Let stand 20 minutes. (Scrape glaze from tray; return to bowl.)
10. Pour over remaining glaze, adding a little more hot water to glaze if it seems too thick. Let stand 1 hour.
11. Meanwhile, melt chocolate and butter together over hot water, mixing well. Let cool.
12. With chocolate mixture in small pastry bag, using small, straight tube for writing, pipe 5 lengthwise stripes on glaze. To make feather effect, pull wooden pick crosswise through stripes, at ½-inch intervals, alternating direction each time. Set aside.
13. To assemble: Place pastry layer, cut side up, on serving platter or tray; spread with one third of Pastry Cream. Place another layer, cut side up, on first; spread with one third of cream. Add third layer, cut side down; spread with rest of cream. Then top with glazed layer.
14. Refrigerate 30 minutes.
15. To serve: With knife with serrated edge, cut crosswise into 10 Napoleons.

PASTRY CREAM

½ cup sugar
Dash salt
1 tablespoon cornstarch
1 cup light cream or milk

3 egg yolks, slightly beaten
1 teaspoon vanilla extract
¼ cup heavy cream

1. In small, heavy saucepan, combine sugar, salt, and cornstarch. Gradually add light cream, stirring until smooth.
2. Over medium heat, cook, stirring often with wire whisk or wooden spoon, till mixture is thick and bubbly. Boil 1 minute, stirring.
3. Remove from heat; stir a little hot mixture into egg yolks, mixing well. Pour back into saucepan. Bring back to boiling, stirring.
4. Pour mixture into small bowl; stir in vanilla. Place sheet of waxed paper directly on surface of filling. Refrigerate until chilled.
5. Whip cream until stiff. Add to pastry cream; beat with rotary beater until smooth.

CORNETS
(Horns)

Puff Pastry
1 egg white, slightly beaten
Granulated sugar

Filling:
2 cups heavy cream

½ cup sifted confectioners'
   sugar
½ teaspoon almond extract
1 teaspoon vanilla extract

1. Line 2 cookie sheets with double thickness of heavy brown paper.
2. Remove chilled pastry from refrigerator. On lightly floured surface, roll out pastry into an 18-by-12-inch rectangle; trim edges. Cut lengthwise into 12 strips, 1 inch wide.
3. For each Cornet: Starting at narrow end of a cone-shape metal form,* spiral pastry strip around form, letting each row overlap the one below by about ½ inch. Do not extend pastry beyond wide end of form. Moisten end of strip with a little water; press gently to seal.
4. Place Cornets, 2 inches apart, on cookie sheets. Refrigerate 30 minutes.
5. Meanwhile, preheat oven to 400F.
6. Bake 20 minutes. Brush lightly with mixture of egg white and 2 tablespoons water. Sprinkle lightly with granulated sugar. Bake 5 minutes longer, or until golden-brown and glazed.
7. Carefully remove to wire rack; cool slightly. Then remove forms; let cool completely.
8. Make Filling: In medium bowl, beat cream with confectioners' sugar just until stiff. Gently fold in extracts. Use to fill cooled Cornets.
* To make your own cone form: Cut a double thickness of heavy-duty foil into a 9-inch square; fold over to form a triangle. Then roll into a cone shape, 4 inches long and 1½ inches in diameter, leaving a small opening at narrow end. Fold top over to make cone secure.

Dessert Sauces

Almost everybody loves desserts; but everyone, without exception, loves desserts dressed up with a delicious sauce. And our sauces, we think, are almost impossible to beat.

ALMOND CREAM

MAKES 2 CUPS

1 cup chilled heavy cream
2 tablespoons
    confectioners' sugar
½ teaspoon almond extract

1. In small bowl, whip cream only until it holds its shape. Fold in sugar and almond extract.
2. Refrigerate until serving.

APRICOT-ORANGE SAUCE

MAKES 1⅔ CUPS

1 jar (1 lb) apricot preserves   ⅓ cup orange juice

1. Combine preserves and orange juice in small saucepan; blend well.
2. Cook, stirring occasionally, over medium heat, 5 minutes, or until preserves are melted.
3. Serve warm, over vanilla ice cream.

FLUFFY BRANDY SAUCE

MAKES 1½ CUPS

1 egg white
Dash salt
1 cup sifted
    confectioners' sugar
1 egg yolk
½ cup heavy cream,
    whipped
3 tablespoons brandy

1. In small bowl of electric mixer, at high speed, beat egg white with salt just until foamy.
2. Add ½ cup sugar, a few tablespoons at a time, beating well after each addition. Continue beating just until egg white forms soft peaks when beater is raised.
3. Beat egg yolk in small bowl (with same beater) until thick and lemon-colored. Gradually add remaining sugar, beating until very thick and light.
4. At low speed, beat into egg-white mixture along with whipped cream and brandy, beating only until combined.
Note: Sauce may be made several hours ahead of time and refrigerated. Before serving, beat with fork, to fluff.

BRANDY SAUCE

4 egg yolks
½ cup sugar

⅓ cup brandy
½ cup heavy cream

1. In top of double boiler, beat egg yolks with sugar until very thick and light. Stir in brandy; cook, stirring, over hot, not boiling, water until thickened.

2. Refrigerate until well chilled.

3. Just before serving, pour cream into small bowl; beat until stiff. Fold into brandy mixture until well combined. Serve with Brandied Apricot Soufflé.*

* See this chapter.

CARAMEL SAUCE

1½ cups sugar
1 tablespoon butter or
    margarine

⅛ teaspoon salt
½ teaspoon vanilla extract

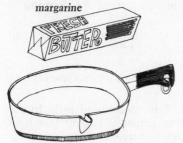

1. In large, heavy skillet, heat sugar, over very low heat and stirring, until melted and light golden-brown.

2. Remove from heat. Very gradually stir in 1 cup hot water; bring to boiling point. Reduce heat, and simmer until it thickens slightly or reaches 228F on candy thermometer.

3. Remove from heat. Add butter, salt, and vanilla. Let cool.

CARDINAL SAUCE

3 tablespoons cornstarch
1 pkg (10 oz) thawed frozen
    raspberries

1 pkg (10 oz) thawed frozen
    sliced strawberries

1. In saucepan, combine cornstarch with 1¼ cups water until smooth. Bring to boiling point; boil, stirring, until thickened and translucent—5 to 8 minutes.

2. Stir in berries. Let cool.

FLAMING CHERRY SAUCE

1 cup currant jelly
1 can (1 lb, 1 oz) pitted
    Bing cherries

3 tablespoons brandy

1. Melt jelly in small saucepan, over low heat, stirring occasionally.

2. Drain cherries, reserving ¼ cup liquid.

3. Add cherries and reserved liquid to jelly; bring to boiling point. Pour into serving dish.

4. Heat brandy gently in small pan. Light with match; pour flaming brandy over cherries. Serve immediately, with hot Vanilla Soufflé.*

* See this chapter.

CHOCOLATE SAUCE

MAKES ABOUT 1⅓ CUPS

3 squares unsweetened
    chocolate
¾ cup sugar
¼ teaspoon salt

4½ tablespoons butter or
    margarine
¾ teaspoon vanilla extract

1. In small saucepan, combine chocolate with ½ cup water. Cook, stirring occasionally, over low heat, until chocolate is melted.
2. Add sugar and salt; cook, stirring, until sugar is melted and mixture is thickened, about 5 minutes.
3. Stir in butter and vanilla.

FLAMING CHOCOLATE SAUCE

MAKES 1¼ CUPS

1 pkg (6 oz) semisweet-
    chocolate pieces
1 tablespoon butter or
    margarine

¼ cup light corn syrup
¼ cup milk
¼ cup dark rum

1. Melt chocolate and butter in top of double boiler, over hot, not boiling, water.
2. Gradually stir in corn syrup and milk, beating until mixture is smooth. Pour into metal serving bowl.
3. Gently warm rum in small saucepan, over very low heat. Ignite with match; pour blazing rum into chocolate mixture. Take flaming to table.
4. When blazing subsides, stir mixture well. Serve over ice cream.

QUICK CHOCOLATE SAUCE

MAKES ABOUT 1 CUP

1 pkg (6 oz) semisweet-
    chocolate pieces

⅔ cup evaporated milk,
    undiluted

1. Combine chocolate pieces and milk in medium saucepan. Stir constantly, over low heat, just until chocolate is melted.
2. Serve warm, over ice cream or cakes.

POUR CUSTARD

MAKES 1½ CUPS

1½ cups milk
3 egg yolks
¼ cup sugar

Dash salt
½ teaspoon vanilla extract

1. Heat milk in top of double boiler, over direct heat, until tiny bubbles appear around edge of pan.
2. Beat yolks, sugar and salt to mix well.
3. Very slowly pour hot milk into egg mixture, beating constantly.
4. Return mixture to double-boiler top; place over hot, not boiling, water. Water in lower part of double boiler should not touch upper part.
5. Cook, stirring constantly, until thin coating forms on metal spoon—8 to 10 minutes.
6. Pour custard immediately into bowl; place sheet of waxed paper directly on surface.
7. Set bowl in cold water, to cool. Stir in vanilla. Refrigerate. Serve over strawberries.

VANILLA HARD SAUCE

⅓ cup soft butter or
    margarine
1 teaspoon vanilla extract

1 cup unsifted
    confectioners' sugar

1. In small bowl of electric mixer, at high speed, cream butter until light.
2. Add vanilla and sugar; beat until fluffy and smooth.

Sherry Hard Sauce: Prepare sauce as above, but substitute 1 teaspoon sherry for vanilla extract.

Orange Hard Sauce: Prepare sauce as above, with these exceptions: Omit vanilla. Add 1 tablespoon grated orange peel, 2 teaspoons orange juice, and ½ teaspoon orange extract.

To Store Hard Sauces: Put them in pretty jars with tight-fitting lids. Keep refrigerated.

HONEY ICE-CREAM SAUCE

¼ cup light raisins
¼ cup apple juice
2 tablespoons butter or
    margarine

¼ cup coarsely chopped
    walnuts
1 cup honey
½ teaspoon rum extract

1. Combine raisins and apple juice in small saucepan; let stand 10 minutes, to plump raisins.
2. Add butter, walnuts, and honey; cook, over medium heat, stirring, 10 minutes. Stir in rum extract.
3. Remove from heat; let cool slightly. Serve warm, over vanilla or coffee ice cream.

Honey-Rum Ice-Cream Sauce: Or use ¼ cup white rum instead of apple juice; omit extract.

LEMON-CREAM SAUCE

1 tablespoon all-purpose
    flour
1 cup sugar
1 egg
1½ teaspoons grated lemon
    peel

⅓ cup lemon juice
1 tablespoon butter or
    margarine
½ cup heavy cream

1. Combine flour and sugar in top of double boiler. With spoon, beat in ⅔ cup water, egg, lemon peel and juice; cook, stirring, over boiling water until slightly thickened—about 10 minutes.
2. Remove from heat. Add butter; refrigerate until well chilled—at least 1 hour.
3. Just before serving, beat cream until stiff. Gently fold into lemon mixture until well combined. Nice over angel-food cake.

SHERRIED-MINCEMEAT ICE-CREAM SAUCE

2½ cups prepared
    mincemeat, undrained
½ cup broken walnuts
½ cup sherry

1. Combine mincemeat and walnuts in saucepan; heat, stirring, to boiling.
2. Remove from heat. Stir in sherry. Serve hot, over ice cream.

RASPBERRY SAUCE

MAKES ABOUT 1¼ CUPS

1 tablespoon cornstarch
¼ cup butter or margarine
1 cup sugar

1 cup fresh raspberries,
    crushed
½ teaspoon lemon juice

1. Combine cornstarch with 1 tablespoon cold water; stir to make a smooth paste.
2. Melt butter in saucepan. Stir in sugar, raspberries, and cornstarch mixture; bring to boiling point, stirring constantly. Boil 1 minute.
3. Remove from heat. Stir in lemon juice; cool. Serve over ice cream, pudding, or cake.

BRANDIED-RASPBERRY SAUCE

MAKES ABOUT 2¼ CUPS

2 cups raspberry preserves
¼ cup brandy

2 tablespoons orange juice

Combine all ingredients in medium bowl; stir until well mixed.

ROSÉ RASPBERRY SAUCE

MAKES 2½ CUPS

2 tablespoons cornstarch
¼ cup sugar

1 pkg (10 oz) thawed frozen
    raspberries, undrained
½ cup rosé wine

1. In small saucepan, combine cornstarch and sugar. Add 1 cup water, stirring until smooth.
2. Bring to boiling, stirring. Reduce heat, and continue cooking, stirring, until thickened and translucent—5 to 8 minutes.
3. Remove from heat. Stir in raspberries; let cool.
4. Add wine; refrigerate, covered, until well chilled. Serve over squares of plain cake.

RUM SAUCE

MAKES 1 CUP

⅓ cup butter or margarine
1 cup light-brown sugar,
    firmly packed

2 tablespoons light corn
    syrup
⅓ cup heavy cream
2 tablespoons white rum

1. Melt butter in small saucepan, over low heat. Stir in sugar, corn syrup, and cream; bring to boiling point.
2. Remove from heat; let cool. Then stir in rum.

VANILLA SAUCE

MAKES ABOUT 1½ CUPS

½ cup butter or margarine
1 cup sugar

½ cup light cream
1 teaspoon vanilla extract

1. Melt butter in medium saucepan.
2. Remove from heat. Add remaining ingredients, mixing well. Simmer, stirring, over low heat, about 5 minutes, or until sugar is dissolved and sauce is heated.
3. Serve hot, over steamed pudding.

14

Eggs, Omelets, and Soufflés

W hat a perfect invention, the egg! And how very thoughtful of the hen
to provide mankind with a food so nutritious, so handy, so inexpensive,
so easy to cook, and so good in any form: scrambled, boiled, fried, baked,
shirred—alone or in the company of other foods. Besides rules on how to make
eggs behave their very best, we give you recipes that should serve you from
the early-morning breakfast hours clear through very-late suppers.

EGGS AND HOW TO TREAT THEM

1. Eggs should always be refrigerated. It is
best to buy only from a market that keeps
eggs under refrigeration, so they lose none
of their freshness.

2. Eggs have a natural protective coating
that keeps them fresh, so don't wash them
until ready to use.

3. Eggs separate best when they are cold.

4. They whip best, attain their greatest volume, at room temperature. In all our recipes
calling for beaten egg whites, this is one of
the essentials.

5. You can't tell a hard-cooked egg from a
fresh egg in the refrigerator. This, however,
is a sure and simple way to tell which is
which: Lay the egg on its side on a flat
surface, and spin it. A hard-boiled egg spins
fast; a fresh egg, hardly at all.

6. The contents of eggs, whether white or
brown, are exactly the same.

KNOW THE EGGS YOU BUY

Nowadays, all eggs on the market have their
grade printed clearly on the box. Most markets have four grades:

Grade AA: Excellent for table use. When broken from the shell, the white covers only a small area; the yolk stands high; there is a large amount of thick white hugging the yolk and a small amount of thin white at the very edge. When hard-cooked, the yolk may be easily centered. When fried, the yolk is round and upstanding; the white is high and thick around the yolk.

Grade A: Good for table use. When broken from the shell, the white spreads over a larger area; the yolk still stands high; there is a large amount of thick white hugging the yolk and a small amount of thin white at the very edge. When hard-cooked, the yolk is slightly off center. When fried, the yolk is round and upstanding; the white is somewhat spread out.

Grade B: Fair for table, good for cooking and baking. When broken from the shell, the white spreads out wide; the yolk is somewhat flat; there is a medium amount of thick white around the yolk, but it looks flat; there is a medium amount of thin white. When hard-cooked, the yolk is far off center. When fried, the yolk looks somewhat flat; the white spreads widely and is pretty thin.

Grade C: All right for cooking and baking. When broken from the shell, the white covers a large area, and it is mostly thin; the yolk is very flat and easily broken. When hard-cooked, the yolk is far off center, in a ragged-looking circle. When fried, the white is thin and spreads over a large area; the yolk is very flat.

HOW TO COOK EGGS

A protein food, eggs should be cooked at a low temperature if you want them to retain their tenderness and delicacy. They are so easy to cook that there's no excuse, we think, for not cooking them perfectly. These simple rules will bring success every time.

Soft-Cooked Eggs: Cover eggs with water to an inch above them; bring rapidly to a boil. Take pan off heat; cover, and let stand 2 to 4 minutes, depending on doneness desired. Cool under cold running water, to prevent further cooking.

Hard-Cooked Eggs: Follow directions for Soft-Cooked Eggs, letting eggs stand 20 minutes. Cool immediately, in cold water, to prevent dark surface on yolks and so shells can be removed easily.

Scrambled Eggs: Allow 1 teaspoon milk to each egg. Mix well eggs, milk, salt and pepper to taste. Heat fat (enough to cover bottom of skillet) until just hot enough to sizzle a drop of water. Pour in egg mixture, and reduce heat. When eggs have set slightly, stir constantly with a fork. Perfectly scrambled eggs should be soft and creamy. Don't overcook.

Poached Eggs: Bring water (about 1 inch deep) in shallow pan to boiling point. Reduce heat to simmer. Break each egg into a saucer; quickly slip egg into water. Cook, covered, 3 to 5 minutes. Lift out of water with slotted pancake turner or spoon. Drain well.

Fried Eggs: Heat 1 to 2 tablespoons butter or margarine in small skillet until just hot enough to sizzle a drop of water. Break eggs directly into pan. Take pan off heat immediately, and baste eggs with hot fat about 3 or 4 minutes.

Or: Melt 1 tablespoon butter or margarine in small skillet. Break eggs directly into pan. Over low heat, fry gently until of desired doneness—about 3 or 4 minutes. Eggs may be covered or turned, to cook yolk.

DEVILED EGGS

12 eggs
2 tablespoons mayonnaise
    or cooked salad
    dressing
1 tablespoon white vinegar
1 teaspoon dry mustard
1½ teaspoons
    Worcestershire sauce

¾ teaspoon salt
⅛ teaspoon pepper
⅛ teaspoon paprika
¼ cup grated sharp
    Cheddar cheese
Parsley sprigs

1. Hard-cook eggs. Remove shells. Cool eggs completely.
2. Halve eggs lengthwise. Take out yolks, being careful not to break whites.
3. Press yolks through sieve into medium bowl. Add remaining ingredients, except parsley; mix with fork until smooth and fluffy.
4. Lightly mound yolk mixture in egg-whites. Garnish each with parsley sprig.

DEVILED EGGS DIVAN

6 hard-cooked eggs
2 pkg (10-oz size) frozen
    asparagus spears
¼ cup butter or margarine
¼ cup finely chopped onion
2 tablespoons flour

¼ teaspoon dry mustard
½ teaspoon salt
Dash pepper
1½ cups milk
½ cup grated Parmesan
    cheese

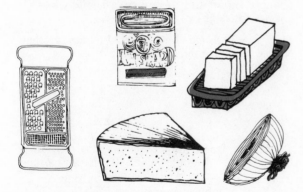

1. Make Deviled Eggs as above, using half of recipe.
2. Cook asparagus as label directs; drain.
3. Meanwhile, preheat oven to 400F.
4. In hot butter in medium saucepan, sauté onion till golden—about 5 minutes. Remove from heat. Add flour, mustard, salt, and pepper, stirring until smooth.
5. Gradually add milk; bring to boiling, stirring. Reduce heat.
6. Add cheese; simmer, stirring, until cheese is melted.
7. Arrange asparagus spears to cover bottom of an 8-by-8-by-2-inch baking dish. Place eggs, stuffing side up, on asparagus. Pour sauce over all.
8. Bake, uncovered, 20 minutes.

HAM-DEVILED EGGS

6 hard-cooked eggs
1 can (2¼ oz) deviled ham
¼ cup mayonnaise or
    cooked salad dressing
Dash liquid hot-pepper
    seasoning

1 tablespoon prepared
    mustard
¼ teaspoon Worcestershire
    sauce
⅛ teaspoon onion powder
1 tablespoon chopped
    parsley

1. Halve eggs lengthwise. Remove yolks to a medium bowl. Reserve whites.
2. Using fork, mash yolks. Add rest of ingredients, except parsley; mix until smooth.
3. Fill each white with yolk mixture, mounding high.
4. Sprinkle tops with parsley.

Should you add water, or milk, or cream to scrambled eggs? Should you add no liquid at all? A controversy rages about this. We belong to the milk-and-cream school. And our scrambled-egg variations for Sunday brunch or a Saturday-night supper belong to this category. We give you recipes for Skillet Scrambled Eggs and a number of variations.

SKILLET SCRAMBLED EGGS

MAKES 2 SERVINGS

1½ tablespoons butter or
    margarine
4 eggs

¼ teaspoon salt
Dash pepper
2 tablespoons light cream

1. Heat butter in small skillet over low heat.
2. Break eggs into skillet; stir with a fork.
3. Add salt, pepper, and cream; mix well.
4. Cook slowly. As eggs start to set at bottom, gently lift cooked portion, with spatula, to form flakes, letting uncooked portion flow to bottom of pan.
5. When eggs are cooked but still shiny and moist, remove from skillet.

Bacon Scrambled Eggs: Sauté 4 bacon slices until crisp; drain well. Crumble bacon; stir into eggs as they cook.

Cheese Scrambled Eggs: Stir 1 teaspoon finely chopped onion and ¼ cup grated mild Cheddar cheese into eggs as they cook.

Sherry Scrambled Eggs: Stir ¼ cup cottage cheese and 1 tablespoon sherry into eggs as they cook.

MUSHROOM SCRAMBLED EGGS

MAKES 6 SERVINGS

½ lb fresh mushrooms, or 1
    can (6 oz) sliced
    mushrooms
5 tablespoons butter or
    margarine
10 eggs
½ cup milk

½ teaspoon salt
¼ teaspoon dried thyme
    leaves
⅛ teaspoon pepper
1 tablespoon chopped
    parsley (optional)

1. Wash fresh mushrooms; slice ¼ inch thick, right through stem. If using canned mushrooms, drain well on paper towels.
2. Heat 2 tablespoons butter in large skillet; in it, sauté mushrooms until golden. Remove from skillet; keep warm.
3. Combine eggs, milk, salt, thyme, and pepper in large bowl; beat, with rotary beater, just until combined—not frothy.
4. Heat remaining butter in same skillet. Add egg mixture; cook over low heat. As eggs cook, lift with spatula, and turn gently; do not stir. Cook until almost set.
5. Stir in mushrooms. Sprinkle with chopped parsley, if desired.

SCRAMBLED EGGS
À LA SUISSE

12 eggs
1 teaspoon salt
⅛ teaspoon pepper
3 drops liquid hot-pepper
    seasoning
¾ cup milk

¼ lb natural Swiss cheese,
    cut in ½-inch cubes
    (1 cup)
3 tablespoons butter or
    margarine

1. In a large bowl, beat eggs, salt, pepper, hot-pepper seasoning, and milk until well combined. Add Swiss-cheese cubes.

2. In large skillet, heat butter until bubbly. Pour in egg mixture; cook over low heat.

3. When bottom of eggs begins to set, stir with spatula to form creamy curds all the way through. Eggs should be slightly soft and cheese melted.

Sometimes called *shirred*, baked eggs are the easiest way to do eggs for a group. The oven takes care of the last-minute watching. Baked eggs are especially good combined with other ingredients, like cheese or ham.

BAKED EGGS FLORENTINE

2 pkg (10-oz size) frozen
    chopped spinach
1¼ teaspoons salt
2 tablespoons light cream
3 tablespoons butter or
    margarine

½ cup grated Swiss cheese
1½ tablespoons flour
Dash pepper
1 cup milk
6 eggs

1. Preheat oven to 350F. Lightly grease an 8-by-8-by-2-inch baking dish.

2. Cook spinach as package label directs; drain well.

3. Stir in 1 teaspoon salt, the cream, and 1 tablespoon butter.

4. Turn spinach into baking dish, making an even layer. Sprinkle with 2 tablespoons cheese.

5. Melt rest of butter in small saucepan. Remove from heat. Add flour, rest of salt, and pepper, stirring until smooth. Gradually stir in milk; bring the sauce to boiling, stirring.

6. Carefully break eggs over spinach. Cover with sauce. Sprinkle with rest of cheese.

7. Bake, uncovered, 15 minutes or until eggs are set and top is golden.

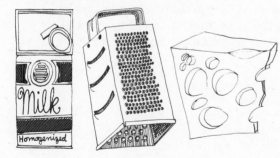

SHIRRED EGGS AND HAM

6 boiled-ham slices
1 cup plus 2 tablespoons
    light cream
12 eggs

Salt
Pepper
6 tablespoons grated
    Cheddar cheese

1. Preheat oven to 325F.

2. Line each of 6 ramekins or 9½-ounce casseroles with boiled-ham slice.

3. Then, into each, pour 3 tablespoons cream. Carefully slip 2 eggs on top of cream; sprinkle with salt, pepper, and 1 tablespoon cheese.

4. Cover each ramekin with foil. Bake 20 to 25 minutes, or until eggs are of desired doneness.

SHIRRED EGGS À LA SUISSE

MAKES 6 SERVINGS

Butter or margarine
6 tablespoons fresh bread
    crumbs
12 slices natural Swiss
    cheese (½ lb)
6 large tomato slices
Dried thyme leaves
¾ cup heavy cream

6 eggs
¼ teaspoon salt
⅛ teaspoon pepper
⅛ teaspoon paprika
2 tablespoons grated
    Parmesan cheese
6 buttered toast slices,
    crusts removed

1. Preheat oven to 325F.

2. Butter bottoms and sides of 6 (5-inch) ramekins. Sprinkle 1 tablespoon bread crumbs in bottom of each.

3. Then cover with 2 slices Swiss cheese, overlapping to cover bottom and side of ramekin. Top with a slice of tomato, sprinkled with a dash of thyme.

4. To each, add 1 tablespoon cream. Break egg on top. Cover each with 1 more tablespoon cream. Sprinkle each with a little salt, pepper, paprika, and 1 teaspoon Parmesan cheese.

5. Bake, uncovered, 15 to 20 minutes, or just until eggs are set.

6. Cut toast into triangular quarters; arrange 4 triangles around edge of each ramekin.

Reputations and even fortunes have been made by omelets. While we don't promise you'll be able to run a wildly successful omelet restaurant, like some women we've heard of, we shall show you how to produce sheer golden perfection, time after time after time. So even if you have chronic omelet trouble, if your omelets are runny, or leathery, or thin, or anything a well-behaved omelet should never be, just look at our recipes. You'll never have that trouble again.

3.

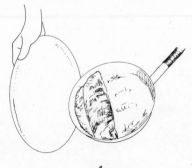

4.

BASIC OMELET

3 eggs
¼ teaspoon salt
1 tablespoon cold water

1 tablespoon butter or
  margarine

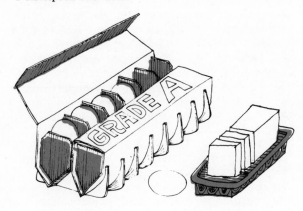

1. In medium bowl, with wire whisk or rotary beater, beat eggs with salt and water just until well mixed. (Mixture should not be too frothy.) Meanwhile, slowly heat a 9-inch heavy skillet or omelet pan. To test temperature, sprinkle a small amount of cold water on skillet; water should sizzle and roll off in drops. Add butter; heat until it sizzles briskly—it should not brown.

2. Quickly turn egg mixture, all at once, into skillet. Cook over medium heat.

3. As omelet sets, run spatula around edge, to loosen. Tilt pan, to let uncooked portion run underneath. Continue loosening and tilting until omelet is almost dry on top and golden-brown underneath.

4. To turn out, loosen edge with spatula. Fold, in thirds, to edge of pan; tilt out onto plate.

MUSHROOM OMELET

Filling:
1 lb small fresh mushrooms
Lemon juice
2 tablespoons flour
¼ teaspoon salt
⅛ teaspoon pepper
1 cup light cream

½ cup butter or margarine
⅓ cup finely chopped
  onion
1 teaspoon Worcestershire
  sauce

4 Basic Omelets

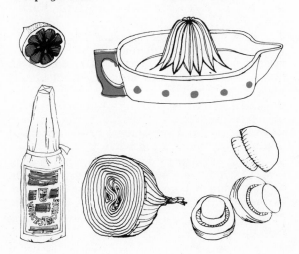

1. Make Filling: Wash mushrooms; remove stems. Chop stems; measure 2½ cups. (Chop some of caps, if necessary.) Toss caps with lemon juice, coating well; set aside.

2. In top of double boiler, over hot water, combine flour, salt, pepper, and cream, stirring until smooth. Cook, stirring occasionally, 10 to 15 minutes, or until mixture thickens.

3. Meanwhile, in ¼ cup hot butter in medium skillet, sauté onion until tender—about 5 minutes.

4. Add mushroom stems; cook 5 minutes longer. Add to thickened mixture along with Worcestershire.

5. Remove from heat; keep warm over hot water.

6. In same skillet, melt remaining butter. Add mushroom caps; sauté until tender—about 5 minutes. Keep warm, and reserve for garnish.

7. Make 4 omelets, one by one.

8. Just before folding each omelet, place ½ cup filling in center. Fold over in thirds; tilt out onto serving plate.

9. Garnish with mushroom caps. Keep warm until serving.

CHEESE OMELET

MAKES 4

Filling:
1 tablespoon flour
¼ teaspoon dry mustard
⅛ teaspoon salt
⅛ teaspoon pepper
½ cup milk

2 cups grated sharp
    Cheddar cheese
1 teaspoon grated onion

4 Basic Omelets
½ cup grated sharp
    Cheddar cheese

1. Make Filling: In top of double boiler, over hot water, combine flour, mustard, salt, pepper, and milk, stirring until smooth.
2. Add 2 cups cheese and the onion; cook, stirring occasionally, 15 to 20 minutes, or until mixture thickens and cheese is melted.
3. Remove from heat; keep warm over hot water.
4. Make 4 omelets, one by one, in omelet pan or skillet with heat-resistant handle.
5. Before pouring into pan, add 1 tablespoon cheese to each.
6. Just before folding each omelet, place ¼ cup filling in center. Fold over in thirds; sprinkle each with 1 tablespoon cheese.
7. Run under broiler, 6 inches from heat, until the cheese is bubbly and golden—about 1 minute.
8. With spatula, lift out onto serving plate; keep warm until serving.

OMELET FINES HERBES

MAKES 1 OR 2 SERVINGS

3 eggs
¼ teaspoon salt
2 tablespoons finely snipped
    fresh parsley
1 teaspoon finely snipped
    fresh tarragon leaves
1 teaspoon finely snipped
    fresh marjoram leaves

½ teaspoon finely snipped
    fresh thyme leaves
1 teaspoon finely chopped
    shallots
1 tablespoon butter or
    margarine
Parsley sprig

1. Combine eggs, salt, and 1 tablespoon cold water in small bowl; beat, with rotary beater, just until combined, not frothy.
2. Combine rest of ingredients, except butter and the parsley sprig; stir into eggs, mixing well.
3. Slowly heat a medium-size heavy skillet. It is ready when small amount of cold water sprinkled over surface sizzles and rolls off in drops. Add butter; heat until it sizzles briskly (not browned).
4. Quickly turn egg mixture into skillet; cook over medium heat. As omelet sets, loosen edge with spatula, and tilt skillet, to let uncooked mixture run under set portion.
5. When omelet is dry on top and golden-brown on bottom, fold it over to edge of pan. Tilt out onto hot serving plate. Serve at once, garnished with parsley sprig.
Note: Or substitute dried herbs for fresh, using half the quantity.

OMELET WITH CHICKEN LIVERS

MAKES 4

Filling:

8 bacon slices

1 pkg (6 oz) frozen chicken livers, thawed

1 cup finely chopped onion

⅛ teaspoon salt

Dash pepper

4 Basic Omelets

1 tablespoon chopped fresh dill or parsley

1. Make Filling: In medium skillet, over low heat, sauté bacon until crisp. Drain on paper towels; crumble. Measure ⅓ cup.
2. In same skillet, over low heat, sauté chicken livers until tender—3 to 4 minutes. Remove from heat; drain, and chop finely.
3. Add onion to skillet; sauté until tender—about 5 minutes. Drain fat from skillet.
4. Add bacon, chicken liver, salt, and pepper; reheat gently. Cover, and keep warm.
5. Make 4 omelets, one by one.
6. Just before folding each omelet, place ¼ cup filling in center. Fold over in thirds, and tilt out onto serving plate.
7. Sprinkle with dill. Keep warm until serving.

Prima donna among foods, the hot soufflé is temperamental and demanding. You MUST follow the recipe precisely; you MUST use the exact-size, straight-side dish called for; you MUST maintain a constant, even oven temperature, without peeking. YOU must wait for IT, not the other way round!

When the soufflé makes its entrance, high-crowned and dramatic, you'll agree, and so will your guests, that it is entirely worth waiting for. The recipes that follow are for main-dish soufflés. See our Desserts Chapter for the best sweet soufflés, hot or cold, that you've ever tasted.

FRESH ASPARAGUS SOUFFLÉ

MAKES 6 SERVINGS

5 eggs, separated

¼ cup butter or margarine

¼ cup unsifted all-purpose flour

1⅓ cups milk

1 teaspoon salt

Dash pepper

1 teaspoon grated onion

2 tablespoons chopped pimiento

¼ cup grated sharp Cheddar cheese

1¼ cups finely chopped fresh asparagus

¼ teaspoon cream of tartar

1. In large bowl of electric mixer, let egg whites warm to room temperature—1 hour.
2. Melt butter in medium saucepan. Remove from heat. Blend in flour.
3. Stir in milk slowly; cook over low heat, stirring, until thickened and smooth.
4. Add salt, pepper, onion, pimiento, and cheese; stir until blended. Set aside to cool.
5. Preheat oven to 350F. Grease well a 1½-quart, straight-side soufflé dish or casserole.
6. Add asparagus to cooled sauce.
7. At high speed of electric mixer, beat egg whites with cream of tartar until stiff peaks form when beater is slowly raised.
8. In small bowl of electric mixer, beat yolks till thick and light. Blend in asparagus sauce.
9. With wire whisk or rubber scraper, using an under-and-over motion, fold asparagus mixture into egg whites. Turn into prepared dish.
10. Set in pan containing about 1 inch hot water; then bake for 60 minutes.
11. Serve at once with Cheese Sauce.*
* See Sauces and Gravies Chapter.

CHEDDAR-CHEESE SOUFFLÉ

4 eggs, separated
2 tablespoons butter or
   margarine
3 tablespoons flour
½ teaspoon salt
Dash cayenne

Dash paprika
¾ cup milk
2 cups (½ lb) grated sharp
   Cheddar cheese
¼ teaspoon cream of tartar

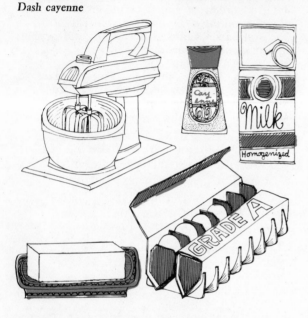

1. Preheat oven to 350F.
2. In large bowl of electric mixer, let egg whites warm to room temperature—1 hour.
3. Melt butter in medium saucepan; remove from heat. Stir in flour, salt, cayenne, and paprika until smooth. Then stir in milk.
4. Over medium heat, bring to boiling point, stirring. Add cheese; stir until it melts. Remove from heat.
5. Let cool. Stir into slightly beaten egg yolks.
6. With mixer at high speed, beat egg whites with cream of tartar just until stiff peaks form when beater is slowly raised.
7. With wire whisk or rubber scraper, using an under-and-over motion, gently fold cheese mixture into egg whites.
8. Turn into ungreased 1½-quart, straight-side soufflé dish.
9. Make top hat: With back of large spoon, make a deep path around soufflé top, about 1 inch from edge.
10. Set dish in pan containing about 1 inch hot water; bake 50 to 55 minutes.
11. Serve at once. Cheddar-Cheese Soufflé is good by itself but may be dressed up with Shrimp-Newburg Sauce.*
* See Sauces and Gravies Chapter.

CHICKEN SOUFFLÉ, HOLLANDAISE

6 egg whites
¼ cup butter or margarine
¼ cup unsifted all-purpose
   flour
1 teaspoon salt
Dash pepper

1 cup milk
¼ teaspoon cream of tartar
4 egg yolks
1¼ cups finely chopped
   cooked chicken

1. Preheat oven to 375F.
2. In large bowl of electric mixer, let egg whites warm to room temperature—1 hour.
3. Melt butter in medium saucepan; remove from heat. Stir in flour, salt, and pepper until smooth. Then stir in milk.
4. Over medium heat, bring to boiling point, stirring. Remove from heat; cool 10 minutes.
5. With mixer at high speed, beat egg whites with cream of tartar just until stiff peaks form when beater is slowly raised.
6. In small bowl of mixer, beat egg yolks until light and fluffy.
7. Stir chicken, then egg yolks into sauce.
8. With wire whisk or rubber scraper, using an under-and-over motion, gently fold chicken mixture into egg whites.
9. Turn into ungreased 1½-quart, straight-side soufflé dish.

(*Chicken Soufflé, Hollandaise continued*)

FISH SOUFFLÉ WITH LOBSTER SAUCE

Soufflé:

5 egg whites
5 tablespoons butter
   or margarine
2 tablespoons packaged dry
   bread crumbs
1 lb fillet of flounder, or
   1 lb thawed frozen
   fillet of flounder
⅓ cup unsifted all-purpose
   flour
2 teaspoons salt
⅛ teaspoon pepper
1½ cups milk
¼ teaspoon cream of tartar
4 egg yolks

Lobster Sauce:

2 tablespoons butter or
   margarine
2 tablespoons flour
¾ cup milk
1 cup light cream
1 cup coarsely chopped
   cooked lobster; or 1
   can (5 oz) lobster,
   drained, cut up
¾ teaspoon salt
Dash cayenne
1 egg yolk, slightly beaten

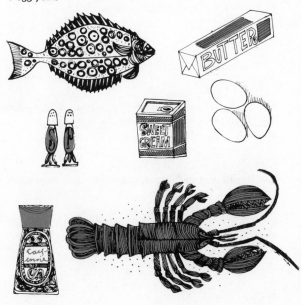

10.   Make top hat: With back of large spoon, make a deep path around soufflé top, about 1 inch from edge.

11.   Set dish in pan containing about 1 inch hot water; bake 55 to 60 minutes.

12.   About 15 minutes before soufflé is done, make Hollandaise Sauce.* Serve at once.

* See Sauces and Gravies Chapter.

MAKES 6 SERVINGS

1.   Preheat oven to 375F.

2.   Let egg whites warm to room temperature in large bowl of electric mixer—1 hour. Grease 1½ quart, straight-side soufflé dish with 1 tablespoon butter. Coat with bread crumbs.

3.   Place fish flat in large skillet with 2 cups water; bring to boiling. Reduce heat; simmer, covered, 5 minutes, or until fish can be easily flaked with fork.

4.   Drain very well, reserving ¼ cup cooking liquid for Lobster Sauce. Flake fish, and measure 2 cups.

5.   Melt rest of butter in medium saucepan. Remove from heat; stir in flour, salt, and pepper until smooth.

6.   Stir in milk; bring to boiling, stirring, over medium heat. Remove from heat; cool 10 minutes.

7.   With mixer at high speed, beat egg whites with cream of tartar just until stiff peaks form when beater is slowly raised.

8.   In small bowl, with mixer at high speed, beat egg yolks until light and fluffy.

9.   Stir fish and egg yolks into white sauce.

10.   Turn mixture into egg whites; with wire whisk or rubber scraper, using an under-and-over motion, gently fold into whites until well combined. Turn into soufflé dish.

11.   Make top hat: With back of large spoon, make deep path around top of soufflé, 1 inch from edge.

12.   Set dish in pan containing about 1 inch hot water; bake 55 minutes.

13.   While soufflé bakes, make Lobster Sauce: Melt butter in small saucepan; remove from heat. Stir in flour until smooth. Then add reserved fish liquid, milk, and cream; bring to boiling, stirring. Remove from heat. Add lobster, salt, cayenne, and egg yolk; cook, stirring, over low heat just until lobster is hot.

14.   Serve soufflé at once, with Lobster Sauce.

Here are such super-elegant egg dishes as Eggs Benedict, so good for any occasion, from extra-special weekend breakfasts through lunch and supper.

EGGS BENEDICT

MAKES 8 SERVINGS

Mock Hollandaise Sauce*
4 English muffins
8 teaspoons butter or
   margarine
1 teaspoon salt
8 eggs

4 slices fully cooked ham
   (¾ lb)
⅛ teaspoon cayenne
8 parsley sprigs

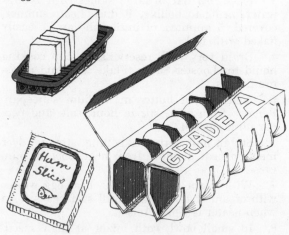

1. Prepare Mock Hollandaise Sauce. Keep warm over hot water.
2. Slice muffins in half, crosswise. Spread each cut side with 1 teaspoon butter. Toast until golden-brown. Arrange, cut side up, on serving platter; cover; keep warm.
3. In large skillet, bring ½ inch water to simmering; add salt.
4. Add eggs carefully, one at a time; poach, covered, 3 to 5 minutes. If possible, use rings to keep shape circular.
5. Meanwhile, in large skillet, sauté the ham about 3 minutes on each side. Cut slices in half.
6. Arrange ham slices on muffins.
7. Remove eggs with slotted utensil; trim if necessary, being careful not to break yolk.
8. Place eggs on ham; top with Mock Hollandaise Sauce.
9. Garnish with cayenne and parsley.

* See Sauces and Gravies Chapter.

EGGS FU YUNG

MAKES 4 TO 6 SERVINGS

1 teaspoon soy sauce
1 teaspoon dark molasses
1 teaspoon cider vinegar
2 teaspoons cornstarch
½ cup canned chicken
   broth, undiluted
1 cup finely chopped
   cooked ham or pork

1 cup canned bean sprouts,
   drained
1 cup finely chopped onion
6 eggs, slightly beaten
1 teaspoon salt
1 tablespoon soy sauce
Salad oil

1. In top of double boiler, combine 1 teaspoon soy sauce, molasses, vinegar, and cornstarch, stirring until smooth.
2. Gradually stir in chicken broth; over direct heat, bring to boiling, stirring.
3. Reduce heat, and simmer 10 minutes. Sauce will be thickened and translucent. Keep warm over hot water.
4. In large bowl, combine ham, bean sprouts, and onion. Add eggs, salt, and 1 tablespoon soy sauce, stirring just until combined.

(*Eggs Fu Yung continued*)

5. Slowly heat a little oil in small skillet. Add egg mixture, about 2 tablespoons at a time (as for pancakes).

6. Sauté, turning once, just until browned on both sides. Remove, and keep warm. Repeat until all egg mixture is used.

7. Arrange "pancakes" on hot platter. Pour the hot sauce over them.

ASPARAGUS AND EGGS GOLDENROD WITH CANADIAN BACON

MAKES 12 SERVINGS

5 lb asparagus, or 4 pkg
    (10-oz size) frozen
    asparagus spears
Boiling water
2 teaspoons salt

Eggs Goldenrod:
6 hard-cooked eggs
1/3 cup butter or margarine
1/3 cup unsifted all-purpose
    flour
2 teaspoons salt
Dash white pepper

2 cups milk
4 teaspoons prepared
    horseradish
1/8 teaspoon liquid hot-
    pepper seasoning
1/4 teaspoon Worcestershire
    sauce
4 teaspoons white vinegar

2 tablespoons lemon juice
2 lb cooked Canadian-
    bacon slices, drained

1. Cook asparagus: Cut off and discard tough ends; wash asparagus well. With vegetable parer, scrape skin and scales from lower part of stalks. Stand stalks upright in bottoms of two double boilers, or in 2 large, deep saucepans. To each, add boiling water to measure 2 inches and 1 teaspoon salt.

2. Bring to boiling; cook, covered, 15 to 20 minutes, or just until tender. (If using frozen asparagus, cook as package label directs.)

3. Meanwhile, make Eggs Goldenrod: Press 2 egg yolks through coarse sieve; set aside for garnish. Press rest of eggs through sieve.

4. Melt butter in medium saucepan; remove from heat. Add flour, salt, and pepper, stirring until smooth. Gradually stir in milk.

5. Bring to boiling, stirring. Reduce heat, and simmer, stirring, until the mixture is thickened and smooth—about 3 minutes. Remove from heat.

6. Add sieved eggs, except reserved yolks, horseradish, hot-pepper seasoning, Worcestershire, and vinegar; mix well.

7. Drain asparagus well. Arrange on serving platter; sprinkle with lemon juice.

8. Pour Eggs Goldenrod over asparagus in a wide band; top with reserved sieved yolk. Surround with Canadian-bacon slices.

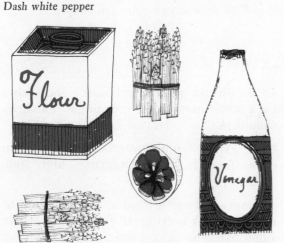

Fish 15
and
Shellfish

That gift from the sea, fresh fish, is good not only for Lent but for all the days of the year when you want a change from meat. McCall's suggests you try our recipes if you like fish-with-a-difference.

Seafoods provide a variety of nutritive factors. Rich in protein and, in some instances, in minerals and vitamins, they are a valuable addition to the diet, especially of the calorie-conscious person. The composition and food value of seafoods vary according to the species and the locality where they are caught.

Purchasing Hints

In selecting fresh fish, observe these points:

Eyes: Should be clean, clear, bright, full, and bulging. Redness is not an indication of spoilage—the eyes may have been bruised when the fish was caught or in packing.

Gills: Reddish-pink, free from odor, slime, and discoloration.

Scales: Should have a characteristic sheen, adhere tightly to the skin, without slime.

Flesh: Should be firm and elastic and spring back under pressure of your finger. The flesh should not be separated from the bones.

Odor: Fish when it's fresh has a clean, fresh odor, free from objectionable and stale smells.

Amounts to buy: A third to a half pound of fresh fish per serving. If you serve a whole small fish, choose one weighing a pound for one serving.

Storage

Fresh fish should be wrapped in moisture-proof, air-tight material or placed in a covered container and stored in the refrigerator immediately. If you intend to keep it for several days, freeze it in moisture-vapor-proof freezer paper or container. Properly wrapped and frozen, it will not spoil as long as it remains frozen solid. Once it has been thawed, do not refreeze. It should remain packaged and refrigerated while thawing. If you want to thaw it quickly, place it under cold running water.

BROILED FISH

1. Let frozen fish thaw completely before broiling. Wash fish in cold water; pat dry with paper towels.

2. Lightly brush broiler rack with salad oil; arrange fish on rack. Brush fish with one of basting sauces, below.

3. Broil, 4 inches from heat, as directed in timetable, below, or until fish flakes easily when tested with fork but is still moist.

4. To serve: Remove fish to heated platter. Garnish with lemon wedges and parsley sprigs. Pass one of sauces* for fish, if desired.

* See Sauces and Gravies Chapter.

Herbed Basting Sauce: Combine 2 tablespoons salad oil, 2 tablespoons lemon juice, ¼ teaspoon paprika, and ¼ teaspoon dried marjoram, basil, or thyme leaves. Use to brush on fish several times during broiling.

Curried Basting Sauce: Combine 2 tablespoons salad oil, 2 tablespoons lemon juice, and ¼ teaspoon curry powder. Use to brush on fish several times during broiling.

Lemony Basting Sauce: Combine 3 tablespoons lemon juice with ⅛ teaspoon dry mustard, and 1 bay leaf, crumbled. Use to brush on fish several times during broiling.

Fish	Approximate Broiling Time
Fillets	5 to 8 minutes on each side
Steaks	5 to 8 minutes on each side
Dressed Whole	5 minutes per lb, each side
Split	5 to 8 minutes on each side

POACHED CODFISH IN MUSTARD SAUCE

MAKES 6 SERVINGS

2½ lb codfish steaks
1 medium onion, cut in
    quarters
1 bay leaf, crumbled
Dash allspice
1¼ teaspoons salt
¼ teaspoon pepper

3 tablespoons butter or
    margarine
3 tablespoons flour
¼ cup prepared English-
    style mustard
1 tablespoon lemon juice

1. Wipe codfish with damp cloth. Arrange in single layer in large skillet with tight-fitting cover.
2. Add 2½ cups water, the onion, bay leaf, allspice, ¾ teaspoon salt, and the pepper; bring to boiling.
3. Reduce heat; simmer, covered, 8 minutes, or until fish flakes easily with fork.
4. Carefully drain fish, reserving liquid. Place fish on heated platter; keep warm.
5. Melt butter in medium saucepan.
6. Remove from heat. Add flour, stirring until smooth. Gradually stir in 2 cups reserved liquid from fish; bring to boiling, stirring.
7. Reduce heat. Stir in mustard, lemon juice, and remaining salt; simmer gently until heated through.
8. Spoon some of sauce over codfish; pass rest.

BAKED STRIPED BASS

MAKES 6 SERVINGS

3- to 4-lb whole striped
    bass, dressed and
    boned
½ teaspoon salt
⅛ teaspoon pepper
1 shallot, thinly sliced
¼ cup thinly sliced onion
2 bay leaves
Dash dried thyme leaves
2 garlic cloves
1 cup thinly sliced fresh
    mushrooms

½ cup parsley sprigs
2 celery stalks, with leaves
1 tablespoon butter or
    margarine
3 cups dry white wine

Sauce:
Cooking liquid from fish
1 teaspoon plus ½ cup
    butter or margarine
1 teaspoon all-purpose flour

1. Preheat oven to 400F. Lightly grease large, shallow baking pan.
2. Wash bass; pat dry with paper towels.
3. Sprinkle bass, inside and out, with salt and pepper.
4. Place in baking pan. Add remaining ingredients, except Sauce, distributing evenly around bass.
5. Bake, basting frequently with liquid in pan, 40 minutes, or until fish flakes easily with fork.
6. Carefully remove fish to heated serving platter; cover, and keep in warm place.
7. Make Sauce: Strain cooking liquid from fish into small saucepan; discard vegetables. Cook liquid, uncovered and over medium heat, until it measures 1 cup—about 15 to 20 minutes. Remove from heat.
8. Combine 1 teaspoon butter with flour; blend into hot liquid.
9. Bring to boiling, stirring; boil 2 minutes.
10. Reduce heat. Add remaining butter, shaking pan from side to side until butter melts. Remove from heat. Pass sauce with fish.

CODFISH CAKES

½ pkg (1-lb size) salt
   codfish
3 medium potatoes, pared
   and cubed (3 cups)
⅛ teaspoon pepper
Dash ginger
1 tablespoon milk

1 egg yolk
1 small onion, peeled and
   grated
1 egg white
3 tablespoons butter or
   margarine

1. Freshen codfish as package label directs.
2. In large saucepan, combine codfish and potatoes with water to cover; bring to boiling. Reduce heat, and simmer, covered, 30 minutes, or until potatoes are tender. Drain well.
3. Return codfish and potatoes to saucepan; cook, uncovered, over low heat, about 5 minutes, or until mixture appears dry.
4. Turn codfish-potato mixture into large bowl. Add pepper, ginger, milk, egg yolk, and onion. With wooden spoon, beat mixture vigorously about 5 minutes, or until very light and fluffy.
5. Beat egg white until stiff peaks form when beater is raised. Gently stir into fish-potato mixture.
6. Shape mixture in 8 flat cakes. Sauté in hot butter, in large skillet, until golden-brown on both sides. Drain well on paper towels.

TARRAGON FILLETS

2 lb flounder fillets
1 cup tarragon vinegar
½ cup yellow cornmeal
½ cup unsifted all-purpose
   flour

¼ teaspoon salt
⅛ teaspoon pepper
¼ cup butter or margarine

1. Arrange flounder in shallow baking dish. Pour on vinegar; let marinate 10 minutes.
2. Meanwhile, combine cornmeal, flour, salt, and pepper. Use to coat fillets evenly on both sides.
3. In hot butter in large skillet, sauté fillets until golden-brown—about 4 minutes on each side. Serve fillets with Cucumber Sauce.*
* See Sauces and Gravies Chapter.

BAKED FISH IN WHITE WINE

1½ cups very thinly sliced
   carrots
Boiling water
1½ cups finely chopped
   onion
½ lb fresh mushrooms,
   sliced; or 1 can (3 oz)
   mushroom caps,
   drained
3 tablespoons chopped
   parsley

½ cup thinly sliced celery
   and leaves
2 teaspoons salt
⅛ teaspoon pepper
1 slice halibut or cod (2 lb)
6 thin lemon slices
3 bacon slices, chopped
¾ cup dry white wine or
   chicken broth

1. Preheat oven to 375F.
2. In small saucepan, cover carrots with boiling water; bring to boiling. Boil, covered, 5 minutes. Drain.
3. Arrange carrots, onion, mushrooms, parsley, and celery in bottom of large, shallow bake-and-serve pan. Sprinkle with 1 teaspoon salt and the pepper.
4. Place fish on vegetables; sprinkle with rest of salt. Overlap lemon slices across fish. Sprinkle with bacon. Pour on wine.
5. Cover top of pan completely with foil; bake 20 minutes.
6. Remove foil; bake 15 to 20 minutes longer, or until fish can be easily flaked with fork. Serve right from pan.

BAKED STUFFED WHOLE FISH

Savory Stuffing:
1 egg, beaten
¼ teaspoon dried thyme
    leaves
½ teaspoon dill seed
2 tablespoons chopped
    parsley
¼ teaspoon salt
Dash pepper
½ cup butter or
    margarine, melted
3 tablespoons finely
    chopped onion

3 cups white-bread crumbs
    (day-old bread,
    grated)

1 (3- to 5-lb) whole fish,
    dressed and split
    (red snapper, bluefish,
    mackerel, whitefish,
    cod, haddock, striped
    bass, or similar fish)
Salt
Pepper
2 tablespoons butter or
    margarine, melted
4 to 8 lemon wedges

1. Preheat oven to 500F.
2. Make Savory Stuffing: Combine egg, thyme, dill seed, parsley, salt, and pepper in a large bowl; mix well.
3. In hot butter, sauté onion until it is golden —about 5 minutes.
4. To seasonings, add onion-butter mixture, 2 tablespoons hot water, and bread crumbs, tossing lightly with a fork, to mix well.
5. Sprinkle inside of fish with salt and pepper. Place fish in large, shallow baking dish; stuff. Close opening with skewers or toothpicks.
6. Brush top with melted butter; then bake, uncovered, 10 minutes.
7. Reduce heat to 400F; bake 10 minutes per pound, or until fish flakes easily with fork. Serve with lemon wedges.

SALMON TIMBALES

1 can (5 oz) deveined
    shrimp, drained
¼ cup butter or margarine
¼ cup unsifted all-purpose
    flour
2 cups milk
2 cans (7-¾-oz size) salmon,
    drained

1 teaspoon salt
¼ teaspoon pepper
2 eggs, slightly beaten
1 tablespoon sherry
1 tablespoon lemon juice
½ teaspoon paprika

1. Preheat oven to 350F.
2. Lightly grease 4 (6-oz) custard cups. Place 1 shrimp in center of each cup.
3. In medium saucepan, melt 2 tablespoons butter. Remove from heat.
4. Add 2 tablespoons flour, stirring until smooth. Gradually stir in ½ cup milk. Bring to boiling, stirring constantly. Remove from heat.
5. Flake salmon with fork. Add to milk mixture, with ½ teaspoon salt, the pepper, and eggs; mix well. Spoon salmon mixture over shrimp in each cup.
6. Set cups in pan containing 1 inch hot water; bake 35 minutes.
7. Meanwhile, make sauce: Melt rest of butter in medium saucepan.
8. Remove from heat. Add rest of flour, stirring until smooth. Gradually stir in rest of milk; bring to boiling, stirring constantly.
9. Reduce heat. Add sherry, lemon juice, paprika, and rest of salt.
10. Coarsely chop remaining shrimp. Add to sauce; stir, over low heat, until hot.
11. Unmold timbales onto warm platter. Top each with some of sauce; pass rest of sauce.

CRISPY SALMON STEAKS

½ cup butter or
    margarine, melted
1 teaspoon salt
⅛ teaspoon paprika
6 (6- to 8-oz) salmon steaks,
    ¾ inch thick

1 cup crushed saltines
1 cup crushed potato chips
6 lemon wedges
6 parsley sprigs

MAKES 6 SERVINGS

1. Combine butter, salt, and paprika.
2. Wipe steaks with damp cloth. Dip each into butter mixture; then roll in combined saltines and potato chips.
3. Arrange steaks on lightly greased broiler rack in broiler pan. Broil, 6 inches from heat, 5 minutes.
4. Turn; broil 5 to 8 minutes, or until fish flakes easily with fork. Serve each steak with a lemon wedge and parsley sprig.

BAKED FILLETS THERMIDOR

2 lb sole fillets
5 tablespoons butter or
    margarine
2 teaspoons salt
¼ teaspoon pepper
½ teaspoon seasoned salt

1¼ cups milk
3 tablespoons flour
1 cup grated sharp Cheddar
    cheese (¼ lb)
3 tablespoons sherry
Paprika

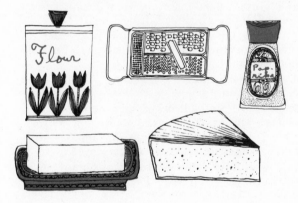

MAKES 6 SERVINGS

1. Preheat oven to 350F.
2. Wash fillets, and dry on paper towels.
3. Melt 2 tablespoons butter. Use to brush dark side of fillets. Sprinkle with salt, pepper, and seasoned salt.
4. Roll up fillets, seasonings inside. Arrange in a 9-by-9-by-1¾-inch baking dish. Pour on ½ cup milk.
5. Bake, uncovered, 30 minutes.
6. Meanwhile, in medium saucepan, melt rest of butter.
7. Remove from heat. Add flour, stirring until smooth. Gradually stir in remaining milk; bring to boiling, stirring constantly.
8. Reduce heat. Add cheese, stirring until it is melted. Then add sherry.
9. Carefully drain liquid from fish; stir into cheese sauce. Pour sauce over fish. Sprinkle with paprika.
10. Place under broiler, 4 inches from heat, until sauce is golden-brown.

SKILLET-FRIED TROUT

2 fresh brook trout; or
    1 pkg (10 oz) frozen
    trout, thawed
2 teaspoons lemon juice
1 teaspoon salt

3 tablespoons all-purpose
    flour
⅛ teaspoon pepper
¼ cup salad oil
1 medium onion, sliced

MAKES 2 SERVINGS

1. Clean and scale trout, if necessary. Sprinkle lemon juice and ½ teaspoon salt in slash.
2. Combine remaining salt, the flour, and pepper on waxed paper. Roll trout in flour mixture, to coat.
3. Slowly heat salad oil, in medium skillet, until a drop of water sizzles when added.
4. Put in trout; sauté 5 minutes, or until golden-brown. Turn; sauté other side 1 minute.
5. Add onion, and cook over medium heat, turning onion often, about 5 minutes, or just until fish is nicely browned.

FILLETS OF SOLE FLORENTINE

MAKES 6 SERVINGS

Hollandaise Sauce:
2 egg yolks
¼ teaspoon salt
Dash cayenne
½ cup butter or margarine, melted
1½ tablespoons lemon juice

2½ lb sole or flounder fillets
¼ cup lemon juice
1 clove garlic, finely chopped
1 shallot, finely chopped
¼ cup chopped fresh mushrooms

1 tablespoon dried tarragon leaves
About 1 cup sauterne or Chablis
2 pkg (10-oz size) frozen chopped spinach
½ teaspoon salt
⅛ teaspoon pepper
1 cup heavy cream

Wine Sauce:
¼ cup butter or margarine
¼ cup unsifted all-purpose flour
½ teaspoon salt
⅛ teaspoon pepper
½ cup light cream

1. Make Hollandaise Sauce: In small bowl, beat egg yolks with rotary beater until thick and light. Add salt and cayenne; turn into double-boiler top.

2. Over hot, not boiling, water, gradually beat ¼ cup butter into yolks, with wire whisk or spoon; beat well after each addition.

3. Combine rest of butter with lemon juice; beat into egg yolks bit by bit. Continue beating, over hot water, just until consistency of mayonnaise. Remove from hot water; set aside.

4. Preheat oven to 350F. Lightly grease large, shallow baking dish.

5. Wash fillets; dry well on paper towels. Brush both sides with lemon juice. (If using flounder or broad fillets, split down center.)

6. Fold fillets into thirds, with dark side inside. Arrange in single layer in baking dish. Sprinkle garlic, shallot, mushrooms, and tarragon over and around fish. Pour on enough sauterne to come halfway up side of dish.

7. Cover top of dish with foil; bake 20 minutes, or just until fish flakes easily with fork. Do not overcook.

8. Meanwhile, cook spinach as package label directs; drain.

9. Then drain well on paper towels. Add salt, pepper, and ⅓ cup heavy cream; mix well.

10. Turn creamed spinach into another shallow baking dish, making an even layer.

11. Carefully remove fish from baking dish; reserve liquid and vegetables. Drain fish very well, and arrange on spinach in single layer. Cover, and keep in warm place.

12. Make Wine Sauce: Over low heat, melt butter in medium saucepan, stirring.

13. Remove from heat. Add flour, salt, and pepper, stirring until smooth. Gradually stir in 1½ cups reserved liquid and vegetables from fish and the light cream.

14. Bring to boiling, stirring. Strain; discard vegetables.

15. Spoon hot Wine Sauce over fillets, covering completely. Gradually add remaining ⅔ cup heavy cream to Hollandaise, stirring until well mixed. Carefully spoon Hollandaise over fillets and Wine Sauce, covering completely.

16. Run under broiler 1 to 2 minutes, or until top is golden-brown.

FILLETS OF SOLE WITH TARRAGON-CHIVE BUTTER

MAKES 6 SERVINGS

2 lb fillets of sole; or 2 pkg
    (1-lb size) frozen
    fillets of sole, thawed
½ cup butter or margarine,
    melted
2 tablespoons lemon juice

1 tablespoon coarsely
    snipped fresh
    tarragon leaves
1 tablespoon snipped chives
¼ teaspoon salt

1. Preheat oven to 350F.

2. Brush fillets with ¼ cup butter. Sprinkle with lemon juice. Arrange in greased 13-by-9-by-2-inch baking dish.

3. Cover dish with foil; bake 30 minutes, or until fish flakes easily with fork.

4. Combine rest of butter with tarragon, chives, and salt; heat slightly.

5. To serve, put fillets on platter; pour warm herb butter over them.

BAKED TUNA LOAVES

MAKES 8 SERVINGS

6 tablespoons butter or
    margarine
1 cup chopped onion
1 cup chopped celery
3 tablespoons finely
    chopped parsley
1 cup packaged dry bread
    crumbs
2 hard-cooked eggs,
    chopped

⅔ cup evaporated milk,
    undiluted
3 tablespoons lemon juice
2 eggs, beaten
1½ teaspoons salt
¼ teaspoon pepper
3 cans (7-oz size) tuna,
    drained and flaked

1. Preheat oven to 350F. In 4 tablespoons hot butter in large skillet, sauté onion, celery, and parsley until onion is golden—about 5 minutes.

2. In large bowl, combine onion mixture with ¾ cup bread crumbs, hard-cooked eggs, milk, lemon juice, beaten eggs, salt, pepper, and tuna; mix thoroughly.

3. On lightly greased 15½-by-10½-by-1-inch jelly-roll pan, shape mixture into 8 loaves, using about ¾ cup for each. Brush with rest of butter, melted. Sprinkle with remaining bread crumbs.

4. Bake 25 minutes, or until lightly browned. Serve tuna loaves on platter with Caper Sauce.*

* See Sauces and Gravies Chapter.

TUNA AMANDINE

MAKES 8 SERVINGS

1 cup packaged sliced
    potatoes
1 can (10½ oz) cream-of-
    celery soup, undiluted
½ cup milk
2 tablespoons lemon juice
½ teaspoon paprika
4 drops liquid hot-pepper
    seasoning

1 tablespoon chopped
    parsley
1 can (5 oz) toasted slivered
    almonds
3 cans (7-oz size) chunk-
    style tuna, drained
4 to 6 stuffed olives, sliced
2 tablespoons butter or
    margarine, melted

1. Cook potatoes as package label directs; drain.

2. Preheat oven to 350F.

3. Meanwhile, in medium saucepan, combine soup, milk, lemon juice, paprika, hot-pepper seasonings, parsley, and ¾ cup almonds. Simmer, stirring, 5 minutes.

4. Layer two thirds of tuna in bottom of 2-quart casserole. Pour on one third almond sauce.

5. Top with potatoes, then one third almond sauce. Cover with remaining tuna, then remaining almond sauce.

6. Garnish edge of casserole with sliced olives. Fill center with rest of almonds.

7. Pour butter over almonds; bake 30 minutes.

Shellfish

Any time of the year, any place you live (whether close to the sea or many miles from it), you can buy protein-rich shrimp, oysters, clams, lobsters, crabs, and scallops. How lucky we are that food so plentiful tastes so good and is so good for us!

H ard-shell clams are large and are used for broth and chowder. Soft-shell clams are usually small and are used for steaming and fritters. Serve clams on the half shell, dipped in Seafood-Cocktail Sauce,* or see Index for other clam recipes.

* See Sauces and Gravies Chapter.

FRIED CLAMS

MAKES 4 TO 6 SERVINGS

1 qt shucked clams
1 egg, slightly beaten
1 teaspoon salt
⅛ teaspoon pepper

Dash paprika
1 cup packaged dry bread
  crumbs
½ cup butter or margarine

1. Drain clams, reserving 2 tablespoons liquid.
2. Combine clam liquid with egg, salt, pepper, and paprika.
3. Dip clams in egg mixture; then roll in bread crumbs, coating completely.
4. In hot butter in medium skillet, sauté clams 3 to 4 minutes on each side, or until golden. Drain well on paper towels.

T he lovely, delicate flavor of crab appeals to almost everybody, so much so that crab is the second most popular shellfish in America. Crabmeat is available in cans and frozen packages. Even though crabmeat may seem expensive, there is absolutely no waste, and one pound serves four adequately. Now, try these recipes.

BOILED CRABS

MAKES ABOUT 2 CUPS CRABMEAT

¼ cup salt

16 live hard-shell crabs

1. In large kettle, bring 4 quarts water and the salt to boiling.
2. Place crabs in collander; wash in cold water until crabs seem clean.
3. Holding crabs by tongs or back feelers, plunge head first into boiling water; return water to boiling. Reduce heat, and simmer, covered, 12 to 15 minutes.
4. Drain; let cool.

(*Boiled Crabs continued*)

5. To remove meat: Twist off claws and legs; crack them with nutcracker or hammer; remove meat.

6. Lay crab on top shell. Insert point of a knife under forward end of the flap that folds under body from rear; break it off, and discard.

7. Pick up crab in both hands; pull upper and lower shells apart. Discard top shell.

8. Hold crab under running water; remove gills and all spongy material.

9. Cut away any hard membrane along outer edge; carefully remove meat with fork.

CRAB MORNAY

MAKES 4 TO 6 SERVINGS

1 pkg (10 oz) frozen
    chopped spinach
3 tablespoons butter or
    margarine
2 tablespoons flour
½ teaspoon salt
Dash cayenne
1½ cups milk
½ cup light cream

1 cup grated Swiss cheese
1 tablespoon lemon juice
2 cans (6½-oz size)
    crabmeat, drained and
    flaked
¼ cup packaged dry bread
    crumbs
Paprika
4 to 6 buttered-toast slices

1. Cook spinach as package label directs; drain. Place in 1½-quart casserole; set aside.

2. Preheat oven to 375F.

3. Melt butter in medium saucepan. Remove from heat.

4. Blend in flour, salt, and cayenne. Gradually stir in milk and cream.

5. Bring to boiling, stirring; boil 1 minute.

6. Add cheese; stir until melted. Add lemon juice and crabmeat.

7. Pour over spinach. Sprinkle with bread crumbs and paprika.

8. Bake 15 minutes, or until crumbs are browned.

9. Serve over toast.

CRAB MOUSSE

MAKES 6 SERVINGS

1 envelope unflavored
    gelatine
¼ cup boiling water
¾ cup heavy cream,
    whipped

½ cup mayonnaise or
    cooked salad dressing
3 tablespoons lemon juice
1¼ teaspoons salt
2 cups cooked crabmeat,
    coarsely chopped
Salad greens

1. Sprinkle gelatine over ¼ cup cold water; let stand 5 minutes to soften.

2. Add boiling water; stir until gelatine is dissolved. Set aside to cool.

3. Combine whipped cream, mayonnaise, lemon juice, and salt. Gently fold in cooled gelatine and crabmeat. Turn into 1-quart mold.

4. Refrigerate until firm—about 2 hours.

5. To unmold: Run a small spatula around edge of mold; invert over serving platter; shake gently to release. If necessary, place a hot, damp cloth over mold; shake again to release. Surround with salad greens.

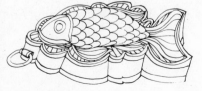

SAUTÉED SOFT-SHELL CRABS

MAKES 3 SERVINGS

6 soft-shell crabs
1 egg
1 teaspoon salt
⅛ teaspoon pepper
⅛ teaspoon paprika

½ cup packaged dry bread
   crumbs
¼ cup unsifted all-purpose
   flour
½ cup butter or margarine

1. To clean crabs: With sharp knife, cut away segment that folds under body from rear; discard.

2. With scissors, remove head, about ¾ inch behind eyes; discard.

3. Lift back shell on either side; scrape away lungs and spongy substance under it. Wash crabs well under cold running water.

4. Beat egg slightly with salt, pepper, and paprika. Combine bread crumbs with flour.

5. Dip crabs in egg mixture, then in crumb mixture, coating completely.

6. In hot butter in large skillet, sauté crabs until golden—about 4 minutes on each side.

SHERRIED CRABMEAT

MAKES 8 SERVINGS

2 cans (6½-oz size)
   crabmeat
¼ cup butter or margarine
3 tablespoons flour
½ teaspoon salt
Dash pepper
Dash cayenne
¾ cup bottled clam juice
½ cup heavy cream
1½ tablespoons dry sherry
1 hard-cooked egg, finely
   chopped

1 tablespoon finely chopped
   onion
½ cup sliced fresh
   mushrooms
1 tablespoon finely chopped
   parsley
1 tablespoon finely chopped
   chives
¼ cup packaged dry bread
   crumbs

1. Drain crabmeat, and remove any cartilage.

2. Melt 3 tablespoons butter in medium saucepan. Remove from heat; stir in flour, salt, pepper, and cayenne until smooth. Gradually stir in clam juice and cream.

3. Bring mixture to boiling, stirring; sauce will be thickened and smooth.

4. Stir in sherry, egg, and crabmeat.

5. Heat rest of butter in small skillet; in it, sauté onion, mushrooms, parsley, and chives until mushrooms are tender—about 5 minutes. Stir in bread crumbs.

6. Fill 8 patty shells or toast cups with crabmeat mixture; top each with mushroom mixture.

Most elegant of shellfish, lobster is represented in our waters by two kinds. The spiny or rock lobster, without claws and with the meat concentrated in the tail; caught in southern waters. The northern lobster, with claws, caught from Maine to Nova Scotia. Native lobsters can be bought alive or boiled whole; or boiled, removed from the shell, then packed in tins or frozen. And don't overlook frozen lobster tails!

Fish *Feast*

Here's fish with a difference. Not just fish-because-it's-a-change-from-meat, but fish you'll be proud to serve either to company or to your family. It's a mistake to think that fish tastes "fishy." As you'll soon see, it can be a dish for the most refined palate.

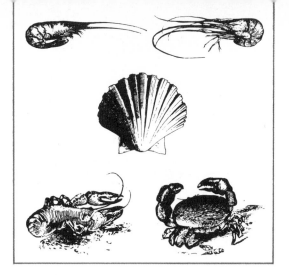

SHELLFISH

They're not very pretty to look at, but many people consider some form of them among the greatest delicacies in the world. They're an "acquired taste," it's said; but, once acquired, this can be a taste that dominates all others. These days, at any time of the year, any place you live (whether close to the sea or many miles from it), you can buy protein-rich shrimp, oysters, clams, lobsters, crabs, and scallops. Serve shellfish hot or cold, with fancy sauces or plain, in casseroles or salads. How lucky we are that food that tastes so good is so plentiful and that it's so good for us, as well!

BOILED LIVE LOBSTERS

MAKES 2 SERVINGS

3 tablespoons salt   Melted butter
2 (1-lb size) live lobsters   Lemon wedges

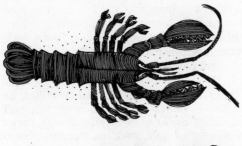

1. In large kettle, bring 3 quarts water with the salt to boiling.

2. Plunge lobsters into water, head first; return water to boiling. Reduce heat, and simmer, covered, 20 minutes. Drain.

To Serve Lobster in Shell:

1. Place lobster on back shell. With sharp knife, split body down middle, cutting through thin undershell and leaving back shell intact.

2. Remove dark intestinal vein running down center of lobster and small sac, about 2 inches long, below head; discard. Crack large claws. Serve hot or cold, with melted butter or lemon wedges.

To Remove Meat from Shell:

1. Lay lobster on back shell; twist off all claws close to body. Slit center of thin shell entire length of lobster. Remove meat from tail in one piece.

2. Lay tail meat red side down. Slit lengthwise down middle; remove and discard dark intestinal vein. Remove meat from body of lobster with pick, discarding stomach (a small sac about 2 inches below head). Green liver (tomalley) may be used if desired.

3. Crack large claws with nutcracker; remove meat.

BROILED LOBSTERS

MAKES 2 SERVINGS

2 (1-lb size) live lobsters   Pepper
Butter or margarine, melted   Paprika
Salt   Lemon wedges

1. Kill lobster: Lay lobster on back shell on wooden board. To sever spinal cord, insert point of knife through to back shell where body and tail of lobster come together.

2. With sharp knife, split body of lobster down middle, cutting through thin undershell just to back shell and leaving back shell intact.

3. Discard dark intestinal vein running down center of lobster; also discard small sac below head.

4. Crack large claws. Lay lobsters on back shell on broiler rack; spread open. Brush with melted butter; sprinkle with salt, pepper, and paprika.

5. Broil, 4 inches from heat, 12 to 15 minutes, or until lightly browned. Serve with lemon wedges and melted butter.

BAKED STUFFED LOBSTERS

MAKES 4 SERVINGS

5½ teaspoons salt

4 (1½-lb size) live lobsters, or 2 pkg (10-oz size) frozen rock-lobster tails

¾ cup butter or margarine, melted

¼ cup finely chopped onion

2¼ cups small day-old white-bread cubes, crust removed

2 tablespoons finely snipped fresh oregano leaves, or 1 tablespoon dried oregano leaves

2 tablespoons finely snipped parsley

⅛ teaspoon pepper

¼ cup light cream

¼ cup sherry

¼ cup grated Parmesan cheese

1. In large kettle, bring to boiling about 5 quarts cold water with 5 teaspoons salt. Plunge lobsters head first into water (water should cover them); bring to boiling again. Reduce heat; simmer, covered, 20 minutes.

2. Run cold water over lobsters. Drain; let cool at room temperature. (If using frozen lobster tails, cook as package label directs. Drain; cool.)

3. In ¼ cup hot butter in small skillet, sauté onion until golden—about 5 minutes. Add to bread cubes in large bowl, along with oregano, parsley, rest of salt, and the pepper; toss with fork until well mixed.

4. Preheat oven to 400F.

5. To remove meat from lobsters: Twist off lobster claws. With nutcracker, crack large claws; remove meat. (Small claws may be saved and used as garnish.)

6. Turn lobsters on backs; with sharp knife or kitchen shears, cut down center from head to tail. Remove and discard membrane; remove and discard small sac, about 2 inches long, just below head. Remove meat with pick. Reserve tomalley (green liver). Remove meat from tail; discard black vein.

7. Cut meat in bite-size pieces. Wash shells, and dry. (If using frozen tails, cut meat in bite-size pieces; wash shells, and dry.)

8. Add lobster meat, with tomalley, to bread mixture, along with cream, sherry, and rest of butter. Toss with fork to combine well. Spoon stuffing into shells. Sprinkle with grated cheese.

9. Place stuffed lobsters in flat baking dish. Cover top of dish with foil; bake 20 to 30 minutes, or until lobsters are thoroughly hot.

LOBSTER NEWBURG

MAKES 3 OR 4 SERVINGS

¾ lb cooked lobster meat, or 2 cans (6-oz size) lobster meat

2 egg yolks, slightly beaten

½ cup heavy cream

¼ cup butter or margarine

2 tablespoons sherry

½ teaspoon salt

Dash cayenne

Dash nutmeg

1. If necessary, break lobster meat into chunks

2. Combine egg yolks with cream.

3. Melt butter in medium saucepan, over low heat. Stir in egg mixture and sherry; cook, stirring constantly, until mixture thickens.

4. Remove from heat. Add salt, cayenne, nutmeg, and lobster; reheat gently.

5. Serve hot, over buttered toast slices.

Oysters are marketed in their shells, out of their shells, canned, and frozen. Each variety has a slightly different flavor and shape.

Probably the most popular way of serving them is on the half shell, with lemon juice and black pepper.

FRIED OYSTERS

MAKES 4 TO 6 SERVINGS

Salad oil or shortening for
    frying
2 eggs, beaten
¼ cup liquid from oysters

½ teaspoon salt
½ teaspoon pepper
3 dozen fresh oysters
Cracker crumbs

1. In large, heavy skillet, heat salad oil (at least one inch) to 375F on deep-frying thermometer.
2. Combine eggs, liquid from oysters, salt, and pepper.
3. Dip oysters in cracker crumbs, then in egg mixture, coating completely.
4. Fry, a few at a time, until golden on both sides—about 3 minutes in all.
5. Drain well on paper towels.

RICH OYSTER STEW

MAKES 6 SERVINGS

2 dozen small fresh oysters
2 tablespoons butter or
    margarine
Dash Worcestershire
    sauce

2 cups milk
2 cups light cream
Salt
Pepper
Celery salt

1. Drain oysters, reserving liquid.
2. In medium saucepan, combine oysters, 2 tablespoons liquid from oysters, butter, and Worcestershire; cook, over low heat, until edges of oysters begin to curl. Remove from heat.
3. Meanwhile, heat remaining liquid from oysters to boiling. In separate saucepan, heat milk and cream until bubbles form around edge of pan.
4. Combine oysters, oyster liquid, and milk mixture. Season with salt, pepper, and celery salt.

There are two varieties of scallops. Happily, one kind or the other is obtainable, fresh or frozen, all year long. The tiny bay scallop, tender and delicately flavored, is favored by gourmets. The larger sea scallop is more available. Each is delicious.

BROILED SEA SCALLOPS

MAKES 3 OR 4 SERVINGS

1 lb sea scallops	Salt
¼ cup butter or margarine, melted	Pepper
1 tablespoon lemon juice	Paprika

1. Rinse scallops. Drain; dry on paper towels.
2. Arrange scallops on broiler rack. Combine butter and lemon juice; brush half of mixture over scallops. Sprinkle with salt, pepper, and paprika.
3. Broil, 5 inches from heat, 3 minutes.
4. Turn scallops; brush with remaining lemon-butter mixture. Broil 2 to 3 minutes longer, or until scallops are tender. Serve garnished with parsley sprigs, if desired.

PAN-FRIED SCALLOPS

MAKES 4 SERVINGS

1½ lb bay scallops (1½ pt)	⅛ teaspoon paprika
½ cup packaged dry bread crumbs	½ cup butter or margarine
¼ teaspoon salt	4 buttered toast slices
⅛ teaspoon pepper	3 tablespoons dry white wine

1. Wash scallops; drain.
2. Combine bread crumbs with salt, pepper, and paprika. Roll scallops in bread-crumb mixture, coating completely.
3. In hot butter in large skillet, sauté scallops, turning frequently, until nicely browned all over—about 5 minutes.
4. With slotted spoon, carefully remove scallops from skillet, and arrange on toast slices.
5. Add wine to fat in skillet; boil gently 1 minute, stirring. Pour over scallops.

SCALLOPS WITH MUSHROOMS

MAKES 6 SERVINGS

1½ lb bay scallops (1½ pt)	1½ cups milk
¼ cup butter or margarine	2 teaspoons salt
½ lb fresh mushrooms, thinly sliced	Dash pepper
	Dash cayenne
¼ cup chopped green pepper	2 canned pimientos, chopped
¼ cup unsifted all-purpose flour	¼ cup sherry

1. Wash scallops in cold water; drain.
2. Place scallops in large skillet; add water to cover; bring to boiling. Reduce heat, and simmer, uncovered, 2 to 3 minutes, or until scallops are tender. Drain, and set aside.
3. In same skillet, in hot butter, cook mushrooms and green pepper 5 minutes, stirring occasionally.
4. Remove from heat. Blend in flour; then add milk, salt, pepper, and cayenne. Bring to boiling, stirring.
5. Remove from heat. Add pimientos, sherry, and scallops; reheat gently. Serve hot over toast.

Most popular shellfish is the shrimp, and we eat about ten times as many shrimp as any other shellfish. Our chief source of supply is the Gulf Coast. Shrimp can be bought green or raw (uncooked and unshelled); cooked, in the shell; cooked, deveined, without the shell; in cans; uncooked, frozen; or partially prepared for cooking, then frozen. You can't beat our shrimp dishes. Try them all, hot or cold.

BOILED SHRIMP

MAKES 2⅓ CUPS

1 tablespoon salt
1 tablespoon lemon juice
1 envelope (¼ oz) shrimp spice*

1½ lb raw shrimp, shelled and deveined

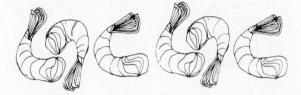

1. In large saucepan, combine salt, lemon juice, and shrimp spice with 1 quart water. Bring to boiling.
2. Add shrimp; return to boiling. Reduce heat, and simmer, covered, 3 to 5 minutes, or until shrimp are tender.
3. Drain; let cool. Then refrigerate, covered, until ready to use in salads or shrimp cocktails.

* Or tie 5 whole black peppers, 1 bay leaf, and ⅛ teaspoon dried thyme leaves in cheesecloth bag. Use instead of shrimp spice.

SHRIMP CREOLE WITH WHITE RICE

MAKES 6 TO 8 SERVINGS

½ lemon, sliced
4 whole black peppers
2 lb raw shrimp, shelled and deveined
4 slices bacon
2 tablespoons butter or margarine
1 clove garlic, finely chopped
1 cup chopped onion
1½ cups chopped green pepper
¼ cup finely chopped parsley

1½ cups thinly sliced celery
1 can (1 lb, 12 oz) tomatoes
1 can (6 oz) tomato paste
1 tablespoon lemon juice
1 tablespoon sugar
1 teaspoon salt
¼ to ½ teaspoon pepper
¼ to ½ teaspoon crushed red pepper
1 bay leaf
½ teaspoon dried thyme leaves
½ teaspoon filé powder
Cooked white rice

1. Bring 1 quart water to boiling in large saucepan. Add lemon slices, black peppers, and shrimp. Reduce heat; simmer, uncovered, 3 minutes.
2. Drain shrimp, reserving 1 cup cooking liquid.
3. In same saucepan, sauté bacon, over low heat, until crisp. Remove bacon; drain on paper towels; crumble.
4. To bacon fat, add butter, garlic, onion, green pepper, parsley, celery; cook, stirring, about 5 minutes, or until vegetables are tender.
5. Add reserved shrimp liquid, bacon, tomatoes, tomato paste, lemon juice, sugar, salt, pepper, red pepper, bay leaf, and thyme; bring to boiling. Reduce heat; simmer, covered, 30 minutes.
6. Just before serving, stir in filé powder and shrimp; bring to boiling. Reduce heat, and simmer 5 minutes.
7. Serve over hot, cooked white rice.

Note: This dish may be made in advance and frozen until ready to use.

343

BAKED STUFFED SHRIMP ON SHELL

MAKES 8 SERVINGS

32 large raw shrimp
¾ cup salad or olive oil
1 clove garlic, crushed
1½ teaspoons salt
¼ cup butter or margarine
½ teaspoon pepper

Stuffing:
1 cup finely chopped onion
½ cup fresh white-bread
    crumbs

2 tablespoons butter or
    margarine, melted
2 tablespoons dairy sour
    cream
1 teaspoon salt
½ teaspoon dried thyme
    leaves
½ teaspoon dried tarragon
    leaves

8 lemon wedges
1 bunch watercress

1. Preheat oven to 350F.
2. Shell shrimp, leaving on tails; devein. Wash under running water. Curl shrimp, fastening with wooden pick.
3. In large, shallow baking dish, combine oil, butter, garlic, salt, and pepper; heat in oven 5 minutes.
4. Make Stuffing: In large bowl, lightly toss all ingredients, mixing with fork. Place ½ teaspoon stuffing in center of each shrimp.
5. Arrange shrimp in single layer in baking dish. Baste with oil mixture.
6. Cover dish with foil; bake 15 to 20 minutes, or until shrimp are tender. (Be careful not to overcook.)
7. Drain on paper towels; remove picks. For each serving, place 4 shrimp on a serving shell; garnish with lemon wedge and watercress.

SHRIMP WITH GREEN PEPPERS

MAKES 4 SERVINGS

1 lb raw shrimp, shelled
    and deveined
6 tablespoons unsifted
    all-purpose flour
2 tablespoons grated
    Parmesan cheese
1¾ teaspoons salt

½ cup olive or salad oil
1 clove garlic, crushed
6 medium green peppers,
    cut into strips
¼ cup dry white wine
Dash pepper

1. Toss shrimp with flour, cheese, and 1 teaspoon salt, coating well.
2. Slowly heat oil in large, heavy skillet. Add shrimp and garlic; cook about 5 minutes, or until shrimp are golden.
3. Remove shrimp from skillet; set aside.
4. Add pepper strips to skillet. Cook, covered, over medium heat, 10 to 15 minutes, or until crisp-tender.
5. Add shrimp, rest of salt, wine, and pepper to skillet. Cook, covered, until heated through. Serve with rice if desired.

SHRIMP MARINARA

MAKES 4 SERVINGS

2 tablespoons olive or salad
    oil
1 clove garlic, crushed
1 teaspoon chopped parsley
1 lb raw shrimp, shelled and
    deveined
Dash cayenne

⅓ cup dry white wine
1 medium tomato, peeled
    and chopped
1 teaspoon salt
Dash pepper
Cooked white rice

1. Slowly heat oil in large, heavy skillet. Add garlic; sauté until golden.
2. Add parsley, shrimp, and cayenne; cook, stirring frequently, 3 minutes.
3. Add wine; cook, covered, 3 minutes.
4. Add tomato, salt, and pepper; cook, covered, 10 minutes.
5. Serve hot, over rice.

16

Freezing

How easily we grow accustomed to miracles! Do you remember, not so many years ago, when you had to wait until spring for fresh strawberries, until summer for corn on the cob or rhubarb pie?

So many new uses have evolved for the freezer that today's meal planning depends on it to yield fruits, vegetables, baked goods. and favorite cuts of meat any time of the year.

This chapter tells you how to shop for a freezer, if you don't already own one; how to wrap and freeze foods properly; and how to enjoy all the benefits of freezer living.

What Kind of Freezer to Buy

How large a freezer does a family need? Size is usually measured in cubic-foot capacity. Most freezers have capacities from 11 to 18 cubic feet; some chest models run larger.

As a guide to the freezer size most appropriate to a particular family, figure from 4 to 6 cubic feet of storage per person, depending on the use that will be made of the freezer. (The freezer sections of two-door refrigerator-freezer combinations are considered freezers. The "freezer" areas of one-door refrigerators, however, rarely maintain temperatures low enough for quick-freezing of fresh foods, although they will keep commercially frozen food or food that is already frozen solid satisfactorily for short periods—about 2 or 3 days.)

Should you choose a chest or upright model? Probable location of the freezer is often a deciding factor. Although they require more floor space, chest models are more economical to operate than uprights. (Since hot air rises, only hot air escapes when a chest model is opened. When an upright freezer is opened, cold air tumbles out, horizontally, from all levels.) The upright, however, is more attractive in a kitchen; it takes up less floor space.

A warranty comes with most freezers. Be sure you know just what yours covers—parts, labor, and possible food spoilage—and for how long. A freezer sometimes has two separate warranties—one for the appliance and one for the food in it.

Care of the Freezer

Defrosting   Freezers, like refrigerators, must be defrosted regularly unless they have nonfrosting mechanisms. They need defrosting less often than refrigerators; just how often depends on how much the freezer is used and on the surrounding room temperature. When packages freeze together or are so frosted over that labels are obscured, when sliding baskets or shelves no longer slide— then it's time to defrost. Too much frost cuts operating efficiency and, of course, reduces storage space. To defrost, follow exact instructions for your model.

In case of power failure, keep freezer closed. Food will remain frozen about 48 hours in a fully loaded box; less time in a half-full one. Call the local utility to find out when power in your area will be restored. If the time will be longer than 48 hours, add enough dry ice to the freezer to keep food frozen solidly. (It's smart to locate a source of dry ice before an emergency and to find nearby food lockers with standby power.) You'll need about 1½ pounds of dry ice per cubic foot of storage space for every 24 hours you are without current.

Packaging and Storing Frozen Foods

Freezer wraps and containers, to be satisfactory, should be airtight, moisture- and vaporproof. Such packaging materials prevent transfer of flavors among foods and the development of off-flavors. They retard spoilage in fatty foods and prevent loss of moisture, so often responsible for "freezer burn" in meats, for toughness of vegetables, for darkening of fruit. Wraps that retain moisture during thawing are good protection for foods that should be thawed before cooking. Don't skimp on these materials—they're inexpensive, and the foods they protect are not. Most wrapping materials are available in supermarkets. You'll find freezer tape, marking pencils, and labels there, too.

When you package foods for the freezer, keep the following points in mind:

Liquids expand when frozen. Always allow ½-inch head space at the top of cartons holding liquids or foods packed in liquid.

Never freeze more food in a container than you expect to serve at one time, particularly when you are freezing cooked foods. It is not safe to refreeze thawed cooked foods, not even when they have been reheated and cooled. If you are packaging complete cooked dinners, select combinations of foods that can be kept frozen for the same length of time.

Accurate labeling is as important as careful packaging. Food in each package should be fully and clearly identified and dated. Some homemakers prefer to label a package with the food's expiration date rather than its processing date. Include on the label such information as number of servings.

An inventory of freezer stock will show at a glance what the freezer holds. This record can be kept in any way that's convenient for you—in a separate notebook or card file, on a wall chart near the freezer. Be sure it includes such information as kind of food, number of servings, processing or expiration date.

Do not try to quick-freeze large amounts of

food at one time. Limit foods to be frozen to 10 per cent of your freezer's capacity, or to no more than 3 pounds of food per cubic foot of freezer capacity. Overloading slows the rate of freezing; foods may lose quality or even spoil.

Once foods are solidly frozen, they can be stored as you wish—according to date, by type of food, perhaps in some combination of the two. In chest models, use the upper portion for foods with rapid turnover—but don't forget the packages on the lower level.

FREEZER WRAPS AND CONTAINERS

Material	Characteristics	Common Uses
Freezer-weight aluminum foil	Flexible; molds tightly to food, preventing air pockets within package	Meats, poultry, fish, sandwiches, pastry, cakes, irregularly shaped foods
Laminated freezer paper	Flexible; molds well to food. Seal ends and seams with freezer tape	Same as above
Saran wrap, freezer cellophane	Flexible; transparent for easy identification. Cellophane needs heat-sealing and stockinette protection	Same as above
Polyethylene wrap or bags (including bags in continuous snap-off rolls)	Flexible; transparent. Bags are often reusable	Same as above
Wax- or plastic-coated or lined pint or quart cartons, with snap-on lids	Stackable; frequently reusable. Square cartons waste no space; maintain contact with freezing surfaces	Fruits, vegetables, juices, soups. Sauces, some meat dishes, such as stews
Aluminum-foil containers	Same as above	Same as above
Polyethylene or styrene containers	Same as above	Same as above
Wide-mouth glass jars; glass casseroles	Same as above. Transparent; reusable. Necessary to thaw food before it can be removed from jars. Casseroles can be used as is in oven	Same as above. Also casserole dishes
Aluminum-foil pie plates	Can go from freezer to oven without transfer of food	Cooked foods, pies
Milk cartons, juice cans	No expense involved	Cookie rolls, liquids

Freezing Vegetables

Home freezing of garden surplus is an excellent and economical method of ensuring vegetable variety. Remember to label clearly and date packages for inventory rotation.

Follow these simple rules:

1. Select fresh, tender vegetables; old, mature vegetables lose texture and flavor on freezing. Salad vegetables—tomatoes, celery, lettuce, cucumbers, etc.—do not freeze well.

2. Wash vegetables in cold water; do not soak. Sort or cut into uniform size or pieces, removing peel wherever necessary.

3. Blanch vegetables according to directions. In large kettle, blanch 1 pound prepared vegetables in 1 gallon rolling, boiling water. (Water may be reused, but must be returned to boiling for each 1 pound vegetables.)

4. Start counting time as soon as vegetables are immersed. For best results and ease of handling, use wire basket, colander, or cheesecloth.

5. Cool vegetables immediately (no time should be lost between blanching and cooling): Put blanched vegetables in large kettle of cold running water, to lower temperature; but do not soak. Then plunge into ice water, for thorough chilling; do not soak. Drain vegetables thoroughly.

6. Pack in clean moisture- and airproof containers or cartons. Freeze immediately. For best results, freeze without seasoning or liquid.

7. French-fried potatoes may be frozen after the first frying of the Double-Frying Method.*

*See Vegetables and Potatoes Chapter.

Preparation of Vegetables

Asparagus: Select young stalks. Sort according to thickness of stalk. Wash well. Cut off tough end of stalk. Spears may be length of package or cut into 2-inch lengths. Heat stalks in boiling water: 2 minutes for small, 3 minutes for medium, 4 minutes for large. Cool rapidly in cold water; drain. Pack into containers, leaving no head space. Alternate tip and stem ends. Freeze as usual.

1 crate (12 2-pound bunches) yields 15 to 22 pints.

Beans (snap, green, wax): Select young, stringless beans that snap when broken. Wash; remove ends; cut into 2-inch pieces, or slice lengthwise into strips. Heat in boiling water 3 minutes. Chill; drain, and freeze as usual. If packing very tightly, leave

½-inch head space.

1 bushel (30 pounds) yields 30 to 45 pints.

Broccoli: Select tight, compact, dark-green heads with tender stalks, free of woodiness. Wash stalks, and peel. Trim to remove insects; soak for ½ hour in a solution of 4 teaspoons salt to 1 gallon cold water. Split lengthwise, so flowerets measure not more than 1½ inches across. Heat in steam 5 minutes or in boiling water 3 minutes. Cool in cold water; drain. Pack, leaving no head space. Freeze as usual.

1 crate (25 pounds) yields 24 pints.

Carrots: Since carrots are available most of the year, freeze them in small quantities. Select young, tender carrots. Peel or scrape;

then slice lengthwise or dice. If carrots are small, they can be frozen whole. Heat carrots in boiling water: 2 minutes for Julienne-style carrots, 3 minutes for diced or sliced carrots, 5 minutes for whole small carrots. Cool; package, and freeze.

To steam carrots: Prepare as for blanching, and steam 3 minutes for Julienne-style carrots, 4 minutes for diced or sliced carrots, 5 to 6 minutes for whole small carrots. Cool; package, and freeze.

Carrots and Peas: Prepare vegetables separately, as directed under individual entries. Combine, and cool as usual. Package, leaving ½-inch head space. Seal and freeze as you would any vegetable.

Corn: Whole ears are not the most economical form in which to freeze corn, but they are fun. Select ears with plump, tender kernels and sweet milk. If milk is thick, it is better to cut corn from cob and then freeze. Husk ears; remove silk; wash, and dry. Heat ears in boiling water 4 minutes. Cool rapidly in cold water; drain.

For whole-kernel: Cut kernels from cob at about ⅔ depth of kernel. Pack, leaving ½-inch head space. Seal; freeze.

For cream-style: Cut kernels from cob about center of kernel. Scrape cobs with back of knife, to remove juice and heart of kernel.

Pack as whole-kernel.

1 bushel (35 pounds) yields 14 to 17 pints.

For on-the-cob: Heat small ears in boiling water 7 minutes; medium ears, 9 minutes; large ears, 11 minutes. Cool promptly in cold water; drain. Pack in containers, or wrap in moisture- vaporproof paper. Seal; freeze.

Peas, green: Choose bright-green, plump pods, with sweet, tender peas. Shell peas. Heat in boiling water 1½ minutes. Cool promptly; drain. Pack, leaving ½-inch head space. Seal; freeze.

1 bushel (30 pounds) yields 12 to 15 pints.

Peppers, green and hot: Don't heat peppers before freezing if you plan to use them uncooked. Heat halves 3 minutes, slices 2 minutes. Cool promptly; drain. Package, leaving ½-inch head space for heated peppers. Seal; freeze. Prepare uncooked peppers as above; package without blanching. Do not keep unblanched peppers longer than 1 month.

3 peppers yield 1 pint.

Squash, summer: Select young squash with small seeds and tender rind. Wash; cut into ½-inch slices. Heat in boiling water 3 minutes. Cool, and drain. Package, leaving ½-inch head space. Seal; freeze.

1 bushel (40 pounds) yields 32 to 40 pints.

Freezing Fruits

Freeze fresh fruits as soon after picking as possible. The sooner they're frozen, the better they'll taste when defrosted. Always select fruits of uniform ripeness, free from spoilage. Wash in cold or ice water.

Most fruits can be successfully frozen in several forms—whole fruit and choice slices to serve at the table, less perfect slices and crushed or puréed fruit for cooking. All can be kept 12 months at 0°F.

The directions on these pages give specific instructions for preparing fruits most often frozen. Most authorities recommend peeling, even for peaches.

Work with small quantities—do only a few containers at a time, especially if you're freezing fruits that darken rapidly. Always pack fruit well. Iron utensils, chipped enameled ware, and tinware can cause metallic off-flavors. For best results, use glass, enamel, stainless steel, or aluminum ware.

Sugar. To add or not to add? Either is perfectly acceptable. Most fruits are best packed in sugar or syrup. When a member of the family requires a low-sugar diet, his fruits must be packed without sugar, of course. Such fruits as gooseberries, currants, cranberries, rhubarb keep as well without sugar. In general, fruits packaged for dessert are best in syrup. Those planned for pies or other cooking are best packed in dry sugar or left unsweetened. When cooking fruits are packed with sugar, each container should show the amount. When the fruit is used, simply subtract this amount from the sugar in the recipe.

When packing fruit in syrup, make syrup in advance by bringing the sugar and water to a full, rolling boil. Chill thoroughly before using. In the directions, syrups are designated as Syrup 1, 2, 3, and 4. For each, use the following proportions:

Syrup	Sugar	Water
No. 1	2 cups	4 cups
No. 2	3 cups	4 cups
No. 3	4 cups	4 cups
No. 4	5 cups	4 cups

For dry-packed fruit, add sugar to fruit, and stir gently until enough juice is drawn from fruit to partly dissolve sugar. Follow amounts specified in individual recipes. Small fruits and berries may be frozen without sugar or syrup.

To keep fruits from darkening, ascorbic acid can be added. Dissolve from ¼ to ¾ teaspoon crystalline ascorbic acid in 1 quart chilled syrup just before packing fruit. (For exact amounts, see directions with individual fruits.) For best results, pour about ½ cup syrup containing ascorbic acid into the container. Slice fruit directly into this syrup, adding more if necessary, to cover. Ascorbic acid can be bought in any drugstore. Commercial ascorbic-acid preparations are also available; with these, follow label instructions for amounts.

Containers should be moisture- and vapor-proof. Select a size that holds only enough fruit for one meal. A quart container of peaches for a small family means defrosted leftovers, not quite as good at the second meal.

Rigid containers, flat on both top and bottom, stack easily. Round containers or those with flared sides or raised bottoms waste freezer space. Fruits can be removed most easily and with less breaking or marring if containers are straight from bottom to top or slightly flared at the top.

Packaging, labeling, storing. Label cartons with the kind of fruit, amount of syrup or of dry sugar, and date. Pack fruits tightly, to cut down on amount of air in the container. When fruits are packed in bags, press air out of unfilled portion; seal at once. Allow head space in cartons, for expansion during freezing. Suggested head space:

Type of Pack	Container with Wide Top		Container with Narrow Top	
	Pint	Quart	Pint	Quart
Dry pack	½"	½"	½"	½"
Syrup pack	½"	1"	¾"	1½"

Keep sealing edges free from moisture or food. Seal carefully.

Pointers on thawing. For highest quality, keep fruits frozen until they are ready to use. Thawed foods spoil more quickly than fresh foods. Fruits may be refrozen if they are not completely thawed; but quality will suffer. Fruits that have defrosted and warmed up to 40°F should never be refrozen. Fermentation and spoilage may already have begun at this temperature.

Apples: Select crisp, firm, full-flavored apples. Wash; peel; core. Slice medium apples into twelfths, large apples into sixteenths.
Syrup pack: Use Syrup 2, adding ½ teaspoon ascorbic-acid crystals per quart. Put ½ cup cold syrup into a pint container; slice apples into syrup. Press fruit down. Add syrup to cover. Leave head space. Seal; freeze.
Sugar pack: To prevent darkening, slice apples into a solution of 2 tablespoons salt per gallon of water. Hold in solution 15 minutes; drain. Then place slices in single layer in steamer; steam 1½ to 2 minutes. Cool in cold water; drain. Sprinkle each quart with ½ cup sugar; stir. Pack, leaving head space. Seal; freeze.
Unsweetened pack: Follow directions for sugar pack, omitting sugar.
1 bushel (48 pounds) yields 32 to 40 pints; 1½ pounds yield 1 pint.

Apricots: Syrup pack is preferred for table fruit; sugar pack for cooking. Sort; wash; halve; pit. Peel and slice, if desired. Treat for darkening. If not peeled, heat in boiling water ½ minute. Cool; drain.
Syrup pack: Use Syrup 2, adding ¾ teaspoon ascorbic-acid crystals per quart. Pack, leaving head space. Seal; freeze.
Sugar pack: Dissolve ¼ teaspoon ascorbic-acid crystals in ¼ cup cold water. Sprinkle over 1 quart apricots. Mix ½ cup sugar with each quart fruit; stir. Pack as usual, leaving ½-inch head space. Seal; freeze.
1 bushel (48 pounds) yields 60 to 70 pints; ¾ pound yields 1 pint.

Berries (blackberries, boysenberries, loganberries, youngberries): Sort; remove leaves and stems. Wash, and drain.
Syrup pack: Pack into containers, and cover with Syrup 2 or 3, depending on your sweet tooth. Leave head space; seal.
Sugar pack: For each quart berries, add ¾ cup sugar. Turn berries over and over gently until most sugar is dissolved. Pack, leaving head space, and seal.
1 crate (24 quarts) yields 32 to 36 pints; 1½ pints yield 1 pint.

Blueberries, huckleberries, and elderberries: Steam 1 minute, for better flavor and more tender skin. Cool.
Syrup pack: Pack into containers, and cover with Syrup 2. Seal, and freeze as usual.
Sugar pack: Not recommended.
1 crate (24 quarts) yields 32 to 36 pints; 1½ pints yield 1 pint.

Cherries, sour: Select bright-red, tree-ripened cherries. Stem; sort; wash; drain; pit.
Syrup pack: Pack into containers. Cover with Syrup 4. Seal.
Sugar pack: To 1 quart, add ¾ cup sugar; mix to dissolve. Pack as usual.

Cherries, sweet: Prepare quickly, to avoid color changes. Red varieties are best. Proceed as with sour cherries.
Syrup pack: Use Syrup 2, adding ½ teaspoon ascorbic-acid crystals per quart syrup.
Sugar pack: Use ½ cup sugar to 1 quart fruit. Pack, and freeze.
1 bushel (56 pounds) yields 36 to 44 pints; 1½ pounds yield 1 pint.

Cranberries: Choose deep-red berries with glossy skins. Stem; sort; wash; drain. Most often packed unsweetened. Or cover with Syrup 2.
Purée: Add 2 cups water for each quart or pound prepared fruit. Cook until skins pop.

Press through sieve. Add about 2 cups sugar per quart purée. Pack, leaving head space; seal, and freeze.

25 pounds yield 50 pints; 1 peck (8 pounds) yields 16 pints.

Melons: Select firm-fleshed, well-colored, ripe melons. Cut in half; remove seeds; peel. Slice, cube, or make into balls. Pack. Cover with Syrup 1. Leave head space; seal, and freeze as usual.

25 pounds yield 20 pints.

Peaches: Best packed in syrup or with sugar; can be packed in water. Select firm, ripe peaches, with no trace of green. Sort; wash; pit; peel. Slice, if desired.

Syrup pack: Use Syrup 2. Add ½ teaspoon ascorbic-acid crystals for each quart syrup. Pack as usual, leaving ½-inch head space; seal, and freeze.

Sugar pack: Dissolve ¼ teaspoon ascorbic-acid crystals in ½ cup water. Sprinkle over peaches. To each quart prepared fruit, add ⅔ cup sugar; mix. Pack as usual; seal, and freeze.

1 bushel (48 pounds) yields 40 to 50 pints; 1 to 1½ pounds yield 1 pint.

Plums: Though syrup or sugar packs are possible, unsweetened pack is preferred. Leave plums whole, or cut in halves or quarters. Pack, and freeze.

At the time of use, dip fruit in cold water for 5 to 10 seconds. Remove skins, and cover with Syrup 2 while thawing.

1 bushel yields 38 to 56 pints; 1 crate (20 pounds) yields 13 to 20 pints; 1 to 1½ pounds yield 1 pint.

Rhubarb: Choose tender stalks with few fibers. Wash; trim; cut in ½-inch lengths. Heat in boiling water 1 minute. Cool in cold water.

Unsweetened pack: Usually preferred. Freeze as any fruit.

Syrup pack: Pack tightly in containers. Cover with Syrup 2. Proceed as usual.

15 pounds yield 15 to 22 pints; ⅔ to 1 pound yields 1 pint.

Strawberries: Choose firm, ripe berries, preferably tart. Sort; wash; drain; remove hulls. Slice or crush large berries. Sugar and syrup packs are best.

Syrup pack: Put berries in containers, and cover with Syrup 2. Continue as with any fruit.

Sugar pack: Add ¾ cup sugar for each quart berries; mix well. Pack. Freeze as usual.

Unsweetened pack: If no sweetening can be used, cover berries in containers with solution of water and ascorbic-acid crystals —1 teaspoon crystals to each quart water. Freeze as usual.

1 crate (24 quarts) yields 38 pints; ⅔ quart yields 1 pint.

Freezing Meats

Always select fresh, high-quality cuts for freezing. Refrigerate them promptly to 40F or below (normal refrigerator temperature). If buying sections of a carcass, separate steaks from roasts, pot roasts from stew meat, etc.

To freeze meats: Plan to package meats in amounts to suit your family's size—only enough in each package for one meal. Wrap in moisture- vaporproof paper; pull paper tight, to force out air. Keep packages as smooth as possible. Seal ends and seams with freezer tape. Label packages with date, kind and cut of meat, number of servings. Freeze promptly at 0°F, leaving enough air around each package to expose all sides to the 0°F temperature. When packages are frozen hard, stack them compactly.

If your home freezer maintains a constant temperature of 0°F or lower, and if several inches of air space are allowed between and around packages, the meat should freeze thoroughly in 8 to 12 hours. The more rapidly meat is frozen solid, the better its flavor and texture will be. But if you open your freezer several times during the initial freezing period, meat may not freeze for 24 hours or even longer, and some quality will be lost.

To store frozen meats: The wise homemaker rotates the meats in her freezer, organizing them so she uses soonest those that have been frozen longest. There's no economy in using meat that has been frozen only a few weeks when the freezer holds similar cuts that have been frozen for months.

To thaw meats: Whether or not to thaw meats before cooking is largely up to the homemaker. The exception is pork. Never cook pork from the hard-frozen state. Because trichinosis is always a danger, pork must be thoroughly defrosted, then thoroughly cooked.

Size can have a bearing. Small cuts are best if cooked from the hard-frozen state; large roasts cook more evenly if they are first thawed. But if some members of your family like rare meat and others prefer it well-done, you might cook a small roast from the frozen state. If you want to coat small cuts for browning, they must first be thawed. Coating will not stick to frozen meats. Ground meat must, of course, be thawed before it can be seasoned or shaped into patties. But before freezing ground meat, you can preseason it and then form it into patties. Wrap them separately or in meal-size quantities. Such patties can be fried or broiled without thawing.

Whether or not to thaw meat before cooking also depends on how much time is available, and when. Cooking meat from a hard-frozen state takes longer and uses more fuel. But unless meat is defrosted early in the day, waiting for a roast to thaw can delay dinner for hours. The Beef Roasting Chart below gives cooking times for hard-frozen and completely thawed beef. In general, the same times apply to comparable amounts of veal and lamb.

TIMETABLE FOR THAWING MEATS

Method*	Temperature	Cut	Thickness (in inches)	Approximate Thawing Time
Refrigerator	40 to	Steaks	1	12 hours
	50F	Roasts {small		3-4 hours per lb
		{large		4-6 hours per lb
Room	70 to	Steaks	1	2-3 hours
temperature	75F	Roasts {small		1-2 hours per lb
		{large		2-3 hours per lb
		Patties	⅝	1 hour

* Because meat tends to absorb water, even when wrapped, thawing in cold running water is not recommended. Nor is the electric-fan method recommended for large roasts; meat would not thaw uniformly, and excessive juice would be lost from outer, thawed portion.

BEEF ROASTING CHART

Cut of Beef	Defrosted	Hard-Frozen
4-lb standing rib (300 to 325F)	Rare: 1½ to 1¾ hours Medium: 1¾ to 2¼ hours Well: 2½ to 3 hours	2 to 2½ hours 2½ to 3 hours 3 to 4 hours
4-lb rolled rib (300 to 325F)	Rare: 2 to 2¼ hours Medium: 2¼ to 2½ hours Well: 2½ to 2¾ hours	2½ to 3 hours 3 to 3½ hours 3½ to 4 hours

Freezing Fish

Chill fresh fish immediately. Pack in ice if it is a warm day. Scale; remove head and entrails; wash thoroughly. Trim fins and tail if fish is small and will be frozen whole. Cut large fish into pan-ready steaks or boneless strips.

To freeze fish: Wrap in moisture- vaporproof paper, following procedure outlined for meat. Freeze promptly at 0°F.

If you prefer to glaze fish and freeze it unwrapped: Dip cleaned, prepared fish in near-freezing water. Freeze until ice film forms. Dip. Freeze hard. Reglaze as needed.

To thaw fish: Unless you plan to boil it, fish is easier to handle if partially thawed before cooking. Hard-frozen fish is likely to spatter and stick to the pan. Cook partly thawed fish a little longer than you would fresh, and at a lower-than-usual temperature. Always cook before fish thaws completely — while there is still some ice in it. (Fish to be used in chowder or soup need not be thawed at all.)

To freeze shellfish: Such shellfish as shrimp, oysters, and clams should be frozen raw, either in the shell or shelled. If shrimp and oysters are cooked first, they toughen during the freezing period. Crab and lobster, however, should be cooked and the meat removed from the shell before freezing.

To defrost shellfish: Crab and lobster should be thawed just enough to separate pieces. Scallops, oysters, and clams should be completely thawed before use and treated as if they were fresh. Thaw cooked shellfish completely before serving it cold.

Freezing Breads

Quick and yeast breads should be baked before freezing. To be sure of success, bake yeast rolls and breads; cool them quickly. Package; label; freeze at once. Baked breads thaw quickly. In fact, they can be sliced and toasted for immediate use. Or they will thaw in the time it takes to prepare dinner.

Rolls can also be half baked, then frozen. Bake them at 275F for 20 minutes. Cool; wrap, and freeze until hard, being careful not to crush them. Then stack. Keep frozen at 0°F or below. To complete the baking of such rolls, let them thaw in the sealed package 10 to 15 minutes. Then open the package, and arrange the rolls on a cookie sheet. If the surface of the rolls seems dry, grease it lightly. Bake in oven preheated to 450F until a delicate brown—5 to 10 minutes. If too low a baking temperature is used, the crust may be too thick, perhaps even tough. *Note:* For information on freezing cakes, cookies, and pies, see individual chapters.

Sandwiches and Sandwich Fillings

Most properly packaged sandwiches freeze and keep well. Fillings to avoid are very moist mixtures (they can make bread soggy), those containing raw vegetables, hard-cooked egg whites, or fruit jellies.

Advice for lunch-box packers: If you make up lunches five days out of every seven, put your freezer to work to keep early mornings from becoming hectic. You can wrap, assemble, seal, and freeze sandwiches a dozen at a time. Or you can freeze fillings in separate containers. Sandwiches removed from the freezer in the morning will be thawed and ready to eat by lunchtime. Nine times out of ten, they will be even fresher than if they had been made that morning.

If you freeze a filling separately, pack it in several small containers, each just large enough to hold filling for one day's lunch-box requirements. Transfer container from freezer to refrigerator the night before. Filling will be ready to spread by morning.

Complete lunch boxes—sandwiches and dessert, all assembled—can also be prepared and frozen, assembly-line fashion. If a soup or beverage is one that freezes well and is served cold, it might also be included. Label each box, or bag, with its complete contents and the date it was packed. Use frozen sandwiches and lunches within two weeks.

Freezing Poultry

Select fresh, clean, high-quality poultry for freezing. Today, with most poultry plucked and dressed before we buy it, little need be said about scalding and plucking. But if you must pluck your chickens: Dip fowl into water heated to 128 to 140F. Do not overscald. As soon as feathers can be removed easily, cool bird quickly in cold running water. Pluck; draw, and wash carefully. Dry thoroughly.

Fryers and broiler-fryers are usually disjointed or cut into serving-size pieces before freezing; broilers, split in two down the back. If freezing whole birds for roasting, tie wings firmly to sides of breast; tie legs together. Never stuff poultry before freezing it.

To freeze poultry: Wrap pieces or whole bird in moisture- vaporproof paper; pull paper tight, to force out air. Keep packages smooth, so they can be packed together compactly in your freezer. Seal ends and seams with freezer tape. Mark each package with the date, number of servings, and kind of bird. Freeze promptly at 0°F, leaving enough air space around each package to expose all sides to the zero temperature. When frozen hard, stack as compactly as possible. Keep frozen at or below 0°F.

TIMETABLE FOR THAWING POULTRY

Method	Temperature	Weight (Ready-to-cook)	Approximate Thawing Time
Refrigerator	40–50F	4- to 10-lb turkey	1–2 days
		10- to 20-lb turkey	2–3 days
		20- to 24-lb turkey	3–4 days
		5-lb roaster	15–30 hours
		3-lb cut-up fryer	10–20 hours
Room temperature	70–75F	5-lb roaster	5–6 hours
		3-lb cut-up fryer	4–5 hours
Running water (use only until bird is pliable)	Cold	4- to 10-lb turkey	4–6 hours
		10- to 20-lb turkey	6–8 hours
		20- to 24-lb turkey	8–12 hours
		5-lb roaster	1–3 hours

To thaw poultry: Though poultry can be cooked directly from the hard-frozen state, most authorities suggest that it first be thawed. Unthawed roasters cook less uniformly than thawed; they are difficult to stuff, and stuffing may not be thoroughly heated by the time roaster is cooked.

Just before bird is thawed, prepare stuffing. We repeat: Never stuff birds before they are frozen.

Thaw poultry in its freezer wrapping—the skin of an uncovered bird might become dry and tough when exposed too long to air. Refrigerator thawing is preferred for a whole bird. To speed thawing, stand the bird in cold running water, but only until it becomes pliable. Do not use an electric fan for thawing—outer portions might dry out before the center had thawed.

To cook poultry: Thawed poultry and poultry parts cook more uniformly and take less total fuel than hard-frozen. It's difficult to get a nice brown crust on frozen fryers. If you plan to dip poultry parts into egg and crumbs or into a flour mixture before browning, you must definitely thaw the pieces and wipe them dry before coating them.

A word about giblets: Except for the quick-cooking liver, which can be frozen with the bird, giblets should be packaged and frozen separately.

When freezing game of any kind, check the game regulations in your state. Many specify the length of time game may legally be frozen and the amount of each kind you are permitted to freeze. Freeze game as you would meat or poultry, depending on which it is.

Care of Purchased Frozen Foods

Correct handling of commercially frozen foods is just as important as the handling of those you freeze at home. The greatest threat to quality lies in permitting temperature to rise above 0°F. This is most likely to occur between the time foods are purchased and the time they are safely in the freezer, so:

· Make your food shopping the last you do;

the frozen items the last you buy. Never let frozen foods stand in the car while you run errands.

· Most supermarkets provide insulated bags for frozen foods. Be sure yours are given this protection before you put them in your shopping cart.

· Put frozen purchases in the freezer as soon as you get them home. Don't let them stand on the kitchen counter. The higher temperature a package reaches, the greater the possibility of changes in quality. Foods stored without fluctuation at 0°F will taste much better than those subjected to higher temperatures for even a very short time before being returned to 0°F.

· Just as with foods you freeze, rotate purchases on a first-in, first-out basis. Put new packages at the back or the bottom of the freezer. Use first those that have been stored longest.

· What about keeping frozen purchases in the ice-cube compartment of your refrigerator? This compartment maintains a maximum low of 15F. Frozen purchases that will be used within 3 days can be stored here, though some quality and flavor can be lost even in that time.

Freezer Tricks

· When you fix family favorites—goulash, spaghetti sauce, or chili, for example—that require a long time to prepare and/or cook, double or triple the recipe. Serve some that night; freeze the remainder, to heat and serve on busy days.

· If you cater to someone on a special diet, prepare his dishes in quantity. Serve one portion, and freeze the rest as individual servings.

· Use your freezer to keep shopping trips to a minimum. Bread and other baked goods can be stored in the freezer for a short time. Day-old bread and cake, frequently a bargain, are actually freshened by 24 hours in the freezer.

· Prepare ahead for parties, holiday meals, dinner on your weekly "busy day." Fancy desserts, decorative canapés, garnishes, dips for tidbits, a novelty ice ring for a buffet can be prepared days ahead. Working mothers can devote a few weekend hours to shopping and cooking ahead for week-night meals.

· It's quite economical to freeze leftover odds and ends. These may vary from rosettes of unused whipped cream, for future garnishes, to slices of roast lamb, frozen with gravy, for a future supper. Cubes of cooked meat might be saved for a salad or casserole. If you've baked an angel-food cake, freeze the unused egg yolks, to use later in a sponge-cake.

· Chop and freeze green pepper, onion, celery, and parsley in individual packages, to save last-minute cutting.

· Leftover bread slices are easy to cube or grate for stuffings if they are frozen first. Use directly from the freezer.

· Freeze Brazil nuts in polyethylene bags. For easier shelling, crack and shell while they're still frozen.

· To freeze chowder, stew, baked beans, chili con carne, and macaroni and cheese: Line a bowl with foil; turn cooled mixture into bowl; fold foil over top of mixture; freeze. When frozen, remove foil-wrapped mixture from bowl; label; freeze until ready to use. To reheat: Remove foil. Place mixture in top of double boiler; cook, covered, over boiling water, until hot—about 40 minutes.

. When making popcorn, double the amount. Let half cool; place in polyethylene bags, and freeze until ready to use.

. To avoid holiday rush, bake fruitcakes, cookies, pies, breads in advance. Freeze.

. Freeze green peppers when they are in season, to use later on. Select large, firm peppers. Wash well; dry. Remove seeds and ribs. Place peppers in polyethylene bag, and store in freezer until ready to use.

To Freeze Cooked Foods

1. Package cooked foods, if possible, in containers in which they can be reheated. Transfer foods as little as possible from one container to another. Seal; label; freeze as rapidly as possible.

2. Plan to use frozen cooked foods within a few weeks. Most well-packaged foods will keep 3 to 4 months or longer; but more rapid turnover is preferable. Make your goal a one-month freezer life for cooked dishes.

3. In general, fried foods do not freeze well. Frozen French-fried potatoes and onion rings are the exceptions.

4. If milk is part of a stew or chowder, add it when you reheat for serving. You can also postpone thickening gravies until reheating time.

5. Never freeze hard-cooked egg white—it would be tough when thawed.

6. Don't freeze vegetables if crispness is important—salad greens, for example.

7. Never freeze cooked potatoes in stews—they might be soggy when reheated.

8. Crumb or cheese toppings should be added when food is reheated.

9. Freeze meat pies and turnovers unbaked.

10. Rice, especially "converted" rice, freezes well. Undercook it slightly, for freezing.

APPROXIMATE MAXIMUM STORAGE LIFE OF SOME COMMON PREPARED AND PRECOOKED FOODS

Biscuits, baked	2 months
Cakes, fruit	12 months
Cakes, nonfat	
angel, baked	4 months
sponge, baked	4 months
Cakes with shortening	
baked	4 to 9 months
Casserole dishes, prepared	1 to 4 months
Cookies, baked or unbaked	12 months
Ice cream, commercial*	2 to 3 weeks
homemade	1 month
Muffins, baked	2 months
Pies, fruit, baked or unbaked	3 to 4 months
Pie shells, baked or unbaked	1½ to 2 months
Sandwiches	1 to 2 months
Soups	6 months
Yeast rolls, baked	12 months
half baked	12 months

* Half-gallon or gallon containers may be economical if ice cream is used within 2 or 3 weeks and stored properly. Each time ice cream is removed, put moisture- vaporproof paper directly on remainder, to keep ice crystals from forming. Never refreeze defrosted ice cream—harmful bacteria may have developed.

You want something special, to set off a simple meal or complete a more elaborate one, so you reach into your freezer, take out a package of rolls or French bread, season it with herbs, and in no time at all, mmmmm, what a savory delight! So are the meats, the garden-fresh vegetables, the summery fruit pies you'll find in this chapter.

FROZEN CLOVERLEAF ROLLS

MAKES 12

1.   Prepare and shape Cloverleaf Rolls as recipe directs.
2.   Meanwhile, preheat oven to 275F. Bake rolls 20 minutes. Remove from pan; cool completely on wire rack. Freezer-wrap; label, and freeze.
3.   To finish baking: Preheat oven to 450F. Unwrap frozen rolls; place on cookie sheet; bake 5 to 10 minutes, or until golden. Serve warm.
* See Yeast Breads Chapter.

FROZEN WAFFLES

MAKES 4 LARGE WAFFLES

2 cups packaged pancake-
    and-waffle mix or
    biscuit mix*

1.   Preheat waffle iron.
2.   Prepare waffle batter as package label directs.
3.   For each waffle, pour batter into center of lower half of waffle iron until it spreads to 1 inch from edge—about ½ cup.
4.   Lower cover on batter; cook as manufacturer directs, or until waffle iron stops steaming. Do not raise cover during baking.
5.   Carefully loosen edge of waffle with fork; remove.
6.   Cool completely on wire rack. Place double thickness of waxed paper between waffles. Freezer-wrap; label, and freeze.
7.   To reheat: Reheat frozen waffles in toaster. Or preheat oven to 450F; bake waffles on oven rack 3 to 5 minutes, or until heated through.
* Or use recipe for HRM's Waffles. See Quick Breads Chapter.

FROZEN PANCAKES

MAKES 8 (4-INCH) PANCAKES

1.   Make Griddlecakes* batter as recipe directs. Cook as directed. Let cool completely on wire rack.
2.   Place double thickness of waxed paper between pancakes. Wrap in foil; label, and freeze.
3.   To reheat: Preheat oven to 450F. Remove waxed paper from between pancakes. Rewrap frozen pancakes in foil. Bake 15 to 20 minutes, or until heated through.
* See Quick Breads Chapter.

GINGER-PEACH JAM

MAKES 4 PINTS

3 lb fresh peaches
2 tablespoons finely
   chopped crystallized
   ginger

5 cups sugar
2 pkg (1¾-oz size)
   powdered pectin

1.   Peel peaches; remove pits; chop peaches finely. Measure 4 cups.
2.   In large bowl, combine chopped peaches with ginger. Gradually stir in sugar until well combined. Set aside.
3.   In small saucepan, combine pectin with 1 cup cold water. Over medium heat, bring to boiling, stirring constantly; boil rapidly 1 minute.
4.   Add pectin to fruit mixture, stirring until well combined. Continue stirring 5 minutes.
5.   Ladle into 4 (1-pint) freezer containers; cover. Let stand at room temperature 24 hours, to set. Label, and freeze until ready to use. Jam may be stored in freezer up to 6 months.
6.   To serve: Let jam stand at room temperature at least 1 hour before serving. To store, keep covered in refrigerator; jam may be kept in refrigerator up to 3 weeks.
Note: Frozen jams and jellies are softer in texture than the boiled type. Delicious used as sauce for ice cream or cake squares.

STRAWBERRY-PINEAPPLE JAM

MAKES 4 PINTS

2 pt boxes fresh
   strawberries
2½ cups finely chopped
   fresh pineapple

7½ cups sugar
2 pkg (1¾-oz size)
   powdered pectin

1.   Gently wash strawberries in cold water; drain; hull. Crush strawberries with potato masher. Measure 2½ cups.
2.   In large bowl, combine crushed strawberries with pineapple. Gradually stir in sugar until well combined. Set aside.
3.   In small saucepan, combine pectin with 1 cup cold water. Over medium heat, bring to boiling, stirring constantly; boil rapidly 1 minute.

(Strawberry-Pineapple Jam continued)

4. Add pectin to fruit mixture, stirring until well combined; continue stirring 5 minutes.

5. Ladle into 4 (1-pint) freezer containers; cover. Let stand at room temperature 24 hours, to set. Label, and freeze until ready to use. Jam may be stored in freezer up to 6 months.

6. To serve: Let jam stand at room temperature at least 1 hour before serving. To store, keep covered in refrigerator; jam may be kept in refrigerator up to 3 weeks.

CHICKEN PIE, COUNTRY STYLE

MAKES 8 SERVINGS

5-lb ready-to-cook stewing
   chicken
2 celery stalks, quartered
1 medium onion, quartered
½ lemon, sliced
2 parsley sprigs
10 whole black peppers
1 bay leaf
2½ teaspoons salt
1½ teaspoons monosodium
   glutamate
1 lb carrots, pared and
   diced

2 lb fresh peas, shelled*
1 can (6 oz) sliced
   mushrooms, drained
1 cup light cream
¼ teaspoon nutmeg
¼ teaspoon celery salt
⅛ teaspoon pepper
½ cup unsifted all-purpose
   flour

Flaky pastry for 2-crust pie

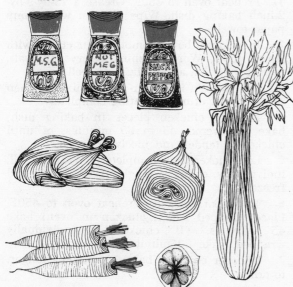

1. In 6-quart kettle, place chicken, 8 cups water, celery, onion, lemon, parsley, black peppers, bay leaf, 2 teaspoons salt, and 1 teaspoon monosodium glutamate; bring to boiling. Reduce heat; simmer, covered, 2 hours, or until chicken is tender. Let chicken cool in broth.

2. Cut off meat in large pieces; cut into cubes. Strain broth, reserving 5 cups.

3. Meanwhile, in 1 inch boiling water, cook carrots and peas, covered, 15 minutes. Drain.

4. Toss vegetables with chicken and mushrooms, to combine. Divide mixture evenly among 8 (5⅜-by-1⅝-inch) deep-dish foil pans.

5. In medium saucepan, combine 4 cups reserved broth with cream, nutmeg, celery salt, pepper, and remaining salt and monosodium glutamate; bring to boiling.

6. Combine flour with remaining broth, stirring to make a smooth paste; stir into boiling broth mixture. Reduce heat, and simmer 2 minutes, stirring constantly. Pour over chicken and vegetables; let cool completely.

7. Divide pastry into 8 parts. On lightly floured surface, roll each part into a 6-inch circle. Arrange a pastry round over filling in each pan; press edge of pastry to rim of pan, to seal. Freezer-wrap; label, and freeze until ready to use.

8. To bake pies: Preheat oven to 450F. Unwrap pies; make several gashes in center of each for steam vents; place on cookie sheet. Bake 40 minutes, or until crust is golden and filling is bubbling and hot.

* Or use 1 package (10 oz) frozen peas, partially thawed; do not cook.

CIOPPINO

½ cup olive or salad oil
3 cloves garlic, finely
   chopped
1¼ cups chopped onion
¾ cup chopped green
   onion
¾ cup chopped green
   pepper
1 jar (11½ oz) whole clams
1 can (1 lb, 12 oz)
   tomatoes, undrained
1 can (6 oz) tomato paste
1¾ cups Burgundy

⅓ cup chopped parsley
2 teaspoons dried oregano
   leaves
½ teaspoon dried basil
   leaves
2 teaspoons salt
¼ teaspoon pepper
1½ lb halibut steaks
½ lb raw shrimp, shelled
   and deveined
3 pkg (6-oz size) frozen
   crabmeat, thawed and
   undrained

1. Slowly heat oil in 6-quart kettle. In hot oil, sauté garlic, onions, and green pepper until tender—about 10 minutes.
2. Meanwhile, drain clams, reserving ¼ cup liquid. Set clams aside.
3. Add reserved clam liquid, tomatoes, tomato paste, Burgundy, parsley, oregano, basil, salt, pepper, and ¾ cup water to sautéed vegetables, mixing well. Bring to boiling; reduce heat, and simmer, uncovered, 10 minutes.
4. Meanwhile, cut halibut into 1-inch pieces; discard skin and bones. Add halibut, shrimp, crabmeat, and clams to tomato mixture; simmer, covered, 15 minutes. Then simmer, uncovered, 15 minutes longer.
5. To freeze: Let Cioppino cool completely. Line a large bowl with foil, letting foil extend about 6 inches above top of bowl. Turn cooled mixture into bowl; fold foil over top. Freeze until firm.
6. Remove foil-wrapped Cioppino from bowl. Cover tightly with foil; label, and freeze until ready to use.
7. To serve: Remove foil. Place Cioppino in large kettle; cook, covered, over boiling water, 40 minutes, or until heated through.

CRISPY OVEN-FRIED CHICKEN

2- to 2½-lb broiler-fryer,
   cut up
¾ cup dairy sour cream
1 tablespoon lemon juice
1 teaspoon Worcestershire
   sauce
1 teaspoon celery salt

1 teaspoon salt
⅛ teaspoon pepper
½ teaspoon paprika
2 cloves garlic, finely
   chopped
1 cup packaged dry bread
   crumbs

1. Preheat oven to 350F. Grease a 13-by-9-by-2-inch baking dish. Wipe chicken with damp paper towels.
2. In medium bowl, combine sour cream with lemon juice, Worcestershire, celery salt, salt, pepper, paprika, and garlic; mix well.
3. Dip chicken into sour-cream mixture; then roll in bread crumbs, coating completely.
4. Arrange chicken pieces in baking dish; bake, uncovered, 45 to 60 minutes, or until chicken is tender and nicely browned.
5. Let chicken cool completely. Wrap in foil, individually or in a single layer; label, and freeze.
6. To reheat chicken: Preheat oven to 450F. Place wrapped frozen chicken in oven; bake 45 minutes. (If chicken is individually wrapped, bake 30 minutes.)
7. Uncover chicken; bake 10 minutes longer, to crisp.

FROZEN MEAT-LOAF MUFFINS

MAKES 6

1.   Prepare and bake Meat-Loaf Muffins* as recipe directs. Remove from pan; cool completely on wire rack. Wrap in foil; label, and freeze.

2.   To reheat: Preheat oven to 450F. Place wrapped and frozen muffins in oven; bake 30 minutes. Uncover, and bake 5 minutes longer.

* See Meats and Game Chapter.

FROZEN MEAT LOAF

MAKES 6 SERVINGS

1.   Prepare Meat-Loaf Muffins* as recipe directs, doubling amount of ingredients.

2.   Line a 9-by-9-by-1¾-inch pan with foil, letting foil extend about 5 inches above top of pan.

3.   Pack meat-loaf mixture into pan; fold foil over top. Refrigerate 2 hours.

4.   Remove wrapped meat loaf from pan; label, and freeze until ready to use.

5.   To bake: Preheat oven to 350F. Remove foil from meat loaf. Return frozen meat loaf to pan; bake 1 hour and 40 minutes. Invert onto serving platter. Cut into squares.

* See Meats and Game Chapter.

FROZEN MEAT PATTIES

MAKES 8

2 lb ground chuck   *Butter or margarine*

1.   Lightly shape meat into 8 (4-inch) patties.

2.   Place a double thickness of waxed paper, or single layer of baking-pan-liner paper, between patties. Freezer-wrap; label, and freeze until ready to use.

3.   To cook: Remove as many patties as desired from freezer. In small amount of hot butter in heavy skillet, cook frozen patties, over medium heat, 5 minutes. Turn, and cook 5 minutes longer, or until of desired doneness.

SCALLOPS AU GRATIN

2 lb fresh sea scallops
    (4 cups)
¼ cup butter or margarine
2 medium green peppers,
    cut into ¾-inch
    squares (2 cups)
2 medium onions, cut up
    (1 cup)

4 celery stalks, cut into ½-
    inch pieces (2 cups)
3 cups soft bread crumbs
1 teaspoon salt
¼ teaspoon pepper
2 cups light cream
1 cup grated sharp Cheddar
    cheese

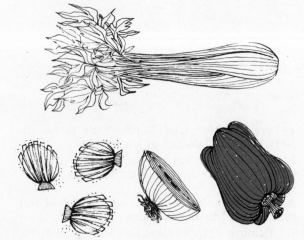

1. Rinse scallops well in cold water; drain. In large saucepan, add water to scallops to cover; bring to boiling, uncovered. Remove from heat; drain, and set aside.

2. In hot butter in large skillet, sauté green pepper, onion, and celery until tender—about 8 minutes.

3. In large bowl, combine sautéed vegetables with scallops, bread crumbs, salt, and pepper; toss lightly to combine.

4. Divide scallop mixture evenly among 6 (5-inch) foil pie pans. Let cool completely.

5. Pour ⅓ cup cream over scallop mixture in each pie pan. Wrap each in foil; label, and freeze until ready to use.

6. To bake: Preheat oven to 450F. Place wrapped pie pans on cookie sheet. Bake scallop mixture, unthawed, 40 minutes. Remove foil; sprinkle each with some of cheese; bake 10 to 15 minutes longer, or until cheese is melted and scallop mixture is heated through.

Note: Or use 2 (9-inch) foil pie pans. Pour 1 cup cream over scallop mixture in each. Bake 50 minutes before removing foil. Sprinkle each with ½ cup cheese; bake 10 to 15 minutes, or until cheese is melted and scallop mixture is heated through.

FROSTED LEMON DESSERTS

¾ cup crushed toasted rice
    cereal
3 egg whites
½ cup sugar
3 egg yolks

1 tablespoon grated lemon
    peel
⅓ cup lemon juice
1 cup heavy cream, whipped

1. Sprinkle 1 tablespoon crushed cereal into bottom of each of 6 (5-oz) paper dessert dishes. Set dishes and rest of crushed cereal aside.

2. In medium bowl, with portable electric mixer at high speed, beat egg whites until soft peaks form when beater is slowly raised. Gradually beat in sugar, 2 tablespoons at a time, until stiff peaks form when beater is slowly raised.

3. With same beaters, beat egg yolks, at medium speed, until thick and lemon-colored. Beat in lemon peel and juice until well combined.

4. With rubber scraper, using an under-and-over motion, fold egg-yolk mixture and whipped cream into egg whites until just combined.

5. Turn mixture onto cereal in dessert dishes. Sprinkle each with 1 tablespoon reserved crushed cereal. Freezer-wrap; label, and freeze.

6. To serve, let stand in refrigerator 30 minutes.

FROZEN PEPPERMINT-ICE-CREAM CAKE

1 pkg (15 oz) angel-food-
   cake mix
1/3 cup coarsely chopped
   thin chocolate-mint
   wafers

3/4 cup chopped walnuts
1/4 teaspoon peppermint
   extract
3 pints soft vanilla ice
   cream*

1. Preheat oven to 375F.

2. Make cake as package label directs. Turn into ungreased 10-inch tube pan.

3. Bake on lowest shelf of oven 30 to 40 minutes, or until surface springs back when gently pressed with fingertip.

4. Invert pan immediately, hanging tube over neck of bottle. Let cool completely—about 1 hour. Remove; split crosswise into 3 layers.

5. In large bowl, add mints, nuts, and peppermint extract to ice cream, stirring until well combined. (If ice cream becomes too soft to spread, return to freezer for a few minutes.)

6. Working quickly, assemble cake on cookie sheet or foil: Spread bottom cake layer with 1/3 ice-cream mixture. Top with second cake layer; spread with 1/3 ice-cream mixture. Top with third cake layer; spread remaining ice-cream mixture over top.

7. Freeze until firm—about 2 hours. To serve: With sharp knife, cut frozen cake into slices.

Note: To store cake in freezer: Freeze as directed. Then freezer-wrap; label, and freeze until ready to serve.

* Or use 3 pints soft peppermint ice cream; omit extract.

ICE-CREAM EASTER EGG

3 pt soft vanilla ice
   cream
1 cup mixed candied fruit
1/4 cup light rum

1 cup heavy cream
2 tablespoons sugar
Few drops red, blue, and
   yellow food color

1. In large bowl, combine ice cream with candied fruit and rum, mixing well. Do not let ice cream melt.

2. Pack ice-cream mixture into a 1½-quart melon mold. Freeze until firm—several hours or overnight.

3. To unmold: Wipe outside of mold with hot, wet dishcloth; unmold ice cream onto chilled serving platter. Freeze 15 minutes.

4. Whip cream with sugar just until stiff. Use half of whipped-cream mixture to frost ice cream. Return ice cream to freezer.

5. Divide remaining whipped cream into 3 parts. Tint one part pink, one blue, and one yellow. Keeping colors separate, pipe whipped cream through desired decorating tip of pastry bag, decorating ice cream like an Easter egg.

6. Freeze until firm. Then, freezer-wrap; label, and freeze until ready to use. To serve, cut crosswise into slices.

MOCHA ICE-CREAM PIE

MAKES 8 TO 10 SERVINGS

⅔ cup butter-flavored
   syrup
2½ cups toasted rice cereal
1 pt chocolate ice cream

1 pt coffee ice cream
⅓ cup chopped nuts
1 cup heavy cream,
   whipped

1. Lightly butter bottom and side of a 9-inch pie plate.
2. In small saucepan, bring syrup to boiling. Reduce heat, and simmer 2 minutes, stirring occasionally.
3. Pour syrup over rice cereal in large bowl; mix well. Turn into prepared pie plate. With spatula, press evenly to bottom and side and on rim of pie plate. Freeze 30 minutes.
4. Meanwhile, let chocolate ice cream soften in refrigerator until of spreading consistency— about 1 hour.
5. Spread chocolate ice cream evenly over cereal in pie shell. Freeze until firm.
6. Meanwhile, let coffee ice cream soften; then combine with nuts. Spread evenly over chocolate layer. Freeze until firm—at least 1 hour. Wrap in foil; label, and store in freezer until ready to use.
7. To serve: Make whipped-cream rosettes around edge of pie, using a pastry bag with a No. 6 decorating tip.

FROZEN WHIPPED-CREAM MOUNDS

MAKES ABOUT 30 MOUNDS

1 pt heavy cream

¼ cup confectioners' sugar
   (optional)

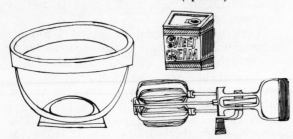

1. In medium bowl, whip cream with sugar just until stiff.
2. Drop whipped cream, by mounds, onto foil-covered cardboard. (If rosettes are desired, put whipped cream through pastry bag, using No. 6 decorating tip.)
3. Freeze about 2 hours, or until firm.
4. Working quickly, remove to polyethylene bags. Label, and freeze until ready to use.
5. When ready to use, place frozen whipped cream on dessert; let stand about 10 minutes, to thaw.

FRUITED ICE RING

4 maraschino cherries,
   quartered

16 orange sections
16 thin lime-peel strips

1. Place a fluted 2-quart ring mold in freezer until well chilled.
2. Rinse inside of chilled mold in cold water. Return to freezer until a thin coating of ice forms on inside of mold.
3. In each indentation in mold, arrange a cherry, orange section, and lime strip in a pretty design, placing lime strip skin side down.

(Fruited Ice Ring continued)

4. Slowly add enough cold water just to cover bottom of mold—about ⅓ cup. (Do not add too much water; fruit would float.) Freeze until firm.

5. Add water to cover fruit completely; freeze until firm.

6. Fill mold to top with water; freeze until firm.

7. When ready to use: Run cold water over mold, to loosen. Unmold ice ring, and float in punch bowl.

Note: You may substitute plastic flowers for fruit. Wash flowers well.

When the summer's at its height, pick the top-of-the-crop purple plums, velvety apricots and raspberries, and crisp, white-fleshed apples. Tuck them in the freezer, and when the frost is on the ground, remember summer in our delectable fruit pies.

FREEZER PIES

MAKES 6 TO 8 SERVINGS

Filling for Fresh-Apricot
    Pie, Raspberry-Apple
    Pie, Peach-Blueberry
    Pie, or Spiced Plum
    Pie*

Flaky pastry for 2-crust pie
2 tablespoons butter or
    margarine

1. To freeze Filling: Line a 9-inch pie plate with heavy-duty foil, making sure foil extends at least 6 inches above rim.

2. Make pie filling as recipe directs. Turn into pie plate; bring foil over top, to cover loosely. Freeze several hours, or until filling is firm.

3. Remove frozen, foil-wrapped filling from pie plate; cover top tightly with foil. Label, and return to freezer until ready to bake. Filling may be stored in freezer as long as 6 months.

4. To bake pie: Preheat oven to 425F. On lightly floured surface, roll out half of pastry into an 11-inch circle. Use to line 9-inch pie plate; trim.

5. Remove filling from freezer; discard foil. Place filling in pie plate. Dot with butter.

6. Roll out remaining pastry into an 11-inch circle. Make several slits near center, for steam vents. Adjust over filling; trim. Fold edge of top crust under bottom crust; crimp edge decoratively.

7. Bake 45 to 50 minutes, or until crust is golden-brown.

8. Cool partially on wire rack; serve slightly warm.

* See Pies and Small Pastries Chapter.

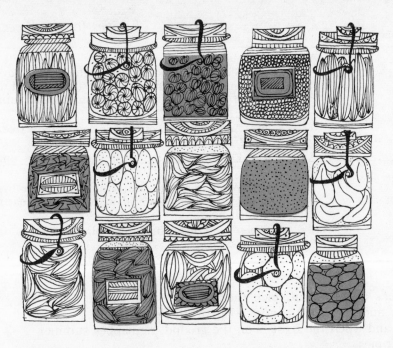

Jams, Jellies, and Relishes

17

Because there is such a wide variety of commercial jams, jellies, and relishes on the market, we have limited our recipes to a gourmet's taste. We tell you frankly that these are no simple fruit preserves to be spread on breakfast toast. No, indeed. Nor are our relishes run-of-the-mill relishes. All are destined to become proud recipes of the house, to serve at special luncheon and dinner occasions.

Always, be sure to sterilize jars properly. To sterilize jars: In soapy water, wash jars and lids; rinse. Place on rack in large kettle; add water to cover. Bring water to boiling. Reduce heat; simmer 10 minutes. When ready to fill jars, remove from water with tongs, one at a time.

FRESH-CRANBERRY JELLY

MAKES 8 TO 10 SERVINGS

4 cups (1 lb) fresh cranberries	2 cups sugar Dash salt

1. Wash cranberries; drain, and remove stems.
2. Turn into 3½-quart saucepan. Add 2 cups water; bring to boiling point over high heat. Reduce heat; simmer, covered, 20 minutes.
3. Press cranberries and liquid through food mill or colander; then strain, to remove seeds.
4. Bring cranberry purée to boiling point; boil, uncovered, 3 minutes. Add sugar and salt; boil 2 minutes.
5. Pour into a 3-cup mold. Refrigerate for 5 hours, or until firm.
6. To unmold, carefully loosen edge of mold with a sharp knife. Turn out onto serving dish.

CRANBERRY-ORANGE JELLY

FILLS ABOUT 8 (8-OZ) JELLY GLASSES

1 qt cranberry juice
6 cups sugar
1 cup orange peel, cut in
  large pieces

1 bottle (6 oz) liquid fruit
  pectin

1. Sterilize 8 (8-oz) jelly glasses; leave in hot water until ready to fill.

2. In large, deep saucepan, combine cranberry juice and sugar. Tie orange peel securely in small, double-thickness cheesecloth bag; add to cranberry mixture.

3. Stir, over high heat, until sugar is dissolved.

4. Then, still over high heat, bring mixture to a full, rolling boil.* Stir in pectin.

5. Again bring to a full, rolling boil; boil 1 minute, stirring constantly.

6. Remove saucepan from heat. Discard orange peel in cheesecloth bag. Skim off any foam from liquid.

7. Ladle jelly into hot, sterilized jelly glasses. Immediately cover with ⅛ inch hot paraffin.

8. Let cool; then cover with lid. A natural for poultry of all kinds.

* Rolling boil is one that cannot be stirred down.

PORT-WINE FESTIVAL JELLY

FILLS ABOUT 4 (8-OZ) JELLY GLASSES

2 cups port wine
3 cups sugar
⅛ teaspoon cinnamon

⅛ teaspoon cloves
½ bottle (6-oz size) liquid
  fruit pectin

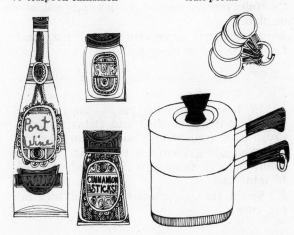

1. Sterilize 4 (8-oz) jelly glasses; leave in hot water until ready to fill.

2. In top of double boiler, combine port, sugar, cinnamon, and cloves. Place over rapidly boiling water; heat 2 minutes, stirring constantly.

3. Then, over direct heat, bring to a full, rolling boil. Stir in pectin.

4. Again bring to a full, rolling boil; boil 1 minute—stir constantly.

5. Remove pan from heat. Skim off any foam from liquid.

6. Ladle jelly into hot, sterilized jelly glasses. Immediately cover with ⅛ inch hot paraffin.

7. Let cool; then cover with lid. Looks beautiful on a buffet table.

SPICED GRAPE JELLY

6½ cups sugar
½ teaspoon cinnamon
½ teaspoon cloves
½ teaspoon allspice

2 cans (6-oz size) frozen
    grape juice
    concentrate, thawed
1 bottle (6 oz) liquid pectin

1. Sterilize 10 (8-oz) jelly glasses; leave in hot water until ready to fill.

2. In large kettle, combine sugar, cinnamon, cloves, and allspice with 3 cups water; mix well.

3. Cook, stirring, over high heat to dissolve sugar. Bring to a full, rolling boil, stirring constantly; boil hard 1 minute, stirring.

4. Remove from heat. Stir in thawed concentrate and pectin, mixing well.

5. Ladle into hot, sterilized jelly glasses. Immediately cover with ⅛ inch hot paraffin.

6. Let cool; then cover with lid.

PARSLEY JELLY

1½ cups Parsley Infusion
    (below)
2 tablespoons lemon juice
Green food color

3½ cups sugar
½ bottle (6-oz size) liquid
    fruit pectin
4 large parsley sprigs

1. Sterilize 4 (8-oz) jelly glasses; keep in hot water until ready to use.

2. In very large, deep saucepan, combine Parsley Infusion, lemon juice, and just enough drops green food color to tint desired shade.

3. Add sugar, and mix well.

4. Then, over high heat, bring mixture to a full, rolling boil. Stir in liquid fruit pectin.

5. Again bring to a full, rolling boil; boil 1 minute, stirring constantly. Remove saucepan from heat. Skim off any foam from liquid.

6. Place parsley sprig in each jelly glass. With sterilized teaspoon, hold parsley stem against side and bottom of glass.

7. Ladle in jelly; let set 15 to 20 minutes. Carefully remove spoon—parsley sprig will stay in place.

8. Immediately cover with ⅛ inch hot paraffin. Let cool; then cover with lid.

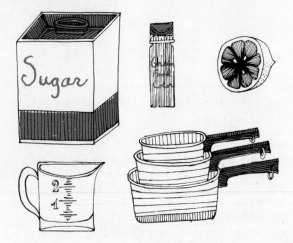

PARSLEY INFUSION

1. In large saucepan, put 2 cups (firmly packed) parsley, washed and stems removed. Crush parsley thoroughly with potato masher.

2. Then add 2¼ cups water; bring to boiling point. Remove from heat; let stand, covered, 10 minutes.

3. Strain through cheesecloth, and measure 1½ cups.

FRUIT PRESERVES

These are no simple fruit preserves to be spread on breakfast toast. No, indeed!
They're gourmet items you won't find in a store, made for special occasions
and to enhance special dishes. These are the proud recipes of the house!

ODE TO A PEACH

They have traveled across the centuries, from the ancient worlds of China and Persia to our far-flung orchards. Peaches are classed as cling or freestone, one adhering to the stone, the other breaking away easily. The varieties are many, both yellow and white, but perhaps the favorite is the golden Elberta. You can use peaches in desserts (wait till you try our peach short-cake or peach ice cream!), with meats, in salads, or just plain. They come frozen or canned the whole year round, but they're at their best tree-ripe fresh!

Relishes, Jams, and Conserves

A relish is something you relish, of course; but it also is something that makes you relish the foods it is served with. And our pretty relishes are guaranteed to make food sparkle —spiced things, peach chutney, brandied pears, conserves, and such excitements.

SPICED BLUEBERRY JAM

1½ qt blueberries
2 tablespoons lemon juice
¼ teaspoon cloves
¼ teaspoon cinnamon
¼ teaspoon allspice
1 pkg (1¾ oz) powdered
    fruit pectin
5 cups sugar

FILLS 8 (6-OZ) GLASSES

1. Sterilize 8 (6-oz) jelly glasses; keep in hot water until ready to fill.
2. Wash and drain blueberries; pick over fruit; remove stems.
3. To purée blueberries, press through a food mill or sieve (or blend in electric blender, covered, about ½ minute). Measure 1 quart purée.
4. In large saucepan, combine purée, lemon juice, cloves, cinnamon, allspice, and pectin; stir to mix well.
5. Over high heat, bring mixture to a full, rolling boil; boil 1 minute, stirring constantly.
6. Add sugar all at once. Again bring mixture to a rolling boil; boil 1 minute, stirring constantly. Skim off any foam on surface.
7. Ladle into hot, sterilized jelly glasses. Immediately cover with ⅛ inch hot paraffin. Let cool; then cover with lid.

SPICED CHERRY JAM

4 cups pitted, tart red
    cherries
¼ cup lemon juice
7½ cups sugar
1 teaspoon cinnamon
½ teaspoon cloves
½ teaspoon allspice
½ bottle (6-oz size) liquid
    fruit pectin

FILLS ABOUT 7 (8-OZ) JELLY GLASSES

1. Sterilize 7 (8-oz) jelly glasses; keep in hot water until ready to fill.
2. Chop cherries very fine (or in electric blender, blend at high speed—a small amount at a time—1 minute).
3. In very large saucepan, stir chopped cherries, lemon juice, sugar, cinnamon, cloves, and allspice until well combined.
4. Then, over high heat, bring to a full, rolling boil; boil 1 minute, stirring constantly.
5. Remove saucepan from heat. Immediately stir in pectin. With metal spoon, skim off any foam from liquid. Stir and skim 5 minutes, to cool slightly and prevent fruit's floating.
6. Ladle into hot, sterilized jelly glasses. Immediately cover with ⅛ inch hot paraffin. Let cool; then cover with lid. Let stand about 2 weeks before using.

BLACK-CHERRY CONSERVE

FILLS ABOUT 4 (8-OZ) JARS

2 medium navel oranges,
    unpeeled and thinly
    sliced
4 cans (1-lb, 1-oz size)
    pitted Bing cherries;
    or 4 cups fresh Bing
    cherries, pitted

3 cups sugar
¼ cup lemon juice
¾ cup slivered blanched
    almonds

1. In very large saucepan, combine orange slices and 2 cups cold water; bring to boiling point. Then reduce heat; simmer, uncovered, 10 minutes, or until orange peel is tender.

2. Add cherries, sugar, and lemon juice; simmer gently, uncovered and stirring occasionally, until mixture is thick and syrupy—about 1½ hours. Stir in almonds; simmer 2 minutes longer. Remove from heat.

3. Sterilize 4 (8-oz) jars; keep in hot water until ready to fill.

4. Ladle conserve into hot, sterilized jars. Cap immediately as manufacturer directs.

BLUEBERRY-APPLE CONSERVE

MAKES 4 PINTS

2 pt fresh blueberries
5 cups coarsely chopped,
    unpared tart apples
6 cups sugar

1 tablespoon grated lemon
    peel
⅓ cup lemon juice
1 cup slivered blanched
    almonds

1. Wash blueberries well in cold water; drain. In large saucepan, combine with apples, sugar, lemon peel and juice.

2. Cook, stirring constantly, over high heat until sugar is dissolved.

3. Reduce heat; simmer, uncovered and stirring occasionally, 1½ hours, or until mixture is very thick. Remove from heat. Add almonds.

4. Meanwhile, sterilize 4 pint jars; leave in hot water until ready to fill.

5. Immediately ladle conserve into hot, sterilized jars, filling to within ½ inch of top. Cap at once as manufacturer directs.

FRESH-FRUIT CONSERVE

MAKES 7 (8-OZ) JARS

2 cups coarsely chopped
    fresh pineapple
1 qt fresh strawberries
4 cups rhubarb, sliced ¼
    inch thick (about
    1¾ lb)

5 cups sugar
½ cup blanched slivered
    almonds

1. In large kettle, combine pineapple with 1 cup water. Bring to boiling; reduce heat, and simmer, covered, 10 minutes.

2. Wash strawberries; drain; hull. Add strawberries, rhubarb, and sugar to pineapple.

3. Stir constantly, over high heat, until sugar is dissolved. Reduce heat; simmer, uncovered and stirring occasionally, about 1 hour, or until thick (mixture should drop from metal spoon in sheets). Skim foam from surface.

4. Meanwhile, sterilize 7 (8-oz) jars; keep in hot water until ready to fill.

5. Remove fruit from heat; stir in almonds.

6. Ladle immediately into hot, sterilized jars, filling to within ½ inch of top. Cap at once as manufacturer directs.

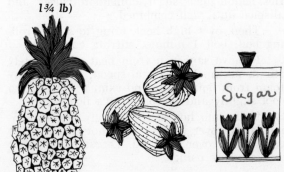

BRANDIED PEACHES

3 cups sugar
2 qt peeled fresh peach
    halves

¾ cup brandy

1. Sterilize 4 pint jars; leave in hot water until ready to fill.
2. Combine sugar and 1 cup water in large saucepan. Over medium heat, bring to boiling point, stirring until sugar is dissolved.
3. Then reduce heat, and simmer 10 minutes.
4. Add peach halves; simmer gently 10 minutes, or just until peaches are tender. Remove saucepan from heat.
5. Meanwhile, put 1 tablespoon brandy in each hot, sterilized jar. Half fill jars with peaches; then add 1 tablespoon brandy to each jar. Fill with remaining peaches; top each with 1 tablespoon brandy, and cover with syrup.
6. Cap at once as manufacturer directs.

PEACH CHUTNEY

1 medium onion
1 small clove garlic
1 cup seedless raisins
2 qt cut-up, peeled peaches
2 tablespoons chili powder
1 cup chopped crystallized
    ginger

2 tablespoons mustard seed
1 tablespoon salt
1 qt vinegar
2¼ cups light-brown sugar,
    firmly packed

1. Put onion, garlic, and raisins through fine blade of food chopper.
2. In large kettle, combine ground-onion mixture with remaining ingredients; mix well. Bring to boiling point, stirring constantly until sugar is dissolved. Reduce heat; simmer, uncovered, stirring occasionally, until quite thick and deep-brown—about 45 to 60 minutes.
3. Meanwhile, sterilize 5 pint jars; leave in hot water until ready to fill.
4. Ladle chutney into hot, sterilized jars. Cap immediately as manufacturer directs.

SPICED PEACHES

4 cups sugar
½ cup cider vinegar
1 tablespoon whole allspice
1 tablespoon whole cloves

4 (2½-inch) cinnamon
    sticks
2 qt peeled fresh peach
    halves

1. Sterilize 4 pint jars; leave in hot water until ready to fill.
2. In medium kettle, combine sugar, vinegar, allspice, cloves, and cinnamon sticks; bring to boiling. Reduce heat; simmer, stirring, until sugar is dissolved.
3. Add peaches to sugar syrup; simmer, uncovered and stirring occasionally, 10 minutes, or until peaches are heated through.
4. With slotted spoon, ladle peaches into hot, sterilized jars. Put a cinnamon stick into each jar. Fill with sugar syrup to within ½ inch of top. Cap at once as manufacturer directs.

BRANDIED PEARS

MAKES 4 PINTS

4½ cups sugar
4 lb fresh pears
¾ cup brandy

Maraschino cherries,
   drained (optional)

1. Combine sugar and 1½ cups water in large saucepan. Over medium heat, bring to boiling, stirring constantly—sugar should be dissolved.
2. Reduce heat; simmer, uncovered, 10 minutes.
3. Meanwhile, cut pears in half; core, and pare. Add to sugar syrup; simmer, uncovered, 30 to 40 minutes, or until pears are tender. Remove from heat.
4. While pears are cooking, sterilize 4 pint jars; leave in hot water until ready to fill.
5. Put 1 tablespoon brandy into each hot, sterilized jar. With slotted spoon, lift pears from syrup. If desired, put a maraschino cherry in each pear half.
6. Half fill jars with pears; add 1 tablespoon brandy to each. Fill jars with rest of pears; add 1 tablespoon brandy to each.
7. Fill with sugar syrup to within ½ inch of top. Cap at once as manufacturer directs.

GINGER PEARS

MAKES 10 PINTS

12 lb firm pears (about 25)
¾ cup lemon juice
6 cups sugar
⅓ cup slivered lemon
   peel

⅓ cup slivered crystallized
   ginger

1. Wash and peel pears; halve each lengthwise; remove core and stem.
2. Put pear halves in large kettle with 2 cups water and lemon juice; bring to a boil. Reduce heat; simmer, uncovered, until pears are almost tender—30 to 40 minutes.
3. Then add sugar, lemon peel, and ginger. Simmer, stirring occasionally, until mixture is slightly thickened—10 to 15 minutes.
4. Meanwhile, sterilize 10 pint jars; keep in hot water until ready to fill.
5. Pack pears into hot, sterilized jars.

LA VELLE'S PLUM CHUTNEY

MAKES ABOUT 10 PINTS

5 lb unpeeled purple plums,
   halved and pitted
2 lb yellow onions, coarsely
   chopped
4 lb McIntosh apples,
   peeled, cored,
   coarsely chopped
3 cups white vinegar

2 lb granulated sugar
2 lb dark-brown sugar
1 tablespoon allspice
1 tablespoon cloves
1 tablespoon ginger
3 tablespoons salt
1 teaspoon cayenne

1. In very large kettle, combine plums, onions, apples, and vinegar; bring to boiling point. Stir in remaining ingredients.
2. Again bring to boiling point. Reduce heat; simmer, uncovered, 1½ hours. Stir occasionally, to prevent scorching.
3. Meanwhile, sterilize 10 pint jars; keep in hot water until ready to fill.
4. Ladle into hot, sterilized jars. Cap immediately as manufacturer directs.

PLUM CONSERVE

5 lb fresh damson plums
½ orange
1 lemon

6 cups sugar
¾ cup broken walnuts

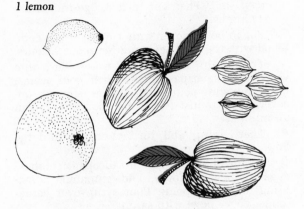

1. Wash plums; remove pits. Chop plums coarsely (makes 7 cups chopped fruit).

2. Cut orange half into 2 wedges. Cut lemon into 4 wedges. With flat side down, cut lemon and orange wedges lengthwise into thin slices.

3. In large kettle, combine fruit and sugar; stir constantly, over high heat, until sugar is dissolved. Reduce heat; simmer, uncovered, 1 hour, or until thick.

4. Meanwhile, sterilize 4 pint jars; leave in hot water until ready to fill.

5. Remove fruit from heat. Stir in walnuts.

6. Ladle immediately into hot, sterilized jars, filling to within ½ inch of top. Cap at once as manufacturer directs.

RHUBARB CONSERVE

4 cups rhubarb, sliced ¼ inch thick (about 1¾ lb)
4 cups sugar
1 tablespoon grated orange peel

½ cup orange juice
1 lemon, thinly sliced
1 cup seedless raisins
1-inch cinnamon stick

1. In 3-quart saucepan, combine rhubarb with remaining ingredients.

2. Stir constantly, over high heat, until sugar is dissolved. Bring to boiling, stirring. Reduce heat; simmer, uncovered and stirring occasionally, 30 to 45 minutes, or until mixture is thick.

3. Meanwhile, sterilize 4 (8-oz) jars; keep in hot water until ready to fill.

4. Remove fruit from heat. Ladle immediately into hot, sterilized jars, filling to within ½ inch of top. Cap at once as manufacturer directs.

TROPICAL JAM

3 pt boxes fresh strawberries
1 can (1 lb, 4 oz) crushed pineapple, drained

2 tablespoons lemon juice
7½ cups sugar
1 bottle (6 oz) liquid fruit pectin

1. Sterilize 10 (6-oz) jelly glasses; keep in hot water until ready to fill.

2. Wash berries gently in cold water. Drain; hull. In large bowl, with potato masher, crush berries. Measure 3⅔ cups.

3. In large kettle, combine berries, pineapple, lemon juice, and sugar; stir to combine well. Place over high heat; stirring constantly, bring to a full, rolling boil. Boil hard for 1 minute.

4. Remove from heat. Stir in pectin. With metal spoon, stir and skim 5 minutes, to cool slightly and prevent fruit's floating.

5. Ladle quickly into hot, sterilized jelly glasses. Top with ⅛ inch hot paraffin. Cool.

CANTALOUPE PICKLES

5 cantaloupes, slightly
    underripe
¼ cup salt
7 cups sugar

2 cups white vinegar
2 whole cloves
3-inch cinnamon stick

1. Cut each melon in 8 wedges; remove seeds and pulp. Remove rind, leaving small amount of green rind. Then cut each wedge into triangular chunks.
2. Put in bowl; cover with 1 quart water combined with the salt. Let stand for about 2 hours.
3. Then drain; rinse in cold water. Turn into very large saucepan; cover with cold water; bring to boiling point. Reduce heat; simmer, uncovered, until just tender but not soft—about 10 minutes.
4. Then drain, and turn chunks into large bowl.
5. Meanwhile, in medium saucepan, combine sugar, vinegar, cloves, and cinnamon stick; bring to boiling point. Pour syrup over cantaloupe; cover bowl with saran.
6. Let stand overnight at room temperature.
7. Next day, drain syrup from cantaloupe. Heat syrup to boiling point. Pour over melon; cover with saran. Let stand overnight at room temperature.
8. Sterilize 7 pint jars; leave in hot water until ready to fill.
9. Bring syrup and melon to boiling point; remove from heat.
10. Ladle into hot, sterilized jars; pour syrup over top. Cap immediately as manufacturer directs. A nice change on the relish dish.

PICKLED CHERRIES

2½ cups light-brown
    sugar, firmly packed
2 cups cider vinegar
2 teaspoons whole cloves

4 (3-inch) cinnamon sticks,
    broken
2 qt pitted, tart red
    cherries

1. Sterilize 3 pint jars; keep in hot water until ready to fill.
2. In very large saucepan, combine sugar, vinegar, and spices; bring to boiling point. Reduce heat; simmer 3 to 4 minutes.
3. Then strain through cheesecloth, to remove cloves and cinnamon.
4. In same saucepan, cook strained liquid with cherries about 5 minutes, or until heated through. Remove from heat.
5. Ladle into hot, sterilized jars; cover with hot juice. Cap immediately as manufacturer directs. Pickled cherries are delightful with roast pork.

DILLED GREEN-TOMATO PICKLES

3 lb medium green
 tomatoes, washed
2 cups white vinegar
2 tablespoons salt

3 cloves garlic, peeled and
 split
5 fresh dill sprigs, or 2½
 teaspoons dried dill

1. Remove stems from tomatoes. Cut each tomato into 6 wedges; set aside.
2. Sterilize 5 pint jars; leave in hot water until ready to fill.
3. In small saucepan, combine vinegar with 1 cup water and the salt; bring to boiling. Reduce heat; simmer, uncovered, 5 minutes.
4. Add tomatoes; bring just to boiling. Remove from heat.
5. With slotted spoon, quickly ladle tomatoes into hot, sterilized jars. To each jar, add ½ clove garlic and 1 dill sprig (or ½ teaspoon dried dill). Fill with vinegar mixture to within ½ inch of top. Cap at once as manufacturer directs.

GREEN-TOMATO PICKLES

7½ lb green tomatoes
Salt
5 small yellow onions
 (½ lb)
2 cups sugar
2 cups white vinegar

1 tablespoon mustard seed
1 teaspoon celery seed
1 teaspoon whole black
 peppers
1 teaspoon ginger
1 teaspoon turmeric

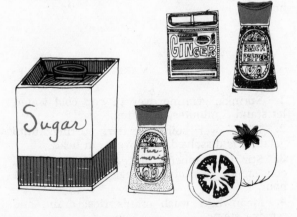

1. Wash tomatoes; remove stems. Cut tomatoes into quarters. In very large bowl, lightly toss tomatoes with ½ cup salt.
2. Slice onions ⅛ inch thick. Lightly toss, in small bowl, with 1 tablespoon salt.
3. Let tomatoes and onions stand 1 hour. Then rinse in cold water, and drain thoroughly.
4. Sterilize 7 pint jars; leave in hot water until ready to fill.
5. In large kettle, combine sugar, 1 teaspoon salt, and remaining ingredients. Cook, stirring and over medium heat, until sugar is dissolved.
6. Add drained tomatoes and onions; bring to boiling point. Remove from heat.
7. Ladle into hot, sterilized jars; cover with hot syrup; stir slightly to remove surface bubbles. Cap immediately as manufacturer directs. A nice accompaniment to hot sandwiches for Sunday-night supper.

Relishes to Serve Right Now

These include relishes and meat accompaniments to be served with a special menu. Some of them should be served hot, some chilled. None requires sterilized jars or canning equipment. And every one of them adds a special touch.

CINNAMON-APPLE WEDGES

½ cup sugar
2 bottles (1¾-oz size) red
   cinnamon candies

6 cups thickly sliced, pared,
   cored apples (about
   2 lb)

1. Combine sugar, candies, and 1 cup water in 2½-quart saucepan; stir, over high heat, to dissolve sugar and candies. Reduce heat.
2. Add apple slices; simmer, covered and stirring occasionally, until apples are just tender (not mushy)—about 10 minutes.
3. With slotted spoon, remove apples to large bowl.
4. Bring cinnamon syrup to boiling; boil, uncovered, until thick, or 220F is reached on candy thermometer—about 5 minutes.
5. Pour syrup over apples; refrigerate about 2 hours. Serve as relish with ham, pork chops, roast pork, sausage, or Canadian bacon.

PICKLED BEETS

1 can (8¼ oz) sliced beets
½ cup vinegar
2 tablespoons sugar
½ teaspoon salt

Dash cloves
1 small bay leaf
1 small onion, thinly sliced

1. Drain beets, reserving ¼ cup liquid; turn beets into small serving dish.
2. In small saucepan, combine beet liquid and remaining ingredients; bring to boiling point. Reduce heat; simmer 5 minutes. Pour over beets.
3. Refrigerate until well chilled—about 1 hour.

CRANBERRY–BRAZIL-NUT RELISH

1 envelope unflavored
   gelatine
1 cup bottled cranberry
   juice
2 cups fresh cranberries

½ cup sugar
¼ teaspoon salt
½ cup chopped Brazil nuts
½ cup diced celery

1. Sprinkle gelatine over ½ cup cold water; let stand 5 minutes, to soften.
2. Place over boiling water, stirring, until gelatine is dissolved. Remove from heat.
3. Stir in cranberry juice; refrigerate until consistency of unbeaten egg white—about 1 hour.
4. Meanwhile, wash cranberries; drain, and remove stems.
5. Put cranberries through medium blade of food chopper. Add sugar and salt; mix well. Gently fold cranberry mixture, Brazil nuts, and celery into gelatine mixture, combining well.
6. Turn into 1-quart serving dish; refrigerate until firm—at least 2 hours. Serve with poultry, ham, or pork.

FRESH-CRANBERRY RELISH

2 large navel oranges
4 cups (1 lb) fresh
    cranberries

2 unpared red apples, cored
2 cups sugar

1. Peel oranges; reserve half of 1 peel. Chop oranges coarsely.

2. Wash cranberries; drain, and remove stems. Put cranberries, apples, and reserved orange peel through coarse blade of food chopper. Add oranges and sugar; mix well.

3. Refrigerate several hours, or overnight, before serving.

FRESH-CRANBERRY SAUCE

4 cups (1 lb) fresh
    cranberries
3 cups sugar

2 cups boiling water
1 tablespoon grated orange
    peel

1. Wash cranberries; drain, and remove stems.

2. Combine with remaining ingredients in 3½-quart saucepan; let stand 5 minutes.

3. Simmer, covered, 5 minutes. Remove from heat. Let stand 5 minutes.

4. Simmer, covered, 5 minutes longer. Remove from heat.

5. Cool; then refrigerate until well chilled— several hours, or overnight.

SPICED CRANBERRIES

4 cups (1 lb) fresh
    cranberries
5 whole cloves

5 whole allspice
2 (3-inch) cinnamon sticks
3 cups sugar

1. Wash cranberries; drain, and remove stems.

2. Turn into 3½-quart saucepan. Add 1½ cups water.

3. Tie spices in a small cheesecloth bag; add to cranberries.

4. Cook, covered and over medium heat, just until cranberries burst—about 10 minutes.

5. Remove from heat; discard cheesecloth bag. Stir in sugar; cook, stirring, over low heat, 5 minutes.

6. Cool; refrigerate covered. Serve cold.

MARINATED CUCUMBERS

2 small cucumbers (or
    1 large cucumber),
    unpeeled, very thinly
    sliced
2 teaspoons salt

¼ cup finely chopped
    parsley
½ cup vinegar
½ teaspoon sugar
Dash pepper

1. In an 8- or 9-inch pie plate, layer cucumber slices with 1 teaspoon salt.

2. With another pie plate, press cucumbers, to extract water and make cucumbers wilt.

3. Refrigerate about 1 hour.

4. Pour off salt water. Sprinkle parsley, vinegar, sugar, pepper, and remaining salt over cucumbers. Toss to mix well.

CURRIED DRIED FRUIT

1 pkg (11 oz) mixed dried
    fruit
1 can (12 oz) apricot nectar
½ cup light raisins
⅔ cup dried figs, halved
1 unpeeled lemon, thinly
    sliced

1 teaspoon salt
4½ teaspoons curry powder
2 tablespoons lemon juice
1 teaspoon Worcestershire
    sauce

1. Remove pits from prunes in mixed dried fruit. Cut pears in half.

2. In large saucepan, combine mixed dried fruit with apricot nectar, raisins, figs, lemon slices, salt, curry powder, and 2 cups water; stir until well mixed.

3. Bring to boiling. Reduce heat; then simmer, covered, 25 minutes.

4. Stir in lemon juice and Worcestershire. Serve warm, as a relish with chicken, lamb, or ham. (May be stored, covered, in refrigerator. Reheat before serving.)

GARDEN RELISH

1 quart (1 lb) chopped
    green cabbage
¾ cup finely chopped
    carrot
¾ cup finely chopped
    green pepper
½ cup finely chopped
    onion

¾ cup vinegar
¾ cup sugar
1 tablespoon salt
½ teaspoon mustard seed
½ teaspoon celery seed

1. In large bowl, combine cabbage, carrot, green pepper, and onion.

2. In jar with tight-fitting lid, combine remaining ingredients; shake well.

3. Pour dressing over vegetables; toss until they are well coated.

4. Refrigerate, covered, about 2 hours before serving.

KIDNEY-BEAN RELISH

2 cans (1-lb size) red kidney
    beans, drained
¼ cup chopped onion
½ cup chopped green
    pepper

½ cup bottled Italian-
    style dressing
¼ lb unsliced process
    American cheese, cut
    in ¼-inch cubes

1. In medium bowl, combine kidney beans, onion, and green pepper. Add dressing, and toss well.

2. Cover, and refrigerate 2 to 3 hours.

3. Before serving, toss with cheese.

GRILLED PEACH HALVES

1 can (1 lb, 14 oz) cling-
    peach halves

¼ cup butter or margarine,
    melted

1. Preheat griddle.

2. Drain peaches; place on paper towels, to absorb excess juice.

3. Brush peaches with butter; grill, hollow side down, 1½ minutes, or until lightly browned. Turn, and grill 1½ minutes longer.

4. If desired, fill centers with jelly or cranberry sauce. A nice garnish for chicken or turkey.

Note: Canned pear halves can be grilled the same way.

JAMS, JELLIES AND RELISHES

HOT GINGERED PEARS

MAKES 12

2 cans (1-lb, 13-oz size)
    pear halves
About 24 whole cloves
2 (2-inch) cinnamon sticks
¼ teaspoon nutmeg
4 teaspoons lemon juice
1 teaspoon grated lemon
    peel

1 teaspoon grated orange
    peel
2½ tablespoons chopped
    crystallized ginger
⅛ teaspoon ground ginger
2 tablespoons butter or
    margarine

1. Drain pears well, reserving 1½ cups syrup.

2. In medium saucepan, combine reserved syrup with 10 cloves, cinnamon sticks, and nutmeg; bring to boiling. Reduce heat; simmer, uncovered, 5 minutes. Remove cloves, and discard.

3. To syrup, add lemon juice, lemon and orange peels, gingers, and butter; simmer, uncovered and stirring occasionally, 10 to 15 minutes, or until slightly thickened.

4. Meanwhile, preheat oven to 350F.

5. Arrange pear halves, hollow side down, in single layer in shallow baking dish. Then insert 1 or 2 cloves in each.

6. Pour hot syrup over pears; bake, uncovered, 15 minutes, basting several times with syrup. Serve hot.

Note: Hot Gingered Pears may be prepared the day before and refrigerated. Bring to room temperature; then, just before serving, reheat at 300F for 10 minutes.

EASY PICKLED PEARS

MAKES 1 PINT

1 can (1 lb, 1 oz) pear
    halves
2 tablespoons cider vinegar

1½ teaspoons pickling
    spice

1. Drain liquid from pears into small saucepan. Turn pears into small serving dish.

2. Stir vinegar and pickling spice into pear liquid.

3. Bring to boiling point; boil, uncovered, 5 minutes. Pour over pears. Serve hot or cold, with meat.

PICKLED PINEAPPLE

MAKES ABOUT 3 CUPS

2 cans (13½-oz size)
    thawed frozen
    pineapple chunks
½ cup red-wine vinegar
¾ cup sugar

⅛ teaspoon salt
8 whole cloves
2½-inch cinnamon stick
¼ teaspoon nutmeg

1. Drain pineapple very well, reserving 1 cup liquid.

2. In medium saucepan, combine reserved pineapple liquid with rest of ingredients, except pineapple.

3. Bring to boiling. Reduce heat; simmer, uncovered, 10 minutes.

4. Add pineapple; bring just to boiling. Remove from heat.

5. Let stand 20 minutes.

6. Pour pineapple and liquid into 1-quart jar; cover tightly. Refrigerate until ready to use.

7. Drain well before using. Nice as a relish with meat.

18

Meats and Game

S ince meat is probably the costliest item on anybody's food budget, it makes good sense to be well informed on how to buy it so you are sure of getting the best for your money; how to store it, whether it is fresh, cured, cooked, frozen, or canned; and how to cook it to get the most in flavor and nutrition.

Meat-Buying Hints

Beef should have fat that is firm and creamy white. Lean meat should be red, well marbled with fat, firm, with a fine grain.

Veal has very little fat; the fat should be firm, clear, and white, not watery. Lean meat should be grayish-pink, firm, and fine grained. It is not marbled with fat.

Lamb should be well covered with clear, white, firm fat. Lean meat is pinkish-red and marbled with fat.

Pork is well covered with fat that is firm, white, free from moisture. Lean meat is grayish-pink to rose; firm, fine grained, well marbled with fat.

Amounts to Buy

Boneless meat: Buy ¼ pound per serving; e.g., lean ground beef, liver.
Bone-in meat: Buy ½ pound per serving; e.g., leg of lamb, steaks, chops.
Bony meat: Buy ¾ to 1 pound per serving; e.g., spareribs, shortribs.

Meat Storage

Fresh Meat: Cover or wrap loosely, and place in the coldest part of the refrigerator. Fresh meat that has been prepackaged (as it is in self-service markets) should have the wrappings loosened before storing. Proper circulation of air is important in storing fresh meats; the slight drying effect retards bacterial action. Most fresh meat can be stored 2 to 3 days; but ground beef and variety meat should be used within a day or two, or wrapped and frozen.

Cured Meat: Lightly cover or wrap, and place in the refrigerator. It will keep slightly longer than fresh meat.

Cooked Meat: Keep lightly covered in refrigerator. It can be held 4 to 5 days safely.

Frozen Meat: Properly packaged in moisture- and vaporproof wrap or in an airtight container, it should be maintained at 0°F or lower. *The ice-cube compartment of a standard refrigerator is not adequate.* Meat should be kept wrapped while it is defrosting.

Canned Meat: Store in a cool place. After you open it, refrigerate what you don't use.

Basic Meat Cookery

For all meat cookery, regardless of method, the best results are obtained with low to moderate heat. Three basic methods are dry-heat, moist-heat, and fat cookery.

COOKING WITH DRY HEAT

Dry-Heat Roasting: This is done in an oven, with heat circulating around the meat placed, fat side up, on a rack in a shallow, open pan. The meat thermometer is placed in the thickest part, not resting on bone or fat. The pan is uncovered, without water or basting. Seasoning is not necessary; salt does not penetrate more than half an inch, anyway. Roast at 325F. See timetables.

Broiling and Grilling: This is cooking by direct heat, over charcoal, under gas flame or electric unit. Low temperatures are obtained by the distance the meat is placed from the source of heat (2 to 5 inches, depending on the meat's thickness). Preheating a broiler pan is not necessary. The fat on chops and steaks should be scored, to prevent curling. Seasoning is done *after* browning. This helps prevent the loss of juices. Broiled meats should be served at once. See timetable.

Pan-Broiling: Meat is placed in a heavy skillet, uncovered, without fat or liquid. This is good for thinly cut steaks and chops, as well as meat patties. The cooking is done slowly; occasionally, the meat is turned. Fat is poured off as it is accumulated. Cook to the desired doneness.

COOKING WITH MOIST HEAT

Braising: This is top-of-range cooking, in a heavy skillet or Dutch oven. Chops, steaks, or roast may be done by this method. The meat can be coated with flour, if you wish. It should be well browned, slowly, in a small amount of fat. Add seasonings and a small amount of liquid. Cover tightly, to allow the formation of steam, and simmer slowly until the meat is tender. The time depends on the cut of meat. This method is often referred to as "pot-roasting." See timetable.

Simmering in Water and Stewing: This is cooking on the top of the range in a large quantity of liquid. The meat can first be floured and then browned, if you wish. The liquid should cover the meat. It is never boiled, but simmered, covered, at low temperature. Seasonings can be added with the liquid. Vegetables are added toward the end of the cooking time and should never be overcooked. This method is best for the less-tender cuts of meat. See timetables.

COOKING WITH FAT

Pan-Frying: This is similar to pan-broiling, with the addition of fat. Meat is often coated with flour or with egg and crumbs. Pan-frying is done uncovered, at moderate heat.

Deep-Fat Frying: Enough fat must be used to cover the meat. A deep-frying thermometer should be used. The fat should be heated to 350 to 360F before the meat is added. Temperature drops with the addition of the meat, so adjust the heat to maintain the proper temperature. Variety meats and croquettes are best done by this method. Cooking time depends on the size of the piece of meat. After the meat has been cooked, drain on paper towels.

GENERAL DIRECTIONS FOR BROILING STEAK

1. Have steak at room temperature. Preheat broiler and broiler pan, with rack, 3 or 4 inches from heat.

2. Trim a little fat from steak to rub over broiler rack. Or brush rack with salad oil.

3. If steak is lean (as an unlarded filet), brush both sides lightly with salad oil.

4. Broil steak on one side; season with salt and pepper. Turn steak with tongs; broil other side.

5. To test for doneness, cut small slit in meat near bone or in center. Broil longer if meat is too rare. Season.

Note: Broiling timetable is to be used as a guide for approximate broiling times.

BROILING OR GRILLING TIMETABLE

| Cut | Thickness | Weight | Approximate Total Time (Minutes) | | |
			Rare	Medium	Well Done
BEEF					
Patties	¾ inch	4 oz each	8	12	15
Steak, Club	1 inch	1½ lb	10 to 12	14	16 to 18
Porterhouse	1 inch	2½ lb	12	16	22 to 24
	1½ inch	2½ to 3 lb	16 to 18	18 to 20	25 to 30
	2 inch	3 to 3½ lb	20 to 25	30 to 35	40 to 45
Rib	1 inch	1½ lb	10 to 12	14	16 to 18
Sirloin	1 inch	2½ to 3½ lb	16 to 18	20	20 to 25
	1½ inch	3½ to 4½ lb	24 to 28	28 to 30	34 to 36
Tenderloin (Filet)	1 inch	————	6 to 8	10	12 to 14
LAMB					
Chops, Rib or Loin (1 rib)	¾ inch	2 to 3 oz each	————	————	14 to 15
Double Rib	1½ inch	4 to 5 oz each	————	————	22 to 25
Shoulder	¾ inch	3 to 4 oz each	————	————	14 to 15
Patties	¾ inch	4 oz each	————	————	14 to 15

BRAISING TIMETABLE

Cut	Weight Range	Approximate Time
BEEF		
Flank Steak	1½ to 2 lb	Brown; then simmer 1½ hours
Pot Roast, Chuck, Rump, or Heel of Round	3 to 5 lb	Brown; then simmer 3½ to 4 hours
Short Ribs	2 to 2½ lb	Brown; then simmer 2 to 2½ hours
Swiss Steak (round) 1 inch thick	2 lb	Brown; then simmer 1½ to 2 hours
Oxtails	1 to 1½ lb	Brown; then simmer 3 to 4 hours
LAMB		
Shanks	1 lb each	Brown; then simmer 1½ hours
Shoulder Chops	4 to 5 oz each	Brown; then simmer 35 to 40 minutes
Shoulder Pot Roast (rolled)	3 to 5 lb	Brown; then simmer 2 to 2½ hours
PORK		
Rib or Loin Chops	4 to 5 oz each (¾ to 1 inch thick)	Brown; then simmer 35 to 40 minutes
Shoulder Steaks	5 to 6 oz each	Brown; then simmer 35 to 40 minutes
VEAL		
Cutlets or Round Steak	2 lb	Brown; then simmer 45 to 50 minutes
Loin or Rib Chops	3 to 5 oz each	Brown; then simmer 45 to 50 minutes
Shoulder Pot Roast (rolled)	4 to 5½ lb	Brown; then simmer 2 to 2½ hours

SIMMERING-IN-WATER TIMETABLE

Cut	Weight Range	Approximate Total Time
BEEF		
Brisket or Plate, fresh	8 lb	4 to 5 hours
Brisket, Corned; half or whole	4 to 8 lb	4 to 6 hours
Shanks, cross-cut	4 lb	3 to 4 hours
Tongue, fresh or smoked	3 to 4 lb	3 to 4 hours
PORK		
Hocks	¾ lb	3 hours

STEWING TIMETABLE

Cut	Weight	Approximate Total Time
Beef— 1½-inch cubes from neck, chuck, plate, or heel of round	2 lb	2½ to 3 hours
Veal or Lamb— 1–1½-inch cubes from shoulder or breast	2 lb	1½ to 2 hours

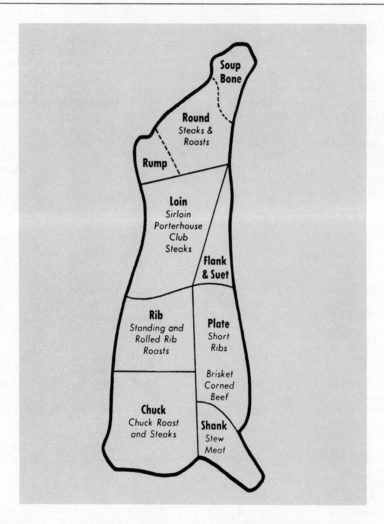

BEEF BUYING AND COOKING GUIDE

Round Steak (Braise)

Rolled Rump (Braise; roast with use of tenderizer)

Sirloin Steak (Broil)

Porterhouse Steak (Broil; pan-broil)

Club Steak (Broil; pan-broil)

Tenderloin Filet from Loin—Filet Mignon (Broil; pan-broil)

Tenderloin from Loin (Roast)

Standing Rib (Roast)—Rib steaks cut from this section are broiled or charcoal grilled

Rolled Rib Boast (Roast)

Chuck Steak (Broil, if meat tenderizer is used; braise)

Round-Bone Pot Roast from Chuck (Braise)

Blade-Bone Pot Roast from Chuck (Braise)

Boston Cut from Chuck (Braise—May be cut into small pieces for stewing)

Shank (Braise; simmer for soup)

Cut from Plate (Simmer; braise)

Short Ribs (Braise)

Brisket (Simmer, corned or fresh)

Flank (Braise; broil)

Standing ribs of beef, richly brown outside, juicy inside, tender to the fork, gratifying to the taste—our time-and-temperature chart will tell you how to achieve exactly the doneness you prefer.

TIMETABLE FOR ROASTING BEEF—AT 325F

Cut	Weight	Approx. roasting time (hours)	Internal temperature
Rib Roast, standing (bone in)*	4 lb	1¾	140F (rare)
		2¼	160F (medium)
		3	170F (well done)
	6 lb	3¼	140F (rare)
		3¾	160F (medium)
		4¼	170F (well done)
	8 lb	3½	140F (rare)
		4½	160F (medium)
		5	170F (well done)
Rib Roast, boned and rolled**	4 lb	2¾	140F (rare)
		3¼	160F (medium)
		3½	170F (well done)
	6 lb	3½	140F (rare)
		4¼	160F (medium)
		4¾	170F (well done)
Sirloin Tip Roast (high quality)	3–5 lb	1¾–2½	140F (rare)
		2¼–3	160F (medium)
		2½–3½	170F (well done)

* Ribs that measure approximately 6 inches from chine bone to tip of the ribs. If ribs are cut longer, allow less roasting time.

** Diameter of roasts: 4 pounds—4½ to 5 inches; 6 pounds—5½ to 6 inches. Thinner roasts of same weight will require less roasting time.

HOW TO ROAST BEEF

1. Preheat oven to 325F. Place beef (taken chilled from refrigerator), fat side up, in shallow, open roasting pan. Use rack for boned roast; omit rack for bone-in roast.

2. Insert meat thermometer through outside fat into thickest part of muscle; point should not rest on fat or bone.

3. Do not add water. Do not sear meat. Do not cover pan. Do not baste.

4. Remove from oven when meat thermometer registers desired degree of doneness. Let the roast stand 20 minutes in a warm place before carving.

SAVORY ROAST OF BEEF

MAKES 2½ CUPS GRAVY,
ABOUT 16 SERVINGS BEEF

Standing 3-rib roast of beef,
bone in* (about 9 lb)

¼ teaspoon dried marjoram
leaves

¼ teaspoon dried thyme
leaves

¼ teaspoon rubbed savory

¼ teaspoon dried basil
leaves

½ teaspoon salt

⅛ teaspoon pepper

1 teaspoon meat-extract
paste

1½ cups Burgundy

6 tablespoons unsifted all-
purpose flour

1. Preheat oven to 325F. Place beef, fat side up, in shallow, open roasting pan. Do not use rack; let beef rest on bones.

2. Mix herbs with salt and pepper.

3. Rub herb mixture into surface of beef on all sides. Insert meat thermometer through outside fat into thickest part of muscle; point should not rest on fat or bone.

4. Dissolve meat-extract paste in ½ cup hot water. Add ½ cup Burgundy. Use some of mixture to baste beef.

5. Roast beef, uncovered, basting several times with remaining Burgundy mixture. Roast until of desired doneness. See timetable.

6. Remove roast to heated platter. Let stand in warm place 20 minutes before carving.

7. Meanwhile, make gravy: Pour off drippings from roasting pan into measuring cup. Pour back 6 tablespoons into pan. Stir in flour to make a smooth mixture.

8. Gradually add 1¼ cups water and remaining 1 cup Burgundy, stirring until smooth and browned bits in pan are dissolved.

9. Bring to boiling, stirring. Reduce heat, and simmer, stirring, 5 minutes longer. Add more salt and pepper, if necessary. Serve with beef.

* Ribs that measure approximately 6 inches from chine bone to tip of the ribs. If ribs are cut longer, allow less roasting time.

Every woman should have at least one great recipe with which to do a great occasion proud. We believe internationally famous Beef Stroganoff, tender, tasty, elegant, is such a one. Though the list of ingredients is long, the cooking time is short, and our way is easy.

1.

2.

PERFECT BEEF STROGANOFF

2-lb filet of beef
6 tablespoons butter or
    margarine
1 cup chopped onion
1 clove garlic, finely
    chopped
½ lb fresh mushrooms,
    sliced ¼ inch thick
3 tablespoons flour
2 teaspoons meat-extract
    paste
1 tablespoon catsup
½ teaspoon salt

⅛ teaspoon pepper
1 can (10½ oz) beef
    bouillon, undiluted
¼ cup dry white wine
1 tablespoon snipped fresh
    dill, or ¼ teaspoon
    dried dill weed
1½ cups dairy sour cream
1½ cups cooked wild rice
    tossed with 4 cups
    cooked white rice
Fresh dill or parsley,
    snipped

1. Trim fat from beef. Cut filet crosswise into ½-inch-thick slices. Cut each slice, across grain, into ½-inch-wide strips.

2. Slowly heat large, heavy skillet. In it, melt 2 tablespoons butter. Add just enough beef strips to cover skillet bottom. Over high heat, sear quickly on all sides. With tongs, remove beef as it browns. (It should be browned outside, rare inside.) Brown rest of beef; set aside.

3. In remaining hot butter in same skillet, sauté onion, garlic, and mushrooms until onion is golden—about 5 minutes. Remove from heat. Add flour, meat-extract paste, catsup, salt, and pepper; stir until smooth. Gradually add bouillon; bring to boiling, stirring. Reduce heat; simmer 5 minutes.

4. Over low heat, add wine, snipped dill, and sour cream, stirring until well combined. Add beef; simmer just until sauce and beef are hot.

5. Serve Stroganoff with rice. Sprinkle 2 tablespoons dill or parsley over top.

3.

4.

What is America's favorite meat? Ask any boy under ninety years of age (or ask any girl, for that matter) and probably you, too, will discover that it's some form of hamburger. So to satisfy the national hunger, we give you savory, delicious, irresistible forms of the hamburger.

BEEF TARTARE

2 lb ground round
½ cup finely chopped
    onion
½ cup capers, drained
8 anchovy fillets, finely
    chopped

4 egg yolks
1 teaspoon salt
⅛ teaspoon pepper
¼ cup finely chopped
    watercress

1. In large bowl and using 2 forks, lightly toss all ingredients until well combined.

2. Shape into 6 patties. Serve at once.

Note: Mixture may be shaped into ¾-inch balls, to serve as hors d'oeuvres.

BEEF-BALL STROGANOFF

Beef Balls:
1¾ lb ground chuck
1 teaspoon salt
¼ teaspoon pepper
½ teaspoon dried dill
   weed
4 teaspoons bottled steak
   sauce
⅓ cup packaged dry bread
   crumbs
1 egg
2 tablespoons butter
   or margarine

Sauce:
½ cup chopped onion
1 can (3 oz) sliced
   mushrooms, drained
2 tablespoons flour
½ teaspoon meat-extract
   paste
1 teaspoon catsup
1 can (10½ oz) beef
   bouillon, undiluted
1 cup dairy sour cream

1. Make Beef Balls: In large bowl, lightly toss chuck with salt, pepper, dill, steak sauce, bread crumbs, and egg until well combined.

2. Gently shape mixture into 18 balls, each about 2 inches in diameter.

3. In hot butter in large skillet, brown beef balls well all over. Reduce heat.

4. Simmer 8 minutes. Remove beef balls.

5. Make Sauce: In pan drippings, sauté onion and mushrooms 3 minutes. Remove from heat. Stir in flour, meat-extract paste, and catsup.

6. Gradually stir in bouillon; bring to boiling, stirring. Then add beef balls; simmer gently 5 minutes, or until heated through.

7. Stir in sour cream; cook, stirring and over low heat, 3 minutes, or until sauce is hot.

GOLDEN BEEF-POTATO PIE FOR A CROWD

1 cup evaporated milk,
   undiluted
½ cup canned tomato
   purée
1¾ cups raw quick-cooking
   oats
1 tablespoon monosodium
   glutamate
3 eggs
2 teaspoons salt
2 teaspoons dry mustard
¾ teaspoon pepper
½ teaspoon dried thyme
   leaves
⅔ cup finely chopped
   onion

3 lb ground chuck

Potato Topping:
2 large pkg (8-serving size)
   instant mashed
   potatoes
Milk
Butter or margarine
Salt
Pepper
¼ cup butter or margarine,
   melted
⅓ cup grated Parmesan
   cheese

1. Preheat oven to 350F.

2. In large bowl, combine milk, tomato purée, and oats, mixing well. Add monosodium glutamate, eggs, salt, mustard, pepper, thyme, and onion, mixing well.

3. Add chuck, stirring lightly, with fork, until thoroughly combined.

4. Turn into a 15½-by-10½-by-2¼-inch baking pan, spreading evenly; bake 30 minutes.

5. Meanwhile, make Potato Topping: Prepare mashed potatoes as package label directs, using amounts of milk, butter, salt, and pepper called for on label.

6. Swirl potatoes over meat; brush top with melted butter, and sprinkle with cheese. Bake 20 minutes.

7. Then, if desired, run under broiler, 4 inches from heat, until golden—about 1 minute. To serve: Cut into 12 squares. Serve topped with Creole Sauce.*

* See Sauces and Gravies Chapter.

SALISBURY STEAK

1½ lb ground chuck
¾ cup raw quick-cooking
   oats
¼ cup chopped onion

2 teaspoons salt
¼ teaspoon pepper
1 egg
½ cup tomato juice

1. Combine all ingredients in large bowl.

2. On rack of broiler pan, shape meat mixture to resemble 1½-inch-thick porterhouse steak.

3. Broil, 4 inches from heat; for medium-rare, broil 7 minutes on one side, 5 minutes on other.

SALISBURY STEAK À LA RITZ

MAKES 6 SERVINGS

1 egg white
½ cup dairy sour cream
½ teaspoon salt

1 tablespoon prepared
    horseradish
Salisbury Steak
Paprika

1. With rotary beater, beat egg white in small bowl until stiff. Gently fold in sour cream, salt, and horseradish until well combined.

2. Broil steak as in Salisbury Steak.

3. Then frost top with sour-cream mixture; place under broiler until golden-brown. Sprinkle with paprika. Serve at once.

ONION BURGERS

MAKES 6 SERVINGS

¼ cup butter or margarine
1 cup chopped celery
½ cup chopped onion
1 lb ground chuck
1 teaspoon chili powder
½ teaspoon salt
Dash pepper

1 teaspoon Worcestershire
    sauce
1 can (10½ oz) onion soup,
    undiluted
1 tablespoon flour
⅛ teaspoon paprika
6 hamburger buns, split

1. In 2 tablespoons hot butter in skillet, sauté celery and onion until golden—about 5 minutes. Add beef, chili powder, salt, and pepper; cook, stirring, until meat is browned.

2. Add Worcestershire and onion soup.

3. Combine flour and 1 tablespoon water, stirring until smooth.

4. Add to meat mixture; simmer, stirring, until heated through and slightly thickened—about 10 minutes.

5. Melt rest of butter with paprika. Use to brush split sides of buns. Toast under broiler. Top with meat mixture.

We know people who'd rather have meat loaf than filet mignon! For sheer eatability, for flavor, for gratifying variety (as our recipes will show you), for economy as well, you can't beat the meat loaf!

BAKED MUSHROOM MEAT LOAF

MAKES 6 TO 8 SERVINGS

1 can (3 oz) sliced
    mushrooms
Milk
2 eggs
½ cup chili sauce
1 teaspoon Worcestershire
    sauce
2 teaspoons salt
½ teaspoon dried thyme
    leaves

1 cup packaged dry bread
    crumbs
1½ lb ground chuck
½ lb ground pork
2 hard-cooked eggs, cut into
    8 wedges
1 tablespoon grated
    Parmesan cheese
1 tablespoon chopped
    parsley

1. Preheat oven to 350F.

2. Drain mushrooms well, reserving liquid; set mushrooms aside. Combine liquid with enough milk to make 1 cup.

3. In large bowl, beat eggs slightly with fork. Stir in milk mixture, chili sauce, Worcestershire, salt, thyme, and bread crumbs. With fork, lightly mix until bread crumbs are thoroughly moistened.

4. Add chuck and pork; mix just until well combined, using hands if necessary.

5. Place half the meat mixture in an 11-by-7-by-1½-inch baking dish. With moistened hands, shape into a 9½-by-5-inch rectangle.

6. Arrange egg wedges and mushroom slices over mixture; sprinkle with cheese and parsley. Top with remaining meat mixture.

7. Shape into a loaf; bake 1 to 1¼ hours. Remove to platter.

GLAZED MEAT LOAVES

1 egg
1 can (6 oz) evaporated
   milk, undiluted
1 cup soft white-bread
   crumbs
2 teaspoons salt
¼ teaspoon pepper

1 teaspoon dried marjoram
   leaves
1½ lb ground chuck

Glaze:
6 tablespoons apricot jam
1 teaspoon lemon juice

1. Preheat oven to 350F.
2. In large bowl, beat egg slightly with fork. Stir in milk, bread crumbs, salt, pepper, and marjoram. Add chuck; mix until combined, using hands if necessary.
3. With moistened hands, shape mixture into 4 to 6 individual loaves.
4. Place in a 15½-by-10½-by-1-inch jelly-roll pan; bake 30 minutes.
5. Meanwhile, make Glaze: In small bowl, combine apricot jam and lemon juice; mix well.
6. Brush tops and sides of meat loaves with glaze; bake 10 minutes longer. Remove to platter.

MEAT-LOAF "MUFFINS"

1 egg
½ cup milk
¾ cup soft white-bread
   crumbs

1½ teaspoons salt
¼ teaspoon pepper
1 lb ground chuck

1. Preheat oven to 350F.
2. In large bowl, beat egg slightly with fork. Stir in milk, bread crumbs, salt, and pepper. Add chuck; mix thoroughly.
3. Spoon into 6 (3-inch) muffin-pan cups. With spatula, round tops to resemble muffins.
4. Bake 30 minutes. Remove to platter. Serve with Mushroom Beef Gravy.*
* See Sauces and Gravies Chapter.

ROAST MEAT LOAF

2 eggs
1 cup milk
¾ cup raw quick-cooking
   oats
1 tablespoon salt
1 teaspoon monosodium
   glutamate
½ teaspoon dried savory
   leaves
¼ teaspoon pepper
1 tablespoon chopped
   parsley

1 tablespoon butter or
   margarine
½ cup coarsely chopped
   onion
2½ lb ground chuck

Glaze:
½ cup chili sauce
2 tablespoons brown sugar
¼ teaspoon dry mustard
½ teaspoon liquid
   gravy seasoning

1. In large bowl, beat eggs slightly with fork. Stir in milk, oats, salt, monosodium glutamate, savory, pepper, and parsley; set aside.
2. In hot butter in skillet, sauté onion until tender—about 5 minutes.
3. Add to egg mixture along with chuck; mix until well combined, using hands if necessary.
4. Line a 9-by-5-by-3-inch loaf pan with waxed paper. Turn meat mixture into pan, packing down well; refrigerate, covered, at least 2 hours.
5. Preheat oven to 350F.
6. Run spatula around edge of meat loaf, to loosen. Carefully turn out into shallow baking pan, keeping original shape as much as possible; bake 30 minutes.
7. Meanwhile, make Glaze: In small bowl, combine all ingredients, mixing well. Brush top and sides of meat loaf with glaze.
8. Bake 45 minutes, brushing several times with glaze. Remove to platter.

Proteins are proteins, and nutrition is nutrition, no matter what price you pay for the meat you buy. It's what you do with it that distinguishes the low-cost meat-and-potatoes dish from the festive, elegant company meal. Our recipes show you how to go grand at low prices.

BEEF À LA DEUTSCH

MAKES 6 SERVINGS

2 lb chuck, well trimmed
1 teaspoon instant meat
   tenderizer
¼ cup butter or margarine
¼ lb mushrooms, thickly
   sliced; or 1 can (3 oz)
   sliced mushrooms,
   drained
½ cup sliced green pepper

½ cup sliced onion
1 can (10½ oz) beef
   bouillon, undiluted
1 teaspoon salt
⅛ teaspoon pepper
3 tablespoons flour
1½ cups dairy sour cream
¼ cup chopped pimiento

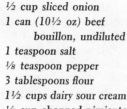

1. Cut chuck into ½-inch-thick slices. Thoroughly moisten one side of each. Sprinkle with tenderizer; pierce with fork. Repeat on other side.

2. In hot butter in large, heavy skillet, sauté beef until browned all over. Remove, and set aside.

3. In same skillet, sauté mushrooms, green pepper, and onion until onion is golden—about 5 minutes.

4. Stir in bouillon, salt, and pepper, along with beef; simmer, uncovered, stirring occasionally, until beef is tender—about 35 minutes.

5. Meanwhile, combine flour and ½ cup sour cream. Stir into beef mixture; bring to boiling, stirring. Mixture will be thickened.

6. Reduce heat. Stir in rest of sour cream and the pimiento. Heat gently until sauce is thoroughly hot.

LONDON BROIL

MAKES 4 TO 6 SERVINGS

2-lb flank steak, U.S. Prime
   or Choice*
1 tablespoon salad oil
1 teaspoon lemon juice
1 teaspoon salt

⅛ teaspoon pepper
1 clove garlic, crushed
2 teaspoons chopped
   parsley
Mushroom Sauce**

1. With sharp knife, trim excess fat from steak. Wipe steak with damp paper towels.

2. Combine oil with lemon juice, salt, pepper, garlic, and parsley. Use half of mixture to brush top of steak.

3. Place steak on lightly greased rack in broiler pan; broil, 4 inches from heat, 5 minutes. Turn; brush with rest of oil mixture; broil 3 to 5 minutes longer.

4. To serve: Slice very thinly, on diagonal, across the grain. Serve the Mushroom Sauce with it.

* To ensure tenderness, use unseasoned meat tenderizer, following package directions and omitting salt.

** See Sauces and Gravies Chapter.

ROLLED, STUFFED FLANK STEAK

MAKES 4 TO 6 SERVINGS

1½-lb flank steak, U.S.
   Prime or Choice*
3 tablespoons butter or
   margarine
½ cup chopped celery
2 tablespoons chopped
   onion
2½ cups white-bread cubes
1 teaspoon dried parsley
   flakes

½ teaspoon salt
¼ teaspoon poultry
   seasoning
¼ teaspoon dried
   marjoram leaves
⅛ teaspoon pepper
1 can (3 oz) sliced
   mushrooms,
   undrained
1½ tablespoons flour

1. Wipe steak with damp paper towels. With sharp knife, trim excess fat. Score surface in diamond pattern, ⅛ inch deep, on both sides.

2. Melt 2 tablespoons butter in Dutch oven or top-stove casserole. Add celery and onion; sauté until tender—about 5 minutes. Remove from heat.

3. Add bread cubes, parsley, salt, poultry seasoning, marjoram, and pepper, tossing lightly with fork until well mixed.

4. Place this stuffing lengthwise down center of steak. Starting at narrow end, roll up steak; secure with skewers.

5. Preheat oven to 350F.

6. Melt remaining butter in Dutch oven. In it, brown steak well on all sides—8 to 10 minutes in all.

7. Spoon mushrooms and their liquid over top; bake, covered, 1½ hours, or until steak is tender. Remove steak to heated platter; keep warm.

8. Pour mushrooms and liquid from Dutch oven into bowl; skim off fat from surface. Measure 1 cup liquid, and return to Dutch oven.

9. Combine flour and 2 tablespoons water, stirring to make a smooth paste. Then stir into liquid, to combine well. Bring mixture to boiling; reduce heat, and simmer 2 minutes.

10. To serve: Slice steak crosswise. Pour gravy over it.

* To ensure tenderness, use unseasoned meat tenderizer, following package directions and omitting salt.

BRAISED SHORT RIBS

MAKES 4 SERVINGS

3½ lb short ribs, in serving-
   size pieces
2 tablespoons flour
1 tablespoon salad oil or
   shortening

2 teaspoons salt
⅛ teaspoon pepper
1 bay leaf

1. Wipe short ribs with damp paper towels. Roll in flour, coating evenly on all sides.

2. Slowly heat large, heavy skillet or Dutch oven. Add oil; heat. In this, brown short ribs well on all sides—about 20 minutes in all.

3. Add rest of ingredients along with ¾ cup water; bring to boiling. Reduce heat; simmer, covered, 2 to 2½ hours, or until meat is fork-tender.

4. Skim fat from surface of liquid in skillet. Serve short ribs with pan liquid.

POLYNESIAN SHORT RIBS

MAKES 4 SERVINGS

Braised Short Ribs with ½
    cup cooking liquid
1 tablespoon salad oil
¾ cup sliced onion
1½ cups sliced celery (on
    diagonal)
1½ cups slivered green
    pepper
1 can (1 lb, 4½ oz)
    pineapple chunks

¼ cup sugar
1 teaspoon monosodium
    glutamate
½ teaspoon salt
¼ teaspoon ginger
1 tablespoon soy sauce
1 tomato, cut in eighths
1 tablespoon cornstarch

1. Remove meat from bones; cut into cubes.

2. Slowly heat salad oil in large, heavy skillet. In it, brown meat, turning, on all sides—about 5 minutes in all. Remove meat, and set aside.

3. In same skillet, sauté onion, celery, and pepper 5 minutes, or until tender.

4. Drain pineapple, reserving ½ cup liquid.

5. Stir pineapple into vegetables along with meat, the ½ cup cooking liquid, and rest of ingredients, except ¼ cup pineapple liquid and the cornstarch. Cook, covered, 5 minutes.

6. In small bowl, combine cornstarch and remaining ¼ cup pineapple liquid, stirring until smooth.

7. Pour into skillet; bring to boiling, stirring. Mixture will be thickened and translucent. Nice served with white rice.

CORNED BEEF AND CABBAGE

MAKES 6 TO 8 SERVINGS

4- to 5-lb corned-beef
    brisket
1 medium clove garlic
1 medium yellow onion,
    halved
2 whole cloves

10 whole black peppers
2 bay leaves
¼ teaspoon mustard seed
1 medium head cabbage,
    cut into wedges

1. Wipe corned beef with damp paper towels. Place in large kettle; cover with cold water. Add remaining ingredients, except cabbage.

2. Bring to boil. Reduce heat; simmer 5 minutes. Skim.

3. Cover; continue to simmer 3 to 4 hours, or until fork-tender.

4. Add cabbage last 15 minutes of simmering time.

5. To serve: Remove corned beef and cabbage from liquid. Slice corned beef; arrange on platter with cabbage wedges.

New England Boiled Dinner: Add 6 medium carrots, pared and quartered; 6 medium white turnips or parsnips, pared and quartered; and 6 medium potatoes, pared and quartered, to Corned Beef and Cabbage during last 25 minutes of cooking.

PERFECT CORNED-BEEF HASH

4 medium potatoes
    (1½ lb), cooked and
    peeled*
1 can (12 oz) corned beef
½ cup chopped onion
1 teaspoon salt

¼ teaspoon pepper
1 teaspoon monosodium
    glutamate
¼ cup butter or margarine
Catsup or chili sauce

1. Finely chop potatoes, corned beef, and onion together.

2. In large bowl, combine mixture with salt, pepper, and monosodium glutamate; mix well.

3. Slowly heat butter in large skillet.

4. Turn hash mixture into skillet, patting down firmly with spatula or pancake turner.

5. Over medium heat, cook hash, uncovered, about 15 minutes, or until a brown crust forms on bottom.

6. Loosen edges; fold in half, like an omelet. Turn out on serving platter. Serve with catsup.

* Use either boiled or baked potatoes.

POT ROAST

6- to 7-lb brisket of beef
½ teaspoon salt
⅛ teaspoon pepper
2 medium onions

2 medium carrots
2 celery stalks
1 large tomato

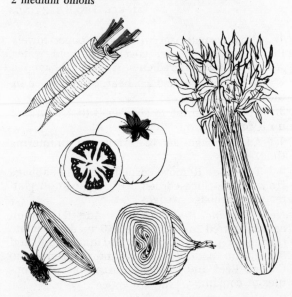

1. Preheat oven to 350F.

2. Sprinkle beef with salt and pepper; place in large skillet. Brown meat on fat side only, over high heat.

3. While meat is browning, prepare vegetables. Slice onions very thin. Pare carrots; cut carrots and celery in 1-inch pieces. Peel tomato, and cut it in chunks.

4. When meat is well browned, remove from skillet; place in roasting pan or large Dutch oven.

5. Add onions to skillet; sauté until golden.

6. Spoon onions over meat; surround meat with prepared vegetables. Add 1 cup water.

7. Roast, covered, 2½ to 3 hours, or until meat is tender.

8. Remove roast to serving platter; keep warm while preparing gravy.

9. Make gravy: Strain pan juices to remove vegetables. Press vegetables through food mill. Skim fat from pan juices.

10. Add vegetables to pan juices; heat thoroughly. Pass along with roast.

BRAISED CHUCK STEAK WITH VEGETABLES

3½- to 4-lb chuck steak,
   1½ inches thick
¼ cup unsifted all-purpose
   flour
1 tablespoon shortening
2 teaspoons salt
⅛ teaspoon pepper
⅛ teaspoon ginger

½ cup chopped onion
½ cup chopped celery
¼ teaspoon liquid gravy
   seasoning (optional)
4 carrots, pared and
   quartered
1 rutabaga, pared and
   cut up (4 cups)

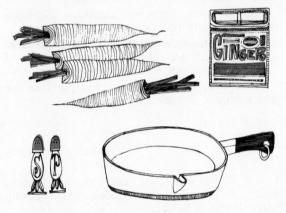

1. Wipe steak with damp paper towels. Roll in 2 tablespoons flour, coating evenly on both sides.
2. Slowly heat large, heavy skillet or Dutch oven. Add shortening; heat. In it, brown steak well on both sides, turning with tongs—15 to 20 minutes in all.
3. Add salt, pepper, ginger, onion, celery, and 1 cup water; bring to boiling. Reduce heat; simmer, covered, 1½ hours, or until meat is fork-tender.
4. Add gravy seasoning, carrots, and rutabaga; bring to boiling. Reduce heat; simmer, covered, 30 minutes, or until vegetables are tender.
5. Remove steak and vegetables to heated platter; keep warm.
6. Pour pan liquid into bowl; skim off fat from surface; measure liquid. For each cup liquid, combine 2 tablespoons flour and ¼ cup water, stirring to make a smooth paste; then stir into liquid to combine well.
7. Return to skillet; bring to boiling. Reduce heat; simmer 2 minutes. Pour over steak.

BROWNED SWISS STEAK

1¼-lb round steak, 1½
   inches thick
3 tablespoons flour
2 tablespoons salad oil or
   shortening
½ cup chopped onion
½ cup grated carrot
2 tablespoons chopped
   parsley

1 teaspoon salt
⅛ teaspoon pepper
¼ teaspoon dried thyme
   leaves
2 bay leaves
3 whole cloves
½ teaspoon liquid gravy
   seasoning

1. Wipe steak with damp paper towels. Roll it in 2 tablespoons flour, coating evenly on both sides.
2. Slowly heat large, heavy skillet. Add oil; heat. In it, brown steak well on both sides, turning with tongs—15 to 20 minutes in all.
3. Add rest of ingredients, except remaining flour, along with 1 cup of water; bring to boiling. Reduce heat; simmer, covered, 2 to 2½ hours, or until meat is fork-tender.
4. Combine rest of flour with ¼ cup water in small bowl, stirring until smooth.
5. Stir into liquid in skillet; bring to boiling. Reduce heat, and simmer 5 minutes.

Swiss Steak With Tomatoes: Prepare and brown Swiss Steak as above. Add 1 can (1 lb, 3 oz) tomatoes (undrained) along with rest of ingredients, except 1 tablespoon flour; omit 1 cup water. Finish cooking as above.

CHUCK-STEAK BROIL

MAKES 4 SERVINGS

3½-lb chuck steak, 1½
    inches thick
Unseasoned meat tenderizer
2 large tomatoes, halved
    crosswise
4 teaspoons packaged
    seasoned dry bread
    crumbs

Butter or margarine
1 pkg (10 oz) thawed
    frozen peas
Salt
Pepper
1 packet (4-serving size)
    instant mashed
    potatoes

1.   Wipe steak with damp paper towels. Sprinkle both sides with meat tenderizer as package label directs.

2.   Place in a 13-by-9-by-2-inch metal baking pan; broil, 5 inches from heat, 10 to 15 minutes, depending on desired doneness. Drain excess fat.

3.   Turn steak; arrange tomato halves around it. Sprinkle each tomato half with 1 teaspoon bread crumbs; then dot with butter.

4.   Spoon peas between tomatoes. Sprinkle lightly with salt and pepper; dot with butter.

5.   Prepare mashed potatoes as package label directs. Spoon potatoes along inside edge of baking pan (or put through pastry bag).

6.   Broil 8 to 10 minutes, or until potatoes are golden-brown. Serve right from pan.

SIRLOIN TIPS EN BROCHETTE

MAKES 8 SERVINGS

¼ cup soy sauce
½ cup sherry
1 can (10½ oz) beef
    bouillon, undiluted
1 clove garlic, split

1½ teaspoons ginger
2 lb sirloin tips, cut into
    1½-inch cubes
1 tablespoon cornstarch
White Rice With Onions*

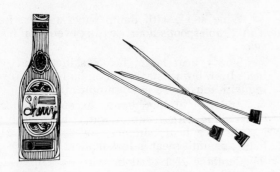

1.   In small saucepan, combine soy sauce, sherry, bouillon, garlic, ginger, and ¼ cup water; bring to boiling.

2.   Reduce heat; simmer, uncovered, 5 minutes. Remove from heat; discard garlic. Let mixture cool to room temperature.

3.   In shallow baking dish, marinate sirloin cubes in soy-sauce mixture 2½ hours, turning occasionally.

4.   Drain cubes, reserving ¾ cup soy-sauce mixture.

5.   Thread cubes on 8 skewers (4 or 5 cubes each). Place skewers across shallow pan, so ends rest on its sides.

6.   In small saucepan, combine reserved soy-sauce mixture with cornstarch; mix well. Bring to boiling, stirring. Reduce heat; simmer, stirring, until thickened and translucent.

7.   Use to brush cubes on all sides, reserving some of sauce for later use.

8.   Broil, 4 inches from heat, about 3 minutes, or until browned. Turn; brush again with soy-sauce mixture. Broil 3 minutes longer, or until nicely browned.

9.   Place a skewer on rice on each plate. Spoon rest of soy-sauce mixture over cubes.

* See Cereals Chapter.

BEEF ROULADES

3 lb beef round, sliced
    ¼ inch thick
2 large dill pickles
Salt
Pepper
6 bacon slices, halved
    crosswise

¾ cup chopped onion
2 tablespoons salad oil
1 can (10½ oz) beef
    bouillon, undiluted
½ teaspoon caraway seed
Flour

1. Cut beef into 12 rectangles, each about 4 by 3 inches. Cut each pickle into 6 lengthwise strips.

2. Sprinkle beef lightly with salt and pepper. Place pickle strip at narrow end of rectangle; then top with bacon strip and 1 tablespoon onion.

3. Roll up beef; tie each with twine.

4. In Dutch oven, or heavy skillet with tight-fitting cover, slowly heat salad oil. In hot oil, brown roulades, turning on all sides, until nicely browned—10 to 15 minutes. (Brown only as many roulades at one time as will cover bottom of Dutch oven.) As they brown, remove roulades to another pan; continue until all are browned. Pour off oil.

5. Return roulades to Dutch oven. Pour bouillon over all. Add caraway seed.

6. Bring to boiling, covered. Reduce heat, and simmer very slowly about 2 hours, or until tender.

7. Remove roulades to serving platter. Remove twine; keep warm.

8. Measure liquid in Dutch oven. For each cup liquid, mix 1½ tablespoons flour with 3 tablespoons water, forming a smooth mixture. Stir into liquid in Dutch oven. Bring to boiling, stirring. Reduce heat, and simmer until thickened.

9. Pour gravy over roulades. Serve with buttered noodles, if desired.

How to Store Frankfurters

Leave them in their original package, or wrap them loosely in waxed paper, saran, or foil. Keep in refrigerator. Use within 3 to 4 days, for peak flavor.

How to Heat Frankfurters

Simmered: Drop frankfurters into a kettle of boiling water. Cover. Remove from heat, or keep heat so low the water never boils. Heat 5 to 8 minutes. Remove with tongs. Never break skins with a fork.

Pan-Broiled: Melt a tablespoon of fat in skillet or griddle. Add frankfurters, and heat, over low temperature, until brown on all sides. Use tongs as a turning tool.

Broiled: Rub each frankfurter with butter, margarine, or salad oil. Arrange on broiler rack, and broil, 3 inches from heat, until evenly browned.

Campfire Grilled: Let the fire burn down to glowing coals. Put frankfurters on long forks or green sticks, and grill over coals until brown.

Pork

Pork is good enough for family or parties. Whenever it is in great abundance, it is one of the best buys in the market. The flesh of good pork is a soft gray-pink, and the fat is white. Remember: Pork must be cooked very thoroughly.

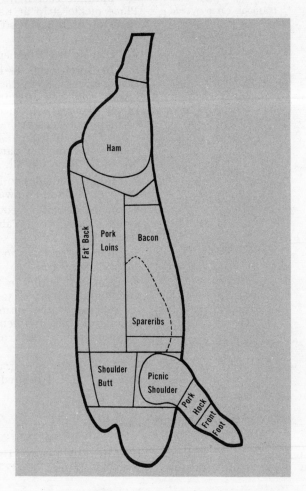

PORK BUYING AND COOKING GUIDE

Whole Ham (Roast; braise)
Fat Back (Salt pork and lard)
Loin Chop (Braise; pan-broil; pan-fry)
Rib Chop (Braise; pan-broil; pan-fry)
Rib and Loin Roast (Roast)
Boston Butt (Roast)
Boned Rolled Butt (Roast)

Shoulder Steak—Round Bone or Blade Bone
  —from Shoulder Butt (Braise)
Picnic (Roast)
Hock (Simmer)
Foot (Simmer)
Spareribs (Braise; roast; simmer)
Bacon (Broil; pan-broil)

TIMETABLE FOR ROASTING FRESH PORK—AT 325F

Cut	Weight	Internal Temperature	Approximate Roasting Time (hours)
Fresh Ham	10 to 14 lb	185F	6 to 7
Fresh Ham (half)	5 to 6 lb	185F	3½ to 4
Loin	4 to 5 lb	185F	3¼ to 3½
Loin End	2½ to 3 lb	185F	2¼ to 2½
Shoulder Butt	4 to 6 lb	185F	3½ to 4

Just the smell of bacon frying is enough to set your mouth watering. And when you taste it, its promise is fulfilled. Wonderful cooked with vegetables, as a side dish with eggs, or as part of a bacon, lettuce and tomato sandwich. 16% of a pig is bacon. A lot of people wish the percentage were higher.

Pan-Fried: Start bacon in cold skillet. Cook, over moderate heat, turning frequently. Remove bacon from pan when desired doneness is reached. Drain on paper towels.

Baked (an ideal method for large quantities): Start oven at 400F, or hot. Use broiling pan and rack, or cake rack over a shallow baking pan. Put bacon on rack over drip pan. (No need to separate slices now.) Bake 5 minutes; then pull slices slightly apart, if necessary, and bake 5 minutes longer. (No need to watch or turn.) Drain on paper towels if crispness is desired.

Broiled: Separate slices; arrange on rack. Broil, 6 inches from heat, 3 to 4 minutes. Turn; broil 1 minute. Drain on paper towels.

GLAZED SMOKED SHOULDER BUTT

MAKES 6 TO 8 SERVINGS

3 lb fully cooked smoked boneless shoulder butt, sliced 1 inch thick

1 can (9 oz) crushed pineapple, undrained

¼ cup light-brown sugar, firmly packed

¼ teaspoon cinnamon

⅛ teaspoon cloves

¼ teaspoon dry mustard

2 tablespoons vinegar

3 maraschino cherries, quartered

1. Preheat oven to 375F.
2. Place butt slices, overlapping, in a 12-by-8-by-2-inch baking dish.
3. Add ½ cup water; bake, uncovered, 30 minutes. Drain off liquid.
4. Meanwhile, combine rest of ingredients in small saucepan; bring to boiling. Reduce heat, and simmer 2 minutes, stirring.
5. Pour over meat; bake 30 minutes. Serve pork slices with the glaze spooned over.

BAKED STUFFED PORK CHOPS

4 rib pork chops, 1 inch
   thick, with pocket
1 tablespoon butter or
   margarine
½ cup diced celery
2 tablespoons minced
   onion

1 cup day-old bread cubes
1 cup diced unpared apple
¼ cup seedless raisins
Dash pepper
¼ teaspoon rubbed sage
1½ teaspoons salt
½ cup apple juice

1. Wipe chops well with damp paper towels.
2. In hot butter in medium skillet, cook celery and onion until tender—about 8 minutes.
3. Remove from heat. Add bread cubes, apple, raisins, pepper, sage, and 1 teaspoon salt; toss lightly with fork to combine. Use mixture to fill pockets in chops.
4. Preheat oven to 350F.
5. In large, heavy skillet, slowly brown chops well on both sides—about 15 minutes in all.
6. Remove chops to 2-quart casserole. Sprinkle with remaining salt; pour on apple juice.
7. Bake, covered, about 1¼ hours, or until chops are tender. Serve with sauce spooned over.

ORANGE-BRAISED PORK CHOPS

6 loin pork chops, 1 inch
   thick
2 tablespoons flour
½ teaspoon salt
2 tablespoons salad oil or
   shortening

1 tablespoon light-brown
   sugar
⅛ teaspoon ginger
1 tablespoon grated orange
   peel
1 cup orange juice
1 cup orange sections

1. Wipe chops with damp paper towels. Coat with mixture of flour and salt.
2. In hot oil in large skillet, brown chops well on both sides—about 10 minutes on each side.
3. Combine remaining ingredients, except orange sections. Pour over chops; cover.
4. Reduce heat; simmer 45 to 50 minutes, or until chops are fork-tender.
5. Add orange sections just before serving.

Orange-Braised Lamb Shanks: Use six lamb shanks (5 lb), cracked, instead of pork chops. Double all other ingredients. Then proceed as above, except simmer lamb shanks 1½ to 2 hours. Makes 6 Generous Servings.

SAVORY STUFFED
PORK CHOPS

6 rib pork chops, 1 inch
   thick, with pocket
½ cup chopped onion
½ cup chopped celery
½ cup grated carrot
½ cup chopped green
   pepper

1 tablespoon butter or
   margarine, melted
1 teaspoon salt
½ teaspoon dried thyme
   leaves
¼ teaspoon pepper
⅔ cup sherry

1. Wipe pork chops well with damp paper towels. Trim off excess fat.
2. In medium skillet, sauté vegetables in butter until onion is tender—about 3 minutes. Remove from heat.
3. Add ½ teaspoon salt, ¼ teaspoon thyme, ⅛ teaspoon pepper, and 1 tablespoon sherry; toss to combine well. Use to fill pockets in chops.
4. In large, heavy skillet, slowly brown chops well on both sides—20 minutes in all.

MEAT

Proteins are proteins, and nutrition is nutrition, no matter
what price you pay for the meat you buy. It's what you do
with it that distinguishes the low-cost meat-and-potatoes
dish from the elegant company meal. Here, you'll find the

POPULAR POULTRY
It doesn't have to be that regal bird pictured above (a turkey, of course); it can be the smallest Cornish hen. No matter what kind, poultry is popular, making any meal a time for thanksgiving.

(Savory Stuffed Pork Chops continued)

5. Sprinkle on half of remaining seasonings. Add rest of sherry.

6. Reduce heat; simmer, covered, 25 minutes. Turn; sprinkle on rest of seasonings. Simmer, covered, 20 minutes, or until well done.

7. Skim fat from pan juices; pour juices over chops.

MAKES 4 SERVINGS

WINE-BRAISED PORK CHOPS

4 rib pork chops, 1 inch thick (1½ lb)	2 teaspoons salt
1 medium green pepper, sliced crosswise	¼ teaspoon pepper
	2 medium tomatoes, quartered
1 clove garlic, crushed	⅓ cup white wine
½ lb fresh mushrooms, sliced through stem; or 1 can (6 oz) sliced mushrooms, drained	

1. Wipe chops with damp paper towels.

2. Slowly heat large, heavy skillet. Brown chops well—10 minutes on each side. Remove.

3. Drain all but ½ tablespoon fat from skillet. Add green pepper, garlic, and mushrooms; sauté, stirring, about 5 minutes.

4. Place chops on green pepper. Sprinkle with salt and pepper; top with tomatoes and wine.

5. Simmer slowly, covered, 40 to 45 minutes, or until chops are tender. Serve with wine sauce.

MAKES 8 SERVINGS

PARTY CROWN ROAST OF PORK WITH APPLE STUFFING

4¾-lb crown roast of pork	¼ cup butter or margarine, melted
2¼ teaspoons salt	
½ teaspoon pepper	2 tablespoons light-brown sugar
4½ tablespoons flour	
1 cup diced, unpared tart apple	1 teaspoon grated lemon peel
2½ cups toasted bread cubes	¼ teaspoon paprika
	¼ teaspoon cinnamon
¼ cup seedless raisins, soaked	¼ cup apple juice
	½ teaspoon liquid gravy seasoning
¼ cup chopped cooked prunes	

1. Preheat oven to 325F.

2. Wipe meat well with damp paper towels.

3. Combine 1 teaspoon salt, ¼ teaspoon pepper, and 2 tablespoons flour; rub meat well with mixture.

4. Insert meat thermometer into center of fleshy part of meat, away from fat and bone. Place roast in shallow roasting pan, without rack; roast 1 hour and 15 minutes.

5. Meanwhile, prepare stuffing. In large bowl, toss apple, bread cubes, raisins, prunes, butter, sugar, lemon peel, paprika, cinnamon, apple juice, and ½ teaspoon salt.

6. Remove roast from oven. Spoon stuffing lightly into center cavity, mounding it. Cover stuffing with 10-inch square of foil.

7. Return roast to oven; roast 1 hour and 25 minutes, or until meat thermometer registers 185F. Place roast on heated platter; keep warm while making gravy.

8. In small saucepan, blend 2 tablespoons pan drippings with 2½ tablespoons flour.

9. Stir in 1½ cups water, gravy seasoning, ¾ teaspoon salt, and ¼ teaspoon pepper; cook, over medium heat and stirring constantly, until mixture boils and thickens. Serve with roast.

BREADED PORK CUTLETS

1 lb lean loin pork cutlets
1 egg, slightly beaten
½ cup packaged seasoned
    dry bread crumbs

2 tablespoons salad oil
1 can (10½ oz) condensed
    cream-of-mushroom
    soup, undiluted

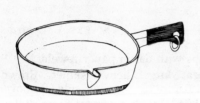

1. Wipe cutlets with damp paper towels. Pound very thin—about ⅛ inch—with mallet or edge of plate.
2. Dip cutlets into egg, then into bread crumbs, to coat well.
3. Slowly heat oil in large skillet. Sauté cutlets, over medium heat, until golden on both sides—15 minutes in all.
4. Combine soup with ¾ cup water; stir to mix well.
5. Add to cutlets. Reduce heat; simmer, covered, 20 minutes. Serve cutlets with sauce.

FRESH PORK HOCKS WITH SAUERKRAUT

4 fresh pork hocks (3½ lb)
½ teaspoon salt
1 bay leaf

1 can (1 lb, 11 oz)
    sauerkraut, undrained
1 teaspoon caraway seed
1 pared tart cooking apple,
    cut into wedges

1. In large kettle, combine pork hocks, salt, and bay leaf with water to cover—about 1 quart. Bring to boiling; simmer, covered, 2½ hours.
2. Add remaining ingredients; cook, uncovered, about 15 minutes longer, or until meat is tender.
3. To serve: With slotted spoon, remove to serving platter.

ROAST PORK WITH HERB GRAVY

3½-lb loin of pork
1 tablespoon finely chopped
    onion
2 tablespoons flour
1 teaspoon salt
⅛ teaspoon pepper
1 teaspoon dried sage leaves

¼ teaspoon dried thyme
    leaves
¼ teaspoon dried oregano
    leaves
¼ teaspoon liquid gravy
    seasoning

1. Preheat oven to 325F.
2. Wipe pork with damp paper towels. Place pork, fat side up, in shallow roasting pan. (Omit rack; pork will rest on bones.) Insert meat thermometer into center of meaty part of pork; it should not rest against bone.
3. Roast 2½ to 3 hours, or to 185F on meat thermometer. Remove to heated platter; keep warm.
4. Pour off fat from pan (leaving any meat juices in pan). Return 1 tablespoon fat to pan.
5. Add onion; sauté, stirring and over direct heat, about 3 minutes, or until onion is golden. Remove from heat.
6. Stir in flour, to form a smooth mixture. Stir in rest of ingredients.
7. Gradually add 1½ cups water; bring to boiling, stirring—mixture will be thickened and smooth.
8. Reduce heat; simmer 2 minutes. Serve gravy with pork.

BAKED PORK LOAF

1¾ cups soft white-bread
    crumbs
½ cup milk
1 egg, slightly beaten
2 tablespoons finely
    chopped onion
1 tablespoon chopped
    parsley
2 lb ground pork

1½ teaspoons salt
⅛ teaspoon pepper
1 teaspoon monosodium
    glutamate
½ teaspoon dried
    marjoram leaves
1 can (8 oz) tomato sauce
¼ teaspoon dried oregano
    leaves

1. Preheat oven to 375F.
2. In large bowl, combine bread crumbs with milk; let stand several minutes.
3. Then add rest of ingredients, except tomato sauce and oregano; mix well.
4. With moistened hands, shape mixture into a loaf in shallow baking dish.
5. Bake, uncovered, 1¼ hours. Remove to serving platter.
6. Heat tomato sauce with oregano. Serve with pork loaf.

MAPLE-BARBECUED SPARERIBS

1½ cups maple syrup
2 tablespoons chili sauce
2 tablespoons cider vinegar
1½ tablespoons finely
    chopped onion
1 tablespoon
    Worcestershire sauce

1 teaspoon salt
½ teaspoon dry mustard
⅛ teaspoon pepper
3 lb spareribs, cut in
    serving-size pieces

1. Preheat oven to 350F.
2. In medium bowl, combine maple syrup with rest of ingredients, except spareribs; mix well.
3. Wipe spareribs with damp paper towels. Brush on both sides with maple basting sauce.
4. Place ribs, in single layer, on rack in shallow, open roasting pan. Roast 1½ hours, or until tender, brushing frequently with sauce and turning occasionally, to glaze evenly.

PORK-AND-SAUERKRAUT GOULASH

2-lb boneless pork-shoulder
    roast, trimmed
2 cups chopped onion
1 clove garlic, finely
    chopped
1 teaspoon dried dill weed
1 teaspoon caraway seed

1 tablespoon salt
1 beef-bouillon cube
½ cup boiling water
1 tablespoon paprika
1 can (1 lb, 11 oz)
    sauerkraut, drained
2 cups dairy sour cream

1. Cut pork into 2-inch cubes.
2. In large Dutch oven or heavy kettle, combine pork, onion, garlic, dill, caraway seed, salt, bouillon cube, and boiling water.
3. Bring to boiling. Reduce heat, and simmer, covered, 1 hour.
4. Add paprika; stir until dissolved. Add sauerkraut; mix well.
5. Simmer, covered, until meat is tender—1 hour longer.
6. Stir in sour cream; heat thoroughly.

Let's have glazed ham. Let's serve the ham with fresh asparagus hollandaise and tiny new potatoes in their jackets; endive-and-tomato salad; and pineapple sherbet, say, for dessert. Let's keep having it, hot or cold—in casseroles, patties, sandwiches—until nothing's left but a scrap for pea soup.

TIMETABLE FOR BAKING HAM—AT 325F

Type	Weight	Internal Temperature	Approximate Baking Time (hours)
Fully Cooked Ham:			
Bone-in whole ham	8 to 12 lb	130F	2¼ to 2¾
Bone-in whole ham	14 to 18 lb	130F	3 to 3½
Bone-in half ham	6 to 8 lb	130F	2 to 2¼
Boneless whole ham	8 to 10 lb	130F	2½ to 3
Boneless quarter or half ham	2½ to 5 lb	130F	1½ to 1¾
Cook-before-Eating-Ham:			
Bone-in whole ham	8 to 12 lb	155F	2¾ to 3¼
Bone-in whole ham	14 to 18 lb	155F	3½ to 4
Bone-in half ham	6 to 8 lb	155F	2 to 2½

GINGER-GLAZED BAKED HAM

MAKES 12 SERVINGS

7- to 8-lb fully cooked,
  bone-in ham butt
6 cups unsifted all-purpose
  flour
2 tablespoons ginger
1 tablespoon ground cloves
½ teaspoon salt

Glaze:
1 cup ginger ale
1 cup orange juice
½ cup light-brown sugar,
  firmly packed
1 tablespoon ginger
1 tablespoon grated orange
  peel
About 24 whole cloves

1. Preheat oven to 325F.

2. Wipe ham with damp paper towels.

3. In large bowl, combine flour, ginger, cloves, and salt; mix well. Gradually add 2 cups cold water, mixing well with fork.

4. On lightly floured board, mold dough around top and side of ham until they are evenly covered.

5. Place on rack in shallow roasting pan; insert meat thermometer in center away from bone. Bake until internal temperature is 130F—about 2 hours.

6. Meanwhile, make Glaze: Combine ingredients in small saucepan; bring to boiling, stirring.

7. Reduce heat; simmer, uncovered and stirring occasionally, 40 to 60 minutes. (Glaze should measure 1 cup.)

8. Remove pastry covering from ham, and discard.

9. With sharp knife, lift off skin. In outside fat layer, make diagonal cuts, 1¼ inches apart, to form a diamond pattern. Stud center of each diamond with a whole clove.

10. Brush ham well with glaze; bake 25 minutes, brushing twice more. Ham will be shiny and glazed.

MAPLE-GLAZED BAKED HAM

MAKES ABOUT 20 SERVINGS

8- to 10-lb fully-cooked
    boneless ham
Whole cloves
¾ cup light-brown sugar,
    firmly packed

1 cup dark corn syrup
2 tablespoons prepared
    mustard
1 tablespoon maple
    flavoring

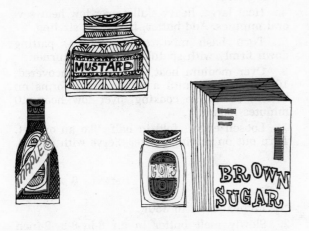

1. Preheat oven to 325F.
2. Place ham, fat side up, on rack in shallow, open roasting pan. Insert meat thermometer in center. Bake, uncovered, 2½ to 3 hours, or until internal temperature is 130F. Remove from oven.
3. To glaze: Turn oven temperature to 450F. Take out meat thermometer; carefully remove rind from ham.
4. With tip of knife, cut fat into diamond pattern; do not cut into ham. Insert a clove in each diamond.
5. In bowl, mix rest of ingredients. Spread half of glaze over ham; bake 10 minutes.
6. Put on rest of glaze; bake 10 minutes.
7. For easy slicing, let ham stand 20 minutes.

BAKED VIRGINIA HAM

MAKES ABOUT 24 SERVINGS

10- to 12-lb country-style
    Virginia ham
Whole cloves
1 cup dark-brown sugar,
    firmly packed

1 teaspoon dry mustard
3 tablespoons pineapple
    juice
1 tablespoon cider vinegar

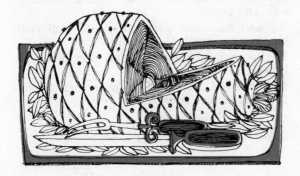

1. Cover ham completely with cold water; let stand 24 hours.
2. Next day, scrub ham with stiff brush. Rinse well in cold water.
3. In large kettle, cover ham with cold water; bring to boiling. Reduce heat; simmer, covered, 4 to 5 hours, or until ham is almost tender.
4. Remove from heat; let cool in liquid.
5. Meanwhile, preheat oven to 325F.
6. Remove cooled ham from liquid; carefully remove skin and excess fat.
7. With tip of knife, cut fat into diamond pattern; do not cut into ham. Insert a clove in each diamond.
8. Place ham, on rack, in shallow roasting pan. Insert meat thermometer in center, away from bone.
9. Bake, uncovered, 2½ hours.
10. Combine remaining ingredients; spread over ham.
11. Bake 15 minutes longer, or until internal temperature is 155F. For easy slicing, let stand 20 minutes.

BROWNED HAM HASH

2 cups cut-up cooked ham
1 cup cut-up pared raw
    potato
1 cup coarsely chopped
    onion
¼ cup coarsely chopped
    green pepper

⅛ teaspoon pepper
⅛ teaspoon dry mustard
1 can (8¾ oz)
    cream-style corn
¼ cup butter or margarine
Catsup or chili sauce

1.   In large bowl, lightly toss ham with potato, onion, and green pepper.

2.   Put mixture through coarse blade of food grinder.

3.   Combine with pepper, mustard, and corn, mixing well.

4.   Heat large, heavy skillet over low heat several minutes. Add butter; heat until sizzling.

5.   Turn hash mixture into skillet, patting down firmly with spatula or pancake turner.

6.   Over medium heat, cook hash, uncovered, 10 minutes, or until a brown crust forms on bottom. Continue cooking, over low heat, 10 minutes longer.

7.   Loosen edges; fold in half, like an omelet. Turn out on serving platter. Serve with catsup.

UPSIDE-DOWN HAM LOAF

1 tablespoon butter or
    margarine
½ cup dark-brown sugar,
    firmly packed
1 can (13½ oz) crushed
    pineapple
3 maraschino cherries,
    quartered
Milk
1 egg

1 cup soft white-bread
    crumbs
2 tablespoons prepared
    mustard
1 teaspoon salt
⅛ teaspoon pepper
1½ lb fully cooked smoked
    ham, ground
½ lb pork, ground

1.   Preheat oven to 350F.

2.   Slowly melt butter in an 8-by-8-by-2-inch pan, over low heat. Stir in sugar until smooth; remove from heat.

3.   Drain pineapple well, reserving liquid. Spread pineapple evenly over sugar mixture in pan.

4.   Arrange cherries in a pretty design on pineapple; set aside.

5.   Combine pineapple liquid with enough milk to measure 1 cup.

6.   In large bowl, beat egg slightly with fork. Stir in milk mixture, bread crumbs, mustard, salt, and pepper.

7.   Add ham and pork; mix until well combined, using hands if necessary.

8.   Spoon meat mixture evenly over pineapple in pan; bake 1 hour.

9.   Drain off excess liquid. Invert loaf on platter, so pineapple is on top.

Glazes For Baked Ham

HOT CRANBERRY GLAZE

1 can (7 oz) jellied
    cranberry sauce
    (⅔ cup)

⅓ cup dark corn syrup
1 tablespoon vinegar

1.   Combine all ingredients in small saucepan.

2.   Cook, over low heat, stirring, until sauce is melted and mixture is smooth.

BURGUNDY GLAZE AND SAUCE

MAKES 2 CUPS

1 can (1 lb, 1 oz) pitted
    Bing cherries
¾ cup liquid from cherries
2 tablespoons cornstarch

¾ cup Burgundy
2 tablespoons wine vinegar
¼ cup light corn syrup
2 teaspoons lemon juice

1. Drain cherries, reserving ¾ cup liquid.
2. In small saucepan, combine cherry liquid and cornstarch, stirring until mixture is smooth.
3. Add Burgundy, vinegar, and corn syrup; bring to boiling, over medium heat, stirring.
4. Stir in lemon juice. Glaze will be thickened and translucent.
5. Measure ½ cup glaze; use to glaze ham.
6. Add cherries to rest of glaze. Just before serving, heat slowly. Use as sauce for baked ham.

ORANGE-MARMALADE GLAZE

MAKES ABOUT 1½ CUPS

½ cup orange marmalade
1 cup dark corn syrup

2 teaspoons dry mustard

In small bowl, combine all ingredients, stirring until well mixed. Use to glaze ham.

PINEAPPLE GLAZE

MAKES ABOUT 1½ CUPS

1 cup pineapple juice
1 tablespoon cornstarch
⅓ cup light corn syrup

¼ cup light-brown sugar,
    firmly packed

1. In small saucepan, combine ¼ cup pineapple juice and the cornstarch; stir till smooth.
2. Add remaining pineapple juice and rest of ingredients; bring to boiling, stirring, over medium heat. Glaze will be slightly thickened and translucent.

RED-CURRANT-JELLY GLAZE

MAKES ABOUT 1 CUP

1 cup red-currant jelly
2 tablespoons dark corn
    syrup

1 teaspoon dry mustard
1 tablespoon white vinegar

1. Combine all ingredients in small saucepan.
2. Cook, over low heat, stirring, until jelly is melted and mixture is smooth.

Pork and Ham Accompaniments

FRIED APPLE RINGS

MAKES 6 SERVINGS

3 large red apples

3 tablespoons butter
    or margarine

1. Wash and core apples; trim ends. Cut each crosswise into 4 slices.
2. Heat butter in large skillet.
3. Sauté apple rings just until tender—4 to 5 minutes—turning them once.

GRILLED APPLE RINGS

3 large cooking apples
¼ cup butter or
    margarine, melted
½ teaspoon lemon juice
1 tablespoon sugar
¼ teaspoon cinnamon

1. Preheat griddle.
2. Wash and core apples; cut each into 4 crosswise slices.
3. Combine 2 tablespoons butter and the lemon juice. Use to brush both sides of apple rings.
4. Grill about 1½ minutes, or until golden on underside; add more butter as needed. Turn; grill 1½ minutes longer, or until tender.
5. While rings are still on grill, sprinkle with sugar combined with cinnamon. Serve with pork, sausage, ham, or bacon.

SAUTÉED BANANAS AND PINEAPPLE

4 large medium-ripe
    bananas
¼ cup butter or
    margarine, melted
1 can (1 lb, 4½ oz)
    pineapple chunks,
    drained
¼ cup light-brown sugar,
    firmly packed
Cinnamon

1. Peel bananas; slice crosswise into 1-inch chunks.
2. Place in butter in large skillet. Add pineapple. Sprinkle sugar over top; then sprinkle very lightly with cinnamon.
3. Cook, over low heat, until fruit is hot.

C omes spring, comes lamb. But this light, tender meat is available all year round, although we'll admit it is especially appealing when the days turn warmer. Broiled, braised, roasted, stewed, served hot, or served in cold, thin slices, lamb has more than taste and texture to recommend it, for it abounds in precious vitamins and minerals.

TIMETABLE FOR ROASTING LAMB—AT 325F

Cut	Weight	Internal Temperature	Approximate Roasting Time (hours)
Leg (whole)	6 to 7 lb	175 to 180F	3½ to 3¾
Leg (half)	3 to 4 lb	175 to 180F	3 to 3½
Boned Rolled Shoulder	4 to 6 lb	175 to 180F	3 to 4
Bone-in, Stuffed	4 to 5 lb	175 to 180F	2½ to 2¾

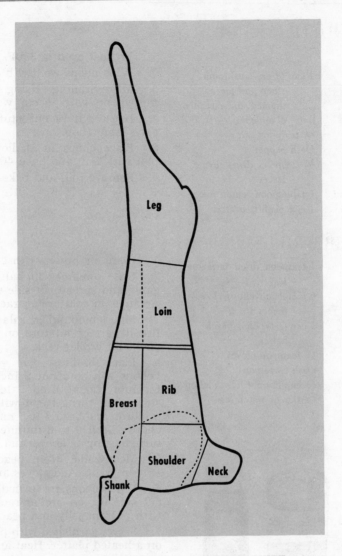

LAMB BUYING AND COOKING GUIDE

Whole Leg of Lamb (Roast)
Shank Half of Leg (Roast)
Butt Half of Leg (Roast) (Center-cut steaks, broil)
Loin Chops (Broil; pan-broil. English Chops and Rolled Loin Roast are made from this cut.)
Breast (Braise; stew. Whole breast may be roasted)
Riblets from Breast (Braise; stew)

Shanks (Braise; stew)
Square-Cut Shoulder (Roast)
Rolled Shoulder (Roast)
Round-Bone Shoulder Chop (Braise)
Blade-Bone Shoulder Chop (Braise)
Neck (Stew)
Rib Chops (Broil; pan-broil. French Chops and Crown Roasts are made from this cut.)
Stew Meat (Braise; stew)

STUFFED SHOULDER LAMB CHOPS

*4 shoulder lamb chops,
      1 inch thick, with
      pocket*

Stuffing:
*1½ cups packaged
      stuffing mix*
*2 tablespoons butter
      or margarine, melted*

*1 can (4 oz) mushroom
      stems and pieces,
      drained and coarsely
      chopped*
¼ teaspoon salt
Dash pepper
*¼ teaspoon dried thyme
      leaves*
1 tablespoon lemon juice
1 egg, slightly beaten

1. Preheat oven to 350F.

2. Wipe chops well with damp paper towels.

3. Make Stuffing: Using hands, blend stuffing ingredients with ⅓ cup water.

4. Use about ½ cup stuffing to fill pocket in each lamb chop.

5. Place chops in shallow, open pan. Cover pan with foil, and bake 40 minutes.

6. Remove foil, and bake 10 minutes longer.

BROILED LAMB GRILL

*6 tablespoons soft butter
      or margarine*
*3 tablespoons grated
      Parmesan cheese*
3 firm tomatoes
*1½ teaspoons dried
      oregano leaves*
¼ cup lemon juice
½ cup salad oil

*1 teaspoon dried tarragon
      leaves*
*6 loin lamb chops, 1½
      inches thick*
*1 can (1 lb) cling-peach
      halves*
¼ teaspoon cloves
Dash cinnamon
⅓ cup currant jelly, melted
Parsley or watercress

1. Combine butter with cheese.

2. Slice tomatoes in half. Sprinkle with oregano, and spread cut side with cheese mixture. Arrange on cold broiler rack.

3. Mix lemon juice, salad oil, and tarragon. Brush part of mixture on chops, and arrange chops on broiler rack.

4. Place broiling pan 4 inches from heat (chops will be about 2 inches from heat). For medium chops: Broil 5 to 6 minutes on first side; then turn; baste with more lemon-juice mixture, and broil 4 to 5 minutes. For well-done chops: Broil 6 to 8 minutes on first side; then turn, basting as above, and broil 5 to 7 minutes.

5. Meanwhile, drain peach halves, reserving ⅓ cup syrup. Add cloves and cinnamon.

6. When chops are turned, place peach halves, cut side up, on broiler rack. Brush generously with currant jelly and peach syrup.

7. Serve, garnished with parsley or watercress, on a heated platter. Heat any remaining lemon-juice mixture, and pour it over chops.

LEG OF LAMB

6-lb leg of lamb
1 clove garlic, slivered
½ cup salad oil
2 cups dry red wine
3 onions, sliced
¼ teaspoon cloves

*2 teaspoons dried oregano
      leaves*
2 teaspoons salt
1 carrot, sliced
3 sprigs parsley

1. Wipe lamb with damp paper towels. Using paring knife, make several small pockets in flesh, and insert garlic slivers.

2. Combine remaining ingredients, to make marinade. In large, shallow glass baking dish, arrange lamb as flat as possible. Pour marinade over it.

3. Refrigerate, covered, at least 24 hours, turning lamb occasionally.

4. Preheat oven to 325F.

(Leg of Lamb continued)

5. Place lamb, fat side up, on rack in shallow roasting pan. In fleshy part, away from bone or fat, insert meat thermometer.
6. Roast, uncovered and basting occasionally with marinade, about 2½ hours, or to 175F on meat thermometer, for medium.
7. Let roast stand 20 minutes before carving, for easier slicing. If desired, some of the marinade may be heated, to pass with roast.

ROAST LEG OF LAMB, SWEDISH STYLE

4- to 4½-lb leg of lamb
2 teaspoons salt
¼ teaspoon pepper
¾ cup black coffee
1 tablespoon light cream

2 teaspoons sugar
2 tablespoons flour
About 1½ cups milk
2 teaspoons currant jelly

MAKES 6 TO 8 SERVINGS

1. Preheat oven to 350F.
2. Wipe lamb with damp cloth; rub with salt and pepper.
3. Place lamb, fat side up, on rack in shallow roasting pan. Insert meat thermometer in fleshy part, away from bone or fat. Roast, uncovered, 1½ hours.
4. Combine coffee, cream, and sugar; pour over lamb. Roast, basting occasionally, about 1 hour, or to 175F on thermometer, for medium.
5. Remove lamb to heated platter. For easier slicing, let stand in warm place 20 minutes before carving.
6. Meanwhile, make gravy: Strain pan drippings. Skim off fat, and measure 2 tablespoons fat into roasting pan.
7. Stir in flour until smooth; cook, stirring, over low heat about 1 minute, to brown flour.
8. Pour pan drippings into 2-cup measure. Add milk to make 2 cups. Gradually stir into flour mixture; bring to boiling, stirring.
9. Remove from heat; add currant jelly. Serve gravy hot, with lamb.

RACK OF LAMB

2-lb rack of lamb
1 teaspoon salt

¼ cup orange marmalade
¼ cup lemon juice

MAKES 2 OR 3 SERVINGS

1. Preheat oven to 300F.
2. Cover tip of each rib bone with aluminum foil, to prevent scorching. Rub lamb with salt. Insert meat thermometer in fleshy part, away from bone or fat.
3. Place lamb, fat side up, on rack in shallow roasting pan; roast, uncovered, 30 minutes.
4. Mix marmalade with lemon juice. Brush half of glaze on lamb.
5. Roast lamb, uncovered, 30 minutes; then brush with rest of glaze. For medium lamb: Roast 15 minutes more, or until meat thermometer reads 175F. For well-done lamb: Roast 30 minutes more, or until thermometer reads 180F.
6. To serve, replace foil tips with paper frills.

LAMB RING WITH CURRIED RICE

1 egg
1 cup milk
1 cup packaged dry bread crumbs
1 cup grated raw carrot
1 tablespoon chopped parsley
1 tablespoon lemon juice
1 tablespoon salt
½ teaspoon garlic powder
½ teaspoon poultry seasoning
¼ teaspoon pepper
2½ lb ground lamb

1. In large bowl, beat egg slightly with fork. Stir in milk. Add remaining ingredients; mix well, using hands if necessary.
2. Line bottom of a 1½-quart ring mold with waxed paper. Turn meat-loaf mixture into mold, packing down well.
3. Refrigerate, covered, at least 2 hours.
4. Meanwhile, preheat oven to 350F.
5. Run spatula around edges of meat loaf, to loosen. Turn out onto a 13-by-9-by-2-inch pan.
6. Bake 1 hour. Remove to serving platter.
7. Fill center with Curried Rice,* mounding it high. Garnish platter with remaining rice.
* See Cereals Chapter.

LEMONY LAMB SHANKS

4 lamb shanks
5 tablespoons flour
1 teaspoon salt
½ teaspoon pepper
½ teaspoon paprika
2 tablespoons shortening or salad oil
2 tablespoons grated lemon peel
½ cup lemon juice
2 bay leaves
4 whole black peppers
1 clove garlic

1. For quicker cooking and easier serving, have meatman crack bone in lamb shanks.
2. Combine 4 tablespoons flour, the salt, pepper, and paprika. Coat lamb with this mixture.
3. Heat shortening in Dutch oven or heavy skillet. Add lamb shanks; brown, turning.
4. Add 1½ cups water and rest of ingredients, except remaining flour; bring to boil. Then reduce heat; cover, and simmer slowly 1½ to 2 hours, or until lamb is tender. Transfer to serving platter, and keep warm.
5. Skim fat from liquid in pan. Make a smooth paste of remaining flour and ¼ cup water.
6. Blend into pan liquid; cook, stirring, until gravy boils and is thick; pour over shanks.

Sure cure for menu monotony: Ring in a welcome change of pace with a savory, sophisticated veal dish, subtle in flavor, smooth in texture. Veal, you know, can be as juicy and delicate as chicken and so tender you can cut it with a fork, whether it's a shank, steak, or shoulder—*if* you follow our suggestions for cooking.

TIMETABLE FOR ROASTING VEAL—AT 325F

Cut	Weight	Internal Temperature	Approximate Roasting Time (hours)
Leg (center cut)	7 to 8 lb	170F	3 to 3½
Loin	4½ to 5 lb	170F	2½ to 3
Boned Rolled Shoulder	5 to 6 lb	170F	3½ to 4
Boned Rolled Shoulder	3 lb	170F	3

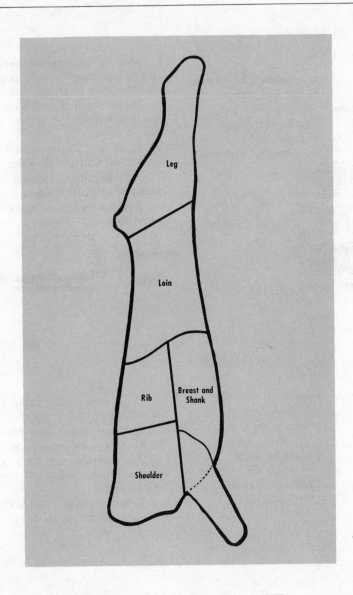

Leg

Loin

Rib

Breast and Shank

Shoulder

VEAL BUYING AND COOKING GUIDE

Center Cut of Leg (Braise)
Round Steak from Leg (Braise)
Sirloin Steak from Leg (Braise)
Rolled Rump from Leg (Braise)
Standing Rump from Leg (Braise)
Loin Chop (Braise)
Rib Chop (Braise)
Blade-Bone Shoulder Steak (Braise)
Arm-Bone Shoulder Steak (Braise)

Blade-Bone Pot Roast from Shoulder (Braise)
Arm-Bone Pot Roast from Shoulder (Braise)
Rolled Shoulder Roast (Braise; may be roasted)
Breast (Braise; stew; whole breast may be roasted)
Riblets from Breast (Braise; stew)
Stew Meat from Breast (Braise; stew)

415

VEAL BIRDS WITH BREAD STUFFING

6 tablespoons butter
    or margarine
1 cup finely chopped onion
3 cups soft bread crumbs
1 teaspoon salt
⅛ teaspoon pepper

¼ teaspoon dried dill weed
12 thin veal scallops
    (1½ lb)
2 tablespoons flour
¾ cup canned beef
    bouillon, undiluted

1. Melt 4 tablespoons butter in large skillet. Add onion, crumbs, salt, pepper, and dill; cook, over medium heat, stirring, about 2 minutes.
2. Place about 2 tablespoons stuffing on each veal slice; roll up; secure with wooden pick. Roll in flour.
3. Heat remaining butter in skillet; brown veal birds well on all sides.
4. Add bouillon; simmer, covered, 30 to 35 minutes, or until tender.
5. Remove wooden picks. Spoon pan juices over birds.

BRAISED VEAL CHOPS

6 veal chops, cut 1½ inches
    thick
1½ teaspoons salt
¼ teaspoon pepper
⅓ cup salad oil
½ cup chopped onion
¾ cup sliced raw carrots

1 can (8 oz) tomatoes,
    undrained
⅓ cup dry sherry or
    chicken bouillon
1 can (6 oz) sliced
    mushrooms, drained
2 tablespoons chopped
    parsley

1. Wipe chops with damp paper towels. Sprinkle with salt and pepper.
2. In large skillet, over medium heat, heat oil. Brown chops on both sides, with onion.
3. Add carrots, tomatoes, and sherry. Reduce heat; simmer, covered, 1 hour, or until meat is fork-tender.
4. Remove cover. Add mushrooms and parsley; heat 5 minutes. Serve chops with sauce.

VEAL POT ROAST

4½-lb veal rump roast
1 tablespoon dry mustard
1 teaspoon poultry
    seasoning
2 tablespoons light-brown
    sugar
1 tablespoon salt

¼ teaspoon pepper
1 tablespoon flour
3 tablespoons salad oil
1 bay leaf
3 tablespoons cider vinegar
⅔ cup sliced onion

1. Wipe roast with damp paper towels.
2. In small bowl, combine mustard, poultry seasoning, sugar, salt, pepper, and flour. Rub well into roast.
3. Heat oil in medium Dutch oven. In it, brown roast well on all sides.
4. Add remaining ingredients and ¼ cup water.
5. Cover; simmer 2½ hours, or until fork-tender, turning twice during cooking.

BAKED VEAL LOAF

2 eggs
¾ cup milk
½ cup catsup
1 cup packaged cracker meal
½ cup chopped stuffed olives
2 teaspoons salt

1 teaspoon monosodium glutamate
¼ teaspoon pepper
1 tablespoon butter or margarine
¼ cup coarsely chopped onion
1½ lb veal, ground
½ lb pork, ground

1. Preheat oven to 350F.
2. In large bowl, beat eggs slightly with fork. Stir in milk, catsup, cracker meal, olives, salt, monosodium glutamate, and pepper; set aside.
3. In hot butter in skillet, sauté onion until tender—about 5 minutes.
4. Add to egg mixture along with veal and pork. Mix just until well combined, using hands if necessary.
5. With moistened hands, shape into loaf in 2-quart flat baking dish; bake, uncovered, 1¼ hours. Remove to platter. Serve with Quick Mushroom Gravy.*
* See Sauces and Gravies Chapter.

VEAL PAPRIKA

2½-lb veal cutlet, cut ½ inch thick
1 teaspoon salt
⅛ teaspoon pepper
¼ cup salad oil

Sauce:
3 tablespoons butter or margarine
¼ cup chopped onion

1 clove garlic, minced
¼ cup unsifted all-purpose flour
1 tablespoon paprika
½ teaspoon salt
1 can (10½ oz) beef bouillon, undiluted
¼ cup dry white wine
¼ cup dairy sour cream
1 tablespoon lemon juice

1. Wipe cutlet with damp paper towels. Cut into serving pieces. With mallet or edge of plate, pound thin. Season with salt and pepper.
2. In hot oil in large skillet, sauté veal until golden.
3. Meanwhile, make Sauce: Melt butter in medium skillet. In it, sauté onion and garlic until onion is limp—about 5 minutes. Remove from heat.
4. Blend in flour, paprika, and salt. Stir in bouillon, 1 cup water, and wine; cook, over low heat and stirring, until thickened—about 5 minutes.
5. Add sour cream and lemon juice; cook just until heated.
6. Place browned cutlets on heated serving dish. Pour paprika sauce over them.

ROAST LEG OF VEAL

4- to 5-lb boneless leg of veal
2 cloves garlic, peeled and split

1 teaspoon salt
¼ teaspoon pepper
2 tablespoons soy sauce
6 slices bacon

1. Preheat oven to 325F.
2. Wipe roast with damp paper towels. Rub it well with garlic; season with salt and pepper; brush with soy sauce. Arrange bacon to cover top.
3. Place veal on rack in shallow roasting pan. Insert meat thermometer into thickest part of meat.
4. Roast 2½ hours, or until thermometer registers 155 to 160F.

VEAL SHOULDER WITH PRUNE STUFFING

3 tablespoons butter
    or margarine

1 large onion, finely
    chopped

1 small clove garlic, finely
    chopped

2 cups fresh bread crumbs

1 can (8¾ oz) crushed
    pineapple, drained

¾ cup cooked prunes,
    pitted and diced

4- to 5-lb boned shoulder of
    veal, with pocket

1 teaspoon salt

¼ teaspoon pepper

1 teaspoon dried tarragon
    or thyme leaves

2 or 3 veal bones

1 small onion, peeled

2 cups dry white wine

1. In 2 tablespoons hot butter in small skillet, sauté chopped onion and garlic until onion is golden—about 5 minutes.

2. In medium bowl, add onion and garlic to crumbs, pineapple, and prunes. Toss to mix well.

3. Wipe veal well with damp paper towels. Rub with salt and pepper.

4. Spoon stuffing into pocket. Roll up; close with skewers or string.

5. In remaining butter in 3-quart Dutch oven, brown roast well on all sides. Sprinkle with tarragon. Add veal bones, small onion, and wine.

6. Reduce heat; cook, covered, 1½ to 2 hours, or until tender.

7. Place roast on hot platter; remove skewers or string. Keep hot. Make gravy as in note, below.

Note: To make gravy: Pour pan juices into small bowl or 1-quart measure. Skim off fat. Measure 2 cups juices. Melt 2 tablespoons butter or margarine in small saucepan. Remove from heat. Stir in 3 tablespoons flour and 2 cups juices; bring to boiling, stirring. Serve with roast.

APPLE-STUFFED VEAL ROLLS

6 tablespoons butter or
    margarine

1 cup finely chopped onion

2½ cups soft bread cubes

1 cup coarsely chopped
    pared apple*

1 teaspoon salt

½ teaspoon poultry
    seasoning

12 thin veal scallops
    (about 1½ lb)

2 tablespoons flour

¾ cup apple cider or
    juice

1. Melt 4 tablespoons butter in large skillet. Add onion; sauté, stirring often, until golden—about 5 minutes.

2. Add bread, apple, salt, and poultry seasoning, cook, stirring, over medium heat, about 4 minutes.

3. Place 1 heaping tablespoon stuffing on each veal slice; roll up; secure with wooden pick.

4. Roll in flour. Heat remaining butter in skillet; brown rolls well on all sides.

5. Add cider; simmer, covered, 30 to 35 minutes, or until tender.

6. Remove picks; spoon juices over veal.

* Or use 1 cup canned apple slices, drained and chopped.

VEAL SHANKS

6 (¾- to 1-lb size) veal shanks
½ cup unsifted all-purpose flour
1½ teaspoons salt
¼ teaspoon pepper
⅓ cup salad oil
1 clove garlic, minced
¾ cup coarsely chopped onion
1 cup sauterne or chicken bouillon
1 can (8 oz) tomato sauce
1½ teaspoons dried basil leaves
⅓ cup chopped parsley
1 tablespoon grated lemon peel

1. Wipe veal with damp paper towels. On waxed paper, combine flour, salt, and pepper; rub well into veal.
2. Heat oil slowly in large, heavy skillet with cover, over medium heat. Brown veal completely, turning often.
3. Add garlic and onion toward end of browning; sauté with veal until onion is golden.
4. Add sauterne, tomato sauce, and basil. Reduce heat; simmer, covered, 1 hour, or until meat is fork-tender.
5. Remove cover. Add parsley and lemon peel; stir well.

VEAL SAUTÉ MARENGO

Boiling water
4 medium tomatoes (about 2 lb)
⅓ cup salad oil
3½ lb thin veal scallops
1 cup chopped onion
1 clove garlic, finely chopped
2 teaspoons salt
⅛ teaspoon pepper
1 teaspoon dried basil leaves
1 tablespoon cornstarch
1½ cups dry white wine
½ cup beef bouillon
2 tablespoons butter or margarine
½ lb fresh mushrooms, sliced
Parsley sprigs

1. Pour boiling water over tomatoes to cover; let stand 1 minute; drain. Cover with cold water; remove skins.
2. Cut tomatoes in half, crosswise. Remove seeds; discard with any juice. Coarsely chop firm flesh of tomatoes. Measure 3 cups tomatoes; set aside.
3. In large skillet with tight-fitting cover, slowly heat 2 tablespoons salad oil. Sauté scallops, a few at a time, until nicely browned—about 5 minutes on each side—adding rest of oil as needed. Remove from skillet; set aside.
4. In same skillet, sauté onion about 3 minutes. Stir in tomatoes, garlic, salt, pepper, and basil; simmer, covered, 5 minutes. Remove from heat.
5. Combine cornstarch with 1 tablespoon cold water. Add to mixture in skillet along with wine and bouillon, mixing well.
6. Bring to boiling, stirring. Boil 3 to 4 minutes, stirring occasionally, or until sauce is thickened.
7. Meanwhile, in hot butter in small skillet, sauté mushrooms until tender—about 5 minutes.
8. Add mushrooms to sauce; simmer 1 minute.
9. Then add veal; simmer, covered, 5 minutes.
10. Serve veal with sauce spooned over. Garnish with parsley sprigs.

In Europe, the so-called variety meats are much better known than they are here. Kidney, sweetbreads, calves' brains, tongue, and the others, well prepared and interestingly seasoned, are a gourmet's delight abroad. We are sure our recipes will make many converts on this side of the ocean. And a good thing, too, because these meats are remarkably high in food value, and many are remarkably low in price. So let variety meats give variety to your family table.

BASIC METHOD FOR COOKING BRAINS

MAKES 4 SERVINGS

1 lb brains
1 teaspoon salt

1 tablespoon lemon juice

1.   In large saucepan, bring 1 quart water to boiling.
2.   Add brains, salt, and lemon juice; return to boiling. Reduce heat, and simmer, covered, 20 minutes.
3.   Drain; plunge into cold water.
4.   Remove outer membrane and veins. Prepare as desired.

SCRAMBLED EGGS AND BRAINS

MAKES 4 SERVINGS

1 lb veal brains, cooked*
3 tablespoons butter
    or margarine
6 eggs, slightly beaten
6 tablespoons milk

1 teaspoon dried parsley
    flakes
½ teaspoon salt
¼ teaspoon pepper
Chopped parsley

1.   Cut brains into uniform pieces.
2.   In hot butter in large skillet, sauté brains until nicely browned—3 to 5 minutes.
3.   In medium bowl, combine eggs, milk, parsley flakes, salt, and pepper, mixing well.
4.   Pour over brains in skillet. Cook, over medium heat, stirring occasionally with fork, until eggs are cooked but still shiny and moist—3 to 5 minutes.
5.   Turn out onto serving platter; sprinkle with chopped parsley.
* Cook according to Basic Method for Cooking Brains.

CREAMED HEART ON BISCUITS

MAKES 4 SERVINGS

1-lb pork or lamb heart
1 tablespoon salad oil
¼ cup lemon juice
1 teaspoon salt
1 teaspoon sugar
¼ teaspoon pepper

¼ teaspoon dried oregano
    leaves
2 tablespoons flour
½ cup evaporated milk,
    undiluted
4 hot biscuits, split

1.   Remove excess fat and large blood vessels from heart. Wash heart well; dry with paper towels. Cut into 1-inch cubes.
2.   In jar with tight-fitting lid, combine salad oil, lemon juice, salt, sugar, pepper, and oregano with ½ cup water; shake vigorously to combine.
3.   Pour over heart cubes in medium bowl. Refrigerate, covered, several hours or overnight.

(Creamed Heart on Biscuits continued)

4. In medium saucepan, bring heart cubes and marinade to boiling. Reduce heat, and simmer, covered, 1½ hours, or until heart is tender. Remove from heat.

5. In small bowl, blend flour with milk.

6. Gradually add to heart mixture, mixing well. Bring to boiling, stirring. Reduce heat, and simmer, covered, 5 minutes. Serve hot over biscuits.

MAKES 6 SERVINGS

STUFFED VEAL HEARTS

2 (1½-lb size) veal hearts
Salt
Pepper
10 dried prunes, pitted
2 medium apples, pared
    and thinly sliced

2 tablespoons butter or
    margarine
1 teaspoon sugar
½ cup light cream

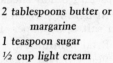

1. Split hearts lengthwise down one side. Remove excess fat and large blood vessels. Wash hearts well; dry with paper towels. Sprinkle with salt and pepper.

2. Stuff each heart cavity with 5 prunes and as many apple slices as possible.

3. Close opening with skewers.

4. In hot butter in heavy skillet or Dutch oven, brown hearts on both sides. Remove from heat.

5. Add remaining apple slices, ¾ teaspoon salt, the sugar, and 1 cup water; mix well.

6. Bring to boiling. Reduce heat, and simmer, covered, 1½ hours, or until hearts are tender.

7. With slotted utensil, remove hearts to heated serving platter; remove skewers. Slice, and keep warm.

8. Add cream to mixture in skillet, mixing well. Reheat gently. Pass along with heart.

MAKES 4 SERVINGS

BRAISED LAMB KIDNEYS

8 lamb kidneys (1 lb)
¼ cup butter or margarine
1 cup sliced green pepper
    (about 1)
½ cup sliced onion
½ cup beef bouillon
1 teaspoon salt

⅛ teaspoon pepper
1 can (3 oz) sliced
    mushrooms
1 tablespoon flour
¼ cup sherry
Cooked white rice

1. Remove fat and white veins from kidneys; cut each in 4 or 6 pieces. Rinse well, and dry with paper towels.

2. In hot butter in large skillet, sauté green pepper and onion until tender—about 5 minutes. Remove; set aside.

3. In same skillet, sauté kidneys until nicely browned—about 5 minutes. Remove from heat. Stir in bouillon, salt, and pepper.

4. Drain mushrooms, reserving liquid. Add mushrooms, green pepper, and onion to skillet; simmer, uncovered, 15 minutes.

5. Add reserved mushroom liquid to flour, stirring until smooth. Add to mixture in skillet, mixing well. Bring to boiling, stirring; boil 2 minutes.

6. Remove from heat; stir in sherry. Serve over rice.

421

MIXED GRILL

4 English kidney chops,
1 inch thick
4 Bermuda-onion slices,
½ inch thick
Melted butter or margarine
Salt
Pepper

Paprika
2 tomatoes, halved
2 tablespoons grated sharp
Cheddar cheese
¼ teaspoon curry powder
4 fresh mushroom caps
4 bacon slices

1. Wipe chops with damp paper towels. Arrange chops and onion slices on broiler pan. Brush with butter; sprinkle with salt and pepper. Sprinkle onion slices with paprika.
2. Broil, 4 inches from heat, 15 minutes.
3. Brush tomato halves with butter; sprinkle with salt and pepper. Top each with some of Cheddar cheese combined with curry powder.
4. Arrange tomatoes on broiler rack. Turn chops and onion slices; broil 10 minutes.
5. Brush mushroom caps with butter; sprinkle with salt and pepper. Place on broiler rack.
6. Broil 3 minutes.
7. Place bacon slices on broiler rack. Broil, turning bacon once, 3 or 4 minutes longer, or until bacon is crisp.
8. On each of 4 heated plates, arrange a chop, onion slice, tomato half, mushroom cap, and bacon slice.

BRAISED LIVER

1 lb beef or pork liver,
sliced ½ inch thick
¼ cup unsifted all-purpose
flour
2 tablespoons butter or
margarine

¼ cup chopped carrot
¼ cup chopped celery
¼ cup chopped onion
1 teaspoon salt
⅛ teaspoon pepper

1. Coat liver well with flour.
2. In hot butter in large skillet, sauté liver until nicely browned—3 minutes on each side.
3. Add remaining ingredients along with ¾ cup water.
4. Bring to boiling. Reduce heat, and simmer, covered, 20 to 30 minutes, or until liver and vegetables are tender.

BROILED LIVER

1 lb calves' or lambs' liver,
sliced ½ inch thick
Melted butter or margarine

Salt
Pepper

1. Brush liver with melted butter; sprinkle with salt and pepper.
2. Broil, 3 inches from heat, 3 minutes on each side.

PAN-FRIED LIVER

¼ cup unsifted all-purpose
flour
½ teaspoon salt
⅛ teaspoon pepper

1 lb calves' or lambs' liver,
sliced ½ inch thick
2 tablespoons butter or
margarine

1. Combine flour, salt, and pepper on sheet of waxed paper. Roll liver in mixture, coating well.
2. Melt butter in large skillet. Sauté liver until nicely browned—about 5 minutes on each side.

LIVER IN WINE

2 lb lambs' liver, sliced ¼ inch thick
½ cup bottled Italian-style dressing
¼ cup unsifted all-purpose flour
6 bacon slices
2 cups sliced onion
1 can (3 oz) sliced mushrooms
Dry white wine
1 teaspoon salt
⅛ teaspoon pepper
1 teaspoon grated lemon peel
2 tablespoons chopped parsley

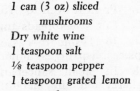

MAKES 6 TO 8 SERVINGS

1. In shallow dish, marinate liver in Italian dressing. Refrigerate, covered, several hours or overnight. Turn occasionally.
2. Drain; coat well with flour.
3. Preheat oven to 325F.
4. In large skillet, sauté bacon until crisp. Drain on paper towels; crumble, and set aside.
5. Add onion to skillet; sauté until tender—about 5 minutes. Remove, and set aside.
6. In same skillet, sauté liver, a few slices at a time, until golden—about 3 minutes on each side. As liver browns, remove to an 8-by-8-by-2-inch baking dish. Reserve drippings.
7. Drain mushrooms, reserving liquid. Set mushrooms aside.
8. In 1-cup measure, combine reserved mushroom liquid with wine to measure ¾ cup.
9. Add to drippings in skillet along with salt, pepper, and lemon peel; bring to boiling, stirring. Remove from heat.
10. Add onion and mushrooms to liver. Pour over wine sauce. Top with bacon and parsley.
11. Bake 30 minutes.

OXTAIL STEW

2 (3-lb size) oxtails
¼ cup unsifted all-purpose flour
3 tablespoons salad oil
1 can (1 lb, 3 oz) tomatoes, undrained
1 tablespoon salt
1 bay leaf
6 whole cloves
¼ teaspoon pepper
1 medium onion, quartered
2 medium potatoes, pared and quartered
2 medium carrots, pared and quartered
¾ cup cubed celery

MAKES 2 QUARTS—6 SERVINGS

1. Trim fat from oxtails; wipe with damp paper towels. Cut into 2-inch pieces. Coat well with flour.
2. In hot oil in large kettle, over low heat, slowly brown oxtails.
3. Add 2 cups water; bring to boiling. Reduce heat, and simmer, covered, 1 hour.
4. Skim off excess fat. Add tomatoes, salt, bay leaf, cloves, and pepper; bring to boiling. Reduce heat, and simmer, covered, 1½ hours, or until meat is almost tender.
5. Add vegetables; simmer, covered, 30 minutes longer, or until meat and vegetables are tender.

BASIC METHOD FOR COOKING SWEETBREADS

1 lb sweetbreads
1 teaspoon salt
1 tablespoon lemon juice

MAKES 3 OR 4 SERVINGS

1. In large saucepan, bring 1 quart water to boiling. Add sweetbreads, salt, and lemon juice; return to boiling.
2. Reduce heat; simmer, covered, 20 minutes.
3. Drain well; plunge into cold water. Remove membrane and veins. Prepare as desired.

CREAMY SWEETBREAD CASSEROLE

1 lb beef sweetbreads,*
  cooked
1 can (1 lb) cut asparagus,
  drained
2 tablespoons slivered
  toasted almonds
2 tablespoons pimiento
  strips

1 can (10½ oz) condensed
  cream-of-mushroom
  soup, undiluted
¼ cup sherry
¼ cup milk
½ cup packaged seasoned
  dry bread crumbs
1 tablespoon butter or
  margarine, melted

MAKES 3 OR 4 SERVINGS

1. Preheat oven to 375F.
2. Cut sweetbreads into uniform pieces.
3. In 1½-quart casserole, layer sweetbread pieces, asparagus, almonds, and pimiento.
4. In small saucepan, combine soup with sherry and milk, blending well. Bring to boiling, stirring. Pour over mixture in casserole.
5. Sprinkle with mixture of bread crumbs and butter.
6. Bake 25 minutes.

* Cook according to Basic Method for Cooking Sweetbreads.

BOILED TONGUE

3- to 4-lb smoked beef
  tongue
1 large onion, quartered
10 whole black peppers

¼ teaspoon mustard seed
2 bay leaves
4 whole cloves

MAKES 7 OR 8 SERVINGS

1. Wash tongue; pat dry with paper towels.
2. In 6-quart kettle, combine tongue and remaining ingredients with water to cover—about 3 quarts.
3. Bring to boiling. Reduce heat; simmer, covered, 2½ to 3 hours, or until tongue is tender.
4. Drain tongue. (If desired, reserve stock for use in sauce.) Plunge tongue into cold water.
5. To remove skin: With sharp knife, gently slit skin on underside from thick end to tip. Peel off skin, and remove and discard root.
6. To serve: Slice tongue thinly, and serve hot or cold with Gingersnap or Raisin Sauce.*

* See Sauces and Gravies Chapter.

PINEAPPLE-GLAZED TONGUE

1. Cook tongue as directed above.
2. Preheat oven to 350F.
3. Combine 1 can (8¾ oz) crushed pineapple, drained, with 2 tablespoons prepared mustard and ¼ cup light-brown sugar, firmly packed; mix well.
4. Pour over tongue in shallow, 2-quart baking dish; bake 30 minutes. Slice, and serve hot. Makes 7 or 8 servings.

GLAZED TONGUE

3½-lb cooked smoked beef
  tongue*
3 envelopes unflavored
  gelatine
2 cups cold tongue stock or
  beef bouillon
1 cup dairy sour cream

1 tablespoon prepared
  horseradish
¼ teaspoon liquid hot-
  pepper seasoning
¼ teaspoon salt
Ripe olives
Pimiento

MAKES 8 TO 10 SERVINGS

1. Remove skin and root from tongue. Refrigerate, covered, until well chilled—2 hours.
2. Meanwhile, in small saucepan, sprinkle 2 envelopes gelatine over 1 cup tongue stock; let stand 5 minutes to soften. Over low heat, cook, stirring, until gelatine is dissolved. Cool.

(Glazed Tongue continued)

3. Add rest of ingredients, except olives and pimiento, to gelatine mixture, mixing well. Refrigerate until consistency of unbeaten egg white—about 45 minutes.

4. Place tongue, root end down, on rack in shallow pan. Pour gelatine mixture evenly over tongue, coating well.

5. With aspic cutters, cut olives and pimiento into fancy shapes; arrange on tongue in decorative design. Refrigerate.

6. In small saucepan, sprinkle remaining gelatine over rest of tongue stock; let stand 5 minutes to soften. Over low heat, cook, stirring, until gelatine is dissolved. Cool.

7. Pour gelatine mixture evenly over glazed tongue, making sure design is entirely covered.

8. Refrigerate until firm—about 2 hours. To serve, cut into thin slices.

* Cook according to directions for Boiled Tongue.

BOILED FRESH TRIPE

Fresh tripe
Salt
10 whole black peppers

1 bay leaf
1 medium onion

EACH POUND OF TRIPE MAKES 4 SERVINGS

1. In large kettle, cover tripe with water. For every quart water, add 1 teaspoon salt. Add remaining ingredients.

2. Bring to boiling. Reduce heat, and simmer, covered, 1½ to 2 hours, or until fork-tender.

3. Drain. Cut into serving pieces; serve hot.

PEPPER POT

1 lb fresh honeycomb tripe
2 lb veal knuckles
1 tablespoon salt
10 whole black peppers
2 bay leaves
1 teaspoon monosodium
    glutamate
1 medium onion, quartered
¼ cup butter or margarine
1 cup diced celery
1 cup diced carrot

1 cup diced green pepper
    (about 1)
1 cup diced sweet red
    pepper (about 1)
1 can (1 lb, 1 oz) tomatoes,
    undrained
¼ teaspoon dried thyme
    leaves
½ cup uncooked elbow
    macaroni

MAKES 6 TO 8 HEARTY SERVINGS

1. In large kettle, combine tripe, veal knuckles, salt, black peppers, bay leaves, monosodium glutamate, and onion. Add water to cover.

2. Bring to boiling. Reduce heat, and simmer, covered, 1½ to 2 hours, or until tripe and veal knuckles are tender.

3. Remove from stock; cut into small pieces, and set aside. Strain stock, reserving 6 cups.

4. In hot butter in large saucepan, sauté celery, carrot, green pepper, and red pepper until tender—about 5 minutes.

5. Remove from heat. Add reserved stock, tomatoes, and thyme, mixing well.

6. Bring to boiling. Add macaroni; reduce heat; simmer, covered and stirring occasionally, 15 minutes, or until macaroni is tender.

7. Add tripe and veal knuckles; reheat gently.

Is there a hunter in your family? Does he triumphantly return home bearing gifts of partridge or pheasant or venison? Flatter him by preparing his prize according to one of McCall's special recipes.

BROILED BUFFALO OR BEAR STEAK

MAKES 1 OR 2 SERVINGS

¾-lb buffalo or bear steak*   Pepper
Salt

1. Wipe meat with damp paper towels. Sprinkle with salt and pepper.
2. Broil, 5 inches from heat, 5 to 6 minutes on each side, or to desired doneness.
* To ensure tenderness, use unseasoned meat tenderizer, following package-label directions and omitting salt.

BROILED WILD DUCK

MAKES 2 SERVINGS

1½-lb ready-to-cook wild Mallard duck, halved
¼ cup butter or margarine, melted
1 teaspoon salt
¼ cup melted currant jelly

1. Rinse duck thoroughly; pat dry with paper towels. (If desired, rub entire surface of duck with 1 tablespoon baking soda; rinse thoroughly.)
2. Place duck, skin side down, on broiler rack. Combine butter and salt with 2 tablespoons water; brush duck with some of mixture.
3. Broil, 6 inches from heat, 5 to 15 minutes, depending on desired doneness; brush occasionally with butter mixture.
4. Turn duck; broil 5 to 15 minutes longer, brushing occasionally with butter mixture.
5. Remove to heated serving platter. Brush with currant jelly.

ROAST WILD DUCK

MAKES 2 SERVINGS

1½-lb ready-to-cook wild Mallard duck
½ teaspoon salt
⅛ teaspoon pepper
3 onion slices, ¼ inch thick
1 celery stalk
1 medium carrot, pared
3 juniper berries (optional)
2 bacon slices
½ cup dry white wine

1. Rinse duck well; pat dry with paper towels. Sprinkle surface and body cavity with salt and pepper. Preheat oven to 450F.
2. Stuff duck cavity with onion, celery, carrot, and juniper berries.
3. Fasten skin of neck to back, with poultry pin. Fold wing tips under body, to secure wings close to it. Then close body cavity with poultry pins. Lace with twine. Tie ends of legs together.
4. Place duck on rack in shallow roasting pan. Secure bacon slices across top; baste with wine. Roast 30 minutes, basting frequently with wine. (Roast longer if a well-done duck is desired.)
5. When duck is done, remove poultry pins and twine. Cut into serving-size pieces, and arrange on platter.

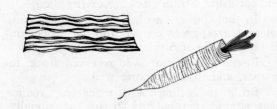

BRAISED PARTRIDGES

2 (¾-lb size) ready-to-cook
   partridges*
¼ cup butter or margarine
⅓ cup sliced onion

1 can (10½ oz) condensed
   cream-of-mushroom
   soup, undiluted
⅓ cup sauterne

1. Rinse partridges; dry with paper towels.
2. In hot butter in heavy skillet or Dutch oven, sauté partridges until nicely browned—about 10 minutes.
3. Add onion; cook, stirring occasionally, until tender—about 5 minutes.
4. Add soup and sauterne, mixing well; bring to boiling. Reduce heat, and simmer, covered, 25 to 30 minutes, or until partridges are fork-tender. Serve with sauce spooned over.

* Grouse may be substituted for partridge and cooked as directed above.

BRANDIED PARTRIDGES

2 (¾-lb size) ready-to-cook
   partridges
¼ cup butter or margarine
1 tablespoon finely
   chopped onion

½ cup chicken bouillon or
   consommé
½ teaspoon salt
1 cup seedless grapes
¼ cup brandy
2 teaspoons cornstarch

1. Rinse partridges; dry with paper towels.
2. In hot butter in large skillet, sauté partridges until nicely browned—10 minutes.
3. Add onion, bouillon, and salt; bring to boiling. Reduce heat, and simmer, covered, 25 to 30 minutes, or until partridges are almost tender.
4. Add grapes; simmer 10 minutes longer. Remove from heat.
5. In small bowl, combine brandy and cornstarch, mixing well. Add to mixture in skillet, blending well. Bring to boiling, stirring; boil ½ minute. Serve partridges with sauce.

PHEASANT WITH WILD-RICE STUFFING

3-lb ready-to-cook pheasant
2 tablespoons butter or
   margarine
¾ cup diced celery
¼ cup chopped onion
2 tablespoons chopped
   parsley
1 teaspoon salt

¼ teaspoon pepper
¾ teaspoon dried rosemary
   leaves
1 can (3 oz) sliced
   mushrooms, drained
1½ cups cooked wild rice
2 or 3 bacon slices

1. Rinse pheasant well; pat dry with paper towels. Preheat oven to 325F.
2. Slowly melt butter in medium skillet. Add celery, onion, and parsley; cook, stirring, over medium heat, until vegetables are tender—about 10 minutes. Remove from heat.
3. Add remaining ingredients, except bacon, tossing gently with fork to combine.
4. Spoon stuffing lightly into neck and body cavity of pheasant. Truss pheasant, following directions for trussing Roast Wild Duck.
5. Place on rack in shallow roasting pan. Place bacon slices over breast.
6. Roast 2 hours, basting occasionally with pan drippings.
7. To serve: Remove pins and twine. Spoon stuffing into a serving dish. Cut pheasant in half or in quarters; arrange on heated platter.

SAVORY PHEASANT PIE

3-lb ready-to-cook
    pheasant, cut up
1 bay leaf
2 celery tops
1 onion, quartered
3 medium carrots, pared
5 whole black peppers
2 teaspoons salt
1 teaspoon monosodium
    glutamate
1 can (3 oz) sliced
    mushrooms

½ pkg (10-oz size) thawed
    frozen peas
6 tablespoons butter or
    margarine
6 tablespoons unsifted
    all-purpose flour
¼ cup dry sherry
1 cup milk
½ pkg (10-oz size) piecrust
    mix

1.   Rinse pheasant well; pat dry with paper towels.

2.   In large kettle, combine pheasant, bay leaf, celery tops, onion, carrots, black peppers, salt, and monosodium glutamate with 6 quarts water.

3.   Bring to boiling. Reduce heat, and simmer, covered, 1¼ hours, or until pheasant is tender.

4.   Preheat oven to 425F. With slotted utensil, remove pheasant and carrots from stock. Place pheasant in 2-quart casserole. Slice carrots; add to pheasant.

5.   Strain stock, reserving 1½ cups. Also, drain mushrooms, reserving liquid.

6.   Add mushrooms along with peas to pheasant.

7.   Slowly melt butter in medium saucepan. Remove from heat. Add flour, stirring to make a smooth paste.

8.   Combine reserved stock, reserved mushroom liquid, sherry, and milk. Gradually add to flour mixture, stirring until smooth.

9.   Over medium heat, bring to boiling, stirring; boil 2 minutes. Pour over mixture in casserole.

10.   Prepare piecrust mix as package label directs. On lightly floured surface, roll out to a 10-inch circle, or circle large enough to fit over casserole. Adjust over top of casserole; trim edge, and flute. Make several gashes in center of crust, for steam vents.

11.   Bake 15 to 20 minutes, or until crust is golden-brown.

SAUTÉED QUAIL

4 ready-to-cook quail
    (1¼ lb)
¼ cup butter or margarine
⅓ cup sliced onion

½ teaspoon salt
⅛ teaspoon pepper
⅓ cup sherry

1.   Rinse quail well; pat dry with paper towels.

2.   In hot butter in large skillet, sauté quail until nicely browned—about 10 minutes.

3.   Add onion; cook, stirring occasionally, until tender—about 5 minutes.

4.   Add salt, pepper, and sherry, mixing well; bring to boiling. Reduce heat, and simmer, covered, 20 minutes, or until quail are tender.

SMOTHERED QUAIL

4 ready-to-cook quail
    (1½ lb)
¼ cup butter or margarine
½ cup sliced shallots

¼ cup cider vinegar
1 tablespoon sugar
½ teaspoon salt

1. Rinse quail well; pat dry with paper towels.
2. In hot butter in large skillet, sauté quail until nicely browned—about 10 minutes.
3. Add shallots; cook, stirring occasionally, until tender—about 5 minutes.
4. Add vinegar, sugar, and salt, mixing well; bring to boiling. Reduce heat, and simmer, tightly covered, 20 to 30 minutes, or until quail are tender.
5. Serve quail with pan juices spooned over.

BRAISED RABBIT

2 (1-lb size) ready-to-cook
    cottontail rabbits, cut
    up
3 bacon slices
¼ cup sliced onion
1 clove garlic, crushed
2 parsley sprigs
1 teaspoon salt

¼ teaspoon pepper
½ teaspoon dried basil
    leaves
½ teaspoon dried oregano
    leaves
1 can (8 oz) tomatoes,
    undrained
¼ cup port

1. Rinse rabbit pieces well; pat dry with paper towels.
2. In large, heavy skillet or Dutch oven, over medium heat, sauté bacon until crisp. Drain well on paper towels; crumble, and set aside.
3. In same skillet, in bacon drippings, sauté rabbit until nicely browned on all sides. Remove from heat.
4. Add remaining ingredients, along with bacon; mix well. Bring to boiling. Reduce heat, and simmer, covered, 45 minutes to 1 hour, or until rabbit is tender.
5. Remove to heated serving platter. Spoon pan juices over rabbit.

SQUAB IN SOUR CREAM

2 (¾-lb size) ready-to-cook
    squab
¼ cup unsifted all-purpose
    flour
2 tablespoons butter or
    margarine
½ cup sliced onion
½ cup tomato juice
1 teaspoon salt

½ teaspoon paprika
½ teaspoon dried basil
    leaves
¼ teaspoon pepper
1 can (3 oz) sliced
    mushrooms,
    undrained
1 cup dairy sour cream

1. Rinse squab well; pat dry with paper towels. Coat well with flour.
2. In hot butter in large skillet, sauté squab until nicely browned—10 to 15 minutes.
3. Add onion; cook, stirring occasionally, until tender—about 5 minutes.
4. Combine tomato juice, salt, paprika, basil, pepper, and mushrooms. Pour over squab; bring to boiling. Reduce heat, and simmer, covered, 20 to 30 minutes, or until squab is tender.
5. Remove squab to heated platter; keep warm.
6. Gradually add sour cream to mixture in skillet, stirring constantly. Reheat gently. Pour over squab.

ROTISSERIE-BROILED SQUAB

2 (¾-lb size) ready-to-cook
    squab
2 tablespoons butter or
    margarine
¼ cup apricot preserves
1 tablespoon lemon juice
½ teaspoon dry mustard
1 teaspoon paprika
¼ teaspoon salt
¼ teaspoon ginger

1. Rinse squab; pat dry with paper towels. Bend wings under birds; tie legs together. Secure on spit.

2. In small saucepan, over low heat, cook butter and preserves, stirring, until both are melted. Remove from heat.

3. Add remaining ingredients, mixing well. Brush squab with some of mixture.

4. Broil 45 minutes, brushing occasionally with remaining mixture.

VENISON POT ROAST

7-lb boned leg-of-venison
    roast
3 to 6 bacon slices
2 cups Burgundy
½ cup cider vinegar
2 celery tops
1 medium onion, sliced
4 lemon slices
1 large carrot, pared and
    sliced
1 tablespoon salt
10 whole black peppers
2 bay leaves
1 clove garlic, crushed
¼ cup unsifted all-purpose
    flour
2 tablespoons salad oil

1. Wipe roast with damp paper towels. Arrange bacon slices over inside surface of meat; roll up, and tie securely.

2. Combine Burgundy, vinegar, celery tops, onion, lemon slices, carrot, salt, black peppers, bay leaves, and garlic with 1 cup water.

3. Pour over roast in large bowl. Refrigerate, covered, 24 hours, turning occasionally.

4. Remove roast from marinade; reserve 2 cups marinade.

5. Coat roast well with flour. Slowly heat oil in Dutch oven. Add roast; cook, over medium heat, until browned all over—about 20 minutes.

6. Add 1 cup reserved marinade; bring to boiling. Reduce heat, and simmer, covered, 4 hours, or until roast is fork-tender. Baste meat occasionally with pan liquid, adding rest of marinade as needed.

7. Remove to heated serving platter.

ROAST VENISON WITH WINE

7½-lb boned leg-of-venison
    roast
9 bacon slices
1 teaspoon salt
¼ teaspoon dried thyme
    leaves
¼ teaspoon pepper
2 tablespoons chopped
    onion
1 clove garlic, crushed
¼ cup lemon juice
1 cup beef bouillon
1 cup Burgundy

1. Preheat oven to 500F. Wipe roast with damp paper towels. Arrange 6 bacon slices on inside surface of roast; roll up, and tie securely. Place 3 bacon slices across top.

2. Place roast on rack in shallow roasting pan. Sear, in oven, 10 to 15 minutes.

3. Remove roast from oven. Lower oven temperature to 425F.

4. Combine remaining ingredients; pour over roast. Cover with foil.

5. Roast, basting occasionally with pan drippings, 2½ to 3 hours, until meat is tender.

6. Remove to heated serving platter. Strain pan drippings, and pass with roast.

T he test of a good cook is a really good pie, with a crisp, golden crust that literally melts in your mouth. Though no one rightly remembers the genius who first invented the pie, nobody ever forgets the woman who bakes a perfect one. An honest-to-goodness American pie is a real contribution to good eating. It may have a crimped edge as prim and precise as a picket fence and a delicately browned crust so tender it crumbles at the first touch of a fork. Our recipes include a great variety of pie shells for single- and double-crust pies, as well as a list of pies as long as your arm. Dumplings, too, and small tarts and turnovers. What wonderful desserts await you and your family—and your lucky guests!

Tips For Pie Bakers

1. Our pie recipes were tested using sifted all-purpose flour. If the unsifted type of flour is substituted, follow manufacturer's directions on the package.

2. When using a pastry cloth, rub flour well into surface, with palm of hand, so no additional flour is rolled into pastry, which would toughen it.

3. Tracing a circle on pastry cloth or waxed paper is a helpful guide in rolling pastry to desired circumference. Or cut a sheet of waxed paper to desired circumference, to use as a guide.

4. A stockinette cover for the rolling pin can be floured to keep pastry from sticking and tearing.

5. Another rolling trick: Roll pastry between two sheets of waxed paper to desired circumference. Chill in waxed paper in refrigerator while preparing pie filling. Waxed paper peels easily from chilled pastry. No additional flour is used.

6. For well-baked, browned bottom crust, select pie plates of heat-resistant glass. Shiny metal pans do not bake bottom crusts as well; use aluminum pans with dull finish.

7. When baking a two-crust fruit pie, place a square of foil on bottom of oven, directly under pie plate, to catch any juices that might bubble through crust.

TO FREEZE PIE SHELLS

Unbaked Pie Shells: Prepare pie shell as recipe directs. Prick pie shell that is going to be baked without filling. Freezer-wrap; label, and freeze.
Baked Pie Shells: Prepare and bake pie shell as recipe directs. Let cool completely on wire rack. Freezer-wrap; label, and freeze.

TO USE FROZEN PIE SHELLS

Unbaked pie shells: Preheat oven to 450F. Remove freezer-wrap. Immediately bake frozen pie shell about 20 minutes, or until golden-brown. Let cool completely on wire rack. Fill as desired.
If pie shell is going to be baked along with filling: Remove freezer-wrap. Let stand in refrigerator or at room temperature to thaw. Then fill as desired, and bake as specific recipe directs.
Baked pie shells: Preheat oven to 375F. Remove freezer-wrap. Heat solidly frozen pie shell 10 minutes, or until thawed. Cool completely on wire rack. Fill as desired.
   Or remove freezer-wrap. Let stand at room temperature until completely thawed.

All Other Pie Shells: Let stand at room temperature to thaw. If necessary to bake pie shell, bake as specific recipe directs.

TO FREEZE PIES

Kinds to Freeze: Fruit pies, baked or unbaked, freeze best. You may also freeze chiffon pies, although filling may toughen slightly. Cream and custard pies do not freeze well.
Unbaked Fruit Pies: Prepare pie as recipe directs. Do not make slits in upper crust. Freeze pie, unwrapped, until firm.
Then wrap pie in freezer-wrap; label, and freeze.
Baked Fruit Pies: Prepare and bake pie as recipe directs. Cool completely on wire rack. Freezer-wrap; label, and freeze.
Chiffon Pies: Prepare pie as recipe directs; omit whipped-cream topping. Freeze pie, unwrapped, until filling is firm. Then wrap in freezer-wrap; label, and freeze.

TO SERVE FROZEN PIES

Unbaked Fruit Pies: Preheat oven to 425F. Remove freezer-wrap. Make slits in upper crust for steam vents. Bake about 1 hour, or until fruit is tender and crust is golden-brown.
If lightweight-aluminum-foil pie pans are used, place on cookie sheet during baking.
Baked Fruit Pies: Preheat oven to 375F. Remove freezer-wrap. Bake solidly frozen pies about 40 minutes, or until filling bubbles through slits in upper crust.
Chiffon Pies: Remove freezer-wrap. Let stand in refrigerator, to thaw, about 1½ hours. Then top as desired.

CHEESE PASTRY FOR 2-CRUST PIE

1⅔ cups sifted all-purpose
    flour
½ teaspoon salt

1 cup grated sharp
    Cheddar cheese
½ cup shortening
¼ to ⅓ cup ice water

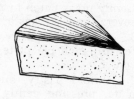

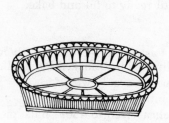

MAKES ENOUGH PASTRY FOR AN
8- OR 9-INCH 2-CRUST PIE

1.   Sift flour with salt into medium bowl.

2.   Add cheese, tossing lightly with fork to mix well.

3.   With pastry blender, using a short, cutting motion, or 2 knives, cut in shortening until mixture resembles coarse cornmeal.

4.   Quickly sprinkle ice water, 1 tablespoon at a time, over all of pastry mixture, tossing lightly with fork after each addition and pushing dampened portion to side of bowl; sprinkle only dry portion remaining. (Pastry should be just moist enough to hold together, not sticky.)

5.   Shape pastry into a ball; wrap in waxed paper, and refrigerate until ready to use. Divide in half; flatten each half with palm of hand.

6.   Make bottom and top crusts as directed in Flaky Pastry for 2-Crust pie.

Note: To make one crust, reduce flour to 1 cup; halve rest of ingredients. Make shell as directed in Flaky Pastry for 1-crust pie. Or, roll to fit top of 1½-quart casserole.

FLAKY PASTRY FOR 1-CRUST PIE

1 cup sifted all-purpose
    flour
½ teaspoon salt
⅓ cup plus 1 tablespoon
    shortening or ⅓ cup
    lard

2 to 2½ tablespoons ice
    water

MAKES ENOUGH PASTRY FOR AN
8- OR 9-INCH PIE SHELL, OR
TOP OF 1½-QUART CASSEROLE

1.   Sift flour with salt into medium bowl.

2.   With pastry blender, using a short, cutting motion, or 2 knives, cut in shortening until mixture resembles coarse cornmeal.

3.   Quickly sprinkle ice water, 1 tablespoon at a time, over all of pastry mixture, tossing lightly with fork after each addition and pushing dampened portion to side of bowl; sprinkle only dry portion remaining. (Pastry should be just moist enough to hold together, not sticky.)

4.   Shape pastry into a ball; wrap in waxed paper, and refrigerate until ready to use. Flatten with palm of hand.

UNBAKED PIE SHELL

1. On lightly floured surface, roll out Flaky Pastry for 1-Crust Pie to an 11-inch circle, rolling with light strokes from center to edge and lifting rolling pin as you reach edge. As you roll, alternate directions, to shape an even circle.
2. If rolled piecrust is too irregular in shape, carefully trim off any bulge and use as patch. Lightly moisten pastry edge to be filled in. Gently press patch in place. Smooth seam with several light strokes of the rolling pin.
3. Fold rolled pastry in half; carefully transfer to 9-inch pie plate, making sure fold is in center.
4. Unfold pastry, and fit carefully into pie plate, pressing gently with fingertips toward center of plate. This eliminates air bubbles under crust and helps reduce shrinkage.
5. Fold under edge of crust, and press into upright rim. Crimp decoratively.
6. Refrigerate until ready to fill and bake.

BAKED PIE SHELL

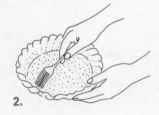

1. Prepare Flaky Pastry for 1-Crust Pie; then make pie shell as directed in Unbaked Pie Shell.
2. Prick entire surface evenly with fork.
3. Refrigerate 30 minutes.
4. Meanwhile, preheat oven to 450F. Bake pie shell 8 to 10 minutes, or until golden-brown.
5. Cool completely on wire rack before filling.

FLAKY PASTRY FOR 2-CRUST PIE

MAKES ENOUGH PASTRY FOR AN
8- OR 9-INCH 2-CRUST PIE

| 2 cups sifted all-purpose flour | ¾ cup shortening or ⅔ cup lard |
| 1 teaspoon salt | 4 to 5 tablespoons ice water |

1. Sift flour with salt into medium bowl.
2. With pastry blender, using a short, cutting motion, or 2 knives, cut in shortening until mixture resembles coarse cornmeal.
3. Quickly sprinkle ice water, 1 tablespoon at a time, over all of pastry mixture, tossing lightly with fork after each addition and pushing dampened portion to side of bowl; sprinkle only dry portion remaining. (Pastry should be just moist enough to hold together, not sticky.)
4. Shape pastry into a ball; wrap in waxed paper, and refrigerate until ready to use. Divide in half; flatten each half with palm of hand.

PERFECT PIES

Now to find out how good a cook you really are. For the really good cook makes really good piecrusts—one of the hardest things a cook can make—and fills them to perfection with fruit or cream or lemon meringue.

TARTS PERSONIFIED

"T" is for Tarts, easily the smartest hostess notion of the season. Dozens of different one-bite confections. What a tantalizing display to bring to the table, with fruit at dinner or for an afternoon tea. Actually, what we've pictured are "tartlets"—tiny tarts served to give the eater a variety of tastes. All are made with pastry, praline paste, and pastry cream; then topped with fruit of your choice and glazed or frosted. Sound good? Yes!

(Flaky Pastry for 2-Crust Pie continued)

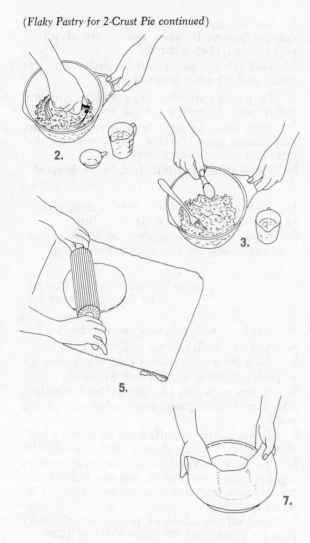

2.

3.

5.

7.

5. To make bottom crust: On lightly floured surface, roll out half of pastry to an 11-inch circle, rolling with light strokes from center to edge and lifting rolling pin as you reach edge. As you roll, alternate directions, to shape an even circle.

6. If rolled piecrust is too irregular in shape, carefully trim off any bulge and use as patch. Lightly moisten pastry edge to be filled in. Gently press patch in place. Smooth seam with several light strokes of the rolling pin.

7. Fold rolled pastry in half; carefully transfer to pie plate, making sure fold is in center.

8. Unfold pastry, and fit carefully into pie plate. Do not stretch pastry. Trim bottom crust even with edge of pie plate.

9. Turn prepared filling into bottom crust.

10. To make top crust: Roll out remaining half of pastry to an 11-inch circle.

11. Fold in half; make several gashes near center, for steam vents.

12. Carefully place pastry on top of filling, making sure fold is in center; unfold.

13. Trim top crust ½ inch beyond edge of pie plate. Fold top crust under bottom crust; press gently together, to seal. Crimp edges decoratively.

14. For a shiny, glazed top, brush top crust with 1 egg yolk beaten with 1 tablespoon water, or with 1 slightly beaten egg white, or with undiluted evaporated milk.

15. To prevent edge of crust from becoming too brown, place 1½-inch strip of foil around crust; bake as recipe indicates. Remove foil last 15 minutes of baking.

Orange Flaky Pastry for 2-Crust Pie

Make pastry as directed, adding 1 tablespoon grated orange peel and 1 teaspoon sugar, before adding ice water.

OIL PASTRY FOR 1-CRUST PIE

1¼ cups sifted all-purpose   ½ teaspoon salt
     flour   ⅓ cup salad oil

MAKES ENOUGH PASTRY FOR AN 8- OR 9-INCH PIE SHELL, OR TOP OF 1½-QUART CASSEROLE

1. Sift flour with salt into medium bowl.

2. Add oil, mixing well with fork.

3. Sprinkle 2 tablespoons cold water over all of pastry mixture, mixing well with fork. If pastry seems too dry to hold together, add 1 to 2 tablespoons more salad oil.

4. Form pastry into a ball; flatten slightly.

UNBAKED PIE SHELL

1. On wet counter top (so paper won't slip), roll out pastry, between two sheets of waxed paper, to an 11-inch circle.
2. Peel off top paper; invert pastry into pie plate; peel off other sheet of paper.
3. Fit pastry carefully into pie plate, pressing gently with fingertips toward center of plate.
4. Trim crust ½ inch beyond edge of plate. Fold under edge of crust, and press into upright rim; crimp decoratively.
5. Fill with desired filling; bake as directed.

BAKED PIE SHELL

1. Preheat oven to 450F. Prick entire surface of unbaked pie shell evenly with fork.
2. Bake 12 to 15 minutes, or until golden. Cool completely on wire rack before filling.

OIL PASTRY FOR 2-CRUST PIE

MAKES ENOUGH PASTRY FOR AN
8- OR 9-INCH 2-CRUST PIE

2 cups sifted all-purpose flour
1 teaspoon salt
½ cup salad oil

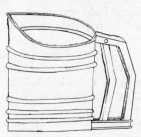

1. Sift flour with salt into medium bowl.
2. Add salad oil, mixing well with fork.
3. Sprinkle 3 tablespoons cold water over all of pastry mixture, mixing well with fork.
4. If pastry seems too dry to hold together, add 1 to 2 tablespoons more salad oil, mixing well.
5. Divide pastry in half; form each into a ball. With palm of hand, flatten each ball slightly.
6. To make bottom crust: On wet counter top (so paper won't slip), roll out half of pastry, between two sheets of waxed paper, to an 11-inch circle.
7. Peel off top sheet of paper; invert pastry into pie plate; peel off other sheet of paper.
8. Fit pastry carefully into pie plate; do not stretch.
9. Trim crust even with edge of pie plate. Turn prepared filling into bottom crust.
10. To make top crust: Roll out remaining half of pastry, between two sheets of waxed paper, to an 11-inch circle.
11. Peel off top sheet of paper; make several slits for steam vents. Invert pastry over filling; peel off paper.
12. Trim crust ½ inch beyond edge of pie plate. Fold top crust under bottom crust; crimp edge decoratively. Bake as specific recipe directs.

COOKIE-CRUST PIE SHELL

MAKES 9-INCH SHELL

1 cup sifted all-purpose
    flour
¼ cup sugar
1 teaspoon grated lemon
    peel

½ cup butter or margarine
1 egg yolk, slightly beaten
¼ teaspoon vanilla extract

1. Preheat oven to 400F.
2. Combine flour, sugar, and lemon peel in medium bowl.
3. With pastry blender or 2 knives, cut in butter until mixture resembles coarse cornmeal.
4. Stir in egg yolk and vanilla.
5. Mix pastry, with hands, until well blended.
6. Pat evenly into 9-inch pie plate; make a small edge on rim.
7. Bake 10 minutes, or until light-golden. Cool on wire rack before filling.

BAKED GRAHAM-CRACKER PIE SHELL

MAKES 9-INCH SHELL

1⅓ cups graham-cracker
    crumbs
    (about 19 crackers)
¼ cup sugar

¼ teaspoon nutmeg
¼ cup soft butter or
    margarine

1. Preheat oven to 375F.
2. In medium bowl, combine crumbs with sugar and nutmeg; mix well.
3. With back of wooden spoon, or fingers, rub in butter until well combined.
4. With fingers, press mixture evenly on bottom and side of 9-inch pieplate, not on rim.
5. Bake 8 minutes, or until golden-brown. Cool on wire rack before filling.

UNBAKED GRAHAM-CRACKER PIE SHELL

MAKES 9-INCH SHELL

1¼ cups graham-cracker
    crumbs
    (about 18 crackers)

¼ cup soft butter or
    margarine
¼ cup sugar
¼ teaspoon cinnamon

1. Combine all ingredients in medium bowl; blend with fingers, fork, or pastry blender.
2. Press evenly on bottom and side of 9-inch pie plate, not on rim. Refrigerate until ready to fill.

VANILLA-WAFER PIE SHELL

MAKES 9-INCH SHELL

1 pkg (4¾ oz) vanilla
    wafers
¼ teaspoon nutmeg

⅓ cup butter or margarine,
    melted

1. Preheat oven to 300F.
2. With rolling pin, crush wafers between 2 sheets of waxed paper. Measure 2 cups crumbs.
3. Toss with nutmeg and butter until well mixed.
4. Press on bottom and side of 9-inch pie plate, not on rim.
5. Bake 10 minutes. Cool on wire rack before filling.

437

HERBED CRUST FOR MEAT PIES

1½ cups sifted all-purpose flour
¾ teaspoon salt
½ teaspoon dried dill weed

½ cup shortening
3 to 4 tablespoons ice water

MAKES ENOUGH TO COVER A 2½-QUART CASSEROLE AND PROVIDE EXTRA TRIM

1. Sift flour and salt into medium bowl. Stir in dill.
2. Cut in shortening, with pastry blender or 2 knives, until mixture resembles coarse cornmeal.
3. Add ice water, and stir briskly.
4. Form pastry into a ball, and chill in refrigerator until ready to use.
5. Roll pastry on floured board or pastry cloth.
6. Cover casserole, sealing pastry securely to moistened edge of dish. Crimp edge; slash top, to release steam.

Fruit Pies

When the bloom is on the apple and the peach and the pear, when dried fruits are newly appealing and nuts simply beg to be cracked, then it's high time for our fruit-pies-plus. Eat them warm, as though they'd recently been taken from the oven; serve them with heavy cream, whipped or poured; or sharp Cheddar cheese; or with vanilla ice cream that melts down into the fruit; or with any of the sauces we'll tell you about.

DEEP-DISH APPLE PIE

Pastry for 1-crust pie
2 lb tart cooking apples
1 tablespoon lemon juice
1 cup sugar
3 tablespoons flour

½ teaspoon nutmeg
¼ teaspoon cloves
¼ teaspoon allspice
½ cup heavy cream
1 egg yolk

MAKES 6 SERVINGS

1. Prepare pastry. Refrigerate, wrapped in waxed paper, until ready to use.
2. Preheat oven to 400F. Lightly grease 1½-quart casserole.
3. Wash apples; core; slice thinly into large bowl. Sprinkle with lemon juice.
4. Combine sugar, flour, and spices; gently toss with apples, mixing well. Add cream; mix well. Turn into prepared casserole.
5. On lightly floured surface, roll out pastry into a 9½-inch circle. Fit over top of casserole; flute edge.
6. Make several cuts in center, for vents.
7. Brush lightly with egg yolk beaten with 1 tablespoon water; bake 50 to 60 minutes. Top should be golden-brown and apples tender. Serve warm—with light cream, if desired.

OLD-FASHIONED APPLE PIE

Pastry for 2-crust pie
1 cup sugar
1 teaspoon cinnamon
4 tablespoons flour
Dash salt

6 cups thinly sliced, pared
    tart cooking apples
    (2 lb)
2 tablespoons butter or
    margarine

1.   On lightly floured surface, roll out half of pastry into an 11-inch circle. Use to line 9-inch pie plate; trim. Refrigerate, with rest of pastry, until ready to use.

2.   Preheat oven to 425F.

3.   In small bowl, combine sugar, cinnamon, flour, and salt, mixing well.

4.   Add to apples in large bowl, tossing lightly to combine.

5.   Turn into pastry-lined pie plate, mounding high in center; dot with butter.

6.   Roll out remaining pastry into an 11-inch circle. Make several slits near center for steam vents; adjust over filling; trim.

7.   Fold edge of top crust under bottom crust; press together with fingertips. Crimp edge decoratively.

8.   Bake 45 to 50 minutes, or until apples are tender and crust is golden-brown.

9.   Cool partially on wire rack; serve warm.

FRESH-APPLE-PEAR PIE

Pastry for 2-crust pie
3 cups thinly sliced, pared
    ripe Bartlett pears
    (about 3 large pears)
3 cups thinly sliced, pared
    tart cooking apples
    (about 4 medium
    apples)
2 tablespoons lemon juice

½ cup light-brown sugar,
    firmly packed
½ cup granulated sugar
⅛ teaspoon salt
3 tablespoons flour
½ teaspoon nutmeg
2 tablespoons butter or
    margarine

1.   On lightly floured surface, roll out half of pastry into an 11-inch circle. Use to line 9-inch pie plate; trim. Refrigerate, with rest of pastry, until ready to use.

2.   Preheat oven to 425F.

3.   In large bowl, combine pears and apples; sprinkle with lemon juice.

4.   In small bowl, combine sugars, salt, flour, and nutmeg. Add to fruit, tossing lightly to combine.

5.   Turn into pastry-lined pie plate, mounding high in center; dot with butter.

6.   Roll out remaining pastry into an 11-inch circle. Make several slits near center for steam vents; adjust over filling; trim.

7.   Fold edge of top crust under bottom crust; press together with fingertips. Crimp edge decoratively.

8.   Bake 45 to 50 minutes, or until fruit is tender and crust is golden-brown. Cool partially on wire rack; serve warm.

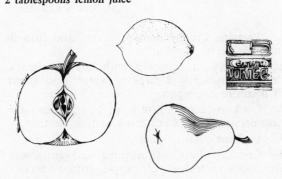

PRALINE GLAZE FOR APPLE PIE

¼ cup light-brown sugar,
   firmly packed
1 tablespoon light cream

2 tablespoons soft butter
   or margarine
¼ cup walnut or pecan
   halves

1. Preheat oven to 425F.
2. In small bowl, combine sugar, cream, and butter, mixing well.
3. Spoon mixture evenly over top of any warm apple pie. Arrange nuts over top.
4. Bake about 5 minutes, or until mixture melts and pie is nicely glazed. Cool on wire rack; serve warm.

FRESH-APRICOT PIE

MAKES 6 TO 8 SERVINGS

1 tablespoon lemon juice
4 cups sliced, pitted,
   unpeeled apricots
   (about 3 lb)
¾ cup light-brown sugar,
   firmly packed
¼ cup granulated sugar

2 tablespoons quick-
   cooking tapioca
½ teaspoon salt
Pastry for 2-crust pie
2 tablespoons butter or
   margarine

1. Sprinkle lemon juice over apricots in large bowl.
2. Combine sugars with tapioca and salt. Add to apricots, tossing lightly to combine. Let stand 15 minutes.
3. Meanwhile, preheat oven to 425F.
4. On lightly floured surface, roll out half of pastry into an 11-inch circle. Use to line 9-inch pie plate; trim.
5. Turn apricot mixture into pie plate, mounding in center; dot with butter.
6. Roll out rest of pastry into a 10-inch circle. With knife or pastry wheel, cut into 11 strips.
7. Slightly moisten rim of shell with cold water. Arrange 6 strips across filling; press ends to rim of shell. At right angles to these, place rest of strips, to form a lattice; press ends to rim of shell.
8. Fold bottom crust over ends of strips, to make a rim; crimp decoratively.
9. Bake 45 to 50 minutes, or until crust is golden and apricots are tender.
10. Cool partially on wire rack; serve slightly warm.

APRICOT-PINEAPPLE PIE

MAKES 8 SERVINGS

Cream-Cheese Pastry
   (recipe follows)
1 package (11 oz) dried
   apricots
½ cup sugar
2 tablespoons flour
½ teaspoon salt

¼ teaspoon nutmeg
¼ teaspoon cinnamon
1 can (8½ oz) crushed
   pineapple
1 tablespoon butter or
   margarine
1 egg yolk

1. Prepare Cream-Cheese Pastry, and line 9-inch pie plate.
2. Coarsely cut apricots, with kitchen shears. Combine apricots, 2 cups of water, and sugar in medium saucepan.
3. Cook, over moderate heat, 15 minutes, stirring occasionally. Cool to room temperature.
4. Preheat oven to 425F.
5. Combine flour, salt, nutmeg, and cinnamon. Stir, with undrained pineapple, into apricots.

(*Apricot-Pineapple Pie continued*)

6. Pour filling into pastry-lined pie plate. Dot with butter. Lay pastry strips over filling, to make lattice. Seal edges, and crimp.

7. Mix egg yolk with 1 tablespoon water, and brush on pastry. Bake 10 minutes. Reduce oven temperature to 350F; bake 25 minutes. Cool on wire rack.

CREAM-CHEESE PASTRY

2 cups sifted all-purpose flour
1 teaspoon salt
½ cup shortening

1 package (3 oz) cream cheese
2 tablespoons ice water

MAKES ENOUGH FOR 2-CRUST 9-INCH PIE

1. Sift flour and salt together into medium bowl.

2. Cut in shortening, with pastry blender or 2 knives, until mixture is like coarse cornmeal.

3. Cut in cream cheese until mixture is again like coarse cornmeal.

4. Gradually sprinkle with ice water, tossing with fork. Shape into ball; divide in half; roll each half, between two sheets of waxed paper, into an 11-inch circle. Refrigerate.

5. Fit one circle into 9-inch pie plate. With pastry wheel, cut other circle into ½-inch-wide strips.

Note: If desired, sprinkle poppy seed on pastry remaining from lattice. Place on cookie sheet; bake, with the pie, 8 to 10 minutes.

FRESH-BERRY PIE

Pastry for 2-crust pie
2 pint boxes fresh blackberries or raspberries (4 cups)
1 tablespoon lemon juice (optional)

1 cup sugar
¼ cup flour
¼ teaspoon cloves
2 tablespoons butter or margarine

MAKES 6 TO 8 SERVINGS

1. On lightly floured surface, roll out half of pastry into an 11-inch circle. Use to line 9-inch pie plate; trim. Refrigerate, with rest of pastry, until ready to use.

2. Preheat oven to 425F.

3. Wash berries gently in cold water; drain.

4. In large bowl, combine berries with lemon juice, mixing well.

5. Combine sugar, flour, and cloves. Add to berries, tossing lightly to combine.

6. Turn into pastry-lined pie plate, mounding high in center; dot with butter.

7. Roll out remaining pastry into an 11-inch circle. Make several slits near center, for steam vents; adjust over filling; trim.

8. Fold edge of top crust under bottom crust; press together. Crimp edge decoratively.

9. Bake 45 to 50 minutes, or until juices start to bubble up through steam vents and crust is golden-brown.

10. Cool partially on wire rack; serve warm.

BEST CHERRY PIE

Pastry for 2-crust pie
2 cans (1-lb size) tart red
  cherries, packed in
  water
1 cup sugar
⅓ cup unsifted all-purpose
  flour

⅛ teaspoon salt
2 tablespoons butter or
  margarine
¼ teaspoon almond extract
¼ teaspoon red food color
1 egg yolk

1. Preheat oven to 425F. Make pastry. Wrap in waxed paper, and refrigerate until ready to use.

2. Drain cherries, reserving 1 cup liquid.

3. Combine sugar, flour, and salt; stir into cherry liquid in saucepan. Bring to boiling, stirring.

4. Reduce heat, and simmer 5 minutes. Mixture will be thickened. Stir in butter.

5. Add almond extract and food color. Add cherries; refrigerate, covered.

6. Roll half of pastry, on lightly floured surface, into an 11-inch circle. Fit into 9-inch pie plate; trim. Roll other half of pastry into an 11-inch circle. With knife or pastry wheel, cut eight ½-inch wide strips.

7. Pour cooled cherry filling into pie shell.

8. Moisten edge of pie shell with cold water. Arrange 4 pastry strips across filling; press ends to rim of shell.

9. Place 4 pastry strips across first ones at right angles, to make lattice. Press ends to rim of shell.

10. Fold overhang of lower crust over ends of strips, to make a rim; crimp decoratively.

11. Lightly brush top, not edge, with egg yolk beaten with 1 tablespoon water.

12. Bake 30 to 35 minutes, or until pastry is nicely browned. Cool partially on wire rack; serve slightly warm.

FRESH-CONCORD-GRAPE PIE

Pastry for 2-crust pie
5½ cups Concord grapes
1 cup sugar
¼ cup flour
⅛ teaspoon salt

1 teaspoon grated lemon
  peel
1 tablespoon grated orange
  peel
2 tablespoons butter or
  margarine

1. On lightly floured surface, roll out half of pastry into an 11-inch circle. Use to line 9-inch pie plate; trim. Refrigerate, with rest of pastry, until ready to use.

2. Preheat oven to 425F.

3. Wash grapes; drain. Remove skin from each grape by pressing between thumb and forefinger until skin breaks and pulp pops out; set skins aside.

4. In medium saucepan, over medium heat, bring pulp to boiling, stirring; boil 2 minutes.

5. Press pulp through sieve, to remove seeds.

6. In large bowl, combine pulp with skins, mixing well.

(*Fresh-Concord-Grape Pie continued*)

7. In small bowl, combine sugar, flour, and salt. Add to grape mixture, along with lemon and orange peel; mix well.

8. Turn into pastry-lined pie plate. Dot with butter.

9. Roll out remaining pastry into an 11-inch circle. Make several slits near center for steam vents; adjust over filling; trim.

10. Fold edge of top crust under bottom crust; press together with fingertips. Crimp edge decoratively.

11. Bake 40 to 45 minutes, or until crust is golden.

12. Cool partially on wire rack; serve warm.

FRESH-CRANBERRY-RAISIN PIE

MAKES 6 TO 8 SERVINGS

Pastry for 2-crust pie
3 cups fresh cranberries
2 tablespoons flour
2 cups sugar
¼ teaspoon salt
⅔ cup boiling water

1 cup seedless raisins
2 teaspoons grated lemon
    peel
2 tablespoons butter or
    margarine
1 egg, beaten

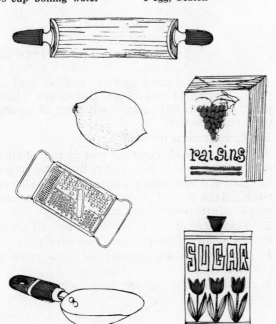

1. Roll out half of pastry, on lightly floured surface, into an 11-inch circle. Use to line 9-inch pie plate; trim. Refrigerate, with rest of pastry, until ready to use.

2. Preheat oven to 400F.

3. Wash cranberries, removing stems.

4. Combine flour, sugar, and salt in 3½-quart saucepan. Stir in cranberries, water, raisins, and lemon peel.

5. Cook, covered, over medium heat until cranberries start to pop—about 10 minutes. Remove from heat.

6. Add butter; cool about 5 minutes.

7. Meanwhile, roll out other half of pastry into an 11-inch circle. With knife or pastry wheel, cut 8 (½-inch-wide) strips.

8. Turn cranberry-raisin filling into pie shell. Moisten edge of shell slightly with cold water. Arrange 4 pastry strips, 1 inch apart, across filling; press ends to rim of pastry. Place 4 pastry strips across first ones, at right angles, to make lattice. Press ends to rim of shell.

9. Fold overhang of lower crust over ends of strips, to make a rim. Crimp rim decoratively. Lightly brush pastry with egg.

10. Bake 45 to 50 minutes, or until crust is nicely browned. Cool partially on wire rack; serve slightly warm.

LATTICE-TOP PEACH PIE

MAKES 6 TO 8 SERVINGS

Pastry for 2-crust pie
6 cups thinly sliced, pared
   ripe peaches (about
   2½ lb)
1 teaspoon lemon juice

¾ cup light-brown sugar,
   firmly packed
2 tablespoons flour
¼ teaspoon salt
¼ teaspoon cinnamon

1. On lightly floured surface, roll out half of pastry into an 11-inch circle. Use to line 9-inch pie plate. Refrigerate.

2. Roll out remaining pastry into a 12-inch circle. With knife or pastry wheel, cut fourteen ¾-inch-wide strips. Refrigerate, on waxed paper, until ready to use.

3. Preheat oven to 425F.

4. In large bowl, sprinkle peaches with lemon juice.

5. In small bowl, combine sugar, flour, salt, and cinnamon, mixing well.

6. Add to peaches, tossing lightly to combine.

7. Turn mixture into pastry-lined pie plate.

8. Moisten edge of shell slightly with cold water. Arrange 7 pastry strips across filling; press ends to rim of pastry.

9. Place 7 pastry strips across first ones, at right angles, to make lattice. Press ends to rim of shell.

10. Fold overhang of lower crust over ends of strips, to make a rim. Crimp decoratively.

11. Bake 45 to 50 minutes, or until peaches are tender and crust is golden.

12. Cool on wire rack.

BRANDIED-MINCEMEAT PIE

MAKES 6 TO 8 SERVINGS

Pastry for 2-crust pie
1 jar (28 oz) prepared
   mincemeat (3 cups)
1 cup coarsely chopped
   walnuts

¼ cup diced candied
   orange peel, chopped
2 tablespoons sliced
   candied cherries
¼ cup brandy or sherry

To Flame Mincemeat Pies:

Cut 4 kumquats in half, lengthwise.
Scoop out inside of each half.
Soak 8 small sugar cubes in lemon extract a few minutes; place one in each kumquat half.
Arrange kumquat halves, on top of crust, near edge of pie.
Take pie to table; light the sugar cubes.

1. On lightly floured surface, roll out half of pastry into an 11-inch circle. Use to line 9-inch pie plate; trim. Refrigerate, with rest of pastry, until ready to use.

2. Preheat oven to 425F.

3. In large bowl, combine rest of ingredients, mixing well. Turn into pastry-lined pie plate.

4. Roll out remaining pastry into an 11-inch circle. Make several slits near center for steam vents; adjust over filling; trim.

5. Fold edge of top crust under bottom crust; press together. Crimp edge decoratively.

6. Bake 40 to 45 minutes, or until crust is golden-brown.

7. Cool partially on wire rack; serve warm.

PEACH-AND-BLUEBERRY PIE

2 tablespoons lemon juice
3 cups sliced, pitted, peeled
    peaches (about
    2¼ lb)
1 cup blueberries
1 cup sugar

2 tablespoons quick-
    cooking tapioca
½ teaspoon salt
Pastry for 2-crust pie
2 tablespoons butter or
    margarine

1. Sprinkle lemon juice over fruit in large bowl.

2. Combine sugar with tapioca and salt. Add to fruit, tossing lightly to combine. Let stand 15 minutes.

3. Meanwhile, preheat oven to 425F.

4. On lightly floured surface, roll out half of pastry into an 11-inch circle. Use to line 9-inch pie plate; trim.

5. Turn fruit mixture into pastry-lined pie plate, mounding in center; dot with butter.

6. Roll out remaining pastry into an 11-inch circle. Make several slits near center, for steam vents; adjust over filling; trim.

7. Fold edge of top crust under bottom crust; press together with fingertips. Crimp edge decoratively.

8. Bake 45 to 50 minutes, or until fruit is tender and crust is golden-brown.

9. Cool partially on wire rack; serve slightly warm.

RASPBERRY-AND-APPLE PIE

1 tablespoon lemon juice
2 cups thinly sliced, pared,
    cored tart cooking
    apples
2 cups raspberries
1 cup sugar

2 tablespoons quick-
    cooking tapioca
½ teaspoon salt
Pastry for 2-crust pie
2 tablespoons butter or
    margarine

1. Sprinkle lemon juice over fruit in large bowl.

2. Combine sugar with tapioca and salt. Add to fruit, tossing lightly to combine. Let stand 15 minutes.

3. Meanwhile, preheat oven to 425F.

4. On lightly floured surface, roll out half of pastry into an 11-inch circle. Use to line 9-inch pie plate; trim.

5. Turn fruit mixture into pastry-lined pie plate, mounding in center; dot with butter.

6. Roll out remaining pastry into an 11-inch circle. Make several slits near center, for steam vents; adjust over filling; trim.

7. Fold edge of top crust under bottom crust; press together with fingertips. Crimp edge decoratively.

8. Bake 45 to 50 minutes, or until fruit is tender and crust is golden-brown.

9. Cool partially on wire rack; serve slightly warm.

FRESH-RHUBARB PIE

Orange Flaky Pastry for
  2-Crust Pie*
1½ cups sugar
⅓ cup unsifted all-purpose
  flour

4 cups fresh rhubarb, cut
  into ½-inch pieces
  (about 1¾ lb)
2 tablespoons butter or
  margarine
Granulated sugar

1. On lightly floured surface, roll out half of pastry into an 11-inch circle. Use to line 9-inch pie plate; trim. Refrigerate, with rest of pastry, until ready to use.

2. Preheat oven to 400F.

3. In small bowl, combine 1½ cups sugar and flour; mix well.

4. Add to rhubarb in large bowl, tossing lightly to combine.

5. Turn into pastry-lined pie plate, mounding high in center; dot with butter.

6. Roll out remaining pastry into an 11-inch circle. Make several slits near center, for steam vents; adjust over filling; trim.

7. Fold edge of top crust under bottom crust; press together with fingertips. Crimp edge decoratively. Sprinkle with sugar.

8. Bake 50 to 55 minutes, or until rhubarb is tender and crust is golden-brown.

9. Cool partially on wire rack; serve slightly warm.

* See this chapter.

SPICED PLUM PIE

2 tablespoons lemon juice
4 cups sliced, pitted,
  unpeeled purple
  plums (about 3 lb)
1 cup sugar
2 tablespoons quick-
  cooking tapioca

½ teaspoon cinnamon
½ teaspoon nutmeg
Pastry for 2-crust pie
2 tablespoons butter or
  margarine

1. Sprinkle lemon juice over plums in large bowl.

2. Combine sugar with tapioca, cinnamon, and nutmeg. Add to plums, tossing lightly to combine. Let stand 15 minutes.

3. Meanwhile, preheat oven to 425F.

4. On lightly floured surface, roll out half of pastry into an 11-inch circle. Use to line 9-inch pie plate; trim.

5. Turn plum mixture into pastry-lined pie plate, mounding in center; dot with butter.

6. Roll out remaining pastry into an 11-inch circle. Make several slits near center, for steam vents; adjust over filling; trim.

7. Fold edge of top crust under bottom crust; press together with fingertips. Crimp edge decoratively.

8. Bake 45 to 50 minutes, or until plums are tender and crust is golden-brown.

9. Cool partially on wire rack; serve slightly warm.

One-crust Pies with Cream Fillings

These delectable, creamy pies make super desserts. Whether it's chocolate cream or butterscotch cream or coconut cream, hidden under a fluffy meringue or whipped cream, do be sure to follow our recipes to the letter. They must be smooth and firm enough to slice neatly. A cream pie that does not hold its shape defeats its purpose as a tempting dessert. Unlike fruit pies, pies with creamy fillings are served cold.

BUTTERSCOTCH MERINGUE PIE

9-inch baked pie shell

Filling:
¾ cup light-brown sugar, firmly packed
¼ cup granulated sugar
¼ cup cornstarch
½ teaspoon salt
2½ cups milk
3 egg yolks, slightly beaten

2 tablespoons butter or margarine
1 teaspoon vanilla extract

Meringue:
3 egg whites, at room temperature
¼ teaspoon cream of tartar
6 tablespoons granulated sugar

MAKES 6 TO 8 SERVINGS

1. Prepare and bake pie shell; let cool.
2. Make Filling: In medium saucepan, combine sugars, cornstarch, and salt; mix well.
3. Gradually stir in milk, mixing until smooth.
4. Over medium heat, bring to boiling, stirring; boil 1 minute, stirring constantly. Remove from heat.
5. Stir half of hot mixture into egg yolks, mixing well; pour back into saucepan.
6. Bring back to boiling, stirring; boil 1 minute longer. Remove from heat.
7. Stir in butter and vanilla; pour immediately into pie shell.
8. Meanwhile, preheat oven to 400F.
9. Make Meringue: In medium bowl, with portable electric mixer at medium speed, beat egg whites and cream of tartar until soft peaks form when beater is raised.
10. Gradually beat in sugar, 2 tablespoons at a time, beating well after each addition. Continue to beat until stiff peaks form when beater is raised.
11. Spread meringue over warm filling, sealing to edge of crust.
12. Bake 7 to 10 minutes, or until meringue is golden.
13. Cool on wire rack, away from drafts, 1 hour before serving.

Butterscotch Cream Pie: Instead of meringue topping, spread ½ cup heavy cream, whipped, combined with 2 tablespoons sifted confectioners' sugar, on top of cooled filling. Refrigerate until ready to serve.

CHOCOLATE MERINGUE PIE

MAKES 6 TO 8 SERVINGS

9-inch baked pie shell

Filling:
1 cup sugar
5 tablespoons cornstarch
2 squares unsweetened
    chocolate, cut up
½ teaspoon salt
2½ cups milk

3 egg yolks, slightly beaten
½ teaspoon vanilla extract
½ teaspoon almond extract

Meringue:
3 egg whites, at room
    temperature
¼ teaspoon cream of tartar
6 tablespoons sugar

1. Prepare and bake pie shell; let cool.
2. Make Filling: In medium saucepan, combine sugar, cornstarch, chocolate, and salt; mix well.
3. Gradually stir in milk, mixing until smooth.
4. Over medium heat, bring to boiling, stirring; boil 1 minute, stirring constantly. Remove from heat.
5. Stir half of hot mixture into egg yolks, mixing well; pour back into saucepan.
6. Bring back to boiling, stirring; boil 1 minute longer. Remove from heat.
7. Stir in extracts; pour immediately into pie shell.
8. Meanwhile, preheat oven to 400F.
9. Make Meringue: In medium bowl, with portable electric mixer at medium speed, beat egg whites and cream of tartar until soft peaks form when beater is raised.
10. Gradually beat in sugar, 2 tablespoons at a time, beating well after each addition. Continue to beat until stiff peaks form when beater is raised.
11. Spread meringue over warm filling, sealing to edge of crust.
12. Bake 7 to 10 minutes, or until meringue is golden.
13. Cool on wire rack, away from drafts, 1 hour before serving.

Chocolate Cream Pie: Instead of meringue topping, spread ½ cup heavy cream, whipped, combined with 2 tablespoons sifted confectioners' sugar, on top of cooled filling. Refrigerate until ready to serve.

FRESH-COCONUT CREAM PIE

MAKES 6 TO 8 SERVINGS

9-inch baked pie shell
1 cup sugar
½ cup cornstarch
¼ teaspoon salt
3 cups hot milk

3 egg yolks, beaten
1 teaspoon vanilla extract
½ teaspoon almond extract
2 cups grated fresh coconut
1 cup heavy cream

1. Prepare and bake pie shell; let cool completely before filling.
2. Combine sugar, cornstarch, and salt; gradually add to milk in medium saucepan, stirring until smooth. Bring to boiling, stirring, over medium heat; boil 2 minutes. Remove from heat.
3. Stir half of hot mixture into egg yolks; then combine with rest in saucepan.

(Fresh-Coconut Cream Pie continued)

4. Cook, stirring and over low heat, until it boils and is thick enough to mound from spoon —about 5 minutes.

5. Turn into bowl; stir in extracts and half of coconut. Place waxed paper directly on filling; refrigerate 1 hour.

6. Turn into pie shell; refrigerate 3 hours.

7. To serve: Whip cream, and spread over filling; top with remaining coconut.

Note: Or use 2 cans (3½-oz size) flaked coconut in place of grated fresh coconut.

LEMON MERINGUE PIE

MAKES 8 SERVINGS

9-inch baked pie shell

Filling:
⅓ cup cornstarch
1½ cups sugar
¼ teaspoon salt
4 egg yolks, slightly beaten
¼ cup lemon juice
2 tablespoons grated lemon
    peel

2 tablespoons butter or
    margarine

Meringue:
4 egg whites (½ cup), at
    room temperature
¼ teaspoon cream of tartar
½ cup sugar

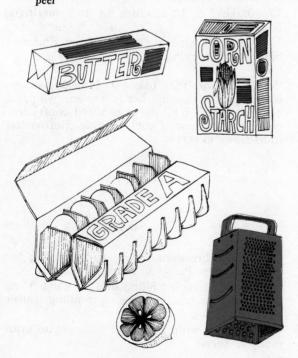

1. Prepare and bake pie shell; let cool.

2. Make Filling: In small saucepan, combine cornstarch, sugar, and salt. Gradually add 1½ cups water, stirring until smooth.

3. Over medium heat, bring to boiling, stirring constantly; boil 1 minute, stirring.

4. Remove from heat; quickly stir half of hot mixture into egg yolks, mixing well. Return to saucepan, blending well.

5. Over medium heat, return to boiling, stirring; boil 1 minute.

6. Remove from heat. Stir in lemon juice, lemon peel, and butter. Pour immediately into pie shell.

7. Meanwhile, preheat oven to 400F.

8. Make Meringue: In medium bowl, with portable electric mixer at medium speed, beat egg whites with cream of tartar until soft peaks form when beater is raised.

9. Gradually beat in sugar, 2 tablespoons at a time, beating well after each addition. Continue to beat until stiff peaks form when beater is raised.

10. Spread meringue over hot filling, carefully sealing to edge of crust.

11. Bake 7 to 9 minutes, or just until meringue is golden.

12. Let cool on wire rack, away from drafts, at least 1 hour before serving.

Fresh-Lime Meringue Pie: Substitute ½ cup fresh lime juice and 1 tablespoon grated lime peel for lemon juice and lemon peel. Add a few drops green food color to filling, if desired.

VANILLA MERINGUE PIE

MAKES 6 TO 8 SERVINGS

9-inch baked pie shell

Filling:
¾ cup sugar
¼ cup cornstarch
2½ cups milk
½ teaspoon salt
3 egg yolks, slightly beaten

1 tablespoon butter or margarine
1 teaspoon vanilla extract

Meringue:
3 egg whites, at room temperature
¼ teaspoon cream of tartar
6 tablespoons sugar

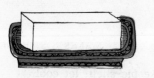

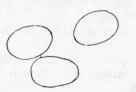

1. Prepare and bake pie shell; let cool.
2. Make Filling: In medium saucepan, combine sugar, cornstarch, and salt; mix well.
3. Gradually stir in milk, mixing until smooth.
4. Over medium heat, bring to boiling, stirring; boil 1 minute, stirring constantly. Remove from heat.
5. Stir half of hot mixture into egg yolks, mixing well; pour back into saucepan.
6. Bring back to boiling, stirring; boil 1 minute longer. Remove from heat.
7. Stir in butter and vanilla; pour immediately into pie shell.
8. Meanwhile, preheat oven to 400F.
9. Make Meringue: In medium bowl, with portable electric mixer at medium speed, beat egg whites and cream of tartar until soft peaks form when beater is raised.
10. Gradually beat in sugar, 2 tablespoons at a time, beating well after each addition. Continue to beat until stiff peaks form when beater is raised.
11. Spread meringue over warm filling, sealing to edge of crust.
12. Bake 7 to 10 minutes, or until meringue is golden.
13. Cool on wire rack, away from drafts, 1 hour before serving.

Vanilla Cream Pie: Instead of meringue topping, spread ½ cup heavy cream, whipped, combined with 2 tablespoons sifted confectioners' sugar, on top of cooled filling. Refrigerate until ready to serve.

BANANA CREAM PIE

MAKES 6 TO 8 SERVINGS

1. Follow directions for preparing filling for Vanilla Cream Pie; cool filling completely.
2. Pour half cooled filling into pie shell. Then slice two bananas; arrange over filling. Cover with remaining filling.
3. Top with whipped cream. Refrigerate until ready to serve.

SOUR-CREAM—RAISIN PIE

MAKES 8 SERVINGS

9-inch baked pie shell
1 cup light-brown sugar,
    firmly packed
2 tablespoons flour
½ teaspoon nutmeg
½ teaspoon cinnamon
¼ teaspoon salt
1 cup dairy sour cream
3 eggs, separated
1 cup seedless raisins
6 tablespoons granulated
    sugar

1. Prepare and bake pie shell; cool on wire rack.
2. Combine brown sugar, flour, spices, salt, and sour cream in top of double boiler; cook, over simmering water, stirring constantly, 5 minutes, or until slightly thickened.
3. In medium bowl, with rotary beater, beat egg yolks until slightly thickened. Beat hot sugar mixture, a small amount at a time, into egg yolks. Return to double-boiler top; cook 5 minutes. Add raisins; cool. Turn into pie shell.
4. Preheat oven to 350F.
5. In large bowl of electric mixer, at high speed, beat egg whites until soft peaks form. Add granulated sugar gradually (a tablespoon at a time), beating until stiff peaks form. Spread meringue over filling, and seal to edge of crust.
6. Bake 15 minutes, or until delicately browned. Cool 1 hour before serving.

One-crust Pies with Baked Fillings

Here we have such old favorites as pecan pie, open-face fruit pie, pumpkin pie, and many others, including Dutch apple pie. There are several things you can do to decorate the open-face baked pie. For instance, Pennsylvania-Dutch cooks serve their pumpkin pie with pastry strips crisscrossed over the top. Mennonite women mix several tablespoons of molasses into whipped cream, and spoon it over pumpkin pie. Women from the Deep South sprinkle chopped Brazil nuts over theirs. And speaking of Southern cooks, whoever created the first pecan pie should get a medal.

DUTCH APPLE PIE

MAKES 6 TO 8 SERVINGS

9-inch unbaked pie shell

Topping:
⅔ cup sifted all-purpose
    flour
⅓ cup light-brown sugar,
    firmly packed
⅓ cup butter or margarine

Filling:
2 lb tart cooking apples
1 tablespoon lemon juice
2 tablespoons flour
¾ cup granulated sugar
Dash salt
1 teaspoon cinnamon

1. Prepare pie shell; refrigerate until used.
2. Make Topping: Combine flour and sugar in medium bowl. Cut in butter, with pastry blender or 2 knives, until mixture is consistency of coarse cornmeal. Refrigerate.
3. Preheat oven to 400F.
4. Make Filling: Core apples, and pare; thinly slice into large bowl. Sprinkle with lemon juice.
5. Combine flour, sugar, salt, and cinnamon, mixing well. Toss lightly with apples.
6. Turn filling into unbaked pie shell, spreading evenly. Cover with topping; bake 40 to 45 minutes, or until apples are tender.

CHERRY PIE SUPREME

9-inch unbaked pie shell
1 can (1 lb, 6 oz) cherry-pie
   filling
4 pkg (3-oz size) soft cream
   cheese

½ cup sugar
2 eggs
½ teaspoon vanilla extract
1 cup dairy sour cream

1. Preheat oven to 425F.
2. Prepare pie shell. Spread half of cherry-pie filling in bottom; set rest aside.
3. Bake shell 15 minutes, or just until crust is golden. Remove from oven.
4. Reduce oven temperature to 350F.
5. Meanwhile, in small bowl, with portable electric mixer, beat cheese with sugar, eggs, and vanilla until smooth.
6. Pour over hot cherry-pie filling: bake 25 minutes. (Filling will be slightly soft in center.)
7. Cool completely on wire rack.
8. To serve: Spoon sour cream around edge of pie. Fill center with remaining cherry-pie filling.

Blueberry Pie Supreme: Follow above recipe, substituting 1 can (1 lb, 6 oz) blueberry-pie filling for cherry-pie filling.

PERFECT CUSTARD PIE

9-inch baked pie shell
4 eggs
⅔ cup sugar
½ teaspoon salt

¼ teaspoon nutmeg
1⅓ cups milk
1 cup heavy cream
1 teaspoon vanilla extract

1. Prepare and bake pie shell; let cool completely.
2. Preheat oven to 350F.
3. Beat eggs slightly; then add remaining ingredients, and beat until well mixed.
4. Pour into buttered 9-inch pie plate; set plate in pan of cold water; bake 30 to 35 minutes, or until silver knife inserted 1 inch from edge of filling comes out clean. The center may look a bit soft, but it will set as custard cools.
5. When filling is completely cool, loosen from pie plate by carefully running a small spatula around edge and shaking plate gently.
6. Holding custard just above far rim of pastry shell, carefully slip it into shell.

PEACH CREAM PIE GLACÉ

9-inch unbaked Cookie-
   Crust Pie Shell*
4 pkg (3-oz size) soft cream
   cheese
½ cup sugar

2 eggs
¼ teaspoon cinnamon
5 fresh ripe peaches (about
   1¾ lb)
¼ cup peach preserves

1. Prepare pie shell; refrigerate until ready to fill.
2. Preheat oven to 375F.
3. In small bowl of electric mixer, at medium speed, beat cheese until light and fluffy.
4. At low speed, beat in sugar, eggs, and cinnamon until smooth.

(Peach Cream Pie Glacé continued)

5. Pour filling into unbaked pie shell. Bake 30 minutes, or until pastry is golden-brown and filling is set. Cool completely on wire rack.

6. Wash peaches; peel. Halve peaches; remove pits, and slice. Arrange sliced peaches over cooled filling.

7. In small saucepan, combine peach preserves with 2 teaspoons water. Cook, stirring, over low heat, until preserves are melted.

8. Press preserve mixture through sieve, to purée. Spoon evenly over peach slices.

9. Refrigerate 1 hour, or until well chilled.

* See this chapter.

GLAZED CHERRY PIE

MAKES 6 SERVINGS

9-inch unbaked pie shell
½ cup finely chopped
    blanched almonds
4 cups fresh pitted red
    cherries; or 2 cans
    (1-lb, 4-oz size) tart
    red cherries, drained
1 cup sugar
⅛ teaspoon salt

¼ cup flour
1 tablespoon lemon juice
2 tablespoons butter or
    margarine
¾ cup red-currant jelly
⅛ teaspoon cloves
⅛ teaspoon cinnamon
¾ cup whipped cream
    (optional)

1. Make pie shell. Sprinkle almonds over bottom.

2. Preheat oven to 375F.

3. In large bowl, combine cherries, sugar, salt, flour, and lemon juice. Pour into unbaked pie shell.

4. Dot with butter; bake 40 minutes. Cool pie on wire rack.

5. Melt jelly in small saucepan. Stir in cloves and cinnamon. Spoon over cherries. Cool. If desired, serve topped with whipped cream.

PEAR PIE WITH STREUSEL TOPPING

MAKES 6 SERVINGS

9-inch Almond-Pastry Shell
    (recipe follows)

Streusel Topping:
⅔ cup sifted all-purpose
    flour
⅓ cup light-brown sugar,
    firmly packed
⅓ cup butter or margarine

Filling:
¼ cup granulated sugar
¼ teaspoon ginger
4 teaspoons flour
5 ripe Bartlett pears (2 lb)
4 teaspoons lemon juice
¼ cup light corn syrup

1. Prepare Almond-Pastry Shell.

2. Make Streusel Topping: In small bowl, combine flour and sugar. Cut in butter, with pastry blender or 2 knives, until mixture is like coarse cornmeal. Refrigerate until ready to use.

3. Preheat oven to 450F.

4. Make Filling: Combine sugar, ginger, and flour; sprinkle about a third of mixture over bottom of pie shell.

5. Peel and core pears; slice thinly into bowl. Arrange half of pears in shell; top with a third of sugar mixture. Arrange remaining pears; top with remaining sugar mixture. Drizzle lemon juice and corn syrup over top.

6. Cover with Streusel Topping; bake 15 minutes. Reduce oven temperature to 350F, and bake 30 minutes.

453

ALMOND-PASTRY SHELL

MAKES 9-INCH SHELL

1 cup sifted all-purpose
    flour
½ teaspoon salt
⅓ cup shortening
¾ cup finely chopped
    toasted almonds
2 tablespoons ice water

1. Sift flour and salt into medium bowl.

2. Cut in shortening, with pastry blender or 2 knives, until mixture is like coarse cornmeal. Stir in almonds.

3. Sprinkle ice water gradually over mixture, tossing with fork. Shape into a ball; roll, between sheets of waxed paper, into an 11-inch circle. Refrigerate until ready to use.

4. Fit pastry into 9-inch pie plate. If it is crumbly, press gently against pie plate, to repair breaks. Form neat rim around edge of pie plate; do not crimp.

PECAN PIE

MAKES 6 TO 8 SERVINGS

9-inch unbaked pie shell
3 eggs
½ cup light-brown sugar,
    firmly packed
1 cup dark corn syrup
½ teaspoon salt
1 teaspoon vanilla extract
¼ cup butter or margarine,
    melted
1 cup pecan halves, cut in
    half
½ cup heavy cream,
    whipped (optional)

1. Prepare pie shell; refrigerate until ready to fill.

2. Preheat oven to 375F.

3. Beat eggs well in medium bowl.

4. Add sugar, corn syrup, salt, and vanilla; beat until well combined.

5. Stir in butter and pecans, mixing well.

6. Turn into unbaked pie shell; bake 45 to 50 minutes, or until filling is set in center when pie is gently shaken. Let cool.

7. Before serving, garnish with rosettes of whipped cream, if desired.

OPEN-FACE PLUM PIE

MAKES 6 TO 8 SERVINGS

9-inch Kuchen Pie Shell
    (recipe follows)
1½ lb Italian plums
2 tablespoons granulated
    sugar
1½ teaspoons grated
    orange peel
Confectioners' sugar

1. Prepare pie shell; refrigerate until ready to fill.

2. Preheat oven to 400F.

3. Wash plums. Cut into quarters; remove pits. Arrange plums, in tight circular rows, in pie shell. Sprinkle with granulated sugar and orange peel.

4. Bake 15 minutes. Reduce oven temperature to 350F; bake 45 minutes longer.

5. Sprinkle with confectioners' sugar. Cool partially on wire rack; serve warm.

KUCHEN PIE SHELL

MAKES 9-INCH SHELL

1½ cups sifted all-purpose flour
¼ teaspoon baking powder
½ cup soft butter or margarine

1 egg
⅓ cup sugar
Dash salt

1. Sift flour, baking powder into medium bowl.
2. With portable electric mixer, or back of spoon, blend in butter until smooth.
3. In small bowl, beat egg until frothy. Gradually beat in sugar and salt, beating until mixture is thick and lemon-colored.
4. Add to flour mixture, mixing until smooth.
5. Turn dough into center of greased 9-inch pie plate. Press dough evenly over bottom and side, not on rim, of pie plate.
6. Refrigerate until ready to fill.

PRALINE-PUMPKIN PIE

MAKES 8 SERVINGS

9-inch unbaked pie shell

Praline Layer:
⅓ cup finely ground pecans, firmly packed
⅓ cup light-brown sugar, firmly packed
2 tablespoons soft butter or margarine

Filling:
2 eggs
1 cup canned pumpkin

⅔ cup light-brown sugar, firmly packed
1 tablespoon flour
¼ teaspoon cloves
⅛ teaspoon mace
½ teaspoon cinnamon
½ teaspoon ginger
½ teaspoon salt
1 cup light cream

1. Prepare pie shell; refrigerate until ready to use.
2. Preheat oven to 400F.
3. Make Praline Layer: Blend all ingredients in small bowl. Press gently onto bottom of pie shell, with back of spoon.
4. Make Filling: In medium bowl, with rotary beater, beat eggs until frothy. Add remaining ingredients, in order; then beat only until well mixed.
5. Pour into unbaked pie shell; bake 50 to 55 minutes, or until tip of sharp knife inserted in center comes out clean. Cool thoroughly on wire rack.

BRANDIED-PUMPKIN PIE

MAKES 6 TO 8 SERVINGS

9-inch Almond-Pastry Shell*

Filling:
1 cup canned pumpkin
1 cup evaporated milk, undiluted
1 cup light-brown sugar, firmly packed

3 eggs, slightly beaten
¼ cup brandy
1 teaspoon pumpkin-pie spice**
¾ teaspoon salt

Heavy cream, whipped

1. Prepare Almond-Pastry Shell.
2. Preheat oven to 400F.
3. Make Filling: Combine pumpkin, milk, and sugar in large bowl, blending until well mixed.
4. Then stir in eggs, brandy, pie spice, and salt; mix well.
5. Pour filling into prepared pie shell; bake 50 to 55 minutes, or until tip of sharp knife inserted in center comes out clean. Cool on wire rack.
6. Just before serving, garnish pie with 6 to 8 rosettes of whipped cream.
* See this chapter.
** Or use 1 teaspoon cinnamon, 1 teaspoon nutmeg, ½ teaspoon ginger, and ½ teaspoon mace.

455

PUMPKIN PIE

Filling:
2 eggs, slightly beaten
¾ cup sugar
1½ teaspoons cinnamon
½ teaspoon nutmeg
½ teaspoon ginger
¼ teaspoon allspice
¼ teaspoon cloves
½ teaspoon salt

1 can (1 lb) pumpkin
3 tablespoons molasses
2 cans (6-oz size)
    evaporated milk,
    undiluted

9-inch unbaked pie shell
1 egg white, unbeaten

1. Preheat oven to 400F.
2. Make Filling: In large bowl, combine eggs, sugar, spices, salt, pumpkin, molasses, and evaporated milk. Stir, with wooden spoon, until mixture is smooth.
3. Lightly brush pie shell with egg white. Fill with pumpkin mixture.
4. Bake 55 to 60 minutes, or until tip of sharp knife inserted in center comes out clean.
5. Let cool on wire rack. Serve garnished with whipped cream, if desired.

PRUNE-WALNUT CREAM PIE

9-inch unbaked Cookie-
    Crust Pie Shell*

Filling:
3 eggs
¼ cup sifted all-purpose
    flour
1 cup sugar
½ teaspoon salt
⅛ teaspoon cinnamon

¾ cup milk
½ cup prune juice
1 teaspoon vanilla extract
1 cup coarsely cut dried
    prunes
¼ cup coarsely chopped
    walnuts

1 cup heavy cream

1. Prepare Cookie-Crust Pie Shell; refrigerate.
2. Preheat oven to 375F.
3. Make Filling: Beat eggs slightly in medium bowl.
4. Sift flour with sugar, salt, and cinnamon over eggs.
5. Stir in milk, prune juice, vanilla, and prunes.
6. Pour into unbaked pie shell, distributing prunes evenly. Sprinkle with walnuts.
7. Bake 50 minutes, or until filling is set in center when pie is shaken gently. Cool to room temperature on wire rack.
8. Whip cream, and serve as topping.
* See this chapter.

SOUTHERN CHESS PIE

9-inch unbaked pie shell
3 eggs
1 cup light-brown sugar,
    firmly packed
½ cup soft butter or
    margarine

1 teaspoon vanilla extract
1 cup seedless raisins
½ cup coarsely chopped
    walnuts or pecans

Whipped cream (optional)

1. Prepare pie shell; refrigerate until ready to fill.
2. Preheat oven to 375F.
3. In medium bowl, with rotary beater, beat eggs slightly.
4. Add sugar, butter, and vanilla; beat until well blended. Stir in raisins and walnuts.
5. Turn into unbaked pie shell; bake 40 to 50 minutes, or just until filling is set in center. (Shake pie gently; center should be firm.)
6. Let cool on wire rack. If desired, serve garnished with whipped cream.

SHOOFLY PIE

MAKES 6 TO 8 SERVINGS

½ pkg (10-oz size) piecrust mix

1 cup sifted all-purpose flour

½ cup light-brown sugar, firmly packed

½ teaspoon salt

½ teaspoon cinnamon

⅛ teaspoon nutmeg

⅛ teaspoon cloves

2 tablespoons butter, margarine, or shortening

½ teaspoon baking soda

½ cup light molasses

1 egg, well beaten

1. Preheat oven to 375F. Make pastry as package label directs.

2. On lightly floured surface, roll out pastry to form an 11-inch circle.

3. Use to line a 9-inch pie plate. Trim edge, and crimp. Refrigerate until ready to use.

4. In medium bowl, combine flour, sugar, salt, and spices, mixing well. Add butter; using fingers, rub into flour mixture to make crumbs.

5. Pour ¾ cup hot water over baking soda in small bowl; stir to dissolve. Beat in molasses and egg, combining well.

6. Sprinkle one fourth crumb mixture in bottom of pie shell. Top with one third molasses mixture. Continue layering, ending with crumb mixture.

7. Bake 35 minutes, or until filling is firm to the touch when lightly pressed with fingertip.

8. Serve pie warm, with vanilla ice cream or whipped cream, if desired.

One-crust Pies with Refrigerated Fillings

These pies have an advantage besides their marvelous taste and appearance. They need not be made at the last minute, but can be done ahead and chilled.

Your husband is going to love the refrigerated chiffon pies. And if you've never made one before, you'll be gratified by how easy they are. Included, besides the chiffon pies, are glazed fruit pies that are as pretty as pictures.

CARIBBEAN RUM PIE

MAKES 8 SERVINGS

9-inch Unbaked Graham-Cracker Pie Shell*

Filling:

1 envelope unflavored gelatine

3 egg yolks

6 tablespoons sugar

¼ cup light rum, or 1 teaspoon rum extract in ¼ cup water

1 cup heavy cream

½ square unsweetened chocolate

1. Prepare pie shell; refrigerate until filled.

2. Make Filling: Sprinkle gelatine over ¼ cup cold water; let soften. Dissolve over hot water; cool.

3. Beat egg yolks until thick and fluffy.

4. Add sugar gradually, beating well after each addition. Stir in rum.

5. Whip cream; fold carefully into egg mixture, along with gelatine. Pour into pie shell.

6. Refrigerate 2 to 3 hours, or until set. Shave unsweetened chocolate over pie, as garnish.

* See this chapter.

457

CHOCOLATE BAVARIAN PIE

MAKES 6 TO 8 SERVINGS

9-inch baked pie shell
2 teaspoons unflavored
    gelatine
½ cup milk
2 egg yolks
¼ cup sugar

Dash salt
1 teaspoon vanilla extract
¾ cup grated sweet
    chocolate
2 cups heavy cream
Chocolate Curls*

1. Prepare and bake pie shell; let cool completely before filling.
2. Sprinkle gelatine over ¼ cup cold water, to soften.
3. In top of double boiler, heat milk until film forms over surface.
4. In small bowl, with rotary beater, beat egg yolks, sugar, salt, and ½ teaspoon vanilla until thick and creamy.
5. Beat a small amount of hot milk into egg mixture. Stir egg mixture quickly into remaining hot milk in top of double boiler.
6. Over boiling water, cook, stirring, about 5 minutes, or until mixture coats a metal spoon.
7. Stir in gelatine and grated chocolate. Continue cooking, over simmering water, 3 minutes, or until chocolate is melted.
8. Remove from heat; cover surface with waxed paper; refrigerate until chilled.
9. In medium bowl, with rotary beater, whip cream with remaining vanilla.
10. Fold half of whipped cream into chocolate mixture. Pour into baked pie shell. Top with remaining whipped cream; garnish with chocolate curls. Chill before serving.

*To Make Chocolate Curls: Let square or bar of chocolate warm to room temperature. With sharp paring knife or vegetable parer, cut thin curls from back of square.

LEMON CHIFFON PIE

MAKES 6 TO 8 SERVINGS

9-inch baked pie shell
1 envelope unflavored
    gelatine
1 cup sugar
¼ teaspoon salt
4 egg yolks
½ cup lemon juice

1 tablespoon grated lemon
    peel
4 egg whites, at room
    temperature
1 cup heavy cream,
    whipped

1. Prepare and bake pie shell; let cool completely before filling.
2. In top of double boiler, combine gelatine with ½ cup sugar and the salt.
3. In small bowl, beat egg yolks with lemon juice and ½ cup water just until combined. Add to gelatine mixture, mixing well.
4. Cook, stirring constantly, over boiling water (water in bottom should not touch base of top of double boiler) until gelatine dissolves and mixture is hot and thickens—about 5 minutes.
5. Remove from hot water. Stir in lemon peel.
6. Set in bowl filled with ice cubes 20 to 30 minutes, stirring occasionally, until gelatine mixture is thick and mounds when dropped from a spoon.

(Lemon Chiffon Pie continued)

7. Meanwhile, in large bowl of electric mixer, at high speed, beat egg whites until soft peaks form when beater is raised.

8. Gradually add remaining ½ cup sugar, 2 tablespoons at a time, beating well after each addition. Continue beating until stiff peaks form when beater is raised.

9. With rubber scraper, using an under-and-over motion, gently fold gelatine mixture into egg whites, just until combined.

10. Turn into pie shell; refrigerate several hours, or until firm.

11. Just before serving, whip cream until stiff. Spread over pie filling.

Lime Chiffon Pie: Make Lemon Chiffon Pie as directed above, substituting ½ cup fresh-lime juice, and 1 tablespoon grated lime peel for lemon juice and lemon peel. Add a few drops green food color when folding gelatine mixture into egg whites.

PUMPKIN CHIFFON PIE

MAKES 6 TO 8 SERVINGS

9-inch Unbaked Graham-
   Cracker Pie Shell*
1 envelope unflavored
   gelatine
½ cup light-brown sugar,
   firmly packed
½ teaspoon salt
1½ teaspoons pumpkin-pie
   spice

2 tablespoons light
   molasses
3 egg yolks, slightly beaten
½ cup milk
1¼ cups canned pumpkin
3 egg whites
½ cup granulated sugar

Whipped cream (optional)

1. Prepare pie shell; refrigerate until needed.

2. In small saucepan, combine gelatine, brown sugar, salt, and spice, mixing well.

3. Add molasses, egg yolks, milk, and pumpkin, mixing well.

4. Bring to boiling, stirring; remove from heat.

5. Transfer to medium bowl; cool; then refrigerate, covered, until firm.

6. Meanwhile, in small bowl, with rotary beater, beat egg whites until foamy.

7. Gradually beat in sugar, 2 tablespoons at a time, beating well after each addition. Continue to beat until stiff peaks form when beater is raised.

8. Then beat pumpkin mixture until smooth.

9. Gradually beat egg-white mixture into pumpkin mixture just until combined.

10. Turn mixture into pie shell; refrigerate until firm—about 2 hours. Serve garnished with whipped cream, if desired.

Note: If filling is too soft to mound when turned into pie shell, refrigerate about 10 minutes. Then turn into pie shell.

* See this chapter.

STRAWBERRY CHIFFON PIE

MAKES 6 SERVINGS

9-inch baked pie shell
3 egg yolks
1 teaspoon lemon juice
¼ teaspoon salt
½ cup plus 2 tablespoons
    sugar

1 envelope unflavored
    gelatine
3 egg whites, at room
    temperature
1 pint box fresh strawberries
Red food color

1.   Prepare and bake pie shell; let cool completely before filling.

2.   In top of double boiler, beat egg yolks until frothy. Add lemon juice, salt, and ½ cup sugar.

3.   Place over hot water; cook, stirring, until thickened—about 7 to 8 minutes. Remove from heat.

4.   Meanwhile, sprinkle gelatine over ½ cup cold water in small bowl; let stand 5 minutes to soften. Then stir into egg mixture to dissolve.

5.   Gently wash berries in cold water. Drain; hull. Set aside ½ cup berries.

6.   In medium bowl, crush remaining berries with potato masher. Stir in egg-gelatine mixture and few drops red food color.

7.   Refrigerate until consistency of unbeaten egg white—about 1 hour.

8.   In large bowl, with rotary beater, beat egg whites until stiff peaks form when beater is slowly raised.

9.   Gradually beat in 2 tablespoons sugar.

10.   Gently fold in strawberry mixture just until combined. (If too thin to mound, refrigerate 10 to 15 minutes, to set slightly.)

11.   Turn into baked pie shell; refrigerate 2 hours, or until set. Before serving, garnish with reserved whole berries.

STRAWBERRY-GLAZED CHEESE PIE

MAKES 6 SERVINGS

8-inch baked pie shell

Glaze:
3 cups fresh strawberries
    (about 1 pint box)
1 cup sugar
2 tablespoons cornstarch

Filling:
1 pkg (8 oz) cream cheese

⅓ cup sugar
1 teaspoon grated orange
    peel
2 tablespoons orange juice
2 tablespoons light cream
3 cups fresh strawberries
    (about 1 pint box)

½ cup heavy cream,
    whipped (optional)

1.   Make pie shell; bake; cool.

2.   Make Glaze: Gently wash berries in cold water. Drain; hull.

3.   In medium saucepan, with potato masher, crush berries. Combine sugar and cornstarch; stir into crushed berries.

4.   Over low heat, stirring constantly, bring to boiling. Mixture will be thickened and translucent. Strain; cool.

5.   Meanwhile, make Filling: Let cheese warm to room temperature.

6.   In medium bowl, with portable electric mixer, beat cheese, sugar, orange peel and juice, and light cream until light and fluffy. Spread in baked, cooled pie shell.

(Strawberry-Glazed Cheese Pie continued)

7. Gently wash berries in cold water. Drain; hull.

8. Arrange evenly over cream-cheese mixture. Pour cooled glaze over berries.

9. Refrigerate until chilled—about 3 hours. Serve with whipped cream, if desired.

FRESH-STRAWBERRY GLACÉ PIE

9-inch baked pie shell

Glaze:
1 pint box fresh
　strawberries
1 cup granulated sugar
2½ tablespoons cornstarch
1 tablespoon butter or
　margarine

Filling:
2 pint boxes fresh
　strawberries
2 tablespoons Cointreau or
　orange juice

1 cup heavy cream,
　whipped
2 tablespoons sifted
　confectioners' sugar

MAKES 6 TO 8 SERVINGS

1. Prepare and bake pie shell; let cool.

2. Make Glaze: Wash strawberries gently in cold water. Drain; hull. In medium saucepan, crush strawberries with potato masher.

3. Combine sugar and cornstarch; stir into crushed strawberries. Add ½ cup water.

4. Over low heat, stirring constantly, bring to boiling. Mixture will be thickened and translucent.

5. Strain; add butter. Cool.

6. Meanwhile, make Filling: Wash strawberries gently in cold water. Drain; hull. Measure 3 cups; reserve rest for garnish.

7. In medium bowl, gently toss strawberries with Cointreau; let stand about 30 minutes. Then arrange in baked pie shell.

8. Pour cooled glaze over strawberries. Refrigerate until well chilled—about 2 hours.

9. Just before serving, whip cream until stiff; fold in confectioners' sugar. To serve, garnish pie with reserved strawberries and whipped cream.

Strawberry Devonshire Glacé Pie: Combine 1 pkg (3 oz) soft cream cheese with 1 tablespoon light cream. Spread over bottom of cooled pie shell before adding strawberries.

Dumplings, Turnovers, and Tarts

These small pastries go something like this: The *dumpling* is a pastry sack containing a whole fruit. It may have a glaze of its own juices as they run into the pan, and it may be served with a separate sauce or pour cream. The *tart* is a miniature open-face pie, and it is usually filled with fruit. The *turnover* is a triangular envelope of pastry with fruit inside; it is sealed on all sides, so that none of the juice escapes. It is served hot, sometimes with a dollop of ice cream or whipped cream on top. And is it good!

GLAZED APPLE DUMPLINGS

MAKES 6

Pastry for 2-crust pie
6 medium baking apples
6 tablespoons granulated
    sugar
½ teaspoon nutmeg

6 tablespoons soft butter
    or margarine

Syrup:
2 cups light-brown sugar,
    firmly packed

1. Make pastry; form into a ball. Wrap in waxed paper, and refrigerate until ready to use.
2. Pare and core apples.
3. Combine sugar and nutmeg.
4. On lightly floured surface, divide pastry into 6 parts.
5. Roll each part into a 7- to 9-inch circle or square.
6. Place apple in center of each. Fill hollow with 1 tablespoon sugar-nutmeg mixture and 1 tablespoon butter. Mold pastry around each apple, covering completely.
7. Place in 13-by-9-by-2-inch baking pan; refrigerate 30 minutes.
8. Meanwhile, preheat oven to 425F.
9. Make Syrup: In small saucepan, combine sugar with 1 cup water. Over medium heat, dissolve sugar, stirring. Bring to boiling; boil gently 5 minutes.
10. Spoon 1 tablespoon syrup over each dumpling; bake, uncovered, 10 minutes.
11. Remove from oven; pour remaining syrup over dumplings. Continue baking 25 to 30 minutes, basting occasionally with syrup, or until apples are tender.
12. Serve warm, with syrup spooned over, and with cream, if desired.

PEACH DUMPLINGS

MAKES 6

Pastry for 2-crust pie
6 medium-ripe, medium-
    size peaches
6 tablespoons granulated
    sugar

6 tablespoons butter or
    margarine
Nutmeg

Syrup:
2 cups light-brown sugar,
    firmly packed

1. Make pastry; form into ball. Wrap in waxed paper, and chill in refrigerator.
2. Peel peaches; remove pits, being careful to keep peaches whole.
3. Fill each cavity with 1 tablespoon granulated sugar and 1 tablespoon butter. Sprinkle top with nutmeg.
4. Roll pastry into rectangle about 15 by 10 inches and ⅛ inch thick. Cut into 6 squares.
5. Place a peach in center of each square, and mold pastry around it, covering peach completely.
6. Place dumplings in deep baking pan, and refrigerate 30 minutes.
7. Preheat oven to 425F.

(*Peach Dumplings continued*)

8. Make Syrup: In saucepan, over medium heat, cook brown sugar with ½ cup water, stirring, about 5 minutes.

9. Spoon some syrup over each dumpling; bake 10 minutes.

10. Reduce oven temperature to 350F, and bake 30 to 40 minutes, basting with syrup at 10-minute intervals. Serve warm or cold, with heavy cream or whipped cream, if desired.

TURNABOUT TURNOVERS

2 pkg (10-oz size) piecrust mix
⅔ cup butter or margarine
Blueberry or Red-Cherry Filling, follows
Blueberry or Red-Cherry Sauce, follows
1 egg yolk
Confectioners' sugar

MAKES 8

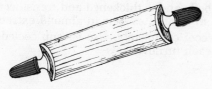

1. Prepare each package of pastry as label directs; form each into a ball. Wrap in waxed paper; chill about 1 hour.

2. Meanwhile, let butter soften to room temperature. On lightly floured surface, roll each ball of pastry into a 12-by-16-inch rectangle.

3. Carefully spread each rectangle with ⅓ cup soft butter, leaving ½-inch margin all around (don't tear pastry).

4. Now fold pastry lengthwise into thirds; with your fingers, pinch ends together to seal. Then fold crosswise into thirds.

5. Wrap in waxed paper; refrigerate about 2 hours (butter should be firm).

6. While pastry chills, make filling and sauce. Preheat oven to 425F.

7. Then, on lightly floured surface, roll each batch of pastry into a 12-inch square. Cut each into four 6-inch squares. (If pastry becomes soft and difficult to handle, refrigerate between sheets of waxed paper about 15 minutes.)

8. Put ½ cup fruit filling on diagonal half of each pastry square. Lightly brush edges with water; fold to form triangle. With floured fork, seal edges firmly.

9. Place turnovers on ungreased cookie sheet; chill 10 minutes.

10. Brush tops with egg yolk beaten with 1 tablespoon water.

11. Bake 20 to 25 minutes, or until nicely browned. Serve warm, sprinkled with confectioners' sugar, and with one of the sauces.

To do ahead: Wrap each unbaked turnover in saran or foil; freeze until ready to use. About an hour before serving, preheat oven to 475F. Lightly brush turnovers with egg yolk beaten with 1 tablespoon water. Bake frozen turnovers 20 to 25 minutes, or until nicely browned.

BLUEBERRY FILLING

2 tablespoons brown sugar
2 tablespoons cornstarch
⅛ teaspoon salt
⅛ teaspoon nutmeg
Dash ground cloves

2 teaspoons lemon juice
4 cups fresh blueberries, or
   3 pkg (12-oz size)
   thawed frozen
   blueberries*

1. In saucepan, thoroughly combine sugar, cornstarch, salt, nutmeg, and cloves.
2. Stir in ¼ cup water and lemon juice until well blended. Add blueberries.
3. Cook mixture, stirring, over medium heat, until it boils and is thickened and translucent —about 5 to 6 minutes.
4. Let cool completely. Use ½ cup cooled filling for each turnover.

* If you use thawed frozen blueberries: Drain, reserving ¼ cup syrup. Use syrup instead of water. Proceed as above.

RED-CHERRY FILLING

3 cans (1-lb size) pitted red
   sour cherries (packed
   in water)
3 tablespoons sugar

3 tablespoons cornstarch
⅛ teaspoon salt
1 teaspoon lemon juice
⅛ teaspoon almond extract

1. Drain cherries, reserving ¼ cup liquid. In saucepan, thoroughly combine sugar, cornstarch, and salt.
2. Stir in cherry liquid and lemon juice until well blended. Add cherries.
3. Cook mixture, stirring, over medium heat, until it boils and is thickened and translucent— about 5 to 6 minutes. Stir in almond extract.
4. Let cool completely. Use ½ cup cooled filling for each turnover.

BLUEBERRY SAUCE

¼ cup sugar
2 tablespoons cornstarch
2 teaspoons lemon juice

1⅓ cups fresh blueberries,
   or 1 pkg (12 oz)
   thawed frozen
   blueberries*

1. In saucepan, thoroughly combine sugar and cornstarch. Stir in 1½ cups water, lemon juice, and blueberries.
2. Cook mixture, stirring, over medium heat, until it boils and is thickened and translucent— about 5 to 6 minutes. Serve warm over turnovers.

* If you use thawed frozen blueberries: Drain, reserving syrup. Add enough water to syrup to measure 1½ cups. Proceed as above, using syrup instead of water.

RED-CHERRY SAUCE

1 can (1 lb) pitted red sour
    cherries, packed in
    water
⅔ cup sugar
3 tablespoons cornstarch

2 tablespoons butter or
    margarine
1 teaspoon lemon juice
Few drops red food color
    (optional)

MAKES ABOUT 2 CUPS

1. Drain cherries, reserving liquid. If necessary, add water to liquid to measure 1⅓ cups.
2. In saucepan, thoroughly combine sugar and cornstarch. Stir in cherry liquid.
3. Cook mixture, stirring, over medium heat, until it boils and is thickened and translucent —about 5 to 6 minutes.
4. Add butter and lemon juice, stirring until butter melts. Add red food color, if desired.
5. Measure ½ cup drained cherries; stir into hot sauce. Serve warm over turnovers.

APPLE-RAISIN TURNOVERS

Pastry for 2-crust pie

Filling:
1 can (1 lb, 4 oz) sliced
    apples, drained and
    chopped
¼ cup sugar
1 tablespoon flour

¼ teaspoon cinnamon
¼ teaspoon nutmeg
¼ cup seedless raisins
1 tablespoon grated orange
    peel (optional)

1 egg white
2 tablespoons sugar

MAKES 8

1. Prepare pastry; form into a ball. Wrap in waxed paper, and refrigerate.
2. Make Filling: In medium bowl, combine all ingredients; mix well.
3. On lightly floured surface, roll pastry into an 18-by-9-inch rectangle. Cut rectangle into eight 4½-inch squares. Moisten edges of each.
4. Spread 2 tablespoons filling on half of each square; fold over; seal edges with tines of fork. Prick top of each in 3 places, with fork.
5. Beat egg white slightly, with 1 tablespoon water; use to brush turnovers. Sprinkle each with a little of the sugar.
6. Bake, on ungreased cookie sheets, about 20 minutes, or until crust is golden-brown.
7. Cool partially on wire rack; serve warm.

Individual Baked Tart Shells

FLUTED TART SHELLS

MAKES 8 OR 10

1. Prepare pastry for 2-crust pie.
2. Divide pastry in half; divide each half into 5 parts.
3. On lightly floured surface, roll each part into a 5-inch circle. Use each circle to line a 3½-inch fluted tart pan, pressing pastry evenly to bottom and side of each pan; trim.
4. Prick each tart shell well with fork; refrigerate 30 minutes.
5. Meanwhile, preheat oven to 450F.
6. Bake shells, on large cookie sheet, 10 to 12 minutes, or until golden-brown.
7. Cool completely on wire racks; then carefully remove shells from pans. Fill as desired.
Note: For thicker shells, divide pastry in half; divide each half into 4 parts. Proceed as above.

PETAL TART SHELLS

1. Prepare pastry for 2-crust pie.
2. Divide pastry in half. On lightly floured surface, roll each half ⅛ inch thick.
3. With 2¼-inch, round cookie cutter, cut 18 circles out of each half.
4. Place 1 circle in bottom of each of 6 (6-oz) custard cups.
5. Then arrange 5 circles, overlapping, around side of each custard cup, moistening edges of each and pressing firmly to side and bottom.
6. Prick shells with fork; refrigerate 30 minutes.
7. Meanwhile, preheat oven to 450F.
8. Bake shells, on large cookie sheet, 10 to 12 minutes, or until golden-brown.
9. Cool completely on wire racks; then carefully remove shells from custard cups. Fill as desired.

PLEATED TART SHELLS

1. Prepare pastry for 2-crust pie.
2. Divide pastry in half; divide each half into 5 parts. On lightly floured surface, roll each part into a 6½-inch circle.
3. Invert saucer over each circle; with sharp knife or pastry wheel, trim to edge of saucer.
4. Fit a circle over outside of each of 10 inverted 3-inch muffin-pan cups or 6-oz custard cups; pinch into pleats, to fit snugly.
5. Prick shells with fork; refrigerate 30 minutes.
6. Meanwhile, preheat oven to 450F.
7. Bake shells 10 to 12 minutes, or until golden-brown.
8. Cool thoroughly on wire racks; then carefully remove shells from muffin-pan cups. Fill as desired.

SANDWICH TARTS

1. Preheat oven to 450F. Prepare pastry for 2-crust pie.
2. Divide pastry in half. On lightly floured surface, roll each half into a 9-inch square. With 3-inch, round cookie cutter, cut 9 circles out of each half (or, with sharp knife, cut into 9 squares).

(Sandwich Tarts continued)

3. Transfer to ungreased cookie sheets; prick each with fork. Bake 10 to 12 minutes, or until golden-brown.

4. Remove to wire rack; let cool. To serve, put together, sandwich fashion, with ice cream or fruit; top with a sauce.

CANAPÉ TART SHELLS

MAKES 64

1. Prepare Cheese Pastry for 2-Crust Pie.*
2. Divide pastry in half. On lightly floured surface, roll each half ⅛ inch thick.
3. With 1¾-inch, round cookie cutter, cut 32 circles out of each half.
4. Fit each circle into a 1¼-inch muffin-pan cup. Prick with fork.
5. Refrigerate 15 minutes.
6. Meanwhile, preheat oven to 425F.
7. Bake shells 12 to 15 minutes, or until golden-brown.
8. Cool completely on wire racks; then carefully remove from muffin-pan cups. Fill as desired.
* See this chapter.

BANBURY TARTS

MAKES 18

Filling:
½ cup finely chopped
    walnuts
1 cup finely chopped
    seedless raisins
1 tablespoon grated lemon
    peel
2 tablespoons lemon juice
1 cup sugar

2 tablespoons butter or
    margarine, melted
1 egg, slightly beaten
2 tablespoons packaged dry
    bread crumbs

Pastry for 2-crust pie
1 egg yolk

1. Make Filling: In medium bowl, combine all ingredients; set aside.
2. Preheat oven to 425F.
3. Prepare pastry; divide in half. Roll each half into a 12-inch square. Cut each square into 9 (4-inch) squares.
4. Spread 1 tablespoon filling, diagonally, over half of each square; moisten edges.
5. Fold pastry over to form a triangle; press edges together with tines of fork.
6. Beat egg yolk with 2 tablespoons water; use to brush top of tarts.
7. Prick top of each tart in three places with fork.
8. Bake, on ungreased cookie sheets, 15 to 18 minutes, or until crust is golden-brown.
9. Cool on wire rack.

MINIATURE COCONUT TARTS

Pastry:
1⅓ cups sifted all-purpose
    flour
⅓ cup sugar
¼ teaspoon salt
¾ cup butter or margarine
1 egg, slightly beaten

Filling:
1 egg
1 pkg (3½ oz) flaked
    coconut
⅔ cup sugar

1. Make Pastry: Sift flour with sugar and salt into medium bowl. With pastry blender or 2 knives, cut in butter until mixture is like coarse cornmeal. With fork, stir in egg.

2. Knead slightly, with hands, until mixture holds together. Wrap in waxed paper; refrigerate several hours, or until firm.

3. Then preheat oven to 375F. Make Filling: With fork, beat egg in small bowl. Add coconut and sugar; mix well.

4. For each tart: Pinch off about 1 teaspoon chilled dough. Press into 2-by-½-inch tartlet pan, to make a lining ⅛ inch thick.

5. Fill each tart with 1 teaspoon filling.

6. Bake tarts (about 24 at a time), set on cookie sheet, 12 minutes, or until coconut filling is golden-brown.

7. Place pans on wire rack; cool slightly. With small spatula, gently remove tarts.

TINY CURRANT TARTS

Pastry for 2-crust pie
½ cup sugar
1 tablespoon flour
¼ teaspoon salt
¼ cup light corn syrup
1 tablespoon lemon juice

1 tablespoon grated lemon
    peel
⅓ cup butter or margarine,
    melted
1 egg, slightly beaten
½ cup currants

1. Prepare pastry; divide in half.

2. On lightly floured surface, roll each half ⅛ inch thick.

3. With 1¾-inch, round cookie cutter, cut out circles. Fit each circle into a 1¼-inch muffin-pan cup; refrigerate 15 minutes.

4. Preheat oven to 400F.

5. In medium bowl, combine sugar, flour, and salt, mixing well.

6. Add remaining ingredients; mix well.

7. Spoon 1 teaspoon filling into each pastry-lined muffin-pan cup.

8. Bake 20 to 25 minutes, or until pastry is golden-brown.

9. Remove immediately from pans; cool completely on wire racks.

STRAWBERRY TARTS

6 baked tart shells, 3½
    inches in diameter
1½ cups washed, hulled,
    sliced strawberries*
¼ cup sugar

1½ cups whole
    strawberries,* washed
    and hulled
½ cup currant jelly
2 drops red food color
½ cup heavy cream,
    whipped

1. Prepare tart shells; bake. Let shells cool.

2. In medium bowl, combine sliced berries and sugar.

3. Cut whole berries in half lengthwise.

4. In small saucepan, over moderate heat, stir jelly with food color until melted; cool.

(Strawberry Tarts continued)

5. Assemble tarts just before serving: Spoon about 3 tablespoons sliced berries into each tart shell.

6. Top with 4 or 5 berry halves, arranged in pattern. Brush with melted jelly. Top with whipped cream.

* Recipe requires 1½ pint boxes fresh strawberries in all.

VIENNA TARTS

½ cup soft butter or margarine

1 pkg (3 oz) soft cream cheese

1 cup sifted all-purpose flour

About 3 tablespoons redcurrant, raspberry, strawberry, or grape jelly

1 egg yolk

2 tablespoons milk

¼ cup finely chopped nuts

Confectioners' sugar

MAKES 3 DOZEN

1. With wooden spoon, cream butter and cheese until light. Stir in flour, mixing well. Refrigerate 1 hour.

2. Meanwhile, preheat oven to 400F.

3. Turn out dough onto lightly floured surface; roll out into 12-inch square. With sharp knife or pastry wheel, cut into 2-inch squares.

4. Place about ¼ teaspoon jelly near center of each square. Fold over to form a triangle; press edges to seal.

5. Brush top of each with mixture of egg yolk beaten with milk; sprinkle with nuts.

6. Bake, on ungreased cookie sheet, 8 to 10 minutes, or until golden. Sprinkle with confectioners' sugar; let cool on wire rack.

B e a famous hostess, and serve our tartlets—at teatime, on a buffet table, or with ice cream. Serve them either glazed or frosted. Recipes for both are given below.

GLAZED TARTLETS TRIUMPHANT

Praline Paste or Easy Praline Paste, below

Tartlet Shells, below

Pastry Cream, below

Assorted fruits (fresh, frozen, or canned)

Apricot Glaze, below

MAKES 65

1. Spoon ¼ teaspoon Praline Paste into each shell.

2. Add ½ teaspoon Pastry Cream to each shell; top with fruit of your choice. (Drain frozen or canned fruit.)

3. Spoon ½ teaspoon Apricot Glaze over fruit in each shell.

FROSTED TARTLETS TRIUMPHANT

Praline Paste or Easy Praline Paste, below

Tartlet Shells, below

Pastry Cream, below

Drained whole maraschino cherries (optional)

Chocolate or Vanilla Frosting, below

MAKES 65

1. Spoon ¼ teaspoon Praline Paste into each shell.

2. Add ½ teaspoon Pastry Cream; top with cherry. (If cherry is omitted, increase amount of cream to 1 teaspoon.)

3. Spoon about 1 teaspoon warm frosting over each tartlet. Decorate as desired.

PRALINE PASTE FOR TARTLETS

MAKES ½ CUP

¼ cup sugar
½ cup coarsely chopped
   pecans or hazelnuts

2 squares semisweet
   chocolate, melted

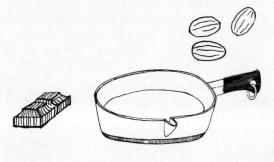

1. Lightly butter an 8-by-1½-inch round layer-cake pan or small cookie sheet.
2. Melt sugar in small, heavy skillet, over low heat, shaking pan from side to side. Continue to cook, stirring, until syrup turns light golden.
3. Remove from heat. Add nuts, stirring until just coated with syrup.
4. Working quickly, turn mixture into prepared pan. (Mixture will harden almost immediately.)
5. When cool, break into 2-inch pieces. Blend in food blender, to grind pieces finely.
6. In small bowl, combine ground nut mixture with chocolate, mixing well.

EASY PRALINE PASTE

MAKES ½ CUP

¼ lb nut brittle

2 squares semisweet
   chocolate, melted

1. Break up brittle into 2-inch pieces.
2. Blend in blender, to grind finely.
3. In small bowl, combine ground nut mixture with melted chocolate, mixing well.

TARTLET SHELLS

MAKES 65

½ cup soft butter or
   margarine
¼ cup sugar
¼ teaspoon salt
1 egg white

¼ teaspoon almond extract
¾ cup blanched almonds,
   ground
1 cup sifted all-purpose
   flour

1. In medium bowl, with spoon, blend butter, sugar, salt, egg white, and almond extract until smooth and well combined.
2. Add ground almonds and flour; mix until smooth. (If dough is very stiff, mix with hands.)
3. Wrap dough in waxed paper; refrigerate 1 hour.
4. Preheat oven to 375F.
5. For each tartlet, use 1 teaspoon dough. Press dough evenly into 2-by-½-inch tartlet pans.
6. Set tartlet pans on cookie sheet; bake about 10 minutes, or until golden-brown.
7. Let cool on wire rack 10 minutes. With small spatula, gently remove tartlets from pans. Let cool completely before filling.

Note: Tartlet Shells may be made day before and stored in an air-tight container.

PASTRY CREAM FOR TARTLETS

MAKES ABOUT 1¼ CUPS

¼ cup sugar
Dash salt
1 tablespoon cornstarch
1 cup milk

2 egg yolks, slightly beaten
½ teaspoon vanilla extract
¼ teaspoon almond extract

1. In small saucepan, mix sugar, salt, and cornstarch. Stir in milk.
2. Cook, stirring constantly, over medium heat, until mixture thickens and begins to boil; boil 1 minute. Remove from heat.
3. Add a little hot mixture to egg yolks, mixing well. Return to saucepan.
4. Cook, stirring constantly, until mixture is thick and bubbly.
5. Stir in extracts. Let cool to room temperature—about 1 hour.

APRICOT GLAZE FOR TARTLETS

MAKES 1 CUP

¾ cup apricot preserves   ¼ cup water

1. Combine preserves and water in small saucepan.
2. Stir, over medium heat, until preserves melt.
3. Press mixture through sieve. Spoon glaze over tartlets while it is still slightly warm.

CHOCOLATE FROSTING FOR TARTLETS

MAKES ⅔ CUP

2 tablespoons butter or
        margarine
⅓ cup sugar

2 squares unsweetened
        chocolate
1 teaspoon vanilla extract

1. In small saucepan, combine butter, sugar, chocolate, and ¼ cup water.
2. Stir, over medium heat, until chocolate melts and mixture is smooth and starts to boil.
3. Add vanilla. Spoon while still warm over tartlets.

VANILLA FROSTING FOR TARTLETS

MAKES ABOUT 1 CUP

2½ cups sifted
        confectioners' sugar
2 tablespoons light corn
        syrup

1 teaspoon vanilla extract
¼ teaspoon almond extract
Few drops red or green
        food color (optional)

1. In top of double boiler, combine all ingredients with 2 tablespoons water.
2. Cook, stirring, over hot water, just until frosting is smooth and shiny and coats a wooden spoon. Spoon while still warm over tartlets.
3. If frosting thickens on standing, thin it with a little water.

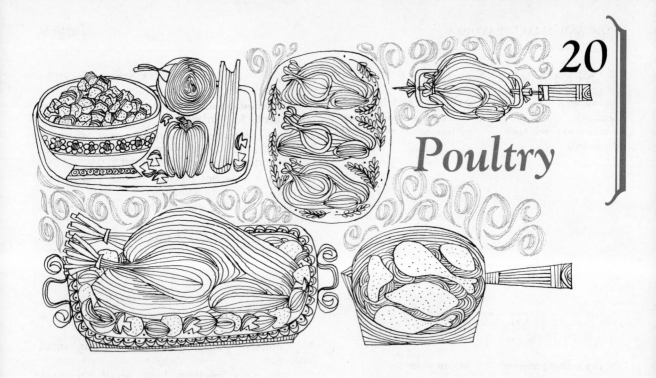

Poultry

Poultry, so plentiful and usually such a good buy any time of the year, is company food at family prices, a good thing to remember if you have to do much entertaining and your budget is limited.

Selection and Storage

When you buy chicken, choose your market for cleanliness. A good market keeps fresh chicken refrigerated and frozen chicken frozen at all times. The birds we buy in our markets today are the most carefully chaperoned in the world. Since January, 1959, virtually all chickens have passed a rigid processing-plant inspection by officials of the U.S. Department of Agriculture. All water and equipment used in processing must also be officially checked. Today, chickens are one of our safest, most carefully controlled foods.

Look for the government inspection mark on wing tags, outer wrappers, boxes, or giblet wrappers. If you do not see the mark on the chicken or its wrapping, check with your re-tailer. Most fresh, ice-packed chickens are shipped from the processor in large wooden boxes, which carry the inspection stamp. Although you will not find a mark on these chickens, you may be sure they traveled to your market in an adequately stamped crate.

How much should you buy? The figures below are amounts to buy for each serving:

Broiling   ½ of one 1½-pound broiler
Frying   ¾ pound
Roasting   ¾ pound
Stewing   ¾ pound

Remember these figures mean *per serving*, not per person served. Gauge your needs by the appetites of those eating. If you expect them to take seconds, figure how many servings you need, not how many people you will feed. Also, if yours is a dark-meat family, take advantage of legs and thighs sold separately. One whole chicken plus several legs will give each his choice.

Often, fresh ready-to-cook poultry arrives at the market in a plastic wrapping, which it wears right into your kitchen. If so, leave it in this wrapping, and keep it in the refrigerator until you are ready to cook it. Today's safe, clean packaging means these birds can be kept under refrigeration for several days or even a bit longer. If your butcher

cuts up your chicken or wraps it whole in his own wrappings, or if you buy parts, remove the butcher's wrappings when you get home. Rewrap loosely in foil, waxed paper, or transparent saran wrap, and keep chicken refrigerated until used. Use within a few days.

If you buy a frozen chicken or packaged frozen parts, keep frozen until 24 hours before cooking. Then unwrap, and leave it in the food compartment of your refrigerator overnight. Or, for quicker defrosting, unwrap, and thaw in running cold water for 1 to 2 hours.

Test Your Terminology

Broiler or broiler-fryer. Chicken about 9 weeks old, weighing 1½ to 3½ pounds. Tender, with smooth-textured skin and flexible breastbone cartilage. Of all chickens sold, 70 to 80 per cent are broiler-fryers.

Roaster. Tender chickens of 3½ to 5 pounds, about 12 weeks old.

Fryer. Same as broiler, but used to mean largest of the broilers, usually those weighing over 2½ pounds.

Stewing chicken. Mature female chickens, less tender than roasters. Can be broiler chickens allowed to grow old or layers past ideal age for laying eggs.

Capon. Desexed (through surgery) male chicken, weighing 4 to 8 pounds. Very tender, with large amount of white meat.

Ready-to-cook or oven-ready. All commercially produced birds are now sold ready to

cook. Pinfeathers are removed, hair singed, bird thoroughly cleaned inside and out; giblets cleaned, wrapped, and placed in cavity; bird shipped to market in iced wooden crates in refrigerated trucks.

New methods of feeding, distribution, and marketing have made the following terms obsolete:

Drawn. Dressed poultry with entrails, head, feet removed. All inspected poultry is shipped this way.

Fowl. Older female chickens, now referred to as stewing chickens.

Milk-fed. Fed rations high in milk to increase fat, bleach skin, soften muscle. Obsolete, since all poultry get milk by-products daily.

Spring chickens. Young cockerel chickens, once sold in the spring as by-product of the egg industry.

Chicken

Chicken boiled or broiled is delicate, tender, undemanding food for the invalid, the young person, the calorie-conscious. Cook it with wine, as the French so often do, and you

have a sophisticated treat. Or with oregano, like the Italians; with orange-almond sauce, like the Chinese; with paprika, as the Hungarians do; with curry, East Indian style.

BAKED CHICKEN BREASTS SUPREME

6 (12-oz size) broiler-fryer
   breasts
2 cups dairy sour cream
¼ cup lemon juice
4 teaspoons Worcestershire
   sauce
4 teaspoons celery salt
2 teaspoons paprika

4 cloves garlic, finely
   chopped
4 teaspoons salt
½ teaspoon pepper
1¾ cups packaged dry
   bread crumbs
½ cup butter or margarine
½ cup shortening

MAKES 12 SERVINGS

1. Cut chicken breasts in half; wipe well with damp paper towels.
2. In large bowl, combine sour cream with lemon juice, Worcestershire, celery salt, paprika, garlic, salt, and pepper.
3. Add chicken to sour-cream mixture, coating each piece well.
4. Let stand, covered, in refrigerator overnight.
5. Next day, preheat oven to 350F.
6. Remove chicken from sour-cream mixture. Roll in crumbs, coating evenly. Arrange in single layer in large, shallow baking pan.
7. Melt butter and shortening in small saucepan. Spoon half over chicken.
8. Bake chicken, uncovered, 45 minutes. Spoon rest of butter mixture over chicken.
9. Bake 10 to 15 minutes longer, or until chicken is tender and nicely browned.

CHICKEN BREASTS IN WINE

15 whole chicken breasts,
   boned and skinned
   (about 5½ lb)
1¾ cups butter or
   margarine
½ cup cognac
2½ lb small fresh
   mushrooms
5 lb small white onions
1½ teaspoons salt

¾ teaspoon pepper
2 bay leaves
⅛ teaspoon dried thyme
   leaves
2⅓ cups sauterne
3 cans (12½-oz size)
   chicken broth,
   undiluted
½ cup cornstarch
2½ cups heavy cream

MAKES 30 SERVINGS

1. Cut chicken breasts in half.
2. In two large skillets, divide 1¼ cups butter; heat. Fry chicken, a few pieces at a time, until golden—about 5 minutes on each side. Remove; set aside until all chicken is browned. Return to skillets.
3. Warm cognac in small saucepan. Divide over chicken; ignite.
4. Heat remaining butter in 2 (5-quart) Dutch ovens. Sauté mushrooms and onions about 10 minutes, stirring several times. Add chicken, salt, pepper, bay leaves, thyme, 2 cups sauterne, and chicken broth.
5. Cover, and simmer over low heat 20 minutes, or until chicken is fork-tender. (This much may be done a day ahead; but refrigerate overnight. Next day, reheat before proceeding.)
6. In small bowl, make a smooth paste of cornstarch and remaining sauterne. Gradually add to chicken; simmer, stirring, 5 minutes.
7. Stir in heavy cream; simmer, covered, 10 minutes.
8. Remove bay leaves. Serve in chafing dish or over candle warmer. Serve with Fluffy White Rice.*

* See Cereals Chapter.

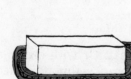

CHICKEN CURRY

5-lb ready-to-cook stewing chicken
1 onion, stuck with 4 whole cloves
3 celery tops
1 tablespoon salt
1 bay leaf

Curry Sauce:
2½ cups hot milk
3 cups packaged grated coconut
½ cup butter or margarine

2 cloves garlic, finely chopped
1½ cups chopped onion
¼ teaspoon ginger
1½ tablespoons curry powder
2 cups broth from chicken
½ cup sifted all-purpose flour
1 teaspoon salt
1 tablespoon lemon juice
1 cup light cream

1. In 6-quart kettle, place chicken, 12 cups water, onion stuck with cloves, celery tops, salt, and bay leaf; bring to boiling.
2. Reduce heat, and simmer, covered, 2 hours, or until chicken is tender.
3. Remove chicken; let cool. Then cut off meat in large pieces.
4. Reserve 2 cups broth; strain.
5. Make Curry Sauce: Pour hot milk over coconut; let stand 45 minutes.
6. In ¼ cup hot butter, sauté garlic, onion, and ginger until onion is tender—about 5 minutes. Stir in curry powder.
7. Turn into top of double boiler. Add chicken broth and coconut mixture.
8. Simmer, covered, over hot water, 1 hour; stir occasionally.
9. Strain mixture, pressing out as much liquid as possible. Discard coconut, garlic, and onion.
10. In medium saucepan, melt rest of butter; remove from heat.
11. Stir in flour, then strained liquid until smooth; bring to boiling, stirring constantly.
12. Reduce heat, and simmer 5 minutes, or until thickened and smooth.
13. Stir in salt, lemon juice, cream, and chicken; heat gently to boiling.
14. Serve over White Rice with Raisins.*

Note: Instead of stewing chicken and broth, you can use 4 cups cooked cut-up chicken and 2 cups canned chicken broth.

* See Cereals Chapter.

CHICKEN LIVERS IN WHITE WINE

½ cup butter or margarine
2 tablespoons finely chopped onion
2 tablespoons finely chopped parsley
2 lb thawed frozen chicken livers

1 teaspoon dried tarragon leaves
1 teaspoon salt
Dash pepper
2 tablespoons white wine

1. Heat butter in large skillet. In it, sauté onion and parsley about 5 minutes.
2. Add chicken livers; cook, stirring occasionally, about 8 minutes (livers should be browned on all sides and cooked through, but not overcooked).
3. Remove to heated platter.
4. Stir remaining ingredients into drippings in skillet; bring to boiling.
5. Pour over livers.

CHICKEN IN ORANGE-ALMOND SAUCE

1¾-lb broiler-fryer, cut in
    serving pieces
½ teaspoon salt
¼ cup butter or margarine
2 tablespoons flour
⅛ teaspoon cinnamon
Dash ginger

1½ cups orange juice
½ cup slivered blanched
    almonds
½ cup seedless raisins
1 cup orange sections
4 cups hot cooked rice

MAKES 4 SERVINGS

1. Wash chicken in cold water; pat dry with paper towels. Sprinkle with ¼ teaspoon salt.
2. Heat butter in large skillet. Brown chicken lightly; remove.
3. Mix flour, remaining salt, cinnamon, and ginger. Blend into pan drippings, to make a smooth paste.
4. Add orange juice; cook, stirring constantly, until sauce bubbles and thickens. Return chicken to skillet along with almonds and raisins.
5. Cover; cook over low heat about 45 minutes, or until chicken is fork-tender.
6. Add orange sections; heat through. Serve chicken and some of sauce on a bed of rice. Pass remaining sauce.

CHICKEN OREGANO

3- to 4-lb broiler-fryer,
    quartered
¼ cup lemon juice
2 tablespoons finely
    chopped parsley
1 clove garlic, finely
    chopped

2 teaspoons dried oregano
    leaves
⅓ cup olive oil
½ teaspoon salt
Dash pepper

MAKES 4 SERVINGS

1. Wash chicken; pat dry with paper towels.
2. In small bowl, combine lemon juice with remaining ingredients, mixing well.
3. Brush chicken on both sides with lemon-juice mixture. Place, skin side down, on rack in broiler pan.
4. Broil, 6 inches from heat, 15 minutes; brush occasionally with lemon-juice mixture.
5. Turn; broil, brushing with remaining lemon-juice mixture, 15 to 20 minutes longer, or until chicken is crisp and nicely browned. Serve chicken with pan juices spooned over.

CHICKEN PAPRIKA

¼ cup butter or margarine
2 tablespoons salad oil
2 (2½- to 3-lb size) broiler-
    fryers, cut up
½ cup sliced onion
½ cup sliced carrot
½ cup sliced celery
2 tablespoons paprika

3 tablespoons flour
1 tablespoon catsup
1½ teaspoons salt
¼ teaspoon pepper
1¾ cups canned chicken
    broth, undiluted
½ cup dairy sour cream

MAKES 6 TO 8 SERVINGS

1. Heat about half of butter and salad oil in Dutch oven or large, heavy skillet.
2. Brown chicken, a few pieces at a time, until golden on all sides (add more butter and oil as needed). Remove chicken as it browns.
3. In Dutch oven, sauté onion, carrot, and celery 5 minutes. Add paprika; cook 1 minute.
4. Remove from heat. Stir in flour, catsup, salt, and pepper. Gradually add chicken broth; bring to boiling point, stirring. Reduce heat; simmer, covered, 10 minutes.
5. Add browned chicken; simmer, covered, 35 to 40 minutes, or until chicken is tender. Remove chicken and vegetables to heated platter.
6. Stir sour cream into sauce; heat gently, stirring—do not boil. Pour some of sauce over chicken; pass rest in bowl.

CHICKEN STEW

5-lb ready-to-cook stewing
   chicken, cut in
   serving pieces
¼ cup butter or margarine
1 small onion, sliced
2 celery stalks, sliced
1 carrot, sliced

½ lemon, quartered
3 whole black peppers
1 bay leaf
Boiling water
2 teaspoons salt
¼ cup unsifted all-purpose
   flour

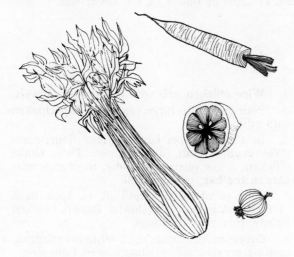

1. Wash chicken pieces; pat dry with paper towels.

2. In hot butter in large kettle, brown chicken pieces on both sides. Remove from heat.

3. Add onion, celery, carrot, lemon, black peppers, and bay leaf to chicken, along with boiling water to cover.

4. Bring to boiling; reduce heat, and simmer, covered, 45 minutes.

5. Add salt; simmer, covered, 1 hour longer, or until chicken is tender.

6. Remove from heat. Let stand until fat forms on surface.

7. Skim fat from chicken broth, reserving ¼ cup. Remove chicken pieces from broth; keep warm. Strain broth, reserving 3 cups.

8. Heat chicken fat in medium saucepan; remove from heat. Add flour, stirring to make a smooth paste. Slowly add chicken broth, stirring until smooth.

9. Bring to boiling, stirring. Reduce heat; simmer 1 minute.

10. Serve chicken with some of sauce spooned over; pass rest. Delicious with hot biscuits.

SWEET-SOUR BAKED CHICKEN

2½- to 3-lb broiler-fryer,
   cut in serving pieces
½ cup unsifted all-purpose
   flour
1 teaspoon salt
¼ teaspoon pepper
⅓ cup salad oil or melted
   shortening

Sauce:
½ cup cider vinegar
3 tablespoons light-brown
   sugar
⅓ cup chopped sweet
   gherkins
1 tablespoon Worcester-
   shire sauce
1 tablespoon catsup

1. Wipe chicken well with damp paper towels.

2. In clean paper bag, combine flour, salt, and pepper. Shake chicken pieces in bag until well coated with flour mixture.

3. Heat oil slowly in large skillet. Brown chicken in oil, a few pieces at a time, turning often. Place, skin up, in 13-by-9-by-2-inch baking dish.

4. Meanwhile, preheat oven to 350F. Make Sauce: In small bowl, combine vinegar and sugar, stirring to dissolve sugar. Blend in remaining ingredients.

5. Brush chicken pieces carefully with sauce. Pour rest over chicken.

6. Bake, covered, 30 minutes.

7. Baste with sauce; bake, uncovered, 15 minutes.

8. Serve with sauce spooned over.

Fried chicken can be crisp and delicate and easy to digest, or it can be greasy, heavy, and utterly unattractive. With our simple recipe, you'll make it perfectly and often—no doubt about that!

One thing about fried chicken— it's right, no matter what the occasion: cold at your next picnic, for instance; hot, at an important company dinner, with your good china and silver.

Incidental tips: Have a supply of paper bags and paper towels, if you plan to fry chicken often. The bag, to simplify flouring the chicken; the towels, to dry the chicken well, so that flour or bread crumbs or batter or whatever will adhere to it.

PERFECT FRIED CHICKEN

MAKES 4 SERVINGS

2½- to 3-lb broiler-fryer,
    cut in serving pieces
⅓ cup undiluted
    evaporated milk
¾ cup unsifted all-purpose
    flour

¾ cup packaged cornflake
    crumbs
2 teaspoons salt
¼ teaspoon pepper
Salad oil

1.   Wipe chicken well with damp paper towels.

2.   Pour milk into large pie plate. Dip chicken into milk.

3.   In a clean paper bag, combine flour, cornflake crumbs, salt, and pepper. Then shake chicken, a few pieces at a time, in crumb mixture in the bag, coating well.

4.   Pour salad oil to depth of ¼ inch in 2 (8-inch) skillets. Heat slowly. Brown chicken lightly, turning with tongs.

5.   Cover; reduce heat; cook 40 to 45 minutes, turning occasionally to ensure even browning.

6.   Remove cover; cook 5 minutes longer, to crisp the crust.

2.

3.

4.

BATTER-FRIED CHICKEN

2½- to 3-lb broiler-fryer,
    cut in serving pieces
½ cup unsifted all-purpose
    flour
Salad oil or shortening

Batter:
1½ cups sifted all-purpose
    flour

2 teaspoons baking powder
2 teaspoons salt
¼ teaspoon pepper
2 eggs
¾ cup milk
1½ tablespoons salad oil

1. Wipe chicken well with damp paper towels. Roll in flour.
2. In deep-fat fryer or deep skillet, slowly heat oil (at least 2 inches deep) to 350F on deep-frying thermometer.
3. Also, preheat oven to 300F.
4. Meanwhile, make Batter: Sift flour with baking powder, salt, and pepper; set aside.
5. In medium bowl, with rotary beater, beat eggs, milk, and oil until combined.
6. Add flour mixture gradually, beating until smooth.
7. Dip floured chicken pieces in batter, to coat evenly.
8. Deep-fry, a few pieces at a time and turning several times, 18 to 20 minutes, or until golden-brown and tender. Drain well on paper towels.
9. Place cooked chicken in shallow pan in oven, to keep warm while rest of chicken cooks.

FRIED CHICKEN HAWAIIAN

2½- to 3-lb broiler-fryer,
    cut in serving pieces
½ cup unsifted all-purpose
    flour
1 teaspoon salt
1 teaspoon ginger

¼ teaspoon pepper
¼ cup butter or margarine
1 can (8¾ oz) crushed
    pineapple, undrained
2 teaspoons soy sauce

1. Wipe chicken well with damp paper towels.
2. In a clean paper bag, combine flour, salt, ginger, and pepper. In it, shake chicken, a few pieces at a time, coating well.
3. Heat butter in large skillet. Add half the chicken pieces; brown well, turning often. Set browned chicken aside; brown remainder. Place all chicken in skillet.
4. In small bowl, combine pineapple, soy sauce, and ½ cup water; pour over chicken.
5. Cover; simmer 30 minutes, or until fork-tender. Serve with white rice.

OVEN-FRIED CHICKEN

2½- to 3-lb broiler-fryer, cut
    in serving pieces
½ cup unsifted all-purpose
    flour
1 teaspoon salt

⅛ teaspoon pepper
½ teaspoon poultry
    seasoning
½ cup melted butter or
    margarine

1. Preheat oven to 400F.
2. Wipe chicken well with damp paper towels.
3. In a clean paper bag, combine flour, salt, pepper, and poultry seasoning. Shake chicken in bag, a few pieces at a time, coating well.
4. Arrange chicken in very shallow pan (such as a 15-by-10-by-1-inch pan). Brush butter over chicken.
5. Cover pan with foil; bake 30 minutes.
6. Remove foil. Increase oven temperature to 450F; bake 15 to 20 minutes, or until fork-tender and golden-brown.

FRIED CHICKEN PROVENCAL

MAKES 4 SERVINGS

2½- to 3-lb broiler-fryer,
   cut in serving pieces
½ cup unsifted all-purpose
   flour
1½ teaspoons salt
½ teaspoon pepper
¼ cup butter or margarine
¼ cup olive or salad oil

¼ cup finely chopped
   onion
1 small clove garlic, finely
   chopped
1 cup finely chopped,
   peeled tomato
2 tablespoons finely
   chopped parsley

1. Wipe chicken well with damp paper towels.

2. In a clean paper bag, combine flour, salt, and pepper. In it, shake chicken, a few pieces at a time, coating well.

3. Slowly heat butter and oil in large skillet. To hot fat, add half the chicken pieces; brown well, turning often. Remove chicken as it browns; set aside. Brown rest of chicken.

4. In same fat in skillet, sauté onion and garlic until golden.

5. Add tomato and chicken; simmer, covered, 30 minutes, or until chicken is tender.

6. Remove chicken to heated platter. To serve: Drain tomato remaining in skillet; spoon over chicken. Sprinkle with parsley. Very nice with white rice.

TIMETABLE FOR ROASTING STUFFED CHICKEN—AT 325F
(Chicken and dressing should be at room temperature)

Chicken	Ready-To-Cook Weight	Approximate Roasting Time (hours)
Broiler-fryer	3 lb	1½*
Roaster	4 lb	3½
Capon	5 lb	2½
	8 lb	4½

* Broiler-fryers are roasted at **375F** for 30 minutes per pound.

ROAST CHICKEN WITH YAM STUFFING

MAKES 6 TO 8 SERVINGS

4-lb ready-to-cook roasting
   chicken

Stuffing:
1½ cups mashed cooked
   yams
¾ cup butter or margarine,
   melted
3 cups toasted bread cubes
1 cup finely chopped onion
¾ cup finely chopped
   celery
¾ teaspoon salt
½ teaspoon dried thyme
   leaves

½ teaspoon dried marjoram
   leaves
¼ teaspoon dried sage
   leaves
¼ teaspoon pepper

Gravy:
2 tablespoons flour
1½ cups canned chicken
   broth, undiluted
½ teaspoon salt
⅛ teaspoon pepper
¼ teaspoon liquid gravy
   seasoning

1. Rinse chicken well under cold water; dry well with paper towels.

2. Preheat oven to 350F.

3. Make Stuffing: In large bowl, with wooden spoon or portable electric mixer, beat yams with ¼ cup butter until light and fluffy.

4. Add rest of stuffing ingredients, except remaining butter, tossing lightly with fork to mix well.

5. Lightly fill neck and body cavities of chicken with stuffing—do not pack in. (Bake any leftover stuffing, in shallow dish, along with chicken the last 30 minutes.)

6. Truss chicken: Bring skin over neck opening; fasten to back with poultry pin. Close body cavity with poultry pins. Pin wings to body; then tie legs together, at ends, with twine.

(*Roast Chicken with Yam Stuffing continued*)

7. Place chicken, breast side up, on rack in shallow, open roasting pan. Cover with cheesecloth dipped in ¼ cup melted butter; roast, uncovered, 1½ hours.

8. Remove cheesecloth. Brush chicken with rest of melted butter; roast 45 minutes longer. Remove to warm platter; remove pins and twine. Keep warm.

9. Make Gravy: Pour drippings from roasting pan. Measure 2 tablespoons, and return to pan. Stir in flour, to make a smooth mixture.

10. Gradually add broth, stirring until smooth; bring to boiling over direct heat.

11. Reduce heat. Add rest of gravy ingredients; simmer 1 minute longer.

12. Serve gravy hot, with chicken and stuffing.

ROAST CHICKENS WITH HERB-MUSHROOM STUFFING

2 (2½-lb size) ready-to-
  cook whole broiler-
  fryers
½ cup butter or margarine,
  melted
1 tablespoon finely chopped
  onion
1½ cups coarsely chopped
  fresh mushrooms
3 cups grated day-old
  white-bread crumbs
2 tablespoons finely snipped
  parsley
2 tablespoons coarsely
  snipped fresh
  marjoram leaves*

2 tablespoons finely snipped
  fresh chives
½ teaspoon salt
⅛ teaspoon pepper
⅛ teaspoon nutmeg

Gravy:
3 tablespoons flour
1½ cups canned chicken
  broth, undiluted
1 teaspoon coarsely snipped
  fresh marjoram
  leaves*
½ teaspoon salt
⅛ teaspoon pepper

MAKES 4 TO 6 SERVINGS

1. Rinse broiler-fryers inside and out under running cold water. Dry well with paper towels.

2. Preheat oven to 325F.

3. In ¼ cup hot butter in medium skillet, sauté onion and mushrooms about 5 minutes.

4. In large bowl, with fork, lightly toss sautéed vegetables and bread crumbs with rest of ingredients, except remaining melted butter, until well mixed. Loosely fill neck and body cavities of broiler-fryers.

5. Truss each chicken: Bring skin over neck opening; fasten to back with skewer. Close cavity with skewers. Bend wings under body. Tie legs together at ends.

6. Place chickens, breast side up, on rack in shallow, open roasting pan. Brush with some of melted butter. Cover loosely with foil.

7. Roast 2 to 2½ hours. Remove foil last half hour, and brush chickens with rest of butter.

8. Place on heated platter; remove skewers. Keep warm while making gravy.

9. Make Gravy: Drain all but 3 tablespoons drippings from roasting pan. Add flour; stir to make a smooth paste. Gradually stir in chicken broth.

10. Add rest of gravy ingredients; bring to boiling, stirring. Mixture will be thickened and smooth. Simmer, stirring, 1 minute longer.

11. Serve gravy hot, with chicken and stuffing.

* Or substitute dried herbs for fresh, using half the quantity.

Rock Cornish Game Hens

Rock Cornish game hens, a cross breed of pure Cornish game hens descended from East Indian jungle birds and our familiar Plymouth Rock hens, are not a self-perpetuating cross. The breeding must be carefully controlled each year.

Available frozen, stuffed or unstuffed, completely boned or partially boned, Rock Cornish game hens weigh 12 to 16 ounces (ready-to-cook weight).

HERB-FLAVORED ROCK CORNISH HENS

4 (1-lb size) frozen Rock
    Cornish hens, thawed
4 cloves garlic, split
4 teaspoons dried thyme
    leaves
1 teaspoon seasoned salt
1 teaspoon salt
½ teaspoon pepper
¾ cup butter or margarine,
    melted
½ cup lemon juice
¼ teaspoon paprika

1. Preheat oven to 450F.

2. In each hen, place 1 clove garlic, ½ teaspoon thyme, ¼ teaspoon seasoned salt, ¼ teaspoon salt, and ⅛ teaspoon pepper.

3. Truss hens: If necessary, bring skin over neck opening, and fasten to back with wooden pick. Tie legs together with string. Bend wings under bird. Close cavity with wooden picks.

4. Make basting sauce: Combine ½ cup butter with the lemon juice, paprika, and remaining thyme; stir well.

5. Heat some of the remaining butter in medium skillet; brown hens, turning to brown well on all sides and adding more butter as needed.

6. Arrange hens in large roasting pan, without rack; brush well with basting sauce. Roast, basting several times with sauce, about 40 minutes, or until nicely browned and tender.

ROCK CORNISH HENS ON-THE-SPIT

1½ cups finely chopped
    onion
1 cup finely chopped celery
½ cup finely chopped
    parsley
½ lb butter or margarine,
    melted
6 cups small day-old bread
    cubes
1 teaspoon dried thyme
    leaves
½ teaspoon dried marjoram
    leaves
½ teaspoon rubbed sage
1 teaspoon salt
¼ teaspoon pepper
1 cup chopped prepared
    chutney, undrained
8 (1-lb size) Rock Cornish
    hens

1. Preheat rotisserie to 400F (or oven to 350F).

2. In medium skillet, sauté onion, celery, and parsley in ½ cup butter until tender. Remove from heat.

3. In large bowl, combine sautéed vegetables with bread cubes, seasonings, and chutney.

4. Stuff each hen with about ¾ cup dressing. Close opening with wooden picks; truss with string.

5. Thread hens on spit; secure with prongs. (Or place, breast side up, in shallow roasting pan without rack.) Brush hens with 4 tablespoons butter.

(Rock Cornish Hens on-the-Spit continued)

6. Secure spit in rotisserie; roast hens 30 minutes, basting once with remaining butter. (Or roast in oven 45 to 50 minutes, basting once with remaining butter.) When done, drumstick can be easily moved.

7. To serve, remove wooden picks and string.

Duckling

Though, truthfully, any season is open season—thanks to the miracle of freezing—ducks seem particularly perfect for late-autumn dining. If duck cooking is new to you, this tip will help you.

To Truss Duckling: Fasten skin of neck to back, with poultry pin. Fold wing tips under body, to secure wings close to it. Then close body cavity with poultry pins. Lace (as for shoe) with twine. Tie ends of legs together.

DUCKLING WITH CHERRIES

MAKES 4 SERVINGS

4- to 5-lb ready-to-cook
    duckling
2 unpeeled oranges,
    quartered
1 clove garlic, chopped
1 teaspoon salt
3 whole black peppers
½ cup butter or margarine,
    melted
1 cup port
1 can (1 lb, 1 oz) pitted
    dark sweet cherries,
    drained

Liver from duckling
1 clove garlic, very finely
    chopped
¼ cup finely chopped
    onion
¼ cup unsifted all-purpose
    flour
2 teaspoons meat-extract
    paste
1¼ cups canned clear
    chicken broth,*
    undiluted
¼ cup currant jelly

1. Preheat oven to 425F.

2. Stuff duckling cavity with orange quarters, garlic, salt, and black peppers. Truss.

3. Place duckling, breast side up, on rack in roasting pan. Brush top well with butter; roast, uncovered, 30 minutes.

4. Reduce oven temperature to 375F; roast 1½ hours, draining fat as it accumulates.

5. Meanwhile, pour wine over cherries in small bowl; let stand about 1 hour.

6. When duckling is almost done, make sauce: Pour ¼ cup pan drippings from duckling into medium saucepan. Add liver; brown well; then chop finely, and set aside.

7. Add garlic and onion to same drippings; sauté until golden—about 5 minutes.

8. Remove from heat. Stir in flour and meat-extract paste until smooth. Then add broth; bring to boiling, stirring.

9. Blend in chopped liver, jelly, and cherries in wine; heat, stirring, until jelly is melted and sauce is heated through.

10. When duckling is done, remove poultry pins and twine. Carve into serving-size pieces, and arrange on platter.

11. Pour some sauce with cherries over duckling. Pass rest of sauce.

* Or simmer duckling giblets (not liver) in 2 cups water, covered, 1½ hours. Strain; measure 1¼ cups.

DUCKLING À L'ORANGE

*4- to 5-lb ready-to-cook
    duckling**
*2 unpeeled oranges,
    quartered*
1 clove garlic, chopped
1 teaspoon salt

3 whole black peppers
*½ cup butter or margarine,
    melted*
¼ cup Burgundy
½ cup orange marmalade

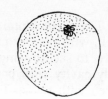

1. Preheat oven to 425F.
2. Stuff duckling cavity with orange quarters, garlic, salt, and peppers. Truss.
3. Place duckling, breast side up, on rack in shallow roasting pan. Brush top well with butter.
4. Pour Burgundy over duckling; roast, uncovered, 30 minutes.
5. Reduce oven temperature to 375F; roast duckling 40 minutes, basting twice with pan drippings.
6. Then turn it over on breast; roast 20 minutes. Turn back again; roast 30 minutes, basting twice with pan drippings.
7. Spread duckling thickly with orange marmalade; roast 10 minutes longer.
8. Remove poultry pins and twine. Carve duckling into serving-size pieces, if desired. Serve with Orange Sauce.**

* Goose of approximately equal weight may be substituted.

** See Sauces and Gravies Chapter.

Turkey

When it's that lovely and savory time of year, time to think of Thanksgiving dinner and what you will serve—though you know perfectly well, and so do we—you'll be grateful for the section on turkeys that follows. Your planning will start with a plump, full-breasted turkey, done to a crisp-skinned gold. Our step-by-step way shows you how.

TIMETABLE FOR ROASTING STUFFED TURKEY†

Ready-To-Cook Weight	Oven Temperature	Approximate Roasting Time (hours)
8 to 12 lb	325F	4 to 4½
12 to 16 lb*	325F	4½ to 5½
16 to 20 lb**	300F	5½ to 7

† For unstuffed turkeys, reduce roasting time approximately 5 minutes per pound.

* Roast breast side down 2½ to 3 hours; then roast breast side up rest of time.

** Brush turkey breast with liquid gravy seasoning as directed on label. Roast breast side down throughout roasting period.

GOLDEN-BROWN TURKEY

MAKES 15 OR 16 SERVINGS;
ABOUT 12 CUPS DRESSING

10- to 12-lb ready-to-cook
  turkey*

*Old-Fashioned Dressing:**
½ cup butter or margarine
1 cup finely chopped onion
3 cups finely chopped celery
¾ cup finely chopped
  parsley

1 tablespoon salt
1 tablespoon poultry
  seasoning
1 teaspoon paprika
½ teaspoon pepper
1 egg, slightly beaten
12 cups fine fresh-white-
  bread crumbs

½ cup butter or margarine,
  melted

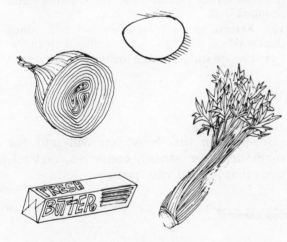

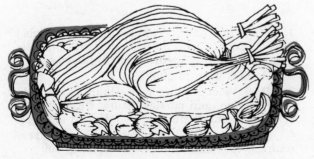

1.   Preheat oven to 325F. Remove giblets from turkey; set aside for gravy. Wash and dry turkey very well inside and out.

2.   Make Old-Fashioned Dressing: Melt ½ cup butter in skillet over low heat. Add onion and celery; sauté until golden—about 5 minutes. Toss lightly with rest of dressing ingredients in large bowl just until well mixed.

3.   Spoon dressing into neck cavity.

4.   Bring skin of neck over back; fasten with poultry pin.

5.   Spoon dressing into body cavity. Do not pack. Bake any leftover dressing in covered casserole.

6.   Insert about 5 poultry pins, at regular intervals, to draw body opening together. With long piece of twine, lace cavity closed, bootlace fashion; tie with knot.

7.   Bend wing tips under body, or fasten wings to body with poultry pins. With twine, tie ends of legs together. Brush turkey all over with some of melted butter.

8.   Insert meat thermometer in inside of thigh at thickest part. Turn, breast side down, on rack in shallow roasting pan.

9.   Roast, uncovered, 2 hours. Turn breast side up. Saturate cheesecloth square with rest of melted butter; place over turkey breast. (Or brush turkey with rest of butter; cover breast loosely with square of foil.) Roast 2 to 2½ hours longer. As cheesecloth dries out, moisten with pan drippings. (Or brush turkey with drippings.)

10.   Turkey is done when meat thermometer registers 185 to 190F; leg joint should move freely when twisted, and fleshy part of drumstick should feel soft.

11.   Place turkey on heated platter; remove cheesecloth or foil, twine, and poultry pins. Let stand 20 to 30 minutes.

12.   Meanwhile, make Giblet Gravy.***

* If frozen, let thaw, still in wrapper, in refrigerator 2 to 3 days.

** You may substitute 2 or 3 (8-oz) packages all-purpose, herb-seasoned stuffing. Follow label directions. Or use one of the stuffings given here.

*** See Sauces and Gravies Chapter.

485

BABY TURKEY MONTMORENCY

4- to 5-lb baby turkey, cut
    in serving pieces*
½ cup butter or margarine,
    melted
Turkey giblets and neck
½ cup finely chopped
    onion

1 clove garlic, crushed
2 tablespoons flour
4 teaspoons meat-extract
    paste
1 cup dry white wine
1 can (1 lb, 6 oz) cherry-pie
    filling

1. Preheat oven to 350F.
2. Wipe turkey with damp paper towels. Arrange, skin side down, in shallow roasting pan; brush with ¼ cup butter.
3. Roast, uncovered, basting now and then with pan juices and turning, until turkey is tender—1¼ to 1½ hours.
4. Meanwhile, in small saucepan, place giblets (reserve liver for sauce), neck, and 2 cups water; bring to boiling. Reduce heat; simmer, covered, 1 hour.
5. Drain; reserve 1½ cups broth. Discard giblets and neck.
6. Make sauce: In rest of hot butter in large skillet, sauté liver until tender—5 minutes.
7. Remove; chop finely; set aside.
8. In same skillet, sauté onion and garlic until golden—about 5 minutes.
9. Remove from heat. Stir in flour and meat-extract paste until smooth. Gradually stir in reserved broth, wine, cherry-pie filling, and chopped liver.
10. Return to heat; simmer, stirring, until thickened—3 minutes. Serve turkey with sauce.
* Or use roasting chicken instead of turkey.

Stuffings

Exactly as important as the chicken or the turkey is the stuffing, and we have provided a great variety that will add a special and scrumptious elegance, appreciated by family and guests alike.

Elsewhere in this book you will find our suggestions for sauces, conserves, and relishes that go well with poultry.

CORNBREAD-DRESSING BALLS

1 pkg (10- or 12-oz)
    cornbread mix
½ cup butter or margarine,
    melted
1½ cups chopped celery
1 cup chopped onion
¼ cup chopped parsley
½ teaspoon rubbed sage

½ teaspoon dried thyme
    leaves
1 teaspoon salt
¼ teaspoon pepper
1 egg
½ cup canned clear
    chicken broth,
    undiluted

1. Make and bake cornbread as package label directs. Cool in pan, on wire rack, 25 minutes; then crumble into medium mixing bowl.
2. Preheat oven to 325F.
3. Heat ¼ cup butter in medium skillet. Add celery, onion, and parsley; sauté, stirring, until celery and onion are tender—about 5 minutes.
4. Add to crumbled cornbread, along with seasonings, egg, and chicken broth; mix well.

(*Cornbread-Dressing Balls continued*)

5. With hands, lightly form mixture into balls, using about ½ cup for each. Arrange in greased shallow baking dish.

6. Brush with rest of butter; bake, covered, 30 minutes.

7. Remove cover; bake 15 minutes longer, or until browned on top.

Note: Dressing balls may be baked in the oven with the turkey.

CHESTNUT-APPLE STUFFING

MAKES ABOUT 12 CUPS
(ENOUGH TO FILL A 10- TO 12-POUND
READY-TO-COOK TURKEY)

¼ cup butter or margarine
½ cup chopped onion
1 cup chopped celery
½ cup raisins
4 cups chopped, pared, cored apples

6 cups fresh-white-bread cubes
4 cups coarsely chopped chestnuts*
1 tablespoon salt
1 teaspoon cinnamon
¼ teaspoon nutmeg

1. In hot butter in large skillet, sauté onion and celery until tender—about 5 minutes.

2. In large bowl, with fork, lightly toss with remaining ingredients until well combined.

* Use 2 lb fresh chestnuts. With sharp knife, make a slit in each shell. Bake chestnuts at 500F for 15 minutes. Remove shells and outer skin. Cover chestnuts with water; simmer, covered, 20 minutes. Drain, and chop coarsely. (Or use 1 can—14½ oz—chestnuts, packed in water. Drain, and chop coarsely.)

SAUSAGE-CORNBREAD DRESSING

MAKES ABOUT 15 CUPS
(ENOUGH TO FILL A 16- TO 18-POUND
READY-TO-COOK TURKEY)

2 pkg (10- or 12-oz size) cornbread mix
1 lb sausage meat
4 cups chopped celery
3 cups chopped onion
1 cup chopped green pepper
¾ cup chopped parsley
1½ teaspoons rubbed savory

1½ teaspoons dried sage leaves
1½ teaspoons dried thyme leaves
1 tablespoon salt
½ teaspoon pepper
1 can (13¾ oz) chicken broth, undiluted
3 eggs, slightly beaten

1. Make cornbread mix as package label directs. Cool.

2. In large skillet, sauté sausage meat, stirring, until lightly browned. Lift out with slotted spoon.

3. In drippings in skillet, sauté celery, onion, green pepper, and parsley until tender—8 to 10 minutes.

4. Meanwhile, crumble cooled cornbread into large bowl or kettle. Add sausage meat, vegetables, savory, sage, thyme, salt, and pepper. Gradually add broth and eggs, tossing lightly with fork.

MUSHROOM-WITH-RICE STUFFING

1 lb Italian-style sausage
   meat
1 cup chopped onion
3 cups finely chopped
   celery
1 can (6 oz) sliced
   mushrooms, drained

1 tablespoon salt
¼ teaspoon pepper
1 teaspoon dried rosemary
   leaves
8 cups cooked white rice

1.   Cook sausage meat in large skillet, stirring, until lightly browned. Remove with slotted spoon; drain, reserving 2 tablespoons drippings.

2.   In reserved drippings, sauté onion and celery until tender—about 5 minutes.

3.   Remove from heat. Add mushrooms, salt, pepper, and rosemary.

4.   In large bowl, with fork, lightly toss rice with sausage and vegetables until well combined.

SAUSAGE STUFFING

1 lb sausage meat
1 cup chopped onion
2 cups chopped celery
1 cup chopped green
   pepper

10 cups fresh-white-bread
   cubes
2 teaspoons salt
1 teaspoon dried tarragon
   leaves
1 egg, slightly beaten

1.   Cook sausage meat in large skillet, stirring, until lightly browned. Remove with slotted spoon; drain, reserving 2 tablespoons drippings.

2.   In reserved drippings, sauté onion, celery, and green pepper until tender—about 5 minutes.

3.   In large bowl, with fork, toss lightly with remaining ingredients and sausage until well combined.

SAVORY HERB STUFFING

6 tablespoons butter or
   margarine
¾ cup chopped onion
1½ cups chopped celery
12 cups white-bread cubes,
   toasted*
2 teaspoons salt
¼ teaspoon pepper

¼ teaspoon dried rosemary
   leaves
¼ teaspoon dried tarragon
   leaves
¼ teaspoon dried
   marjoram leaves
1 cup canned chicken
   broth**
½ cup raisins

1.   In hot butter in skillet, sauté onion and celery until tender—about 5 minutes.

2.   Add to rest of ingredients in large bowl, tossing lightly with fork until well combined.

* To toast bread cubes: Place on cookie sheet; toast at 300F for 25 to 35 minutes, turning cubes several times.

** Or use 1 cup broth from the turkey giblets.

A salad is much more than a chunk of head lettuce with a spoonful of dressing poured over it. Today, the markets are full of the most tempting greens, from the palest, almost white Belgian endive to crisp, tangy dark-green watercress. A salad can open a meal or close it. It can give a fresh, clean taste to complement a hearty dinner. It can serve as the main course of a summer luncheon or supper. And it can also serve as a dessert.

Green Salads

Three things are needed to make a good green salad—crisp greens, thoroughly dried and refrigerated until they crackle when you eat them; an interesting dressing tossed with the salad just before serving, so the leaves don't get soggy and limp; and just the right amount of dressing, not so stingy that the leaves are left undressed nor so lavish that they almost drown in it. How to keep lettuce crisp? Wash it thoroughly, under cold running water, long before you intend to use it, and wrap in a clean towel. If you have a salad basket, the kind so widely used abroad, shake off the moisture after you have washed the leaves. Some women dry the individual leaves with paper towels.

Whatever you do, see that the greens are dry, so the salad dressing will cling to every leaf. If you plan to keep greens for any length of time, you'll find the vegetable crisper of your refrigerator is a good place to store them. Or put them in a plastic bag in the bottom of your refrigerator.

Know Your Salad Greens

Curly endive, or chicory, has a maze of narrow, thin, twisted leaves, shading from dark green at the edges to a pale-yellow heart. It is often used with grapefruit and orange sections or tomatoes. It has an almost bitter tang.

Belgian endive can be sliced lengthwise or crosswise into a salad. Although it is a member of the chicory and escarole family, it is a straight, pale, slender leaf, six inches or more in length. Endive can be eaten alone or served with other greens. Some people enjoy eating it as they do celery.

Escarole. This green tastes a little like Belgian endive, though not as bitter. It is often called the broad-leaf endive. It resembles chicory, but its leaves are broader and not as curly. They are dark green, edging into yellow.

Bibb lettuce, or limestone lettuce, is smaller and more delicate than Boston lettuce, but has something of the same shape and delicious flavor. Use the whole leaf in a salad. This lettuce gets its name from Jack Bibb, of Frankfort, Kentucky, who introduced it to his friends shortly after the Civil War. Still fairly expensive, it is growing less so, now that it has begun to reach the markets in greater quantity.

Boston lettuce, also known as "butterhead" and "big Boston," has velvety, spreading leaves, which can be easily separated. This tender lettuce will do much for a salad. It is available throughout most of the year. However, its distribution is rather limited.

Head lettuce, or iceberg lettuce, or Simpson lettuce is the most familiar of lettuces. It is the firm, tight, compact head of light-green leaves. Separated, the leaves make a lettuce cup as a container for potato salad, fruit salad, and so on. Cut in wedges, it is a favorite of men, particularly those who like to pour blue-cheese dressing over it.

Leaf lettuce is a favorite with the home gardener. It is crisp and has a curly edge. It is a lovely green and has a good flavor, and it grows in large, leafy bunches.

Oak-leaf lettuce. So-called because of the deeply notched leaves, which look so much like true oak leaves. Its flavor is delicate. Bronze Beauty is another variety of this plant, with reddish-tinted leaves instead of green.

Romaine lettuce is more strongly flavored than several other varieties of lettuce. It can be recognized by its long head and spoon-shape leaves, coarser and crisper than head lettuce. Good served with tomatoes and avocados.

Spinach is not a lettuce; but the tender young leaves of spinach give an interesting taste and color to a tossed green salad.

Watercress. This dark-green, leafy plant, with the unexpected bite in its taste, grows along the edges of brooks and springs. It gives an interesting color and taste contrast to a tossed green salad, adds a bright-green note as a garnish, and looks particularly attractive with the contrast of red tomatoes sliced over it.

CAESAR SALAD

1 clove garlic
¾ cup salad oil
2 cups white-bread cubes
2 eggs
3 tablespoons fresh lemon juice
2 teaspoons Worcestershire sauce
½ teaspoon salt

¼ teaspoon pepper
8 anchovy fillets, chopped
2 heads romaine lettuce, washed and chilled
¼ cup crumbled blue cheese
¼ cup grated Parmesan cheese

1. Crush garlic in small bowl; cover with oil. Refrigerate, covered, 30 minutes.
2. In ¼ cup garlic oil in medium skillet, fry bread cubes until brown on all sides. Set aside.
3. If desired, cook eggs only 1 minute in boiling water. Remove, and cool. (Eggs may be used raw.)
4. In small bowl, combine the lemon juice, Worcestershire, salt, pepper, and anchovies; mix well.
5. Into large salad bowl, tear lettuce into bite-size pieces.
6. Drain remaining oil from garlic. Pour over lettuce; toss to coat evenly.
7. Break eggs over salad; toss well.
8. Pour on lemon mixture; toss well.
9. Add bread cubes and cheeses; toss well. Serve at once.

CHEF'S SALAD

Dressing:
3 tablespoons wine vinegar
1 tablespoon lemon juice
½ cup salad oil
½ teaspoon salt
Dash pepper
1 teaspoon sugar

Salad:
1 cut clove garlic
6 leaves Boston lettuce
6 leaves chicory
6 sprigs watercress
¼-lb piece bologna, cubed

¼-lb piece liverwurst, cubed
2 stalks celery, sliced diagonally
2 tomatoes, peeled and quartered
4 scallions, chopped in ¼-inch pieces
4 hard-cooked eggs, chopped coarsely
2 tablespoons chopped parsley

1. Make Dressing: Combine all ingredients in jar with tight-fitting lid; shake vigorously. Chill until ready to use. Shake again before adding to salad.
2. Make Salad: Rub large wooden salad bowl with garlic. Into bowl, tear lettuce, chicory, and watercress in bite-size pieces.
3. Add bologna, liverwurst, celery, tomatoes, and scallions.
4. Pour on dressing, and toss gently until each piece of leaf is coated.
5. Sprinkle with chopped eggs and parsley.

CONTINENTAL CHEF'S SALAD

1 large head romaine
1 pkg (1½ oz) blue cheese
1 can (8 oz) artichoke hearts, drained
1 can (3 oz) mushroom caps, drained
1 can (1 lb) kidney beans, drained

1 tomato, cut in 8 wedges
½ cucumber, sliced
8 onion rings
½ lb boiled tongue, cut in julienne strips
Caper French Dressing*
Salt and pepper (optional)

1. Break romaine into bite-size pieces in a large salad bowl. Crumble cheese over it; toss to combine.
2. Arrange vegetables and tongue in groups on romaine-cheese bed.
3. To serve: Toss with Caper French Dressing. Sprinkle with salt and pepper, if desired.

* See this chapter.

RAW-SPINACH SALAD

MAKES 6 TO 8 SERVINGS

Salad:
1 lb spinach
6 green onions, thinly sliced
4 hard-cooked eggs, coarsely
     chopped
8 crisp-cooked bacon slices,
     crumbled
Dash pepper

Dressing:
1 clove garlic, quartered
½ cup salad or olive oil
½ teaspoon salt
3 tablespoons lemon juice
¼ cup cider vinegar

1. Make Salad: Wash spinach; remove stems; break leaves into bite-size pieces.

2. In salad bowl, lightly toss spinach with onions, eggs, bacon, and pepper.

3. Refrigerate, covered, about 2 hours.

4. Make Dressing: Marinate garlic in salad oil at least 1 hour. Just before serving, remove garlic; discard.

5. Combine garlic oil and salt in small bowl.

6. Mix lemon juice and vinegar; gradually add to oil, beating well with rotary beater.

7. Pour dressing over salad; toss to coat spinach. Serve at once.

RUSSIAN SALAD

MAKES 8 SERVINGS

½ cup mayonnaise
¼ cup catsup
½ teaspoon bottled steak
     sauce
⅛ teaspoon salt
Dash pepper
Dash garlic salt

1 hard-cooked egg, chopped
1 tablespoon chopped
     parsley
1 medium head iceberg
     lettuce
1 tomato

1. Combine all ingredients, except lettuce and tomato, in medium bowl. Cover; refrigerate at least 1 hour before serving.

2. Tear lettuce in bite-size pieces into large salad bowl.

3. Cut tomato in small cubes; add to lettuce.

4. Just before serving, add dressing; toss thoroughly.

SALAD OF FRESH HERBS

MAKES 4 TO 6 SERVINGS

1 medium head Boston
     lettuce
3 tablespoons salad oil
1 tablespoon tarragon
     vinegar
½ teaspoon sugar
¼ teaspoon salt
1 clove garlic, split
2 tablespoons snipped
     parsley

1 tablespoon snipped chives
1 tablespoon snipped dill,
     or 1 teaspoon dried
     dill weed
1 teaspoon thyme leaves, or
     ½ teaspoon dried
     thyme leaves
½ cucumber, thinly sliced
1 medium tomato,
     quartered

1. Cut core from lettuce, and discard. Wash leaves; dry on paper towels.

2. Refrigerate in crisper several hours, or until ready to use.

3. In jar with tight-fitting lid, combine oil, vinegar, sugar, and salt; shake until well combined.

4. Refrigerate about 1 hour.

5. Rub inside of wooden salad bowl with cut sides of garlic; discard garlic.

6. Tear lettuce in bite-size pieces into salad bowl. Toss lightly with parsley, chives, dill, and thyme. Add cucumber and tomato.

7. Shake dressing; pour over salad. Toss until well coated. Serve at once.

Vegetable Salads

Salads like these are a nice change from tossed green salads. The vinaigrettes, in particular, are ideal for a hostess, since they marinate ahead of time and can be served straight out of the refrigerator. They should be well seasoned and pungent—like ours.

ASPARAGUS VINAIGRETTE

MAKES 6 SERVINGS

2 to 2½ lb fresh asparagus,
  cooked and drained*
3 tablespoons cider vinegar
¼ cup salad oil
2 tablespoons olive oil

2 teaspoons salt
Dash pepper
½ teaspoon sugar
1 hard-cooked egg, chopped
2 sweet gherkins, chopped

1.   Arrange cooked, drained asparagus spears in shallow glass baking dish.
2.   In jar with tight-fitting lid, combine vinegar, oils, salt, pepper, and sugar; shake to combine.
3.   Pour dressing over asparagus.
4.   Refrigerate at least 1 hour, turning spears several times.
5.   Arrange asparagus on a platter. Sprinkle with chopped egg and pickle.
* To retain freshness, plunge freshly cooked spears into cold water. Drain.

CUCUMBERS VINAIGRETTE

MAKES 8 SERVINGS

1 bottle (8 oz) Italian-style
  salad dressing
2 tablespoons lemon juice
1 tablespoon chopped
  capers

1 teaspoon Worcestershire
  sauce
¼ teaspoon crushed garlic
2 cucumbers, quartered and
  sliced ¼ inch thick
8 Boston-lettuce leaves

1.   In large bowl, combine dressing, lemon juice, capers, Worcestershire, and garlic; mix well.
2.   Pour over cucumbers in shallow dish; refrigerate, covered, at least 30 minutes.
3.   To serve: With slotted spoon, lift and drain cucumbers; sprinkle dressing over lettuce.
4.   Arrange lettuce on 8 salad plates; top with cucumbers.

FIESTA COLESLAW

MAKES 8 SERVINGS

2 cups finely shredded green
  cabbage
2 cups finely shredded red
  cabbage
2¼ teaspoons salt
⅔ cup mayonnaise or
  cooked salad dressing

2 teaspoons vinegar
2 teaspoons sugar
½ cup shredded carrot
½ cup thinly sliced ripe
  olives
¼ cup finely chopped
  green pepper

1.   Cover green and red cabbage with cold water combined with 1 teaspoon salt; let soak about 1 hour. Drain.
2.   In large bowl, combine mayonnaise, vinegar, sugar, and remaining salt.
3.   Add drained cabbage, carrot, olives, and green pepper; toss lightly until vegetables are well coated with dressing.
4.   Refrigerate, covered, several hours before serving.

SOUR-CREAM COLESLAW

1½ cups dairy sour cream
2 egg yolks
2 tablespoons lemon juice
3 tablespoons prepared
    horseradish, drained
¼ teaspoon paprika

2 teaspoons prepared
    mustard
1 teaspoon sugar
1 teaspoon salt
2 qt (2 lb) finely shredded
    green cabbage

1. Combine sour cream and egg yolks in medium bowl; mix well. Blend in remaining ingredients, except cabbage.
2. Pour dressing over cabbage; toss until it is well coated.
3. Refrigerate 30 minutes.

HARVEST SALAD BOWL

2 cups thinly sliced,
    unpared zucchini
    (about ½ lb)
4 cups thinly sliced, cored,
    unpared red apples
    (about 1¼ lb)
1 medium green pepper,
    cut into thin strips
    (1 cup)

Dressing:
⅓ cup salad oil
¼ cup cider vinegar
¼ cup lemon juice
1 tablespoon sugar
2 teaspoons salt

1. In large bowl, lightly toss zucchini with apples and green pepper.
2. Make Dressing: Combine all ingredients in jar with tight-fitting cover; shake to mix well. Pour over salad, tossing to coat well.
3. Refrigerate, covered, at least 3 hours, tossing occasionally to mix well.

PEPPER SALAD

3½ cups thinly sliced green
    peppers (1¼ lb)
1½ cups thinly sliced fresh
    mushrooms

3 tablespoons vinegar
¼ cup salad oil
½ teaspoon salt
Dash pepper

1. In medium bowl, toss peppers and mushrooms with remaining ingredients.
2. Cover; refrigerate at least 30 minutes.

KIDNEY-BEAN SALAD

2 cans (1-lb size) kidney
    beans, drained
⅓ cup vinegar
2 tablespoons salad oil
1 teaspoon salt
Dash pepper

¼ teaspoon dry mustard
2 large onions
Few sprigs parsley
1 clove garlic
1 jar (4 oz) pimientos

1. Mix beans with vinegar, oil, salt, pepper, and mustard.
2. Chop onions, parsley, and garlic fine; chop pimientos coarsely.
3. Add chopped vegetables to bean mixture; chill about 1 hour before serving.

VEGETABLES VINAIGRETTE

1 lb large carrots
Boiling water
1 pkg (10 oz) frozen peas
5 cherry tomatoes
5 hard-cooked eggs
1½ cups cauliflowerets

1 teaspoon paprika
2 small white onions
1 can (8½ oz) artichoke
    hearts, drained

Vinaigrette Dressing*

1. Pare carrots. Cut into 1½-inch pieces. Trim each piece to make four straight sides; cut each piece, lengthwise, into strips ¼ inch thick.
2. Place carrots in medium saucepan; add boiling water to measure 1 inch. Cook, covered, 5 minutes. Drain thoroughly; let cool.
3. Cook peas as package label directs; drain, and let cool.
4. Meanwhile, prepare other vegetables: With tip of paring knife, cut a zigzag line around middle of each tomato, cutting to center. Gently separate tomato halves.
5. Also, cut a zigzag line around middle of each egg, cutting just to yolk. Separate eggs carefully; remove yolks. (Refrigerate yolks for later use in sandwich fillings.)
6. Place tomato halves inside egg halves.
7. Halve cauliflowerets lengthwise. Dip tops lightly in paprika.
8. Peel onions; cut crosswise into slices ⅛ inch thick. Separate slices into rings; fill the onion rings with carrot strips.
9. Rinse artichoke hearts carefully in cold water; drain. Halve hearts lengthwise; remove 2 or 3 leaves from center of each half. Fill each with 1 teaspoon peas; reserve remaining peas.
10. Assemble vegetables: Place egg-and-tomato halves across center of large, round platter. Make a row of artichokes and carrot strips at each side. Sprinkle remaining peas here and there between rows. Arrange cauliflowerets around edge of platter.
11. Sprinkle vegetables with some of Vinaigrette Dressing; refrigerate at least 1 hour before serving.
12. Serve rest of dressing with vegetables.
* See this chapter.

SUMMER SALAD BOWL

1 medium head Boston
    lettuce, cored, washed
½ lb spinach, washed
1 bunch watercress, washed
¼ lb zucchini, washed
1 cup thin onion rings

½ cup sliced fresh mush-
    rooms; or 1 can (3 oz)
    sliced mushrooms,
    drained
1 cup canned sliced
    pickled beets,
    drained
Roquefort Dressing*

1. Refrigerate greens in crisper until ready to use. With waffle vegetable cutter, thinly slice zucchini crosswise.
2. Tear lettuce and spinach in bite-size pieces into bowl. Toss with rest of ingredients.
* See this chapter.

Potato Salads

The perfect potato salad is tangy but not sour, creamy but not gooey. You couldn't ask more of a potato salad! However, since potato salad is a family favorite, we've given you a choice of several, hot and cold, and every one of them good.

SAVORY HOT POTATO SALAD

MAKES 6 SERVINGS

3 lb medium potatoes
1½ teaspoons salt
⅛ teaspoon pepper
⅔ cup chopped onion
½ cup sliced radishes
½ teaspoon celery seed

2 tablespoons chopped parsley
9 bacon slices, finely cut up
1 tablespoon flour
½ cup white vinegar
2 tablespoons sugar

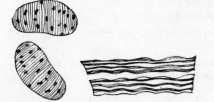 

1. Cook unpeeled potatoes, covered, in boiling water just until tender—about 30 minutes.
2. Drain potatoes; cool; peel, cut into cubes.
3. Toss lightly with salt, pepper, onion, radishes, celery seed, and parsley.
4. Sauté bacon in skillet, over low heat, until crisp; remove from heat. With slotted spoon, remove bacon; add to potatoes.
5. Drain from skillet all except 1 tablespoon bacon fat. Stir in flour until smooth.
6. Gradually add vinegar and ½ cup water. Stir in sugar; bring to boiling point, stirring.
7. In serving bowl, toss lightly with potato mixture until combined. Serve warm.

PERFECT POTATO SALAD

MAKES 6 SERVINGS

2¼ lb unpared medium potatoes
½ cup bottled Italian-style salad dressing
¾ cup thinly sliced celery
½ cup thinly sliced radishes
¼ cup finely chopped cucumber

¼ cup finely chopped onion
2 tablespoons finely chopped pimiento
2 hard-cooked eggs, coarsely chopped
1¼ cups Creamy Dressing*
1 scallion with green top, thinly sliced
Salad greens

1. Cook scrubbed potatoes in small amount of boiling, salted water, covered, just until tender —about 35 minutes. Drain, and let cool slightly.
2. Peel potatoes; cut into ½-inch cubes. In large bowl, using a fork, lightly toss potato cubes with Italian-style dressing. Refrigerate, covered, 1½ to 2 hours.
3. Add rest of ingredients, except scallion and greens. Toss gently to mix well; refrigerate, covered, until well chilled—at least 2 hours.
4. Turn into serving bowl; sprinkle scallion slices over top. Garnish bowl with greens.

* See this chapter.

POTATO SALAD IN SOUR-CREAM DRESSING

MAKES 6 SERVINGS

3 medium potatoes, peeled
1 cup finely chopped celery
2 tablespoons finely chopped onion
1 cup (8 oz) creamed cottage cheese

1 cup dairy sour cream
1 teaspoon finely chopped chives
1 teaspoon salt
Dash pepper
Salad greens

1. In boiling, salted water to cover, cook potatoes, covered, just until tender—about 35 minutes. Drain; refrigerate until cold.
2. Meanwhile, combine remaining ingredients, except salad greens.
3. Dice chilled potatoes. Toss with sour-cream mixture; refrigerate until very well chilled— about 1 hour. Arrange on salad greens.

TRADITIONAL POTATO SALAD

MAKES 6 TO 8 SERVINGS

2 lb unpared medium
    potatoes*
2 tablespoons salad oil
2½ tablespoons cider
    vinegar
1 tablespoon chopped
    parsley
2 tablespoons finely
    chopped onion

¼ cup finely chopped
    green pepper
¾ cup diced celery
1 teaspoon salt
½ teaspoon dill seed
¾ cup mayonnaise or
    Creamy Dressing**
Salad greens

1. Cook scrubbed potatoes in small amount of boiling, salted water, covered, just until tender —about 35 minutes.
2. Drain; let cool slightly. Peel potatoes; dice.
3. In large bowl, combine all ingredients, except salad greens. Refrigerate, covered, until well chilled—several hours.
4. Spoon into serving bowl; garnish with salad greens.

* Or use 2½ cups packaged precooked potatoes. Cook as label directs; drain. Proceed as above.

** See this chapter.

THREE-BEAN SALAD BOWL

MAKES 6 SERVINGS

1 pkg (10 oz) frozen cut-up
    green beans
1 pkg (10 oz) frozen cut-up
    wax beans
1 can (1 lb) red kidney
    beans, drained
½ cup thinly sliced red
    onion
1 green pepper, slivered
    (1 cup)

½ cup salad oil
⅔ cup wine vinegar
½ teaspoon
    Worcestershire sauce
½ cup sugar
1 clove garlic, split
1 teaspoon salt
⅛ teaspoon pepper
Salad greens

1. Cook green and wax beans as package labels direct. Drain; let cool.
2. In large salad bowl, lightly toss with kidney beans, onion, and green pepper.
3. In jar with tight-fitting lid, shake oil, vinegar, Worcestershire, sugar, garlic, salt, and pepper until well mixed. Discard garlic.
4. Pour dressing over beans; mix to coat well.
5. Refrigerate 2 to 3 hours. Serve on salad greens.

OUR BEST CUCUMBERS IN SOUR CREAM

MAKES 4 TO 6 SERVINGS

2 large cucumbers, peeled
    and very thinly sliced
1½ teaspoons salt
1 cup dairy sour cream
2 tablespoons lemon juice
1 tablespoon finely chopped
    onion, or 1 teaspoon
    instant minced
    onion*

2 tablespoons chopped dill
    pickle
¼ teaspoon sugar
Dash pepper
3 radishes, thinly sliced
Lettuce
1½ teaspoons finely
    chopped parsley

1. Lightly toss cucumbers with 1 teaspoon salt; refrigerate until well chilled.
2. Meanwhile, combine sour cream, lemon juice, remaining salt, onion, dill pickle, sugar, pepper, and radishes. Reserve ½ cup sour-cream mixture for garnish.
3. Toss cucumbers with remaining sour-cream mixture; refrigerate.
4. To serve: Arrange well-chilled cucumbers in sour cream on a bed of lettuce. Garnish with reserved sour-cream mixture; sprinkle with chopped parsley.

* Soak 1 teaspoon instant minced onion in 2 teaspoons water for 5 minutes before using.

497

Fruit Salads

Let's thank the Californians for their great idea—serving fruit salad as a first course. So fresh and good, and such a wonderful opener for a meal.

Fruit salads can be sweet or bland or sharp, depending on the dressings used.

The light, pretty fruit salad can accompany a luncheon. Or, fragrant and opulent, with the proper dressing, it makes a rich, creamy dessert.

FRESH-APPLE SLAW

MAKES 6 TO 8 SERVINGS

4½ cups thinly sliced, cored, unpared red apples (about 1½ lb)
3 cups finely shredded green cabbage
1 cup dairy sour cream
3 tablespoons lemon juice
1 tablespoon sugar
¾ teaspoon salt
⅛ teaspoon pepper
1 tablespoon poppy seed

1. In large bowl, lightly toss all ingredients until well combined.
2. Refrigerate at least 1 hour before serving.

AVOCADOS WITH CHICKEN SALAD

MAKES 4 SERVINGS

2 cans (5-oz size) boned chicken, coarsely chopped
¼ cup chopped green pepper
1 medium orange, peeled and sectioned
¼ cup slivered blanched almonds
¼ cup mayonnaise or cooked salad dressing
½ teaspoon salt
1½ tablespoons lemon juice
2 large ripe avocados (about 1½ lb)
Salad greens

1. In medium bowl, combine chicken, pepper, orange, almonds, mayonnaise, salt, and 1 tablespoon lemon juice; mix well.
2. Refrigerate, covered, until well chilled—at least 1 hour.
3. Just before serving, cut avocados in half lengthwise; remove pits. Sprinkle with remaining lemon juice.
4. Top each half with about ⅓ cup chicken salad, mounding high. Serve on salad greens.

CURRIED COTTAGE CHEESE WITH FRUIT

MAKES 4 SERVINGS

1 lb cottage cheese
2 tablespoons chopped seedless raisins
1 tablespoon chopped walnuts
½ teaspoon curry powder
¼ teaspoon salt
2 large unpared red apples, sliced
2 large ripe peaches, peeled and sliced
2 large oranges, peeled and sectioned
1 can (8¾ oz) pineapple tidbits, drained
½ cup fresh blueberries
Salad greens
Mayonnaise or cooked salad dressing

1. In medium bowl, combine cottage cheese, raisins, walnuts, curry powder, and salt, stirring to mix well.
2. Refrigerate, covered, until chilled.
3. On platter, arrange fruits and berries in circle on bed of salad greens. Pile cottage-cheese mixture in center.
4. Serve with mayonnaise.

AVOCADOS WITH CRABMEAT

MAKES 6 SERVINGS

2 cans (6½-oz size)
  crabmeat, drained
½ cup finely chopped
  celery
2 tablespoons bottled
  capers, drained
½ teaspoon salt

⅓ cup mayonnaise or
  cooked salad dressing
1 tablespoon chili sauce
4 teaspoons lemon juice
3 large ripe avocados
  (about 2¼ lb)
Salad greens

1. Separate crabmeat; remove membrane.
2. Add other ingredients, except 3 teaspoons lemon juice, avocados, and greens; toss well.
3. Refrigerate, covered, until chilled—1 hour.
4. Before serving, cut avocados in half lengthwise; remove pits. Sprinkle with rest of lemon juice.
5. Top each half with about ½ cup crabmeat mixture, mounding it high.
6. Serve on salad greens.

CHERRY FRUIT SALAD

MAKES 6 SERVINGS

1½ cups fresh pitted sweet
  cherries
1½ cups melon balls
1 cup diced avocado

1 cup sliced peaches
½ cup Poppy-Seed
  Dressing*
Salad greens

1. In medium bowl, combine fruits and dressing; toss gently.
2. Refrigerate 1 hour, or until well chilled.
3. Toss again. Serve on greens.
* See this chapter.

FABULOUS FRUIT SALAD

MAKES 6 TO 8 SERVINGS

Dressing:
½ cup cranberry juice
2 tablespoons cider vinegar
1 tablespoon orange juice
½ teaspoon grated orange
  peel
¼ cup salad oil
⅛ teaspoon salt
Dash pepper
½ teaspoon sugar
1 pkg (1¼ oz) American
  blue cheese, crumbled

Salad:
1 cup fresh-peach slices
1 cup seedless green grapes
1 cup fresh-pear slices
1 cup fresh-apricot halves
1 cup fresh-pineapple
  chunks
6 leaves Boston lettuce
6 leaves romaine
¼ cup slivered toasted
  almonds

1. Make Dressing: Combine ingredients in jar with tight-fitting lid; shake well. Refrigerate until ready to serve.
2. Make Salad: Peel and prepare fresh fruit; set aside.
3. Tear greens in bite-size pieces into large salad bowl.
4. Arrange each fruit in a separate mound on greens. Sprinkle with almond slivers.
5. Shake chilled dressing, and pour over salad. Toss, and serve immediately.

HONEY-FRUIT SALAD

MAKES 6 TO 8 SERVINGS

Fruit:
1 cup diced pared fresh
  pears
1 cup orange sections
1 cup sliced peeled
  peaches; or 1 can (1
  lb) sliced peaches,
  drained
1 cup fresh blueberries; or
  1 pkg (12 oz) frozen
  blueberries, thawed

2 bananas, peeled and sliced

Syrup:
¾ cup honey
1 tablespoon grated lemon
  peel
2 tablespoons lemon juice
2 tablespoons orange juice
¼ cup sherry

Golden-Gate Dressing*

1. Prepare Fruit: In large bowl, gently toss fruit to combine well; refrigerate.
2. Meanwhile, make Syrup: Combine all ingredients in small saucepan; cook, stirring, over low heat, 5 minutes. Remove from heat; let cool slightly.
3. Pour over fruit; mix gently. Refrigerate at least 1 hour.
4. Serve with Golden-Gate Dressing.
* See this chapter.

HONEYDEW-FRUIT-SALAD PLATE

MAKES 6 SERVINGS

1 medium honeydew melon
3 large bananas
2 tablespoons lemon juice
3 large peaches, peeled, pitted, and quartered
9 sweet red plums, halved and pitted
1 pint cottage cheese
12 fresh strawberries

½ cup blueberries
1 cup dairy sour cream
2 drops liquid hot-pepper seasoning
½ teaspoon salt
2 teaspoons poppy seed
1 tablespoon confectioners' sugar
6 fresh mint sprigs

1. With sharp knife, cut melon crosswise into 8 (½-inch) slices; discard end slices. Remove rind and seeds. Cut bananas into 1-inch chunks; sprinkle with lemon juice.

2. Place honeydew rings on 6 salad plates. In center of each, place 1 banana chunk, 2 peach quarters, and 1 plum half. Top each with ⅓ cup cottage cheese; garnish with 3 banana chunks, 2 plum halves, 2 strawberries, and 1 heaping tablespoon blueberries.

3. Cover with saran; refrigerate 1 hour.

4. In small bowl, combine sour cream and remaining ingredients, except mint sprigs. Refrigerate, covered.

5. To serve: Garnish salad plates with mint sprigs; pass sour-cream dressing.

ORANGE-AND-ONION SALAD

MAKES 4 SERVINGS

4 large oranges
1 medium red onion, peeled

French dressing
Salad greens

1. Peel oranges; remove white membrane. With sharp knife, cut in thin slices.

2. Cut onion in thin slices.

3. In medium bowl, toss onion and orange slices with French dressing.

4. Refrigerate until chilled—at least 1 hour.

5. Serve on salad greens.

TOSSED FRUIT SALAD

MAKES 4 SERVINGS

1 medium head Boston or Bibb lettuce
½ head romaine
8 watercress sprigs
4 plums
4 fresh peaches; or 1 pkg (12 oz) frozen sliced peaches, thawed and drained

1 banana
⅓ cup lemon juice
1 pint box fresh strawberries, washed and hulled
Lime Salad Dressing*
6 small clusters seedless green grapes

1. Wash lettuce, romaine, and watercress; dry well. Store in crisper until ready to use.

2. Refrigerate rest of ingredients.

3. Line shallow salad bowl with crisp, chilled outer lettuce leaves. Break rest of lettuce and romaine into bite-size pieces to measure 3 cups. Turn into center of bowl.

4. Just before serving, prepare fruit: Slice plums into 8 sections. Peel peaches; cut into 8 sections. With tines of fork, flute banana lengthwise; cut into ¾-inch diagonal pieces. Sprinkle plums, peaches, and bananas with lemon juice, to keep fruit from darkening. Reserve 6 strawberries for garnish; cut rest in half.

5. To serve: Add fruit to greens. Toss with Lime Salad Dressing until well coated.

6. Garnish with watercress sprigs, whole strawberries, and grape clusters.

* See this chapter.

PEACH WALDORF SALAD

3 fresh ripe peaches (about 1 lb)	1 teaspoon sugar
1 cup diced celery	1 tablespoon mayonnaise or cooked salad
½ cup chopped pecans	dressing
½ cup heavy cream	Salad greens

1. Wash peaches; peel. Cut in halves; remove pits. Dice peaches.
2. In large bowl, combine diced peaches with celery and pecans. Refrigerate, covered, until well chilled—about 1 hour.
3. Just before serving, whip cream, in medium bowl, until stiff. Combine sugar, salt, and mayonnaise. Add to whipped cream, mixing gently until well combined.
4. With rubber scraper, gently fold whipped-cream mixture into peach mixture.
5. Serve on salad greens.

PERSIMMON-AND-GRAPEFRUIT SALAD

3 grapefruit	Chicory
6 large persimmons	French dressing

1. Peel grapefruit; remove white membrane. Section carefully.
2. Wash persimmons. Place stem end down; with sharp knife, cut each into 6 sections without cutting all the way through.
3. Place persimmons on bed of chicory. Spread open, petal fashion.
4. Arrange grapefruit sections in center of each. Serve with French dressing.

FROZEN FRUIT SALAD

1 can (8¾ oz) pineapple tidbits	1 can (8¾ oz) white seedless grapes, drained; or ¾ cup fresh seedless grapes
3 tablespoons lemon juice	
1 envelope unflavored gelatine	½ cup drained maraschino cherries, halved
1 pkg (3 oz) soft cream cheese	½ cup coarsely chopped walnuts
¼ cup dairy sour cream	1 cup heavy cream, whipped
	1 large bunch watercress

1. Drain pineapple, reserving liquid. Add lemon juice to liquid to measure ½ cup.
2. Sprinkle gelatine over pineapple liquid in measuring cup; let stand 5 minutes, to soften. Set in pan of boiling water; heat, stirring to dissolve gelatine. Let cool slightly.
3. Meanwhile, in large bowl, with wooden spoon, beat cream cheese and sour cream until smooth. Add pineapple, grapes, cherries, walnuts, and gelatine mixture; mix well.
4. Refrigerate 30 to 45 minutes—till mixture mounds slightly when dropped from spoon.
5. Gently fold in whipped cream until well combined.
6. Turn into ice-cube tray lined with waxed paper; freeze until firm—at least 4 hours.
7. To serve: turn out of ice-cube tray. Slice into ½-inch slices. Place on bed of watercress. Let stand 10 minutes before serving.
Note: Follow manufacturer's directions for freezing in your refrigerator.

FROZEN TOMATO-PINEAPPLE SALAD

1 pkg (3 oz) soft cream
    cheese
½ cup sieved creamed
    cottage cheese
1 cup mayonnaise or
    cooked salad dressing
1½ teaspoons salt
¼ teaspoon pepper
⅛ teaspoon ginger

Dash liquid hot-pepper
    seasoning
2 tablespoons grated onion
1 can (1 pt, 2 oz) tomato
    juice
1 cup canned crushed
    pineapple, drained
8 lettuce cups

1. In large bowl of electric mixer, at medium speed, beat cream cheese with cottage cheese until smooth.
2. Add mayonnaise, salt, pepper, ginger, hot-pepper seasoning, onion, and tomato juice; beat until well combined.
3. Stir in pineapple. Pour into 2 ice-cube trays. Refrigerate until firm around edges—2 hours. just until thick and smooth, not melted.
4. Turn into bowl; beat, at medium speed,
5. Return to trays; freeze until firm.
6. Cut into 8 servings. Serve on lettuce cups— with mayonnaise, if desired.

Main-Dish Salads

In the good new summertime, a hearty salad made with meat, poultry, or fish is substantial enough to serve as a main dish. You could accompany it with hot vegetables. If your family tires of cold cuts on hot days, try one of these salads. They'll hit the spot.

BOLOGNA SALAD WITH MUSTARD DRESSING

1 egg, slightly beaten
½ cup vinegar
1 tablespoon butter or
    margarine
1 tablespoon sugar
2 tablespoons prepared
    mustard

1½ teaspoons paprika
1½ lb sliced bologna
1 cup sliced ripe olives
½ cup thinly sliced celery
¼ cup sliced scallions

1. In small saucepan, combine egg, vinegar, butter, sugar, mustard, and paprika. Cook, stirring and over low heat, until slightly thickened —about 5 minutes. Cool.
2. Slice bologna into ¼-inch strips.
3. In large bowl, combine bologna strips, olives, celery, scallions, and cooled dressing. Toss lightly until well combined.
4. Refrigerate at least 1 hour before serving.

HAM-MACARONI SALAD

½ pkg (8-oz size) elbow
    macaroni
2 cups cooked ham, cut in
    julienne strips
¼ cup chopped celery
2 tablespoons chopped
    onion
½ cup mayonnaise or
    cooked salad dressing

¼ cup light cream or milk
1 teaspoon prepared
    horseradish
1 teaspoon salt
Dash pepper
6 lettuce cups
6 tomato slices
12 green-pepper strips

1. Cook macaroni as package label directs. Drain; rinse in cold water.
2. In large bowl, combine cooled macaroni, ham, celery, and onion.
3. In small bowl, blend mayonnaise with cream, horseradish, salt, and pepper.
4. Toss dressing with macaroni mixture.
5. Refrigerate until well chilled—several hours.
6. To serve: Arrange macaroni salad on lettuce. Garnish with tomato and green pepper.

GOURMET TURKEY-AND-RICE SALAD

Dressing:
½ cup salad oil
½ cup vinegar
2 tablespoons lemon juice
1 teaspoon salt
⅛ teaspoon pepper
Dash sugar

Salad:
1 pkg (10 oz) frozen
    artichoke hearts
2 pkg (10-oz size) frozen
    asparagus spears

1 cup cold cooked rice
1 cup diced cucumber
¼ cup mayonnaise or
    cooked salad dressing
¼ teaspoon salt
Dash liquid hot-pepper
    seasoning
½ teaspoon curry powder
1½ lb sliced turkey or
    chicken (about 5
    cups)

1. Make Dressing: Combine all ingredients in jar with tight-fitting lid; shake to mix well.
2. Make Salad: Cook artichoke hearts and asparagus as package labels direct.
3. Drain; then arrange each in separate shallow baking dish. Pour ¼ cup dressing over each vegetable; refrigerate, covered, 1 hour.
4. Meanwhile, in medium bowl, combine rice, cucumber, mayonnaise, salt, hot-pepper seasoning, and curry powder. Toss well, with fork; refrigerate, covered.
5. To serve: Arrange turkey in center of large platter. Group drained artichoke hearts and asparagus spears, separately, at one end of platter. Spoon curried rice at other end.

MOLDED CRANBERRY RING WITH CHICKEN SALAD

1 cup boiling water
1 pkg (6 oz) lemon-flavored
    gelatin
1 pt bottled cranberry juice
2 tablespoons cider vinegar
2 tablespoons sugar
1½ cups finely shredded
    cabbage

¼ cup thinly sliced green
    onion
1 carrot, pared and thinly
    sliced
1 small cucumber, diced
½ teaspoon salt
Dash pepper
Chicken Salad, below
Watercress or parsley sprigs

1. Pour boiling water over gelatin in large bowl; stir till gelatin dissolves. Stir in 1 cup cold water, cranberry juice, vinegar, and sugar.
2. Refrigerate until consistency of unbeaten egg white—about 1 hour.
3. Add rest of ingredients, except Chicken Salad and watercress; mix well.
4. Turn into 5-cup ring mold; refrigerate until firm—about 1½ hours.
5. To unmold: Run a small spatula around edge of mold. Invert over platter; shake gently to release. If necessary, place a hot, wet dishcloth over inverted mold, and shake again to release.
6. Fill center with Chicken Salad. Garnish with watercress.

CHICKEN SALAD

3 cups diced cooked
    chicken
1½ cups celery, in ½-inch
    slices
2 tablespoons chopped
    parsley
1 teaspoon salt
½ teaspoon pepper

½ cup heavy cream,
    whipped
1 cup mayonnaise or
    cooked salad dressing
2 tablespoons lemon juice
½ cup toasted almonds,
    coarsely chopped

1. In large bowl, toss chicken with celery, parsley, salt, and pepper to mix well.
2. Gently fold in whipped cream, mayonnaise, lemon juice, and almonds until well combined.
3. Refrigerate until well chilled—about 1 hour.

PEAS-AND-CRABMEAT SALAD

1 can (6½ oz) crabmeat, drained
1 cup cooked peas
1 cup cooked white rice
½ teaspoon salt
¼ teaspoon curry powder
¼ cup mayonnaise or cooked salad dressing
Crisp salad greens

MAKES 2 OR 3 SERVINGS

1. In medium bowl, separate crabmeat pieces, removing membrane.
2. Add remaining ingredients, except salad greens, mixing gently to combine.
3. Refrigerate, covered, 1 hour. Serve on salad greens.

SENATE SALAD BOWL

Salad:
1 cup torn iceberg lettuce
1 cup torn romaine
½ cup watercress, stems removed
1 cup diced celery
¼ cup chopped green onion
1½ cups cubed cooked lobster or shrimp
2 medium tomatoes, diced
1 avocado, peeled and sliced
½ medium grapefruit, sectioned
5 large pitted ripe olives, sliced
¼ cup lemon juice

Cream Dressing:
1 cup (8 oz) creamed cottage cheese
¼ cup dairy sour cream
¼ teaspoon salt
Dash pepper

MAKES 4 SERVINGS

1. Make Salad: Toss lettuce, romaine, watercress, celery, and onion in large salad bowl.
2. On top, in clusters, arrange lobster, tomatoes, avocado, grapefruit, and olives. Sprinkle lemon juice over all. Refrigerate until well chilled—about 1 hour.
3. Meanwhile, make Cream Dressing: Press cottage cheese through sieve. Add sour cream, salt, and pepper; refrigerate. Serve with salad.

SWISS-CHEESE SALAD

½ lb natural Swiss cheese, cut in ¼-inch cubes
6 hard-cooked eggs, finely chopped
½ cup dairy sour cream
1½ teaspoons dry mustard
1 teaspoon prepared horseradish
½ teaspoon salt
⅛ teaspoon pepper
Salad greens
4 tomato wedges

MAKES 4 SERVINGS

1. In medium bowl, toss cheese and eggs.
2. Combine sour cream, mustard, horseradish, salt, and pepper; stir until well mixed.
3. Then gently, but thoroughly, fold sour-cream mixture into cheese mixture; refrigerate until well chilled—about 1 hour.
4. To serve: Arrange cheese mixture on bed of shredded salad greens. Garnish with tomato wedges.

TOSSED CHICKEN SALAD

1 head Boston lettuce
½ head romaine
1 cup sliced celery, ⅛ inch thick
2 cans (6-oz size) boned chicken; or 2 cups leftover cooked chicken, well chilled
1 can (8¾ oz) pineapple tidbits, drained
Special French Dressing*
3 tablespoons toasted slivered almonds
3 fresh peaches; or 1 can (1 lb, 1 oz) cling-peach halves, drained
Small bunch seedless green grapes

MAKES 4 SERVINGS

1. Wash lettuce and romaine; dry well. Store in crisper until ready to use.
2. Line shallow salad bowl with crisp, chilled outer lettuce and romaine leaves. Break rest of greens into bite-size pieces to measure 3 cups. Turn into center of bowl with celery.
3. Cut chicken into bite-size pieces. Add to greens along with ½ cup pineapple and about ½ cup dressing; toss lightly to combine well, adding more dressing if necessary.
4. Sprinkle salad with almonds. Peel and halve peaches; arrange on top of salad. Fill with rest of pineapple and the grapes.

* See this chapter.

JELLIED VEAL LOAF

3¼-lb boned veal rump
    roast
1 medium onion, quartered
1 stalk celery, cut into
    cubes
2 bay leaves
1 tablespoon salt
2 teaspoons monosodium
    glutamate
10 whole black peppers
2 envelopes unflavored
    gelatine

2 tablespoons chopped
    parsley
¼ teaspoon prepared
    horseradish
⅛ teaspoon liquid hot-
    pepper seasoning
Pimiento strips
Pitted ripe olives
Whipped Horseradish
    Sauce*

1. Wipe veal with damp paper towels. In 6-quart kettle, combine veal, onion, celery, bay leaves, salt, monosodium glutamate, and peppers with 4 cups water; bring to boiling, covered.
2. Reduce heat, and simmer 1½ to 2 hours, or until veal is tender.
3. Remove veal. Strain broth. Let veal and broth cool; then refrigerate both until well chilled—about 1 hour. Skim fat from broth.
4. In small saucepan, sprinkle gelatine over 1 cup cold broth; let stand 5 minutes, to soften.
5. Over low heat, cook, stirring constantly, until gelatine is dissolved. Remove from heat.
6. Stir in remaining veal broth (if necessary, add enough water to measure 3 cups), parsley, horseradish, and hot-pepper seasoning.
7. Refrigerate until consistency of unbeaten egg white—about 1 hour.
8. Meanwhile, trim fat from veal; dice veal finely. Fold into gelatine mixture.
9. Turn into a 9-by-5-by-3-inch loaf pan; refrigerate until firm—at least 1 hour.
10. To unmold: Run a small spatula around edge of pan. Invert over platter; shake gently to release. If necessary, place a hot, damp dishcloth over inverted pan; shake again to release.
11. Decorate top with pimiento and olives.

* See Sauces and Gravies Chapter.

MARINATED-BEEF SALAD PLATTER

Dressing:
½ cup salad oil
½ cup red-wine vinegar
½ teaspoon salt
⅛ teaspoon pepper
3 tablespoons catsup
½ teaspoon Worcestershire
    sauce

2 tablespoons finely
    chopped, fresh
    tarragon

1 lb medium-rare sliced
    roast beef
1 medium tomato, cut in 8
    wedges
1 medium cucumber, thinly
    sliced

1. Make Dressing: In jar with tight-fitting lid, combine dressing ingredients; shake vigorously to combine.
2. Sprinkle 1 teaspoon dressing over each roast-beef slice. Roll up each slice. Arrange, seam side down, in center of large platter.
3. In medium bowl, toss tomato and cucumber with ⅓ cup dressing, coating well; drain. Arrange attractively on platter around beef.
4. Sprinkle 2 tablespoons dressing over beef. Refrigerate, covered, 3 hours.
5. Just before serving, sprinkle 2 more tablespoons dressing over beef. (Refrigerate remaining dressing for later use in a tossed green salad.)

CHEF'S SALAD BOWL

MAKES 6 SERVINGS

½ head iceberg lettuce
½ head romaine
2 cups spinach leaves
1 can (12 oz) luncheon
   meat, slivered; or 2
   cups slivered cooked
   ham
¾ cup slivered cooked
   tongue
¾ cup slivered cooked
   turkey

¼ lb Swiss cheese, slivered
2 radishes, sliced
1 medium cucumber, thinly
   sliced
½ cup bottled herb
   dressing
12 cherry tomatoes
6 radish roses
1 cup garlic-flavored
   croutons*

1. Wash lettuce, romaine, and spinach; dry well. Store in crisper until ready to use.

2. Refrigerate rest of ingredients, except croutons, until ready to use.

3. Line salad bowl with crisp, chilled outer lettuce leaves. Break rest of greens into bite-size pieces to measure 1 quart. Turn into center of bowl.

4. Add luncheon meat, tongue, turkey, cheese, radishes, half of cucumber, and ½ cup croutons.

5. Toss salad with dressing, to coat well. Top with rest of croutons.

6. Garnish salad with rest of cucumber, the cherry tomatoes, and radish roses. Serve at once.

* *Garlic-flavored croutons:* Cut 2 slices white-bread toast into small cubes. Sauté cubes lightly in 2 tablespoons melted butter with 1 clove garlic until lightly browned. Discard garlic. Makes 1 cup.

Molded Salads

They may be more trouble to make than a tossed green salad, but you can do it all in advance of your party. All you do at the last minute is garnish it and serve.

MOLDED COLESLAW RING

MAKES 5 SERVINGS

1 envelope unflavored
   gelatine
1 cup milk
⅔ cup mayonnaise or
   cooked salad dressing
1 teaspoon prepared
   mustard
1½ teaspoons grated onion

1½ teaspoons celery seed
1 teaspoon salt
⅓ cup light cream
1½ cups finely shredded
   cabbage
½ cup finely shredded
   carrot

1. Sprinkle gelatine over ½ cup milk in measuring cup; let stand 5 minutes, to soften. Set in pan of boiling water; heat, stirring to dissolve gelatine. Let cool slightly.

2. In large bowl, combine salad dressing, mustard, onion, celery seed, and salt, mixing well. Gradually stir in cream, rest of milk, and the gelatine mixture.

(Molded Coleslaw Ring continued)

3. Refrigerate until consistency of unbeaten egg white—about 45 minutes.

4. Fold cabbage and carrot into gelatine mixture, combining well. Turn into 3-cup ring mold. Refrigerate until firm—about 2 hours.

5. To unmold: Run a spatula around edge of mold, to loosen. Invert onto serving platter; shake gently to release. If necessary, place a hot, damp dishcloth over inverted mold; shake again to release. Refrigerate until ready to serve.

ASPARAGUS IN ASPIC

MAKES 6 SERVINGS

2 to 2½ lb fresh asparagus
1 pimiento, drained and slivered
½ cup bottled Italian-style salad dressing
2 envelopes unflavored gelatine
2 chicken-bouillon cubes
2 cups boiling water
1 teaspoon salt
⅛ teaspoon pepper
1 teaspoon grated onion
3 drops liquid hot-pepper seasoning
1 teaspoon prepared horseradish
2 tablespoons lemon juice
¼ teaspoon dry mustard
4 hard-cooked eggs
Salad greens

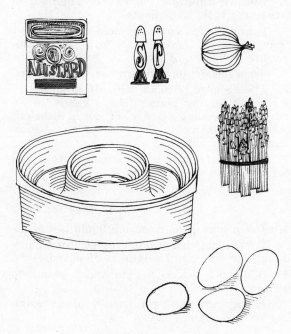

1. Cut or break off tough ends of asparagus stalks. Wash asparagus tips well with cold water; if necessary, use a soft brush to remove grit. With vegetable parer, scrape skin and scales from lower part of stalk only.

2. In saucepan, cook asparagus in boiling, salted water to cover until just tender-crisp—about 10 minutes. Drain.

3. Slice thinly on diagonal.

4. In medium bowl, combine asparagus and pimiento. Add salad dressing; toss to coat well. Set aside.

5. In medium bowl, sprinkle gelatine over 1 cup cold water; let soften 5 minutes.

6. Dissolve bouillon cubes in boiling water. Add hot bouillon to gelatine; stir until dissolved.

7. Add salt, pepper, onion, hot-pepper seasoning, horseradish, lemon juice, and mustard; stir well.

8. Lightly oil a 5½-cup ring mold. Pour in enough gelatine mixture to cover bottom; refrigerate until almost set.

9. Slice eggs; make a circle of overlapping slices on gelatine in mold. Top with just enough gelatine mixture to cover; refrigerate until firm.

10. Drain asparagus and pimiento; fold into remaining gelatine mixture. Pour into mold; refrigerate several hours, or until firm.

11. To unmold: Run a small spatula carefully around edge of mold; invert over platter; shake to release. If necessary, place a hot, damp dishcloth over inverted mold; shake again to release. Garnish with salad greens.

507

AVOCADO MOLD

3 envelopes unflavored
    gelatine
2 cups mashed ripe avocado
    (about 3)
1 cup dairy sour cream
1 cup mayonnaise
2 tablespoons grated onion

1 tablespoon grated green
    pepper
1 teaspoon salt
⅛ teaspoon pepper
¼ cup lemon juice
Salad greens

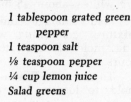

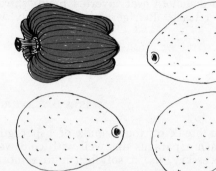

1. Sprinkle gelatine over 1 cup cold water in top of double boiler, to soften; stir over hot water until gelatine is dissolved.
2. Refrigerate until consistency of unbeaten egg white—about 1 hour.
3. Meanwhile, in medium bowl, combine remaining ingredients, except salad greens. Fold gently into gelatine, mixing well.
4. Turn into 5½-cup ring mold that has been rinsed in cold water. Cover with saran; refrigerate until set—about 3 hours.
5. To serve: Run spatula around edge of mold, to loosen it. Invert over serving plate; shake gently to release. If necessary, place a hot, damp dishcloth over mold; shake again.
6. Serve on salad greens with Crab Salad.*
Note: Avocado Mold will discolor if stored in refrigerator longer than 1½ hours after it has been unmolded.

* See this chapter.

CONFETTI RING MOLD

Ring Mold:
1½ tablespoons unflavored
    gelatine
1½ cups ice water
6 tablespoons lemon juice
¼ teaspoon liquid hot-
    pepper seasoning
¾ teaspoon salt
¼ cup finely chopped
    pimiento
¼ cup finely chopped
    onion

¼ cup finely chopped
    green pepper
½ cup diced cucumber
½ cup canned pineapple
    tidbits, drained
1 cup diced avocado

Lettuce leaves
1 cup mayonnaise or cooked
    salad dressing
1 teaspoon lemon juice
2 tablespoons finely
    chopped parsley

1. Make Ring Mold: Sprinkle gelatine over ¾ cup cold water in saucepan, to soften.
2. Place over low heat, stirring constantly, until gelatine is dissolved.
3. Add ice water, to cool quickly. Then stir in remaining mold ingredients.
4. Pour into 5½-cup ring mold; refrigerate 1 hour, stirring several times to keep solids from settling to bottom of mold.
5. Then refrigerate until firm—at least 3 hours.
6. Loosen edge of mold, with sharp knife; invert onto serving platter; shake gently to release. If necessary, place a hot, damp dishcloth over inverted mold; shake again to release. Garnish with lettuce.
7. Combine mayonnaise, lemon juice, and parsley. Serve with salad mold.

RHUBARB-STRAWBERRY SALAD

1 can (8¾ oz) pineapple
    tidbits
1 pkg (3 oz) pineapple-
    flavored gelatin

1 cup very thinly sliced raw
    rhubarb
2 cups sliced fresh
    strawberries
Salad greens

1. Drain pineapple, reserving liquid; set aside.
2. Pour 1 cup hot water over gelatin in medium bowl; stir until gelatin is dissolved.
3. Add cold water to pineapple liquid to measure 1 cup; stir into gelatin.
4. Refrigerate until consistency of unbeaten egg white—about 1 hour.

(Rhubarb-Strawberry Salad continued)

5. Meanwhile, in medium bowl, layer rhubarb, pineapple, and strawberries, so juice from sweeter fruit will marinate rhubarb.

6. Gently fold fruit into gelatin. Turn into 1½-quart mold, or 8 individual molds.

7. Refrigerate until firm—at least 2 hours.

8. To unmold: Run a small spatula around edge of mold; invert over serving platter; shake gently to release. If necessary, place a hot, damp dishcloth over inverted mold, and shake again to release.

9. Garnish with salad greens.

MAKES 4 TO 6 SERVINGS

PINEAPPLE–GINGER-ALE SALAD MOLD

1 can (8¾ oz) pineapple tidbits
1 pkg (3 oz) pineapple-flavored gelatin
¼ cup lemon juice
1 cup ginger ale

1 medium apple, pared and cut into strips
⅓ cup halved seedless green grapes
1 tablespoon finely chopped crystallized ginger

1. Drain pineapple, reserving liquid. If necessary, add water to liquid to measure ¾ cup.

2. Bring liquid to boiling; pour over gelatin in large bowl, stirring to dissolve gelatin.

3. Add lemon juice and ginger ale, mixing well.

4. Refrigerate until consistency of unbeaten egg white—30 to 45 minutes. Stir in rest of ingredients.

5. Turn into 5½-cup ring mold. Refrigerate until firm—about 1 hour.

6. To unmold: Run a spatula around edge of mold, to loosen. Invert onto serving platter; shake gently to release. If necessary, place a hot, damp dishcloth over inverted mold; shake again to release. Refrigerate until serving.

7. Serve with salad greens, if desired.

MAKES 12 SERVINGS

PERFECTION SALAD

3 envelopes unflavored gelatine
½ cup sugar
½ teaspoon salt
½ teaspoon seasoned salt
4 cups boiling water
1 beef-bouillon cube, dissolved in ½ cup boiling water
½ cup tarragon vinegar
3 tablespoons lemon juice
⅛ teaspoon liquid hot-pepper seasoning

1 cup coarsely chopped pared carrot
½ cup coarsely chopped green pepper
½ cup finely chopped celery
½ cup sweet-pickle relish, drained
2 pimientos, drained and cut up
12 lettuce cups
Mayonnaise

1. In large bowl, combine gelatine, sugar, and salts, mixing well.

2. Add boiling water, stirring until gelatine mixture is dissolved.

3. Stir in bouillon, vinegar, lemon juice, and hot-pepper seasoning.

4. Refrigerate until consistency of unbeaten egg white—about 1 hour.

5. Fold in rest of ingredients, except lettuce and dressing, combining well. Turn into a 10-by-6-by-2-inch pan.

6. Refrigerate until firm—several hours.

7. To serve: Cut into 12 pieces; place each on lettuce cup. Serve with mayonnaise.

LAYERED TONGUE-AND-CHEESE SALAD MOLD

2 envelopes unflavored
    gelatine
1 beef-bouillon cube,
    crumbled
½ cup cider vinegar
½ lb sliced cooked tongue

2 cups grated sharp
    Cheddar cheese
    (½ lb)
½ cup diced celery
½ cup sliced gherkins

1. Sprinkle gelatine over 1 cup cold water in measuring cup; let stand 5 minutes, to soften.

2. Add bouillon cube. Set in pan of boiling water; stir to dissolve gelatine and bouillon cube.

3. Add gelatine mixture to vinegar combined with 1½ cups cold water; mix well.

4. Pour ⅓ cup gelatine mixture into bottom of 5½-cup ring mold. Refrigerate 8 to 10 minutes, or until consistency of unbeaten egg white. Let rest of gelatine stand at room temperature until ready to use.

5. Roll up 6 to 8 tongue slices. Arrange in single layer over gelatine in mold. Pour ⅓ cup gelatine over tongue. Refrigerate 20 minutes, or until firm.

6. Chop remaining tongue; set aside.

7. In medium bowl, combine cheese, celery, and gherkins with 1⅓ cups gelatine mixture; pour into mold. Refrigerate until firm—about 45 minutes.

8. Combine rest of gelatine with chopped tongue, mixing well. Pour into mold. Refrigerate 30 minutes, or until firm.

9. To unmold: Run a spatula around edge of mold, to loosen. Invert onto serving platter; shake gently to release. If necessary, place a hot, damp dishcloth over inverted mold; shake again to release. Refrigerate until serving time.

10. To serve, garnish with tomato slices, if desired.

TOMATO ASPIC

1 envelope unflavored
    gelatine
1 teaspoon sugar
1 can (13½ oz) tomato
    juice
¼ teaspoon salt
¼ teaspoon celery salt
½ teaspoon Worcestershire
    sauce

Dash liquid hot-pepper
    seasoning
2 tablespoons lemon juice
Lettuce leaves
Mayonnaise or cooked
    salad dressing

1. In small saucepan, combine gelatine and sugar, mixing well. Slowly add 1 cup tomato juice, stirring until well combined.

2. Cook, over medium heat, stirring constantly, until gelatine dissolves.

3. Remove from heat. Stir in rest of tomato juice, salt, celery salt, Worcestershire, hot-pepper seasoning, and lemon juice.

4. Turn mixture into 4 (4-oz) individual molds or custard cups.

5. Refrigerate 1½ hours, or until firm.

6. To serve, run a small spatula around edge of molds; turn out aspic onto lettuce leaves. Serve with mayonnaise.

TOMATO-EGG ASPIC WITH MARINATED SHRIMP

2 envelopes unflavored
    gelatine
1 beef-bouillon cube,
    dissolved in ½ cup
    boiling water
2 cups tomato juice
1 tablespoon finely chopped
    onion
1 tablespoon chopped
    parsley
¾ teaspoon salt

½ teaspoon prepared
    horseradish
½ teaspoon Worcestershire
    sauce
¼ teaspoon liquid hot-
    pepper seasoning
2 hard-cooked eggs,
    chopped
Salad greens
Marinated Shrimp, below

1. In large bowl, sprinkle gelatine over ½ cup cold water; let stand 5 minutes, to soften.
2. Add hot bouillon, stirring until gelatine is dissolved. Stir in tomato juice, onion, parsley, salt, horseradish, Worcestershire, and hot-pepper seasoning.
3. Refrigerate until consistency of unbeaten egg white—about 1 hour.
4. Carefully fold in eggs. Turn into 1-quart mold.
5. Refrigerate until firm—2 to 3 hours.
6. To unmold: Run a small spatula around edge of mold. Invert over platter; shake gently to release. If necessary, place a hot, damp dishcloth over inverted mold, and shake again to release.
7. Surround with salad greens and Marinated Shrimp.

MARINATED SHRIMP

1 pkg (12 oz) frozen ready-
    to-cook shrimp
¼ cup olive oil
2 tablespoons lemon juice

1 tablespoon chopped
    parsley
½ teaspoon salt
1 clove garlic, crushed

1. Cook shrimp according to package directions. Plunge into cold water. If necessary, devein with sharp, pointed knife. Rinse in cold water; drain.
2. In medium bowl, combine with remaining ingredients.
3. Cover; refrigerate 6 to 8 hours. Stir occasionally.

JELLIED WALDORF SALAD

Boiling water
2 pkg (3-oz size) lemon-
    flavored gelatin
½ cup light or dark raisins
½ cup grated raw carrot
½ cup diced unpared red
    apple

½ cup coarsely chopped
    walnuts
1 teaspoon salt
Salad greens
Mayonnaise or cooked
    salad dressing

1. Pour 1½ cups boiling water over gelatin in medium bowl; stir to dissolve gelatin. Add 1½ cups cold water.
2. Set bowl in pan of ice; leave in ice, stirring occasionally, until mixture is consistency of unbeaten egg white—about 30 minutes.
3. Meanwhile, let raisins stand 10 minutes in boiling water to cover. Drain.
4. Stir raisins, carrot, apple, walnuts, and salt into gelatin mixture until well combined.
5. Pour into 5½-cup ring mold; refrigerate until firm—about 1 hour.
6. To unmold: Run a small spatula around edge of mold. Invert over platter; shake gently to release. If necessary, place a hot, damp dish cloth over inverted mold; shake to release.
7. Surround with salad greens. Serve with mayonnaise.

WINE FRUIT SALAD

2 envelopes unflavored
    gelatine
¼ cup sugar
¼ teaspoon salt
1⅔ cups boiling water
1 teaspoon grated lemon
    peel
2 tablespoons lemon juice
1½ cups rosé wine
5 drops red food color
    (optional)

¾ cup diced orange
    sections
¾ cup diced unpared red
    apple
½ cup slivered pitted dates
¼ cup diced grapefruit
    sections
¼ cup thinly sliced celery
Salad greens

1. Combine gelatine, sugar, and salt in large bowl. Add water; stir until gelatine mixture is dissolved. Then stir in lemon peel, lemon juice, and wine. Add food color, a drop at a time; mix well.

2. Refrigerate about 1 hour, or just until mixture mounds slightly when dropped from spoon.

3. Meanwhile, lightly toss fruit and celery until well mixed. Stir into gelatine mixture.

4. Turn into 5½-cup ring mold; refrigerate until firm—about 2 hours.

5. To serve: Run a small spatula around edge of mold; carefully unmold fruit ring on salad greens.

Seafood Salads

What to serve on a simmering Friday night in summer? One of our seafood salads— chilled, hearty, and different—will tempt a heat-jaded appetite.

CARIBBEAN LOBSTER SALAD

6 (8-oz size) frozen rock-
    lobster tails
3½ teaspoons salt
1 bottle (8 oz) Italian-style
    salad dressing
⅓ cup mayonnaise
½ teaspoon soy sauce
Dash pepper

Dash cayenne
1½ cups fresh-pineapple
    wedges; or 1 can (1 lb,
    4½ oz) pineapple
    chunks, drained
1½ cups sliced celery
Salad greens
6 lime wedges

1. Bring 3 quarts water to boiling. Add unthawed lobster tails and 2 teaspoons salt; return to boiling. Reduce heat; simmer, covered, 10 minutes. Drain; cool.

2. With scissors, cut undershells from lobster tails, reserving shells.

3. Remove lobster meat in one piece; cut into ¾-inch pieces.

4. In medium bowl, toss lobster with salad dressing, coating well.

5. Refrigerate, covered, at least 30 minutes, stirring occasionally.

6. Drain; reserve dressing.

7. In large bowl, combine mayonnaise with soy sauce, pepper, cayenne, and remaining salt; blend well.

8. Add lobster, pineapple, and celery, mixing gently.

9. Mound lobster salad in shells. Serve on greens, tossed with reserved dressing. Garnish with lime wedges.

CRAB SALAD

4 cans (6½-oz size)
    crabmeat
⅔ cup finely chopped
    celery
½ teaspoon salt

¼ cup finely chopped
    pimiento
2 tablespoons lemon juice
½ cup mayonnaise or
    cooked salad dressing

1. In medium bowl, separate crabmeat pieces, removing membrane.

2. Add remaining ingredients; toss well.

3. Cover; refrigerate until serving time.

4. To serve, mound in center of Avocado Mold,* and put rest on greens around mold.

* See this chapter.

TUNA-MACARONI SALAD

1 cup uncooked elbow
    macaroni
¼ cup bottled French
    dressing
1 can (7 oz) chunk-style
    tuna, drained
½ cup diced green pepper

½ cup diced cucumber
¼ cup sliced radishes
1 teaspoon onion salt
⅛ teaspoon pepper
2 tablespoons lemon juice
¼ cup dairy sour cream
Salad greens

1. Cook macaroni as label directs. Drain well.

2. In large bowl, toss with French dressing; refrigerate, covered, 2 to 3 hours.

3. Add remaining ingredients, except salad greens; toss to combine well.

4. Refrigerate until well chilled—at least 1 hour. Serve garnished with salad greens.

SALMON MOUSSE WITH CUCUMBER VINAIGRETTE

1 can (16 oz) red salmon
¼ cup vinegar
¼ cup dairy sour cream
1 tablespoon prepared
    horseradish
1 envelope unflavored
    gelatine
¼ cup lemon juice
1 teaspoon salt
1 teaspoon prepared
    mustard
½ cup heavy cream,
    whipped

Cucumber Vinaigrette:
1 medium unpared
    cucumber, very thinly
    sliced (about 2 cups)
1 medium green pepper,
    cut into thin strips
    (about 1 cup)
¼ cup vinegar
¼ cup lemon juice
¼ cup salad oil
½ teaspoon salt
¼ teaspoon Worcestershire
    sauce
⅛ teaspoon pepper

1. Drain salmon; remove any bones and skin.

2. Turn salmon into medium bowl; with fork, break into small pieces.

3. In electric blender at high speed, blend salmon with vinegar, one third at a time, 1½ minutes, to make a purée.

4. Turn into large bowl; fold in sour cream and horseradish.

5. In measuring cup, sprinkle gelatine over lemon juice combined with ¼ cup water. Let stand 5 minutes. Set in pan of boiling water; stir to dissolve gelatine.

6. Gradually stir into salmon mixture along with salt and mustard. Fold in whipped cream.

7. Turn into 6 (4-oz) individual molds. Refrigerate at least 4½ hours, or until firm.

8. Meanwhile, make Cucumber Vinaigrette: In medium bowl, combine cucumber slices with green-pepper strips.

9. In measuring cup, combine rest of ingredients, mixing well. Pour over cucumber mixture, tossing to coat well.

10. Refrigerate, covered, until well chilled— about 1 hour—tossing occasionally.

11. To serve: Drain dressing from vegetables. Arrange vegetables attractively on large platter.

12. To unmold mousse: Run a spatula around edge of molds; invert onto vegetables. Serve at once.

Salad Dressings

The soul of a salad is its dressing. And though literally hundreds of bottled dressings are available in the market, many of them excellent, a homemade dressing has the extra something that family and guests appreciate.

BASIC COOKED SALAD DRESSING

MAKES 1½ CUPS

2 tablespoons all-purpose
    flour
2 tablespoons sugar
1 teaspoon salt
1 teaspoon dry mustard
Dash cayenne or paprika

1 cup milk
⅓ cup lemon juice or
    vinegar
2 egg yolks, well beaten
2 tablespoons butter or
    margarine

1. In small saucepan, combine flour with sugar, salt, mustard, and cayenne. Gradually stir in milk.
2. Cook, stirring, over low heat, until mixture begins to boil; boil 1 minute. Remove from heat.
3. In small bowl, gradually stir lemon juice into egg yolks; then stir in hot mixture, a little at a time. Pour back into saucepan.
4. Cook, stirring, over low heat, until mixture boils; boil 1 minute. Remove from heat.
5. Stir in butter. Let cool.
6. Store, covered, in refrigerator.

For Fruit Salads: To ½ cup chilled Basic Cooked Salad Dressing, fold in ½ cup heavy cream, whipped. Makes 1½ cups.

For Vegetable Salads: To ½ cup chilled Basic Cooked Salad Dressing, fold in 1 cup dairy sour cream. Makes 1½ cups.

BASIC MAYONNAISE

MAKES 1¼ CUPS

2 egg yolks, or 1 whole egg
½ teaspoon dry mustard
1 teaspoon salt
Dash cayenne

1 cup salad or olive oil
2 tablespoons lemon juice
    or vinegar

1. In small bowl, with portable electric mixer at medium speed, beat egg yolks, mustard, salt, and cayenne until thick and lemon-colored.
2. Add ¼ cup oil, one drop at a time, beating until thick.
3. Gradually add 1 tablespoon lemon juice, beating after each addition. Then add ½ cup oil, in a steady stream, beating constantly.
4. Slowly add remaining lemon juice and then remaining oil, beating constantly.
5. Refrigerate, covered, until ready to use.

Watercress Dressing: Combine 1 cup Basic Mayonnaise with ½ cup finely chopped watercress; mix well. Refrigerate, covered, until ready to use.

BLENDER MAYONNAISE

2 egg yolks, or 1 whole egg
½ teaspoon dry mustard
1 teaspoon salt
2 tablespoons vinegar*
1 cup salad or olive oil

MAKES 1¼ CUPS

1. In blender container, combine egg yolks, mustard, salt, vinegar, and ¼ cup oil. Cover; turn motor to high speed; turn off. Remove cover.
2. Turn motor to high speed. Immediately add remaining oil in a steady, gradual stream. Turn off motor.
3. Refrigerate, covered, until ready to use.
* For flavor variations, substitute wine vinegar or lemon juice.

CHIFFONADE DRESSING

1 cup mayonnaise or cooked salad dressing
1 tablespoon snipped chives
¼ cup finely chopped green pepper
1 hard-cooked egg, finely chopped
¼ cup finely chopped cooked beets

MAKES 1¾ CUPS

1. In small bowl, combine all ingredients, mixing well.
2. Refrigerate, covered, until ready to use.

CHIVE DRESSING

1 cup mayonnaise or cooked salad dressing
½ cup heavy cream, whipped
½ cup snipped chives
2 tablespoons prepared horseradish

MAKES 1½ CUPS

1. In small bowl, combine all ingredients, mixing well.
2. Refrigerate, covered, until ready to use.

CUCUMBER DRESSING

½ small cucumber
1 cup mayonnaise or cooked salad dressing
¼ teaspoon cayenne

MAKES 1½ CUPS

1. Peel cucumber. Halve lengthwise; remove seeds from center, and discard. Chop cucumber finely; measure ½ cup.
2. Combine cucumber with remaining ingredients, mixing well.
3. Refrigerate, covered, until ready to use.

EASY RUSSIAN DRESSING

1 cup mayonnaise or cooked salad dressing
⅔ cup chili sauce
½ cup finely chopped green onion
¼ cup finely chopped green pepper
2 tablespoons lemon juice
Dash salt

MAKES 2¼ CUPS

1. In small bowl, combine mayonnaise with rest of ingredients; mix well.
2. Refrigerate, covered, until ready to use.

SPECIAL FRENCH DRESSING

1 teaspoon salt
Dash pepper
2 tablespoons cider vinegar
¼ cup orange juice
1 tablespoon lemon juice
¾ cup salad oil
1 teaspoon bottled capers

MAKES ABOUT 1 CUP

1. Combine all ingredients in pint jar with tight-fitting lid. Shake vigorously to combine well.
2. Refrigerate until ready to use. Shake well just before using.

HONEY-LIME DRESSING

1 cup mayonnaise or cooked
    salad dressing
½ cup honey
1 cup heavy cream,
    whipped
¼ cup lime juice

1. In small bowl, combine all ingredients well.
2. Refrigerate, covered, until ready to use. Delicious on fruit salad.

LIME SALAD DRESSING

¾ cup salad oil
2 tablespoons cider vinegar
3 tablespoons lime juice
¼ cup orange juice
2 tablespoons sugar
½ teaspoon salt
⅛ teaspoon paprika
3 tablespoons chopped
    fresh mint

1. Combine all ingredients in pint jar with tight-fitting lid. Shake vigorously to combine well.
2. Refrigerate until ready to use. Shake well just before serving.

LORENZO DRESSING

½ cup mayonnaise or
    cooked salad dressing
¼ cup chili sauce
¼ cup finely chopped
    watercress
1 tablespoon catsup
1 tablespoon horseradish
¼ teaspoon salt
Dash pepper

1. In small bowl, combine all ingredients, mixing well.
2. Refrigerate, covered, at least 1 hour before serving.

ROQUEFORT DRESSING

½ cup salad oil
2 tablespoons wine
    vinegar
2 tablespoons lemon juice
½ teaspoon salt
½ teaspoon celery seed
⅛ teaspoon pepper
½ teaspoon sugar
½ teaspoon paprika
⅓ cup crumbled
    Roquefort cheese

1. Combine all ingredients in jar with tight-fitting lid. Shake vigorously to combine.
2. Refrigerate until ready to use. Shake again just before using.

RUSSIAN DRESSING

1½ cups mayonnaise or
    cooked salad dressing
½ cup finely chopped
    cooked beets
1 tablespoon drained
    prepared horseradish
½ teaspoon salt
2 tablespoons caviar
    (optional)

1. Combine all ingredients in small bowl; stir until well blended.
2. Refrigerate, covered, at least 2 hours before serving.

THOUSAND ISLAND DRESSING

¼ cup finely chopped
    stuffed olives
2 tablespoons finely
    chopped green pepper
2 tablespoons finely
    chopped onion
1 cup mayonnaise or
    cooked salad dressing
2 tablespoons chili sauce
¼ cup milk

1. Combine all ingredients in small bowl; stir until well blended.
2. Refrigerate, covered, at least 2 hours before serving.

BASIC FRENCH DRESSING

MAKES 1 CUP

⅓ cup vinegar* or lemon
    juice
⅔ cup salad or olive oil
1½ teaspoons salt

¼ teaspoon pepper
1 teaspoon sugar (optional)
1 clove garlic (optional)

1. Combine all ingredients in jar with tight-fitting lid; shake vigorously to blend.
2. Refrigerate, covered, at least 2 hours before using.
3. Remove garlic; shake just before using.

* You may use white, cider, wine, or herb-flavored vinegar.

ROQUEFORT OR BLUE-CHEESE DRESSING

MAKES 1¼ CUPS

1. Crumble a package (about 3 oz) Roquefort or blue cheese into a small bowl.
2. Add 2 tablespoons Basic French Dressing; mix well with fork. Add rest of dressing.
3. Store, covered, in refrigerator. Mix again just before using.

ANCHOVY DRESSING

MAKES 1¼ CUPS

1. Add 2 tablespoons anchovy paste, 1 tablespoon finely chopped parsley, and 1 tablespoon snipped chives to Basic French Dressing. Shake vigorously to combine.
2. Store, covered, in refrigerator. Shake again just before using.

CAPER FRENCH DRESSING

MAKES 1 CUP

⅔ cup olive or salad oil
⅓ cup cider vinegar
2 tablespoons bottled
    capers, drained

½ teaspoon salt
½ teaspoon paprika
¼ teaspoon garlic powder

1. Combine all ingredients in jar with tight-fitting lid. Shake vigorously.
2. Refrigerate, covered, until chilled. Shake well before using.

FRENCH DRESSING

MAKES 2½ CUPS

1 cup salad oil
½ cup olive oil
¼ cup dry white wine
½ cup red-wine vinegar
2 teaspoons salt
½ teaspoon pepper

½ teaspoon dry mustard
½ teaspoon dried basil
    leaves
½ cup chopped parsley
1 clove garlic, finely
    chopped

1. Combine all ingredients in medium bowl; beat, with rotary beater, until well blended. Pour into jar with tight-fitting lid.
2. Refrigerate, covered, at least 2 hours. Shake well just before serving.

GOLDEN-GATE DRESSING

MAKES 1¼ CUPS

2 eggs, slightly beaten
¼ cup honey
¼ cup canned pineapple
    juice
½ cup orange juice

1 tablespoon grated orange
    peel
½ cup heavy cream,
    whipped

1. Combine all ingredients, except cream, in top of double boiler. Cook, stirring, over hot, not boiling, water 15 minutes, or until thickened.
2. Refrigerate, covered, until well chilled.
3. Just before serving, fold in whipped cream until well combined.

ITALIAN SALAD DRESSING

MAKES 2¾ CUPS

½ cup finely chopped
    onion
1 clove garlic, finely
    chopped
¼ cup sugar
1 cup red-wine vinegar
1 cup olive oil

1 cup catsup
2 teaspoons salt
1 teaspoon dry mustard
1 teaspoon paprika
1 teaspoon dried oregano
    leaves

1. Combine all ingredients in jar with tight-fitting lid; shake to mix well.
2. Refrigerate, covered, at least 2 hours, to blend flavors.
3. Strain, to remove onion and garlic. Shake well just before using.

CREAMY DRESSING

MAKES 1 CUP

1 tablespoon flour
1 tablespoon sugar
1½ teaspoons salt
½ teaspoon dry mustard
2 tablespoons salad oil

3 tablespoons cider vinegar
1 egg, slightly beaten
½ teaspoon celery seed
¼ cup dairy sour cream

1. In top of double boiler, combine flour, sugar, salt, mustard, oil, and ½ cup water. Bring to boiling, stirring, over medium heat. Mixture will be smooth and thickened.
2. In small bowl, gradually stir vinegar into egg; then stir in hot mixture, a little at a time.
3. Pour back into double-boiler top; cook, stirring, over hot, not boiling, water (water should not touch bottom of top part), until thickened—about 5 minutes. Remove from heat.
4. Stir in celery seed and sour cream. Refrigerate, covered, until ready to use.

MAPLE DRESSING FOR FRUIT SALAD

MAKES ABOUT 1 CUP

1 cup maple-flavored syrup
2 tablespoons salad oil
1 tablespoon lemon juice
½ teaspoon paprika

¼ teaspoon salt
¼ teaspoon celery seed
¼ teaspoon onion powder
Dash dry mustard

1. Combine all ingredients in jar with tight-fitting lid. Shake well.
2. Refrigerate, covered, until well chilled. Shake well before using.

POPPY-SEED DRESSING

MAKES 1⅔ CUPS

¾ cup sugar
1 teaspoon dry mustard
1 teaspoon salt
⅓ cup cider vinegar

1 tablespoon onion juice
1 cup salad oil
1½ tablespoons poppy
    seed

1. In medium bowl, combine sugar, mustard, salt, vinegar, and onion juice.
2. Using portable electric mixer or rotary beater, gradually beat in oil until mixture is thick and smooth. Stir in poppy seed.
3. Store, covered, in refrigerator. This dressing is good with any fruit salad.

VINAIGRETTE DRESSING

MAKES 1½ CUPS

1 cup olive or salad oil
⅓ cup red-wine vinegar
1 teaspoon salt
⅛ teaspoon pepper

2 tablespoons chopped
    capers
2 tablespoons chopped
    chives

1. Combine all ingredients in jar with tight-fitting lid. Shake vigorously.
2. Refrigerate the dressing until ready to use. Shake it again just before using.

I t was John Montagu, the fourth Earl of Sandwich, who discovered how much good eating could be tucked away between two slices of bread. Wouldn't he be surprised to see the institution his invention has become?

Just a few tips when you make them: Keep spreads fairly soft. Use ready-sliced bread. Spread with a flexible spatula. Cut a stack of sandwiches at a time. Wrap each sandwich separately, to prevent the mingling of odors.

FESTIVE RIBBONS

EACH LOAF MAKES ABOUT 34 SANDWICHES

*1 loaf (1 lb) unsliced whole-
   wheat bread
1 loaf (1 lb) unsliced white
   bread*

*Fillings, below:
Deviled Ham
Cream Cheese and Green
   Pepper
Mushroom Pâté
Cream Cheese and
   Pimiento*

1. Trim crusts from bread. From each loaf, cut four ½-inch-thick slices, lengthwise. Cover with damp towel.

2. Assemble 2 sandwich loaves: For first loaf, spread a whole-wheat slice with half the Deviled-Ham Filling. Top with white slice; spread with Cream-Cheese and Green-Pepper Filling. Top with whole-wheat slice; spread with rest of Deviled-Ham Filling. Cover with white slice.

3. For second loaf, spread a white slice with half the Mushroom-Pâté Filling. Top with whole-wheat slice; spread with all the Cream-Cheese and Pimiento Filling. Top with white slice; spread with rest of Mushroom-Pâté Filling. Cover with whole-wheat slice.

4. Wrap loaves in saran; cover with damp towel. Refrigerate at least 3 hours.

5. To serve: Using serrated knife, cut each loaf into 17 slices; cut each slice in half crosswise.

519

DEVILED-HAM FILLING

2 cans (4½-oz size)
    deviled ham
1 tablespoon chili sauce

1 teaspoon grated onion
¼ teaspoon Worcestershire
    sauce

Combine ingredients in small bowl, mixing well.

CREAM-CHEESE AND GREEN-PEPPER FILLING

½ pkg (3-oz size) soft
    cream cheese
4 teaspoons mayonnaise

⅔ cup finely chopped
    green pepper
¼ cup sweet-pickle relish,
    drained

In small bowl, mix cream cheese with mayonnaise until smooth. Add pepper and relish; mix well.

MUSHROOM-PÂTÉ FILLING

½ cup finely chopped
    fresh mushrooms
1 tablespoon butter or
    margarine

2 cans (4½-oz size) liver
    pâté
2 tablespoons mayonnaise
¼ teaspoon salt
¼ teaspoon onion powder

Sauté mushrooms in hot butter until tender—about 5 minutes. Remove from heat. Add rest of ingredients; mix well.

CREAM-CHEESE AND PIMIENTO FILLING

2 pkg (3-oz size) soft cream
    cheese
1½ tablespoons mayonnaise
2 tablespoons finely
    chopped green
    pepper

1 tablespoon chopped
    pimiento
1 tablespoon finely
    chopped parsley

In small bowl, mix cream cheese with mayonnaise until smooth. Add rest of ingredients; mix well.

PINWHEEL SANDWICHES

1 Roll Makes About 6 Pinwheel Sandwiches.

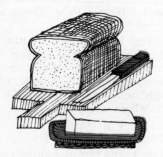

1. With sharp knife, trim crusts from 1-pound loaf of unsliced white bread.
2. Cut loaf, lengthwise, into ¼-inch-thick slices. Run rolling pin lightly over each slice.
3. Spread each slice with 1 tablespoon soft butter or margarine; then spread with 2 tablespoons filling. (Use any one of the fillings.)
4. Place 2 large stuffed olives or gherkins across short end of bread slice. From same end, roll bread tightly, as for jelly roll.
5. Wrap each roll securely in waxed paper or saran; twist ends of paper.
6. Refrigerate several hours or overnight.
7. To serve: With sharp knife, cut each roll into ⅓-inch slices.

Fillings for Pinwheel Sandwiches

PÂTÉ AND ONION FILLING

2 cans (2¼-oz size) liver
pâté
2 tablespoons finely
chopped green onion

1 tablespoon mayonnaise or
cooked salad dressing

MAKES ⅔ CUP

Combine all ingredients, mixing until smooth.

PÂTÉ AND CREAM-CHEESE FILLING

2 cans (2¼-oz size) liver
pâté
1 pkg (3 oz) soft cream
cheese

2 tablespoons sweet-pickle
relish

MAKES 1 CUP

Combine all ingredients, mixing until smooth.

SAVORY CREAM-CHEESE FILLING

1 pkg (3 oz) soft cream
cheese
2 tablespoons finely
chopped cooked ham

¼ teaspoon prepared
mustard or onion
juice
3 tablespoons light cream

MAKES ½ CUP

Combine all ingredients, mixing until smooth.

NUT-PINEAPPLE CREAM-CHEESE FILLING

1 pkg (3 oz) soft cream
cheese
2 tablespoons grated
orange peel

¼ cup finely chopped
walnuts or pecans
2 tablespoons drained
crushed pineapple

MAKES ⅔ CUP

Combine all ingredients, mixing until smooth
and fluffy.

SANDWICH LOAF*

MAKES 1 LOAF; 32 SERVINGS

1 whole-wheat sandwich
loaf (2 lb, 14¼ oz),
unsliced

1 white sandwich loaf (2 lb,
14¼ oz), unsliced

Chicken Filling:
4 cans (5-oz size) boned
chicken
¼ cup chopped celery
½ teaspoon salt
1 tablespoon lemon juice
⅓ cup mayonnaise

Ham Filling:
3 cups ground cooked ham
(about 1 lb)
⅓ cup sweet-pickle relish
2 tablespoons prepared
mustard
2 tablespoons light-brown
sugar
½ cup mayonnaise

Egg Filling:
12 hard-cooked eggs,
coarsely chopped
4 teaspoons capers, drained
1 teaspoon salt
1 tablespoon cider vinegar
⅔ cup mayonnaise

Frosting:
4 pkg (8-oz size) cream
cheese
1 cup milk

Watercress sprigs

1. With sharp knife, remove all crusts from loaves. Cut four ½-inch slices lengthwise from each loaf. Cover slices with damp towel.
2. Make fillings.
3. To assemble loaf: Use whole-wheat slice as base. Spread with even layer of Chicken Filling. Cover with white slice; spread with even layer of Egg Filling. Cover with whole-wheat slice; spread with even layer of Ham Filling. Top with white slice.
4. If desired, loaf may be covered with waxed paper and damp towel, refrigerated overnight, and frosted the next day.
5. To frost: In large bowl of electric mixer, let cream cheese warm to room temperature. At medium speed, beat until light and fluffy. Gradually add milk, beating well after each addition. Reserve ½ cup frosting for decoration.
6. Arrange loaf on serving platter. Carefully frost entire surface. To decorate edges, press reserved frosting through pastry bag. Refrigerate overnight.
7. Garnish top with watercress.

* Bread is sufficient for 2 Sandwich Loaves. Fillings and frosting are enough for one Sandwich Loaf.

Hearty Sandwiches

If sandwiches had a sex, certainly these super-sandwiches would be masculine. For example, there is McCall's Magnifique. This is a sandwich of the century. The other sandwiches, both hot and cold, are equally impressive, in their own ways.

McCALL'S MAGNIFIQUE

MAKES 6 LARGE SERVINGS

1 loaf Italian bread (18
inches long)
¼ cup soft butter or
margarine
½ lb sliced salami
¼ lb sliced natural Swiss
cheese
2 large tomatoes, thinly
sliced
½ lb sliced capocollo or
boiled ham
2 green peppers, sliced
crosswise into rings

2 pkg (6-oz size) sliced
olive loaf
1 can (4 oz) pimientos,
drained and halved
½ small cucumber, cut in
thin slices
⅛ lb fresh mushrooms,
sliced (¼ inch thick)
lengthwise
4 or 5 lettuce leaves
2 tablespoons prepared
mustard
String

1. Halve bread lengthwise. Spread bottom half with butter.
2. On it, layer in order salami, Swiss cheese, tomatoes, capocollo, green peppers, and olive loaf.
3. Then make one more layer by alternating pimientos, cucumber slices, and mushrooms.
4. Cover with lettuce.
5. Spread other half of bread with mustard; place on top.
6. Tie ends with string. Cut across in 6 sections.

BROWN-DERBY SPECIAL

3 cups finely shredded
    cabbage
⅔ cup mayonnaise
3 tablespoons chili sauce
1 tablespoon finely chopped
    onion
¼ teaspoon salt

12 rye-bread slices
Butter or margarine
1 lb thinly sliced baked
    Virginia ham
1 lb thinly sliced natural
    Swiss cheese
6 kosher-style dill pickles

MAKES 6 SANDWICHES

1. Lightly toss cabbage, mayonnaise, chili sauce, onion, and salt.
2. Refrigerate about 1 hour, or until well chilled.
3. For each sandwich, lightly spread 2 slices bread with butter. On one slice, generously layer ham and cheese slices; then spread with some of cabbage mixture. Top with second bread slice.
4. Cut sandwich crosswise into thirds. Serve with a dill pickle.

DEVILED-HAM AND SWISS-CHEESE BUNS

4 hamburger buns, split
4 teaspoons mayonnaise or
    cooked salad dressing
1 can (2½ oz) deviled ham
4 Swiss-cheese slices

4 thin tomato slices
4 thin onion slices
4 large stuffed olives
4 sweet gherkins

MAKES 4 SANDWICHES

1. Spread bottom halves of buns with mayonnaise, then with deviled ham.
2. Top each with cheese slice, tomato slice, onion slice, and other half of bun.
3. Put olives and gherkins on 4 wooden picks, and stick one in each bun.

HERO SANDWICHES

2 loaves brown-and-serve
    French bread (about
    8 inches long)
¼ teaspoon dried oregano
    leaves
¼ cup soft butter or
    margarine
¼ lb sliced boiled ham

1 tomato, thinly sliced
¼ lb sliced Swiss cheese
Prepared mustard
¼ lb sliced pork roll
Lettuce leaves
Salt
Pepper

MAKES 2 SANDWICHES, OR 4 SERVINGS

1. Bake bread according to package directions.
2. Meanwhile, blend oregano into butter.
3. Cool loaves slightly; slice in half lengthwise. Spread with oregano butter.
4. ·On bottom halves, arrange in order ham, tomato, Swiss cheese. Spread cheese with mustard.
5. Add pork and lettuce; sprinkle with salt and pepper.
6. Top with upper halves of loaves.

TUNA-AND-CHEESE CLUB SANDWICHES

1 can (7 oz) chunk-style
    tuna, drained
½ cup stuffed olives,
    chopped
1 hard-cooked egg, finely
    chopped
2 teaspoons lemon juice
⅓ cup mayonnaise or
    cooked salad dressing

16 white-bread slices,
    toasted
8 whole-wheat-bread slices,
    toasted
½ cup soft butter or
    margarine
Lettuce
2 pkg (8-oz size) American-
    cheese slices (16
    slices)

MAKES 8 SANDWICHES

1. Combine tuna, olives, egg, lemon juice, and mayonnaise, tossing until well mixed.
2. Spread all toast slices with butter.
3. Spread 8 white-toast slices with tuna mixture. Top each with lettuce leaf, then whole-wheat slice.
4. Cover each with 2 slices cheese, then white-toast slice.
5. Cut in half diagonally.

BARBECUED SPOONBURGERS

MAKES 4 SERVINGS

3 tablespoons salad oil or
    melted shortening
¼ cup chopped onion
¼ cup chopped green
    pepper
1 lb ground chuck
1 teaspoon salt

¼ teaspoon pepper
1 cup catsup
1 can (1 lb, 1 oz) cream-
    style corn
4 hamburger buns, split,
    toasted, and lightly
    buttered

1. Heat oil in large skillet. Add onion and green pepper; sauté, stirring and over medium heat, until golden and tender—about 5 minutes.
2. Add chuck; cook, stirring, until no longer red.
3. Stir in salt, pepper, catsup, and corn; heat 5 minutes more, or until mixture is bubbly. Serve on hamburger buns.

BUNSTEADS

MAKES 10 SANDWICHES

¼ lb American cheese, cut
    into ½-inch cubes
1 can (7 oz) tuna, drained
    and flaked
3 hard-cooked eggs, finely
    chopped
2 tablespoons finely
    chopped onion
2 tablespoons finely
    chopped green
    pepper

2 tablespoons finely
    chopped stuffed
    olives
3 tablespoons sweet-pickle
    relish, drained
½ cup mayonnaise or
    cooked salad dressing
10 frankfurter rolls, split

1. Preheat oven to 325F.
2. In medium bowl, combine all ingredients, except rolls; mix well.
3. Spoon into rolls. Wrap each in foil; place on cookie sheet; bake 25 minutes.
4. Serve hot, right in foil.

HAMBURGERS À LA CARTE

MAKES 6 SERVINGS

1½ lb ground chuck
2 teaspoons salt
½ teaspoon pepper
1 tablespoon
    Worcestershire sauce

6 hamburger buns, split
3 tablespoons butter or
    margarine, melted
Toppings, below

1. Lightly toss beef, salt, pepper, and Worcestershire. Gently shape into 6 patties, each about ½ inch thick.

2. Arrange on broiler rack, 4 inches from heat. Broil 3 minutes on one side and 2 minutes on other side, for medium rare.

3. Meanwhile, brush cut sides of buns with butter. When meat is done, toast buns under broiler 1 minute.

4. Serve hamburgers in buns, and pass an assortment of toppings.

TOPPINGS

Blue-Cheese Spread: Combine ¼ cup crumbled blue cheese, 4 tablespoons soft butter or margarine, and ½ teaspoon Worcestershire sauce.

Olive Butter: Combine 4 tablespoons chopped pimiento-stuffed olives and ½ cup soft butter or margarine.

Sour-Cream Horseradish: Combine 1 cup dairy sour cream, 1 tablespoon prepared horseradish, ½ teaspoon salt, and ⅛ teaspoon paprika.

Sour-Cream Onion: Combine 1 cup dairy sour cream and 2 tablespoons packaged dry onion-soup mix.

Sour-Cream Chili Sauce: Combine 1 cup dairy sour cream, 2 tablespoons chili sauce, 5 drops liquid hot-pepper seasoning, dash pepper, and ¼ teaspoon seasoned salt.

MONTE CRISTO SANDWICH

Sandwich:
2 tablespoons soft butter or margarine
½ teaspoon prepared mustard
3 slices white bread
3 slices turkey, cut thin
3 slices baked ham, cut thin

Shortening or oil for deep-frying

Batter:
1 egg white
1 egg
2 tablespoons milk
Dash salt
Dash pepper

Currant jelly

1. Make Sandwich: In small bowl, blend butter with mustard.
2. Spread on bread, buttering one slice on both sides.
3. Arrange turkey on one slice of bread; top with slice buttered on both sides, then with ham and third slice, buttered side down.
4. Cut sandwich in half diagonally, and secure with wooden picks.
5. In deep skillet or deep-fat fryer, heat shortening (about 2 inches deep) to 400F on deep-frying thermometer.
6. Meanwhile, make Batter: In small bowl, with rotary beater, beat egg white until stiff peaks form. In medium bowl, beat remaining batter ingredients. Gently fold in egg white.
7. Dip sandwich halves into batter, coating thoroughly. Fry in hot fat until golden—about 2 minutes.
8. Serve with tart currant jelly.

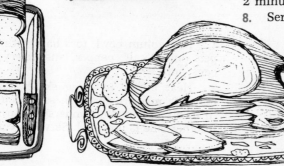

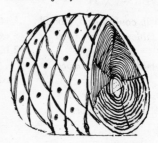

FRANKFURTERS CON CARNE

1 tablespoon salad oil or melted shortening
1⅓ cups finely chopped onion
½ lb ground chuck
1 can (8 oz) tomato sauce
1 teaspoon salt

1 teaspoon chili powder
½ teaspoon cumin seed
1½ teaspoons light-brown sugar
6 frankfurters
6 buttered, split frankfurter rolls

1. Slowly heat oil in large skillet. Add onion, and sauté until tender—about 5 minutes.
2. Add chuck to skillet; cook, stirring occasionally, until meat loses its red color.
3. Add tomato sauce, salt, chili powder, cumin seed, and sugar. Mix well.
4. Cook, uncovered, over low heat and stirring occasionally, 20 minutes, or until most of liquid is absorbed.
5. Meanwhile, broil frankfurters, 4 inches from heat, 3 minutes; turn once.
6. Place rolls, cut side up, on broiler rack; broil 30 seconds, or just until toasted.
7. To serve, place a frankfurter inside each roll; top each with some of chili mixture.

525

HOT CRABMEAT-SALAD SANDWICHES

1 can (6½ oz) crabmeat
¼ cup dairy sour cream
1 tablespoon capers, drained
½ teaspoon Worcestershire sauce
½ teaspoon seasoned salt

Dash liquid hot-pepper seasoning
3 tomato slices, ¼ inch thick
3 white-bread slices
¾ cup grated sharp Cheddar cheese

1. Into small saucepan, separate crabmeat pieces, removing membrane. Add sour cream, capers, Worcestershire, ¼ teaspoon seasoned salt, hot-pepper seasoning; mix well.
2. Heat the mixture, stirring occasionally.
3. Meanwhile, place tomato slices on bread slices; sprinkle tomato with remaining seasoned salt. Run under broiler, 6 inches from heat, 1 minute.
4. Spread one third hot crabmeat mixture over each sandwich; sprinkle each with ¼ cup cheese.
5. Run under broiler, 6 inches from heat, until cheese is bubbly and melted. Serve hot.

DENVERS

¼ lb cooked ham, ground
2 tablespoons chopped green pepper
2 tablespoons chopped onion
Dash salt
⅛ teaspoon pepper

¼ teaspoon celery seed
3 eggs, beaten
2 tablespoons butter or margarine
4 packaged toaster corn muffins, toasted

1. In medium bowl, toss ham with green pepper, onion, salt, pepper, and celery seed. Add eggs; mix well.
2. Heat butter in large skillet. Use ⅓ cup ham-egg mixture for each sandwich. Cook until nicely browned on underside; turn; cook until other side is browned. Serve on corn muffins.

GRILLED TUNA SANDWICHES

1 can (7 oz) tuna, drained and flaked
¼ cup stuffed olives, coarsely chopped
¼ cup chopped celery

⅓ cup mayonnaise or cooked salad dressing
2½ teaspoons lemon juice
6 white-bread slices
¼ cup soft butter or margarine

1. Preheat griddle as manufacturer directs.
2. In medium bowl, combine tuna with olives, celery, mayonnaise, and 1 teaspoon lemon juice, tossing until well mixed.
3. Spread filling on 3 bread slices; top with rest of slices.
4. In small bowl, gradually add remaining lemon juice to butter, mixing well. Spread on both sides of sandwiches.
5. Grill sandwiches about 5 minutes, or until nicely browned on underside. Turn; grill about 5 minutes longer, or until they are browned on other side.

Supper Sandwiches

You'd call these hearty, hot sandwiches a meal in one. Of course, you could serve a tossed green salad and a simple dessert with them.

OUR STEAK SANDWICH

MAKES 1 GENEROUS SERVING

1 tablespoon soft butter
1 teaspoon chopped parsley
½ teaspoon lemon juice
½ lb eye of sirloin (½ inch thick)
Salt

Pepper
2 buttered toast slices
3 tomato wedges
3 thin Spanish-onion slices
Watercress sprigs

1. In small bowl, using rubber scraper, cream butter with parsley and lemon juice until well combined. Form into a pat; refrigerate.
2. Slowly heat large, heavy skillet. Trim a piece of fat from the sirloin steak; rub inside of skillet with fat.
3. Over high heat, brown the sirloin well on one side about 3 minutes; turn; brown other side 3 to 5 minutes, or until of desired doneness.
4. Sprinkle lightly with salt and pepper; place on toast on small heated platter, with tomato and Spanish onion.
5. Top with butter pat. Garnish with watercress sprigs.

DEVILED-CHEESE SANDWICHES

MAKES 6 SANDWICHES

1½ cups grated sharp Cheddar cheese (6 oz)
¼ cup finely chopped celery
3 tablespoons sweet-pickle relish, drained

¼ teaspoon onion salt
⅛ teaspoon bottled steak sauce
¼ cup mayonnaise or cooked salad dressing
6 white-bread slices

1. In medium bowl, combine all ingredients, except bread.
2. Put bread on cookie sheet; toast, in broiler, on one side.
3. Spread cheese mixture on untoasted side; broil, about 4 inches from heat, until cheese begins to melt—about 1 minute. Serve hot.

SATURDAY-NIGHT SPECIAL

MAKES 10 SANDWICHES

6 crisp-cooked bacon slices
½ lb mild Cheddar cheese
1 small onion, peeled
1 medium green pepper
½ cup pitted ripe olives, drained
2 hard-cooked eggs

Dash pepper
⅛ teaspoon garlic powder
¼ cup catsup
1 tablespoon prepared mustard
10 hamburger buns, split

1. Put bacon, cheese, onion, green pepper, olives, and eggs through coarse blade of food chopper.
2. Turn into bowl. Add pepper, garlic powder, catsup, and mustard; mix well.
3. Spoon mixture onto bottom halves of buns on cookie sheet.
4. Broil, about 4 inches from heat, until cheese begins to melt—about 1 minute.
5. Top with other halves of buns. Serve hot.

CORNED BEEF AND HOT SLAW ON RYE

Hot Slaw:
1½ cups shredded cabbage
¼ cup white vinegar
½ teaspoon caraway seed
½ teaspoon salt
Dash pepper

Horseradish Sauce:
⅓ cup dairy sour cream
1 teaspoon prepared horseradish, drained
Dash Worcestershire sauce
Dash salt

¼ lb hot sliced corned beef
4 seedless-rye-bread slices

1. Make Hot Slaw: In medium skillet, combine cabbage, vinegar, caraway seed, salt, and pepper with ½ cup water.
2. Bring to boiling; reduce heat, and simmer, covered, 5 minutes, stirring occasionally. Drain.
3. Meanwhile, make Horseradish Sauce: In small bowl, combine sour cream with horseradish, Worcestershire, and salt; mix well.
4. Place half of the corned beef on one bread slice, half on another. Top each with half of slaw and sauce, then bread slice.

HAMBURGERS WITH CHILI BEANS

Hamburgers:
1 lb ground chuck
3 tablespoons hot catsup
3 tablespoons finely
   chopped onion
½ teaspoon salt
¼ teaspoon Worcestershire
   sauce
⅛ teaspoon pepper

Chili Beans:
1 can (15½ oz) kidney
   beans, drained
⅓ cup bottled tomato
   relish
¼ cup hot catsup
½ teaspoon chili powder

4 hamburger buns, split
3 tablespoons butter or
   margarine, melted
Dried thyme leaves

1. Make Hamburgers: Toss all ingredients in medium bowl until well combined. Lightly shape into 4 patties about ½ inch thick.
2. Broil hamburgers, 4 inches from heat, 5 minutes for medium rare. Turn; broil 5 minutes longer.
3. Meanwhile, make Chili Beans: Combine all ingredients in medium saucepan; heat thoroughly.
4. Brush buns with melted butter; sprinkle with thyme. Broil 30 seconds, or until golden.
5. Place hamburgers in buns. Serve beans along with hamburgers.

BROILED CHICKEN-AND-HAM SANDWICH À LA RITZ

1½ jars (5-oz size) boned
   chicken, diced
1 can (4½ oz) deviled ham
¼ cup mayonnaise or
   cooked salad dressing
½ teaspoon Worcestershire
   sauce

Topping:
2 egg whites

Dash cream of tartar
2 tablespoons mayonnaise
   or cooked salad
   dressing
2 tablespoons prepared
   mustard

2 English muffins, split
Melted butter or margarine

1. In medium saucepan, heat chicken, ham, mayonnaise, and Worcestershire. Keep hot.
2. Make Topping: In small bowl, with rotary beater, beat egg whites with cream of tartar until stiff peaks form when beater is raised.
3. Combine mayonnaise and mustard. Gently fold into egg-white mixture.
4. Brush muffins with butter; broil, four inches from heat, until nicely browned.
5. Spoon hot chicken mixture on muffins, mounding high in center. Cover with egg-white mixture.
6. Run under broiler 2 to 3 minutes, or until topping is golden.

Lunch-Box Sandwiches

The lunch you carry can, and should, be as appealing and satisfying as the lunch you eat at home. And if you're the one to pack a lunch box for a schoolchild, a calorie-conscious teen-ager, an office worker who is an eat-and-run luncher, or a husband with a man-size job, you'll be interested in our next group of sandwiches.

APPLE–PEANUT-BUTTER SANDWICHES

8 whole-wheat-bread slices
Soft butter or margarine
⅔ cup creamy-style peanut butter
⅓ cup applesauce
¼ cup finely chopped unpared red apple
4 crisp-cooked bacon slices, crumbled
Lettuce

MAKES 4 SANDWICHES

1. Lightly spread bread with butter.
2. In small bowl, combine peanut butter and applesauce, mixing until smooth. Stir in apple and bacon.
3. Spread 4 bread slices with filling. Top with lettuce and remaining slices.

Note: Or make sandwiches, omitting lettuce. Then freezer-wrap; label; freeze until ready to use.

CHICKEN-SALAD SANDWICHES

1½ cups cut-up cooked chicken
1 hard-cooked egg, finely chopped
1 tablespoon finely chopped onion
2 tablespoons finely chopped celery
2 tablespoons finely chopped stuffed olives
1 tablespoon sweet-pickle relish
1 teaspoon lemon juice
⅛ teaspoon salt
Dash pepper
¼ cup mayonnaise or cooked salad dressing
12 white-bread slices
Soft butter or margarine

MAKES 6 SANDWICHES

1. In medium bowl, combine all ingredients, except bread and butter. Toss with fork until well mixed.
2. Spread bread lightly with butter. Put slices together with chicken-salad filling.

DAILY SPECIAL

1 can (7 oz) chunk-style tuna, drained
⅓ cup finely chopped celery
¼ cup mayonnaise or cooked salad dressing
3 tablespoons finely chopped ripe olives
2 teaspoons lemon juice
1 teaspoon grated onion
Dash pepper
10 white-bread slices
Soft butter or margarine

MAKES 5 SANDWICHES

1. In small bowl, combine all ingredients, except bread and butter. Toss to combine well.
2. Spread bread lightly with butter. Put together with filling. Cut in half diagonally.
3. If desired, freezer wrap (2 halves together); label, and freeze until ready to use.

ZESTY PEANUT-BUTTER SANDWICHES

8 white-bread slices
8 teaspoons butter or margarine
½ cup peanut butter
6 tablespoons sweet-pickle relish, drained
4 lettuce leaves

MAKES 4 SANDWICHES

1. Spread each bread slice with 1 teaspoon butter.
2. Spread each of 4 slices with 2 tablespoons peanut butter and 1½ tablespoons pickle relish.
3. Top each with lettuce and bread slice.

529

DEVILED-EGG SANDWICHES

MAKES 5 SANDWICHES

10 white-bread slices
Soft butter or margarine
5 hard-cooked eggs, finely
　chopped
1 teaspoon prepared
　mustard
¼ teaspoon onion salt
⅛ teaspoon bottled steak
　sauce

1 tablespoon chopped
　parsley
2 tablespoons chopped
　pimiento
2 teaspoons cider vinegar
¼ cup mayonnaise or
　cooked salad dressing

1. Spread bread lightly with butter.
2. Combine eggs and rest of ingredients, tossing with fork until well mixed.
3. Use to fill 5 sandwiches.

PEANUT-BUTTER 'N' BACON SANDWICHES

MAKES 6 SANDWICHES

½ cup creamy- or chunk-
　style peanut butter
½ cup chopped crisp-
　cooked bacon
3 tablespoons sweet-pickle
　relish, drained
2 tablespoons chopped
　stuffed olives

2 tablespoons mayonnaise
　or cooked salad
　dressing
12 slices white or whole-
　wheat bread, lightly
　buttered

1. Combine all ingredients, except bread; mix well.
2. Use to fill 6 sandwiches. Cut in quarters; put in sandwich bags.
3. Keep refrigerated until packing in lunch box.

SPICY HAM-AND-CHEESE SANDWICHES

MAKES 8 SANDWICHES

2 cans (2¼-oz size) deviled
　ham
3 cups grated Cheddar
　cheese (¾ lb)
¼ cup chili sauce
¼ cup chopped green
　pepper

¼ cup sweet-pickle relish,
　drained
2 teaspoons grated onion
16 bread slices, lightly
　buttered

1. Combine ham and cheese, stirring until smooth. Stir in chili sauce, green pepper, relish, and onion; mix thoroughly.
2. Use to fill 8 sandwiches. Cut in half. Freezer-wrap individually; label, and freeze.
3. Remove from freezer just in time to pack lunch box (sandwiches will be thawed by lunchtime).

TUNA ROLLS

MAKES 4 SANDWICHES

1 can (7 oz) chunk-style
　tuna, drained
½ cup chopped celery
¼ cup sweet-pickle relish,
　drained
2 tablespoons chopped
　onion
2 tablespoons chopped
　parsley

1 hard-cooked egg, chopped
1 tablespoon lemon juice
½ teaspoon salt
⅛ teaspoon pepper
½ cup mayonnaise or
　cooked salad dressing
4 lightly buttered
　frankfurter rolls

1. In medium bowl, combine all ingredients, except rolls; mix well.
2. Fill rolls with tuna mixture.

It's the sauce, the absolutely right sauce, that lifts a dish from the routine to the spectacular. If you want to win a reputation as a gourmet cook, this chapter is a good place to start.

A basic white sauce is one of the first lessons given in cooking class—for good reason, too.

The trick in making a really smooth white sauce lies in melting the butter and taking the pan *off the range* before blending in the flour; then, gradually, blending in the milk. The sauce is *then* returned to the heat. (When flour is blended in over heat, it tends to cook in lumps, which no amount of stirring will remove afterward.)

When white sauce—or, for that matter, almost any other sauce—is made in advance, it is best reheated in a double boiler, to prevent sticking and scorching. Cover it, to prevent the formation of a skin on the surface.

When you add wine to a white sauce, be careful not to let the sauce boil—you might ruin the delicate flavor of the wine. Nor should it be subjected to prolonged heating after the wine has been added.

BASIC WHITE SAUCE

(MEDIUM)

¼ cup butter or margarine
¼ cup unsifted all-purpose
    flour

1 teaspoon salt
⅛ teaspoon pepper
2 cups milk

1. In medium saucepan, slowly heat butter just until melted and golden, not browned, stirring all the while. Remove from heat.

2. Add flour, salt, and pepper; stir until smooth. Add milk, a small amount at a time, stirring after each addition. Return to heat.

3. Over medium heat, bring to boiling, stirring constantly. Reduce heat; simmer 1 minute.

Thin White Sauce: Reduce butter and flour to 2 tablespoons each. Proceed as in Basic White Sauce. Use for soups.

Thick White Sauce: Increase butter to 6 tablespoons and flour to 6 or 8 tablespoons. Proceed as in Basic White Sauce. Use as binder in croquettes or as base for soufflés.

Parsley Sauce: Add ½ cup chopped parsley and ¼ cup lemon juice to Basic White Sauce. Makes 2½ cups.

CHEESE SAUCE

Medium White Sauce
½ teaspoon dry mustard

2 cups grated sharp
    Cheddar cheese
    (½ lb)

1. Make Medium White Sauce.

2. Add mustard and grated cheese; stir, over low heat, just until cheese is melted and sauce is hot.

3. Serve over such vegetables as broccoli, and asparagus; or use in casseroles.

HOT HORSERADISH SAUCE

Medium White Sauce
2 tablespoons prepared
    horseradish

Dash liquid hot-pepper
    seasoning
2 teaspoons lemon juice

1. Make Medium White Sauce.

2. Add horseradish and hot-pepper seasoning; reheat slowly, stirring.

3. Add lemon juice just before serving. Serve with boiled brisket of beef or tongue.

ALMOND SAUCE FOR POULTRY

MAKES 1½ CUPS

1 tablespoon butter or
    margarine
¼ cup blanched almonds,
    finely chopped
2 tablespoons all-purpose
    flour
1 cup chicken stock; or 2
    bouillon cubes, dis-
    solved in 1 cup
    boiling water

¼ teaspoon salt
Dash pepper
Dash mace
¼ teaspoon grated lemon
    peel
½ teaspoon lemon juice
2 tablespoons heavy cream

1. In hot butter in small skillet, sauté nuts, stirring frequently, until golden.

2. Remove from heat. Add flour, stirring to make a smooth mixture. Gradually add chicken stock.

3. Over medium heat, bring to boiling, stirring constantly. Reduce heat; simmer 3 minutes.

4. Remove from heat. Add remaining ingredients; bring back to boiling. Delicious with roast chicken, turkey, and duck.

BORDELAISE SAUCE

MAKES 1 CUP

2 tablespoons butter or
    margarine
1 shallot, finely chopped
1 clove garlic, finely
    chopped
1 onion slice
2 carrot slices
Parsley sprig
6 whole black peppers
1 whole clove

1 bay leaf
2 tablespoons flour
1 cup canned beef
    bouillon, undiluted
¼ teaspoon salt
⅛ teaspoon pepper
⅓ cup Burgundy
1 tablespoon finely
    chopped parsley

1. Slowly heat butter in medium skillet.

2. Add shallot, garlic, onion and carrot slices, parsley sprig, black peppers, clove, and bay leaf.

3. Sauté until onion is golden—about 3 minutes. Remove from heat.

4. Add flour, stirring until smooth.

5. Over very low heat, cook, stirring, until flour is lightly browned—about 5 minutes.

6. Remove from heat. Gradually stir in bouillon.

7. Over medium heat, bring to boiling point, stirring constantly. Reduce heat; simmer gently 10 minutes, stirring occasionally.

8. Strain, and discard vegetables. Add salt, pepper, Burgundy, and chopped parsley.

9. Reheat slowly. This sauce is very good with roast beef, steak, hamburgers, and other beef dishes.

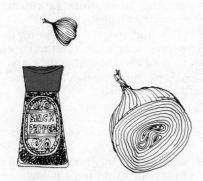

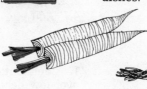

MUSHROOM SAUCE

1. Prepare Bordelaise Sauce as directed.

2. Meanwhile, in small skillet, sauté 1 cup thickly sliced fresh mushrooms in 1 tablespoon hot butter, stirring, until tender—about 5 minutes.

3. Add to Bordelaise Sauce; reheat gently. Makes 1⅓ cups.

BLENDER BÉARNAISE SAUCE

MAKES ¾ CUP

2 tablespoons dry white
wine
1 tablespoon tarragon
vinegar
1 teaspoon dried tarragon
leaves

2 teaspoons chopped onion
or shallots
¼ teaspoon pepper
¾ cup Hollandaise Sauce*

1. In medium skillet, combine wine, vinegar, tarragon, onion, and pepper.
2. Over moderate heat, bring to boiling. Cook until most of liquid is evaporated.
3. In blender container, combine cooked mixture with hollandaise. Cover; blend at high speed 4 seconds. Serve warm, with steak.

* See this chapter.

SAUCE BÉARNAISE

MAKES ABOUT 1 CUP

½ cup tarragon vinegar
¼ cup dry white wine
1 tablespoon finely
chopped shallot

½ teaspoon dried tarragon
leaves
3 egg yolks
½ cup butter or margarine

1. In small saucepan, combine vinegar, wine, shallot, and tarragon leaves.
2. Over medium heat, bring just to boiling. Reduce heat, and simmer, uncovered, until the liquid is reduced to ⅓ cup—8 to 10 minutes.
3. Strain mixture into top of double boiler, discarding shallot and tarragon leaves.
4. With wire whisk or rotary beater, beat egg yolks into liquid. Cook over hot, not boiling, water, beating constantly, until mixture becomes as thick as mayonnaise.
5. Beat in butter, 1 tablespoon at a time, beating well after each addition, to melt butter. Serve at once with steak.

CAPER SAUCE

MAKES ABOUT 2 CUPS

3 tablespoons butter or
margarine
3 tablespoons flour
¾ teaspoon salt
¼ teaspoon paprika
Dash liquid hot-pepper
seasoning

2 cups milk
2 hard-cooked eggs,
quartered
1 tablespoon bottled
capers, drained

1. Melt butter, stirring, in medium saucepan over low heat. Remove from heat.
2. Add flour, salt, and paprika; stir until smooth. Add hot-pepper seasoning, then milk— a small amount at a time—stirring constantly.
3. Over medium heat, bring to boiling point, stirring constantly. Reduce heat.
4. Add eggs and capers; simmer 1 minute.

CURRY SAUCE

MAKES 2¼ CUPS

¼ cup butter or margarine
⅓ cup finely chopped
onion
¼ cup unsifted all-purpose
flour
4 teaspoons curry powder

2 teaspoons sugar
1 teaspoon salt
¼ teaspoon ginger
⅛ teaspoon pepper
2 cups milk
2 teaspoons lemon juice

1. Melt butter, stirring, in medium saucepan over low heat. Add onion; sauté until golden— about 5 minutes.
2. Remove from heat. Add flour, curry powder, sugar, salt, ginger, and pepper; stir until smooth. Add milk, a small amount at a time, stirring after each addition.
3. Over medium heat, bring to boiling point, stirring constantly. Reduce heat; simmer 1 minute. Stir in lemon juice.

CUCUMBER SAUCE

MAKES ABOUT 2 CUPS

1 cup dairy sour cream
1 cup grated pared
    cucumber
¼ teaspoon salt
Dash pepper
¼ teaspoon onion salt

¼ teaspoon paprika
½ teaspoon Worcester-
    shire sauce
1 teaspoon lemon juice
Dash liquid hot-pepper
    seasoning

1. In medium bowl, combine all ingredients, mixing well.
2. Refrigerate until serving.

GINGERSNAP SAUCE

MAKES ABOUT 2¾ CUPS

3 bacon slices
½ cup chopped onion
½ cup crumbled ginger-
    snaps (about 6)
½ cup wine vinegar
½ cup light-brown sugar,
    firmly packed
2½ cups tongue stock or
    beef bouillon

1 bay leaf
1 teaspoon salt
½ cup seedless raisins
1 teaspoon grated lemon
    peel
1 tablespoon Worcester-
    shire sauce

1. In medium skillet, sauté bacon until crisp. Drain on paper towels; crumble; set aside.
2. Add onion to skillet; sauté until tender—about 5 minutes.
3. Stir in gingersnaps, vinegar, sugar, tongue stock, bay leaf, salt, and raisins.
4. Bring to boiling, stirring; boil, stirring, until mixture is clear—about 5 minutes.
5. Remove from heat. Add bacon, lemon peel, and Worcestershire, mixing well. Serve hot, over hot sliced tongue or ham.

WHIPPED HORSERADISH SAUCE

MAKES 1½ CUPS

1 pkg (8 oz) cream cheese
1 tablespoon confectioners'
    sugar
1 tablespoon lemon juice
1 tablespoon Worcester-
    shire sauce

2 tablespoons prepared
    horseradish
½ cup heavy cream,
    whipped

1. In small bowl, let cream cheese soften to room temperature—takes about 1 hour.
2. Blend in sugar, lemon juice, Worcestershire, and horseradish. Then fold in whipped cream.
3. Refrigerate until serving time. Delicious with cold beef.

MINT SAUCE FOR LAMB

MAKES ⅔ CUP

½ cup white vinegar
⅓ cup sugar

Fresh mint leaves

1. Heat vinegar and sugar in small saucepan, stirring until sugar is dissolved.
2. With scissors, snip enough mint leaves coarsely to measure ½ cupful. Pour hot vinegar over mint in small bowl; let stand, covered, several hours.
3. Before serving, strain sauce; discard mint.
4. Snip more fresh mint leaves coarsely to measure ¼ cupful. Add to sauce. Serve sauce, at room temperature, with roast lamb or lamb chops.

535

MUSTARD SAUCE

1 tablespoon butter or
   margarine
1 egg
¼ cup light-brown sugar,
   firmly packed

3 tablespoons granulated
   sugar
3 tablespoons prepared
   mustard
1 teaspoon paprika
½ cup cider vinegar

1. Melt butter in small saucepan. Set aside.
2. In small bowl, with rotary beater, beat egg, sugars, mustard, and paprika.
3. Add vinegar, and beat again. Blend into cooled butter.
4. Cook, stirring and over low heat, just until thickened—4 to 5 minutes. Cool. Good with cold ham or pork.

ORANGE SAUCE FOR DUCKLING

3 tablespoons butter or
   margarine
Liver from duckling
3 tablespoons brandy
2 tablespoons grated
   orange peel
½ teaspoon minced garlic
3 tablespoons flour
⅛ teaspoon pepper
½ teaspoon catsup

1 teaspoon meat-extract
   paste
½ cup orange juice
1 cup canned clear chicken
   broth,* undiluted
¼ cup Burgundy
¼ cup orange marmalade
3 large navel oranges,
   sectioned

1. Heat 2 tablespoons butter in medium skillet. Add liver; brown well.
2. Heat brandy slightly in small saucepan. Light with match; pour over liver.
3. Add remaining butter, the orange peel, and garlic; simmer 2 to 3 minutes.
4. Remove from heat. Chop liver finely, and set aside.
5. Into same skillet, stir flour, pepper, catsup, and meat-extract paste. Gradually add orange juice, broth, Burgundy, and marmalade.
6. Bring to boiling point. Reduce heat; simmer, stirring, 15 minutes. Add orange sections and chopped liver. Serve over duckling.

* Or simmer duckling giblets (not liver) in 1¾ cups water, covered, 1½ hours. Strain; measure 1 cup.

RAISIN SAUCE

¼ cup sugar
1 tablespoon cornstarch
¼ teaspoon salt
Dash cloves
Dash dry mustard
2 cups tongue stock or
   beef bouillon

½ cup currant jelly
¾ cup seedless raisins
1 teaspoon lemon juice
¼ teaspoon Worcestershire
   sauce

1. In medium saucepan, combine sugar, cornstarch, salt, cloves, and mustard.
2. Gradually add tongue stock, stirring until smooth. Add jelly and raisins.
3. Over medium heat, bring to boiling, stirring. Boil 1 minute, or until jelly is melted and mixture is thickened and translucent.
4. Remove from heat. Stir in lemon juice and Worcestershire. Serve hot, over sliced tongue.

SEAFOOD-COCKTAIL SAUCE

¾ cup chili sauce or catsup
2 tablespoons prepared
   horseradish, drained
1 tablespoon lemon juice
½ teaspoon salt

⅛ teaspoon pepper
½ teaspoon Worcestershire
   sauce
Dash cayenne

1. Combine all ingredients.
2. Refrigerate until well chilled.

SHRIMP-NEWBURG SAUCE

MAKES ABOUT 2½ CUPS

3 tablespoons butter or
   margarine
1½ tablespoons flour
Dash nutmeg
Dash paprika
½ teaspoon salt

1 cup light cream
½ cup milk
2 egg yolks, slightly beaten
2 tablespoons sherry
1½ cups cut-up cooked or
   canned shrimp

1. Melt butter in medium saucepan.
2. Remove from heat. Stir in flour, nutmeg, paprika, and salt until smooth. Add light cream and milk.
3. Over medium heat, bring to boiling point, stirring. Remove from heat.
4. Meanwhile, in medium bowl, combine egg yolks with sherry.
5. Stir in a little hot white sauce, beating well. Then pour egg-yolk mixture back into saucepan. Add shrimp.
6. Cook, stirring and over low heat, until mixture is slightly thickened and shrimp is heated through.

SOUR-CREAM TARTAR SAUCE

MAKES ABOUT 1 CUP

1 cup dairy sour cream
2 tablespoons sweet-pickle
   relish, drained
½ teaspoon salt

Dash liquid hot-pepper
   seasoning
1 teaspoon grated onion

1. Thoroughly combine all ingredients in a small bowl.
2. Refrigerate until well chilled. Serve with shrimp or clam fritters.

TARRAGON–SOUR-CREAM SAUCE

MAKES 1 CUP

2 egg yolks
¼ teaspoon dried tarragon
   leaves
1 cup dairy sour cream
1 bay leaf, crumbled

¼ teaspoon finely chopped
   garlic
½ teaspoon salt
1 tablespoon bottled
   capers, drained

1. In small bowl, with rotary beater, beat egg yolks with tarragon until thick and lemon-colored.
2. In saucepan, slowly heat sour cream, bay leaf, and garlic just until bubbles form around edge.
3. Strain; discard garlic and bay leaf. Pour sour cream back into saucepan.
4. Pour a little hot sour cream into egg yolks, stirring; return to saucepan.
5. Over low heat, bring just to boiling point, stirring constantly. Add salt and capers. Delicious served with salmon, or chicken.

SPANISH SAUCE

MAKES 2 CUPS

2 tablespoons butter or
   margarine
⅔ cup chopped onion
2 tablespoons chopped
   green pepper
1 clove garlic, finely
   chopped
2 cans (8-oz size) tomato
   sauce

¼ cup chopped mixed
   sweet pickles
1 tablespoon sugar
¼ teaspoon dried oregano
   leaves
1 teaspoon salt
⅛ teaspoon pepper

1. In hot butter in medium saucepan, sauté onion, green pepper, and garlic until tender—about 5 minutes.
2. Stir in remaining ingredients; bring to boiling.
3. Reduce heat; simmer gently 15 minutes, stirring occasionally.
4. Serve with omelet, or over meat loaf.

537

CREOLE SAUCE

MAKES ABOUT 3 CUPS

2 tablespoons bacon fat or
   salad oil
½ cup chopped onion
1 clove garlic, finely
   chopped
¼ cup chopped green
   pepper
1 can (1 lb, 12 oz)
   tomatoes, undrained

1 teaspoon celery seed
1 bay leaf
1 teaspoon salt
2 teaspoons sugar
½ teaspoon chili powder
1 tablespoon chopped
   parsley

1. In hot bacon fat in medium saucepan, sauté onion, garlic, and pepper until tender—about 5 minutes.
2. Add remaining ingredients; simmer, uncovered, 45 minutes, or until mixture is thickened; stir occasionally. Strain, if desired.

Sauces for Vegetables

One of the easiest ways to vary a favorite, but sometimes monotonous, vegetable is to serve it with a sauce. Sauces high in butter and egg yolks, like hollandaise, require careful technique to prevent curdling. The blender method is a simplification that results in perfect sauce every time. McCall's shiny, lemon-color, lemony-tart hollandaise is a sauce you'll wish to make a permanent part of your repertory.

When you make sauces in a double boiler, make sure that the water in the lower section never reaches the boiling point. You may add a little cold water to prevent this.

DEVILED-HAM SAUCE

MAKES 1⅓ CUPS

1 can (4½ oz) deviled ham
½ cup dairy sour cream
2 egg yolks

3 tablespoons lemon juice
¼ teaspoon paprika

1. Combine all ingredients in small saucepan.
2. Cook over very low heat, stirring constantly with wire whisk or wooden spoon, until thickened—about 5 minutes.

HERBED GARLIC BUTTER FOR VEGETABLES

MAKES ABOUT ½ CUP

1 teaspoon dried basil
   leaves
¼ teaspoon dried thyme
   leaves
½ teaspoon dried tarragon
   leaves
2 teaspoons chopped
   parsley

½ teaspoon grated lemon
   peel
1 clove garlic, crushed
1 green onion, chopped
Dash cayenne
Dash salt
½ cup soft butter or
   margarine

1. Combine basil, thyme, tarragon, parsley, lemon peel, garlic, onion, cayenne and salt. With back of wooden spoon (or with mortar and pestle), press herbs and seasonings together.
2. Add butter; mix to combine well. Serve over hot, cooked vegetables as carrots, broccoli, green beans or cauliflower.

HOLLANDAISE SAUCE

2 egg yolks
¼ cup butter or margarine,
   melted
¼ cup boiling water

1½ tablespoons lemon
   juice
¼ teaspoon salt
Dash cayenne

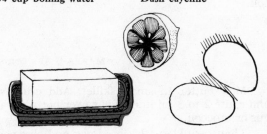

MAKES ABOUT ⅔ CUP

1. In top of double boiler, with wire whisk or fork, slightly beat egg yolks.
2. Slowly stir in butter. Gradually add water, beating constantly.
3. Cook, stirring, over hot water (hot water in double-boiler base should not touch pan above) just until thickened.
4. Remove double-boiler top from hot water. Gradually stir lemon juice, salt, and cayenne into sauce.
5. Cover, and keep hot over warm water until serving. Serve with cooked vegetables or fish.

BLENDER HOLLANDAISE SAUCE

3 egg yolks
2 tablespoons lemon juice
¼ teaspoon salt

Dash cayenne
½ cup hot, melted butter
   or margarine

MAKES 1 CUP

1. In blender container, combine egg yolks, lemon juice, salt, and cayenne. Cover; turn motor on and off; remove cover.
2. Turn motor to high speed; gradually add butter in steady stream. Turn off motor.
3. Serve immediately, or keep warm by placing blender container in 2 inches of hot (not boiling) water.

MOCK HOLLANDAISE SAUCE

½ cup butter or margarine
2 tablespoons flour
¼ teaspoon salt
⅛ teaspoon pepper

Dash cayenne
1 cup milk
2 egg yolks, slightly beaten
2 tablespoons lemon juice

MAKES 1½ CUPS

1. In medium saucepan, slowly melt ¼ cup butter; remove from heat. Stir in flour to make a smooth paste. Add salt, pepper, and cayenne.
2. Gradually add milk, stirring until smooth. Over medium heat, bring mixture to boiling, stirring; boil 1 minute.
3. Remove from heat. Stir in remaining butter.
4. Combine egg yolks and lemon juice. Add a little hot mixture to egg-yolk mixture. Pour back into mixture in saucepan.
5. Bring back to boiling, stirring. Serve over vegetables.

LEMON-CHIVE SAUCE

⅓ cup butter or margarine
2 tablespoons finely
   chopped chives
1 tablespoon lemon juice

1 teaspoon grated lemon
   peel
½ teaspoon salt
Dash pepper

MAKES ABOUT ½ CUP

1. Melt butter in small saucepan. Add remaining ingredients.
2. Beat thoroughly. Serve sauce hot. Delicious served over boiled potatoes, asparagus, broccoli, carrots, or baked fish.

539

SAUCE AMANDINE

½ cup butter or margarine   ½ cup toasted sliced
                             almonds

1. Melt butter in small skillet. Add almonds; sauté, stirring, about 1 minute.
2. Pour over asparagus, green beans or broccoli.

SAUCE POLONAISE

6 tablespoons butter or   1 hard-cooked egg, sieved
  margarine   2 tablespoons chopped
¼ cup packaged dry bread   parsley
  crumbs

1. Melt butter in small skillet. Add crumbs, and sauté 2 to 3 minutes. Pour over hot asparagus or broccoli.
2. Then sprinkle with sieved egg and chopped parsley.

SWEET-AND-SOUR SAUCE FOR CABBAGE

1 egg yolk   1 teaspoon prepared
1 tablespoon sugar   horseradish
¼ teaspoon salt   2 tablespoons white vinegar
¼ teaspoon paprika   ½ cup dairy sour cream

1. In top of double boiler, slightly beat egg yolk with sugar, salt, and paprika. Stir in remaining ingredients.
2. Cook, stirring constantly, over hot water (water in double-boiler base should not touch pan above) until slightly thickened—about 5 minutes. Serve hot, over steamed red- or green-cabbage wedges.

SOUR CREAM AND CHIVES

1 cup dairy sour cream   ¼ teaspoon bottled steak
1 teaspoon chopped fresh   sauce
  chives   Dash pepper
¼ teaspoon dried dill
  weed

1. Combine all ingredients.
2. Let stand at room temperature at least 1 hour. Spoon over baked potatoes.

CARAWAY–CHEDDAR-CHEESE SAUCE

2 tablespoons butter or   Dash liquid hot-pepper
  margarine   seasoning
2 tablespoons flour   1½ cups grated natural
½ teaspoon salt   sharp Cheddar cheese
1 cup milk   1 teaspoon caraway seed

1. Melt butter in small saucepan; remove from heat.
2. Stir in flour, salt, and milk; cook, over medium heat and stirring, until mixture boils and is thickened and smooth.
3. Add hot-pepper seasoning, cheese, and caraway seed; stir until cheese melts. Serve hot, over baked potatoes.

Today's low-temperature methods of roasting meats have reduced the amount of drippings in the roast pan. For this reason, bottled gravy flavorings are frequently used to make the flavor richer. The use of beef bouillon, in cans or cubes, helps enrich the taste. A wire whisk is an invaluable tool in stirring up a smooth gravy. Be careful to *stir* it with a flat, circular motion.

RICH MEAT GRAVY

MAKES 2 CUPS

¼ cup meat drippings
3 tablespoons flour
2 cups water or beef
    bouillon

½ teaspoon salt
Dash pepper

1. Lift roast from pan, and place on heated platter. Let stand 20 minutes.
2. Pour off drippings in roasting pan. Return ¼ cup drippings to pan.
3. Stir in flour, to make a smooth mixture; brown it slightly over low heat, stirring to loosen any brown bits in pan.
4. Gradually stir in water, salt, and pepper.
5. Stir gravy until smooth, and bubbly.

BEEF GRAVY

MAKES 2 CUPS

¼ cup roast-beef drippings
¼ cup unsifted all-purpose
    flour
1 teaspoon salt
⅛ teaspoon pepper

2 cups beef stock or canned
    beef bouillon,
    undiluted
1 teaspoon meat-extract
    paste

1. After roast beef has been removed from roasting pan, pour off drippings. Measure ¼ cup; return to roasting pan.
2. Add flour, salt, and pepper; stir until smooth. Over very low heat, cook, stirring, until flour is lightly browned—about 5 minutes. (Stir in any browned bits left in pan.) Remove from heat.
3. Gradually add beef stock, stirring after each addition; bring to boiling, stirring constantly. Reduce heat.
4. Add meat-extract paste; stir until dissolved. Simmer 1 minute longer.

MUSHROOM BEEF GRAVY

MAKES 3 CUPS

Beef Gravy, above
¼ cup dry red wine

1 can (6 oz) sliced
    mushrooms, drained

1. Make Beef Gravy.
2. Just before serving, stir in wine and mushrooms. Simmer slowly, stirring, until hot.

CHICKEN GRAVY

MAKES 1½ CUPS

3 tablespoons roast-chicken
    drippings
3 tablespoons flour
1½ cups canned chicken
    broth, undiluted

½ teaspoon salt
⅛ teaspoon pepper
1 teaspoon coarsely snipped
    fresh marjoram
    leaves, or ½ teaspoon
    dried marjoram
    leaves (optional)

1. Pour off drippings from roasting pan. Return 3 tablespoons drippings to pan.
2. Add flour; stir to make a smooth paste.
3. Gradually stir in chicken broth. Add rest of ingredients.
4. Bring to boiling, stirring. Mixture will be thickened and smooth. Simmer, stirring, 1 minute longer. Serve hot, with roast chicken.

541

QUICK MUSHROOM GRAVY

MAKES 1½ CUPS

1 tablespoon butter or
  margarine
¼ cup thinly sliced onion
1 tablespoon chopped
  green pepper
2 tablespoons pimiento
  strips

1 can (10½ oz) condensed
  cream-of-mushroom
  soup, undiluted
⅓ cup dry white wine or
  bouillon

1. Slowly heat butter in medium skillet.
2. Add onion and pepper; sauté until tender—about 5 minutes. Remove from heat.
3. Add remaining ingredients; mix well.
4. Simmer, uncovered, 5 minutes, stirring occasionally.

GIBLET GRAVY

MAKES ABOUT 5 CUPS

Giblets and neck from
  turkey
1 celery stalk, cut up
1 bay leaf
1 onion, peeled and thinly
  sliced
1 small carrot, pared and
  cut up

2½ teaspoons salt
4 whole black peppers
½ cup roast-turkey
  drippings
½ cup unsifted all-purpose
  flour
¼ teaspoon pepper

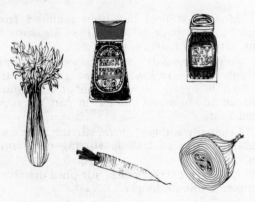

1. Split gizzard with sharp knife; if necessary, remove inner sac; scrape gizzard lining. Wash giblets very well under cold water. Refrigerate liver until ready to use.
2. Place giblets (except liver) in medium saucepan with neck, celery, bay leaf, onion, carrot, ½ teaspoon salt, black peppers, and 6 cups water; bring to boiling.
3. Reduce heat; simmer, covered, 2½ hours, or until giblets are tender. Add liver; simmer 15 minutes longer.
4. Strain broth, pressing vegetables through sieve along with broth. Measure; add water to make 5 cups.
5. Chop giblets coarsely; set aside.
6. When turkey has been removed to heated platter, pour off drippings in roasting pan. Return ½ cup drippings to pan.
7. Stir in flour, to make a smooth mixture; brown it slightly over low heat, stirring to loosen any brown bits in pan. Remove from heat. Gradually stir in broth.
8. Return to heat; bring to boiling, stirring. Reduce heat; simmer 5 minutes, stirring.
9. Add 2 teaspoons salt, pepper, and giblets; simmer 5 minutes.

BASE FOR QUICK GRAVY

MAKES 1⅓ CUPS

(BROWN ROUX)

½ cup unsifted all-purpose
  flour
½ cup soft shortening
1 tablespoon liquid gravy
  seasoning

½ teaspoon instant minced
  onion
1 can (10½ oz) condensed
  beef bouillon,
  undiluted

1. Lightly brown flour in small skillet over low heat. Remove from heat.
2. In small bowl, blend flour and shortening well. Stir in gravy seasoning and onion.
3. Store, covered, in refrigerator until ready to use.
4. To use, mix 4 tablespoons roux with beef bouillon in small saucepan. Refrigerate remaining roux.
5. Bring mixture to boiling, stirring constantly. Reduce heat; simmer till thick and smooth.

24

SOUPS

Whether you make it at home or buy it in a can or package, there is a soup for every taste and diet need. To the overweight, clear broths and consommés offer low-calorie nourishment. Rich cream soups build up the underweight, and even the ulcer patient can find in such soups the soothing food he requires. If yours is a low-salt, low-fat, or diabetic diet, you can eat like a gourmet by accenting soup with the herbs and spices your diet permits.

Serve a cup of conviviality, right in your living room, just as you might a cocktail before dinner. Make it a mug of good hot soup, to be sipped and savored slowly, interspersed with pleasant talk. It's nourishment for body, and for spirit, too.

Good accompaniments to "cocktail" soups are cheese wafers, individual pizzas, or crackers with a variety of cheeses from a handy cheese board.

HERBAL BOUILLON

MAKES 6 TO 8 SERVINGS

3 medium carrots, unpared
2 medium potatoes,
    unpared
1 medium onion, peeled
3 outer green lettuce leaves

Green tops from 1 bunch
    celery
2 medium tomatoes
½ cup finely chopped
    parsley
2 fresh thyme sprigs

1. Wash vegetables well.

2. In 4-quart kettle, combine carrots, potatoes, onion, lettuce, celery tops, and tomatoes. Add 2 quarts cold water.

3. Bring to boiling, covered. Reduce heat, and simmer 1 hour.

4. Add parsley and thyme; simmer, covered, 30 minutes.

5. Strain through sieve, discarding vegetable pulp. Serve hot.

BEEF BROTH

1 lb marrow bones,*
    cracked
2 lb beef shin, cut into
    cubes
1 large onion, peeled
1 stalk celery and leaves
3 medium unpared carrots,
    scrubbed

2 tablespoons finely
    chopped parsley
2 teaspoons salt
4 whole black peppers
2 whole cloves
½ bay leaf
⅛ teaspoon dried marjoram
    leaves
⅛ teaspoon dried thyme
    leaves

1. Scrape marrow (fat inside bones) into a 4-quart kettle; set bones aside. Melt marrow over low heat.
2. In it, slowly brown half of beef until it becomes a dark, rich brown—about 30 minutes. Do not scorch.
3. Add remaining meat and bones with 7 cups of water; cover.
4. Over low heat, slowly bring to boiling, skimming often with slotted metal spoon to remove foam from surface.
5. Add vegetables and seasonings. Cover; simmer 3 hours, skimming occasionally.
6. Line large strainer with double thickness of dampened cheesecloth. Strain broth mixture into metal bowl or pan.
7. Cool strained broth quickly by placing bowl in ice water. Chill until fat rises to surface and solidifies. Skim off fat. Serve broth hot or as an ingredient in other soups.

Note: If richer flavored stock is desired, return strained broth to kettle; simmer, uncovered, to reduce volume and concentrate flavor.

To clarify stock: Slightly beat 1 egg white with 2 tablespoons water; add to cold stock along with crushed eggshell. Over moderate heat, bring to boiling, stirring constantly; boil 2 minutes. Remove from heat; add 1 cup cold water; let stand 30 minutes. Strain again as directed.

* If marrow bones are unavailable, brown meat in 2 tablespoons shortening.

BORSCH

1 can (1 lb) julienne beets
⅓ cup finely chopped
    onion
1 can (10½ oz) condensed
    beef bouillon, un-
    diluted

1 teaspoon salt
2 tablespoons sugar
¼ cup lemon juice
2 eggs
½ cup dairy sour cream
Fresh dill (optional)

1. In medium saucepan, combine beets and liquid, onion, bouillon, salt, sugar, and lemon juice with 2 cups water.
2. Over medium heat, bring to boiling, covered. Reduce heat; simmer 5 minutes.
3. In small bowl, with wire whisk or rotary beater, beat eggs well. Gradually pour ½ cup hot beet liquid over eggs, continuing to beat.
4. Return to beet mixture in saucepan. Stir quickly, to combine smoothly.
5. Serve at once in warm bowls. (Do not reheat; mixture might curdle.) Top each serving with a heaping tablespoon sour cream; sprinkle with snipped fresh dill, if desired.

Note: Borsch may also be served chilled.

CARDINAL CUP

2 cans (10½-oz size)
  condensed tomato
  soup, undiluted
2 cans (10½-oz size) con-
  densed beef bouillon,
  undiluted
⅓ cup thinly sliced onion

4 whole black peppers
½ teaspoon salt
1 tablespoon lemon juice
¼ teaspoon nutmeg
½ cup sherry
1 tablespoon chopped
  parsley

1. In 3½-quart saucepan, combine all ingredients except sherry and parsley.
2. Stir in 1 cup water, mixing well; bring to boiling. Reduce heat, and simmer, covered, 30 minutes.
3. Strain; discard onion and peppers.
4. Return to saucepan along with sherry; heat, stirring. Serve topped with parsley.

HOMEMADE CHICKEN OR VEAL BROTH

4½-lb chicken, cut up, or
  knuckle of veal
1 stalk celery and leaves
1 large onion, peeled
3 medium carrots, unpared
  and scrubbed
2 tablespoons finely
  chopped parsley

2 teaspoons salt
3 whole black peppers
2 whole cloves
1 blade mace
¼ bay leaf
½ teaspoon monosodium
  glutamate

1. In 6-quart kettle, combine all ingredients with 6 cups water.
2. Over low heat, slowly bring to boiling, skimming with slotted metal spoon to remove any foam from surface.
3. Cover; simmer 3 hours.
4. Line large strainer with double thickness of dampened cheesecloth. Strain broth mixture into metal bowl or pan.
5. Cool strained broth quickly by placing bowl in ice water. Chill until fat rises to surface and solidifies. Skim off fat.
6. May be stored, covered, in refrigerator. Serve hot or as an ingredient in other soups.
Note: Chicken may be removed from bones and used in sandwiches or salads.

HOT BUTTERED TOMATO JUICE

1 can (1 qt, 14 oz) tomato
  juice
¼ cup butter or margarine

½ teaspoon bottled steak
  sauce or Worcester-
  shire sauce

1. Combine all ingredients in medium saucepan; bring to boiling.
2. Serve hot, in mugs.

On a hot, bright summer evening, serve a velvety avocado soup, to sip from a goblet; or jellied borsch, sparkling like garnets; or tomato soup with dill, with toasted cheese sandwiches; serve smooth-textured curry soup, or Vichyssoise—to name a few of our refreshing cold soups. But whatever you serve, do see that it is glacially cold.

CHILLED AVOCADO SOUP

MAKES 4 TO 6 SERVINGS

3 large ripe avocados (about 2 lb)
1 can (14 oz) clear chicken broth
1 tablespoon lemon juice
½ to 1 teaspoon salt
Dash pepper
½ cup light cream
3 crisp-cooked bacon slices, coarsely chopped

1. Cut avocados in half lengthwise; remove pits; peel. Mash; measure 1⅔ cups.
2. In medium bowl, combine avocado, chicken broth, lemon juice, salt to taste, pepper, and 1½ cups water.
3. Press through sieve, or purée in electric blender.
4. Refrigerate until well chilled—2 hours.
5. Just before serving, stir in cream. Sprinkle each serving with chopped bacon.

CRAB BISQUE

MAKES 6 SERVINGS

2 cans (10½-oz size) condensed cream-of-celery soup, undiluted
1 soup can (10½ oz) milk
1 soup can (10½ oz) water
2 cans (6½-oz size) crabmeat, drained
⅔ cup finely chopped celery

1. In medium bowl, with rotary beater, beat soup, milk, and water until well mixed.
2. Remove any cartilage from crabmeat. Stir crabmeat and celery into soup mixture.
3. Refrigerate until well chilled—3 to 4 hours. Pour into soup bowls.

Note: Or remove cartilage from crabmeat; with electric blender, covered, at low speed, blend ingredients till smooth—1 minute.

JELLIED BORSCH

MAKES 8 SERVINGS

1 can (1 lb) julienne beets
2½ cups canned consommé madrilène
2 tablespoons finely chopped onion
⅛ teaspoon cloves
½ teaspoon salt
Dash pepper
1 cup finely shredded green cabbage
1 envelope unflavored gelatine
2 tablespoons vinegar
½ cup dairy sour cream

1. Drain beets, reserving liquid; set beets aside. Measure beet liquid; add water, if necessary, to make ⅔ cup.
2. In small saucepan, combine beet liquid, 1¾ cups water, consommé madrilène, onion, cloves, salt, pepper, and cabbage. Bring mixture to boiling point; then reduce heat, and simmer, covered, 10 minutes.
3. Meanwhile, sprinkle gelatine over ½ cup cold water in small bowl; let stand 5 minutes.
4. Add softened gelatine to cooked cabbage mixture; stir until gelatine is dissolved.
5. Add the beets and vinegar. Turn mixture into large bowl.
6. Refrigerate until well chilled and slightly jellied—about 4 hours.
7. Serve in bowls; garnish with sour cream.

ICED CURRY SOUP

MAKES 6 SERVINGS

2 cans (14-oz size) clear
  chicken broth
  (3½ cups)
3 teaspoons curry powder

1½ teaspoons lemon juice
2 egg yolks
1 cup heavy cream

1. In large bowl, refrigerate chicken broth several hours, or until well chilled.
2. Skim off fat. Stir curry powder and lemon juice into broth.
3. In small bowl, with rotary beater, beat egg yolks and cream until well combined but not frothy.
4. Add to broth mixture; beat, with rotary beater, to blend well.
5. Refrigerate several hours. Beat again just before serving.

TOMATO SOUP WITH DILL

MAKES 6 SERVINGS

¼ cup salad oil
4 medium onions, finely
  chopped
2 lb tomatoes, coarsely
  chopped
¼ cup catsup
4 cups crushed ice

2½ tablespoons finely
  chopped dill
2½ teaspoons salt
¼ teaspoon liquid hot-
  pepper seasoning
½ cup heavy cream

1. In hot oil in medium saucepan, sauté onions until golden and tender—about 5 minutes.
2. Add tomatoes; cook, stirring and over moderate heat, until soft.
3. Strain mixture, and discard tomato and onion pieces.
4. Into tomato-onion liquid, stir catsup, ice, 2 tablespoons dill, 2 teaspoons salt, and the liquid hot-pepper seasoning.
5. Refrigerate until mixture is well chilled— 3 to 4 hours.
6. At serving time, whip cream until it's slightly stiff. Fold in remaining dill and salt. Beat soup with rotary beater; pour into cream-soup bowls.
7. Garnish each with a tablespoon of whipped-cream mixture.

EASY VICHYSSOISE

MAKES 6 TO 8 SERVINGS

2 cans (10¼-oz size)
  frozen condensed
  cream-of-potato soup,
  unthawed

2 soup cans (10¼-oz size)
  milk
¼ cup snipped chives
1 cup dairy sour cream

1. Combine soup, milk, and chives in medium saucepan.
2. Heat slowly, stirring, until soup is thawed.
3. With rotary beater, beat until smooth (or blend in electric blender, covered and at high speed, until smooth—about 1 minute).
4. Then beat in (or blend in) sour cream.
5. Refrigerate until very well chilled—about 4 hours.

BLENDER VICHYSSOISE

MAKES 4 SERVINGS

½ small onion, sliced
1 can (14 oz) clear chicken
  broth, chilled
1 teaspoon salt
Dash pepper

1½ cups diced cooked
  potatoes, chilled
1 cup dairy sour cream
Chopped chives

1. In blender container, combine onion, broth, salt, pepper, and potatoes. Cover; blend at high speed about 8 seconds.
2. Add sour cream; cover; blend 10 seconds.
3. Refrigerate until well chilled—about 1 hour.
4. Serve in chilled bowls. Garnish with chives.

J ust the thing for a special luncheon when the P.T.A. board meets at your home, or for a first course at a sit-down dinner, these cream soups have an elegant touch. Try the Cream-of-Curry Soup or the Sherried Mushroom Bisque—they're delicious.

CREAM-OF-ASPARAGUS SOUP

MAKES 6 SERVINGS

2 to 2½ lb fresh asparagus
¼ cup chopped onion
1 cup light cream
1 cup milk

2 tablespoons butter or
  margarine
2 tablespoons flour
1½ teaspoons salt
Dash pepper

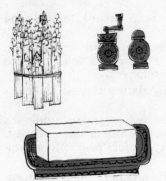

1. Break or cut off tough ends of asparagus stalks. Wash asparagus tips well with cold water; if necessary, use a soft brush to remove grit. With vegetable parer, scrape skin and scales from lower part of stalk only. With sharp knife, cut into ½-inch pieces.
2. In medium saucepan, bring asparagus, onion, and 1 cup water to boiling. Reduce heat; simmer, covered, 15 minutes, or until very tender.
3. Rub cooked asparagus and liquid through a sieve. Measure 2 cups into medium bowl. Blend in cream and milk.
4. Melt butter in medium saucepan. Remove from heat. Add flour, stirring until smooth. Slowly stir in asparagus mixture.
5. Cook over medium heat, stirring, just until bubbles form around edge. Season with salt and pepper.

CREAM-OF-CHICKEN SOUP

MAKES 4 SERVINGS

2 egg yolks
1 can (12½ oz) chicken
  consommé
1¼ cups heavy cream
1 teaspoon salt

¼ teaspoon pepper
3 tablespoons dry sherry
1 tablespoon coarsely
  chopped watercress

1. In top of double boiler, combine egg yolks and consommé; mix well.
2. Cook, over hot water and stirring constantly, until mixture thickens and forms coating on metal spoon—8 to 10 minutes.
3. Remove from heat. Stir in cream, salt, and pepper.
4. Cook, over hot water and stirring occasionally, about 5 minutes, or until very hot. Stir in sherry.
5. Serve at once. Garnish with watercress.

CREAM-OF-CURRY SOUP

2 tablespoons butter or
    margarine
2 tablespoons finely
    chopped onion
2 teaspoons curry powder
1 tablespoon flour

2 cans (14-oz size) clear
    chicken broth
4 egg yolks, slightly beaten
1 cup heavy cream
1 cup canned crushed pine-
    apple, well drained

1. In hot butter in large skillet, sauté onion until golden—about 5 minutes.
2. Remove from heat. Stir in curry powder and flour until smooth. Add chicken broth; bring to boiling, stirring.
3. Blend some of hot broth mixture into egg yolks; then stir into broth in skillet.
4. Cook, stirring, over low heat, about 1 minute, or until slightly thickened.
5. Strain into large bowl; let cool.
6. Refrigerate, covered, several hours. Just before serving, stir in cream and pineapple.

SHERRIED MUSHROOM BISQUE

2 pkg (2-oz size) dried
    cream-of-mushroom-
    soup mix
2 cans (12½-oz size)
    chicken consommé

¾ cup milk
½ teaspoon nutmeg
Dash cayenne
⅛ teaspoon dry mustard
½ cup sherry

1. Combine all ingredients, except sherry, with 2¼ cups water in medium saucepan.
2. With wire whisk or rotary beater, beat until well mixed.
3. Over high heat, bring to boiling, uncovered; stir occasionally. Reduce heat; simmer 5 minutes, stirring occasionally. Remove from heat.
4. Stir in sherry. Serve at once.

OYSTER BISQUE

2 cans (10¼-oz size) frozen
    condensed oyster
    stew,* undiluted
3 cups milk
2½ teaspoons instant
    minced onion
2 tablespoons dried celery
    flakes

2 bay leaves
¼ teaspoon garlic powder
⅛ teaspoon mace
Dash pepper
½ cup sherry
2 tablespoons dried parsley
    flakes

1. In medium saucepan, combine all ingredients, except sherry and parsley, with ¾ cup water; stir until well mixed.
2. Over high heat, bring to boiling, uncovered; stir occasionally.
3. Reduce heat; simmer 10 minutes, stirring occasionally.
4. Remove from heat. Stir in sherry and parsley. Serve at once.
* Partially thaw as label directs.

SOUR-CREAM SOUP

2 cans (10½-oz size) con-
    densed beef bouillon,
    undiluted
½ teaspoon salt
½ teaspoon caraway seed

1½ cups dairy sour cream
⅓ cup unsifted all-purpose
    flour
Croutons

1. Add water to bouillon to measure 1 quart.
2. In large saucepan, bring bouillon, salt, and caraway seed to boiling. Reduce heat.
3. Meanwhile, in small bowl, combine sour cream and flour, stirring until smooth.
4. Slowly pour into bouillon, stirring constantly until well blended. Bring just to boiling. Serve at once. Garnish with croutons.

WATERCRESS CREAM CONSOMMÉ

Consommé:

2 tablespoons butter or margarine

2 tablespoons flour

4 cups watercress, with stems (packed)

4 cans (10½-oz size) condensed beef bouillon, undiluted

⅛ teaspoon pepper

1 cup heavy cream

Garnish:

8 French-roll slices, ½ inch thick, toasted*

Watercress sprigs

1. Several hours before serving, make Consommé: Combine half of butter, flour, watercress, and bouillon in electric blender.

2. Blend, at high speed, covered, 1 minute; pour into large saucepan. Repeat with remaining butter, flour, watercress, and bouillon. Refrigerate covered, until just before serving.

3. To serve: Bring to boiling over medium heat, stirring. Reduce heat; add pepper and cream; heat, stirring, several minutes longer.

4. For Garnish: In center of each roll slice, make a hole ¼ inch wide.

5. Insert several watercress sprigs through each hole; trim stems.

6. Float a garnish on each serving of consommé.

* Toast at 300F for 15 to 20 minutes, turning once.

These hearty, stick-to-the-ribs soups need only a green salad and crusty bread to make a whole meal. Best known in this country is the chowder, or what the French call La Chaudière, named for the huge cauldron in which peasant soups and stews were cooked.

HEARTY BEEF-AND-VEGETABLE SOUP

3¼ lb beef shanks, cut crosswise

3 teaspoons salt

10 whole black peppers

1 bay leaf

2 celery stalks, with green tops

1 onion, quartered

3 parsley sprigs

1 can (1 lb, 12 oz) tomatoes (3½ cups)

1½ cups cut-up pared potatoes

¾ cup cut-up pared carrots

¼ teaspoon dried tarragon leaves

¼ teaspoon curry powder

1 teaspoon monosodium glutamate

½ pkg (10-oz size) frozen peas

½ cup sliced leek (optional)

1 cup shredded cabbage

1. In large kettle, combine beef shanks, 2 teaspoons salt, peppers, bay leaf, celery, onion, parsley, and 1½ quarts water. Bring to boiling; reduce heat, and simmer, covered, 1¾ hours, or until beef is fork-tender.

2. Remove shanks. Strain stock; let cool slightly; then skim fat from surface. Remove beef from bones; cut into 1-inch pieces.

3. In same kettle, combine beef stock, beef, tomatoes, potatoes, carrots, tarragon, curry, monosodium glutamate, and rest of salt. Bring to boiling; reduce heat, and simmer, covered, 20 minutes, or until potatoes and carrots are almost tender.

4. Add peas, leek, and cabbage; simmer, covered, 10 minutes, or until peas and cabbage are tender.

BLACK-BEAN SOUP

MAKES 6 SERVINGS

2 cups dried black beans
2 cups coarsely chopped
celery
1 medium onion, sliced
4 whole cloves
½ lb salt pork, cut in
chunks

1 teaspoon Worcestershire
sauce
2 teaspoons lemon juice
2 teaspoons salt
¼ teaspoon pepper
¼ cup sherry
6 thin lemon slices

1. Cover beans with cold water; refrigerate, covered, overnight.
2. Next day, drain. Turn into 6-quart kettle. Add celery, onion, cloves, salt pork, and 2 quarts water. Bring to boil; then reduce heat, and simmer, covered, 3 hours, or until beans are very tender.
3. Press bean mixture (including liquid) through a sieve, to purée.
4. Add Worcestershire, lemon juice, salt, and pepper; heat gently—about 5 minutes.
5. Just before serving, stir in sherry. Garnish each serving with a lemon slice.

BURGUNDY BEAN SOUP

MAKES 6 SERVINGS

2 cans (11¼-oz size)
condensed bean-with-
bacon soup, undiluted
1 can (10½ oz) condensed
beef bouillon,
undiluted

1 teaspoon instant minced
onion
1 teaspoon Worcestershire
sauce
¾ cup Burgundy

1. Pour bean soup into medium saucepan; with fork, mash whole beans. Add remaining ingredients, except Burgundy, along with 2 cups water; stir until well combined.
2. Over high heat, bring to boiling, uncovered; stir occasionally. Reduce heat; simmer, covered, 15 minutes, stirring occasionally.
3. Remove from heat. Stir in Burgundy. Serve at once.

OLD-FASHIONED CHICKEN SOUP

MAKES 4 SERVINGS

3½-lb stewing chicken,
cut up
2½ teaspoons salt
⅛ teaspoon pepper
¼ teaspoon dried basil
leaves
1 bay leaf

4 medium carrots
½ lb small white onions
1 cup fine noodles,
uncooked
1 tablespoon finely
chopped parsley

1. Wash chicken. Place in large kettle, and cover with 5 cups water. Add seasonings.
2. Simmer, covered, 1½ hours, or until chicken is just tender.
3. While chicken is cooking, prepare vegetables: Wash carrots; peel; cut in 1-inch chunks. Wash and peel onions.
4. When chicken is done, remove it, along with bay leaf, from stock. Skim off as much fat as possible from stock.
5. Bring back to boiling. Add carrots and onions; simmer 45 minutes.
6. While vegetables are cooking, remove skin and bones from chicken, leaving chicken in large pieces. Save the scraps for sandwiches or salad.
7. Ten minutes before vegetables are done, add noodles and chicken pieces. Cook 10 minutes longer.
8. Sprinkle with parsley.

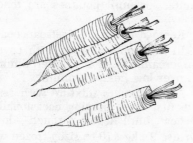

551

MANHATTAN CLAM CHOWDER

4 bacon slices, diced
1 cup sliced onion (about 4)
1 cup diced carrots
   (about 4)
1 cup diced celery
1 tablespoon chopped
   parsley
1 can (1 lb, 12 oz) tomatoes

2 jars (11½-oz size) clams
2 teaspoons salt
4 whole black peppers
1 bay leaf
1½ teaspoons dried thyme
   leaves
3 medium potatoes, pared
   and diced (3½ cups)

MAKES 8 LARGE SERVINGS

1.   In large kettle, sauté bacon until almost crisp.
2.   Add onion; cook until tender—about 5 minutes.
3.   Add carrots, celery, and parsley; cook over low heat 5 minutes, stirring occasionally.
4.   Drain tomatoes; reserve liquid in 1-quart measure. Add tomatoes to vegetables in kettle.
5.   Drain clams; set clams aside. Add clam liquid to tomato liquid. Add water to make 1½ quarts liquid. Pour into kettle. Add salt, peppers, bay leaf, and thyme.
6.   Bring to boiling. Reduce heat; cover, and simmer 45 minutes.
7.   Add potatoes; cover, and cook 20 minutes.
8.   Chop clams; add to chowder. Simmer, uncovered, 15 minutes. Serve hot.

NEW ENGLAND CLAM CHOWDER

2 bacon slices, diced
½ cup chopped onion
   (1 medium)
1 cup cubed, pared potato
   (1 medium)
1½ teaspoons salt
Dash pepper

3 cans (7½-oz size) minced
   clams
2 cups milk
2 tablespoons butter or
   margarine
8 soda crackers, crushed

MAKES 8 SERVINGS

1.   In medium kettle, sauté bacon until almost crisp.
2.   Add onion; cook until tender—about 5 minutes.
3.   Add potatoes, salt, pepper, and 1½ cups water; cook 10 minutes.
4.   Add clams and liquid, milk, and butter; cook 3 minutes.
5.   Sprinkle in crackers; heat through—do not boil. Serve hot.

CORN CHOWDER

4 slices bacon, finely
   chopped
1 medium onion, thinly
   sliced
4 cups cubed, pared
   potatoes (about 4
   medium)

4 cups fresh corn kernels,*
   cut from cob
1 cup heavy cream
1 teaspoon sugar
¼ cup butter or margarine
2½ teaspoons salt
¼ teaspoon white pepper
2 cups milk

MAKES 8 TO 10 SERVINGS

1.   In large saucepan with cover, sauté bacon, over moderate heat, until golden.
2.   Add onion, potatoes, and 1 cup water. Cover; bring to boiling, and simmer about 10 minutes, or until potatoes are tender but not mushy.
3.   Remove cover, and set saucepan aside.
4.   In medium saucepan with cover, combine corn, cream, sugar, and butter. Simmer, covered and over low heat, 10 minutes.
5.   Add to potato mixture with remaining ingredients. Cook, stirring occasionally and over low heat, until heated through—do not boil.
* Or use 2 pkg (10-oz size) frozen whole kernel corn, thawed.

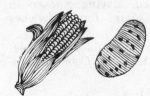

NEW ENGLAND FISH CHOWDER

2 lb halibut fillets
2½ teaspoons salt
3 cups cut-up pared
    potatoes
6 bacon slices, chopped

1 cup chopped onion
2 cups milk
2 cups light cream
¼ teaspoon pepper

1. Place halibut, with 2 cups water, in large saucepan; bring to boiling.

2. Reduce heat; simmer, covered, 15 minutes, or until fish flakes easily with fork. Remove fish; set aside.

3. To fish broth, add 1 teaspoon salt and the potatoes; boil, covered, about 8 minutes, or until potatoes are almost tender.

4. Meanwhile, sauté bacon until crisp; remove, and drain on paper towels.

5. Sauté onion in bacon fat until tender—about 5 minutes.

6. Flake fish. Add, along with bacon, onion, remaining salt, and rest of ingredients, to potatoes; slowly bring to boiling.

7. Reduce heat; simmer, uncovered, 15 minutes.

SOUTHERN GUMBO

1 lb boneless veal, cut in
    1-inch cubes
¼ cup unsifted all-purpose
    flour
¼ cup butter or margarine
½ cup finely chopped
    onion
2 pkg (12-oz size) frozen
    okra, thawed and cut
    into 1-inch pieces*

1 can (1 lb, 12 oz)
    tomatoes, undrained
1 cup finely chopped green
    pepper
4 teaspoons salt
¼ teaspoon pepper
½ teaspoon dried thyme
    leaves
1 teaspoon fines herbes

1. Coat veal cubes well in flour.

2. Slowly heat butter in 8-quart kettle. In it, brown veal cubes well, turning on all sides.

3. Add onion, okra, and tomatoes; cover; cook 15 minutes.

4. Add 2 quarts water and remaining ingredients; cover; bring to boiling. Reduce heat; simmer 2 hours, stirring occasionally.

* Or use 1 quart fresh okra, washed and cut into 1-inch pieces.

HAMBURGER SOUP

3 tablespoons butter or
    margarine
1½ lb ground chuck
1 can (1 lb, 12 oz)
    tomatoes, undrained
2 cans (10½-oz size)
    condensed beef
    consommé, undiluted
1 can (10½ oz) condensed
    onion soup, undiluted

4 carrots, pared, sliced ¼
    inch thick
¼ cup chopped celery tops
¼ cup chopped parsley
1 bay leaf
½ teaspoon Italian
    seasoning
10 whole black peppers

1. Melt butter in large kettle. Add beef; cook, stirring and over medium heat, 5 minutes, or until browned.

2. Add remaining ingredients, along with 2 cups water; bring to boiling.

3. Reduce heat; simmer, covered, 45 minutes, stirring occasionally.

MULLIGATAWNY SOUP

½ cup butter or margarine
2 lb lamb shoulder, cut
    into 1-inch cubes
1 cup thinly sliced onion
1 cup thinly sliced carrot
1 cup thinly sliced celery
3 cups thinly sliced, pared
    tart apples
2 tablespoons flour

1 teaspoon curry powder
2 teaspoons salt
¼ teaspoon pepper
½ teaspoon dried thyme
    leaves
3 tablespoons finely
    chopped parsley
1 bay leaf
2 tablespoons lemon juice

1. In hot butter in large kettle, brown lamb well on all sides; remove.

2. Add onion, carrot, celery, and apples; cook, stirring, about 5 minutes. Remove from heat.

3. Combine flour, curry powder, salt, and pepper; stir into vegetable mixture. Add lamb, thyme, parsley, bay leaf, and 2 quarts water; bring to boiling. Reduce heat, and simmer, covered, 2 hours.

4. Remove lamb. Strain vegetables, and press through coarse sieve.

5. Return lamb and puréed vegetables to broth. Stir in lemon juice; reheat gently.

FRENCH ONION SOUP

¼ cup butter or margarine
4 cups thinly sliced onion
4 cans (10½-oz size)
    condensed beef
    bouillon, undiluted

1 teaspoon salt
4 to 6 French-bread slices,
    1 inch thick
2 tablespoons grated
    Parmesan cheese

1. Heat butter in large skillet. Add onion, and sauté, stirring, until golden—about 8 minutes.

2. Combine onion, bouillon, and salt in medium saucepan; bring to boiling. Reduce heat, and simmer, covered, 30 minutes.

3. Meanwhile, toast bread slices in broiler until browned on both sides.

4. Sprinkle one side of each with grated cheese; run under broiler about 1 minute, or until cheese is bubbly.

5. To serve: Pour soup into a tureen or individual soup bowls. Float toast, cheese side up, on soup.

OLD-FASHIONED
SPLIT-PEA SOUP

1½ cups quick-cooking
    split green peas
1 ham bone
⅔ cup coarsely chopped
    onion
¼ cup cut-up carrot
½ cup coarsely chopped
    celery
2 parsley sprigs
1 clove garlic

1 bay leaf, crumbled
½ teaspoon sugar
¼ teaspoon salt
⅛ teaspoon dried thyme
    leaves
⅛ teaspoon pepper
2 cans (14-oz size)
    clear chicken broth
1 cup slivered cooked ham

1. In 3½-quart kettle, combine peas and 1 quart water; bring to boiling. Reduce heat; simmer, covered, 45 minutes. Add more water if necessary.

2. Add ham bone and rest of ingredients, except ham; simmer, covered, 1½ hours.

3. Remove ham bone, and discard.

4. Press vegetables and liquid through coarse sieve.

5. Return to kettle. Add ham; reheat slowly until thoroughly hot.

CHICKEN-AND-CORN SOUP

MAKES 6 TO 8 SERVINGS

4-lb ready-to-cook
    roasting chicken,
    cut up
2 teaspoons salt
Dash pepper
¼ teaspoon saffron,
    (optional)
1 stalk celery, with leaves

1 whole onion, peeled
2 cups medium noodles
2 pkg (10-oz size) frozen
    whole-kernel corn
2 teaspoons chopped
    parsley
2 hard-cooked eggs,
    coarsely chopped

1. Rinse chicken well in cold water. Place in 4-quart kettle along with 2 quarts water, the salt, pepper, saffron, celery, and onion.

2. Bring to boiling; reduce heat, and simmer, covered, 1 hour, or until chicken is tender. Skim off fat.

3. Lift out chicken; let cool slightly. Remove celery and onion, and discard.

4. Remove chicken from bones; cut into bite-size pieces.

5. Return chicken to broth; bring to boiling. Add noodles and corn; boil, uncovered, 20 minutes, or until noodles are tender.

6. If necessary, add a little more salt and pepper. Just before serving, add parsley and egg.

Garnishes For Soups

· Thin strip of canned pimiento.
· Paper-thin slices of lemon, orange, or lime.
· Slices or tiny cubes of avocado.
· Salted, buttered popcorn.
· Any of the unsweetened, dry cereals.
· Very thin strips of celery, green onion, carrot, white turnip, radishes, cucumber, or green pepper.
· Sliced or chopped olives, green or ripe.
· Crumbled potato or corn chips.
· Grated or crumbled cheese.
· Sour cream mixed with lemon juice.

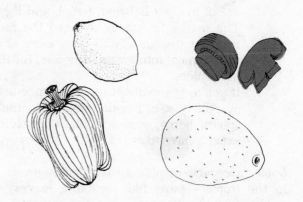

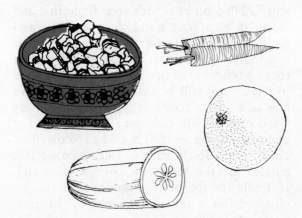

· Whipped cream with horseradish or with catsup.
· Thin slices of buttered, toasted bread—French or rye—sprinkled with celery, poppy, or sesame seed.
· Thin slices of raw mushroom.
· Finely chopped, salted nuts.
· Finely chopped watercress, parsley, or chives.
· Tiny cream puffs filled with deviled ham.
· Croutons sprinkled with melted butter, dipped in Parmesan cheese, and toasted in the oven.
· Grated hard-cooked egg.

Spices and Herbs

25

Solomon sang of them. Marco Polo wrote of them. The mightiest monarchs of ancient Babylon, Israel, and Egypt prized them as highly as rare jewels. The search for spices changed the face of history. Now here they are, these fragrant treasures, only a grocer's shelf away from you, ready to change a simple meal into an exciting one, for there's no denying that cooking is livelier with spices.

If you're vague about the difference between a spice and an herb, so is almost everybody else! For the most part, the word *spice* covers the whole gamut of spices, herbs, seeds, vegetable seasonings, and blends. But here's what the experts have to say:

Spices are parts of plants that usually grow in the tropics—parts like the bark, leaves, seeds, stamens, shells, or any other aromatic part suitable for seasoning or preserving.

Herbs, on the other hand, are *always* leaves of temperate-zone plants. Not only are rosemary and basil herbs, but so are such familiar favorites as parsley and mint.

First step to fine cooking is a knowledge of herbs and spices—and our Herb and Spice Chart in this chapter will help you. Herbs are an accessory, and like all accessories, they should be chosen with care and used with discretion, so they accent but do not overwhelm. At first, it's better to be over-cautious than reckless. If an herb is new to you, crush a bit of it with your fingertips and warm it with your hand. Now sniff it, and taste it. If it is strong and pungent, use it sparingly—quite literally, as many of our recipes tell you, by the pinch. If it is delicate in flavor, you will be safe in using more. No one can know precisely how much of any spice or herb will suit *your* taste. Since the pungency of spices differs and a spice's effect on different foods varies, and since no two palates are the same, there is no hard-and-fast rule for the perfect amount. At the beginning, follow our recipes exactly. In time, your nose and your taste buds will be your best guides in the use of herbs and spices.

Fresh herbs from the garden can be used in cooking just as successfully as handy dried herbs; but you should use less of the dried than of the fresh. Just keep in mind that half a teaspoonful of a dried herb is equivalent to approximately two scant teaspoonfuls of a freshly minced herb. One part of instant minced onion or parsley flakes is

equal in seasoning strength to about four parts of the raw product. One part of celery or sweet-pepper flakes is equivalent to about two parts of the raw vegetable. Fresh herbs should always be minced, cut, or crushed before using, to bring out volatile oils and true flavors. Spices and herbs are perishable and should be used soon after purchasing them, while their flavors are at their strongest and best.

Buying, Storing, and Using Spices and Herbs

Look for strength and color when you buy spices and herbs. Your best guarantee of freshness and flavor is the brand name of the distributor. Since spices and herbs gradually lose color and flavor, you'll get no bargain when you buy a large quantity in a paper bag. Small, tightly sealed containers, of glass or tin, are best.

Spices and herbs should be stored in a cool, dry place—definitely not right over or too near the range. They keep best in their airtight containers, as they come from the store. But once even the best container is opened, its contents will inevitably deteriorate in time. Small apothecary jars make attractive spice-shelf containers, as do small canisters with tight-fitting lids. In hot or humid climates, keep paprika and red-pepper blends in the refrigerator, to guard them against molding or infestation.

Herbs tend to lose flavor a little faster than ground pepper, ginger, cinnamon, and cloves. But we use herbs more generously than we do pungent spices. Properly stored, the few ounces of herbs in the average container retain good flavor and color for several months. Whole spices, on the other hand, keep their flavor almost indefinitely. Therefore, it is safe to buy stick cinnamon,

whole cloves, and such spices in larger quantity. The same spices ground, however, should be used up and replenished within six months, if you want their flavor at the maximum.

Whole spices are best in slow-cooking dishes, like stews. They should be added at the beginning of the cooking, so the long simmering can extract the full flavor and aroma.

Ground spices are soon dissipated, so add them only about 15 minutes before you are ready to serve.

If you use herbs slowly, buy them packaged in the leaf form, and crush them as you use them. The flavor and aroma last longer when leaves are whole and tightly sealed.

Flavoring seeds include sesame, poppy, dill, mustard, and caraway seeds. Seeds like poppy and sesame may be toasted before they are used, to enhance the flavor.

Seasoning blends—like chili powder, curry powder, *fines herbes*, mixed pickling spice, poultry seasoning, and pumpkin-pie spice— are available at your grocer's. *Fines herbes* refers to a combination of certain fresh herbs, which are chopped separately, combined, and sprinkled over stews, soups, omelets and fish sauces. Some combinations are: Parsley, chives, watercress and tarragon; or parsley, chives and chervil. *Bouquet garni* is one blend, however, that you usually make yourself. To make such a blend, tie together, in a small cheesecloth bag, the fresh or dried herbs and spices you will use. Like a tea bag, the sack of seasonings should be removed and discarded after it has imparted its flavor in cooking. A variety of combinations is possible for different dishes. For lamb stew, for instance, a good garni might include leaf thyme, a clove, parsley. The recipe may suggest what to use, but you will have fun experimenting.

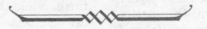

HERB AND SPICE CHART

HERB, SPICE, OR BLEND	USE
ALLSPICE	**Whole:** Pickling spice mixtures, pot roast, stews, and ham. **Ground:** Mincemeat and pumpkin pies, plum pudding, cookies, cakes, and some vegetables (squash, turnips, carrots).
ANISE	Cookies, candies, sweet pickles, beverage flavoring. Also used in coffeecakes and sweet rolls.
BASIL	An important seasoning in tomato dishes. Also good in soups, stews and as a seasoning for beans, peas, squash. Often sprinkled on lamb before cooking.
BAY LEAVES	Pickling spice mixtures, soups, stews. They make an excellent addition to fish chowder, tomato and seafood aspics, and such variety meats as kidney and heart.
CARAWAY	Caraway gives rye bread its distinctive flavor. A frequent addition to rolls, cakes, and cheeses. Also good in cottage cheese, sauerkraut, and coleslaw. Add to turnips and asparagus when cooking.
CARDAMOM	**Whole:** Pickling spice mixtures and in a demitasse of hot, strong coffee. **Ground:** Danish pastry, coffeecakes, custards, cookies, and fruits.
CELERY SEED	Excellent in pickling spice mixtures, sauces, salads, salad dressings, fish, and vegetables. Or sprinkle over cheese, crackers, or rolls.
CHERVIL	Frequently included in "fines herbes" blends. Use in soups, sauces, salads, and in poultry and fish stuffings.
CHILI POWDER	Good in seafood-cocktail sauces and barbecue sauces. Try it in meat loaf, hamburger, and stews.

HERB AND SPICE CHART
(Continued)

HERB, SPICE, OR BLEND	USE
CHIVES	Recommended in salads and salad dressings, scrambled eggs, omelets. Or add to cream cheese, cottage cheese, or soft butter.
CINNAMON	**Whole:** Pickling, preserving, flavoring puddings and stewed fruits. As a muddler for coffee, tea, and hot wine drinks. **Ground:** Good in combination with apples in any baked dish. Sprinkle over puddings and hot cereals. Combine with mashed sweet potatoes, and with sugar for cinnamon toast.
CLOVES	**Whole:** Roast pork, ham, pickled fruits, spicy syrups, and meat gravies. **Ground:** Baked goods, chocolate pudding, stews, and vegetables.
CORIANDER	**Whole:** Pickling mixtures, Spanish rice. **Ground:** In curry blends.
CRAB BOIL AND SHRIMP SPICE	Add one envelope to a quart of water when boiling shellfish.
CUMIN	**Whole:** Chili con carne, hot tamales, soups, cheese, meat and rice dishes. **Ground:** Deviled eggs, meat loaf, croquettes, cheese spreads, canapes.
CURRY POWDER	Used in curry sauces for curried eggs, vegetables, fish, and meat. Try a dash in French dressing, scalloped tomatoes, clam and fish chowders, and split pea soup.
DILL SEED	Adds a bright touch to pickles, rye and pumpernickel bread, soups, salads, sauces, meat and fish dishes, potatoes, and coleslaw.
FENNEL	Comes both whole and ground. Used extensively for bread, rolls, and pastry. Also used in sweet pickles, and as a seasoning for soups, fruit dishes and sauces.
FENUGREEK	Used commercially, both ground and whole, for making chutney and curry powder.
FILE	Used mainly in Creole cookery for gumbos.
GARLIC (Dehydrated)	A little garlic does wonders for most soups, salads, sauces, meats, fish, and casserole dishes.
GINGER	**Whole:** Preserves and pickling mixtures. **Ground:** Used widely in cookies, spicecakes, gingerbread. Also good in pot roasts, stews, chicken, soups, and fish dishes.
MACE	Can be added to poundcakes for flavoring. Also excellent in fish and meat stuffings, peach and cherry pies, fruitcakes and cobblers. Add a dash to oyster stew, creamed eggs, or whipped cream.

HERB AND SPICE CHART
(Continued)

HERB, SPICE, OR BLEND	USE
MARJORAM	Available both whole and ground. Excellent seasoning for vegetables (green beans, lima beans, and peas). Enhances the flavor of lamb, mutton, sausage, stews, and poultry stuffing. Many processed foods, such as head cheese, liverwurst, and bologna use it for seasoning.
MINT	Used most often fresh, in drinks, fruit cups, jellies, salads, fish sauces, vegetables, and meat sauces (especially lamb).
MIXED PICKLING SPICE	Primarily for pickle making, this spice also is especially suited to long-cooking dishes.
MUSTARD	**Whole:** Add to pickles, cabbage, sauerkraut, coleslaw, relishes, and potato salad. **Ground:** Adds zip to cream soups, cheese, egg, and seafood dishes. **Prepared:** Frankfurters, hamburgers, meat loaf, salad dressings.
NUTMEG	Available whole and ground. Used in flavoring baked goods, rice and custard puddings, vegetables, and in beverages (particularly eggnog). Add to creamed vegetables and soups, beef and fish dishes.
OREGANO	Comes whole and ground. An essential ingredient in chili powder. A classic addition to almost any tomato dish, vegetable, or salad.
PAPRIKA	Used as a garnish for colorless foods. Important ingredient in chicken paprika and Hungarian goulash. It brightens fish, salads, and canapes.
PARSLEY	Goes perfectly with cheese, eggs, fish, meats, poultry, salads, sauces, and vegetables.
BLACK PEPPER	**Whole:** Pickling mixtures, soups, and meats. **Ground and Cracked:** In meats, sauces, gravies, many vegetables, soups, salads, and eggs.
CAYENNE PEPPER	Use in deviled ham and eggs, cheese canapes, Welsh rabbit, creamed dishes, and stews.
RED PEPPER	**Whole:** Pickles, relishes, hot sauces. **Crushed:** Sauces, pickles, highly spiced meats. **Ground:** Meats, sauces, fish, and egg dishes.
POPPY SEED	Used as topping for cookies, pastries, rolls, and bread. Excellent sprinkled over noodles and salad greens.
POULTRY SEASONING	For poultry, veal, pork, and fish stuffings. Good with paprika for meat loaf.

HERB AND SPICE CHART
(Continued)

HERB, SPICE, OR BLEND	USE
ROSEMARY	Available whole and ground. Wonderful with boiled potatoes, turnips, and cauliflower. Sprinkle on beef and fish before cooking.
SAFFRON	Adds a distinctive flavor to rolls and cakes. Particularly good with rice.
SAGE	Available whole and ground. Perfect accompaniment for pork and poultry.
SAVORY	An excellent flavoring for meats, poultry, and fish dishes, in scrambled eggs, sauerkraut, cabbage, peas, and salads.
SESAME SEED	Use for cookies, rolls, scones, and candies. Nice in chicken dishes and on French bread and sprinkled over green beans and asparagus.
TARRAGON	Good in chicken dishes and stuffings, green and seafood salads, and lamb chops.
THYME	Available whole and ground. Use in clam chowder, fish sauces, croquettes, fresh-tomato salads, and egg dishes.
TURMERIC	Used as flavoring and coloring in prepared mustard and in combination with mustard as flavoring for meats, dressing, and salads. Used in pickling, chowchow, and other relishes.

The Wassail Bowl is the forerunner of our modern toast. The word wassail is derived from two Anglo-Saxon words: "wes," meaning "be thou," and "hal," meaning "whole."

WASSAIL BOWL

MAKES 36 (4-OZ) SERVINGS

Whole cloves
6 oranges
1 gallon apple cider
1½ cups lemon juice
10 (2-inch) cinnamon
    sticks
2 cups vodka
¼ cup brandy

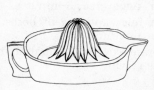

1. Preheat oven to 350F.
2. Insert cloves, ¼ inch apart, in oranges. Bake, uncovered, in shallow pan, 30 minutes.
3. Meanwhile, heat cider in large kettle until bubbles form around edge.
4. Remove from heat. Add lemon juice, cinnamon sticks, and oranges. Heat, covered, over very low heat, 30 minutes.
5. Add vodka and brandy, mixing well; pour into punch bowl. Serve warm.

MAI BOWLE

MAKES 6 SERVINGS

10 fresh sweet-woodruff
    sprigs
1 bottle (⅘ qt) Rhine
    wine, chilled

1 teaspoon crushed
    strawberries
1 teaspoon brandy
1 tablespoon sugar
6 whole strawberries

1. In small bowl, with wooden spoon, lightly bruise 4 woodruff sprigs while stirring in 1 cup wine.

2. Refrigerate, covered, overnight, or at least 3 hours.

3. Just before serving, strain into small punch bowl. Remove woodruff, and discard.

4. Add rest of wine, the crushed strawberries, brandy, and sugar; stir to mix well.

5. Serve in punch cups or goblets, with whole strawberry and woodruff sprig in each.

ROSE-GERANIUM LEMONADE

MAKES 4 SERVINGS

4 small sprigs, or 4 large
    leaves, rose geranium
2 teaspoons sugar
4 maraschino cherries

4 teaspoons maraschino-
    cherry juice
1 can (6 oz) frozen
    lemonade concentrate
Ice cubes

1. In each of 4 (12-oz) glasses, using back of wooden spoon, crush 1 rose-geranium sprig with ½ teaspoon sugar.

2. Then add 1 cherry and 1 teaspoon cherry juice to each glass.

3. Make lemonade as label directs.

4. Pour over ice in glasses, stirring to mix well. Garnish each with rose-geranium sprig, if desired.

Note: Or make Fresh-Mint Lemonade by using mint sprigs in place of rose-geranium sprigs.

HERBED TOMATO JUICE

MAKES 5 OR 6 SERVINGS

2 cans (1-pt, 2-oz size)
    tomato juice
¼ cup orange juice
1 tablespoon lemon juice
1 teaspoon sugar
½ teaspoon salt

1 teaspoon dried basil
    leaves
½ teaspoon dried
    marjoram leaves
¼ teaspoon dried parsley
¼ teaspoon instant minced
    onion

1. Combine 3½ cups tomato juice, the orange juice, lemon juice, sugar, and salt in a 1½-quart pitcher; stir to mix well.

2. Combine herbs and onion in small cheese-cloth bag; tie with string.

3. In small saucepan, bring rest of tomato juice to boiling. Add bag of herbs; reduce heat, and simmer, uncovered, 5 minutes.

4. Stir hot juice and bag of herbs into other tomato-juice mixture.

5. Refrigerate, covered, several hours. Remove herbs before serving.

HOT SOUP

Ideal for a cold winter's eve. Ideal, in fact, just about any time. Whether it's chowder, bouillon, broth, or "cream of"—whether it serves as a first course or a meal-in-itself—there's nothing as good as soup—if you prepare it right. As a special idea, serve it in your living room as it's pictured below, much as you might a cocktail before dinner. That's right. Make it a mug of good, hot soup, to be sipped and savored slowly. Or serve it in the conventional way in bowls at the dinner table. But serve it often —and serve it piping hot!

Spices of Life

Spices and herbs. Without them, life's hardly worth living. Use them, and any meal becomes a feast. From earliest times, men have sought them to enliven their dinners. Solomon sang of spices; Marco Polo wrote of them; monarchs of old prized them as highly as jewels. The leaves and seeds of such herbs as thyme, marjoram, sage, and basil have left a fragrant trail through history. We tell you how to use them well. Live!

PRIVATE-LABEL SEASONED SALT

1 cup salt
1 teaspoon dried thyme
    leaves
1½ teaspoons dried oregano
    leaves
1 teaspoon garlic salt

2½ teaspoons paprika
1 teaspoon curry powder
2 teaspoons dry mustard
½ teaspoon onion powder
¼ teaspoon dried dill
    (optional)

Combine all ingredients in medium bowl; mix very well.

To store: Pour into handsome jars with tight-fitting lids. Keep in cool, dry place.

FRESH-TARRAGON VINEGAR

1 cup coarsely chopped
    fresh tarragon

½ cup sugar
2 cups cider vinegar

1. Sterilize a pint jar; keep in hot water until ready to fill.

2. In medium saucepan, combine tarragon, sugar, and vinegar. Cook, stirring, over high heat, until sugar is dissolved.

3. Reduce heat; bring to boiling, stirring.

4. Pour into hot, sterilized jar; cap as manufacturer directs. Let stand in cool, dry place, 4 to 6 weeks, before using.

Fresh-Dill Vinegar: Make vinegar as above, substituting 2 sprigs fresh dill for tarragon.

Fresh-Chive or Fresh-Mint Vinegar: Make vinegar as above, omitting sugar and substituting 1 cup chopped fresh chives or 1 cup snipped fresh mint leaves for tarragon.

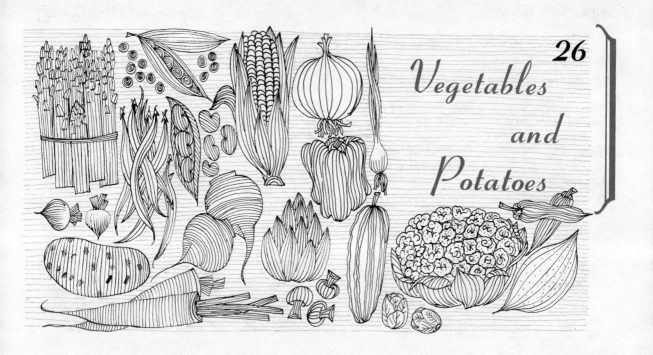

26

Vegetables and Potatoes

I s there a vegetable hater in your home? Most likely there is; there seems to be one in almost every family.

Frequently, we've tasted vegetables in the homes of avowed vegetable haters and found them overcooked or devoid of taste or color. Properly cooked and well-seasoned vegetables will be gobbled up by the very ones who think they don't like them. With spices and herbs, with sauces and combinations of vegetables to add variety, the vegetable hater can become a vegetable lover, scraping every plate clean.

When you plan vegetables for a meal, remember that contrast in color and texture are almost as important as flavor. One strongly flavored vegetable, like cauliflower or brussels sprouts, is enough for a single menu. So is one green vegetable. Put sprouts and potatoes on the same plate. They balance each other in taste, color, and texture. And cauliflower in company with fresh-cooked green peas looks inviting, tastes interesting.

McCall's Vegetable Chart tells you when your favorite vegetables are in season, how to prepare them, and how to cook them. It starts with artichokes and goes almost the full length of the alphabet down to turnips. Familiarize yourself with the information it contains. It will save you money, time, and trouble.

VEGETABLE CHART

VEGETABLE	BUYING GUIDE	PREPARATION	BASIC COOKERY
All vegetables	Best buys are in season	Wash all vegetables before cooking	Approximate number of servings per pound and cooking time. Simmer, tightly covered, in 1 inch boiling water with ½ to 1 teaspoon salt per pound. Vegetables are done when tender-crisp
Artichokes (French or Italian)	Compact, firm, heavy globes; free from brown blemishes. Good green color. Fleshy, tightly closed leaf scales. Season: September-May	Cut 1 inch from top. Cut stem close to base. Remove lower tough outer leaves. With scissors, cut thorny tip of each leaf	1 per serving 20 to 45 minutes, standing upright in saucepan
(Jerusalem)	Free from blemishes	Pare thinly. Leave whole, dice, or slice	3 or 4 servings 15 to 35 minutes
Asparagus	Green, firm stalk with close, compact tips; tender stalk is brittle and easily punctured. Should not be woody. Free from blemishes. Season: March-June	Break off woody end of stalk. Remove tough scales. Leave stalk whole, or cut into 1-inch lengths	3 or 4 servings 10 to 20 minutes
Beans, Green or Wax	Clean, firm, crisp, tender pods. Should snap when broken. Free from blemishes Season: All year Peak: March-August	Remove ends. Cut, into lengthwise strips, for French-style. Cut on diagonal, into 1-inch pieces; or serve whole	4 to 6 servings French style: 10 to 20 minutes Cut or whole: 15 to 30 minutes
Beans, Lima	Unshelled limas should be well filled, clean, free from blemishes; dark-green, firm pods. Shelled limas are very perishable; should be light-green or green-white; plump, with tender skins. Season: July-November	Shell just before cooking	2 servings 20 to 25 minutes

VEGETABLE CHART
(Continued)

VEGETABLE	BUYING GUIDE	PREPARATION °	BASIC COOKERY (See page 565)
Beets	Sold in bunches. Smooth, free from blemishes or cracks; fairly clean, firm roots with green tops. Small to medium in size. Season: All year	Remove tops (use as green vegetable); leave 1-inch stems. Scrub well. Peel and slice after cooking	3 servings Cover with cold water. Cook, covered, 30 to 45 minutes (Cook greens just with water that clings to leaves, 5 to 15 minutes)
Broccoli	Firm, tender stems with compact cluster of flower buds. Dark-green or purple-green (depending on variety), free from bruises or yellow. Season: All year Peak: October-March	Trim stem end; split heavy stalks. (Entire stalk is edible)	3 servings 10 to 15 minutes
Brussels Sprouts	Firm, compact, bright-green. Avoid yellow or worm-eaten leaves. Season: November-January	Cut off stem end. Soak in cold water 15 minutes	4 servings 10 to 20 minutes
Cabbage	Firm, heavy heads; crisp, tender leaves. Avoid yellowing or worm-eaten leaves. Season: All year Peak: October-March	Remove outer leaves; wash. Cut into wedges and remove most of core; or shred	3 or 4 servings Green, in wedges: 10 to 15 minutes Shredded: 3 to 10 minutes; Red, shredded: 8 to 12 minutes
Carrots	Firm, clean, smooth, well-shaped, with good color. Free from bruises and cracks. Season: All year	Remove tops. Scrape or pare thinly, or scrub well with brush. Cook whole or cut	4 servings Whole: 15 to 25 minutes Cut: 10 to 20 minutes
Cauliflower	Clean, heavy, compact head. White flowerets with green, crisp leaves. Avoid bruises or brown spots. Season: All year Peak: October-December	Remove outer leaves. Leave whole, removing stem, or cut into flowerets.	3 or 4 servings Whole: 15 to 20 minutes Flowerets: 8 to 15 minutes

VEGETABLE CHART
(Continued)

VEGETABLE	BUYING GUIDE	PREPARATION	BASIC COOKERY (See page 565)
Corn on Cob	Plump, firm, milky kernels with bright color. Husks should be green; dried-out, yellow discolorations indicate stale corn. Immature corn lacks flavor. Season: May-October	Just before cooking, remove husks and silk	1 or 2 per serving 5 to 10 minutes
Eggplant	Heavy, firm, free from blemishes; shiny, smooth purple skin. Season: All year Peak: July-September	Pare, if necessary. Do not soak in salted water. Cut as desired	4 or 5 servings Cook as directed in recipes
Greens (Collards Dandelions Kale Spinach)	Young, tender, crisp leaves. Free from bruises, excess dirt, and coarse stems. Season: Some type available all year round	Cut off root ends. Wash several times, lifting out of water, letting sand sink to bottom of vessel	3 or 4 servings Thin leaf greens are cooked just with water that clings to leaves. Thick leaf greens need only ½ inch water
Onions, Small White	Firm, clean, white, dry skins, free from sprouts. Season: All year	Remove outer skins under cold, running water.	4 servings 15 to 25 minutes
Parsnips	Smooth, firm, clean, well-shaped, free from rot. Small to medium in size. Season: August-May	Scrape or peel. Cut as desired, or leave whole	3 or 4 servings Cut: 10 to 20 minutes Whole: 20 to 40 minutes
Peas	Bright-green, filled pods, free from yellow or mildew, moisture or bruises. Season: All year Peak: May-August	Shell just before cooking	2 servings 8 to 20 minutes
Potatoes, Sweet (or yams)	Firm, plump, free from soft spots. Purchase small quantities; perishable. Sweets skins are pale to deep yellow. Flesh is light orange. Yams: skins are white to reddish. Flesh is deep orange. Season: All year	Remove bruised spots and root ends. Do not pare	2 or 3 servings Cover with boiling water. Cook, covered, 25 to 35 minutes, or until tender

VEGETABLE CHART
(Continued)

VEGETABLE	BUYING GUIDE	PREPARATION	BASIC COOKERY (See page 565)
Potatoes White (mature or new)	Firm, uniform in shape (medium-size). Free from cuts and blemishes. Color varies with variety. Eyes should be shallow	Pare; remove eyes; leave whole. Pare; cut into quarters. Pare; cut into 1-inch cubes; or slice ⅛ inch thick. Whole, small new potatoes. Pare or scrape. Unpared, whole potatoes (medium size)	2 or 3 servings 35 to 40 minutes 20 to 25 minutes 20 to 25 minutes 20 to 25 minutes Cover with boiling water. Cook, covered, 35 to 40 minutes
Squash Acorn	Dark-green, ribbed. Hard rind. Season: All year Peak: October-December	Cut in half, lengthwise. Remove seeds. Do not peel	2 servings (1 large) 20 to 30 minutes (Cook cut side down)
Summer (Zucchini included)	Heavy for size, free from blemishes. Thin, tender skin. Season: May-August	Remove stem and blossom ends. Paring not necessary. Cut as desired	2 or 3 servings 10 to 20 minutes
Winter	Heavy for size, free from blemishes and bruises. Hard rind. Season: October-December	Cut as desired. Remove seeds. Remove rind, if desired	2 servings 25 to 30 minutes
Turnips (Rutabagas)	Firm, smooth, clean, free from bruises, with few fibrous roots. Heavy for size. Season: All year Peak: October-November	Peel thinly just before cooking. Cut as desired	3 or 4 servings 20 to 30 minutes
White	Firm, smooth, clean, free from bruises, with few fibrous roots. Small to medium in size. Season: All year Peak: October-November	Peel thinly just before cooking. Leave whole, or cut	3 or 4 servings Whole: 20 to 30 minutes Cut: 10 to 20 minutes

Canned Vegetables

To cook such canned vegetables as green beans, green limas, peas, carrots, asparagus, etc., drain liquid from can into a saucepan, and boil down to half the original quantity. Then add vegetables, and heat through only.

Do not cook further—these vegetables are already cooked. Season, and serve.

To cook tomatoes, cream-style corn, squash, etc., pour vegetables into a saucepan, and heat through only. Season, and serve.

Frozen Vegetables

Always follow package directions exactly. Remember, the correct amount of water and correct cooking time are of the utmost importance for perfect vegetables.

In general, drop the frozen vegetable, un-thawed, into a small amount of boiling, salted water. Bring to a brisk boil; cover tightly; cook quickly until vegetables are tender but not mushy. Season, and serve immediately.

FRESH ARTICHOKES

MAKES 4 SERVINGS

4 large artichokes
1 teaspoon salt
2 tablespoons salad
    or olive oil
1 tablespoon lemon juice
1 clove garlic

1. Trim stems from artichokes; remove tough outer leaves; discard. Cut a 1-inch slice, crosswise, from top of each; discard. Wash artichokes well; drain.

2. In large saucepan, place artichokes in 1 inch water; add remaining ingredients.

3. Bring to boiling; reduce heat, and simmer, covered, about 45 minutes, or until a leaf may be pulled out easily.

4. Remove artichokes; drain on paper towels. Serve with melted butter or Hollandaise Sauce.*

* See Sauces and Gravies Chapter.

How to eat artichokes: Pull off each leaf separately with fingers; dip into sauce. With teeth, scrape off fleshy portion at base of each leaf. Cut away and discard the choke (thistle-like center). Then eat the heart (base of artichoke) with fork.

ARTICHOKES FLORENTINE

MAKES 6 SERVINGS

2 pkg (9-oz size) frozen
    artichoke hearts
1/4 cup olive or salad oil
3/4 cup dry white wine
2 cloves garlic, finely
    chopped
1 teaspoon salt
Dash pepper
1/2 teaspoon dried oregano
    leaves
1 can (8 oz) tomato sauce

1. Preheat oven to 350F.

2. Cook artichoke hearts as package label directs; drain.

3. In 2-quart casserole, combine artichoke hearts with remaining ingredients, except tomato sauce.

4. Bake, covered, 35 minutes.

5. Stir tomato sauce into casserole. Bake, uncovered, 10 minutes longer.

ARTICHOKE HEARTS IN WINE

MAKES 6 SERVINGS

2 pkg (9-oz size) frozen
    artichoke hearts,
    unthawed
2 cups dry white wine
2 teaspoons salt
2 teaspoons grated onion

1 teaspoon lemon juice
2 tablespoons butter or
    margarine, melted
1 tablespoon chopped
    parsley

1. In medium saucepan, combine artichoke hearts, wine, salt, onion, and lemon juice; bring to boiling.

2. Reduce heat; simmer, covered, 5 to 8 minutes, or until artichokes are just tender.

3. Drain artichokes; turn into serving dish. Toss gently with butter; sprinkle with parsley.

In the spring, a gourmet's fancy fondly turns to thoughts of crisp, tender, green, freshly cut asparagus—cooked quickly to preserve its delicate flavor, and served, hot or cold. And remember this: In any other season, when fresh asparagus is not available in the market, there are the frozen and the canned.

CHINESE-STYLE ASPARAGUS

MAKES 6 SERVINGS

2 to 2½ lb fresh asparagus
⅓ cup butter or margarine

½ teaspoon salt
Dash pepper

1. Break or cut off tough ends of asparagus stalks. Wash asparagus tips well with cold water; if necessary, use a soft brush to remove grit. With a vegetable parer, scrape skin and scales from lower part of stalk only.

2. With a sharp knife, cut stalks on the diagonal, making bias slices about 1 inch long and ¼ inch thick.

3. In large skillet with tight-fitting cover, heat butter with ⅓ cup water to boiling. Add asparagus, salt, and pepper; cook, covered and over high heat, 5 to 8 minutes, adding a little more water if necessary. Asparagus should be tender when pierced with fork, and water should be evaporated.

FRESH ASPARAGUS

MAKES 4 TO 6 SERVINGS

2 to 2½ lb asparagus
Boiling water
1½ teaspoons salt

¼ cup butter or margarine,
    melted
Lemon wedges (optional)

1. Break or cut off tough ends of asparagus stalks. Wash asparagus tips well with cold water; if necessary, use a brush to remove grit. With a vegetable parer, scrape skin and scales from lower part of stalk only.

2. Stand stalks upright in bottom of double boiler; form into a bunch, securing with a rubber band or tying with string. Add boiling water, to depth of 2 inches, and the salt.

3. Bring to boiling; cook, covered, 15 to 20 minutes, or just until tender. Do not overcook.

4. Drain asparagus well. Pour melted butter over it. Serve hot, with lemon wedges or with a sauce.*

* See Sauces and Gravies Chapter.

SKILLET FRESH ASPARAGUS

MAKES 4 TO 6 SERVINGS

2 to 2½ lb asparagus
1 teaspoon salt

⅓ cup butter or margarine,
    melted
Lemon juice (optional)

1. Break or cut off tough ends of asparagus stalks. Wash asparagus tips well with cold water; if necessary, use a brush to remove grit. With vegetable parer, scrape skin and scales from lower part of stalk only.

2. In large skillet, add salt to 1½ inches of water; bring to boiling. Add asparagus spears; cover; boil vigorously 8 to 10 minutes (depending on size and tenderness of asparagus)—just until, when pierced with fork, it is cooked as you prefer. Do not overcook.

3. Drain well. Serve hot, topped with melted butter. Sprinkle with lemon juice, if desired.

SPRING-GARDEN MEDLEY

MAKES 6 SERVINGS

1¼ lb fresh asparagus
1 lb fresh peas, shelled
1 cup shredded lettuce
1 green onion, thinly sliced

2 teaspoons salt
⅛ teaspoon pepper
6 tablespoons butter or
    margarine

1. Break or cut off tough ends of asparagus stalks. Wash asparagus tips well with cold water; if necessary, use a soft brush to remove grit. With vegetable parer, scrape skin and scales from lower part of stalk only.

2. With sharp knife, thinly slice stalks on the diagonal. Combine all ingredients, except butter, in large bowl.

3. Cut 6 (6-inch) squares aluminum foil. Place about ⅔ cup vegetables in center of each square. Top each with 1 tablespoon butter. Wrap securely, using a drugstore or sandwich wrap.

4. Place 1 inch boiling water in bottom of a steamer. Arrange foil packages in basket. (You can improvise a steamer by using a large saucepan and, as a basket, a colander or strainer.)

5. Cover; steam 30 minutes. Serve, if desired, right in foil packages.

ASPARAGUS-ON-THE-BIAS

MAKES 6 TO 8 SERVINGS

2 pkg (10-oz size) thawed
    frozen whole
    asparagus spears

3 tablespoons salad oil
1 teaspoon salt

1. Slice asparagus on extreme diagonal (slices will be about ¼ inch thick).

2. Heat oil in large skillet. Add asparagus; cook, over high heat and stirring frequently, until tender-crisp—about 2 minutes. Add salt. Serve at once.

Kidney beans. Black beans. Green beans. Lima beans. White beans. How many beans do you know and use? Most of us are inclined to limit our bean cookery to baked beans and black-bean soup. Good as these are (and it's hard to think of anything better than baked beans with catsup and brown bread on a Saturday night, or bean soup, black as your hat, garnished with pale lemon slices), bean cookery offers many other tantalizing, hearty, and economical dishes. We include dried beans as well as fresh in this section.

BARBECUE BAKED BEANS

MAKES 8 SERVINGS

2 medium onions, coarsely chopped
1 clove garlic, finely chopped
2 tablespoons salad oil
4 cans (1-lb size) baked beans, undrained
¼ cup light molasses
½ cup catsup
1 cup grated sharp Cheddar cheese
½ cup packaged dry bread crumbs
2 tablespoons melted butter or margarine

1. Preheat oven to 350F.
2. In 2-quart top-stove casserole, sauté onion and garlic in hot salad oil until golden and tender—about 5 minutes.
3. Remove from heat. Stir in beans, molasses, and catsup.
4. In small bowl, toss together cheese, bread crumbs, and butter. Spoon over bean mixture.
5. Bake, uncovered, 30 minutes, or until mixture is bubbly and top is browned.

BARBECUED KIDNEY BEANS

MAKES 6 SERVINGS

2 cups dried kidney beans
¼ lb salt pork or bacon, chopped
¼ cup salad oil or melted shortening
1 cup chopped onion
1 clove garlic, finely chopped
1 can (1 lb, 3 oz) tomatoes, undrained
2 teaspoons dry mustard
2 tablespoons Worcestershire sauce
1½ teaspoons chili powder
2 teaspoons salt
¼ teaspoon pepper
¼ cup cider vinegar

1. Combine beans with water to cover; refrigerate, covered, overnight.
2. Next day, drain beans; turn into 6-quart kettle. Add salt pork with 3 cups cold water.
3. Bring to boiling; reduce heat, and simmer, covered, 1½ hours, or until beans are tender. Drain.
4. Meanwhile, preheat oven to 350F.
5. In Dutch oven, slowly heat salad oil. Add onion and garlic; cook, stirring, until tender—about 8 minutes.
6. Add drained beans, along with rest of ingredients and 1 cup water, to Dutch oven, mixing well.
7. Bake, uncovered, 45 minutes.

KIDNEY BEANS WITH CHEESE

MAKES 6 SERVINGS

3 bacon slices
1 cup coarsely chopped onion
2 cans (1-lb size) kidney beans, drained
1 can (1 lb, 3 oz) tomatoes, undrained
1½ teaspoons chili powder
1 teaspoon salt
Dash pepper
1 cup grated sharp Cheddar cheese

1. In large skillet, sauté bacon slices until crisp. Remove; drain on paper towels; crumble, and set aside.
2. Add onion to bacon drippings in skillet; cook, stirring occasionally, until tender—about 10 minutes.
3. Add beans, tomatoes, chili powder, salt, and pepper, mixing well. Cook, uncovered, over low heat, stirring occasionally, 20 minutes.
4. Stir in cheese; cook until cheese is melted.
5. To serve: Turn into serving dish. Sprinkle bacon over top.

BLACK BEANS WITH RUM

1 lb dried black beans
1 medium onion, sliced
1 bay leaf
*¼ teaspoon dried thyme
  leaves*
1 celery stalk, chopped
Few sprigs parsley
*¼ lb salt pork, cut in
  chunks*

*1 tablespoon butter or
  margarine*
1 tablespoon flour
1 tablespoon salt
*Dash liquid hot-pepper
  seasoning*
¼ cup dark rum
Dairy sour cream

1. Cover beans with cold water; refrigerate, covered, overnight.

2. Next day, drain. Turn into 6-quart kettle. Add onion, bay leaf, thyme, celery, parsley, salt pork, and 5 cups cold water.

3. Bring mixture to boiling point; reduce heat, and simmer, covered, about 2 to 2½ hours, or until beans are tender. Stir several times during cooking.

4. Drain beans; reserve liquid. Turn beans into 2-quart casserole.

5. Preheat oven to 350F.

6. Melt butter in small saucepan; remove from heat. Stir in flour, salt, hot-pepper seasoning, and 2 cups reserved bean liquid.

7. Cook, stirring and over low heat, until mixture bubbles. Stir in rum, and pour mixture over beans in casserole.

8. Bake, uncovered, 30 to 40 minutes. Serve topped with sour cream.

KIDNEY BEANS WITH CHILI

1 lb dried kidney beans
*¼ lb salt pork, cut into
  small pieces*
*3 cloves garlic, finely
  chopped*
*½ cup finely chopped
  onion*

*½ teaspoon dried oregano
  leaves*
Pinch ground cumin
*2 cans (10½-oz size)
  tomato purée*
2 tablespoons chili powder
1½ teaspoons salt
Dash pepper

1. Cover beans with cold water; refrigerate, covered, overnight.

2. Next day, drain. Turn into 6-quart kettle; cover with 5 cups cold water. Bring to boiling point. Reduce heat; simmer, covered, 1 hour. Drain thoroughly.

3. In medium saucepan, sauté salt pork until crisp on all sides. Add garlic and onion; sauté until golden—about 5 minutes.

4. Then stir in rest of ingredients, along with drained beans.

5. Simmer, covered and over very low heat, 1½ hours, or until beans are tender. Stir several times during cooking.

SPANISH BEAN CASSEROLE

MAKES 6 SERVINGS

1 pkg (1 lb) large dried
    lima beans
½ cup finely chopped
    carrot
1 cup finely chopped
    onion
1 cup finely chopped
    celery
2 cups finely chopped
    tomato
2 teaspoons salt

¼ teaspoon pepper
2 tablespoons butter or
    margarine
2 tablespoons salad oil
1 clove garlic, finely
    chopped
Pinch dried thyme leaves
1 teaspoon dry mustard
1 teaspoon paprika
2 tablespoons dry white
    wine

1. Cover beans with cold water; refrigerate, covered, overnight.

2. Next day, drain. Turn into large kettle. Add carrot, onion, celery, tomato, salt, pepper, and 3 cups cold water.

3. Bring to boiling point. Reduce heat; simmer, covered, 1 hour; stir frequently. Drain.

4. Meanwhile, preheat oven to 300F.

5. Turn bean mixture into 2-quart casserole. Stir in butter, salad oil, garlic, thyme, mustard, and paprika; bake, covered, 2 hours, or until beans are tender (stir several times during baking). Just before serving, stir in wine.

WHITE BEANS, COUNTRY STYLE

MAKES 6 SERVINGS

1 lb dried white beans
2 teaspoons salt
½ teaspoon pepper
1 clove garlic
1 bay leaf
6 tablespoons butter or
    margarine
2 medium onions, finely
    chopped

1 green pepper, finely
    chopped
3 peeled tomatoes, coarsely
    chopped
½ teaspoon dried oregano
    leaves
¼ cup finely chopped
    parsley

1. Cover beans with cold water; refrigerate, covered, overnight.

2. Next day, drain. Turn into 6-quart kettle; cover with 5 cups cold water. Add salt, pepper, garlic, and bay leaf.

3. Bring to boiling point. Reduce heat; simmer, covered, 2 hours, or until beans are tender. Stir several times during cooking. Drain.

4. Meanwhile, in 4 tablespoons hot butter in saucepan, sauté onion until golden—about 5 minutes.

5. Then add green pepper and tomato; cook 5 minutes. Stir in oregano and parsley.

6. Stir vegetable mixture and remaining butter into drained beans.

LENTILS WITH ONIONS

MAKES 4 TO 6 SERVINGS

2 cups lentils
1 tablespoon salt
½ cup butter or margarine
3 cups chopped onion
1 teaspoon curry powder
    (optional)

2 tablespoons chopped
    parsley
1 hard-cooked egg, finely
    chopped

1. Cover lentils with cold water; refrigerate, covered, overnight.

2. Next day, drain. Turn into large kettle; cover again with cold water, and add salt.

3. Bring to boiling point. Reduce heat; simmer, covered, about 2 hours, or until lentils are tender. Stir several times during cooking. Drain very well.

4. Meanwhile, in hot butter in large skillet, sauté onion until golden—about 5 minutes.

5. Stir in curry powder and lentils; cook, stirring and over low heat, until mixture appears dry. To serve: Sprinkle with parsley and egg.

BAKED LENTILS WITH HONEY

2 cups lentils
6 bacon slices, cut into
    small pieces
½ cup finely chopped
    onion
1 teaspoon salt

Dash pepper
¼ cup finely chopped
    chutney
1 teaspoon dry mustard
½ cup honey

1. Put lentils in large saucepan; add 4 cups cold water; bring to boiling point. Reduce heat; simmer, covered, 1 hour. Drain excess liquid.
2. Meanwhile, preheat oven to 325F.
3. Into lentils, stir bacon, onion, salt, pepper, chutney, mustard, and 1 cup water.
4. Turn into 2-quart shallow baking dish. Pour honey over top; bake, covered, 45 minutes.
5. Remove cover; bake 30 minutes more.

LIMA BEANS WITH SOUR CREAM

1 lb large dried lima beans
3 teaspoons salt
¼ cup butter or margarine
¾ cup finely chopped
    onion
½ lb fresh mushrooms,
    thinly sliced

1 tablespoon flour
1 tablespoon paprika
2 cups dairy sour cream
2 tablespoons chopped
    parsley

1. Cover beans with cold water; refrigerate, covered, overnight.
2. Next day, drain. Turn into large saucepan; cover with cold water; add 1 teaspoon salt.
3. Bring to boiling point. Reduce heat; simmer about 1½ hours, or until beans are tender, stirring several times during cooking. Drain well.
4. Meanwhile, in hot butter in large skillet, sauté onion until golden—about 5 minutes.
5. Add mushrooms; cook, stirring, 5 minutes. Then remove from heat.
6. Stir in flour and paprika until smooth. Return to heat; cook till bubbling—3 minutes.
7. Add drained beans, remaining salt, and sour cream; heat gently—do not boil. Before serving, sprinkle top with the chopped parsley.

NEW ENGLAND BAKED BEANS

3 cups dried navy or pea
    beans
½ lb sliced bacon
1 teaspoon salt
1 clove garlic, finely
    chopped

¼ cup light-brown sugar,
    firmly packed
2 teaspoons dry mustard
1 cup dark molasses
Boiling water

1. Cover beans with cold water; refrigerate, covered, overnight.
2. Next day, drain. Turn into 6-quart kettle; cover with 2 quarts cold water.
3. Bring to boiling point. Reduce heat; simmer, covered, 30 minutes. Drain thoroughly.
4. Preheat oven to 300F.
5. Cut bacon into chunks; put into 3-quart casserole or bean pot. Add beans; stir until well combined.
6. Mix remaining ingredients, except water; pour over bean mixture. Add about 1 cup boiling water—just enough to cover beans.
7. Bake, covered, 6 hours. (Stir once every hour, so beans cook evenly. If they seem dry after stirring, add a little more boiling water.)
8. To brown top of beans, remove cover 30 minutes before end of baking time.

GREEN BEANS LYONNAISE

1 lb fresh green beans, or
    1 pkg (10 oz) frozen
    French-style green
    beans
Boiling water
½ teaspoon salt
¼ cup butter or margarine
¼ cup chopped onion

2 tablespoons chopped
    parsley
¾ teaspoon salt
⅛ teaspoon pepper
Dash cloves
⅛ teaspoon nutmeg
Pimiento strips (optional)

1. Wash fresh beans; drain. Trim ends; cut lengthwise into slivers.
2. Place beans in medium saucepan; add boiling water to measure 1 inch and the salt. Cook, covered, 15 to 20 minutes, or until tender. (Cook frozen beans as package label directs.) Drain.
3. In hot butter in same pan, sauté onion until golden—about 5 minutes.
4. Add drained beans and rest of ingredients except pimiento strips. Reheat gently.
5. Turn beans into serving dish; top with pimiento strips.

GREEN BEANS WITH MUSHROOMS

2 pkg (10-oz size) frozen
    French-style green
    beans
2 tablespoons finely
    chopped onion
2 tablespoons olive or salad
    oil

3 pimientos, cut in strips
1 tablespoon finely
    chopped parsley
½ teaspoon salt
¼ teaspoon pepper
1 can (3 oz) sliced mushrooms, undrained

1. Cook beans as package label directs; drain.
2. In large skillet, sauté onion in hot oil until tender—about 3 minutes.
3. Add beans and remaining ingredients; heat thoroughly.

HERBED GREEN BEANS

1 lb fresh green beans, or 1
    pkg (10 oz) frozen
    French-style green
    beans
Boiling water
½ teaspoon salt
4 bacon slices, cut crosswise into ¼-inch pieces
¼ cup chopped onion

2 tablespoons chopped
    green pepper
2 tablespoons chopped
    parsley
⅛ teaspoon dried
    marjoram leaves
Dash dried rosemary leaves
¼ teaspoon monosodium
    glutamate
⅛ teaspoon pepper

1. Wash fresh beans; drain. Trim ends; cut lengthwise into slivers.
2. Place in medium saucepan; add boiling water to measure 1 inch and the salt. Cook, covered, 15 to 20 minutes, or until tender. (Cook frozen beans as package label directs.) Drain beans.
3. Meanwhile, in large skillet, sauté bacon until crisp. Remove; drain on paper towels. Crumble; set aside.
4. In bacon drippings in same skillet, cook onion and green pepper until tender—about 5 minutes.
5. Add drained beans along with parsley and seasonings to skillet, mixing well.
6. Cook, covered, over low heat, 5 minutes, stirring occasionally.
7. Turn into serving dish; sprinkle with bacon.

LIMA-BEAN CASSEROLE

1½ lb fresh lima beans,
    shelled; or 1 pkg (10
    oz) frozen lima beans
Salt
Boiling water
4 bacon slices, cut in 1-inch
    pieces
3 tablespoons chopped
    onion

¼ cup chopped celery
2 tablespoons chopped
    parsley
1 can (10½ oz) condensed
    tomato soup,
    undiluted
½ cup packaged dry bread
    crumbs

1. In medium saucepan, cover lima beans with lightly salted, boiling water to measure 1 inch. Cook, covered, about 20 minutes, or until beans are tender. (Cook frozen lima beans as package label directs.) Drain.
2. Meanwhile, preheat oven to 350F. Lightly grease 1-quart casserole.
3. Partially cook bacon in small skillet. Remove; drain on paper towels; set aside.
4. To bacon drippings in skillet, add onion, celery, and parsley; cook, stirring occasionally, until vegetables are tender—about 5 minutes.
5. Turn drained beans into prepared casserole. Add onion, celery, parsley, tomato soup, and ¼ cup bread crumbs, mixing well.
6. Sprinkle remaining bread crumbs and bacon over top. Bake, uncovered, 30 minutes.

Beets

BEETS IN ORANGE-AND-LEMON SAUCE

2 lb beets
½ cup orange juice
½ cup lemon juice
2 tablespoons cider vinegar
1½ tablespoons cornstarch
2 tablespoons sugar

1 teaspoon salt
¼ cup butter or margarine
1 teaspoon grated orange
    peel
1 teaspoon grated lemon
    peel

1. Gently wash beets, leaving skins intact; remove leaves.
2. Place beets in large saucepan; cover with cold water; bring to boiling. Reduce heat; simmer, covered, 45 minutes, or until tender.
3. Drain; cool. Peel; cut into ¼-inch slices.
4. In the same saucepan, combine orange and lemon juices, vinegar, and cornstarch; stir until smooth. Bring to boiling, stirring; mixture will be thickened and translucent.
5. Add sugar, salt, and beets; cook gently, uncovered, 10 minutes, or until heated through.
6. Stir in butter and orange and lemon peels.

HARVARD BEETS

3 lb beets
¼ cup butter or margarine
3 tablespoons sugar
2 tablespoons cornstarch
¾ cup cider vinegar

1 teaspoon Worcestershire
    sauce
½ teaspoon salt
¼ teaspoon crushed garlic
⅛ teaspoon pepper

1. Gently wash beets, leaving skin intact; remove leaves.
2. Place beets in large saucepan; cover with cold water; bring to boiling. Reduce heat; simmer, covered, 45 minutes, or until tender.
3. Drain; let cool. Peel; cut into ⅓-inch cubes.
4. In same saucepan, melt butter over medium heat. Add sugar and cornstarch; cook, stirring, ½ minute. Remove from heat.
5. Slowly stir in vinegar and ¼ cup water. Add rest of ingredients, except beets; bring to boiling, stirring constantly. Reduce heat.
6. Add beets; heat 10 minutes; stir occasionally.

Broccoli

BROCCOLI AMANDINE

MAKES 8 SERVINGS

2 pkg (10-oz size) frozen
    broccoli spears
½ cup butter or margarine
3 tablespoons lemon juice

½ teaspoon salt
½ cup slivered blanched
    almonds

1. Cook broccoli as package label directs.
2. Meanwhile, melt butter in small saucepan. Add rest of ingredients; simmer, stirring occasionally, 5 minutes.
3. Drain broccoli; arrange in serving dish; top with the sauce.

BROCCOLI WITH PIMIENTO

MAKES 4 SERVINGS

1 bunch broccoli (about
    2 lb)
Boiling water
2 tablespoons butter or
    margarine
½ cup sliced green onions,
    with tops

2 canned pimientos,
    drained and chopped
1 teaspoon grated lemon
    peel
2 tablespoons lemon juice
1 teaspoon salt
⅛ teaspoon pepper

1. Remove from broccoli and discard large leaves and tough portions of stalks. Wash broccoli thoroughly; drain. Split each stalk lengthwise into halves (or quarters, depending on size). Make gashes, lengthwise, along stalks.
2. Place broccoli in medium saucepan. Add boiling water to measure 1 inch; cook, covered, 10 minutes, or until stalks are tender.
3. Meanwhile, in hot butter in small skillet, cook onions until tender—about 5 minutes.
4. Remove from heat; stir in remaining ingredients.
5. Drain broccoli; arrange in serving dish. Pour pimiento mixture over top.

Brussels Sprouts

BAKED BRUSSELS SPROUTS AU GRATIN

MAKES 6 SERVINGS

1 cup boiling water
1 teaspoon salt
2 pkg (10-oz size) frozen
    brussels sprouts
½ cup process sharp-cheese
    spread

¼ cup butter or margarine
¼ cup packaged dry bread
    crumbs
⅓ cup chopped walnuts

1. Preheat oven to 400F.
2. In boiling, salted water in 1½-quart saucepan, simmer brussels sprouts, covered, 4 to 5 minutes, or until fork-tender.
3. Drain; turn into greased 1½-quart casserole. Dot with cheese spread.
4. Melt butter in small skillet. Add bread crumbs and walnuts; cook, stirring, until lightly browned.
5. Sprinkle over brussels sprouts; bake 10 minutes.

SAVORY BRUSSELS SPROUTS

2 pkg (10-oz size) frozen
    brussels sprouts
2 tablespoons butter or
    margarine
½ cup crushed* bite-size
    shredded-wheat
    biscuits
½ teaspoon seasoned salt
¼ cup wine vinegar

1. Cook brussels sprouts as package label directs, just until tender. Drain thoroughly.
2. Meanwhile, heat butter in small skillet. Add crushed biscuits and seasoned salt; sauté, stirring, 3 minutes.
3. Turn sprouts into serving dish. Pour vinegar over them. Then sprinkle with sautéed crushed biscuits.
* To crush: Place biscuits between 2 sheets of waxed paper; roll with rolling pin.

Cabbage

BRAISED CABBAGE

3 bacon slices
2 qt (2 lb) finely
    shredded cabbage
1½ teaspoons salt
Dash pepper
3 tablespoons white-wine
    vinegar

1. In 12-inch skillet, sauté bacon over low heat until crisp. Remove; drain on paper towels; crumble.
2. In skillet, toss bacon fat with cabbage, salt, pepper, and vinegar; coat cabbage well.
3. Cook, covered and over high heat, about 3 minutes, or until cabbage is tender. Sprinkle with bacon.

CARAWAY RED CABBAGE

¼ cup butter or margarine
½ cup chopped onion
2 qt (2 lb) shredded red
    cabbage
½ cup sugar
1 tablespoon lemon juice
½ cup cider vinegar
1 tablespoon salt
¼ teaspoon pepper
¼ teaspoon caraway seed

1. In hot butter in large skillet, sauté onion until golden—about 5 minutes.
2. Add remaining ingredients, mixing well. Cook, covered, over medium heat, about 20 minutes, or until cabbage is tender.

RED CABBAGE AND APPLES

2 tablespoons butter or
    margarine
2 qt (2 lb) shredded
    red cabbage
2 tablespoons dark molasses
2 tart cooking apples,
    peeled and sliced
2 tablespoons chopped
    onion
3 tablespoons lemon juice
¼ cup dry red wine
1½ teaspoons salt

1. Melt butter in Dutch oven or heavy kettle. Add cabbage and molasses; cook, over medium heat, stirring constantly, until cabbage is limp —about 5 minutes.
2. Add remaining ingredients; simmer, covered, 1½ hours, stirring occasionally.

PENNSYLVANIA PEPPER CABBAGE

1 small head green cabbage
 (1¼ lb)
1 medium green pepper,
 cut into very thin
 strips (¾ cup)

Salt
1 egg, beaten
1 tablespoon sugar
Dash pepper
¼ cup cider vinegar

1. Grate cabbage on medium grater, or slice fine with long, sharp knife. (Grated cabbage should measure about 7 cups, packed.)
2. In 3-quart saucepan, toss cabbage with green pepper; sprinkle lightly with salt.
3. Over very low heat, steam vegetables, covered, 15 to 18 minutes, or until tender.
4. In small bowl, combine egg, 1 teaspoon salt, and rest of ingredients; beat well.
5. Add to hot cabbage, tossing with fork until well combined.
6. Heat slowly 5 minutes, stirring.

SAUERKRAUT WITH APPLES

2 tablespoons butter or
 margarine
3 tablespoons chopped
 onion
2 cans (1-lb size) sauerkraut
 (1 qt), drained
2 cups pared, sliced tart
 cooking apples

1 can (10½ oz) condensed
 beef bouillon,
 undiluted
2 tablespoons vinegar
1 tablespoon flour
½ cup grated raw potato
⅛ teaspoon caraway seed

1. In hot butter in large skillet, sauté onion until golden—about 3 minutes.
2. Add sauerkraut, apples, bouillon, and vinegar; simmer, uncovered, 15 minutes.
3. Mix flour with 2 tablespoons water until smooth. Stir into sauerkraut, along with potato and caraway seed.
4. Cook, over medium heat and stirring, 5 minutes, or until slightly thickened.

Carrots

CARROTS IN MUSTARD GLAZE

3 lb carrots
Boiling water
¼ cup butter or margarine
½ cup light-brown sugar,
 firmly packed

¼ cup prepared mustard
2 tablespoons chopped
 chives, mint, or
 parsley

1. Wash carrots; pare; cut diagonally into 1-inch slices.
2. Place in large saucepan. Add boiling water to measure 1 inch; simmer, covered, 20 minutes, or until tender. Drain, if necessary (most of liquid will be evaporated).
3. Meanwhile, in small saucepan, combine butter, sugar, and mustard. Cook, stirring, until butter melts and sugar is dissolved; continue cooking 3 minutes.
4. Pour mixture over carrots, tossing gently to combine. Heat several minutes, and then add chopped chives.

CARROT-AND-CELERY CASSEROLE

MAKES 4 TO 6 SERVINGS

3 cups diagonally sliced
    pared carrots (½ inch
    thick)
2 cups diagonally sliced
    celery (¼ inch thick)
¼ cup butter or margarine,
    melted

1 teaspoon sugar
1 teaspoon salt
⅛ teaspoon pepper
1 tablespoon chopped
    parsley

1. Preheat oven to 350F.
2. Combine carrots and celery in lightly greased 1½-quart casserole. Add 2 tablespoons butter, the sugar, salt, pepper, and ¼ cup water; mix well.
3. Bake, covered, 45 minutes, or until vegetables are tender.
4. Drain off any liquid. Add rest of butter; toss. Sprinkle with parsley.

BUTTERY GRATED CARROTS

MAKES 4 TO 6 SERVINGS

2 lb carrots
1 tablespoon salad oil
¼ teaspoon finely chopped
    garlic

½ teaspoon salt
⅛ teaspoon pepper
¼ cup butter

1. Pare carrots; grate on medium grater into large skillet with tight-fitting cover.
2. Toss with oil, garlic, salt, pepper, and 2 tablespoons water. Cook, covered, over medium heat, stirring occasionally, 10 to 12 minutes, or until tender.
3. Remove from heat. Toss lightly with butter until carrots are coated.

BUTTERY GRATED TURNIPS

MAKES 4 TO 6 SERVINGS

1. Use 3 lb white turnips instead of carrots. Proceed as above, but cook turnips 15 minutes, or until tender.
2. Then, to evaporate liquid, cook, uncovered, over very low heat, 5 minutes.
3. Remove from heat. Toss with the butter, 2 tablespoons lemon juice, ¼ cup chopped parsley until turnips are coated.

BUTTERY GRATED BEETS

MAKES 4 TO 6 SERVINGS

1. Use 2 lb beets instead of carrots. Proceed as above, but cook beets 20 minutes, or until tender.
2. Remove from heat. Toss lightly with butter and 2 tablespoons lemon juice until beets are coated.

Cauliflower

CAULIFLOWER, ITALIAN STYLE

1 head cauliflower
    (1¾ lb)
Salt
Boiling water
3 tablespoons olive or salad
    oil
1 clove garlic

½ teaspoon salt
1 cup chopped, peeled
    tomato
¼ cup grated Parmesan
    cheese
1 tablespoon chopped
    parsley

MAKES 4 SERVINGS

1. Wash cauliflower thoroughly; cut into flowerets. Cook, covered, in 1 inch lightly salted, boiling water until tender—about 10 minutes. Drain well.
2. Slowly heat oil in large, heavy skillet. Add garlic; sauté until golden—about 3 minutes. Remove garlic, and discard.
3. In same skillet, combine cauliflower, salt, and tomato. Cook, stirring, about 3 minutes, or until vegetables are hot.
4. Turn into serving dish; sprinkle with cheese and parsley.

CAULIFLOWER WITH LEMON BUTTER

1 head cauliflower
    (1¾ lb)
Salt
Boiling water
¼ cup butter or margarine,
    melted
⅓ cup lemon juice

3 tablespoons bottled
    capers, drained
1 tablespoon chopped
    parsley
1 tablespoon chopped
    chives (optional)

MAKES 4 SERVINGS

1. Wash cauliflower thoroughly; cut into flowerets. Cook, covered, in 1 inch lightly salted, boiling water, until tender—about 10 minutes. Drain well.
2. Meanwhile, combine butter, lemon juice, and capers.
3. Turn cauliflower into serving dish; pour lemon butter over top. Sprinkle with parsley and chives.

Celery

BRAISED CELERY AND MUSHROOMS

1 lb fresh mushrooms
4 cups sliced celery (sliced
    diagonally 1 to 1½
    inches thick)
¾ cup Burgundy
1 beef-bouillon cube,
    crumbled

¼ cup lemon juice
¼ cup butter or margarine,
    melted
1 teaspoon salt
¼ teaspoon pepper
1 tablespoon finely chopped
    parsley

MAKES 4 TO 6 SERVINGS

1. Preheat oven to 350F.
2. Wash mushrooms; then remove stems.
3. In lightly greased 2-quart casserole, layer half the mushrooms. Cover with celery; top with rest of mushrooms.
4. Pour Burgundy over all; sprinkle with bouillon cube, lemon juice, butter, salt, and pepper.
5. Bake, covered, 1 hour, or until vegetables are tender. Before serving, sprinkle with parsley.

The Indians loved it. The Pilgrims loved it. Everybody loves it. Plump, tender corn, well buttered, salted, and peppered, is, without a doubt, a favorite American vegetable. Boil it, roast it, scrape it, eat it straight, or combine it with other foods. Only, get it from garden to pot as rapidly as possible, to preserve that heavenly, heart-of-summer taste.

CORN CUSTARD

MAKES 6 TO 8 SERVINGS

3 tablespoons butter or
    margarine
3 tablespoons flour
1 teaspoon salt
Dash pepper
1 tablespoon sugar
½ cup light cream

¾ cup milk
1 can (12 oz) whole-kernel
    corn, drained
1 cup cream-style corn,
    undrained
3 eggs, well beaten

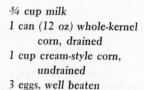

1. Preheat oven to 350F. Lightly grease 1-quart casserole.
2. Melt butter in medium saucepan; remove from heat.
3. Stir in flour, salt, pepper, and sugar until smooth; blend in cream and milk. Cook, stirring, over medium heat, until mixture boils and is thickened and smooth.
4. Stir corn into sauce until well combined; then thoroughly blend in eggs.
5. Turn mixture into prepared casserole; set in pan containing 2 inches of hot water. Bake, uncovered, 1 hour and 30 minutes, or until silver knife inserted in center comes out clean.

CORN OFF THE COB

MAKES 6 SERVINGS

4 cups fresh corn kernels,
    cut from cob
1 cup heavy cream
1 teaspoon sugar

½ teaspoon salt
Dash pepper
¼ cup butter or margarine

1. Combine all ingredients in medium saucepan.
2. Simmer, covered, 10 minutes.

CORN OYSTERS

MAKES 4 TO 6 SERVINGS

½ cup sifted all-purpose
    flour
1 teaspoon salt
¼ teaspoon monosodium
    glutamate

2 cups fresh corn kernels,
    cut from cob
2 eggs, separated
⅓ cup salad oil

1. Sift dry ingredients into large bowl. Combine corn kernels and egg yolks, and blend into flour mixture.
2. With rotary beater, beat egg whites until stiff but not dry; fold gently into corn mixture.
3. Heat oil in heavy skillet. Drop batter by tablespoonfuls into hot oil. Fry until golden-brown; then turn, and fry on other side—about 5 minutes in all.

ROAST CORN

1. Preheat oven to 400F.
2. Dot husked ears of corn with butter; sprinkle with salt, pepper, and seasoned salt.
3. Wrap each ear in foil. Roast about 30 minutes, or until tender.

FRESH CORN MEXICANA

MAKES 6 SERVINGS

3 tablespoons butter or
    margarine
¼ cup chopped onion
¼ cup chopped green
    pepper
3 cups fresh corn kernels,
    cut from cob

1 teaspoon salt
⅛ teaspoon pepper
2 tablespoons chopped
    pimiento
4 slices crisp-cooked
    bacon, crumbled

1. Melt butter in medium skillet with cover; in it, sauté the onion and green pepper until tender—about 5 minutes.

2. Add corn, ⅓ cup water, seasonings, and pimiento.

3. Cover, and cook 10 minutes, over low heat, stirring several times. Serve hot, with bacon.

Cucumbers

CUCUMBERS WITH PARSLEY SAUCE

MAKES 4 TO 6 SERVINGS

3 pared cucumbers, sliced
    1 inch thick (4 cups)
Boiling water
1 tablespoon butter or
    margarine
2 tablespoons finely
    chopped onion

2 tablespoons flour
1½ teaspoons salt
⅛ teaspoon pepper
1½ cups milk
1 egg, beaten
2 tablespoons finely
    chopped parsley

1. Cook cucumbers, covered, in 1 inch boiling water 10 minutes; drain well.

2. Meanwhile, in hot butter in medium skillet, sauté onion until golden—about 5 minutes.

3. Remove from heat. Add flour, salt, and pepper, stirring until smooth. Gradually stir in milk; bring to boiling, stirring till thickened.

4. Stir small amount of hot sauce into egg; then pour back into skillet. Add cucumbers.

5. Over low heat, bring cucumbers and sauce just to boiling, stirring. Sprinkle with parsley.

FRIED CUCUMBERS

MAKES 6 SERVINGS

1½ lb cucumbers
2 eggs
2 teaspoons salt
¼ teaspoon pepper

1 teaspoon prepared
    horseradish
½ cup packaged dry bread
    crumbs
½ cup butter or margarine

1. Pare cucumbers; slice ¼ inch thick.

2. Beat eggs with salt, pepper, and horseradish in small bowl. Dip cucumber slices in egg mixture, then in crumbs, coating well.

3. Meanwhile, heat butter in large skillet. Fry slices, a few at a time, until golden—about 2 minutes on each side.

4. Drain on paper towels; keep warm while frying rest.

Eggplant

PERFECT FRIED EGGPLANT

MAKES 4 SERVINGS

2 eggs, beaten
1 teaspoon salt
Dash pepper
1 cup packaged dry bread
    crumbs

2 tablespoons grated
    Parmesan cheese
1 medium eggplant
    (about 1 lb)
Salad oil or shortening for
    frying

1. In shallow dish, mix eggs, salt, and pepper.

2. Combine crumbs and cheese on waxed paper.

3. Cut unpeeled eggplant, crosswise, into ⅛-inch-thick slices. Dip in egg, then in crumb mixture, coating completely.

4. Meanwhile, in large, heavy skillet, slowly heat salad oil (at least ¼ inch).

5. Sauté eggplant until golden-brown—about 3 minutes on each side. Drain on paper towels.

EGGPLANT-AND-TOMATO CASSEROLE

2 medium eggplants
Boiling water
Salt
¼ cup salad oil
2 cloves garlic, finely
    chopped
2 tablespoons flour
2 cans (1-lb size) stewed
    tomatoes, undrained

2 teaspoons sugar
1 teaspoon paprika
⅛ teaspoon pepper
⅛ teaspoon dried basil
    leaves
½ cup grated
    Parmesan cheese

MAKES 6 TO 8 SERVINGS

1. Preheat oven to 375F. Lightly grease 2-quart casserole.
2. Wash and peel eggplants; cut into 2-inch cubes. Simmer, covered, in small amount of boiling, salted water 10 minutes; drain.
3. Meanwhile, in hot oil in skillet, sauté garlic until golden—3 minutes. Remove from heat.
4. Into skillet, stir flour, tomatoes, 2 teaspoons salt, sugar, paprika, pepper, and basil. Cook, stirring, over medium heat until mixture boils and is slightly thickened.
5. In prepared casserole, layer eggplant cubes alternately with tomato mixture; top with grated cheese.
6. Bake 20 minutes until lightly browned.

The Greeks called mushrooms food of the gods, and the Roman poets sang of their exquisite flavor. But it was a dictator, Julius Caesar, who thought common man so unworthy of this fragile fungus that he restricted its sale to the aristocracy.

Now cooks all over the world sing mushrooms' praises, and happily for all of us, mushrooms—fresh, canned, or dried—are available to everybody everywhere the year round.

Before you delve into these delicious mushroom recipes, we think it would be helpful for you to know these facts:
Fresh mushrooms should always be refrigerated and used within two or three days of purchase.
You don't need to peel fresh mushrooms. Just snip off tips of stems.

Use both caps and stems in cooking unless recipe calls for caps only—in which case, save stems for use in other cooking.
To clean fresh mushrooms: Wipe with a damp cloth, or wash quickly in cold water. Drain thoroughly.
Slight discolorations due to oxidation do not affect flavor.

BAKED MUSHROOMS IN CREAM

1½ lb fresh mushrooms
½ teaspoon salt
Dash pepper

2 tablespoons butter or
    margarine
⅔ cup heavy cream

MAKES 6 SERVINGS

1. Preheat oven to 425F. Lightly grease a shallow baking dish.
2. Wash mushrooms; remove ends of stems. Arrange in prepared baking dish.
3. Sprinkle mushrooms with salt and pepper; dot with butter. Pour cream over all.
4. Bake, uncovered, 10 minutes. Serve over toast.

MUSHROOMS IN SOUR CREAM

3 tablespoons butter or
   margarine
1 cup chopped onion
1¼ lb fresh mushrooms,
   sliced ¼ inch thick

1 teaspoon salt
1 teaspoon paprika
½ teaspoon pepper
¼ cup chopped parsley
1 cup dairy sour cream

1. In hot butter in medium skillet, sauté onion until golden—about 5 minutes.

2. Add mushrooms and ½ cup water; simmer, covered (adding more water, if necessary), until mushrooms are tender—about 15 minutes.

3. Add salt, paprika, pepper, 2 tablespoons parsley, and the sour cream. Heat very slowly, stirring, until thoroughly hot. Before serving, sprinkle with rest of parsley.

SAVORY STUFFED MUSHROOMS

12 to 16 fresh medium
   mushrooms
½ cup butter or margarine
3 tablespoons finely
   chopped green
   pepper

3 tablespoons finely
   chopped onion
1½ cups fresh-bread cubes
   (¼ inch)
½ teaspoon salt
⅛ teaspoon pepper
Dash cayenne

1. Preheat oven to 350F.

2. Wipe mushrooms with damp cloth. Remove stems, and chop stems fine; set aside.

3. Heat 3 tablespoons butter in large skillet. Sauté mushroom caps only on bottom side 2 to 3 minutes; remove. Arrange, rounded side down, in shallow baking pan.

4. Heat rest of butter in same skillet. Sauté chopped stems, green pepper, and onion until tender—about 5 minutes.

5. Remove from heat. Stir in bread cubes and seasoning. Use to fill mushroom caps, mounding mixture high in center.

6. Bake 15 minutes.

Okra

OKRA AND TOMATOES

1 pkg (10 oz) frozen okra,
   thawed
1 cup chopped onion
2½ cups cubed, peeled
   tomatoes

2 tablespoons butter or
   margarine
2 teaspoons salt
Dash pepper

1. Cut okra crosswise into ½-inch pieces.

2. In medium saucepan, combine okra with remaining ingredients.

3. Cook, covered and over low heat, stirring occasionally, 10 to 15 minutes, or until vegetables are tender.

I t would be difficult to imagine any vegetable that would be missed more than the onion and its family if suddenly they were withdrawn from our markets. As a flavoring agent in stews, soups, salads, meat and fish dishes, as an accompaniment to meats, even as a main dish in some cases, the onion has no peer.

BAKED STUFFED ONIONS

MAKES 6 SERVINGS

6 large yellow onions,
    peeled (about 4 lb)
1½ teaspoons salt
1 can (3 oz) chopped
    mushrooms, drained
    and finely chopped
½ cup fine fresh-white-
    bread crumbs
¼ cup cooked crumbled
    bacon

⅛ teaspoon pepper
2 teaspoons dried thyme
    leaves
2 tablespoons butter or
    margarine, melted
1 cup grated sharp Cheddar
    cheese (¼ lb)
3 tablespoons chopped
    parsley

1. In large saucepan, place onions, ½ teaspoon salt, and enough cold water to cover; bring to boiling.

2. Reduce heat; simmer, covered, 30 minutes, or until onions are tender. Drain, and let cool.

3. With spoon, scoop out center of onions, leaving several outside layers as a shell. Chop scooped-out onion very fine; measure 2 cups.

4. Preheat oven to 400F.

5. In medium bowl, combine 2 cups chopped onion, the mushrooms, bread crumbs, bacon, remaining salt, pepper, thyme, and butter; toss to mix well. Add ½ cup cheese and 2 tablespoons parsley, mixing well. Use to fill onion shells, mounding high.

6. Place onions in shallow baking dish; pour ½ cup water around them; bake 20 minutes.

7. Sprinkle with rest of cheese; bake 10 minutes longer. Serve sprinkled with rest of parsley.

COMPANY CREAMED ONIONS

MAKES 6 SERVINGS

2 cans (15½-oz size) small
    white onions
2 tablespoons butter or
    margarine
2 tablespoons flour
1¼ cups milk

½ teaspoon salt
¼ teaspoon mace
Dash pepper
2 tablespoons packaged dry
    bread crumbs

1. Drain onions, reserving ½ cup liquid.

2. Melt butter in medium saucepan; remove from heat. Stir in flour until smooth.

3. Gradually add reserved onion liquid and milk; bring mixture to boiling point, stirring; boil gently 1 minute.

4. Add onions, salt, mace, and pepper; heat thoroughly; turn into 1-quart casserole.

5. Sprinkle with bread crumbs, and run under broiler about 2 minutes, just to brown the top.

FRIED ONIONS, SWISS STYLE

MAKES 6 SERVINGS

¼ cup butter or margarine
8 medium onions, peeled
    and thinly sliced
    (1¾ lb)

⅛ teaspoon salt

1. Slowly melt butter in large skillet. Add onion slices and salt.

2. Cook, over low heat, stirring occasionally, until onions are nicely browned about 35 minutes. Delicious with steak, liver, chops, or hamburgers.

FRIED ONION RINGS

1 large Bermuda onion
  (¾ lb)

Batter:
1 cup sifted all-purpose
  flour
2 teaspoons salt
1½ teaspoons baking
  powder

1 egg yolk
⅔ cup milk
1 tablespoon salad oil
1 egg white

Shortening or oil for deep-
  fat frying

1. Peel onion; slice about ¼ inch thick; sep-arate into rings. Cover with cold water, and let stand 30 minutes. Drain, and spread out on paper towels.

2. Meanwhile, make Batter: Sift flour, salt, and baking powder into medium bowl; set aside.

3. Beat egg yolk slightly in bowl; then stir in milk and salad oil. Add to flour mixture, stir-ring until smooth.

4. Beat egg white until soft peaks form. Fold into batter.

5. Heat 1 inch of melted shortening in sauce-pan or skillet to 375F on deep-frying thermom-eter.

6. Dip onion rings in batter (let excess batter drip into bowl); drop several rings at a time into hot fat, and fry until golden. Drain on pa-per towels. Keep warm while frying rest.

F resh out of the garden, the freezer, the can, sweet, tender peas give you their delicate taste, their nutritive virtues, their staccato color. No wonder, each year, more and more people love them more and more!

FRESH PEAS OREGANO

¼ cup butter or margarine
2 lb fresh peas, shelled; or
  1 pkg (10 oz) frozen
  peas
½ teaspoon salt
1 tablespoon lemon juice

1 tablespoon dried onion
  flakes
½ teaspoon dried oregano
  leaves
½ teaspoon monosodium
  glutamate

1. Slowly melt butter in medium skillet. Add remaining ingredients.

2. Cook, covered and over medium heat, 10 to 15 minutes, or until just tender.

MINTED PEAS AND CARROTS

1 lb carrots, pared
½ teaspoon salt
1 pkg (10 oz) frozen peas
1 tablespoon chopped fresh
  mint leaves

1 teaspoon sugar
1½ tablespoons butter or
  margarine, melted

1. Slice carrots ½ inch thick, on diagonal. In 1 inch boiling water, in medium saucepan, cook carrots with salt, covered, 10 to 15 minutes, or until fork-tender.

2. Also, cook peas as package label directs.

3. Meanwhile, combine mint and sugar in small bowl, stirring to coat mint well.

4. Drain carrots and peas; toss lightly with mint mixture and butter until well combined. Serve hot.

PEAS À LA FRANÇAIS

3 to 6 lettuce leaves*
2 lb fresh peas, shelled
1 teaspoon sugar
½ teaspoon salt

⅛ teaspoon pepper
2 tablespoons butter or
    margarine

1. Line medium skillet with lettuce leaves. Add peas, sugar, salt, and pepper; dot with butter.

2. Cook, tightly covered and over medium heat, 10 to 15 minutes, or just until peas are tender.

* Two tablespoons water may be substituted for lettuce leaves. Proceed as directed.

PEAS WITH BACON

2 bacon slices, diced
¼ teaspoon salt

2 lb fresh peas, shelled; or
    1 pkg (10 oz) frozen
    peas

1. In medium skillet, over low heat, sauté bacon until crisp. Remove skillet from heat.

2. Add salt and peas; cook, covered and over medium heat, 10 to 15 minutes, or until peas are just tender.

PEAS WITH GREEN ONIONS

2 tablespoons butter or
    margarine
½ cup sliced green onions
⅛ teaspoon pepper

2 lb fresh peas, shelled; or
    1 pkg (10 oz) frozen
    peas
½ teaspoon salt

1. Slowly melt butter in medium skillet. Add remaining ingredients.

2. Cook, covered and over medium heat, 10 to 15 minutes, or until peas are just tender.

A native American, the sweet green pepper is popularly known as the bell pepper. Peppers are green at first, changing to red as they ripen, except for one variety that turns bright yellow. They are delicious and picturesque either raw or cooked. Hot peppers, such as the long red cayenne, are used, fresh or dried, for sauces and for pickling. They should be used cautiously.

GREEN-PEPPER RINGS

2 lb green peppers (about
    6 medium), cut into
    ¼-inch rings

3 tablespoons salad oil
½ teaspoon garlic salt
½ teaspoon salt

1. Remove ribs from pepper rings.

2. Heat oil in large skillet. Add pepper rings; cook, over high heat and stirring frequently, until tender-crisp—about 5 minutes.

3. Sprinkle with garlic salt and salt. Serve at once.

QUICK STUFFED PEPPERS

2 large green peppers
(about 1 lb)
¾ teaspoon salt
1 tablespoon butter
or margarine
1 can (3 oz) sliced
mushrooms, drained

1 can (10½ oz)
condensed tomato
soup, undiluted
1 can (15 oz) Spanish
rice
¼ cup dairy sour
cream

1. Preheat oven to 350F.
2. Cut peppers in half, crosswise; remove ribs and seeds. Trim thin slice from base of each.
3. In medium saucepan, bring 2 cups water to boiling. Add peppers and salt; simmer, covered, 8 to 10 minutes, or until peppers are just tender. Drain.
4. Meanwhile, in hot butter in small skillet, sauté mushrooms 3 minutes. Gradually add tomato soup, mixing well. Bring to boiling, stirring constantly. Remove from heat.
5. Fill pepper halves with Spanish rice. Arrange in 1½-quart shallow baking dish. Pour tomato-soup mixture around peppers.
6. Bake, uncovered, 15 minutes. Top each pepper half with 1 tablespoon sour cream.

ROASTED PEPPERS

8 medium-size sweet red
peppers (about
2½ lb)
1 cup olive or salad oil

¼ cup lemon juice
2 teaspoons salt
1 small clove garlic

1. Preheat oven to 450F.
2. Wash and drain peppers well.
3. Place peppers on baking sheet. Bake about 20 minutes, turning every 5 minutes with tongs, or until skin of peppers becomes blistered and charred.
4. Place hot peppers in large kettle; cover. Let stand 15 minutes.
5. With sharp knife, peel off charred skin. Cut each pepper into fourths.
6. Remove ribs and seeds; cut out any dark spots. Wash and drain peppers well.
7. In large bowl, combine olive oil, lemon juice, salt, and garlic. Add pepper strips; toss lightly to coat peppers.
8. Pack mixture into 1-quart jar; cap. Refrigerate several hours or overnight. Serve as an appetizer or in a tossed salad.

EASY PEPPER RELISH

2 cups coarsely chopped
red peppers (1 lb)
2 cups coarsely chopped
green peppers (1 lb)
1 small clove garlic, slivered
1 cup white vinegar

½ cup salad oil
¼ cup sugar
1½ teaspoons salt
¼ teaspoon pepper
1 teaspoon dried basil
leaves

1. In large bowl, combine red and green peppers with rest of ingredients; mix well.
2. Pack mixture into quart jar.
3. Refrigerate several hours or overnight. Nice with cold meats and hamburgers.

Underground vegetables, roots and tubers, bring you rich, solid nourishment long after the green and leafy things of summer have waned. Among them, none is more beloved, none more popular than the potato.

Baked Potatoes

To bake potatoes perfectly: Scrub skin; dry thoroughly; prick skin with fork, to let steam escape during cooking. Then put in a 425F preheated oven, and bake 50 to 60 minutes. You can tell they're done when they are easily pierced with a fork or feel soft when squeezed gently. If you don't like a hard skin, oil potatoes before placing in oven—this keeps skin soft and tender.

As soon as potatoes are baked, slash top in an X; then gently squeeze, so steam can escape and potatoes fluff up.

The traditional way to serve baked potatoes

is to add a chunk of butter with salt, pepper, and paprika. However, we suggest that you try these good variations:

Baked Potatoes with Sour Cream: Spoon about 1 tablespoon sour cream on each potato. Sprinkle with chopped chives or parsley or finely chopped green onions.

Cheesed Baked Potatoes: Sprinkle grated Parmesan cheese on each potato. Then, if you like, run them under the broiler for just a second or so.

Baked Potatoes with Bacon: Crumble crisp-cooked bacon on each potato.

DILLED NEW POTATOES

1 lb small new potatoes, pared	½ teaspoon paprika
	¼ teaspoon salt
Boiling water	1 tablespoon snipped fresh
3 tablespoons butter or margarine, melted	dill, or 1 teaspoon dried dill

1. Cook potatoes in 1 inch boiling water in medium saucepan, covered, 10 minutes. Drain.
2. Turn potatoes into shallow baking pan. Brush well with 2 tablespoons butter; sprinkle all over with paprika and salt.
3. Broil, 6 inches below heat, turning frequently, 10 to 15 minutes, or until fork-tender. Potatoes should have a golden outer crust.
4. Add dill to rest of butter; roll potatoes in mixture, coating well.

FLUFFY MASHED POTATOES

8 medium potatoes (about 2½ lb)	1 tablespoon salt
	1 cup milk
Boiling water	¼ cup butter or margarine

1. Pare potatoes; cut in quarters. Cook in 1 inch boiling water with salt, covered, until tender—20 minutes. Drain well; set aside.
2. In saucepan, heat milk and butter until butter melts—don't let milk boil.
3. Mash potatoes smoothly. Gradually beat in hot milk mixture until potatoes are smooth, light, and fluffy.

Mashed Pimiento Potatoes: Fold in 1 can (4 oz) pimientos, drained and coarsely chopped.

FRENCH-FRIED POTATOES

(SINGLE-FRYING METHOD)

1.   Pare as many Idaho potatoes as desired. Cut lengthwise into ⅜-inch-thick slices. Then cut slices lengthwise into strips ⅜ inch wide. Rinse in cold water; drain well on paper towels.

2.   Meanwhile, heat salad oil or shortening in deep-fat fryer* (filling at least one third full) to 385F on deep-frying thermometer.

3.   Cover bottom of fryer basket with a single layer of potatoes; lower basket slowly into fat. Fry 5 or 6 minutes, or until potatoes are golden-brown and tender.

4.   Remove potatoes; drain well on paper towels. Sprinkle with salt. Keep warm while frying rest of potatoes.

* Or use an electric skillet, following manufacturer's directions.

FRENCH-FRIED POTATOES

(DOUBLE-FRYING METHOD)

1.   Pare as many Idaho potatoes as desired. Cut lengthwise into ⅜-inch-thick slices. Then cut slices into strips ⅜ inch wide. Rinse in cold water; drain thoroughly on paper towels.

2.   Meanwhile, heat salad oil or shortening in deep-fat fryer* (filling at least one third full) to 360F on deep-frying thermometer.

3.   Cover bottom of fryer basket with a single layer of potatoes; lower basket slowly into fat. Fry 4 minutes, or until potatoes are tender but not browned.

4.   Remove potatoes; drain well on paper towels. Keep at room temperature until ready to complete cooking. Reserve oil.

5.   Before serving, reheat oil to 375F on deep-frying thermometer.

6.   Cover bottom of fryer basket with 2 layers of potatoes; fry 1 minute, or until potatoes are golden.

7.   Remove potatoes; drain well on paper towels. Sprinkle with salt. Keep warm while frying rest of potatoes.

* Or use an electric skillet, following manufacturer's directions.

GERMAN-FRIED POTATOES

4 medium potatoes (about 1¼ lb), pared
¼ cup butter or margarine
Salt
Pepper

MAKES 4 SERVINGS

1.   Slice potatoes, crosswise, into ⅛-inch-thick slices.

2.   In hot butter in large skillet, sauté potato slices, turning occasionally, until golden-brown and tender.

3.   Sprinkle with salt and pepper.

LYONNAISE POTATOES

⅓ cup butter or margarine
6 medium potatoes (about 2 lb), pared and thinly sliced
1½ cups sliced onion

1 teaspoon salt
Dash pepper
2 tablespoons chopped parsley

1. In hot butter in large, heavy skillet, sauté potato and onion slices, turning frequently, until golden-brown and tender—15 to 20 minutes.
2. Sprinkle with salt, pepper, and parsley.

POTATOES ANNA

6 medium potatoes (about 2 lb), pared and thinly sliced
1½ teaspoons salt

¼ teaspoon pepper
6 tablespoons butter or margarine

1. Preheat oven to 425F. Lightly grease 10-inch skillet with heat-resistant handle, or shallow casserole, with tight-fitting cover.
2. Gently toss potatoes with salt and pepper.
3. Layer a third of potato slices circular-fashion around bottom of prepared skillet. Dot with 2 tablespoons butter. Repeat twice.
4. Bake, covered, 30 minutes. Remove cover; bake 5 minutes. To serve: invert on platter.

SCALLOPED POTATOES

3 lb potatoes
4 medium onions, thinly sliced
Boiling water
3 teaspoons salt
3 tablespoons butter or margarine

2 tablespoons flour
⅛ teaspoon pepper
⅛ teaspoon paprika
2¼ cups milk
2 tablespoons chopped parsley

1. Preheat oven to 400F. Lightly grease 2-quart casserole.
2. Wash, pare, and thinly slice potatoes; measure 8 cups.
3. Cook potatoes and onions, covered, in small amount of boiling water, with 2 teaspoons salt, about 5 minutes, or until slightly tender. Drain.
4. Melt butter in saucepan. Remove from heat. Stir in flour, pepper, paprika, and remaining salt until smooth. Blend in milk.
5. Cook, stirring, over medium heat, to boiling point, or until thickened and smooth.
6. In prepared casserole, layer one third of potatoes and onions. Sprinkle with 1 tablespoon parsley; top with one third of sauce. Repeat. Then add remaining potatoes and onions, and top with remaining sauce.
7. Bake, uncovered, 35 minutes, or until top is browned and potatoes are tender when pierced with fork.

AMELIA'S POTATO PANCAKES

4 large potatoes,
      pared
¼ cup grated onion
2 eggs, slightly
      beaten

2 tablespoons flour
¾ teaspoon salt
Dash pepper
Oil or shortening
      for frying

1.   Using medium grater, grate potatoes. Drain very well; measure 3 cups.

2.   In large bowl, combine grated potato with onion, egg, flour, salt, and pepper; mix gently.

3.   Add oil to large, heavy skillet to depth of ⅛ inch. Heat slowly, until bread cube dropped into oil becomes golden-brown.

4.   For each pancake, drop 2 tablespoons potato mixture into hot fat. With spatula, flatten to a 4-inch pancake. Fry 2 or 3 minutes on each side, or until golden-brown.

5.   Drain well on paper towels. Serve hot. Nice with pot roast.

Note: For 24 smaller pancakes, proceed as directed above, using 1 tablespoon potato mixture for each pancake; flatten to a 2-inch circle.

GLAZED SWEET POTATOES

6 sweet potatoes (about
      2 lb)
Boiling water
¼ cup butter or margarine

½ teaspoon salt
½ cup light-brown sugar,
      firmly packed
¼ cup chopped pecans

1.   Wash potatoes. Place in large saucepan; cover with boiling water; bring back to boiling. Reduce heat; simmer, covered, 30 minutes, or until tender.

2.   Drain; let cool. Peel, and halve lengthwise.

3.   In large skillet, combine butter, salt, sugar, and ¼ cup water; stir, over low heat, until butter melts and sugar is dissolved. Then boil, uncovered, 3 minutes.

4.   Reduce heat. Add potato halves and pecans; simmer, uncovered, 5 minutes, basting often with syrup.

5.   Serve potatoes with syrup and nuts spooned over them.

YAMS FLAMBÉS

2 lb large yams (2 or 3)
½ teaspoon salt
¾ cup light-brown sugar,
      firmly packed

¼ cup butter or margarine
⅓ cup dark rum

1.   Scrub yams well with vegetable brush. Place in medium saucepan; add water to cover and the salt. Over medium heat, bring to boiling. Reduce heat; simmer, covered, 30 minutes, or just until fork-tender.

2.   Drain; let cool. Then peel, and slice crosswise ½ inch thick. Lightly coat each slice with brown sugar.

3.   In hot butter in medium skillet, sauté slices until browned—about 2 minutes on each side. With slotted utensil, lift to serving dish. Drain fat from skillet.

4.   In same skillet, gently heat rum just until steaming. Ignite; pour over yams.

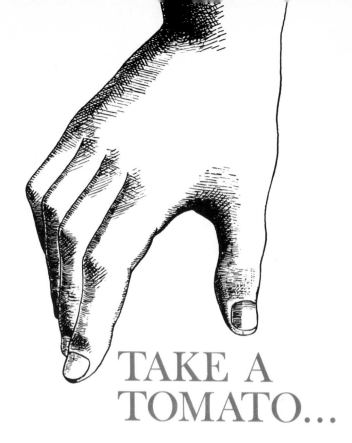

TAKE A TOMATO...

Let it ripen in a dry, dark place (some cooks use a paper bag), then slice it, peel it, stew it, boil it, or eat it as is with a little salt. Tomatoes are among the most delicious fruits in the world. When you serve them sliced, sprinkle them lightly with sugar (along with other seasonings) to bring out their full flavor. And always keep fully ripe tomatoes in the refrigerator.

...or any VEGETABLE

from artichokes to zucchini. If you prepare it well, it can become as important a part of your meal as the meat dish or dessert. Most people say they simply "don't like vegetables." They'd rather eat ice cream, say, or hot dogs. They think a vegetable is just something that's good for them, a duty to eat rather than a pleasure. Well, we believe that properly cooked and well-seasoned vegetables will be gobbled up by the very people who claim distaste for them. There's no excuse for monotony in the vegetable diet, especially now that modern methods of preparation and shipping make almost every vegetable available at your market at any season. Start enjoying them today.

Pumpkin

BAKED PUMPKIN CASSEROLE

MAKES 6 TO 8 SERVINGS

1 can (1 lb, 13 oz) pumpkin
   (3 cups)
2 tablespoons granulated
   sugar
2 tablespoons butter or
   margarine, melted
¼ teaspoon mace
½ teaspoon salt
Dash pepper

2 eggs, slightly beaten
½ cup coarsely chopped
   pecans

Glaze:
½ cup light-brown sugar,
   firmly packed
¼ cup maple syrup

½ cup pecan halves

1. Preheat oven to 350F. Lightly grease 1-quart casserole.
2. Combine pumpkin, granulated sugar, butter, mace, salt, pepper, eggs, and chopped pecans in large bowl; mix well. Turn into casserole.
3. Make Glaze: Mix brown sugar and syrup in small saucepan. Heat, stirring, until sugar is dissolved; then bring to boiling. Cool slightly.
4. Arrange pecan halves around edge of casserole. Cover pumpkin and pecans with glaze; bake 40 minutes.

Parsnips

CHEESE-BUTTERED PARSNIPS

MAKES 6 SERVINGS

2 lb parsnips
Boiling water
2 tablespoons butter or
   margarine
1 cup grated sharp Cheddar
   cheese (¼ lb)

½ cup light-brown sugar,
   firmly packed
1¼ teaspoons salt
2 tablespoons finely
   chopped fresh dill, or
   3 teaspoons dried dill
   weed

1. Wash parsnips. Pare; cut lengthwise into quarters; cut quarters into 3-inch pieces.
2. Place in medium saucepan. Add boiling water to measure 1 inch; simmer, covered, 20 minutes, or just until tender.
3. Drain, if necessary (most of liquid will have evaporated). Cool slightly; remove core from parsnips.
4. Melt butter in same saucepan, over medium heat. Stir in cheese, sugar, and salt.
5. Add parsnips; stir gently, over low heat, until cheese is melted and parsnips are well coated. Stir in dill, and serve at once.

Turnips

SAVORY RUTABAGA

MAKES 6 SERVINGS

1 medium rutabaga (2½ to
   3 lb)
Boiling water
1 can (10½ oz) condensed
   cream-of-mushroom
   soup, undiluted

½ cup crumbled cooked
   bacon
1 teaspoon salt
½ teaspoon pepper
¼ cup chopped parsley

1. Wash rutabaga. Pare; cut into ⅓-inch cubes.
2. Place in large saucepan. Add boiling water to measure 1 inch; simmer, covered, 25 minutes, or until tender. Drain, if necessary (most of liquid will have evaporated).
3. Stir in soup, bacon, salt, and pepper. Heat gently 5 minutes. Stir in parsley.

TURNIPS WITH SHERRY

1 lb white turnips
Boiling water
¾ teaspoon salt

2 tablespoons sherry
¼ cup butter or margarine
⅛ teaspoon nutmeg

1. Wash turnips; pare. Cut into ½-inch cubes.
2. In 1 inch boiling water, in medium saucepan, combine turnips with salt.
3. Cook, covered, over medium heat, 20 minutes, or until turnips are tender.
4. Drain turnips. Toss with butter and sherry. Turn into serving dish. Sprinkle with nutmeg.

TURNIPS FLORENTINE

1 lb white turnips (about 4 medium)
Boiling water
½ teaspoon salt
1 teaspoon instant minced onion
1 tablespoon lemon juice
2 tablespoons butter or margarine
½ cup finely chopped raw spinach

1. Wash turnips; pare. Cut each into quarters.
2. In 1 inch boiling water, in small saucepan, combine turnips with salt and onion.
3. Cook, covered, 25 to 30 minutes, or until turnip is tender.
4. Drain turnips well. Mash till smooth.
5. Return mashed turnips to heat. Cook, over low heat, 1 to 2 minutes to dry out.
6. Add lemon juice, butter, and spinach, mixing well. Serve at once.

SKILLET TURNIPS

1½ lb white turnips
3 tablespoons butter or margarine
1 teaspoon salt
¼ teaspoon sugar
2 tablespoons lemon juice
1 cup finely chopped onion
1 tablespoon chopped parsley

1. Wash turnips; pare. Cut into ¼-inch cubes.
2. In medium skillet, with tight-fitting lid, combine turnips, 1 tablespoon butter, salt, sugar, and ½ cup water. Cook, covered, over medium heat, 10 to 15 minutes, or until turnips are tender and water is absorbed.
3. Meanwhile, in small skillet, slowly heat rest of butter. Add lemon juice, onion, and parsley. Cook, stirring, until onion is tender.
4. Gently toss onion mixture with turnips.

WHITE TURNIPS WITH ONION RINGS

2 lb small white turnips
1½ teaspoons salt
Boiling water
1 lb small white onions
¼ cup butter or margarine
½ teaspoon pepper

1. Wash turnips. Pare; cut into ¼-inch-thick slices.
2. Place in medium saucepan with ½ teaspoon salt. Add boiling water to measure 1 inch; simmer, covered, 20 to 25 minutes, or until turnips are just tender. Drain.
3. Meanwhile, peel onions, and slice crosswise.
4. In hot butter in large skillet, sauté onions until tender and golden—about 10 minutes.
5. Add hot turnips, rest of salt, and the pepper; toss gently.

Spinach

SPINACH GOURMET

1 pkg (10 oz) frozen spinach or 1 lb fresh spinach*
1 can (3 oz) sliced mushrooms
⅛ teaspoon pepper
1 tablespoon butter or margarine
1 tablespoon chopped onion
1 clove garlic, crushed
½ cup dairy sour cream

1. Cook spinach as package label directs. Drain, and keep warm.
2. Meanwhile, drain mushrooms, reserving liquid. In small skillet, cook mushroom liquid until it measures ¼ cup—about 5 minutes.
3. Remove from heat. Add pepper, butter, onion, garlic, and mushrooms; cook, over low heat, 2 minutes.

(Spinach Gourmet continued)

4. Stir some of hot liquid into sour cream. Return to mixture in skillet; reheat gently.

5. Pour sauce over spinach, tossing gently to combine.

* Wash spinach; remove and discard stems. Cook spinach in large saucepan, covered, over medium heat, stirring frequently, 5 minutes, or until spinach is tender. (Do not add water.) Drain if necessary. Continue as directed.

SPINACH WITH CROUTONS

MAKES 6 SERVINGS

2 pkg (10-oz size) frozen chopped spinach	1¼ teaspoons salt Dash pepper
2 tablespoons butter or margarine	⅛ teaspoon nutmeg ⅔ cup heavy cream
¼ cup chopped onion	2 cups croutons*
1 tablespoon flour	

1. Cook spinach as package label directs; drain.

2. In hot butter in medium saucepan, sauté onion until golden and tender—5 minutes.

3. Remove from heat. Add spinach along with flour, salt, pepper, nutmeg, and cream; reheat gently.

4. Turn into serving dish; sprinkle with croutons.

* To make croutons: In 2 tablespoons hot butter in medium skillet, sauté 2 cups bread cubes until golden-brown all over.

Squash

STUFFED ACORN SQUASH

MAKES 4 SERVINGS

2 medium acorn squash Salt	¾ cup finely chopped pared apple
½ lb sausage meat, sliced	¼ teaspoon dried oregano leaves
2 tablespoons finely chopped onion	

1. Preheat oven to 375F.

2. Scrub squash. Cut in half crosswise; scoop out seeds and stringy portion.

3. Sprinkle squash with salt. Place, cut side down, in shallow baking pan. Add hot water to measure ½ inch.

4. Bake, uncovered, 30 minutes, or until squash is tender when tested with fork.

5. Meanwhile, in medium skillet, sauté sausage meat until nicely browned on all sides, breaking it into small chunks with fork as it browns.

6. Remove sausage from skillet; set aside. Drain all except 2 tablespoons drippings from skillet. Add onion; sauté until golden—about 3 minutes.

7. Return sausage, with remaining ingredients, to skillet, tossing lightly to combine.

8. Fill squash halves with sausage mixture; bake, uncovered, 30 minutes longer.

HONEY-SPICE ACORN SQUASH

MAKES 6 SERVINGS

3 medium acorn squash
¼ cup butter or margarine, melted
¼ teaspoon cinnamon
½ teaspoon salt
¼ teaspoon ginger
⅓ cup honey

1. Preheat oven to 375F.
2. Scrub squash. Cut in half lengthwise; remove seeds and stringy fibers.
3. Arrange, cut side down, in shallow baking pan. Surround with ½ inch hot water.
4. Bake 30 minutes.
5. Combine remaining ingredients. Pour off excess liquid from baking pan; turn squash cut side up.
6. Pour sauce into cavities; bake 15 minutes, basting now and then with sauce.

SQUASH WITH ORANGE

MAKES 4 SERVINGS

2 pkg (12-oz size) frozen Hubbard squash
¼ teaspoon grated orange peel
2 tablespoons orange juice
¼ cup butter or margarine
2 tablespoons light-brown sugar
½ teaspoon salt
Dash nutmeg

1. Cook squash as package label directs.
2. Add remaining ingredients, mixing well. Cook, over low heat, 5 minutes, stirring occasionally.

HERB-BAKED SUMMER SQUASH

MAKES 6 SERVINGS

1 can (10½ oz) condensed beef bouillon, undiluted
2 lb yellow summer squash (about 3)
2 tablespoons butter or margarine, melted
½ teaspoon salt
1 teaspoon finely snipped fresh rosemary or oregano leaves*

1. Preheat oven to 350F.
2. Heat bouillon with 1 can water until thoroughly hot. Cut stem ends from squash. Cut squash in half lengthwise. Place halves, cut side down, in large, shallow baking dish.
3. Pour bouillon around squash; bake, uncovered, 20 minutes.
4. Turn squash; brush cut sides with butter combined with salt and rosemary.
5. Bake 15 minutes longer, or until squash is fork-tender. Before serving, brush with more butter, if desired.
* Or use ½ teaspoon dried rosemary or oregano leaves.

YELLOW SQUASH WITH SOUR CREAM

MAKES 8 SERVINGS

2¾ lb small summer squash
Salt
¾ cup butter or margarine
⅔ cup finely chopped onion
1½ teaspoons paprika
½ teaspoon salt
¼ teaspoon pepper
2 tablespoons chopped fresh dill
2 teaspoons vinegar
1 cup dairy sour cream

1. Wash squash. Cut in quarters lengthwise; scoop out seeds. Cut squash into long, thin strips.
2. Sprinkle with a little salt; let stand 1 hour.
3. Drain squash; squeeze gently in a clean towel, to remove excess moisture.
4. In ½ cup hot butter in large skillet, sauté onion until golden and tender—about 5 minutes.

(Yellow Squash with Sour Cream continued)

5. Remove from heat. Stir in squash along with remaining butter, paprika, salt, pepper, dill, and vinegar.

6. Cook, uncovered, over medium heat, stirring occasionally, until squash is tender—about 15 minutes.

7. Stir in sour cream; reheat gently.

HERB-BUTTERED ZUCCHINI AND CARROTS

1½ lb small carrots
1½ lb small zucchini
½ cup boiling water
1 teaspoon salt

1 teaspoon dried thyme
   leaves
2 tablespoons butter or
   margarine

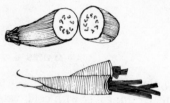

MAKES 8 SERVINGS

1. Scrub carrots and zucchini well with vegetable brush. Pare carrots. Slice carrots and zucchini, on diagonal, ⅛ inch thick.

2. To boiling water in 2½-quart saucepan, add salt, thyme, and carrots; bring to boiling, covered tightly. Reduce heat, and simmer 10 minutes. Carrots should be slightly underdone.

3. Add zucchini, tossing to mix well; bring to boiling, covered tightly. Reduce heat; simmer about 5 minutes, or until vegetables are tender. Let cook, uncovered, a few minutes longer, to evaporate liquid.

4. Add butter, tossing gently to coat vegetables.

Tomatoes

Here are some helpful hints to guide you in the care and preparation of tomatoes: *To ripen:* Place tomatoes in a dry, dark place away from the light (some cooks use a brown-paper bag). It is not good practice to place green tomatoes in the sun to ripen. *To peel:* Drop them in boiling water for a minute or two, then in cold, and the skin will come off easily.

When you buy tomatoes, look for those that are mature yet firm, well formed, plump, smooth, a good red color, and free from blemishes. You should always keep fully ripe tomatoes in the refrigerator.

BAKED STUFFED TOMATOES

6 medium tomatoes
½ cup butter or margarine
⅓ cup finely chopped
   onion
2 tablespoons chopped
   parsley

1 teaspoon dried basil
   leaves
1 teaspoon salt
¼ teaspoon pepper
1 cup packaged dry bread
   crumbs

MAKES 6 SERVINGS

1. Preheat oven to 375F.

2. Cut ½-inch-thick slice from stem end of each tomato. With spoon, scoop out a hollow, about 1 inch deep, in each tomato. Arrange tomatoes in shallow baking pan.

3. In hot butter in skillet, sauté onion, parsley, and basil 1 to 2 minutes. Add salt, pepper, and bread crumbs; mix thoroughly, with a fork.

4. Lightly fill tomatoes with stuffing, mounding it high in center.

5. Bake about 30 minutes, or until browned.

PENNSYLVANIA TOMATOES

6 large tomatoes (about 3 lb)
½ cup unsifted all-purpose flour
¼ lb butter or margarine
Light-brown sugar
1 teaspoon salt
¼ teaspoon pepper
1½ cups heavy cream

1. Trim a thin slice from top and bottom of each tomato. Cut each tomato, crosswise, into 3 slices.

2. Dip cut sides of slices in flour, coating completely.

3. In hot butter in large skillet, sauté slices until nicely browned on underside. Sprinkle each with ½ teaspoon brown sugar.

4. Turn slices; sprinkle with some of salt, pepper, and a little more brown sugar. When other side is nicely browned, turn slices again.

5. Pour cream into skillet; cook, over medium heat, uncovered, 5 minutes, or until tomato slices are tender.

STEWED TOMATOES

Boiling water
3 large tomatoes (about 1½ lb)
1 bay leaf
1 tablespoon butter or margarine
1 tablespoon sugar
½ teaspoon salt
⅛ teaspoon pepper

1. Pour boiling water over tomatoes; let stand for 1 minute. Drain; cover with cold water. Carefully peel skin. Cut tomatoes into cubes; measure 3½ cups.

2. In medium saucepan, combine tomatoes with remaining ingredients; bring to boiling. Reduce heat, and simmer, covered, about 8 minutes, or until tomatoes are tender.

TOMATOES PROVENCALE

6 medium tomatoes
Salt
Pepper
1 cup soft bread crumbs
2 tablespoons finely chopped parsley
1 clove garlic, crushed
Olive oil or salad oil

1. Preheat oven to 450F. Lightly grease a shallow baking pan.

2. Wash tomatoes; cut each in half horizontally. If necessary, drain on paper towels.

3. Arrange tomato halves, cut side up, in prepared pan. Sprinkle with salt and pepper.

4. Combine bread crumbs, parsley, and garlic; sprinkle over tomatoes. Drizzle a little olive oil over each.

5. Bake 10 to 15 minutes, or until breadcrumb mixture is golden.

M̲ost romantic kind of cooking is chafing-dish cooking. It has the air, somehow, of a ritual: the live heat glowing under the blazer pan, copper or steel or whatever; the cook bending over it, intent and content, adding a bit of this, a dash of that, pouring a ladleful of blazing cognac on the mixture and watching the blue flame ripple across it. Whether it is a fragrant Café Brûlot, hot as blazes; a hot appetizer, kept hot and appetizing; a main dish of uncommon distinction; a fabulous flaming dessert; or even such a simple thing as oyster stew or scrambled eggs served at midnight—make it in a chafing dish, and secure your reputation as a hostess of style and sophistication. Our recipes, we say without a bit of modesty, are worthy of your finest chafing dish.

About Chafing Dishes

Chafing dishes may be purchased in many styles and sizes—from very small to large ones for serving more than twenty.

Most chafing dishes are actually double boilers. They consist of a stand, burner, water pan, cooking pan (blazer), and lid. The blazer pan is generally used over direct heat for cooking; then placed over boiling water, in the water pan, to keep foods warm. Another kind of chafing dish is the deep-skillet type. It consists of a stand, burner, cooking pan (skillet), and lid. Cook in the skillet as you would in a blazer pan; or use the skillet to keep foods warm.

Chafing dishes are heated by alcohol, electricity, or canned heat. When you cook in blazer pan or skillet over direct heat, alcohol is recommended because of its high heat intensity. To keep foods in skillet warm, reduce heat in alcohol burner to a warming flame. Any recipe prepared in a chafing dish may also be prepared in an electric skillet.

Be familiar with your chafing dish. Read manufacturer's directions carefully. Since chafing dishes vary as to capacity and kind of heat used, cooking times given in our recipes are approximate.

CAFÉ BRÛLOT

MAKES 12 SERVINGS

2 (1½-inch) cinnamon sticks
2 whole cloves
¼ teaspoon grated nutmeg
¼ teaspoon whole allspice

Peel of 1 small orange, removed in a spiral
1 lemon slice
12 sugar cubes
1 cup cognac
5 cups hot, strong coffee*

1. In chafing dish, over direct heat, combine all ingredients, except coffee. Heat until hot throughout—about 10 minutes.
2. In heated ladle, ignite a little of hot cognac mixture. Pour back into cognac in chafing dish, to ignite.
3. While cognac is flaming, pour in hot coffee. Serve in brûlot or demitasse cups.

* Coffee made from dark-roast Italian coffee, fine grind, in a special caffè-espresso pot is preferred. Follow manufacturer's directions.

OYSTER STEW WITH SHERRY

MAKES 4 APPETIZER SERVINGS,
2 LUNCHEON SERVINGS

2 tablespoons butter or margarine
1 pint shucked oysters, well drained
½ teaspoon salt
½ teaspoon Worcestershire sauce

¼ teaspoon liquid hot-pepper seasoning
1¾ cups light cream
¼ cup sherry
Dash paprika

1. Melt butter in chafing dish, over direct heat. Add oysters; cook until edges begin to curl—about 5 minutes.
2. Add salt, Worcestershire, hot-pepper seasoning, cream, and sherry. Heat until hot throughout, stirring occasionally—about 15 minutes. Sprinkle with paprika.
3. Serve in soup bowls, as an appetizer or a luncheon dish.

LIVERWURST COCKTAIL MEATBALLS

MAKES 36

1 egg, slightly beaten
¼ cup chili sauce
½ cup packaged dry bread crumbs
½ teaspoon salt
½ teaspoon monosodium glutamate

¼ lb ground chuck
½ lb liverwurst
1 tablespoon flour
¼ cup butter or margarine
1 cup beef bouillon

1. In medium bowl, combine egg, chili sauce, bread crumbs, salt, and monosodium glutamate, mixing well.
2. Add beef and liverwurst, mixing until well combined.
3. Using 1 level tablespoon for each, shape mixture into 36 meatballs. Roll meatballs lightly in flour, coating completely.
4. In hot butter in heavy skillet, sauté meatballs until browned all over, shaking skillet occasionally so meatballs will brown evenly.
5. Remove from heat. Add bouillon to skillet, mixing well; bring to boiling. Reduce heat, and simmer, uncovered, 15 minutes. Turn into chafing dish.

CURRIED BEAN DIP

MAKES 2¾ CUPS

1 can (1 lb) barbecue beans
1 can (11 oz) condensed
    Cheddar-cheese soup,
    undiluted

1 teaspoon curry powder
Chopped parsley

1. Combine all ingredients, except parsley, in medium saucepan. Over medium heat, bring to boiling, stirring.

2. Turn into chafing dish; sprinkle with parsley. Serve with corn chips or crackers.

HOT SHRIMP COCKTAILS

MAKES 6 TO 8 SERVINGS

2 tablespoons butter or
    margarine
3 tablespoons lemon juice
¾ teaspoon salt
¼ teaspoon liquid hot-
    pepper seasoning

1½ lb raw shrimp, shelled
    and deveined
Chopped parsley

Seafood-Cocktail Sauce*

1. Heat butter in large, heavy skillet. Remove from heat; add lemon juice, salt, hot-pepper seasoning, and shrimp, stirring until well combined.

2. Cook, uncovered, over medium heat, 5 minutes, or until shrimp is pink; stir occasionally.

3. Turn into chafing dish; sprinkle with parsley. Serve with Seafood-Cocktail Sauce.

* See Sauces and Gravies Chapter.

PRUNE-CHUTNEY HORS D'OEUVRES

MAKES 18

18 large dried prunes
6 wedges (1-oz size) process
    Gruyère cheese

1 jar (9 oz) chutney

1. Using scissors, carefully remove pits from prunes.

2. Cut each cheese wedge into 3 wedges, to make 18 in all.

3. Insert a cheese wedge in center of each prune. Place in chafing dish.

4. In small saucepan, gently heat chutney; pour over prunes.

BLUE CHEESE AND CRABMEAT

MAKES 10 SERVINGS

2 tablespoons butter or
    margarine
⅔ cup finely chopped
    onion
½ cup chopped green
    pepper
1 cup diced celery
1 cup milk
1 cup light cream

2 pkg (3-oz size) blue
    cheese, crumbled
1 cup sliced pitted ripe
    olives
4 pkg (6-oz size) frozen
    crabmeat, thawed and
    drained
1 teaspoon paprika
2 tablespoons chopped
    parsley

1. In hot butter in large skillet, sauté onion, green pepper, and celery, stirring, over medium heat until vegetables are just tender—8 to 10 minutes. Remove from heat.

2. Meanwhile, in top of double boiler, combine milk, cream, and cheese. Over hot water, heat until cheese is melted and mixture is smooth, stirring occasionally.

3. Add cheese mixture to vegetables in skillet, along with olives and crabmeat, stirring until well combined. Heat slowly, stirring, until hot —about 20 minutes.

4. To serve: Turn into chafing dish. Sprinkle with paprika; circle edge with chopped parsley. Serve on toast or Golden-Noodle Nests.*

* See Cereals Chapter.

603

BEEFBURGERS IN WINE

MAKES 4

1 lb ground chuck
1½ teaspoons salt
4 whole cloves

2-inch cinnamon stick,
   broken
½ teaspoon nutmeg
1 cup Burgundy

1. Lightly shape chuck into 4 patties.

2. Sprinkle salt in bottom of large, heavy skillet. Add patties to skillet; cook, uncovered, over medium heat, 4 minutes on each side, for medium rare.

3. Meanwhile, tie spices in cheesecloth bag. Add to wine in small saucepan; bring just to boiling. Reduce heat, and simmer, uncovered, 5 minutes.

4. Place patties in chafing dish. Remove and discard spices from wine. Pour wine over patties.

Miniature Beefburgers in Wine: Proceed as directed in Beefburgers in Wine, shaping chuck into 16 meatballs. Cook meatballs, uncovered and turning occasionally, until browned all over. Then proceed as directed above. Serve as hors d'oeuvres. Makes 16.

BENGAL CURRY

MAKES 4 SERVINGS

2 tablespoons shortening
2 lb boneless shoulder of
   lamb, cut into 1-inch
   cubes
½ cup sliced onion
1 tablespoon curry powder
1 teaspoon salt
⅛ teaspoon pepper
⅛ teaspoon cloves
2 tablespoons slivered
   crystallized ginger

1 tablespoon chopped
   fresh mint, or ½
   teaspoon dried mint
   leaves
2 cups milk
2 tablespoons flour
½ cup flaked coconut
2 tablespoons lime juice
1 cup light cream
3 cups cooked white rice

1. Heat shortening in large, heavy skillet. In hot shortening, sauté lamb until browned all over.

2. Add onion; sauté, stirring occasionally, about 5 minutes, or until onion is tender. Remove from heat.

3. Combine curry powder, salt, pepper, and cloves. Stir into mixture in skillet, along with ginger, mint, and milk.

4. Bring mixture to boiling. Reduce heat, and simmer, covered, 1 hour, or until lamb is tender. (Mixture will appear curdled.)

5. Combine flour with ¼ cup cold water until smooth. Slowly stir into mixture in skillet; bring to boiling, stirring.

6. Remove from heat. Add coconut, lime juice, and cream, mixing well. Reheat gently.

7. Turn curry into chafing dish. Serve over rice. If desired, serve chopped peanuts, chopped hard-cooked eggs, chopped crisp bacon, chopped onion, grated fresh coconut, and chutney, in individual bowls, along with curry, as accompaniments. Let guests make their own selection.

CHICKEN LIVERS WITH WILD RICE

¼ cup butter or margarine
1 lb chicken livers
2 bacon slices, diced
2 tablespoons chopped
 shallots or green
 onions
½ cup sliced celery
1½ cups cooked wild rice
1 cup cooked white rice
1 teaspoon salt

½ teaspoon monosodium
 glutamate
½ teaspoon dried rosemary
 leaves
⅛ teaspoon pepper
1 can (3 oz) sliced
 mushrooms
About ¾ cup chicken
 bouillon

MAKES 4 SERVINGS

1. In hot butter in large skillet, sauté chicken livers until tender—about 5 minutes. Remove from heat; set aside.
2. In chafing dish, over direct heat, cook bacon 5 minutes. Add shallots and celery; cook 5 minutes longer, stirring occasionally.
3. Stir in rice, salt, monsodium glutamate, rosemary, and pepper.
4. Drain mushrooms, reserving liquid. Add bouillon to mushroom liquid to measure 1 cup. Add to mixture in chafing dish, along with mushrooms and chicken livers, mixing well.
5. Simmer, covered, 5 minutes.

CHIPPED BEEF IN SOUR CREAM

1 jar (5 oz) sliced dried
 beef
1 tablespoon butter or
 margarine
1 pint dairy sour cream
¼ cup dry white wine

1 tablespoon grated
 Parmesan cheese
Dash cayenne
1 can (8½ oz) artichoke
 hearts, drained and
 halved

MAKES 4 TO 6 SERVINGS

1. If desired, rinse dried beef. Let dry on paper towels.
2. Slowly heat butter in medium skillet. Remove from heat; add sour cream, wine, cheese, and cayenne, mixing well. Gently stir in dried beef and artichoke hearts.
3. Heat to serving temperature, stirring occasionally. Turn into chafing dish. Serve over toast points or cooked white rice.

CREAMED DEVILED EGGS

6 hard-cooked eggs
2 tablespoons prepared
 mustard
1 tablespoon mayonnaise
 or cooked salad
 dressing
½ teaspoon Worcestershire
 sauce
½ teaspoon prepared
 horseradish

⅛ teaspoon liquid hot-
 pepper seasoning
¼ cup butter or margarine
1 tablespoon prepared
 anchovy paste
¼ cup unsifted all-purpose
 flour
2 cups milk
1 tablespoon bottled
 capers, drained
Chopped parsley

MAKES 4 SERVINGS

1. Cut eggs in half lengthwise; carefully remove yolks, leaving whites intact. Set whites aside; press yolks through sieve.
2. In small bowl, combine egg yolks with mustard, mayonnaise, Worcestershire, horseradish, and hot-pepper seasoning until smooth and light.
3. Pile egg-yolk mixture lightly into egg whites, mounding in center. Arrange eggs in chafing dish.
4. Slowly heat butter in medium saucepan. Remove from heat; stir in anchovy paste and flour until smooth. Gradually stir in milk and capers until blended.
5. Bring to boiling, stirring; boil 1 minute. Pour over eggs in chafing dish. Heat gently; sprinkle with parsley. Serve hot with toast.

DEVILED-HAM–CHEESE RABBIT

¼ cup butter or margarine
¼ cup unsifted all-purpose
   flour
1¼ cups milk
¾ cup tomato juice

2 cups grated sharp
   Cheddar cheese
   (½ lb)
1 can (4½ oz) deviled ham
¼ cup sliced pimiento-
   stuffed olives

MAKES 4 TO 6 SERVINGS

1. Melt butter in blazer pan of chafing dish, over direct heat. Remove from heat.

2. Stir in flour to make a smooth paste. Gradually stir in milk until smooth.

3. Return to heat; bring to boiling, stirring— takes about 15 minutes. Boil, stirring constantly, 5 minutes, or until sauce thickens.

4. Stir in tomato juice; cook 5 minutes. Add cheese and ham; cook, stirring occasionally, 5 minutes longer.

5. Remove chafing dish from direct heat; place over boiling water in water pan. Garnish with olives, and serve over toast.

HAM AND SWEETBREADS SUPREME

1 lb veal sweetbreads
¼ cup butter or margarine
1 cup finely diced celery
⅓ cup chopped green
   pepper
2 tablespoons chopped
   onion
2 tablespoons chopped
   pimiento

¼ cup unsifted all-purpose
   flour
1 teaspoon salt
⅛ teaspoon pepper
1½ cups milk
¾ cup dry white wine
2 cups diced cooked ham
6 warm patty shells

MAKES 6 SERVINGS

1. Cook sweetbreads according to Basic Method for Cooking Sweetbreads.* Cut into uniform pieces; set aside.

2. In hot butter in large skillet, sauté celery, green pepper, onion, and pimiento about 5 minutes, or until tender.

3. Remove from heat. Add flour, salt, and pepper to sautéed vegetables, mixing well. Gradually stir in milk and ½ cup wine.

4. Bring mixture to boiling, stirring constantly. Add sweetbreads and ham; reduce heat, and simmer, uncovered, 10 minutes.

5. Stir in remaining wine. Turn mixture into chafing dish. Serve over patty shells.

* See Meats and Game Chapter.

MEATBALLS MOLE

1 lb ground chuck
1 egg, slightly beaten
½ cup milk
¾ cup crushed corn chips
2½ teaspoons salt
2½ tablespoons flour
2 tablespoons shortening
2 cups sliced onion
1 clove garlic, crushed
2 tablespoons sugar

1 tablespoon chili powder
1 teaspoon ground cumin
1 teaspoon ground
   coriander
1 teaspoon dried oregano
   leaves
1 can (1 lb, 3 oz) tomatoes,
   undrained
1 square unsweetened
   chocolate
3 cups cooked white rice

MAKES 4 TO 6 SERVINGS

1. In large bowl, lightly toss chuck with egg, milk, corn chips, and 1 teaspoon salt to combine. Refrigerate, covered, 1 hour.

2. Gently shape into 20 meatballs, using 2 tablespoons meat mixture for each. Roll meatballs, lightly, in 2 tablespoons flour, coating completely.

3. Slowly heat shortening in large, heavy skillet with tight-fitting lid. In hot shortening, sauté meatballs, a few at a time, until nicely browned all over. Remove meatballs from skillet as they are browned.

4. In same skillet, cook onion and garlic, stirring occasionally, about 5 minutes, or until tender. Remove from heat.

(Meatballs Molé continued)

5. Combine sugar, chili powder, cumin, coriander, oregano, and rest of salt and flour. Stir into skillet along with tomatoes, chocolate, and 1 cup water, mixing well.

6. Bring mixture to boiling, stirring constantly. Reduce heat; simmer, covered and stirring occasionally, 45 minutes.

7. Add meatballs to skillet; simmer, covered, 15 minutes. Uncover; simmer 15 minutes.

8. Turn meatballs and sauce into chafing dish. Serve over hot rice.

MAKES 6 SERVINGS

ORIENTAL CHICKEN BALLS

1 egg, slightly beaten	5 tablespoons butter or
¾ cup milk	margarine
¼ cup packaged dry bread	½ cup sliced onion
crumbs	½ cup sliced celery
¼ cup finely chopped	½ cup sliced green pepper
toasted blanched	1½ cups chicken bouillon
almonds	½ teaspoon monosodium
1 teaspoon salt	glutamate
½ teaspoon hickory-	1 tablespoon sugar
smoked salt	1 tablespoon cornstarch
⅛ teaspoon pepper	1 tablespoon lemon juice
3 cans (5-oz size) boned	½ cup seedless green
chicken, ground	grapes
(4 cups)	4½ cups cooked white rice
1 tablespoon flour	

1. In large bowl, combine egg, milk, bread crumbs, almonds, ½ teaspoon salt, hickory-smoked salt, and pepper; mix well. Add chicken, tossing lightly to combine.

2. Using 2 level tablespoons for each, shape chicken mixture into 24 balls. Roll balls lightly in flour, coating completely.

3. In 4 tablespoons hot butter in large skillet, sauté chicken balls until browned on all sides. Remove from heat; keep warm.

4. In blazer pan of chafing dish, over direct heat, heat rest of butter. In hot butter, sauté onion, celery, and green pepper about 5 minutes, or until vegetables are tender.

5. Add bouillon, monosodium glutamate, sugar, and remaining salt; cook, stirring occasionally, until mixture starts to simmer—about 15 minutes.

6. Combine cornstarch with lemon juice until smooth. Stir into mixture in chafing dish; continue to simmer, stirring constantly, until mixture is thickened and translucent—about 5 minutes.

7. Add chicken balls and grapes; simmer 5 minutes longer. Place over boiling water in water pan, to keep warm. Serve over hot rice.

MAKES 4 SERVINGS

POACHED FILLETS WITH TOMATO

1 tablespoon butter or	½ cup slivered ripe olives
margarine	¼ cup dry white wine
½ cup sliced onion	½ teaspoon salt
1 tablespoon flour	½ teaspoon dried oregano
1 can (1 lb, 3 oz) tomatoes,	leaves
undrained	¼ teaspoon pepper
2 pkg (1-lb size) frozen sole	Chopped parsley
fillets, thawed and	
cut into serving	
pieces	

1. In hot butter in medium skillet with tight-fitting lid, cook onion 3 minutes.

2. Remove from heat; stir in flour until smooth. Gradually add tomatoes, mixing well. Then add rest of ingredients, except parsley.

3. Bring to boiling, stirring. Reduce heat; simmer, covered, 10 minutes. Turn into chafing dish. Sprinkle with parsley.

QUICK CHOW MEIN

2 tablespoons butter or margarine
2 cups sliced celery
1 cup green-pepper strips
½ cup sliced onion
1 can (1 lb) bean sprouts, drained
1 cup beef bouillon

2 teaspoons soy sauce
½ teaspoon monosodium glutamate
1 can (12 oz) roast beef, diced*
1 tablespoon cornstarch
3 cups cooked white rice

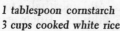

1. In hot butter in large skillet, cook celery, green pepper, and onion until tender—about 5 minutes.

2. Add bean sprouts, bouillon, soy sauce, monosodium glutamate, and beef, mixing until well combined. Bring just to boiling; remove from heat.

3. Combine cornstarch with 1 tablespoon cold water until smooth. Slowly stir into beef mixture.

4. Bring to boiling; boil 1 minute. Reduce heat, and simmer, uncovered, stirring occasionally, 5 minutes.

5. Turn into chafing dish. Serve over hot rice, along with Chinese noodles, if desired.

* Or use 2 cups diced, cooked roast beef, pork or chicken.

SAVORY SCRAMBLED EGGS

1 tablespoon butter or margarine
½ cup finely diced cooked ham
¼ cup finely chopped green pepper

¼ cup finely chopped onion
4 eggs
2 tablespoons milk
¼ teaspoon salt
Dash pepper

1. Melt butter in blazer pan of chafing dish, over direct heat. Add ham, green pepper, and onion; cook 5 minutes.

2. Meanwhile, in medium bowl, with rotary beater, beat eggs with milk, salt, and pepper. Pour into chafing dish.

3. Cook, stirring occasionally, until eggs are set but still shiny and moist—about 5 minutes.

4. Remove chafing dish from direct heat. Place over boiling water in water pan, to keep warm.

SCRAMBLED EGGS WITH OYSTERS

1 tablespoon butter or margarine
4 eggs
2 tablespoons milk

¼ teaspoon salt
Dash pepper
1 can (3⅔ oz) smoked oysters

1. Melt butter in blazer pan of chafing dish, over direct heat.

2. Meanwhile, in medium bowl, with rotary beater, beat eggs with milk, salt, and pepper. Pour into chafing dish.

3. Cook, stirring occasionally, until eggs are set but still shiny and moist—about 5 minutes. Gently stir in oysters.

4. Remove chafing dish from direct heat. Place over boiling water in water pan, to keep warm. Sprinkle with chopped parsley, if desired.

SCRAMBLED EGGS WITH CHICKEN LIVERS

1. In 2 tablespoons hot butter in small skillet, sauté ½ lb chicken livers with ¼ cup sliced onion about 5 minutes, or until tender.
2. Proceed as directed in Scrambled Eggs with Oysters, substituting chicken livers and onion for oysters.

TOMATO-CHEESE SCRAMBLED EGGS

Proceed as directed in Scrambled Eggs with Oysters, substituting 1 cup diced, peeled tomato and ¼ cup grated sharp Cheddar cheese for oysters.

SPAGHETTI AND CRAB

¼ cup olive or salad oil
2 cloves garlic, chopped
1 tablespoon chopped parsley
⅔ cup chopped onion
1 can (6 oz) tomato paste
1 can (1 lb, 3 oz) tomatoes, undrained
1½ teaspoons salt
¼ teaspoon pepper
1½ teaspoons dried oregano leaves
2 cans (6½-oz size) King-crab meat, drained
¼ cup sherry
1½ pkg (8-oz size) spaghetti
Grated Parmesan cheese

1. Slowly heat oil in heavy, 3-quart saucepan. In hot oil, sauté garlic, parsley, and onion until tender—about 5 minutes.
2. Combine tomato paste with 1 cup water, mixing until smooth. Add to garlic mixture along with tomatoes, salt, pepper, and oregano; bring to boiling. Reduce heat; simmer, uncovered, stirring occasionally, 45 minutes.
3. Add crabmeat and sherry; simmer, uncovered, 15 minutes longer.
4. Meanwhile, cook spaghetti as package label directs; drain well.
5. In large bowl, toss spaghetti with sauce until spaghetti is well coated. Turn into chafing dish. Sprinkle with cheese.

TUNA WITH MUSHROOMS

1 tablespoon butter or margarine
1 tablespoon finely chopped onion
2 tablespoons finely chopped celery
2 tablespoons finely chopped green pepper
1 can (4 oz) button mushrooms, drained
1 can (10½ oz) condensed cream-of-asparagus soup, undiluted
1 can (7 oz) tuna, drained
½ cup grated sharp Cheddar cheese
Hot, cooked noodles

1. Melt butter in chafing dish, over direct heat. Add onion, celery, green pepper, and mushrooms; cook, uncovered, until tender—about 8 minutes.
2. Stir in soup, tuna, and cheese; mix well.
3. Cook, uncovered, until heated through—about 15 minutes. Serve over noodles.

APRICOTS FLAMBÉS

1 can (1 lb, 14 oz) whole
    apricots
½ teaspoon grated lemon
    peel
1 tablespoon lemon juice

Dash allspice
2 tablespoons dark-brown
    sugar
¼ cup cognac

1.   Drain apricots, reserving ½ cup syrup. Carefully remove pits, keeping apricots as whole as possible.

2.   Place apricots in 9-inch pie plate. Sprinkle with lemon peel and lemon juice.

3.   Mix reserved syrup with allspice and sugar, in small saucepan; bring to boiling, stirring. Reduce heat; simmer, uncovered, 3 minutes. Pour over apricots.

4.   Run under broiler, 5 inches from heat, about 5 minutes, or until apricots are glazed; baste frequently with syrup. Turn into chafing dish.

5.   Slowly heat cognac in small saucepan. Ignite; pour over apricots.

6.   Serve as dessert or as sauce over ice cream.

CHOCOLATE SAUCE AUX MARRONS

1 jar (9½ oz) marrons in
    heavy syrup

1 pkg (6 oz) semisweet-
    chocolate pieces
¼ cup light rum

1.   Drain marrons, reserving 2 tablespoons syrup; slice marrons.

2.   Melt chocolate over hot, not boiling, water. Add marrons, reserved syrup, and rum; mix well.

3.   Pour into chafing dish. Serve warm, over chocolate or vanilla ice cream.

FRESH-STRAWBERRY SAUCE

1 pint box fresh
    strawberries
¼ cup sugar

⅓ cup Grand Marnier or
    orange juice

1.   Wash strawberries gently in cold water. Drain; hull.

2.   In blazer pan of chafing dish, over direct heat, combine all ingredients. Heat, stirring occasionally, about 10 minutes, or until sugar dissolves.

3.   Place chafing dish over boiling water in water pan. Serve sauce warm, over ice cream or meringue shells.

28

Convenience Foods

Want to be an Escoffier in a matter of minutes? Take a can from your shelves or a package from your freezer, do a little something extra to it, and make magic in your kitchen. The convenience foods are wonderful in themselves, goodness knows, but combined with other convenience foods and ingredients, there's no limit to the imaginative, tasty dishes you can create.

SUNDAY-SUPPER SOUP

MAKES 6 SERVINGS

1 tablespoon butter or margarine
2 tablespoons chopped onion
1 can (11¼ oz) condensed bean-with-bacon soup, undiluted
1 can (10¾ oz) condensed minestrone soup, undiluted
¼ teaspoon dried thyme leaves
1 teaspoon Worcestershire sauce

1. In hot butter in large saucepan, sauté the onion until it is golden—about 3 minutes.

2. Stir in bean-with-bacon soup, along with 2 soup cans water. Add remaining ingredients; simmer, stirring occasionally, over low heat about 10 minutes.

SWISS LEEK SOUP WITH WHITE WINE

MAKES 4 OR 5 SERVINGS

½ cup grated natural Swiss cheese (⅛ lb)
½ cup chablis or light white wine
1 envelope (1⅞ oz) dried cream-of-leek-soup mix
¾ cup milk

1. Combine cheese and wine in top of double boiler. Cook over hot water, stirring, just until cheese melts.

2. Make cream-of-leek soup as package label directs, using milk and 2¼ cups water.

3. Stir wine-and-cheese mixture into soup. Cook, stirring, just until heated through.

POTATO-CORN CHOWDER

MAKES 4 SERVINGS

4 slices bacon
¼ cup chopped onion
2 tablespoons finely
    chopped green
    pepper

1 can (10¼ oz) frozen
    condensed cream-of-
    potato soup,
    undiluted
2 soup cans (10¼-oz size)
    milk
1 can (8 oz) cream-style
    corn

1. In large saucepan, sauté bacon until crisp. Drain; crumble. Reserve 2 tablespoons drippings.

2. In this, sauté onion and green pepper until tender. Add soup and milk.

3. Over low heat, cook until soup thaws, stirring occasionally. Do not boil.

4. Add corn; heat thoroughly. Sprinkle with bacon.

SOUTH SEA SOUP

MAKES 6 SERVINGS

1 pkg (4 oz) dried green-
    pea-soup mix
2 tablespoons finely grated
    orange peel

⅓ cup orange juice
1½ cups milk
½ teaspoon mace
Popcorn

1. In medium saucepan, combine all ingredients, except popcorn, with 4 cups water; stir until well mixed.

2. Cook, uncovered, over medium heat and stirring occasionally, 10 minutes.

3. Serve at once. Top each serving with several kernels of popcorn.

QUICK ONION-CLAM CHOWDER

MAKES 6 SERVINGS

1 pkg (1⅞ oz) dried cream-
    of-leek-soup mix
2 cans (10¼-oz size) frozen
    condensed clam
    chowder,* undiluted
2 cups milk

Dash pepper
¼ teaspoon dried parsley
    flakes
2 canned pimientos,
    drained and cut into
    small shapes

1. In medium saucepan, combine soup mix, chowder, milk, pepper, and parsley with 1½ cups water; stir until well mixed.

2. Over high heat, bring to boiling, uncovered; stir occasionally.

3. Reduce heat; simmer 5 minutes, stirring occasionally. Serve at once. Top each serving with several pimiento cutouts.

* Partially thaw as label directs.

CRANBERRY FRENCH TOAST WITH CHICKEN SAUCE

MAKES 4 SERVINGS

Chicken Sauce:
1 can (10¾ oz) condensed
    cream-of-vegetable
    soup, undiluted
1 can (5 oz) boned chicken,
    cut in 1-inch pieces
⅔ cup milk

½ teaspoon poultry
    seasoning

1 can (7 oz) jellied
    cranberry sauce
8 white-bread slices
1 egg, slightly beaten
½ cup milk
¼ cup butter or margarine

1. Make Chicken Sauce: In medium saucepan, combine soup with chicken, milk, and poultry seasoning.

2. Over medium heat, bring to boiling, stirring. Remove from heat; cover, and keep warm.

3. Cut cranberry sauce, crosswise, into 4 slices. Place each slice between 2 bread slices.

4. Combine egg and milk in shallow dish. Dip sandwiches in egg-milk mixture, coating completely on both sides.

5. In hot butter in medium skillet, sauté sandwiches until golden—about 2 minutes on each side.

6. Serve with warm sauce spooned over.

EASY BORDELAISE SAUCE

1 tablespoon butter or
   margarine
2 tablespoons chopped
   onion
1 can (3 oz) sliced
   mushrooms, drained

1 can (10¾ oz) beef gravy
   (1¼ cups)
1 cup Bordeaux or
   Burgundy

1. In hot butter in medium saucepan, sauté onion until tender—about 3 minutes.

2. Add mushrooms; simmer 2 minutes.

3. Add beef gravy and wine; simmer, uncovered and stirring occasionally, 40 minutes, or until thickened. Nice with roast beef, hamburger, and other beef dishes.

TUNA-MACARONI CASSEROLE

2 cans (15¼-oz size)
   macaroni with cheese
   sauce
1 can (7 oz) chunk-style
   tuna, drained
1 tomato, peeled, coarsely
   chopped
½ teaspoon dried thyme
   leaves

⅛ teaspoon pepper
3 tablespoons fresh bread
   crumbs
1 tablespoon butter or
   margarine, melted
1 tablespoon chopped
   parsley

1. Preheat oven to 375F.

2. Combine macaroni, tuna, tomato, thyme, and pepper in 2-quart casserole; toss gently until well mixed.

3. Toss bread crumbs with butter and parsley; sprinkle over casserole.

4. Bake 20 minutes.

SAUERBRATEN STEW

2 cans (24-oz size) beef
   stew
8 gingersnaps, crushed
   (¾ cup)
2 tablespoons vinegar
2 tablespoons brown sugar

1 teaspoon instant minced
   onion
¼ teaspoon cloves
Dash pepper
1 bay leaf, crumbled
1 tablespoon chopped
   parsley

1. Preheat oven to 375F.

2. In 2-quart casserole, combine all ingredients, except parsley; stir to mix well.

3. Bake 30 minutes.

4. Sprinkle with chopped parsley. Serve, if desired, with hot, buttered noodles.

ORANGE-GLAZED LUNCHEON MEAT

1 can (12 oz) luncheon
   meat
1 orange, unpeeled
½ cup raisins

1 tablespoon cornstarch
2 tablespoons sugar
½ cup orange juice
1 tablespoon lemon juice

1. Preheat oven to 350F.

2. Cut meat crosswise into 8 slices. Cut orange into 4 slices; halve each slice crosswise.

3. In 9-inch round baking dish, alternate meat slices and orange slices, overlapping.

4. Add raisins to 1 cup water in medium saucepan; bring to boiling.

5. In small bowl, combine cornstarch, sugar, and orange and lemon juices; stir until smooth. Add to raisins; cook, stirring, over low heat until mixture boils and is thickened and translucent.

6. Pour over meat and oranges; bake 30 minutes.

 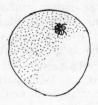

613

CHEESE PUFFLE

MAKES 4 TO 6 SERVINGS

4 egg whites
¼ cup soft butter or
    margarine
1 small clove garlic,
    crushed
7 white-bread slices, crusts
    removed
⅓ cup dry white wine
1 tablespoon flour

1 teaspoon dry mustard
Dash salt
½ teaspoon Worcester-
    shire sauce
¼ teaspoon pepper
4 egg yolks, slightly beaten
1 can (10 oz) condensed
    cheese soup,
    undiluted
⅛ teaspoon cream of tartar

1. In large bowl of electric mixer, let egg whites warm to room temperature—1 hour.

2. Meanwhile, in small bowl, combine butter with garlic, mixing well. Spread bread slices with garlic butter; then cut into 1-inch strips.

3. Line bottom and side of 1-quart, straight-side soufflé dish with bread strips, buttered side out. Trim bread even with top edge of dish. Sprinkle wine evenly over bread; set aside. Preheat oven to 400F.

4. In medium saucepan, combine flour, mustard, salt, Worcestershire, pepper, and egg yolks, mixing well. Gradually stir in soup until smooth.

5. Cook, stirring constantly, over very low heat, 8 to 10 minutes, or until thickened and smooth. Cool slightly.

6. At high speed, beat egg whites with cream of tartar until stiff peaks form when beater is slowly raised.

7. With wire whisk or rubber scraper, gently fold cheese mixture into egg whites, just until combined.

8. Turn into soufflé dish; bake 20 to 25 minutes, or until Puffle seems firm when gently shaken and is puffed and golden. Serve at once.

LIMA-BEAN–MEATBALL PIE

MAKES 4 SERVINGS

2 pkg (10-oz size) frozen
    Fordhook lima beans
    with tomatoes
3 tablespoons butter or
    margarine
½ teaspoon seasoned salt
1 can (15¼ oz) meatballs
    in beef gravy
¼ cup catsup

1 teaspoon Worcestershire
    sauce
1 packet (4-serving size)
    instant mashed
    potatoes
½ cup milk
½ teaspoon salt
⅛ teaspoon pepper
¼ cup grated Parmesan
    cheese

1. Prepare lima beans as package directs. Drain. Toss with 1 tablespoon butter and the seasoned salt. Cover, and keep warm.

2. In small saucepan, combine meatballs and gravy with catsup and Worcestershire; bring to boiling, stirring. Reduce heat; simmer, covered, 8 minutes.

3. Meanwhile, prepare mashed potatoes as package label directs, using milk, 1½ cups water, salt, pepper, and rest of butter.

4. Add cheese to potatoes, mixing well. Turn into an 8-inch pie plate. Spread potatoes evenly over bottom and side of plate, extending onto rim. With tip of knife, make decorative edge.

5. Run under broiler, 6 inches from heat, until edge is golden—about 7 minutes.

6. To serve: Fill potato crust with lima-bean mixture. With slotted spoon, lift meatballs from gravy; pile in center of lima beans. Pass gravy with pie.

DEVILED-HAM CASSEROLE

MAKES 4 SERVINGS

1 can (15¼ oz) macaroni
    with cheese sauce
1 can (4½ oz) deviled ham
1 can (8 oz) stewed
    tomatoes
1 tablespoon chopped
    parsley
1 teaspoon instant minced
    onion

1 teaspoon prepared
    mustard
1 cup ready-to-eat corn
    cereal
1 pkg (2 oz) shredded
    Cheddar cheese
2 tablespoons butter or
    margarine

1. Preheat oven to 400F.
2. Lightly grease 1-quart casserole.
3. In bowl, combine macaroni, deviled ham, tomatoes, parsley, onion, mustard, ½ cup cereal, and cheese.
4. Pour macaroni mixture into casserole.
5. In hot butter in skillet, sauté remaining cereal until lightly browned; spoon over top of casserole.
6. Bake 20 minutes.

QUICK MEATBALLS STROGANOFF

MAKES 4 SERVINGS

1 pkg (8 oz) medium
    noodles
1 tablespoon butter or
    margarine
¼ cup chopped onion
1 can (15¼ oz) meatballs
    in beef gravy
½ cup dairy sour cream

1 can (3 oz) sliced
    mushrooms, drained
1 tablespoon catsup
¼ teaspoon meat-extract
    paste
Dash pepper
¼ teaspoon dried dill weed

1. Cook noodles as package label directs; drain.
2. Meanwhile, in hot butter in medium saucepan, sauté onion until golden—2 to 3 minutes.
3. Add all remaining ingredients except the noodles and the dried dill; mix well.
4. Cook 5 minutes, over medium heat, stirring occasionally.
5. Turn noodles onto platter; toss with dill.
6. Spoon meatballs and sauce over noodles. Serve hot.

FRIDAY SKILLET HASH

MAKES 4 SERVINGS

¼ cup butter or margarine
¼ cup chopped onion
1 pkg (12 oz) frozen potato
    patties
1 pkg (8 oz) frozen
    precooked fish sticks

½ teaspoon salt
⅛ teaspoon pepper
1 tablespoon lemon juice
2 tablespoons chopped
    parsley

1. Heat butter in large, heavy skillet. Add onion and potato patties; sauté, turning frequently, about 5 minutes, or until patties can be broken up with fork.
2. Crumble fish sticks into potato mixture. Add remaining ingredients; mix well.
3. Over medium heat, cook about 12 minutes, turning with spatula as hash browns. Serve with tomato sauce or catsup.

HOT TUNA SALAD

MAKES 6 SERVINGS

2 tablespoons butter or
    margarine
½ cup thinly sliced celery
1 cup thinly sliced onion
½ cup chopped green
    pepper
2 cans (7-oz size) tuna,
    drained

½ cup French dressing
2 tablespoons vinegar
⅛ teaspoon dried basil
    leaves
½ teaspoon salt
Dash pepper
1 can (1 lb) white potatoes,
    drained and sliced

1. In hot butter in large skillet, sauté celery, onion, and green pepper until tender—about 5 minutes.
2. Flake tuna into bite-size pieces. Stir into skillet, along with rest of ingredients, being careful not to break up potatoes.
3. Simmer gently, uncovered, 5 minutes, or until heated through.

615

SHRIMP NEWBURG IN PATTY SHELLS

MAKES 6 SERVINGS

1 pkg (10 oz) frozen patty shells
1 pkg (12 oz) frozen ready-to-cook shrimp
1 can (10 oz) frozen condensed cream-of-shrimp soup, undiluted
¼ cup milk
1 teaspoon grated onion
½ cup grated sharp Cheddar cheese
¼ cup sherry

1. Preheat oven to 450F.
2. Bake patty shells according to package directions.
3. Cook shrimp according to package directions; drain. If necessary, devein with sharp, pointed knife; rinse. Set aside.
4. Meanwhile, in medium saucepan, heat soup and milk, over low heat, until soup is thawed. Stir in onion and cheese; heat until cheese is melted.
5. Add sherry and cooked shrimp; heat 5 minutes. Do not boil.
6. Fill warm patty shells with Shrimp Newburg.

HOT MACARONI SALAD

MAKES 6 SERVINGS

1 pkg (14 oz) macaroni-and-cheese dinner
½ cup chopped green pepper
½ cup mayonnaise or cooked salad dressing
3 tablespoons sweet-pickle relish, drained
2 tablespoons cider vinegar
1 teaspoon onion salt
⅛ teaspoon pepper
½ teaspoon Worcestershire sauce
Pimiento strips

1. Cook macaroni as package label directs; drain.
2. In large saucepan, combine macaroni and cheese, mixing well. Add rest of ingredients, except pimiento strips, stirring gently to combine.
3. Cook, stirring, over low heat, until macaroni mixture is heated through. Serve hot, garnished with pimiento strips.

QUICK KIDNEY-BEAN SALAD

MAKES 4 TO 6 SERVINGS

1 can (12 oz) luncheon meat
1 can (1 lb) red kidney beans, drained
½ cup tomato relish, drained
½ cup mayonnaise or cooked salad dressing
1 tablespoon vinegar
⅛ teaspoon pepper
Crisp salad greens

1. Cut luncheon meat into ½-inch cubes.
2. In large bowl, lightly toss cubes with beans and relish. Refrigerate, covered, 1 hour.
3. Meanwhile, in small bowl, combine remaining ingredients, except salad greens, to mix well. Fold into meat mixture.
4. Serve on crisp greens.

SWEET-POTATO-AND-APPLE CASSEROLE

MAKES 8 SERVINGS

2 cans (1 lb, 2-oz size) sweet potatoes
1 can (1 lb, 4 oz) sliced apples
¼ cup light-brown sugar, firmly packed
½ teaspoon allspice
¼ cup butter or margarine, melted
2 teaspoons lemon juice

1. Preheat oven to 400F.
2. Slice potatoes ¼ inch thick.
3. In 1½-quart casserole, alternately layer potatoes and apples, ending with potatoes and sprinkling each layer with some of sugar, allspice, butter, and lemon juice.
4. Bake 20 minutes, or until nicely browned.

616

GREEN BEANS MORNAY

MAKES 6 SERVINGS

1 can (1 lb) cut green
   beans, drained
1 can (3½ oz) French-fried
   onions
1 can (10½ oz) condensed
   cream-of-celery soup,
   undiluted

½ cup milk
¼ teaspoon dried
   marjoram leaves
⅓ cup grated sharp
   Cheddar cheese

1. Preheat oven to 375F.
2. Alternately layer beans and onions in 1½-quart casserole.
3. Combine soup, milk, and marjoram; pour over beans and onions.
4. Sprinkle top with cheese; bake, uncovered, 25 to 30 minutes.

POTATO-PATTY DUMPLINGS

MAKES 6 SERVINGS

1 pkg (12 oz) frozen
   potato patties,
   thawed
⅓ cup unsifted all-purpose
   flour

1 teaspoon salt
⅛ teaspoon pepper
¼ teaspoon nutmeg
1 egg, beaten
Flour

1. In medium bowl, break up patties with fork. Add ⅓ cup flour, salt, pepper, nutmeg, and egg, mixing until well combined.
2. Shape into 6 balls; roll in additional flour.
3. In large saucepan, bring about 2 quarts lightly salted water to boiling point.
4. Drop dumplings into rapidly boiling water; cover tightly. Reduce heat; boil 18 to 20 minutes (center of dumplings should be dry).
5. With slotted spoon, transfer to paper towels; drain. Serve at once, with pot roast and gravy.

CARAWAY CORN MUFFINS

MAKES 6

1 pkg (9¼ oz) frozen corn
   muffins

1 tablespoon butter or
   margarine, melted
½ teaspoon caraway seed

1. Preheat oven to 400F.
2. Bake muffins as package label directs.
3. After 18 minutes, remove from oven. Brush with butter. Sprinkle with caraway seed; bake 3 to 5 minutes longer. Serve hot.

HONEY BUNS

MAKES 8 SERVINGS

⅓ cup butter or margarine,
   melted
½ cup honey
2 tablespoons grated
   orange peel

2 pkg (8-oz size)
   refrigerator biscuits
⅓ cup chopped walnuts,
   or ⅓ cup light raisins

1. Preheat oven to 375F. Brush a 9-inch ring mold (5½-cup size) with 1 tablespoon butter. Pour in honey.
2. In shallow dish, combine remaining butter and orange peel.
3. Separate biscuits; shape each into a ball. Dip into butter mixture to coat; then dip top into nuts.
4. Arrange irregularly, nut side down, on honey in mold. Place foil under mold in oven, to catch possible runover.
5. Bake buns 20 to 25 minutes, or until golden. Cool in pan 5 minutes; turn out on plate. Serve immediately.

SPICY BLUEBERRY MUFFINS

MAKES 6

1 pkg (9¼ oz) frozen
 blueberry muffins
1 tablespoon butter or
 margarine, melted

1 tablespoon sugar
⅛ teaspoon cinnamon

1. Preheat oven to 400F.
2. Bake muffins according to package directions.
3. After 18 minutes, remove from oven. Brush with butter. Sprinkle with combined sugar and cinnamon; bake 3 to 5 minutes longer. Serve hot.

DANISH-PASTRY RING

MAKES 7 OR 8 SERVINGS

2 pkg (9.5-oz size)
 refrigerator Danish
 pastry

½ cup toasted sliced
 almonds
2 preserved kumquats, cut
 into eighths

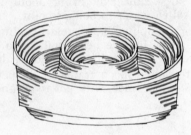

1. Preheat oven to 375F. Separate each of the packages of Danish pastry into 8 portions, to make 16 pastries in all.
2. Arrange 8 of the pastries, barely touching, flat side down, around bottom of an ungreased 5½-cup ring mold.
3. Then arrange 8 remaining pastries on top of first layer, so that each overlaps 2 pastries on bottom layer.
4. Bake 20 to 25 minutes, or until ring is golden-brown.
5. Invert pastry on wire rack; remove pan. Spread top and side of warm pastry with frosting from both packages.
6. Decorate ring with sliced almonds and kumquat strips. Best served still slightly warm.

HOT CHEESE ROLLS

MAKES 12

1 pkg (8 oz) refrigerator
 butterflake rolls
3 tablespoons butter or
 margarine, melted

⅓ cup packaged grated
 American cheese

1. Preheat oven to 375F.
2. Separate dough into 12 rolls. Coat each completely with butter, then with cheese; bake as package label directs. Serve hot.

SESAME CRESCENT

MAKES 1 SMALL LOAF

2 pkg (8-oz size)
 refrigerator biscuits

1 egg white, slightly beaten
4 teaspoons sesame seed

1. Preheat oven to 350F.
2. Place both packages of unseparated biscuits, on edge and end to end, on ungreased cookie sheet; lightly press together, to make one loaf. Taper ends slightly; bend into crescent.
3. Brush lightly with egg white. Sprinkle with sesame seed; then bake about 25 minutes, or until bread is nicely browned.

QUICK APPLESAUCE CRISP

1 can (1 lb, 1 oz)
   applesauce
½ cup seedless raisins
½ cup light-brown sugar,
   firmly packed
½ cup broken walnuts

½ teaspoon cinnamon
¼ teaspoon nutmeg
1 cup packaged biscuit mix
½ cup granulated sugar
¼ cup butter or margarine

MAKES 6 SERVINGS

1.   Preheat oven to 400F.
2.   Combine applesauce, raisins, brown sugar, walnuts, cinnamon, and nutmeg. Turn into a 9-inch pie plate.
3.   Combine biscuit mix and granulated sugar in medium bowl. With pastry blender, cut in butter until like coarse cornmeal.
4.   Sprinkle over applesauce; bake 25 minutes.
5.   Serve warm, with light cream, if desired.

BAKED PEACHES AND CREAM

1 can (1 lb, 13 oz) peach
   halves
½ cup light-brown sugar,
   firmly packed
⅛ teaspoon cinnamon

6 tablespoons cornflakes
1 tablespoon butter or
   margarine
1 pint vanilla ice cream

MAKES 6 SERVINGS

1.   Preheat oven to 375F.
2.   Drain peaches, reserving ½ cup liquid. Arrange peaches, cut side up, in an 8-by-8-by-2-inch baking pan. Add reserved liquid.
3.   Combine sugar and cinnamon; sprinkle evenly over peaches.
4.   Top each peach half with 1 tablespoon cornflakes and a dot of butter; bake 15 minutes.
5.   Serve warm, with ice cream spooned over.

PLUM CRUMBLE

5 tablespoons butter or
   margarine
1 can (1 lb, 14 oz) purple
   plums, drained
½ cup sifted all-purpose
   flour

½ cup sugar
¼ teaspoon salt
¼ teaspoon nutmeg
1 cup cornflakes
Light cream

MAKES 4 SERVINGS

1.   Preheat oven to 350F. Lightly grease 4 (6-oz) custard cups with 1 tablespoon butter.
2.   Cut plums in half; remove pits. Divide plums equally into prepared custard cups.
3.   Combine flour, sugar, salt, and nutmeg in medium bowl. With pastry blender, cut in rest of butter until crumbly. Stir in cornflakes.
4.   Sprinkle over plums; bake 40 minutes.
5.   Serve warm, with light cream.

QUICK BUTTERSCOTCH BROWNIES

½ cup sifted all-purpose
   flour
¼ cup sugar
½ teaspoon baking powder
¼ teaspoon salt
2 eggs
2 pkg (4-oz size)
   butterscotch-pudding
   and pie-filling mix

⅓ cup butter or margarine,
   melted
½ teaspoon vanilla extract
½ cup chopped walnuts
½ cup semisweet-
   chocolate pieces

MAKES 24

1.   Preheat oven to 325F. Lightly grease a 9-by-9-by-1¾-inch pan.
2.   Sift flour with sugar, baking powder, and salt; set aside.
3.   In large bowl, with rotary beater, beat eggs until very thick. Add flour mixture and rest of ingredients; stir to mix well.
4.   Turn into prepared pan; bake 35 to 40 minutes, or until cake tester inserted in center comes out clean.
5.   Let cool slightly in pan, placed on wire rack. Cut into 24 pieces.

PEACHES IN WINE JELLY

MAKES 5 SERVINGS

1 pkg (3 oz) raspberry-
   flavored gelatin
1 cup boiling water
⅔ cup Burgundy

1 pkg (12 oz) frozen peach
   slices, drained
Whipped cream
   (optional)

1. Dissolve gelatin in boiling water in medium bowl. Add Burgundy and ⅓ cup cold water.

2. Refrigerate until consistency of unbeaten egg white—about 1 hour.

3. Stir in peach slices. Pour into 5 (4-oz) molds. Refrigerate until firm—about 1 hour.

4. To unmold, loosen edge of each mold with spatula. Invert over individual serving plates; shake gently to release. If necessary, place a hot, damp dishcloth over inverted molds, and shake again to release.

5. Garnish with whipped cream.

NUT-BREAD TORTE

MAKES 8 TO 10 SERVINGS

1 pkg (1 lb, 1 oz) nut-bread
   mix
1 egg
1 cup seedless black-
   raspberry preserves

¾ cup apricot preserves
1 tablespoon lemon juice
1 cup heavy cream,
   whipped

1. Preheat oven to 350F. Line bottoms of two 8-by-1½-inch round layer-cake pans with waxed paper.

2. Make nut-bread mix, as package label directs, using egg and 1 cup water.

3. Turn into prepared pans; bake 25 minutes, or until cake tester inserted in center comes out clean.

4. Let cool in pans 5 minutes. Then turn out on wire rack; peel off paper. Let cool completely.

5. With sharp knife, split each layer in half horizontally.

6. In small bowl, combine raspberry and apricot preserves with lemon juice; mix well.

7. Put torte layers together with preserve mixture, using a scant ½ cup between layers and on top.

8. Frost side of torte with some of whipped cream. Put rest of cream through pastry bag, using a No. 2 decorating tip. Decorate top edge of torte. Refrigerate until serving.

Quick Tricks with Frozen Dinners

Scallop Dinner: Carefully remove cover. Mix 3 tablespoons melted butter or margarine, 4 teaspoons lemon juice, and ½ teaspoon bottled capers. Spoon over scallops. Sprinkle with 1 tablespoon grated Parmesan cheese. Replace cover. Heat according to package directions.

Chicken Dinner: Carefully remove cover. Spoon 1 tablespoon chopped chutney with syrup over chicken. Replace cover. Heat according to package directions.

Beef Dinner: Carefully remove cover. Spread 1 teaspoon horseradish over beef. Replace cover. Heat according to package directions.

Swiss-Steak Dinner: Carefully remove cover. Spread 1 tablespoon canned chopped mushroom stems and pieces over meat. Replace cover. Heat according to package directions.

Meat-Loaf Dinner: Carefully remove cover. Sprinkle meat loaf and sauce with ⅛ teaspoon dried oregano leaves and ⅛ teaspoon garlic powder. Replace cover. Heat according to package directions.

Creamed-Chicken Dinner: In 1 tablespoon butter or margarine in small skillet, sauté 1 tablespoon slivered almonds until golden. Carefully remove cover. Spread almonds over chicken. Replace cover. Heat according to package directions.

Any Dinner: Carefully remove cover. Sprinkle vegetable with ⅛ teaspoon seasoned salt. Replace cover. Heat as package directs.

Quick Tricks with Frozen Pies

Individual Turkey Pie: Just before serving, spread 1 tablespoon canned cranberry sauce over top of hot pie.

Individual Chicken Pie: Five minutes before end of baking period, remove pie from oven. Sprinkle 2 tablespoons grated Cheddar cheese over crust. Complete baking.

Individual Tuna Pie: Melt 1 tablespoon butter or margarine. Stir in ¼ teaspoon celery seed. Brush over crust of pie. Bake as label directs.

Individual Beef Pie: Melt 1 tablespoon butter or margarine. Stir in ½ teaspoon sesame seed. Brush over crust of pie. Bake as label directs.

Family-size Apple Pie: Combine 2 tablespoons sugar, ¼ teaspoon cinnamon, and ⅛ teaspoon nutmeg. Five minutes before end of baking period, remove pie from oven. Brush crust with 2 tablespoons melted butter or margarine. Sprinkle with sugar mixture. Complete baking.

Family-Size Pumpkin Pie: Bake pie according to package directions. Sift ¼ cup light-brown sugar over hot pie. Sprinkle with ¼ cup chopped pecans. Return to oven for 3 minutes. Cool.

Family-Size Blueberry Pie: Combine 2 tablespoons sugar, ¼ teaspoon nutmeg, and ½ teaspoon grated lemon peel. Five minutes before end of baking period, remove pie from oven. Brush crust with 2 tablespoons melted butter or margarine. Sprinkle with sugar mixture. Complete baking.

29
Cooking
for
Children

The best cooks begin early in childhood, and almost always by watching their mothers. At first, perhaps, there is the magic of the egg beater turning an egg white into a little mountain peak of shiny white snow, or the smell of breakfast bacon in the pan, or the lick and promise of chocolate icing in the making. Later, there is the actual participation—maybe a small one to begin with—and gradually the children become real working partners in the creation of food.

Cooking is fun. It opens the child's door to a whole new world, a creative, challenging world. Do be sure that your children's first cooking venture is a success, that it rewards them with a sense of accomplishment. Let them cook what they wish or help when they wish to. The experience should be a pleasant one, not a job assignment.

The preschool child is usually content to help stir a batter or cut out cookies. Older children take pleasure in measuring and adding ingredients and feeling that the finished product is their own. Teach them how to read a recipe completely through before they start to prepare it. See that they understand and follow safety rules; until a child is experienced enough to know the danger in handling knives and matches, their use should be carefully supervised. Other precautions to be stressed are the proper use of pot holders, the proper way to set a pot on the range, so that the handle cannot be hit accidentally.

Also (and this can avoid messiness and clutter and a big clean-up job) establish standards of cleanliness and good working habits. Teach them to wash the dishes and utensils as they go along, so there is a minimum of cleaning up to do afterward.

Now, on to the recipes.

Easy Recipes for Children to Make

Easiest of the easy and quickest to reward are these no-cutting, no-cooking drinks. Chocolate milk is a good place to start. Later on, as they progress, what fun they'll have making soups and main dishes and yummy desserts for their friends and families!

CHOCOLATE-FLAVORED MILK

MAKES 2 SERVINGS

2 cups cold milk
2 tablespoons prepared
   chocolate syrup
¼ teaspoon peppermint
   extract

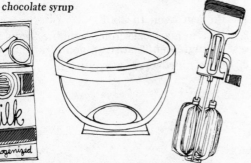

1. Beat all ingredients together in small bowl, with rotary beater, until well combined.
2. Pour into 2 chilled glasses.

Cherry-Flavored Milk: Proceed as directed above, substituting ¼ cup maraschino-cherry juice for chocolate syrup. Omit peppermint extract.

Strawberry-Flavored Milk: Proceed as directed above, substituting ½ cup frozen strawberries, partially thawed and undrained, for chocolate syrup. Omit peppermint extract.

CRANBERRY-APPLE PUNCH

MAKES 18 TO 20 SERVINGS

1 bottle (1 pt, 12 oz)
   apple juice, chilled
1 bottle (1 pt, 12 oz)
   ginger ale, chilled
1 bottle (1 pt) cranberry
   juice, chilled
1 small orange, thinly
   sliced

1. Combine all ingredients in large bowl, stirring to mix well.
2. Serve over ice cubes in punch cups.

Grape-Apple Punch: Make Cranberry-Apple Punch, substituting 1 bottle (1 pt) grapejuice for cranberry juice.

HEARTY PEA SOUP

MAKES 3 OR 4 SERVINGS

1 can (11¼ oz) condensed
   pea soup, undiluted
1 cup milk
2 frankfurters, thinly sliced
2 white-bread slices,
   toasted and buttered

1. Place soup in medium saucepan. Gradually add milk, stirring until well combined.
2. Bring to boiling, over medium heat, stirring constantly.
3. Reduce heat. Add frankfurters; simmer, uncovered, 3 minutes longer.
4. Trim off crusts from bread; cut bread into cubes.
5. Serve soup in individual bowls, topped with bread cubes.

623

MEATBALL SUPPER SOUP

MAKES 4 TO 6 SERVINGS

1 can (10½ oz) condensed
    cream-of-mushroom
    soup, undiluted
1 cup milk
1 teaspoon instant minced
    onion

1 can (15¼ oz) meatballs
    in beef gravy
1 tablespoon finely
    chopped parsley

1. In medium saucepan, combine all ingredients except parsley.
2. Bring to boiling, stirring. Serve in bowls, sprinkled with parsley.

CAMPFIRE BEANS

MAKES 8 SERVINGS

2 cans (1-lb size)
    barbecue beans
¼ cup light molasses

1 teaspoon Worcestershire
    sauce
2 tablespoons prepared
    mustard

1. Preheat oven to 350F.
2. In 1½-quart casserole, combine beans with rest of ingredients, stirring gently to mix well.
3. Bake, uncovered, 30 minutes.

CHEESY FRENCH FRIES

MAKES 3 SERVINGS

1 pkg (9 oz) frozen French-
    fried potatoes
¼ teaspoon salt

Dash pepper
½ cup grated sharp
    Cheddar cheese

1. Preheat oven to 450F.
2. Arrange potatoes in lightly greased 9-inch pie plate. Sprinkle with salt and pepper.
3. Bake, uncovered, 15 minutes.
4. Sprinkle cheese over potatoes. Bake 2 to 3 minutes longer, or until cheese is melted.

CHICKEN-CORN PILAF

MAKES 4 TO 6 SERVINGS

¼ cup butter or margarine
1½ cups packaged
    precooked rice
1 chicken-bouillon cube
1 cup boiling water
½ teaspoon salt

1 can (5 oz) boned chicken,
    coarsely chopped
1 can (7 oz) whole-kernel
    corn, drained
2 tablespoons finely
    chopped pimiento

1. In hot butter in medium skillet, sauté rice, stirring frequently, until golden-brown.
2. Add remaining ingredients, mixing well. Cook, tightly covered and over low heat, 5 minutes. Serve with sliced tomatoes, if desired.

STUFFED CELERY PLUS

For a special treat, stuff chilled crisp celery stalks with one of the following:

1. Combine 1 cup creamed cottage cheese with 1 tablespoon chopped stuffed olives. Makes 1 cup.

2. Combine 1 (3-oz) package soft cream cheese with 2 tablespoons drained crushed pineapple. Makes ½ cup.

3. Mix ½ cup creamed cottage cheese with ¼ cup grated raw carrot and 2 tablespoons seedless raisins. Makes ⅔ cup.

4. Blend ½ cup pasteurized process cheese spread with 2 teaspoons drained sweet-pickle relish. Makes ½ cup.

5. Or use crunchy-style peanut butter.

EASY TUNA CASSEROLE

MAKES 4 TO 6 SERVINGS

1 can (10½ oz) condensed
    cream-of-mushroom
    soup, undiluted
½ cup milk
1 can (7 oz) tuna, drained

1 can (8 oz) peas, drained
2 tablespoons sliced
    pimiento-stuffed
    olives
2 cups corn chips, crushed

1. Preheat oven to 375F.

2. In 1½-quart casserole, combine soup with milk, mixing until smooth.

3. Add tuna, peas, and olives, mixing well. Top with corn chips.

4. Bake, uncovered, 25 minutes.

EGGS À LA KING

MAKES 4 SERVINGS

1 can (10½ oz) condensed
    cream-of-mushroom
    soup, undiluted
½ cup milk

4 hard-cooked eggs,
    coarsely chopped
4 packaged toaster corn
    muffins, toasted
Chopped parsley

1. In medium saucepan, combine soup and milk, mixing well. Bring to boiling, stirring constantly.

2. Carefully stir in eggs; reheat gently. Serve hot, over corn muffins. Sprinkle with parsley.

SLOPPY JOES

MAKES 6 SERVINGS

½ lb ground beef
1 can (1 lb) beans and
    ground beef in
    barbecue sauce

¼ cup catsup
3 hamburger buns, split
    and toasted

1. In medium skillet, sauté meat, stirring, until it loses its red color.

2. Add beans and catsup, mixing well. Simmer, uncovered, 5 minutes. Spoon mixture over buns.

SPAGHETTI MEAT LOAF

MAKES 8 SERVINGS

1 lb ground chuck
½ cup finely chopped
   onion
1 egg, slightly beaten

1 teaspoon seasoned salt
1 can (15¼ oz) spaghetti
   in tomato sauce

1.   Preheat oven to 350F. Lightly grease an 8-by-8-by-2-inch baking dish.
2.   Lightly toss chuck with onion, egg, salt, and spaghetti, to combine.
3.   Pack mixture into prepared pan; bake, uncovered, 1 hour.
4.   To serve, cut into squares.

FUDGE COTTAGE PUDDING

MAKES 8 SERVINGS

1½ cups sifted cake flour
1 cup sugar
⅓ cup sifted unsweetened
   cocoa
1 teaspoon baking soda

¾ teaspoon salt
⅓ cup salad oil
1 teaspoon vanilla extract
1 teaspoon white vinegar
1 qt soft vanilla ice cream

1.   Preheat oven to 350F.
2.   Sift flour with sugar, cocoa, baking soda, and salt into ungreased 8-by-8-by-2-inch pan.
3.   Shake pan, to distribute flour mixture evenly. Make 3 wells in center of flour mixture. Pour oil into one, vanilla into second, and vinegar into third.
4.   Pour 1 cup cold water over mixture; stir until smooth and well combined. Batter will be thin.
5.   Bake 30 to 35 minutes, or until cake tester inserted in center comes out clean. Let cool slightly on wire rack. Cut into squares while still warm, and serve with ice cream.

STUFFED DATES

MAKES ABOUT 21

¾ cup pitted dates
About 21 miniature
   marshmallows, ¼
   cup walnut or pecan
   halves, or ¼ cup
   creamy peanut butter

Flaked coconut or
   confectioners' sugar

1.   Stuff each date with a marshmallow, a nut, or ½ teaspoon peanut butter.
2.   Then roll in coconut or confectioners' sugar.

PEANUT-BUTTER CUSTARD

MAKES 6 SERVINGS

½ cup crunchy-style
   peanut butter

1 pkg (2¼ oz) custard-
   flavored dessert mix
2 cups milk

1.   In medium saucepan, combine peanut butter and dessert mix. Gradually add milk, stirring until smooth.
2.   Cook, over medium heat, stirring constantly, until custard comes to full boil.
3.   Pour into bowl; let stand 2 minutes.
4.   Place a sheet of waxed paper directly on surface of custard. Refrigerate at least 1 hour, or until well chilled.

SPICY APPLE BETTY

MAKES 6 SERVINGS

1 can (1 lb, 4 oz) sliced
    apples, undrained
6 tablespoons light-brown
    sugar
⅛ teaspoon salt

¼ teaspoon cinnamon
2 cups cornflakes
¼ cup butter or margarine,
    melted
Soft vanilla ice cream

1. Preheat oven to 400F.
2. In a 1½-quart casserole, combine apples with 2 tablespoons sugar, the salt, and cinnamon, mixing well.
3. Toss cornflakes with rest of sugar and the butter. Spoon over apples.
4. Bake, uncovered, 15 minutes. Serve warm, topped with ice cream.

Recipes Mother Makes for Children

This chapter is dedicated not only to recipes that children can make but also to dishes that mothers may prepare for their children. Ours are imaginative and gay and so appetizing that we're sure they'll turn any child into an Eager Eater!

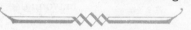

BANANA EGGNOG

MAKES 2 CUPS

1 small, ripe banana
1 egg
1 tablespoon sugar

1 cup cold milk
½ teaspoon vanilla extract

1. Peel banana. Cut into small pieces. In 1-quart measure, with rotary beater, beat banana with egg and sugar until smooth and well combined.
2. Add milk and vanilla; continue to beat until just combined. Pour into chilled glasses.

VARIATIONS

Chocolate-Banana Eggnog: Make Banana Eggnog, substituting chocolate milk for milk.

Maple-Flavored Banana Eggnog: Make Banana Eggnog, omitting vanilla; add 2 tablespoons maple-flavored syrup.

Peanut-Butter Banana Eggnog: Make Banana Eggnog, adding ¼ cup creamy peanut butter.

Raspberry-Banana Eggnog: Make Banana Eggnog, adding ½ cup raspberry sherbet. Makes about 2¼ cups.

MEXICAN CHOCOLATE

MAKES 8 SERVINGS

¼ lb sweet chocolate
1 cup hot water
5½ cups milk
½ cup heavy cream
1 tablespoon cinnamon

⅛ teaspoon nutmeg
1 teaspoon vanilla extract
8 (2½-inch) cinnamon
    sticks (optional)

1. Combine chocolate and hot water in top of double boiler; melt, over hot water, stir.
2. Meanwhile, in 3-quart saucepan, combine milk, cream, cinnamon, and nutmeg; beat with rotary beater or wire whisk until well combined.
3. Over medium heat, heat milk mixture until bubbles form around edge of pan; stir occasionally.
4. Remove from heat. Stir in melted chocolate and vanilla; beat with rotary beater until foamy. Serve with cinnamon stick in each cup.

BLACK-EYED-SUSAN SALAD

MAKES 4 SERVINGS

4 large dried prunes,
    cooked and pitted
½ cup creamed cottage
    cheese
4 crisp lettuce leaves

1 can (1 lb, 1 oz) peach
    slices, drained
3 tablespoons grated carrot
2 ripe olives, halved

1. Stuff each prune with 2 tablespoons cottage cheese. Arrange a lettuce leaf on each of 4 individual salad plates; place a prune in center of each.
2. Arrange 5 peach slices, petal fashion, around each prune.
3. Sprinkle a little grated carrot over each prune; top with olive half.

BUNNY SALAD

MAKES 1 SERVING

1 canned pear half
1 crisp lettuce leaf

4 orange sections
1 maraschino cherry

1. Place pear half, cut side down, on lettuce leaf. Add 2 orange sections for each ear.
2. Cut cherry into 6 slivers; use to make eyes, nose, mouth, and centers for ears. Serve with mayonnaise, if desired.

JACK-BE-NIMBLE SALAD

MAKES 2 SERVINGS

2 crisp lettuce leaves
2 pineapple slices, drained
1 large banana, halved
    crosswise

2 maraschino cherries
Mayonnaise

1. Place lettuce leaves on individual salad plates. Arrange a pineapple slice in center of each.
2. Stand a banana half, cut side down, on each pineapple slice. Fasten a cherry to the tip of each banana with a wooden pick. Serve with mayonnaise.

PETER RABBIT SALAD

MAKES 3 SERVINGS

1 pkg (3 oz) cream cheese
⅓ cup grated carrot*
3 parsley sprigs

Spinach leaves
1 can (8¾ oz) pineapple
    tidbits, drained

1. Divide cream cheese into 3 parts. With hands, shape each part to resemble a carrot 3 inches long.
2. Roll "carrots" in grated carrot, coating completely. Insert a parsley sprig in top of each.
3. Serve on spinach leaves; garnish with pineapple tidbits. Serve with mayonnaise, if desired.
* Grate carrot directly onto paper towel; pat dry with another paper towel.

CARROT-RAISIN SALAD

MAKES 4 SERVINGS

1 cup grated raw carrot
1 cup shredded cabbage
¼ cup seedless raisins
½ teaspoon salt

2 tablespoons lemon juice
1 tablespoon sugar
¼ cup mayonnaise or
    cooked salad dressing

1. Lightly toss carrot, cabbage, raisins, salt, lemon juice, and sugar until well combined. Refrigerate until ready to serve.
2. Just before serving, toss with mayonnaise.

SANDWICH CUTOUTS

MAKES 6 SANDWICHES

1 pkg (3 oz) soft cream
    cheese
¼ cup orange marmalade
6 white-bread slices

6 whole-wheat-bread slices
3 tablespoons soft butter or
    margarine

1. In small bowl, combine cheese with marmalade, mixing until well combined.
2. With sharp knife, trim crusts from bread. With animal-shape cookie cutter, cut out center of 3 white-bread slices and 3 whole-wheat bread slices. Set cutouts and cutout bread slices aside.
3. Spread remaining bread slices with butter; then spread with cream-cheese mixture. Top with cutout bread slice; fit in animal cutout of contrasting-color bread.

VEGETABLE ROLL-UPS

MAKES 10

10 fresh-white-bread slices
¼ cup soft butter or
    margarine
½ cup grated sharp
    Cheddar cheese

Fillings:
10 (3-inch) carrot sticks,
    celery sticks, green-
    pepper strips, or
    cooked asparagus
    spears

1. Trim crusts from bread; flatten each slice with rolling pin.
2. In small bowl, mix butter with cheese. Use to spread on bread slices. Place one of Fillings along one side; roll up as for a jelly roll.
3. Wrap each roll securely in waxed paper. Refrigerate, seam side down on tray, at least 1 hour before serving.

Toasted Vegetable Roll-Ups: Make Vegetable Roll-Ups, as directed above. Run under broiler, 4 inches from heat, until golden-brown. Serve immediately.

BLUSHING BUNNY

MAKES 4 SERVINGS

1 can (8 oz) tomato sauce
1 can (11 oz) condensed
    Cheddar-cheese
    soup, undiluted
¼ teaspoon dry mustard

4 white-bread slices,
    toasted
4 crisp bacon slices,
    crumbled

1. In small saucepan, combine tomato sauce with cheese soup and mustard, mixing well. Over medium heat, bring to boiling, stirring constantly.
2. Serve over toast. Sprinkle with bacon.

MILK TOAST

MAKES 4 SERVINGS

2 cups milk

4 white-bread slices,
    toasted and buttered

1. Heat milk in small saucepan just until bubbles form around edge of pan. Remove from heat; let cool slightly.
2. Serve toast slices in individual soup plates with ½ cup warm milk poured over each.

Cinnamon-Sugar Milk Toast: Combine ¼ cup sugar with ½ teaspoon cinnamon, mixing well. Proceed as directed for Milk Toast, sprinkling toast slices with cinnamon-sugar mixture.

Banana Milk Toast: Proceed as directed for Milk Toast, arranging a few banana slices over each toast slice.

EGG IN A FRAME

1 white-bread slice
1 tablespoon soft butter or
    margarine
1 egg
Salt

1. Spread both sides of bread with butter. With round 2½-inch cookie cutter, cut out center.
2. In small skillet with tight-fitting lid, sauté bread slice and bread round, uncovered, until golden on both sides.
3. Remove bread round from skillet; keep warm. Carefully break egg into center of bread slice; cook, covered, 4 to 5 minutes, or until egg is set.
4. With pancake turner, remove to serving plate; sprinkle egg lightly with salt. If desired, spread bread round with deviled ham; place on top of egg.

PEANUTBURGERS

1 lb ground chuck
½ teaspoon salt
⅛ teaspoon pepper
¼ cup crunchy-style
    peanut butter

1. Lightly toss chuck with rest of ingredients, in large bowl, to combine.
2. Gently shape into 6 patties.
3. Broil, 4 inches from heat, 6 minutes on one side. Turn; broil 4 minutes on other side, for medium.

Relishburgers: Proceed as directed above, substituting 2 tablespoons mustard-pickle relish for peanut butter.

Chiliburgers: Proceed as directed above, omitting peanut butter; add 2 tablespoons chili sauce and ½ teaspoon instant minced onion.

Oliveburgers: Proceed as directed above, substituting 2 tablespoons chopped stuffed olives for peanut butter.

SCRAMBLED EGGS IN TOAST CUPS

4 white-bread slices
2 tablespoons butter or
    margarine, melted
4 eggs
¼ cup milk
¼ teaspoon salt
Dash pepper
2 tablespoons butter or
    margarine

1. Preheat oven to 350F.
2. Trim crusts from bread slices. Brush both sides with melted butter.
3. Press a slice into each of 4 (6-oz) custard cups. Place on cookie sheet; bake 15 to 20 minutes, or until bread is toasted.
4. Meanwhile, in small bowl, with rotary beater, beat eggs with milk, salt, and pepper until well combined.
5. Heat butter in medium skillet until a little cold water sizzles when dropped on it.
6. Pour egg mixture into skillet; cook slowly until eggs start to set. Then stir constantly with fork until eggs are soft and creamy.
7. To serve: Fill toast cups with egg mixture. If desired, sprinkle with crumbled, cooked bacon or chopped parsley.

CHOCOLATE ICE-CREAM CONES

2 pkg (6-oz size) semisweet-
    chocolate pieces or
    butterscotch pieces
12 ice-cream cones
Decorations, below
3 pt assorted ice cream

 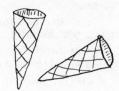

MAKES 12

1. Melt chocolate over hot, not boiling, water.
2. With small spatula, spread 1 tablespoon melted chocolate inside each cone. Swirl top edge of cone in chocolate; spread to make a ¾-inch-deep border.
3. Decorate as desired. Refrigerate until serving.
4. Top with ice cream.

PEANUT-BUTTER ICE-CREAM CONES

½ cup creamy peanut
    butter, softened
12 ice-cream cones
Decorations, below
3 pt assorted ice cream

MAKES 12

1. With small spatula, spread peanut butter around top edge and side of cones to make a border ¾ inch deep.
2. Decorate or sprinkle with one or more decorations.
3. Top each with scoop of ice cream. Serve at once.

Decorations for Ice-Cream Cones: Chocolate-covered peanuts; miniature marshmallows, halved crosswise; miniature nonpareils; chocolate sprinkles; colored sprinkles; chopped walnuts; red and green sugar; flaked coconut; light or dark raisins.

CRISPY-CARAMEL LOLLIPOPS

½ pkg (14-oz size) vanilla
    caramels (25)
4 cups oven-toasted rice
    cereal

MAKES 5

1. In top of double boiler, combine caramels with 3 tablespoons water.
2. Cook, over hot water, stirring occasionally, until caramels are melted.
3. Pour caramel mixture over cereal in medium bowl; stir with wooden spoon until cereal is well coated.
4. Pack cereal mixture into 5 (5-oz) paper dessert dishes. Insert wooden skewer into center of each.
5. Refrigerate at least 30 minutes. To serve, gently remove lollipops from paper dishes.

EASY RICE-CUSTARD PUDDING

½ cup packaged
   precooked rice
3 tablespoons sugar
1 teaspoon vanilla
   extract
1 pkg (2¼ oz) custard-
   flavor dessert mix

2½ cups milk
½ cup light raisins
½ cup heavy cream,
   whipped

1. Cook rice as package label directs. Stir in sugar and vanilla. Set aside, covered.
2. Meanwhile, in medium saucepan, combine dessert mix with milk. Bring to boiling, stirring occasionally.
3. Stir in rice and raisins. Let cool, uncovered, stirring occasionally.
4. Spoon into 6 custard cups. Refrigerate until firm—about 1½ hours.
5. To serve, garnish with whipped cream.

GINGERBREAD-AND-APPLESAUCE ICE-CREAM CONES

12 flat-bottom ice-cream
   cones
1 pkg (14½ oz) ginger-
   bread mix

1½ pt soft vanilla ice
   cream
1 cup applesauce

1. Preheat oven to 350F. Arrange ice-cream cones on large cookie sheet.
2. Make gingerbread mix as package label directs, using amount of water specified.
3. Fill each cone with 3 level tablespoons gingerbread batter. Bake 25 minutes, or until cake tester inserted in center comes out clean. Then remove cones to wire rack; let cool.
4. Meanwhile, in large bowl, combine ice cream with applesauce; mix well. Turn into ice-cube tray. Freeze until firm—about 1 hour.
5. To serve: Top each gingerbread cone with scoop of applesauce ice cream.

HEAVENLY HASH

2 cups cold cooked white
   rice, loosely packed
1 can (8¾ oz) pineapple
   tidbits, drained
¼ cup maraschino cherries,
   drained and sliced

12 marshmallows,
   quartered*
1 cup heavy cream,
   whipped

1. In medium bowl, lightly toss rice with pineapple, cherries, and marshmallows, to combine. Refrigerate, covered, 1 hour.
2. Fold in whipped cream just before serving. Top with additional cherries, if desired.
* Or use 1½ cups miniature marshmallows.

RAGGEDY ANN PUDDINGS

1 pkg (3¾ oz) instant
   vanilla pudding
2 cups milk
4 chocolate wafers, crushed

1 maraschino cherry,
   slivered
10 seedless raisins

1. Prepare vanilla pudding with milk as package label directs.
2. Pour into 4 or 5 shallow, round dessert dishes. Refrigerate 30 minutes, or until well chilled.
3. To decorate pudding: From tip of spoon, sprinkle some of crushed wafers halfway around edge of each pudding, for hair. Use cherry sliver for mouth, raisins for eyes and nose. Serve immediately.

For years, we've been making all sorts of charming favors out of marshmallows. We've made them for parties, to brighten sickrooms, to beguile children. Sometimes we've made them just to surprise and delight our families at dinner. Favors are fun to make; but the real reward comes when you see the faces of the people (big and little) you have set out to please.

MARSHMALLOW FAVORS

Glue:	Soft licorice candy
1½ cups unsifted	Licorice string
confectioners' sugar	Small soft gumdrops
1 egg white, unbeaten	Wooden picks
	Paper plates
Large marshmallows	Stiff brown and white
Miniature marshmallows	paper

1. To make Glue: In small bowl of electric mixer at medium speed, beat sugar with egg white until mixture is thick enough to hold a definite shape.

2. Keep glue covered with damp cloth until ready to use. Makes about ½ cup.

Note: When making favors, let glue dry completely on each part of animal before assembling next part.

MARY'S LITTLE LAMB

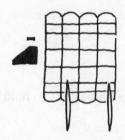

1. Insert 4 wooden picks in side of large marshmallow, for legs; insert legs into inverted paper plate, for support.

2. Glue 2 rows of miniature marshmallows (use about 10 for each row) around side of a large marshmallow. Then glue more miniature marshmallows over front and back, leaving space in front for nose.

3. Glue pieces of licorice candy to marshmallow, for nose; add 2 pieces of licorice string to right and left of nose, for eyes.

FROSTY THE SNOWMAN

1. First make top hat: Use a thin, flat piece of licorice candy for brim. Glue a larger piece of licorice candy to brim for crown.

2. Attach 2 large marshmallows, ends together, with wooden pick, to resemble a snowman. Insert one end of wooden pick into top hat; insert other end of wooden pick into inverted paper plate, for support.

3. Make eyes, mouth, and buttons for snowman with pieces of licorice string.

TIMMY THE TURTLE

1. Use large marshmallow for body. With wooden pick, attach small gumdrop (flat side down) to bottom edge of body, for head.

2. Cut another small gumdrop into slivers. Make 4 slits around bottom edge of marshmallow; insert gumdrop slivers, for feet. Add 2 pieces licorice string, for eyes.

What to serve on festive occasions is a common problem. So here are McCALL's suggestions for any event from a back-yard social to a big party.

Back-Yard Ice-Cream Social

Pack a colored plastic pail with ice cubes; fill with bottled carbonated drinks. Tie a bottle opener to handle of pail.

Cut 1-inch holes in bottom of a large, round hatbox; cut as many holes as guests. Cover side of hatbox with adhesive-back plastic or crepe paper. Fill ice-cream cones with any flavor ice cream desired. Insert cones in holes. Let each guest select his own. Have small napkins to fold around cones.

MENU

Chocolate, and Peanut-Butter
Ice-Cream Cones*
Assorted Carbonated Drinks

Easter-Egg Hunt

Hide decorated Easter eggs or colored jelly beans around the house or garden. As guests arrive, provide them with baskets to hold the eggs they find.

MENU

Sandwich Cutouts*
Bunny Salads*
Crispy-Caramel Lollipops*
Milk

Halloween Party

No other time of year provides a better opportunity for the colorful decorations children love so well. Halloween cutouts of witches, owls, and black cats may be hung in the living room. (Purchase decorations, or make your own.)

Use Halloween paper plates and napkins. Fill small paper cups with assorted Halloween candy; set at each place.

Let your child help make the invitations— orange jack-o-lanterns or round black cats, cut out of construction paper.

Make costumes mandatory. Have a prize for the best.

MENU

Sloppy Joes*
Halloween Cake (Chocolate Cake
with Fudge Frosting, Decorated
with Candy Corn)
Ice Cream
Hot Cocoa

Children's Thanksgiving

A table just for children at Thanksgiving is an old custom in many homes. It eliminates a great deal of confusion at traditionally large family gatherings. The children love helping to make decorations for their own table. Make sure the children's table looks like more fun than the adults'.

Set up the table in the same room as the adults' table—or choose an out-of-the-way spot, away from the main kitchen traffic. Also, provide special food surprises for the children: Hollow out orange halves, to make baskets for cranberry sauce. Or with animal-shape cutters, cut out cranberry jelly. Or cut celery stalks into 5-inch pieces; stuff with cheese spread. Spear an olive and radish on a wooden pick; insert into each piece of celery.

Children's Birthday Parties

A child's introduction to the world of party-going and giving is almost certain to be a birthday party. Make it very gay and very traditional, with ribbon-tied packages, paper hats, bright balloons, and noisy snap crackers.

To make the occasion happily memorable, let the young host or hostess answer the door.

Plan plenty of games, in case one or two fail to hold youngsters' interest. Sure-fire for pre-schoolers: pin the tail on the donkey, musical chairs, a tub of water and floating toys, bubble pipes. If outdoor activities are on the agenda, be sure to have rainy-day substitutes. Plan a story to read or coloring books and crayons for everybody.

LITTLE GIRL'S BIRTHDAY PARTY

Tiny Chicken-Salad Sandwiches
Strawberry Ice Cream   Pink Posy Cake†
Ginger Ale

LITTLE BOY'S BIRTHDAY PARTY

Peanutburgers*
Ice Cream   Wagon-Train Birthday Cake†
Carbonated Drinks

† See Cake Decorating Chapter for recipes.
* See this chapter.

30

COOKING FOR TWO

S ince it happens that most women who cook for two are either brides who are not too familiar with cooking, or mothers who must adjust, once more, to a small household, now that their children are married or living away from home, we have made this chapter especially useful by including advice on how to market for two, how to plan good breakfasts, lunches, dinners and suppers, and even party meals—though, as a matter of fact, recipes for two are easy to double, triple, or quadruple, to accommodate as large a company as you may have.

Marketing Information

1. Plan meals ahead. If freezer space allows, cook double the amount needed for one meal; freeze remainder for another meal. Stews, soups, and sauces keep well in the freezer.

2. Take advantage of products packed in smaller quantities; *e.g.*, individual boxes of cereal, small loaves of bread.

3. Buy only as much as you can store with ease and use without waste.

4. Keep in mind the many kinds of processed food that will save you time and work. See our recipes in Convenience Foods Chapter.

5. Plan foods with second uses. See our recipes in Leftovers Chapter.

636

Cooking for Two

If there are just two of you, and you are stymied or bored, at times, by the limitations imposed upon a small family's menus, if you fervently wish that someone would invent a miniature turkey or prime ribs of beef or leg of lamb, or something that didn't entail endless leftovers, well, we do the next best thing—provide you with a variety of menus and cut-to-size recipes, all of them really interesting and some even on the gourmet side! So, brides and mothers, here's cooking the intimate way!

BRUNCH OR BREAKFAST MENUS

Chilled Pineapple-Grapefruit Juice
Puffy French Toast*
Crisp Bacon
Icy Crème-de-Menthe Pears*
Coffee

* Recipes given for starred dishes.

PUFFY FRENCH TOAST

MAKES 2 SERVINGS

Batter:
½ cup milk
1 egg
¾ cup packaged pancake mix

4 day-old white-bread slices, crusts removed
½ cup shortening
Warm maple syrup

1. Make Batter: In medium bowl, with rotary beater, beat milk, egg, and pancake mix just until combined.
2. Cut each bread slice in half, on diagonal. Dip bread into batter, coating completely. Then let bread stand in batter 1 minute.
3. Meanwhile, slowly heat shortening in heavy, 8-inch skillet.
4. In hot shortening, sauté bread slices, 2 at a time, until golden-brown and puffy—about 3 minutes on each side. Serve warm, with maple syrup.

ICY CRÈME-DE-MENTHE PEARS

MAKES 2 SERVINGS

1 can (1 lb) pear halves
1 tablespoon lemon juice
3 to 4 tablespoons green crème de menthe
½ pt lemon sherbet

1. Drain pear halves, reserving liquid. Pack pear halves into pint jar with tight-fitting lid.
2. In small saucepan, bring reserved pear liquid to boiling. Remove from heat; stir in lemon juice and crème de menthe.
3. Pour hot liquid over pears; cap. Let cool; refrigerate overnight.
4. To serve: Place a pear half in each of 2 dessert dishes. Top with lemon sherbet. Spoon 1 tablespoon syrup over each.

Note: Remaining pears may be stored in refrigerator 2 or 3 days. Serve as accompaniment to lamb or as first course.

Broiled Grapefruit with Rum*
Scrambled Eggs with
Crabmeat-Mushroom Sauce*
Popovers for Two*   Strawberry Preserves
Coffee

BROILED GRAPEFRUIT WITH RUM

MAKES 2 SERVINGS

1 large grapefruit, halved
2 tablespoons apricot or
    peach preserves

1 tablespoon butter or
    margarine, melted
1 teaspoon dark rum

1. Cut out centers and remove seeds from each grapefruit half. With grapefruit knife, cut around each section, to loosen.
2. Combine preserves with butter. Sprinkle each grapefruit half with rum; then spread with preserve mixture.
3. Run under broiler, 4 inches from heat, about 3 minutes, or until top is bubbly.

SCRAMBLED EGGS WITH CRABMEAT-MUSHROOM SAUCE

MAKES 2 SERVINGS

Crabmeat-Mushroom
Sauce:
1 can (6½ oz) king-crab-
    meat, drained
½ cup condensed cream-
    of-mushroom soup,*
    undiluted
¼ cup light cream
1 teaspoon lemon juice
2 tablespoons sherry
    (optional)

Scrambled Eggs:
4 eggs
¼ cup milk
¼ teaspoon salt
Dash pepper
2 tablespoons butter or
    margarine
1 tablespoon finely
    chopped parsley

1. Make Crabmeat-Mushroom Sauce: Separate crabmeat, remove membrane. Set aside.
2. In small saucepan, combine soup and cream, mixing well. Bring mixture to boiling, stirring.
3. Stir in crabmeat, lemon juice, and sherry; reheat gently. Cover, and keep warm.
4. Make Scrambled Eggs: In medium bowl, with rotary beater, beat eggs, milk, salt, and pepper until combined.
5. Slowly heat butter in medium skillet. Pour in egg mixture. As eggs start to set at bottom, gently lift cooked portion with spatula, letting uncooked portion flow to bottom of pan.
6. When eggs are cooked but still shiny and moist, remove to heated serving platter. Sprinkle with parsley. Surround eggs with toast points, if desired. Pass sauce along with eggs.

* Serve rest of soup, diluted as label directs, at another meal.

POPOVERS FOR TWO

MAKES 4

½ cup sifted all-purpose
    flour
¼ teaspoon salt

½ cup milk
1 egg

1. Preheat oven to 425F. Generously grease 4 (6-oz) custard cups.
2. In small bowl, with rotary beater, beat all ingredients just until batter is smooth.
3. Pour batter evenly into prepared custard cups. Place on cookie sheet; bake 40 to 45 minutes, or until popovers are a deep golden-brown. Serve hot, with butter.

LUNCHEON OR SUPPER MENUS

Corn-Clam Chowder*
Crisp Crackers
Iced Carrot Sticks, Cucumber Sticks,
and Radish Roses
Individual Boysenberry Pies*
Coffee   Tea

CORN-CLAM CHOWDER

MAKES 2 SERVINGS

1 bacon slice
2 tablespoons diced onion
1 tablespoon diced green
   pepper
1 can (8¾ oz) cream-style
   corn
1 can (7 oz) whole-kernel
   corn, undrained
1 can (7½ oz) minced
   clams, drained

1 tablespoon chopped
   pimiento
⅔ cup milk
¼ teaspoon salt
¼ teaspoon celery salt
Dash pepper
⅛ teaspoon dried thyme
   leaves

1. In medium saucepan, sauté bacon until crisp. Drain bacon well on paper towels; crumble, and set aside.
2. In bacon drippings, sauté onion and green pepper until tender—about 3 minutes.
3. Add bacon and rest of ingredients. Over low heat, bring chowder to boiling, stirring occasionally. Serve hot.

Note: If a thinner chowder is desired, add a little more milk.

INDIVIDUAL BOYSENBERRY PIES

MAKES 2 SERVINGS

Pastry for 1-crust pie

Filling:
1 can (8¾ oz) boysen-
   berries
2 tablespoons sugar

Dash salt
1½ teaspoons cornstarch
1 teaspoon butter or
   margarine
1 teaspoon vanilla extract

1. Preheat oven to 450F. Prepare pastry; divide into 4 parts. Roll each part into 6-inch circle; use to line 4 individual pie pans, 4½ inches in diameter. Prick pastry shells all over.
2. Bake 10 to 12 minutes, or until golden. Let cool completely on wire rack. (Freezer-wrap; label, and freeze two shells for later use.)
3. Meanwhile, make Filling: Drain berries, reserving syrup. Set berries aside.
4. In small saucepan, combine sugar, salt, and cornstarch. Stir in reserved syrup until smooth.
5. Over medium heat, bring to boiling, stirring constantly. Reduce heat; simmer 1 minute.
6. Remove from heat. Stir in berries and butter; then stir in vanilla. Refrigerate filling until chilled. (Filling may be refrigerated overnight, if desired.)
7. Just before serving, spoon filling into pie shells. Top with sweetened whipped cream, if desired.

Hamburger Chop Suey*
Iced Cherry Tomatoes
Pineapple Slices with Coconut*
Coffee   Tea

HAMBURGER CHOP SUEY

MAKES 2 SERVINGS

1 tablespoon butter or
  margarine
1 cup thinly sliced celery
¼ cup sliced onion
½ pkg (9-oz size) French-
  style green beans,
  partially thawed
½ lb ground chuck

1 cup drained canned bean
  sprouts*
1 beef-bouillon cube
1 tablespoon soy sauce
¼ teaspoon salt
⅛ teaspoon pepper
1 tablespoon cornstarch
1 cup cooked white rice
Chinese noodles

1. In hot butter in heavy skillet, cook celery, onion, and green beans, stirring, 2 minutes.
2. Add beef; cook about 5 minutes longer, or until beef loses its red color.
3. Remove from heat. Stir in bean sprouts, bouillon cube, soy sauce, salt, pepper, and ½ cup water; cook, stirring, about 3 minutes, or until bouillon cube dissolves.
4. Combine cornstarch with ¼ cup cold water. Stir into beef mixture; cook, stirring constantly, until mixture boils and becomes thickened and translucent. Serve over rice; top with Chinese noodles.

* Use rest of bean sprouts in can to make Egg Fu Yung for two. See Leftovers Chapter for recipe.

PINEAPPLE SLICES WITH COCONUT

MAKES 2 SERVINGS

1 can (8½ oz) pineapple
  slices, chilled

2 tablespoons flaked
  coconut

1. Arrange pineapple slices in 2 dessert dishes; spoon some of liquid over them.
2. Sprinkle each with 1 tablespoon coconut.

Fruit-Salad Plate*
Date-Nut-Bread-and-Butter Sandwiches
Fluffy Cinnamon Tapioca*
Coffee   Tea

FRUIT-SALAD PLATE

MAKES 2 SERVINGS

1 can (8½ oz) pineapple
  slices
Crisp lettuce leaves
1 cup creamed cottage
  cheese (8 oz)
3 tablespoons chopped
  parsley

6 cooked pitted prunes
6 whole strawberries
1 navel orange, peeled and
  thinly sliced
¼ cup mayonnaise or
  cooked salad dressing

1. Drain pineapple, reserving 2 tablespoons liquid; set aside.
2. Arrange lettuce leaves on each of 2 individual plates. Place ½ cup cottage cheese on each.
3. Dip edges of pineapple slices in parsley. Arrange 2 pineapple slices, 3 prunes, 3 strawberries, and half the orange slices on each plate.
4. For dressing, combine mayonnaise with reserved pineapple liquid. Serve along with salad.

FLUFFY CINNAMON TAPIOCA

1 egg yolk
3 tablespoons sugar
¼ teaspoon cinnamon
Dash salt
1 cup milk

1½ tablespoons quick-
    cooking tapioca
½ teaspoon vanilla extract
1 egg white

1. In medium saucepan, with rotary beater, beat egg yolk with sugar, cinnamon, and salt, to combine.

2. Stir in milk and tapioca; let stand 5 minutes.

3. Over medium heat, bring mixture to a full boil, stirring constantly; mixture will be slightly thickened. Remove from heat.

4. Let stand 10 minutes, to cool; stir in vanilla.

5. Beat egg white until stiff peaks form. Gently fold into tapioca mixture.

6. Turn mixture into 2 sherbet glasses. Refrigerate until well chilled—about 1 hour. To serve, top with whipped cream or unpeeled apple slices, if desired.

DINNER MENUS

Swedish Meatballs* with Dilled Noodles*
Marinated Green-Pepper and Cucumber
Salad Bowl
Poppy-Seed Rolls*
Lemon Sherbet with Raspberry-Rum Sauce*
Coffee   Tea

SWEDISH MEATBALLS

¾ lb ground chuck
½ teaspoon salt
½ teaspoon pepper
¼ teaspoon Worcestershire
    sauce
¼ teaspoon dried thyme
    leaves
⅓ cup butter or margarine
1½ teaspoons flour

½ cup heavy cream
1 beef-bouillon cube,
    crumbled
¼ teaspoon meat-extract
    paste
¼ teaspoon bottled gravy
    seasoning
1 tablespoon chopped fresh
    dill (optional)

1. Preheat oven to 350F.

2. In medium bowl, lightly toss chuck with salt, ¼ teaspoon pepper, the Worcestershire, and thyme, mixing well. Gently shape mixture into 18 meatballs.

3. In hot butter in large skillet, sauté meatballs until browned on all sides. Remove skillet from heat; place meatballs in 2-quart casserole.

4. Remove all but 1 tablespoon drippings from skillet; stir in flour until smooth. Gradually stir in cream and ½ cup water; bring to boiling, stirring.

5. Add bouillon cube, meat-extract paste, gravy seasoning, and remaining pepper; simmer, uncovered, 3 minutes, stirring occasionally. Pour over meatballs.

6. Bake, covered, 25 minutes, or until meatballs are tender. Sprinkle with dill.

DILLED NOODLES

1 teaspoon salt
1½ cups broad noodles
½ cup cottage cheese

2 tablespoons chopped
    fresh dill
Dash pepper

1. In 2-quart saucepan, bring 1 quart water and the salt to boiling.
2. Gradually pour in noodles; water should not stop boiling. Boil, uncovered and stirring occasionally, 10 to 12 minutes, or until noodles are tender.
3. Drain noodles; return to hot saucepan.
4. Add cheese, dill, and pepper, tossing lightly to combine. Reheat gently.

POPPY-SEED ROLLS

MAKES 6

1 pkg (8.6 oz) refrigerator
    butterflake rolls

1 tablespoon poppy seed

1. Preheat oven to 375F. Separate dough into 6 rolls.
2. Dip top of each in poppy seed, coating well.
3. Bake as package label directs. Serve hot or cold.
Note: To reheat rolls, wrap in foil; place in preheated 300F oven 7 to 10 minutes, or until heated through.

LEMON SHERBET WITH RASPBERRY-RUM SAUCE

MAKES 2 SERVINGS

1 pkg (10 oz) thawed
    frozen raspberries,
    undrained

1¼ teaspoons cornstarch
¼ cup white rum
½ pt lemon sherbet

1. In medium saucepan, mix raspberries with cornstarch until smooth. Bring to boiling, stirring constantly. Reduce heat, and simmer, stirring occasionally, 5 minutes.
2. Let cool; then refrigerate 1 hour.
3. Just before serving, stir rum into sauce. Serve over sherbet.
Note: If desired, sauce may be served warm. Stir in rum just before serving.

Curry-Broiled Chicken*
Fruited Rice Pilaf*
Buttered Green Beans*
Marinated-Mushroom Salad*
Sesame Rolls
Cold Lemon Soufflé*
Champagne

CURRY-BROILED CHICKEN

MAKES 2 SERVINGS

2-lb broiler-fryer, split in
    half
½ cup butter or margarine,
    melted

1 teaspoon curry powder
½ teaspoon salt
Dash pepper

1. Wipe chicken with damp paper towels. With long skewers, secure wings and legs of chicken close to body.
2. Place chicken, skin side down, in broiler pan, without rack. Brush surface with ¼ cup melted butter.

(Curry-Broiled Chicken continued)

3. Broil chicken, 8 inches from heat, 15 minutes, or until browned, brushing every 5 minutes with drippings.

4. Turn chicken skin side up. Brush with pan drippings; broil 5 minutes longer. Meanwhile, in small bowl, combine rest of butter with the curry, salt, and pepper.

5. Brush chicken again, using half the curry butter.

6. Broil chicken 5 minutes more. Then brush with rest of curry-butter mixture; broil 5 minutes longer, or until nicely browned and chicken is crisp and tender.

7. To serve: Carefully remove skewers. Place each chicken half on a serving plate.

FRUITED RICE PILAF

MAKES 2 SERVINGS

⅔ cup packaged precooked rice
½ teaspoon salt
1 can (8 oz) fruit cocktail, drained
1 tablespoon butter or margarine

1. Prepare rice with salt as package label directs.

2. Fluff up rice with a fork. Gently toss with the fruit.

3. Reheat gently. Toss with butter.

BUTTERED GREEN BEANS

MAKES 2 GENEROUS SERVINGS

1 pkg (9 oz) frozen whole green beans
1 tablespoon butter or margarine
¼ teaspoon salt
⅛ teaspoon pepper
Dash nutmeg

1. Cook beans as package label directs. Drain very well.

2. Add butter, salt, pepper, and nutmeg; toss lightly to combine.

MARINATED-MUSHROOM SALAD

MAKES 2 SERVINGS

10 small whole mushroom caps

Marinade:
¼ cup salad oil
¼ cup cider vinegar
1 tablespoon finely chopped onion
1 tablespoon finely chopped parsley
1 clove garlic, crushed
¼ teaspoon salt
¼ teaspoon sugar

Boston-lettuce leaves
Watercress sprigs

1. Wash mushroom caps well. Dry on paper towels.

2. Make Marinade: In medium bowl, combine all marinade ingredients. Toss mushroom caps with marinade, coating well.

3. Refrigerate, covered, at least 1½ hours.

4. To serve: Arrange lettuce and watercress on 2 salad plates. With slotted spoon, remove mushroom caps from marinade. Place 5 on each salad plate. Pour over remaining marinade, if desired.

COLD LEMON SOUFFLÉ

MAKES 2 SERVINGS

¼ cup milk
2 tablespoons sugar
2 egg yolks, well beaten
1 teaspoon unflavored
   gelatine
3 tablespoons lemon juice
¾ teaspoon grated lemon
   peel

2 egg whites
⅛ teaspoon cream of tartar
¼ cup heavy cream,
   whipped
2 tablespoons finely
   chopped pecans

1. Lightly grease bottoms and sides of 2 (4-oz) individual soufflé dishes. Make paper collars: For each soufflé dish, tear sheet of waxed paper 10 inches long. Fold lengthwise into thirds; lightly grease one side. With string, tie collar (buttered side inside) around top of dish, to form rim 2 inches above edge.

2. Heat milk and sugar in small saucepan just until sugar is dissolved.

3. Remove from heat. Gradually add mixture to egg yolks, in small bowl, beating constantly with fork. Let cool.

4. Sprinkle gelatine over lemon juice in custard cup; let stand 5 minutes to soften. Set in pan of hot water; stir until gelatine dissolves. Stir in lemon peel.

5. Add gelatine mixture to egg-milk mixture, mixing well. Refrigerate until consistency of unbeaten egg white—about 30 minutes.

6. In medium bowl, with portable electric mixer at high speed, beat egg whites with cream of tartar until stiff peaks form when beater is slowly raised.

7. With rubber scraper, using an under-and-over motion, fold gelatine mixture and whipped cream into egg whites until well combined.

8. Turn mixture into soufflé dishes. Refrigerate until firm—about 2 hours.

9. Before serving, gently remove collars. Press nuts against side of each soufflé.

Orange-Glazed Stuffed Pork Chops*
Artichoke Hearts with Onions*
Zucchini-and-Tomato Salad*
Hot French Bread
Fruit with Cheese Tray
Coffee   Tea

ORANGE-GLAZED STUFFED PORK CHOPS

MAKES 2 SERVINGS

2 double loin pork chops, with pocket (about 1 lb)

Stuffing:
¼ cup prepared stuffing mix
¾ teaspoon finely chopped parsley
½ teaspoon grated orange peel
¼ teaspoon salt

¼ teaspoon Worcestershire sauce
⅛ teaspoon pepper
2 tablespoons boiling water

Glaze:
¼ cup orange juice
2 tablespoons light-brown sugar
2 tablespoons orange marmalade
1 tablespoon cider vinegar

1. Preheat oven to 375F. Wipe pork chops well with damp paper towels.
2. Make Stuffing: Combine all ingredients in small bowl; toss lightly until well mixed. Use to stuff pork chops.
3. Place chops in small, shallow baking pan; bake 15 minutes. Turn, and bake 15 minutes longer.
4. Meanwhile, make Glaze: Combine all ingredients in small saucepan, mixing well. Bring to boiling, stirring. Reduce heat; simmer, uncovered, 10 minutes, stirring occasionally.
5. Brush chops with some of glaze; bake 30 minutes longer. Brush with rest of glaze every 10 minutes.

ARTICHOKE HEARTS WITH ONIONS

MAKES 2 SERVINGS

½ teaspoon salt
1 cup thinly sliced onion
1 pkg (9 oz) frozen artichoke hearts

1 tablespoon white vinegar
1 tablespoon butter or margarine

1. In medium saucepan, bring 1 cup water and the salt to boiling.
2. Add onion and artichoke hearts; simmer, covered, 8 to 10 minutes, or until vegetables are just tender.
3. Drain well. Toss with vinegar and butter.

ZUCCHINI-AND-TOMATO SALAD

MAKES 2 SERVINGS

½ cup diced raw zucchini
½ cup diced peeled tomato
¼ cup mayonnaise or cooked salad dressing
1 tablespoon chopped chives

1 teaspoon prepared mustard
½ teaspoon salt
⅛ teaspoon pepper
Crisp salad greens

1. In medium bowl, combine all ingredients except salad greens; mix gently.
2. Refrigerate at least 1 hour, stirring occasionally.
3. Serve on salad greens.

645

Tangy Tomato-Juice Cocktail*
Savory Skillet Lamb Chops*
Spinach   Browned Potatoes in Cream*
Toasted Garlic-Bread Strips*
Cinnamon-Glazed Baked Apples*
Coffee   Tea

TANGY TOMATO-JUICE COCKTAIL

MAKES 2 SERVINGS

2 cans (5½-oz size) tomato juice
½ teaspoon Worcestershire sauce

2 lemon wedges
2 parsley sprigs

1.   Combine tomato juice and Worcestershire, mixing well. Refrigerate until well chilled—about 1 hour.
2.   Just before serving, pour into 2 chilled glasses. Garnish each with lemon wedge and parsley sprig.

SAVORY SKILLET LAMB CHOPS

MAKES 2 SERVINGS

2 teaspoons salad oil
2 shoulder lamb chops (1 lb)
¼ teaspoon salt
⅛ teaspoon pepper

½ teaspoon dried oregano leaves
1 teaspoon instant minced onion
1 teaspoon lemon juice

1.   Slowly heat salad oil in skillet with tight-fitting lid. Add chops; brown well on both sides —about 5 minutes in all.
2.   Add rest of ingredients along with ½ cup water, mixing well; bring to boiling. Reduce heat; simmer, covered, 40 minutes, or until chops are tender. (Add more water if necessary.)

BROWNED POTATOES IN CREAM

MAKES 2 SERVINGS

1 tablespoon butter or margarine
1 can (8 oz) small whole potatoes, drained and sliced

⅛ teaspoon salt
Dash pepper
¼ cup light cream

1.   Slowly heat butter in small skillet. Add potatoes, salt, and pepper; cook, stirring occasionally, until potatoes are lightly browned.
2.   Add cream, mixing well; simmer 2 minutes. Serve hot.

TOASTED GARLIC-BREAD STRIPS

MAKES 12

2 tablespoons butter or margarine, melted

¼ teaspoon garlic salt
4 white-bread slices

1.   Preheat oven to 300F.
2.   Combine butter with garlic salt. Brush on one side of each bread slice. Cut each slice into 3 strips.
3.   Place strips, buttered sides up, on ungreased cookie sheet; bake 30 minutes. Serve hot.

CINNAMON-GLAZED BAKED APPLES

Glaze:
½ cup sugar
2 tablespoons cinnamon
    candies

2 large baking apples
    (about 1 lb)
1 teaspoon lemon juice
½ teaspoon butter or
    margarine

1.   Preheat oven to 375F. Lightly grease a small baking dish.

2.   Make Glaze: In small saucepan, combine sugar and cinnamon candies with ½ cup water; bring to boiling, stirring until sugar dissolves. Reduce heat; simmer, uncovered, 2 minutes. Remove from heat.

3.   Pare each apple one third way down side. Core apples, leaving bottom intact.

4.   Brush apples with lemon juice; arrange in baking dish. Dot centers with butter; brush generously with some of glaze.

5.   Bake apples, uncovered, 1 hour, brushing frequently with rest of glaze. Serve warm or cold, with cream, if desired.

Timed Menus

McCALL's mail is heavy with plaintive cries for help, like this one from a brand-new bride: "When my roast is hot, my vegetables are not. Please tell me how to get them *all* to the table piping hot."

The answer is planning—a procedure that experienced cooks get strictly from experience—and that inexperienced ones may get from our step-by-step work plans for breakfast and dinner—a valuable guide that tells you when to set the table, prepare the aspic, put the chicken in the oven, the vegetables on the range, and so on, down to the very last detail. When you have mastered our master plan, not only will your meals taste better but you yourself will feel better.

BREAKFAST FOR EVERY DAY

Sliced Bananas
Scrambled Eggs   Toast
Coffee

WORK PLAN

1. Set table the night before.

2. Use 4-cup percolator; start coffee 20 minutes before serving.

3. Place sugar, cream and butter on table.

4. After coffee starts to perk, let perk 7 minutes.

5. While coffee is perking, slice bananas directly into dishes. Place on table.

6. Make scrambled eggs. Turn out onto plates.

7. Pour coffee. Make toast at table.

CELEBRATION DINNER

Roast Chicken for Two*
Mashed Potatoes
Asparagus with Lemon Butter*
Molded Fruit Medley*
Hot Rolls   Radish Roses and Ripe Olives
Butterscotch-Rum Sundae*
Cake Fingers
Coffee   Tea

WORK PLAN

Day before Dinner

1. Prepare Molded Fruit Medley. Do not make dressing. Refrigerate overnight.

2. Wash and dry chicken; rub inside with salt. Wrap in saran or foil; refrigerate.

3. Make stuffing for chicken. Cover, and refrigerate.

4. Make radish roses. Refrigerate in ice water.

Day of Dinner

1. About 2¾ hours before dinner is served: Stuff and truss chicken. Preheat the oven to 325F. Roast as recipe directs.

2. Make chicken broth, if desired, while chicken is roasting.

3. Make dressing for Molded Fruit Medley. Unmold salad. Refrigerate both.

4. If asparagus is fresh, wash it, and cut up.

5. Cut cake into fingers. Arrange on tray; cover with waxed paper.

6. Arrange radish roses and olives in dish. Refrigerate.

7. Combine ingredients for Butterscotch-Rum Sundae in small saucepan. Heat just before serving.

8. Set table.

9. About 20 minutes before dinner is served: Remove chicken to heated serving platter; keep warm. Also, make gravy; keep warm.

10. About 10 minutes before serving: Cook asparagus. Prepare mashed potatoes. (Use instant mashed potatoes, following recipe on package for fluffier mashed potatoes.)

11. Put rolls in oven to warm. Start coffee in electric percolator, or heat water for tea or instant coffee.

12. Place butter and ice water on table.

13. At serving time: Remove salad from refrigerator; top with dressing. Also, remove relishes from refrigerator.

14. Turn mashed potatoes and asparagus into serving dishes. Remove rolls from oven: place in napkin-lined basket. Turn gravy into gravy boat.

ROAST CHICKEN FOR TWO

2½-lb whole broiler-fryer
½ teaspoon salt

2 tablespoons soft butter
    or margarine
Paprika

Stuffing:
¼ cup butter or margarine
¼ cup finely chopped
    onion
1 cup packaged herb-
    seasoned stuffing

Gravy:
2 tablespoons flour
1 cup chicken broth,* or
    1 cup canned clear
    chicken broth

1. Preheat oven to 325F. Remove giblets and neck from chicken; set aside to make chicken broth* for Gravy, if desired. Wash and dry chicken inside and out; rub inside with salt.

2. Make Stuffing: In hot butter in medium skillet, cook onion until tender—about 5 minutes. Add ¼ cup water and the herb-seasoned stuffing, fluffing up with fork.

3. Lightly fill body cavity of chicken with stuffing. Bring skin over neck opening; fasten to back with poultry pin. Close body cavity with pins. Pin wings to body; then tie legs together at ends, with twine.

4. Place chicken on rack, breast side down, in shallow, open roasting pan. Brush with 1 tablespoon butter. Roast, uncovered, 45 minutes.

5. Turn chicken breast side up. Brush with remaining butter; sprinkle with paprika. Roast 1¼ hours longer, or until leg moves freely when twisted and fleshy part of drumstick feels soft.

6. Remove chicken to warm serving platter; remove pins and twine. Keep warm.

7. Make Gravy: To pan drippings, add flour, stirring to make a smooth mixture. Gradually add chicken broth, stirring until smooth; bring to boiling over direct heat. Reduce heat; simmer 1 minute.

8. To serve chicken: With poultry shears, cut lengthwise through backbone and breastbone, to make 2 halves. Serve gravy hot, along with chicken.

* To make Chicken Broth:

1. In small saucepan, combine giblets (except liver) and neck, 1 teaspoon instant minced onion, ¼ teaspoon salt, 1 cup cut-up carrots, and 1 cup cut-up celery with 2 cups water; bring to boiling.

2. Reduce heat; simmer, covered, 1 hour and 45 minutes. Add liver and 1 chicken-bouillon cube; simmer 15 minutes longer.

3. Strain broth, pressing vegetables through sieve along with broth. Measure 1 cup.

ASPARAGUS WITH LEMON BUTTER

1 lb fresh asparagus*
¼ teaspoon salt

2 tablespoons soft butter or
    margarine
1 teaspoon lemon juice

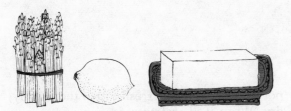

1. Break off tough ends of asparagus stalks. Wash asparagus tips well with cold water; if necessary, use a brush to remove grit. With vegetable parer, scrape skin and scales from lower part of stalk only.

2. With sharp knife, cut stalks on the diagonal, making bias slices about 1 inch long.

3. In medium skillet, with tight-fitting cover, bring ⅓ cup water to boiling. Add asparagus and salt; cook, covered and over high heat, 5 to 8 minutes, adding more water if necessary.

4. Drain, if necessary. Add butter and lemon juice, tossing until butter is melted.

* Or use 1 pkg (10 oz) frozen asparagus cuts. Cook as package label directs.

MOLDED FRUIT MEDLEY

MAKES 6 SERVINGS

1 can (8¾ oz) fruit cocktail
1 pkg (3 oz) orange-
    pineapple-flavored
    gelatin
1 cup boiling water
½ cup cubed fresh orange
4 maraschino cherries,
    halved

Dressing:
1 tablespoon mayonnaise or
    cooked salad dressing
1 tablespoon bottled
    French dressing
Crisp lettuce leaves

1.   Drain fruit cocktail, reserving syrup. Set fruit cocktail aside.

2.   In medium bowl, dissolve gelatin in boiling water. Add cold water to reserved syrup to measure 1 cup; stir into gelatin.

3.   Refrigerate until consistency of unbeaten egg white—30 to 40 minutes.

4.   Fold fruit cocktail, orange, and cherries into gelatin. Turn into 6 (5-oz) custard cups; refrigerate until firm.

5.   Meanwhile, make Dressing: Combine mayonnaise with French dressing; refrigerate until ready to use.

6.   To unmold: Quickly dip 2 molds in warm water. Run a small spatula around edge of mold; invert onto lettuce leaves; shake gently to release. Spoon half of dressing over each mold.

Note: Serve remaining molds for dessert another day. Top them with sweetened whipped cream.

BUTTERSCOTCH-RUM SUNDAE

MAKES 2 SERVINGS

½ cup butterscotch sauce
1 tablespoon light rum
1 tablespoon butter or
    margarine

½ pt vanilla ice cream
6 pecan halves (optional)

1.   In small saucepan, combine butterscotch sauce with rum and butter.

2.   Heat, stirring, over medium heat, just until butter melts.

3.   Serve sauce warm, over ice cream. Garnish with pecan halves, if desired.

FRIDAY-NIGHT SPECIAL

Chilled Grapefruit Sections
Broiled Bass with Grilled Tomatoes*
Garlic Potato Balls*
Tossed Green Salad
Hot Rolls
Baked Custard for Two*   Cookies
Coffee   Tea

WORK PLAN

Day before Dinner

1. Prepare Baked Custard for Two. Let cool; refrigerate.

2. If fish is frozen, place in refrigerator. Do not unwrap. If fish is fresh, wash thoroughly; dry. Wrap well; refrigerate.

Day of Dinner

1. In morning, spoon grapefruit sections (fresh or frozen) into sherbet glasses. Cover with saran; refrigerate.

2. About 40 minutes before serving: Prepare greens for tossed salad; turn into salad bowl. Refrigerate.

3. Arrange cookies on plate.

4. Set table.

5. Arrange fish and tomato halves on broiler rack.

6. Fifteen minutes before serving: Broil fish

and tomato halves as recipe directs. Wrap rolls in foil; place in oven to heat. Start coffee in electric percolator, or heat water for instant coffee or tea.

7. Cook Garlic Potato Balls.

8. Just before serving: Place butter, grapefruit, and ice water on table.

9. Remove fish and tomato halves to platter. Turn potato balls into small bowl.

10. Place rolls in napkin-lined basket. Toss salad greens lightly with dressing.

BROILED BASS WITH GRILLED TOMATOES

MAKES 2 SERVINGS

1½-lb whole sea bass, dressed	1 teaspoon salt
1 large tomato, halved	¼ teaspoon pepper
¼ cup butter or margarine, melted	½ teaspoon monosodium glutamate

1. Wash bass; pat dry with paper towels. With sharp knife, make 2 gashes, ¼ inch deep, on each side. Arrange fish and tomato halves on well-oiled broiler rack.

2. Combine butter with salt, pepper, and monosodium glutamate. Use some of butter mixture to brush tomato halves and fish.

3. Broil, 5 inches from heat, 10 minutes, brushing occasionally with butter mixture. Turn fish; brush with rest of butter mixture; broil 5 minutes longer.

GARLIC POTATO BALLS

MAKES 2 SERVINGS

1 tablespoon butter or margarine	1 can (8 oz) small whole potatoes, drained
	¼ teaspoon garlic salt

1. Slowly heat butter in small skillet. Add potatoes; sprinkle with garlic salt.

2. Cook potatoes, stirring occasionally, until golden-brown—about 5 minutes.

BAKED CUSTARD FOR TWO

MAKES 2 SERVINGS

1 egg, slightly beaten	1 cup milk
Dash salt	¾ teaspoon vanilla extract
3 tablespoons sugar	Dash nutmeg

1. Preheat oven to 350F.

2. Beat egg with salt, sugar, milk, and vanilla just until combined. Turn into 2 (6-oz) ungreased custard cups. Sprinkle with nutmeg.

3. Set in pan containing 1 inch hot water; bake 30 to 35 minutes, or until knife inserted in center comes out clean.

4. Let cool; then refrigerate until well chilled.

31

Entertaining

No party can be a complete success unless the hostess has as much fun as the guests. A successful party doesn't just happen: It is planned—and the more casual and effortless it seems, the more planning has usually gone into it.

Organize your party in this fashion:

Two weeks ahead, invite the guests.

Three days before the party: Plan the menu and check against your card file, to avoid repeats. Make a grocery list. Plan flowers; check the linens; polish silver; and wash seldom-used glassware and dishes.

Two days before: Order groceries—except perishables. Prepare foods that can be safely refrigerated.

One day before: Order cream, salad greens, and other perishable food.

Day of the party: Set the table, mixing or matching china and silver, and arrange flowers or centerpiece. Check on these: cigarettes, hand towels, ashtrays. Complete all food preparation. Do develop a specialty that guests can anticipate with pleasure, but don't overdo it till it gets boring. Do serve at least one surprise—but don't let the surprise be on you; try it out on the family beforehand.

Do get the children and yourself dressed with some time left over to relax. Allow for such time-takers as stockings that run and zippers that jam.

The focus of attention on a buffet table should be an eye-catching conversation-making centerpiece—e.g., a Victorian hand holding an arrangement of tiny mums, dried flowers, and grapes swagged with ribbon; a classic Greek bust crowned with cornflowers, grapes, and ivy.

652

The Informal Dinner

The Table Setting: Allow 18 to 20 inches of table space for each place setting. Arrange knives, forks, and spoons in the order in which they will be used, from the outside in toward the plate. Knives and spoons are placed at the right of the plate, with sharp edge of knife toward the plate; all forks (except cocktail or oyster fork) are placed at the left. Bread-and-butter plate with spreader is placed at tip of fork; salad plate at left of fork. Water glass or goblet is placed at tip of knife; wine glass or goblet at right of water glass. Napkin is placed on serving plate or at left of place setting.

Controversial rules may often be resolved by one's own good judgment. Examples: The fold of the napkin is governed by the design of the napkin as well as personal preference; the butter spreader may be placed in any position except in center of butter plate.

The Service: When it is time to serve, hostess goes unobtrusively to the kitchen and brings food to the table.

If one of the guests is a good friend, she might quietly get up, with no comment, and help with the last-minute preparations. When the candles are lit, announce dinner in any way that seems natural; lead guests to the table, and show them where to sit.

The table should be set so that the meat is in front of the host, who carves and serves it, and the vegetables in front of the hostess. Or the host may serve both. All extras, such as bread and relishes, should be on the table, to be passed from hand to hand.

If there is wine with dinner, the host may open it at the table. If he opens a new bottle, he pours a little into his own glass first, to get rid of any bits of cork that might be floating on the top, then fills the glass of the woman on his right and so on, walking straight around the table, ending with his own glass. It is not necessary to serve all the women first.

For second helpings, the host asks each guest whether he would like another serving, starting with the woman on his right and going around the table. Each plate is refilled with both meat and vegetables. At the end of the course, hostess gets up quietly and clears the table, removing plates in the most convenient way. She may take them two at a time to the kitchen or have a tray on a side table to carry a larger number at a time. Remove all the dishes and any silver on the table not needed for dessert or coffee.

Dessert may be served in individual dishes in the kitchen and brought to the dining table, or can be served from a serving bowl or plate in front of host or hostess, with dessert plates placed nearby for serving. In either case, it is simpler to have dessert silver already placed on the table. Coffee may be served with dessert or in the living room after dinner.

The Buffet

Avoid a traffic jam at the buffet table by arranging food and service logically; there should be no criss crossing, no reaching across the table, and no traffic congestion. Stack plates at the "starting" end of the table. Menu should be simple, so that the complete meal can be placed on a large dinner plate. Place silver and napkins close to each other at the "finishing" end of the table, ready to be picked up.

The beverage—water or wine—is sometimes at the far end of the buffet table, or on a side table, for the guests to take as they go by. Or you can wait until everyone is seated and pass the filled beverage glasses on a tray. At a card-table dinner, the water would be on the tables before service begins.

Give your guests a place to put plates down. Individual snack tables set with silver, glass, salt and pepper on a pretty mat are fine for small parties. Or for large affairs, use card tables for four, all decked in the same color, with matching or contrasting napkins.

While the guests eat, the serving dishes should be refilled for second helpings. As guests finish, they get up and serve themselves. A man may offer to refill a woman's plate.

Dessert and coffee may be set up on a dessert cart, or on a side table, or on the same buffet table after the main course has been removed.

Dessert plates and silver are on the table, and guests serve themselves, or the hostess may fill plates and pass one to each guest. Coffee may be served along with or after dessert. Coffeepot, coffee cups, saucers, silver, sugar, and cream are arranged on the side table. When dessert and coffee are finished, the dessert plates, coffee cups, napkins, dirty ashtrays, and little tables are taken away.

If desired, a liqueur or cordial may be served. A tray with liqueurs and small cordial glasses is placed on a coffee table. Host or hostess serves each guest his preference.

The Cocktail Party

A good cocktail party should have good drinks, good food, compatible people, and enough room to circulate a bit.

The food should never be sweet, but should certainly be highly seasoned. We favor a "menu" hearty enough to substitute for a meal, since cocktail parties often span the dinner hour. It should be well-balanced, something hot, something cold; meat, cheese, relishes; a spread, a finger food.

Have lots of ashtrays, and put them everywhere. And, if possible, have about twice as many glasses as guests; otherwise, you will be washing glasses during most of the party. Put coasters on every flat surface that could be harmed by alcohol.

If possible, have separate tables for the drinks and for the food. Try to put the drink table in a place where traffic can move freely.

Start freezing ice cubes several days ahead, or buy them in quantity.

A nice touch is to serve coffee later on for your helpers and any stragglers.

Beauty Tips for Your Table

. Your cloth should be gay, fascinating, colorful, rather than merely safe and proper. Though sometimes, of course, only a proper cloth will do.

. Collect printed, plain, striped, or woven dress fabric, bed sheeting, upholstery material, dyed burlap, whatever you see that you're crazy about. They make stunning and unusual cloths for table or buffet.

. If your cloth is patterned, use napkins in one or more solid colors, to accent colors in the design or to contrast sharply with it. Or you could use plaid, striped, or flowered napkins with a solid-color cloth.

. Choose a theme for your table. The party itself may dictate the theme if it's a holiday like Christmas or New Year's. The picture hanging above your table may inspire the setting. Or your cloth may suggest the décor.

. Food, silver, linen, and decorative objects should form a pleasant still-life that blends with the character of the room.

. Avoid the cluttered look of too many objects, too much color, too many flowers.

. Collect good-looking, though not necessarily costly, serving pieces that will do double duty: an urn that will hold flowers or sugar; a basket for rolls or a group of potted plants; a salad bowl that could be used for your folded napkins.

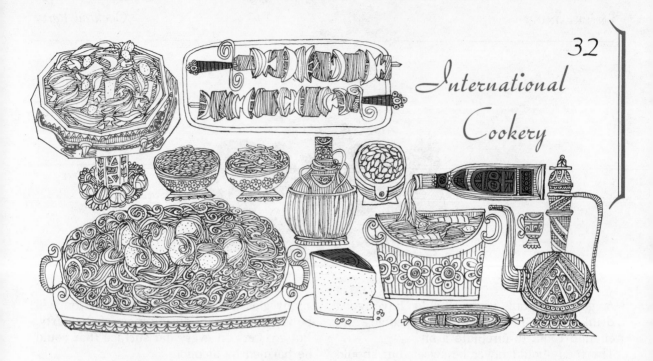

Maybe it's the increased activity in travel (real or arm-chair type) that has stimulated such an interest in foreign cookery; never have so many Americans wanted so many recipes from so many other countries. We've gathered ours from France, Italy, China, Spain, Germany, the South Seas, and other distant glamour places. Here they are:

Indian food, for all its many flavors (coriander, cloves, cumin, and other spices), is quite uncomplicated to prepare. If you like really distinctive food, this is IT.

ROAST LAMB INDIENNE

MAKES 6 SERVINGS

4- to 5-lb leg of lamb
2 tablespoons lemon juice
*¼ teaspoon crushed whole
    cardamom*
½ teaspoon pepper
*¼ teaspoon ground
    coriander*

½ pt yoghurt
1 cup finely chopped onion
1 cup butter or margarine
½ teaspoon ginger
*½ teaspoon saffron,
    crumbled*
½ cup light cream

1.   Wipe lamb with damp paper towels. With sharp knife, score deeply in diamond pattern. In small bowl, combine lemon juice, cardamom, pepper, coriander, and yoghurt into a paste. Rub well into lamb; let stand 1 hour.

2.   Meanwhile, preheat oven to 325F. Insert meat thermometer into thickest part of lamb, away from bone and fat. Place in shallow baking pan without rack.

3.   Roast until meat thermometer registers 180F—about 3½ hours.

4.   About 45 minutes before end of roasting period, sauté onion in butter in small skillet. Add ginger.

(*Roast Lamb Indienne continued*)

5. Thirty minutes before end of roasting period, baste lamb with onion mixture.

6. In small bowl, combine saffron and cream. Brush meat with this mixture twice during last 10 minutes of roasting time.

7. Serve lamb with White Rice with Raisins and Almonds or with Sweet Pilau.*

* See this chapter.

LAMB KARMA

MAKES 4 TO 6 SERVINGS

1½-lb boneless leg or
  shoulder of lamb
½ cup yoghurt
½ teaspoon ground cumin
½ teaspoon ground
  turmeric
¼ teaspoon ground
  cardamom
¼ cup salad oil
1⅓ cups chopped onion
1 clove garlic, finely
  chopped

½ teaspoon ginger
½ teaspoon dry mustard
¼ teaspoon pepper
¼ teaspoon cayenne
¼ teaspoon cinnamon
⅛ teaspoon cloves
2½ teaspoons salt
1 teaspoon lemon juice
2 tablespoons flaked
  coconut
4½ cups cooked white rice,
  drained

1. With sharp knife, trim excess fat from lamb. Cut lamb into 1-inch cubes. In large bowl, combine yoghurt, cumin, turmeric, and cardamom. Add lamb; toss to coat well. Let marinate 1 hour; drain.

2. In 1 tablespoon hot oil in medium saucepan, brown lamb well on all sides; remove lamb.

3. In rest of hot oil, sauté onion and garlic until tender—about 5 minutes.

4. Add remaining spices; cook, stirring, until well blended—about 2 minutes.

5. Add browned lamb, salt, and 1 cup water; simmer, covered but stirring several times, 40 minutes, or until lamb is tender.

6. Just before serving, add lemon juice and coconut. Serve the lamb with hot rice.

DUCK VINDALAO

MAKES 4 SERVINGS

4- to 5-lb ready-to-cook
  duckling, quartered
4 teaspoons salt
2 cups finely chopped onion
1 clove garlic, crushed
¼ cup salad oil or
  shortening
1½ teaspoons crushed
  coriander seed
½ teaspoon ground
  turmeric

¼ teaspoon ginger
¼ teaspoon ground
  cardamom
¼ teaspoon ground cumin
¼ teaspoon pepper
⅛ teaspoon cayenne
¼ teaspoon dry mustard
3 tablespoons cider vinegar
1½ cups hot water

1. Preheat oven to 425F.

2. Wipe duckling with damp paper towels. Trim off excess fat. Prick skin well with fork; rub with salt.

3. Arrange duckling on rack in shallow roasting pan; roast, uncovered, 30 minutes.

4. Reduce heat to 375F; roast, uncovered, 1 hour and 25 minutes. Drain.

5. Meanwhile, in large skillet, sauté onion and garlic in hot oil about 3 minutes.

6. Combine remaining ingredients, except hot water, to form a smooth paste. Add to onion mixture; cook slowly 3 minutes.

7. Stir in hot water; simmer, covered, 35 minutes, adding more water if necessary.

8. Place duckling, skin side down, in sauce; simmer, covered, 35 minutes.

9. Serve duckling on platter or in shallow casserole; spoon sauce over it.

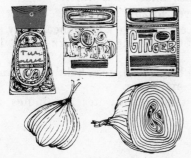

SOUTH INDIA CHUTNEY

MAKES 1⅓ CUPS

½ cup finely chopped
    onion
2 tablespoons grated
    radish
⅓ cup finely chopped
    green pepper

½ teaspoon salt
⅛ teaspoon ginger
1 tablespoon lemon juice
½ cup flaked coconut

1. Combine all ingredients, tossing to mix well.
2. Serve with meat dishes or any curry.

SWEET PILAU

MAKES 6 SERVINGS

1½ cups raw long-grain
    white rice
¼ cup butter or margarine
6 cloves
2-inch cinnamon stick
½ teaspoon saffron,
    crumbled
3 teaspoons salt

¼ cup light raisins*
¼ cup shelled pistachio
    nuts, blanched
¼ cup cashew nuts
½ cup toasted slivered
    almonds
1½ tablespoons sugar

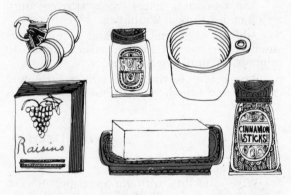

1. Soak rice in 4 cups cold water for 30 minutes; then drain well.
2. Heat butter in 3-quart heavy saucepan or skillet. Add rice; sauté, stirring, 3 minutes.
3. Combine cloves, cinnamon, and saffron in small cheesecloth bag. Place in another saucepan with 3 cups water and the salt. Bring to boiling; boil 3 minutes, or until water is well colored. Remove bag.
4. Pour seasoned water over rice, stirring well with fork.
5. Cook, tightly covered and over low heat, until rice is tender and all water is absorbed—about 15 minutes. (Do not stir during cooking. If necessary, lift rice several times, with fork, from bottom of pan.)
6. Add raisins, nuts, and sugar, mixing lightly with fork.

* Let raisins stand in hot water 10 minutes, to plump them.

WHITE RICE WITH RAISINS AND ALMONDS

MAKES 6 SERVINGS

1½ teaspoons salt
2 cups raw long-grain white
    rice
¼ cup light raisins*

½ cup toasted slivered
    almonds
1½ tablespoons sugar

1. In medium saucepan, bring 6 cups water with salt to boiling.
2. Add rice; cover; bring to boiling. Boil rapidly 8 to 10 minutes, or just until rice is tender.
3. Drain; rinse under cold water.
4. Preheat oven to 250F.
5. Spread rice on 2 large cookie sheets. Dry in oven 30 minutes, tossing with fork every 10 minutes.
6. Turn into large bowl; toss lightly with raisins, almonds, and sugar.

* Let raisins stand in hot water 10 minutes, to plump them.

PURIS (Fried Bread Puffs)

MAKES 16

2 cups sifted all-purpose
   flour
1 teaspoon salt

¼ cup butter or margarine,
   melted
Salad oil or shortening

1. Sift flour with salt into large bowl. Add butter, mixing well with fork.

2. Stir in about 6 tablespoons water, mixing to make a soft, pliable dough.

3. On lightly floured surface, knead dough 5 to 7 minutes, or until it is shiny and satiny. (Or put dough through medium blade of food chopper about 10 times, or until it is shiny and satiny.)

4. Roll out dough about ⅛ inch thick. Cut into 3-inch rounds.

5. Meanwhile, in deep skillet or deep-fat fryer, slowly heat salad oil (at least 2 inches) to 360F on deep-frying thermometer.

6. Deep-fry dough rounds, a few at a time, 30 seconds, or until they puff and are golden-brown. Turn; fry 1 minute on other side, or until golden-brown. Drain on paper towels. Serve hot.

Cocktail Nibblers: Cut dough into 1½-inch rounds. Proceed as above. Just before serving, sprinkle with seasoned salt. Makes 32.

Chinese cooking is subtle and makes use of many ingredients, but it is surprisingly quick. Our dishes include some familiar favorites and others destined to become so.

EGG-DROP SOUP

MAKES 8 SERVINGS

4 cans (14-oz size) clear
   chicken broth
   (7 cups)
3 tablespoons cornstarch
½ teaspoon sugar

1 teaspoon salt
¼ teaspoon pepper
2 eggs, beaten
1 cup chopped green onions
   (with tops)

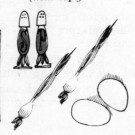

1. Heat broth to boiling point in large saucepan.

2. Meanwhile, in small bowl, make a smooth paste of cornstarch and ¼ cup cold water.

3. Into hot broth, slowly stir cornstarch mixture, with sugar, salt, and pepper. Heat to boiling point, stirring constantly—mixture should be slightly thickened and translucent.

4. Reduce heat. Add eggs, a small amount at a time, stirring to separate them into shreds.

5. Remove from heat; add green onions. Serve at once.

659

FIVE-FLAVOR BEEF

¼ cup salad oil
4 lb boned chuck or rump pot roast
1 cup soy sauce
1-inch cinnamon stick

2 anise seeds
½ cup sugar
1 cup sherry
3 tablespoons cornstarch

1. Slowly heat oil in Dutch oven. In it, brown meat well on all sides—about 15 minutes.
2. Meanwhile, combine soy sauce, 2 cups water, cinnamon stick, anise seeds, and sugar.
3. Pour over meat; simmer, covered, 3 hours, or until meat is tender. After 2 hours, add sherry.
4. Remove meat to heated platter.
5. Reserve 2½ cups liquid in Dutch oven, and discard rest; bring to boil.
6. Meanwhile, in small bowl, make a smooth mixture of cornstarch and ½ cup water.
7. Stir into boiling liquid in Dutch oven; simmer, stirring, until thickened and translucent. Serve over beef.

SWEET-AND-SOUR PORK

2¾ lb pork shoulder, cut into ½-inch cubes
3 tablespoons sherry
1½ teaspoons soy sauce
1 teaspoon monosodium glutamate
½ teaspoon ground ginger
1 qt salad oil

Batter:
3 eggs
¾ cup sifted all-purpose flour
3 tablespoons cornstarch

Sauce:
1 can (13½ oz) thawed frozen pineapple chunks
1 cup sugar
1 cup vinegar
2 large green peppers, cut in ½-inch strips
½ cup thinly sliced gherkins
2 tablespoons cornstarch
2 teaspoons soy sauce
2 large tomatoes, cut in eighths
½ cup slivered crystallized ginger

Cooked white rice

1. In large, shallow dish, toss pork with sherry, soy sauce, monosodium glutamate, and ginger; let stand 10 minutes.
2. Meanwhile, in 3-quart saucepan or deep-fat fryer, slowly heat oil to 375F on deep-frying thermometer.
3. Make Batter: In medium bowl, with rotary beater, beat eggs very well. Add flour and cornstarch; beat until smooth.
4. Drain pork cubes well. Pour batter over them; mix well, to coat evenly.
5. Drop cubes (about one fourth at a time—do not crowd) into hot fat; fry about 5 minutes, turning, until golden on all sides. With slotted spoon, remove pork; drain on paper towels.
6. Keep warm in oven set at very low temperature.
7. Make Sauce: Drain pineapple chunks, reserving juice. Add water to juice to make 1 cup.
8. In large saucepan, combine juice, sugar, and vinegar; heat, stirring, until sugar is dissolved. Then bring to boiling point.
9. Add green peppers and gherkins; boil 2 minutes. Remove from heat.
10. In small bowl, combine cornstarch and ¼ cup water; stir until smooth. Add to pineapple-juice mixture, with soy sauce, tomatoes, ginger, and pineapple chunks.
11. Cook, stirring and over moderate heat, until thickened and translucent.
12. Arrange pork cubes in serving dish. Pour on the sweet-sour sauce. Serve with hot rice.

BEEF AND PEPPERS

1½-lb sirloin steak, 1 inch
    thick
Boiling water
4 cups thinly sliced green-
    pepper rings
3 tablespoons salad oil
3 cups thinly sliced onions
¾ teaspoon salt
2 cloves garlic
5 green onions, with their
    tops, sliced
2 teaspoons monosodium
    glutamate

1½ teaspoons sugar
Dash pepper
⅓ cup sherry
1½ teaspoons finely
    chopped crystallized
    ginger
¾ cup canned beef
    bouillon
3 tablespoons cornstarch
2 tablespoons soy sauce
Cooked white rice

1. To make beef easier to slice, store in freezing compartment until partially frozen. Slice into ⅛-inch slivers; thaw completely at room temperature.

2. Pour just enough boiling water over green-pepper rings to cover. Let stand about 3 minutes; then rinse in cold water.

3. Heat oil in large skillet. Add green-pepper rings, onion slices, salt, garlic, and green onions; cook, stirring and over high heat, 3 minutes.

4. Then add beef slivers; cook, stirring and over high heat, 2 minutes.

5. Add monosodium glutamate, sugar, pepper, sherry, and ginger; cook, stirring, 1 minute.

6. Add bouillon, and bring mixture to boiling point.

7. Meanwhile, in small bowl, combine cornstarch, soy sauce, and ¾ cup water. Stir into skillet; cook, stirring, until sauce is thickened and translucent. Serve with hot rice.

LOBSTER CANTONESE

6 (6- to 8-oz size) thawed
    frozen rock-lobster
    tails
¼ cup salad oil
1 clove garlic, very finely
    chopped
½ lb pork shoulder,
    ground
2 tablespoons cornstarch

¼ cup soy sauce
1 teaspoon sugar
1 teaspoon salt
½ teaspoon pepper
2¼ cups boiling water
2 eggs
½ cup slivered green
    onion

1. With kitchen shears, cut shell away from lobster meat. Remove meat in one piece, and cut it crosswise in 2-inch sections.

2. Heat oil in large skillet with cover. Add garlic and pork; sauté, stirring, until pork is no longer pink—takes about 10 minutes.

3. Meanwhile, in small bowl, make a smooth mixture of cornstarch and ⅓ cup water.

4. Stir into pork the soy sauce, sugar, salt, pepper, boiling water, and cornstarch mixture; bring to a boil. Reduce heat; simmer, stirring, until thickened and translucent—about 10 minutes.

5. Add lobster pieces; cook, covered and over low heat, until lobster is tender—takes about 8 to 10 minutes (don't overcook).

6. In small bowl, beat eggs slightly with fork. Stir, all at once, into lobster mixture (eggs will form shreds). Add green onion. Serve at once.

CHICKEN WITH TOASTED ALMONDS

3 (2-lb size) broiler-fryers
5 tablespoons salad oil
2 tablespoons soy sauce
2 teaspoons salt
1½ teaspoons sugar
Dash pepper
¼ cup cornstarch
1 can (14 oz) clear chicken
　　broth

1 can (5 oz) water
　　chestnuts, drained
　　and chopped
½ cup thawed frozen, or
　　canned, peas, drained
1 cup thinly sliced celery
1 can (4 oz) whole
　　mushrooms, drained
½ cup toasted slivered
　　almonds

MAKES 6 SERVINGS

1.　Have meatman bone and skin broiler-fryers. To make them easier to slice, store in freezing compartment until partially frozen. Then slice into long, thin slivers; let thaw completely at room temperature.

2.　Heat oil in large skillet. Add chicken slivers, soy sauce, salt, sugar, and pepper; cook, stirring, a few minutes, or just until chicken is no longer pink.

3.　In small bowl, make a smooth paste of cornstarch and ⅓ cup water. Stir into chicken mixture, with chicken broth, water chestnuts, peas, celery, and mushrooms; cook, stirring, until slightly thickened and translucent. Sprinkle top with almonds.

SHRIMP WITH APRICOT SAUCE

2 lb fresh or thawed frozen
　　uncooked shrimp
2 eggs
½ cup milk
¾ cup sifted all-purpose
　　flour

2 tablespoons cornstarch
1 teaspoon baking powder
1 teaspoon salt
2 teaspoons salad oil
1 quart salad oil
Apricot Sauce, below

MAKES 6 SERVINGS

1.　Leaving shell on tail, remove rest of shell from each shrimp. Devein shrimp; rinse in cold water; drain well on paper towels.

2.　In medium bowl, with rotary beater, beat eggs slightly. Add milk, flour, cornstarch, baking powder, salt, and 2 teaspoons oil. Beat until batter is smooth.

3.　In deep-fryer or heavy kettle, slowly heat 1 quart oil to 375F on deep-frying thermometer.

4.　While oil is heating, make Apricot Sauce.

5.　Then dip shrimp in batter, coating thoroughly. Fry, a few at a time, until golden-brown —takes about 4 minutes. Drain on paper towels. Serve shrimp with hot Apricot Sauce.

APRICOT SAUCE

½ cup pineapple juice
2 to 4 tablespoons dry
　　mustard
2 tablespoons soy sauce

1 cup apricot jam
2 teaspoons grated lemon
　　peel
¼ cup lemon juice

MAKES ABOUT 1¾ CUPS

1.　In medium skillet, stir pineapple juice into mustard until mixture is smooth.

2.　Add remaining ingredients. Heat, stirring over low heat, until jam is melted.

FRIED RICE

¼ cup salad oil
2 cups cold cooked white
　　rice
3 eggs, beaten
2 cooked bacon slices,
　　crumbled

2 tablespoons soy sauce
⅛ teaspoon pepper
3 green onions with tops,
　　sliced

MAKES 6 SERVINGS

1.　Heat oil in heavy skillet. In hot oil, sauté rice, over medium heat, stirring with metal spoon, about 5 minutes, or until golden.

2.　Stir eggs into rice; cook, stirring constantly and over medium heat, until eggs are cooked— about 3 minutes.

3.　Then stir in bacon, soy sauce, and pepper; combine well. Garnish with green onions.

CHINESE ALMOND CAKES

MAKES 3 DOZEN

2½ cups sifted all-purpose
    flour
¾ cup sugar
¼ teaspoon salt
1 teaspoon baking powder
¾ cup butter or margarine

1 egg
1 teaspoon almond extract
About 36 whole blanched
    almonds
1 egg yolk

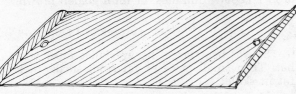

1. Sift flour with sugar, salt, and baking powder into large bowl.

2. Using pastry blender or 2 knives, cut in butter until mixture resembles coarse cornmeal.

3. Beat egg with 2 tablespoons water and the almond extract. Add to flour mixture, mixing with fork until dough leaves side of bowl.

4. On lightly floured surface, knead dough until smooth. Wrap in waxed paper; refrigerate 1 hour.

5. Meanwhile, preheat oven to 350F.

6. Form dough into balls 1 inch in diameter. Place, 3 inches apart, on ungreased cookie sheets.

7. With palm of hand, flatten each cookie to a circle ¼ inch thick; press almond into center of each.

8. Combine egg yolk with 1 tablespoon water. Brush on cookies.

9. Bake cookies 20 to 25 minutes, or until golden-brown. Remove to wire rack; let cool.

How come a French cook can take the same (well, nearly the same) ingredients as anyone else and with a dash of something or other—magic, most likely—turn out dishes that linger in the memory forever? Our recipes let you in on the secret.

BEEF IN BURGUNDY WITH GNOCCHI

MAKES 8 SERVINGS

¼ cup butter or margarine
¼ cup salad oil
1¼ lb small white onions
4 lb chuck, trimmed, cut
    in 2-inch cubes
2½ tablespoons potato
    flour, or ¼ cup
    unsifted all-purpose
    flour
1 teaspoon meat-extract
    paste
1 tablespoon tomato paste

3 cups Burgundy
¼ teaspoon pepper
2 bay leaves
½ teaspoon dried thyme
    leaves
½ teaspoon dried marjoram
    leaves
4 parsley sprigs
¾ lb mushrooms, washed
Chopped parsley
Gnocchi

1. Preheat oven to 325F.

2. In 4-quart Dutch oven, heat butter and oil. In fat, sauté onions 5 minutes; remove.

3. Add beef, a third at a time, to fat; brown well on all sides, and remove.

4. Remove Dutch oven from heat; discard all but 1 tablespoon fat. Stir in the flour, meat-extract paste, and tomato paste until smooth.

5. Gradually add Burgundy, stirring until smooth. Then add beef, pepper, herbs, parsley sprigs, and mushrooms, stirring until well mixed.

6. Bake, covered, 1½ hours.

7. Add onions; bake 1 hour longer, or until meat is tender. Sprinkle with chopped parsley. Serve with Gnocchi.

663

GNOCCHI

1 pkg (8½ oz) cream-puff
    mix
1 cup boiling water
4 eggs
¼ cup grated Parmesan
    cheese

1 teaspoon dry mustard
1 teaspoon salt
¼ cup butter or margarine,
    melted

1. Prepare cream-puff mix as package directs, using boiling water and eggs. Then stir in cheese and mustard.

2. Turn into large pastry bag, using a large, plain tube.

3. Meanwhile, fill 2-quart saucepan with water. Add salt; bring just to boiling. Reduce heat to very low.

4. Pipe cream-puff mixture in a stream into hot water, cutting into 1-inch lengths as it drops into water. Gnocchi will rise to top as they are cooked.

5. Drain well on paper towels; let cool.

6. Just before serving, arrange in shallow baking dish. Pour butter over top; run under broiler about 3 minutes, or until golden brown.

PEPPER STEAK

2-lb sirloin steak, 1½ inches
    thick
2 teaspoons coarsely ground
    black pepper
1 teaspoon arrowroot or
    cornstarch

1½ teaspoons salt
½ cup canned beef
    bouillon, undiluted
½ cup brandy

1. Slowly heat large, heavy skillet until very hot. Trim small piece of fat from steak; melt fat in skillet.

2. Meanwhile, rub 1 teaspoon pepper into each side of steak. Over high heat, sear steak in hot fat about 2 minutes on each side, or until well browned.

3. Reduce heat to medium; pan-broil steak 8 to 10 minutes on each side, for medium rare.

4. Meanwhile, in small saucepan, combine arrowroot and rest of ingredients, stirring until smooth. Bring to boiling, stirring constantly. Remove from heat.

5. Place steak on heated platter; keep warm.

6. Drain all but 2 tablespoons drippings from skillet. Stir in bouillon mixture; simmer 5 minutes. Pour over steak.

LOBSTER IN TOMATO SAUCE

6 (5-oz size) frozen rock-
    lobster tails,
    unthawed; or 3½
    cups cut-up cooked
    lobster
2 tablespoons butter or
    margarine
1½ cups finely chopped
    onion
1 clove garlic, finely
    chopped

1 can (6 oz) tomato paste
¼ cup finely chopped
    parsley
1 teaspoon dried thyme
    leaves
1 bay leaf, crumbled
1 teaspoon salt
¼ teaspoon pepper
1 cup dry white wine
¼ cup brandy (optional)

1. Cook lobster tails as package label directs; let cool.

2. Remove meat from shell; cut into large chunks.

3. In hot butter in large skillet, sauté onion and garlic until golden—about 5 minutes.

4. Remove from heat. Stir in remaining ingredients, except lobster; bring to boiling. Reduce heat; simmer, covered, 15 minutes.

5. Add lobster; simmer gently 5 minutes longer, or until lobster is heated through.

CHICKEN IN WHITE WINE

¼ cup salad oil
½ lb small white onions, peeled
1 clove garlic, finely chopped
3-lb broiler-fryer, cut up
2 tablespoons flour
1 cup dry white wine
1 tablespoon brandy (optional)
1 teaspoon salt

⅛ teaspoon pepper
1 teaspoon dried thyme leaves
2 tablespoons finely chopped parsley
¼ lb fresh mushrooms, sliced; or 1 can (3 oz) sliced mushrooms, drained
Chopped parsley

1. In large, heavy skillet or Dutch oven with tight-fitting cover, slowly heat salad oil. In this, sauté onions and garlic until golden—about 5 minutes. Remove onions, and set aside.

2. Add chicken; sauté until browned on all sides. Remove skillet from heat.

3. Remove chicken, and set aside. Drain all but 2 tablespoons fat from skillet.

4. Stir in flour until smooth. Gradually stir in wine. Add brandy, salt, pepper, thyme, and 2 tablespoons finely chopped parsley, along with chicken and onions; simmer, covered, 30 minutes, or until chicken is almost tender.

5. Add mushrooms; simmer, covered, 10 minutes.

6. To serve: Put chicken, with sauce, on warm platter. Sprinkle with chopped parsley.

MADELEINES

2 eggs
1 cup granulated sugar
1 cup sifted all-purpose flour

¾ cup butter or margarine, melted and cooled
1 teaspoon grated lemon peel
Confectioners' sugar

1. Preheat oven to 350F. Grease and lightly flour madeleine pans.

2. In top of double boiler, over hot, not boiling, water (water in bottom of double boiler should not touch base of pan above), with portable electric mixer at medium speed, beat eggs and granulated sugar just until lukewarm —about 2 minutes.

3. Set top of double boiler into cold water. Beat egg mixture, at high speed, 5 minutes, or until very light and fluffy.

4. With wire whisk or rubber scraper, gently fold flour into egg mixture until well combined.

5. Stir in cooled butter and lemon peel.

6. Pour into prepared madeleine pans, using 1 tablespoon batter for each form.

7. Bake 12 minutes. Cool 1 minute; then remove from pans with a small spatula.

8. Cool completely. Sprinkle with confectioners' sugar.

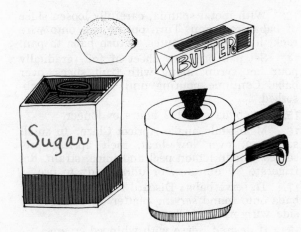

665

BABA AU RHUM

¾ cup warm water
(105 to 115F)
2 pkg active dry yeast
¼ cup sugar
1 teaspoon salt
6 eggs
3¾ cups sifted all-purpose flour
¾ cup soft butter or margarine
½ cup finely chopped citron
¼ cup currants or seedless raisins

Rum Syrup:
2½ cups sugar
1 medium unpeeled orange, sliced crosswise
½ unpeeled lemon, sliced crosswise
1 to 1½ cups light rum

Apricot Glaze:
1 cup apricot preserves
1 teaspoon grated lemon peel
2 teaspoons lemon juice

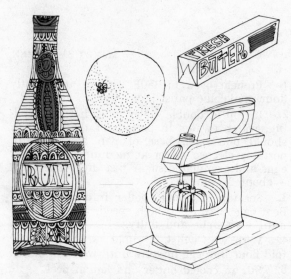

1. Lightly grease a 10-by-4-inch tube pan. If possible, check temperature of warm water with thermometer.

2. Sprinkle yeast over water in large bowl of electric mixer; stir until dissolved.

3. Add sugar, salt, eggs, and 2¼ cups flour. At medium speed, beat 4 minutes, or until smooth, scraping side of bowl and guiding mixture into beater with rubber scraper.

4. Add butter; beat 2 minutes, or until very well blended.

5. At low speed, beat in rest of flour; beat until smooth—about 2 minutes.

6. Stir in citron and currants. Batter will be thick.

7. Turn batter into prepared pan, spreading evenly. Cover with towel.

8. Let rise in warm place (85F), free from drafts, 1 hour and 10 minutes, or until baba has risen to within ½ inch of top of pan.

9. Meanwhile, preheat oven to 400F. Gently place baba on oven rack (do not jar; baba may fall).

10. Bake 40 to 45 minutes, or until deep golden-brown and cake tester inserted in center comes out clean.

11. Meanwhile, make Rum Syrup: In medium saucepan, combine sugar with 2 cups water; bring to boiling, stirring, until sugar is dissolved. Boil, uncovered, 10 minutes.

12. Reduce heat. Add orange and lemon slices; simmer 10 minutes. Remove from heat; add rum.

13. With metal spatula, carefully loosen sides of baba from pan. Turn out of pan onto wire rack; let cool 15 minutes. Return baba to pan.

14. Set pan on large sheet of foil; gradually pour hot syrup, along with fruit slices, over baba. Continue pouring until all syrup is absorbed.

15. Let baba stand 2 hours or longer.

16. Meanwhile, make Apricot Glaze: In small saucepan, over low heat, melt apricot preserves. Stir in lemon peel and juice; strain. Refrigerate 30 minutes, or until ready to use.

17. To serve baba: Discard fruit slices. Invert baba onto round serving platter. Brush top and side with Apricot Glaze.

18. If desired, serve with whipped cream.

Holiday Baba au Rhum: In small saucepan, combine 1 cup sugar with ½ cup water. Bring to boiling, stirring, until sugar is dissolved. Add 1 cup cranberries. Cook, uncovered, 5 minutes. Let cool completely. Use, instead of Apricot Glaze, to brush top of baba, letting it run down side.

MOUSSE AU CHOCOLAT

MAKES 6 SERVINGS

1 pkg (6 oz) semisweet-
*   chocolate pieces*
2 teaspoons instant coffee
½ cup sugar

½ teaspoon vanilla extract
3 egg yolks
3 egg whites
Whipped cream (optional)

1. In medium saucepan, combine chocolate, coffee, ¼ cup sugar, and 2 tablespoons water. Stir constantly, over low heat, until chocolate is melted and sugar is dissolved.

2. Remove from heat. With wooden spoon, beat until smooth; let cool slightly.

3. Add vanilla. Beat in egg yolks, one at a time, beating well after each addition.

4. In medium bowl, with rotary beater or portable electric mixer, beat egg whites just until soft peaks form when beater is slowly raised. Add remaining sugar, 1 tablespoon at a time, beating well after each addition. Beat until stiff peaks form.

5. With rubber scraper or wire whisk, gently fold chocolate mixture into egg-white mixture until well combined.

6. Spoon into 6 sherbet dishes. Refrigerate until well chilled—1 hour—or until serving time. If desired, garnish with whipped cream.

G erman cooking, at its best, is flavorful and deeply satisfying. The following recipes give you a generous sampling.

LENTIL SOUP

MAKES 6 SERVINGS

½ lb (1½ cups) lentils
4 bacon slices
1 cup chopped leek
½ cup chopped onion
¼ cup chopped carrot
¾ cup chopped green
*   pepper*
¾ cup chopped tomato

3 tablespoons butter or
*   margarine*
3 tablespoons flour.
1 can (10½ oz) condensed
*   beef bouillon,*
*   undiluted*
2 teaspoons salt
2 tablespoons vinegar

1. Put lentils in 5 cups cold water in large kettle; bring to boil. Reduce heat; simmer, covered, 1 hour.

2. Meanwhile, cut bacon in small pieces; sauté, in large skillet, until crisp.

3. To bacon in skillet, add leek, onion, carrot, pepper, and tomato; sauté over low heat about 5 minutes. Combine with lentils in kettle.

4. Melt butter in same skillet; remove from heat. Stir in flour until smooth; then gradually stir in bouillon. Add salt and vinegar; bring to boiling point, stirring.

5. Pour into lentils; cook, over low heat and stirring occasionally, about 30 minutes.

667

SAUERKRAUT AND PORK

(Alsatian)

2 onions
8 whole cloves
2 carrots, pared
2 lb unsliced bacon,
    halved
2-lb smoked boneless butt
10 whole black peppers
6 juniper berries (optional)

4 cans (1-lb size) sauerkraut
    (2 qt), drained
1 tablespoon butter or
    margarine
2 cans (14-oz size) clear
    chicken broth
    (3½ cups)
1 cup white wine
¼ cup lemon juice

1. Stud each onion with 4 cloves. Put onions, carrots, bacon, and smoked butt in large kettle.
2. Add peppers and berries, tied in cheesecloth bag. Cover with sauerkraut. Add butter.
3. Combine broth, wine, and lemon juice. Pour over mixture in kettle; bring to boiling point.
4. Reduce heat; simmer, covered, 1½ to 2 hours, or until butt is tender when pierced with fork. Discard onions and cheesecloth bag.
5. To serve: Cut each piece of bacon into 4 slices, butt into 8 slices. Arrange on large platter, with sauerkraut. Slice carrots crosswise, and use as garnish.

SAUERBRATEN

1 cup red-wine vinegar
½ cup cider vinegar
½ cup Burgundy
2 onions, sliced
1 carrot, sliced
1 stalk celery, chopped
Few sprigs parsley
1 bay leaf
2 whole allspice
4 whole cloves

1 tablespoon salt
1 tablespoon pepper
4 lb chuck pot roast
⅓ cup shortening or salad
    oil
6 tablespoons unsifted
    all-purpose flour
1 tablespoon sugar
½ cup crushed gingersnaps

1. In large glass or ceramic bowl, combine vinegars, Burgundy, onion, carrot, celery, parsley, bay leaf, allspice, cloves, salt, and pepper.
2. Wipe meat with damp cloth. Add meat to marinade; refrigerate, covered, 3 days. Turn several times, to marinate evenly.
3. Remove meat from marinade; wipe dry.
4. Heat marinade in small saucepan.
5. Heat Dutch oven or large, heavy kettle very slowly. Add shortening, and heat.
6. Dredge meat in 2 tablespoons flour; brown very well on all sides in hot fat in Dutch oven.
7. Pour in marinade; simmer meat, covered, 2½ to 3 hours, or until tender.
8. Then strain liquid from meat into 1-quart measure; skim fat from surface. Measure 3½ cups liquid into saucepan; heat.
9. In small bowl, make paste of ½ cup cold water, rest of flour, and sugar. Stir into liquid; bring to boiling point, stirring.
10. Add gingersnaps. Pour over meat; simmer, covered, 20 minutes.
11. Remove meat to heated platter; pour some of gravy over it. Serve in thin slices, with more gravy and Potato Dumplings.*

* See Quick Breads Chapter.

GERMAN POTATO SALAD

MAKES 6 SERVINGS

2 lb potatoes, pared and
   sliced*
Salt
⅓ cup bacon drippings
¼ cup cider vinegar

1 teaspoon instant minced
   onion
½ teaspoon paprika
6 slices crisp-cooked bacon,
   crumbled

1. In medium saucepan, cook potatoes in 1 inch of boiling, salted water, covered, just until tender. Drain.

2. Meanwhile, in small saucepan, heat bacon drippings, vinegar, onion, ½ teaspoon salt, and paprika.

3. In large bowl, combine hot potato slices, bacon, and dressing; toss lightly, being careful not to break potatoes. Serve at once.

* Or use 2½ cups packaged precooked potatoes. Cook as label directs; drain. Proceed as above.

HAZLENUT TORTE

MAKES 10 TO 12 SERVINGS

Cake:
Confectioners' sugar
6 eggs
6 tablespoons granulated
   sugar
1 teaspoon grated lemon
   peel
1 tablespoon lemon juice
1⅓ cups ground hazelnuts
2 tablespoons packaged dry
   bread crumbs

¾ cup granulated sugar
1 cup ground hazelnuts

Frosting:
2 egg yolks
2 tablespoons granulated
   sugar
¼ cup soft butter
   or margarine
2 squares semisweet
   chocolate, melted

Filling:
3 cups heavy cream,
   whipped

1 tablespoon ground
   hazelnuts

1. Make Cake: Preheat oven to 325F. Lightly grease 2 (8-by-1½-inch) layer-cake pans; then coat lightly with confectioners' sugar.

2. Separate eggs, putting whites into large bowl of electric mixer and yolks into the small bowl.

3. With mixer at high speed, beat whites just until stiff peaks form when beater is slowly raised. Then, with same beater, beat yolks, at high speed, until thick and lemon-colored.

4. Gradually add granulated sugar (2 tablespoons at a time) to yolks, beating well after each addition. Add lemon peel and juice, hazelnuts, and bread crumbs; beat well.

5. With wire whisk or rubber scraper, using an under-and-over motion, gently fold yolk mixture into whites until well combined.

6. Pour into prepared pans; bake 40 minutes, or just until surface springs back when gently pressed with fingertip.

7. Cool completely in pans, on wire rack—takes about 1 hour.

8. Make Filling: Combine all ingredients in medium bowl.

9. Make Frosting: In small bowl, with rotary beater, beat egg yolks and sugar until thick and light. Add butter and chocolate; beat until smooth and blended.

10. Gently remove cooled torte layers from pans. Split each crosswise, making 4 layers.

11. Put together with two thirds of the filling. Cover top with frosting; then cover sides with rest of filling.

12. Sprinkle top with 1 tablespoon ground hazelnuts. Refrigerate until ready to serve.

Our Polynesian recipes are delicate and exotic things like ginger-scented pork, bananas baked in orange juice, and other unusual dishes.

LOMI SALMON

¾ lb salted or smoked salmon
5 green onions
1 teaspoon coarse salt

3 large tomatoes, peeled and chilled
¼ cup ice water

1. Wipe salmon with damp cloth; cover with water, and soak 3 to 4 hours.
2. Drain; remove skin and bones. With large knife, shred salmon.
3. Finely chop onions; add salt. With a rolling pin, mash onions and salt to a smooth paste.
4. Slice tomatoes vertically from stem end.
5. Toss together salmon, onion mixture, and tomatoes, combining well. Add ice water; refrigerate until thoroughly chilled. Serve in small salad bowls.

ISLAND BAKED SHRIMP

3 lb deveined uncooked shrimp
Dash cayenne
2 tablespoons prepared mustard
1 teaspoon brown sugar
1 tablespoon bottled steak sauce

½ cup melted butter or margarine
3 drops liquid hot-pepper seasoning
1 teaspoon salt
½ cup buttered fresh bread crumbs

1. Preheat oven to 375F.
2. In boiling water to cover, simmer shrimp, with cayenne, 5 minutes.
3. Drain, and dice. Arrange in 8-by-8-by-2-inch baking dish.
4. Combine mustard, sugar, steak sauce, butter, hot-pepper seasoning, and salt; spread over shrimp. Sprinkle with bread crumbs.
5. Bake 15 to 20 minutes, or until crumbs are golden.

ROAST LOIN OF PORK, POLYNESIAN

3½-lb loin of pork
2 tablespoons finely chopped crystallized ginger

¼ cup soy sauce
Watercress

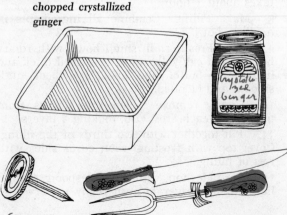

1. Preheat oven to 325F.
2. With paring knife, make several slits at intervals in pork. Insert 1 tablespoon ginger.
3. Combine rest of ginger and soy sauce.
4. Place pork loin, fat side up (let loin rest on bones), in shallow roasting pan, without rack. Insert meat thermometer in meatiest part, away from bone and fat.
5. Brush pork with part of soy-sauce mixture. For well-done roast, cook about 1 hour and 45 minutes, or until meat thermometer reads 185F (brush with soy-sauce mixture several times).
6. Remove from oven; wait 20 minutes; carve.
7. To serve: Put pork loin on wooden board or serving platter; garnish with watercress. Arrange Bananas Baked in Orange Juice around roast.

BANANAS BAKED IN ORANGE JUICE

6 to 8 medium bananas
1 medium orange, peeled
    and cut in chunks
2 tablespoons orange juice

2 tablespoons lemon juice
⅓ cup sugar
Dash cinnamon
Dash nutmeg

1. Preheat oven to 325F.
2. Peel bananas (use slightly underripe ones —green-tipped or yellow, not flecked with brown). Arrange in shallow baking dish. Add remaining ingredients.
3. Bake 25 to 30 minutes, or until bananas are golden and tender. Serve hot.

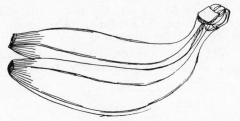

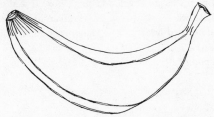

When you taste the wonderful food that follows, you'll think of Italy (whether you've been there or just dreamed of it), of lunch in a sun-drenched piazza or dinner at a breeze-swept table, and you enjoying it all.

SPAGHETTI WITH MEATBALL SAUCE

4 white-bread slices
1 lb ground beef
1 tablespoon grated
    Parmesan cheese
1 egg
1 tablespoon chopped
    parsley
½ teaspoon grated onion
¼ teaspoon crushed garlic
2 teaspoons salt
¼ teaspoon pepper

3 tablespoons salad or
    olive oil
1 can (1 lb) stewed
    tomatoes, undrained
2 cans (8-oz size) tomato
    sauce
2 bay leaves, crumbled
½ teaspoon dried basil
    leaves
1 pkg (8 oz) spaghetti

1. In small bowl, add enough water to bread slices to cover; let stand 2 minutes. Remove slices, and squeeze out excess water.
2. In medium bowl, combine bread with beef, cheese, egg, parsley, onion, garlic, 1 teaspoon salt, and ⅛ teaspoon pepper; toss lightly, with fork, to combine.
3. With moistened hands, shape meat mixture into balls, ¾ inch in diameter.
4. Slowly heat salad oil in large skillet. Add meatballs; over medium heat, sauté, turning occasionally, until browned all over.
5. With slotted utensil, remove meatballs from skillet; set aside.
6. To same skillet, add tomatoes and tomato sauce. Over medium heat, bring to boiling, stirring. Remove from heat.
7. Add bay leaves, basil, meatballs, and remaining salt and pepper; mix well.
8. Cook, covered, over low heat and stirring occasionally, 1 hour.
9. Meanwhile, cook spaghetti as package label directs; drain well.
10. Serve spaghetti with hot sauce poured over.

MINESTRONE ALLA MILANESE

MAKES ABOUT 3½ QUARTS—12 SERVINGS

3 tablespoons olive or salad oil

½ cup finely chopped onion

¼ cup finely chopped parsley

3 beef-bouillon cubes

1½ teaspoons meat-extract paste

1 teaspoon dried basil leaves

1 tablespoon salt

¼ teaspoon pepper

1½ cups diced pared potatoes (2 medium)

2 cups diced zucchini (1 lb)

1 cup sliced celery

1 cup shredded cabbage

1 cup sliced carrots

1 pkg (9 oz) frozen cut green beans, thawed

½ cup raw regular white rice

1. Heat oil in large kettle. Add onion and parsley; sauté for 5 minutes.

2. Add 3 quarts water; bring to boiling.

3. Add bouillon cubes and meat-extract paste; stir until dissolved. Add basil, salt, and pepper; simmer, uncovered, 5 minutes.

4. Remove from heat. Add rest of ingredients, except rice; bring to boiling. Reduce heat; simmer, covered, 20 minutes.

5. Add rice; simmer, covered, 25 minutes longer, or just until rice is tender. Serve hot.

VEAL TETRAZZINI

MAKES 6 SERVINGS

3-lb boned shoulder-of-veal roast

2 carrots, pared

1 large onion, sliced

5 or 6 celery tops

1 tablespoon salt

4 whole black peppers

1 pkg (8 oz) thin spaghetti

Sauce:

⅓ cup butter or margarine

⅓ cup finely chopped green pepper

⅓ cup finely chopped onion

⅓ cup unsifted all-purpose flour

2½ cups reserved veal stock

1½ teaspoons salt

1 can (6 oz) sliced mushrooms, drained

½ cup light cream

½ cup sherry

1½ cups grated Parmesan cheese

1. Wipe veal with damp paper towels.

2. Place in 6-quart kettle with 2 quarts water, the carrots, onion, celery, salt, and peppers; bring to boiling.

3. Reduce heat; simmer, covered, 1½ to 1¾ hours, or until veal is tender.

4. Remove from heat; let veal cool in liquid.

5. When veal has cooled, strain liquid, reserving 2½ cups for sauce. Cut veal into ½-inch cubes.

6. Meanwhile, cook spaghetti as package label directs; drain.

7. Preheat oven to 350F.

8. Make Sauce: In hot butter in medium saucepan, sauté green pepper and onion until tender—about 5 minutes.

9. Remove from heat. Add flour, stirring until smooth. Slowly stir in reserved veal stock; then bring to boiling, stirring. Reduce heat, and simmer 1 minute. Sauce will be thickened and smooth.

10. Add salt, mushrooms, cream, and sherry; simmer, stirring, 3 minutes longer.

11. In a 12-by-8-by-2-inch baking dish, layer half the spaghetti; top with half the veal, then with half the sauce and ½ cup cheese. Repeat layering rest of spaghetti, veal, and sauce; top with rest of cheese.

12. Bake 20 to 25 minutes, or until Tetrazzini is bubbly and cheese is golden.

BAKED LASAGNA

MAKES 6 SERVINGS

Meatballs:
½ lb ground chuck
¼ lb ground veal
2 tablespoons finely
    chopped onion
1 clove garlic, finely
    chopped
2 tablespoons finely
    chopped parsley
1 teaspoon dried oregano
    leaves
½ teaspoon dried basil
    leaves
¾ teaspoon salt
Dash pepper
2 tablespoons grated
    Parmesan cheese
1 egg

Tomato Sauce:
¼ cup olive or salad oil
¼ cup finely chopped
    onion

1 clove garlic, finely
    chopped
2 tablespoons finely
    chopped parsley
1 can (1 lb, 12 oz) whole
    tomatoes, undrained
    (3½ cups)
2 cans (6-oz size) tomato
    paste
2 teaspoons dried oregano
    leaves
1 teaspoon dried basil
    leaves
2 teaspoons salt
1 teaspoon garlic powder
¼ teaspoon pepper
⅛ teaspoon cayenne

½ pkg (1-lb size) lasagna
1 lb Mozzarella cheese,
    diced
1 lb ricotta cheese
1 cup grated Parmesan
    cheese

1. Make Meatballs: In medium bowl, combine all ingredients; toss lightly to mix well.

2. With teaspoon, shape mixture into 30 balls, each ¾ inch in diameter.

3. Make Tomato Sauce: Slowly heat oil in large, heavy skillet. Brown meatballs in hot oil; remove.

4. Add onion, garlic, and parsley; sauté until tender—about 5 minutes. Add rest of sauce ingredients, along with ½ cup water and meatballs; stir to mix well.

5. Bring to boiling. Reduce heat; simmer, uncovered, 1½ hours, stirring occasionally.

6. Preheat oven to 350F. Lightly grease a 13-by-9-by-2-inch baking dish.

7. Meanwhile, cook lasagna as package label directs. Drain; rinse with hot water.

8. In prepared baking dish, layer half the ingredients, in this order: lasagna, Mozzarella, ricotta, tomato sauce with meatballs, and Parmesan cheese; then repeat. Bake 30 to 35 minutes, or until cheese is melted and lasagna is heated through.

EGGPLANT PARMESAN

MAKES 6 SERVINGS

1 large eggplant (1½ lb)
3 eggs, beaten
1½ cups packaged dry
    bread crumbs
1 cup olive or salad oil
2 teaspoons dried oregano
    leaves

2 teaspoons salt
½ lb sliced Mozzarella or
    pizza cheese
4 cans (8-oz size) tomato
    sauce
½ cup grated Parmesan
    cheese

1. Preheat oven to 350F. Lightly grease a 9-by-9-by-1¾-inch baking dish.

2. Cut eggplant crosswise into ¼-inch-thick slices. Dip into beaten eggs, then into bread crumbs, coating completely.

3. Meanwhile, slowly heat oil in large skillet. Sauté eggplant until golden-brown—about 2 minutes on each side. Drain.

4. In prepared baking dish, layer, in order, half the eggplant, 1 teaspoon oregano, 1 teaspoon salt, half the Mozzarella-cheese slices, half the tomato sauce, and ¼ cup Parmesan cheese; repeat.

5. Bake, uncovered, 25 to 30 minutes, or until cheese is melted and eggplant is tender.

ZABAIONE

6 egg yolks   ⅓ cup Marsala
3 tablespoons sugar

1.   In top of double boiler, with portable electric mixer at high speed (or with rotary beater), beat egg yolks with sugar until light and fluffy.
2.   Gradually add Marsala, beating until well combined.
3.   Over hot, not boiling, water, beat at medium speed 8 minutes, or until mixture begins to hold its shape.
4.   Turn into 4 dessert glasses. Serve at once, or while still slightly warm. (Zabaione separates on standing.)

BISCUIT TORTONI

2 egg yolks   1 cup heavy cream,
½ cup confectioners' sugar   whipped
2 tablespoons sherry   ½ cup plus 2 tablespoons
½ teaspoon vanilla extract   crushed Italian-type
2 egg whites   macaroons

1.   In small bowl, with rotary beater, beat egg yolks with sugar until smooth and fluffy.
2.   Stir in sherry and vanilla, mixing well.
3.   In medium bowl, beat egg whites just until stiff peaks form.
4.   Gently fold egg-yolk mixture into whites. Then gently fold in whipped cream until well combined.
5.   Stir in ½ cup crushed macaroons.
6.   Turn into 6 to 8 (4- or 5-oz) paper dessert dishes. Sprinkle each with crushed macaroons.
7.   Freeze until firm—about 4 hours. Serve right from paper dishes.

To the Japanese, the look of food is as important as the taste of it. Each of these dishes, therefore, is a picture, and each is fascinating to eat.

TEMPURA

½ lb large fresh shrimp,   ¾ lb sweet potatoes, pared
   shelled and deveined   and sliced ⅛ inch
1 pkg (10 oz) frozen rock-   thick
   lobster tails   1 large green pepper, sliced
2 pkg (10-oz size) frozen   lengthwise in ¼-inch
   scallops   strips
6 large parsley sprigs   Salad oil
½ small eggplant, cut in   Batter, below
   2-by-¼-inch strips   Sauce, below

1.   Drop shrimp into boiling, salted water to cover; bring back to boiling. Reduce heat; simmer, covered, 5 minutes. Then drain, and let cool.
2.   Cook lobster tails as package label directs. Drain; cool. With scissors, cut shell away from meat; halve meat crosswise.
3.   Drop unthawed scallops into boiling, salted water to cover; bring back to boiling. Reduce heat; simmer, covered, 5 minutes. Then drain, and let cool.

(Tempura continued)

4. On platter, arrange shrimp, lobster, and scallops in attractive pattern with parsley, eggplant, sweet potatoes, and green pepper.

5. Refrigerate, covered, until you are ready to cook Tempura.

6. Tempura is best served immediately, cooked at table. In electric skillet or deep-fryer, heat oil (at least 3 inches deep) to 350F on deep-frying thermometer.

7. With tongs, dip shrimp, lobster, scallops, and vegetables into batter, to coat lightly.

8. Deep-fry, a few pieces at a time, until lightly browned—about 3 minutes.

9. Serve a combination of seafood and vegetables to each guest, along with a small bowl of sauce for dipping.

MAKES 2⅓ CUPS

BATTER FOR TEMPURA

3 eggs
2½ teaspoons shoyu or soy
    sauce
1⅔ cups sifted all-purpose
    flour
2 tablespoons sugar
1 teaspoon salt

1. Make batter just before using: Beat eggs, in medium bowl, with rotary beater.

2. Add shoyu and 1¼ cups water. Gradually add flour, sugar, and salt, beating until smooth.

MAKES ENOUGH FOR 6 SERVINGS

SAUCE FOR TEMPURA

½ cup sherry
½ cup beef bouillon
1 cup shoyu or soy sauce
1 teaspoon monosodium
    glutamate
Radishes, freshly grated
Horseradish, freshly grated
Ginger root, freshly grated

1. In small saucepan, combine sherry, bouillon, shoyu, and monosodium glutamate; bring to boiling.

2. Divide into 6 individual serving bowls. Place on tray, along with 3 small bowls filled with grated radishes, horseradish, and ginger root.

3. Each guest adds radish, horseradish, or ginger root to dipping sauce to suit his own taste.

MAKES 8 SERVINGS

RICE WITH MUSHROOMS

2 cups raw long-grain white
    rice
¼ lb fresh mushrooms,
    washed and finely
    chopped
1½ teaspoons salt
⅛ teaspoon pepper
1 tablespoon shoyu or soy
    sauce

1. Place rice in heavy, 2½-quart saucepan. Add about 1 cup cold water; wash rice well, using fingers.

2. Pour off water, and wash rice again. Repeat until water is clear.

3. Add fresh cold water to cover rice about ½ inch—takes about 1½ cups. Let rice soak 1 hour.

4. Add remaining ingredients. Cover saucepan tightly; place over high heat.

5. When steam appears around edge of cover, reduce heat; simmer 15 minutes.

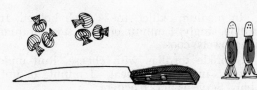

SUKIYAKI

(TO BE COOKED AT TABLE)

2 lb boneless sirloin steak,
    sliced ⅛ inch thick*
2 onions
2 bunches green onions
12 large fresh mushrooms
1 can (5 oz) bamboo
    shoots, drained
½ lb fresh spinach
½ small head cabbage
1 can (8¾ oz) shirataki,
    drained (optional)

¾ cup shoyu or soy sauce
2 tablespoons sugar
2 beef-bouillon cubes, dis-
    solved in 1½ cups
    boiling water
1 teaspoon monosodium
    glutamate
¼ lb beef suet or
    shortening
Cooked white rice

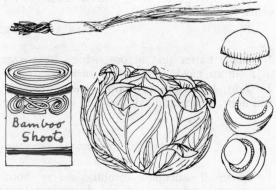

1. Cut beef into 2-inch strips.
2. Prepare vegetables: Peel onions, and slice very thin. Diagonally slice green onions and tops into 1-inch pieces. Slice mushrooms and bamboo shoots ¼ inch thick. Cut spinach in 1-inch strips. Shred cabbage.
3. Arrange all these ingredients and the shirataki attractively on a large serving platter.
4. In small saucepan, combine shoyu, sugar, bouillon, and monosodium glutamate; heat, stirring, until sugar is dissolved.
5. Preheat electric skillet to 350F. Fry suet in skillet to lubricate pan; remove.
6. Add onion and green onion slices, sauté, stirring occasionally, until golden. Add remaining vegetables and shirataki.
7. Cover with beef strips, overlapping if necessary. Pour on sauce mixture; simmer, uncovered, 10 minutes.
8. Turn meat; simmer just until vegetables are tender—about 5 minutes.
9. Serve at once, with hot rice.
* Have meatman slice on meat slicer.

JAPANESE TEA

5 cups boiling water

¼ cup green Japanese tea

1. Rinse teapot with 1 cup boiling water. Place tea in pot; add 2 cups boiling water.
2. Let stand 1 minute. Strain the tea immediately into 4 cups. Do not let tea steep; it will become bitter.
3. Add 2 cups boiling water to the same leaves. (Leaves may be used several times.)

Our South-of-the-Border recipes are not fiery, but of a pleasant warmth. Frank adaptations, they nevertheless capture the gay, sunny essence of Mexican cookery.

ANNIE'S SPECIAL TOSTADOS

Salad oil for frying
10 tortillas

1 cup grated
    Cheddar cheese

1. In medium skillet, in ¾ inch hot oil, fry tortillas, singly, 1 minute on each side. Drain on paper towels; cool.
2. Sprinkle tortillas with cheese. Run under broiler, 5 inches from heat—1 minute or until bubbly. Serve as hors d'oeuvre.

BEEF ENCHILADAS

Meat Filling:
1 lb ground chuck
1 clove garlic, finely
    chopped
2 teaspoons salt
1 tablespoon vinegar
1 tablespoon tequila,
    cognac, or water
1 tablespoon chili powder
1 can (1 lb) kidney beans,
    undrained

Tomato Sauce:
3 tablespoons salad oil
1 clove garlic, very finely
    chopped
¼ cup chopped onion
2 tablespoons flour
2 cans (10½-oz size)
    tomato purée

1 tablespoon vinegar
1 beef-bouillon cube
1 cup boiling water
2 tablespoons finely
    chopped canned
    green chiles
Dash ground cumin
½ teaspoon salt
Dash pepper

Enchiladas:
10 tortillas, canned or
    frozen
1 cup grated sharp Cheddar
    cheese, or 1 cup
    cubed Monterey Jack
    cheese

1. Prepare Meat Filling: In medium skillet, over low heat, sauté chuck with garlic, salt, vinegar, tequila, and chili powder until chuck is browned. Then stir in kidney beans. Set aside.

2. Make Tomato Sauce: In hot oil in skillet, sauté garlic and onion until golden.

3. Remove from heat. Stir in flour until smooth; then stir in tomato purée, vinegar, and bouillon cube, dissolved in boiling water.

4. Bring mixture to boiling point, stirring, over medium heat.

5. Add chiles, cumin, salt, and pepper; simmer, uncovered and stirring occasionally, about 5 minutes. Set aside.

6. To assemble Enchiladas: Preheat oven to 350F.

7. Place about ⅓ cup filling in center of each tortilla; roll up. Arrange, seam side down, in a 13-by-9-by-2-inch baking dish. Pour tomato sauce over all; sprinkle with cheese.

8. Bake 25 minutes.

Note: Meat filling and tomato sauce may be made ahead of time and refrigerated. Reheat slightly when ready to use.

CHILES RELLENOS

1 can (4 oz) sweet green
    chiles (4), or 2
    medium green
    peppers
4 pieces Monterey Jack or
    process Swiss cheese
2 eggs, separated

2 tablespoons all-purpose
    flour
Shortening or oil for deep-
    frying
All-purpose flour
Sauce, see next page

1. Carefully remove seeds and ribs from chiles. (If using green peppers: Wash; cut in half; remove seeds and ribs; parboil 8 to 10 minutes.)

2. Place a 2-by-1-by-½-inch piece of cheese in each chile.

3. In small bowl, beat egg yolks slightly. In medium bowl, with rotary beater, beat whites until they hold soft peaks.

4. Gently fold yolks into whites, using an under-and-over motion. Add 2 tablespoons flour, and continue to fold until no patches of white remain.

5. In deep-fryer or skillet, heat 3 inches of shortening to 400F on deep-frying thermometer.

6. Roll cheese-stuffed chiles in flour. Then, with large kitchen spoon, dip chiles in batter, coating generously.

7. Place in hot fat, and fry until golden on all sides—3 to 4 minutes.

8. Serve at once, with sauce.

SAUCE FOR CHILES RELLENOS

MAKES 2 CUPS

1 can (1 lb) stewed
   tomatoes
2 tablespoons finely
   chopped onion
½ teaspoon salt
¼ teaspoon dried oregano
   leaves
Dash pepper

1. Combine all the ingredients in a medium saucepan.
2. Simmer, stirring occasionally, 10 minutes.

GUACAMOLE-TOMATO SALAD

MAKES 6 SERVINGS

6 medium tomatoes, peeled
2 teaspoons salt
1 medium onion, finely
   chopped
1 or 2 canned green chiles,
   finely chopped
2 teaspoons lemon juice
2 very ripe medium
   avocados
6 lettuce leaves
3 crisp-cooked bacon slices,
   crumbled

1. Core tomatoes; scoop out centers, and chop finely. Sprinkle inside of tomato cups with ½ teaspoon salt; turn upside down on paper towels, to drain. Chill.
2. To chopped tomato, add onion, green chiles to taste, lemon juice, and remaining salt. Chill.
3. Just before serving, mash avocados (they will turn dark if allowed to stand). Blend in tomato mixture.
4. Arrange tomato cups on lettuce leaves. Fill with guacamole; top with crumbled bacon.

FLAN

MAKES 6 TO 8 SERVINGS

¾ cup sugar
4 eggs
1 can (14 oz) sweetened
   condensed milk
1 teaspoon vanilla extract

1. Preheat oven to 350F.
2. Put sugar in heavy skillet, over low heat, stirring constantly with a wooden spoon, until sugar melts and turns golden.
3. Pour into a 1-quart casserole. With wooden spoon, spread caramelized sugar around casserole, to coat bottom and sides evenly. Let cool while preparing custard.
4. Beat eggs. Add condensed milk, 1 cup water, and vanilla.
5. Pour into caramel-coated casserole. Place casserole in pan containing 1 inch hot water.
6. Bake 1 hour, or until silver knife inserted ½ inch into center comes out clean. Cool completely—about 2 hours.
7. Run spatula around edge of flan, and turn out on serving dish. Pour caramel over flan.
8. Chill before serving.

Our recipes from the Middle-East are fit for a prince. They're gently and subtly seasoned to bring out, and never mask, natural flavors of foods.

LAMB WITH VEGETABLES, ARMENIAN STYLE

MAKES 6 SERVINGS

6 whole carrots, pared
8 medium potatoes, pared and halved
1 small eggplant, cut in large chunks
2 onions, peeled and sliced
1 lb zucchini, cut in ½-inch slices
4 fresh tomatoes, halved; or 1 can (1 lb, 12 oz) tomatoes

Few sprigs parsley, chopped
1 bay leaf
1 clove garlic, minced
2 teaspoons salt
½ teaspoon pepper
6 shoulder lamb chops, 1 inch thick
¼ cup unsifted all-purpose flour

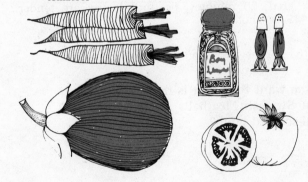

1. Preheat oven to 375F.
2. In deep baking dish (with cover) or Dutch oven, arrange carrots, potatoes, eggplant, onions, zucchini. Top with tomatoes. (If using canned tomatoes, drain; reserve ½ cup liquid.)
3. Combine parsley, bay leaf, half of garlic, 1 teaspoon salt, ¼ teaspoon pepper; sprinkle over vegetables.
4. Rub lamb chops with mixture of remaining garlic, salt, and pepper. Arrange on top of vegetables.
5. Bake, with cover on, 1 hour. Remove from oven.
6. Combine flour and ½ cup water (or reserved tomato liquid) to make a smooth paste.
7. Lifting chops in several places, stir flour mixture into pan juices.
8. Bake, uncovered, 20 minutes longer, or until gravy is thickened and chops are brown.
9. To serve: Arrange meat on platter, and surround with vegetables. Pass the gravy separately.

SHISH KEBAB

MAKES 4 SERVINGS

Kebabs:
2-lb boned leg of lamb, cut in 1½-inch cubes
3 medium onions, peeled and quartered
1 large green pepper, cut into squares
4 cherry tomatoes

Marinade:
½ cup lemon juice
½ cup lime juice
½ cup olive oil
1 teaspoon salt
⅛ teaspoon pepper
½ teaspoon dried rosemary leaves

1. Prepare Kebabs: On 4 long skewers, thread lamb alternately with onion and green pepper. Lay flat in large roasting pan.
2. Make Marinade: Combine all ingredients in medium bowl; mix well.
3. Pour marinade over kebabs in pan; cover with foil. Refrigerate several hours, or overnight, turning several times.
4. Broil kebabs, 4 inches from heat, 12 to 15 minutes, or until browned.
5. Turn; brush with marinade; broil 10 minutes. Place tomato on one end of each skewer; broil 5 minutes longer. Serve at once.

STUFFED GRAPE LEAVES

MAKES 7 OR 8 SERVINGS

⅓ cup raw long-grain white rice

3 tablespoons dried split peas

¼ cup olive oil

⅓ cup chopped onion

¼ cup chopped celery

¾ lb ground lamb

1½ teaspoons salt

¼ teaspoon pepper

½ teaspoon turmeric

½ teaspoon cloves

36 to 40 grape leaves, packed in brine

1 chicken-bouillon cube

¾ cup boiling water

¼ cup vinegar

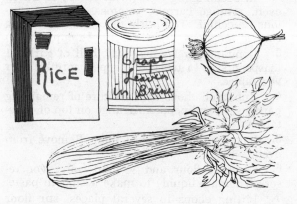

1. Cook rice as package label directs; drain, and set aside.

2. To peas in small saucepan, add enough cold water to cover; bring to boiling. Reduce heat; simmer, covered, 10 minutes. Drain.

3. In hot oil in large skillet, sauté onion, celery, and lamb, stirring occasionally, 8 to 10 minutes, or until vegetables are tender and lamb is browned.

4. Remove from heat. Stir in salt, pepper, turmeric, cloves, rice, and peas.

5. Drain grape leaves well on paper towels. Then overlap edges of 2 leaves; place 2 table-spoons meat mixture in center; fold edges over, to form packets. Carefully place stuffed leaves, folded edges down, in large saucepan. Continue until all leaves and the meat mixture are used.

6. Dissolve bouillon cube in boiling water; stir in vinegar. Pour over stuffed leaves.

7. Bring to boiling. Reduce heat; simmer, covered, 20 minutes, or until leaves are tender. Serve hot.

Include the Scandinavian any time you want food that is notable and good, fragrant and nourishing. How about Swedish Meatballs soon, f'rinstance? Or a delicious soup, hot or cold? Or dill-scented lamb?

YELLOW-SPLIT-PEA SOUP

MAKES 6 SERVINGS

1 lb quick-cooking dried yellow split peas, washed

2 quarts boiling water

1 bay leaf

2 lb pork shoulder, bone in

1 cup finely chopped onion

1 teaspoon dried marjoram leaves

¼ teaspoon dried thyme leaves

¼ teaspoon ginger

3 teaspoons salt

¼ teaspoon pepper

1. Combine peas, boiling water, and bay leaf in 4½-quart kettle or Dutch oven; bring to boiling. Reduce heat; simmer, covered, 1 hour; stir occasionally.

2. Add pork, onion, marjoram, thyme, and ginger; bring to boiling. Reduce heat, and boil gently, covered, 1 hour and 15 minutes; stir occasionally. Peas and pork should be tender.

3. Stir in salt, pepper, and ½ cup water.

4. Remove pork. Strain soup through coarse strainer. Pour back into kettle, and gently reheat. Meanwhile, slice pork.

5. Serve bowls of soup, along with pork slices and, if desired, sliced pumpernickel.

SWEDISH DILLED LAMB

MAKES 4 TO 6 SERVINGS

2-lb boned shoulder of lean
    lamb, cut in 1½-inch
    cubes
1 tablespoon salt
4 whole black peppers
1 bay leaf
1 teaspoon dried dill weed

Dill Sauce:
3 tablespoons butter or
    margarine
¼ cup flour
2 cups lamb broth
1½ tablespoons vinegar
1 to 2 teaspoons sugar
1 egg yolk

1. In heavy saucepan, bring lamb slowly to boil in 3 cups water. Skim off any brown film from surface.

2. Add salt, peppers, bay leaf, and dill. Simmer, covered and over low heat, 1¼ hours, or until tender.

3. Strain 2 cups broth, and set aside. Keep lamb warm in remaining broth.

4. Make Dill Sauce: Melt butter in saucepan, over low heat; remove from heat.

5. Stir in flour until smooth; then cook over low heat 1 minute.

6. Slowly add reserved lamb broth, the vinegar, and sugar.

7. Simmer, stirring, about 5 minutes, or until thickened.

8. Slightly beat egg yolk. Add some of broth mixture, beating vigorously. Return this to rest of hot sauce; cook, stirring, until heated through—do not boil.

9. Drain lamb. Arrange on warm serving platter, and cover with Dill Sauce.

SWEDISH MEATBALLS

MAKES 6 TO 8 SERVINGS

Meatballs:
5 tablespoons butter or
    margarine
3 tablespoons finely
    chopped onion
¾ cup light cream
¾ cup packaged dry bread
    crumbs
1½ lb ground chuck
½ lb ground pork
2 eggs, slightly beaten
2 teaspoons salt
¼ teaspoon pepper

¼ teaspoon allspice
Dash cloves

Sauce:
2 tablespoons flour
½ cup light cream
1 teaspoon salt
Dash pepper
½ teaspoon bottled gravy
    seasoning

Parsley sprigs

1. Make Meatballs: In 1 tablespoon hot butter in skillet, sauté onion 3 minutes, or until golden.

2. In large bowl, combine cream, ¾ cup water, and the bread crumbs. Add onion, ground meats, eggs, salt, pepper, allspice, and cloves; toss lightly, to mix well.

3. With teaspoon, shape into 75 meatballs, about ¾ inch in diameter.

4. In 2 tablespoons hot butter in same skillet, sauté meatballs, a few at a time, until browned on all sides. Add more butter as needed. Remove meatballs, and set aside.

5. Make Sauce: Remove all but 2 tablespoons drippings from skillet. Stir in flour until smooth.

6. Gradually stir in cream and 1½ cups water; bring to boiling, stirring. Add salt, pepper, and gravy seasoning.

7. Add meatballs; heat gently 5 minutes, or until heated through. Serve garnished with parsley.

ROAST LOIN OF PORK WITH PRUNES

10 pitted prunes
4- to 4½-lb loin of pork
1¾ teaspoons salt
½ teaspoon pepper

3 tablespoons flour
½ cup light cream or milk
1 teaspoon currant jelly

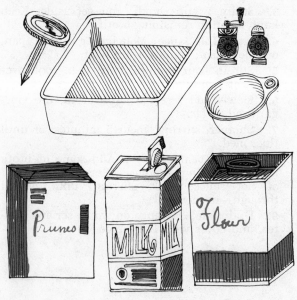

1. Preheat oven to 325F.
2. Soak prunes in hot water 30 minutes, to soften; drain well.
3. Wipe pork with damp paper towels. With sharp knife, make tiny slits between meat and bone; insert prunes. Then tie with twine, to hold meat to bone.
4. Combine 1 teaspoon salt, ¼ teaspoon pepper, and 1 tablespoon flour; rub into meat.
5. Place, fat side up, in shallow roasting pan without rack. Insert meat thermometer in fleshy part, away from bone or fat.
6. Roast, uncovered, 3 to 3½ hours, or to 185F on meat thermometer, for well done.
7. Remove pork to heated platter. For easier slicing, let stand in warm place 20 minutes before carving.
8. Meanwhile, make gravy: Pour pan drippings into 2-cup measure. Skim off fat; measure 2 tablespoons fat into roasting pan. Stir in remaining flour until smooth.
9. Add water to drippings to make 1¼ cups. Gradually stir into flour mixture, along with cream; bring to boiling, stirring.
10. Add rest of salt and pepper and the currant jelly. Serve hot, with pork.

SWEDISH-STYLE BROWN BEANS

2 cups dried Swedish
    brown beans
2 teaspoons salt
¾ cup cider vinegar

¾ cup dark corn syrup
¼ cup light-brown sugar,
    firmly packed

1. Wash beans; turn into 3-quart saucepan with 6 cups water. Refrigerate, covered, overnight.
2. Next day, bring to boiling. Reduce heat; simmer, covered, 1 hour.
3. Add remaining ingredients; simmer, covered, about 4 hours, or until beans are tender and mixture is thick; stir occasionally.

SCANDINAVIAN CABBAGE

2 quarts (2 lb) coarsely
    shredded green
    cabbage
3 cups boiling water

1 cup dairy sour cream
1 teaspoon caraway seed
1½ teaspoons salt
¼ teaspoon pepper

1. Cook cabbage in boiling water, covered, 6 to 8 minutes, or until tender but still slightly crisp. Drain very well.
2. In top of double boiler, toss cabbage with rest of ingredients; cook, covered, over boiling water, 15 minutes (cabbage will still be slightly crisp).

SCANDINAVIAN FRUIT SOUP

MAKES 8 SERVINGS

1 cup pitted dried prunes
1 cup dried apricots
¼ cup light or dark raisins
½ lemon, sliced
3 (4-inch) cinnamon sticks

¼ cup sugar
3 tablespoons quick-cooking
   tapioca
1 cup pared cubed apple

1. Combine all ingredients, except apple cubes, in 3-quart saucepan. Add 6 cups water; bring to boiling, stirring.

2. Reduce heat; simmer, covered, 20 minutes, or until fruit is tender and tapioca is cooked. Stir occasionally.

3. Add apple cubes; simmer, covered, 5 minutes. Remove cinnamon.

4. Serve, warm or cold, as a dessert.

S panish food, you may be surprised to learn, does not burn the tongue. It is gentle, well seasoned, "natural" food, with a character better savored than described—hint of garlic, dash of lemon, sprinkling of herbs.

PAELLA VALENCIANA AND SAFFRON RICE

MAKES 8 GENEROUS SERVINGS

2 (2-lb size) broiler-fryers,
   cut up
1 carrot, pared
1 small onion, peeled
1 bay leaf
2 sprigs parsley
4 teaspoons salt
4 whole black peppers
½ cup salad oil
4 cloves garlic, slivered
2 cups coarsely chopped
   green pepper

3 cups chopped onion
¼ cup chopped parsley
1 teaspoon saffron,
   crumbled
1 tablespoon paprika
1 teaspoon dried oregano
   leaves
¼ teaspoon pepper
1 jar (11½ oz) whole clams
1½ cups raw regular white
   rice
1 lb cooked shrimp, shelled
   and deveined

1. In 3 cups water in 2-quart saucepan, combine chicken necks, hearts, livers, gizzards with carrot, whole onion, bay leaf, parsley sprigs, ½ teaspoon salt, and black peppers.

2. Cover; bring to boiling; simmer 45 minutes.

3. In 6-quart Dutch oven, slowly heat salad oil. In this, brown cut-up chicken pieces well; remove.

4. Add garlic, green pepper, chopped onion, and chopped parsley to hot oil; cook, stirring, until onion is limp.

5. Stir in saffron, paprika, remaining salt, oregano, and pepper.

6. Arrange chicken pieces in Dutch oven.

7. Preheat oven to 350F.

8. Drain clam liquid into 1-quart measure. Strain chicken stock; add enough to clam liquid to make 3 cups.

9. Pour into Dutch oven; bring to boiling over direct heat.

10. Add rice, stirring to make sure it is in the liquid; cover; bring again to boiling.

11. Then bake, covered, about 1 hour, or until rice is done.

12. Add clams and shrimp; cover.

13. Return to oven; bake 10 minutes.

683

GAZPACHO
(Andalusian Soup)

2 large tomatoes, peeled
    (1¾ lb)
1 large cucumber, pared
1 medium onion
1 medium green pepper
1 pimiento, drained
2 cans (12-oz size) tomato
    juice
⅓ cup olive oil

⅓ cup red-wine vinegar
¼ teaspoon liquid hot-
    pepper seasoning
1½ teaspoons salt
⅛ teaspoon coarsely ground
    black pepper
2 cloves garlic, split
½ cup packaged croutons
¼ cup chopped chives

1.   In electric blender, combine 1 tomato, ½ cucumber, ½ onion, ¼ green pepper, pimiento, and ½ cup tomato juice. Blend, covered, at high speed, 30 seconds, to purée the vegetables.

2.   In a large bowl, mix puréed vegetables with the remaining tomato juice, ¼ cup olive oil, vinegar, hot-pepper seasoning, salt, and pepper.

3.   Refrigerate mixture, covered, until well chilled—2 hours. Refrigerate 6 serving bowls.

4.   Meanwhile, rub inside of skillet with garlic; reserve garlic. Add rest of oil; heat. Sauté the croutons until they are browned; set aside.

5.   Chop separately remaining tomato, cucumber, onion, and pepper. Place in separate bowls, along with separate bowls of croutons and chopped chives. Serve as accompaniments.

6.   Just before serving time, crush the reserved garlic; then add to the chilled soup, mixing well. Serve in chilled bowls.

CHICKEN NAVARESA

3- to 4-lb roasting
    chicken
¼ cup olive oil
1 lb small white onions,
    peeled

1 lb carrots, pared and cut
    into quarters
1 cup white wine
1½ teaspoons flour
½ teaspoon salt
⅛ teaspoon pepper

1.   Preheat oven to 350F. Wash chicken under cold water; dry on paper towels.

2.   Tie ends of legs together with twine. Bend wings under body of chicken.

3.   Slowly heat olive oil in large Dutch oven. Sauté chicken, breast side down, until golden-brown. Turn breast side up; roast, uncovered, in oven, 15 minutes.

4.   Arrange onions around chicken; then baste onions and chicken with pan drippings. Roast 15 minutes longer.

5.   Remove from oven. Place carrots under chicken; pour white wine over it. Roast, covered, 1 to 1½ hours, or until chicken and vegetables are fork-tender.

6.   Remove chicken to warm platter; surround with vegetables. Keep warm.

7.   Measure liquid in Dutch oven; if necessary, add water to measure 1 cup.

8.   In small saucepan, combine flour, liquid, salt, and pepper; bring to boiling, stirring constantly. Reduce heat, and simmer 1 minute.

9.   Serve sauce with chicken and vegetables.

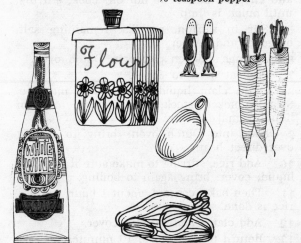

MARZIPAN-STUFFED APRICOTS

MAKES 6 SERVINGS

1 can (1 lb, 14 oz) whole
    apricots (12)
1 can (8 oz) almond paste
12 blanched whole almonds
1½ teaspoons cornstarch

¾ cup coarsely cut orange
    sections
¼ cup toasted sliced
    almonds
2 teaspoons brandy

1. Preheat oven to 325F. Drain apricots, reserving liquid. If necessary, slit each apricot, on one side only, to remove pit.
2. Divide almond paste evenly into 12 pieces.
3. Insert 1 whole almond in each piece of almond paste. Roll into a ball, being careful to cover almond completely.
4. Put an almond-paste ball inside each apricot. Arrange apricots in a 10-by-6-inch baking dish.
5. Bake for 20 to 25 minutes, or until the apricots are heated through and the almond paste is slightly browned.
6. Meanwhile, in small saucepan, combine reserved apricot liquid (if necessary, add water to measure 1⅓ cups) with cornstarch.
7. Over medium heat, bring to boiling, stirring. Add oranges; reduce heat, and simmer, stirring, 2 minutes.
8. Stir in the toasted sliced almonds and the brandy; pour over apricots. Serve warm.

CHURROS

(Spanish Doughnuts)

MAKES ABOUT 24

¼ cup butter or margarine,
    cut into small pieces
⅛ teaspoon salt
1¼ cups sifted all-purpose
    flour

3 eggs
¼ teaspoon vanilla extract
Salad oil for deep-frying
½ teaspoon cinnamon
½ cup sugar

1. In medium saucepan, combine butter with ½ cup water. Stir, over low heat, until butter is melted. Bring just to boiling; add salt, and remove from heat.
2. Add flour all at once; beat very hard with wooden spoon. Over low heat, beat until very smooth—about 2 minutes.
3. Remove from heat; let cool slightly. Beat in eggs, one at a time, beating well after each addition. Add vanilla. Continue beating until mixture has satinlike sheen.
4. Meanwhile, in deep skillet or deep-fat fryer, slowly heat salad oil (at least 1½ inches) to 380F on deep-frying thermometer.
5. Press the doughnut mixture through a large pastry bag with a large, fluted tip, ½ inch wide. With wet scissors, cut batter into 2-inch lengths as it drops into hot oil.
6. Deep-fry, a few at a time, 2 minutes on a side, or until golden-brown.
7. Lift out with slotted spoon; drain well on paper towels.
8. Meanwhile, combine cinnamon and sugar in medium bowl.
9. Toss drained doughnuts in sugar mixture to coat well. Serve warm.

685

33

Leftovers

The French have a masterful way with leftovers, and we gladly take our inspiration from them. The dishes in this chapter have a "better than ever" quality, and they can be served with pride at any party—our Lamb Curry in a Hurry, for example, or our Turkey Tetrazzini. Even the members of your family who may sniff disdainfully at most leftovers will sniff blissfully at ours. Try them, and see.

An Important Hint

Remove any leftover meat or poultry from the bones as soon as possible, to prevent the meat from drying out.

If meat is not to be used within a day or two, freezer-wrap in meal-size portions; label, and freeze. Use the bones to make stock.

BARBECUED BEEF ON BUNS

MAKES 8 SERVINGS

¼ cup butter or margarine
1 cup thinly sliced onion
1 teaspoon chili powder
1 teaspoon charcoal
*   seasoning*
1 can (8 oz) tomato sauce

¼ teaspoon salt
2 cups slivered cooked
*   roast beef or pot roast*
8 hamburger buns,
*   split, toasted, and*
*   buttered*

1. In hot butter in medium skillet, sauté onion until golden—about 5 minutes.

2. Add chili powder, charcoal seasoning, tomato sauce, and salt, mixing well; simmer, covered, 10 minutes.

3. Add roast beef; simmer 5 minutes longer.

4. Place about ½ cup roast-beef mixture on bottom halves of hamburger buns; top with other halves. Serve hot.

ROAST-BEEF HASH

Hash:

2 cups finely chopped
    cooked roast beef*

2½ cups finely chopped
    cold cooked potatoes

2 tablespoons finely
    chopped green pepper

¼ cup finely chopped
    onion

½ teaspoon salt

⅛ teaspoon pepper

1 teaspoon Worcestershire
    sauce (optional)

¼ cup beef bouillon, beef
    gravy, or milk

3 tablespoons butter or
    margarine

Sauce:

1 can (8 oz) tomato sauce

1 to 2 tablespoons prepared
    horseradish,
    undrained

1 teaspoon Worcestershire
    sauce

1 tablespoon finely
    chopped parsley

1.   Make Hash: In medium bowl, toss roast beef with potatoes, green pepper, onion, salt, pepper, Worcestershire, and bouillon until well combined.

2.   Slowly heat butter in heavy, 10-inch skillet. Spread hash in skillet; cook, over medium heat, about 10 minutes, or until hash is heated through and most of liquid is absorbed. Turn hash over occasionally, with pancake turner, scraping bottom to remove brown bits; then spread evenly in skillet.

3.   Reduce heat; cook, uncovered, about 40 minutes, without stirring, or until hash is very brown and crusty on underside. (Occasionally lift edge of hash with turner, to test.)

4.   Meanwhile, make Sauce: Combine all ingredients in small bowl. Refrigerate until ready to serve.

5.   To turn out hash: Carefully run turner under hash, to loosen; fold in half. Tilt out onto serving platter. Sprinkle with parsley. Pass sauce along with hash.

* Do not trim fat from roast beef.

STUFFED PEPPERS

2 large green peppers

1 teaspoon salt

Filling:

½ cup leftover beef gravy*

1 teaspoon instant minced
    onion

½ cup grated raw carrots

1½ cups packaged herb-
    seasoned stuffing

½ cup boiling water

1 cup coarsely chopped
    cooked roast beef

Sauce:

1 can (8 oz) tomato sauce

½ cup leftover beef gravy*

1 teaspoon instant minced
    onion

¼ cup grated sharp
    Cheddar cheese

1.   Wash peppers. Cut in half, lengthwise; remove seeds and ribs.

2.   In medium saucepan, bring 4 cups water and the salt to boiling. Add peppers; reduce heat; simmer, uncovered, 15 minutes, or just until peppers are tender. Drain.

3.   Meanwhile, preheat oven to 350F. Make Filling: In small bowl, lightly toss all ingredients, to combine.

4.   Make Sauce: In small saucepan, combine tomato sauce with gravy, onion, and ½ cup water; bring to boiling, over medium heat, stirring constantly.

5.   Fill each pepper half with about ½ cup filling. Place in 2-quart casserole. Pour hot sauce into bottom of casserole.

6.   Bake peppers, uncovered, 20 minutes. Baste with sauce; sprinkle with cheese; bake 10 minutes longer.

* Or use ½ cup canned beef gravy.

Leftover ham can be used down to the last smidgeon, and always tastefully, as you'll see, starting with our Caramel Ham Loaf and ending with our Tangy Ham Dip.

CARAMEL HAM LOAF

MAKES 8 SERVINGS

⅓ cup dark-brown sugar, firmly packed
½ teaspoon cloves
½ lb cooked ham, ground
1 lb beef chuck or round, ground
⅔ cup packaged dry bread crumbs

1 tablespoon finely-chopped parsley
1 teaspoon grated onion
¼ teaspoon salt
⅛ teaspoon pepper
1 cup milk
1 egg, slightly beaten
1 teaspoon prepared mustard

1. Preheat oven to 350F.
2. Combine sugar and cloves; sprinkle on bottom of an 8½-by-4½-by-2½-inch loaf pan.
3. In large bowl, combine ham with rest of ingredients, mixing well.
4. Turn mixture into loaf pan, pressing firmly; bake 1½ hours.
5. Let loaf stand in pan about 5 minutes. Invert on serving platter, so caramel is on top. Cut crosswise into 8 slices.

CARAWAY COLESLAW WITH HAM

MAKES 8 SERVINGS

3 cups finely shredded green cabbage
2 cups diced, pared tart cooking apples
2 tablespoons lemon juice
½ cup sliced pitted ripe olives
1 cup cubed cooked ham or corned beef

1 cup thinly sliced celery
½ cup mayonnaise or cooked salad dressing
¼ cup bottled French dressing
1 teaspoon caraway seed
½ teaspoon salt
2 teaspoons finely chopped chives or green onion

1. In large bowl, toss cabbage with rest of ingredients, except chives, until it is well coated.
2. Refrigerate 30 minutes. To serve, sprinkle with chives.

HAM HASH WITH POACHED EGGS

MAKES 4 SERVINGS

2 cups packaged sliced potatoes for frying
3 tablespoons salad oil
1 teaspoon salt
1 cup thinly sliced onion

½ cup thinly sliced green pepper
1 cup diced cooked ham or corned beef
4 eggs
Chopped parsley

1. In large, heavy skillet with tight-fitting lid, combine potatoes, salad oil, salt, onion, and green pepper with 2 cups hot water; bring to boiling. Cover; boil 10 minutes, over medium heat.
2. Remove cover; cook, turning potatoes occasionally with wide spatula, until most of water is absorbed.
3. Add ham, mixing well. With back of large spoon, make 4 indentations, about 4 inches wide and 1 inch deep, in potato-ham mixture.
4. Carefully, break egg into each indentation; cook, covered, over low heat, 5 minutes, or until eggs are set. Sprinkle with parsley.

HAM PATTIES WITH SOUR-CREAM SAUCE

2 cups ground cooked ham
2 tablespoons grated onion
½ cup packaged dry bread
    crumbs
2 eggs, slightly beaten
1½ tablespoons finely
    chopped parsley

1 teaspoon prepared
    mustard
⅛ teaspoon salt
2 tablespoons shortening
¼ teaspoon paprika
¼ cup boiling water
1 cup dairy sour cream

1. Lightly toss ham, in large bowl, with onion, bread crumbs, eggs, 1 tablespoon parsley, mustard, and salt until well combined.
2. Shape into 6 patties.
3. Heat shortening in large skillet, over medium heat. Brown patties well on both sides.
4. Transfer to serving platter; keep warm.
5. Add paprika to boiling water. Pour into skillet; bring to boiling, stirring, until paprika is dissolved.
6. Reduce heat. Stir in sour cream; heat thoroughly.
7. Spoon sour-cream sauce over ham patties. Sprinkle with remaining parsley.

TANGY HAM DIP

1 cup ground cooked ham
2 teaspoons prepared
    horseradish
1 teaspoon instant minced
    onion
1 tablespoon finely
    chopped parsley

¼ teaspoon salt
Dash cayenne
Dash pepper
¼ cup mayonnaise or
    cooked salad dressing

1. In small bowl, combine all ingredients; mix until well combined.
2. Refrigerate several hours before serving. Delicious with corn chips.

EGG FU YUNG FOR TWO

Sauce:
1 teaspoon cornstarch
1 bouillon cube
1 teaspoon soy sauce
1 teaspoon sugar
1 teaspoon vinegar

3 eggs, slightly beaten
¼ cup chopped onion

1 cup drained canned bean
    sprouts
½ cup chopped cooked
    ham
2 teaspoons soy sauce
⅛ teaspoon salt

1 teaspoon salad oil

1. Make Sauce: In small saucepan, combine cornstarch with ½ cup cold water. Add bouillon cube, soy sauce, sugar, and vinegar, stirring to combine.
2. Bring mixture to boiling, stirring. Reduce heat; simmer 1 minute. Remove from heat; cover, and keep hot.
3. Combine eggs with onion, bean sprouts, ham, soy sauce, and salt, stirring just until combined.
4. Slowly heat oil in small skillet. Add egg mixture, ¼ cup at a time (as for pancakes). Sauté, turning once, just until browned on both sides. Remove, and keep warm. Repeat until egg mixture is used. Serve "pancakes" with hot sauce spooned over.

L amb lends itself to some real gourmet food. Now we invite you to try our Lamb Curry in a Hurry, and other lamb dishes.

LAMB CURRY IN A HURRY

MAKES 4 SERVINGS

2 tablespoons butter or
    margarine
¼ cup coarsely chopped
    onion
¼ cup thinly sliced celery
¼ cup chopped green
    pepper
1 cup leftover lamb gravy*

1½ cups cubed cooked
    lamb (½-inch cubes)
½ teaspoon curry powder
½ cup diced, peeled tart
    cooking apple
¼ teaspoon salt
White Rice with Raisins**

1. In hot butter in medium skillet with tight-fitting lid, sauté onion, celery, and green pepper until tender—about 5 minutes.
2. Add gravy, lamb, curry powder, apple, and salt, mixing well.
3. Bring mixture to boiling. Reduce heat; simmer, covered, 10 minutes, or until apple is tender.
4. Serve with White Rice with Raisins.
* Or use 1 cup canned chicken gravy.
** See Cereals Chapter.

QUICK LAMB STEW WITH DUMPLINGS

MAKES 6 SERVINGS

Stew:
1 cup diagonally sliced
    carrots, ¼ inch thick
1 cup sliced onion
1 cup cubed raw potato
1 teaspoon salt
1 cup leftover lamb gravy*
2 cups cubed cooked lamb
    (1-inch cubes)

⅛ teaspoon pepper

Dumplings:
1½ cups packaged biscuit
    mix
2 tablespoons finely
    chopped parsley
½ cup milk

1. Make Stew: In medium skillet with tight-fitting lid, combine carrots, onion, potato, and salt with 1½ cups water; bring to boiling. Reduce heat; simmer, covered, 20 minutes, or just until vegetables are tender.
2. Add gravy, lamb, and pepper, mixing well; bring mixture back to boiling.
3. Meanwhile, make Dumplings: In medium bowl, combine all ingredients; beat with fork until smooth and well blended.
4. Drop dumpling batter, by slightly rounded teaspoonfuls, onto boiling stew. Reduce heat; simmer, uncovered, 10 minutes. Cover; simmer 10 minutes longer. Serve at once.
* Or use 1 cup canned chicken gravy.

SHEPHERD'S PIE

MAKES 8 SERVINGS

Filling:
1 pkg (10 oz) frozen
    Fordhook lima beans
1 cup leftover lamb gravy*
¼ cup finely chopped
    onion
½ cup finely chopped
    celery
¼ teaspoon dried
    marjoram leaves
¼ teaspoon salt
2 cups cubed cooked
    lamb (1-inch cubes)

Potato Crust:
2 packets (4-serving size)
    instant mashed
    potatoes
1 teaspoon salt
2 teaspoons instant minced
    onion
2 tablespoons butter or
    margarine
¼ cup finely chopped
    pimiento
1 egg, slightly beaten

2 tablespoons grated
    Parmesan cheese

1. Preheat oven to 350F. Lightly grease a 2-quart casserole.
2. Make Filling: Cook lima beans as package label directs; drain.
3. Meanwhile, combine gravy with onion, celery, marjoram, and salt; bring to boiling, stirring. Remove from heat. Add lima beans and lamb, mixing well; cover, and keep warm.
4. Make Potato Crust: Prepare potatoes as package label directs, using amount of liquid specified on package, the salt, onion, and butter. Add pimiento and egg, beating with fork until well combined.

(*Shepherd's Pie continued*)

5. Spoon half of potato mixture into bottom of prepared casserole; add filling. Swirl rest of potato mixture over filling; sprinkle with cheese.

6. Bake, uncovered, 30 minutes, or until crust is golden.

* Or use 1 cup canned chicken gravy.

The beauty of these pork recipes is that they would take you hours if you had to start with uncooked pork. But with leftovers, you can have pork dishes in no time at all. If you like your pork cold and sliced, we'll show you how to make some excellent sauces to go with it.

PORK CHOP SUEY

MAKES 6 SERVINGS

2 tablespoons salad oil
1 cup thinly sliced onion
2 cups sliced celery
½ cup leftover pork gravy*
1 can (10½ oz) condensed cream-of-mushroom soup, undiluted
¼ cup soy sauce

1½ cups slivered roast pork
1 can (16 oz) bean sprouts, drained
1 tablespoon cornstarch
3 cups cooked white rice, or 1 can (3 oz) Chinese noodles

1. In hot oil in large skillet, sauté onion and celery, stirring, until onion is golden—about 10 minutes.

2. Add gravy, soup, and soy sauce; bring to boiling, stirring. Add pork and bean sprouts; return to boiling. Reduce heat; simmer, covered, 5 minutes.

3. Combine cornstarch with ½ cup cold water, stirring until smooth. Add some of hot mixture to cornstarch; pour back into skillet, mixing well.

4. Bring to boiling, stirring, until mixture is thickened and translucent—about 5 minutes. Serve over rice.

* Or use ½ cup canned chicken gravy.

PORK WITH CARAWAY SAUERKRAUT

MAKES 6 SERVINGS

2 tablespoons butter or margarine
¼ cup light-brown sugar, firmly packed
1½ cups sliced, unpared tart cooking apples
½ cup coarsely chopped onion

1 cup leftover pork gravy*
1 can (16 oz) sauerkraut, drained
½ teaspoon salt
1 teaspoon caraway seed
8 roast-pork slices, about ⅛ inch thick

1. In large skillet with tight-fitting lid, combine butter with sugar; cook, stirring, over low heat, until sugar melts.

2. Add apples and onion, mixing well; simmer, covered, 5 minutes.

3. Stir in gravy, sauerkraut, salt, and caraway seed; bring to boiling. Reduce heat. Arrange pork slices on sauerkraut; simmer, covered, 10 minutes longer.

* Or use 1 cup canned chicken gravy.

691

Sauces for Cold Roast Pork

CREAMY HORSERADISH SAUCE

1 jar (8 oz) applesauce
  (1 cup)
3 tablespoons prepared
  horseradish, drained

Dash cayenne
¼ teaspoon salt
½ cup heavy cream,
  whipped

1. In small bowl, combine applesauce with horseradish, cayenne, and salt, mixing well.
2. Gently fold in whipped cream just until combined.
3. Refrigerate until well chilled—about 1 hour.

TANGY APPLESAUCE

MAKES 1 CUP

1 jar (8 oz) applesauce
  (1 cup)

3 to 4 tablespoons prepared
  horseradish, drained

1. In small bowl, combine applesauce and horseradish, mixing well.
2. Refrigerate until well chilled—about 1 hour.

CURRIED APPLESAUCE

MAKES 1 CUP

1 jar (8 oz) applesauce
  (1 cup)

½ to 1 teaspoon curry
  powder

1. In small bowl, combine applesauce and curry, mixing well.
2. Refrigerate until well chilled—about 1 hour.

Turkey is another leftover with endless possibilities, endless treats. And after you've enjoyed the meat in every possible form, there's always the most heavenly soup to be made from the bones.

SAVORY TURKEY HASH

MAKES 4 TO 6 SERVINGS

2 tablespoons butter or
  margarine
1 cup sliced onion
¼ cup chopped celery
½ to 1 teaspoon salt
⅛ teaspoon pepper
⅛ teaspoon poultry seasoning (optional)

1 cup leftover turkey gravy*
½ cup turkey stock or milk
2 cups chopped cooked po-
  tatoes
2 cups chopped cooked
  turkey

1. In hot butter in medium skillet, sauté onion and celery until golden—about 8 minutes.
2. Remove from heat. Add remaining ingredients, mixing until well combined; bring to boiling. Reduce heat; simmer, uncovered and stirring frequently, about 20 minutes, or until most of liquid is evaporated. Serve hot, with catsup.

* Or use 1 cup canned chicken gravy.

CRISPY TURKEY HASH

1. Turn Savory Turkey Hash into greased 9-inch pie plate.
2. Run under broiler, 4 inches from heat, about 3 minutes, or until hash is crispy and brown. Serve hot, with catsup.

SCALLOPED TURKEY

MAKES 6 SERVINGS

2 tablespoons butter or
    margarine
1½ cups packaged herb-
    seasoned stuffing
¼ cup finely chopped pars-
    ley

1 can (10½ oz) condensed
    cream-of-chicken
    soup, undiluted
1 cup leftover turkey gravy*
2 cups cubed cooked turkey

1. Preheat oven to 350F. Grease a 1½-quart casserole.

2. In medium saucepan, combine butter with ½ cup water; cook, over medium heat, just until butter melts.

3. Remove from heat. Add stuffing and parsley, tossing lightly until stuffing is moistened; set aside.

4. In small saucepan, combine soup with gravy, mixing until smooth; over medium heat, bring to boiling, stirring. Remove from heat.

5. In prepared casserole, layer in order: half the turkey, half the soup-gravy mixture, and half the stuffing. Repeat with rest of ingredients.

6. Bake, uncovered, 30 minutes. Serve hot.

* Or use 1 cup canned chicken gravy.

TURKEY CHOWDER

MAKES ABOUT 1 QUART

3 cups turkey stock
1 cup diced raw potato
2 teaspoons minced onion
½ to 1 teaspoon salt
Dash pepper
1 can (10½ oz) condensed
    cream-of-celery soup,
    undiluted

¼ cup crumbled cooked
    bacon
2 tablespoons chopped pars-
    ley
½ cup diced cooked turkey
    (optional)

1. In a 3½-quart saucepan, combine turkey stock with potato, onion, salt, and pepper; bring to boiling. Reduce heat; simmer, covered, about 20 minutes, or until potatoes are tender.

2. Remove from heat. Add cream-of-celery soup, stirring until well combined. Add remaining ingredients; reheat gently.

TURKEY STOCK

MAKES 1 OR MORE QUARTS

Turkey carcass
1 bay leaf
½ teaspoon dried
    marjoram leaves
½ teaspoon dried
    thyme leaves

½ teaspoon dried
    basil leaves
1 medium onion, chopped
½ cup chopped celery
½ cup sliced carrot
Salt
Pepper

1. Remove any meat from carcass; set meat aside for later use.

2. Break up turkey carcass, cracking large bones.

3. Place bones in large kettle. Add remaining ingredients and cold water to cover.

4. Bring to boiling. Reduce heat; simmer, covered, 3 hours.

5. Let stock cool slightly; strain.

6. Store stock, covered, in refrigerator. Skim off fat before using.

693

TURKEY TETRAZZINI

½ pkg (8-oz size) spaghetti
1 pkg (10 oz) frozen peas

Sauce:
1 can (10½ oz) cream-of-
mushroom or chicken
soup, undiluted
1 cup turkey stock*
1 cup grated sharp Cheddar
cheese

½ teaspoon Worcestershire
sauce
1 teaspoon salt
Dash pepper

2 cups cubed cooked turkey
¼ cup whole toasted
almonds (optional)
½ cup grated Parmesan
cheese
Paprika

1. Cook spaghetti as package label directs. Drain, and keep hot.
2. Also, cook peas as package label directs. Drain, and keep hot.
3. Meanwhile, make Sauce: In small saucepan, combine all sauce ingredients, mixing well. Over medium heat, bring mixture to boiling, stirring. Remove from heat.
4. Toss spaghetti with peas, turkey, almonds, and half the sauce, just until combined. Turn mixture into shallow, 2-quart baking dish. Pour over rest of sauce; sprinkle with cheese and paprika.
5. Run under broiler, 4 inches from heat, about 4 minutes, or until Tetrazzini is brown and bubbly. Serve hot.

* Or use 1 cup canned clear chicken broth.

The delicate taste of veal lends itself to a number of fine dishes, which are the kind you could serve to guests with pride.

VEAL À LA KING IN NOODLE RING

Noodle Ring:
2 tablespoons soft butter or
margarine
1 pkg (6 oz) medium
noodles
1 tablespoon butter or
margarine, melted
3 eggs
¾ cup milk
½ teaspoon salt
Dash pepper
½ teaspoon instant minced
onion
1 tablespoon finely chopped
parsley or green pep-
per

Veal à la King:
¼ cup butter or margarine

¼ cup thinly sliced green
pepper
¼ cup flour
¾ teaspoon salt
⅛ teaspoon pepper
1 cup canned clear chicken
broth
1 can (10½ oz) condensed
cream-of-chicken or
mushroom soup, un-
diluted
2 cups cubed cooked veal
(1-inch cubes)*
2 egg yolks, slightly beaten
½ cup milk
2 tablespoons slivered pimiento
2 tablespoons sherry (op-
tional)

1. Preheat oven to 350F. Make Noodle Ring: Using the soft butter, generously grease a 5½-cup ring mold.
2. Cook noodles as package label directs; drain. Toss with the melted butter.
3. Beat eggs with milk, salt, pepper, onion, and parsley until just combined. Add to hot noodles, tossing lightly.
4. Turn noodle mixture into prepared ring mold. Set in pan containing 1 inch hot water; bake, uncovered, 40 minutes, or just until knife inserted 1 inch from edge comes out clean.
5. Meanwhile, make Veal à la King: In hot butter in medium saucepan, sauté green pepper, stirring, until tender—about 5 minutes.
6. Remove from heat. Stir in flour, salt, and pepper. Then gradually stir in broth, mixing well.
7. Bring to boiling, stirring. Reduce heat; simmer 1 minute. Add soup and veal, mixing well; bring back to boiling.

(*Veal à la King in Noodle Ring continued*)

8. Remove from heat. Combine egg yolks with milk. Stir into hot veal mixture; cook, stirring, over medium heat, 5 minutes, or until heated through.

9. Remove from heat. Stir in pimiento and sherry. Cover, and keep hot.

10. To unmold Noodle Ring: Carefully run a small spatula around edge of mold, to loosen. Invert over serving platter; shake gently to release. (Remove any noodles that may adhere to bottom of mold, and replace on ring.)

11. Fill center of ring with some of Veal à la King; keep rest warm until ready to use.

* Or use turkey, chicken, or ham.

QUICK VEAL MARENGO

MAKES 6 SERVINGS

Sauce:
1 can (1 lb, 3 oz) tomatoes, undrained
1 pkg (1½ oz) dried spaghetti-sauce mix with mushrooms
½ cup leftover veal gravy*
1 teaspoon instant minced onion
¼ teaspoon salt

Dash pepper
2 tablespoons salad oil
2 cups cut-up cooked veal
½ teaspoon dried basil leaves
1 cup raw regular white rice
1 cup finely chopped raw spinach

1. Make Sauce: In medium saucepan, combine tomatoes with spaghetti-sauce mix, gravy, onion, salt, pepper, and salad oil; bring to boiling. Reduce heat; simmer, uncovered, 30 minutes, stirring occasionally.

2. Add veal and basil; simmer 5 minutes longer.

3. Meanwhile, cook rice as package label directs; drain. Add spinach, tossing to combine.

4. To serve, pour veal mixture over rice.

* Or use ½ cup canned chicken gravy.

Uses for Leftover Bread

Use bread slices that are several days old to make crumbs. To make crumbs: Preheat oven to 300F. Bake bread slices on cookie sheet until hard and dry—but not brown. Place in clean paper bag, and crush with rolling pin. Or break bread slices into pieces, and put through blender. Store crumbs in jar with tight-fitting lid. Keep in cool, dry place until ready to use.

FRENCH TOAST

MAKES 3 SERVINGS

2 eggs, well beaten
3 tablespoons milk
½ teaspoon sugar
Dash salt

Dash nutmeg
6 day-old white-bread slices
Butter or margarine
Maple syrup

1. In shallow dish, combine eggs with milk, sugar, salt, and nutmeg.

2. Add bread slices, one at a time, to egg mixture; let stand about 30 seconds on each side to coat completely.

3. In medium skillet, using about 1 tablespoon butter for each, sauté bread slices until golden on both sides—about 1½ minutes in all.

4. Serve hot, with maple syrup.

695

FRENCH-TOAST WAFFLES

MAKES 3 SERVINGS

1. Preheat waffle iron.
2. Prepare French Toast as directed; do not cook.
3. Place bread slices, 2 at a time, in lower half of waffle iron. Bake until waffle iron stops steaming, or until "waffles" are golden. Serve hot, with maple syrup.

Leftover Eggs

HOW TO USE RAW EGG YOLKS

1. To enrich pudding and pie-filling mixes, add one slightly beaten egg yolk to amount of milk specified on package. Then make pudding as package label directs.
2. Beat one or two egg yolks into hot, seasoned mashed potatoes.
3. When making eggnogs or scrambled eggs, add one or two egg yolks along with whole eggs.
4. To make a richer Basic White Sauce;* Prepare white sauce as recipe directs. Add a little of the hot mixture to one or two slightly beaten egg yolks, mixing well. Pour back into mixture in saucepan. Over low heat, bring just to boiling, stirring.
5. Beat one or two yolks into cooked cereals.
6. Combine one egg yolk with ¼ cup bottled French dressing. Toss with crisp salad greens.
7. Prepare condensed cream soups as label directs. Add a little hot soup to a slightly beaten egg yolk, mixing well. Pour into saucepan; over low heat, bring just to boiling, stirring.
8. Substitute two egg yolks for one whole egg when making baked or boiled custards.
* See Sauces and Gravies Chapter.
Note: If you are using broken egg yolks, 1 yolk measures 1 tablespoon.

TO COOK EGG YOLKS

Whole Yolks:

1. In small saucepan, bring 3 cups water and ½ teaspoon salt to boiling.
2. Gently slip an egg yolk into boiling water. Reduce heat; simmer, uncovered, 5 minutes, or until yolk is firm.
3. Remove yolk with slotted utensil. Let cool; refrigerate, covered, until ready to use. (Do not store yolks in refrigerator longer than 2 days.)
4. Press yolks through coarse sieve, for garnish. Or chop yolks, and use in sandwich fillings.

Broken Yolks:

1. Lightly grease a 6-ounce custard cup.
2. Place egg yolks (not more than 2 at a time) in custard cup. Set in 1 inch simmering water.
3. Cook, uncovered, over medium heat, about 10 minutes, or until yolks are firm.
4. Let cool; refrigerate, covered, until ready to use. (Do not store yolks in refrigerator longer than 2 days.)
5. Press yolks through coarse sieve, for garnish. Or chop yolks, and use in sandwich fillings.

TO USE RAW EGG WHITES

1. Beat one egg white with 2 tablespoons sugar until stiff. Fold into hot cooked puddings just until combined.
2. See Index for recipes using egg whites; *e.g.,* McCall's Best Angel-Food Cake, Baked Meringue Shell, Seven-Minute Frosting, and many others.

TO STORE WHOLE RAW EGG YOLKS

Place yolks in jar with tight-fitting lid. Add water to cover yolks. Refrigerate, covered, until ready to use. Drain before using. Do not keep longer than 3 days.

TO STORE RAW EGG WHITES

Refrigerate egg whites in jar with tight-fitting lid until ready to use. Egg whites may be held a week to 10 days.

34

Low-Calorie Cooking

S erious dieters should familiarize themselves with the many nationally available dietetic foods on the market, for they are generally low in calories. With the caloric value clearly marked on packages and cans, it is easier to keep track of your total daily calorie count.

Below are recipes—referred to in the 500 Calorie Dinners, Meal Planning and Menus Chapter—in which the calorie count has been reduced from that normally found in the individual recipe. The dishes are nourishing—and you lose weight.

TOMATO BOUILLON

MAKES 6 SERVINGS; 1 CUP, 63 CALORIES, EACH

2 teaspoons butter or
  margarine
¾ cup chopped onion
6 cups tomato juice
1 bay leaf
½ cup chopped celery, with
  leaves
½ teaspoon dried oregano
  leaves
¼ teaspoon seasoned salt
⅛ teaspoon pepper

1. In hot butter in medium saucepan, sauté onion, stirring, until golden—3 minutes.

2. Add other ingredients; simmer 15 minutes. Stir occasionally.

3. Strain. Taste for seasoning. Serve hot or cold.

HEARTY VEGETABLE SOUP

MAKES 6½ QUARTS
1 SERVING: 1½ CUPS, 181 CALORIES

2 lb shin beef
Large soupbone
1 tablespoon salt
4 cups thinly sliced cabbage
    (1 lb)
1½ cups chopped onion
6 carrots (½ lb), pared and
    cut in 3-inch pieces
¾ cup chopped celery
¼ cup chopped green
    pepper
1 can (1 lb, 12 oz) toma-
    toes, undrained
    (3½ cups)
½ pkg (10-oz size)
    frozen lima beans
½ pkg (9-oz size) frozen
    cut green beans
½ pkg (10-oz size) frozen
    peas
1 can (12 oz) whole-kernel
    corn, drained
1 pared potato, cubed
    (1 cup)
2 tablespoons chopped
    parsley
1 can (6 oz) tomato paste
½ teaspoon cloves
1 teaspoon sugar
2 teaspoons salt
½ teaspoon pepper

1. Place beef, soupbone, salt, and 4 quarts water in very large kettle. Cover; bring to boiling. Skim surface.
2. Add cabbage, onion, carrots, celery, green pepper, and tomatoes.
3. Bring to boiling; simmer, covered, 30 minutes.
4. Add other ingredients; simmer, covered, 3½ hours.
5. Remove meat and bone; discard bone.
6. Let meat cool. Cut into cubes; add to soup. Refrigerate several hours.
7. Just before serving soup, skim fat from surface. Slowly heat soup to boiling. Store leftover soup, covered, in refrigerator.

BRAISED SWISS STEAK

MAKES 6 SERVINGS; 1 SLICE WITH 2 TABLE-
SPOONS PAN JUICES, 311 CALORIES, PER SERVING

¼ cup packaged dry bread
    crumbs
2 teaspoons salt
¼ teaspoon pepper
2 lb round steak
2 tablespoons butter or
    margarine, melted
1 can (1 lb) tomatoes, un-
    drained
2 medium onions, thinly
    sliced
¼ cup chopped celery
1 clove garlic, finely
    chopped
1 tablespoon Worcester-
    shire sauce

1. Combine bread crumbs, salt, and pepper.
2. Trim fat from steak; wipe meat with damp cloth.
3. Sprinkle one side with half of crumb mixture; pound into steak, using rim of saucer. Repeat on other side.
4. Brush both sides with butter; place under broiler, turning once, until browned on both sides.
5. Meanwhile, in Dutch oven or heavy skillet with tight-fitting cover, combine remaining ingredients.
6. Add steak; simmer, covered, 2 hours, or until meat is tender.

BOILED BRISKET OF BEEF

MAKES 6 SERVINGS; 4 PIECES (EACH 1½-BY-1-
BY-1 INCH), 280 CALORIES, PER SERVING

1 onion, stuck with 2 whole
    cloves
4-lb brisket of beef,
    trimmed of fat
1 cup cut-up celery, with
    tops
1 cup cut-up carrots
¼ cup coarsely chopped
    parsley
1 bay leaf
3 whole black peppers
1 tablespoon salt
Few sprigs parsley

1. Bring 2 quarts water to boiling in large kettle. Add all ingredients, except parsley sprigs; bring to boiling.
2. Reduce heat; simmer, covered, 3 hours, or until meat is tender.
3. Garnish with parsley sprigs; serve with Horseradish Sauce.*
* See this chapter.

CHINESE BEEF

2-lb flank steak
1 tablespoon salad oil
1 clove garlic, finely
    chopped
1 teaspoon salt
Dash pepper
¼ teaspoon ginger
¼ cup soy sauce

3 drops noncaloric liquid
    sweetener
2 large green peppers
2 medium tomatoes, quar-
    tered
1 can (1 lb) bean sprouts,
    drained
1 tablespoon cornstarch

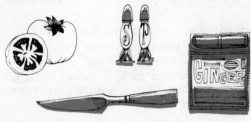

MAKES 8 SERVINGS; ¾ CUP, 335 CALORIES, EACH

1. Slice beef, across grain, into thin strips.
2. In hot oil in large, heavy skillet, over high heat, sauté beef with garlic, salt, pepper, and ginger until browned all over—5 minutes.
3. Add soy sauce and sweetener; cook, covered, 5 minutes.
4. Remove seeds and ribs from peppers. Cut peppers into 1-inch strips; add, with tomatoes and bean sprouts, to beef.
5. Bring to boiling; cook, covered and over high heat, 5 minutes.
6. Meanwhile, make a smooth paste of cornstarch and ¼ cup water. Stir into beef mixture; bring to boiling, stirring.

BAKED CHICKEN AND PINEAPPLE

2 (3-lb size) broiler-fryers,
    cut up
2 teaspoons dried rosemary
    leaves
2 teaspoons salt
½ teaspoon pepper

10 shallots, peeled
2 cups unsweetened pine-
    apple juice
1 teaspoon ginger
Paprika

MAKES 6 SERVINGS; 3 SMALL PIECES (AS ½ BREAST, THIGH, AND WING), 315 CALORIES, PER SERVING

1. Preheat oven to 350F.
2. Wash chicken; drain well on paper towels.
3. Combine rosemary, salt, and pepper; rub into chicken.
4. Arrange chicken, skin side up, in two 9-by-9-by-1½-inch baking dishes. Add shallots.
5. Combine pineapple juice and ginger; pour over chicken. Sprinkle with paprika.
6. Bake, uncovered, 55 to 60 minutes, or until tender.

LOW-CALORIE CHICKEN PAPRIKA

2 (2½- to 3-lb size) broiler-
    fryers, cut up
2½ teaspoons salt
4 teaspoons paprika

½ cup chopped onion
1 cup yoghurt
2 tablespoons chopped
    parsley

MAKES 6 SERVINGS; 282 CALORIES, EACH

1. Wash chicken well; drain on paper towels.
2. Sprinkle with 2 teaspoons salt and 2 teaspoons paprika.
3. Arrange in broiler pan without rack; broil, about 6 inches from heat, 5 minutes on each side, or until nicely browned.
4. Place chicken and onion in large skillet with tight-fitting cover. Add 1½ cups water; simmer, covered, 40 minutes, or until chicken is tender. Remove chicken to serving platter.
5. Stir yoghurt and rest of salt and paprika into liquid in skillet; heat slowly, stirring, until hot. Do not boil.
6. Pour over chicken. Sprinkle with parsley.

BROILED CALVES' LIVER

6 slices (1½ lb) calves'
    liver
¼ cup low-calorie French
    dressing

1 can (3 oz) sliced mush-
    rooms, drained

MAKES 6 SERVINGS; 1 SLICE, 176 CALORIES, EACH

1. Brush both sides of liver with dressing.
2. Place on broiler rack; broil, 4 inches from heat, 4 minutes.
3. Turn; then broil 2 minutes on other side.
4. Cover with mushrooms; broil 2 minutes.

HERB-BROILED LAMB CHOPS

12 rib lamb chops, 1 inch
    thick
2 teaspoons dried basil
    leaves

2 teaspoons dried marjoram
    leaves
2 teaspoons dried thyme
    leaves
2 teaspoons salt

MAKES 6 SERVINGS; 2 CHOPS, 256 CALORIES,
PER SERVING

1. Wipe chops with damp cloth.
2. Mix other ingredients; rub into both sides of chops. Chill, covered, 1 hour.
3. Place on broiler rack, 4 inches from heat; for medium rare, broil 6 minutes on one side, 4 minutes on other.

ROAST SHOULDER OF LAMB

4 to 4½ lb (boned and
    rolled) lamb shoulder
1 clove garlic, cut
2 teaspoons salt

¼ teaspoon pepper
1 teaspoon dried basil
    leaves

MAKES 6 SERVINGS; 2 SLICES,
257 CALORIES, PER SERVING

1. Preheat oven to 325F.
2. Wipe meat with damp cloth. Unroll lamb; rub inside portion with garlic, and sprinkle with combined salt, pepper, and basil. Roll up; tie with twine.
3. Place on rack in shallow roasting pan. Insert meat thermometer, away from fat, in center of lamb.
4. For well-done lamb, roast 2½ hours, or until meat thermometer reads 182F.

VEAL RAGOUT PARISIENNE

1 tablespoon butter or
    margarine
1½ lb veal shoulder, cut
    into 2-inch cubes
1 clove garlic, finely
    chopped
1 tablespoon flour
1½ teaspoons salt
¼ teaspoon pepper

1½ cups boiling water
1½ cups sliced carrots
1 cup sliced celery
2 medium potatoes, pared
    and quartered
½ teaspoon dried mar-
    joram leaves
1 pkg (10 oz) frozen peas

MAKES 6 SERVINGS; 1 SCANT CUP,
393 CALORIES, EACH

1. In hot butter in Dutch oven or heavy skillet, brown veal well on all sides (in several batches, if necessary).
2. Add garlic; sauté 3 minutes.
3. Sprinkle flour, salt, and pepper over veal. Gradually stir in boiling water; bring to boiling, stirring.
4. Reduce heat; simmer, covered, 1 hour, stirring occasionally.
5. Add carrots, celery, potatoes, and marjoram; simmer, covered, about 25 minutes, or until vegetables are almost tender. (If mixture seems dry, stir in a little boiling water.)
6. Break frozen peas into chunks. Add to veal; simmer, covered, 10 minutes.

SHRIMP IN GARLIC SAUCE

2 tablespoons salad oil
2 lb uncooked deveined
   shrimp
2 small cloves garlic, finely
   chopped
1 can (6 oz) tomato paste

2 teaspoons salt
½ teaspoon pepper
½ teaspoon dried basil
   leaves
½ cup chopped onion

MAKES 6 SERVINGS; 1 SCANT CUP,
206 CALORIES, EACH

1. In hot oil in large skillet, over medium heat, sauté shrimp, turning several times, about 5 minutes, or just until they turn pink. Remove from heat.

2. Stir in other ingredients, along with 1 cup water; simmer, covered, until heated through.

BABY LOBSTERS MARINIÈRE

4 (1-lb size) live lobsters*
Boiling water
2 tablespoons salt

¾ cup bottled low-calorie
   Italian dressing
2 tablespoons lemon juice

MAKES 4 SERVINGS,
164 CALORIES, EACH

1. Plunge lobsters into large kettle of boiling, salted water. Return to boiling; boil, covered, 15 to 20 minutes. Drain.

2. Serve hot or cold, with this dip: Combine dressing and lemon juice, stirring to mix well. Allow 3½ tablespoons per serving.

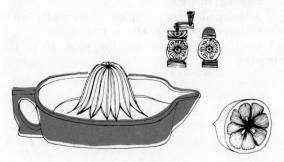

MAKES 4 SERVINGS,
180 CALORIES, EACH

* Or use 4 (5-oz size) frozen rock-lobster tails. Plunge, unthawed, into large kettle of boiling, salted water. Return to boiling; boil, covered, 6 to 8 minutes. Drain; then proceed as above.

TUNA-MACARONI CASSEROLE

1 cup elbow macaroni
¾ cup chopped onion
2 tablespoons chopped
   parsley
½ cup chopped celery,
   with tops
1 clove garlic, chopped
1 can (1 lb, 12 oz) toma-
   toes, undrained
1 bay leaf, crumbled
1 teaspoon salt
⅛ teaspoon pepper
½ teaspoon dried basil
   leaves

½ teaspoon dried oregano
   leaves
Dash noncaloric liquid
   sweetener
2 tablespoons butter or
   margarine, melted
1 tablespoon grated Parmesan cheese
3 tablespoons packaged dry
   bread crumbs
2 cans (6½-oz size) dietetic
   tuna, drained

MAKES 6 SERVINGS;
221 CALORIES, EACH

1. Cook macaroni as package label directs; drain.

2. Meanwhile, preheat oven to 375F. In 2-quart saucepan, combine onion, parsley, celery, garlic, tomatoes, bay leaf, salt, pepper, basil, oregano, and sweetener.

3. Bring to boiling, stirring.

4. Reduce heat; simmer, uncovered, 20 minutes.

5. Combine butter, cheese, and bread crumbs in small bowl.

6. Lightly toss macaroni, tomato mixture, and tuna until well combined.

7. Turn into 6 individual baking dishes; top with crumb mixture.

8. Place on cookie sheet; bake 20 minutes, or until crumbs are golden-brown.

ARTICHOKE HEARTS CONTINENTAL

MAKES 4 SERVINGS;
6 ARTICHOKE-HEART HALVES,
150 CALORIES, PER SERVING

2 pkg (9-oz size) frozen
   artichoke hearts

1 teaspoon dried oregano
   leaves
Garlic salt

1. Cook artichoke hearts as package label directs, adding oregano at beginning of cooking.
2. Drain well, and serve sprinkled with garlic salt.

BRAISED FRESH CUCUMBERS

MAKES 6 SERVINGS;
¾ CUP, 35 CALORIES, EACH

4 cucumbers, pared and
   thinly sliced (6 cups)
2 teaspoons salt
3 bacon slices, diced
1 teaspoon sugar

¼ teaspoon noncaloric
   liquid sweetener
⅛ teaspoon pepper
1 tablespoon cider vinegar

1. In small bowl, layer cucumbers, sprinkling with salt. Refrigerate, covered, 30 minutes.
2. Meanwhile, in large skillet, sauté bacon until crisp; drain well.
3. Add cucumbers, drained thoroughly, and remaining ingredients; stir to mix well.
4. Cook, covered and over low heat, 10 to 12 minutes.

BROWN-RICE PILAF

MAKES 6 SERVINGS;
½ CUP, 66 CALORIES, EACH

1¼ cups boiling water
1 chicken-bouillon cube
½ cup raw brown rice
½ cup chopped onion
1 can (3 oz) sliced mush-
   rooms, drained

1 teaspoon salt
¼ teaspoon pepper
Dash dried thyme leaves
½ cup thinly sliced celery

1. Preheat oven to 350F.
2. Add water to bouillon cube in 1-quart casserole, stirring until dissolved.
3. Add remaining ingredients, except celery.
4. Bake, covered, 1 hour and 10 minutes.
5. Stir in celery, with fork; bake 10 minutes.
6. Just before serving, fluff up rice with fork.

GREEN PEPPER SAUTÉ

MAKES 6 SERVINGS;
½ CUP, 50 CALORIES, EACH

1 tablespoon salad oil
1 cup sliced onion
3 green peppers (1½ lb),
   sliced in ¼-inch rings
½ lb fresh mushrooms,
   sliced; or 2 cans (3-oz
   size) sliced mush-
   rooms, drained

1 teaspoon salt
⅛ teaspoon crushed dried
   red pepper
⅛ teaspoon dried oregano
   leaves

1. In hot oil in skillet, sauté onion, stirring, until golden—about 5 minutes.
2. Add remaining ingredients; cook, covered, over medium heat, 5 minutes, stirring occasionally.

MARINATED CARROTS

1 cup white vinegar
¼ cup chopped onion
1 teaspoon salt

1 teaspoon mixed pickling
    spice
9 carrots, quartered length-
    wise (¾ lb)

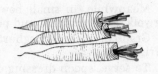

MAKES 6 SERVINGS; 6 QUARTERS,
65 CALORIES, PER SERVING

1. In medium saucepan, heat vinegar, onion, salt, and pickling spice to boiling.
2. Add carrots; bring to boiling. Reduce heat; simmer, covered, 5 minutes.
3. Pour into shallow baking dish. Let cool; refrigerate 2 hours.
4. Drain just before serving.

SAUERKRAUT IN WHITE WINE

3 cups sauerkraut, drained
    (1½ lb)
1 cup dry white wine

1 jar (7¾ oz) junior apri-
    cot-applesauce

MAKES 6 SERVINGS;
¾ CUP, 57 CALORIES, EACH

1. Run sauerkraut under cold water, to wash it thoroughly; then drain once more.
2. Combine all ingredients in 2-quart saucepan; cook, covered and over low heat, 40 minutes, stirring occasionally.

CREAMY COLESLAW

1 lb cabbage, finely
    shredded (1 qt)
¾ teaspoon salt
Ice water

Dressing:
1½ tablespoons dairy sour
    cream
¼ cup yoghurt

3 tablespoons low-calorie
    mayonnaise
1 teaspoon noncaloric
    liquid sweetener
1 tablespoon cider vinegar
½ teaspoon salt
⅛ teaspoon pepper
Dash paprika

MAKES 4 SERVINGS;
½ CUP, 48 CALORIES, EACH

1. Let cabbage stand 1 hour in salted ice water to cover.
2. Meanwhile, make Dressing: Combine sour cream and remaining ingredients in large bowl; mix well.
3. Drain cabbage. Rinse in cold water; drain again. Let dry on paper towels.
4. Add cabbage to dressing; toss to coat well. Refrigerate 1 hour.

MARINATED
GREEN-BEAN SALAD

2 pkg (9-oz size) frozen
    French-style green
    beans
3 tablespoons cider vinegar
1½ tablespoons salad oil

1 teaspoon salt
Dash pepper
½ teaspoon chopped
    parsley

MAKES 6 SERVINGS;
¾ CUP, 50 CALORIES, EACH

1. Cook beans as package label directs; drain.
2. Turn into shallow serving dish; refrigerate until well chilled—about 1 hour.
3. Combine remaining ingredients in jar with tight-fitting lid; shake vigorously.
4. Pour over beans; toss gently, to coat them well.
5. Refrigerate until ready to serve; then toss once more.

GREEN-BEAN SALAD WITH YOGHURT DRESSING

2 pkg (9-oz size) frozen cut
    green beans
1 egg yolk
¼ teaspoon salt

¼ teaspoon dry mustard
¼ teaspoon paprika
¾ cup yoghurt
1 tablespoon lemon juice

MAKES 6 SERVINGS; ¾ CUP BEANS
WITH 2 TABLESPOONS DRESSING,
38 CALORIES, PER SERVING

1. Cook beans as package label directs; drain. Refrigerate until well chilled—about 1 hour.
2. Meanwhile, in small bowl, with fork, beat egg yolk, salt, mustard, and paprika until fluffy.
3. Gradually beat in yoghurt and lemon juice. Refrigerate.
4. To serve, spoon dressing over chilled beans.

BUTTERMILK DRESSING

1 cup buttermilk
½ teaspoon onion juice
¾ teaspoon salt

1½ tablespoons lemon
    juice

MAKES 1 CUP;
3 CALORIES, PER TABLESPOON

1. Combine all ingredients in jar with tight-fitting lid; shake vigorously to blend.
2. Store in refrigerator until ready to use. Shake again just before using.

CREAMY CUCUMBER DRESSING

1 cup finely chopped, pared
    cucumber
½ cup chopped green
    pepper
1 clove garlic, finely
    chopped
½ teaspoon salt

¼ cup yoghurt
¼ cup low-calorie
    mayonnaise
¼ cup chili sauce
1 tablespoon prepared
    horseradish

MAKES 2 CUPS; 2 TABLESPOONS,
12 CALORIES, PER SERVING

1. Combine all ingredients in medium bowl; mix well.
2. Refrigerate 30 minutes, or until well chilled.

HORSERADISH SAUCE

1 cup (8 oz) yoghurt
½ teaspoon salt
⅛ teaspoon pepper

1 teaspoon prepared horse-
    radish

MAKES 1 CUP; 2 TABLESPOONS,
14 CALORIES, PER SERVING

1. Combine all ingredients in small bowl.
2. Refrigerate, covered, until well chilled—about 1 hour. Serve cold.

LOW-CALORIE CREOLE SAUCE

½ cup chopped onion
½ cup chopped green
    pepper
2 tablespoons chopped
    parsley

1 can (1 lb) tomatoes,
    undrained
1 teaspoon salt
⅛ teaspoon pepper
1 bay leaf, crumbled
Dash cloves

MAKES 2 CUPS; ⅓ CUP,
32 CALORIES, PER SERVING

1. Combine all ingredients in 2-quart saucepan; bring to boiling.
2. Reduce heat, and simmer, uncovered, 20 minutes.

ALMOND-PEACH PUDDING

6 canned dietetic peach
    halves, drained
2 cups skim milk
½ teaspoon almond extract

1 pkg (1½ oz) vanilla
    rennet custard
Nutmeg

1. Put peach halves in 6 sherbet glasses.
2. Heat milk and extract just to lukewarm (110F).
3. Stir in custard until dissolved.
4. Pour immediately into sherbet glasses (peaches will rise to top).
5. Let stand 10 minutes; then refrigerate until well chilled.
6. Sprinkle with nutmeg.

APPLE SNOW PUDDING

1 envelope unflavored gela-
    tine
2 cans (8½-oz size) dietetic
    applesauce (2 cups)
1 tablespoon grated lemon
    peel

3 tablespoons lemon juice
2 teaspoons noncaloric
    liquid sweetener
¼ teaspoon cinnamon
¼ teaspoon nutmeg
2 egg whites

1. Sprinkle gelatine over ½ cup cold water in small bowl, to soften.
2. Combine applesauce, lemon peel and juice, sweetener, and spices in saucepan; bring to boiling, stirring.
3. Add softened gelatine, stirring until dissolved.
4. Pour into bowl; refrigerate 1 hour.
5. Meanwhile, let egg whites warm to room temperature in small bowl.
6. Beat, with rotary beater, just until stiff peaks form.
7. Gently fold into gelatine mixture; refrigerate until well chilled.

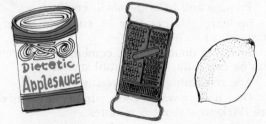

BAKED PEARS MELBA

3 fresh pears, halved, cored,
    and pared
1 cup canned unsweetened
    pineapple juice

1 teaspoon noncaloric
    liquid sweetener
¼ teaspoon ginger
2 tablespoons dietetic red-
    raspberry preserves

1. Preheat oven to 350F.
2. Arrange pears in 2-quart casserole.
3. In small saucepan, heat pineapple juice, sweetener, and ginger to boiling. Pour over pears.
4. Bake, covered, 45 minutes, or until pears are tender.
5. Spoon warm pear halves, with liquid, into 6 serving dishes. Top each with 1 teaspoon preserves.

LOW-CALORIE COFFEE MOUSSE

1 envelope unflavored gelatine
1 cup nonfat-dry-milk
   powder
2 tablespoons instant coffee

2 teaspoons noncaloric
   liquid sweetener
¼ teaspoon almond extract
½ cup ice water

MAKES 6 SERVINGS;
72 CALORIES, EACH

1. Sprinkle gelatine over ½ cup cold water in small saucepan; let stand 5 minutes to soften. Stir, over low heat, until gelatine is dissolved. Remove from heat.

2. Dissolve ½ cup dry-milk powder in ¾ cup water. Add to dissolved gelatine along with coffee, sweetner, and almond extract; mix well.

3. Refrigerate until consistency of unbeaten egg white—takes about 30 minutes.

4. Meanwhile, with rotary beater or portable electric mixer, beat rest of dry-milk powder with ice water until stiff peaks form when beater is raised.

5. Fold into gelatine mixture until well combined. Spoon into 6 sherbet dishes.

6. Refrigerate 1 hour, or until well chilled. If desired, garnish with shaved chocolate.

LOW-CALORIE RUM CHIFFON PIE

9-inch baked pie shell
1 envelope unflavored gelatine
3 tablespoons cornstarch
1½ cups skim milk
1½ tablespoons noncaloric
   liquid sweetener

¼ teaspoon salt
3 egg yolks, slightly beaten
3 egg whites
1 teaspoon vanilla extract
1 teaspoon rum flavoring

MAKES 8 SERVINGS;
142 CALORIES, EACH

1. Prepare and bake pie shell; cool.

2. Sprinkle gelatine over ¼ cup cold water; let stand, to soften.

3. In top of double boiler, combine cornstarch with ¾ cup milk, stirring until smooth.

4. Add remaining milk, sweetner, and salt.

5. Over boiling water, cook, stirring, until mixture thickens—about 5 minutes.

6. Add small amount of hot mixture to egg yolks, mixing well. Return to mixture in double boiler.

7. Cook, stirring, 2 minutes longer. Remove from boiling water.

8. Add gelatine, stirring until dissolved. Refrigerate until consistency of unbeaten egg white—about 30 minutes.

9. Meanwhile, in small bowl of electric mixer, at high speed, beat egg whites until stiff peaks form when beater is raised.

10. At low speed, gradually beat in gelatine mixture, vanilla and rum just until smooth and well combined.

11. Pour filling into pie shell; refrigerate until firm—about 2 hours.

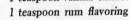

LIME-PINEAPPLE PARFAIT

1½ cups boiling water
1 package (21 grams) dietary lime gelatin
1½ cups bottled unsweetened apple juice

1 cup canned dietetic sliced pineapple, drained and diced
½ cup dessert-topping mix
¼ cup milk
¼ cup grated coconut
¼ teaspoon vanilla extract

1. Pour boiling water over gelatin, stirring to dissolve.
2. Stir in apple juice; refrigerate until consistency of unbeaten egg white—about 1 hour.
3. Fold pineapple into gelatin.
4. Pour into 6 parfait glasses or serving dishes. Refrigerate until firm.
5. In small bowl, combine dessert-topping mix and milk; beat, with rotary beater, until stiff peaks form.
6. Fold in coconut and vanilla.
7. Garnish each with 1 tablespoon topping.

VANILLA BLANCMANGE WITH FRUIT SAUCE

2 envelopes unflavored gelatine
3 cups skim milk
1 tablespoon sugar
¼ teaspoon salt

1 teaspoon noncaloric liquid sweetener
2 teaspoons vanilla extract
1 can (1 lb) dietetic fruit cocktail, drained

1. Sprinkle gelatine over ½ cup milk in medium bowl; let stand, to soften.
2. Meanwhile, slowly heat rest of milk just until bubbly around edge of pan.
3. Pour over gelatine, stirring until dissolved. Add sugar, salt, sweetener, and vanilla.
4. Refrigerate until consistency of unbeaten egg white—about 1 hour.
5. With rotary beater, beat until very frothy and almost double in bulk.
6. Pour into 6 individual molds or 8-inch (5½-cup) ring mold. Refrigerate several hours.
7. To serve: Loosen edge with sharp knife. Invert onto serving plates or platter.
8. Spoon fruit cocktail over molds.

WARM FRUIT COMPOTE

1 can (1 lb) dietetic peach halves
2 whole cloves
2 (4-inch) cinnamon sticks
1 tablespoon noncaloric liquid sweetener

1 can (1 lb) dietetic pear halves, drained
1 can (1 lb) packed-in-water sour red cherries, drained

1. Drain peach halves, reserving liquid.
2. Combine peach liquid, cloves, cinnamon, and sweetener in 1½-quart saucepan; bring to boiling. Reduce heat; simmer, uncovered, 5 minutes.
3. Quarter peach and pear halves; combine with cherries in medium bowl.
4. Pour hot syrup over fruit; let stand 15 minminutes. Serve compote warm.

What is a menu? A menu is a meal plan. As a meal plan, it should provide a well-balanced diet, which will include all the necessary nutrients without additional concentrates. With very little extra effort, family meals can be just as tempting as company meals.

From the thousands of foods in today's supermarket, it is possible to devise an almost endless variety of menus.

Here are some random hints, to make family meals easier to plan and to enjoy.

1. Make a shopping list from your menu plan, and you will shop more quickly and economically.

2. Keep your menu flexible. Take advantage of good buying tips in newspaper food columns, grocers' advertisements, and specials you find at the market.

3. Take advantage of foods that are in season and are plentiful.

4. Don't repeat the same food or flavor in one meal. Variety is the keynote of appealing meals.

5. Try to vary the texture, flavor, color, and methods of preparation involved in a single meal.

Combine soft and crisp, tart and sweet, hot and cold foods.

Be sure hot foods are served hot, and cold foods served cold. Heat and/or refrigerate plates as needed.

This does not mean, however, that you should serve a great number of foods at one meal. The happiest menu is achieved by serving a few carefully selected foods.

6. Arrange foods attractively, to heighten eye appeal. A simple garnish can add a note of elegance to an ordinary food.

7. Try a new food occasionally, and see if your family approves.

8. Try a new recipe. Don't be afraid to give a family favorite a new look. Keep a card file of the recipes that have been popular with your family, with your friends.

9. Cost alone is not an indication of a good meal. Low-cost foods can be enhanced with seasonings or spices, or can be combined with other foods in unusual ways.

10. Give children small servings, remembering that big amounts may be discouraging. It's best for a child to form the habit of cleaning his plate and then asking for a second helping.

11. Introduce a new food to a young child in sample-size tastes at the start of a meal, when he is hungry. If he doesn't like it the first time, try again another day.

12. Make meal planning a family project. When they all have a chance to make suggestions, they'll enjoy mealtime more.

13. Make mealtime an interesting and pleasant family association.

14. Good cooking and a well-planned meal deserve a pleasing table setting. It doesn't take much to decorate the table—a touch of color in napkins, your favorite house plant, or a figurine.

15. Be a good manager. Plan to use all the leftovers. Serve them to your family in a different form. Imagination is your most important ingredient.

Note: For starred recipes used in menus, see Index.

The word "breakfast" comes from two Anglo-Saxon words, "brecan" and "faesten," meaning to break a fast. When you sit down to breakfast—and a well-balanced breakfast fortifies you for the busy morning ahead—you are usually breaking a fast of more than ten hours.

Ideally, breakfast should be a quarter to a third of one's daily calorie and protein intake. Such foods as cereals (with milk), enriched breads with butter or margarine, meat, milk, and eggs meet these requirements. Fruit, too, of course, because without it the vitamin-C intake tends to lag behind nutritional standards.

EVERYDAY BREAKFASTS

Tomato Juice
Soft-Cooked Eggs*
Whole-Wheat Toast   Butter
Coffee   Tea   Milk

Melon (Cantaloupe or Honeydew)
Sausages
Buttermilk Bran Muffins*
Strawberry Jam   Butter
Coffee   Tea   Milk

Breakfast-in-a-Bowl*
Coffee   Milk

Prunes with Lemon
French Toast* with Spiced Cherry Jam*
Bacon
Coffee   Milk

Grapefruit
Blueberry Pancakes* with Butter and Syrup
Coffee   Milk

Frozen Pineapple Chunks
Basic Omelet* with Jelly
Butter-Toasted French Rolls
Coffee   Milk

Homemakers are notorious lunch skippers and/or lunch skimpers. Here's a week of luncheon menus for you (and for your family, too). And they're to be eaten sitting down at the table, not a snatch-as-snatch-can while you're doing a dozen things.

Hamburgers à la Carte*
Kidney-Bean Salad*
Milk
Cookies and Fruit

Vegetable Soup
Grilled Cheese Sandwiches
Carrot Sticks
Coconut Jelly Cupcakes*
Milk

Bouillon in Mugs
Welsh Rabbit* with Bacon on Baked Tomato
Peach Cobbler*
Milk

Egg and Green-Bean Casserole*
Sliced Tomatoes
Toasted French Rolls
Dream Bars*
Milk

Hamburger Soup*
Fiesta Coleslaw*
Toasted Crackers
Warm Country Applesauce* with
Sour Cream and Brown Sugar
Milk

Perfect Potato Salad* in Lettuce Cups
Cold Cuts
Melon
Soft Drinks

You *can* take it with you—and we mean our good box lunches, designed for hard-working men and women of all ages, including the kindergarten crowd.

Slices of Sunday's Roast Beef with
Horseradish on White Bread
Dill Pickles
Fresh Sauerkraut
Hot Buttered Tomato Juice*
(in vacuum bottle)
Glazed Chocolate Cookies*

Chili con Carne*
(in vacuum bottle)
Buttered Corn-Bread Square
(from a mix)
Celery Sticks, Olives, Cherry Tomatoes
Packet of Dried Figs
Milk

Cold Oven-Fried Chicken*
Roll with Mayonnaise and Lettuce
Watermelon Pickles
Individual Apple Pie with
Cheddar-Cheese Wedge
Hot Coffee

Sliced-Ham or Sliced-Tongue Sandwich on
Cheese Bread*
Corn or Sweet-Pickle Relish
Fresh-Apple Slaw*
Honey-Spicecake Square
(from a mix)
Hot Coffee   Milk

Cream-of-Green-Pea Soup
(canned; in vacuum bottle)
Meat-Loaf-and-Lettuce Sandwich
Hermits*
Applesauce (in a plastic cup)
Milk

———

Peanut-Butter-'N'-Bacon Sandwich*
Celery Hearts
Small Box of Raisins
Gingerbread
(from a mix; cut into fancy shapes with a
cookie cutter)
Chocolate Milk

Spicy-Ham-and-Cheese Sandwich*
Baked Apple with Raisins*
Toasted Oatmeal Cookies*
(saran-wrapped and tied with a red ribbon)
Hot Cocoa
(with miniature marshmallows,
to float on top)

———

Deviled-Egg Sandwich*
Small Tomato   Salt
Brownie*
Packet of Dried Apricots and Prunes
Strawberry Milk
(from a mix)

A family dinner should be interesting, nutritious, and economical. And our dinner menus for a week are just that. They include such delicious company touches as hot breads and biscuits, flavorful side dishes, and desserts to remember.

Sour Cream Soup*
Browned Swiss Steak*   Buttered Noodles
Julienne Carrots
Cheese Biscuits*
Orange-Pineapple Jubilee*
Coffee

———

Maple-Glazed Baked Ham*
Scalloped Potatoes*
Buttered Zucchini
Marinated Sliced Tomatoes
Hot Rolls
Apple-Raisin Turnovers*
Coffee

———

Perfect Fried Chicken*
Honey-Spice Acorn Squash*
Buttered Green Beans
Fruit Salad
Double Cornbread*
Rhubarb-Strawberry Tapioca*
Coffee

Roast Meat Loaf
Baked Potatoes*
Raw-Spinach Salad*
Old-Fashioned Apple Pie*   Coffee

———

Shrimp Creole with White Rice*
Peas à la Francais
Sour-Cream Coleslaw*
Rolls
Lemon Chiffon Pie*   Coffee

———

Shepherd's Pie*
Tossed Green Salad
French Bread, Toasted with
Parmesan Cheese
Jellied Prunes with Walnuts*
Whipped Cream
Coffee

———

Broiled Lamb Chops
Peach Halves with Chutney
Broiled Tomatoes
Buttered Asparagus with Lemon
Celery Sticks
Butterflake Rolls
Flan*   Coffee

Since that pause in the day's occupation that is known as the dinner hour offers more enticements to the dieter than you could shake a resolution at, we've concentrated on the big meal of the day—dinner. Here are two weeks' worth of dinner menus, each 500 calories, very little more or less. The starred recipes are in our Low-Calorie Cooking Chapter.

	CALORIES
Veal ragout Parisienne*	393
Lettuce wedge with	8
Creamy cucumber dressing*	12
½ slice French bread, toasted	30
Almond-peach pudding*	58
Coffee	0
Total	**501**
Beef bouillon (1 cup)	25
2 plain crackers (2-inch square)	30
Roast shoulder of lamb*	257
Brown-rice pilaf*	66
Braised fresh cucumbers*	35
Vanilla blancmange with fruit sauce*	81
Tea	0
Total	**494**
Broiled calves' liver*	176
Baked winter squash (¾ cup)	71
½ pat butter or margarine	37
Green-bean salad with yoghurt dressing*	38
Fresh pear	63
Edam cheese (1 oz), 2 plain crackers	
(2-inch square)	115
Coffee	0
Total	**500**
Tomato juice (½ cup)	21
Braised Swiss steak*	311
Medium baked potato	98
Brussels sprouts (½ cup), lemon wedge	33
Canned dietetic applesauce (⅓ cup)	35
Coffee	0
Total	**498**
Hearty vegetable soup*	181
2 small slices French bread	106
Butter or margarine (½ thin pat)	25
Cheddar cheese (1 oz)	113
Low-calorie chocolate pudding (from a mix)	54
Ladyfinger	18
Coffee	0
Total	**497**

	CALORIES
Tomato bouillon*	63
5 oyster crackers	15
2 herb-broiled lamb chops	256
Green-pepper saute*	50
Marinated carrots*	65
Baked pears melba*	53
Tea	0
Total	**502**
Shrimp in garlic sauce,*	206
with white rice (½ cup)	100
Green peas (½ cup)	56
2 celery hearts, 3 radishes	9
Hard roll	95
2 chilled canned dietetic pear halves	31
Tea	0
Total	**497**
Low-calorie chicken paprika*	282
on poppy-seed noodles (½ cup)	54
Cooked frozen mixed vegetables (½ cup)	30
Fresh pineapple (½ cup)	52
Angel-food cake (½ average piece)	78
Coffee	0
Total	**496**
Boiled brisket of beef*	280
Horseradish sauce*	14
½ small baked potato	40
Sauerkraut in white wine*	57
Marinated green-bean salad*	50
Warm fruit compote*	58
Coffee	0
Total	**499**
Chinese beef*	335
on cooked white rice (½ çup)	68
3 celery sticks, 2 radishes	13
Fresh-orange sections (½ cup)	44
2 coconut bars	36
Tea	0
Total	**496**

	CALORIES		CALORIES
Baked chicken and pineapple*	315	Chilled pineapple juice (½ cup)	60
Steamed broccoli (1½ large stalks), with		Chive cream cheese (2 teaspoons) on	
lemon wedge	45	2 plain crackers (2-inch square)	66
Tossed green salad (2 lettuce leaves,		Tuna-macaroni casserole*	221
6 cucumber slices, ½ tomato, 2		Tossed green salad (3 leaves lettuce, 1 scallion,	
tablespoons low-calorie dressing)	32	2 tablespoons low-calorie French dressing)	19
Rye wafer, ½ pat butter or margarine	56	Orange milk sherbet (½ cup)	118
Apple snow pudding*	48	Sugar wafer	15
Tea	0	Coffee	0
Total	496	Total	499
Baby lobster mariniere*	164		
Artichoke hearts continental*	150		
Creamy coleslaw*	48		
Rye wafer	20		
Lime-pineapple parfait*	118		
Coffee	0		
Total	500		

A late-late breakfast (call it brunch, if you wish) is a nice, easy way to entertain friends, on Christmas-Day-in-the-morning, or after church on Easter Sunday, or any other official or personal holiday. Wheel in a serving cart with something hot in the chafing dish, something cold, something sweet, something tart, something like the menus that follow. For starred dishes, see Index.

BRUNCHES OR SUNDAY BREAKFASTS

Broiled Grapefruit
Savory Stuffed Mushrooms*
Bacon
Toasted English Muffins
Strawberry Preserves
Cottage Cheese
Coffee

Winter Pears in Wine*
Sautéed Cornmeal Slices*   Hot Maple Syrup
Grilled Sausage Patties
Fried Apple Rings*
Streusel Cinnamon Coffeecake*
Coffee

Mulled Pineapple Juice*
Mushroom-Scrambled Eggs*
Broiled Ham Steak
Ginger Pears*
Crumb-Topped Coffeecake*
Coffee

Tomato Juice
Ham and Sweetbreads Supreme*
Blueberry Muffins*
Winter-Fruit Compote*
Coffee

Fresh Strawberries
Scrambled Eggs à la Suisse*
Canadian Bacon
Corn Sticks*   Currant Jelly
Coffee

PARTY LUNCHEONS

Beef-Ball Stroganoff*
Casserole of Wild Rice*
Asparagus Vinaigrette*
Lemon Sherbet with Raspberries*
Pecan Balls*
Tea

Avocados with Crabmeat*
Olives   Relishes
Buttermilk Biscuits*
Open-Face Plum Pie*
Tea

Chicken Soufflé Hollandaise*
Salad of Fresh Herbs*
Corn Muffins*   Butter
Fresh Pineapple with Mixed Fruits
Coffee

Veal Sauté Marengo*
Orange-and-Onion Salad*
Hot Buttered Rye Toast
Brandied Peach Melba*
Coffee

Cardinal Cup*
Curried Cottage Cheese with Fruit*
Perfect Baking-Powder Biscuits*
Coconut Chiffon Loaf Cake*
Tea

SPECIAL-OCCASION MENUS

Afternoon Reception	*Afternoon Tea*
Sherry Punch Bowl*	Pinwheel Sandwiches*
Tray of Miniature Coconut Tarts*	Fondant-Filled Fruits*
Fruitcake Slices	Spiced Walnuts*
Shortbread Stars*	Decorated Petits Fours*
Candied Grapefruit Peel*	Hot Tea Coffee
Coffee for a Crowd*	———
	Poundcake*
	Mints
	Hot Spiced Tea

THE COFFEE BREAK

Morning	*Late Evening*
Cinnamon-Sugar Muffins*	Whole-Wheat Doughnuts*
Coffee	Coffee
	———
Afternoon	Spiced Coffee Cream*
Brownies*	Mixed Salted Nuts
Coffee	

BRIDAL BUFFETS

Sandwich Loaf*	Chicken Breasts in Wine*
Wedding Cake*	Fluffy White Rice*
Nuts Mints	Tiny Rolls and Butter
Hot Tea For 50* Golden Punch*	Pickled Pineapple*
———	Apricot Ice-Cream Mold*
Avocado Mold* with Crab Salad*	Wedding Cake*
Assorted Sandwiches	Coffee Champagne
Wedding Cake*	
Nuts Mints	
Coffee Pink Party Punch*	

Buffet food should be notable. For hot buffets, there are many marvelous things to serve as a change from the good, but too familiar, Boston baked beans and spaghetti with meat sauce. However, if spaghetti is what you want, serve it in special style, with a brand-new sauce. For starred dishes, see Index.

Baked Chicken Breasts Supreme*
Savory Stuffed Mushrooms*
Peach Waldorf Salad*
Hot Cheese Biscuits*
Crème-de-Menthe Parfait
Coffee

———

Our Best Cucumbers in Sour Cream*
Sirloin Tips en Brochette*
White Rice with Onions*
Carrots in Mustard Glaze*
Fresh Peas Oregano*
Baba au Rhum*
Tea

Beef in Burgundy with Gnocchi*
Herb-Buttered Zucchini and Carrots*
Green-Salad Bowl
Rolls
Pears Sabayon*
Jewel Cookies*
Coffee   Tea

———

Chicken Curry* on White Rice with Raisins*
Curry Accompaniments
(chutney, salted peanuts, coconut, kumquats)
Sesame Rolls
Raspberry Sherbet
Coffee   Tea

HOLIDAY MENUS

Easter

Melon Cup
Ginger-Glazed Baked Ham*
Buttered New Potatoes
Artichoke Hearts in Wine*
Asparagus Vinaigrette* with Deviled Eggs*
Rolls
Four-Seasons Flan*
Coffee

Traditional Thanksgiving

Golden-Brown Turkey*
Peas and Little Onions
Buttery Grated Carrots*
Cranberry-Brazil-Nut Relish*
Rolls
Brandied Pumpkin Pie*
Coffee

Thanksgiving

Roast Loin of Pork, Polynesian*
Yams Flambés*
Green Beans with Mushrooms*
Wine Fruit Salad*
Rolls
Cranberries Jubilee*
Coffee   Wine

Christmas

Savory Roast of Beef*
Fluffy Mashed Potatoes*
Braised Celery with Mushrooms*
Tomato Aspic* Served on Green-Pepper Rings
Rolls
Mincemeat Glacé*
Coffee

36

Nutrition

Basic Nutrition For Your Family

Each year brings advances in our knowledge of nutrition. New information reveals that reactions taking place within the human body each day, even each second, are extremely complicated. We are also told about the extensive study of the role of nutrition in the prevention and treatment of many chronic disorders.

With nutrition facts seeming to change so frequently, many homemakers wonder whether it is possible for them to feed their families adequately. Yet it is really quite easy for menus to add up to good nutrition. Keep in mind that we need nutrients for three purposes: to provide materials for growth and replacement of muscle tissue, to provide a source of energy (measured as calories), and to provide materials for regulating body processes. Some nutrients help in only one of these functions. Others can (and do) provide materials that participate in more than one. Sometimes they take part in all three functions.

Which nutrients are needed daily? Are there certain amounts that we should have, and do we need more of some than of others? It is easy to remember that we need five groups: protein, fat, carbohydrate, vitamins, and minerals.

Protein is essential because it contains materials for all three nutritive functions. The proteins in our foods are composed of even smaller units, known as amino acids. It is through amino-acid activity that proteins function. Some amino acids can be synthesized within our bodies from materials in other foods. But there are others that our bodies cannot manufacture; these are called "essential amino acids." Sources of these should be included in the diet each day.

We have also learned that the amino acids we can synthesize (known as "nonessential") function better in the presence of the essential amino acids. And we know that all the essential amino acids must be present at the same time, to obtain the most benefit from all. So one might easily wonder if the foods selected meet all these qualifications. Yet there are simple guides to help you get the most nutrition from foods for your family.

Carbohydrates and fats are necessary as energy-givers. However, there are also essential fatty acids (part of some fats) that many believe we need each day. So sources of these should be included in the diet.

Minerals are important as sources of materials that regulate body functions. They may also become part of the structure of the body. Calcium, for example, is an essential component of the skeletal frame. Although this function takes place primarily during growth, there is a continued calcium exchange within the body. So we need calcium as adults. And calcium is necessary for the coagulation of blood. This mineral has other important functions, too.

It is believed that we must have certain amounts of calcium and iron each day. Other minerals equally important to health are needed in such small quantities that we apparently obtain adequate amounts. Some of these are: sodium, potassium, chlorine, phosphorus, copper, zinc, magnesium, manganese, cobalt, iodine, sulfur, fluorine, and others.

Even the youngest family member is soon familiar with the idea that vitamins are important. But again, how much and which ones to include can become a nagging worry to the homemaker.

The National Research Council's Food and Nutrition Board has published a Table of Daily Recommended Allowances for those nutrients that its members consider necessary to include in the diet each day. The vitamins specified are: vitamin A, thiamine (B-1), riboflavin (B-2), niacin, ascorbic acid (vitamin C), and vitamin D. Other vitamins are equally essential and perform vital roles in our body's metabolism. However, either we are able to synthesize adequate amounts or our need for them is so small that we obtain enough from our food. Chief among these additional vitamins are: pyridoxine, biotin, pantothenic acid, folic acid, vitamin B-12. You have probably seen these names on labels.

The possibility is realized that some factor, unknown at present, remains to be identified as an essential nutrient.

Even though you require some twenty to thirty nutrients daily, your menu planning need not resemble a complex calculator. The United States Department of Agriculture has developed an easy-to-follow menu plan.

A DAILY FOOD GUIDE

Milk Group

Some milk for everyone.
Children, 3 to 4 cups
Teen-agers, 4 or more cups
Adults, 2 or more cups

Vegetable, Fruit Group

4 or more servings. Include:
A citrus fruit or other fruit or vegetable important for vitamin C. A dark-green or deep-yellow vegetable for vitamin A—at least every other day. Other vegetables and fruits, including potatoes

Meat Group

2 or more servings. Beef, veal, pork, lamb, poultry, fish, eggs. As alternatives— dry beans, dry peas, nuts

Bread, Cereal Group

4 or more servings. Whole grain, enriched, or restored

The guide is flexible. You can adapt it to fit family preferences. Even though you have freedom of choice, keep in mind that foods within each group are similar but not identical. Thus, to safeguard your nutrient intake, plan to have variety within each group. The foods listed in the guide probably will provide you with your nutritive needs—except for calories. So you may select additional foods, from the four food groups or from other foods, such as desserts, fats, oils, and sweet foods, to provide the necessary calories.

Each food group makes certain contributions to the diet. For example, fruits and vegetables supply vitamins and minerals. They are especially rich in vitamin A and vitamin C. Dark-green leafy vegetables, like spinach, kale, chard, provide vitamin A; while citrus fruits and other fresh fruits, such as strawberries and cantaloupe, and vegetables, like green pepper and broccoli, provide significant amounts of vitamin C (ascorbic acid).

Milk supplies many nutrients. Several studies have indicated that if we do not have enough milk (or its substitutes), our diet may be low in protein, calcium, and riboflavin. You may have the following, instead of 1 cup of milk, to obtain approximately the same amount of calcium:

1 cup fluid skim milk or buttermilk
1¼ cups dairy sour cream
1¼ ounces process Cheddar cheese
1⅓ cups cottage cheese
2 cups (approximately) ice cream

The meat group is especially important for its protein value. It, as well as the milk group, contains high-quality protein. This means that a good supply of all the essential amino acids is found in meat foods— eggs, fish of all varieties, and poultry are included.

Other nutrients found here are the B vitamins and iron.

Breads and cereals, the fourth group, often reflect ethnic cultures, as types of bread vary from country to country. Rice, noodles, macaroni, crackers, grits, and baked goods are among the foods in this group. They can be a good source of the B vitamins and iron *if* they are whole grain or enriched. You may also obtain some amino acids to supplement those from the meat and milk groups. Read the label to see if the food has been enriched.

The same basic rules can be used for the whole family—children and parents need the same nutrients, just different amounts. And, of course, there will be different needs for foods that supply calories primarily.

Diets Restricted in Sodium

When the doctor hands you or some member of your family a diet list and says you will have to cut down on your sodium for a while, you may feel lost. And as you read his directions, as clear as they are, the task may seem almost hopeless. Surely, food can't be appetizing if all the salt is removed!

Don't despair! First of all, realize that the doctor is serious about his order. Be sure you treat it just as you would any other prescription, for it is just as important to your medical treatment. You can't "cheat" if you expect sodium restriction to help you. A diet restricted in sodium is used as part of the medical treatment for a variety of conditions. It is wise not to impose such a diet on yourself, however. Self-medication is a foolhardy practice.

The degree and level of sodium restriction can vary for different individuals. In addition, some people are advised to reduce calorie intake, for weight loss. Others may be given diets with various modifications among the types and amounts of fat. In spite of such differences, all sodium-restricted diets have many points in common. Because of this, ideas for purchasing, seasoning, and preparing food for this type of diet may make it easier to follow.

When your doctor orders a low-sodium diet for you or a family member, you might become aware of how little you know about this essential substance. You might wonder how such small amounts of it can affect health.

Sodium is a mineral element. It is found in many items we consume in a number of forms. It is important for normal body function. It is soluble and thus is in solution within our bodies. It is possible to measure the amount of sodium in foods and other materials. So whenever we need to restrict sodium, we can estimate the amount consumed.

We usually ingest far more sodium than we need. But our bodies are equipped with a regulating mechanism that keeps the amount of sodium within a fairly consistent range. Thus, if we ingest more than we need, which is usually the case, it is excreted quickly. This is called "maintaining the sodium balance." Excess sodium is lost through the urine (by far the greatest amount), the sweat glands, and the feces. Sodium is in solution in body water and is an important part of many intestinal secretions. For example, sodium exchange within the small intestine is constantly taking place as it is reabsorbed after being secreted in the digestive fluids, such as bile, saliva, the pancreatic juice, and other intestinal secretions. Thus we can conserve our present supply of sodium, retain what we need from the amount ingested, and then cast out the excess.

Fifty-five to sixty-five per cent of man's body weight is due to its water content. The primary function of sodium is to participate in maintaining the body's water balance. Other functions are related to the composition of the blood, the conduction of impulses of the nervous system, and the contraction of muscles (especially the heart muscle). When the proper water and mineral balance within the body is maintained, the tissue cells are able to function normally.

Sodium is restricted in an individual's diet when the physician believes that such restriction would improve normal body function. Usually the diet order indicates the amount of sodium the patient is to have. For example, the physician may recommend "no added salt," or "1,000 mg. sodium per day," or a smaller amount.

Even though the diet is low in sodium, you must be sure to have a nutritionally adequate menu. By following the Daily Food Guide, you can easily plan nutritionally sound meals. Even though you plan meals carefully, they may not be appetizing to your patient (accustomed as he is to salt), and food may be left on the plate. One study reported that the important nutrients calcium, riboflavin, and protein were in short supply in a patient's diet, due it was thought, to decreased milk intake. Low-sodium milk did not satisfy the patient. Other reports have shown that the nutrients iron, thiamine, niacin, and protein might be low in a diet. This could be due to reduced intake of meat and eggs.

It is possible to have an adequate diet *if* the suggestions of the Daily Food Guide are followed and *if* you make every effort to prepare attractive and tasty food.

Because the approximate sodium content of foods is known, you can follow your doctor's prescription for sodium restriction by omitting or cutting down on certain foods or substances. If you also must have a low-calorie diet and/or one further modified by its specific fat content, you might have to add even more items to your "don't" list.

As you restrict sodium, you actually are counting the amount you take into your body. If asked to name the chief source of sodium, you would immediately answer "food." The answer is correct, yet two other sources add significant amounts of sodium: water and medicaments. These are often troublesome, as they are hidden sources and you may be including more sodium than you realize.

Sodium occurs naturally in most foods. As you would expect, the amount varies considerably. Each food group will be discussed separately; but, in general, fruits contain very little, vegetables contain more (some are excluded from most diets), meats have larger amounts (some are excluded, and the portion size of others is controlled), milk and its substitutions (forms of cheese) are considerably rich in sodium. Usually, your doctor will allow most of these foods, though he may eliminate certain ones and limit the amount of others.

Salt, one of the chief forms of sodium in the diet, is composed of sodium (40 per cent) and chloride. We add considerable amounts of sodium by our use of table salt. Salt is also used in many ways in commercial processing. It is added to most canned vegetables, to many canned and frozen prepared foods, such as chili, stews, TV dinners, and so on. Brine—salt and water—is used as a preservative to inhibit the growth of bacteria in some foods and for flavoring in others. You cannot eat foods so treated. These include such things as pickles, corned beef, sauerkraut, tongue, and ham. Other foods are immersed in brine in cleaning, blanching, or a flotation process. So certain fruits and vegetables and some frozen ones, as well as frozen fish fillets, would be eliminated.

As sodium is used as a leavening agent, any item containing baking powder or baking soda would need to be replaced. This includes baked goods items, such as quick breads, cookies, and cakes. Commercial bakeries usually add baking soda, baking powder, or salt to their products. However, low-sodium baking powders are available, and you can use them for home baking. If you cannot obtain such baking powder locally, ask your pharmacist to prepare the following for you:

Potassium bicarbonate .... 39.8 gm
Cornstarch .... 28.0 gm
Tartaric acid .... 7.5 gm
Potassium bitartrate .... 56.1 gm

Use 1½ teaspoons of this mixture in place of 1 teaspoon of regular baking powder. It is suggested that, to obtain best results, you add it toward the end of the mixing and avoid overbeating.

Sodium compounds are frequently used commercially for various reasons. They can add considerable amounts of sodium to a diet, and such foods are usually eliminated from your list of allowed foods. The most common of these practices are:

Di-sodium phosphate: Used in the preparation of some quick-cooking cereals and processed cheeses.

Monosodium glutamate: Used to enhance flavor. Added to many packaged, canned, and frozen foods. Also, it can be purchased for home use under several brand names.

Sodium alginate: Used to obtain a smooth texture in such foods as chocolate milks and ice creams.

Sodium benzoate: Used as a preservative. Chiefly found in such foods as relishes and salad dressings.

Sodium hydroxide: Used to soften skins of some foods during processing. Examples: Some fruits, vegetables, olives.

Sodium proprionate: Used as a preservative to inhibit the growth of mold. Chiefly found in some cakes, breads, pasteurized cheeses.

Sodium sulfite: Used to prepare certain foods for further processing or as a preservative in others. Foods so treated: Glazed or crystallized fruits, some dried fruits, maraschino cherries.

Water is frequently a hidden source of sodium. In some cities, the sodium content is so low that it is of little concern. In others, it becomes a dietary factor. We use water for cooking vegetables, for baking, and for such meat dishes as stews.

Medicines often contain sodium and, if used frequently, can add undesirable amounts to your diet. Some of the most common ones to watch for are: sedatives, pain-relievers, cough medicines, alkalizers (taken for "indigestion"), and antibiotics. Many dentifrices contain sodium. You may be inadvertently increasing your sodium intake by using sodium-containing compounds—for instance, cleaning dentures with baking soda. The only way to prevent these occurrences is to become alert to unsuspected sources of sodium. Begin to think sodium and become detection-minded. Read every label carefully before you purchase (an excellent practice, in any event!). Learn to recognize the labeling of sodium: salt, sodium compounds, and the chemical symbol Na. Only through such vigilance can you keep unwanted sodium from slipping into your diet.

Foods are usually considered in relation to others in the same groups. We usually plan menus with substitutions in mind, so it is helpful to consider sodium content from this standpoint.

Foods containing milk are quite high in sodium. Processing and elimination of cream, as in skim milk or buttermilk, do not reduce the sodium content. So, as far as a diet is concerned, evaporated milk, nonfat-dry-milk powder, fluid milk, skim milk, and buttermilk contain approximately the same amount of sodium.

Special products are helpful in substituting. Low-sodium milk can be obtained in either liquid or powder form. If the latter is used, reconstituting it (adding water) and thoroughly chilling it before drinking greatly enhance its flavor. In some areas, you may be able to buy low-sodium cheeses, both cottage and Cheddar.

You will probably have to eliminate all commercial foods made with milk. Such items as ice cream, milk shakes, condensed milk must be omitted. Many people have the mistaken notion that sherbets are "ices" and could be included; but they, too, must be eliminated.

Apart from those so high in sodium that they are usually restricted in *any* diet, vegetables and fruits are permitted in most low-sodium diets. Fresh fruits and vegetables, canned fruits, and frozen fruits are usually acceptable. However, most canned vegetables have been salted, and sodium may have been used in processing frozen vegetables (outstanding examples are frozen lima beans and frozen peas). However, you may be allowed to include others; it depends on your diet prescription.

What meats, then, are prohibited? Obviously, those prepared or preserved with some form of salt. Many popular foods are thus ruled out. Trying to find a substitute sometimes presents a problem. Bologna, frankfurters, ham, luncheon meats, sausages, smoked tongue, and so on are among those not permitted.

Besides being canned or smoked, fish is often preserved with salt. Caviar, salted and dried cod and herring, canned salmon and tuna are favorites that must be excluded from most low-sodium diets. Shellfish are especially high in sodium content, so such items as shrimp, crabs, clams, oysters, lobsters, and scallops must be omitted. Also, salt is added during the processing of frozen fish fillets.

A few fish—salmon and tuna, for example—sometimes are canned without salt. These can be used as if they were fresh.

Eggs are often regarded as a substitute for meat. If the diet's fat content, as well as its sodium, is being modified, eggs may be limited to one or two a week. However, since most of the sodium is in the egg white, you may be able to use the yolks for certain desserts.

Most commercially prepared bread and cereal products contain sodium in some form. A few without it are available, such as Melba toast, matzoth, and unsalted saltine crackers. In some communities, commercial bakeries sell low-sodium breads.

Your doctor probably will pay special attention to this food group. He will either limit the servings of "regular" bread or suggest you prepare your own. Foods in this group that are relatively free of sodium are usually allowed as desired.

You may have some dry cereals: puffed rice, puffed wheat, and shredded wheat. Cooked cereals are limited to farina, grits, oatmeal, and rolled wheat. Other foods allowed: flour, macaroni, noodles, rice (brown or white), spaghetti. You may bake with cornmeal, cornstarch, and tapioca. And you can have popcorn if it is unsalted.

Many prepared or partially prepared foods in this group contain sodium. Be sure to read the labels. For example, dry cereals except the three mentioned above contain sodium. So do quick-cooking and enriched cereals. Quick breads are usually made with baking powder or baking soda and salt. Commercial mixes and self-rising flours contain sodium. Almost all crackers (except those labeled as dietetic) contain sodium. And, of course, many popular "nibble foods" are high in salt. You will have to forget about such things as potato chips, pretzels, and salted popcorn.

What can you do? If you are not allowed *some* commercial bread and cereal, you may have to prepare your own. Low-sodium baking powders are available for quick breads. If you cannot buy low-sodium bread, you can make it, using yeast as a leavening agent.

If your diet is limited in calories, too, foods not in the four food groups may be reduced to a minimum. However, since they add flavor and satisfaction to menus, they are usually allowed in varying amounts. Some are relatively sodium-free; others, especially prepared foods, are rich in the forbidden element.

Butter (unsalted), avocado, cooking oil (unsalted), margarine (unsalted), and shortenings (unsalted) are relatively free of sodium. Your doctor may limit cream, light and heavy, sweet and sour, because its sodium content is rather high.

Commercially prepared French dressing, mayonnaise, and other specialty dressings are high in sodium. Needless to say, foods like bacon, salted butter, olives, and salted nuts are usually excluded.

Many sweet foods are allowed on a low-sodium diet, if the doctor permits the calories; *e.g.*, sugar (brown and white), homemade candy without salt, syrup, honey, jelly, jam, marmalade. If you purchase the last three, check the labels to see they were made without sodium.

Many other popular foods you can have as desired—for example, instant and regular coffee, tea, lemonade, fruit juices, alcoholic beverages (if your doctor permits), and cocoa made with the milk allowance.

But you must be sure not to have carbonated beverages, instant cocoa mixes, fountain beverages, molasses, and prepared beverage mixes. All contain sodium. Other commercial mixes, such as cake, muffin, and pudding mixes, are not allowed, either.

You may use rennet dessert powder, but not rennet tablets. If you want gelatin, use plain, unflavored gelatine, and add it to fruit juice.

As you plan your menus, it's a good idea to become adept at seasoning food, so you won't miss the flavor of salt.

There are two ways to avoid cooking a double set of meals: Cook all foods without seasoning; remove portions for the person on the low-sodium diet; then season the rest for the family. Or use various flavors so skillfully that your meals satisfy everyone. You may even become well known for your gourmet dishes, and no one will suspect they are sodium-free.

Many seasonings, low in sodium or containing negligible amounts, can be used to enhance natural food flavors. The following spices and herbs lend themselves to many dishes.

SPICES	HERBS	EXTRACTS	MISCELLANEOUS		
Allspice	Basil	Almond	Cocoa	Horseradish	Pimiento
Anise seed	Bay leaf	Lemon	(limited	(without	Saccharin
Caraway seed	Chives	Maple	amounts)	salt)	Sugar
Chili powder	Dill	Orange	Coconut	Lemon juice	Vinegar
Cinnamon	Marjoram	Peppermint	Garlic, fresh	Onion, fresh	Wine (if
Cloves	Mint	Vanilla		Peppers	allowed)
Cumin	Oregano	Walnut		(green or	
Curry	Parsley			red)	
Fennel	Rosemary				
Ginger	Sage				
Mace	Savory				
Mustard	Tarragon				
(dry)	Thyme				
Nutmeg					
Paprika					
Pepper					
(black,					
white, or					
red)					
Poppy seed					
Saffron					
Sesame seed					
Turmeric					

A few foods and flavorings are high in sodium; consequently, they are not allowed on a low-sodium diet. Chief among these:

Bouillon cubes (unless low-sodium)
Catsup
Celery leaves, celery salt, celery seed
Chili sauce
Garlic salt
Meat extracts and tenderizers
Mustard, prepared
Onion salt
Pickles
Relishes
Soy sauce

Before you use any sugar substitute or any salt substitute, check with your doctor, to be sure there is no sodium compound in it. Once you understand the need for and the importance of your sodium-restricted diet you will look upon food preparation as a challenging task. It will actually be a game to try to make your best meals taste even better. If you can cook the same meals for the whole family, your lot will be an easier one.

Be creative. Look over your recipe file, and note how many recipes can be prepared without salt. Some may need additional flavorings. Our chapter on herb cookery may give you many ideas useful for a low-sodium diet.

Also, a fruit pie can be made without using salt in the piecrust dough. You can bake custard without egg whites. Vegetables can be cooked in many ways: in combinations with other foods; lightly seasoned with butter, nuts, or one or two herbs. Each family will discover combinations that suit everyone best.

You may not be allowed desserts. This is understandable when you realize that dishes that combine foods might complicate your diet. Milk and eggs, for example, contain high amounts of sodium, and even though you had only one portion of a dessert containing both, the sodium content might exceed your allowance. Perhaps you will be allowed to have some on special occasions. If so, any techniques you can use to lower the sodium content will help. You might try low-sodium milks and baking powders.

Investigate the low-sodium preparations in your locality. Then ask your doctor if you may use any of them. You will be surprised at the wide variety available.

Your own diet prescription will determine just how venturesome you may be. But try some of the following recipes, to see how easy it is to adapt old favorites to your new pattern.

CURRY NIBBLERS

MAKES 3 CUPS

6 tablespoons unsalted butter or margarine
½ teaspoon curry powder
⅛ teaspoon ginger
3 cups bite-size shredded-wheat cereal

1. Slowly heat butter in large skillet.
2. Remove from heat. Add rest of ingredients; toss to coat cereal.
3. Cook, over low heat, 3 minutes. Serve as hors d'oeuvre.

FISH

Suggested fish for low-sodium diets:

Bass	Halibut
Blue	Rockfish
Catfish	Salmon
Cod	Sole
Flounder	Trout

Broil fish as directed in Broiled Fish,* basting it with any of suggested basting sauces. Serve on heated platter, with lemon wedge and parsley sprig.

* See Fish and Shellfish Chapter.

DUTCH-OVEN BEEF

1 tablespoon salad oil
1½ lb lean chuck, cut in 2-inch cubes
1½ cups thinly sliced onion
1 clove garlic, crushed
½ cup sliced fresh mushrooms

1 tablespoon finely chopped parsley
Dash pepper
¼ teaspoon dried thyme leaves
1 can (8 oz) dietetic-pack tomatoes, undrained

MAKES 6 SERVINGS

1. In hot oil in Dutch oven, sauté beef cubes until browned all over.
2. Add onion, garlic, and mushrooms; cook 2 minutes.
3. Add remaining ingredients, mixing well; simmer, covered, 1½ hours, or until beef is tender. Serve over salt-free noodles or rice.

HERBED OVEN-FRIED CHICKEN

2- to 2½-lb broiler-fryer, cut up
2 tablespoons salad oil
1 cup crushed shredded-wheat biscuits

¼ teaspoon dried rosemary leaves
¼ teaspoon paprika

MAKES 3 OR 4 SERVINGS

1. Preheat oven to 425F. Lightly oil a 13-by-9-by-2-inch baking pan.
2. Wipe chicken with damp paper towels. Brush lightly with salad oil.
3. Combine cereal with rosemary and paprika. Roll chicken pieces in mixture, coating completely.
4. Arrange chicken in prepared pan; bake, uncovered, 30 minutes. Turn chicken; bake 15 minutes longer.

LOW-SODIUM CREOLE SAUCE

1 tablespoon salad oil
¼ cup coarsely chopped onion
¼ cup coarsely chopped green pepper
1 tablespoon flour
1 can (1 lb) dietetic-pack tomatoes, undrained

⅛ teaspoon dried thyme leaves
¼ teaspoon dried basil leaves
¼ teaspoon dried oregano leaves
1 tablespoon chopped parsley
Dash pepper

MAKES 2 CUPS

1. Slowly heat oil in large skillet. Add onion and green pepper; cook, over medium heat, stirring occasionally, until vegetables are tender—about 5 minutes.
2. Remove from heat. Add flour, stirring until well combined. Stir in rest of ingredients.
3. Bring mixture to boiling. Reduce heat; simmer, uncovered, 5 minutes. Serve sauce hot, over fish or omelet.

SHERRIED-CREAMED TUNA

¼ cup unsalted butter or margarine
2 tablespoons chopped green pepper
¼ cup unsifted all-purpose flour
1¾ cups reconstituted low-sodium high-protein food powder*

¼ cup sherry
2 cans (6½-oz size) dietetic-pack tuna, drained and flaked
1 can (8 oz) dietetic-pack green beans, drained

MAKES 4 SERVINGS

1. In hot butter in medium saucepan, sauté green pepper until tender. Remove from heat. Stir in flour until smooth.
2. Gradually add reconstituted food powder, stirring after each addition. Over medium heat, bring mixture to boiling, stirring constantly. Reduce heat; simmer 1 minute.
3. Add rest of ingredients, mixing well; reheat gently. Serve hot, over salt-free toast slices.

* Available at pharmacies.

NOODLES AND COTTAGE CHEESE

1 pkg (8 oz) noodles
¼ cup unsalted butter or
    margarine

1½ cups skim-milk low-
    sodium cottage
    cheese
1 tablespoon caraway seed

1. Cook noodles in unsalted, boiling water as package label directs. Drain.
2. Slowly heat butter in large skillet. Add noodles; cook, over medium heat, stirring constantly, until noodles are lightly browned—about 20 minutes.
3. Remove from heat. Stir in cottage cheese and caraway seed, mixing well. Serve warm.

LOW-SODIUM BROWNIES

2 squares unsweetened
    chocolate
½ cup unsalted butter or
    margarine
2 eggs

1 cup sugar
⅔ cup sifted cake flour
1 teaspoon vanilla extract
1 cup chopped walnuts or
    pecans

1. Preheat oven to 350F. Lightly butter an 8-by-8-by-2-inch baking pan.
2. In top of double boiler, over hot water, melt chocolate and butter. Remove from hot water; let cool.
3. In medium bowl, beat eggs with rotary beater. Add sugar and cooled chocolate mixture, mixing well. Add flour, beating until smooth and well combined. Stir in vanilla and nuts.
4. Pour batter into prepared pan; bake 35 minutes, or until surface springs back when gently pressed with fingertip.
5. Let cool completely in pan on wire rack. To serve, cut into squares.

LOW-SODIUM CAKE

2 cups sifted cake flour
2 teaspoons low-sodium
    baking powder
1½ -cups sugar
½ cup unsalted butter or
    margarine

¾ cup reconstituted high-
    protein low-sodium
    food powder*
1 teaspoon vanilla extract
2 eggs

1. Preheat oven to 350F. Butter and flour a 9-by-9-by-1¾-inch baking pan.
2. Sift flour with baking powder and sugar into large bowl of electric mixer. Add butter, reconstituted food powder, and vanilla; beat 2 minutes, at medium speed, cleaning beaters and side of bowl with rubber scraper.
3. Add eggs; beat 1½ minutes longer.
4. Turn batter into prepared pan; bake about 40 minutes, or until surface springs back when gently pressed with fingertip.
5. Let cake cool in pan 10 minutes. Turn out of pan; cool completely on wire rack. Frost, if desired, with Orange Cupcake Butter Frosting.** To serve, cut cake into squares.

* Available at pharmacies.

** See Cake Frostings and Fillings Chapter for recipe. Use unsalted butter or margarine.

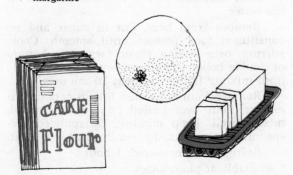

BUTTERSCOTCH BROWNIES

½ cup sifted all-purpose
flour
½ teaspoon low-sodium
baking powder
1 egg

¼ cup unsalted butter or
margarine, melted
1 cup light-brown sugar,
firmly packed
½ cup chopped walnuts or
pecans

MAKES 16

1. Preheat oven to 350F. Butter an 8-by-8-by-2-inch baking pan.
2. Sift flour with baking powder; set aside.
3. In medium bowl, beat egg with butter. Add sugar, beating until well combined. Stir in flour mixture until smooth; add nuts.
4. Pour batter into prepared pan; bake 30 minutes, or until cake tester inserted in center comes out clean.
5. Let cool completely in pan on wire rack. To serve, cut into squares.

VANILLA REFRIGERATOR COOKIES

2 cups sifted all-purpose
flour
1½ teaspoons low-sodium
baking powder
⅔ cup soft unsalted butter
or margarine

1 cup sugar
1 egg
1 teaspoon vanilla extract
1 cup finely chopped
pecans

MAKES ABOUT 9 DOZEN IN ALL

1. Sift flour with baking powder; set aside.
2. In large bowl, with wooden spoon or portable electric mixer at medium speed, beat butter, sugar, egg, and vanilla until light and fluffy.
3. Gradually stir in flour mixture and nuts; mix, with hands, to form a stiff dough.
4. Turn out dough onto lightly floured surface. Divide in half. With hands, shape each into a roll 8 inches long.
5. Wrap each in waxed paper or foil. Refrigerate until firm—several hours or overnight—before baking. (Rolls may be refrigerated for a week or ten days; bake fresh as desired.)
6. Preheat oven to 375F. With sharp knife, cut as many ⅛-inch slices as desired for one baking. Rewrap roll; refrigerate.
7. Place slices, 2 inches apart, on ungreased cookie sheet; bake 10 to 12 minutes, or until lightly browned. Remove to wire rack; cool.

PEPPERMINT CRUNCHIES

2 squares unsweetened
chocolate
½ cup sugar
¼ cup reconstituted low-
sodium high-protein
food powder*

¼ teaspoon peppermint
extract
2½ cups puffed rice

MAKES 40

1. Melt chocolate in top of double boiler over hot water.
2. Remove from heat. Stir in sugar and reconstituted food powder until smooth. Cook, stirring, over boiling water (water in bottom of double boiler should not touch base of top) until mixture is thick—about 10 minutes.
3. Remove from hot water. Stir in peppermint extract. Pour over puffed rice in large bowl, mixing well. Drop mixture, by rounded teaspoonfuls, onto waxed-paper-lined cookie sheet.
4. Refrigerate, uncovered, 1 hour.

* Available at pharmacies.

37

Outdoor Cooking

We dedicate these recipes to the Great American Mister, who stands, chef's cap on head, fork in hand, on terrace or back porch, in patio or back-yard, anywhere in the land, watching his roast turning on the spit. And to his wife, without whom (sometimes) the barbecue could never be the smashing summer success it undoubtedly is.

How to Build a Charcoal Fire

1. A fire base, usually recommended for the bottom of the fire bowl, permits your fire to "breathe," or draft, more easily and absorbs meat drippings (if your unit has openings in the side or bottom, they accomplish this purpose). Generally, the base is made of small, smooth or crushed stones, ⅜ to ½ inch in diameter. Use enough gravel to make the base level to the edge of the bowl.

2. Charcoal briquets are the most popular fuel. They're considered the best, too: They give an abundance of intense heat, are long-lasting, and don't crackle and pop. Most people use too much charcoal, so learn to use a modest amount. Store the briquets in a dry place, so they won't absorb moisture and become difficult to light.

3. It's a wise barbecue chef who lights his fire early enough (about 20 to 30 minutes before cooking time) to get a good bed of coals before he begins to cook. If you use a fluid to start the fire, saturate a pyramid of charcoal; after it has soaked about 30 seconds, ignite it. *Always follow the directions*

on the can. If you use an electric starter, pile the charcoal around it, and plug it in. It will take about 10 minutes for the fuel to catch fire. Then disconnect and remove the electric starter.

Cylinder starters are a good way to start a fire. You can even make one yourself. Cut out top and bottom of a 46-ounce juice can. With a triangular beer-can opener, punch a strip of holes around one edge, pushing the metal all the way through to form a row of legs. Set the can (or cans—you'll need two or three for a large fire) on the gravel, and fill it with charcoal. Light the charcoal, with a liquid fire starter if you wish, and when the coals are ashy, remove the can and spread the coals.

4. That gray ash on the coals means your fire is ready. Just before putting meat on the grill or spit, knock off the ash with a fire rake or poker. Knock it off periodically during cooking; it tends to hold back the heat.

5. For grilling, arrange hot coals in an even layer over the gravel, leaving about a half-inch space between coals, to prevent a flame-up. If your grill is one that slants and directs the fat into a drip pan, it isn't necessary to space the coals so carefully. When you barbecue on a spit, arrange the coals toward the rear of the fire bowl.

6. With grill cooking, spit barbecuing, or covered cooking, it's fun to experiment with nut- or fruitwood chunks or chips, to get new flavors. Soak wood chips (be sure they have sap in them, or leftover meat may turn rancid) in water about 20 minutes. Soaking increases smoke penetration and extends the life of the chips. Drop a few soaked chips directly on the hot coals. If they begin to flame, remove with tongs; drop into water; replace with more dampened chips.

7. The accurate way to tell when a roast or large piece of meat is done is to use a barbecue-meat thermometer. Insert it into the thickest part of the meat, making sure it doesn't touch a bone or the barbecue spit, and leave it in place as the meat cooks.

8. If you think you may need more charcoal, put some briquets at the edge of the fire bed, to warm up as cooking progresses. Add these warm briquets about 15 minutes before you need them. Dumping cold briquets on hot ones reduces the fire's temperature and slows up cooking.

9. When cooking is finished, just let the coals die. Don't throw water on the fire—it's not good to subject the grill to sharp changes in temperature, and it would make a great deal of unpleasant smoke.

Barbecuing Hints

Since, basically, cooking over charcoal is a dry-heat method similar to broiling, meats must be tender cuts or must be made tender by the use of a meat tenderizer or by precooking.

In barbecuing pork, take care to adjust the grill so the meat will be well done without scorching the surface.

For less costly meat dishes, try some of our chicken and fish suggestions. It's helpful to cook vegetables and fruits on the grill as accompaniments to the main dish. Then, with a large salad, the meal is complete with a minimum of effort.

BARBECUED CHUCK STEAK

4- to 4½-lb boneless chuck steak, 2 inches thick (U.S. Choice)

Unseasoned meat tenderizer

Sauce:

2 tablespoons salad or olive oil

1 medium onion, finely chopped

1 clove garlic, finely chopped

½ teaspoon dried basil leaves

½ teaspoon hickory salt (optional)

½ teaspoon salt

⅛ teaspoon pepper

1 teaspoon sugar

1 can (1 lb) tomatoes, undrained

1 can (8 oz) tomato sauce

1. Sprinkle steak evenly on all sides with meat tenderizer, following label directions (use 2 to 2¼ teaspoons). With fork, pierce meat at 1-inch intervals, to ensure tenderizer's penetration.

2. Meanwhile, make Sauce: In hot oil in large skillet, sauté onion and garlic until golden and tender. Stir in remaining ingredients.

3. Cook, stirring, to boiling point; reduce heat, and simmer 10 minutes. Keep warm.

4. For medium-rare steak: On outdoor grill and 3 inches from prepared coals, broil steak 20 minutes on one side; turn, and grill 20 minutes on other side.

5. To serve: Slice thinly on diagonal; top each serving with some of sauce.

BURGUNDY BEEFBURGERS

2 lb ground chuck

2 green onions, sliced

1½ teaspoons salt

Dash pepper

¼ cup Burgundy

1 egg

1 cup fresh bread crumbs

Burgundy Sauce:

¼ cup Burgundy

2 green onions, sliced

½ cup butter or margarine

1. With fork and in large bowl, toss chuck with onions, salt, pepper, Burgundy, egg, and bread crumbs until well combined. Shape beef into 8 patties.

2. Combine ingredients for sauce.

3. Adjust grill 4 inches from prepared coals. Grill beefburgers 8 to 10 minutes on each side, basting frequently with sauce.

4. Heat remainder of sauce to serve with beefburgers.

DE LUXE HAMBURGERS

2 lb ground chuck

¼ cup prepared hamburger relish

2 tablespoons prepared mustard

2 tablespoons catsup

1. Lightly toss chuck with the other ingredients. Shape into 8 patties.

2. Adjust grill 4 inches from prepared coals. For medium rare, grill hamburgers 4 minutes on each side. Or grill until of desired doneness.

To cook indoors: Make patties as above. Pan-broil, in skillet, about 4 minutes on each side. Or broil, on rack in broiler pan, 4 inches from heat, 4 to 6 minutes on each side.

BARBECUED SHORT RIBS OF BEEF

3 lb short ribs, cut in pieces
1 teaspoon monosodium
    glutamate
1 bay leaf
¼ teaspoon whole
    black peppers
½ teaspoon salt
½ cup vinegar

Basting Sauce:
¼ cup salad oil
2 tablespoons vinegar
2 tablespoons brown sugar
1 pkg (1½ oz) dried onion-
    soup mix
¼ teaspoon liquid hot-pep-
    per seasoning

1. In large kettle, combine short ribs, mono-sodium glutamate, bay leaf, peppers, salt, and vinegar with water to cover.

2. Bring to boiling, covered. Reduce heat; simmer 60 minutes, or until ribs are almost tender. Drain.

3. Make Basting Sauce: In small saucepan, combine all ingredients with ⅓ cup water; bring to boiling, stirring.

4. Remove short-rib meat from bones. Thread meat chunks on skewers.

5. Place foil drip pan under meat, to catch drippings. Grill meat, 5 inches from prepared coals, 10 minutes on each side; baste frequently with sauce.

To cook indoors: Prepare short ribs as above. Broil on rack in broiler pan, 5 inches from heat, about 8 minutes on each side, basting frequently with sauce.

CHUTNEY-GRILLED LAMB CHOPS

1 cup prepared chutney,
    finely chopped
2 tablespoons lemon juice
2 teaspoons curry powder

1 teaspoon ginger
½ cup butter or margarine
8 shoulder lamb chops,
    1 inch thick

1. In small saucepan, combine chutney, lemon juice, curry powder, ginger, and butter; cook slowly, over low heat, stirring, 10 minutes.

2. Adjust grill 4 inches from prepared coals. Grill chops 10 minutes, brushing several times with chutney sauce. Turn; grill 10 minutes longer, brushing with sauce. Serve with any remaining sauce.

LAMB KEBABS

1 lb lamb shoulder, cut into
    1-inch cubes
2 tablespoons salad or olive
    oil
¼ cup vinegar
½ teaspoon dried oregano
    leaves

1 teaspoon salt
1 tablespoon sugar
¼ teaspoon pepper
1 clove garlic, very finely
    chopped
4 small tomatoes, quartered

1. Arrange lamb in shallow glass baking dish. In jar with tight-fitting lid, shake oil, vinegar, oregano, salt, sugar, pepper, and garlic until well combined.

2. Pour mixture over lamb; refrigerate, covered, 3 hours, turning lamb occasionally.

3. Adjust grill 4 inches from prepared coals. Remove lamb from oil mixture. Arrange cubes alternately with tomato quarters on 4 long (about 10-inch) skewers; brush with oil mixture.

4. Grill kebabs, turning and brushing several times with oil mixture, about 20 minutes, or until of desired doneness.

MINT-BARBECUED LEG OF LAMB

5¼-lb boned leg of lamb
1 teaspoon salt
1 clove garlic, cut into 8
   slivers

Mint Sauce:
½ cup mint jelly
½ cup cider vinegar
1 tablespoon butter or
   margarine

¼ cup light-brown sugar,
   firmly packed
1 teaspoon grated
   lemon peel
1 tablespoon lemon juice
¼ cup granulated sugar
½ teaspoon salt
½ teaspoon dry mustard

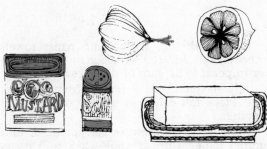

MAKES 6 TO 8 SERVINGS

1. Have butcher flatten lamb to 2-in. thickness.
2. With sharp knife, score fell (skin) side of lamb crisscross fashion. Wipe with damp cloth. Sprinkle with 1 teaspoon salt.
3. With tip of knife, make 8 gashes in meat, and insert garlic slivers. Arrange lamb in large, shallow baking dish.
4. Make Mint Sauce: In small saucepan, combine mint jelly with remaining ingredients; stir, over low heat, until jelly is melted; bring to boiling point. Let cool; pour over lamb.
5. Marinate for ½ hour; turn once.
6. Adjust grill 5 inches from prepared coals. Remove lamb from sauce; lay flat on grill.
7. Then grill, basting several times with sauce and turning several times, 1 to 1½ hours.
8. After 1 hour, test for doneness with a sharp knife; if too rare, continue grilling until of desired doneness. Serve with any remaining sauce.

BARBECUED FRANKFURTERS

1 envelope (2¼ oz) dried
   tomato-soup mix
1 tablespoon lemon juice
1 teaspoon dried marjoram
   leaves

2 tablespoons light-brown
   sugar
⅛ teaspoon dry mustard
2 lb frankfurters (12 to 16)
12 to 16 frankfurter rolls
   (optional)

MAKES 6 TO 8 SERVINGS

1. Adjust grill 4 inches from prepared coals.
2. In small saucepan, combine soup mix, 1¾ cups water, lemon juice, marjoram, sugar, and mustard.
3. Simmer on grill, stirring occasionally, 4 minutes. Move to edge of grill, to keep hot.
4. Arrange frankfurters on grill. Baste with sauce; grill 8 minutes on each side; baste often.
5. Serve on plate, or, if desired, in rolls. Top frankfurters with remaining sauce.

To cook indoors: Simmer sauce ingredients, stirring, over medium heat, 4 minutes. In broiler pan without rack, broil frankfurters until well browned, basting several times with sauce.

BARBECUED SPARERIBS

4-lb spareribs cut in 2 pieces
1 onion, quartered
2 teaspoons salt
¼ teaspoon pepper

Barbecue Sauce:
¾ cup cider vinegar
½ teaspoon dry mustard
2 tablespoons chopped
   onion

1 tablespoon light-brown
   sugar
¼ cup Worcestershire
   sauce
½ cup catsup
¼ cup chili sauce
1 tablespoon lemon juice
1 clove garlic, finely
   chopped
Dash cayenne

MAKES 6 SERVINGS

1. In large kettle, combine ribs with onion, salt, and pepper. Add water to cover; bring to boiling. Reduce heat, and simmer, covered, 1½ hours, or until very tender.
2. Meanwhile, make Barbecue Sauce: In medium saucepan, combine all ingredients except cayenne. Simmer, uncovered, 1 hour, stirring occasionally. Add cayenne.
3. Drain ribs; thread, accordion-fashion, on spit. Brush well with sauce.
4. Roast 25 to 30 minutes, 6 inches from prepared coals, brushing with sauce several times during roasting. Cut into serving-size pieces.

HAM STEAK SAN JUAN

MAKES 6 TO 8 SERVINGS

1 cup light rum
1 tablespoon dry mustard
2 tablespoons honey
¼ teaspoon cloves

2 slices fully cooked ham, 1 inch thick (about 1-lb, 8-oz size)
¼ cup soft butter or margarine

1. Combine rum, mustard, honey, and cloves.
2. Lay ham slices flat, not overlapping, in shallow dish. Add marinade; let stand at least 30 minutes.
3. Adjust grill to 4 inches from prepared coals. Remove ham from marinade. Grill 8 minutes, spreading with 2 tablespoons butter and basting several times with marinade.
4. Turn; grill 8 minutes longer, spreading with remaining butter and basting several times with marinade. Serve with any remaining marinade.

SWEET-AND-PUNGENT LOIN OF PORK
(USE A MOTOR-DRIVEN SPIT)

MAKES 8 TO 10 SERVINGS

6-lb loin of pork
½ cup catsup
1 can (6 oz) frozen pineapple-juice concentrate, undiluted
¼ teaspoon salt
½ teaspoon ginger

1 tablespoon lemon juice
1 tablespoon prepared mustard
¼ cup honey; or ¼ cup light-brown sugar, firmly packed

1. Wipe pork loin with damp paper towels. Secure on spit. Insert a barbecue-meat thermometer in pork, to be sure of doneness.
2. Adjust spit about 8 inches from prepared coals. Place foil drip pan under pork, to catch drippings.
3. Roast 15 to 20 minutes per pound, or until internal temperature is 185F—2½ to 3 hours.
4. Meanwhile, combine remaining ingredients in small saucepan; simmer, stirring, 5 minutes.
5. Use to brush pork generously during last half hour of roasting.

HICKORY-SMOKED CHICKEN

MAKES 8 SERVINGS

8 hickory chips or rings
½ cup butter or margarine, melted
1 teaspoon salt

½ teaspoon paprika
¼ teaspoon pepper
4 (2½-lb size) broiler-fryers, halved

1. Soak hickory chips in water to cover for 30 minutes; drain.
2. Adjust grill 3 inches from prepared coals.
3. In small bowl, combine butter, salt, paprika, and pepper. Brush both sides of broiler-fryers with butter mixture.
4. Grill, skin side down, 20 minutes, basting frequently with butter mixture. Turn; baste well again.
5. Place drained hickory chips on coals. Pull down door of smoke oven* to let smoke flavor broilers.
6. Grill 20 minutes in smoke oven; do not baste. Serve smoked broilers with any remaining basting sauce.

* To improvise a smoke oven: Crush heavy-duty aluminum foil to bowl shape, and place over broilers on grill.

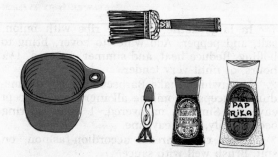

ITALIAN BARBECUED CHICKEN

3 cloves garlic, finely chopped

1 cup chopped parsley

1 bay leaf

1 tablespoon dried oregano leaves

3 cans (1-lb size) tomatoes, undrained

2 teaspoons salt

½ teaspoon pepper

¾ cup grated Parmesan cheese

4 (2- to 2½-lb size) broiler-fryers, halved

½ cup salad oil

1. Adjust grill 3 inches from coals.

2. Combine garlic, parsley, bay leaf, oregano, tomatoes, salt, and pepper in medium saucepan; bring to boil. Reduce heat; simmer 15 minutes.

3. Stir in cheese. Keep sauce warm.

4. Brush each broiler half on each side with ½ tablespoon salad oil. Arrange on grill, skin side up.

5. Grill 15 to 20 minutes, basting several times with sauce. Turn; fill broiler cavities with sauce; grill 15 to 20 minutes longer, basting several times with sauce.

SPIT-BROILED CHICKEN

2 (3-lb size) whole broiler-fryers

2 cans (8¾-oz size) pineapple tidbits

1 cup raw regular white rice

¼ cup finely chopped green pepper

2 tablespoons finely chopped onion

1½ teaspoons salt

¼ teaspoon pepper

¾ teaspoon ginger

2 teaspoons butter or margarine

1 can (6 oz) thawed frozen pineapple-juice concentrate, undiluted

1. Wash chickens thoroughly inside and out; dry well with paper towels.

2. Drain pineapple, reserving liquid. Add water to liquid to measure 2 cups.

3. In medium saucepan, combine pineapple liquid with rice, green pepper, onion, salt, pepper, ¼ teaspoon ginger, and butter.

4. Bring to boiling, uncovered. Reduce heat; simmer, covered, 12 to 14 minutes, or until rice is tender and liquid is absorbed.

5. Add pineapple tidbits, fluffing up rice with fork. Use to stuff chickens.

6. Truss chickens. Secure on spit; skewer wings in place, and tie legs together.

7. Adjust spit 8 inches from prepared coals. Roast chickens 1¼ hours, basting often during last ½ hour with thawed frozen pineapple juice combined with rest of ginger.

To cook indoors: Roast chickens on rotisserie about 1¼ hours.

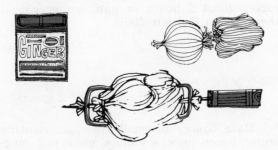

ROCK-CORNISH HENS

(USE A MOTOR-DRIVEN SPIT)

2 (1-lb size) frozen Rock-Cornish hens, thawed

Salt

2 tablespoons butter or margarine, melted

¼ teaspoon poultry seasoning

½ teaspoon garlic salt

½ teaspoon monosodium glutamate

½ cup sauterne

½ teaspoon paprika

1. Rub hens with salt; secure on spit. Bend wings under birds; tie legs together.

2. Adjust spit 8 inches above prepared coals. Roast hens about 1 hour.

3. Meanwhile, combine remaining ingredients in small saucepan. Use to brush hens often during last 45 minutes of roasting time.

To cook indoors: Roast hens on rotisserie about 1 hour. Meanwhile, proceed as above.

TURKEY ON A SPIT
(USE A MOTOR-DRIVEN SPIT)

MAKES 6 TO 8 SERVINGS

6-lb Beltsville turkey

Apricot-Rice Stuffing:
1 cup raw regular white
  rice
1 cup boiling water
½ cup dried apricots
½ cup butter or margarine
1½ cups finely chopped
  onion
2 cups finely chopped
  celery

½ teaspoon salt
½ teaspoon pepper
½ teaspoon poultry
  seasoning

Apricot Glaze:
¼ cup canned apricot
  nectar
¼ cup lemon juice
½ cup honey

1. Wash turkey well inside and out; dry thoroughly with paper towels.
2. Make Apricot-Rice Stuffing: Cook rice according to package directions. Meanwhile, pour boiling water over apricots; let stand 5 minutes. Drain, and chop fine.
3. Then, in hot butter in large skillet, cook onion and celery until golden—about 5 minutes.
4. Add salt, pepper, poultry seasoning, apricots, and cooked rice; toss with fork until well combined. Use to stuff body and neck cavities of turkey about three fourths full.
5. Make Apricot Glaze: Combine nectar, lemon juice, and honey.
6. Truss turkey; fold wings, and skewer or tie close to body. Tie legs together tightly, bringing cord under tail and up over breast.
7. Insert spit rod through center of body cavity, balancing turkey carefully. Tighten skewer at each end, to hold turkey securely. Insert barbecue-meat thermometer in center of inner thigh muscle.
8. Place spit about 8 inches from prepared coals.
9. Roast turkey 10 minutes; then brush with glaze. Brush with glaze every 20 minutes. Roast turkey about 2 hours, or until barbecue-meat thermometer registers 290F.

GRILLED WHOLE FISH

MAKES 2 OR 3 SERVINGS

Sauce:
¼ cup butter or margarine,
  melted
¼ cup lemon juice
2 tablespoons soy sauce
½ teaspoon garlic salt
½ teaspoon dried oregano
  leaves

½ teaspoon monosodium
  glutamate

1½- to 2-lb whole fish: bass,
  flounder, bluefish, or
  trout
Salad oil

1. Make Sauce: In small saucepan, combine butter, lemon juice, soy sauce, garlic salt, oregano, monosodium glutamate, and 2 tablespoons water. Heat on edge of grill.
2. Clean fish, and score.
3. Adjust grill 5 inches from prepared coals.
4. Place fish on well-oiled strip of foil; grill 12 to 15 minutes per pound, turning once and brushing frequently with sauce.

To cook indoors: Heat sauce ingredients, stirring, over medium heat, until hot. On greased rack in broiler pan, broil fish, 5 inches from heat, 10 minutes per pound, brushing frequently with sauce.

SOY-BARBECUED SHRIMP

2 lb fresh or thawed frozen
    large shrimp

Soy Marinade:*
2 cloves garlic
½ teaspoon salt
½ cup salad or olive oil

¼ cup soy sauce
½ cup lemon juice
3 tablespoons finely
    chopped parsley
2 tablespoons finely
    chopped onion
½ teaspoon pepper

1. Shell and devein shrimp, leaving tails on. Arrange shrimp in shallow dish.

2. Make Marinade: In small bowl, mash garlic with salt. Stir in remaining ingredients.

3. Pour marinade over shrimp; refrigerate, covered, 2 to 3 hours.

4. Adjust grill 3 inches from prepared coals. Remove shrimp from marinade, and thread on skewers.

5. Grill 3 minutes, basting with marinade. Turn; grill 5 minutes more, basting several times.

6. Use any remaining marinade as a dip.

* For variety, try this Herb Marinade: Combine 1 cup salad or olive oil, 1 teaspoon salt, 3 tablespoons chopped parsley, 1 tablespoon dried basil leaves, 2 cloves garlic (very finely chopped), 1 tablespoon catsup, 1 teaspoon pepper, and 1 tablespoon red-wine vinegar.

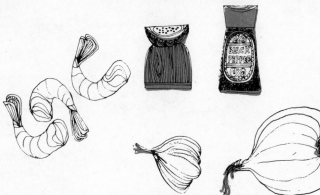

GRILLED ROCK-LOBSTER TAILS

6 (5-oz size) frozen rock-
    lobster tails, thawed
¼ cup butter or margarine,
    melted
Garlic salt

Lemon-Butter Sauce:
½ cup butter or margarine,
    melted
2 tablespoons lemon juice
1 teaspoon salt
Dash cayenne

1. Adjust grill 3 inches from prepared coals.

2. To make lobster easier to eat: With sharp knife, carefully loosen meat from undershell all the way around; leave lobster in shell. Then bend each shell backward until it cracks.

3. Brush lobster meat with butter; sprinkle with garlic salt.

4. Grill, shell side down, 15 minutes. Turn; grill 15 minutes longer.

5. Meanwhile, make Lemon-Butter Sauce: Heat butter with remaining ingredients. Serve with lobster.

737

CALORIE CHART

Food	Approximate Measure	Calories
Almonds, salted	10 to 12 nuts	95
Anchovy	1 medium fillet	10
Angel-food cake	1 piece (1/10 of an average cake)	145
Apple	1 small, 2¼" diam.	60
Apple, baked	1 large, 2 tbsp sugar	215
Apple butter	1 tbsp	35
Apple juice	½ cup	60
Apple pie	1/6 of med. pie	375
Applesauce, no sugar	½ cup	50
Applesauce, sweetened	½ cup	90
Apricot juice	½ cup	60
Apricots, canned, sweetened	4 halves, 2 tbsp juice	95
Apricots, dried	4 to 6 halves, raw	80
Apricots, fresh	3 medium	55
Artichoke, French	1 medium	45
Asparagus, fresh, canned, or frozen	6 medium stalks, drained	20
Asparagus soup, cream of	1 can, condensed	180
Avocado	½ small pear	245
Bacon, Canadian	2½" diam. x 3/10" slice	70
Bacon, fried	1 strip, 6" long	50
Bacon, lettuce, tomato sandwich	2 slices white bread, 3 slices tomato, 2–3 leaves lettuce, 2 strips bacon, 1 tbsp mayonnaise	300
Baked beans and pork, molasses	½ cup, canned	160
Baking-powder biscuits	1 av., 2" diam.	110
Banana, fresh	1 medium	130
Bass, baked	1 serving, 3" x 3" x ½"	285
Bean soup and bacon	1 can, condensed	436
Bean soup and pork	1 can, condensed	399
Beans, dried	½ cup, cooked	115
Bean, snap; fresh, canned, or frozen	½ cup, drained	15
Beef flank, cooked	3 slices, 4½" x 4" x ¼"	250
Beef, rib roast	4½" x 3" x ½" slice	265
Beef, rump roast	3½" x 2½" x ½" slice	320
Beef, shank	3½" x 2½" x ⅝" slice	170
Beef soup	1 can, condensed	275
Beef soup, noodle	1 can, condensed	155
Beef steak, sirloin	4½" x 2" x 1" piece	260
Beef stew, chuck, and gravy	1 av. serving, 2 small potatoes, 1 carrot, 1 onion	530
Beer	1 bottle, 12 oz	170
Beets, canned	½ cup, diced, drained	35
Blackberries, canned	½ cup, with syrup	110
Blackberries, fresh	1 cup	60

CALORIE CHART (Continued)

Food	Approximate Measure	Calories
Blackberry pie	⅙ of med. pie	365
Blueberries, canned	½ cup, with syrup	125
Blueberries, fresh	½ cup	45
Blueberries, frozen	½ cup, with sugar	90
Blueberry pie	⅙ of med. pie	370
Bluefish, baked	1 piece, 3½″ x 3″ x ½″	195
Bluefish, fried	1 piece, 3½″ x 3″ x ½″	245
Bologna	4½″ x ⅛″ slice	65
Boston brown bread	1 slice, 3″ x ¾″	105
Bouillon	1 cup	25
Bouillon cube	1, vegetable-extract type	10
Bourbon whisky	1 jigger, 1½ oz	120
Bran bread	1 slice, av.	75
Bran, dry cereal	½ cup	75
Bran flakes	1 cup	120
Bran muffin	1 med.	105
Bran, raisin	1 cup	150
Brandy	1½ oz	105
Brazil nuts	2 med.	60
Bread crumbs, dry, grated	1 cup	340
Bread pudding	¾ cup, with raisins	315
Broccoli	⅔ cup, or 1 large stalk	30
Brown Betty	½ cup	255
Brownie	2″ x 2″ x ¾″ piece	140
Brussels sprouts	6 av.	35
Butter	1 tbsp	100
Butter	1 tsp	35
Butter	1 pat, av.	70
Butter	1 pat, thin	50
Butterfish, fried	1 6¼″ long	210
Buttermilk	½ pt	85
Butterscotch candy	1″ x 1″ x ¼″ piece	20
Butterscotch sauce	1 tbsp	100
Cabbage	½ cup, shredded	10
Cake, cup, iced	1 med., vanilla icing	230
Cake, plain	2½″ sq.	230
Cake, plain, iced	2½″ sq., chocolate icing	300
Camembert cheese	1 oz	85
Candies, bulk	2 oz peanut clusters, almonds, raisins, or nut caramels	290
Cantaloupe or muskmelon	½ of 5″ melon	35
Caramel, plain	1 med.	45
Carrots, canned	½ cup cubes, drained	22
Carrot, raw	1, 5½″ x 1″	20
Cashew nuts	8 med.	90
Catsup	1 tbsp	15
Cauliflower	1 cup	25
Celery	2 stalks or hearts	10
Celery soup, cream of	1 can, condensed	215
Celery soup, cream of, homemade	⅔ cup	155

CALORIE CHART (Continued)

Food	Approximate Measure	Calories
Champagne	3½ oz	90
Chard, Swiss	½ cup leaves and stalks, cooked	15
Cheddar cheese, natural	1 oz	115
Cheese, processed, pasteurized	1 slice, 3½" x 3½" x 1/16"	70
Cheese sauce	¼ cup	130
Cherries, canned, red	½ cup, with syrup	105
Cherries, canned, white	½ cup, with syrup	85
Cherries, fresh, sweet	20 to 25 small	60
Cherry pie	⅙ of med. pie	360
Chewing gum	1 stick	8
Chewing gum, candy-covered	1 piece	10–15
Chicken, broiler, fried	½ med.	465
Chicken, canned	½ cup, scant	200
Chicken, creamed	½ cup	210
Chicken-gumbo soup	1 can, condensed	153
Chicken livers	3 small	140
Chicken-noodle soup	1 can, condensed	209
Chicken pie, homemade	4 tbsp chicken, peas, potatoes, gravy; 1 biscuit	335
Chicken pie, individual	3¾" diam., pastry topping	460
Chicken, roasted	3 slices, 3½" x 2½" x ¼"	200
Chicken salad	3 heaping tbsp	185
Chicken-salad sandwich	2 slices white bread, butter; 2 tbsp salad with mayonnaise	245
Chicken soup with rice	1 can, condensed	110
Chicken, stewed	½ breast or 1 thigh	200
Chicory or endive, curly	10 small inner leaves	5
Chili con carne	1 cup, canned	510
Chili sauce	1 tbsp	15
Chocolate, all milk	1 cup, 6 oz milk	210
Chocolate, half milk	1 cup, 3 oz milk	150
Chocolate, no milk	1 cup, 1 tbsp whipped cream	135
Chocolate bar, plain	1 oz	154
Chocolate bar, plain	1¾ oz	270
Chocolate cake, one layer	2" sq., chocolate icing	185
Chocolate cookie	1 large	75
Chocolate cupcake	1 med., chocolate icing	280
Chocolate frosted	1, 8 oz milk, vanilla ice cream	420
Chocolate fudge	1¼" sq.	120
Chocolate ice cream	1 av. serving (⅙ of 1 qt)	240
Chocolate malted-milk shake	1, 8 oz milk	500
Chocolate milk	½ pt	185
Chocolate milk shake	1, 8 oz milk	420
Chocolate mint	3" diam.	180
Chocolate pie	⅙ of med. pie (no whipped cream)	295
Chocolate sauce	2 tbsp	90
Chocolate syrup	1 tbsp, commercial	40
Chop suey	1 cup, chicken, pork	350–400
Cider, sweet or fermented	1 glass, 6 oz	75
Cinnamon bun	1 av.	160
Cinnamon bun, with raisins	1 av.	185

CALORIE CHART (Continued)

Food	Approximate Measure	Calories
Clam chowder	1 can, condensed, av.	200
Clams, raw	5 to 10	80
Cocoa, all milk	1 cup, 6 oz milk	175
Cocoa, half milk	1 cup	110
Coconut-custard pie	⅙ of med. pie	310
Coconut, dried	2 tbsp, shredded	85
Coconut, fresh	1" x 1" x ½" piece	55
Coconut, moist	2 tbsp, shredded	50
Cod, dried, creamed	⅔ cup	265
Codfish Cake	1 large cake, or 2 balls	200
Coffee, black	———	———
Coffeecake, nuts and icing	1 small, 4½" diam.	245
Cola beverages	1 bottle, 6 oz	80
Coleslaw	1 cup	100
Collards, cooked	1 cup	76
Condensed milk, sweetened	1 tbsp	65
Consommé	1 can, condensed	101
Cordial	1 oz	100
Corn, canned	½ cup, drained	70
Corn, cream-style, canned	½ cup	85
Corn, fresh	1 med. ear	90
Corn syrup	1 tbsp	55
Cornbread	2" sq.	140
Corned beef, canned	3" x 2¼" x ¼" slice	70
Corned-beef hash	½ cup	145
Cornflakes	1⅓ cups, or 1-oz box	110
Cornmeal, cooked	1 cup	120
Cornstarch pudding, chocolate	½ cup	220
Cottage cheese, cream-style	1 rounded tbsp	40
Cottage cheese, dry	1 rounded tbsp	30
Crab, canned	3 oz	90
Crab, deviled	1 med. crab	185
Crab salad	3 heaping tbsp	140
Cracked-wheat bread	1 av. slice	60
Cracker, butter type	1 av.	20
Cracker, oyster	1	5
Cracker, salted	2" sq.	15
Cracker, soda	2½" sq.	25
Cranberry jelly	1 tbsp	50
Cranberry sauce	1 tbsp	40
Cream cheese	1 oz	105
Cream-cheese-and-jelly sandwich	2 slices white bread, 1 oz cream cheese, 2 tbsp jelly	330
Cream, heavy	1 tbsp	50
Cream, light	1 tbsp	30
Cream-of-chicken soup	1 can, condensed	210
Cream pie	⅙ of med. pie	300
Cream puff	1 av. cream filling	315
Cream, whipped	1 tbsp, sweetened	55
Croquette, beef	3¼" x 1¾" diam.	205
Cruller, sugared	2½" diam.	150

CALORIE CHART (Continued)

Food	Approximate Measure	Calories
Cucumber	½ med., or 6 slices	5
Custard, baked	½ cup	205
Custard pie	⅙ of med. pie	265
Daiquiri cocktail	1 av.	125
Dates	3 to 4	85
Deviled ham	1 rounded tbsp	95
Doughnut, yeast	3″ diam.	120
Doughnut, yeast, with jelly	1 av.	225
Dried beef	5 to 6 slices, 4″ x 5″	205
Dried beef, creamed	½ cup scant	210
Duck, roasted	3 slices, 3½″ x 3″ x ¼″	310
Éclair, chocolate icing	1 av., custard filling	315
Éclair, no icing	1 av., whipped-cream filling	300
Edam cheese	1 oz	85
Egg, boiled	1 med.	80
Egg, fried	1 med., 1 tsp fat	110
Egg, poached	1 med.	80
Egg, raw, whole	1 med.	80
Egg-salad sandwich	2 slices white bread, 1 hard-cooked egg, 1 tbsp mayonnaise, 2 tbsp minced celery and onion	275
Egg, scrambled	1 med., 1 tbsp milk, 1 tsp fat	120
Eggnog, all milk	1 large, 8 oz milk	290
Eggplant, fried	2 slices, 4″ diam.	200–250
Endive, Belgian	10 long leaves; 15 to 20 small leaves	10
Escarole	2 large leaves	10
Evaporated milk	1 tbsp	20
Farina, cooked	1 cup	105
Fig bars	1 small	55
Figs, canned	3 figs, 2 tbsp juice	130
Fig, dried	1 large	60
Figs, fresh	3 small, 1½″ diam.	90
Finnan haddie, creamed	⅔ cup	265
Flounder, fried	3″ x 2″ x ¾″ serving	200
Flour, white, enriched	1 cup	400
Frankfurter, boiled	5½″ x ¾″	125
French bread	1″ slice	55
French dressing, commercial	1 tbsp	60
French dressing, homemade	1 tbsp	85
Fruit cocktail, canned	6 tbsp fruit and juice	70
Fruit salad, canned	3 heaping tbsp, 2 leaves lettuce	155
Fruit salad, fresh	3 heaping tbsp, 2 leaves lettuce	175
Fruitcake	3″ x 2¾″ x ½″ slice	140
Gelatin	3-oz box dessert powder, any flavor	325
Gelatin dessert	½ cup, any flavor	80
Gelatine salad with fruit	2½″ sq., or 1 cup	170
Gelatine, salad with vegetables	2½″ sq.	115
Gelatine, unflavored	1 tbsp	35

Food	Approximate Measure	Calories
Gin, dry	1 jigger, 1½ oz	105
Ginger ale	1 glass, 6 oz	60
Gingerbread	2" x 2" x 2" piece	205
Gingersnap	1 small	15
Goose, roasted	3 slices, 3" x 3" x ¼"	325
Graham cracker	1 small, 2½" sq.	15
Grape juice	½ cup	85
Grapefruit, fresh	½ medium	75
Grapefruit juice, canned, sweetened	½ cup scant	65
Grapefruit juice, canned, unsweetened	½ cup scant	45
Grapefruit juice, fresh	½ cup	45
Grapes, American	22 to 24, or 1 cup	70
Grapes, Malaga or Tokay	22 grapes	100
Grapes, seedless white	60 grapes	100
Gravy, brown	1 tbsp	40
Griddlecake, buckwheat	4" diam.	50
Griddlecake, white	4" diam.	60
Haddock, fried	4" x 3" x ½" fillet	160
Halibut steak, baked	3½" x 3½" x ½"	220
Halibut steak, fried	4" x 3" x ½"	250
Ham, boiled	4" x 2½" x ⅛" slice	90
Ham-salad sandwich	3 tbsp chopped ham, 1 tbsp salad dressing, 2 slices white bread, 1 pickle	320
Ham sandwich	1 slice ham 4" x 2½" x ⅛", 2 slices rye bread, 1 tsp butter or margarine, mustard	270
Ham sandwich	1 slice ham 4" x 2½" x ⅛", 2 slices white bread, 1 tsp butter or margarine, mustard	280
Ham, smoked, lean, fried	4" x 4" x ⅜" slice	390
Ham, spread	1 rounded tbsp	95
Hamburger	1 patty (5 per lb)	245
Hamburger in a bun	⅛ lb hamburger, 1 bun, 1 tsp butter or margarine	300
Hard sauce	1 tbsp	50
Hash, beef	1 cup	290
Heart, braised	¼ beef heart, lean	110
Herring, kippered	½ fish	210
Herring, pickled	1	110
Hollandaise sauce	1 tbsp	45
Hominy or grits	½ cup, cooked	120
Honey	1 tbsp	60
Honeydew melon	1 slice, 2" x 7"	50
Ice-cream soda	1 regular	260
Irish whisky	1 jigger, 1½ oz	120
Jams	1 tbsp	55
Jellies	1 tbsp	50
Kale	1 cup	45
Kidney, braised	3 slices, 3¼" x 2½" x ¼"	170

CALORIE CHART (Continued)

Food	Approximate Measure	Calories
Lamb breast, stewed	6 pieces, 2" x 1" x ⅜"	275
Lamb chop, rib, broiled	1 chop	130
Lamb chop, shoulder	1 chop, 4" x 3½" x ½"	215
Lamb leg, roasted	2 slices, 3" x 3¼" x ⅛"	205
Lamb, shoulder	2 slices, 3" x 3½" x ⅛"	255
Lard	1 tbsp	125
Lemon, fresh	1 medium	20
Lemon-meringue pie	⅙ of med. pie	280
Lemon milk sherbet	½ cup	240
Lemonade, fresh	1 large glass (1 oz lemon juice)	105
Lentils, dried	½ cup cooked	100
Lettuce	2–3 leaves	5
Lifesaver	1	10
Lima beans, fresh, canned, or frozen	½ cup, drained	75
Limburger cheese	1 oz	85
Lime, fresh	1 medium	20
Liver, beef	1 slice, 3" x 2¼" x ⅜"	85
Liver, calves'	1 slice, 3" x 2¼" x ⅜"	75
Liver, spread	1 rounded tbsp	50
Liverwurst sandwich	1 slice liverwurst, 3" x ¼", 2 slices rye bread, 1 tbsp mayonnaise	255
Liverwurst sandwich	1 slice liverwurst, 3" x ¼", 2 slices white bread, 1 tbsp mayonnaise	265
Lobster, canned	½ cup scant	50
Lobster, fresh, boiled or broiled	¾ lb, 2 tbsp butter or margarine	310
Luncheon meat	4" x 8½" x ⅛" slice	80
Macaroni, baked	1 cup, with cheese	465
Macaroni, cooked (stick or elbow type)	1 cup, plain	210
Macaroon	1 large or 2 small	110
Mackerel, fresh, broiled	4" x 2" x ¾"	275
Manhattan cocktail	1 av.	165
Maple syrup	1 tbsp	50
Margarine	1 tbsp	100
Marmalade, orange, commercial	1 tbsp	55
Marshmallow	1 av.	25
Martini cocktail	1 av.	145
Matzoth	6" in diam.	60
Mayonnaise, commercial	1 tbsp	60
Meat loaf	4" x 3" x ⅜" slice	265
Melba toast	1 slice	20
Milk, skim	½ pt	85
Milk, whole	½ pt	165
Mince pie	⅙ of med. pie	400
Molasses	1 cup	760
Molasses cookie	3½" diam.	70
Muffin, cornmeal	1 medium	130
Muffin, plain	1 medium	120
Mushroom soup, cream of	1 can, condensed	320
Mushrooms, canned	½ cup, drained	15

CALORIE CHART (Continued)

Food	Approximate Measure	Calories
Mushrooms, fresh	4 large, or 10 small	15
Mutton, leg, roasted	2 slices, 3" x 3¼" x ⅛"	205
Nectarines	2 medium	60
Noodles	1 cup, cooked	105
Nuts, mixed	8 to 12	95
Oatmeal, cooked	1 cup	150
Oatmeal cookie	1 large, 3½" diam.	115
Okra	8 pods	30
Old-fashioned cocktail	1 av.	185
Olive oil	1 tbsp	125
Olive, green	1 medium	7
Olive, ripe	1 medium	10
Omelet, plain	2 eggs	225
Onions, creamed	3 small, with sauce	150
Onion, raw	1, 2½" diam.	50
Onions, green (scallions)	5 small	25
Orange	1 medium, 3" diam.	70
Orange-and-grapefruit juice, canned, sweetened	½ cup	65
Orange-and-grapefruit juice, canned, unsweetened	½ cup	50
Orange ice	½ cup	145
Orange juice, canned, sweetened	½ cup	70
Orange juice, fresh	½ cup	50
Orange juice, frozen	½ cup, reconstituted	50
Ovaltine	1 cup, 8 oz milk	220
Oyster stew	1 serving (8 oz milk, 1 pat butter or margarine, 4–5 oysters)	320
Oysters, raw	4 to 6, medium	70
Parmesan cheese	1 oz	115
Parsley	10 sprigs	5
Parsnips, cooked	1 cup	95
Pea soup, green	1 can, condensed	330
Pea soup, green, cream of	1 can, condensed	215
Peach ice cream	1 serving, ⅙ qt	280
Peach pie	⅙ of med. pie	405
Peach shortcake, biscuit	3" biscuit, 2 tbsp whipped cream	400
Peaches, canned	2 halves, 1 tbsp juice	70
Peaches, dried, cooked	3 halves, 2 tbsp juice	125
Peach, fresh	1 medium	45
Peaches, frozen	½ cup	90
Peanut brittle	2½" x 2½" x ⅜" piece	110
Peanut butter	1 tbsp	90
Peanut-butter sandwich	2 slices white bread, 2 tbsp peanut butter	300
Peanuts, roasted	16 to 17	85
Pears, canned	2 halves, 1 tbsp juice	68
Pear, fresh	1 medium	65
Peas, canned	½ cup, drained	75

CALORIE CHART (Continued)

Food	Approximate Measure	Calories
Peas, dried	½ cup, cooked	110
Peas, fresh or frozen	½ cup, cooked	55
Pecans	12 halves	105
Pepper, green or red	1 medium	20
Pickle, dill or sour	1 large	15
Pickles, mixed sweet	4 small pieces	25
Pickle, sweet	1 small	20
Pimiento, canned	1 medium	10
Pineapple, chunks, canned	½ cup, with juice	95
Pineapple, chunks, frozen	½ cup, with juice	95
Pineapple, crushed, canned	½ cup, with juice	100
Pineapple, fresh, with sugar	½ cup, diced	60
Pineapple, fresh, without sugar	½ cup, diced	35
Pineapple, juice	½ cup	60
Pineapple, sliced, canned	¾" thick slice, 2 tbsp juice	95
Plums, canned	3 med., 2 tbsp juice	90
Plum, fresh	1, 2" diam.	30
Popover	1 av.	90
Popped corn	1 cup, no fat	55
Pork chop, loin, fried	1 med. chop	235
Pork chop, shoulder, fried	1 med. chop	310
Pork liver, cooked	1 slice, 3" x 2¼" x ⅜"	85
Pork loin, roasted	2 slices, 3½" x 3" x ¼"	285
Port wine	3½ oz	160
Postum	1 cup	35
Pot roast and gravy	1 slice, 5" x 3½" x ¼"	320
Potato chips	10 med. pieces, 2" diam.	110
Potato salad	½ cup	185
Potatoes, scalloped	½ cup	130
Potato, white, baked, no butter or margarine	1, 3¼" diam.	145
Potato, white, boiled	1, 2⅜" diam.	85
Potatoes, white, creamed	½ cup	115
Potatoes, white, French-fried	10 pieces	200
Potatoes, white, mashed	½ cup, scant	125
Poundcake	2¾" x 3" x ⅝" slice	130
Pretzel	1 large	140
Pretzel	1 medium	70
Pretzel	1 small	30
Pretzel sticks	7	35
Protein bread	1 slice, ⅜" thick	45
Prune juice	½ cup	85
Prunes	4 to 5 med., 2 tbsp juice	120
Puffed rice	1 cup	55
Puffed wheat	1 cup	45
Pumpkin pie	⅙ of med. pie	330
Radish	1" diam.	2
Raisin bread	1 slice, av.	65
Raisin pie	⅙ of med. pie	435
Raisins	¼ cup	110
Raspberries, canned	½ cup, 2 tbsp juice	100

Food	Approximate Measure	Calories
Raspberries, fresh, red	½ cup	35
Raspberries, frozen	½ cup	85
Raspberry ice	½ cup	120
Rennet pudding	½ cup	110
Rhubarb pie	⅙ of med. pie	430
Rhubarb, stewed	½ cup, sweetened	175
Rice, converted	½ cup, cooked	100
Rice pudding	½ cup, with raisins	250
Rice, white or brown	½ cup, cooked	100
Rice, wild	½ cup, cooked	90
Roast-beef sandwich	2 slices white bread, 2 thin slices beef, no gravy	340
Roast-pork sandwich	2 slices white bread, 1 thin slice pork, no gravy	435
Roll, white, hard	1 av.	95
Roll, white, soft	1 av.	120
Rolled oats	½ cup, cooked	75
Romaine	1 large leaf	2
Roquefort cheese	1 oz	110
Rum	1 jigger, 1½ oz	105
Rusk	1 piece	60
Rutabaga	½ cup	25
Rye bread, light	1 slice, thin	55
Rye wafer	1 double square wafer	20
Rye whisky	1 jigger, 1½ oz	120
Salad dressing	1 tbsp cooked type	60
Salad oil	1 tbsp	125
Salami	3¾" x ¼" thick	130
Salmon, baked	4" x 3" x ½" piece	205
Salmon, boiled	4" x 3" x ½" piece	170
Salmon, canned	½ cup	100
Salmon, fried	4" x 3" x ½" piece	205–225
Salmon loaf	½ cup	190
Sardine, packed in oil	1 sardine, drained	110
Sauerkraut, canned	½ cup, drained	15
Sausage, pork	3" x ½" link	95
Sauterne	3½ oz	85
Scallops, fried	5 to 6 pieces	300
Scotch whisky	1 jigger, 1½ oz	105
Scrapple	3½" x 2¼" x ¼" slice	210
Sherbet	1 cup	235
Sherry	3½ oz	140
Shortbread	1 piece, 1¾" sq.	40
Shortening	1 tbsp	125
Shredded wheat	1 biscuit	100
Shredded-wheat wafer	1 av. sq.	25
Shrimp, canned	5 to 6	65
Soda water, plain	——	——
Sole, fried	3" x 2" x ¾" piece	200
Sour ball, candy	1	25

CALORIE CHART (Continued)

Food	Approximate Measure	Calories
Sour cream	1 tbsp	30
Soybeans, fresh, cooked	1 cup	180
Spaghetti and cheese	1 serving	435
Spaghetti and meat sauce	1 serving	400
Spaghetti and tomato sauce	1 serving	245
Spaghetti, canned	¾ cup	100
Spaghetti, cooked, plain	1 cup	110
Spareribs, roasted	6 pieces, 4" x 1"	245
Spinach, canned or cooked	½ cup	25
Spinach, fresh	⅔ cup	25
Split-pea soup	1 can, condensed	357
Split-pea soup, homemade	¾ cup, no milk	200
Spongecake	1 med. piece (1/10 of av. cake)	145
Squash, summer	½ cup, cooked	20
Squash, winter	½ cup, cooked	45
Strawberries, fresh	10 large	40
Strawberries, frozen	½ cup	90
Strawberry ice cream	1 serving, ⅙ qt	260
Strawberry pie, one crust	⅙ of med. pie	275
Strawberry shortcake, spongecake	3" sq. cake, 2 tbsp whipped cream	400
Succotash	½ cup	145
Sugar, brown, light or dark	1 tbsp	50
Sugar cookie	3" diam.	65
Sugar, confectioners'	1 tbsp	40
Sugar, white, granulated	1 tbsp	50
Sweet potato, baked	1 medium	185
Sweet potato, candied	1 med., 2 halves, 3¾" x 2¼"	358
Swiss cheese	1 slice, 3½" x 3½" x 1/16"	65
Tangerine	1 large or 2 small	45
Tapioca pudding	½ cup	135
Tartar sauce	1 rounded tbsp	95
Tea, plain	———	———
Tokay wine	3½ oz	120
Tom Collins	1 av.	180
Tomato juice	½ cup	25
Tomato paste	1 tbsp	10
Tomato purée	1 tbsp	5
Tomato sauce	¼ cup	80
Tomato soup	1 can, condensed	220
Tomato soup, cream of, homemade	¾ cup	195
Tomatoes, canned	½ cup	25
Tomato, fresh	1 medium	30
Tongue, fresh, boiled	3 slices, 3" x 2" x ⅛"	160
Tonic water	1 bottle	5
Tuna	½ cup scant, no oil	150
Tuna-salad sandwich	2 slices white bread, 3 tbsp tuna, 1 tbsp mayonnaise, onion, celery	340
Turkey, cooked	2 slices, 4½" x 2½" x ¼"	185
Turnip greens	½ cup, cooked	25
Turnips, white	½ cup cubes, cooked	25

CALORIE CHART (Continued)

Food	Approximate Measure	Calories
Vanilla ice cream	1 av. serving, ⅙ qt	200
Vanilla wafer	1 small, thin	20
Veal chop, loin	⅜" thick	185
Veal cutlet, breaded	4" x 2¼" x ½"	220
Veal leg, roasted	2 slices, 3" x 2" x ⅛"	190
Vegetable-beef soup	1 can, condensed	230
Vegetable-juice cocktail	½ cup	20
Vegetable soup	1 can, condensed	205
Vegetable soup, homemade	¾ cup	95
Vegetable soup, without meat	1 can, condensed	245
Waffle, homemade	6" diam.	220
Walnuts, English	8 to 12 halves	100
Watercress	10 sprigs	2
Watermelon	½ slice, ¾" x 10"	45
Wheat cereal, dry	1 oz	100
White bread, enriched	1 slice, av.	65
White sauce, medium	¼ cup	105
Whitefish, fried	3" x 3" x 1" piece	185
Whole-wheat bread, 100%	1 slice, av., ½" thick	55
Whole-wheat, wafer	2" sq.	25
Wine, red and white, domestic	3½ oz	75
Yam, baked	1 small, no butter	120
Yeast	1-oz pkg. or cake	25
Yoghurt	1 cup	130
Zwieback	1 piece	30

GENERAL SHOPPING GUIDE

Food	Weight as Purchased	Approximate Measure	Approximate Number of Servings	Miscellaneous Equivalents—Comments
Beverages				
Chocolate, unsweetened	8 oz pkg	8 squares, 1 oz each		1 square, grated = ¼ cup
Cocoa, unsweetened	½ lb	2 cups		
Coffee, regular grind	1 lb	5 cups	40 to 45	
Coffee, instant	2 oz jar	1 cup	25	1 teaspoon per cup
Tea, regular	¼ lb	1½ to 2 cups	75	1 teaspoon per cup
Cereals and Cereal Products				
Bread cubes, soft		1 (⅝ inch) slice fresh, untrimmed		makes 1 cup soft bread cubes (¾ cup toasted)
Bread crumbs, soft		1 (⅝ inch) slice fresh, untrimmed		makes 1 cup soft bread crumbs
Bread cubes, dry		1 (⅝ inch) slice dry, untrimmed		makes ¾ cup dry bread cubes
Bread crumbs, dry		1 (⅝ inch) slice dry, untrimmed		makes ⅓ cup dry bread crumbs
Bread stuffing, prepared	8 oz bag	3 cups		1 bag makes enough stuffing for 5-lb chicken; 2 bags—for 10-lb turkey
Cornflakes	18 oz pkg	16 to 20 cups	18 (1 cup)	1 oz = 1 serving
Cornmeal, white or yellow	1 lb, 8 oz pkg	4⅓ cups	26 (⅔ cup)	1 cup uncooked = 4 cups cooked
Crackers, graham	1 lb pkg	about 66 crackers		15 crackers, crushed = 1 cup crumbs
Crackers, soda	3½ oz pkg	33 (2-inch square crackers)		22 crackers crushed = 1 cup crumbs
Farina	1 lb, 12 oz pkg	4⅓ cups	26 (⅔ cup)	
Hominy grits	1 lb, 8 oz pkg	3¾ cups	25 (⅔ cup)	
Macaroni, elbow or shell	8 oz pkg	2 to 2½ cups	4 to 6	1 cup uncooked (4 oz) = 2 cups cooked

GENERAL SHOPPING GUIDE (Continued)

Food	Weight as Purchased	Approximate Measure	Approximate Number of Servings	Miscellaneous Equivalents—Comments
Noodles, one-inch pieces	8 oz pkg	3 cups	4	1 cup uncooked (2½ oz) = 1¼ cups cooked
Oatmeal, rolled (quick-cooking)	1 lb, 2 oz pkg	5⅔ cups	15 (⅔ cup)	1 cup uncooked = 1¾ cup cooked
Rice, precooked	4⅝ oz pkg	1⅓ cups		2⅔ cups prepared
Rice, white polished	1 lb pkg	2¼ to 2½ cups	12 (⅔ cup)	1 cup uncooked = 3 cups cooked
Spaghetti	1 lb pkg	4 to 5 cups	8	1 cup uncooked (4 oz) = 2 cups cooked
Tapioca, quick-cooking	8 oz pkg	1½ cups	24	1 oz = 3 tablespoons
Dairy Products				
Butter	1 lb	2 cups	48 squares (⅓ oz each)	¼ lb (½ cup) = 1 bar 1 oz = 2 tablespoons
Cheese				
Cheddar	8 oz	2 cups, grated		
Cottage	1 lb carton	2 cups		
Cream	8 oz pkg	1 cup		
	3 oz pkg	6 tablespoons		
Cream				
Heavy (30-35% fat)	½ pt	1 cup		Doubles in volume when whipped (2 cups whipped)
Light or coffee (20% fat)	½ pt	1 cup	16 table-spoons	Not recommended for whipping
Ice cream	1 qt		6 to 8	
Milk				
Condensed	1 can (15 oz)	1⅓ cups		Sweetened
Evaporated	14½ oz can	1⅔ cups		Equals 3⅓ cups milk
	6 oz can	⅔ cups		Equals 1⅓ cups milk
Fresh, whole	1 qt	4 cups	4 (8 oz) glasses	
Instant nonfat dry milk	about 9½ oz pkg	makes 3 qts	12 (1 cup)	1⅓ cups instant nonfat dry milk and 3¾ cups water make about 1 qt liquid skim milk
Eggs, fresh				
Large	2 oz each	1 dozen		Whole, 5 per cup; whites, 8 to 9 per cup; yolks, 10 to 12 per cup
Medium	1¾ oz each	1 dozen		Whole, 6 per cup
Small	1½ oz each	1 dozen		Whole, 7 per cup
Fats and Oils				
Butter and margarine	1 lb	2 cups	48 squares (⅓ oz each)	¼ lb (½ cup) = 1 bar 1 oz = 2 tablespoons

GENERAL SHOPPING GUIDE (Continued)

Food	Weight as Purchased	Approximate Measure	Approximate Number of Servings	Miscellaneous Equivalents—Comments
Lard	1 lb	2 cups		
Shortening, hydrogenated	1 lb can	2½ cups		
Salad oil	1 pint bottle	2 cups		
Suet	1 lb	3¾ cups, chopped		

Fish and Shellfish—(See Fish and Shellfish Chapter)

Flours

All-purpose flour	2 lb pkg	1 lb (4 cups, sifted)		
Cake flour	1 lb	4½ cups, sifted		
Rye flour	2 lb pkg	1 lb (5 cups, sifted)		
Whole wheat or graham	2 lb pkg	1 lb (3½ cups, unsifted)		stirred before measuring

Fruits, dried

Apples	8 oz pkg	2 cups		5 cups, cooked
Apricots	1 lb	3 cups		5 cups, cooked
Currants	11 oz pkg	2 cups		
Dates, pitted	8 oz pkg	1⅓ cups (loosely packed)		1½ cups, cut-up (loosely packed)
Dates, whole, unpitted	8 oz pkg	1½ cups (loosely packed)		1¼ cups, pitted, cut-up (loosely packed)
Figs, whole	1 lb	2¾ cups		2⅔ cups, cut-up
Peaches, halved	1 lb	3 cups	12 (½ cup)	6 cups, cooked
Prunes, medium	1 lb	2½ cups	8 (½ cup)	4 cups, cooked
Raisins, seedless	15 oz pkg	3 cups (loosely packed)		2 cups, chopped

Fruit Juice

Orange, etc., frozen concentrate	6 oz can	1½ pts, reconstituted	6 (½ cup)	keep frozen until ready to use
	12 oz can	1½ qts, reconstituted	12 (½ cup)	
Lemonade, frozen concentrate	6 oz can	1 qt, reconstituted	8 (½ cup)	
	12 oz can	2 qts, reconstituted	16 (½ cup)	

Fruits, fresh

Apples	1 lb	3 medium	3	3 cups, sliced and pared; 2½ cups, cubed
Apricots	1 lb	8 to 12	5	
Avocado	¾ lb	1	2 (½ per serving)	2 cups, cubed (½ inch)

GENERAL SHOPPING GUIDE (Continued)

Food	Weight as Purchased	Approximate Measure	Approximate Number of Servings	Miscellaneous Equivalents—Comments
Bananas	1 lb	3 medium	3	2½ cups, sliced; 2 cups, mashed
Berries				
Blueberries	1 pt		4	
Cranberries	1 lb	4¾ cups		makes 3 to 3½ cups sauce
Strawberries	1 pt		3	1½ to 2 cups, hulled
Cherries, red	1 lb	2 cups, pitted	4 (½ cup)	
Grapefruit	1 lb	1 medium	2 (½ per serving)	makes ¾ cup juice; 1¼ cups cubed pulp
Grapes				
Concord	1 lb	1 qt	4	
Tokay	1 lb	2¾ cups, halved and seeded		
Lemons	1 dozen (medium)	3 lbs		makes 2 cups juice 1 lemon, grated = 1½ to 2 teaspoons peel 1 lemon = 2 to 3 tablespoons juice
Oranges	1 dozen (medium)	6 lbs	8 (½ cup)	makes 4 cups juice 1 orange, grated = 1 to 2 tablespoons peel 1 orange = ⅓ cup juice
Peaches	1 lb	4 medium	4	2½ cups peeled, sliced
Pears	1 lb	4 medium	4	2½ cups peeled, sliced
Pineapple	2 lbs	1 medium	6 (½ cup)	
Plums	1 lb	8 to 20	4	
Rhubarb	1 lb	4 to 8 stalks	4 (½ cup)	2 cups cut into ½-inch pieces
Fruits, frozen	10 to 16 oz package	1 to 2 cups	2 to 4	
Meats—(See Meat and Game Chapter)				
Miscellaneous				
Coconut, flaked	3½ oz can	1⅓ cups		
Coconut, shredded	4 oz can	1½ cups		
Gelatine, unflavored	1 oz pkg	3 envelopes		1 envelope = 1 tablespoon
Marshmallows	¼ lb	16 large		10 miniature = 1 large marshmallow
Peanut butter	8 oz jar	1 cup		
Nuts				
Nuts, shelled				
Almonds, whole, blanched	1 lb	4 cups		1 lb in shell = ¼ lb nutmeats
Brazil nuts	1 lb	3 cups		1 lb in shell = ½ lb nutmeats
Filberts	1 lb	3⅓ cups		1 lb in shell = ½ lb nutmeats
Peanuts	1 lb	3¼ cups		1 lb in shell = ⅔ lb nutmeats
Pecan halves	1 lb	4¼ cups		1 lb in shell = ⅓ lb nutmeats
chopped	1 lb	3¾ cups		
Walnut halves	1 lb	4½ cups		1 lb in shell = ½ lb nutmeats
chopped	1 lb	3⅔ cups		

GENERAL SHOPPING GUIDE (Continued)

Food	Weight as Purchased	Approximate Measure	Approximate Number of Servings	Miscellaneous Equivalents—Comments
Peels and Candied Fruits				
Cherries, whole candied	6½ oz jar	1⅛ cups		
Citron, lemon or orange peel	4 oz jar	½ cup, chopped		
Mixed candied peels	1 lb jar	2½ cups, chopped		
Poultry—(See Poultry Chapter)				
Sugars				
Brown	1 lb pkg	2¼ cups, firmly packed		light or dark
Confectioners'	1 lb pkg	4 to 4½ cups, sifted		
Granulated	1 lb pkg	2¼ cups		
Superfine	1 lb pkg	2⅓ cups		
Syrups				
Corn syrup	1½ lbs (1 pint bottle)	2 cups		light or dark
Honey	1 lb jar	1½ cups		
Maple-blended	12 oz bottle	1½ cups		table syrup
Molasses	1 lb	1⅓ cups		light or dark
Vegetables, dried				
Kidney beans	1 lb	2½ cups	9 (¾ cup)	
Lima beans	1 lb	2½ cups	8 (¾ cup)	
Navy beans	1 lb	2⅓ cups	8 (¾ cup)	
Split peas	1 lb	2 cups	7 (¾ cup)	
Vegetables, fresh				
Asparagus	1 lb	16 to 20 stalks	4	
Beans, lima, in pod	1 lb	⅔ cup shelled	2 (⅓ cup)	
shelled	1 lb	2 cups	6 (⅓ cup)	
Beans, snap	1 lb	3 cups	5 (½ cup)	
Beets	1 lb	2 cups, diced	4 (½ cup)	
Broccoli	1 lb		3	
Brussels sprouts	1 lb	1 qt or less	5	
Cabbage, raw	1 lb	½ small head 4 cups, shredded	7	
cooked	1 lb		4 (½ cup)	
Carrots	1 lb	2½ cups, diced or shredded	5 (½ cup)	
Cauliflower	1 lb	1½ cups	3 (½ cup)	
Celery	1 lb	2 medium bunches, or 2 cups diced	4 (½ cup, cooked)	
Corn, cut	1 lb		5	
ears	12 medium	3 cups, cut	6	
Eggplant	1 lb	2½ cups, diced	5 (½ cup)	

GENERAL SHOPPING GUIDE (Continued)

Food	Weight as Purchased	Approximate Measure	Approximate Number of Servings	Miscellaneous Equivalents—Comments
Greens, beet	1 lb		4	
Mushrooms, medium	1 lb	35 to 45	6	
Onions	1 lb	3 large	4	
Parsnips	1 lb	4 medium	4	
Peas, in pod	1 lb	1 cup shelled	2	
Potatoes, sweet	1 lb	3 medium	3	
white	1 lb	3 medium	3	
		2½ cups, diced	5 (½ cup)	
Rutabaga	1 lb	2⅔ cups, diced	4	
Squash, Hubbard	1 lb		2	
summer	1 lb		3	
Tomatoes	1 lb	4 small	4	
Turnips	1 lb	3 medium	4 (½ cup)	

APPROXIMATE SUBSTITUTIONS OF ONE INGREDIENT FOR ANOTHER

1 tablespoon all-purpose flour ....½ tablespoon
(for thickening)   cornstarch,
                                                potato flour;
                                                or 2 teaspoons
                                                quick-cooking
                                                tapioca

1 cup cake flour ....1 cup all-purpose
                                                flour, less 2
                                                tablespoons

1 ounce (1 square)
unsweetened chocolate ....3 tablespoons
                                                unsweetened cocoa
                                                plus 1 tablespoon fat

1 cup butter ....1 cup margarine

1 cup whole milk ....½ cup evaporated
                                                milk plus ½ cup
                                                water

1 cup whole milk ....1 cup reconstituted
                                                nonfat dry milk plus
                                                2 teaspoons butter or
                                                margarine

1 cup buttermilk or
sour milk ....1 tablespoon lemon
                                                juice plus milk to
                                                make 1 cup (let stand
                                                5 minutes)

Index

Mace

Mace, the scarlet covering of the nutmeg seed, has a clean fragrance and delicate, exotic flavor.

Marjoram

Versatile marjoram, member of the mint family, grows in France, Chile, Peru, and California.

Mint

A sweet, tangy, and refreshing herb, mint is grown in many gardens in the United States.

Mixed Pickling Spice

This handy blend is a mixture of several whole spices from as many as 14 different countries.

Mustard

This hot, pungent spice in its prepared form is one of the most widely used condiments in America.

Nutmeg

Nutmeg, once sold as a charm, has a warm and spicy flavor. It is tropical in origin.

Oregano

Similar to marjoram in flavor, oregano is a must in the preparation of many spicy Italian dishes.

Paprika

Bright in color, usually mild in flavor, paprika is ground from dried pods of a red-colored pepper.

Parsley

Rich in vitamins and minerals, parsley is justly famous as a garnish, adding lovely garden freshness.

Black Pepper

Pepper, imported from India and Indonesia, was one of the most valuable in the spice trade.

Cayenne Pepper

Made from capsicum red peppers, cayenne has a fiery bite that makes it the most pungent spice.

Red Pepper

Made from a larger variety of red pepper than cayenne, this spice is less fiery, has slightly less bite.